UNDERSTANDING

MANAGEMENT

SECOND EDITION

UNDERSTANDING

MANAGEMENT

SECOND EDITION

RICHARD L. DAFT
Vanderbilt University

DOROTHY MARCIC
University of Economics—Prague

THE DRYDEN PRESS

HARCOURT BRACE COLLEGE PUBLISHERS

FORT WORTH   PHILADELPHIA   SAN DIEGO   NEW YORK   ORLANDO   AUSTIN   SAN ANTONIO

TORONTO   MONTREAL   LONDON   SYDNEY   TOKYO

Publisher	GEORGE PROVOL
Acquisitions Editor	JOHN WEIMEISTER
Product Manager	LISÉ JOHNSON
Developmental Editor	TRACI KELLER
Project Editor	REBECCA DODSON
Production Manager	LOIS WEST
Art Director	BURL DEAN SLOAN
Picture & Rights Editor	ADELE KRAUSE
Compositor	GTS GRAPHICS, INC.
Text Type	10/12 NEW BASKERVILLE
Part Opening Art	BURL DEAN SLOAN

ISBN: 0-03-024593-1
Library of Congress Catalog Card Number: 97-065945

Address for Orders
The Dryden Press, 6277 Sea Harbor Drive, Orlando, FL 32887
1-800-782-4479, or 1-800-433-0001 (in Florida)

Address for Editorial Correspondence
The Dryden Press, 301 Commerce Street, Suite 3700, Fort Worth, TX 76102

Website address:
http://www.hbcollege.com

The Dryden Press
Harcourt Brace College Publishers

THE DRYDEN PRESS SERIES IN MANAGEMENT

Anthony, Perrewé, and Kacmar
Strategic Human Resource Management
Second Edition

Bereman and Lengnick-Hall, Mark
*Compensation Decision Making: A
Computer-Based Approach*
Second Edition

Bergmann, Scarpello, and Hills
Compensation Decision Making
Second Edition

Bourgeois
*Strategic Management: From Concept to
Implementation*

Bracker, Montanari, and Morgan
Cases in Strategic Management

Brechner
*Contemporary Mathematics for Business
and Consumers*

Calvasina and Barton
*Chopstick Company: A Business
Simulation*

Costin
Readings in Total Quality Management

Costin
*Managing in the Global Economy: The
European Union*

Costin
Economic Reform in Latin America

Costin
*Management Development and Training:
A TQM Approach*

Costin
*Readings in Strategy and Strategic
Management*

Czinkota, Ronkainen, and Moffett
International Business
Fourth Edition

Czinkota, Ronkainen, Moffett, and
Moynihan
Global Business
Second Edition

Daft
Management
Fourth Edition

Daft and Marcic
Understanding Management
Second Edition

DeSimone and Harris
Human Resource Development
Second Edition

Foegen
Business Plan Guidebook
Revised Edition

Gatewood and Feild
Human Resource Selection
Fourth Edition

Gold
*Exploring Organizational Behavior:
Readings, Cases, Experiences*

Greenhaus and Callanan
Career Management
Second Edition

Higgins and Vincze
Strategic Management: Text and Cases
Fifth Edition

Hodgetts
Modern Human Relations at Work
Sixth Edition

Hodgetts and Kroeck
*Personnel and Human Resource
Management*

Hodgetts and Kuratko
Effective Small Business Management
Sixth Edition

Holley and Jennings
The Labor Relations Process
Sixth Edition

Jauch and Coltrin
*The Managerial Experience: Cases and
Exercises*
Sixth Edition

Kindler and Ginsburg
Strategic & Interpersonal Skill Building

Kirkpatrick and Lewis
*Effective Supervision: Preparing for the
21st Century*

Kuratko and Hodgetts
*Entrepreneurship: A Contemporary
Approach*
Fourth Edition

Kuratko and Welsch
Entrepreneurial Strategy: Text and Cases

Lengnick-Hall, Cynthia, and Hartman
Experiencing Quality

Lewis
Io Enterprises Simulation

Long and Arnold
The Power of Environmental Partnerships

Morgan
Managing for Success

Ryan, Eckert, and Ray
Small Business: An Entrepreneur's Plan
Fourth Edition

Sandburg
Career Design Software

Vecchio
Organizational Behavior
Third Edition

Walton
*Corporate Encounters: Law, Ethics, and
the Business Environment*

Zikmund
Business Research Methods
Fifth Edition

ABOUT THE AUTHORS

Richard L. Daft, Ph.D., holds the Ralph Owen Chair in Management and is Director of the Center for Leadership and Organizational Transitions at Vanderbilt University, where he specializes in the study of organization theory and leadership. Dr. Daft is a Fellow of the Academy of Management and has served on the editorial boards of *Academy of Management Journal, Administrative Science Quarterly,* and *Journal of Management Education.* He is the Associate Editor-in-Chief of *Organization Science* and served for three years as associate editor of *Administrative Science Quarterly.*

Professor Daft has authored or co-authored six books including *Organization Theory and Design* (West Publishing, 1995) and *What to Study: Generating and Developing Research Questions* (Sage, 1982). He is currently finishing *The Fourth Way: Harnessing the Forces of Fusion Leadership* (with Robert Lengel). He has also authored dozens of scholarly articles, papers, and chapters. His work has been published in *Administrative Science Quarterly, Academy of Management Journal, Academy of Management Review, Strategic Management Journal, Journal of Management, Accounting Organizations and Society, Management Science, MIS Quarterly, California Management Review,* and *Organizational Behavior Teaching Review.* Professor Daft has been awarded several government research grants to pursue studies of organizational design, organizational innovation and change, strategy implementation, and organizational information processing.

Dr. Daft also is an active teacher and consultant. He has taught management, organizational change, organizational behavior, organizational theory, and leadership. He has been actively involved in management development and consulting for many companies and government organizations including the American Banking Association, Bell Canada, NL Baroid, Tenneco, the United States Air Force, The U.S. Army, J. C. Bradford & Co., Central Parking System, and the Vanderbilt University Medical Center.

Dorothy Marcic, Ed.D., M.P.H., is a former Fulbright Scholar at the University of Economics in Prague and the Czech Management Center, where she taught courses and did research in leadership, organizational behavior, and cross-cultural management. Currently she teaches courses at the Peabody School of Vanderbilt University, Monterey Institute of International Studies, and the University of Economics in Prague. While in Europe, she also taught courses or gave presentations at the Helsinki School of Economics, Slovenian Management Center, College of Trade in Bulgaria, City University in Slovakia, Landegg Institute in Switzerland, the Swedish Management Association, Technion University in Israel, and the London School of Economics. Other international work includes projects at the Autonomous University in Guadalajara, Mexico, and a training program for the World Health Organization in Guatemala. She has served on the boards of the Organizational Behavior Teaching Society, the Health Administration Section of the American Public Health Association, and the *Journal of Applied Business Research.*

Dr. Marcic has authored eleven books, including *Organizational Behavior: Experiences and Cases* (Southwestern Publishing, Fifth edition, 1998), *Management International* (West Publishing, 1984), *Women and Men in Organizations* (George Washington Univeristy, 1984), and *Managing with the Wisdom of Love: Uncovering Virtue in People and Organizations* (Jossey-Bass, 1997). In addition, she has had dozens of articles printed in such publications as *Journal of Management Development, International Quarterly of Community Health Education, Psychological Reports,* and *Executive Development.*

Dr. Marcic has conducted hundreds of seminars on various topics and done consulting for executives at AT&T Bell Labs; the Governor and Cabinet of North Dakota; the U.S.

Department of State; United Parcel Service; Aerial Beauty Supply Company; the U.S. Air Force; Slovak Management Association; Eurotel; Czech Ministry of Finance; the Cattaraugus Center, two arts organizations in the Twin Cities, and the Salt River-Pima Indian Tribe in Arizona. In addition, Dorothy worked to develop a three-week management training program on empowerment for Hallmark Corporation and has served as an advisor to the U.S. Ambassador of the Czech Republic. She served as delegate to the UN Economic and Social Development Summit in Copenhagen and gave workshops on ethical management at the NGO Forum.

PREFACE

Revealing the Nature of Management

Our vision for the second edition of *Understanding Management* is to create the best and most relevant textbook available for students and teachers who are interested in small and medium-sized organizations. Unlike traditional management textbooks, this book does not rely on abstract theories and company examples applicable only to top managers of billion-dollar corporations. To achieve the vision of appealing to students who "work for a living in typical companies," this textbook contains two distinctive qualities:

- Management concepts are absolutely current and up-to-date, and they are selected for relevance to the large student audience interested in real management problems in local companies. The management concepts are also applicable to readers with interests in small business and entrepreneurship. The concepts have been enhanced with an easy-to-understand writing style, and many practical examples are woven into the text.

- Case applications, boxed items, photo captions, and end-of-chapter materials are heavily oriented toward middle management and supervisory issues in smaller companies and away from the "top management of Fortune 500 companies" perspective applicable to M.B.A. students in select schools. Vivid illustrations of real organizational issues appeal to people at all levels in companies of all sizes. Not only are these teaching aids current and practical, they reinforce the vision of the book by illustrating companies and management situations with which students can identify.

A revolution is occurring in the field of management. The traditional view of management's purpose as that of controlling people, seeking stability and efficiency, and using rules and regulations to create a top-down hierarchy no longer works to create healthy and thriving organizations in the present fast-paced global environment. More current thinking sees management's purpose as harnessing employees' enthusiasm and creativity; finding shared vision, norms, and values; sharing information and power; and encouraging teamwork and participation. Both paradigms are guiding management actions in the world today.

Our vision for the second edition of *Understanding Management* is to introduce the new paradigm in a way that is interesting and valuable to students, while retaining the best of traditional management ideas. To achieve this vision, we have included the most recent management thinking and research as well as the contemporary application of management ideas in organizations. We have worked together with the Dryden Press to provide a textbook better than any other for capturing the excitement and adventure of organizational management.

Any textbook is limited as a medium for teaching management. A textbook about management is like a music video of the Boston Pops Orchestra—the listener isn't really there, and much of the music's impact is lost. We revised *Understanding Management* to provide a visual recording of utmost quality that will create in students both respect for the changing field of management and confidence that they can understand and master it.

The "audio," or textual, portion of this book has been enhanced through the easy-to-understand writing style and the many in-text examples and boxed items that make the concepts realistic and relevant to students. The "visual," or graphical, component has been enhanced with a new set of photo essays that illustrate specific management concepts. The well-chosen photographs provide vivid illustrations and intimate glimpses of management scenes, events, and people. The photos are combined with brief written essays that explain how a specific management concept looks and feels. Both the textual and graphical portions of the textbook help students grasp the often abstract and distant world of management.

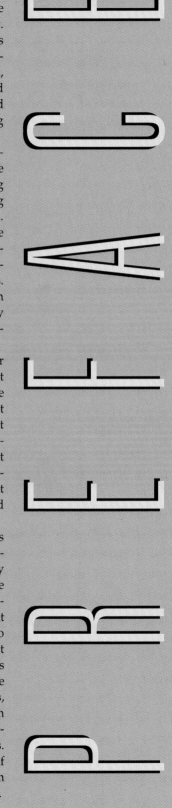

In this second edition of *Understanding Management*, we have purposely chosen examples of companies (both in in-text and boxed items) that tend to embody this new paradigm of management, demonstrating with ample empirical evidence the groundswell developing toward this new way of organizing and managing companies. Therefore, this second edition is especially focused on the future of management education by identifying and describing elements and examples of the new management paradigm. New materials in the book include the following:

- Chapters 1 and 2 introduce the management revolution and learning organizations and explain how the management paradigm shift contributes to the concept of a learning organization.

- Each chapter contains a boxed item called "Leading the Management Revolution" that describes real people and companies who are leading the change toward the new management paradigm. Examples of leadership are drawn from companies that include Hewlett-Packard, Eastman Kodak, Rykodisc, Taco Bell, Globe Metallurgical, General Electric, Yahoo!, J. Peterman, Amazon Books, Rebel Shoes, Starbucks, Gateway 2000, Relax the Back, Yakima, Blue Bird Buses, Granite Rock, Harbor Sweets, Knowaste, Nucor Steel, Texas Instruments, Nu Skin International, and Jostens.

- Each chapter contains a boxed item called "Technology for Today" that illustrates how technological innovations and products are reshaping the workplace.

- New material on creativity has been added to Chapter 8 on decision making, and a discussion of interactive leadership and servant leadership has been added to Chapter 13 on leadership.

- New concepts such as chaos theory have been added to explain the need for the management revolution toward the learning organization.

- The content of the chapters on teamwork, communication, and organization structure has been updated to reflect the trend toward empowerment and participation in organizations.

- Additional material on total quality management has been added to Chapter 2 on management history as well as Chapter 17 on quality control.

- End-of-chapter discussion materials have been enriched with the addition of an ethical dilemma, two experiential exercises, and an Internet assignment.

- Chapter 6 on small business has been moved to the second section of the book about the environment of organizations.

- Updated material on NAFTA, the EU, and GATT has been added to Chapter 4 on the global environment.

- The appendix on organizational behavior has been retained to increase the coverage of OB and show students how OB concepts apply to them.

In addition, Dryden has provided the resources necessary to bring together a team of experts to create and coordinate color photographs, video cases, beautiful artwork, and supplementary materials for the best management textbook and package on the market.

Organization

The chapter sequence in *Understanding Management* is organized around the management functions of planning, organizing, leading, and controlling. These four functions effectively encompass both management research and characteristics of the manager's job.

Part I introduces the world of management, including the nature of the manager's job, the revolution in management, the new paradigm, learning organizations, and historical perspectives on management.

Part II examines the environments of management and organizations. This section includes material on the business environment and corporate culture, the global environment, ethics and social responsibility, the natural environment, and the environment of small business and entrepreneurship.

Part III presents two chapters on planning, which include organizational goal setting and planning, strategy formulation and implementation, and the decision-making process, as well as information technology.

Part IV focuses on organizing processes. These chapters describe the dimensions of structural design, the design alternatives managers can use to achieve strategic objectives, structural designs for promoting innovation and change, the design and use of the human resource function, and the impact diverse employees have on the organizing function.

Part V is devoted to leadership. This section begins with a description of leadership and paves the way for the subsequent topics of employee motivation, communication, and management of teams.

Part VI describes the controlling function of management, including basic principles of total quality management, the design of control systems, management information systems, and techniques for control of operations management.

The appendixes include supplementary material on organizational behavior and management science aids for decision making. Appendix A, "Insights into Individual Behavior," provides material for instructors who like to expand the amount of OB concepts used in the management course. Moreover, Appendix A shows students how concepts apply specifically to them, giving them a more intimate feeling for the concepts. Appendix B, "Management Science Aids for Planning and Decision Making," contains the quantitative material that many instructors use to expand on the more qualitative decision approaches described in Chapter 8. The quantitative approaches of linear programming, breakeven analyses, forecasting, PERT charting, and decision tree analysis are all covered in Appendix B.

Special Features

One major goal of this book is to offer better ways of using the textbook medium to convey management knowledge to the reader. To this end, the book includes several special features.

Chapter Outline and Learning Objectives. Each chapter begins with a clear statement of its learning objectives and an outline of its contents. These devices provide an overview of what is to come and can also be used by students to see whether they understand and have retained important points.

Management Problem/Solution. The text portion of each chapter begins with a real-life problem faced by organization managers. The problem pertains to the topic of the chapter and will heighten students' interest in chapter concepts. The questions posed in the Management Problem are resolved in the Summary and Management Solution at the end of the chapter, where chapter concepts guiding the management's actions are highlighted.

Photo Essays. Another feature of the book is the use of photographs accompanied by detailed captions that describe management events and the ways they relate to the chapter material. While the photos are beautiful to look at, they also convey the vividness, immediacy, and concreteness of management events in today's business world.

Contemporary Examples. Every chapter of the text contains a large number of written examples of management incidents. These are placed at strategic points in the chapter and are designed to demonstrate the application of concepts to specific companies. These in-text examples—indicated by an icon in the margin—include well-known companies such as J. Peterman, Beech-Nut, Southwest Airlines, Blue Bird Buses, Prudential Insurance, Compaq, and Hewlett-Packard, as well as less well-known companies and not-for-profit organizations such as Marmot Mountain Works, Raymond Corp., Retrieva Fabrics, Urgences Santé, ServiceMaster, and Blackberry

Stores. These examples put students in immediate touch with the real world of organizations so that they can appreciate the value of management concepts.

Leading the Management Revolution Boxes.
These boxes illustrate a major theme of the second edition: the learning organization in practice. This feature explores how companies, when faced with chaotic environments, use new paradigm ideas to compete successfully in both the domestic and global marketplace.

Technology for Today Boxes.
These boxes show the speed and unpredictability of technological changes and how managers are harnessing these innovations, causing tremendous changes in the workplace. These boxed items contain issues of special interest to management students. They may describe a contemporary topic or problem that is relevant to chapter content, or they may contain a diagnostic questionnaire or a special example of how managers handle a problem. These boxes will heighten student interest in the subject matter and provide an auxiliary view of management issues not typically available in textbooks.

Focus on. . . Boxes.
These boxed items highlight topics such as ethics, change, management, quality, diversity, and teamwork. Their purpose is to help students integrate these topics with other concepts in the book. Too often such topics are presented in discrete chapters that have no connection with other materials. Yet concepts in almost every chapter have implications for these topics. The Focus boxes are referenced in the chapter to help students understand the relevance of the chapter material for these important management concepts.

Video Cases.
The parts of the text conclude with video cases that illustrate the concepts presented in that part. The sixteen videos enhance class discussion because students can see the company and more directly apply the management theories they have learned. A detailed description of each video, classroom activities, and discussion questions and answers are provided in the *Instructor's Manual*.

Exhibits.
Many aspects of management are research based, and some concepts tend to be abstract and theoretical. To enhance students' awareness and understanding of these concepts, many exhibits have been included throughout the book. These exhibits consolidate key points, indicate relationships among variables, and visually illustrate concepts. They also make effective use of color to enhance their imagery and appeal.

Glossaries.
Learning the management vocabulary is essential to understanding contemporary management. This process is facilitated in three ways. First, key concepts are boldfaced and completely defined where they first appear in the text. Second, brief definitions are set out in the margin for easy review and follow-up. Third, a Glossary summarizing all key terms and definitions appears at the end of the book for handy reference.

Summary and Management Solution and Discussion Questions.
Each chapter closes with a summary of key points that students should retain. In addition, the questions raised in the Management Problem are answered. The discussion questions are a complementary learning tool that will enable students to check their understanding of key issues, to think beyond basic concepts, and to determine areas that require further study. The summary and discussion questions help students discriminate between main and supporting points and provide mechanisms for self-teaching.

Management Exercises.
End-of-chapter exercises called "Manager's Workbook," "Manager's Workshop," and "Surf the 'Net" provide self-tests for students, group exercises, and an opportunity to experience management issues in a personal way. Also, the "Ethical Dilemma" exercises place stu-

dents in real-life situations in which they must take action. All of these exercises take the form of questionnaires, scenarios, and activities, and many also provide an opportunity for students to work in teams.

Case for Critical Analysis. Also appearing at the end of each chapter is a brief but substantive case that provides an opportunity for student analysis and class discussion. Many of these cases are about companies whose names students will recognize; others are based on real management events but the identities of companies and managers have been disguised. These cases allow students to sharpen their diagnostic skills for management problem solving.

Supplementary Materials

Dryden has once again spared no expense to make *Understanding Management* the premier textbook in the market today. Many instructors face large classes with limited resources, and supplementary materials provide a way to expand and improve the students' learning experience. The learning package provided with *Understanding Management* was specifically designed to meet the needs of instructors facing a variety of teaching conditions and to enhance management students' experience of the subject.

Instructor's Manual/Video Teaching Notes. The *Instructor's Manual* has been prepared to provide fundamental support to new professors teaching the course and innovative new materials for experienced professors. Prepared by Thomas Lloyd of Westmoreland County Community College, the manual features Chapter Outlines, Annotated Learning Objectives, and detailed "Lecture Outlines." A section called Company Examples poses questions and provides answers to the in-text examples that are highlighted in each chapter. These additional questions and answers provide instructors new material for class discussion or assignments. The manual also contains answers to chapter discussion questions, teaching notes for the end-of-chapter Ethical Dilemmas, and answers to the case questions.

Prepared by Carol Cirulli, the Video Teaching Notes provide a video outline, references to concepts within the chapter that are discussed in the video, answers to video case discussion questions, individual and group exercises, and a multiple-choice quiz about the video.

Computerized Instructor's Manual. A disk is available to instructors that contains most elements of the *Instructor's Manual.* Teachers can electronically cut and paste together the parts of the manual they desire for customized lecture outlines.

Test Bank. Another important part of the teaching package is the *Test Bank.* This ancillary was given special attention during the preparation of the second edition because instructors desire test questions that accurately and fairly assess student competence in the subject material. The *Test Bank* provides over 1,700 true/false, multiple-choice, short answer, essay, and scenario questions. Each question has been rated for level of difficulty and is designated either as factual or application so that instructors can provide a balanced set of questions for student exams. Also, page numbers where answers may be found are provided for objective questions. The *Test Bank* was prepared by Amit Shah, Frostburg State University.

Computerized Test Bank. The *Computerized Test Bank* is available for Windows- and DOS-based and Macintosh computers and is free to adopters. This item allows instructors to select and edit test items from the printed *Test Bank* as well as add an unlimited number of their own questions. Up to 99 versions of each test can be custom printed.

Study Guide. This guide is invaluable for helping students master management concepts. Prepared by Harold Babson of Columbus State Community College and

Murray Brunton of Central Ohio Technical College, the *Study Guide* provides a chapter outline with a list of corresponding learning objectives, discussion of key chapter concepts, matching questions for key terms, and multiple-choice questions tied to real-life situations. In addition, the Study Guide includes Skill Practice Exercises that are based on "Just Suppose" scenarios. Each chapter also contains Personal Learning Experience exercises that can be assigned as homework or used in class. Students are also encouraged to keep journal entries throughout the course. An Integrated Case with questions completes the chapters.

Transparency Acetates and Masters.
Seventy-five full-color acetates are available to adopters. The acetates are bound and three-hole punched for easy removal and organization in a binder. The 100 Transparency Masters comprise selected art from the textbook for effective display and discussion. Detailed teaching notes accompany the acetates and masters and include summaries of key concepts and discussion questions for in-class use. The transparencies and notes were developed by Charles Beem of Bucks County Community College.

Laser Disc. The laser disc from the first edition of *Understanding Management* is still available to adopters. The disc includes graphic and textual elements from the textbook and support materials integrated with video and animation sequences to provide a dynamic, easy-to-use multimedia presentation of the principles of management.

The Dryden Press will provide complimentary supplements or supplement packages to those adopters qualified under our adoption policy. Please contact your sales representative to learn how you may qualify. If as an adopter or potential user, you receive supplements you do not need, please return them to your sales representative or send them to:

Attn: Returns Department

Troy Warehouse

465 South Lincoln Drive

Troy, MO 63379

ACKNOWLEDGMENTS

A gratifying experience for us was working with the Fort Worth team of dedicated professionals at The Dryden Press who were committed to the vision of producing the best management text ever. We are grateful to Ruth Rominger, whose enthusiasm and ideas kept the book's spirit alive, and to her successor, John Weimeister, for his creative ideas, assistance, and vision for this text. Lisé Johnson provided keen market knowledge and innovative ideas for instructional support. Traci Keller provided superb project coordination and offered excellent ideas and suggestions to help the team meet a demanding and sometimes arduous schedule. Lois West and Becky Dodson coordinated the production team. Burl Sloan successfully blended visual expertise and practical knowledge to produce a quality text design that appeals to both students and instructors. Adele Krause orchestrated the voluminous job of permissions. Jeff Beckham provided the right touch of copyediting. These people brought enormous caring and commitment to this textbook, and I thank each of them very much.

Four other people who made a special contribution to this text are Mara Winick,

Susan Halfhill, Dan Farrell, and Kathy Wohlert. Mara Winick contributed the material on information systems and technology and did a superb job integrating recent developments and applications. Susan Halfhill drafted materials for Appendix A. The expansion of organizational behavior concepts and applications to individual students is a significant contribution to this text. Dan Farrell suggested changes to the history chapter, and Kathy Wohlert suggested changes to the ethics chapter. Their suggestions were excellent, and we gratefully adopted them.

From Dick: Here at Vanderbilt I want to extend special appreciation to my secretary and assistant, Linda Roberts, and my research assistant, Mike Dallas. Linda provided excellent typing and other assistance that gave us time to write. Mike made many trips to the library and provided special help with the ethical dilemmas. I also want to acknowledge an intellectual debt to my colleagues, Alice Andrews, Bruce Barry, Ray Friedman, Tom Mahoney, Rich Oliver, Barry Gerhart, and Greg Stewart. Thanks also to Dean Marty Geisel who supported a variety of my projects and maintained a positive scholarly atmosphere in the school.

From Dorothy: This project was a work of intense proportions, and I could not have managed without a great deal of support from some colleagues. They are Joe Seltzer, Carol and Bill Pendergast, Judith White, Peter Vaill, Bob Rosenfeld, and Eva Jarosova.

Another group of people who made a major contribution to this textbook are the management experts who provided advice, reviews, answers to questions, and suggestions for changes, insertions, and clarifications. We want to thank each of these colleagues for their valuable feedback and suggestions:

Jack Cichy
Davenport College

Martin Lecker
Rockland Community College

Thomas W. Lloyd
Westmoreland County Community College

Amit Shah
Frostburg State University

We also want to thank participants in the focus group in which many of the ideas that shape this textbook were first discussed and fine-tuned. We consider them our advisory panel and deeply appreciate their commitment to excellence:

Judy Bullin
Monroe Community College

Barry Burns
Houston Community College

Bonnie Chavez
Santa Barbara City College

Phyllis Goodman
College of DuPage

Rudy Stippec
Tarrant County Junior College-South Campus

Understanding Management also benefited from the valuable input of management instructors throughout the country. We would especially like to thank those who responded to our questions about how they teach management and who reviewed various parts of the manuscript:

Hal Babson
Columbus State Community College

Barbara Barrett
Merrimac Community College

Kathy Daruty
Pierce College

Helen Davis
University of Kentucky

Joe Galdiano
Normandale Community College

Jenna Johannpeter
Belleville Area College–Granite City Campus

Betty Ann Kirk
Tallahassee Community College

Chad Lewis
Everett Community College

Tom Shaughnessy
Illinois Central Community College

Darrell Thompson
Mountainview College

Bill Vincent
Santa Barbara City Collge

James H. White
North Lake College

We would like to extend a personal word of thanks to the many dedicated authors who contributed to the extensive supplement package for the second edition. Amit Shah has written a wonderful *Test Bank*. Tom Lloyd has made the *Instructor's Manual* a valuable teaching tool with innovative new features. Hal Babson and Murray Brunton have worked hard to ensure that the *Study Guide* reflects the chapter material in the textbook. Charles Beem enhanced the teachability of the Teaching Acetates and Transparency Masters with instructive notes.

We also want to acknowledge our daughters. First, Danielle and Amy, and their husbands, Brian and Gary, for their love and support this past year. We don't live in the same city, but we have developed a wonderful understanding and appreciation for one another, reached in part through the joy of traveling and skiing together. Thanks also to B. J. and Kaitlyn, and Kaci and Matthew for their warmth, silliness, and smiles that brighten our lives during our days together. Finally, Roxanne, Solange, and Elizabeth, who have been closer geographically (i.e, in the same house) and therefore in our daily lives. They have extended patience to us when ours was thin, and have given important emotional balance. Even though Roxanne went back to her school in Southern Bohemia (Czech Republic), she is still in our hearts and thoughts—and on the phone often.

We'd like to pay special tribute to our editorial associate, Pat Lane. This revision is our second project together, and she has spoiled us to the point that we can't imagine how we ever got along on our own. Pat provided truly outstanding help throughout every step of the revision of this text. She skillfully drafted materials for a variety of cases and topics, researched topics when new sources were lacking, and did an absolutely superb job with the copyedited manuscript, galleys, and page proofs. Her commitment to this text enabled us to achieve our dream for its excellence. We also want to thank Chris Atcher and DeeGee Lester. Both pitched in to help with the revision when the time schedule got tight, and Chris also helped with other activities that kept our lives in order during periods of high pressure.

RICHARD L. DAFT
DOROTHY MARCIC
NASHVILLE, TENNESSEE
JULY 1997

BRIEF CONTENTS

CONTENTS

UNDERSTANDING

MANAGEMENT

SECOND
EDITION

In an increasingly competitive environment, organizations today must adapt for survival. The structure of organizations is being reshaped by new challenges, opportunities, and workforces. The impact of technology has also been profound. Together, these changes are nothing short of revolutionary.

The role of managers is changing as swiftly as the face of business. No longer isolated in the organizational hierarchy, managers currently work in teams and share information and decision making with their co-workers. Today's manager must plan well, be flexible, and work within limited resources to meet organizational goals.

In Chapter 1 we explore the changing paradigm of management—both for today and the next century. Chapter 2 presents the current influences on learning organizations and the trends and forces that have shaped and are shaping managers' roles.

Introduction to Management

PART I

The Changing Paradigm of Management

LEARNING OBJECTIVES

After studying this chapter, you should be able to

- Explain the management revolution and how it will affect you as a future manager.

- Describe the four management functions and the type of management activity associated with each.

- Explain the difference between efficiency and effectiveness and their importance for organizational performance.

- Define functional, general, and project managers.

- Describe conceptual, human, and technical skills and their relevance for managers and nonmanagers.

- Define ten roles that managers perform in organizations.

- Describe the learning organization and the issues managers must prepare for in the future.

CHAPTER 1

MANAGEMENT PROBLEM

Sitting in their cramped and windowless warehouse/ office, Kellee McCormack and Eyal Balle crouch behind their makeshift desks of a nightstand and a pile of shoeboxes. Looking at them in these surroundings, wearing their casual denims and T-shirts, it is hard to believe they are entrepreneurs who have built a shoe company from literally nothing in 1993 to one with projected sales of $7 million in 1996.

Rebel Shoes began as a dream by two people who had no experience in the shoe business, but had the instinct to see an opportunity. Eyal's bravado helped him convince a U.S. shoe manufacturer to feature his as-yet-unmade shoe. Armed with only an idea for a comfortable and stylish shoe, Eyal made a trip to his native Israel, where his only contact was his accountant father. He came back with an agreement for $45,000 worth of shoes, with no down payment, and without knowing so much as what a size run was.

With complementary skills of design and accounting, Kellee and Eyal were bound together in the early days by the rush of selling all those shoes. For a while, the office was in Eyal's bedroom and to make deliveries, they jammed up to 17 cases of shoes in the back of Kellee's two-door Volvo.

Rebel's success comes from sticking to the knitting and staying close to customers. They keep on the cutting edge of the fashion shoe business by making twice-yearly trips to shoe shows in Europe, thereby getting a jump on what likely will be popular in the U.S. market. But even every six months is not enough to keep up with the chaotic environment, so they hired a designer in Italy to cruise more shows. Customers are nurtured carefully. Eyal and Kellee make regular calls to buyers and Eyal talks to them "like they're his friends." They learned through hard experience that when a buyer is replaced, they cannot depend on recent sales to continue. Another trip to develop a relationship with the new buyer is crucial. Trust is a key element in their business and customers respond positively to that.

Rebel's makeshift look of cramming six people into two offices does not represent the true picture of a successful company with a national sales manager and 13 sales representatives. Their success is partly attributed to getting good people who had jumped out of sinking companies, thereby "learning from bitter experience." With a tight cash-flow, Eyal managed to barter salaries for some employees and even their advertising photographer—with shoes.[1]

• In the high-flash business of fashion shoes, they could be gone tomorrow. In fact, they have been told to sell the company and get out while they can. What would you do?

Many people may have heard of Rebel Shoes, but few students have heard of Kellee McCormack and Eyal Balle. Most are unfamiliar with the management actions needed to keep a company or a department healthy, inspired, and productive. Today's companies are struggling to remain competitive in the face of increasingly tough global competition, uncertain environments, cutbacks in personnel and resources, and massive worldwide economic, political, and social shifts. The growing diversity of the workforce brings new challenges: maintaining a strong corporate culture while supporting diversity; balancing work and family concerns; and coping with the conflict brought about by the demands of women and ethnic minorities for increased power and responsibility. Workers are asking that managers share rather than hoard power. Organizational structures are becoming flatter, with power and information pushed down and out among fewer layers and with teams of frontline workers playing new roles as decision makers.

Because of these changes, a revolution is taking place in the field of management. A new kind of leader is needed who can guide businesses through this turbulence—a strong leader who recognizes the complexity of today's world and realizes there are no perfect answers.[2] The revolution asks managers to do more with less, to engage whole employees, to see change rather than stability as the nature of things, to consider the needs of the customer as primary, and to create vision and cultural values that allow people to create a truly collaborative workplace. This new management approach is very different from a traditional mind-set that emphasizes tight top-down control, employee separation and specialization, and management by impersonal measurements and analysis. Kellee McCormack and Rebel Shoes are excellent examples of a manager and company that are leading this revolution toward a new management paradigm, or way of thinking.

Making a difference as a manager today and tomorrow requires a different approach from yesterday. Successful departments and organizations don't just happen—they are managed to be that way. Managers in every organization today face major challenges and have the opportunity to make a difference.

Lee Iacocca made a difference at Chrysler Corporation when he rescued it from bankruptcy by reducing internal costs, developing new products, and gaining concessions from lenders, the union, and government. Iacocca transformed Chrysler again by implementing a strategy for developing a new generation of LH cars that appeared beginning in 1993. General William Creech made a difference to the huge Tactical Air Command of the U.S. Air Force when he reversed a sortie rate (number of flights flown with tactical aircraft) that had been declining 7.8 percent a year. Within a year of his appointment as TAC commander, the sortie rate increased 11.2 percent and continued to rise at that rate for five years with no additional people or resources.[3] Jack Stack made a difference at Missouri's Springfield Remanufacturing Company (SRC). In 1980, SRC, an engine remanufacturing subsidiary of what was then International Harvester (IH), was close to folding because of a crippling 172-day strike at the parent company. Stack, a plant manager at IH, organized a group of investors for a $9 million buyout. At the end of its first fiscal year, the company had lost $61,000 on sales of $16 million. Stack thought the only way to turn things around was by getting every worker to think like an owner and to really understand how every nickel saved could make a difference—for the company and for everyone's paycheck. Each week, the company shuts down the machines for 30 minutes while its 800 employees break into small groups and study the latest financial statements. Stack's open-book management paid off. In an industry with millimeter-sized margins, SRC earned 6 percent pretax on sales of $100 million in 1994; SRC employees earned $1.4 million in bonuses.[4] On the international level, Chanut Piyaoui made a difference by changing the somewhat unsavory reputation of Thailand hotels as "places of entertainment," as she delicately phrased it. With little initial capital, Chanut's vision and management skills created Thailand's leading hotel chain. Her Dusit Thani Group was ranked by *Asiamoney* magazine as one of the 100 best-managed companies in Asia.[5]

These managers are not unusual. Every day managers solve difficult problems, turn organizations around, and achieve astonishing performances. Every organization needs skilled managers to be successful.

This textbook introduces and explains the process of management and the changing ways of thinking and perceiving the world that are becoming increasingly critical for managers of today and tomorrow. By reviewing examples of successful and not-so-successful managers, you will learn the fundamentals of management. The challenges Eyal Balle and Kellee McCormack face at Rebel Shoes are not unusual for managers. By the end of this book, you will un-

derstand fundamental management skills for planning, organizing, leading, and controlling a department or an entire organization. In the remainder of this chapter, we will define management and look at the ways in which roles and activities are changing for today's managers. The final section of the chapter talks about the trend toward the learning organization and provides more detail about some of the challenges managers will face in the coming years.

THE DEFINITION OF MANAGEMENT

What do managers like Lee Iacocca, General Creech, and Eyal Balle have in common? They get things done through their organizations. One management scholar, Mary Parker Follett, described management as "the art of getting things done through people."[6] Peter Drucker, a noted management theorist, explains that managers give direction to their organizations, provide leadership, and decide how to use organizational resources to accomplish goals.[7] Getting things done through people and other resources and providing direction and leadership are what managers do. These activities apply not only to top executives such as Lee Iacocca, General Creech, or Eyal Balle but also to a new lieutenant in charge of a TAC maintenance squadron, a supervisor in the Ontario plant that makes Plymouth minivans, and a sales manager at Rebel Shoes. Moreover, management often is considered universal because it uses organizational resources to accomplish goals and attain high performance in all types of profit and not-for-profit organizations. Thus, our definition of management is as follows:

> **Management** is the attainment of organizational goals in an effective and efficient manner through planning, organizing, leading, and controlling organizational resources.

There are two important ideas in this definition: (1) the four functions of planning,

management
The attainment of organizational goals in an effective and efficient manner through planning, organizing, leading, and controlling organizational resources.

E X H I B I T   I . I
The Process of Management

Management Functions

organizing, leading, and controlling and (2) the attainment of organizational goals in an effective and efficient manner. Managers use a multitude of skills to perform these functions. Management's conceptual, human, and technical skills are discussed later in the chapter. Exhibit 1.1 illustrates the process of how managers use resources to attain organizational goals. Although some management theorists identify additional management functions, such as staffing, communicating, or decision making, those additional functions will be discussed as subsets of the four primary functions in Exhibit 1.1. Chapters of this book are devoted to the multiple activities and skills associated with each function, as well as to the environment, global competitiveness, and ethics, which influence how managers perform these functions. The next section begins with a brief overview of the four functions.

THE FOUR MANAGEMENT FUNCTIONS

Planning

Planning defines where the organization wants to be in the future and how to get there. **Planning** means defining goals for

future organizational performance and deciding on the tasks and use of resources needed to attain them. Senior managers at Hewlett-Packard defined a specific plan: over a period of less than a year, to transform a division making microwave test gear into a leader in the hot market for digital video, a transformation James Olson, manager of the division, called "from gearheads into gladiators." In 1994 alone, HP's Video Communications Division signed deals to supply video computers to Pacific Telesis Video Services, BellSouth, Southern New England Telephone, and the government of Singapore. Senior managers at Home Depot have devised extensive plans to increase the number of its stores by 25 percent a year and open 460 new stores in Canada, Mexico, and the United States by 1998.[8]

A lack of planning—or poor planning—can hurt an organization's performance. For example, Ashton-Tate Corporation, a PC software giant ranked in the big three of the industry, tumbled sharply as a result of planning errors attributed to chief executive Edward Esber, Jr. Critics cite Esber's lack of vision in perceiving market direction and a weak planning effort that left too many bugs in the dBASE V software introduction along with failed efforts to develop other software products. Poor planning is a major reason for the sharp decline in Ashton-

planning
The management function concerned with defining goals for future organizational performance and deciding on the tasks and resource use needed to attain them.

Tate's market share and revenue growth rate, producing the company's first net loss of $30 million.[9]

Organizing

Organizing typically follows planning and reflects how the organization tries to accomplish the plan. **Organizing** involves the assignment of tasks, the grouping of tasks into departments, and the allocation of resources to departments. For example, Hewlett-Packard, Sears Roebuck, Xerox, and Digital Equipment have all undergone structural reorganizations to accommodate their changing plans. Semco, a Brazilian company making industrial pumps, mixers, propellers, and other products, reorganized from a highly structured, autocratic business into a company run on trust, freedom, and democracy. Six people, including one woman, rotate as CEO, each putting in six-month stints. Employees set their own work schedules, organizing themselves to accomplish their tasks. Semco's loose organization has been so successful that Mobil, IBM, and hundreds of other U.S. companies have traveled to São Paulo to see the operation firsthand. After meeting CEO Ricardo Semler in 1988, Noel Ginsburg decided to remake Container Industries of Denver in Semco's image. Since then, Container Industries' annual sales have more than doubled, and the money-losing company has become profitable.[10] Honeywell managers reorganized new product development into "tiger teams" consisting of marketing, engineering, and design employees. The new structural design reduced the time to produce a new thermostat from 4 years to 12 months.[11] Many companies today are following Honeywell's lead by reorganizing into teams that have more responsibility for self-management.

Leading

Providing leadership is becoming an increasingly important management function. **Leading** is the use of influence to motivate employees to achieve organizational goals. Leading means creating a shared culture and values, communicating goals to employees throughout the organization, and infusing employees with the desire to perform at a high level. Leading involves motivating entire departments and divisions as well as those individuals working immediately with the manager. In an era of uncertainty, downsizing, international competition, and a growing diversity of the workforce, the ability to shape culture, communicate goals, and motivate employees is critical to business success.

Managers such as Lee Iacocca are exceptional leaders. They are able to communicate their vision throughout the organization and energize employees into action. General Creech was a leader when he improved the motivation of aircraft maintenance technicians in hundreds of maintenance squadrons. Maintenance people previously had been neglected in favor of pilots. Creech set up highly visible bulletin boards displaying pictures of the maintenance crew chiefs, improved their living quarters, and established decent maintenance facilities, complete with paintings and wall murals. He introduced competition among the newly independent maintenance squadrons. He created trophy rooms to hold plaques and other prizes won in maintenance competitions. This prominent display of concern for maintenance specialists greatly increased their motivation to keep the planes flying.

Herb Kelleher, CEO of Southwest Airlines, is a master leader, though some might not think so to see him impersonating Elvis or dressing up as a leprechaun to amuse employees and customers on St. Patrick's Day. Kelleher has built a strong culture at Southwest based on simple, fundamental principles of giving customers what they want and being happy in the work you do. Kelleher thinks the best way to handle stiff competition in the increasingly complex world of business is to get back to the basics. Communication, he says, "must proceed directly from the heart. . . . [It doesn't mean] getting up and giving formal speeches." Kelleher believes each employee

organizing
The management function concerned with assigning tasks, grouping tasks into departments, and allocating resources to departments.

leading
The management function that involves the use of influence to motivate employees to achieve the organization's goals.

must be treated as an individual, and he's been known to visit sick workers from the lowest levels of the company. Southwest's employees are highly productive, largely thanks to Kelleher's philosophy that it's the people on the front lines, not in the front office, who are the heroes. Every employee is encouraged to accept responsibility, solve her own problems, and be a leader. A baggage handler who does his job well is recognized as a leader just as much as a manager would be.[12]

Kelleher's style impacts other managers in the company. Rita Bailey, manager of corporate employment, knows that the main reason Southwest is the best performer in the airline industry is its people. The mission of her 125-member department is to hire and promote to managers the best people available. During the two-hour "conversation" she uses to interview candidates, Bailey studies subtle clues to find out which candidates could relate well to anybody or anything that comes along, which would be good team players, and how willing each would be to pitch in on any job—even blowing up balloons for a festive event. Southwest Treasurer John D. Owen has said the People Department at Southwest "is like the keeper of the flame."[13]

Leadership can have a negative impact, too. Contrast Kelleher's leadership with that of Harding Lawrence of Braniff Airlines. Lawrence's leadership of Braniff was said to contribute to employees' *demotivation*. Lawrence won notoriety on Braniff's Flight 6, which he took weekly to visit his wife, who worked in New York City:

> His tantrums on Flight 6 are legend. On one flight a stewardess served him an entire selection of condiments with his meal instead of asking him which one he preferred. He slammed his fist into the plate, splattering food on the surrounding seats of the first-class cabin. "Don't you ever assume what I want!" he screamed.
>
> "On several occasions flight attendants came to me in tears, fearful of losing their jobs," says Ed Clements,

former director of flight attendant services at Braniff. "I was sickened by what he was doing to the employees."

Lawrence's appearance on an aircraft was likely to arouse two emotions in the crew: fear and hatred.[14]

Inevitably, dissatisfied employees led to dissatisfied customers. Marketing surveys indicated that Braniff was unpopular with many of its passengers. Without a loyal customer base, successful expansion and high performance proved impossible.[15]

Controlling

Controlling is the fourth function in the management process. **Controlling** means monitoring employees' activities, determining whether the organization is on target toward its goals, and making corrections as necessary. Managers must ensure that the organization is moving toward its goals. New trends toward empowerment and trust of employees have led many companies to place less emphasis on top-down control and more emphasis on training employees to monitor and correct themselves. At ISS (International Service System), the Danish company that grew from a local office-cleaning contractor to a $2 billion multinational business, the entire control system is built on the belief that people at all levels will make the right decisions if they are provided with the appropriate information. Frontline employees are thoroughly trained to measure their own performance against company standards and make corrections as needed. Ongoing training programs at Andersen Consulting instill in every employee the company's core values and standards of expected performance, enabling the company to give its employees great freedom without endangering the firm's high standards.[16]

However, managers must realize that what works in one company or one situation may not work in another. C. R. England, a long-haul refrigerated trucking company in Salt Lake City, instituted a strict, computerized control system because

controlling
The management function concerned with monitoring employees' activities, keeping the organization on track toward its goals, and making corrections as needed.

the company was losing money and future prospects were dim. The system monitors about 500 procedures a week, and truckers can earn up to $9,000 a year extra if they meet safety and fuel consumption goals. Every employee is graded weekly based on computerized data. Although such strict control opposes recent trends toward trust and empowerment, it has brought C. R. England from the brink of destruction to be one of the top five companies in its industry. Although workers don't particularly like such close monitoring, turnover actually dropped when the new system was implemented.[17]

Organization failure can occur when managers are not serious about control or lack control information. Robert Fomon, longtime autocratic chief executive of E. F. Hutton, refused to set up control systems because he wanted to supervise senior management personally. At one time he reviewed the salaries and bonuses of more than 1,000 employees, but Hutton grew too big for his personal supervision. To achieve profit goals managers got involved in an undetected check-kiting scheme, and the firm pleaded guilty to 2,000 counts of mail and wire fraud. Other undetected behaviors were the $900,000 in travel and entertainment expenses for one executive in one year and the listing of women from escort services as temporary secretarial help. The lack of control led to Fomon's demise. E. F. Hutton never fully recovered.[18]

ORGANIZATIONAL PERFORMANCE

The other part of our definition of management is the attainment of organizational goals in an efficient and effective manner. Management is so important because organizations are so important. In an industrialized society where complex technologies dominate, organizations bring together knowledge, people, and raw materials to perform tasks no individual could do alone. Without organizations, how could 17,000 airline flights a day be accomplished without an accident, electricity produced from large dams or nuclear power generators, millions of automobiles manufactured, or hundreds of films, videos, and compact disks made available for our entertainment? Organizations pervade our society. Most college students will work in an organization—perhaps Federated Department Stores, Boise Cascade, an Internet company, or a start-up of their own. College students already are members of several organizations, such as a university, junior college, YMCA, church, fraternity, or sorority. College students also deal with organizations every day: to renew a driver's license, be treated in a hospital emergency room, buy food from a supermarket, eat in a restaurant, or buy new clothes. Managers are responsible for these organizations and for seeing that resources are used wisely to attain organizational goals.

Our formal definition of an **organization** is a social entity that is goal directed and deliberately structured. *Social entity* means being made up of two or more people. *Goal directed* means designed to achieve some outcome, such as make a profit (LA Gear, Mack Trucks), win pay increases for members (AFL-CIO), meet spiritual needs (Methodist church), or provide social satisfaction (college sorority). *Deliberately structured* means that tasks are divided and responsibility for their performance assigned to organization members. This definition applies to all organizations, including both profit and not-for-profit. Vickery Stoughton runs Toronto General Hospital and manages a $200 million budget. He endures intense public scrutiny, heavy government regulation, and daily crises of life and death. Hamilton Jordan, formerly President Carter's chief of staff, created a new organization called the Association of Tennis Professionals that has taken control of the professional tennis circuit. John and Marie Bouchard launched a small business called Wild Things that sells goods for outdoor activities. Small, offbeat, and not-for-profit organizations are more numerous than large, visible corporations—and just as important to society.

organization
A social entity that is goal directed and deliberately structured.

effectiveness
The degree to which the organization achieves a stated goal.

efficiency
The use of minimal resources—raw materials, money, and people—to produce a desired volume of output.

performance
The organization's ability to attain its goals by using resources in an efficient and effective manner.

Based on our definition of management, the manager's responsibility is to coordinate resources in an effective and efficient manner to accomplish the organization's goals. Organizational **effectiveness** is the degree to which the organization achieves a stated goal. It means that the organization succeeds in accomplishing what it tries to do. Organizational effectiveness means providing a product or service that customers value. Organizational **efficiency** refers to the amount of resources used to achieve an organizational goal. It is based on how much raw material, money, and people are necessary for producing a given volume of output. Efficiency can be calculated as the amount of resources used to produce a product or service.

Efficiency and effectiveness can both be high in the same organization. For example, Chrysler has reinvented itself from the executive office to the shop floor, enabling the company to cut costs and speed up the introduction of new models such as the popular Neon. The leadership of Dick Dauch, vice president of manufacturing, has contributed to the startling increase in efficiency. Chrysler can now build 8,000 cars and trucks a day compared with 4,500 a few years ago, and the number of worker-hours per vehicle has shrunk from 175 to 102. Likewise, management efforts to decentralize decision making and stay on top of technological developments enable Nucor Steel's Crawfordsville, Indiana, plant to produce a ton of flat-rolled steel in less than one worker-hour, compared with an average of four worker-hours elsewhere.[19] In addition to increasing efficiency, managers at Chrysler and Nucor improved effectiveness, shown in better product quality, increased revenues, and higher profits.

Managers in other organizations, especially service firms, are improving efficiency and effectiveness, too. Labor shortages in the Midwest and northeastern United States have prompted managers to find laborsaving tricks. Burger King and Taco Bell restaurants let customers serve themselves drinks. Sleep Inn hotels have a washer and dryer installed behind the desk so that clerks can launder sheets and towels while waiting on customers.[20] Susan O'Malley dramatically improved effectiveness when she took over as president of the Washington Bullets (now the Washington Wizards) basketball team. Through a combination of intense nurturing of season ticketholders and shrewd marketing, O'Malley led the team from only one sellout crowd during the 1988–89 season to 25 sellouts in 1994–95. The organization is once again making money rather than losing it.[21]

The ultimate responsibility of managers, then, is to achieve high **performance,** which is the attainment of organizational goals by using resources in an efficient and effective manner. One example of extraordinary performance in the entertainment industry is the Grateful Dead rock band.

■ BUSINESS AT THE GRATEFUL DEAD

News of Jerry Garcia's death in August 1995 stunned the music industry, and millions of Grateful Dead fans mourned the loss of a consummate artist whose words and music spanned generations. Few people remember the other side of Garcia—the leader who helped manage a successful business. Garcia rotated with each band member to share responsibility as chief financial and executive officer of Grateful Dead Productions (GDP). The carefully managed business behind the Grateful Dead was largely responsible for the group's financial success and its almost unmatched 29 years of performing the same program to sellout crowds.

Perhaps the service GDP's customers appreciated most was the band's ticketing business, which distributed nearly half of all Dead concert tickets directly to fans. The group listened to customers and gave them what they wanted. Most rock bands forbid tape-recording at concerts to prevent copyright infringement, yet the Dead would rope off a portion of the concert floor just for "tapeheads."

The band members jointly made major management decisions, but they empowered GDP's 60 or so employees to run the day-to-day business of the group. GDP employees, who earned good salaries and enjoyed extensive benefits, profit sharing, bonuses, and say so, did everything from moving the band from concert to concert to handling catalog merchandising, a publishing company, and a non-profit foundation. Employees felt like part of the business, and staff turnover was low in an industry known for its instability.

Management counts. The Grateful Dead successfully balanced control and delegation to run a thriving business and keep doing what they loved to do for nearly three decades. They created an organization with a powerful culture, a significant vision, and the motivation of human energy that set a great orgnization apart from the crowd.[22] ■

Whether managers are responsible for the organization as a whole, such as the Grateful Dead, or for a single department or division, such as Rita Bailey at Southwest Airlines, their ultimate responsibility is performance.

MANAGEMENT SKILLS

A manager's job is complex and multidimensional and, as we shall see throughout this book, requires a range of skills. Although some management theorists propose a long list of skills, the necessary skills for managing a department or an organization can be summarized in three categories: conceptual, human, and technical.[23] As illustrated in Exhibit 1.2, the application of these skills changes as managers move up in the organization. Though the degree of each skill necessary at different levels of an organization may vary, all managers must possess skills in each of these important areas to perform effectively.

Conceptual Skills

Conceptual skill is the cognitive ability to see the organization as a whole and the relationship among its parts. Conceptual skill involves the manager's thinking, information processing, and planning abilities. It involves knowing where one's department fits into the total organization and how the organization fits into the industry, the community, and the broader business and social environment. It means the ability to "think strategically"—to take the broad, long-term view.

Conceptual skills are needed by all managers but are especially important for managers at the top. They must perceive significant elements in a situation and broad, conceptual patterns. For example, Microsoft Corporation, the giant software company, reflects the conceptual skills of its founder and chairman, Bill Gates. Overall business goals are clearly stated and effectively communicated throughout the company, contributing to Microsoft's leadership reputation and billion-dollar revenues. While actively participating in and coordinating small units devoted to functional areas such as programming and marketing, Gates spreads his concept for Microsoft by delegating to a cadre of strong managers. As Scott Oki, senior vice president for U.S. sales and marketing, pointed out, "Each part of the company has a life of its own now, but Bill [Gates] is the glue that holds it all together."[24]

As managers move up the hierarchy, they must develop conceptual skills or their promotability will be limited. A senior engineering manager who is mired in technical matters rather than thinking strategically will not perform well at the top of the orga-

conceptual skill
The cognitive ability to see the organization as a whole and the relationship among its parts.

Management Level			
Top Managers	Conceptual Skills		
Middle Managers		Human Skills	
First-Line Managers			Technical Skills
Nonmanagers (Personnel)			

EXHIBIT 1.2
Relationship of Conceptual, Human, and Technical Skills to Management Level

John Dasburg, president and CEO of Northwest Airlines, knows that *human skills* become even more important with the increase in globalization and workforce diversity. A recent trip to Asia strengthened relationships with the Japanese government and Pacific-region personnel. Dasburg thanked employees such as Sachiko Takeda, Tokyo passenger sales, and Jun Mokudai, vice president of marketing and sales, Japan, for their valuable contributions to Northwest's success.

nization. Many of the responsibilities of top managers, such as decision making, resource allocation, and innovation, require a broad view.

Human Skills

human skill
The ability to work with and through other people and to work effectively as a group member.

Human skill is the manager's ability to work with and through other people and to work effectively as a group member. This skill is demonstrated in the way a manager relates to other people, including the ability to motivate, facilitate, coordinate, lead, communicate, and resolve conflicts. A manager with human skills allows subordinates to express themselves without fear of ridicule and encourages participation. As manager of corporate employment for Southwest Airlines, a company that relies heavily on the quality of its people for its success, Rita Bailey uses human skills daily to communicate effectively with other employees in the department as well as to gauge the abilities of applicants to work within Southwest's strong culture. Her ability to lead comfortable yet informative group interviews requires immense human skills. A manager with human skills likes other people and is liked by them. Barry

Merkin, chairman of Dresher, Inc., the largest U.S. manufacturer of brass beds, is a cheerleader for his employees. He visits the plant floor and uses humor and hoopla to motivate them. Employees may have buckets of fried chicken served to them by supervisors wearing chef's hats.

In recent years, awareness of the importance of human skills has increased. Such books as *In Search of Excellence* and *A Passion for Excellence* were among the first to stress the need for managers to take care of the human side of the organization. As globalization and workforce diversity increase, human skills become even more crucial. To encourage Singaporean workers who make paging devices to collaborate with a sister plant in Florida, Motorola, Inc., managers flew the workers to a Colorado resort for bonding and team-building exercises. Excellent managers do not take people for granted. John Vanderpoel, a team leader at American Express Financial Advisors, occasionally takes his 20-member team out to dinner to celebrate team accomplishments. Former auto racer Roger Penske, who purchased struggling Detroit Diesel Corporation from General Motors, focused on people to turn the company around. He answered questions from hundreds of employees and met regularly with union workers to solve problems. Penske used his human skills to motivate workers toward speedy and courteous response to customers. The result was a 25 percent increase in Penske's share of heavy-truck engine sales during the first year.[25] Effective managers are cheerleaders, facilitators, coaches, and nurturers. They build through people. Effective human skills enable managers to unleash subordinates' energy and help them grow as future managers.

Technical Skills

Technical skill is the understanding of and proficiency in the performance of specific tasks. Technical skill includes mastery of the methods, techniques, and equipment involved in specific functions such as engineering, manufacturing, or finance. Technical skill also includes specialized knowledge, analytical ability, and the competent use of tools and techniques to solve problems in that specific discipline. Rodney Mott, plant manager at Nucor Corp.'s new Hickman, Arkansas, steel mill, needed technical skills to decide on the installation of a new $50 million caster, which turns liquid metal into bands of steel. The move nearly doubled the Hickman plant's capacity, to 36,000 tons a week.[26] Technical skills are particularly important at lower organizational levels. Many managers get promoted to their first management job by having excellent technical skills. However, technical skills become less important than human and conceptual skills as managers move up the hierarchy.

MANAGEMENT TYPES

Managers use conceptual, human, and technical skills to perform the four management functions of planning, organizing, leading, and controlling in all organizations—large and small, manufacturing and service, profit and not-for-profit. But not all managers' jobs are the same. Managers are responsible for different departments, work at different levels in the hierarchy, and meet different requirements for achieving high performance. For example, Mary Lee Bowen is a middle manager at Rubbermaid, responsible for teams that create new home organization and bath accessories products. Phillip Knight is chief executive officer for Nike, world leader in sports shoe design and manufacturing.[27] Both are managers, and both must contribute to planning, organizing, leading, and controlling their organizations—but in different amounts and ways.

Vertical Differences

An important determinant of the manager's job is hierarchical level. Three levels in the hierarchy are illustrated in Exhibit 1.3. **Top managers** are at the top of the hierarchy and are responsible for the entire organization. They have such titles as president, chairperson, executive director, chief executive officer (CEO), and executive vice president. Top managers are responsible for setting organizational goals, defining strategies for achieving them, monitoring and interpreting the external environment, and making decisions that affect the entire organization. They look to the long-term future and concern themselves with general environmental trends and the organization's overall success. Among the most important responsibilities for top managers are communicating a shared vision for the organization, shaping corporate culture, and nurturing an entrepreneurial spirit that can help the company keep pace with rapid change. Today more than ever before, top managers must engage the unique knowledge, skills, and capabilities of each employee.[28]

Middle managers work at middle levels of the organization and are responsible for business units and major departments. Examples of middle managers are department head, division head, manager of quality control, and director of the research lab. Middle managers typically have two or more management levels beneath them. They are responsible for implementing the

technical skill
The understanding of and proficiency in the performance of specific tasks.

top manager
A manager who is at the top of the organizational hierarchy and is responsible for the entire organization.

middle manager
A manager who works at the middle levels of the organization and is responsible for major departments.

EXHIBIT 1.3
Management Levels in the Organizational Hierarchy

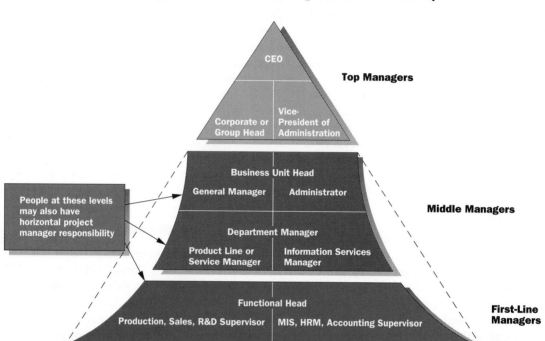

SOURCE: Adapted from Thomas V. Bonoma and Joseph C. Lawler, "Chutes and Ladders: Growing the General Manager," *Sloan Management Review* (Spring 1989), 27–37.

overall strategies and policies defined by top managers. Middle managers are concerned with the near future, are expected to establish good relationships with peers around the organization, encourage teamwork, and resolve conflicts.

Recent trends in corporate restructuring and downsizing have made the middle manager's job difficult. Many companies have become lean and efficient by laying off middle managers and by slashing middle management levels. Traditional pyramidal organization charts are flattening, allowing information to flow quickly from top to bottom and decisions to be made with the greater speed necessary in today's highly competitive global marketplace. The shrinking middle management is illustrated in Exhibit 1.3. For example, Eastman Kodak recently cut middle management by 30 percent and reduced its middle management levels from seven to three. The Medical Systems Group at General Electric cut middle management by 35 percent. These cuts have improved the efficiency and performance of many corporations via improved responsiveness to customers, speed in new product development, and increased profits.[29] The decline in middle management and the simultaneous improvement in corporate efficiency are partly due to the increased use of project managers, or team managers. A **project manager** is responsible for a temporary work project that involves the participation of other people at a similar level in the organization. Project managers manage horizontally and give up their management responsibilities when the project is finished. Also, a manager of one project may be a team member on another project. The participation of managers in different projects and managing horizontally without adding positions to the hierarchy enable an organization to get the most from its middle management resources.

First-line managers are directly responsible for the production of goods and services. They are the first or second level of management and have such titles as supervisor, line manager, section chief, and office manager. They are responsible for groups of nonmanagement employees. Their primary concern is the application of rules and procedures to achieve efficient production, provide technical assistance, and motivate subordinates. The time horizon at this level is short, with the emphasis on accomplishing day-to-day goals.

Horizontal Differences

The other major difference in management jobs occurs horizontally across the organization. **Functional managers** are responsible for departments that perform a single functional task and have employees with similar training and skills. Functional departments include advertising, sales, finance, human resources, manufacturing, and accounting. Line managers are responsible for the manufacturing and marketing departments that make or sell the product or service. Staff managers are in charge of departments such as finance and human resources that support line departments.

General managers are responsible for several departments that perform different functions. A general manager is responsible for a self-contained division, such as a Dillard's department store, and for all of the

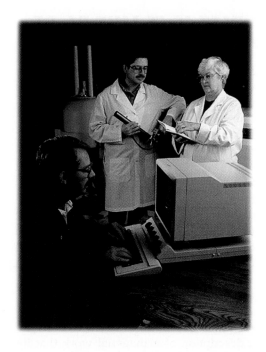

Project manager Francis Timmers (standing), coordinated the cross-functional team that developed Dow Chemical's new catalyst technology, called Insite, which dramatically improves the value of the company's polyolefin products. To develop new ideas into products and bring them to market more effectively, Dow assigns a leader to stay with each project from the idea stage through commercial launch, working with people throughout the organization to meet project goals.

functional departments within it. Project managers also have general management responsibility, because they coordinate people across several departments to accomplish a specific project.

Project management is a vital role in today's flatter, delayered organizations and enables middle managers to contribute significantly to corporate success.[30] As executive vice president William Kelvie, chief information officer for the Federal National Mortgage Association (FannieMae), said, "Automation and empowerment take away the need to have managers oversee the day-to-day work. Everything has become projects. This is the way FannieMae does business today."[31] Companies as diverse as consumer products and aerospace firms use project managers to coordinate people from marketing, manufacturing, finance, and production when a new product is developed. As corporations continue to reduce hierarchical levels and move toward flatter, more horizontal structures, more people with project management skills will be needed. Project managers need significant human skills, because they coordinate diverse people to attain project goals.

project manager
A manager responsible for a temporary work project that involves the participation of other people at a similar level in the organization.

first-line manager
A manager who is at the first or second management level and is directly responsible for the production of goods and services.

functional manager
A manager who is responsible for a department that performs a single functional task and has employees with similar training and skills.

general manager
A manager who is responsible for several departments that perform different functions.

WHAT IS IT LIKE TO BE A MANAGER?

So far we have described how managers at various levels perform four basic functions that help ensure that organizational resources are used to attain high levels of performance. These tasks require conceptual, human, and technical skills. Unless someone has actually performed managerial work, it is hard to understand exactly what managers do on an hour-by-hour, day-to-day basis. The manager's job is so diverse that a number of studies have been undertaken in an attempt to describe exactly what happens. The question of what managers actually do to plan, organize, lead, and control was answered by Henry Mintzberg, who followed managers around and recorded all their activities.[32] He developed a description of managerial work that included three general characteristics and ten roles. These characteristics and roles have been supported in subsequent research.[33]

Manager Activities

One of the most interesting findings about managerial activities is how busy managers are and how hectic the average workday can be. For Hugh Murphy, operations manager of O'Hare International Airport, the nature of managerial work means he is picking up litter and tossing out cups left on windowsills one minute, then virtually the next minute making complex arrangements for an unexpected landing of Vice President Al Gore in Air Force Two. Immediately after greeting the vice president, Murphy zips back to his office to check his phone messages and return any urgent ones, then consults with computer technicians to make sure a critical malfunction of five security checkpoints has been corrected.[34]

Managerial Activity is Characterized by Variety, Fragmentation, and Brevity.[35] The manager's involvements are so widespread and voluminous that there is little time for quiet reflection. The

average time spent on any one activity is less than nine minutes. Managers shift gears quickly. Significant crises are interspersed with trivial events in no predictable sequence.[36] One example of just two hours for a typical general manager, Janet Howard, follows. Note the frequent interruptions, brevity, and variety.

> 7:30 A.M. Janet arrives at work and begins to plan her day.
>
> 7:37 A.M. A subordinate, Morgan Cook, stops in Janet's office to discuss a dinner party the previous night and to review the cost-benefit analysis for a proposed microcomputer.
>
> 7:45 A.M. Janet's secretary, Pat, motions for Janet to pick up the telephone. "Janet, they had serious water damage at the downtown office last night. A pipe broke, causing about $50,000 damage. Everything will be back in shape in three days. Thought you should know."
>
> 8:00 A.M. Pat brings in the mail. She also asks instructions for typing a report Janet gave her yesterday.
>
> 8:14 A.M. Janet gets a phone call from the accounting manager, who is returning a call from the day before. They talk about an accounting report.
>
> 8:25 A.M. A Mr. Nance is ushered in. Mr. Nance complains that a sales manager mistreats his employees and something must be done. Janet rearranges her schedule to investigate this claim.
>
> 9:00 A.M. Janet returns to the mail. One letter is from an irate customer. Janet dictates a helpful, restrained reply. Pat brings in phone messages.
>
> 9:15 A.M. Janet receives an urgent phone call from Larry Baldwin. They go back and forth talking about lost business, unhappy subordinates, a potential promotion, and what should be done.[37]

The Manager Performs a Great Deal of Work at an Unrelenting Pace.[38]
Managers' work is fast paced and requires great energy. The managers observed by Mintzberg processed 36 pieces of mail each

day, attended eight meetings, and took a tour through the building or plant. As soon as a manager's daily calendar is set, unexpected disturbances erupt. New meetings are required. During time away from the office, executives catch up on work-related reading and paperwork.

At O'Hare, an unofficial count one October Friday found operations manager Hugh Murphy interacting with about 45 airport employees. In addition, he listened to complaints from local residents about airport noise, met with disgruntled executives of a French firm who built the airport's new $128 million people-mover system, attempted to soothe a Hispanic city alderman who complained that Mexicana Airlines passengers were being singled out by overzealous tow-truck operators, toured the airport's new fire station, and visited the construction site for the new $20 million tower. Hugh Murphy's unrelenting pace is typical for managers. Said Aviation Commissioner David Mosena, Murphy's boss, "There are days I've had to tell him to go home and go to bed."[39]

Manager Roles

Mintzberg's observations and subsequent research indicate that diverse manager activities can be organized into ten roles.[40] A **role** is a set of expectations for a manager's behavior. Exhibit 1.4 provides examples of each of the ten roles. These roles are divided into three conceptual categories: informational (managing by information); interpersonal (managing through people); and decisional (managing action). Each role represents activities that managers undertake to ultimately accomplish the functions of planning, organizing, leading, and controlling. Although it is necessary to separate the components of the manager's job to understand the different roles and activities of a manager, it is important to remember that the real job of management cannot be practiced as a set of independent parts; all the roles interact in the real world of management. As Mintzberg says, "The manager who only communicates or only conceives

never gets anything done, while the manager who only 'does' ends up doing it all alone."[41]

Informational Roles. Informational roles describe the activities used to maintain and develop an information network. General managers spend about 75 percent of their time talking to other people. The *monitor* role involves seeking current information from many sources. The manager acquires information from others and scans written materials to stay well informed. One manager at a Canadian insurance company takes a turn at the switchboard every 40 days, plugging directly into customer and employee satisfaction.[42] The *disseminator* and *spokesperson* roles are just the opposite: The manager transmits current information to others, both inside and outside the organization, who can use it. With the trend toward empowerment of lower-level employees, many managers are sharing as much information as possible. At Oticon, a $100 million company that has revolutionized the hearing aid industry, CEO Lars Kolind sees the dissemination of knowledge as vital to the company's ability to innovate. For an interesting example of the spokesperson role, consider the Danish captain of an SAS airplane as "manager" of the flight. Just after takeoff, the plane experienced engine trouble and the crew and passengers spent a harrowing 25 minutes to get safely back on the ground. Captain Ebbe Starcke did something unique: during the descent, acting as spokesperson for the airline and the crew, Starcke never stopped talking to the passengers—in both Danish and English—explaining exactly what was happening and what was being done to solve the problem. By the time the plane landed, Captain Starcke was a hero to a lot of people—some of whom determined to always fly SAS whenever they had a choice.[43]

Interpersonal Roles. Interpersonal roles pertain to relationships with others and are related to the human skills described earlier. The *figurehead* role involves

role
A set of expectations for one's behavior.

E X H I B I T   1 . 4
Ten Manager Roles

Category	Role	Activity
Informational	**Monitor**	Seek and receive information, scan periodicals and reports; maintain personal contacts.
	Disseminator	Forward information to other organization members; send memos and reports; make phone calls.
	Spokesperson	Transmit information to outsiders through speeches, reports, memos.
Interpersonal	**Figurehead**	Perform ceremonial and symbolic studies such as greeting visitors, signing legal documents.
	Leader	Direct and motivate subordinates; train, counsel, and communicate with subordinates.
	Liaison	Maintain information links both inside and outside organization; use mail, phone calls, meetings.
Decisional	**Entrepreneur**	Initiate improvement projects; identify new ideas; delegate idea responsibility to others.
	Disturbance handler	Take corrective action during disputes or crises; resolve conflicts among subordinates; adapt to environmental crises.
	Resource allocator	Decide who gets resources; schedule, budget, set priorities.
	Negotiator	Represent department during negotiation of union contracts, sales, purchases, budgets; represent departmental interests.

SOURCES: Adapted from Henry Mintzberg, *The Nature of Managerial Work* (New York: Harper & Row, 1973), 92–93; and Henry Mintzberg, "Managerial Work: Analysis from Observation," *Management Science* 18 (1971), B97–B110.

handling ceremonial and symbolic activities for the department or organization. The manager represents the organization in his or her formal managerial capacity as the head of the unit. The presentation of employee awards by a division manager at Taco Bell is an example of the figurehead role. The *leader* role encompasses relationships with subordinates, including motivation, communication, and influence. The *liaison* role pertains to the development of information sources both inside and outside the organization. An example is a face-to-face discussion between a controller and plan supervisor to resolve a misunderstanding about the budget.

Decisional Roles.   Decisional roles pertain to those events about which the manager must make a choice and take action. These roles often require conceptual as well as human skills. The *entrepreneur* role involves the initiation of change. Managers and entrepreneurs are constantly thinking

about the future and how to get there.[44] An example of such an entrepreneur is Zubair M. Kazi.

 HIGH FLYING FRANCHISEE SOARS ON THE (CHICKEN) WINGS OF SUCCESS

Zubair M. Kazi may own four different homes—one worth $4 million—and six Mercedes-Benz cars, but 25 years ago he earned $2.00 an hour or less as a cook's helper at Kentucky Fried Chicken. Zubair's determination and hard work led to his current ownership of 50 KFC franchises.

What is the "secret recipe" to his success? New ideas and motivated workers who always, always put the needs of the customer on the highest pedestal of serving plates.

Zubair says it generally takes 12–18 months to turn around a store, for that is how long it takes customers to realize the change. He has learned the route to success in a new store: replace feeble kitchen equipment, re-train workers, and remodel the front of the store. Dark colors go and more lighting is added. Workers are trained to be pleasant to customers and greet them as they enter. Essential to re-engineering managers is giving them autonomy. Even if they do something that he does not think is such a great idea—such as suspending a TV so diners can watch sports events—he keeps his mouth shut, figuring even if the idea fails, the manager will have learned an important lesson.

Zubair still scouts for new locations. Now the motive is less one of improving his financial portfolio as it is providing for his employees, half of whom are minorities. Getting this far has taken him so long, "because the foundation of the business has to be very strong and solid," he says. "Now I am ready for real growth."[45] ∎

Managers become aware of problems and search for improvement projects that will correct them. One manager studied by Mintzberg had 50 improvement projects going simultaneously. The *disturbance handler* role involves resolving conflicts among subordinates or between the manager's department and other departments. For example, the division manager for a large furniture manufacturer got involved in a personal dispute between two section heads. One section head was let go because he did not fit the team. The *resource allocator* role pertains to decisions about how to allocate people, time, equipment, budget, and other resources to attain desired outcomes. The manager must decide which projects receive budget allocations, which of several customer complaints receive priority, and even how to spend his or her own time. The *negotiator* role involves formal negotiations and bargaining to attain outcomes for the manager's unit of responsibility. For example, the manager meets and formally negotiates with others—a supplier about a late delivery, the controller about the need for additional budget resources, or the union about a worker grievance—during the normal workday.

MANAGING IN SMALL BUSINESSES AND NOT-FOR-PROFIT ORGANIZATIONS

Small businesses are growing in importance. Hundreds of small businesses are opened every month by people who have found themselves squeezed out of the corporation due to downsizing or who voluntarily leave the corporate world to seek a slower pace and a healthier balance between work and family life. Many small businesses are opened by women or minorities who found limited opportunities for advancement in large corporations.

As even the smallest businesses become increasingly complicated due to globalization, government regulation, and customer demands for better quality at lower prices, managerial dexterity is critical to success. A 1994 survey on trends and future developments in small business found that nearly half of the respondents saw inadequate management skills as a threat to their companies, as compared to less than 25 percent in larger companies.[46]

One interesting finding is that managers in small businesses tend to emphasize roles different from those of managers in large corporations. Managers in small companies often see their most important role as spokesperson, because they must promote the small, growing company to the outside world. The entrepreneur role is also very important in small businesses, because managers must be creative and help their organizations develop new ideas to be competitive. Small-business managers tend to rate lower on the leader role and on information-processing roles compared with counterparts in large corporations.

Not-for-profit organizations also represent a major application of management talent. The Salvation Army, the Girl Scouts, universities, city governments, hospitals, public schools, symphonies, and art museums all require excellent management. Sometimes managers in not-for-profit organizations have been leaders in creating a sense of purpose and mission that motivates employees, empowering workers to try new ideas, and trimming overlong vertical hierarchies.[47] We might expect managers in not-for-profits to place more emphasis on the roles of figurehead (to deal with the public), leader (to motivate employees with fewer financial incentives), and resource allocator (to distribute government resources that often are assigned top down).

As the world of small and not-for-profit organizations becomes increasingly complex, managers should carefully integrate the three categories of roles: They must simultaneously manage by information, manage through people, and manage through action to keep their organizations healthy. Chapter 6 provides an in-depth look at the world of small business management.

paradigm
A mind-set that presents a fundamental way of thinking about, perceiving, and understanding the world.

LEADING THE MANAGEMENT REVOLUTION

One final question: How do you learn to be a manager for the year 2000 in an uncertain and rapidly changing world? How can a course in management or a college degree in business prepare you to face the challenges of the twenty-first century?

Management is both an art and a science. It is an art because many skills cannot be learned from a textbook. Management takes practice, just like golf, tennis, or skating. Management is also a science because a growing body of knowledge and objective facts describes management and how to obtain organizational effectiveness. This knowledge can be conveyed through teaching and textbooks. Becoming a successful manager requires a blend of formal learning and practice, of art and science.

Students today will be leaders tomorrow, leading the management revolution that will change organizations for the twenty-first century. One of the most important contributions a textbook or a management course can make today is to define for students some of the forces that will affect their jobs as managers tomorrow.

Preparing for the Year 2000

Over the next few years, managers will have to rely heavily on human skills and conceptual skills, but they will apply them in new ways. Major changes on the horizon for which managers must prepare include paradigm shifts, chaos theory, workplace diversity, and globalization.

Paradigm Shifts. A **paradigm** is a mind-set that presents a fundamental way of thinking about, perceiving, and understanding the world. Our beliefs and understandings direct our behavior. Shifts in ways of thinking are occurring in our society, and these in turn are associated with shifts in understanding and behavior in organizations. Changing one's management paradigm is not easy, but it is becoming increasingly important in a world of rapidly changing products, technologies, and management techniques. In a recent survey, change emerged as the most common problem facing today's organizations.[48] Not too many years ago, Swiss companies made the best watches in the world, cornering 65 percent of sales and 80 percent of profits. A paradigm shift in the fundamental rules of watchmaking from mechanical to electronic dropped Swiss market share to 10 percent and profits to less than 20 percent. Another shift is in the speed with which work must be accomplished. Ford, Honda, and Chrysler have cut the time to develop a new car from five years to three, thus demanding new ways of thinking and organizing. In the new paradigm, organizations are based more on teamwork, face-to-face interaction, frequent innovations, and continuous learning and improvement rather than on hierarchy and strict schedules and procedures. Managers must become facilitators, partners, and risk takers who help all employees find and use their own power and energy responsibly. The paradigm that dominated the latter part of the twentieth century is compared to the twenty-first-century paradigm in Exhibit 1.5.

Chaos Theory. The new science of chaos theory reveals the existence of ran-

	Late-Twentieth-Century Paradigm	**Twenty-First-Century Paradigm**
Culture	Stability, efficiency	Change, problem solving
Technology	Mechanical	Electronic
Tasks	Physical	Mental, idea-based
Hierarchy	Vertical	Horizontal
Power/Control	Top management	Widely dispersed
Career Goals	Security	Personal growth/Mastery
Leadership	Autocratic	Transformational
Workforce	Homogeneous	Culturally diverse
Doing Work	By individuals	By teams
Markets	Local, domestic	Global
Focus	Profits	Customers
Resources	Capital	Information
Quality	What's affordable	No exceptions

EXHIBIT 1.5
The Shifting Management Paradigm

SOURCES: John A. Byrne, "Paradigms For Postmodern Managers," *Business Week/Reinventing America* (1992), 62–63; and George Land and Beth Jarman, *Breakpoint and Beyond* (New York: Harper Business, 1992).

domness and disorder within larger patterns of order. This means that day-to-day events for most organizations are random and unpredictable. Chaos theory will be associated with a paradigm shift away from the belief that managers can predict and control future events toward a management philosophy that organizations must become fluid and adaptable and stay connected to customers and the environment on a day-to-day basis. Recent television commercials by companies such as Honda and AT&T have incorporated elements of chaos theory to sell their products and services, reminding customers that today's business world is uncertain and that seemingly insignificant changes can have far-reaching impact. In this climate, managers may become less concerned with detailed planning and control, orienting themselves instead toward facilitating teams and managing overall patterns, not day-to-day events.[49]

Workplace Diversity. The increasing diversity of people within organizations is reflected in several ways. The number of male students in business education has been stable since the mid-1970s. The increase of students has been accounted for by women, who now constitute 45 percent of all bachelor degrees in business. Recent studies project that in the twenty-first century, Asian Americans, African Americans, and Latinos will make up 85 percent of U.S. population growth and will constitute about 30 percent of the total workforce.[50] Diversity will be not only a public relations issue but also a strategic one, and the ability to attract and keep a talented, diverse workforce may become the most competitive advantage a company has.[51] People from diverse ethnic and cultural backgrounds offer varying styles, and organizations must learn to welcome and incorporate this diversity into the upper ranks. Some research indicates, for example, that women have a different, and often superior, management style, as discussed in the Focus on Diversity box. Managers must learn to motivate and lead different types of people and to attract the best people from these groups. U.S.-born white males will make up only about 15 percent of the new entrants into the labor force.[52]

Globalization. Among the many factors influencing business in the coming years, globalization may have the greatest repercussions. Managers in U.S. companies will have their work cut out for them as trade barriers continue to fall, opening up new markets and spurring the growth of new competitors both at home and internationally.[53] Goods, money, and people are crossing borders as never before. Some large U.S. companies, like Johnson & Johnson, Gillette, Corning, Coca-Cola, and Xerox, now generate more than half their revenues

FOCUS ON DIVERSITY
DO WOMEN MANAGE DIFFERENTLY?

CEO Linda Wachner acquired Warnaco, Inc., in the mid-1980s, increasing sales to $563 million in 1991. Under her leadership, the lingerie company is achieving her vision of becoming the "Coca-Cola of the bra business." Despite her success, however, Wachner, like other women managers, cannot escape the "too soft or too strident" assessment trap. Her tough leadership style has drawn the complaint that she is "very, very difficult to work for." If she is not tough, she is perceived as too soft to run a large corporation.

Buoyed by reputations as nurturing, inclusive, and natural sharers of information, women managers are touted by many as being ideally suited to the flattened organization of the 1990s. Women are comfortable persuading, encouraging, and motivating, while men often want to issue orders and have them followed. Enthusiastic proponents of a female managerial style argue that early socialization and skills that grew from home and family experiences give women somewhat better human skills than men. Indeed, people often expect these skills, and when a woman manages aggressively she may be unfairly criticized as too tough.

"Feminine" qualities such as openness, encouragement, understanding, sensitivity, and consensus building appear to fit the requirements of leaders who are facilitators and coaches rather than autocrats. Modern human-oriented techniques, such as MBWA (managing by wandering around) easily combine with feminine qualities such as "stroking" people that enable top managers to achieve positive results from employees.

The traditional "male" command-and-control style is suited to hierarchical organizations of the past. "Masculine" qualities such as aggression, assertiveness, rational analysis, and competitiveness grew out of male-dominated military and sports traditions. Research by a number of people supports the argument that women's managerial styles, on average, differ from those of their male counterparts.

Other researchers question whether male and female stereotypes should apply to management. Masculine and feminine traits, including those needed for human skills, they say, can be developed in both sexes to manage modern corporations. As more women move into important management positions, they can be valued for assertiveness as well as nurturing. Indeed, women have already succeeded in many companies, including General Mills, Hewitt Associates, Neiman-Marcus, and PepsiCo.

Although women appear to manage somewhat differently on average, the final answer may be for companies to value the diversity of management styles held by both men and women to find the strength and flexibility to survive in a highly competitive global environment.

SOURCES: "Feminine Management Styles Are Here to Stay," *Personnel Journal* 75, no. 5 (May 1996), 16; Bernard M. Bass and Bruce J. Avolio, "Shatter the Glass Ceiling: Women May Make Better Managers," *Human Resource Management* 33, no. 4 (Winter 1994), 549–560; Sharon Nelton, "Men, Women and Leadership," *Nation's Business*, May 1991, 16–22; Laurie Kretchmar, "Do Women Manage Differently?" *Fortune*, December 17, 1990, 115–118; Judy B. Rosener, "Ways Women Lead," *Harvard Business Review* (November–December 1990), 119–125; and Gary N. Powell, "One More Time: Do Female and Male Managers Differ?" *Academy of Management Executive* 4 (August 1990), 68–75.

outside the United States, and both Ford Motor and Matsushita Electronics employ nearly half their workers outside their respective borders.[54] A South Korean company recently bought out Zenith, the last U.S. company still manufacturing television sets in the United States.

Not only large corporations but also even the smallest businesses will soon be enmeshed with foreign competitors, suppliers, and customers. Diversity will be a real advantage in the global marketplace; skillful employees who speak the language and understand the culture of international competitors, partners, and customers can provide a competitive edge. By one estimate, industrial countries on average import nearly 40 percent of the parts used in domestic manufacturing. Foreign companies have strong influence in the United States and Canada, with many citizens working for foreign employers. Some experts feel that globalization presents a huge management challenge because the United States is losing worldwide market share in important product areas.

Successful managers of tomorrow will be able to cross borders, will be good at languages, and will understand cultural differences. Right now executive recruiting organizations are searching worldwide for managers to take assignments in global organizations. Global experience is a prize asset of tomorrow's managers.[55]

The Learning Organization

The preceding changes have caused the revolution taking place in management thinking. Globalization, diversity, and increased competition are changing both the nature of managerial work and the paths to career advancement. In the new paradigm, the primary responsibility of management is to create learning capability throughout the organization. Many companies are reinventing themselves toward something called the *learning organization.* There is no single model of the learning organization; it is a philosophy or attitude about what an organization is and the role of employees. Everyone in the organization participates in identifying and solving problems, enabling the organization to continuously experiment, improve, and increase its capability. The focus is on quality and customer satisfaction. The learning organization emphasizes teams and systems rather than hierarchy to maximize performance.

Vision and Culture.   In the learning organization, top managers must be leaders who create a vision for the future that is widely understood and imprinted throughout the organization. Such managers develop the governing ideas of purpose, mission, and core cultural values that guide employees' behavior and attitudes. The vision represents desired long-term outcomes, freeing employees to identify and solve problems on their own. Core cultural values set the guidelines within which employees work, clarifying the acceptable ways for attaining company goals and long-term outcomes.[56]

Empowered Workers.   The model of managers controlling workers no longer works in a world of rapidly changing technologies, shifting demographics, global competition, and increased emphasis on

quality and flexibility. Far from being a fad, empowerment of workers at all levels of the company is a significant means of coping with challenges and problems. Empowerment means not so much giving people power but recognizing the power they have and unleashing it to help the company operate more effectively.[57] At Granite Rock Company, for example, virtually all decisions are made by teams of low-level workers. The company uses more than 100 teams to share knowledge and make decisions.[58] Through trust, Harbor Sweets manages to demonstrate the value of each worker, as described in the Leading the Management Revolution box.

New Structures.   The traditional top-down hierarchical organization is giving way to flatter organizations focused on self-directed teams collaborating across levels and departments. Quality takes center stage at all levels, no longer the province of quality-control specialists. Workers monitor and improve the quality of their own work and products. Engineers, planners, and accountants work side by side with production personnel to find quick solutions to problems.[59] Monsanto, a large chemical company, achieved excellent results by tapping the power of teams. Teams of workers at Monsanto's chemical and nylon plant near Pensacola, Florida were responsible for hiring, purchasing, job assignments, and production. Management was reduced from seven levels to four, and both profitability and safety increased.[60]

Open-Book Management.   A key to effective teams of empowered workers is information sharing. Without complete information, workers cannot identify needs and solve problems. In a learning organization, data about budgets, profits, and departmental expenses, once the province of top management, are available to anyone. In the new paradigm, managers believe that too much information sharing is better than too little. At the Danish company Oticon, all incoming mail is scanned into a computer and, with few exceptions, anyone can access

LEADING THE MANAGEMENT REVOLUTION
HARBOR SWEETS

Benneville Strohecker created Harbor Sweets candy company in his Salem, Massachusetts basement in 1973. Today it is a $2.6 million business, and Strohecker is proud to have built a company that ignores convention. Most of the workforce is part-time, with flexible hours, and is composed of a diverse group of teenagers, old-agers, the handicapped, and immigrants from places like Laos and the Dominican Republic.

Strohecker pays his 150 employees similar to a McDonald's and they receive no benefits except paid vacation, but they are part of a company profit-sharing plan and receive discounted candy. In a seasonal business centered around holidays, summer layoffs are common.

If you think these workers feel like exploited stepchildren, think again. Harbor Sweets attracts smart, dedicated people who stay around. Strohecker sums up the the key to the company's success and the essence of his management style: "Trust still remains the most important ingredient in our recipes. But I believe it is not just being nice. Relying on trust is good business."

A lofty sentiment, and Strohecker means it. In an age of background checks and integrity profiles, he still "hires by gut." Trust extended to allowing employees to fill out their own time cards until time clocks were recently installed at the request of employees.

On occasion, Strohecker has deviated from reliance on trust. He once brought in a consultant group to increase plant efficiency. What at first seemed prudent and reasonable turned out to be self-defeating, and the system was discarded. "The very fact that we were measuring is not the culture of Harbor Sweets," says Strohecker. Instead, he told his employees to work as hard as they could; they responded with many suggestions of their own, and the former sense of freedom was restored. A similar scenario evolved when a financial consultant wanted to present Strohecker some benefit options, but the boss suggested going directly to the employees. The astonished consultant was certain Strohecker had lost his mind and that the employees would plunder him. He was wrong on both counts. They decided on a package that was probably more conservative than even Strohecker would have chosen.

Some would say Strohecker's style is an anachronism, not likely to be duplicated elsewhere. But he is confident his company and its philosophy will survive without him and, though he remains CEO, has turned over day-to-day management to chief operating officer Phyllis Leblanc.

"As long as we keep in mind that there's more to this company than making a lot of money, hiring faster people, or buying fancier equipment," he says, "I think our success will always be sweet."

SOURCE: Ben Strohecker, "A Business Built on Trust," *Guideposts,* August 1996, 6–9; Leslie Brokaw, "Like Money for Chocolate: Harbor Sweets," *Hemisphere,* Dec. 1995, 35–38; Anne Driscoll, "Candy Man of the People," *Boston Globe,* March 29, 1992; Tracy E. Benson, "In Trust We Manage," *Industry Week,* March 4, 1991, 26–27; and Martha Mangelsdorf, "Managing the New Work Force," *Inc.,* January 1990, 78–83. Company sources.

anyone else's mail. The same applies to financial documents, and employees are encouraged to tap into each other's files whenever possible.[61] Open-book management helps build trust and gives workers a sense of ownership in the company.

New Career Paths. All of this clearly means that the role of managers is changing. Planning to work one's way up through the levels of a bureaucracy no longer makes sense. In a learning organization, managers will more often move horizontally. Strong project managers will be increasingly important in flatter organizations.[62] Although the delayering and downsizing of organizations is frightening to many managers and business students, some researchers believe these trends will create more opportunities and more exciting jobs. There will no longer be a single career path but multiple paths: the entrepreneurial path, the small-business path, and freelancing opportunities.[63] William Wickham got a reputation as a change expert at Occidental Petroleum, Xerox, and Amax. Three years ago, he went on his own, working as a project manager for various companies. He's currently helping Coca-Cola reorganize its New York metropolitan area distribution. Lucie Fjeldstad, a rising star at IBM, left the company in 1993 to work as an independent multimedia consultant when she discovered the perils of trying to introduce innovations in a giant,

TECHNOLOGY FOR TODAY
BARON MESSENGER

Miami's 70-degree December temperature isn't the most pleasant experience for a red-suited Santa with black boots. But Larry Schwartz, president and co-owner of Baron Messenger Service, Inc., is personally delivering packages as St. Nick.

Laurie Baron launched Baron Messenger in 1981 from her father's transmission shop in the booming Miami area, which then had no local messenger service. She had no venture capital, only a pad of paper, a 1972 Chevy Impala and her smarts, but she managed to secure 300 customers by 1983.

When Laurie's husband, Larry Schwartz, joined the company full-time, paper was the mode of communication. An unwieldy system of writing down orders from the phone and placing them in cardboard boxes for dispatchers proved nearly unmanageable, not only for orders, but especially for complaints and billing.

Realizing their growth depended on radical action, they invested $6,000 in their first computer to automate the billing process, something nearly unheard of at that time. After that, Schwartz was hooked. Even though their annual income was only $300,000 he quickly spent another $60,000 for six more PCs to have a central file server, which gave them not only an efficient billing system, but faster dispatching and handling of complaints.

Now their annual revenues have grown to $1.5 million, largely because they invested in an array of computer systems that match the capabilities of their bigger competitors, such as FedEx and United Parcel Service. Such big companies typically spend hundreds of millions of dollars on their sophisticated information systems, while Baron Messenger has spent less than $100,000 in the past ten years.

Not one to sit idly, Schwartz is thinking of linking the phone system with the computers, so that customers' records would flash on the screen even before the operator says "Hello. Baron Messenger."

SOURCE: "Speed Demon," *Inc. Technology*, 1996, 34–38.

---

bureaucratic company.[64] Larry Schwartz, president of Baron Messenger, started on a career path as a salesman for Minolta Corp. and then jumped ship to his wife's start-up, as described in the Technology for Today box. The managers of tomorrow must be willing to take charge of their own careers; they can no longer expect the security of climbing the corporate ladder and retiring with a gold watch.

It's an exciting time to be entering the field of management. More than ever before, managers have the opportunity to shape the course of business in the twenty-first century.

SUMMARY AND MANAGEMENT SOLUTION

This chapter introduced a number of important concepts and described the changing nature of management. High performance requires the efficient and effective use of organizational resources through the four management functions of planning, organizing, leading, and controlling. To perform the four functions, managers need three skills—conceptual, human, and technical. Conceptual skills are more important at the top of the hierarchy; human skills are important at all levels; and technical skills are most important for first-line managers.

Two characteristics of managerial work also were explained in the chapter: (1) Managerial activities involve variety, fragmentation, and brevity and (2) managers perform a great deal of work at an unrelenting pace. Managers also are expected to perform activities associated with ten roles: the informational roles of monitor, disseminator, and spokesperson; the interpersonal roles of figurehead, leader, and liaison; and the decisional roles of entrepreneur, disturbance handler, resource allocator, and negotiator.

For new companies and small businesses, the entrepreneur and spokesperson roles are particularly important, as managers at Rebel Shoes realized. Eyal Balle and Kellee McCormack in the Management Problem decided not to sell the business, risky though it be. To Balle that would be almost like not breathing anymore. Instead the pair continue to scour malls and shoe stores, looking at the competition in every free moment. They pay calls on old and new customers, whether large or small accounts, keeping the trust strong in the relationships. And they have regular dialogue with their Italian designer, mostly by fax, letting him know about any new ideas they have or what the competition is doing. He likewise keeps them informed. Success is evidenced by sales volume 300 percent of last year's. Not one to stay with the status quo, Balle is think-ing of installing a state-of-the-art $50,000 inventory management system, which would hopefully allow for more growth. They may also add a sales rep in Chicago.

The management characteristics described in the first part of this chapter are still accurate, but they are being applied in a new world of increasing chaos, diversity, and global competition. Thus, a management revolution is changing management toward the concept of the learning organization. Creating learning organizations is the challenge that will face leaders in the future. In the next chapter learning organizations will be discussed in more depth.

DISCUSSION QUESTIONS

I Assume you are a research engineer at a petrochemical company, collaborating with a marketing manager on a major product modification. You notice that every memo you receive from her has been copied to senior management. At every company function, she spends time talking to the big shots. You are also aware that sometimes when you are slaving away over the project, she is playing golf with senior managers. What is your evaluation of her behavior?

2 What do you think the text means by a management revolution? Do you expect to be a leader or follower in this revolution? Explain.

3 What similarities do you see among the four management functions of planning, organizing, leading, and controlling? Do you think these functions are related—that is, is a manager who performs well in one function likely to perform well in the others?

4 Why did a top manager such as Harding Lawrence at Braniff fail to motivate employees while a top manager such as General Creech of Tactical Air Command succeeded? Which of the four management functions best explains this difference? Discuss.

5 What is the difference between efficiency and effective-ness? Which is more important for performance? Can an organization succeed in both simultaneously?

6 What changes in management functions and skills occur as one is promoted from a nonmanagement to a management position? How can managers acquire the new skills?

7 If managerial work is characterized by variety, fragmentation, and brevity, how do managers perform basic management functions such as planning, which would seem to require reflection and analysis?

8 A college professor told her students, "The purpose of a management course is to teach students *about* management, not to teach them to be managers." Do you agree or disagree with this statement? Discuss.

9 Describe the characteristics of a learning organization. How do these characteristics compare to those of an organization in which you have worked? Would you like to work or manage in a learning organization? Discuss.

10 How could the teaching of management change to prepare future managers to deal with workforce diversity? With empowerment? Do you think diversity and empowerment will have a substantial impact on organizations in the future? Explain.

MANAGEMENT EXERCISES

MANAGER'S WORKBOOK

Rate each of the following questions according to this scale:

5 I always am like this.
4 I often am like this.

3 I sometimes am like this.
2 I rarely am like this.
I I never am like this.

____ **1** When I have a number of tasks or homework to do, I set priorities and organize the work around the deadlines.   C

____ **2** Most people would describe me as a good listener.   H

____ **3** When I am deciding on a particular course of action for myself (such as which hobbies to pursue, languages to study, job to take, special projects to be involved in), I typically consider the long-term (three years or more) implications of what I would choose to do.   C

____ **4** I prefer technical or quantitative courses rather than those involving literature, psychology, or sociology.   T

____ **5** When I have a serious disagreement with someone, I hang in there and talk it out until it is completely resolved.   H

____ **6** When I have a project or assignment, I really get into the details rather than the "big picture" issues.*   C

____ **7** I would rather sit in front of my computer than spend a lot of time with people.   T

____ **8** I try to include others in activities or when there are discussions.   H

____ **9** When I take a course, I relate what I am learning to other courses I have taken or concepts I have learned elsewhere.   C

____ **10** When somebody makes a mistake, I want to correct the person and let her or him know the proper answer or approach.*   H

____ **11** I think it is better to be efficient with my time when talking with someone, rather than worry about the other person's needs, so that I can get on with my real work.   T

____ **12** I know my long-term vision for career, family, and other activities and have thought it over carefully.   C

____ **13** When solving problems, I would much rather analyze some data or statistics than meet with a group of people.   T

____ **14** When I am working on a group project and someone doesn't pull a full share of the load, I am more likely to complain to my friends rather than confront the slacker.*   H

____ **15** Talking about ideas or concepts can get me really enthused and excited.   C

____ **16** The type of management course for which this book is used is really a waste of time.   T

____ **17** I think it is better to be polite and not to hurt people's feelings.*   H

____ **18** Data or things interest me more than people.   T

Scoring key

*Add the total points for the following sections. Note that starred * items are reverse scored, as such:*

1 I always am like this.
2 I often am like this.
3 I sometimes am like this.
4 I rarely am like this.
5 I never am like this.

1, 3, 6, 9, 12, 15   **Conceptual skills total score**   ——
2, 5, 8, 10, 14, 17   **Human skills total score**   ——
4, 7, 11, 13, 16, 18   **Technical skills total score**   ——

The above skills are three abilities needed to be a good manager. Ideally, a manager should be strong (though not necessarily equal) in all three. Anyone noticeably weaker in any of the skills should take courses and read to build up that skill. For further background on the three skills, please refer to the model in this chapter.

*reverse scoring item

MANAGER'S WORKSHOP

The Worst Manager

1 By yourself, think of two managers you have had—the best and the worst. Write down a few sentences to describe each.

The best manager I ever had was . . .   _____

_____

_____

The worst manager I ever had was . . . _____

_____

_____

2 Divide into groups of five to seven members. Share your experiences. Each group should choose a couple of examples to share with the whole group. Complete the table below as a group.

	Management principle followed or broken	Skills evident or missing	Lessons to be learned	Advice you would give managers
The best managers				
The worst managers				

3 What are the common problems managers have?

4 Prepare a list of "words of wisdom" you would give as a presentation to a group of managers. What are some basic principles they should use to be effective?

SURF THE 'NET

Use at least two Web browsers and look for information on issues in management, such as management practices, bureaucracy, supervision, new paradigm, etc. Write a few paragraphs on what you found and include addresses for the Web sites.

ETHICAL DILEMMA

Can Management Afford to Look the Other Way?

Harry Rull had been with Shellington Pharmaceuticals for 30 years. After a tour of duty in the various plants and seven years overseas, Harry was back at headquarters, looking forward to his new role as vice president of U.S. Marketing.

Two weeks into his new job, Harry received some unsettling news about one of the managers under his supervision. Over casual lunch conversation, the director of human resources mentioned that Harry should expect a phone call about Roger Jacobs, Manager of New Product Development. Jacobs had a history of being "pretty horrible" to his subordinates, she said, and one disgruntled employee had asked to speak to someone in senior management. After lunch, Harry did some follow-up work. Jacobs's performance reviews had been stellar, but his personnel file also contained a large number of notes documenting charges of Jacobs's mistreatment of subordinates. The complaints ranged from "inappropriate and derogatory remarks" to subsequently dropped charges of sexual harassment. What was more disturbing was that the amount as well as the severity of complaints had increased with each of Jacobs's ten years with Shellington.

When Harry questioned the company president about the issue, he was told, "Yeah, he's had some problems, but you can't just replace someone with an eye for new products. You're a bottom-line guy; you understand why we let these things slide." Not sure how to handle the situation, Harry met briefly with Jacobs and reminded him to "keep the team's morale up." Just after the meeting, Sally Barton from HR called to let him know the problem she'd mentioned over lunch had been worked out. However, she warned, another employee had now come forward demanding that her complaints be addressed by senior management.

What Do You Do?

1 Ignore the problem. Jacobs's contributions to new product development are too valuable to risk losing him, and the problems over the past ten years have always worked themselves out anyway. No sense starting something that could make you look bad.

2 Launch a full-scale investigation of employee complaints about Jacobs, and make Jacobs aware that the documented history over the past ten years has put him on thin ice.

3 Meet with Jacobs and the employee to try to resolve the current issue, then start working with Sally Barton and other senior managers to develop stronger policies regarding sexual harassment and treatment of employees, including clear-cut procedures for handling complaints.

SOURCE: Based on Doug Wallace, "A Talent for Mismanagement," *What Would You Do? Business Ethics*, Vol. II (November–December 1992), 3–4.

CASE FOR CRITICAL ANALYSIS

SportsGear

George Marlow, a manufacturing vice president, walked into the monthly companywide meeting with a light step and a hopefulness he hadn't felt in a long time. The company's new, dynamic CEO was going to announce a new era of empowerment at SportsGear, an 80-year-old publicly held company that had once been a leading manufacturer and retailer of recreational clothing and footwear. In recent years, the company experienced a host of problems: market share was declining in the face of increased foreign and domestic competition; new product ideas were few and far between; departments like manufacturing and sales barely spoke to one another; morale was at an all-time low, and many employees were actively seeking other jobs. Everyone needed a dose of hope.

Martin Griffin, who had been hired to revive the failing company, briskly opened the meeting with a challenge: "As we face increasing competition, we need new ideas, new energy, new spirit to make this company great. And the source for this change is you—each one of you." He then went on to explain that under SportsGear's new empowerment campaign, employees would be getting more information about how the company was run and would be able to work with their fellow employees in new and creative ways. Martin proclaimed a new era of trust and cooperation at SportsGear. George felt the excitement stirring within him; but as he looked around the room, he saw many of the other employees, including his friend Harry, rolling their eyes. "Just another pile of corporate crap," Harry said later. "One minute they try downsizing, the next reengineering. Then they dabble in restructuring. Now Martin wants to push empowerment. Garbage like empowerment isn't a substitute for hard work and a little faith in the people who have been with this company for years. We made it great once, and we can do it again. Just get out of our way." Harry had been a manufacturing engineer with SportsGear for more than 20 years. George knew he was extremely loyal to the company, but he—and a lot of others like him—were going to be an obstacle to the empowerment efforts.

Top management assigned selected managers to several problem-solving teams to come up with ideas for implementing the empowerment campaign. George loved his assignment as team leader of the manufacturing team, working on ideas to improve how retail stores got the merchandise they needed when they needed it. The team thrived, and trust blossomed among the members. They even spent nights and weekends working to complete their report. They were proud of the ideas they had come up with, which they believed were innovative but easily achievable: permit a manager to follow a product from design through sales to customers; allow salespeople to refund up to $500 worth of merchandise on the spot; make information available to salespeople about future products; and swap sales and manufacturing personnel for short periods to let them get to know one another's jobs.

When the team presented their report to department heads, Martin Griffin was enthusiastic. But shortly into the meeting he had to excuse himself because of a late-breaking deal with a major department store chain. With Martin absent, the department heads rapidly formed a wall of resistance. The director of human resources complained that the ideas for personnel changes would destroy the carefully crafted job categories that had just been completed. The finance department argued that allowing salespeople to make $500 refunds would create a gold mine for unethical customers and salespeople. The legal department warned that providing information to salespeople about future products would invite industrial spying.

The team members were stunned. As George mulled over the latest turn of events, he considered his options:

keep his mouth shut; take a chance and confront Martin about his sincerity in making empowerment work; push slowly for reform and work for gradual support from the other teams; or look for another job and leave a company he really cared about. He realized there would be no easy choices and no easy answers.

Questions

1 How might top management have done a better job changing SportsGear into a learning organization? What might they do now to get the empowerment process back on track?

2 Can you think of ways George could have avoided the problems his team faced in the meeting with department heads?

3 If you were George Marlow, what would you do now? Why?

SOURCE: Based on Lawrence R. Rothstein, "The Empowerment Effort That Came Undone," *Harvard Business Review* (January–February 1995), 20–31.

ENDNOTES

1 Edward O. Welles, "Basic Instincts," *Inc.,* September 1996, 39–50.
2 Nicholas Imparato and Oren Harari, *Jumping the Curve: Innovation and Strategic Choice in an Age of Transition* (San Francisco: Jossey-Bass Publishers, 1994); Tom Broersma, "In Search of the Future," *Training and Development,* January 1995, 38–43; Rahul Jacob, "The Struggle to Create an Organization for the Twenty-First Century," *Fortune,* April 3, 1995, 90–99; and Charles Handy, *The Age of Paradox* (Boston: Harvard Business School Press, 1994).
3 Kathleen Kerwin and James B. Treece, "Detroit's Big Chance," *Business Week,* June 29, 1992, 82–90; Wendy Zellner, "Chrysler's Next Generation," *Business Week,* December 19, 1988, 52–55; and Tom Peters and Nancy Austin, *A Passion for Excellence: The Leadership Difference* (New York: Random House, 1985).
4 Jaclyn Fierman, "Winning Ideas from Maverick Managers," *Fortune,* February 6, 1995, 66–80.
5 Louis Kraar, "Iron Butterflies," *Fortune,* October 7, 1991, 143–154.
6 James A. F. Stoner and R. Edward Freeman, *Management,* 4th ed. (Englewood Cliffs, N.J.: Prentice-Hall, 1989).
7 Peter F. Drucker, *Management Tasks, Responsibilities, Practices* (New York: Harper & Row, 1974).
8 Greising, "Home Depot," and Hof, "Hewlett-Packard," in Wendy Zellner, Robert D. Hof, Richard Brandt, Stephen Baker, and David Greising, "Go-Go Goliaths," *Business Week,* February 13, 1995, 64–70.
9 G. Pascal Zachary, "How Ashton-Tate Lost Its Leadership in PC Software Arena," *The Wall Street Journal,* April 11, 1990, A1, A12.
10 Ricardo Semler, *Maverick: The Success Story Behind the World's Most Unusual Workplace* (New York: Warner Books, 1993); Ricardo Semler, "All for One, One for All," *Harvard Business Review* (Sep-

tember–October 1989), 76–84; and Fierman, "Winning Ideas from Maverick Managers."
11 John Bussey and Douglas R. Sease, "Manufacturers Strive to Slice Time Needed to Develop Products," *The Wall Street Journal,* February 23, 1988, 1, 13.
12 "Southwest Airlines' Herb Kelleher: Unorthodoxy at Work" *Management Review,* January 1995, 9–12; James Campbell Quick, "Crafting an Organizational Culture: Herb's Hand at Southwest Airlines," *Organizational Dynamics* (autumn 1992), 45–56; and Edward O. Welles, "Captain Marvel," *Inc.,* January 1992, 44–47.
13 Wendy Zellner, Robert D. Hof, Richard Brandt, Stephen Baker, and David Greising, "Go-Go Goliaths," *Business Week,* February 13, 1995, 64–70; and "Southwest Airlines' Herb Kelleher: Unorthodoxy at Work," *Management Review,* January 1995, 9–12.
14 Byron Harris, "The Man Who Killed Braniff," *Texas Monthly,* July 1982, 116–120, 183–189.
15 Ibid.
16 Christopher A. Bartlett and Sumantra Ghoshal, "Changing the Role of Top Management: Beyond Systems to People," *Harvard Business Review* 73 (May–June 1995), 132–142.
17 Fierman, "Winning Ideas from Maverick Managers."
18 Brett Duval Fromson, "The Slow Death of E. F. Hutton," *Fortune,* February 29, 1988, 82–88.
19 Zellner et al., "Go-Go Goliaths"; and Alex Taylor III, "Lee Iacocca's Production Whiz," *Fortune,* June 22, 1987, 36–44.
20 David Wessel, "With Labor Scarce, Service Firms Strive to Raise Productivity," *The Wall Street Journal,* June 1, 1989, A1, A8.
21 Amy Barrett, "Meet the Fastest Five-Footer in the NBA," *Business Week,* January 16, 1995, 91.

22 Leslie, Brokaw, "The Dead Have Customers, Too," *Inc.,* September 1994, 90–92; David E. Bowen and Caren Siehl, "Sweet Music: Grateful Employees, Grateful Customers, 'Grate' Profits," *Journal of Management Inquiry* (June 1992), 154–156; and Janice C. Simpson, "The Bands of Summer," *Time,* August 3, 1992, 66–67.

23 Robert L. Katz, "Skills of an Effective Administrator," *Harvard Business Review* 52 (September–October 1974), 90–102.

24 Brenton Schlender, "How Bill Gates Keeps the Magic Going," *Fortune,* June 18, 1990, 82–89.

25 Jacob, "The Struggle to Create an Organization for the Twenty-First Century"; and Joseph B. White, "How Detroit Diesel, Out from Under GM, Turned Around Fast," *The Wall Street Journal,* August 16, 1991, A1, A8.

26 Baker, "Nucor," in Zellner et al., "Go-Go Goliaths," 70.

27 Eric Calonius, "Smart Moves by Quality Champs," *Fortune,* special 1991 issue—The New American Century, 24–28.

28 Bartlett and Ghoshal, "Changing the Role of Top Management"; and Sumantra Ghoshal and Christopher A. Bartlett, "Changing the Role of Top Management: Beyond Structure to Processes," *Harvard Business Review* 73 (January–February 1995), 86–96.

29 Carol Hymowitz, "When Firms Slash Middle Management, Those Spared Often Bear a Heavy Load," *The Wall Street Journal,* April 5, 1990, B1.

30 Steven W. Floyd and Bill Wooldridge, "Dinosaurs or Dynamos? Recognizing Middle Management's Strategic Role," *Academy of Management Executive* 8, no. 4 (1994), 47–57.

31 Thomas A. Stewart, "The Corporate Jungle Spawns a New Species: The Project Manager," *Fortune,* July 10, 1995, 179–180.

32 Henry Mintzberg, *The Nature of Managerial Work* (New York: Harper & Row, 1973); and Mintzberg, "Rounding Out the Manager's Job," *Sloan Management Review* (fall 1994), 11–26.

33 Robert E. Kaplan, "Trade Routes: The Manager's Network of Relationships," *Organizational Dynamics* (spring 1984), 37–52; Rosemary Stewart, "The Nature of Management: A Problem for Management Education," *Journal of Management Studies* 21 (1984), 323–330; John P. Kotter, "What Effective General Managers Really Do," *Harvard Business Review* (November–December 1982), 156–167; and Morgan W. McCall, Jr., Ann M. Morrison, and Robert L. Hannan, "Studies of Managerial Work: Results and Methods" (Technical Report No. 9, Center for Creative Leadership, Greensboro, N.C., 1978).

34 Anita Lienert, "A Day in the Life: Airport Manager Extraordinaire," *Management Review,* January 1995, 57–61.

35 Henry Mintzberg, "Managerial Work: Analysis from Observation," *Management Science* 18 (1971), B97–B110.

36 Alan Deutschman, "The CEO's Secret of Managing Time," *Fortune,* June 1, 1992, 135–146.

37 Based on Carol Saunders and Jack William Jones, "Temporal Sequences in Information Acquisition for Decision Making: A Focus on Source and Medium," *Academy of Management Review* 15 (1990), 29–46; Kotter, "What Effective General Managers Really Do"; and Mintzberg, "Managerial Work."

38 Mintzberg, "Managerial Work."

39 Lienert, "A Day in the Life."

40 Lance B. Kurke and Howard E. Aldrich, "Mintzberg Was Right!: A Replication and Extension of *The Nature of Managerial Work,*" *Management Science* 29 (1983), 975–984; Cynthia M. Pavett and Alan W. Lau, "Managerial Work: The Influence of Hierarchical Level and Functional Specialty," *Academy of Management Journal* 26 (1983), 170–177; and Colin P. Hales, "What Do Managers Do?

A Critical Review of the Evidence," *Journal of Management Studies* 23 (1986), 88–115.

41 Mintzberg, "Rounding Out the Manager's Job."

42 Wendy Trueman, "CEO Isolation and How to Fight It," *Canadian Business,* July 1991, 28–32.

43 Oren Harari, "Open the Doors, Tell the Truth," *Management Review,* January 1995, 33–35.

44 Harry S. Jonas III, Ronald E. Fry, and Suresh Srivastva, "The Office of the CEO: Understanding the Executive Experience," *Academy of Management Executive* 4 (August 1990), 36–48.

45 Jeffrey A. Annenbaum, "Chicken and Burgers Create New Hot Class: Powerful Franchisees," *The Wall Street Journal,* CCXXVII (100), May 21, 1996, A1, A8; and Thomas Peters and Robert Waterman, *In Search of Excellence.*

46 Edward O. Welles, "There Are No Simple Businesses Anymore," *The State of Small Business,* 1995, 66–79.

47 John A. Byrne, "Profiting from the Nonprofits," *Business Week,* March 26, 1990, 66–74; and Michael Ryval, "Born-Again Bureaucrats," *Canadian Business,* November 1991, 64–71.

48 Eileen Davis, "What's on American Managers' Minds?" *American Management Association,* April 1995, 14–20.

49 James Gleick, *Chaos: Making a New Science* (New York: Viking, 1987).

50 Octave V. Baker, "Meeting the Challenge of Managing Cultural Diversity," in *Managing in the Age of Change: Essential Skills to Manage Today's Diverse Workforce,* ed. Roger A. Ritvo, Anne H. Litwin, and Lee Butler (Burr Ridge, Ill.: Irwin, 1995).

51 Imparato and Harari, *Jumping the Curve.*

52 Janice Castro, "Get Set: Here They Come!" *Time,* fall 1990 special issue, 50–51; Carol Hymowitz, "Day in the Life of Tomorrow's Manager," *The Wall Street Journal,* March 20, 1989, B1; and Amanda Troy Segal, "Corporate Women," *Business Week,* June 8, 1992, 74–78.

53 Davis, "What's on American Managers' Minds?"

54 Richard A. Luecke, *Scuttle Your Ships Before Advancing, and Other Lessons from History on Leadership and Change for Today's Managers* (New York: Oxford University Press, 1994), 108–109.

55 Bob Hagerty, "Firms in Europe Try to Find Executives Who Can Cross Borders in a Single Bound," *The Wall Street Journal,* January 25, 1991, B1; and Shawn Tully, "The Hunt for the Global Manager," *Fortune,* May 21, 1990, 140–144.

56 Richard L. Daft, *Organization Theory and Design,* 5th ed. (Minneapolis/St. Paul: West Publishing Company, 1995).

57 W. Alan Randolph, "Navigating the Journey to Empowerment," *Organizational Dynamics,* spring 1995, 19–31.

58 John Case, "The Change Masters," *Inc.,* March 1992, 58–70.

59 Broersma, "In Search of the Future."

60 Jeffrey Pfeffer, "Producing Sustainable Competitive Advantage through the Effective Management of People," *Academy of Management Executive* 9, no. 1 (1995), 55–72.

61 Harari, "Open the Doors, Tell the Truth."

62 Arno Penzias, "New Paths to Success," *Fortune,* June 12, 1995, 90–94.

63 Judith H. Dobrzynski, "New Secrets of Success: Getting Off the Ladder," an interview with John P. Kotter, *The New York Times,* March 19, 1995, F14.

64 Thomas A. Stewart, "Planning a Career in a World without Managers," *Fortune,* March 20, 1995, 72–80; and Andrea Gabor, "The True Tale (and Happy Ending) of a Career Crisis," *Executive Female,* November–December 1994, 42–47.

Foundations of Learning Organizations

CHAPTER OUTLINE

The Revolution in Management
Chaotic Environment
Paradigm Shift

The Learning Organization
The Learning Manager
The Learning Organization
Leadership
Horizontal Structure
Employee Empowerment
Communication/Information Sharing
Emergent Strategy
Strong Culture

Historical Forces Leading Up to the Learning Organization

Classical Perspective
Scientific Management
Bureaucratic Organizations
Administrative Principles

Humanistic Perspective
The Human Relations Movement
The Human Resources Perspective
The Behavioral Sciences Approach

Management Science Perspective

Contemporary Extensions
Systems Theory
Contingency View

Recent Historical Trends
Globalization
Total Quality Management

LEARNING OBJECTIVES

After studying this chapter, you should be able to

- Discuss the causes of the current revolution in management thinking.

- Describe the concept of the learning organization as it relates to managers and to organizations.

- Discuss how a learning organization is designed through changes in leadership, structure, empowerment, information sharing, strategy, and culture.

- Understand how historical forces in society have influenced the practice of management.

- Identify and explain major developments in the history of management thought.

- Describe the major components of the classical management perspective.

- Describe the major components of the humanistic management perspective.

- Discuss the quantitative management perspective.

- Explain the major concepts of systems theory.

- Discuss the basic concepts underlying contingency views.

- Describe the recent influences of global competition on management in North America.

CHAPTER 2

MANAGEMENT PROBLEM

The outlook for Behlen, a manufacturer of steel agricultural buildings, was upbeat. Located in Columbus, Nebraska, Behlen had several hundred employees and a factory spanning the length of 17 football fields, and it couldn't keep up with orders for its steel silos and prefabricated buildings. Uncle Sam provided grain-storage subsidies to farmers, and Behlen profited handsomely, earning some $3 million on $50 million in revenues. Everything was on track, until the government announced it would no longer subsidize grain storage. Suddenly half the market for grain-storage buildings was gone. Tony Raimondo, in the middle of that crisis, took over Behlen. With revenues down 50 percent and workers afraid of losing their jobs, Raimondo had a dream that new products could be made for new markets. Raimondo also knew he couldn't save the company alone. Somehow he had to create a new kind of company to survive in a rapidly shifting environment.[1]

• If you were Tony Raimondo, how would you go about turning around this company? What advice would you give him for the kind of company he might create?

Behlen is faced with a situation similar to many companies. Everything is going along fine, and then suddenly the bottom drops out. Everything changes. Managers then face a seemingly impossible situation and have to create a new kind of company, one with which they have little experience or skill.

Many organizations, like Behlen, succeeded by developing centralized structure and control. These companies use a strict hierarchy to achieve efficiency and profitability. This works fine as long as the world is stable. But the emerging world of the twenty-first century is one of chaos and rapid change. The emerging world is asking far more of managers, which is what this book is about. This book describes elements of the management revolution now under way, from open-book management to empowerment, international competition, changing environments, the need for ethics and diversity, continuous quality improvement, and new leadership. This all adds up to a new paradigm for management.

Some companies have taken up the challenge of reinventing themselves, of becoming more than status quo companies. For example, Disney's theme parks have become known for people management and creative leadership. Johnsonville Foods and Saturn have moved to self-managing teams and a culture of employee empowerment. Motorola has achieved extraordinary quality. Federal Express achieves excellence through treating its people and customers well. Springfield Remanufacturing has led the way with open-book management, sharing all financial information with every employee. Rubbermaid has excelled by learning to create a flood of new products that are nearly always successful in the marketplace. These companies go beyond the norm to succeed in an increasingly difficult world.[2]

All this means that we are currently experiencing the emergence of a new world, a new kind of organization, and a new approach to management. Managers headed into the twenty-first century face the ultimate paradox: (1) Keep everything running efficiently and profitably, and, at the same time, (2) change everything.[3] It's no longer enough just to learn how to measure and control things. Success accrues to those who learn how to be leaders, to initiate change, and to participate in and even create organizations with fewer managers and less hierarchy that can change quickly.

This chapter consolidates the new management themes that describe the organization for the twenty-first century, called the learning organization, and the conditions that create it. After describing the learning organization, we will look at the historical factors that have led up to its development. This chapter provides an overview of how managers' philosophies have changed over the years. This foundation of management understanding illustrates that the value of studying management lies not in learning current facts and research but in developing a perspective that will facilitate the broad, long-term view needed for management success.

THE REVOLUTION IN MANAGEMENT

What is causing leading-edge companies to change so much? What is causing the revolution in management thinking? Actually there are two things: the increasingly chaotic nature of the environment and a paradigm shift in the way people think about organizations.

Chaotic Environment

The world is becoming turbulent and chaotic. Chapter 1 introduced the concept of chaos theory, which reveals the randomness and disorder that exists in most systems, especially organizations. Day-to-day events for most organizations are random and unpredictable.

Yet most managers have been trained to think of the world as in equilibrium. Following World War II, there was no global competition for U.S. companies. The war had ravaged Europe, the Soviet Union, and

Japan. With its technological and manufacturing base intact, the United States would have enjoyed great economic success no matter what system it used. The United States adopted a mass-production mind-set that organizations could be managed with statistical analysis and engineering control.

Things went along fine until the OPEC oil embargo of 1972–1973. Americans suddenly realized that they had limited control of their own destiny. During the 1980s and 1990s, intrusions by global companies caused American managers to rethink their beliefs. Perhaps they had to be more concerned with quality, encourage workers to participate, and become more people and customer oriented, because this seemed to be working in other countries.

Changes and shocks were hitting companies, similar to what happened to Behlen, described at the beginning of this chapter. For example, Digital Equipment Corporation launched an internal revolution as a matter of survival after rapidly changing market forces devastated the world's number-three computer maker. Corporate culture was redesigned. Products, processes, customers, and ways of thinking were all examined and refashioned in an effort to survive.[4] Of course, similar events happened at IBM. Thousands of managers were laid off, a new management team was hired, and the company once thought to be the most successful in the world was humbled by its falling reputation, market share, and stock price. It seems as if no company can withstand the onslaught of the chaotic environment.

Paradigm Shift

A **paradigm** was described in Chapter 1 as a fundamental way of thinking about, perceiving, and understanding the world. The paradigm during the twentieth century has been a belief in equilibrium, that things can be stable and efficient. A new way of viewing the world—the new paradigm—is based on far-from-equilibrium thinking. Far from equilibrium means that in a chaotic world, things will never stabilize. Surprises,

disturbances, failures, and stress are always hitting organizations. Consequently, managers who try to control things back into stable equilibrium find their task impossible. Instead, new paradigm thinking is to get comfortable with continuous change. Organizations have to find ways to embrace the twenty-first-century paradox of keeping everything running and at the same time changing everything. To do so means to look at the world through a different lens.

The world that most of today's managers were trained to work in included cultural values of stability and efficiency, mechanical technology, physical tasks, vertical hierarchies, top-management power and control, careers designed to maintain financial security, autocratic leadership, a homogeneous workforce, individually oriented work, and a local market orientation, with an effort to achieve profits through the use of capital resources to make products of modest quality.

What a change today's students are going to face in the twenty-first century. The existence of continuous change has started the management revolution described in this book. The new management paradigm involves a big shift. New corporate cultures value change and problem solving, technologies are electronic, people's tasks are mental and idea based, hierarchies are becoming horizontal, power and control are widely dispersed, and people want career opportunities for personal growth and mastery of complex tasks. Moreover, leadership is more inspirational and transformational, the workforce is more diverse, and work is performed by teams rather than by individuals. This new world is characterized by concern with global markets and supplies, a greater concern for customers than for profits, information as the primary resource, and the best possible quality as the norm.[5]

Seen through this new paradigm, the world is awesomely complex. Changes are occurring that no individual or company can control. Yet, many managers have become dependent on the traditional vertical hierarchy, stability, financial security, a homogeneous workforce, and the belief that

paradigm
A fundamental way of thinking about, perceiving, and understanding the world.

profits and capital are the goals of success. Making the necessary paradigm change is frustrating and difficult. This realization has prompted a company like Tenneco, prodded by former CEO Michael Walsh, to completely remake itself. One division president admitted, "Corporate arrogance was our culture. We said, 'Here are the services we think our customers need,' but we never asked them. The hierarchy suppressed new ideas." As companies revitalize themselves, management becomes a blank page, a chance to do everything over. It's exciting and scary at the same time. And many managers can't handle it. At least 15 percent, and perhaps as many as 30 percent, of people cannot adapt to the new paradigm and will leave a company that undergoes this kind of change.[6]

The kind of organization Tenneco and other companies are trying to become goes by a variety of names. It has been called the twenty-first-century organization, the collaborative organization, the empowered organization, and even the new-age organization. The term we will use to describe this new organization form is the learning organization.

THE LEARNING ORGANIZATION

Managers began thinking about the concept of learning organization after the publication of Peter Senge's book, *The Fifth Discipline: The Art and Practice of Learning Organizations.*[7] Senge described the kinds of changes managers needed to undergo to help their organizations adapt to an increasingly chaotic world.

The Learning Manager

In Senge's original concept, building a learning organization is a matter of managers developing five disciplines.

I *Systems thinking.* All employees should understand how the company really works and have the big picture in their mind as well as a picture of their own job and department. This lets each person act in ways that support the whole company.

2 *Shared vision.* The organization must develop a common purpose and commitment, as well as an overall plan on which everyone can agree.

3 *Challenging mental models.* This means questioning current ways of thinking and uncovering the deep assumptions that prevent people from adopting new behaviors. People are often stuck in the old paradigm and don't realize it.

4 *Team learning.* People pitch in to help the group succeed and work collectively to achieve the overall vision rather than pursue individual goals.

5 *Personal mastery.* Employees know the job, people, and processes they are responsible for at a very deep level; they experience intimacy with their work rather than detachment.

These five disciplines enable managers to make the shift from old-style thinking and organizing to a new paradigm. The most difficult part is breaking free of the old ways of thinking, as the Massachusetts Department of Revenue learned.

MASSACHUSETTS DEPARTMENT OF REVENUE

By thinking about the job in new ways, the Massachusetts Department of Revenue reorganized its methods for collecting delinquent child-support payments. The number of paying cases increased by 41 percent, from 37,000 to 52,000, in only two years. Amazingly, these results were achieved with only 10 percent of the staff previously used, a reduction from 200 caseworkers pursuing delinquent parents to 20 people working as accountants.

With the state headed into recession and department layoffs imminent, Commissioner Bob Melia saw the need for a new mental model. Going after delinquent people case by case was not working. After three months of meetings and flow charting the work process,

As pilots play out various combat scenarios at the Virtual Warfare Center of McDonnell Douglas Aerospace, observers watch big-screen monitors to gain perspective into the complex interactions of key technologies. The purpose of the center is to improve *focus on the customer.* By being able to rapidly simulate aircraft, sensors, weapons, and scenarios, both MDA and its customers can find the best and most cost-efficient solutions to meet specific needs.

the team developed a shared vision: a collection system that would make use of computer technology. The new system would compare social security numbers of all new hires in Massachusetts against the data on deadbeat parents. Now, 75 percent of all money collected comes from employers, increasing the rate of collections with far fewer revenue employees. Developing a systems perspective on the old collection method allowed the department to change it as a new mental model evolved. Every employee receives two weeks of training per year to increase personal mastery, reflecting a budget increase from $5 to $500 a year for each person on the staff. The training specifically teaches people to think "outside the box."[8] ■

The Learning Organization

Senge's original approach has worked very well, and the concept of learning organization has evolved to describe characteristics of the organization itself. There is no single view of what a learning organization looks like. The learning organization is an attitude or philosophy about what an organization can become.

The **learning organization** can be defined as one in which everyone is engaged in identifying and solving problems, enabling the organization to continuously experiment, change, and improve, thus increasing its capacity to grow, learn, and achieve its purpose. The essential idea is problem solving, in contrast to the traditional organization designed for efficiency. In the learning organization all employees look for problems, such as understanding special customer needs. Employees also solve problems, which means putting things together in unique ways to meet a customer's needs.

The learning organization reflects concepts described in this book. Companies generally evolve into learning organizations in three stages. The first stage is the traditional hierarchy, in which top managers maintain central control for actions within the organization and also maintain control of strategy, including relationships with customers and the environment. In the second stage of development, top managers move toward empowerment, giving employees responsibility for workflow decisions and actions. This action has been

learning organization
An organization in which everyone is engaged in identifying and solving problems, enabling the organization to continuously experiment, improve, and increase its capability.

described by such terms as horizontal or network organization, empowerment, and creating people-oriented corporate cultures. Stage three occurs when employees are also engaged in setting strategic direction. Employees who work with customers or other parts of the environment make choices about company strategy and tactics for succeeding in that environment. Employees are no longer factors of efficient production to be assigned to routine tasks that do not change. Strategy emerges from the accumulated activities of employee teams. Employees work within the overall vision, and different parts of the organization are adapting and changing independently while at the same time contributing to the company mission.

In one sense, becoming a learning organization increases the size of a company's brain. Employees participate in all thinking activities, including strategy, with few boundaries among employees in different departments or between the top and bottom. Everyone communicates and works together, creating enormous intelligence and flexibility to deal with a rapidly changing environment.

Designing a learning organization means making specific changes in the areas of leadership, horizontal structure, empowerment, communications/information sharing, emergent strategy, and strong culture. These six characteristics are illustrated in Exhibit 2.1, and each is described in the following sections.

Leadership

Leadership is the only means through which a company can change into a learning organization. The traditional view of leaders who set goals, make decisions, and direct the troops reflects an individualistic view. Leadership in learning organizations requires something more. Leaders are designers, teachers, and stewards. Leaders need the ability to build a shared vision, help people see the whole system, work together, design the horizontal structure, initiate change, and expand the capacity of people

to shape the future.[9] Leaders who understand the learning organization can help other people build it. Leaders in a learning organization have three distinct roles.

I *Create a shared vision.* The shared vision is a picture of an ideal future for the organization. The vision includes what the organization will look like, performance outcomes, and underlying values. A vision may be created by the leader or with employee participation, but this purpose must be widely understood and imprinted in people's minds. The vision represents desired long-term outcomes; hence, employees are free to identify and solve problems that help achieve that vision. Without a shared vision, employee action may not add to the whole because decisions are fragmented and take people in different directions.

Robert Allen, when appointed CEO of AT&T, helped transform AT&T toward a learning organization by pushing the shared vision. His vision included turning the organization chart upside down to put the customer on top. The people close to the customer make customer-based decisions. Allen's vision included the company values of respect for individuals and dedication to helping customers. He also improved ties with unions and built linkages with companies that have critical technologies for AT&T's future. Because all employees understood the vision, they were able to carry it out without direct supervision from the top.[10]

2 *Design structure.* The leader puts in place an organization structure, including policies, strategies, and formats that support the learning organization. The learning organization takes advantage of horizontal relationships, including teams, task forces, and frequent meetings that involve cross-sections of employees. The structure works toward boundarylessness, with people reaching out to each other across departments rather than competing.

EXHIBIT 2.1
**The Web of
Interacting Elements
in a Learning
Organization**

The leader also helps people understand that reorganization is continuous, with people taking on new roles and learning new skills. For example, when Robert Allen turned AT&T's organization chart upside down, putting the customer on top, this became the prevailing view of structure. He also encouraged cooperation among independent business units. He created a team of leaders from four major business groups to run the organization and developed additional cross-unit teams at lower levels that collaborate to seek new strategic opportunities. In all this design, the leader is more transformational than transactional, as we will describe in Chapter 13. The leader is always pushing the organization to transform and renew itself. The owners of Book Binding, Inc., realized they had to radically change their mode of operation or they would not survive.

BOOK BINDING, INC.

Thomas A. Patrevito and John Z. Kosowski, owners of Book Binding Inc., sat in their Broadview, Illinois, offices and faced a hard reality. Their 1976 start-up began with only $20,000 capital, but by 1992 sales had reached $9.5 million. Yet, even though sales were up 30 percent, profits had remained exactly the same. They realized they were working harder, but with no obvious reward.

Competitors had copied Book Binding's high quality and great service model, and they had lost the edge in the marketplace. The only solution seemed obvious but painful. Downsize. Cut one-third of the 180-person workforce.

Yet something inside Kosowski churned at this idea. There had to be some other way, he reasoned, to wring better productivity out of their employees, especially the sales force.

Because of past mediocre experiences, they reluctantly brought in a corporate trainer. Mark N. Landiak of Corporate Dynamics Inc. challenged every assumption they had about customer relationships, markets, employees and services. Soon they realized the disturbing truth: They had lost sight of why they started the business, and they simply didn't know how to turn a profit anymore. Book Binding has gone down the common road of surrendering to the "beast" of commoditization by increasing volumes and decreasing margins. In the grips of the beast, companies often lay off valuable workers and hire less qualified and cheaper ones, reducing the very expertise they need.

Rather than downsizing, Kosowski and Patrevito decided on culture change—transform the sales force. At first, there was great resistance to these changes, but the two partners persisted, demanding cooperation in the training programs. Salespeople were taught to analyze the market, the customer, and their own services. It was not long before the sales-people realized these new skills were giving them more control. They developed business plans, action steps, and agendas for customer meetings (which were faxed to the client be-forehand). Later they did everything they could to understand each customer's business, including doing in-depth research in areas such as folding and saddlestitching, and then giving two-hour presentations to their peers. Perhaps the most important thing they learned was to listen to the customer rather than jump into a sales pitch.

Was all this worth the effort? In 1995, Book Binding posted profits double the industry av-erage. Their experiencies prove that culture change can be more effective than jumping on the "corporate anorexia" bandwagon.[11] ■

3 *Servant leadership.* Learning organiza-tions are built by servant leaders who devote themselves to others and to the organization's vision. Servant leaders give things away—power, ideas, infor-mation, recognition, credit for accom-plishments. The leader is devoted to building the organization rather than acquiring things for herself or himself. The leader who wants to be a single actor, a hero, seeking personal recognition and resources, cannot build a learning orga-nization. Servant leaders are devoted to the organizational community rather than to themselves. A servant leader encourages participation, shares power, enhances other people's self-worth, en-courages contact among staff members, and gets others excited about their work.[12]

One example of a servant leader is George Sztykiel, chairman of Spartan Motors. Sztykiel's attitude is reflected in his statements to new employees: "Wel-come. We think this is a good corpora-tion. It is run on the same principles that a family is, because we think that's the most effective way human beings have managed to get along." He adds, "I am not the boss. I am the number one ser-vant of this corporation." He makes sure

everyone has equal opportunity and shares in the gains of continuous learn-ing. He takes only a small salary, setting an example for resource sharing.[13] More about Sztykiel and Spartan Motors will be discussed in Chapter 13.

Once leaders are ready to take on the new role of leadership, the other parts of the learning organization can be put into place.

Horizontal Structure

The learning organization breaks down the former vertical structure that separated managers and workers. The learning orga-nization uses the newest ideas for achieving collaboration, including teams, horizontal linkages, task forces, and such concepts as the network organization, in which groups are given profit center autonomy. Large staff departments at headquarters are elimi-nated, and people are sent out to the field. The trend of reengineering, in which hori-zontal processes are brought together into a single unit for speed and efficiency, reflects horizontal organizing. New organization structures represent a revolution in man-agement thinking. The team is more impor-tant than the individual, and teams are given major responsibilities, such as pro-ducing a product or service while also deal-ing with customers. The boss no longer makes the decisions. Team members take responsibility for training, safety, schedul-ing vacations, and sometimes making deci-sions about work and pay.

One organization that has redesigned it-self on the basis of both leadership and hor-izontal structure is Xerox Corporation.

 XEROX CORPORATION

Paul Allaire, CEO of Xerox Corporation, is an example of a new leader who started a revo-lution that not all his managers would survive. Xerox's business environment was so volatile that the functional hierarchy no longer worked. Technology was changing rapidly, and so were customer demands. Indeed, both were moving targets, so Xerox had to be changing also.

Xerox's redesign went far beyond traditional reorganization—moving boxes around on the organization chart—to change what Allaire believed were the three major design components: hardware, people, and software. Hardware includes the traditional boxes on the organization chart, and these were redesigned into small, entrepreneurial business units. This huge company had to become more entrepreneurial, more innovative, and more responsive to the marketplace. People achieved speed, flexibility, accountability, and creativity by being part of small, highly focused divisions.

The changes in people improved the personal mastery and confidence of managers and employees. A new type of manager was required, one who could see not only his or her responsibility but the company as a whole. Everyone needed a total business focus to participate in strategic thinking and implementation. Training was provided to help managers achieve these abilities as well as the qualities of character and personal consistency needed when managers have so much autonomy.

The third element was software, which is the underlying culture, including informal communication networks, values, social relationships, and ways of doing things. The new software placed a high value on teamwork and the ability to delegate to and empower subordinates. The new cultural values also encouraged personal integrity, courage, and elements of servant leadership, such as being able to support and encourage others.

Allaire and a few top managers did an inventory of potential leaders and promoted people who had the ability to implement the hardware, people, and software necessary to put Xerox on the road to becoming a learning organization. Its success has been due to the leadership of CEO Paul Allaire and the new structural architecture.[14] ∎

Employee Empowerment

How is it possible to maintain a sustainable competitive success in a world that is increasingly volatile and chaotic? Companies that are succeeding, like Hewlett-Packard,

Southwest Airlines, Wal-Mart, and Plenum Publishing, sustain top performance through people. They pay attention to employees and empower them to an extraordinary degree. *Empowerment* means giving employees the power, freedom, knowledge, and skills to make decisions and perform effectively. Traditional management tries to limit employees, while empowerment expands their behavior. Empowerment may be reflected in self-managing work teams, quality circles, job enrichment, and employee participation groups as well as through decision-making authority, training, and information so that people can perform jobs without close supervision. Empowerment will be discussed in more detail in Chapter 14.

Attaining competitive success through people means that leaders work with people rather than replace them or limit their scope of activities. People are a leader's primary source of strength, not a cost to be minimized. Firms that adopt this perspective often employ the following practices: Treat employees well. Provide employment security and good wages. Provide a sense of employee ownership by sharing gains in productivity and profits. Commit to education for all members' growth and development. Help employees become world-renowned experts. Cross-train to help people acquire multiple skills. Promote from within.[15]

How do companies implement participation and empowerment? It starts by encouraging the decentralization of decision making and broader worker participation. Again, the leaders set the standard. Nordstrom, a department store chain, for example, uses the following rule:

> Rule #1. Use your good judgment in all situations. There will be no additional rules.[16]

Another example is in Exhibit 2.2, which shows the continuum of skills for which teams take responsibility as they increase in empowerment. Teams typically start out by taking responsibility for technical skills, such as housekeeping, equipment

EXHIBIT 2.2
Continuum of Team Empowerment

SOURCES: Based on Lawrence Holpp, "Applied Empowerment," *Training*, February 1994, 39–44; and Richard S. Wellins, William C. Byham, and Jeanne M. Wilson, *Empowered Teams: Creating Self-Directed Work Groups That Improve Quality, Productivity, and Participation* (San Francisco: Jossey-Bass Publishers, 1991), 26.

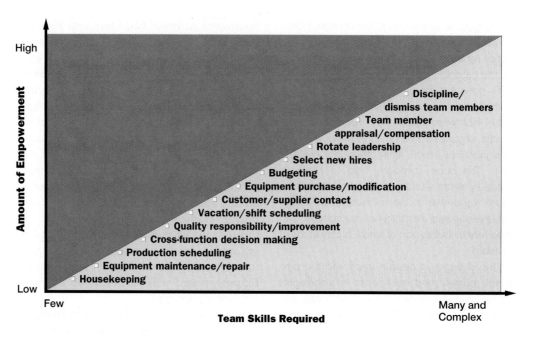

maintenance, and quality. As teams reach higher levels of empowerment, they take over management responsibilities, including budgeting, selecting new employees to join the group, rotating team leadership, and even deciding their own compensation and disciplining team members. Delegating these responsibilities to employees truly increases the brain capacity of the organization, enabling it to deal with unexpected changes and solve whatever problem comes up to achieve the company's vision. At Granite Rock Company, virtually all decisions are made by teams at low levels. A team of drivers and mechanics makes decisions about buying trucks. A team of workers selected the quarry's $850,000 bulldozer.[17]

Communication/ Information Sharing

A learning organization is flooded with information. To identify needs and solve problems, people have to be aware of what's going on. They must understand the whole organization as well as their part in it. Formal data about budgets, profits, and departmental expenses are available to everyone. Described in detail in Chapter 17, this approach is called open-book management. Every employee is free to look at the books and exchange information with anyone in the company. As organizations work with ideas and information rather than products and things, information sharing reaches extraordinary levels. Like the oil in a car's engine, information is not allowed to get low. Leaders in learning organizations know that too much information is better than too little. Employees can select whatever they need for their tasks.

The learning organization also utilizes open communication, which will be described in Chapter 15, and electronic communication, such as e-mail, to be described in Chapter 8. Open communication means getting people talking face-to-face, with the emphasis on listening. It means people talking across departmental lines and talking about the company's vision and values. "Coffee talks" are held in every department at Hewlett-Packard, where the senior manager discusses with employees what's happening not only in their fiefdom but also in the greater $20 billion company. This discussion includes financial results, new products, and whatever employees want to ask. Some companies are using dialogue, which takes people away from work in

The move to *open communication* and *information sharing* usually involves training to bring workers up to speed on company performance. Maytag uses Learning Maps to train employees to understand key business issues and the competitive challenges the company must overcome to remain profitable. The open-forum nature of Maytag's training sessions allows employees to ask specific questions about the corporation's business decisions as well as provide input on how to improve product quality and overall efficiency.

groups of 30 to 40 to communicate deeply and honestly. Back at the workplace, employees are encouraged to call one another directly, crossing levels of hierarchy and departments. Face-to-face meetings are encouraged, with notes taken and circulated to people not attending. Project teams are encouraged to use each other's files.

At companies such as Intel and Microsoft, electronic mail is the primary mechanism of communication. E-mail greatly accelerates the pace of work. Leaders sometimes hold electronic meetings without even knowing where people are located. E-mail overcomes barriers of time and space, enabling people to send highly detailed messages without having to track down intended receivers. People get to the point more quickly.[18]

The move to open communication and information sharing usually involves training. People have to be brought up to speed on computers, and they are given training to interpret profit statements and balance sheets. Whether a secretary or salesperson, a software designer or telephone operator or engineer, each person is part of the business and all are accountable to each other for performance.[19] At Globe Metallurgical, managers have daily, weekly, monthly, and quarterly meetings with employees. These meetings examine details of performance, productivity, and finances. Even senior executive quarterly review meetings are open to all employees. More often than not, leaders go to employees, holding meetings on the plant floor rather than in conference rooms.[20]

Raymond Corporation found it had to restructure its communication process, both inside and outside of the organization, in order to solve a difficult and potentially devastating problem, as described in the Leading the Management Revolution box.

Emergent Strategy

Strategy and planning have traditionally been the domain of top management, for only they had the big picture, knowledge, and expertise to direct the corporation. In the learning organization, leaders still influence overall vision and direction, but they do not control or direct strategy alone.

LEADING THE MANAGEMENT REVOLUTION
EVERY WORKER A STUDENT

Some of the world's smartest and most sophisticated forklifts are made by Raymond Corp., but without a forklift, you can't carry their repair manuals. Chairman Ross Colquhoun realized Raymond was manufacturing too many forklift models and decided to design an integrated circuit universal forklift that could be programmed uniquely for each customer. Constantly displaying its vital signs on an electronic screen, the forklift could also generate daily use reports. It was an innovation and the industry was excited. Orders flooded in. Everything looked good until the forklifts were delivered.

Customers got confused with the continual blinking computer codes. The downside of infinite possibilities for programming was the complexity of the necessary codes. It was more a computer than a forklift, and Raymond's 1,000 trained mechanics did not see themselves as computer techies. "It was a traumatic shock," noted Colquhoun.

Issuing more service manuals and offering more training programs only made the situation worse, for these were people who had chosen a career that involved minimal ongoing study.

Instead, Raymond intentionally became a "learning organization." By tracking mechanics who were making breakthroughs and dispatchers who were becoming skilled phone diagnosticians, consultant Diane Gayeski helped create a knowledge network to record these "best practices." Raymond had to learn not merely to *give* information *to* dealerships, but more importantly to *access* data *from* the dealerships as well.

Dealers were hooked up to a company "intranet," which contained scanned manuals in its database. Dealers, engineers, and mechanics could communicate on problems and troubleshooting, and the worst of the crisis was past. However, such a knowledge bank is only as good as the readiness of participants to make deposits and withdrawals.

Time will tell if Raymond Corp. will maintain the energy and enthusiasm for its newfound learning organization.

SOURCE: Adapted from Thomas Petzinger, Jr., "Two Educators Turn a Forklift Factory into Corporate School." *The Wall Street Journal,* May 17, 1996, B1.

Everyone helps. After all, the core competency of the learning organization is its employees. Strategy emerges from discussions among employees. Information is gathered by employees who work directly with customers, suppliers, and other organizations. Employees develop sensitive antennae for technological and market change. Salespeople look at what customers ask for today, and they look at what customers may need tomorrow. Perhaps thousands of people are in touch with the environment, providing data about external changes in technology and customer needs. They are the ones to identify needs and solutions, passing these ideas into the organization for discussion.[21]

Emergent strategy relies on an experimental mind-set. People are encouraged to try new things, and failure is accepted. Changes in work processes, policies, and products are a series of learning opportunities. Employees contribute their ideas. For example, Ralph Stayer, CEO of Johnsonville Foods, did not make the decision to accept an invitation to make products to be sold under a grocery store chain's own label. He turned the decision over to employees who met in teams for an entire day, investigating every aspect of this opportunity and whether it would be a benefit to the company. Employees saw they could do it. They decided strategy. In another example, Nucor Steel developed the strategy of low-cost production that reflected the vision of CEO Ken Iverson, who took a $270 million chance on new technology for a thin-slab minimill. But employees helped him acquire the new technology and provided ideas for new products and processes that used it. The result was astonishing, with Nucor producing a ton of sheet steel in forty-five worker-minutes versus three worker-hours for big steelmakers.[22]

Strong Culture

Corporate culture is the set of key values, beliefs, understandings, and norms shared by members of the organization. The culture is the foundation of a learning organization. The culture of a learning organization is strong and typically includes strong values in the following three areas.

1 *The whole is more important than the part, and boundaries among parts are minimized.*[23] People in the learning organization are aware of the whole system and how parts fit together. Only by understanding the overall vision and how each part adds to the whole can the learning organization succeed. The emphasis on the whole reduces boundaries. People no longer hoard information or ideas for themselves. The move toward a "boundaryless organization" means reducing barriers among departments, divisions, and external organizations. The free flow of people, ideas, and information allows coordinated action to occur in an uncertain and changing environment. A climate of openness means accessible information for everyone, and open communications. Problems, failures, and lessons are shared, not hidden. Debate and conflict among groups are acceptable ways to solve problems. Everything is in the open, and people have access to any information they need.

2 *The culture is egalitarian.* The culture of a learning organization creates a sense of community, compassion, and caring for one another. People count. Every person has value. The learning organization becomes a place for creating a web of relationships that nurtures and develops each person to his or her maximum potential. Activities that create differences among people are discarded. At a company like Intel, everyone has a small, open cubicle, including CEO Andy Grove. He, and everyone else, can see over the dividers to call out to colleagues across the open space. In a learning organization there are no private dining rooms or reserved parking spots. Everyone gets the same amount of vacation, regardless of position. Everyone may share in stock options or performance bonuses, too. The orientation toward people provides safety for experimentation, frequent mistakes, and failures that enable learning. People are treated with respect and thereby contribute their best to the company.

3 *The culture values improvement and adaptation.* A basic value is to question the status quo, the current way of doing things. Can we do this any better? Why do we do this job that way? Constant questioning of assumptions and challenging the status quo open the gates to creativity and improvement. The philosophy of total quality management is everywhere. People examine other companies and compare themselves to the best, called *benchmarking,* in order to surpass competitors. The organization learns to do things faster and to improve everything on an ongoing basis. An adaptive culture means that people care about important stakeholders, including employees, customers, and stockholders. Managers pay close attention to stakeholders and initiate change when needed. The culture also celebrates the creators of new ideas, products, and work processes. People who contribute to improvement and change are highly rewarded. The organization may pay particular attention to demanding, dissatisfied customers, knowing that improvements to satisfy these customers may lead to the next generation of new products. People in the culture know that the world is by nature chaotic and far from equilibrium, and they do not try to maintain the status quo. The learning organization is always moving forward.

In the learning organization, the culture heroes, stories, symbols, and slogans encourage openness, boundarylessness, equality, continuous improvement, and change. Although no company represents a perfect example of a learning organization, one excellent example is Chaparral Steel, which has been called a learning laboratory because of its clear vision and universal participation of empowered employees to solve problems. Only two levels of hierarchy exist and employees are rewarded for learning new skills and for performance. Maximum communication among all employees is encouraged.[24] Another example of a learning organization is Granite Rock Company, which had to learn a totally new way of doing business in order to survive.

■ GRANITE ROCK COMPANY

Granite Rock Company of Watsonville, California, has been owned and operated by the Wilson/Woolpert family for more than 90 years, but the company was hit with big changes ten years ago. The threat of absorption into a conglomerate was added to California's tightening industrial regulations, while customers were clamoring for high quality materials and more responsive service. Computer technology to automate quarry work was new and expensive. Granite Rock would have to find new ways of doing business amid a host of changes and well-financed predators.

Bruce Woolpert, a joint CEO with brother Steve, and eight-year veteran of Hewlett-Packard, wanted to be as efficient and customer-oriented as HP. First, he got maximum information flowing into the company. Instead of the industry standard of a dozen internal process controls, Granite Rock kept track of one hundred. Then Bruce started asking customers to rate the company against competitors on "report cards."

Bruce went out and "benchmarked" within the company, identifying "best practices" by visiting cement plants and the quarry. Asking workers what they liked and disliked about their jobs and the company, he set up a model for two-way communication up and down the entire organization. He organized teams of managers and hourly workers to analyze problems. Both groups also attended many seminars together. Merging the two groups increased input and united the company's now 535 employees.

Technology and training have made Granite Rock the region's low-cost producer of crushed rock with annual sales of more than $90 million. Quality and service levels are high enough to allow charging a 6 percent premium and still increase market share. Granite Rock inspires fierce loyalty among workers. Former CEO Betsy Wilson Woolpert, Bruce's mother and daughter of founder Arthur Wilson, says, "Most Granite Rock people remain with us for their entire career. We like that and hope it can be maintained."[25] ■

Chaparral Steel and Granite Rock Company have become true learning organizations. The leadership provides flat, horizontal designs, a shared vision, and an attitude of serving employees. The cultures stress egalitarian values, providing support for risk taking. There are no boundaries separating departments. People are empowered to the point where no one has to take orders if he or she feels the order is wrong. The strategy emerges through the experiences of employees who work with customers and new technologies. Chaparral and Granite Rock are flooded with information from experiments and travel, and that information is liberally shared. The flat structure reinforces horizontal teams and company performance.

HISTORICAL FORCES LEADING UP TO THE LEARNING ORGANIZATION

The paradigm shift spoken of earlier has led to many changes in organizations. Yet it should not be forgotten that these innovations were possible in part because of the trial and error experiments in organizations during the past century. We are now benefiting from the accumulated wisdom of many men and women who have either studied or practiced management.[26]

History is important to managers because a study of the past contributes to understanding both the present and the future. It is a way of learning: learning from others' mistakes so as not to repeat them; learning from others' successes so as to repeat them in the appropriate situation; and, most of all, learning to understand why things happen to improve things in the future.

For example, such companies as Polaroid, AT&T, International Harvester, Consolidated Edison, and Wells Fargo Bank have all asked historians to research their pasts. Managers want to know their corporate roots. Polaroid's W-3 plant in Waltham, Massachusetts, started out as a model of efficiency, but over the years productivity dropped and relations with workers soured. A corporate historian was hired to interview employees and examine old records. He pieced together how managers had imposed ever tighter controls over the years that lowered workers' morale.[27] Or consider the signing of Randy Travis, now a country music superstar, by Warner Brothers. Country music had been invaded by pop music influence, and industry managers wanted more pop in the country sound to appeal to younger audiences. Martha Sharp, a vice president for Warner Brothers, loved Travis's voice and used a cycle-of-history argument on her bosses. She argued that, based on historical patterns, a traditional country sound would reemerge, and Travis would be in the forefront. Her argument won, Travis was signed, and he led a resurgence in country music.[28]

Studying history does not mean merely arranging events in chronological order; it means developing an understanding of the impact of societal forces on organizations. Studying history is a way to achieve strategic thinking, see the big picture, and improve conceptual skills. We will start by examining how social, political, and economic forces have influenced organizations and the practice of management.[29]

Social forces refer to those aspects of a culture that guide and influence relationships among people. What do people value? What do people need? What are the standards of behavior among people? These forces shape what is known as the *social contract,* which refers to the unwritten, common rules and perceptions about relationships among people and between employees and management. Expressions such as "a man's as good as his word" and "a day's work for a day's pay" convey such perceptions.

Political forces refer to the influence of political and legal institutions on people and organizations. Political forces include basic assumptions underlying the political system, such as the desirability of self-government, property rights, contract rights, the definition of justice, and the determination of innocence or guilt of a crime. The end of the Cold War and the spread of capitalism throughout the world are political forces that will dramatically affect business in coming years. Recent moves to establish a free market system in Eastern Europe underscore the growing interdependence among the world's countries. This interdependence requires managers to think in different ways. In addition, the empowerment of citizens throughout the world is a dramatically energetic political force. Power is being diffused both within and among countries as never before.[30] People are demanding empowerment, participation, and responsibility in all areas of their lives, including their work. Managers must learn to share rather than hoard power.

Economic forces pertain to the availability, production, and distribution of resources in a society. Governments, military agencies, churches, schools, and business organizations in every society require resources to achieve their goals, and economic forces influence the allocation of scarce resources. Resources may be human or material, fabricated or natural, physical or conceptual, but over time they are scarce and must be allocated among competing users. Economic scarcity is often the stimulus for technological innovation with which to increase resource availability. The perfection of the moving assembly line at Ford in 1913 cut the number of worker-hours needed for assembling a Model T from 12 to 1.5. Ford doubled its daily pay rate to $5, shortened working hours, and cut the price of Model Ts until its market share reached 57 percent in 1923.

political forces
The influence of political and legal institutions on people and organizations.

economic forces
Forces that affect the availability, production, and distribution of a society's resources among competing users.

social forces
The aspects of a culture that guide and influence relationships among people—their values, needs, and standards of behavior.

CLASSICAL PERSPECTIVE

The practice of management can be traced to 3000 B.C. to the first government organizations developed by the Sumerians and Egyptians, but the formal study of management is relatively recent.[31] The early study of management as we know it today began with what is now called the *classical perspective.*

classical perspective
A management perspective that emerged during the nineteenth and early twentieth centuries that emphasized a rational, scientific approach to the study of management and sought to make organizations efficient operating machines.

The **classical perspective** on management emerged during the nineteenth and early twentieth centuries. The factory system that began to appear in the 1800s posed management challenges that earlier organizations had not encountered. Problems arose in tooling the plants, organizing managerial structure, training employees (many of them non-English-speaking immigrants), scheduling complex manufacturing operations, and dealing with increased labor dissatisfaction and resulting strikes.

In response to the myriad new problems facing management throughout industrial America, managers developed and tested solutions to the mounting challenges. The evolution of modern management, called the classical perspective, thus began. This perspective contains three subfields, each with a slightly different emphasis: scientific management, bureaucratic organizations, and administrative principles.[32]

Frederick Winslow Taylor (1856–1915) Taylor's theory that labor productivity could be improved by scientifically determined management practices earned him the status of "father of scientific management."

Scientific Management

scientific management
A subfield of the classical management perspective that emphasized scientifically determined changes in management practices as the solution to improving labor productivity.

Organizations' somewhat limited success in achieving improvements in labor productivity led a young engineer to suggest that the problem lay more in poor management practices than in labor. Frederick Winslow Taylor (1856–1915) insisted that management itself would have to change and, further, that the manner of change could be determined only by scientific study; hence, the label **scientific management** emerged. Taylor suggested that decisions based on rules of thumb and tradition be replaced with precise procedures developed after careful study of individual situations.[33]

Taylor's approach is illustrated by the unloading of iron from rail cars and reloading finished steel for the Bethlehem Steel plant in 1898. Taylor calculated that with correct movements, tools, and sequencing, each man was capable of loading 47.5 tons per day instead of the typical 12.5 tons. He also worked out an incentive system that paid each man $1.85 a day for meeting the new standard, an increase from the previous rate of $1.15. Productivity at Bethlehem Steel shot up overnight.

Although known as the "father of scientific management," Taylor was not alone in this area. Henry Gantt, an associate of Taylor's, developed the *Gantt Chart*—a bar graph that measures planned and completed work along each stage of production by time elapsed. Two other important pioneers in this area were the husband-and-wife team of Frank B. and Lillian M. Gilbreth. Frank B. Gilbreth (1868–1924) pioneered time and motion study and arrived at many of his management techniques independently of Taylor (the Gilbreth family was featured in the movie *Cheaper By the*

Dozen). Gilbreth stressed efficiency and was known for his quest for the "one best way" to do work. Although he is known for his early work with bricklayers, his work had great impact on medical surgery by drastically reducing the time patients spent on the operating table. Surgeons were able to save countless lives through the application of time and motion study. Lillian M. Gilbreth (1878–1972) was more interested in the human aspect of work. When her husband died at the age of 56, she had 12 children ages 2 to 19. The undaunted "first lady of management" went right on with her work. She presented a paper in Prague in place of her late husband, continued their seminars and consulting, lectured, and eventually became a professor at Purdue University.[34] She pioneered in the field of industrial psychology and made substantial contributions to personnel management.

The basic ideas of scientific management are shown in Exhibit 2.3. To use this approach, managers should develop standard methods for doing each job, select workers with the appropriate abilities, train workers in the standard methods, support workers and eliminate interruptions, and provide wage incentives.

Although scientific management improved productivity, its failure to deal with the social context and workers' needs led to increased conflict between managers and

Lillian M. Gilbreth (1878–1972) Frank B. Gilbreth (1868–1924) Shown here using a "motion study" device, this husband-and-wife team contributed to the principles of *scientific management.* His development of time and motion studies and her work in industrial psychology pioneered many of today's management and human resource techniques.

employees. Under this system, workers often felt exploited. This was in sharp contrast to the harmony and cooperation that Taylor and his followers had envisioned.

Bureaucratic Organizations

A systematic approach developed in Europe that looked at the organization as a whole is the **bureaucratic organizations** approach, a subfield within the classical perspective. Max Weber (1864–1920), a German theorist, introduced most of the concepts on bureaucratic organizations.[35]

During the late 1800s, many European organizations were managed on a "personal," family-like basis. Employees were loyal to a single individual rather than to the organization or its mission. The

bureaucratic organizations
A subfield of the classical management perspective that emphasized management on an impersonal, rational basis through such elements as clearly defined authority and responsibility, formal record-keeping, and separation of management and ownership.

General Approach
- Developed standard method for performing each job.
- Selected workers with appropriate abilities for each job.
- Trained workers in standard method.
- Supported workers by planning their work and eliminating interruptions.
- Provided wage incentives to workers for increased output.

Contributions
- Demonstrated the importance of compensation for performance.
- Initiated the careful study of tasks and jobs.
- Demonstrated the importance of personnel selection and training.

Criticisms
- Did not appreciate the social context of work and higher needs of workers.
- Did not acknowledge variance among individuals.
- Tended to regard workers as uninformed and ignored their ideas and suggestions.

EXHIBIT 2.3
Characteristics of Scientific Management

Max Weber
(1864–1920)
The German theorist's concepts on *bureaucratic organizations* have contributed to the efficiency of many of today's corporations.

5 Management is separate from the ownership of the organization.
6 Managers are subject to rules and procedures that will ensure reliable, predictable behavior. Rules are impersonal and uniformly applied to all employees.

Weber believed that an organization based on rational authority would be more efficient and adaptable to change. The term *bureaucracy* has taken on a negative meaning in today's organizations and is associated with endless rules and red tape. We have all been frustrated by waiting in long lines or following seemingly silly procedures. On the other hand, rules and other bureaucratic procedures provide a standard way of dealing with employees. Everyone gets equal treatment, and everyone knows what the rules are. This has enabled many organizations to become extremely efficient. Consider United Parcel Service (UPS), also called the "Brown Giant."

dysfunctional consequence of this management practice was that resources were used to realize individual desires rather than organizational goals. Employees in effect owned the organization and used resources for their own gain rather than to serve customers. Weber envisioned organizations that would be managed on an impersonal, rational basis. This form of organization was called a *bureaucracy*. The six characteristics of bureaucracy as specified by Weber are:

1 Labor is divided, with clear definitions of authority and responsibility that are legitimized as official duties.
2 Positions are organized in a hierarchy of authority, with each position under the authority of a higher one.
3 All personnel are selected and promoted based on technical qualifications, which are assessed by examination or according to training and experience.
4 Administrative acts and decisions are recorded in writing. Recordkeeping provides organizational memory and continuity over time.

UNITED PARCEL SERVICE

United Parcel Service took on the U.S. Postal Service at its own game—and won. UPS specializes in the delivery of small packages. Why has the Brown Giant been so successful? One important reason is the concept of bureaucracy. UPS is bound up in rules and regulations. There are safety rules for drivers, loaders, clerks, and managers. Strict dress codes are enforced—no beards; hair cannot touch the collar; mustaches must be trimmed evenly; and no sideburns. Rules specify cleanliness standards for buildings and other properties. No eating or drinking is permitted at employee desks. Every manager is given bound copies of policy books and expected to use them regularly.

UPS also has a well-defined division of labor. Each plant consists of specialized drivers, loaders, clerks, washers, sorters, and maintenance personnel. UPS thrives on written records. Daily worksheets specify performance goals and work output. Daily employee quotas and achievements are reported on a weekly and monthly basis.

Technical qualification is the criterion for hiring and promotion. The UPS policy book says the leader is expected to have the knowledge and capacity to justify the position of leadership. Favoritism is forbidden. The bureaucratic model works just fine at UPS, "the tightest ship in the shipping business."[36] ■

Administrative Principles

Another major subfield within the classical perspective is known as the **administrative principles** approach. Whereas scientific management focused on the productivity of the individual worker, the administrative principles approach focused on the total organization. The contributors to this approach included Henri Fayol, Mary Parker Follett, and Chester I. Barnard.

Henri Fayol (1841–1925) was a French mining engineer who worked his way up to become head of a major mining group known as Comambault. Comambault survives today as part of Le Creusot-Loire, the largest mining and metallurgical group in central France. In his later years, Fayol wrote down his concepts on administration, based largely on his own management experiences.[37]

In his most significant work, *General and Industrial Management,* Fayol discussed 14 general principles of management, several of which are part of management philosophy today. For example:

- *Unit of command.* Each subordinate receives orders from one—and only one—superior.

- *Division of work.* Managerial and technical work are amenable to specialization to produce more and better work with the same amount of effort.

- *Unity of direction.* Similar activities in an organization should be grouped together under one manager.

- *Scalar chain.* A chain of authority extends from the top to the bottom of the organization and should include every employee.

Mary Parker Follett (1868–1933) Follett was a major contributor to the *administrative principles* approach to management. Her emphasis on worker participation and shared goals among managers was embraced by many businesspeople of the day and has been recently "rediscovered" by corporate America.

Fayol felt that these principles could be applied in any organizational setting. He also identified five basic functions or elements of management: planning, organizing, commanding, coordinating, and controlling. These functions underlie much of the general approach to today's management theory.

Mary Parker Follett (1868–1933) was trained in philosophy and political science at what today is Radcliffe College. She applied herself in many fields, including social psychology and management. She wrote of the importance of common superordinate goals for reducing conflict in organizations.[38] Her work was popular with businesspeople of her day but was often overlooked by management scholars.[39] Follett's ideas served as a contrast to scientific management and are reemerging as applicable for modern managers dealing with rapid changes in today's global environment. Her approach to leadership stressed the importance of people rather than engineering techniques. She offered the pithy admonition "Don't Hug Your Blueprints" and analyzed the dynamics of management–organization interactions. Follett addressed issues that are timely in the 1990s,

administrative principles
A subfield of the classical management perspective that focused on the total organization rather than the individual worker, delineating the management functions of planning, organizing, commanding, coordinating, and controlling.

such as ethics, power, and how to lead in a way that encourages employees to give their best. The concepts of empowerment, facilitating rather than controlling employees, and allowing employees to act depending on the authority of the situation opened new areas for theoretical study by Chester Barnard and others.[40]

Chester I. Barnard (1886–1961) studied economics at Harvard but failed to receive a degree because he lacked a course in laboratory science. He went to work in the statistical department of AT&T and in 1927 became president of New Jersey Bell. One of Barnard's significant contributions was the concept of the informal organization. The *informal organization* occurs in all formal organizations and includes cliques and naturally occurring social groupings. Barnard argued that organizations are not machines and informal relationships are powerful forces that can help the organization if properly managed. Another significant contribution was the *acceptance theory of authority*, which states that people have free will and can choose whether to follow management orders. People typically follow orders because they perceive positive benefit to themselves, but they do have a choice. Managers should treat employees properly because their acceptance of authority may be critical to organization success in important situations.[41]

The overall classical perspective as an approach to management was very powerful and gave companies fundamental new skills for establishing high productivity and effective treatment of employees. Indeed, America surged ahead of the world in management techniques, and other countries, especially Japan, borrowed heavily from American ideas.

HUMANISTIC PERSPECTIVE

Mary Parker Follett and Chester Barnard were early advocates of a more **humanistic perspective** on management that empha-

sized the importance of understanding human behaviors, needs, and attitudes in the workplace as well as social interactions and group processes.[42] We will discuss three subfields based on the humanistic perspective: the human relations movement, the human resources perspective, and the behavioral sciences approach.

The Human Relations Movement

America has always espoused the spirit of human equality. However, this spirit has not always been translated into practice when it comes to power sharing between managers and workers. The human relations school of thought considers that truly effective control comes from within the individual worker rather than from strict, authoritarian control.[43] This school of thought recognized and directly responded to social pressures for enlightened treatment of employees. The early work on industrial psychology and personnel selection received little attention because of the prominence of scientific management. Then a series of studies at a Chicago electric company, which came to be known as the **Hawthorne studies,** changed all that.

Beginning about 1895, a struggle developed between manufacturers of gas and electric lighting fixtures for control of the residential and industrial market.[44] By 1909 electric lighting had begun to win, but the increasingly efficient electric fixtures used less total power. The electric companies began a campaign to convince industrial users that they needed more light to get more productivity. When advertising did not work, the industry began using experimental tests to demonstrate their argument. Managers were skeptical about the results, so the Committee on Industrial Lighting (CIL) was set up to run the tests. To further add to the tests' credibility, Thomas Edison was made honorary chairman of the CIL. In one test location—the Hawthorne plant of the Western Electric Company—some interesting events occurred.

Hawthorne studies
A series of experiments on worker productivity begun in 1924 at the Hawthorne plant of Western Electric Company in Illinois; attributed employees' increased output to managers' better treatment of them during the study.

humanistic perspective
A management perspective that emerged around the late nineteenth century that emphasized understanding human behavior, needs, and attitudes in the workplace.

The major part of this work involved four experimental and three control groups. In all, five different "tests" were conducted. These pointed to the importance of factors *other* than illumination in affecting productivity. To more carefully examine these factors, numerous other experiments were conducted.[45] These were the first Relay Assembly Test Room, the second Relay Assembly Group, the Mica Splitting Group, the Typewriting Group, and the Bank Wiring Observation Room. The results of the most famous study, the first Relay Assembly Test Room (RATR) experiment, were extremely controversial. Under the guidance of two Harvard professors, Elton Mayo and Fritz Roethlisberger, the RATR studies lasted nearly six years (May 10, 1927 to May 4, 1933) and involved 24 separate experimental periods. So many factors were changed and so many unforeseen factors uncontrolled that scholars disagree on the factors that truly contributed to the general increase in performance over that period. Most early interpretations, however, agreed on one thing: Money was not the cause of the increased output.[46] Recent analyses of the experiments, however, suggest that money may well have been the single most important factor.[47] An interview with one of the original participants revealed that just getting into the experimental group had meant a huge increase in income.[48]

These new data clearly show that money mattered a great deal at Hawthorne, but it was not recognized at the time of the experiments. Then it was felt that the factor that best explained increased output was "human relations." Employees' output increased sharply when managers treated them in a positive manner. These findings were published and started a revolution in worker treatment for improving organizational productivity. To be historically accurate, money was probably the best explanation for increases in output, but at that time experimenters believed the explanation was human relations. Despite the inaccurate interpretation of the data, the findings provided the impetus for the **human relations movement.** That movement shaped management theory and practice for well over a quarter-century, and the belief that human relations is the best approach for increasing productivity persists today. See Exhibit 2.4 for a number of management innovations that have become popular over the years.

The Human Resources Perspective

The human relations movement initially espoused a "dairy farm" view of management—contented cows give more milk, so satisfied workers will give more work. Gradually, views with deeper content began to emerge. The human resources perspective maintained an interest in worker participation and considerate leadership but shifted the emphasis to consider the daily tasks that people perform. The **human resources perspective** combines prescriptions for design of job tasks with theories of motivation.[49] In the human resources view, jobs should be designed so that tasks are not perceived as dehumanizing or demeaning but instead allow workers to use their full potential. Two of the best-known contributors to the human resources perspective were Abraham Maslow and Douglas McGregor.

Abraham Maslow (1908–1970), a practicing psychologist, observed that his patients' problems usually stemmed from an inability to satisfy their needs. Thus, he generalized his work and suggested a hierarchy of needs. Maslow's hierarchy started with physiological needs and progressed to safety, belongingness, esteem, and, finally, self-actualization needs. Chapter 16 discusses his ideas in more detail.

Douglas McGregor (1906–1964) had become frustrated with the early simplistic human relations notions while president of Antioch College in Ohio. He challenged both the classical perspective and the early human relations assumptions about human behavior. Based on his experiences as a manager and consultant, his training as a psychologist, and the work of Maslow,

human relations movement
A movement in management thinking and practice that emphasized satisfaction of employees' basic needs as the key to increased worker productivity.

human resources perspective
A management perspective that suggests jobs should be designed to meet higher-level needs by allowing workers to use their full potential.

EXHIBIT 2.4
Ebbs and Flows of Management Innovations, 1950–1995

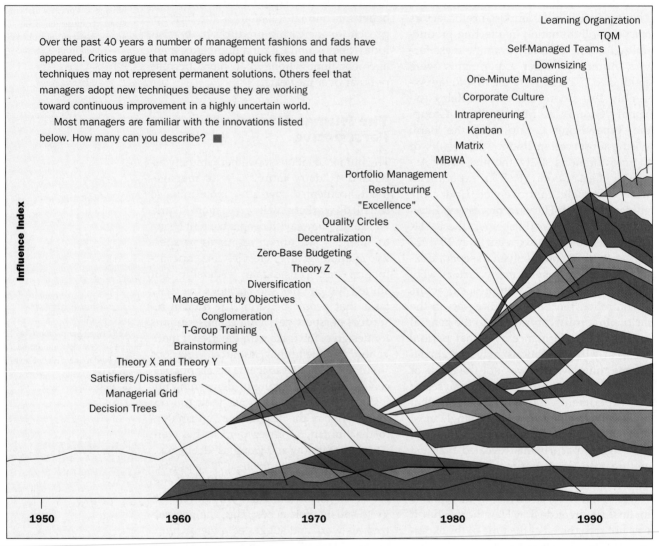

Over the past 40 years a number of management fashions and fads have appeared. Critics argue that managers adopt quick fixes and that new techniques may not represent permanent solutions. Others feel that managers adopt new techniques because they are working toward continuous improvement in a highly uncertain world.

Most managers are familiar with the innovations listed below. How many can you describe? ■

SOURCE: Reprinted with the permission of Simon & Schuster from *Managing on the Edge* by Richard Tanner Pascale. Copyright © 1990 by Richard Pascale.

McGregor formulated his Theory X and Theory Y, which are explained in Exhibit 2.5.[50] McGregor believed that the classical perspective was based on Theory X assumptions about workers. He also felt that a slightly modified version of Theory X fit early human relations ideas. In other words, human relations ideas did not go far enough. McGregor proposed Theory Y as a more realistic view of workers for guiding management thinking.

The point of Theory Y is that organizations can take advantage of the imagination and intellect of all their employees. Employees will exercise self-control and will contribute to organizational goals when given the opportunity. A few companies today still use Theory X management, but many are trying Theory Y techniques. Saturn Corp., with one of the greatest success stories in the auto industry, has practiced Theory Y from its beginning.

EXHIBIT 2.5
Theory X and Theory Y

Assumptions of Theory X

- The average human being has an inherent dislike of work and will avoid it if possible....
- Because of the human characteristic of dislike for work, most people must be coerced, controlled, directed, or threatened with punishment to get them to put forth adequate effort toward the achievement of organizational objectives....
- The average human being prefers to be directed, wishes to avoid responsibility, has relatively little ambition, wants security above all.

Assumptions of Theory Y

- The expenditure of physical and mental effort in work is as natural as play or rest. The average human being does not inherently dislike work....
- External control and the threat of punishment are not the only means for bringing about effort toward organizational objectives. A person will exercise self-direction and self-control in the service of objectives to which he or she is committed....
- The average human being learns, under proper conditions, not only to accept but to seek responsibility....
- The capacity to exercise a relatively high degree of imagination, ingenuity, and creativity in the solution of organizational problems is widely, not narrowly, distributed in the population.
- Under the conditions of modern industrial life, the intellectual potentialities of the average human being are only partially utilized.

SOURCE: Douglas McGregor, *The Human Side of Enterprise* (New York: McGraw-Hill, 1960), 33–48.

SATURN CORPORATION

For years, General Motors poured billions of dollars into the Spring Hill, Tennessee, Saturn plant while critics claimed GM would never be able to build a small car that would compete with the Japanese. The critics didn't understand the extent to which Saturn Corp. would trust employees, engaging their hearts and minds in the production of a world-class automobile. Organized into teams, assembly line workers hire new employees, approve parts from suppliers, choose their own equipment, and handle administrative matters such as the budget. Worker teams keep costs down and pass the savings to customers. And the teams have the responsibility to achieve quality targets, which they will not compromise. Saturn's revolutionary labor agreement makes full partners of union members and managers, giving everyone the authority to solve quality problems. Line workers have the authority, for example, to telephone the supplier when defective parts are discovered to get them fixed. The 14-member door assembly team recently suggested rearranging machinery to improve quality and productivity, which meant using two fewer people. The two extra employees were transferred to another part of the plant, reflecting the trust employees have that they won't be worked out of a job.

Saturn has been so successful at taking advantage of the imagination, creativity, and ability of its employees that it has jumped to the top of the customer approval ratings, joining Lexus and Infiniti, which cost tens of thousands more. The cars almost race out of dealer showrooms.[51] ∎

The Behavioral Sciences Approach

The **behavioral sciences approach** develops theories about human behavior based on scientific methods and study. Behavioral science draws from sociology, psychology, anthropology, economics, and other disciplines to understand employee behavior and interaction in an organizational setting. The approach can be seen in practically every organization. When General Electric conducts research to determine the best set of tests, interviews, and employee profiles to use when selecting new employees, it is employing behavioral science techniques. Emery Air Freight has utilized reinforcement theory to improve the incentives given to workers and increase the performance of many of its operations. When Westinghouse trains new managers in the techniques of employee motivation, most of

behavioral sciences approach
A subfield of the humanistic management perspective that applies social science in an organizational context, drawing from economics, psychology, sociology, and other disciplines.

the theories and findings are rooted in behavioral science research.

In the behavioral sciences, economics and sociology have significantly influenced the way today's managers approach organizational strategy and structure. Psychology has influenced management approaches to motivation, communication, leadership, and the overall field of personnel management.

Remaining chapters of this book contain research findings and applications that can be attributed to the behavioral sciences approach to the study of organizations and management. Exhibit 2.4 shows the trend of new management concepts from the behavioral sciences. Note the increase in concepts about 1970 and then again from 1980 until the present. The increasing intensity of global competition has produced great interest in improved behavioral approaches to management. The continued development of new management techniques can be expected in the future.

MANAGEMENT SCIENCE PERSPECTIVE

World War II caused many management changes. The massive and complicated problems associated with modern global warfare presented managerial decision makers with the need for more sophisticated tools than ever before. The **management science perspective** emerged to treat those problems. This view is distinguished for its application of mathematics, statistics, and other quantitative techniques to management decision making and problem solving. During World War II, groups of mathematicians, physicists, and other scientists were formed to solve military problems. Because those problems frequently involved moving massive amounts of materials and large numbers of people quickly and efficiently, the techniques had obvious applications to large-scale business firms.[52]

Operations research grew directly out of the World War II groups (called *operational research teams* in Great Britain and *operations research teams* in the United States).[53] It consists of mathematical model building and other applications of quantitative techniques to managerial problems.

Operations management refers to the field of management that specializes in the physical production of goods or services. Operations management specialists use quantitative techniques to solve manufacturing problems. Some of the commonly used methods are forecasting, inventory modeling, linear and nonlinear programming, queuing theory, scheduling, simulation, and break-even analysis.

Management information systems (MIS) is the most recent subfield of the management science perspective. These systems are designed to provide relevant information to managers in a timely and cost-efficient manner. The advent of the high-speed digital computer opened up the full potential of this area for management.

Many of today's organizations have departments of management science specialists to help solve quantitatively based problems. When Sears used computer models to minimize its inventory costs, it was applying a quantitative approach to management. When AT&T performed network analysis to speed up and control the construction of new facilities and switching systems, it was employing management science tools.

One specific technique used in many organizations is queuing theory. *Queuing theory* uses mathematics to calculate how to provide services that will minimize the waiting time of customers. Queuing theory has been used to analyze the traffic flow through the Lincoln Tunnel and to determine the number of toll booths and traffic officers for a toll road. Queuing theory was used to develop the single waiting line for tellers used in many banks. Wesley Long Community Hospital in Greensboro, North Carolina, used queuing theory to analyze the telemetry system used in wireless cardiac monitors. The analysis helped the hospital acquire the precise number of telemetry units needed to safely monitor all patients without overspending scarce resources.[54]

management science perspective A management perspective that emerged after World War II and applied mathematics, statistics, and other quantitative techniques to managerial problems.

CONTEMPORARY EXTENSIONS

Management is by nature complex and dynamic. Elements of each of the perspectives we have discussed are still in use today. The most prevalent is the humanistic perspective, but even it has been undergoing change in recent years. Two major contemporary extensions of this perspective are systems theory and the contingency view. Examination of each will allow a fuller appreciation of the state of management thinking today.

Systems Theory

A **system** is a set of interrelated parts that function as a whole to achieve a common purpose.[55] A system functions by acquiring inputs from the external environment, transforming them in some way, and discharging outputs back to the environment. Exhibit 2.6 shows the basic **systems theory** of organizations. Here there are five components: inputs, a transformation process, outputs, feedback, and the environment. *Inputs* are the material, human, financial, or information resources used to produce goods or services. The *transformation process* is management's use of production technology to change the inputs into outputs. *Outputs* include the organization's products and services. *Feedback* is knowledge of the results that influence the selection of inputs during the next cycle of the process. The *environment* surrounding the organization includes the social, political, and economic forces noted earlier in this chapter.

Some ideas in systems theory have had substantial impact on management thinking. These include open and closed systems, entropy, synergy, and subsystem interdependencies.[56]

Open systems must interact with the environment to survive; **closed systems** need not. In the classical and management science perspectives, organizations were frequently thought of as closed systems. In the management science perspective, closed system assumptions—the absence of external disturbances—are sometimes used to simplify problems for quantitative analysis. In reality, however, all organizations are open systems, and the cost of ignoring the environment may be failure.

Entropy is a universal property of systems and refers to their tendency to run

system
A set of interrelated parts that function as a whole to achieve a common purpose.

systems theory
An extension of the humanistic perspective that describes organizations as open systems that are characterized by entropy, synergy, and subsystem interdependence.

open system
A system that interacts with the external environment.

closed system
A system that does not interact with the external environment.

entropy
The tendency for a system to run down and die.

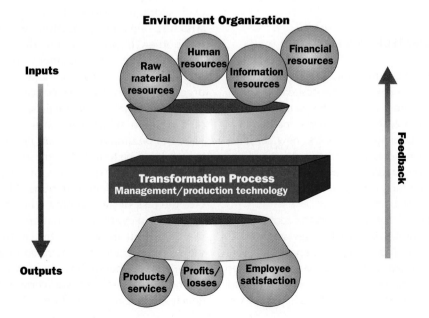

EXHIBIT 2.6
The Systems View of Organizations

down and die. If a system does not receive fresh inputs and energy from its environment, it will eventually cease to exist. Organizations must monitor their environments, adjust to changes, and continuously bring in new inputs in order to survive and prosper. Managers try to design the organization/environment interfaces to reduce entropy.

Synergy means that the whole is greater than the sum of its parts. When an organization is formed, something new comes into the world. Management, coordination, and production that did not exist before are now present. Organizational units working together can accomplish more than those same units working alone. The sales department depends on production and vice versa.

Subsystems are parts of a system that depend on one another. Changes in one part of the organization affect other parts. The organization must be managed as a coordinated whole. Managers who understand subsystem interdependence are reluctant to make changes that do not recognize the subsystem impact on the organization as a whole. Because of this, some large organizations are spinning off their subsystems in order to allow them to be more successful. Consider the case of Ultratech.

synergy
The concept that the whole is greater than the sum of its parts.

subsystems
Parts of a system that depend on one another for their functioning.

contingency view
An extension of the humanistic perspective in which the successful resolution of organizational problems is thought to depend on managers' identification of key variables in the situation at hand.

■ ULTRATECH CORPORATION

Freedom from the big, bureaucratic corporation can be great. But the cost can be pretty high and the transition brutal, as many spinoffs fail miserably. No longer under the thumb of the overbearing structure, the new company also is without its protection. Employees skilled at working organizational politics suddenly find the extremely competitive entrepreneurial world a different story.

Arthur W. Zafiropoulo and his company, Ultratech, make one of the success stories. Manufacturing products called "steppers" that are used to make integrated circuits, Ultratech bled red ink under its previous owner, giant General Signal Corporation. In 1990, Zafiropoulo was brought in to whip the division into shape to be sold. He moved quickly, slashing about one-third of the workforce, down to 230. Realizing he needed to get back the entrepreneurial spirit, he re-established Ultratech's independent sales force, getting away from the mingled one with General Signal. Even though the big company had tried to make Ultratech profitable, it was, after all, just a small part of their business.

By 1993 the division was beginning to show profit, but no buyers were found for the still-shaky venture. Anxious to shed its albatross, General Signal asked Zafiropoulo to lead a buyout on his own, which he did with $5,000 and some loans. Accelerating changes he had already begun, Zafiropoulo oversaw an increase in sales of 350 percent and the workforce expanded to 700.

Spinoffs are still risky, though, and require "seat-of-the-pants" decision making. That's why large bureaucracies are often not user-friendly to small divisions.[57] ■

Contingency View

The second contemporary extension to management thinking is the contingency view. The classical perspective assumed a *universalist* view. Management concepts were thought to be universal; that is, whatever worked—leader style, bureaucratic structure—in one organization would work in another. It proposed the discovery of "one-best-way" management principles that applied the same techniques to every organization. In business education, however, an alternative view exists. This is the *case* view, in which each situation is believed to be unique. There are no universal principles to be found, and one learns about management by experiencing a large number of case problem situations. Managers face the task of determining what methods will work in every new situation.

To integrate these views the **contingency view** has emerged, as illustrated in Exhibit 2.7.[58] Here neither of the other views is seen as entirely correct. Instead, certain contingencies, or variables, exist for helping man-

EXHIBIT 2.7
**The Contingency
View of Management**

agement identify and understand situations. The contingency view means that a manager's response depends on identifying key contingencies in an organizational situation. For example, a consultant may mistakenly recommend the same management-by-objectives (MBO) system for a manufacturing firm that was successful in a school system. A central government agency may impose the same rules on a welfare agency that it did in a workers' compensation office. A large corporation may take over a chain of restaurants and impose the same organizational charts and financial systems that are used in a banking division. The contingency view tells us that what works in one setting may not work in another. Management's job is to search for important contingencies. When managers learn to identify important patterns and characteristics of their organizations, they can then fit solutions to those characteristics. One such pattern emerging recently is the advantage of small companies over large ones in the use of technology, as shown in the Technology for Today box.

Industry is one important contingency. Management practice in a rapidly changing industry will be very different from that in a stable one. Other important contingencies that managers must understand are manufacturing technology and international cultures. For example, several major banks, such as Manufacturers Hanover Corporation, misunderstood the nature of making loans to developing countries. As these big banks raised loan-loss reserves to cope with the prospect of bad international loans, their balance sheet was weakened to the extent that they had to stop expansion into new regions and new business activities.

Having been through this experience, managers in the future will know how to handle this contingency in the international financial environment.[59]

RECENT HISTORICAL TRENDS

The historical forces that influence management perspective continue to change and influence the practice of management. The most striking change now affecting management is international competition. This important trend has major impact on the total quality management and learning organization movements in North America and Europe.

Globalization

The domain of business now covers the entire planet, where Reeboks, stock markets, fax machines, television, personal computers, and T-shirts intermingle across national boundaries. The world of commerce is becoming wired like an integrated circuit, with no nation left out of the loop.

The impact on firms in the United States and Canada has been severe. International competition has raised the standard of performance in quality, cost, productivity, and response times.[60] As a result, the United States and Canada have seen a decline in worldwide market share in traditional products. Moreover, in 1975, the U.S. balance of payments was close to zero. In recent years it has been hundreds of billions of dollars in the red.[61] Likewise, the business world is reeling under the impact of recent historical events—the breakup of the

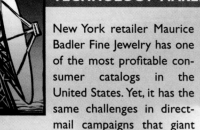

TECHNOLOGY FOR TODAY
TECHNOLOGY MAKES THE SMALL BEAUTIFUL

New York retailer Maurice Badler Fine Jewelry has one of the most profitable consumer catalogs in the United States. Yet, it has the same challenges in direct-mail campaigns that giant American Express does. That is, in order to reduce waste, they must know which clients are more likely to purchase from the expensive catalogs sent. But the two companies have the same problem for the *opposite* reasons. As a small company, Badler suffers from too little information, while American Express has too much. Badler solves the problem by buying demographic databases and loading them onto PCs, ending with a typical order of $1,000, or five times the average catalog order. American Express, on the other hand, pours its vast sea of customer information into potent mainframes that churn away.

The technology war between large and small companies is raging and so far it looks like small businesses will win. Research by Morgan Stanley Bank shows that small companies have an edge in profiting from technology. For example, small manufacturing companies can use technology to produce faster, smaller and more customized runs. Small companies are more able to use technology to offer flexible and efficient services. Results indicate that the smaller the company, the greater the gains.

Using technology to learn new ways of doing things is the secret to the edge small companies have. Big companies, on the other hand, use technology almost obsessively to increase efficiency of existing performance.

The advantages of smaller-scale technology have not been lost on big companies, who have been downsizing so hawkishly that they now look like giant dying stars, shrunk to lumps of glowing gas. No one yet knows if these "white dwarf" companies still have too much of their large-company baggage to gain the small-company technology advantage.

Who's winning the technology war?

Benefit of technology	Who wins?	Why?	What can big companies do?
Customized products	Small companies	Require smaller runs	Reorganize around small units
Better service	Small companies	Cultural constraints	Force cultural change and shift focus from replacement to service
Ability to react to change	Small companies	Complexity of giant systems	Move to PC-based systems
Productivity	Small companies	Have much less developmment overhead than large companies	Shrink

SOURCE: Reprinted with permission, *Inc.* magazine, (SOSB 1996). Copyright 1996 by Goldhirsh Group, Inc., 38 Commercial Wharf, Boston, MA 02110.

Soviet Union and the opening of markets among its former republics and throughout the former Eastern bloc; the long-awaited arrival of Europe '92 with its lowering of internal trade boundaries; and the implementation of the North American Free Trade Agreement. All of this means a new set of opportunities and upheavals for companies that strive to meet global competitive standards.

Globalization causes the need for innovation and new levels of customer service. Companies must shorten the time for developing new products, and new products must account for a larger percentage of total income because international competitors are relentless innovators.[62] Globalization has also triggered the need for new management approaches that emphasize empowerment of workers and involvement of employees.

The success of Japanese and other foreign firms that emphasize employee involvement has encouraged many U.S. companies to adopt more participatory management practices in response to growing international competition. Employee involvement has been a rapidly growing trend since the late 1980s, and a majority of large companies have by now introduced some form of employee involvement in their organizations.[63]

The success of Japanese firms is often attributed to their group orientation. The Japanese culture focuses on trust and intimacy within the group and family. In North America, in contrast, the basic cultural orientation is toward individual rights and achievements. These differences in the two societies are reflected in how companies are managed.

Exhibit 2.8 illustrates differences in the management approaches used in America and Japan. American organizations are characterized as Type A and Japanese organizations as Type J. However, it is impractical to take a management approach based on the culture of one country and apply it directly to that of another country. **Theory Z** proposes a hybrid form of management that incorporates techniques from both Japanese and North American management practices. Type Z management, shown in the center of Exhibit 2.8, is a blend of American and Japanese characteristics that can be used to revitalize and strengthen corporate cultures in North America.[64]

Total Quality Management

The quality movement in Japan emerged partly as a result of American influence after World War II. Yet Japanese companies achieved a significant departure from the American model by gradually shifting from an inspection-oriented approach to quality control toward an approach emphasizing employee involvement in the prevention of quality problems.[65]

Today, **total quality management (TQM),** which focuses on managing the total organization to deliver quality to customers, is at the forefront in helping managers deal with global competition. The approach infuses quality values throughout every activity within a company, with front-line workers intimately involved in the process. Four significant elements of quality management are employee involvement, focus on the customer, benchmarking, and continuous improvement. These elements will be discussed in more depth in Chapter 17.

| Employee involvement. TQM requires companywide participation in quality control.[66] Workers must be trained, involved, and empowered. For example, after product quality suffered following

total quality management (TQM)
A concept that focuses on managing the total organization to deliver quality to customers. Four significant elements of TQM are employee involvement, focus on the customer, benchmarking, and continuous improvement.

Theory Z
A management perspective that incorporates techniques from both Japanese and North American management practices.

EXHIBIT 2.8
Characteristics of Theory Z Management

Type A (American)
Short-term employment
Individual decision making
Individual responsibility
Rapid evaluation and promotion
Explicit, formalized control
Specialized career path
Segmented concern

Type Z (Modified American)
Long-term employment
Consensual decision making
Individual responsibility
Slow evaluation and promotion
Implicit, informal control with explicit, formalized measures
Moderately specialized career path
Holistic concern, including family

Type J (Japanese)
Lifetime employment
Consensual decision making
Collective responsibility
Slow evaluation and promotion
Implicit, informal control
Nonspecialized career path
Holistic concern

SOURCE: Adapted from William G. Ouchi and Alfred M. Jaeger, "Type Z Organizations: Stability in the Midst of Mobility," *Academy of Management Review 3* (1978), 308–314.

rapid sales growth in 1991, Precision Industries, Inc., a distributor of industrial parts, organized workers into quality groups assigned to identify operational problems, set higher production goals, and meet customer quality expectations.[67]

2 *Focus on the customer.* TQM companies find out what the customer wants. When Standard Aero, Inc., a Winnipeg aircraft-engine repair company, instituted a quality management program, top managers spent $100,000 to find out what customers actually expected. Some customers were so happy to be asked for their opinions that the fact-finding mission itself yielded $7 million in unsolicited new business.[68]

3 *Benchmarking.* Benchmarking is a process whereby companies find out how others do something better than they do and then try to imitate or improve on it. Through research and field trips by teams of workers, companies compare their products, services, and business practices with those of their competitors and other companies and then change practices to beat the competition. Companies like AT&T, Motorola, Xerox, Du Pont, and Eastman Kodak are constantly benchmarking.[69]

4 *Continuous improvement.* Total quality management is not a quick fix; it relies on continuous improvement to produce long-term results. Continuous improvement is the implementation of small, incremental improvements in all areas of the organization on an ongoing basis. The basic philosophy is that improving things a little bit at a time, all the time, has the highest probability of success. Companies like Motorola and Procter & Gamble have achieved astonishing results in efficiency, quality, and customer satisfaction through long-term, continuous improvement.[70]

SUMMARY AND MANAGEMENT SOLUTION

This chapter has described important ideas about the revolution taking place in management. This revolution has been caused by rapid changes in the external environment, changes in technology, and increased global competition. The result has been a shift in the basic management paradigm from one of stability and efficiency to one of change and problem solving.

The paradigm is reflected in the organizational change from traditional vertical hierarchy, with top managers firmly in control, to organizations designed with horizontal relationships, where employees work in teams and are empowered. Some organizations are moving all the way toward a learning organization, in which employees are involved in all activities. The learning organization is characterized by visionary leadership, a horizontal structure, an emergent strategy, a strong culture, empowered employees, and shared information. The learning organization represents a substantial departure from the traditional management hierarchy.

Volatile environments that lead to rapid organizational changes, including downsizing and movement toward horizontal and learning organization forms, have severe implications for managers and employees. The old social contract of the employee being loyal to the company and the company taking care of the employee until retirement no longer holds. Employees are responsible for themselves.

In order to understand the forces shaping the current management revolution, it is important to study historical trends which have led us to the current situation. The evolution of management perspectives is summarized in Exhibit 2.4.

Three major forces that affect management are social, political, and economic. These forces have influenced management from ancient times to the present.

The three major perspectives on management that have evolved since the late 1800s are the classical perspective, the humanistic perspective, and the management science perspective. Each perspective has several specialized subfields. Two recent extensions of management perspectives are systems theory and contingency views. The most recent historical force affecting management is industrial globalization. The higher standards of quality, productivity, and responsiveness have caused a renewed concern for the full participation of people within organizations. The most recent trend in management has been to adopt participatory management practices and to create the widespread desire for achieving excellence and continuous learning in North American organizations.

Recall from the management problem at the beginning of this chapter that Tony Raimondo was faced with a sudden shift in the environment of Behlen, and the company suddenly lost 50 percent of its business. Raimondo took action similar to that described for becoming a horizontal or learning organization. He replaced the authoritative structure with participative management and stripped away layers of vice presidents and middle managers. He created autonomous business units, each responsible for a specific market. He searched out natural leaders to replace traditional supervisors. He resolved to share all information and news—good and bad—with employees. A program the employees named "Awareness Is Money" produced a flood of ideas for reducing costs. A strategy emerged that enabled Behlen to expand from reliance on grain-storage buildings to livestock equipment. A gain-sharing plan was installed so that employees shared in improved productivity. Time clocks were removed. Everyone was invited to call Raimondo or walk into his office. Teams were created. Employees now do what it used to take four supervisors to do. Employees know it's okay to take action on their own.[71]

Becoming a learning organization took Behlen almost ten years. The change was difficult because it affected the lifelong habits and behaviors of employees and managers. But it was clearly worth it.

DISCUSSION QUESTIONS

1 What is a paradigm? Have you seen evidence of a paradigm shift in your university or where you work?

2 Which of the six characteristics of learning organizations do you find most appealing? Which would be the hardest for you to adopt? Why?

3 Some experts believe that leadership is more important than ever in learning organizations. Do you agree? Explain.

4 Why is it important to understand the different perspectives and approaches to management theory that have evolved throughout the history of organizations?

5 How do social, economic, and political forces influence the practice and theory of management? Do you think management trends are a response to these forces?

6 What is the behavioral sciences approach? How does it differ from earlier approaches to management?

7 Explain the basic idea underlying the contingency view and provide an example.

8 Why can an event such as the Hawthorne studies be a major turning point in the history of management even if the idea is later shown to be in error? Discuss.

9 Identify the major components of systems theory. Is this perspective primarily internal or external?

10 Which approach to management thought is most appealing to you? Why?

11 Do you think management theory will ever be as precise as theories in the fields of physics, chemistry, or experimental psychology? Why or why not?

MANAGEMENT EXERCISES

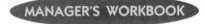
MANAGER'S WORKBOOK

Creating a Learning Organization

Imagine you are working in the "ideal" learning organization. What would it be like and how is that different from a recent work experience you have had (or your experience in the "job" of a student)? What keeps your workplace from becoming more learning-oriented? Complete the following table:

Aspects of ideal learning organization	List behaviors for this aspect	What would be the result of these behaviors?	What are blocks to achieving these?	How will I know if progress has been made?
1. (Example): Employees feel what they do has some meaning	Energy and enthusiasm when work is being done	The team is more motivated, new ideas are generated	Lack of clarity on how tasks help fulfill overall mission	When employees start to talk about how they are filling an important mission
2.				
3.				
4.				
5.				
6.				

Further work

1 Choose the three aspects that are the most compelling to you and the organization.
2 How can the organization achieve these? What are the major blocks?
3 (optional) Compare your table and top three entries with other students in groups. Are there some common themes? What is most important in creating a learning organization? What are reasons for not having a learning organization—what are the blocks?

SOURCE: Adapted from "Defining Your Learning Organization," in Peter Senge, et al, *The Fifth Discipline Fieldbook* (New York: Doubleday, 1994), 50–52.

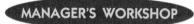

MANAGER'S WORKSHOP

Shifting Paradigms

1 Divide into groups of five to seven members.
2 Below is a list of the types of paradigm shifts companies have been experiencing in recent years as they move toward the learning organization model. As a group, discuss the impact of these shifts on management and the impact on your future career.

Paradigm shift	The impact on management	Impact on you and your career	How you feel about changes required of you
1. Flatter hierarchy			
2. Less formal rules and procedures			
3. More service orientation to customer			

Paradigm shift	The impact on management	Impact on you and your career	How you feel about changes required of you
4. From autocratic to more participative decision making			
5. From individual to teamwork and self-directed teams			
6. Less control and more empowerment			
7. Open-book management			
8. Less career path and more freelancing			
9. More diversity of employees and managers			
10. Globalization of business			

SURF THE 'NET

Find Web pages for two companies in the same industry. Choose one giant company and one small one. Compare the quality of their Web pages and see if you would have been able to tell which company is larger and has a (presumably) much larger advertising budget. What does this tell you about the common belief that size brings advantages in the marketplace? Can you see any evidence of the small-company advantage in technology? Or at least indi-

cations of the leveling that the World Wide Web does between large and small companies?

Here are two to try before you select your own two:

Godiva Chocolatier (large company)
  http://www.godiva.com
Esther Price Candies (small company)
  http://www.estherprice.com

ETHICAL DILEMMA

Dreaded Decline

You manage a 12-member product design department in a midsized company. Your department has an excellent reputation as a top place to work. Over the years, your department has been especially successful in developing new talent. A special "family" relationship has emerged, and many designers have gone on to careers in middle management throughout the company.

Now a general downturn within the industry is forcing major cutbacks. Your company is preparing for major changes. A new CEO is downsizing every department and wants to create a new structure and corporate culture based on teamwork and horizontal relationships. You

have received word to cut three employees. One member of the department is nearing retirement, so that will count as one reduction. But two more jobs must be cut, and seniority does not have to be the deciding factor. Friendly employees suddenly are competitors for the remaining positions, and you foresee terrible consequences for the department—not only for the people who will lose their jobs but also for the "family" relationship.

What Do You Do?

1 Pick the two people who have least seniority. Although this is not required, it provides an objective criterion and will cause the least damage to the department, which already has a team culture.

2 Pick the two people you consider the poorest performers and would like to replace. This will enable you to replace them and improve the department when it grows back to normal size.

3 Try to get around the rule. Discuss the situation with departmental employees, and see if they are willing to take pay reductions so that no one has to lose his or her job.

4 Turn the decision over to employees. This will maintain a family atmosphere, and employees who might have been planning to leave anyway will be identified.

CASE FOR CRITICAL ANALYSIS

Pierre Dux

Pierre Dux sat quietly in his office considering the news. A third appointment to regional management had been announced and, once again, the promotion he had expected had been given to someone else. . . .

Four years earlier, the INCO manufacturing plant had been one of the least productive of the 13 facilities operating in Europe. Absenteeism and high employee turnover were symptoms of the low morale among the work group. . . . Pierre Dux had been in his current position one year and had derived his only satisfaction from the fact that these poor results might have been worse had he not instituted minor reforms in organizational communication. These allowed workers and supervisors to vent their concerns and frustrations. Although nothing substantial had changed during that first year, operating results had stabilized, ending a period of rapid decline. . . .

[The next step in] the change process, which had begun three years before, had centered on a redesign of production operations from a single, machine-paced assembly line to a number of semi-autonomous assembly teams. . . .

After lengthy discussions among the management group [led by Dux], the final design began to emerge. Equally lengthy discussions (often referred to as negotiations) with members of the workforce, supervisors, and representatives of the local unions were part of the design process. The first restructuring into smaller work groups was tried in an experimental project that received tentative approval from top management in INCO headquarters and a "wait and see" response from the union. The strongest initial resistance had come from the plant engineers. They were sold neither on the new structure nor on the process of involving the workforce in the design of operating equipment and production methods. . . .

The initial experiment met with limited success. . . . However, even this limited success attracted the attention of numerous people at INCO headquarters and in other plants. All were interested in visiting the new "experiment." Visits soon became a major distraction, and Dux declared a temporary halt to permit the project to proceed, although this produced some muttering at headquarters about his "secretive" and "uncooperative" behavior.

Because of the experiment's success, Dux and his staff prepared to convert the entire production operation to the new system. The enthusiasm of workers in the plant grew as training for the changeover proceeded. In fact, a group of production workers asked to help with the installation of the new equipment as a means of learning more about its operation.

Dux and his staff were surprised at the difficulties encountered at this phase. Headquarters seemed to drag their feet in approving the necessary funding for the changeover. Even after the funding was approved, there was a stream of challenges to minor parts of the plan. "Can't you lay the workers off during the changeover?" "Why use workers on overtime to do the changeover when you could hire temporary workers more cheaply?" These criticisms reflected a lack of understanding of the basic operating principles of the new system, and Dux rejected them.

The conversion of the entire assembly line to workgroups was finally achieved, with the local management group making few concessions from their stated plans. The initial change and the first days of operation were filled with crisis. The design process had not anticipated many of the problems that arose with full-scale operations. However, Dux was pleased to see managers, staff, and workers clustered together at the trouble areas, fine-tuning the design when problems arose. Just as the start-up finally appeared to be moving forward, a change in product specifications from a headquarters group dictated additional changes in the design of the assembly process. The new change was handled quickly and with enthusiasm by the workforce. While the period was exhausting and seemingly endless to those who felt responsible for the change, the new design took only six months to reach normal operating levels. . . .

Within a year, Dux was secure that he had a major success on his hands. Productivity and product quality measures for the plant had greatly improved. In this relatively short period his plant had moved from the worst, according to these indicators, to the third most productive in the INCO system. Absenteeism had dropped only slightly, but turnover had been reduced substantially. Morale was not measured formally but was considered by all members of the management team to be greatly improved. Now, after three years of full operations, the plant was considered the most productive in the entire INCO system.

Dux was a bit surprised when no other facility in INCO initiated a similar effort or called upon him for help. Increases of the early years had leveled off, with the peak being achieved in the early part of year three. . . . For Dux it provided the time to reflect on his accomplishment and think about his future career.

It was in this context that he considered the news that he had once again been bypassed for promotion to the next level in the INCO hierarchy.

Questions

1 How would you characterize the paradigm of Pierre Dux compared to the rest of INCO? Dux has been successful, so why do you think other parts of the company have not shifted toward his view?

2 Which of the six elements of a learning organization described in the text are illustrated in Dux's plant? Do you believe they were implemented correctly?

3 If you were Pierre Dux, what would you do now about your career? Why?

SOURCE: This case was prepared by Michael Brimm, associate professor at IN-SEAD. It is intended to be used as a basis for class discussion rather than to illustrate either effective or ineffective handling of an administrative situation. Adaptation reprinted with the permission of INSEAD. Copyright © 1983 INSEAD, Fontainebleau, France. Revised 1987.

ENDNOTES

1 Susan Greco, "The Decade-Long Overnight Success," *Inc.,* December 1994, 73–79.

2 John A. Byrne, "Management Meccas," *Business Week,* September 18, 1995, 122–132.

3 John Huey, "Managing in the Midst of Chaos," *Fortune,* April 5, 1993, 38–48.

4 Ibid.

5 This discussion is based on John A. Byrne, "Paradigms for Postmodern Managers," *Business Week/Reinventing America* (1992), 62–63; and George Land and Beth Jarman, *Breakpoint and Beyond* (New York: HarperBusiness, 1992).

6 Huey, "Managing in the Midst of Chaos."

7 Peter Senge, *The Fifth Discipline: The Art and Practice of Learning Organizations* (New York: Doubleday/Currency, 1990).

8 Marcie Schorr Harsch, "Learning Organizations: The Latest Management Craze," *Working Woman,* June 1995, 21–22.

9 Peter M. Senge, "The Leader's New Work: Building Learning Organizations," *Sloan Management Review* (fall 1990), 7–22.

10 David Kirkpatrick, "Could AT&T Rule the World?" *Fortune,* May 17, 1993, 55–66.

11 Joshua Hyatt, "Hot Commodity," *Inc.,* February 1996, 50–62.

12 Senge, "The Leader's New Work."

13 Edward O. Welles, "The Shape of Things to Come," *Inc.,* February 1992, 66–74.

14 Robert Howard, "The CEO as Organizational Architect: An Interview with Xerox's Paul Allaire," *Harvard Business Review,* September, 1992, 106; and Rob Walker, "Rank Xerox-Management Revolution," *Long Range Planning* 25, no. 1 (1992), 9–21.

15 Jeffrey Pfeffer, "Producing Sustainable Competitive Advantage through the Effective Management of People," *Academy of Management Executive* 9, no. 1 (1995), 55–69.

16 Ibid.

17 John Case, "The Change Masters," *Inc.,* March 1992, 58–70.

18 Alan Deutschman, "The Managing Wisdom of High-Tech Superstars," *Fortune,* October 17, 1994, 197–206.

19 John Case, "The Open-Book Revolution," *Inc.,* June 1995, 26–43.

20 Catherine Romano, "When Money Talks," *Management Review,* November 1994, 44–47.

21 Edwin C. Nevis, Anthony J. DiBella, and Janet M. Gould, "Understanding Organizations as Learning Systems," *Sloan Management Review* (winter 1995), 73–85.

22 Myron Magnet, "Meet the New Revolutionaries," *Fortune,* February 24, 1992, 94–101.

23 Mary Anne Devanna and Noel Tichy, "Creating the Competitive Organization of the Twenty-First Century: The Boundaryless Corporation," *Human Resource Management* 29 (winter 1990), 455–471; and Fred Kofman and Peter M. Senge, "Communities of Commitment: The Heart of Learning Organizations," *Organizational Dynamics* (autumn 1993), 4–23.

24 Dorothy Leonard-Barton, "The Factory as a Learning Laboratory," *Sloan Management Review* (fall 1992), 23–38.

25 Adapted from: "Granite Rock: A Family Operation Nears Its Centennial," *Stone Review,* October 1996, 6–7; David Franceschi, *Quality Director,* 1996; Edward Welles, "How're We Doing?" *Inc.,* May 1991, 80–83; John Case, "The Change Masters," *Inc.,* March 1992, 58–70.

26 Alan M. Kantro, ed., "Why History Matters to Managers," *Harvard Business Review* 64 (January–February 1986), 81–88.

27 Susan Dentzer, "Profiting from the Past," *Newsweek,* May 10, 1982, 73–74.

28 Kim Heron, "Randy Travis: Making Country Music Hot Again," *The New York Times Magazine,* June 25, 1989, 28–58.

29 Daniel A. Wren, *The Evolution of Management Thought,* 2d ed. (New York: Wiley, 1979), 6–8. Much of the discussion of these forces comes from Arthur M. Schlesinger, *Political and Social History of the United States, 1829–1925* (New York: Macmillan, 1925); and Homer C. Hockett, *Political and Social History of the United States, 1492–1828* (New York: Macmillan, 1925).

30 Robin Wright and Doyle McManus, *Flashpoints: Promise and Peril in a New World* (New York: Alfred A. Knopf, 1991).

31 Daniel A. Wren, "Management History: Issues and Ideas for Teaching and Research," *Journal of Management* 13 (1987), 339–350.

32 The following is based on Wren, *Evolution of Management Thought*, Chapters 4, 5; and Claude S. George, Jr., *The History of Management Thought* (Englewood Cliffs, N.J.: Prentice-Hall, 1968), Chapter 4.

33 Charles D. Wrege and Ann Marie Stoka, "Cooke Creates a Classic: The Story behind F. W. Taylor's Principles of Scientific Management," *Academy of Management Review* (October 1978), 736–749.

34 Wren, *Evolution of Management Thought*, 171; and George, *History of Management Thought*, 103–104.

35 Max Weber, *General Economic History*, trans. Frank H. Knight (London: Allen & Unwin, 1927); Max Weber, *The Protestant Ethic and the Spirit of Capitalism*, trans. Talcott Parsons (New York: Scribner, 1930); and Max Weber, *The Theory of Social and Economic Organizations*, ed. and trans. A. M. Henderson and Talcott Parsons (New York: Free Press, 1947).

36 "UPS," *The Atlanta Journal and Constitution*, April 26, 1992, H1; Richard L. Daft, *Organization Theory and Design*, 3d ed. (St. Paul, Minn.: West, 1989), 181–182; and Kathy Goode, Betty Hahn, and Cindy Seibert, "United Parcel Service: The Brown Giant" (unpublished manuscript, Texas A&M University, 1981).

37 Henri Fayol, *Industrial and General Administration*, trans. J. A. Coubrough (Geneva: International Management Institute, 1930); Henri Fayol, *General and Industrial Management*, trans. Constance Storrs (London: Pitman and Sons, 1949); and W. J. Arnold and the editors of *Business Week*, *Milestones in Management* (New York: McGraw-Hill, vol. I, 1965; vol. II, 1966).

38 Mary Parker Follett, *The New State: Group Organization: The Solution of Popular Government* (London: Longmans, Green, 1918); and Mary Parker Follett, *Creative Experience* (London: Longmans, Green, 1924).

39 Henry C. Metcalf and Lyndall Urwick, eds., *Dynamic Administration: The Collected Papers of Mary Parker Follett* (New York: Harper & Row, 1940); Arnold, *Milestones in Management*.

40 Follett, *The New State*; Metcalf and Urwick, *Dynamic Administration*.

41 William B. Wolf, *How to Understand Management: An Introduction to Chester I. Barnard* (Los Angeles: Lucas Brothers, 1968); and David D. Van Fleet, "The Need-Hierarchy and Theories of Authority," *Human Relations* 9 (spring 1982), 111–118.

42 Gregory M. Bounds, Gregory H. Dobbins, and Oscar S. Fowler, *Management: A Total Quality Perspective* (Cincinnati: South-Western College Publishing, 1995), 52–53.

43 Curt Tausky, *Work Organizations: Major Theoretical Perspectives* (Itasca, Ill.: F. E. Peacock, 1978), 42.

44 Charles D. Wrege, "Solving Mayo's Mystery: The First Complete Account of the Origin of the Hawthorne Studies—The Forgotten Contributions of Charles E. Snow and Homer Hibarger" (paper presented to the Management History Division of the Academy of Management, August 1976).

45 Ronald G. Greenwood, Alfred A. Bolton, and Regina A. Greenwood, "Hawthorne a Half Century Later: Relay Assembly Participants Remember," *Journal of Management* 9 (fall/winter 1983), 217–231.

46 F. J. Roethlisberger, W. J. Dickson, and H. A. Wright, *Management and the Worker* (Cambridge, Mass.: Harvard University Press, 1939).

47 H. M. Parson, "What Happened at Hawthorne?" *Science* 183 (1974), 922–932.

48 Greenwood, Bolton, and Greenwood, "Hawthorne a Half Century Later," 219–221.

49 Tausky, *Work Organizations: Major Theoretical Perspectives*, 55.

50 Douglas McGregor, *The Human Side of Enterprise* (New York: McGraw-Hill, 1960), 16–18.

51 Leah Nathans Spiro and Michele Galen, "Saturn," *Business Week*, August 17, 1992, 86–91.

52 Mansel G. Blackford and K. Austin Kerr, *Business Enterprise in American History* (Boston: Houghton Mifflin, 1986), Chapters 10, 11; and Alex Groner and the editors of *American Heritage* and *Business Week*, *The American Heritage History of American Business and Industry* (New York: American Heritage Publishing, 1972), Chapter 9.

53 Larry M. Austin and James R. Burns, *Management Science* (New York: Macmillan, 1985).

54 Tom Scott and William A. Hailey, "Queue Modeling Aids Economic Analysis at Health Center," *Industrial Engineering* (February 1981), 56–61.

55 Ludwig von Bertalanffy, Carl G. Hempel, Robert E. Bass, and Hans Jonas, "General Systems Theory: A New Approach to Unity of Science," *Human Biology* 23 (December 1951), 302–361; and Kenneth E. Boulding, "General Systems Theory—The Skeleton of Science," *Management Science* 2 (April 1956), 197–208.

56 Fremont E. Kast and James E. Rosenzweig, "General Systems Theory: Applications for Organization and Management," *Academy of Management Journal* (December 1972), 447–465.

57 Jeffrey A. Tannenbaum, "On Their Own," *The Wall Street Journal*, May 23, 1996, R20.

58 Fred Luthans, "The Contingency Theory of Management: A Path Out of the Jungle," *Business Horizons* 16 (June 1973), 62–72; Fremont E. Kast and James E. Rosenzweig, *Contingency Views of Organization and Management* (Chicago: Science Research Associates, 1973).

59 Robert Gunther, "Major Banks' Increases in Loan-Loss Reserves May Cramp Expansion," *The Wall Street Journal*, July 29, 1987, 1, 10.

60 Koh Sera, "Corporate Globalization: A New Trend," *Academy of Management Executive* 6, no. 1 (1992), 89–96; and B. Joseph White, "The Internationalization of Business: One Company's Response," *Academy of Management Executive* 2 (1988), 29–32.

61 Arnoldo C. Hax, "Building the Firm of the Future," *Sloan Management Review* (spring 1989), 75–82.

62 Tom Peters, "Prometheus Barely Unbound," *Academy of Management Executive* 4 (November 1990), 70–84.

63 David I. Levine, *Reinventing the Workplace: How Business and Employees Can Both Win* (Washington, D.C.: The Brookings Institution, 1995), 6–7.

64 William G. Ouchi and Alfred M. Jaeger, "Type Z Organizations: Stability in the Midst of Mobility," *Academy of Management Review* 3 (1978), 305–314; and William Ouchi, *Theory Z: How American Business Can Meet the Japanese Challenge* (Reading, Mass.: Addison-Wesley, 1981).

65 Mauro F. Guillen, "The Age of Eclecticism: Current Organizational Trends and the Evolution of Managerial Models," *Sloan Management Review* (fall 1994), 75–86.

66 Bounds, Dobbins, and Fowler, *Management*; and Daft, *Organization Theory and Design*, 5th ed. (St. Paul, Minn.: West, 1995).

67 Bradford McKee, "Turn Your Workers into a Team," *Nation's Business*, July 1992, 36–38.

68 Ted Wakefield, "No Pain, No Gain," *Canadian Business*, January 1993, 50–54.

69 Jeremy Main, "How to Steal the Best Ideas Around," *Fortune*, October 19, 1992, 102–106.

70 Brian Dumaine, "Distilled Wisdom: Buddy, Can You Paradigm?" *Fortune*, May 15, 1995, 205–206; and Main, "How to Steal the Best Ideas Around."

71 Greco, "The Decade-Long Overnight Success."

Herb Kelleher—Leadership at Southwest Airlines

Can a man who appears in public dressed as Elvis Presley and the Easter Bunny be an effective leader of the only U.S. airline that has been consistently profitable throughout the late '80s and '90s? Let's take a look at the leader of Southwest Airlines and see!

Herb Kelleher, CEO of Southwest Airlines in Dallas, provides an unusual leadership profile in the airline industry—an industry that has experienced all of the turbulence associated with deregulation and intense competition. Since the founding of the company in 1967, Kelleher has been the primary force in developing and maintaining a vision and strategy that have enabled his underdog airline to grow and be profitable. Southwest was designed as a low-fare, low-frills, high-frequency, short-haul, single-class, fun-loving airline, and it has expanded by doing the same thing at each new airport. Elements of this different approach include doing their own ticketing rather than using travel agents, and seating passengers on a first come, first served basis.

Many airline industry analysts have credited Southwest's success to Kelleher's unique personality and management style, in addition to his ability to construct successful business strategies. Kelleher has developed a culture at Southwest that treats employees the way it wants its passengers treated—management pays attention, is responsive, and involves employees in decisions. Part of Kelleher's management philosophy is "fun in the workplace." Besides his Elvis impersonations, which are legendary, he has acted in a company rap video, encouraged employees to come in costume to work on Friday "Fun Days," and insisted that a sense of humor be a Southwest hiring criterion for all jobs.

While using humor and joking as a way of interacting with his employees, and encouraging them in turn to demonstrate this fun attitude to the Southwest customer, Kelleher does not treat the performance of his airline lightly at all. Southwest has grown to a nearly $3 billion business with close to 20,000 employees. It has repeatedly won the coveted Triple Crown—with best on-time record, best baggage handling, and fewest customer complaints—based on U.S. Department of Transportation data. But perhaps the best example of Herb Kelleher's astuteness as an executive is the recent battle between United Airlines and Southwest.

In 1994, United Airlines faced off against Southwest Airlines in a battle for the California market. United's strategy was to create an airline-within-an-airline in order to beat Southwest at what it does every day—offer low fares, few frills, and frequent service on short-haul routes. Of course, to do this and to make a profit, United would have to substantially lower its operating costs. When asked to comment on the likely outcome, Herb Kelleher predicted that United's new Shuttle would not succeed in taking away Southwest's customers. He emphasized that his employees thrive on competition and that "their marshaled vigor will ultimately prevail."

By early 1996, Kelleher's predictions were verified; not only had United retreated from many of the California routes, but Southwest had managed to increase its share of California business! Southwest had responded to United's siege with the addition of new planes and more daily flights on the routes that United tried to pick off. Kelleher toured the California airports delivering going-into-battle speeches to his employees. Southwest even cut fares and placed its own ads inside the United terminal.

Although Southwest lost an initial 10 percent of its California business, it rapidly turned the trend around. Unsuccessful in its attempts to cut costs, United increased its fares by $10 and eliminated some routes in April, 1995. By January of 1996, more routes were vacated and Southwest posted growing profits in the California market. Although Herb Kelleher's public persona may be that of a jokester full of good humor, he is an honest, forthright, and tough leader who has maintained a profitable business in a difficult industry while continuing to build a loyal employee following.

QUESTIONS

1. Describe Herb Kelleher's leadership skills as illustrated in the case (conceptual, human, and technical).
2. What primary management functions or roles does Kelleher appear to perform at Southwest Airlines?
3. Do you believe that Southwest is a *learning organization*? Why or why not?

REFERENCES

A. Bryant, "United's Bid to Rule Western Skies," *The New York Times* (September 16, 1994), C1.

S. McCartney and M. McCartney, "Southwest Flies Circles around United's Shuttle," *The Wall Street Journal* (February 20, 1996), B1.

James Campbell Quick, "Crafting an Organizational Culture: Herb's Hand at Southwest," *Organizational Dynamics*, 21 (1992), 45–56.

VIDEO CASE

anagers do not operate in a vacuum. Their decisions and daily tasks are affected by the environment inside their organizations and the broader external environment. By examining their environments, organizations can assess their challenges, opportunities, and strengths.

Also, small businesses drive a large portion of the U.S. economy. Downsized workers and people who have left the corporate world are turning to entrepreneurship to gain control and satisfaction in their work lives.

In Part II, we look at the environment of management: both within and outside an organization. The four chapters in this part discuss the role of external and internal environments, with special emphasis on corporate culture; the global environment; ethics and corporate social responsibility; and the challenges of entrepreneurship and small-business management.

The Environment
of Management

P A R T   I I

The Environment and Corporate Culture

LEARNING OBJECTIVES

After studying this chapter, you should be able to

- Describe the general and task environments and the dimensions of each.

- Explain how organizations adapt to an uncertain environment and identify techniques managers use to influence and control the external environment.

- Define corporate culture and give organizational examples.

- Explain organizational symbols, stories, heroes, slogans, and ceremonies and how they relate to corporate culture.

- Describe how corporate culture relates to the environment.

- Define a symbolic leader and explain the tools a symbolic leader uses to change corporate culture.

CHAPTER 3

MANAGEMENT PROBLEM

It's enough to make you click your mouse until your hand is stiff. As the cyberspace world grows, more new companies enter this revenue-rich field. C/net Online is a brash new company trying to take on the most robust in the computer trade publication business. By offering technical support, technology news, game reviews, product reviews, and bulletin boards, along with 190,000 shareware titles, founder and CEO 31-year-old Halsey Minor hopes to "gut" and siphon off advertising dollars from giant magazines such as *PC Magazine* and *InfoWorld*.

Though online advertising is new, C/net is making $525,000 per month in advertising revenue from companies such as Hewlett-Packard, Intel, Apple, and IBM. It's still not enough to cover the cost of running a 100-employee business, but C/net has nothing to lose and everything to gain by gambling on the Internet. The reward of computer trade advertising C/net is after is worth a fight. The U.S. market was $1.42 billion last year. Ziff-Davis, publisher of *PC Magazine, Computer Shopper,* and 20 other periodicals, took in almost 40 percent of that. One computer industry expert says this may be the year electronic media break the "stranglehold on the computer advertising market."[1]

• If you were a Ziff-Davis manager, would you be worried about companies like C/net? Would you try to compete with C/net on the Internet? What would you do to predict and adapt to future changes in your industry? If you were a manager at C/net, how would you go about taking on the technological media giants?

The environment for publishing and online services has changed dramatically since the early 1990s because of increased competition, rapid changes in technology, and demands from customers for enhanced networking services. Other high-tech companies around the world are waging war on a new level because of increased competition and advancing technology. In Thailand, Sony and Matsushita are battling for the consumer electronics market. Microsoft is facing challenges that may threaten the company's preeminence in the software industry. Today, no company can rest on its laurels. The environment surprises many companies. Dow Corning, which dominated the silicone breast implant industry in 1991, faced an unexpected crisis a year later, when faulty implants and reports of severe health problems caused by leaking silicone led to widespread fear, a barrage of lawsuits, and a ban on cosmetic silicone implants. A gas leak that killed more than 2,000 people in Bhopal, India, damaged Union Carbide's ability to compete for international contracts and by 1992 had reduced the company to half its prior size.[2]

Government actions, regulations, and red tape can also affect an organization's environment and foment a crisis. Passage of the Americans with Disabilities Act forced companies to evaluate existing conditions that required compliance and make adjustments in a number of areas—from promotion practices to parking and restroom access. Changes in Medicare payments may force many rural hospitals to close.

Although few companies experience a crisis as serious as the one resulting from a gas leak, unexpected events that can seriously harm performance occur in the environment of every organization. During the lingering recession in the early 1990s, companies such as H. J. Heinz, Sears, TRW, and General Electric underwent major internal changes—restructuring, discarding product lines, and trimming workforces. Without these major changes, the companies would no longer fit the reality of the changing external environment.

The study of management traditionally has focused on factors within the organization—a closed systems view—such as leading, motivating, and controlling employees. The classical, behavioral, and management science schools described in Chapter 2 focused on internal aspects of organizations over which managers have direct control. These views are accurate but incomplete. Globalization and the trend toward a borderless world affect companies in new ways. Even for those companies that try to operate solely on the domestic stage, events that have greatest impact typically originate in the external environment. To be effective, managers must monitor and respond to the environment—an open systems view.

This chapter explores in detail components of the external environment and how they affect the organization. We will also examine a major part of the organization's internal environment—corporate culture. Corporate culture is shaped by the external environment and is an important part of the context within which managers do their jobs.

THE EXTERNAL ENVIRONMENT

The world as we know it is undergoing tremendous and far-reaching change. This change can be understood by defining and examining components of the external environment.

The external **organizational environment** includes all elements existing outside the boundary of the organization that have the potential to affect the organization.[3] The environment includes competitors, resources, technology, and economic conditions that influence the organization. It does not include those events so far removed from the organization that their impact is not perceived.

The organization's external environment can be further conceptualized as having two layers: general and task environments as illustrated in Exhibit 3.1.[4]

organizational environment
All elements existing outside the organization's boundaries that have the potential to affect the organization.

The **general environment** is the outer layer that is widely dispersed and affects organizations indirectly. It includes social, demographic, and economic factors that influence all organizations about equally. Increases in the inflation rate or the percentage of dual-career couples in the workforce are part of the organization's general environment. These events do not directly change day-to-day operations, but they do affect all organizations eventually. The **task environment** is closer to the organization and includes the sectors that conduct day-to-day transactions with the organization and directly influence its basic operations and performance. It is generally considered to include competitors, suppliers, and customers.

The organization also has an **internal environment,** which includes the elements within the organization's boundaries. The internal environment is composed of current employees, management, and especially corporate culture, which defines employee behavior in the internal environment and how well the organization will adapt to the external environment.

Exhibit 3.1 illustrates the relationship among the general, task, and internal environments. As an open system, the organization draws resources from the external environment and releases goods and services back to it. We will now discuss the two layers of the external environment in more detail. Then we will discuss corporate culture, the key element in the internal environment. Other aspects of the internal environment, such as structure and technology, will be covered in Parts 4 and 5 of this book.

General Environment

The general environment represents the outer layer of the environment. These dimensions influence the organization over time but often are not involved in day-to-day transactions with it. The dimensions of the general environment include international, technological, sociocultural, economic, and legal-political.

International. The **international dimension** of the external environment represents events originating in foreign countries as well as opportunities for American companies in other countries. Note in Exhibit 3.1 that the international dimension represents a context that influences all other aspects of the external environment. The international environment provides new competitors, customers, and suppliers, as well as shapes social, technological, and economic trends.

One study identified 136 U.S. industries—including automobiles, accounting services, entertainment, consumer electronics, and publishing—that will have to compete on a global basis or disappear. The high-quality, low-priced automobiles from Japan and Korea have permanently changed the American automobile industry. Many companies have parts supplied from countries such as Mexico because of low-priced labor. A drop in the dollar's foreign exchange rate lowers the price of U.S.

international dimension
Portion of the external environment that represents events originating in foreign countries as well as opportunities for American companies in other countries.

general environment
The layer of the external environment that affects the organization indirectly.

task environment
The layer of the external environment that directly influences the organization's operations and performance.

internal environment
The environment within the organization's boundaries.

EXHIBIT 3.1
Location of the Organization's General, Task, and Internal Environments

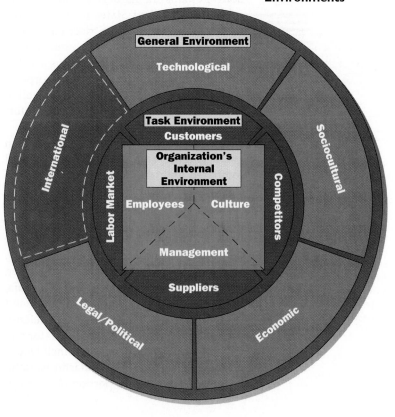

products overseas, increasing export competitiveness.

Today, every company must think internationally. Managers who are used to thinking only about the domestic environment must learn new rules to cope with goods, services, and ideas circulating around the globe. For example, products and services exist in a one-world market. A better machine built in Oklahoma City will find buyers from Europe and Asia. Moreover, competitors in a global village come from all over. A company that does not export will still run into competitors in its own marketplace, including some from developing nations. The world is also a source of supply as well as a market. For example, new products such as liquid Tide are composed of materials and ideas from around the world.

Chapter 4 describes how today's businesses are operating in an increasingly borderless world and examines in detail how managing in a global environment differs from the management of domestic operations. Perhaps the hardest lesson for managers in the United States to learn is that they do not know best. U.S. decision makers know little about issues and competition in foreign countries. U.S. arrogance is a shortcut to failure. To counter this, Pall Corporation keeps a team of Ph.D.s traveling around the world gathering current information on markets and issues.[5]

The global environment represents an ever-changing and uneven playing field compared with the domestic environment. Changes in the international domain can abruptly turn the domestic environment upside down. Consider, for example, the "peace dividend" brought on by the end of the cold war, and the fall of communism. Despite the need for periodic military action in areas such as the Persian Gulf or Bosnia, the peace dividend has increased demand for military cuts, pushing smaller defense contractors out of business and forcing large companies such as McDonnell Douglas, General Dynamics, and Martin Marietta to convert a significant portion of their op-

erations into nonmilitary production.[6] Top industry scientists and engineers are switching to civilian developments such as high-definition television and new areas of transportation such as electric cars.[7]

Technological. The **technological dimension** includes scientific and technological advancements in a specific industry as well as in society at large. In recent years, the most striking advances have been in the computer industry. A greeting card that plays "Happy Birthday" holds more computing power than existed in the entire world before 1950. Today's home video cameras wield more processing power than the old IBM 360, the wonder machine that launched the age of mainframe computers. Millions of households own personal computers (PCs), while the business world has jumped to the next step, with many small computers linked by a network.[8] Revolutionary discoveries in biomimetics (the use of nature as models) and atomscompics (molecular architecture) are leading to high-performance materials that are lighter, stronger, and more resistant to temperature extremes. Smart composite materials, embedded with sensors that enable them to think for themselves, promise new strides for the space program and the aircraft industry.[9] Aircraft surface materials can be embedded with fiber-optic sensors that can feel the weight of ice or the "touch" of enemy radar.[10] These and other technological advances can change the rules of the game; thus, every organization must be ready to respond.

Sociocultural. The **sociocultural dimension** of the general environment represents the demographic characteristics as well as the norms, customs, and values of the general population. Important sociocultural characteristics are geographical distribution and population density, age, and education levels. Today's demographic profiles are the foundation of tomorrow's workforce and consumers. Forecasters see increased globalization of both consumer

technological dimension
The dimension of the general environment that includes scientific and technological advancements in the industry and society at large.

sociocultural dimension
The dimension of the general environment representing the demographic characteristics, norms, customs, and values of the population within which the organization operates.

markets and the labor supply, with increasing diversity both within organizations and consumer markets.[11] For example, U.S. census reports the following key demographic trends:

1 African Americans are the largest ethnic group with a median age in the 18–35 range.
2 In 1994, the number of births fell below the 4 million mark for the first time since 1988, while the elderly population continues to increase.
3 The United States will continue to receive a flood of immigrants, largely from Asia (35.2 percent) and Mexico (23.7 percent).[12]

Blue Bird Bus Company has kept a keen eye on demographic changes and customer needs to maintain its position.

■ BLUE BIRD BUS COMPANY

Blue Bird Bus Company has been a family-run business with a firm hold on its leading position in the highly competitive school bus manufacturing business. A. Laurence Luce founded Blue Bird in 1932, and his sons George, Albert, and Joe assumed control in 1962. The sons learned the business, and the value of a dollar, from their Depression-era father. In an industry where flinty-eyed state or local school boards scrutinize bids for the lowest-cost producer, such lessons helped earn Blue Bird one sale in three in the U.S. market.

Still, the company had a dichotomy. Engineers at Blue Bird availed themselves of the latest computer-aided technology systems. On their way to lunch they passed by the company's ten "Beliefs of the Blue Bird Company," opening with, "We will continue to build our companies on the foundations of Christianity and the free enterprise system."

The brothers saw the declining number of school-age children. Realizing the number of retirees with more disposable income would continue to increase, they began producing the Blue Bird Wanderlodges, or "Birds." These luxury vehicles contain amenities such as microwaves and satellite dishes and are 31 to 40 feet long. Making up nearly half the company's profits, they are priced around $350,000 and have also been sold to kings and princes around the world.

After George's death in 1991, the other brothers sold the company to Merrill Lynch, with the agreement that current management would stay on. Even without the Luces, the company still holds its place in innovation to customers. At Earth Day 1996, Blue Bird unveiled its new ultra-safe, ultra-low-emission school bus, featuring an innovative application of alternative fuel, as well as sophisticated on-board electronics, such as sensors that alert the driver to activity on the bus's sides. It is said to be the safest heavy-duty vehicle ever made. A. Laurence Luce would be proud.[13] ■

The *technological dimension* of the *general environment* plays a major role in Ford Motor Company's push for quality. A vast array of modern technologies in assembly, safety testing, quality assurance, manufacturing, environmental controls, and design keeps Ford on the technological cutting edge. Here, Ford's Emeline King uses an electronic pen to design a new car, which is then projected on a life-size, high-definition screen for evaluation and modification. New technology will keep quality high and Ford competitive in the 1990s.

Demography also shapes society's norms and values. Recent sociocultural trends that are affecting many companies include the trend toward no smoking, the anticholesterol fervor, the greater purchasing power of young children, and the increased diversity of consumers, with specialized markets for groups such as Hispanics and women over age 30. For example, the *Miami Herald* responded to changes in the sociocultural environment by launching a Spanish-language newspaper, *El Nuevo Herald*, with articles emphasizing

Hispanic, Cuban, and Latin American news and sports. Introducing the new paper greatly boosted the *Herald*'s earnings and subscriptions.[14]

economic dimension
The dimension of the general environment representing the overall economic health of the country or region in which the organization functions.

Economic. The **economic dimension** represents the general economic health of the country or region in which the organization operates. Consumer purchasing power, unemployment rate, and interest rates are part of an organization's economic environment. Not-for-profit organizations such as the Red Cross and the Salvation Army find a greater demand for their services during economic decline but receive smaller contributions. They must adapt to these changes in economic conditions. One significant recent trend in the economic environment is the frequency of mergers and acquisitions. The corporate economic landscape is being altered. In the media industry, Disney and ABC Television negotiated the biggest entertainment merger in history, and Westinghouse acquired CBS Television. AT&T purchased McCaw Cellular Communications to enhance the company's link to local customers. In the toy industry, which was once made up of numerous small to medium-sized companies, the three largest toy makers—Hasbro, Mattel, and Tyco—have gobbled up at least a dozen smaller competitors within the past few years. The impact of these deals on employees can be overwhelming, creating uncertainty about future job security. The merger is just the beginning of employee uncertainty, because about half of the acquired companies are resold.[15] In recent years the health care industry has gone through mergers, restructuring, and new finance methods, creating a turbulent environment for any organization in or near it. In the Technology for Today box, you can see how Woods Memorial used technology to become more efficient, thereby coping with these radical changes in the economic dimension.

pressure group
An interest group that works within the legal-political framework to influence companies to behave in socially responsible ways.

legal-political dimension
The dimension of the general environment that includes federal, state, and local government regulations and political activities designed to control company behavior.

Legal-Political. The **legal-political dimension** includes government regulations at the local, state, and federal levels as well as political activities designed to influence company behavior. The U.S. political system encourages capitalism, and the government tries not to overregulate business. However, government laws do specify rules of the game. The federal government influences organizations through the Occupational Safety and Health Administration (OSHA), Environmental Protection Agency (EPA), fair trade practices, libel statutes allowing lawsuits against businesses, consumer protection legislation, product safety requirements, import and export restrictions, and information and labeling requirements. Although designed to solve problems, the influx of regulations often creates problems for organizations. For example, well-publicized lawsuits and problems with devices such as heart valves and silicone breast implants have significantly slowed the FDA's rate of reviewing and approving new-product applications. Businesses like ISS, a company that manufactures surgical assistant systems that use 3-D computer imaging and a robotic tool to aid in performing total hip-replacement procedures, could once develop a new product and bring it to market in two or three years. They're now lucky to make it in six years because of the changed legal-political environment.[16]

Managers must recognize a variety of **pressure groups** that work within the legal-political framework to influence companies to behave in socially responsible ways. Automobile manufacturers, toy makers, and airlines have been targeted by Ralph Nader's Center for Responsive Law. Tobacco companies today are certainly feeling the far-reaching power of antismoking groups. Middle-aged activists who once protested the Vietnam War have gone to battle to keep Wal-Mart from "destroying the quality of small-town life." Some groups have also attacked the giant retailer on environmental issues, which will likely be one of the strongest pressure points in the coming years. Environmental groups put pressure on the lumber industry in the Northwest in the early 1990s because of the

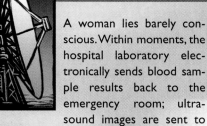

TECHNOLOGY FOR TODAY
CRISIS CARE

A woman lies barely conscious. Within moments, the hospital laboratory electronically sends blood sample results back to the emergency room; ultrasound images are sent to the radiologist, who sends a report to the surgeon's voice-mail box. Ninety minutes after the woman is rushed to the hospital, she is on the operating table. Nothing extraordinary for high-tech health organizations. But this is rural, 72-bed Woods Memorial Hospital in Etowah, Tennessee, part of the group of small hospitals struggling to survive in the current chaotic health care environment.

When CEO Phil Campbell arrived a few years ago, the hospital was $200,000 short of making payroll and had a poor prognosis for survival. Inefficiency was ingrained everywhere, whether it was patient intake, blood work, or billing. Campbell's job became one of changing the culture towards efficiency.

Currently, Woods Memorial is thriving and patient revenues have increased 75 percent. All because of the four-year-old transformation, focusing on cost containment through automation. Campbell's principles were: "Improve quality. Lower costs. Increase volume." He slashed prices on lab work, the hospital's largest profit center. But he knew the key was automation, so he persuaded a vendor to install a new UNIX-based system for one-fourth the going rate. Then he divided the whole medical staff into teams, each responsible for using its PC to search for waste in hospital services.

Computers now use a patient's ID number to instantly add charges so bills are always current, while food service can track every aspect of a patient's eating habits in order to serve preferred foods in desired quantities. Medicare logs are done automatically. Amazingly, not only has the hospital not raised rates in five years, but it has not added any clerical positions, even with the increase in billing due to the doubled patient load.

Woods Memorial's experience proves that even tiny organizations stuck in the downward spiral of an industry can reverse the trend—if they are willing to transform themselves.

SOURCE: Adapted from Joshua Macht, "Critical Care," *Inc. Technology,* 1996 (2), 61–65.

industry's threat to the spotted owl, and Greenpeace has managed to make significant changes in the whaling, tuna fishing, and seal fur industries.[17]

Task Environment

As described earlier, the task environment includes those sectors that have a direct working relationship with the organization, among them customers, competitors, suppliers, and the labor market.

Customers. Those people and organizations in the environment who acquire goods or services from the organization are **customers.** As recipients of the organization's output, customers are important because they determine the organization's success. Patients are the customers of hospitals, students the customers of schools, and travelers the customers of airlines. Companies such as AT&T, General Foods, and Beecham Products have all designed special programs and advertising campaigns to court their older customers, who are, with the aging of baby boomers, becoming a larger percentage of their market.[18] To survive in competition with mass merchandisers like Wal-Mart, small retailers have been forced to come up with new ways to win and keep customers. Baum's, in Morris, Illinois, was started in 1874 as a dry-goods store selling everything from fabrics to grain. Jim Baum, grandson of the founder, has survived by focusing his customer base—he now sells only large-size women's apparel—and investing heavily in advertising and customer service efforts. One of Baum's most-appreciated touches is the comfortable bathrobe in the changing room; shoppers don't have to keep putting their street clothes on to venture onto the shopping floor and select another garment.[19]

customers
People and organizations in the environment who acquire goods or services from the organization.

competitors
Other organizations in the same industry or type of business that provide goods or services to the same set of customers.

labor market
The people available for hire by the organization.

suppliers
People and organizations who provide the raw materials the organization uses to produce its output.

Competitors. Other organizations in the same industry or type of business that provide goods or services to the same set of customers are referred to as **competitors.** Each industry is characterized by specific competitive issues. The recording industry differs from the steel industry and the pharmaceutical industry. Competition in the steel industry, especially from international producers, caused some companies to go bankrupt. Companies in the pharmaceutical industry are highly profitable because it is difficult for new firms to enter it. Despite the competitive wars being waged worldwide, competitors in some industries are finding that they can cooperate to achieve common goals. By the 1990s, Apple, IBM, and Compaq were locked in a titanic power struggle to dominate the personal computer hardware industry as well as to break Microsoft Corporation's domination of the software industry. In a flanking action against Microsoft, Apple and IBM entered a joint venture called Taligent, Inc., for the development of new operating systems software.[20] The Focus on Cooperation box reveals the extent to which some of today's most competitive companies are cooperating to achieve common goals.

Suppliers. The raw materials the organization uses to produce its output are provided by **suppliers.** A steel mill requires iron ore, machines, and financial resources. A small, private university may utilize hundreds of suppliers for paper, pencils, cafeteria food, computers, trucks, fuel, electricity, and textbooks. Large companies such as General Motors, Westinghouse, and Exxon depend on as many as 5,000 suppliers. However, many companies are now using fewer suppliers and trying to build good relationships with them so that they will receive high-quality parts at low prices. The relationship between manufacturers and suppliers has traditionally been an adversarial one, but many companies are finding that cooperation is the key to saving money, maintaining quality, and speeding products to market. Cooperation with suppliers is be-

coming the rule rather than the exception, as discussed in the Focus on Cooperation box.

Labor Market. The **labor market** represents people in the environment who can be hired to work for the organization. Every organization needs a supply of trained, qualified personnel. Unions, employee associations, and the availability of certain classes of employees can influence the organization's labor market. Two labor market factors having an impact on organizations right now are (1) the necessity for continuous investment through education and training in human resources to meet the competitive demands of the borderless world and (2) the effects of international trading blocs, automation, and shifting plant location upon labor dislocations, creating unused labor pools in some areas and labor shortages in others.[21]

SAS Institute maintains a worker-friendly culture and thereby is able to recruit and retain qualified employees in a sometimes-tight high-tech labor market.

■ SAS INSTITUTE

Webmaster Alex Bost is hotly pursued by numerous high-tech companies who offer lucrative salaries, but she is fiercely loyal to her boss, James H. Goodnight, president and cofounder of SAS (Statistical Analysis Systems) Institute in Cary, North Carolina. As the mother of a three-year-old, Alex does not want to give up a work environment with on-site child care and lunch with her son every day in the company's inexpensive gourmet cafeteria. SAS also provides a 26,000-square-foot fitness center, "free snack" rooms, intramural sports, time for "mind-clearing" walks around the company lake, help with aging parents, plus an annual merit bonus. One result of these policies is a turnover rate of only 4 percent, while the industry average is 15 percent.

Alex credits Goodnight for shaping a work environment that is not only personally rewarding, but also professionally stimulating. An

FOCUS ON COOPERATION
THE NEW GOLDEN RULE: COOPERATE!

Worldwide, research and development managers are under pressure as their budgets shrink and technological complexity grows by leaps and bounds. In this new environment, the hottest trend is collaboration—and it's sweeping every field, from autos to aircraft to biotechnology. GM, Ford, and Chrysler are "carpooling" to avoid duplicating R&D efforts. The Big Three have formed 12 consortiums on such projects as electric car batteries and better crash dummies. In biotechnology, an AIDS therapy from a small Quebec company, BioChem Pharma, is being shepherded through clinical trials by Britain's Glaxo Holdings and will be marketed by Burroughs Wellcome. The goal of the threesome's deal is to reduce costs, spread risk, and promote cross-fertilization of ideas. Even Hewlett-Packard and Japan's

Canon, which compete fiercely in low-priced ink-jet printers, have teamed up on higher priced laser printers. With technology getting ever more complex, companies realize that no one can do it all alone.

Suppliers are also a part of this new collaborative business world. At Honeywell's factory in Golden Valley, Minnesota, where thermostats and other building controls are made, supplier sales reps have cubicles right next to the factory floor. Some in-plant suppliers do their own research on products and sales forecasts, are allowed to write sales orders for the company, and look for ways to trim costs. Honeywell's payoff has been inventory levels measured in days rather than weeks or months and 25 percent fewer purchasing agents. Motorola has come to value its suppliers' ingenuity so much that it

established a 15-member council of suppliers to rate Motorola's own practices and offer suggestions for improvement. That reduces costs, according to Motorola's procurement chief, Tom Slaninka, "because every time we make an error it takes people at both ends to correct it." While manufacturers win with lower costs, suppliers gain in higher volume, and transaction costs go down for everyone. In the quest for speed and efficiency, collaboration is a trend that's likely to go even further in the coming years.

SOURCES: Peter Coy with Neil Gross, Silvia Sansoni, and Kevin Kelly, "What's the Word in the Lab? Collaborate," *Business Week*, June 27, 1994, 78–80; Fred R. Bleakley, "Some Companies Let Suppliers Work on Site and Even Place Orders," *The Wall Street Journal*, January 13, 1995, A1; Neal Templin and Jeff Cole, "Manufacturers Use Suppliers to Help Them Develop New Products," *The Wall Street Journal*, December 19, 1994, A1; and Myron Magnet, "The New Golden Rule of Business," *Fortune*, February 21, 1994, 60–64.

---

enormous 31 percent of revenues are put back into R&D, more than any other software developer. Perhaps he values creativity so much because the beginnings of the company came from his own inventiveness. A software program Goodnight developed in the 1970s became the embryo for SAS, which now has more than 30 business decision modules that run on PCs to mainframes.

Goodnight's vision of a worker-friendly culture is partly a result of his earlier negative experiences working with General Electric, where guards were everywhere and a cup of coffee required a long walk down to the vending machine. Even though his company sells sophisticated software for business decisions, Goodnight doesn't use one to decide on a new company benefit, but rather looks at the proposal and says, "This makes sense." He trusts his gut and follows the personal code of "If you do right by people, they'll do right by you."[22] ∎

THE ORGANIZATION-ENVIRONMENT RELATIONSHIP

Why do organizations care so much about factors in the external environment? The reason is that the environment creates uncertainty for organization managers, and they must respond by designing the organization to adapt to the environment or to influence the environment.

Environmental Uncertainty

Organizations must manage environmental uncertainty to be effective. *Uncertainty* means that managers do not have sufficient information about environmental factors to understand and predict environmental needs and changes.[23] As indicated in Exhibit 3.2, environmental characteristics that

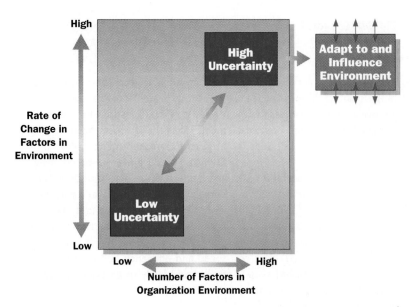

EXHIBIT 3.2
The External Environment and Uncertainty

boundary-spanning roles
Roles assumed by people and/or departments that link and coordinate the organization with key elements in the external environment.

influence uncertainty are the number of factors that affect the organization and the extent to which those factors change. A large multinational like Northern Telecom has thousands of factors in the external environment creating uncertainty for managers. When external factors change rapidly, the organization experiences very high uncertainty; examples are the electronics and aerospace industries. Firms must make efforts to adapt to these changes. When an organization deals with only a few external factors and these factors are relatively stable, such as for soft-drink bottlers or food processors, managers experience low uncertainty and can devote less attention to external issues.

Two basic strategies for coping with high environmental uncertainty are to adapt the organization to changes in the environment and to influence the environment to make it more compatible with organizational needs.

Adapting to the Environment

If the organization faces increased uncertainty with respect to competition, customers, suppliers, or government regu-

lation, managers can use several strategies to adapt to these changes, including boundary-spanning roles, increased planning and forecasting, a flexible structure, and mergers or joint ventures.

Boundary-Spanning Roles. Departments and **boundary-spanning roles** link and coordinate the organization with key elements in the external environment. Boundary spanners serve two purposes for the organization: They detect and process information about changes in the environment, and they represent the organization's interest to the environment.[24] People in departments such as marketing and purchasing span the boundary to work with customers and suppliers, both face-to-face and through market research. For example, Houston-based Characters, Inc., a prepress company, surveys customers twice a year about the desktop-publishing technology they use or plan to use within the next 12 months. In addition, they recently did a blind survey to determine if the company should enter digital, short-run color printing, which is expected to be a $15 billion to $25 billion industry by the year 2000. Results convinced CEO David Steitz that the $2 million investment in new technology would pay off.[25] Perhaps the largest growth area in boundary spanning is competitive intelligence, also known as snooping and spying. McDonnell Douglas used competitive intelligence to get the jump on Boeing with its new prop-fan airliner. Mary Kay executives cried "foul" after discovering rival Avon had hired Dallas private detectives to dig through its trash.[26] Xerox buys rival copiers for its engineers, who take them apart and design a better product component by component. Eighty percent of the *Fortune* 1000 companies maintain in-house snoops, also known as *competitor intelligence professionals*. Most of their work is strictly legal, relying on commercial databases, news clippings, help-wanted advertisements, trade publications, product literature, and personal contacts. Computerizing a company's network of intelligence gatherers, as

AT&T did several years ago, helps employees learn what they need to know about competitors.[27]

Forecasting and Planning. Forecasting and planning for environmental changes are major activities in many corporations. Planning departments often are created when uncertainty is high.[28] Forecasting is an effort to spot trends that enable managers to predict future events. Forecasting techniques range from quantitative economic models of environmental business activity to newspaper clipping services. One of these services, called Burrelle's Information Services, Inc., monitors 16,000 newspapers and magazines and predicts future trends. Chase investors used information about rapidly multiplying television channels in Western Europe to invest in MCA, Inc., which had a valuable film library.

Control Data, Heinz, United Airlines, and Waste Management Inc. have devised specific management plans for handling crises. Whether the crisis is a hostile takeover attempt or product tampering, an organization that does not have a plan will make mistakes. Planning can soften the adverse effect of rapid shifts in the environment.

Flexible Structure. An organization's structure should enable it to effectively respond to shifts in the environment. Research has found that a loose, flexible structure works best when organizations experience uncertainty created by shifts in the external environment or by innovation within the organization, while a tight structure is most effective in a certain environment.[29] The term **organic structure** characterizes an organization that is free flowing, has few rules and regulations, encourages teamwork among employees, and decentralizes decision making to employees doing the job. This type of structure works best when the environment changes rapidly. Dow Chemical and Star-Kist Foods set up "SWAT" teams that can swing into action if an unexpected disaster strikes.

These teams include members from multiple departments who can provide the expertise needed for solving an immediate problem, such as a plant explosion. Organic organizations create many teams to handle changes in raw materials, new products, government regulations, or marketing. A **mechanistic structure** is just the opposite, characterized by rigidly defined tasks, many rules and regulations, little teamwork, and centralization of decision making. Although this is fine for a stable environment, few organizations today exist in a stable environment. Organizational structures are shifting toward the image of the networked structure of advanced, worldwide information systems—an organic web rather than a hierarchy.[30]

Mergers and Joint Ventures. As we discussed, mergers are a major factor in a company's external environment. A merger is also a way to reduce uncertainty. A **merger** occurs when two or more organizations combine to become one. For example, General Host acquired Hickory Farms, a retail chain, to become an outlet for General Host's meat products, thereby reducing uncertainty in the customer sector.

A **joint venture** involves a strategic alliance or program by two or more organizations. This typically occurs when the project is too complex, expensive, or uncertain for one firm to do alone. Oil companies have used joint ventures to explore for oil on the continental shelf or in inaccessible regions of Alaska and Canada. Many small businesses are turning to joint ventures with large firms or with international partners.[31] Recall from the Focus on Cooperation box that a small Canadian pharmaceuticals company has teamed up with two giant companies to promote a new AIDS therapy. A larger partner can provide sales staff, distribution channels, financial resources, or a research staff. Small businesses seldom have the expertise to deal internationally, so a company such as Nypro, Inc., a plastic injection-molding manufacturer in Clinton, Massachusetts, joins with overseas experts

mechanistic structure
An organizational structure characterized by rigidly defined tasks, many rules and regulations, little teamwork, and centralized decision making.

merger
The combination of two or more organizations into one.

joint venture
A strategic alliance or program by two or more organizations.

organic structure
An organizational structure that is free flowing, has few rules and regulations, encourages employee teamwork, and decentralizes decision making to employees doing the job.

who are familiar with the local rules. Nypro now does business in four countries.

Marlene Conway used strategic alliances to provide necessary knowledge in the complicated recycling industry.

ENVIROLUTIONS

Canadian fast-tracker Marlene Conway came home one day to a crisis: Her husband had left her with huge debts and two children to support. "Do what you know best," she was told. So within seven hours she had a plan. Noticing that one-half of her garbage was disposable diapers, she realized there was a need to recycle diapers.

Within 18 months, in 1989, she had scraped together enough capital to launch the Mississauga, Ontario, company, Knowaste, an R&D company to develop environmental resources for sustainable benefit. Lacking a knowledge base in the field, she read books and talked to anyone she could. Needing lab space, she made arrangements to use extra space at Ecolab and Harco. There, Conway, staff, and sponsors spent hours garbed in rubber gloves and boots while they scrubbed, ripped, and destroyed diapers.

Because her staff lacked technological expertise to survive with all the chaotic changes, Conway began looking for strategic partnerships with Procter & Gamble, Hercules Canada, DuPont, and Beloit Corp. By 1990 Knowaste had a major investor with New York Caithness Resources Inc., which saw the business opportunity of North America's landfills bulging with 5 million tons of disposable diapers a year. Currently Knowaste has a suburban Toronto 20,000-square-foot diaper recycling factory, which processes 500 tons of diapers a month, though capacity is four times that. By 1996, plans were being made to have companies ship diapers from Boston and other cities to Mississauga for recycling.

Because her years working on recycling have given her more interest and broad contacts in environmental projects, Conway has used the expertise gained to start a new venture, Envirolutions. Now she works on recycling carpets into bricks, turning pesky zebra mussels into fertilizer, and waste water management. "There's no such thing as garbage," says Conway. "Only materials in process."[32] ■

Influencing the Environment

The other major strategy for handling environmental uncertainty is to reach out and change those elements causing problems. Widely used techniques for changing the environment include advertising and public relations, political activity, and trade associations. Exhibit 3.3 summarizes the techniques organizations can use to adapt to and influence the external environment.

Advertising and Public Relations. Advertising has become a highly successful way to manage demand for a company's products. Companies spend large amounts of money to influence consumer tastes. Hospitals have begun to advertise through billboards, newspapers, and radio commercials to promote special services. Increased competitiveness among CPA firms and law firms has caused them to start advertising for clients, a practice unheard of until recent years. Advertising is an important way to reduce uncertainty about clients.

Public relations is similar to advertising except that its goal is to influence public opinion about the company itself. Most companies care a great deal about their public image. Each year *Fortune* rates more than 300 companies to see which are the most and least admired in each of 32 industries. Public relations and a good public image are accomplished through advertising as well as speeches and press reports. Companies in the tobacco industry have launched an aggressive public relations campaign touting smokers' rights and freedom of choice in an effort to survive in this antismoking era.[33] Dow Chemical became infamous in the 1960s and 1970s for supplying napalm and Agent Orange to the military for use in Vietnam. Even when it stopped making these products, the image persisted. Dow Chemical attempts to change this view with an upbeat advertising campaign—

"Dow Lets You Do Great Things"—and other external communications emphasizing Dow Chemical research and the humanitarian use of its products. Dow Chemical also has a strong in-house ethics program, a model for the industry.[34]

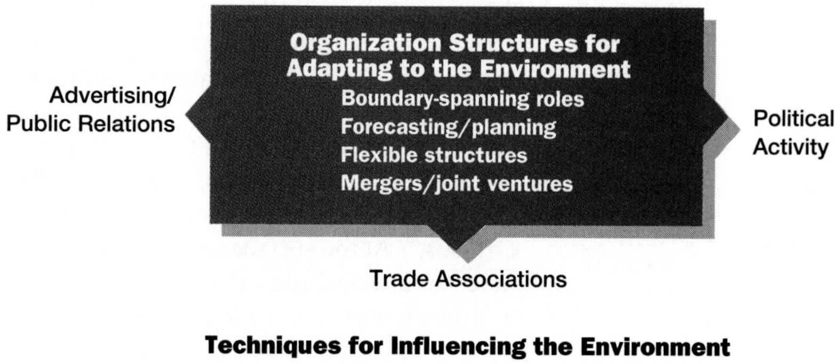

Political Activity.   Political activity represents organizational attempts to influence government legislation and regulation. GM enlisted political bigwigs in its successful effort to settle a battle with the U.S. Transportation Department over the safety of certain models of its pickup trucks. The settlement saved GM the cost of a $1 billion recall, basically allowing the company to buy its way out of the dispute by spending $51 million on safety programs over a five-year period.[35] Many corporations pay lobbyists to express their views to federal and state legislators. Foreign companies are becoming increasingly savvy in U.S. political maneuvering. For example, Japanese companies have placed former key U.S. political insiders on their payrolls as Washington lobbyists and advisers. Under pressure from U.S. companies about government-business collaboration in foreign countries, Washington has warmed to a technology policy that provides government policy support to critical technologies and industry study groups.[36]

Trade Associations.   Most organizations join with others having similar interests; the result is a **trade association.** In this way, organizations work together to influence the environment, including federal legislation and regulation. The number and variety of trade associations is staggering. Although many students have heard of the National Rifle Association or the National Association of Manufacturers, few are aware that there is a National Academy of Nannies, a National Coil Coaters Association, or a National Association of Nameplate Manufacturers. One effective association is the National Tooling and Machining Association (NTMA). The NTMA functions primarily as a center of knowledge. In a recent year, NTMA fielded 16,000

Techniques for Influencing the Environment

queries from members on everything from technical and marketing matters to taxes and labor problems. Since most tooling and machining companies are small, the association lobbies heavily on issues that affect small business, like taxes, health insurance, and government mandates. Recognizing that its members are competing with low-priced competitors in Europe and Japan, the NTMA provides statistics and information to help U.S. companies set competitive prices, and the association has recently committed itself to expanding ties with industry counterparts in Mexico and Canada.[37]

THE INTERNAL ENVIRONMENT: CORPORATE CULTURE

The internal environment within which managers work includes corporate culture, production technology, organization structure, and physical facilities. Of these, corporate culture has surfaced as extremely important to competitive advantage. The internal culture must fit the needs of the external environment and company strategy. When this fit occurs, highly committed employees create a high-performance organization that is tough to beat.[38]

Culture can be defined as the set of key values, beliefs, understandings, and norms shared by members of an organization.[39] The concept of culture helps managers understand the hidden, complex aspects of organizational life. Culture is a pattern of shared values and assumptions about how

EXHIBIT 3.3
Organizational Responses to Environmental Changes

political activity
Organizational attempts, such as lobbying, to influence government legislation and regulation.

trade association
An association made up of organizations with similar interests for the purpose of influencing the environment.

culture
The set of key values, beliefs, understandings, and norms that members of an organization share.

things are done within the organization. This pattern is learned by members as they cope with external and internal problems and taught to new members as the correct way to perceive, think, and feel. Culture can be analyzed at three levels, as illustrated in Exhibit 3.4, with each level becoming less obvious.[40] At the surface level are visible artifacts, which include such things as manner of dress, patterns of behavior, physical symbols, organizational ceremonies, and office layout. Visible artifacts are all the things one can see, hear, and observe by watching members of the organization. At a deeper level are the expressed values and beliefs, which are not observable but can be discerned from how people explain and justify what they do. These are values that members of the organization hold at a conscious level. They can be interpreted from the stories, language, and symbols organization members use to represent them. Some values become so deeply embedded in a culture that members are no longer consciously aware of them. These basic, underlying assumptions and beliefs are the essence of culture and subconsciously guide behavior and decisions. In some organizations, a basic assumption might be that people are essentially lazy and will shirk their duties whenever possible; thus, employees are closely supervised and given little freedom, and colleagues are frequently suspicious of one another. More enlightened organizations operate on the basic assumption that people want to do a good job; in these organizations, employees are given more freedom and responsibility, and colleagues trust one another and work cooperatively. Basic assumptions in an organization's culture often begin with strongly held values espoused by a founder or early leader, as in the case of the giant retailer Wal-Mart, which illustrates how elements of culture can provide competitive advantage.

■ WAL-MART

One organization with a strong culture is Wal-Mart, where folksy values continue to reflect its small-town beginnings and the personality and principles of its late founder, Sam Walton. Walton and other senior managers used fun-loving motivational tactics that included hog calls, songs, hulas, and the Wal-Mart cheer, "W-A-L-M-A-R-T." These antics, merged with Walton's "break-the-rules" philosophy, formed the cultural core of this unbelievable company. The culture stresses the personal touch, and associates are urged to provide community involvement and individual attention. Sam believed, "If you want your people to take care of the customer, you have to take care of your people." Department buyers are urged to "get their noses in it" by working with customers

EXHIBIT 3.4
Levels of Corporate Culture

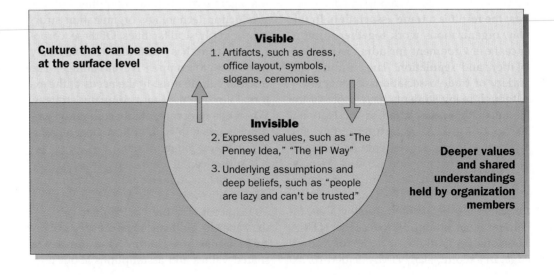

Culture that can be seen at the surface level

Visible
1. Artifacts, such as dress, office layout, symbols, slogans, ceremonies

Invisible
2. Expressed values, such as "The Penney Idea," "The HP Way"
3. Underlying assumptions and deep beliefs, such as "people are lazy and can't be trusted"

Deeper values and shared understandings held by organization members

on the sales floor once a week. CEO David Glass continues the policy of daily experimentation and change. Individual empowerment, continuous improvement, and profit sharing contribute to that small-town culture of "belonging" that is so easily picked up by Wal-Mart's loyal customers.[41,42] ■

In comparing 18 companies that have experienced long-term success with 18 similar companies that have not done so well, James C. Collins and Jerry I. Porras found the key determining factor in successful companies to be a culture in which employees share such a strong vision that they know in their hearts what is right for the company. Their book, *Built to Last: Successful Habits of Visionary Companies*, describes how companies like Hewlett-Packard, Walt Disney, and Procter & Gamble have successfully adapted to a changing world without losing sight of the core values that guide the organization. Some companies put values in writing so they can be passed on to new generations of employees. Hewlett-Packard created a list of cultural concepts called "The HP Way." At Levi Strauss, a set of corporate "aspirations" written by top management is to guide all decisions. Retailer Nordstrom has built so strong a culture around serving the customer that the entire employee manual is a 5-by-8-inch card with one rule on it: "Use your good judgment in all situations."[43]

The fundamental values that characterize cultures at Nordstrom, Wal-Mart, and Hewlett-Packard can be understood through the visible manifestations of symbols, stories, heroes, slogans, and ceremonies. Any company's culture can be interpreted by observing these factors.

Symbols

A **symbol** is an object, act, or event that conveys meaning to others. Symbols associated with corporate culture convey the organization's important values. For example, John Thomas, CEO of a mechanical contractor in Andover, Massachusetts, wanted to imprint the value of allowing mistakes and risk tak-

ing. He pulled a $450 mistake out of the dumpster, mounted it on a plaque, and named it the "No-Nuts Award" for the missing parts. The award is presented annually and symbolizes the freedom to make mistakes but not to make the same mistake twice.[44] Symbolizing his commitment to a true open-door policy, Bill Arnold, president of Nashville's Centennial Medical Center, ripped his office door from its hinges and suspended it from the lobby ceiling for all employees to see.[45] Randall Larrimore, president of MasterBrand Industries, Inc., wanted to break down the vertical walls that isolated departments and develop a team culture. Faced with skeptical managers who felt incapable of leading such a change process, Larrimore gave a motivational speech and then symbolized his message by giving each manager a copy of *Oh, The Places You'll Go*, by Dr. Seuss. The managers now proudly display the book as a symbol of their own pioneering efforts and achievements.[46]

Stories

A **story** is a narrative based on true events that is repeated frequently and shared among organizational employees. Stories are told to new employees to keep the

Standing in the snow, these First Security Corporation employees serve as living *symbols* of company values and employee commitment to giving 110 percent. This Salt Lake City, Utah–based financial services company is focused on superior customer service and has invested thousands of hours in the training of employees. The result: giving 110 percent is a way of life, and surveys of 60,000 customers rated First Security performance an astonishing 6.2 overall (on a 7-point scale) in 30 categories. Whether going the extra mile or standing in the snow, First Security employees pride themselves on a culture in which more is expected.

symbol
An object, act, or event that conveys meaning to others.

story
A narrative based on true events that is repeated frequently and shared by organizational employees.

organization's primary values alive. At Nordstrom, Inc., management does not deny the story about a customer who got his money back on a tire. Nordstrom does not sell tires. The story reinforces the store's no-questions-asked return policy. A story at Dayton Hudson about Ken Macke, CEO, tells how he gave a woman a new washing machine because she complained about needing a broken belt replaced. The story still serves to improve complaint handling at the lowest company levels. For years, workers at U.S. Paper Mills Corporation have told a story about the company's founder and principal stockholder Walter Cloud. One morning, when Cloud saw a worker trying to unclog the drain of a blending vat using an extension pole, he quickly climbed over the edge of the vat and reached through the 3-feet-deep slurry of paper fiber to unclog the drain with his hand. As he wiped the muck from his dress pants, Walter asked the worker, "Now, what are you going to do the next time you need to unclog a drain?" By telling and retelling this story, workers at the mill communicate the importance of jumping in to do whatever needs to be done.[47]

Heroes

A **hero** is a figure who exemplifies the deeds, character, and attributes of a strong culture. Heroes are role models for employees to follow. Sometimes heroes are real, such as Lee Iacocca, who proved the courage of his convictions by working for $1 a year when he first came to Chrysler. Other times they are symbolic, such as the mythical sales representative at Robinson Jewelers who delivered a wedding ring directly to the church because the ring had been ordered late. The deeds of heroes are out of the ordinary but not so far out as to be unattainable by other employees. Heroes show how to do the right thing in the organization. Companies with strong cultures take advantage of achievements to define heroes who uphold key values.

At Minnesota Mining and Manufacturing (3M), top managers keep alive the he-roes who developed projects that were killed by top management. One hero was a vice president who was fired earlier in his career for persisting with a new product even after his boss had told him, "That's a stupid idea. Stop!" After the worker was fired, he would not leave. He stayed in an unused office, working without a salary on the new product idea. Eventually he was re-hired, the idea succeeded, and he was promoted back to vice president. The lesson of this hero as a major element in 3M's culture is to persist at what you believe in.[48]

Slogans

A **slogan** is a phrase or sentence that succinctly expresses a key corporate value. Many companies use a slogan or saying to convey special meaning to employees. H. Ross Perot of Electronic Data Systems established the philosophy of hiring the best people he could find and noted how difficult it was to find them. His motto was "Eagles don't flock. You gather them one at a time." A variation used at PepsiCo to describe the value of turning bright young people into strong managers is "We take eagles and teach them to fly in formation." At Sequins International, where 80 percent of the employees are Hispanic, words from W. Edwards Deming, "You don't have to please the boss; you have to please the customer," are embroidered in Spanish on the pockets of workers' jackets.[49]

Ceremonies

A **ceremony** is a planned activity that makes up a special event and is conducted for the benefit of an audience. Managers hold ceremonies to provide dramatic examples of company values. Ceremonies are special occasions that reinforce valued accomplishments, create a bond among people by allowing them to share an important event, and anoint and celebrate heroes.[50]

The value of a ceremony can be illustrated by the presentation of a major award. Mary Kay Cosmetics Company holds elabo-

---

slogan
A phrase or sentence that succinctly expresses a key corporate value.

hero
A figure who exemplifies the deeds, character, and attributes of a corporate culture.

ceremony
A planned activity that makes up a special event and is conducted for the benefit of an audience.

rate awards ceremonies, presenting gold and diamond pins, furs, and pink Cadillacs to high-achieving sales consultants. The setting is typically an auditorium, in front of a large, cheering audience, and everyone dresses in glamorous evening clothes. The most successful consultants are introduced by film clips, like the kind used to present award nominees in the entertainment industry. These ceremonies recognize and celebrate high-performing employees and emphasize the rewards for performance.[51] An award can also be bestowed secretly by mailing it to the employee's home or, if a check, by depositing it in a bank. But such procedures would not make the bestowal of rewards a significant organizational event and would be less meaningful to the employee.

In summary, organizational culture represents the values, understandings, and basic assumptions that employees share, and these values are signified by symbols, stories, heroes, slogans, and ceremonies. Managers help define important symbols, stories, and heroes to shape the culture.

ENVIRONMENT AND CULTURE

A big influence on internal corporate culture is the external environment. Corporate culture should embody what it takes to succeed in the environment. If the external environment requires extraordinary customer service, the culture should encourage good service; if it calls for careful technical decision making, cultural values should reinforce managerial decision making.

Adaptive Cultures

Research at Harvard on 207 U.S. firms illustrated the critical relationship between corporate culture and the external environment. The study found that a strong corporate culture alone did not ensure business success unless the culture encouraged healthy adaptation to the external environment. As illustrated in Exhibit 3.5, adaptive corporate cultures have different values and behavior from unadaptive corporate cultures. In adaptive cultures, managers are concerned about customers and those internal people and processes that bring about useful change. In the unadaptive corporate cultures, managers are concerned about themselves, and their values tend to discourage risk taking and change. Thus a strong culture alone is not enough, because an unhealthy culture may encourage the organization to march resolutely in the wrong direction. Healthy cultures help companies adapt to the environment.[52]

	Adaptive Corporate Cultures	Unadaptive Corporate Cultures
Visible Behavior	Managers pay close attention to all their constituencies, especially customers, and initiate change when needed to serve their legitimate interests, even if it entails taking some risks.	Managers tend to behave somewhat insularly, politically, and bureaucratically. As a result, they do not change their strategies quickly to adjust to or take advantage of changes in their business environments.
Expressed Values	Managers care deeply about customers, stockholders, and employees. They also strongly value people and processes that can create useful change (e.g., leadership initiatives up and down the management hierarchy).	Managers care mainly about themselves, their immediate work group, or some product (or technology) associated with that work group. They value the orderly and risk-reducing management process much more highly than leadership initiatives.

EXHIBIT 3.5
Environmentally Adaptive versus Unadaptive Corporate Cultures

SOURCE: John P. Kotter and James Heskett, *Corporate Culture and Performance* (New York: The Free Press, 1992), 51.

Types of Cultures

One way to think about corporate cultures was suggested by Jeffrey Sonnenfeld and included four types of culture—baseball team, club, academy, and fortress. Each culture has somewhat different potential for supporting a healthy, successful company and has a different impact on the satisfaction and careers of employees.[53]

The *baseball team culture* emerges in an environmental situation with high-risk decision making and fast feedback from the environment. Decision makers quickly learn whether their choice was right or wrong. Talent, innovation, and performance are valued and rewarded. Top performers see themselves as "free agents," and companies scramble for their services. Performers with "low batting averages" are quickly dropped from the lineup. Baseball team cultures are found in fast-paced, high-risk companies involved in areas such as movie production, advertising, and software development where futures are bet on a new product or project.

The *club culture* is characterized by loyalty, commitment, and fitting into the group. This stable, secure environment values age and experience and rewards seniority. As in the case of career military personnel, individuals start young and stay. Club cultures promote from within, and members are expected to progress slowly, proving competence at each level. Individuals tend to be generalists and may have vast experience in a number of organizational functions. Top executives in commercial banks, for example, frequently began as tellers. While many club qualities contribute to flexibility within the organization, they can also contribute to the perception of a closed company, reluctant to change.

The *academy culture* also hires young recruits interested in a long-term association and a slow, steady climb up the organization. Unlike the club culture, however, employees rarely cross from one division to another. Each person enters a specific "track" and gains a high level of expertise in that area. Job and technical mastery are the bases for reward and advancement. Many long-established organizations such as universities, Coca-Cola, Ford, and GM maintain strong academy cultures. Although specialization provides job security, this culture may limit broad individual development and interdepartmental collaboration, but it works very well in a stable environment.

The *fortress culture* may emerge in an environmental survival situation. Textile firms and savings and loan organizations are examples of former dominant industries that are now retrenching for survival. The fortress culture offers little job security or opportunity for professional growth while companies restructure and downsize to fit the new environment. This culture is perilous for employees but also offers tremendous turnaround opportunities for individual managers with confidence and love of challenge. Those who succeed, such as Lee Iaccoca (Chrysler) or William Crouse (president of Ortho Diagnostic Systems, Inc.), earn recognition nationally or within their industry.[54]

SHAPING CORPORATE CULTURE FOR THE TWENTY-FIRST CENTURY

Changing and Merging Corporate Cultures

A corporation's culture may not always be in alignment with its needs and environment. Cultural values may reflect what worked in the past. The difference between desired cultural norms and values and actual norms and values is called the **culture gap.**[55]

Culture gaps can be immense, especially in mergers and acquisitions.[56] Despite the popularity of mergers and acquisitions as a corporate strategy, many fail. Almost one-half of acquired companies are sold within five years, and some experts claim that 90 percent of mergers never live up to expectations.[57] One reason for failure is that although managers are able to integrate the

culture gap
The difference between an organization's desired cultural norms and values and actual norms and values.

acquired firm's financial systems and production technologies, they typically are unable to integrate the unwritten norms and values that have an even greater impact on a company's success.[58] These problems increase in scope and frequency with global companies and cross-cultural mergers and acquisitions. After acquiring Pre-Press Graphics to move their company into the digital age, managers at Harty Press learned the hard way that trying to put two cultures together can be a killer. Harty workers wear smudged aprons, have ink under their fingernails, and carry union cards. At Pre-Press, people in running shoes and jeans sit before the glow of computer screens. The pace at Harty is hurried, but the style is loose and flexible. At Pre-Press, everything is precisely measured, employees are forbidden from making personal phone calls, and lunch is held strictly to 30 minutes. The two cultures clashed from the beginning, but the most damaging tensions were related to employee anxiety and fear of losing their jobs. Pre-Press employees were reluctant to share their knowledge for fear that once Harty employees learned the new skills, they might no longer be needed. Harty employees with conventional printing skills saw the digital future and worried that they were about to become obsolete in a craft they had cultivated for years. Harty managers' early failure to pay attention to the human side of things didn't kill the company, but it seriously wounded it. Said general manager Michael Platt, "I thought all that stuff people said about culture when it came to mergers was a bunch of fluff—until it happened." Managers often forget that the human systems of a company are what make or break any change initiative.[59]

Culture gaps can also exist in companies that have not gone through merger or acquisition. When Chuck Mitchell took over at GTO, Inc., a nearly bankrupt maker of automatic gate openers in Tallahassee, Florida, he quickly realized that the most damaging inefficiencies were not in the company's products or processes but in the hearts of its employees. As described in the Leading the Management Revolution box, transforming an unadaptive culture requires leaders who are in tune with their own inner values and are motivated by seeing others learn and grow to their full potential.

Symbolic Leadership

One way managers change norms and values toward what is adaptive to the external environment or for smooth internal integration is through symbolic leadership. Managers can use symbols, stories, slogans, and ceremonies to change corporate culture. Managers literally must overcommunicate to ensure that employees understand the new culture values, and they must signal these values in actions as well as words. As described in the Leading the Management Revolution box, Chuck Mitchell didn't just tell workers that the new GTO culture was one in which employees were valued; he put the new values into action.

A **symbolic leader** defines and uses signals and symbols to influence corporate culture. Symbolic leaders influence culture in the following manner:

1 *The symbolic leader articulates a vision for the organizational culture that generates excitement and that employees can believe in.* This means the leader defines and communicates central values that employees believe in and will rally around.
2 *The symbolic leader heeds the day-to-day activities that reinforce the cultural vision.* The symbolic leader makes sure that symbols, ceremonies, and slogans match the new values. Even more important, actions speak louder than words. Symbolic leaders "walk their talk."[60]

The reason symbolic leadership works is that executives are watched by employees. Employees attempt to read signals from what executives do, not just from what they say. For example, a senior manager told a story of how employees always knew in advance when someone was to be laid off in his company. He finally picked up the pattern. Employees noticed that he always dressed in his favorite pink shirt and matching tie when layoffs were to be announced.

symbolic leader
A manager who defines and uses signals and symbols to influence corporate culture.

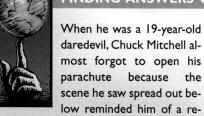

LEADING THE MANAGEMENT REVOLUTION
FINDING ANSWERS WITHIN THE PEOPLE AROUND YOU

When he was a 19-year-old daredevil, Chuck Mitchell almost forgot to open his parachute because the scene he saw spread out below reminded him of a recurring dream he'd had at the age of 12. Chuck Mitchell took another daring leap into treacherous terrain more than 20 years later. After his friend and the founder of GTO, Inc., Lester M. Taub, suffered a fatal heart attack, Mitchell stepped in at the behest of the 16-member board. It didn't take a financial genius to know that GTO, a small company that manufactures automatic gate openers, was in trouble. Average monthly sales were $35,000 short of the break-even point. Most suppliers would send wares only on a COD basis. Morale was terrible on the shop floor. Taub had insisted that being a good manager meant he bicycled through the factory barking epithets at hapless workers, ordering them to work faster or scolding them for filing claims on the company's health insurance policy.

Chuck Mitchell had a powerful vision to transform GTO's culture. His opening speech to the employees amounted to a plea for help. "The bottom line," he said, "is that you've got to look within yourself and within the people around you to come up with answers." To Mitchell's way of thinking, the company's overriding inefficiency was its inability to tap into the inner reserves of its workers. One by one he trotted employees into his office. The more he listened, the more they talked. Linda Williams, who had quit several months earlier, returned to the company and suggested that GTO expand its product line and carry items made by other companies. Last year, out of the 15 products GTO added, only 5 were actually made there. Concerns over the company's minimal health insurance plan led Mitchell to change the policy, which doubled GTO's expenses. But "making people comfortable frees them to come up with ideas for making this business better," he says. "I need their help."

Mitchell also took other steps— some little and some big—to symbolize that he cared. Before he even negotiated a salary with GTO's board, he insisted that the company agree to put aside 5 percent of net profits in a profit-sharing plan. He went out and bought coffee and sugar, which Taub had neglected because he didn't consume it. He hired a roofer to fix the badly leaking roof. To promote a sense of ownership, he freely gives employees keys to the building and tells them they can use GTO tools to repair their cars on weekends. He hands over a blank check when an employee needs to buy a part. Mitchell knows there's risk in such freedom. Yet he also knows that "any company in which there isn't trust is a company with one hand tied behind its back. . . . But to have that kind of trust, you need to make yourself vulnerable."

GTO as a company and a culture has seen big changes. Sales have increased by 10 percent, and net profit has gone from −$311,287 in 1993 to +$475,821 in 1994. The number of employees who submit substantive ideas for improvements has tripled. What matters most to Chuck Mitchell is that by now GTO workers know that he cares, and they have started a culture to care about each other and the company.

SOURCE: Joshua Hyatt, "Real-World Reengineering," *Inc.,* April 1995, 40–53.

When Les Tiffany, director of production at Physio-Control, Inc., saw falling production and rising employee tension, he developed a vision to increase production levels and to celebrate the achievement of each $500,000 level. Upon attainment of each level, a manager, beginning with Tiffany himself, donned a clown costume and pedaled a tricycle through the plant, towing a siren-screaming red wagon with a banner proclaiming the accomplishment. Employees loved it. A "parade route" developed over the three-month period of the celebrations, and although production was interrupted for several minutes each day, motivation ran high to reach the next level and witness the "clowning" of yet another manager.[61]

Jack Welch transformed General Electric—a huge corporation—by defining a new type of senior manager. His demand was for symbolic leaders, which he described as follows: "Somebody who can develop a vision of what he or she wants their . . . activity to do and be. Somebody who is able to articulate what the business is, and gain through a sharing of the discussion—listening and talking—an acceptance of the vision. And someone who then can relentlessly drive implementation of that vision to a successful conclusion."[62]

Even well-established companies with strong cultures may implement changes through symbolic leadership. When IBM chief Lou Gerstner officially relaxed the company's unofficial straitlaced dress code, he was choosing a common symbol for lightening up a "traditional" business atmosphere. Gerstner has used symbolic leadership in other ways, too. On his first day on the job, Gerstner called a dozen top managers into his office and asked them to write a five-page report that answered such questions as What business are you in? Who are your customers? What are your strengths and weaknesses? He asked for the report in two days. In a company known for meetings steeped in ritual, requiring extensive and elaborate preparations, accompanied by massive reports in blue binders, the message was clear: It was no longer business as usual at Big Blue.[63]

Symbolic leaders search for opportunities. They make public statements, including both oral and written communications, to the organization as a whole. After articulating a vision, symbolic leaders change corporate culture through hundreds of small deeds, actions, statements, and ceremonies. A strong leader who articulated a clear vision accounted for the extraordinary success of Wal-Mart, Disney, McDonald's, and Levi Strauss. Harold Geneen, former CEO of ITT, captured his corporate value in a few words: "Search for the unshakeable facts." Herb Kelleher of Southwest Airlines has developed a strong, adaptive culture by sticking to the basics: "Do what your customer wants; be happy in your work."[64]

Scott Kohno, managing director of Chaix & Johnson, shocked and revitalized his 30 employees by hauling his desk from a comfortable executive office with 18-foot ceilings to the middle of the work floor. Kohno compared the move to the "difference between being on the basketball floor instead of the bleachers." The increased contact with staff was soon matched by a supercharged employee energy level.[65]

Another story involving a desk illustrates Mars executives' concern for employees and began when Mr. Mars made a midsummer visit to a chocolate factory:

He went up to the third floor, where the biggest chocolate machines were placed. It was hotter than the hinges of hell. He asked the factory manager, "How come you don't have air conditioning up here?" The factory manager replied that it wasn't in his budget, and he darn well had to make the budget. While Mr. Mars allowed that was a fact, he nonetheless went over to the nearby phone and dialed the maintenance people downstairs and asked them to come up immediately. He said, "While we (he and the factory manager) stand here, would you please go downstairs and get all (the factory manager's) furniture and other things from his office and bring them up here? Sit them down next to the big chocolate machine up here, if you don't mind." Mr. Mars told him that once the factory had been air conditioned, he could move back to his office any time he wanted.[66]

Stories such as these can be found in most companies and used to enhance the desired culture. The value of stories depends not on whether they are precisely true but whether they are repeated frequently and convey the correct values.

To summarize, symbolic leaders influence culture through the use of artifacts such as public statements, ceremonies, stories, heroes, symbols, and slogans. When cultural change is needed to adapt to the external environment or to bring about smoother internal integration, managers must become symbolic leaders and learn how to use speech, symbols, and stories to influence underlying cultural assumptions. Changing culture is not easy, but through their words—and particularly their actions—symbolic leaders let other organization members know what really counts in the company.

SUMMARY AND MANAGEMENT SOLUTION

This chapter discussed several important ideas about internal and external organizational environments. Events in the external environment are considered important influences on organizational behavior and performance. The external environment consists of two layers: the task environment and the general environment. The task environment includes customers, competitors, suppliers, and the labor market. The general environment includes technological, sociocultural, economic, legal-political, and international dimensions. Management techniques for helping the organization adapt to the environment include boundary-spanning roles, forecasting and planning, a flexible structure, and mergers and joint ventures. Techniques managers can use to influence the external environment include advertising and public relations, political activities, and trade associations.

Recall C/net at the beginning of the chapter, which is trying to capitalize on rapid changes in the external environment of the communications industry. Halsey Minor has vowed of his print magazine competition—such as *PC Week, InfoWorld*—that he will "eat [them] for lunch" and one of them will be out of business by the year 2000. Top brass at the publishers don't see C/net's online ads as much of a threat, and they aren't going all out on the Internet. However, though Minor's style is brash and seen as "obnoxious" by some editors, Minor likens his upstart company to another scrappy start-up not so long ago—Microsoft. Minor seems to understand online potential better than the others, which often do no more than dump print advertising into cyberspace. C/net's innovative use of TV/online has attracted a large and youthful audience, which has convinced some advertisers to go with C/net. The small company is also competing by developing new products, such as DREAM, which delivers messages from advertisers based on demographic information, browser type, and online affiliation. A second offering, Product Finder, also "zippy and fun," proves to be the fastest way for users to get information on product updates and new technologies. Minor's vision is to become the "biggest media company serving computers in the world."

Part of Minor's strategy involves tailoring his company's culture (a major element of the internal environment) to the needs of a fast-paced, rapidly changing external environment. For an organization to be effective, corporate culture—which includes the key beliefs, values, understandings, and norms that organization members share—should be aligned with the needs of the external environment. Four types of culture are baseball team, club, academy, and fortress, each of which suits a specific environment. C/net can be most effective using a baseball team culture.

Organizational activities that illustrate corporate culture include stories, symbols, heroes, slogans, and ceremonies. Symbolic leaders can strengthen or change corporate culture by (1) communicating a vision to employees and (2) reinforcing the vision with day-to-day public statements, ceremonies, stories, symbols, and personal actions.

DISCUSSION QUESTIONS

1 Some scientists predict major changes in the earth's climate, including a temperature rise of 8°F over the next 60 years. Should any companies be paying attention to this long-range environmental trend? Explain.

2 Would the task environment for a bank contain the same elements as that for a government welfare agency? Discuss.

3 What forces influence organizational uncertainty? Would such forces typically originate in the task environment or the general environment?

4 *In Search of Excellence*, described in Chapter 2, argued that customers were the most important element in the external environment. Are there company situations for which this may not be true?

5 Caterpillar Corporation was thriving until the mid-1980s, when low oil prices, high interest rates, a worldwide recession, a soaring U.S. dollar, and Japanese competition stunned the giant equipment builder. Discuss the type of response Caterpillar's management might take.

6 Define corporate culture and explain its importance for managers.

7 Why are symbols important to a corporate culture? Do stories, heroes, slogans, and ceremonies also have symbolic value? Discuss.

8 Describe the cultural values of a company for which you have worked. Did those values fit the needs of the external environment? Of employees?

9 What type of environmental situation is associated with a baseball team culture? How does this culture differ from the academy culture?

10 Do you think a corporate culture with strong values is better for organizational effectiveness than a culture with weak values? Are there times when a strong culture might reduce effectiveness?

MANAGEMENT EXERCISES

MANAGER'S WORKBOOK

What Economic Culture Is Your Company In?

According to *Inc.* magazine, the U.S. economy is dividing into three separate worlds. These economies are the Networked, the Kluge, and the Provincial.

In the Networked economy are dense urban concentrations of companies and entrepreneurs that generate most of the country's high-wage jobs in globally competitive industries. Examples are high-tech developers in Silicon Valley, the biomedical Research Triangle in North Carolina, and Midwestern auto developers.

The Kluge economy consists of public bureaucracies, universities, and quasi-government industries such as defense or utilities. Kluge (pronounced "klooj") is software slang for an ill-assigned collection of code that is poorly matched and forms a distressing whole.

The Networked and Kluge economies generate 45 percent (or 50 million) of the nation's non-agricultural jobs.

On the sidelines is the Provincial economy, clustered in the U.S.'s southern and intermountain western regions, which includes low-wage and low-skilled manufacturers, and back-office service providers. This economy makes up about 35 percent of the total.

The Kluge economy, though the least able to survive into the next century, nonetheless tries to attack the healthier and more formidable Networked economy, through government regulation and subsidies, as well as holding on to any monopoly status.

Which economy does your company fit?

1 Think of a company. Choose either one you have worked or studied in, or else interview a friend or family member about their workplace. Answer questions 1–15 that follow.

2 Score the questionnaire.

3 What is the prognosis for the company you chose? How will its economic culture impact on its future survival?

Questions

1 Which does your company value most?
 a. constant interaction with other companies and individuals to define new products and services.
 b. locating in regions with the lowest wage, regulatory, and tax burdens.
 c. gaining access to key public officials.

2 Which best describes your company's staff?
 a. individuals whose responsibilities are constantly evolving and among whom lines of authority are blurred.
 b. a kingdom where the CEO's word is law.
 c. tenured senior employees administering teams of untenured underlings.

3 Which best describes the business-development activities your company would pursue?
 a. a daily diet of telephone calls, meetings, and chance encounters with previous collaborators or new contacts they recommend.
 b. offering to cut the price of core products or services to stimulate sales.
 c. a detailed response to an RFP (request for proposal).

4 Which best describes what your management would most like to achieve?
 a. teaming up with other specialized businesses to develop new products no one ever thought of before.
 b. Doing big mail-order turnover from a converted barn in Kalispell, Montana.
 c. getting a 25 percent surcharge for your products approved by the relevant bureaucracy.

5 How would you describe your suppliers and customers?
 a. partners that change every day or week depending on the project.
 b. stable relationships governed largely by the price of what's bought or sold.

c. organizations defined by what government agencies require.

6 How would you describe your markets?

a. they're always changing.

b. they closely correspond to double-digit standard industrial codes.

c. they seem to vary only with major electoral changes.

7 Whom would your company be most likely to hire?

a. someone who will one day function as a skilled partner in your company's business-development network.

b. someone trustworthy and reliable, who can answer telephones in English.

c. someone who helps meet state or federal regulatory requirements and has good political contacts.

8 Your business is being recruited to move to a new state. What's the primary concern?

a. the depth of the businesses and the skill base in the new region.

b. the tax breaks and incentive package the new state is willing to offer.

c. potential long-term relations and cooperation with state and local officials.

9 Which best describes your company's view of American urban areas?

a. a challenging environment but one offering an intellectual pulse and skill mix that is essential for maintaining a competitive edge.

b. an anti-business, unsafe, regulatory quagmire.

c. a public-contract heaven.

10 Which best describes your company's view of American rural areas?

a. a great place to take ski trips and entertain clients.

b. clean, homogenous communities perfect for building a new plant and raising the kids.

c. an agricultural and public-power contract paradise.

11 What does "diversity" mean to your company?

a. a gateway to world markets and an essential resource for fashioning new products or services.

b. a complicated and contentious issue that can be avoided by moving to Idaho.

c. a critical contract compliance requirement.

12 Which best describes your company's view of technology?

a. whatever's exciting that can be integrated into new or existing products or services.

b. something that comes in discrete waves and is bought when your customers demand it.

c. something produced by a public institution named with an acronym.

13 You've come up with a new product idea. To bring it to market, your company would . . .

a. start a new company, staff it with the most creative people you could find, and jointly try to find as many creative applications of your ideas as possible.

b. look for investors to back your idea or sell out to an Asian consortium.

c. Write a grant proposal for a feasibility study.

14 What's more attractive to your company?

a. getting a piece of the action on a new deal.

b. boosting margins from 4 percent to 5 percent (or maybe 5.14 percent if South Carolina is serious about that tax break).

c. a check imprinted with the words "State of" or signed by the Secretary of the Treasury.

15 Which best describes where the CEO would probably like to be in 20 years?

a. the respected founder of a major new industry.

b. fishing in Utah.

c. chair of a national technology-policy commission.

Scoring

Give yourself 0 points for each A, 5 points for each B, and 10 points for each C.

0–30: Your company is a solid member of the Networked economy.

31–60: Your company has many characteristics in common with Networked companies, but it is also tending toward the low-skill, low-wage Provincial-economy model.

61–90: Your company is a solid member of the Provincial economy. Expect increasing wage and price pressures not just from businesses in other Provincial regions but from low-skill, low-wage launching platforms throughout the world.

91–120: Your company is midway between the Provincial and Kluge economies—hardly a happy mix for the twenty-first century, with global price competition increasing and the public sector shrinking.

121–150: Your company is a core Kluge-economy participant. You are probably in more trouble than an endangered species.

SOURCE: Reprinted with permission, *Inc.* magazine, (February 1996). Copyright 1996 by Goldhirsh Group, Inc., 38 Commercial Wharf, Boston, MA 02110.

Scavenger Hunt: Looking for the University's Culture

1 Divide into groups of four to seven members. These may be ad hoc or ongoing groups.
2 You are asked to find examples of the university's culture. Use 4- by 8-inch notecards. Put one symbol on each card, with the category listed at the top in capital letters. During a future class session, you will be asked to give a five-minute presentation of your findings to the class. You must find all four items from the required list and any four items from the elective list (except if you choose the cartoon option; then you need only two from the elective list).
3 Do NOT steal anything and do not buy any item. Your group is limited to $7 to make copies or take photos.

What Is Needed for Scavenger Hunt

Required list of symbols

1 Mission of university (teaching, research, service).
2 Customer/clients (students, researchers, business, community, country).
3 Locational information (e.g., city, county, state, U.S. or world map indicates local or cosmopolitan orientation).
4 Constituents (students, faculty, administrators, support staff, athletic teams, taxpayers, board of trustees).

Elective list (choose any four)

1 Leadership (respresentation, roles, administration or faculty or student).
2 The future of the university (short-term or long-term).
3 Inappropriate elements on campus (anything which is a mismatch between item and university culture).
4 Rules and policies (organizational policies on Americans with Disabilities Act, sexual harassment, etc.).
5 Pranks or jokes (may be funny or hurtful masked as funny).
6 List of unique language to university and the meanings of words.
7 Cartoons hung on faculty doors and bulletin boards. If you do this one, find enough of them to make comparisons between faculty levels and departments or schools. Are there different types of cartoons, for example, in the business school versus liberal arts? This one counts as three electives, since it is more time-consuming.
8 The value of a college education (technical skills, employability, increased income, life-long learning, intellectual heritage).

SOURCE: Lizabeth Barclay and Kenneth M. York, "The Scavenger Hunt Exercise," (Journal of Management Education, Vol. 20 No. 1) pp. 125–128, copyright © 1996 by Sage Publications. Adapted by permission of Sage Publications, Inc.

Find Web sites for ten companies, five high-tech and five low-tech. From the information on the Web sites, determine what differences in structure and culture you see between the high- and low-tech companies. Use the following concepts in your analysis and comparison:

Mechanistic vs. organic structure.
Symbols, stories, ceremonies, heroes, and slogans.
Culture types: baseball team, club, academy, or fortress.

ETHICAL DILEMMA

Watching Out for Larry

It was the end of the fourth quarter, and Holly Vasquez was completing the profitability statement for her division's regional manager. She was disturbed to see that, for the first time during her tenure as a sales manager for Wallog Computers, her group was not in the top 10 percent of the region. She had watched sales slip during the past year but hoped the fourth quarter might save their numbers. The company was under pressure from stockholders to increase sales. Vasquez was afraid that Wallog would be cutting staff and altering the "people culture" that had kept her there for the past ten years.

As she entered the individual results in the spreadsheet, she saw her main problem: Larry Norris. After 27 years with the company, Norris had more career sales than anyone in the region, but, for the past 3 years, he had not even met his quota. Unlike some of her newer salespeople, Norris was uninformed on new products, and his old-style selling techniques didn't seem to be working. Vasquez had suggested he consult with the "new guys" on technical information and new sales techniques, but Norris was stubborn.

Vasquez knew she had the performance information to move him out of his position, but there was nowhere for him to go at Wallog. At 56, he was too young for retirement but too old to find a job elsewhere at his current

salary. Not only was Larry Norris a friend, but also he was well-liked in her department, and Vasquez wondered what effect his replacement would have on morale. She didn't want to fire him, but she couldn't risk her team's standing or her own reputation by protecting him anymore.

What Do You Do?

1   Fire Larry Norris with two weeks' notice, a generous severance package, and all the help you can provide him in his job hunt.

2   Give him an ultimatum to meet his sales quota or else, and let him find the way. It is his responsibility to stay current and meet his quota.

3   Assign him to study the new products and the sales techniques of the top salespeople—then hope he improves and the others don't slip.

CASE FOR CRITICAL ANALYSIS

Society of Equals

Ted Shelby doesn't make very many mistakes, but . . .

"Hey Stanley," says Ted Shelby, leaning in through the door, "you got a minute? I've just restructured my office. Come on and take a look. I've been implementing some great new concepts!"

Stanley is always interested in Ted Shelby's new ideas, for if there is anyone Stanley wants to do as well as, it is Edward W. Shelby IV. Stanley follows Ted back to his office and stops, nonplussed.

Restructured is right! Gone are Ted's size B (Junior Exec.) walnut veneer desk and furniture, and his telephone table. In fact, the room is practically empty save for a large, round, stark white cafeteria table and the half-dozen padded vinyl swivel chairs that surround it.

"Isn't it a beauty! As far as I know, I'm the first executive in the plant to innovate this. The shape is the crucial factor here—no front or rear, no status problems. We can all sit there and communicate more effectively."

We? Communicate? Effectively? Well, it seems that Ted has been attending a series of Executive Development Seminars given by Dr. Faust. The theme of the seminars was—you guessed it—"participative management." Edward W. Shelby IV has always liked to think of himself as a truly democratic person.

"You see, Stanley," says Ted, managing his best sincere/intense attitude, "the main thing wrong with current mainstream management practice is that the principal communication channel is down-the-line oriented. We on the top send our messages down to you people, but we neglect the feedback potential. But just because we have more status and responsibility doesn't mean that we are necessarily (Stanley duly noted the word, "necessarily") better than the people below us. So, as I see the situation, what is needed is a two-way communication network: down-the-line and up-the-line."

"That's what the cafeteria table is for?" Stanley says.

"Yes!" says Ted. "We management people don't have all the answers, and I don't know why I never realized it before that seminar. Why . . . let's take an extreme example . . . the folks who run those machines out there. I'll bet that any one of them knows a thing or two that I've never thought of. So I've transformed my office into a full-feed-back communication net."

"That certainly is an innovation around here," says Stanley.

A few days later Stanley passed by Ted Shelby's office and was surprised that Ted's desk, furniture, and telephone table were back where they used to be.

Stanley, curious about the unrestructuring, went to Bonnie for enlightenment. "What," he asked, "happened to Shelby's round table?"

"That table we were supposed to sit around and input things?" she said. "All I know is, about two days after he had it put in, Mr. Drake came walking through here. He looked in that office, and then he sort of stopped and went back—and he looked in there for a long time. Then he came over to me, and you know how his face sort of gets red when he's really mad? Well, this time he was so mad that his face was absolutely white. And when he talked to me, I don't think he actually opened his mouth; and I could barely hear him, he was talking so low. And he said, 'Have that removed. Now. Have Mr. Shelby's furniture put back in his office. Have Mr. Shelby see me.'"

My, my. You would think Ted would have known better, wouldn't you? But then, by now you should have a pretty firm idea of just why it is those offices are set up as they are.

Questions

1 How would you characterize the culture in this company? What are the dominant values?

2 Why did Ted Shelby's change experiment fail? To what extent did Ted use the appropriate change tools to increase employee communication and participation?

3 What would you recommend Ted do to change his relationship with subordinates? Is it possible for a manager to change cultural values if the rest of the organization, especially top management, does not agree?

SOURCE: R. Richard Ritti and G. Ray Funkhouser, *The Ropes to Skip & The Ropes to Know*, 3d. ed. (New York: Wiley, 1987), 176–177. Reprinted by permission of John Wiley & Sons, Inc.

ENDNOTES

1 Richard Rapaport, "C/net's Paper Chase," *Forbes ASAP*, June 3, 1996, 62–66.

2 Scott McMurray, "Wounded Giant: Union Carbide Offers Some Sober Lessons in Crisis Management," *The Wall Street Journal*, January 28, 1991, A1, A9; and Jaclyn Fierman, "When Genteel Rivals Become Mortal Enemies," *Fortune*, May 15, 1994, 90–100.

3 Richard L. Daft, *Organization Theory and Design*, 5th ed. (St. Paul, Minn.: West, 1995).

4 L. J. Bourgeois, "Strategy and Environment: A Conceptual Integration," *Academy of Management Review* 5 (1980), 25–39.

5 Richard I. Kirkland, Jr., "Entering a New Age of Boundless Competition," *Fortune*, March 14, 1988, 40–48; and Kenichi Ohmae, "Managing in a Borderless World," *Harvard Business Review* (May–June 1989), 152–161.

6 Nancy J. Perry, "The Arms Makers' Next Battle," *Fortune*, August 27, 1990, 84–88.

7 Eric Schine, Amy Borrus, John Carey, and Geoffery Smith, "The Defense Whizzies Making It in Civvies," *Business Week*, September 7, 1992, 88–90.

8 John Huey, "Waking Up to the New Economy," *Fortune*, June 27, 1994, 36–46.

9 Naomi Frundlich, Neil Gross, John Carey, and Robert D. Hof, "The New Alchemy: How Science Is Molding Molecules into Miracle Materials," *Business Week*, July 29, 1991, 48–52.

10 Otis Port, "Materials That Think for Themselves," *Business Week*, December 5, 1988, 166–167.

11 William B. Johnston, "Global Work Force 2000: The New World Labor Market," *Harvard Business Review* (March–April 1991), 115–127.

12 Maria Mallory and Stephanie Anderson Forest, "Waking Up to a Major Market," *Business Week*, March 23, 1992, 70–73; Michael Mandel, Christopher Farrell, Dori Jones Yang, Gloria Lau, Christina Del Valle, and S. Lynne Walker, "The Immigrants: How They're Helping to Revitalize the U.S. Economy," *Business Week*, July 13, 1992, 114–122; and Population Profile of the United States 1995, United States Department of Commerce, Bureau of the Census, July 1995.

13 "Ultrasafe, Ultra Low-emission School Bus," *Transportation Technologies*, U.S. Dept. Of Energy, 1996; Scott Thurston, "Bus Maker Severs Ties to Founder," *Atlanta Journal & Constitution*, July 19, 1992; and Rita Koselka, "It Was Important to Father and Mother, and It's Important to Us," *Forbes*, Oct. 6, 1986, 88–95.

14 Nicholas Imparato and Oren Harari, *Jumping the Curve: Innovation and Strategic Choice in an Age of Transition* (San Francisco: Jossey-Bass, 1994), 121.

15 David Lieverman, "Keeping Up with the Murdochs," *Business Week*, March 20, 1989, 32–34; Don Lee Bohl, ed., *Tying the Corporate Knot* (New York: American Management Association, 1989); Fierman, "When Genteel Rivals Become Mortal Enemies"; and Joseph Pereira, "The Toy Industry, Too, Is Merging Like Crazy to Win Selling Power," *The Wall Street Journal*, October 28, 1994, A1, A13.

16 Bela L. Musits, "When Big Changes Happen to Small Companies," *Inc.*, August 1994, 27–28.

17 Linda Himelstein and Laura Zinn, with Maria Mallory, John Carey, Richard S. Dunham, and Joan O'C. Hamilton, "Tobacco: Does It Have a Future?" *Business Week*, July 4, 1994, 24–29; Bob Ortega, "Aging Activists Turn, Turn, Turn Attention to Wal-Mart Protests," *The Wall Street Journal*, October 11, 1994, A1, A8; and Richard L. Daft, *Management*, 3d ed. (Fort Worth, Texas: The Dryden Press, 1994), 44.

18 Walecia Konrad and Gail DeGeorge, "U.S. Companies Go for the Gray," *Business Week*, April 3, 1989, 64–67.

19 Jenny C. McCune, "In the Shadow of Wal-Mart," *Management Review*, December 1994, 10–16.

20 Peter H. Lewis, "Apple-IBM Venture, with New Leaders, Searches for a Soul," *The New York Times*, March 8, 1992, F8; and Mark Ivey and Geoff Lewis, "Compaq vs. IBM: Peace Comes to Shove," *Business Week*, May 1, 1989, 132.

21 Michael R. Czinkota and Ilkka A. Ronkainen, "Global Marketing 2000: A Marketing Survival Guide," *Marketing Management* (winter 1992), 37–42.

22 Adapted from Sharon Overton, "And to All a Goodnight," *Sky*, October 1996, pp. 37–40.

23 Robert B. Duncan, "Characteristics of Organizational Environment and Perceived Environmental Uncertainty," *Administrative Science Quarterly* 17 (1972), 313–327; and Daft, *Organization Theory and Design*.

24 David B. Jemison, "The Importance of Boundary Spanning Roles in Strategic Decision-Making," *Journal of Management Studies* 21 (1984), 131–152; and Marc J. Dollinger, "Environmental Boundary Spanning and Information Processing Effects on Organizational Performance," *Academy of Management Journal* 27 (1984), 351–368.

25 David Steitz, "Let the Customer Be Your Guide," *Nation's Business*, March 1995, 4.

26 Wendy Zellner and Bruce Hager, "Dumpster Raids? That's Not Very Ladylike, Avon," *Business Week*, April 1, 1991, 32.

27 Brian Dumaine, "Corporate Spies Snoop to Conquer," *Fortune*, November 7, 1988, 68–76; Dody Tsiantar and John Schwartz, "George Smiley Joins the Firm," *Newsweek*, May 2, 1988, 46–47; James E. Svatko, "Analyzing the Competition," *Small Business Reports*, January 1989, 21–28; and Richard S. Teitelbaum, "The New Race for Intelligence," *Fortune*, November 2, 1992, 104–107.

28 R. T. Lenz and Jack L. Engledow, "Environmental Analysis Units and Strategic Decision-Making: A Field Study of Selected 'Leading Edge' Corporations," *Strategic Management Journal* 7 (1986), 69–89; and Mansour Javidan, "The Impact of Environmental Uncertainty on Long-Range Planning Practices of the U.S. Savings and Loan Industry," *Strategic Management Journal* 5 (1984), 381–392.

29 Tom Burns and G. M. Stalker, *The Management of Innovation* (London: Tavistock, 1961); J. C. Spender and Eric Kessler, "Managing the Uncertainties of Innovation: Extending Thompson (1967)," *Human Relations* 48, no. 1 (1995), 35–56; and Stephen Ackroyd, "On the Structure and Dynamics of Some Small, UK-based Information Technology Firms," *Journal of Management Studies* 32, no. 2 (March 1995), 141–161.

30 Huey, "Waking Up to the New Economy."

31 James E. Svatko, "Joint Ventures," *Small Business Reports*, December 1988, 65–70; and Joshua Hyatt, "The Partnership Route," *Inc.*, December 1988, 145–148.

32 Katrina Onstad, "If You Have a Lemon, Make Lemonade," *Canadian Business*, Sept. 1996, 49–54.

33 Linda Himelstein et al., "Tobacco: Does It Have a Future?"

34 John A. Byrne, "The Best-Laid Ethics Program . . . ," *Business Week*, March 9, 1992, 67–69; and "Dow Chemical: From Napalm to Nice Guy," *Fortune*, May 12, 1986, 75–78.

35 Daniel Pearl and Gabriella Stern, "How GM Managed to Wring Pickup Pact and Keep on Truckin'," *The Wall Street Journal*, December 5, 1994, A1, A8.

36 Edmund Faltermayer, "The Thaw in Washington," *Fortune* (The New American Century), 1991, 46–51; David B. Yoffie, "How an Industry Builds Political Advantage," *Harvard Business Review* (May–June 1988), 82–89; and Douglas Harbrecht, "How to Win Friends and Influence Lawmakers," *Business Week*, November 7, 1988, 36.

37 David Whitford, "Built by Association," *Inc.*, July 1994, 71–75.

38 Yoash Wiener, "Forms of Value Systems: A Focus on Organizational Effectiveness and Culture Change and Maintenance," *Academy of Management Review* 13 (1988), 534–545; V. Lynne Meek, "Organizational Culture: Origins and Weaknesses," *Organization Studies* 9 (1988), 453–473; and John J. Sherwood, "Creating Work Cultures with Competitive Advantage," *Organizational Dynamics* (winter 1988), 5–27.

39 Ralph H. Kilmann, Mary J. Saxton, and Roy Serpa, "Issues in Understanding and Changing Culture," *California Management Review* 28 (winter 1986), 87–94; and Linda Smircich, "Concepts of Culture and Organizational Analysis," *Administrative Science Quarterly* 28 (1983), 339–358.

40 Based on Edgar H. Schein, *Organizational Culture and Leadership*, 2d ed. (San Francisco: Jossey-Bass, 1992), 3–27.

41 Wendy Zellner, "Mr. Sam's Experiment Is Alive and Well," *Business Week*, April 20, 1992, 39; Sam Walton (with John Huey), *Sam Walton: Made in America* (New York: Doubleday, 1992); John Huey, "America's Most Successful Merchant," *Fortune*, September 23, 1991, 46–59; and Bill Saporito, "And the Winner Is Still . . . Wal-Mart," *Fortune*, May 2, 1994, 62–70.

42 "Friendly Service Has Its Rewards," *Discount Store News*, Vol. 35 (9), May 6, 1996, pp. 64–68; and Jennifer Pellett, "Wal-Mart: Yesterday and Today," *Discount Merchandise*, Vol. 35 (9), September 1995, 66–67.

43 James C. Collins, "Change is Good—But First Know What Should Never Change," *Fortune*, May 29, 1995, 141; Brian Dumaine, "Why Great Companies Last," *Fortune*, January 16, 1995, 129; and Russell Mitchell with Michael Oneal, "Managing by Values," *Business Week*, August 1, 1994, 46–52.

44 "Make No Mistake," *Inc.*, June 1989, 115.

45 Nancy K. Austin, "Wacky Management Ideas That Work," *Working Woman*, November 1991, 42–44.

46 Patrick Flanagan, "The ABCs of Changing Corporate Culture," *Management Review*, July 1995, 57–61.

47 Joan O'C. Hamilton, "Why Rivals Are Quaking as Nordstrom Heads East," *Business Week*, June 15, 1987, 99–100; Charlotte B. Sutton, "Richness Hierarchy of the Cultural Network: The Communication of Corporate Values" (unpublished manuscript, Texas A&M University, 1985); and Gregory M. Bounds, Gregory H. Dobbins, and Oscar S. Fowler, *Management: A Total Quality Perspective* (Cincinnati: South-Western College Publishing, 1995), 353–354.

48 Terrence E. Deal and Allan A. Kennedy, *Corporate Cultures: The Rites and Rituals of Corporate Life* (Reading, Mass.: Addison-Wesley, 1982).

49 Brian Dumaine, "Those Highflying PepsiCo Managers," *Fortune*, April 10, 1989, 78–86; and Barbara Ettorre, "Retooling People and Processes," *Management Review*, June 1995, 19–23.

50 Harrison M. Trice and Janice M. Beyer, "Studying Organizational Cultures through Rites and Ceremonials," *Academy of Management Review* 9 (1984), 653–669.

51 Alan Farnham, "Mary Kay's Lessons in Leadership," *Fortune*, September 20, 1993, 68–77.

52 John P. Kotter and James L. Heskett, *Corporate Culture and Performance* (New York: The Free Press, 1992).

53 Jeffrey Sonnenfeld, *The Hero's Farewell: What Happens When CEOs Retire* (New York: Oxford University Press, 1988).

54 William A. Schiermann, "Organizational Change: Lessons from a Turnaround," *Management Review*, April 1992, 34–37.

55 Ralph H. Kilmann, Mary J. Saxton, Roy Serpa, and Associates,

Gaining Control of the Corporate Culture (San Francisco: Jossey-Bass, 1985).

56 Ralph Kilmann, "Corporate Culture," *Psychology Today*, April 1985, 62–68.

57 Morty Lefkoe, "Why So Many Mergers Fail," *Fortune*, June 20, 1987, 113–114.

58 Ibid.; and Afsaneh Nahavandi and Ali R. Malekzadeh, "Acculturation in Mergers and Acquisitions," *Academy of Management Review* 13 (1988), 79–90.

59 Edward O. Welles, "Mis-Match," *Inc.*, June 1994, 70–79; and Thomas A. Stewart, "Rate Your Readiness to Change," *Fortune*, February 7, 1994, 106–110.

60 Thomas J. Peters and Robert H. Waterman, Jr., *In Search of Excellence* (New York: Warner, 1988).

61 Charles A. Jaffe, "Management by Fun," *Nation's Business*, January 1990, 58–60.

62 Russell Mitchell, "Jack Welch: How Good a Manager?" *Business Week*, December 14, 1987, 92–103.

63 Bob Filipczak, "Are We Having Fun Yet?" *Training*, April 1995, 48–56; and Steve Lohr, "On the Road with Chairman Lou," *The New York Times*, June 26, 1994, Section 3, p. 1.

64 "Southwest Airlines' Herb Kelleher: Unorthodoxy at Work," an interview with William G. Lee, *Management Review*, January 1995, 9–12.

65 Ellyn E. Spragins, "Motivation: Out of the Frying Pan," *Inc.*, December 1991, 157.

66 Tom Peters and Nancy Austin, *A Passion for Excellence: The Leadership Difference* (New York: Random House, 1985), 278.

Managing in a Global Environment

LEARNING OBJECTIVES

After studying this chapter, you should be able to

- Describe the emerging borderless world.

- Define international management and explain how it differs from the management of domestic business operations.

- Indicate how dissimilarities in the economic, sociocultural, and legal-political environments throughout the world can affect business operations.

- Describe market entry strategies that businesses use to develop foreign markets.

- Describe the characteristics of a multinational corporation and the generic strategies available to it.

- Explain the strategic approaches used by multinational corporations.

CHAPTER 4

MANAGEMENT PROBLEM

Federal Express has spruced up its logo and developed a new slogan, "The world on time," to reflect the Federal Express commitment to being a global company. Frederick W. Smith created an "overnight" sensation when he founded Federal Express, which quickly established itself as the giant in America's fledgling express mail service. Smith's first bold attempt to duplicate that success overseas, however, foundered on the rocks of reality. Federal Express's North American system of centralized controls and hub-and-spoke delivery was a disaster overseas, and, by the time the company began its global strategy, competitors like Brussels-based DHL Worldwide Express had already established loyal followings throughout Europe and Asia. Federal Express executives' brash approach didn't fly in Europe's tradition-steeped business culture. The company's attempts at tight control also ran headlong into cultural problems, such as late office hours in Spain and the penchant among Russian workers faced with shortages to take home the soap used for daily truck cleaning. After losing $1.5 billion in five years, Federal Express closed its Brussels hub and shut down operations in more than 100 European cities in 1992. As one competitor glibly noted, "Federal Express is one of the finest examples that the rest of the world is not the United States of America."[1]

• Why do you think Federal Express had such difficulty duplicating its U.S. success overseas? What recommendations would you have for Fred Smith as he continues his quest to "deliver the world on time"?

Federal Express is a well-established company facing enormous challenges developing a successful international business. Companies such as McDonald's, IBM, Coca-Cola, Kellogg, Boeing, General Motors, and Caterpillar Tractor all rely on international business for a substantial portion of sales and profits. These companies face special problems in trying to tailor their products and business management to the unique needs of foreign countries—but if they succeed, the whole world is their marketplace.

How important is international business to the study of management? *If you are not thinking international, you are not thinking business management.* It's that serious. As you read this page, ideas, takeover plans, capital investments, business strategies, Reeboks, services, and T-shirts are traveling around the planet by telephone, computer, fax, and overnight mail. Fred Smith knows that, despite the risks, Federal Express must become a global company, and he has recently taken aggressive steps to tap China's huge market as part of the company's long-term international strategy.[2]

The international dimension is becoming an increasingly important part of the external environment discussed in Chapter 3, and its impact on the business world grows with the rapid advances in technology and communications. Montague Corporation designs unique folding mountain bikes in Cambridge, Massachusetts, makes them in Taiwan, and sells most of them in Europe. Design changes are sent back and forth across three continents, sometimes on a daily basis. Nu Skin International, a Utah-based direct sales company, uses a computer network and special software to help its 300,000 independent distributors sell personal care and health products in any of eight different countries.[3]

If you think you are isolated from global influence, think again. Even if you will not budge from your hometown, your company may be purchased by the English,

Japanese, or Germans tomorrow. People who work for Standard Oil, any of the Federated Department Stores, Pillsbury, Shell Oil, Chesebrough-Pond's, Carnation, Celanese, Firestone, or CBS Records are already working for foreign bosses. In addition, the Japanese alone can be expected to purchase about 200 small and medium-sized American companies each year while also hiring additional American workers in expanding U.S.-owned plants.

Or consider this: You arrive at work tomorrow, and your CEO puts globalization in the company's mission statement and orders promotion of employees who have international experience and foreign-language ability. Or worse yet, a foreign competitor may be launching a competitive assault on your company. A few years ago, U.S. firms made 85 percent of the world's memory chips and were unassailable, or so they thought. Soon Japan had a 75 percent share of the world market, with the U.S. share shrunk to 15 percent. With this kind of competition, is it any surprise that foreign-born people with international experience have been appointed to run such companies as Du Pont, Coca-Cola, Revlon, Gerber, NCR, and Heinz?[4]

This chapter introduces basic concepts about the global environment and international management. First, we consider the difficulty managers have operating in an increasingly borderless world. We will address challenges—economic, legal-political, and sociocultural—facing companies within the global business environment. Then we will discuss multinational corporations and touch upon the various types of strategies and techniques needed for entering and succeeding in foreign markets.

A BORDERLESS WORLD

Why would Federal Express CEO Fred Smith want to pursue a global strategy despite previous failures and losses? Conventional wisdom is that companies involved in global industries must play the global game. If a company doesn't think globally, someone else will. Companies failing to keep up will be swallowed up. As Federal Express competitors rush toward globalization with acquisitions, mergers, and alliances, Federal Express risks significant losses in its domestic market share unless it has the capacity to meet the expanding global express mail needs of clients.

Companies find that thinking globally can provide a competitive edge. Consider Hong Kong's Johnson Electric Holdings Ltd., a $195 million producer of micromotors that power hair dryers, blenders, and automobile power windows and door locks. With factories in South China and a research and development lab in Hong Kong, Johnson is thousands of miles away from a leading automaker. Yet the company has cornered the market for electric gizmos for Detroit's Big Three by using new information technology. Via videoconferencing, Johnson design teams meet "face-to-face" for two hours each morning with their customers in the United States and Europe. The company's processes and procedures are so streamlined that Johnson can take a concept and deliver a prototype to the United States in six weeks.[5] Alex Trotman, chairman of Ford Motor Company, announced the birth of Ford 2000, a sweeping remake that will tear apart the company's regional structure and combine operations into one huge, global company designing and making cars to be sold around the world. Ford already has one prototype of a global vehicle—the midsize car known as the Mondeo in Europe and the Ford Contour and Mercury Mystique in America—and is working on the global Escort.[6]

The reality of today's borderless companies also means consumers can no longer tell from which country they're buying. Your Mercury Tracer may have come from Mexico, while a neighbor's Nissan may have been built in Tennessee. A Gap polo shirt may be made from cloth cut in the United States but sewn in Honduras. Eat an all-American Whopper and you've just purchased from a British company.[7]

Corporations can participate in the international arena on a variety of levels, and the process of globalization typically passes through four distinct stages.

1 In the *domestic stage,* market potential is limited to the home country with all production and marketing facilities located at home. Managers may be aware of the global environment and may want to consider foreign involvement.

2 In the *international stage,* exports increase, and the company usually adopts a *multidomestic* approach, probably using an international division to deal with the marketing of products in several countries individually.

3 In the *multinational stage,* the company has marketing and production facilities located in many countries, with more than one-third of its sales outside the home country. Companies typically have a single home country, although they may opt for a *binational* approach, whereby two parent companies in separate countries maintain ownership and control. Examples are Unilever and the Royal Dutch/Shell Group, both of which are based in the United Kingdom and the Netherlands.

4 Finally, the *global* (or *stateless*) *stage* of corporate international development transcends any single home country. These corporations operate in true global fashion, making sales and acquiring resources in whatever country offers the best opportunities and lowest cost. At this stage, ownership, control, and top management tend to be dispersed among several nationalities.[8]

As the number of "stateless" corporations increases, so too the awareness of national borders decreases, as reflected by the frequency of foreign participation at the management level. Rising managers are expected to know a second or third language and to have international experience. The need for global managers with cross-cultural sensitivity is intense, as discussed in the Focus on Diversity box. Consider the makeup of global companies in today's environment. Nestlé (Switzerland) personifies the stateless corporation with 98 percent of

FOCUS ON DIVERSITY
CROSS-CULTURAL COMMUNICATION

American managers are often at a disadvantage when doing business overseas. Part of the disadvantage comes from a lack of foreign language skills, as well as inexperience in dealing with other cultures and less-than-ideal living conditions. Consequently, many mistakes are made—mistakes that could easily be avoided.

The manager's attitude is perhaps the most important factor in success. Those who go abroad with a sense of "wonder" about the new culture are better off than those with a judgmental view of "If it is different, then my culture must be better." Seeing differences as new and interesting is more productive than being critical. Such evaluations lead to an "us versus them" approach, which never sits well with the locals.

Though every culture has its own way of communicating, here are some basic principles to follow in international business relations:

1. Always listen carefully. Don't be in a hurry to finish the "business." Many other cultures value the social component of these interactions.

2. Try to gain an appreciation for the differences between Hofstede's "masculine" and "feminine" cultures. (See Hofstede's work later in this chapter under "Sociocultural Environment," on pp. 116–117.) American masculine business behaviors include high achievement, acquisition of material goods, and efficiency, while other more feminine cultures value relationships, leisure time with family, and developing a sense of community. Don't mistake this more feminine approach with lack of motivation. Similarly, cultures that value "being and inner spiritual development" rather than compulsively "doing" are not necessarily inferior.

3. Try hard not to feel your way is the best. This can come across as arrogance and rubs salt in deep wounds in some lesser-developed countries.

4. Emphasize points of agreement.

5. When there are disagreements, check on the perceived definitions of words. Often there may be a huge or subtle shade of meaning that is causing the problem. You may actually both be trying to say the same thing.

6. Save face and "give" face as well, for this can be a way of showing honor to others.

7. Don't go alone. Take someone who knows the culture or language better than you. If you are discussing in English and the others "know" the language, you might be surprised how much they miss. Often taking an excellent translator along is a good investment.

8. Don't assume the other country sees leadership the same as you do. In many other cultures, "empowerment" seems more like anarchy and the result of an ineffectual manager.

9. Don't lose your temper.

10. Don't embarrass anyone in front of others. Even if you meant it as a "joke," it likely won't be taken that way.

11. Remember you are talking to a person, not a country, so eliminate stereotypes.

12. Avoid clique-building and try to interact with the locals as much as possible. Often, Americans tend to hang together in packs or tribes, which is not welcoming to the locals.

13. Always show respect.

14. If you travel to out-of-the-way locations, learn to tolerate unpredictability and to go without what you may consider basic amenities. Avoid complaining to business clients about poor phone service, lack of hot water (or any water, for that matter), erratic availability of electricity, or unsavory food. Just remember you are a guest and should act with the grace that goes along with that role.

SOURCE: Lorna Wright, "Building cultural competence," *Canadian Business Review*, Spring 1996, pp. 29–33; Lisa Miller, "Why business travel is such hard work, *The Wall Street Journal*, Oct. 30, 1996, p. B1; Dorothy Marcic, "Challenges and opportunities of teaching management in a post-socialist society," *Executive Development*, Vol. 8, no. 5, 1995, pp. 26–31; Geert Hofstede, "Motivation, leadership and organization: Do American theories apply abroad?" *Organizational Dynamics*, Summer 1980, pp. 42-63; Linda Beamer, "Learning intercultural communication competence," *Journal of Business Communication*, vol. 29 (3), 1992, pp. 285–302; Rosemary Neale and Richard Mindel, "Rigging up muilicultural teamworking," *Personnel Management*, January 1992, pp. 36–39.

sales and 96 percent of employees outside the home country. Nestlé's CEO is German-born Helmut Maucher, and half of the company's general managers are non-Swiss. Maucher puts strong faith in regional managers who are native to the region and know the local culture. The combination of strong brands and autonomous regional managers has made Nestlé the largest branded food company in Mexico, Brazil, Chile, and Thailand, and the company is on its way to becoming the leader in Vietnam and China as well. U.S. firms also show a growing international flavor. The global media giant News Corporation, owner of Fox Broadcasting Company, is run by Rupert Murdoch, who was born in Australia and educated in Britain and is now an American citizen. At a British firm, ICI, 40 percent of the top 170 executives are non-British. Meanwhile, German companies such as Hoechst and BASF rely on local managers to run foreign operations.[9]

Both Ford Motor Company and IBM are working to globalize their management structures. To aid its efforts, IBM has studied power equipment giant Asea Brown Boveri Ltd. (ABB), a major player in the global game. ABB generates more than $25 billion in revenues and employs 240,000 in Europe, North and South America, Asia, and India. CEO Percy Barnevik points out that ABB has no geographical center. With a Swedish CEO, a Zurich headquarters, a multinational board, and financial results posted in American dollars, ABB is "a company with many homes."[10]

THE INTERNATIONAL BUSINESS ENVIRONMENT

International management is the management of business operations conducted in more than one country. The fundamental tasks of business management, including the financing, production, and distribution of products and services, do not change in any substantive way when a firm is transacting business across international borders. The basic management functions of planning, organizing, leading, and controlling are the same whether a company operates domestically or internationally. However, managers will experience greater difficulties and risks when performing these management functions on an international scale. For example:

- Wal-Mart has encountered difficulties in translating the warehouse club concept to Hong Kong. As a young accountant eyed a four-pound jar of peanut butter, he said, "The price is right, but where would I put it?"[11]

- When Coors Beer tried to translate a slogan with the phrase "Turn It Loose" into

Spanish, it came out as "Drink Coors and Get Diarrhea." Budweiser goofed when its Spanish ad promoted Bud Lite as "Filling, less delicious."

- Nike ran a commercial with people from various countries supposedly saying "Just Do It" in foreign languages, but a Samburu tribesman was actually saying, "I don't want these; give me big shoes."

- United Airlines discovered that even colors can doom a product. The airline handed out white carnations when it started flying from Hong Kong, only to discover that to many Asians such flowers represent death and bad luck.[12]

Although these examples may seem humorous, there's nothing funny about them to managers trying to operate in a competitive global environment. The complexities of cross-cultural global management are further demonstrated in the Focus on Diversity box. What should managers of emerging global companies look for to avoid obvious international mistakes? When they are comparing one country with another, the economic, legal-political, and sociocultural sectors present the greatest difficulties. Key factors to understand in the international environment are summarized in Exhibit 4.1.

THE ECONOMIC ENVIRONMENT

The economic environment represents the economic conditions in the country where the international organization operates. This part of the environment includes such factors as economic development; infrastructure; resource and product markets; exchange rates; and inflation, interest rates, and economic growth.

Economic Development. Economic development differs widely among the countries and regions of the world. Countries can be categorized as either "developing" or "developed." The developing countries are referred to as *less-developed*

international management
The management of business operations conducted in more than one country.

Economic
- Economic development
- Resource and product markets
- Per capita income
- Infrastructure
- Exchange rates
- Economic conditions

Legal-Political
- Political risk
- Laws, restrictions
- Government takeovers
- Tariffs, quotas, taxes
- Terrorism, political instability

Organization

Sociocultural
- Social values, beliefs
- Language
- Religion (objects, taboos, holidays)
- Kinship patterns
- Formal education, literacy
- Time orientation

EXHIBIT 4.1
Key Factors in the International Environment

infrastructure
A country's physical facilities that support economic activities.

countries (LDCs). The criterion traditionally used to classify countries as developed or developing is *per capita income,* which is the income generated by the nation's production of goods and services divided by total population. The developing countries have low per capita incomes. LDCs generally are in the southern hemisphere, including Africa, Asia, and South America, whereas developed countries tend to be in the northern hemisphere, including North America, Europe, and Japan.[13]

Most international business firms are headquartered in the wealthier, economically advanced countries. However, based on the number of prospective customers, developing countries constitute an immense market that many companies are beginning to tap. Major U.S. retailers like Wal-Mart and Toys 'R' Us are moving across borders to take advantage of the burgeoning demand for convenience, wider selection, and better prices in such countries as China, Mexico, and Brazil. Although they may face challenges today, these companies

are positioning themselves for the future in emerging economies where most of the population is still at least ten years away from their peak buying years.[14] One company looking to the future of high-tech needs in China is SinoAmerican Telecom.

■ SINOAMERICAN TELECOM

Trying to get a company excited about pagers in the West is like talking about the "hot new technology" of laser printers. But in China it is a different story. There, only one person in twenty has a telephone, and already one-third that number have pagers. When you're talking about a nation of one billion people, the numbers are astounding.

Allan Yuen, pager inventor and founder of SinoAmerican Telecom, managed to get China to use his products in their first national paging system. Though he had been an employee of large companies such as ITT, Yuen struck out on his own in 1991. He built a factory in the Shenzen economic zone, just across from Hong Kong, to make phones and audio equipment. One of his first customers was the People's Liberation Army, the operator of perhaps the largest group of Chinese businesses. One of their companies was a pager networker, which liked Yuen's technology and invited his company to build up the network.

In order to equip the massive Chinese network, Yuen will need $30 million worth of equipment. As part of his growth strategy, Yuen took over a NASDAQ-listed concern last year and will now look to Wall Street for financing.[15] ■

Infrastructure. A country's physical facilities that support economic activities make up its **infrastructure,** which includes transportation facilities such as airports, highways, and railroads; energy-producing facilities such as utilities and power plants; and communication facilities such as telephone lines and radio stations. Companies operating in LDCs must contend with lower levels of technology and perplexing logistical, distribution, and communication problems. Mike Mazzola, an executive for Reuters Ltd., found that, in Mexico, getting a telephone installed could take up to a year. Even after he got one, he often had to dial several times before the call would go through. Undeveloped infrastructures represent opportunities for some firms, like Hartford, Connecticut-based United Technologies Corporation, whose businesses include jet engines, air conditioning and heating systems, and elevators. As countries such as China, Russia, and Vietnam open their markets, new buildings need elevators and air and heat systems; opening remote regions for commerce requires more jet engines and helicopters.[16]

Resource and Product Markets. When operating in another country, company managers must evaluate the market demand for their products. If market demand is high, managers may choose to export products to that country. To develop plants, however, resource markets for providing needed raw materials and labor must also be available. For example, the greatest challenge for McDonald's, which now sells Big Macs on every continent except Antarctica, is to obtain supplies of everything from potatoes to hamburger buns to plastic straws. At McDonald's in Cracow, the burgers come from a Polish plant, partly owned by Chicago-based OSI Industries; the onions come from Fresno, California; the buns come from a production and distribution center near Moscow; and the potatoes come from a plant in Aldrup, Germany. McDonald's tries to contract with local suppliers when possible. In Thailand, McDonald's actually helped farmers cultivate Idaho russet potatoes of sufficient quality to produce their golden french fries.[17]

Exchange Rates. *Exchange rate* is the rate at which one country's currency is exchanged for another country's. Changes in the exchange rate can have major implications for the profitability of international operations that exchange millions of dollars into other currencies every day.[18] For example, assume that the American dollar is exchanged for 8 French francs. If the dollar increases in value to 10 francs, U.S. goods will be more expensive in France because it will take more francs to buy a dollar's worth of U.S. goods. It will be more difficult to export American goods to France, and profits will be slim. If the dollar drops to a value of 6 francs, on the other hand, U.S. goods will be cheaper in France and can be exported at a profit.

THE LEGAL-POLITICAL ENVIRONMENT

Businesses must deal with unfamiliar political systems when they go international, as well as with more government supervision and regulation. Government officials and the general public often view foreign companies as outsiders or even intruders and are suspicious of their impact on economic independence and political sovereignty. Some of the major legal-political concerns affecting international business are political risk, political instability, and laws and regulations.

Political Risk. A company's **political risk** is defined as its risk of loss of assets, earning power, or managerial control due to politically based events or actions by host governments.[19] Political risk includes government takeovers of property and acts of violence directed against a firm's properties or employees. Because such acts are not uncommon, companies must formulate special plans and programs to guard against unexpected losses. For example, Hercules, Inc., a large chemical company, has increased the number of security guards at several of its European plants. Because of a rumored protest, Monsanto Corporation canceled a ceremony to celebrate the opening of a new plant in England. Some companies actually buy political risk insurance, especially as they move into high-risk areas like Eastern Europe, China, and Brazil.[20]

political risk
A company's risk of loss of assets, earning power, or managerial control due to politically motivated events or actions by host governments.

Political Instability.   Another frequently cited problem for international companies is political instability, which includes riots, revolutions, civil disorders, and frequent changes in government. Political instability increases uncertainty. Companies moving into former Soviet republics face continued instability because of changing government personnel and political philosophies. For example, Czech hero and playwright Vaclav Havel, initially selected president by voters in a celebration of freedom, had already been replaced by mid-1992, only to be re-elected after the country split in 1993. The Czech government peacefully coped with nationalist tensions in Slovakia and separated into two countries. The former Yugoslavia, by contrast, has been beset by a war among ethnic groups. Doing business in the former Soviet Union has problems both for current instability and remnants of the past, as Ispat Steel found out when it bought a plant in Kazakhstan.

ISPAT STEEL

Little did Ispat Steel realize when it bought the newly privatized Kazakhstani steel plant Karmet, it would get the KGB in the bargain. It took months of negotiations for the KGB "spooks" to leave their electronically sophisticated offices, and the plant manager is still not sure they're all gone.

Manufacturing tin cans and refrigerators, Karmet has become a metaphor for the problems Western companies have doing business in the former Soviet Union. Here on the edge of Siberia, hundreds of workers report to work drunk and the largest customer (the former Soviet Union) is broke. Chechen gunmen have been threatening suppliers and trying to extort bribes from customers, and they reportedly murdered one of the recent directors.

For Ispat Steel, a company down to 50 percent production with still ten layers of management, Karmet's success is desperately needed in this otherwise shrinking economy. At the same time Karmet loitered near death, however, its directors built lavish guests houses and

spas, spending $1 million on armchairs alone.

Ispat faces a tough road. Cutting back one-third of its bloated 38,000-member workforce will occur partly through a new discipline. About 100 workers a week are being fired for drunkenness and for cheating by having a side job on company time. Ispat took on enormous debt and has paid out millions in back pay and notes to suppliers. To change workers, Ispat has started intensive courses in capitalism, from market forces to profits.

The biggest problem is the dearth of orders. Two-thirds go to China and further increase is thwarted by shipping bottlenecks caused by different-size rail tracks into the area. With the nearest waterway half a continent away, expansion to other countries is expensive. To ward off disaster, Ispat is considering going into consumer goods and is trying to buy coal and steel mines as well as power plants.

Citizens are not happy about this. Though unable to manage these industries themselves, they nonetheless feel their resources were "given away" to foreigners.[21] ■

Although most companies would prefer to do business in stable countries, some of the greatest growth opportunities lie in areas characterized by instability. The greatest threat of violence is in countries experiencing political, ethnic, or religious upheaval. In China, for example, political winds have shifted rapidly, and often dangerously. Yet it is the largest potential market in the world for the goods and services of developed countries; and companies like Xerox, AT&T, Motorola, and Kodak are busy making deals there.

U.S. firms or companies linked to the United States are often subject to major threats in countries characterized by political instability. Peruvian revolutionaries have targeted companies such as Pizza Hut and Kentucky Fried Chicken. Sixteen foreign managers were murdered in Russia in 1993 alone, and others working there often hire bodyguards. In 1991, Detleve Rohwedder, chairman of the German Treuhand, the institution in charge of privatizing the state-owned firms of the former East Germany, was assassinated by the Red Army Faction because of his "representation of capitalism." Even in countries that seem safe, like Spain and Great Britain, terrorists have bombed tourist attractions.[22]

Laws and Regulations. Government laws and regulations differ from country to country and make manufacturing and sales a true challenge for international firms. Host governments have myriad laws concerning libel statutes, consumer protection, information and labeling, employment and safety, and wages. International companies must learn these rules and regulations and abide by them. For example, in the United Kingdom, employees are allowed to take up to 40 weeks of maternity leave, and employers are required to provide a government-mandated amount of pay for at least 18 of those weeks. Government inspectors made a surprise visit to Wal-Mart's Supercenter in Mexico City and charged that more than 10,000 of the store's items were improperly labeled or lacked instructions in Spanish. When Kmart's two Mexico City stores were under construction, inspectors ordered one site shut down for lack of an environmental impact study. Company executives were later able to produce evidence of such a study, but by then the workers had been sent home and construction was delayed for nearly two weeks. Santa Clara, California-based Synergy Semiconductors has found its partnership efforts in what used to be East Germany complicated by German labor laws.[23]

The most visible changes in legal-political factors grow out of international trade agreements and the emerging international trade alliance system. Consider, for example, the impact of the General Agreement on Tariffs and Trade (GATT), the European Union (EU), and the North American Free Trade Agreement (NAFTA).

General Agreement on Tariffs and Trade

The General Agreement on Tariffs and Trade (GATT), signed by 23 nations in 1947, started as a set of rules to ensure nondis-

crimination, clear procedures, the settlement of disputes, and the participation of lesser developed countries in international trade. GATT has evolved into an international organization that serves as the governing body for settling international trade disputes. Today, more than 100 member countries abide by the rules of GATT. The primary tools GATT uses to increase trade are tariff concessions, through which member countries agree to limit the level of tariffs they will impose on imports from other GATT members, and the **most favored nation** clause, which calls for each member country to grant to every other member country the most favorable treatment it accords to any country with respect to imports and exports.[24]

GATT has sponsored various rounds of international trade negotiations aimed at reducing trade restrictions. Most recently, the Uruguay Round (the first to be named for a developing country) involved 125 countries and cut more tariffs than ever before. The Round's multilateral trade agreement, which took effect January 1, 1995, is the most comprehensive pact since the original 1947 agreement. Companies like Caterpillar will benefit from tariff reductions on construction equipment. Japanese companies in the steel, agricultural, processed food, and dairy industries will face increased competition following the elimination of Japan's protective barriers. Most experts believe the potential benefits for each country far outweigh the temporary costs. The goal of GATT negotiations is to encourage closer relationships among member nations and help the global marketplace operate more efficiently.[25]

European Union

Formed in 1958 to improve economic and social conditions among its members, the European Economic Community, now called the European Union (EU), has expanded to a 15-nation alliance illustrated in Exhibit 4.2. Countries in Central and Eastern Europe hope economic and political conditions there will stabilize enough for them to begin joining by the year 2000.[26]

most favored nation
A term describing a GATT clause that calls for member countries to grant other member countries the most favorable treatment they accord any country concerning imports and exports.

EXHIBIT 4.2
The Fifteen Nations within the EU

In the early 1980s, Europeans initiated steps to create a powerful single market system called *Europe '92*. The initiative called for creation of open markets for Europe's 340 million consumers. Europe '92 consisted of 282 directives proposing dramatic reform and deregulation in such areas as banking, insurance, health, safety standards, airlines, telecommunications, auto sales, social policy, and monetary union.

Initially opposed and later embraced by European industry, the increased competition and economies of scale within Europe will enable companies to grow large and efficient, becoming more competitive in U.S. and other world markets. Some observers fear that the EU will become a trade barrier, creating a "fortress Europe" that will be difficult to penetrate by companies in other nations.

Implementation of directives regarding the elimination of border controls and deregulations has proceeded on schedule. The deregulation of banking (1993) and insurance (1994) is expected to be followed by investment services by 1999. New open competition in telecommunications will lead to deregulation of cross-border calling. The airlines now enjoy free pricing and the licensing of new carriers as a result of deregulation.

An average of 90 percent of the directives necessary for completion of the single market are now in place.[27] However, other directives languish amid stiff opposition from member countries. In particular, efforts toward economic and monetary union, calling for the establishment of a European central bank and a single currency, have caused deep divisions within the EU. EU members have also been unable to agree on a common immigration policy, hindering progress toward free movement of people throughout Europe.[28]

These divisions and disagreements within the European Union show the difficulty of building alliances among countries. Despite the uncertainties, hopes are still high that solutions to these complex issues can be found and that the EU will become an even more powerful trading alliance. Meanwhile, Canada, Mexico, and the United States have established what is expected to be an equally powerful alliance.

North American Free Trade Agreement (NAFTA)

The North American Free Trade Agreement, which went into effect on January 1, 1994, merged the United States, Canada, and Mexico into a $6 trillion megamarket with more than 360 million consumers. The

agreement breaks down tariffs and trade restrictions on most agricultural and manufactured products over a 15-year period. The treaty builds upon the 1989 U.S.–Canada agreement and is expected to spur growth and investment, increase exports, and expand jobs in all three nations.[29]

The 14-month negotiations climaxed August 12, 1992, with agreements in a number of key areas.

- *Agriculture.* Immediate removal of tariffs on half of U.S. farm exports to Mexico with phasing out of remaining tariffs over 15 years.
- *Autos.* Immediate 50 percent cut of Mexican tariffs on autos, reaching zero in 10 years. Mandatory 62.5 percent North American content on cars and trucks to qualify for duty-free status.
- *Transport.* U.S. trucking of international cargo allowed in Mexican border area by mid-1990s and throughout Mexico by the end of the decade.
- *Intellectual property.* Mexico's protection for pharmaceutical patents boosted to international standards and North American copyrights safeguarded.

NAFTA has spurred the entry of small businesses into the global arena. Jeff Victor,

J. B. Hunt, a diversified transportation company, is poised to reap the benefits of *NAFTA*, which extends the U.S.–Canadian free trade agreement to Mexico. The largest U.S. carrier in Canada, Hunt expanded service into Mexico, joining Transportacion Maritima Mexicana to provide truckline service throughout Mexico and ocean shipping container services from all Mexican ports. Hunt's expanded railway service agreement with Union Pacific will offer eventual interline service to FNM, the Mexican national railroad. Taking advantage of international opportunities such as NAFTA will enable J. B. Hunt to reach its goal of being the premier North American container carrier.

general manager of Treatment Products, Ltd., which makes car cleaners and waxes, credits NAFTA for his surging export volume. Prior to the pact, Mexican tariffs as high as 20 percent made it impossible for the Chicago-based company to expand its presence south of the border. Similarly, last year StoneHeart, Inc., of Cheney, Washington, began selling its scooters for people with leg or foot injuries to a distributor in Canada.[30] However, many groups in the United States oppose the agreement, warning of job loss to Mexico and the potential for industrial "ghost towns." Some environmentalists fear weakened pollution standards and the potential for toxic dumping. Treaty advocates admit there may be short-term problems but stress the long-term benefits in job creation and heightened standard of living within all three trading partners. Many experts also believe NAFTA will enable companies in all three countries to compete more effectively with rival Asian and European companies.[31]

Trade Alliances: Promise or Pitfall?

The future will probably see full implementation of most NAFTA and EU agreements, Eastern European countries possibly joining the EU, and the development of new trade alliances in Central and South America and Southeast Asia. These developments will provide cheaper Mexican watermelons in the United States, more Israeli shoes in Central Europe, and more Colombian roses in Venezuela. These agreements entail a new future for international companies and pose a range of new questions for international managers.

- Will the creation of multiple trade blocs lead to economic warfare among them?

- Will trade blocs gradually evolve into three powerful trading blocs composed of the American hemisphere, Europe (from Ireland across the former Soviet Union), and the "yen bloc" encompassing the Pacific Rim?

- Will the expansion of global, stateless corporations bypass trading zones and provide economic balance among them?[32]

Only the future will provide answers to these questions. International managers and global corporations will both shape and be shaped by these important trends.

THE SOCIOCULTURAL ENVIRONMENT

A nation's **culture** includes the shared knowledge, beliefs, and values, as well as the common modes of behavior and ways of thinking, among members of a society. Cultural factors are more perplexing than political and economic factors in foreign countries. Culture is intangible, pervasive, and difficult to learn. It is absolutely imperative that international businesses comprehend the significance of local cultures and deal with them effectively.

Social Values.   Research done by Geert Hofstede on 116,000 IBM employees in 40 countries identified four dimensions of national value systems that influence organizational and employee working relationships.[33] Examples of how countries rate on the four dimensions are shown in Exhibit 4.3.

- *Power distance.* High **power distance** means that people accept inequality in power among institutions, organizations, and people. Low power distance means that people expect equality in power. Countries that value high power distance are Malaysia, the Philippines, and Panama. Countries that value low power distance are Denmark, Austria, and Israel.

- *Uncertainty avoidance.* High **uncertainty avoidance** means that members of a society feel uncomfortable with uncertainty and ambiguity and thus support beliefs that promise certainty and conformity. Low uncertainty avoidance

culture
The shared knowledge, beliefs, values, behaviors, and ways of thinking among members of a society.

power distance
The degree to which people accept inequality in power among institutions, organizations, and people.

uncertainty avoidance
A value characterized by people's intolerance for uncertainty and ambiguity and resulting support for beliefs that promise certainty and conformity.

Country	Power Distance[a]	Uncertainty Avoidance[b]	Individualism[c]	Masculinity[d]
Australia	7	7	2	5
Costa Rica	8 (tie)	2 (tie)	10	9
France	3	2 (tie)	4	7
West Germany	8 (tie)	5	5	3
India	2	9	6	6
Japan	5	1	7	1
Mexico	1	4	8	2
Sweden	10	10	3	10
Thailand	4	6	9	8
United States	6	8	1	4

[a] 1=highest power distance, 10=lowest power distance
[b] 1=highest uncertainty avoidance, 10=lowest uncertainty avoidance
[c] 1=highest individualism, 10=lowest individualism
[d] 1=highest masculinity, 10=highest femininity

EXHIBIT 4.3
Rank Orderings of Ten Countries along Four Dimensions of National Value Systems

SOURCE: From Dorothy Marcic, *Organizational Behavior and Cases*, 5th ed. (Southwestern Publishing Co., 1998). Based on Geert Hofstede, *Culture's Consequences* (London: Sage Publications, 1984); and *Cultures and Organizations: Software of the Mind* (New York: McGraw-Hill, 1991).

means that people have high tolerance for the unstructured, the unclear, and the unpredictable. High uncertainty avoidance countries include Greece, Portugal, and Uruguay. Countries with low uncertainty avoidance values are Singapore and Jamaica.

■ *Individualism and collectivism.* **Individualism** reflects a value for a loosely knit social framework in which individuals are expected to take care of themselves. **Collectivism** means a preference for a tightly knit social framework in which individuals look after one another and organizations protect their members' interests. Countries with individualist values include the United States, Canada, Great Britain, and Australia. Countries with collectivist values are Guatemala, Ecuador, and Panama.

■ *Masculinity/femininity.* **Masculinity** stands for preference for achievement, heroism, assertiveness, work centrality (with resultant high stress), and material success. **Femininity** reflects the values of relationships, cooperation, group decision making, and quality of life. Societies with strong masculine values are Japan, Austria, Mexico, and Germany. Countries with feminine values are Sweden, Norway, Denmark, and the former Yugoslavia. Both men and women subscribe to the dominant value in masculine and feminine cultures.

Social values influence organizational functioning and management styles. For example, organizations in France and Latin and Mediterranean countries tend to be hierarchical bureaucracies. Germany and other central European countries have organizations that strive to be impersonal, well-oiled machines. In India, Asia, and Africa, organizations are viewed as large families. Effective management styles differ in each country, depending on cultural characteristics.[34]

Other Cultural Characteristics. Other cultural characteristics that influence international organizations are language, religion, attitudes, social organization, and education. Some countries, such as India, are characterized by *linguistic pluralism*, meaning that several languages exist there. Other countries rely heavily on spoken versus written language. Religion includes sacred objects, philosophical attitudes toward life, taboos, and rituals. Attitudes toward achievement, work, and time can all affect organizational productivity. An attitude called **ethnocentrism** means that people have a tendency to regard their own culture as superior and to downgrade other cultures. Ethnocentrism within a country makes it difficult for foreign firms to operate there. Social organization includes status systems, kinship and families, social institutions, and opportunities for social

individualism
A preference for a loosely knit social framework in which individuals are expected to take care of themselves.

collectivism
A preference for a tightly knit social framework in which individuals look after one another and organizations protect their members' interests.

masculinity
A cultural preference for achievement, heroism, assertiveness, work centrality, and material success.

femininity
A cultural preference for cooperation, group decision making, and quality of life.

ethnocentrism
A cultural attitude marked by the tendency to regard one's own culture as superior to others.

Global companies such as LSI Logic Corporation, a leading manufacturer of high-performance semiconductors, appreciate the diverse elements in the *sociocultural environment.* Here, LSI company executives participate in an ancient Korean ritual for luck, wealth, and fortune. By placing cash in the pig's mouth on the traditional Korean Gosa table, these executives please the spirits and ensure prosperity for the company's expanded Korean design center. Participation in cultural ceremonies offers special insight for managers and plays an integral part in intercultural understanding.

mobility. Education influences the literacy level, the availability of qualified employees, and the predominance of primary or secondary degrees.

Managers in international companies have found that cultural differences cannot be ignored if international operations are to succeed. For example, Coke withdrew its two-liter bottle from the Spanish market after discovering that compartments of Spanish refrigerators were too small for it.[35] Even the powerful Disney organization seriously misjudged per-person food and souvenir spending and accommodation needs at EuroDisney in France, forcing the temporary seasonal closing of its 1,100-room Newport Bay Club in the winter of 1992.[36] On the other hand, organizations that manage cultural differences report major successes. Kellogg introduced breakfast cereals into Brazil, where the traditional breakfast is coffee and a roll. Through carefully chosen advertising, many Brazilians were won over to the American breakfast. Many families now start the day with Kellogg's Sucrilhos (Frosted Flakes) and Crokinhos (Cocoa Krispies).[37]

When firms from different countries work together on a project, managers may find that culture provides more barriers than any other factor to successful collaboration. Consider how cultural differences have affected one of the most ambitious cross-cultural business projects of all time.

■ SIEMENS/TOSHIBA/IBM

It was a great idea: Bring together scientists with diverse backgrounds to develop a revolutionary memory chip. Siemens AG of Germany, Toshiba Corporation of Japan, and the U.S. corporation IBM did just that—Triad, as it was known, was supposed to generate creative leaps, yield new approaches, and lead to dazzling discoveries. But culture got in the way. The Siemens scientists were shocked to find Toshiba colleagues closing their eyes and seeming to sleep during meetings, a common practice of overworked Japanese managers when talk doesn't directly concern them. The Japanese, who normally work in large, informal groups, found it almost painful to have to schedule meetings in small, individual offices. The Germans were appalled by the offices, saying that no one in their country would be asked to work in an office without a window. IBMers complained that the Germans plan too much and that the Japanese, who like to constantly review ideas, won't make a decision. Some of the researchers (who were working at IBM's facility in Fishkill, New York) found their greatest difficulty to be communicating ideas clearly in English. Most of the Japanese began communicating among themselves in their native language, and suspicions began to circulate that some researchers were withholding information. Triad participants admit that results have been disappointing because many cultural differences have to be worked through.

In an effort to build friendships outside the office, project organizers tried a number of ideas for cross-cultural socializing. One effort, a softball game, backfired. Although the Americans and the Japanese know the game well, the Germans do not—one of the Siemens scientists fractured a hip when he hit first base stiff-legged. Maybe there's hope for cross-cultural cooperation: A Japanese coworker took him to the hospital, and an American colleague later loaned him a laptop to use at home while he recuperated. The softball project, however, was canceled.[38] ■

GETTING STARTED INTERNATIONALLY

Small and medium-sized companies have a couple of ways to become involved internationally. One is to seek cheaper sources of supply offshore, which is called *outsourcing.* Another is to develop markets for finished products outside their home country, which may include exporting, licensing, and direct investing. These are called **market entry strategies,** because they represent alternative ways to sell products and services in foreign markets. Most firms begin with exporting and work up to direct investment. Exhibit 4.4 shows the strategies companies can use to enter foreign markets.

Outsourcing

Global outsourcing, sometimes called *global sourcing,* means engaging in the international division of labor so that manufacturing can be done in countries with the cheapest sources of labor and supplies. A company may take away a contract from a domestic supplier and place it with a company in the Far East, 8,000 miles away. With advances in telecommunications, service providers can outsource as well. For example, Citibank taps low-cost skilled labor in India, Hong Kong, Australia, and Singapore to manage data and develop products for its global financial services. M. W. Kellogg, a Houston-based company that builds power and chemical plants around the world, farms out the detailed architectural-engineering work to a partner in Mexico.[39]

A unique variation is the *Maquiladora* industry along the Texas–Mexico border. In the beginning, twin plants were set up, with the U.S. plant manufacturing components with sophisticated machinery and the Mexican plant assembling components using

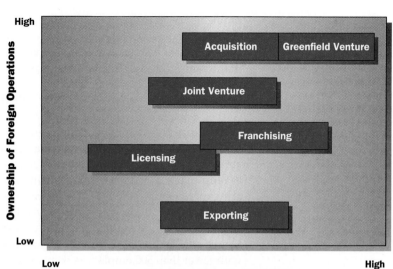

cheap labor. With increasing sophistication in Mexico, new factories with sophisticated equipment are being built farther south of the border, with assembled products imported into the United States at highly competitive prices. The Blue Bird Corporation, a bus manufacturer based in Macon, Georgia, is building a plant in Mexico. The auto industry took advantage of the *Maquiladora* industry throughout the 1980s to combat the Japanese price challenge. By 1992, more than 100,000 Mexicans were employed by U.S. auto companies in towns such as Hermosillo, giving the area the nickname "Detroit South." The low-cost, high-quality Mexican workforce has also attracted manufacturers from other countries, firms such as Nissan, Renault, and Volkswagen.[40] Asian companies in particular are fast establishing *Maquiladoras* in Mexican border towns, with more than 30 Japanese companies already assembling there.

Exporting

With **exporting,** the corporation maintains its production facilities within the home nation and transfers its products for sale in foreign countries.[41] Exporting enables a country to market its products in other countries at modest resource cost and with limited risk. Exporting does entail numerous

EXHIBIT 4.4
Strategies for Entering International Markets

market entry strategy
An organizational strategy for entering a foreign market.

global outsourcing
Engaging in the international division of labor so as to obtain the cheapest sources of labor and supplies regardless of country; also called global sourcing.

exporting
An entry strategy in which the organization maintains its production facilities within its home country and transfers its products for sale in foreign markets.

franchising
A form of licensing in which an organization provides its foreign franchisees with a complete assortment of materials and services.

countertrade
The barter of products for other products rather than their sale for currency.

licensing
An entry strategy in which an organization in one country makes certain resources available to companies in another in order to participate in the production and sale of its products abroad.

direct investing
An entry strategy in which the organization is involved in managing its production facilities in a foreign country.

joint venture
A variation of direct investment in which an organization shares costs and risks with another firm to build a manufacturing facility, develop new products, or set up a sales and distribution network.

problems based on physical distances, government regulations, foreign currencies, and cultural differences, but it is less expensive than committing the firm's own capital to building plants in host countries. For example, a high-tech equipment supplier called Gerber Scientific Inc. prefers not to get involved directly in foreign country operations. Because machinery and machine tools are hot areas of export, executives are happy to ship overseas. Indeed, small businesses are experiencing great success in international markets. A survey by Arthur Andersen & Co. and National Small Business United found that 20 percent of companies with fewer than 500 employees were exporting products and services in 1994, compared to only 11 percent two years earlier.[42]

A form of exporting to less-developed countries is called **countertrade,** which is the barter of products for products rather than the sale of products for currency. Many less-developed countries have products to exchange but have no foreign currency. An estimated 20 percent of world trade is countertrade.

Licensing

With **licensing,** a corporation (the licensor) in one country makes certain resources available to companies in another country (the licensee). These resources include technology, managerial skills, and/or patent and trademark rights. They enable the licensee to produce and market a product similar to what the licensor has been producing. This arrangement gives the licensor an opportunity to participate in the production and sale of products outside its home country at relatively low cost. Hasbro has licensing agreements with companies in several Latin American countries and Japan. Hasbro builds brand identity and consumer awareness by contracting with toy companies to manufacture products locally. Heineken, which has been called the world's first truly global brand of beer, usually begins by exporting to help boost familiarity with its product; if the market looks

enticing enough, Heineken then licenses its brands to a local brewer.

Franchising is a form of licensing in which the franchisor provides foreign franchisees with a complete package of material and services, including equipment, products, product ingredients, trademark and trade name rights, managerial advice, and a standardized operating system. Some of the best-known international franchisors are the fast-food chains. Kentucky Fried Chicken, Burger King, Wendy's, and McDonald's outlets are found in almost every large city in the world. The story is often told of the Japanese child visiting Los Angeles who excitedly pointed out to his parents, "They have McDonald's in America."

Licensing and franchising offer a business firm relatively easy access to international markets at low cost, but they limit its participation in and control over the development of those markets.

Direct Investing

A higher level of involvement in international trade is direct investment in manufacturing facilities in a foreign country. **Direct investing** means that the company is involved in managing the productive assets, which distinguishes it from other entry strategies that permit less managerial control.

Currently, the most popular type of direct investment is to engage in strategic alliances and partnerships. In a **joint venture,** a company shares costs and risks with another firm, typically in the host country, to develop new products, build a manufacturing facility, or set up a sales and distribution network.[43] A partnership is often the fastest, cheapest, and least risky way to get into the global game. Entrepreneurial companies such as Molex, a manufacturer of connectors, and Nypro, a maker of industrial components, have used partnerships to gain overseas access to several countries. In its quest to become the dominant brand in an expanded European market, Heineken Breweries is teaming up with smaller rivals in Hungary, Poland, and Switzerland. In Asia, Heineken has entered into a joint venture with Singapore's Asia Pacific Breweries, makers of Tiger Beer. Coca-Cola has taken Romania by storm after it entered into a joint venture with that country's largest bottler of soft drinks, Ci-Co S.A. Auburn Farms, a Sacramento, California, manufacturer of all-natural snack foods, recently entered into a joint venture with South Africa's Beacon Sweets & Chocolates.[44] An important consideration for both companies in this venture was that they share similar ethics and policies. Business ethics is becoming an increasingly important yet highly complicated consideration for managers as corporations move into developing countries.

The other choice is to have a **wholly owned foreign affiliate,** over which the company has complete control. Direct *acquisition* of an affiliate may provide cost savings over exporting by shortening distribution channels and reducing storage and transportation costs. Local managers

also have heightened awareness of economic, cultural, and political conditions. For example, General Electric purchased Hungarian bulbmaker Tungsram in 1990. By 1994 the company was turning a profit, and quality was so good that GE shifted all European lightbulb production there.[45] Another company that bought a factory in Hungary was Danube Knitwear, as described in the Leading the Management Revolution box.

The most costly and risky direct investment is called a **greenfield venture,** which means a company builds a subsidiary from scratch in a foreign country. The advantage is that the subsidiary is exactly what the company wants and has the potential to be highly profitable. The disadvantage is that the company has to acquire all market knowledge, materials, people, and know-how in a different culture, and mistakes are possible. An example of a greenfield venture is the Mercedes-Benz plant being constructed in Vance, Alabama. This is the first

greenfield venture
The most risky type of direct investment, whereby a company builds a subsidiary from scratch in a foreign country.

wholly owned foreign affiliate
A foreign subsidiary over which an organization has complete control.

LEADING THE MANAGEMENT REVOLUTION
DANUBE KNITWEAR

After the Berlin Wall fell in 1989 and the former Soviet empire collapsed, much of the former trade was discontinued. In many eastern-bloc countries, whole industries were at great risk and some even disappeared. Hungary was hit hard in its textile manufacturing, where production of fabric and yarn dropped by 60 percent and layoffs reduced the workforce by one-third.

One person's grief is another's opportunity. Or so believed Michael Smolens, who started a new company and invested heavily in the country, eventually providing almost 1,000 jobs and providing new technologies for mill operations. Initially, he bought a run-down factory in Baja and thus was born Danube Knitwear. Recently, they opened a new factory in Romania.

"We wanted to put something together in a part of the world where there was no competition," says Smolens. "Somewhere with unlimited upside potential." Market size or financing have not been problems, but resolving cultural differences has.

He has a difficult time finding nationals with experience and willingness to conform to company standards, and training younger managers takes two to five years. In the mill, the problems have centered around motivation. The low pay level had seemed good at first, but then managers found out about the high rates of absenteeism, and turnover has been around 120 percent. Trying to find out how to motivate workers and fill their needs is not as easy as in the West, for these people were used to keeping their mouths shut (or else) under communism.

Even with all these problems, Danube Knitwear was profitable before its third year of operation, with revenues about $45 million, from such T-shirt clients as The Gap, Hanes, Levi's, and Nike.

"We plan to be the dominant knitwear manufacturer in this region," says Smolens.

SOURCE: Kristin Dunlap Godsey, "Thread by thread," *Success,* April 1996, 8.

time the company has built a plant outside Germany. The venture is considered high risk because the new plant will build a new product (sport utility vehicle) with a new workforce, to be sold in a foreign country.[46]

THE MULTINATIONAL CORPORATION

The size and volume of international business are so large that they are hard to comprehend. The revenue of General Motors is comparable to the gross domestic product (GDP) of Finland, that of General Electric is comparable in size to Israel's GDP, Toyota revenues to Hong Kong's GDP, and those of the Royal Dutch/Shell Group to the GDP of Norway.[47]

As discussed earlier in this chapter, a large volume of international business is being carried out in a seemingly borderless world by very large international businesses that can be thought of as *global corporations, stateless corporations,* or *transnational corporations.* In the business world, these large international firms typically are called *multinational corporations (MNCs),* which have been the subject of enormous attention and concern. MNCs can move a wealth of assets from country to country and influence national economies, politics, and cultures.

Characteristics of Multinational Corporations

multinational corporation (MNC)
An organization that receives more than 25 percent of its total sales revenues from operations outside the parent company's home country; also called *global corporation* or *transnational corporation.*

Although there is no precise definition, a **multinational corporation (MNC)** typically receives more than 25 percent of its total sales revenues from operations outside the parent's home country. MNCs also have the following distinctive managerial characteristics:

1 An MNC is managed as an integrated worldwide business system. This means that foreign affiliates act in close alliance and cooperation with one another. Capital, technology, and people are trans-

ferred among country affiliates. The MNC can acquire materials and manufacture parts wherever in the world it is most advantageous to do so.

2 An MNC is ultimately controlled by a single management authority that makes key strategic decisions relating to the parent and all affiliates. Although some headquarters are binational, such as the Royal Dutch/Shell Group, some centralization of management is required to maintain worldwide integration and profit maximization for the enterprise as a whole.

3 MNC top managers are presumed to exercise a global perspective. They regard the entire world as one market for strategic decisions, resource acquisition, location of production, advertising, and marketing efficiency.

In a few cases, the MNC management philosophy may differ from that just described. For example, some researchers have distinguished among *ethnocentric companies,* which place emphasis on their home countries, *polycentric companies,* which are oriented toward the markets of individual foreign host countries, and *geocentric companies,* which are truly world oriented and favor no specific country.[48] In general, a multinational corporation can be thought of as a business enterprise that is composed of affiliates located in different countries and whose top managers make decisions primarily on the basis of global business opportunities and goals.

MANAGING IN A GLOBAL ENVIRONMENT

Managing in a foreign country is particularly challenging. Before undertaking a foreign assignment, managers must understand that they will face great personal challenges. Managers working in foreign countries must be sensitive to cultural subtleties and understand that the ways to provide proper leadership, decision making, motivation, and control vary in different cultures. When companies operate internationally, the need for personal learning and growth is critical.

Personal Challenges for Global Managers

Managers will be most successful in foreign assignments if they are culturally flexible and easily adapt to new situations and ways of doing things. A tendency to be ethnocentric—to believe that your own country's cultural values and ways of doing things are superior—is a natural human condition. Managers can learn to break down those prejudices and appreciate another culture. As one Swedish executive of a large multinational corporation put it, "We Swedes are so content with . . . the Swedish way, that we forget that 99 percent of the rest of the world isn't Swedish."[49] Managers working in foreign countries may never come to understand the local culture like a native; the key is to be sensitive to cultural differences and understand that other ways of thinking and doing are also valid.

Most managers in foreign assignments face a period of homesickness, loneliness, and culture shock from being suddenly immersed in a culture with completely different languages, foods, values, beliefs, and ways of doing things. *Culture shock* refers to the frustration and anxiety that result from constantly being subjected to strange and unfamiliar cues about what to do and how to do it. Even simple, daily events can become sources of stress.[50]

Preparing managers to work in foreign cultures is essential. Some companies try to give future managers exposure to foreign cultures early in their careers. American Express Company's Travel-Related Services unit gives American business-school students summer jobs in which they work outside the United States for up to 10 weeks. Colgate-Palmolive selects 15 recent graduates each year and then provides up to 24 months of training prior to multiple overseas job stints.[51]

Managing Cross-Culturally

To be effective on an international level, managers can first understand their own cultural values and assumptions, as discussed in Chapter 3; then they can interpret the culture of the country and organization in which they are working and develop the sensitivity required to avoid making costly cultural blunders.[52] The following examples illustrate how cultural differences can be significant for foreign managers.

Leading.   In relationship-oriented societies such as those in Asia, the Arab world, and Latin America, leaders should use a warm, personalized approach with employees. In Latin America and China, managers are expected to have periodic social visits with workers, inquiring about morale and health. Leaders should be especially careful about criticizing others. To Asians, Africans, Arabs, and Latin Americans, the loss of self-respect brings dishonor to themselves and their families. One researcher tells of a Dutch doctor managing a company clinic who had what he considered a "frank discussion" with a Chinese subordinate. The subordinate, who perceived the doctor as a father figure, took the criticism as a "savage indictment" and committed suicide.[53] Though this is an extreme example, the principle of "losing face" is highly important in some cultures.

Decision Making.   In America, mid-level managers may discuss a problem and give the boss a recommendation. German managers, on the other hand, expect the boss to issue specific instructions. East Indian and Latin American employees typically do not understand participatory decision making. Deeply ingrained social customs suggest that a supervisor's efforts toward participation signify ignorance and weakness. In contrast, managers in Arab and African nations are expected to use consultative decision making in the extreme. In negotiating with Japanese counterparts, American managers must recognize the importance of consulting all relevant parties to a decision.[54]

Motivating. Motivation must fit the incentives within the culture. In Japan, employees are motivated to satisfy the company. A financial bonus for star performance would be humiliating to employees from Japan, China, or the former Yugoslavia. An American executive in Japan offered a holiday trip to the top salesperson, but employees were not interested. After he realized that Japanese are motivated in groups, he changed the reward to a trip for everyone if together they achieved the sales target. They did. Managers in Latin America, Africa, and the Middle East must show respect for employees as individuals with needs and interests outside of work.[55]

Controlling. When things go wrong, managers in foreign countries often are unable to get rid of employees who do not work out. In Europe, Mexico, and Indonesia, to hire and fire on performance seems unnaturally brutal. Workers are protected by strong labor laws and union rules.

In foreign cultures, managers also should not control the wrong things. A Sears manager in Hong Kong insisted that employees come to work on time instead of 15 minutes late. The employees did exactly as they were told, but they also left on time instead of working into the evening as they had previously. A lot of work was left unfinished. The manager eventually told the employees to go back to their old ways. His attempt at control had a negative effect.

Some cross-cultural differences are epitomized in the following poem.

An Asian View of Cultural Differences

We live in time. You live in space.
We are always at rest. You are always on the move.

We are passive. You are aggressive.
We like to contemplate. You like to act.

We accept the world as it is. You try to change the world according to your blueprint.

We live in peace with nature. You try to impose your will in her.

Religion is our first love. Technology is your passion.
We delight to think about the meaning of life. You delight in physics.

We believe in freedom of silence. You believe in freedom of speech.
We lapse into meditation. You strive for articulation.

We marry first, then love. You love first, then marry.
Our marriage is the beginning of a love affair. Your marriage is the happy end of a romance.
It is an indissoluble bond. It is a contract.

Our love is mute. Your love is vocal.
We try to conceal it from the world. You delight in showing it to others.

Self-denial is the secret to our survival. Self-assertiveness is the key to your success.

We are taught from the cradle to want less and less. You are urged every day to want more and more.

We glorify austerity and renunciation. You emphasize gracious living and enjoyment.

In the sunset years of life we renounce the world and prepare for the hereafter. You retire to enjoy the fruits of your labor.

SOURCE: Dr. Mai Van Trang, Indochinese Resources Center.

Global Learning

Managing across borders calls for organizations to learn across borders. One reason Japanese companies have been so successful internationally is that their culture encourages learning and adaptability. In Asia generally, teaching and learning are highly regarded, and the role of managers is seen as one of teaching or facilitating—of helping those around them to learn.[56] It is partly this emphasis on continuous learning that has helped Matsushita Electric master markets and diverse cultures in 38 countries, from Malaysia to Brazil, from Austria to China, from Iran to Tanzania. One of Matsushita's top lessons for going global is to be a good corporate citizen in every country, respecting cultures, customs, and languages. In countries with Muslim religious practices, for example, Matsushita provides special prayer rooms and allows two prayer sessions per shift.[57]

Corporations can use the concept of continuous learning to become global-thinking, culturally sensitive organizations.

SUMMARY AND MANAGEMENT SOLUTION

This chapter has stressed the growing importance of an international perspective on management. Successful companies are preparing to expand their business overseas and to withstand domestic competition from foreign competitors. Business in the global arena involves special risks and difficulties because of complicated economic, legal-political, and sociocultural forces. Moreover, the global environment changes rapidly, as illustrated by the emergence of the European Union, the North American Free Trade Agreement, and the shift in Eastern Europe to democratic forms of government.

International markets provide many opportunities but are fraught with difficulty, as Federal Express, described at the beginning of this chapter, discovered. Major alternatives for serving foreign markets are exporting, licensing, franchising, and direct investing through joint ventures or wholly owned subsidiaries. Federal Express attempted to shortcut local regulations from freight weight to landing rights in European and Asian countries through a series of acquisitions. The purchase of Flying Tigers opened unrestricted cargo routes to several European and Japanese cities. But international competitors

such as TNT and DHL had already established loyal followings and negotiated new deals with Lufthansa and Japan Airlines. UPS purchased Seaborne European Express Parcels and laid plans for a European trucking business. When Federal Express's system of controls and management methods did not work in foreign cultures, the intense competition took its toll, causing Federal Express to fall back and regroup.[58]

Much of the growth in international business has been carried out by large businesses called MNCs. These large companies exist in an almost borderless world, encouraging the free flow of ideas, products, manufacturing, and marketing among countries to achieve the greatest efficiencies. Managers in MNCs as well as those in much smaller companies doing business internationally face many challenges. Managers often experience culture shock when transferred to foreign countries. They must learn to be sensitive to cultural differences and tailor their management style to the culture. For managers and organizations in an increasingly borderless world, learning across borders is critical.

DISCUSSION QUESTIONS

1 Why do you think international businesses traditionally prefer to operate in industrialized countries? Discuss.

2 What considerations in recent years have led international businesses to expand their activities into less-developed countries?

3 What policies or actions would you recommend to an entrepreneurial business wanting to do business in Europe?

4 What steps could a company take to avoid making

product design and marketing mistakes when introducing new products into a foreign country?

5 Compare the advantages associated with the foreign-market entry strategies of exporting, licensing, and wholly owned subsidiaries.

6 Should a multinational corporation operate as an integrated, worldwide business system, or would it be more effective to let each subsidiary operate autonomously?

7 What does it mean to say that the world is becoming "borderless"? That large companies are "stateless"?

8 What might managers do to avoid making mistakes concerning control and decision making when operating in a foreign culture?

9 What is meant by the cultural values of individu-alism and masculinity/femininity? How might these values affect organization design and management processes?

MANAGEMENT EXERCISES

MANAGER'S WORKBOOK

State of the World Test

How aware are you of the rest of the planet? If you will be working internationally, the more you know about the world, the more successful you are likely to be.

1 Six countries contain one-half the total population of the world. What are the six countries?

1.   4.
2.   5.
3.   6.

2 Another 19 countries account for 25 percent of the world's people. What are those countries?

1.   10.
2.   11.
3.   12.
4.   13.
5.   14.
6.   15.
7.   16.
8.   17.
9.   18.
          19.

3 The 10 most commonly spoken first languages are:

1.   6.
2.   7.
3.   8.
4.   9.
5.   10.

4 How many languages are there in the world that have at least one million speakers?

a. 73
b. 123
c. 223

5 How many nations were there in 1992?

a. 288
b. 188
c. 88

6 Which nation is home to the largest number of commercial banks?

7 Which nation is home to the most transnational corporations?

8 Between 1970 and 1986, global agricultural (plant and livestock) production:

a. declined substantially
b. declined slightly
c. remained about the same
d. increased slightly
e. increased substantially

9 Between 1970 and 1985, the number of people in the world suffering from malnutrition:

a. declined
b. remained about the same
c. increased

10 Let one dot represent all the firepower used in World War II: This would be the equivalent of 200 Hiroshima-sized A-bombs. How many dots would you need to represent the firepower held in the U.S. and the former USSR (before it dissolved) combined?

a. 60
b. 600
c. 6,000
d. 60,000

11 Between 1960 and 1987, the world spent approximately $10 trillion on health care. How much did the world spend on military?

a. $7 trillion
b. $10 trillion
c. $17 trillion
d. $25 trillion

12 According to the United Nations, what percentage of the world's work (paid and unpaid) is done by women?

a. 33%

b. 50%

c. 67%

d. 75%

13 According to the United Nations, what percentage of the world's income is earned by women?

a. 10%

b. 30%

c. 50%

d. 70%

14 The nations of Africa, Asia, Latin America, and the Middle East, often referred to as the Third World, contain about 78 percent of the world's population. What percentage of the world's monetary income do they possess?

a. 10%

b. 20%

c. 30%

d. 40%

15 Americans constitute approximately 5 percent of the world's population. What percentage of the world's resources do Americans consume?

a. 15%

b. 25%

c. 35%

d. 45%

Answers

1 China (1.1b)

India (882 m)

United States (256 m)

Indonesia (185 m)

Brazil (151 m)

Russia (149 m)

2
1. Japan (124)
2. Pakistan (122)
3. Bangladesh (111)
4. Nigeria (90)
5. Mexico (88)
6. Germany (88)
7. Vietnam (69)
8. Phillippines (64)
9. Iran (60)
10. Turkey (59)
11. Italy (58)
12. United Kingdom (58)
13. France (57)
14. Thailand (56)
15. Egypt (56)
16. Ethiopia (54)
17. Ukraine (52)
18. South Korea (44)
19. Myanmar (Burma) (43)

3
1. Mandarin (885)
2. English (450)
3. Hindi (367)
4. Spanish (353)
5. Russian (294)
6. Arabic (202)
7. Bengali (187)
8. Portuguese (174)
9. Malay-Portuguese (145)
10. Japanese (126)

4 *c.* 223

5 *b.* 188

6 Japan

7 United States

8 *e.* increased substantially (by about 35 percent, though since then changes have been more erratic due to a number of political, economic, and climatic factors).

9 *c.* increased (from 5 to 15 percent, and has continued to increase since 1985).

10 *c.* 6,000

11 *c.* $17 trillion

12 *c.* 67%

13 *a.* 10%

14 *b.* 20%

15 *c.* 35%

SOURCE: Jan Drum, Steve Hughes, and George Otere. "State-of-the-World Test," from *Global Winners*, reprinted with permission of Intercultural Press, Inc. Yarmouth, ME, 1994.

MANAGER'S WORKSHOP

Chinese, Indian, and American Values

1 Complete the rankings on the next page prior to class. Rank the 15 values for Chinese, Indian, and American.

2 Break into small groups of four to six members and discuss, trying to achieve consensus on the ranking of values for both Chinese and American cultures, as well as Indian if time permits.

3 Group presentations (optional). Each group presents its rankings and discusses rationales for making those decisions.

4 Discussion of whole class on the differences between Chinese and American value systems, while the instructor gives out the correct rankings.

Background

In the 1950s and 1960s a number of value orientation studies were conducted using university students in various countries. The data presented here come from some studies that used the Edwards Personal Preference Schedule. Groups tested included 1,504 American, 2,876 Chinese, and 288 Indian students.

Value Ranking

Rank each of the 15 values below according to what you think it is in the Chinese, Indian (from India), and American cultures. Use "1" to be the most important value for the culture and "15" to be the least important value for that culture.

Value	American	Chinese	Indian
Achievement			
Deference			
Order			
Exhibition			
Autonomy			
Affiliation			
Intraception			
Succorance			
Dominance			
Abasement			
Nurturance			
Change			
Endurance			
Heterosexuality			
Aggression			

Some definitions:

Succorance: willingness to come to the aid of another or to offer relief.

Abasement: to lower oneself in rank, prestige, or esteem.

Intraception: the other side of extraception, where one is governed by concrete, clearly observable physical conditions. Intraception, on the other hand, is the tendency to be governed by more subjective factors, such as feelings, fantasies, speculations, and aspirations.

Internal/External Locus of Control

Considering American and Chinese groups, which would be more internal locus of control (tend to feel in control of one's destiny, that rewards come as a result of hard work, perseverence, responsibility) and which would be more external control (fate, luck, or other outside forces control destiny)?

Machiavellianism

This concept was defined by Christie and Geis as the belief one can manipulate and deceive people for personal gain. Do you think Americans or Chinese would score higher on the Mach scale?

Questions

1 What are some main differences between the cultures? Did any patterns emerge?
2 Were you surprised by the results?
3 What behaviors could you expect in business dealings with Chinese (or Indians) based on their value system?
4 How do American values dictate Americans' behaviors in business situations?

SOURCE: Exercise copyright 1996 by Dorothy Marcic. Value Rankings table: Table 4.1 from The Psychology of the Chinese People, edited by Michael Harris Bond (Oxford University Press, 1986), p. 110. Reprinted by permission.

MANAGER'S WORKSHOP

Global Economy Scavenger Hunt

In order to get a perspective on the pervasiveness of the global economy, you will be asked to find a number of things and bring them back to class.

1. Divide into teams of four to six members.
2. Each team is to bring the following items to a future class from the list below.
3. On the day in class, each team will give a short, two-minute presentation on the items that were the most difficult to find or the most interesting.
4. How many countries did your team get items from? How many for the entire class?

List for scavenger hunt:

1. Brochures or annual reports of four multinational corporations.
2. Evidence from three local businesses to show they do business internationally.
3. Locate a retail store that sells only "Made in America."
4. Ten toys or games that originated in other countries.
5. Five toys or games that had components from one country and were assembled in another—or somehow developed in more than one country.
6. Food items from 15 different countries.
7. Articles of clothing from 15 different countries.
8. List books sold in your town from authors from 12 different countries. Where were the books published? Who translated them?
9. List of 12 films in the past five years that starred someone from another country.
10. List of five films in the past five years that had multinational crews and locations. Include at least one that was co-produced by two or more countries.
11. Descriptions of interviews from five foreigners (not from your team or the class) asking them six things they like about the United States and six things they don't like.
12. A list of eight places where a language other than English is displayed (on a bulletin board, poster, etc.).
13. Two maps of the world drawn before 1900.
14. Five items in your town that were manufactured in another country and that were not made in that country six years ago.

SOURCE:　Copyright 1996 by Dorothy Marcic; adapted from Jan Drum, Steve Hughes, and George Otere, "Global Scavenger Hunt," in *Global Winners*, Yarmouth, Maine: Intercultural Press, 1994, pp. 21–23.

SURF THE 'NET

Choose a country in the developing world. Then use the Internet to find out as much as you can about that country's economy. What does it produce and where does it export? Does it import raw materials? Which countries are major trade partners? What problems does it experience in the global marketplace?

ETHICAL DILEMMA

Quality or Closing?

On the way home from the launch party celebrating Plaxcor Metals' entrance into the international arena, Donald Fields should have been smiling. He was part of the team that had closed the deal to sell component parts to Asian Business Machine, after his company had spent millions trying to break into this lucrative market. There were several more deals riding on the successful outcome of the first international venture.

The expansion into new markets was critical to Plaxcor's survival. As President Leslie Hanson had put it, "If we aren't global within five years, we may as well close up shop." Fields was tense because of news he learned tonight: intense bidding for the first sale and several last-minute changes requested by the customer had forced Plaxcor to heavily modify its production process. The production manager had confided that "the product is a mess but still better than most of the competition." He went on to assure him that, although well below normal standards, the variability would "probably not cause any problems" and could be worked out after a few more orders.

Fields had spent the last few months selling Plaxcor on its quality reputation. He knew they could probably get by with the first runs and meet the opening deadline. He was afraid that telling the customer of the potential problems or extending the deadline would risk not only this deal but pending projects as well. But he knew if problems arose with the products, Plaxcor's future in the Asian market would be bleak. Donald Fields wasn't sure Plaxcor could afford to gamble its entrance in the international market on a sub-standard product.

What Do You Do?

1 Ask the customer for an extension of the deadline and bring the products up to standard.
2 Gamble on the first runs and hope the products don't fail.
3 Inform the customer of the problem and let it make the call.

CASE FOR CRITICAL ANALYSIS

Coca-Cola

For Coca-Cola, globalization is the real thing. At corporate headquarters in Atlanta, "foreign" and "domestic" aren't even part of the vocabulary. As of 1994, Coca-Cola owned and operated businesses of all sizes in 195 countries. According to Cuban-born CEO Roberto C. Goizueta, "we are increasingly global because 95 percent of the world's consumers are outside [the United States]. It's that simple." Part of the reason Coke has been so successful globally is strategy. Consider Coke's latest adventure in Romania, where the company has gone from having no presence in 1991 to being the biggest soft-drink maker. Coke has rolled past archrival Pepsi not only in Romania but throughout most of Eastern Europe and the rest of the former communist world, where Pepsi once had a strong lead.

The Romanian adventure began in 1990 when Ion Stamanichi, the head of Romania's largest bottler of soft drinks, Ci-Co S.A., invited Coke to enter into a joint venture, one that Coke could control, unlike previous arrangements with state bottlers. In three years, Romanians went from drinking no Coke to an average of 47 8-ounce servings a year, the fastest rate of growth for a country in the company's history.

Coke's advances offer lessons to other companies trying to make inroads in the tantalizing markets of the former Soviet bloc. Starting with the fall of the Berlin Wall in October 1989, Coke severed most of its relations with state bottlers and invested quickly and heavily to import its own manufacturing, distribution, and marketing techniques. Coke has invested $1.5 billion in Eastern Europe, $150 million in Romania alone. By contrast, Pepsi remained tied for some time to the creaky operations of state bottlers and has never come close to Coke's investment levels. Coke's investment has had a multiplier effect. Since it sells soft drinks primarily through small retailers and kiosk owners, the company has helped to create a class of micro-entrepreneurs. One study estimates that for every job Coke has created directly, 11 jobs were created indirectly.

According to a grocery store owner in the Black Sea

city of Constanta, "Pepsi carried the image of the Communist regime, and you never knew whether you would get a bottle with carbonation or not." An operator of a state-owned pastry shop added that kiosk owners selling Pepsi had to line up at state bottlers to get supplies. When Coke came, they were amazed to have company trucks making deliveries once or twice a week.

Coke's international workforce makes the company a truly global organization. Two-thirds of the company's 31,000 employees work outside the United States. To oversee its Romanian operations, Coke chose Nick Constantinescu, a Romanian native who had fled the country in 1972. Ion Stamanichi became general manager of Coke's Bucharest operations. Coke then brought in two of its outside bottlers, one based in Turkey and one in London, to divide the rest of the country.

The soft-drink war in Eastern Europe is probably just beginning, but Coke has made sure Pepsi will have to run twice as hard to catch up.

Questions

1 In what stage of globalization would you classify Coca-Cola? Why?
2 What elements of Coke's strategy have helped it overtake Pepsi throughout Eastern Europe?
3 Discuss the interaction between Coca-Cola and the economic and political environment in Eastern Europe.

SOURCES: Based on Nathaniel C. Nash, "Coke's Great Romanian Adventure," *The New York Times,* February 26, 1995, F1; and "Company Close Up: Coca-Cola," in Luis R. Gómez-Mejía, David B. Balkin, and Robert L. Cardy, *Managing Human Resources* (Englewood Cliffs, N. J.: Prentice-Hall, 1995), 616.

ENDNOTES

1 Chuck Hawkins, "FEDEX: Europe Nearly Killed the Messenger," *Business Week,* May 25, 1992, 124–126; Daniel Pearl, "Innocence Abroad: Federal Express Finds Its Pioneering Formula Falls Flat Overseas," *The Wall Street Journal,* April 15, 1991, A1, A8; Eric Calonius, "Federal Express's Battle Overseas," *Fortune,* December 3, 1990, 137–140; Alan Salomon, "International Emphasis Is Behind New Look for FedEx," *Advertising Age,* June 27, 1994; and Vance Trimble, *Overnight Success* (New York: Crown Publishers, 1993).

2 Michael Mecham, "FedEx to Take Over Evergreen's China Rights," *Aviation Week & Space Technology,* March 6, 1995, 26.

3 Alan Farnham, "Global—or Just Globaloney?" *Fortune,* June 27, 1994, 97–100.

4 Yao-Su Yu, "Global or Stateless Corporations Are National Firms with International Operations," *California Management Review* 34 (winter), 107–126; Jonathan P. Hicks, "Foreign Owners Are Shaking Up the Competition," *The New York Times,* May 28, 1989, sec. 3, 9; and Ira C. Magaziner and Mark Patinkin, *The Silent War* (New York: Random House, 1989).

5 Pete Engardio, with Robert D. Hof, Elisabeth Malkin, Neil Gross, and Karen Lowry Miller, "High-Tech Jobs All over the Map," *Business Week/21st Century Capitalism,* November 18, 1994, 112–117.

6 James B. Treece, with Kathleen Kerwin and Heidi Dawley, "Ford: Alex Trotman's Daring Global Strategy," *Business Week,* April 3, 1995, 94–104.

7 Richard L. Daft, *Management,* 3d ed. (Fort Worth, Texas: The Dryden Press, 1994), 80; James L. Gibson, John M. Ivancevich, and James H. Donnelly, Jr., *Organizations,* 8th ed. (Burr Ridge, Ill.: Irwin, 1994), 54–55.

8 Nancy J. Adler, *International Dimensions of Organizational Behavior* (Boston: PWS-Kent, 1991), 7–8; William Holstein, Stanley Reed, Jonathan Kapstein, Todd Vogel, and Joseph Weber, "The Stateless Corporation," *Business Week,* May 14, 1990, 98–105; and Richard Daft, *Organization Theory and Design* (St. Paul, Minn.: West, 1992).

9 Holstein et al., "The Stateless Corporation"; Carla Rapoport, "Nestlé's Brand Building Machine," *Fortune,* September 19, 1994, 147–156; and Mark Landler, with Joyce Barnathan, Geri Smith, and Gail Edmondson, "Think Globally, Program Locally," *Business Week/21st Century Capitalism,* November 18, 1994, 186–189.

10 William Taylor, "The Logic of Global Business: An Interview with ABB's Percy Barnevik," *Harvard Business Review* (March–April 1991), 91–105; Holstein et al., "The Stateless Corporation"; and John A. Byrne and Kathleen Kerwin, with Amy Cortese and Paula Dwyer, "Borderless Management," *Business Week,* May 23, 1994, 24–26.

11 Carla Rapoport, with Justin Martin, "Retailers Go Global," *Fortune,* February 20, 1995, 102–108.

12 "Slogans Often Lose Something in Translation," *The New Mexican*, July 3, 1994, F1, F2.

13 Karen Paul and Robert Barbarto, "The Multinational Corporation in the Less Developed Country: The Economic Development Model versus the North-South Model," *Academy of Management Review* 10 (1985), 8–14.

14 Rapoport, "Retailers Go Global."

15 "A World of Cool Companies," *Fortune*, October 28, 1996, 163–168.

16 Jennifer Farley, "Negotiating the Border," *American Way*, July 1, 1994, 48–51; and Amal Kumar Jaj, "United Technologies Looks Far from Home for Growth," *The Wall Street Journal*, May 26, 1994, B4.

17 Kathleen Deveny, "McWorld?" *Business Week*, October 13, 1986, 78–86; and Andrew E. Serwer, "McDonald's Conquers the World," *Fortune*, October 17, 1994, 103–116.

18 Bruce Kogut, "Designing Global Strategies: Profiting from Operational Flexibility," *Sloan Management Review* 27 (fall 1985), 27–38.

19 Mark Fitzpatrick, "The Definition and Assessment of Political Risk in International Business: A Review of the Literature," *Academy of Management Review* 8 (1983), 249–254.

20 "Multinational Firms Act to Protect Overseas Workers from Terrorism," *The Wall Street Journal*, April 29, 1986, 31; and Robert J. Bowman, "Are You Covered?" *World Trade*, March 1995, 100–104.

21 Kyle Pope, "A Steelmaker Built up by Buying Cheap Mills Finally Meets Its Match," *The Wall Street Journal*, May 2, 1996, pp. A1; A10.

22 Patricia Sellers, "Where Killers and Kidnappers Roam," *Fortune*, September 23, 1991, 8; Michael R. Czinkota, Ilkka A. Ronkainen, Michael H. Moffett, and Eugene O. Moynihan, *Global Business* (Fort Worth, Texas: The Dryden Press, 1995); and Paul Hofheinz, "Rising in Russia," *Fortune*, January 24, 1994, 92–97.

23 Shari Caudron, "Lessons from HR Overseas," *Personnel Journal*, February 1995, 88–93; Geri Smith, "NAFTA: A Green Light for Red Tape," *Business Week*, July 25, 1994, 48; and Ed Fishbein, "Kultur Klash," World Trade, March 1995, 53–56.

24 Czinkota et al., *Global Business*, 151; and Robert D. Gatewood, Robert R. Taylor, and O. C. Ferrell, Management (Burr Ridge, Ill.: Irwin, 1995), 131–132.

25 "For Richer, for Poorer," *The Economist*, December 1993, 66; Richard Harmsen, "The Uruguay Round: A Boon for the World Economy," *Finance & Development*, March 1995, 24–26; and Czinkota et al., *Global Business*.

26 Mark M. Nelson, "Extra Accommodations," *The Wall Street Journal*, September 30, 1994, R13, R14.

27 "EU Policy," *Business Europe*, March 13, 1995, 5–6.

28 "A Funny New EMU," *The Economist*, March 4, 1995, 49–50; Caspar W. Weinberger, "Commentary on Events at Home and Abroad," *Forbes*, March 13, 1995, 35; and Czinkota et al., *Global Business*, 118.

29 Barbara Rudolph, "Megamarket," *Time*, August 10, 1992, 43–44.

30 Amy Barrett, "It's a Small (Business) World," *Business Week*, April 17, 1995, 96–101.

31 Amy Borrus, "A Free-Trade Milestone, with Many More Miles to Go," *Business Week*, August 24, 1992, 30–31.

32 Keith Bradsher, "As Global Talks Stall, Regional Trade Pacts Multiply," *The New York Times*, August 23, 1992, F5.

33 Geert Hofstede, "The Interaction between National and Organizational Value Systems," *Journal of Management Studies* 22 (1985), 347–357; and Geert Hofstede, "The Cultural Relativity of the Quality of Life Concept," *Academy of Management Review* 9 (1984), 389–398.

34 Ellen F. Jackofsky, John W. Slocum, Jr., and Sara J. McQuaid, "Cultural Values and the CEO: Alluring Companions?" *Academy of Management Executive* 2 (1988), 39–49.

35 Orla Sheehan, "Managing a Multinational Corporation: Tomorrow's Decision Makers Speak Out," *Fortune*, August 24, 1992, 233.

36 Stewart Toy, Patrick Oster, and Ronald Grover, "The Mouse Isn't Roaring," *Business Week*, August 24, 1992, 38.

37 Kenneth Labich, "America's International Winners," *Fortune*, April 14, 1986, 34–46.

38 E. S. Browning, "Computer Chip Project Brings Rivals Together, but the Cultures Clash," *The Wall Street Journal*, May 3, 1994, A1.

39 Engardio et al., "High-Tech Jobs All over the Map."

40 Gary Jacobson, "The Boom on Mexico's Border," *Management Review* (July 1988), 21–25; Stephen Baker, David Woodruff, and Elizabeth Weiner, "Detroit South," *Business Week*, March 16, 1992, 98–103; "Magic Bus," *World Trade*, March 1995, 106; and James H. Donnelly, Jr., James L. Gibson, and John M. Ivancevich, *Fundamentals of Management*, 9th ed. (Burr Ridge, Ill.: Irwin, 1995), 86.

41 Jean Kerr, "Export Strategies," *Small Business Reports* (May 1989), 20–25.

42 William J. Holstein and Brian Bremmer, "The Little Guys Are Making It Big Overseas," *Business Week*, February 27, 1989, 94–96; Iris Lorenz-Fife, "Resource Guide: Small-Business Help from the Government," *Entrepreneur*, December 1989, 168–174; and Barrett, "It's a Small (Business) World."

43 Kathryn Rudie Harrigan, "Managing Joint Ventures," *Management Review* (February 1987), 24–41; and Therese R. Revesz and Mimi Cauley de Da La Sierra, "Competitive Alliances: Forging Ties Abroad," *Management Review* (March 1987), 57–59.

44 Julia Flynn with Richard A. Melcher, "Heineken's Battle to Stay Top Bottle," *Business Week*, August 1, 1994, 60–62; Nathaniel C. Nash, "Coke's Great Romanian Adventure," *The New York Times*, February 26, 1995, F1; and "Importing Can Help a Firm Expand and Diversify," *Nation's Business*, January 1995, 11.

45 Karen Lowry Miller, with Bill Javetski, Peggy Simpson, and Tim Smart, "Europe: The Push East," *Business Week*, November 7, 1994, 48–49.

46 David Woodruff, with Karen Lowry Miller, "Mercedes' Maverick in Alabama," *Business Week*, September 11, 1995, 64–65; and Michael A. Hitt, R. Duane Ireland, and Robert E. Hoskisson, *Strategic Management: Competitiveness and Globalization* (St. Paul, Minn.: West, 1995).

47 "How Revenues of the Top Ten Global Companies Compare with Some National Economies," *Fortune*, July 27, 1992, 16.

48 Howard V. Perlmutter, "The Tortuous Evolution of the Multinational Corporation," *Columbia Journal of World Business* (January–February 1969), 9–18; and Youram Wind, Susan P. Douglas, and Howard V. Perlmutter, "Guidelines for Developing International Marketing Strategies," *Journal of Marketing* (April 1973), 14–23.

49 Robert T. Moran and John R. Riesenberger, *The Global Challenge* (London: McGraw-Hill, 1994), 260.

50 Gibson et al., *Organizations*, 83.

51 Joann S. Lublin, "Younger Managers Learn Global Skills," *The Wall Street Journal*, March 31, 1992, B1.

52 Moran and Riesenberger, *The Global Challenge*, 251–262.

53 Fons Trompenaars, *Riding the Waves of Culture: Understanding Diversity in Global Business* (Burr Ridge, Ill.: Irwin, 1994).

54 Stephen E. Weiss, "Negotiating with 'Romans'—Part 2," *Sloan Management Review* (spring 1994), 85–99.

55 Caudron, "Lessons from HR Overseas."

56 Moran and Riesenberger, *The Global Challenge,* 255; and Caudron, "Lessons from HR Overseas."

57 Brenton R. Schlender, "Matsushita Shows How to Go Global," *Fortune,* July 11, 1994, 159–166.

58 Hawkins, "FEDEX: Europe Nearly Killed the Messenger."

Management Ethics and Corporate Social Responsibility

LEARNING OBJECTIVES

After studying this chapter, you should be able to

■ Define ethics and explain how ethical behavior relates to behavior governed by law and free choice.

■ Explain the utilitarian, individualism, moral-rights, and justice approaches for evaluating ethical behavior.

■ Describe how both individual and organizational factors shape ethical decision making.

■ Define corporate social responsibility and how to evaluate it along economic, legal, ethical, and discretionary criteria.

■ Describe four corporate responses to social demands.

■ Explain the concept of stakeholder and identify important stakeholders for organizations.

■ Describe structures managers can use to improve their organizations' ethics and social responsiveness.

CHAPTER 5

MANAGEMENT PROBLEM

Tatra Inc. makes the world's heaviest and most durable trucks. They are able to start and run without any supplemental equipment in temperatures as low as −58 degrees Fahrenheit, making them the only viable vehicles for such locations as the oil fields of Siberia. After the collapse of the Soviet Union, the Czech company suffered heavy losses and had a bleak future.

Three successful American auto executives, under a company called GSR and led by Gerald Greenwald, entered into a contract in March 1993 with Tatra for $130,000 per month. Each was to work five days, for a total of fifteen days each month (in a country where average wages were $150 per month). Greenwald, who had been instrumental in the Chrysler turnaround, promised to make Tatra profitable within two years.

Soon Greenwald was appointed to run UAL Corp. in the United States, but insisted he could fulfill his obligations at Tatra. After eighteen months, though, the Tatra board grew weary. Losses for 1993 had been $24 million, up from $6.2 million in 1992. GSR executives were asked to resign. As one board member said, "We have determined that their style of management, basically management by fax, has not served Tatra well." Another member said though their intentions may have been good, they were just not around enough to have a positive impact, especially in an unfamiliar culture and a region going through such dramatic changes. A business analyst in Vienna noted that Americans often came into such ventures with "delusions of grandeur."

The Americans were surprised by the Board's reaction, voicing their intention to continue until contract-end in March 1995. They said the problems were a result of a worsening world economy, especially for trucks. Eventually, GSR and Tatra worked out a settlement and the Americans were gone. They had earned over $2 million in the 18 months, plus more in the settlement.

• Did GSR contribute to the problems of Tatra's losses? Was the original agreement ethical and realistic? If you had been one of the GSR executives, what would you have done when the board asked you to resign?[1]

Other companies have had problems internationally, as well. Consider Shell Oil in Nigeria, where one region has become ravaged and a 20-year-old oil spill remains polluted, though Shell claims it has invested heavily in community projects there.[2]

Shell's advertisements in Western countries promote the company as environmentally conscious; yet the situation in Nigeria has damaged Shell's reputation and pressured executives to reexamine policies and practices internationally. This situation symbolizes the rising importance of the need to discuss ethics and social responsibility. The growing importance of international business is only one reason ethics and social responsibility issues are in the forefront of corporate concerns. Corporations are rushing to adopt codes of ethics and develop socially responsible policies. Ethics consultants are doing a land-office business. Unfortunately, the trend is necessary. In a 1994 Gallup Poll asking about the perceived trustworthiness of six American institutions, only the U.S. government scored lower marks than U.S. corporations.[3]

The state of California charged that 72 Sears, Roebuck and Co. tire and auto centers defrauded customers with unnecessary repairs. The findings followed a two-year undercover investigation and resulted in a public apology by Sears chairman Edward Brennan and abandonment of commission sales for auto service departments. In an even farther-reaching scandal, the federal government charged the Bank of Credit and Commerce International (BCCI) with a number of criminal counts, including the laundering of drug money and influence peddling. Exxon faced public anger, enormous fines, and a massive cleanup effort following the Valdez oil spill. These instances of fraud, criminal activity, and pollution illustrate the negative side of ethics issues.[4]

There is also positive news to report. In the wake of the 1992 Los Angeles riots, McDonald's fed burned-out citizens, firefighters, police, and National Guard troops and delivered free lunches to 300 students at a nearby school. H. J. Heinz has funded infant nutrition studies in China and Thailand through its Institute of Nutritional Sciences. Nynex Corporation, embarrassed by scandal when a group of managers was discovered to have attended supplier-sponsored parties that included paid sexual services, is working overtime to prevent future ethical problems. Nynex has trained 95,000 employees in ethical behavior over the past 4 years, created a 60-page "Code of Business Conduct," started a monthly ethics newsletter, and set up a toll-free ethics hotline.[5]

This chapter expands on the ideas about environment, corporate culture, and the international environment discussed in Chapters 3 and 4. We will first focus on specific ethical values that build on the idea of corporate culture. Then we will examine corporate relationships to the external environment as reflected in social responsibility. Ethics and social responsibility are hot topics in corporate America, but this interest should be viewed as more than a fad. More and more companies are beginning to recognize the vast benefits of contributing to the community. This chapter discusses fundamental approaches that help managers think through ethical issues. Understanding ethical approaches helps managers build a solid foundation on which to base future decision making.

WHAT IS MANAGERIAL ETHICS?

Ethics is difficult to define in a precise way. In a general sense, **ethics** is the code of moral principles and values that govern the behaviors of a person or group with respect to what is right or wrong. Ethics sets standards as to what is good or bad in conduct and decision making.[6] Ethics deals with internal values that are a part of corporate culture and shapes decisions concerning social responsibility with respect to the external environment. An ethical issue is present in a situation when the actions of a person or organization may harm or benefit others.[7]

Ethics can be more clearly understood when compared with behaviors governed by laws and by free choice. Exhibit 5.1 illustrates that human behavior falls into three categories. The first is codified law, in which values and standards are written into the legal system and enforceable in the courts. In this area, lawmakers have ruled that people and corporations must behave in a certain way, such as obtaining licenses for cars or paying corporate taxes. The domain of free choice is at the opposite end of the scale and pertains to behavior about which law has no say and for which an individual or organization enjoys complete freedom. An individual's choice of religion or a corporation's choice of the number of dishwashers to manufacture are examples of free choice.

Between these domains lies the area of ethics. This domain has no specific laws, yet it does have standards of conduct based on shared principles and values about moral conduct that guide an individual or company. In the domain of free choice, obedience is strictly to oneself. In the domain of codified law, obedience is to laws prescribed by the legal system. In the domain of ethical behavior, obedience is to unenforceable norms and standards about which the individual or company is aware. An ethically acceptable decision is both legally and morally acceptable to the larger community.

Many companies and individuals get into trouble with the simplified view that choices are governed by either law or free choice. It leads people to mistakenly assume that "If it's not illegal, it must be ethical," as if there were no third domain.[8] A better option is to recognize the domain of ethics and accept moral values as a powerful force for good that can regulate behaviors both inside and outside corporations. As principles of ethics and social responsibility are more widely recognized, companies can use codes of ethics and their corporate cultures to govern behavior, thereby eliminating the need for additional laws and avoiding the problems of unfettered choice.

Because ethical standards are not codified, disagreements and dilemmas about proper behavior often occur. An **ethical dilemma** arises in a situation when each alternative choice or behavior is undesirable because of potentially harmful ethical consequences. Right or wrong cannot be clearly identified.

The individual who must make an ethical choice in an organization is the *moral agent*.[9] Consider the dilemmas facing a moral agent in the following situations:

A top employee at your small company tells you he needs some time off because he has AIDS. You know the employee needs the job as well as the

ethics
The code of moral principles and values that govern the behaviors of a person or group with respect to what is right or wrong.

ethical dilemma
A situation that arises when all alternative choices or behaviors have been deemed undesirable because of potentially negative ethical consequences, making it difficult to distinguish right from wrong.

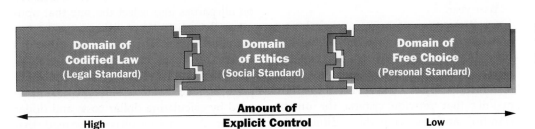

Domain of Codified Law (Legal Standard)	Domain of Ethics (Social Standard)	Domain of Free Choice (Personal Standard)

Amount of Explicit Control

High ←→ Low

EXHIBIT 5.1
Three Domains of Human Action

health insurance benefits. Providing health insurance has already stretched the company's budget, and this will send premiums through the roof. You recently read of a case in which federal courts upheld the right of an employer to modify health plans by putting a cap on AIDS benefits. Should you investigate whether this is a legal possibility for your company?

As a sales manager for a major pharmaceuticals company, you've been asked to promote a new drug that costs $2,500 per dose. You've read the reports saying the drug is only 1 percent more effective than an alternate drug that costs less than one-fourth as much. Can you in good conscience aggressively promote the $2,500-per-dose drug? If you don't, could lives be lost that might have been saved with that 1 percent increase in effectiveness?

Your company has been asked to pay a gratuity in India to speed the processing of an import permit. This is standard procedure, and your company will suffer if you do not pay the gratuity. Is this different from tipping a maitre d' in a nice restaurant?

You are the accounting manager of a division that is $15,000 below profit targets. Approximately $20,000 of office supplies were delivered on December 21. The accounting rule is to pay expenses when incurred. The division general manager asks you not to record the invoice until February.

Your boss says he cannot give you a raise this year because of budget constraints, but he will look the other way if your expense accounts come in a little high because of your good work this past year.

These are the kinds of dilemmas and issues with which managers must deal that fall squarely in the domain of ethics. Now let's turn to approaches to ethical decision making that provide criteria for understanding and resolving these difficult issues.

utilitarian approach
The ethical concept that moral behaviors produce the greatest good for the greatest number.

CRITERIA FOR ETHICAL DECISION MAKING

Most ethical dilemmas involve a conflict between the needs of the part and the whole—the individual versus the organization or the organization versus society as a whole. For example, should a company install mandatory alcohol and drug testing for employees, which may benefit the organization as a whole but reduce the individual freedom of employees? Or should products that fail to meet tough FDA standards be exported to other countries where government standards are lower, benefiting the company but being potentially harmful to world citizens? Sometimes ethical decisions entail a conflict between two groups. For example, should the potential for local health problems resulting from a company's effluents take precedence over the jobs it creates as the town's leading employer?

Managers faced with these kinds of tough ethical choices often benefit from a normative approach—one based on norms and values—to guide their decision making. Normative ethics uses several approaches to describe values for guiding ethical decision making. Four of these that are relevant to managers are the utilitarian approach, individualism approach, moral-rights approach, and justice approach.[10]

Utilitarian Approach

The **utilitarian approach,** espoused by the nineteenth-century philosophers Jeremy Bentham and John Stuart Mill, holds that moral behavior produces the greatest good for the greatest number. Under this approach, a decision maker is expected to consider the effect of each decision alternative on all parties and select the one that optimizes the satisfaction for the greatest number of people. Because actual computations can be very complex, simplifying them is considered appropriate. For example, a simple economic frame of reference could be used by calculating dollar costs and dollar benefits. Also, a decision could be made that considers only the people who are directly affected by the decision, not those who are indirectly affected. When GM chose to continue operations at its Arlington, Texas, plant while shutting down its Ypsilanti, Michigan, plant, managers justified the decision as producing the greater good for the corporation as a whole. The utilitarian ethic is cited as the basis for the recent trend among companies to police employee personal habits such as alcohol and tobacco consumption on the job, and in some cases after hours as well, because such behavior affects the entire workplace.[11]

The utilitarian ethic was the basis for the state of Oregon's decision to extend Medicaid to 400,000 previously ineligible recipients by refusing to pay for high-cost, high-risk procedures such as liver transplants and bone-marrow transplants. Although a few people needing these procedures have died because the state would not pay, many people have benefited from medical services they would otherwise have had to go without.[12] Critics of the utilitarian ethic fear a developing tendency toward a "Big Brother" approach and question whether the common good is squeezing the life out of the individual. Critics also claim that the Oregon decision does not fully take into account the concept of justice toward the unfortunate victims of life-threatening diseases.[13]

Individualism Approach

The **individualism approach** contends that acts are moral when they promote the individual's best long-term interests. Individual self-direction is paramount, and external forces that restrict self-direction should be severely limited.[14] Individuals calculate the best long-term advantage to themselves as a measure of a decision's goodness. The action that is intended to produce a greater ratio of good to bad for the individual compared with other alternatives is the right one to perform. With everyone pursuing self-direction, the greater good is ultimately served because people learn to accommodate each other in their own long-term interest. Individualism is believed to

lead to honesty and integrity because that works best in the long run. Lying and cheating for immediate self-interest just causes business associates to lie and cheat in return. Thus, individualism ultimately leads to behavior toward others that fits standards of behavior people want toward themselves.[15] One value of understanding this approach is to recognize short-term variations if they are proposed. People might argue for short-term self-interest based on individualism, but that misses the point. Because individualism is easily misinterpreted to support immediate self-gain, it is not popular in the highly organized and group-oriented society of today. Individualism is closest to the domain of free choice described in Exhibit 5.1.

Moral-Rights Approach

The **moral-rights** approach asserts that human beings have fundamental rights and liberties that cannot be taken away by an individual's decision. Thus an ethically correct decision is one that best maintains the rights of those people affected by it.

Moral rights that could be considered during decision making are

1 The right of free consent—individuals are to be treated only as they knowingly and freely consent to be treated.
2 The right to privacy—individuals can choose to do as they please away from work and have control of information about their private life.
3 The right of freedom of conscience—individuals may refrain from carrying out any order that violates their moral or religious norms.
4 The right of free speech—individuals may criticize truthfully the ethics or legality of actions of others.
5 The right to due process—individuals have a right to an impartial hearing and fair treatment.
6 The right to life and safety—individuals have a right to live without endangerment or violation of their health and safety.

moral-rights approach
The ethical concept that moral decisions are those that best maintain the rights of those people affected by them.

individualism approach
The ethical concept that acts are moral when they promote the individual's best long-term interests, which ultimately leads to the greater good.

To make ethical decisions, managers need to avoid interfering with the fundamental rights of others. Thus a decision to eavesdrop on employees violates the right to privacy. Sexual harassment is unethical because it violates the right to freedom of conscience. The right of free speech would support whistle-blowers who call attention to illegal or inappropriate action within a company.

Justice Approach

justice approach
The ethical concept that moral decisions must be based on standards of equity, fairness, and impartiality.

The **justice approach** holds that moral decisions must be based on standards of equity, fairness, and impartiality. Three types of justice are of concern to managers. **Distributive justice** requires that different treatment of people not be based on arbitrary characteristics. Individuals who are similar in respects relevant to a decision should be treated similarly. Thus men and women should not receive different salaries if they are performing the same job. However, people who differ in a substantive way, such as job skills or job responsibility, can be treated differently in proportion to the differences in skills or responsibility among them. This difference should have a clear relationship to organizational goals and tasks.

distributive justice
The concept that different treatment of people should not be based on arbitrary characteristics. In the case of substantive differences, people should be treated differently in proportion to the differences among them.

Procedural justice requires that rules be administered fairly. Rules should be clearly stated and be consistently and impartially enforced. **Compensatory justice** argues that individuals should be compensated for the cost of their injuries by the party responsible. Moreover, individuals should not be held responsible for matters over which they have no control.

procedural justice
The concept that rules should be clearly stated and consistently and impartially enforced.

The justice approach is closest to the thinking underlying the domain of law in Exhibit 5.1, because it assumes that justice is applied through rules and regulations. This theory does not require complex calculations such as those demanded by a utilitarian approach, nor does it justify self-interest as the individualism approach does. Managers are expected to define attributes on which different treatment of employees is acceptable. Questions such as how minority workers should be compensated for past

compensatory justice
The concept that individuals should be compensated for the cost of their injuries by the party responsible and also that individuals should not be held responsible for matters over which they have no control.

discrimination are extremely difficult. However, this approach does justify as ethical behavior efforts to correct past wrongs, playing fair under the rules, and insisting on job-relevant differences as the basis for different levels of pay or promotion opportunities. Most of the laws guiding human resource management (Chapter 11) are based on the justice approach.

The challenge of applying these ethical approaches is illustrated by decisions facing companies considering moving operations to cheaper locations.

■ YAKIMA PRODUCTS

Dumping 45 minimum-wage jobs into an already underemployed region did not fit with the values on which Yakima Products had been based. But when Don Banducci and Steve Cole sold their business to John Bowes, that is just what happened.

Outdoor enthusiasts Banducci and Cole built the business from nothing in 1979 to the world's foremost provider of cartop carrying systems for various sporting gear, such as bikes and skis. The two co-founders had purposely chosen the economically sluggish region of Arcasta in northern California. Priding themselves in giving back more than they took from this tight-knit community, they were willing to pay the extra $300,000 per year it cost to be far from suppliers and dealers.

But after Bowes took over, Ford, Isuzu, and Subaru selected Yakima as the official supplier for all their roof racks. Moving manufacturing to Mexico and shipping to San Diego were seen as survival techniques by current CEO Bruce Hamilton. Arcasta still maintains all the high skill, higher-paying jobs of $30,000–50,000.

Compare that with a Midwestern company where 500 jobs were leaving for Mexico. The president flew to Mexico to see the "competition" and negotiated for more time with the CEO. Union representatives were eager to keep the plant running, so they identified some "best practice" operations around the country. This helped the local employees to accept and work on major restructuring and reorganizing of the production process. For now, their jobs are safe.

A third way to cope with lost jobs was exhibited by Milwaukee-area Briggs & Stratton Corp., announcing that 2,000 jobs would be moved to nonunion plants in the South. *The National Catholic Reporter* questioned whether such actions were moral. The response? Briggs & Stratton sued the Catholic newspaper for $30 million.

Which of the three methods do you think is most effective? Most ethical?[16] ■

Consider for a moment how you think the ethics approaches support and refute these companies' actions.

FACTORS AFFECTING ETHICAL CHOICES

When managers are accused of selfishly putting financial concerns over people, or of lying, cheating, or stealing, the blame is usually placed on the individual or on the company situation. Most people believe that individuals make ethical choices because of individual integrity, which is true,

but it is not the whole story. Ethical or unethical business practices usually reflect the values, attitudes, beliefs, and behavior patterns of the organizational culture; thus, ethics is as much an organizational as a personal issue.[17] Let's examine how both the manager and the organization shape ethical decision making.[18]

The Manager

Managers bring specific personality and behavioral traits to the job. Personal needs, family influence, and religious background all shape a manager's value system. Specific personality characteristics, such as ego strength, self-confidence, and a strong sense of independence may enable managers to make ethical decisions.

One important personal trait is the stage of moral development.[19] A simplified version of one model of personal moral development is shown in Exhibit 5.2. At the *preconventional* level, individuals are concerned with external rewards and punishments and obey authority to avoid detrimental personal consequences. In an organizational context, this level may be

E X H I B I T   5 . 2
Three Levels of Personal Moral Development

Level 3: Postconventional

Follows self-chosen principles of justice and right. Aware that people hold different values and seeks creative solutions to ethical dilemmas. Balances concern for individual with concern for common good.

Level 2: Conventional

Lives up to expectations of others. Fulfills duties and obligations of social system. Upholds laws.

Level 1: Preconventional

Follows rules to avoid punishment. Acts in own interest. Obedience for its own sake.

Leadership Style:	Autocratic/coercive	Guiding/encouraging, team oriented	Transforming, or servant leadership
Employee Behavior:	Task accomplishment	Work group collaboration	Empowered employees, full participation

SOURCES: Based on L. Kohlberg, "Moral Stages and Moralization: The Cognitive-Development Approach," In *Moral Development and Behavior: Theory, Research, and Social Issues,* ed. T. Lickona (New York: Holt, Rinehart, and Winston, 1976); and Jill W. Graham, "Leadership, Moral Development and Citizenship Behavior," *Business Ethics Quarterly* 5, no. 1 (January 1995), 43–54.

associated with managers who use an autocratic or coercive leadership style, with employees oriented toward dependable accomplishment of specific tasks. At level two, called the *conventional* level, people learn to conform to the expectations of good behavior as defined by colleagues, family, friends, and society. Meeting social and interpersonal obligations is important. Work group collaboration is the preferred manner for accomplishment of organizational goals, and managers use a leadership style that encourages interpersonal relationships and cooperation. At the *postconventional,* or *principled* level, individuals are guided by an internal set of values and standards and will even disobey rules or laws that violate these principles. Internal values become more important than the expectations of significant others. At this highest level of development, managers use transformative or servant leadership, focusing on the needs of followers and encouraging others to think for themselves and to engage in higher levels of moral reasoning. Employees are empowered and given opportunities for constructive participation in governance of the organization.

The great majority of managers operate at level two. A few have not advanced beyond level one. Only about 20 percent of American adults reach the level-three stage of moral development. People at level three are able to act in an independent, ethical manner regardless of expectations from others inside or outside the organization. Managers at level three of moral development will make ethical decisions whatever the organizational consequences for them. The Focus On Ethics box lists some general guidelines to follow for making ethical decisions.

One interesting study indicates that most researchers have failed to account for the different ways in which women view social reality and develop psychologically and have thus consistently classified women as being stuck at lower levels of development. Researcher Carol Gilligan has suggested that the moral domain be enlarged to include responsibility and care in relationships. Women may, in general, perceive moral complexities more astutely than men and make moral decisions based not on a set of absolute rights and wrongs but on principles of not causing harm to others.[20] Women's sense of integrity seems to be entwined with an ethic of care; hence, they may be ideally suited for the servant leadership needed in today's organizations.

One reason higher levels of ethical conduct are increasingly important is the impact of globalization on organizational ethics and corporate culture. American managers need to develop sensitivity and openness to other systems. Cross-cultural alliances and mergers create the need to work out differences involving ethical values. For example, bribery is an accepted way of conducting business in many developing countries. "Grease" payments to customs officials are considered part of their living wage. Failure to play the game could result in loss of outlets, suppliers, and foreign revenues. On the other hand, foreign bribery is illegal under the U.S. Foreign Corrupt Practices Act. Fortunately, the value system for doing business in foreign countries is slowly changing and grinding away at the practice of bribery. Although the tolerance of bribery by overseas countries is waning, it is still widespread, and managers must use mature ethical judgment in resolving these difficult international issues.[21]

The Organization

The values adopted within the organization are important, especially when we understand that most people are at the level-two stage of moral development, which means they believe their duty is to fulfill obligations and expectations of others. As discussed in Chapter 3, corporate culture can exert a powerful influence on behavior in organizations. For example, an investigation of thefts and kickbacks in the oil business found that the cause was the historical acceptance of thefts and kickbacks. Employees were socialized into those values and adopted them as appropriate. In most companies, employees believe that if they do

FOCUS ON ETHICS
GUIDELINES FOR ETHICAL DECISION MAKING

If Mike Wallace and a "60 Minutes" crew were waiting on your doorstep one morning, would you feel comfortable justifying your actions to the camera? One young manager, when confronted with ethical dilemmas, gives them the "60 Minutes" test. Others say they use such criteria as whether they would be proud to tell their parents or grandparents about their decision or whether they could sleep well at night and face themselves in the mirror in the morning. Managers often rely on their own personal integrity in making ethical decisions. But knowing what to do is not always easy. As a future manager, you will almost surely face ethical dilemmas one day. The following guidelines will not tell you exactly what to do, but, taken in the context of the text

discussion, they will help you evaluate the situation more clearly by examining your own values and those of your organization. The answers to these questions will force you to think hard about the social and ethical consequences of your behavior.

1. Is the problem/dilemma really what it appears to be? If you are not sure, *find out.*
2. Is the action you are considering legal? Ethical? If you are not sure, *find out.*
3. Do you understand the position of those who oppose the action you are considering? Is it reasonable?
4. Whom does the action benefit? Harm? How much? How long?
5. Would you be willing to allow everyone to do what you are considering doing?
6. Have you sought the opinion of oth-

ers who are knowledgeable on the subject and who would be objective?
7. Would your action be embarrassing to you if it were made known to your family, friends, coworkers, or superiors?

There are no correct answers to these questions in an absolute sense. Yet, if you determine that an action is potentially harmful to someone or would be embarrassing to you, or if you do not know the ethical or legal consequences, these guidelines will help you clarify whether the action is socially responsible.

SOURCES: Anthony M. Pagano and Jo Ann Verdin, *The External Environment of Business* (New York: Wiley, 1988), Chapter 5; and Joseph L. Badaracco, Jr., and Allen P. Webb, "Business Ethics: A View from the Trenches," *California Management Review* 37, no. 2 (winter 1995), 8–28.

---

not go along with the ethical values expressed, their jobs will be in jeopardy or they will not fit in.[22]

Culture can be examined to see the kinds of ethical signals given to employees. Exhibit 5.3 indicates questions to ask to understand the cultural system. Heroes provide role models that can either support or refute ethical decision making. Founder Sam Walton stood for integrity at Wal-Mart, and his values are ingrained in the organizational culture. With respect to company rituals, high ethical standards are affirmed and communicated through public awards and

---

1   Identify the organization's heroes. What values do they represent? Given an ambiguous ethical dilemma, what decision would they make and why?
2   What are some important organizational rituals? How do they encourage or discourage ethical behavior? Who gets the awards, people of integrity or individuals who use unethical methods to attain success?
3   What are the ethical messages sent to new entrants into the organization—must they obey authority at all costs, or is questioning authority acceptable or even desirable?
4   Does analysis of organizational stories and myths reveal individuals who stand up for what's right, or is conformity the valued characteristic? Do people get fired or promoted in these stories?
5   Does language exist for discussing ethical concerns? Is this language routinely incorporated and encouraged in business decision making?
6   What informal socialization processes exist, and what norms for ethical/unethical behavior do they promote?

EXHIBIT 5.3
Questions for Analyzing a Company's Cultural Impact on Ethics

SOURCE: Linda Klebe Trevino, "A Cultural Perspective on Changing and Developing Organizational Ethics," in *Research in Organizational Change and Development,* ed. R. Woodman and W. Pasmore (Greenwich, Conn.: JAI Press, 1990), 4.

ceremonies. Myths and stories can reinforce heroic ethical behavior. For example, a story at Johnson & Johnson describes its reaction to the cyanide poisoning of Tylenol capsule users. After seven people in Chicago died, the capsules were removed from the market voluntarily, costing the company more than $100 million. This action was taken against the advice of external agencies—FBI and FDA—but was necessary because of Johnson & Johnson's ethical standards.

Culture is not the only aspect of an organization that influences ethics, but it is a major force because it defines company values. Other aspects of the organization, such as explicit rules and policies, the reward system, the extent to which the company cares for its people, the selection system, emphasis on legal and professional standards, and leadership and decision processes, can also all have an impact on ethical values and manager decision making.[23] At Levi Strauss, for example, the selection system is aimed at promoting diversity of background and thought among workers, a set of "corporate aspirations" written by top management is to guide all major decisions, and one-third of a manager's raise can depend on how well he or she toes the values line.[24]

WHAT IS SOCIAL RESPONSIBILITY?

Now let's turn to the issue of social responsibility. In one sense, the concept of corporate social responsibility, like ethics, is easy to understand: It means distinguishing right from wrong and doing right. It means being a good corporate citizen. The formal definition of **social responsibility** is management's obligation to make choices and take actions that will contribute to the welfare and interests of society as well as the organization.[25]

As straightforward as this definition seems, social responsibility can be a difficult concept to grasp, because different people have different beliefs as to which actions improve society's welfare.[26] To make mat-

ters worse, social responsibility covers a range of issues, many of which are ambiguous with respect to right or wrong. For example, if a bank deposits the money from a trust fund into a low-interest account for 90 days, from which it makes a substantial profit, has it been unethical? How about two companies' engaging in intense competition, such as that between Cleveland Electric Illuminating Co. and Cleveland Public Power? Is it socially responsible for the stronger corporation to drive the weaker one into bankruptcy? Or consider companies such as A. H. Robins, maker of the Dalkon shield; Manville Corporation, maker of asbestos; Eastern Airlines; or Texaco, the oil company, all of which declared bankruptcy—which is perfectly legal—to avoid mounting financial obligations to suppliers, labor unions, or competitors. These examples contain moral, legal, and economic considerations that make socially responsible behavior hard to define. A company's environmental impact must also be taken into consideration.

ORGANIZATIONAL STAKEHOLDERS

One reason for the difficulty understanding social responsibility is that managers must confront the question "responsibility to whom?" Recall from Chapter 3 that the organization's environment consists of several sectors in both the task and general environment. From a social responsibility perspective, enlightened organizations view the internal and external environment as a variety of stakeholders.

A **stakeholder** is any group within or outside the organization that has a stake in the organization's performance. Each stakeholder has a different criterion of responsiveness, because it has a different interest in the organization.[27]

Investors and shareholders, employees, customers, and suppliers are considered primary stakeholders, without whom an organization cannot survive. Investors, shareholders, and suppliers' interests are served

social responsibility
The obligation of organization management to make decisions and take actions that will enhance the welfare and interests of society as well as the organization.

stakeholder
Any group within or outside the organization that has a stake in the organization's performance.

by managerial efficiency—that is, use of resources to achieve profits. Employees expect work satisfaction, pay, and good supervision. Customers are concerned with decisions about the quality, safety, and availability of goods and services. When any primary stakeholder group becomes seriously dissatisfied, the organization's viability is threatened. For example, the inability of Dow Corning to keep customers satisfied with the safety of its breast implants seriously damaged the company.[28]

Other important stakeholders are the government and the community. Most corporations exist only under the proper charter and licenses and operate within the limits of safety laws, environmental protection requirements, and other laws and regulations in the government sector. The community includes local government, the natural and physical environments, and the quality of life provided for residents. Special-interest groups, still another stakeholder, may include trade associations, political action committees, professional associations, and consumerists. Socially responsible organizations consider the effects of their actions upon all stakeholders.

Enlightened corporations invest in a number of philanthropic causes that benefit stakeholders. Today's leading companies are also paying close attention to the needs of employees. For example, Du Pont executive Faith Wohl is a corporate pioneer in the area of work-family coordination—attempting to meet the personal and social needs of employees. Wohl's division established child care centers, job sharing for working mothers, and workshops addressing such issues as rape prevention, racial bias, and sexual harassment.[29]

Well-meaning companies sometimes run afoul of stakeholders anyway but can take actions to appease them. For example, Fina, Inc., established an oil refinery in Port Arthur, Texas, in 1937. Over the years, subdivisions of attractive ranch-style homes grew up in the shadow of the Fina plant. Homeowners became unhappy with the plant in their midst because of its noise and odor. Residents expected the company to

purchase their homes at top market price. Fina made several good faith efforts to resolve problems and then agreed to purchase the homes because the residents had legitimate gripes.[30] Companies such as Fina and Du Pont are acting in a socially responsible way by helping stakeholders.

Today, special-interest groups continue to be one of the largest stakeholder concerns that companies face. Environmental responsibility has become a primary issue in the 1990s as both business and the public acknowledge the damage that has been done to our natural environment.

THE NATURAL ENVIRONMENT

When the first Earth Day celebration was held in 1970, environmentalists were considered by most business leaders to be an extremist fringe group, and few managers felt the need to respond to environmental concerns.[31] By the 25th anniversary of the celebration on April 22, 1995, the world had changed dramatically. Environmental issues have become a hot topic among business leaders, and large corporations as well as small businesses are targeting marketing efforts to woo the environmentally conscious consumer. McDonald's has reached its $1 billion milestone for purchases of recycled products. In addition, the company joined the Environmental Defense Fund and the Ad council to deliver "Buy Recycled and Save" information to more than 200 million consumers through trayliners, cups, and bags. Jeffrey Hollender built a small business, Seventh Heaven, by targeting the "green" consumer with environmentally friendly products.[32] Companies like Aveda and John Paul Mitchell are responding to growing concerns for animal welfare by not testing on animals, and activists recently targeted Procter & Gamble for a boycott due to the company's continued use of animal testing. Linda Bavaro built her company by seeking customers from large corporations with environmentally-friendly policies.

GLOBAL GREEN

Next time you take a sip of soft drink from that plastic two-liter bottle, consider that someday it may end up as a T-shirt on your back. That's thanks to CEO Linda Bavaro, whose Global Green, Inc. makes fabric out of plastic thread from the melted bottles.

Linda and her husband started the Norcross, Georgia, company in 1992 when she learned that recycled bottles could be turned into fabric that feels like a soft cotton blend. After much research, she located a mill that could produce it and took out a trademark on Retrieva fiber.

Hunting for large companies that had recycling as a priority and needed fabrics, she made her first call to Disney. Timing was important, for the managers were planning an in-house environmental exposition and they ordered 37,000 T-shirts. Even though the shirts were 15 percent more expensive than regular cotton, the company felt their commitment to the environment warranted it. Because of the shirt's popularity with employees, the next year Disney ordered give-away baseball caps for workers.

Disney ordered more, too. The company was concerned about the wastefulness of its uniforms, which were disposed of in landfills. To be able to produce a uniform made of material that could be recycled again and again was intriguing.

Turner Broadcasting System, Inc. has given Global Green more business, by developing a line of retail-sale Retrieva clothes based on its "Captain Planet" TV show.

Such arrangements with large companies offer the starting "green" entrepreneur a good opportunity to launch the business. A word of warning, though. Just calling it "green" is no longer enough. Bavaro says that certification by an independent laboratory helps keep consumer trust in the product and sets the company apart from the others.

Thanks to companies like Global Green, those ugly bottles may someday become attractive clothing.[33]   ■

The ranks of environmentally conscious consumers are growing, as revealed by a recent study conducted by the New York–based research firm Roper Starch Worldwide, Inc. Roper divides consumers into five categories.[34]

■ *True-Blue Greens*, 14 percent of the population, up from 11 percent in 1990, are highly committed and make buying decisions and change their personal behavior to help the natural environment.

■ *Greenback Greens*, 6 percent of the population, aren't usually willing to make substantial changes in their purchasing behavior, but they support environmental causes and often vote for pro-environment political candidates.

■ *Sprouts*, who shot up from 26 percent in 1990 to 35 percent, make a few environmentally friendly purchases and become involved in environmental causes from time to time.

■ *Grousers*, 13 percent, only grudgingly acknowledge environmental mandates.

■ *Basic Browns*, 32 percent, are the least environmentally active and generally do not recycle or support governmental regulation designed to help the natural environment.

Although the apathetic Basic Brown group still represents a large percentage of the population, its ranks are thinning. Most observers agree that the direction of society is toward a greater concern for the natural environment and all living things and that managers must be ready for the next "green" wave.[35] Environmentalism has become an integral part of organizational strategy for leading companies. Johnson & Johnson, Hewlett-Packard, Pitney Bowes, IBM, and Colgate Palmolive have all integrated environmentalism into their business planning and operations in ways that translate into bottom-line profits. Over a four-year period, Hewlett-Packard eliminated all ozone-depleting agents from its manufacturing process.[36] Patagonia, a California-based outdoor apparel company, has developed a list of nine environmental goals to be met over five years, including eliminating all solid waste sent to landfills, reducing the use of nonrenewable energy, and including environmental costs in company accounting and production systems. For 11 years, Patagonia has donated 10 percent of pretax profits or 1 percent of sales to environmental causes. Founder Yvon Chouinard believes all companies should adopt an "earth tax" and give a percentage of sales or profits to such causes. Although managers concerned with the bottom line might wince at such a suggestion, Chouinard says, "In almost every case where we've decided to do the right thing, it's turned out to make us more money."[37]

As we've discussed throughout this chapter, companies and managers often walk a fine line in their efforts to do the right thing, make money, and satisfy numerous stakeholders. In the following section, we will look at criteria that can be used to evaluate a company's social performance.

EVALUATING CORPORATE SOCIAL PERFORMANCE

One model for evaluating corporate social performance is presented in Exhibit 5.4. The

As part of its "Project Earth" program, A&P Stores urges customers to take an Earth Pledge and get involved in efforts to improve the natural environment. *Environmental responsibility* has become a primary issue for businesses in the 1990s. A&P adopted the turtle and frog, which are disappearing all over the world, as the company's mascots to roll out a new program aimed at building environmental awareness. One way A&P contributes directly to conservation efforts is its Energy Conservation System, which monitors and adjusts operating equipment to ensure maximum energy efficiency.

model indicates that total corporate social responsibility can be subdivided into four criteria—economic, legal, ethical, and discretionary responsibilities.[38] The responsibilities are ordered from bottom to top based on their relative magnitude and the frequency with which managers deal with each issue.

Note the similarity between the categories in Exhibit 5.4 and those in Exhibit 5.1.

Total Corporate Social Responsibility

EXHIBIT 5.4
Criteria of Corporate Social Performance

SOURCES: Archie B. Carroll, "A Three-Dimensional Conceptual Model of Corporate Performance," *Academy of Management Review* 4 (1979), 499; and "The Pyramid of Corporate Social Responsibility: Toward the Moral Management of Corporate Stakeholders," *Business Horizons* 34 (July–August 1991), 42.

In both cases, ethical issues are located between the areas of legal and freely discretionary responsibilities. Exhibit 5.4 also has an economic category, because profits are a major reason for corporations' existence.

Economic Responsibilities

The first criterion of social responsibility is *economic responsibility*. The business institution is, above all, the basic economic unit of society. Its responsibility is to produce the goods and services that society wants and to maximize profits for its owners and shareholders. Economic responsibility, carried to the extreme, is called the *profit-maximizing view*, advocated by Nobel economist Milton Friedman. This view argues that the corporation should be operated on a profit-oriented basis, with its sole mission to increase its profits so long as it stays within the rules of the game.[39]

The purely profit-maximizing view is no longer considered an adequate criterion of performance in Canada, the United States, and Europe. This approach means that economic gain is the only social responsibility and can lead companies into trouble. A notorious example was Salomon Brothers' attempt to corner the Treasury securities market. Corporate greed, fostered by former chairman John Gutfreund's "win-at-all-costs" culture, resulted in mistakes that led to record penalties of $280 million.[40]

Legal Responsibilities

All modern societies lay down ground rules, laws, and regulations that businesses are expected to follow. *Legal responsibility* defines what society deems as important with respect to appropriate corporate behavior.[41] Businesses are expected to fulfill their economic goals within the legal framework. Legal requirements are imposed by local town councils, state legislators, and federal regulatory agencies.

Organizations that knowingly break the law are poor performers in this category. Intentionally manufacturing defective goods or billing a client for work not done is illegal. An example of the punishment given to one company that broke the law is shown in Exhibit 5.5.

Ethical Responsibilities

Ethical responsibility includes behaviors that are not necessarily codified into law and may not serve the corporation's direct economic interests. As described earlier in this chapter, to be *ethical*, organization decision makers should act with equity, fairness, and impartiality, respect the rights of individuals, and provide different treatment of individuals only when relevant to the organization's goals and tasks.[42] *Unethical* behavior occurs when decisions enable an individual or company to gain at the expense of society.

When Finast took a chance in 1990 and opened a supermarket in Cleveland's inner-city neighborhood of Glenville, it per-

EXHIBIT 5.5
One Company's Punishment for Breaking the Law

SOURCES: Barry C. Groveman and John L. Segal, "Pollution Police Pursue Chemical Criminals," *Business and Society Review* 55 (fall 1985), 41.

February 12, 1985

American Caster Corporation

Dear Businesses & Residents of the City & County of Los Angeles

Pollution of our environment has become a crisis.
Intentional clandestine acts of illegal disposal of hazardous waste, or "midnight dumping" are violent crimes against the community.
Over the past 2 years almost a dozen Chief Executive Officers of both large and small corporations have been sent to jail by the L.A. Toxic Waste Strike Force.
They have also been required to pay huge fines; pay for clean-ups; speak in public about their misdeeds; and in some cases place ads publicizing their crime and punishment.

THE RISKS OF BEING CAUGHT ARE TOO HIGH—
AND THE CONSEQUENCES IF CAUGHT ARE NOT WORTH IT!

We are paying the price. *TODAY,* while you read this ad our President and Vice President are serving time in *JAIL* and we were forced to place this ad.

PLEASE TAKE THE LEGAL ALTERNATIVE AND PROTECT OUR ENVIRONMENT.

Very Truly Yours,

American Caster Corporation
141 WEST AVENUE 34
LOS ANGELES, CA 90031

formed an ethical act. Residents of the neighborhood, which was burned out during the 1968 riots, previously had to ride the bus eight miles to a suburban supermarket or shop at high-priced corner markets. The opening of the supermarket led to further development in the area, including a Rite-Aid drugstore, a condominium development, and 75 new homes. Today, Finast's 11 inner-city stores account for more than a quarter of the company's $800 million in sales. Finast has managed to meet both ethical goals and economic goals. Web Industries, a company headquartered in Westborough, Massachusetts, shows its ethical stance by hiring more than 50 former prisoners, who symbolize Web's commitment to giving people a second chance.[43]

Discretionary Responsibilities

Discretionary responsibility is purely voluntary and guided by a company's desire to make social contributions not mandated by economics, law, or ethics. Discretionary activities include generous philanthropic contributions that offer no payback to the company and are not expected. An example of discretionary behavior occurred when Pittsburgh Brewing Company helped laid-off steelworkers by establishing and contributing to food banks in the Pittsburgh area. Discretionary responsibility is the highest criterion of social responsibility, because it goes beyond societal expectations to contribute to the community's welfare.

CORPORATE ACTIONS TOWARD SOCIAL DEMANDS

Confronted with a specific social demand, how might a corporation respond? If a stakeholder such as the local government places a demand on the company, what types of corporate action might be taken? Management scholars have developed a scale of response actions that companies use when a social issue confronts them.[44] These

"The Vietnam Wall Experience," a project launched in 1990 by Service Corporation International (SCI), is an example of *discretionary responsibility*. SCI is the largest owner and operator of funeral homes and cemeteries in North America. The 100-city tour of the 240-foot replica of the Vietnam Veteran Memorial expands SCI's grief-counseling program by assisting thousands of Americans in the national grief and healing process following the Vietnam War. The girl pictured here might never have the opportunity to travel to Washington, D.C. SCI uses its discretionary responsibility to meet the needs of these people

actions are obstructive, defensive, accommodative, and proactive and are illustrated on the continuum in Exhibit 5.6.

Obstructive. Companies that adopt **obstructive responses** deny all responsibility, claim that evidence of wrongdoing is misleading or distorted, and place obstacles to delay investigation. During the Watergate years, such obstruction was labeled *stonewalling*. A. H. Robins Company reportedly used obstructive actions when it received warnings about its Dalkon shield, an intrauterine device. The company built a wall around itself. It stood against all evidence and insisted to the public that the product was safe and effective. The company spared no effort to resist investigation. As word about injuries caused by the Dalkon shield kept pouring in, one attorney was told to search the files and destroy all papers pertaining to the product.[45]

Defensive. The **defensive response** means that the company admits to some

discretionary responsibility
Organizational responsibility that is voluntary and guided by the organization's desire to make social contributions not mandated by economics, law, or ethics.

obstructive response
A response to social demands in which the organization denies responsibility, claims that evidence of misconduct is misleading or distorted, and attempts to obstruct investigation.

defensive response
A response to social demands in which the organization admits to some errors of commission or omission but does not act obstructively.

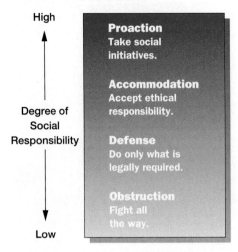

E X H I B I T   5 . 6
Corporate Responses to Social Demands

High

Degree of
Social
Responsibility

Proaction
Take social
initiatives.

Accommodation
Accept ethical
responsibility.

Defense
Do only what is
legally required.

Obstruction
Fight all
the way.

Low

errors of omission or commission. The company cuts its losses by defending itself but is not obstructive. Defensive managers generally believe that "these things happen, but they are nobody's fault." Goodyear adopted a defensive strategy by deciding to keep its South Africa plants open and provided an intelligent argument for why that was the proper action.

accommodative response
A response to social demands in which the organization accepts—often under pressure—social responsibility for its actions to comply with the public interest.

Accommodative. An **accommodative response** means that the company accepts social responsibility for its actions, although it may do so in response to external pressure. Firms that adopt this action try to meet economic, legal, and ethical responsibilities. If outside forces apply pressure, managers agree to curtail ethically questionable activities. Exxon's decision to clean up the oil spill in Prince William Sound was an accommodative decision based largely on the public's outcry.

proactive response
A response to social demands in which the organization seeks to learn what is in its constituencies' interest and to respond without pressure from them.

Proactive. The **proactive response** means that firms take the lead in social issues. They seek to learn what is in the public interest and respond without coaxing or pressure from stakeholders. One example of proactive behavior is the Potlatch Corporation. Potlatch makes milk cartons and came up with the idea of printing photographs of

missing children on them. The company reported that within days after the Alta-Dena Dairy of Los Angeles placed a missing-kids carton in grocery stores, one of the youngsters returned home.[46] Another proactive response is corporate philanthropy. Many companies, including Miller Brewing, Coca-Cola, and Westinghouse, make generous donations to universities, United Way, and other charitable groups as a way of reaching out and improving society.

These four categories of action are similar to the scale of social performance described in Exhibit 5.4. Obstructiveness tends to occur in firms whose actions are based solely on economic considerations. Defensive organizations are willing to work within the letter of the law. Accommodative organizations respond to ethical pressures. Proactive organizations use discretionary responsibilities to enhance community welfare.

Beech-Nut Nutrition Corporation was accused of unethical and socially irresponsible behavior. How would you evaluate its response?

■ **BEECH-NUT NUTRITION CORPO-
RATION**

To Beech-Nut, feeding babies is a sacred trust. Bottles of fruit juice say "100% fruit juice." Yet Beech-Nut was found to have adulterated its best-selling line of apple juice products. A member of the research department became suspicious that the concentrate acquired from suppliers contained nothing more than sugar water and chemicals. When he voiced his concerns, top management accused the employee of not being a team player and wrote in his annual performance review that his judgment was "colored by naivete and impractical ideals." The top managers were not hardened criminals trying to swindle customers. They were honest and well-respected but under great financial pressure. The cheap concentrate from the new supplier saved millions of dollars, and managers simply did not want to recognize that they were receiving a poor product. Beech-Nut was running on a shoestring, and enormous financial pressure forced managers to stay with the low-cost supplier.

Beech-Nut learned its lesson the hard way after an FDA investigation. Had the company admitted its error, payment of a fine would have closed the issue. But management stonewalled, and Beech-Nut found itself in the middle of a nightmare as the case changed from civil to criminal. The company's strategy was to stall investigations and avoid publicity until it could unload the diluted apple juice. After two years and two criminal trials, Beech-Nut's two top executives were sentenced to one year and a day in prison and fined $100,000. The total cost to the company, including fines, legal expenses, and lost sales, was an estimated $25 million.[47] ■

MANAGING COMPANY ETHICS AND SOCIAL RESPONSIBILITY

Many managers are concerned with improving the ethical climate and social responsiveness of their companies. They do not want to be surprised or be forced into an obstructionist or defensive position. As one expert on the topic of ethics said, "Management is responsible for creating and sustaining conditions in which people are likely to behave themselves."[48] Managers must take active steps to ensure that the company stays on an ethical footing. Management methods for helping organizations be more responsible include leadership by example, codes of ethics, ethical structures, and supporting whistle-blowers.

Leadership by Example.   The Business Roundtable, an association of chief executives from 250 large corporations, issued a report on ethics policy and practice in companies such as Boeing, Chemical Bank, General Mills, GTE, Xerox, Johnson & Johnson, and Hewlett-Packard.[49] The report concluded that no point emerged more clearly than the crucial role of top management. The chief executive officer and senior managers need to be openly and strongly committed to ethical conduct. They must give constant leadership in renewing the ethical values of the organization. They must be active in communicating that commitment in speeches, directives, company publications, and especially in actions. The company "grapevine" quickly communicates situations in which top managers chose an expedient action over an ethical one, and subsequent pronouncements of top executives' commitment to ethics count for very little.[50] Top managers set the tone of the organization most clearly by their behavior.

Code of Ethics.   A **code of ethics** is a formal statement of the company's values concerning ethics and social issues; it communicates to employees what the company stands for. Codes of ethics tend to exist in two types: principle-based statements and policy-based statements. *Principle-based statements* are designed to affect corporate culture; they define fundamental values and contain general language about company responsibilities, quality of products, and treatment of employees. General statements of principle are often called *corporate credos*. Examples are GTE's "Vision and Values," Johnson & Johnson's "The Credo," and Hewlett-Packard's "The HP Way."[51]

Policy-based statements generally outline the procedures to be used in specific ethical situations. These situations include marketing practice, conflicts of interest, observance of laws, proprietary information, political gifts, and equal opportunities. Examples of policy-based statements are Boeing's "Business Conduct Guidelines," Chemical Bank's "Code of Ethics," GTE's "Code of Business Ethics" and "Anti-Trust and Conflict of Interest Guidelines," and Norton's "Norton Policy on Business Ethics."[52]

Codes of ethics state the values or behaviors that are expected and those that will not be tolerated, backed up by management's action. A recent study by the Center for Business Ethics found that 90 percent of *Fortune* 500 companies and almost half of all other companies now have codes of ethics. When top management supports and enforces these codes, including rewards for compliance and discipline for violation,

code of ethics
A formal statement of the organization's values regarding ethics and social issues.

ethics codes can uplift a company's ethical climate. When top management doesn't support them, ethics codes are worth little more than the paper on which they're written.[53] The code of ethics at Starbucks reflects an early goal of the company to be a positive force in the community, as discussed in the Leading the Management Revolution box.

Ethical Structures. Ethical structures represent the various systems, positions, and programs a company can undertake to implement ethical behavior. An **ethics committee** is a group of executives appointed to oversee company ethics. The committee provides rulings on questionable ethical issues. The ethics committee assumes responsibility for disciplining wrongdoers, which is essential if the organization is to directly influence employee behavior. For example, Motorola has an Ethics Compliance Committee that is charged with interpreting, clarifying, and communicating the company's code of ethics and with adjudicating suspected code violations. An **ethics ombudsman** is an official given the responsibility of corporate conscience who hears and investigates ethical complaints and points out potential ethics failures to top management. Pitney Bowes has an ethics ombudsman and offers training seminars and a conduct guide on ethics for employees.

Other structures are ethics training programs and hot lines. For example, Chemical Bank has extensive education programs. All new employees attend an orientation session at which they read and sign off on Chemical's code of ethics. Another part of the program provides vice presidents with training in ethical decision making. Both McDonnell Douglas and General Dynamics have used scenario training to transform their ethics codes from pieces of paper to tools for training and education about ethical standards.[54] A hot line is a toll-free number to which employees can report questionable behavior as well as possible fraud, waste, or abuse. For example, Boeing has a toll-free number for employees to report any kind of ethical violation. LTV Corporation uses a hot line to

supplement existing procedures for reporting violations. No reprisals will be taken against anyone using it.

A strong ethics program is important, but it is no guarantee against lapses. Dow Corning, whose faulty silicone breast implants shocked the business community, pioneered an ethics program that was looked upon as a model. Established in the mid-1970s, Dow's ambitious ethics program included the Business Conduct committee, training programs, regular reviews and audits to monitor compliance, and reports to the Audit and Social Responsibility committee. What went wrong? The ethics program dealt with the overall environment, but specific programs such as product safety were handled through normal channels—in this case the Medical Device Business Board, which slowed further safety studies.[55] Dow Corning's problems sent a warning to other industries. It is not enough to *have* an impressive ethics program. The ethics program must be merged with day-to-day operations, encouraging ethical decisions to be made throughout the company.

Whistle-Blowing. Employee disclosure of illegal, immoral, or illegitimate practices on the employer's part is called **whistle-blowing**.[56] No organization can rely exclusively on codes of conduct and ethical structures to prevent all unethical behavior. Holding organizations accountable depends to some degree on individuals who are willing to blow the whistle if they detect illegal, dangerous, or unethical activities. Whistle-blowers often report wrongdoing to outsiders, such as regulatory agencies, senators, or newspaper reporters. Some firms have instituted innovative programs to encourage and support internal whistle-blowing. For this to be an effective ethical safeguard, companies must view whistle-blowing as a benefit to the company and make dedicated efforts to protect whistle-blowers.[57]

When there are no effective protective measures, whistle-blowers suffer, and the company may continue its unethical or illegal activities. Mark Jorgensen thought he was just being an honest guy when he ex-

---

ethics committee
A group of executives assigned to oversee the organization's ethics by ruling on questionable issues and disciplining violators.

ethics ombudsman
An official given the responsibility of corporate conscience who hears and investigates ethics complaints and points out potential ethical failures to top management.

whistle-blowing
The disclosure by an employee of illegal, immoral, or illegitimate practices by the organization.

LEADING THE MANAGEMENT REVOLUTION
STARBUCKS

Not too long ago activists handed out anti-Starbucks leaflets, protesting its alleged contracting of Guatemalan coffee pickers at $.02 a pound for coffee that was sold in its stores for $8 a pound.

Starbucks' management knew that it was already doing more than any other coffee company. Management thought its $100,000+ donations for relief programs in coffee-growing regions was enough, but consumers thought otherwise. Finally, in 1995, Starbucks came out with a code on working conditions, wages, child labor, and the local environment that could change the coffee industry. "There is nothing else like this code of conduct in the coffee or agri-cultural industries," says Starbucks manager Eric Hahn.

Pushing past the norm is nothing new for Starbucks, though. Since Howard Schultz and a group of investors bought it in 1987, it has grown from 11 Seattle stores to nearly 900 stores serving three million cups of coffee per week. But growth did not come at the expense of the idealism of the owners, who believed Starbucks could be their vehicle to a better society.

In order to do this, they realized they had to slightly change an old business adage to: "The employee always comes first." The result is great benefits and profit-sharing ("Bean Stock") for workers, which translates into more security for the employer. Starbucks turnover rate is one-eighth the industry average. The respected and satisfied employees keep customers coming back for more, with sales increasing at double the rate of competitors. And, each Starbucks store is given authority to donate products and money to community groups.

Starbucks could have grown faster with more profits, if Schultz hadn't been concerned about employees or the environment. "Growth," he says, "is not the driving force. Rather it's the passion for quality and respect."

SOURCE: Seanna Browder, "Starbucks Does Not Live by Coffee Alone," *Business Week,* Aug. 5, 1996, 76; Mary Scott, "Interview with Howard Schultz," *Business Ethics,* Nov/Dec 1995, 26–29.

posed fraud in the real-estate funds he managed for the Prudential Insurance Company of America. After all, Prudential top management encouraged its employees to speak up about misdeeds. But soon after blowing the whistle, Jorgensen's world fell apart. His immediate supervisor turned against him, his colleagues shunned him, and company lawyers accused him of breaking the law. Finally, a middle manager at Prudential called to tell him he had been dismissed. Jorgensen and his wife realized the only way they could survive without his salary and health benefits was to sell their home. Jorgensen's willingness to fight for his convictions impressed some of Prudential's largest institutional investors, and the company eventually offered him an apology and his job back (which he declined). Jorgensen became an industry hero, but that likely did not make up for the months of agony and despair Jorgensen and his family suffered.[58] It is not enough for top managers to encourage internal whistle-blowing. Managers can be trained to view whistle-blowing as a benefit rather than a threat, and systems can be set up to effectively protect employees who report illegal or unethical activities.

ETHICS AND THE MANAGEMENT REVOLUTION

Many of today's best companies realize that success can be measured in many ways, not all of which show up on the financial statement. However, the relationship of a corporation's ethics and social responsibility to its financial performance concerns both managers and management scholars and has generated a lively debate.[59] One concern of managers is whether good citizenship will hurt performance—after all, ethics programs cost money. A number of studies have been undertaken to determine whether heightened ethical and social responsiveness increases or decreases financial performance. Studies have provided varying results but generally have found that there is a small positive relationship between social responsibility and financial performance. For example, James Burke, former CEO of Johnson & Johnson (J&J), put together a list of companies known for their high ethical standards, including J&J, Xerox, and Eastman Kodak. In the period from 1950 to 1990, Burke found that the market value of companies that made the list grew at 11.3 percent annually, almost double the 6.2 percent rate achieved by Dow Jones industrials as a group. Although results from these studies are not proof, they do provide an indication that use of resources for ethics and social responsibility does not hurt companies.[60] Hewlett-Packard, Digital Equipment Corporation, and Silicon Graphics, winners of the Sixth Annual Business Ethics Awards, have proven that financial success and social responsibility can go hand in hand.[61] Enlightened companies realize that integrity and trust are essential elements in sustaining successful and profitable business relationships. Although doing the right thing may not always be profitable in the short run, it develops a level of trust that money can't buy and that will ultimately benefit the company. One company that firmly believes this and has made a strong commitment to business ethics for more than 30 years is Texas Instruments, a high-tech electronics firm, described in the Technology for Today box.

A related finding is that firms founded on spiritual values usually perform very well. These firms succeed because they have a clear mission, employees seldom have alcohol and drug problems, and a strong family orientation exists. One of the largest and

---

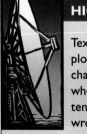

TECHNOLOGY FOR TODAY
HIGH-TECH CAN HELP BUILD TRUST

Texas Instruments (TI) employees work in a rapidly changing environment where difficult decisions, often with no clear right or wrong answer, have to be made on a daily basis. In a company as large and complex as TI, maintaining high ethical standards requires more than lip service. Texas Instruments developed a code of ethics in 1961 but has now gone far beyond that initial step to hold the company and its employees to high standards of integrity. Currently, a staff of seven at TI's Dallas headquarters oversees ethics programs for the company's 60,000 employees worldwide. Carl Skooglund, ethics director, spends most of his time and his $700,000 annual budget on ethics awareness. In addition to regular newsletters and supplemental publications, weekly news articles are sent throughout the world on the company's electronic mail system. Top-

ics include how to determine if a gift is acceptable, patent awards in other countries, the many faces of theft, and software copying. The company has also produced a series of more than 50 short videotapes on ethical dilemmas, which managers can use as a way to encourage discussion of ethical issues among employees.

Perhaps the most remarkable aspect of TI's ethics operation is how successfully the ethics office maintains direct dialog with a global workforce. Employees most frequently contact Skooglund's office through a toll-free telephone line, where anonymity is optional and confidentiality is guaranteed. Employees can also send a message to an ethics post office box, separate from the corporate mail system, or communicate via E-mail through a secure terminal connected to the company's other 30,000 terminals.

Skooglund says Texas Instruments stresses ethics for solid, strategic rea-

sons: "We believe our reputation for integrity is every bit as important as the technology base we've developed." Investing in ethics has paid off for TI. Employees say they are proud to work for a company that holds them to the highest standards. Texas Instruments hasn't experienced the same legal troubles many other large defense contractors have, and the company has earned a string of awards for its ethics operation. So firm is TI's commitment to maintaining its integrity that it has often gone the extra mile. After delivering products to one of its contractors, TI discovered a slight technical variation that had an infinitesimal chance of causing problems in use. TI paid for the product to be recalled and adjusted. The company lost on the deal financially but gained the undying trust of the contractor.

SOURCES: Dorothy Marcic, *Management with the Wisdom of Love* (San Francisco: Jossey-Bass, 1997); and Mark Henricks, "Ethics in Action," *Management Review*, January 1995, 53–55.

most successful companies is Chick-fil-A, Inc., which refuses to open on Sunday. The Sunday closing costs some sales and has gotten the chain frozen out of some shopping malls, but the policy helps attract excellent workers, and this offsets any disadvantages. When Tom Chappell, co-founder with his wife Kate, of Tom's of Maine, became concerned about how to stick to his respect for humanity while keeping his company successful, he went to divinity school. In the writings of the great philosophers, Chappell says he learned that you don't have to sell your soul to make your numbers. Tom's of Maine, a highly successful maker of all-natural personal care products, thrives on spiritual values.[62]

Being ethical and socially responsible does not hurt a firm. Managers and companies can use their discretion to contribute to society's welfare and improve organizational performance at the same time. The public is tired of unethical and socially irresponsible business practices. Companies that make an uncompromising commitment to maintain integrity may well lead the way to a brighter future for both business and society.

SUMMARY AND MANAGEMENT SOLUTION

Ethics and social responsibility are hot topics for managers in the 1990s. The ethical domain of behavior pertains to values of right and wrong. Ethical decisions and behavior are typically guided by a value system. Four value-based approaches that serve as criteria for ethical decision making are utilitarian, individualism, moral-rights, and justice. For an individual manager, the ability to make correct ethical choices will depend on both individual and organizational characteristics. An important individual characteristic is level of moral development. Corporate culture is an organizational characteristic that influences ethical behavior.

Corporate social responsibility concerns a company's values toward society. How can organizations be good corporate citizens? The model for evaluating social performance uses four criteria: economic, legal, ethical, and discretionary. Organizations may use four types of response to specific social pressures: obstructive, defensive, accommodative, and proactive. Evaluating corporate social behavior often requires assessing its impact on organizational stakeholders. Techniques for improving social responsiveness include leadership, codes of ethics, ethical structures, and whistle-blowing. Companies that are socially responsible perform as well as—and often better than—companies that are not socially responsible.

Recall the Tatra case at the beginning of the chapter. It is not clear how much of the responsibility for the company's losses should go to GSR and how much can be attributed to the economy. However, it did seem that the original agreement was overly optimistic and both sides can take blame for that. The Czechs were too naive, wanting too much for a "white knight" to rescue them as perhaps in a fairy tale. And the GSR executives, on the heels of an astounding success with the UAL employee buyout, were perhaps too sure of themselves, especially since it was in a new country and culture. Americans often go to other countries and assume they can do "business as usual," but instead make many mistakes and lose a lot of money. Some would argue that not taking enough time to study relevant parts of the culture could be considered unethical. When asked to resign, GSR balked and felt they had the remaining million dollars or so coming to them, regardless of whether they worked out the end of the contract. Some might argue that was not right. Again, it is a grey area. There are often no easy answers to these ethical dilemmas. Each side believes they are in the right, because each side has its own perspective. The important thing is to clearly and thoughtfully evaluate each possible scenario using sound ethical standards.

DISCUSSION QUESTIONS

1 Dr. Martin Luther King, Jr., said, "As long as there is poverty in the world, I can never be rich. . . . As long as diseases are rampant, I can never be healthy. . . . I can never be what I ought to be until you are what you

ought to be." Discuss this quote with respect to the material in this chapter. Would this be true for corporations, too?

2 Environmentalists are trying to pass laws for oil spills that would remove all liability limits for the oil companies. This would punish corporations financially. Is this the best way to influence companies to be socially responsible?

3 Compare and contrast the utilitarian approach with the moral-rights approach to ethical decision making. Which do you believe is the best for managers to follow? Why?

4 Imagine yourself in a situation of being encouraged to inflate your expense account. Do you think your choice would be most affected by your individual moral development or by the cultural values of the company for which you worked? Explain.

5 Is it socially responsible for organizations to undertake political activity or join with others in a trade association to influence the government? Discuss.

6 The criteria of corporate social responsibility suggest that economic responsibilities are of the greatest magnitude, followed by legal, ethical, and discretionary responsibilities. How do these four types of responsibility relate to corporate responses to social demands? Discuss.

7 From where do managers derive ethical values? What can managers do to help define ethical standards for the corporation?

8 Have you ever experienced an ethical dilemma? Evaluate the dilemma with respect to its impact on other people.

9 Lincoln Electric considers customers and employees to be more important stakeholders than shareholders. Is it appropriate for management to define some stakeholders as more important than others? Should all stakeholders be considered equal?

10 Do you think a code of ethics combined with an ethics committee would be more effective than leadership for implementing ethical behavior? Discuss.

MANAGEMENT EXERCISES

MANAGER'S WORKBOOK

What's Your Environmental IQ?

Mark the one answer you think is correct for each of the following questions. The average U.S. citizen in a study by the Roper Organization received a grade of 33 percent. How does your score compare? Are you more "Green" than "Brown"? (Note: This quiz was devised in 1991; please answer as you would have at that time.)

1 The U.S. government allows most aerosol products to contain chlorofluorocarbons (CFCs), which are known ozone depleters.   **T F**

2 About 50 percent of the world's wild plant, animal, and insect species live in rain forests.   **T F**

3 Most of the biodegradable packaging we throw away in this country decomposes within 10 years.   **T F**

4 The worldwide average temperature for 1990 was the warmest on record.   **T F**

5 The installation of modern sewer systems has eliminated the pollution of drinking water by human wastes.   **T F**

6 You may have heard that populations of American ducks and geese have been declining over the past decade. This is primarily because of

a. parasites and diseases.
b. loss of wilderness habitat.
c. hunger.
d. air pollution.
e. Don't know

7 Which of the following materials was the most widely recycled in the United States last year—that is, having the highest percentage of the amount used being recycled for other purposes?

a. Steel
b. Plastics
c. Paper
d. Glass
e. Don't know

8 In 1989, the Exxon Valdez oil tanker spilled 10 million to 11 million gallons of oil off the coast of Alaska. Compared to this amount, how much used motor oil is dumped by car owners in drains and sewers each year?

a. Less than one-tenth the amount of the Valdez oil spill
b. About half the amount of the Valdez oil spill
c. Twice as much as the Valdez oil spill
d. More than ten times as much as the Valdez oil spill
e. Don't know

9 In terms of volume or tonnage, which of the following is the top source of solid waste disposed of in landfills in this country?
  a. Paper and paperboard
  b. Metal
  c. Food scraps
  d. Plastics
  e. Don't know

10 Sulphur dioxide emitted by Midwestern coal-burning utilities is said to produce acid rain. From what you know, which one of the following is affected most by acid rain?
  a. Black bears in the Great Smoky Mountains
  b. Schoolchildren in the Midwest
  c. Fish in New England streams
  d. Central American rain forests
  e. Don't know

Answers

1 False
2 True
3 False
4 True
5 False
6 b
7 a
8 d
9 a
10 c

SOURCE: From the Roper Organization and S. C. Johnson Company, Inc.

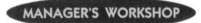

MANAGER'S WORKSHOP

The Power of Ethics

This exercise will help you better understand ethics and what it means to you.

1 Answer the questions below individually for about five minutes.
2 Divide into groups of four to six members.
3 Each group tries to achieve consensus with answers to each of the four questions. For question c, choose one scenario to highlight. You will have 20–40 minutes for this, depending on how much time the instructor assigns.
4 Groups share their answers with the whole class, after which the instructor leads a discussion on ethics and its power in business.

Questions

a In your own words, define ethics in one or two sentences.
b If you were a manager, how would you motivate your employees to follow ethical behavior? Use no more than two sentences.
c Describe a situation where you had an ethical dilemma. What was your decision and behavior? How did you decide to do that? Can you relate your decision to any concept in the chapter?
d What do you think is a powerful ethical message for others? Write it down in one or two sentences. Where did you get it from? How will that influence your behavior in the future?

SOURCE: Copyright 1996 Dorothy Marcic; adapted from Allayne Barrilleaux Pizzolatto's "Ethical Management: An Exercise in Understanding its Power," in *Journal of Management Education,* 17 (1), Feb. 1993, pp.107–109.

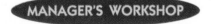

MANAGER'S WORKSHOP

Ethics Investigation

1 Divide into groups of four to six members and choose a real ethical dilemma that members of some organiza-

tion faced. Similar examples include the Nestlé infant formula controversy, HB Fuller and glue-sniffing in Honduras, Kathie Lee Gifford and sweatshops, Silkwood, Nuremburg Trials, Valdez oil spill, CIA involvement in crack, Iran-Contra, trial behavior in the O.J. Simpson case, Whitewater, West Point honor code, sexual harrassment cases in the Army or Navy, admission of women to South Carolina's Citadel military academy, CEO salaries, Shell Oil in Nigeria, corporate downsizing, etc.

2 Consider that you have been hired as a consultant to a major ethics think tank. Conduct thorough research on the subject and collect articles, which may include interviews, eyewitness reports, news magazines, editorials, etc. Try to find any movie or video clips that may be relevant, as well.

3 Write up a case study/report, keeping in mind the time frame and the historical context of this situation. Explicity identify ethical issues and conflicts as they occur. Remember, the think tank is very concerned with these issues and wants you to particularly highlight them. Refer back to ethical concepts in the chapter and see which are relevant. In your case study, include what happened and what the major "actors" did. How did they handle the dilemmas? Finally, describe how you would "rewrite the script" to make the behaviors more ethical. How would that change the outcome?

4 Develop an ethical "code of behavior" based on the events in your dilemma.

5 (optional) Be prepared to hand out copies of your case study and code of behavior to the rest of the class and to conduct a discussion. You may be asked to show the video clips, as well.

SOURCE: Copyright 1996 Dorothy Marcic; adapted from Karen L. Vinton and Melody M. Zajdel, "The ethics packet assignment," *The Organizational Behavior Teaching Review*, Vol. 12, no. 2, pp. 108–110.

SURF THE 'NET

Find a "chat room" or discussion group on the Internet or your E-mail service. Pose an ethical dilemma to them, something real that you or an organization has faced. Ask them what they think should be (or should have been) done? Put all their responses together and summarize what they said. Does it agree with your position?

ETHICAL DILEMMA

What Is Right?

It is often hard for a manager to determine what is "right" and even more difficult to put ethical behavior into practice. A manager's ethical orientation often brings him or her into conflict with people, policies, customers, or bosses. Consider the following dilemmas. How would you handle them?

1 A well-liked member of your staff with an excellent record confides to you that he has Acquired Immune Deficiency Syndrome (AIDS). Although his illness has not affected his performance, you're concerned about his future health and about the reactions of his coworkers. You

   a. tell him to keep you informed about his health and say nothing to his coworkers.

   b. arrange for him to transfer to an area of the organization where he can work alone.

   c. hold a staff meeting to inform his coworkers and ask them how they feel about his continued presence on your team.

   d. consult your human resources officer on how to proceed.

2 During a reorganization, you're told to reduce staff in the department you manage. After analyzing staffing requirements, you realize the job would be a lot easier if two professionals, who are both over age 60, would retire. You

   a. say nothing and determine layoffs based purely on performance and length of service.

   b. schedule a meeting with both employees and ask if they'd consider early retirement.

   c. schedule a meeting with all staff and ask if anyone is interested in severance or early retirement.

   d. lay off the older workers.

3 One of your colleagues has recently experienced two personal tragedies—her husband filed for divorce and her mother died. Although you feel genuine sympathy for her, her work is suffering. A report you completed, based on inaccurate data she provided, has been criticized by management. Your manager asks you for an explanation. You

   a. apologize for the inaccuracies and correct the data.

b. tell your manager that the data supplied by your colleague was the source of the problem.

c. say your colleague has a problem and needs support.

d. tell your manager that because of your work load, you didn't have time to check the figures in the report.

4 Your firm recently hired a new manager who is at the same level you are. You do not like the man personally and consider him a rival professionally. You run into a friend who knows your rival well. You discover this man did not attend Harvard as he stated on his résumé and in fact has not graduated from any college. You know his supposed Harvard background was instrumental in getting him hired. You

a. expose the lie to your superiors.

b. without naming names, consult your human resources officer on how to proceed.

c. say nothing. The company obviously failed to check him out, and the lie will probably surface on its own.

d. confront the man with the information and let him decide what to do.

5 During a changeover in the accounting department, you discover your company has been routinely overcharging members of the public for services provided to them. Your superiors say repayment of charges would wreak havoc on company profits. Your company is federally regulated, and the oversight commission has not noticed the mistake. Your bosses say the problem will never come to light and they will take steps to correct the problem so it never happens again. You

a. contact the oversight commission.

b. take the matter public, anonymously or otherwise.

c. say nothing. It is now in the hands of the bosses.

d. work with the bosses on a plan to recognize the company's error and set up a schedule of rebates that would not unduly penalize the company.

6 In this morning's mail, you received plans and samples for a promising new product from a competitor's disgruntled employee. You

a. throw the plans away.

b. send the samples to your research department for analysis.

c. notify your competitor about what is going on.

d. call the FBI.

Questions

1 Use the guidelines described in Focus On Ethics: "Guidelines for Ethical Decision Making" to determine the appropriate behavior in these cases. Do you have all the information you need to make an ethical decision? How would family or friends react to each alternative if you were in these situations?

2 Which approach to ethical decision making—utilitarian, individualism, justice, or moral-rights—seems most appropriate for handling these situations?

SOURCE: Game developed by Katherine Nelson, "Board Games," *Owen Manager*, spring 1990, 14–16; Craig Dreilinger and Dan Rice, "Office Ethics," *Working Woman*, December 1991, 35–39; and Kevin Kelly and Joseph Weber, "When a Rival's Trade Secret Crosses Your Desk . . . ," *Business Week*, May 20, 1991, 48.

CASE FOR CRITICAL ANALYSIS

Baby-Friendly Hospitals

Jason Rutledge sat in his office and wondered what to recommend in his report. As assistant administrator of 180-bed Babcock Memorial Hospital, he was charged with evaluating a proposal by a U.S. Committee for UNICEF group to become a "Baby-Friendly Hospital." Many U.S. hospitals tend to encourage bottle feeding through a combination of giving away free formula supplied by pharmaceutical companies and employing underskilled staff; and this committee was appealing to hospitals to reverse the trend.

Their arguments were compelling. Breastfed babies cry less, and they are healthier, with reduced risk for ear infections, juvenile diabetes, allergies, dental caries, and Sudden Infant Death Syndrome. Every year, 200,000 U.S. children are hospitalized for diarrhea; most of them are bottle-fed babies. By six months, only 20 percent of mothers breastfeed. Though low-income mothers are 40% less likely to breastfeed as middle income women, they feel a heavier burden with the $1,000 yearly cost of formula. Costs to HMOs and other insurers for basic health care are about 70 percent more for bottle-fed babies than those breastfed.

Still, Babcock Memorial was not an insurer nor even a parent. Jason's responsibilities were to help the hospital continue to trim unnecessary costs. Any help they could get was usually appreciated. Currently, formula companies were paying the hospital about $14,000 a year for formula, bottles, nipples, and feeders. If Babcock became a baby-friendly hospital, it would mean they would have to stop taking these "freebies" from the formula companies and would seriously start to encourage breastfeeding.

It was up to Jason to recommend either accepting the proposal or passing on it, and he realized what a difficult choice it was.

Questions

1 Which of the normative approaches to ethical decision making is most relevant for Jason to use?

2 Give examples of the four decisions Jason would make using each of the four possible responses to social demands.

3 If you were Jason, what would you recommend?

SOURCE: Margaret Kyenkya-Isabirye, "UNICEF launches Baby-friendly hospital initiative," *Maternal and Child Nursing*, Vol. 17, 1992, pp. 177–179; "Baby-friendly expert work group in the United States: Blowing the whistle," *Birth*, Vol. 22, June 1995, pp. 59–62; various hospital sources.

ENDNOTES

1 Dorothy Marcic, *Management with the Wisdom of Love,* San Francisco: Jossey-Bass, 1997; Jay Branegan, White Knights Need Not Apply, *Time,* October 31, 1994, 70–73; Czech Privatization; But Custer Lost, *The Economist,* Vol. 331, June 25, 1993, 66–67, Fleet Sheet, 1993; Neil King, Jr. "Tatra Board to Ponder Fate of U.S. Managers," *The Wall Street Journal Europe,* May 25, 1994, p. 3. Tatra: A Detroit Rescue, *The Economist,* Vol. 327 (7812), May 22, p. 74, Shawn Tully. Who's Who in the East? *Fortune,* July 29, 1991, 155–60.

2 Geraldine Brooks, "Shell's Nigerian Fields Produce Few Benefits for Region's Villagers," *The Wall Street Journal,* May 6, 1994, A1.

3 John A. Byrne, "Businesses Are Signing Up for Ethics 101," *Business Week,* February 15, 1988, 56–57; Don L. Boroughs, "The Bottom Line on Ethics," *U.S. News & World Report,* March 20, 1995, 61–66; and William J. Morin, "Silent Sabotage: Mending the Crisis in Corporate Values," *Management Review,* July 1995, 10–14.

4 Kevin Kelly and Eric Schine, "How Did Sears Blow This Gasket?" *Business Week,* June 29, 1992, 38; and David Dishneau, "Use of Sales Commissions under Scrutiny," *The State,* Columbia, S.C., July 17, 1992, 12B.

5 Edwin M. Raingold, "America's Hamburger Helper," *Time,* June 29, 1992, 66–67; Michael Schroeder and Jonathan Kapstein, "Charity Doesn't Begin at Home Anymore," *Business Week,* February 25, 1991, 91; and Mark Henricks, "Ethics in Action," *Management Review,* January 1995, 53–55.

6 Gordon F. Shea, *Practical Ethics* (New York: American Management Association, 1988); and Linda K. Trevino, "Ethical Decision Making in Organizations; A Person-Situation Interactionist Model," *Academy of Management Review* 11 (1986), 601–617.

7 Thomas M. Jones, "Ethical Decision Making by Individuals in Organizations: An Issue-Contingent Model," *Academy of Management Review* 16 (1991), 366–395.

8 Rushworth M. Kidder, "The Three Great Domains of Human Action," *Christian Science Monitor,* January 30, 1990.

9 Jones, "Ethical Decision Making."

10 This discussion is based on Gerald F. Cavanagh, Dennis J. Moberg, and Manuel Velasquez, "The Ethics of Organizational Politics," *Academy of Management Review* 6 (1981), 363–374; Justin G. Longenecker, Joseph A. McKinney, and Carlos W. Moore, "Egoism and Independence: Entrepreneurial Ethics," *Organizational Dynamics* (winter 1988), 64–72; and Carolyn Wiley, "The ABCs of Business Ethics: Definitions, Philosophies, and Implementation," *IM,* February 1995, 22–27.

11 Zachary Schiller, Walecia Conrad, and Stephanie Anderson Forest, "If You Light Up on Sunday Don't Come in on Monday," *Business Week,* August 26, 1992, 68–72.

12 Ron Winslow, "Rationing Care," *The Wall Street Journal,* November 13, 1989, R24.

13 Alan Wong and Eugene Beckman, "An Applied Ethical Analysis System in Business," *Journal of Business Ethics* 11 (1992), 173–178.

14 John Kekes, "Self-Direction: The Core of Ethical Individualism," *Organizations and Ethical Individualism,* ed. Konstanian Kolenda (New York: Praeger, 1988), 1–18.

15 Tad Tulega, *Beyond the Bottom Line* (New York: Penguin Books, 1987).

16 Howard Rothman, "A Growing Dilemma," *Business Ethics,* July/August 1996, 18–21; Timothy Schellhardt, "Are Lay-Offs Moral? One firm's answer: You Ask, We'll Sue," *The Wall Street Journal,* August 1, 1996, A1; Doug Wallace, "Southern Discomfort," *Business Ethics,* March/April 1996, 52–53.

17 Lynn Sharp Paine, "Managing for Organizational Integrity," *Harvard Business Review* (March–April 1994), 106–117.

18 This discussion is based on Trevino, "Ethical Decision Making in Organizations."

19 L. Kohlberg, "Moral Stages and Moralization: The Cognitive-Developmental Approach," in *Moral Development and Behavior: Theory, Research, and Social Issues,* ed. T. Lickona (New York: Holt, Rinehart & Winston, 1976); L. Kohlberg, "Stage and Sequence: The Cognitive-Developmental Approach to Socialization," in *Handbook of Socialization Theory and Research,* ed. D. A. Goslin (Chicago: Rand McNally, 1969); and Jill W. Graham, "Leadership, Moral Development, and Citizenship Behavior," *Business Ethics Quarterly* 5, no. 1 (January 1995), 43–54.

20 Carol Gilligan, *In a Different Voice: Psychological Theory and Women's Development* (Cambridge, Mass.: Harvard University Press, 1982).

21 Wong and Beckman, "An Applied Ethical Analysis System in Business"; Kent Hodgson, "Adapting Ethical Decisions to a Global Marketplace," *Management Review,* May 1992, 53–57; and Barbara Ettorre, "Why Overseas Bribery Won't Last," *Management Review,* June 1994, 20–24.

22 This discussion is based on Linda Klebe Trevino, "A Cultural Perspective on Changing and Developing Organizational Ethics," in *Research and Organizational Change and Development,* ed. R. Woodman and W. Pasmore (Greenwich, Conn.: JAI Press, 1990), 4.

23 Ibid.; John B. Cullen, Bart Victor, and Carroll Stephens, "An Ethi-

cal Weather Report: Assessing the Organization's Ethical Climate," *Organizational Dynamics* (autumn 1989), 50–62; and Bart Victor and John B. Cullen, "The Organizational Bases of Ethical Work Climates," *Administrative Science Quarterly* 33 (1988), 101–125.

24 Russell Mitchell with Michael Oneal, "Managing by Values," *Business Week*, August 1, 1994, 46–52; and Alan Farnham, "State Your Values, Hold the Hot Air," *Fortune*, April 19, 1993, 117–124.

25 Eugene W. Szwajkowski, "The Myths and Realities of Research on Organizational Misconduct," in *Research in Corporate Social Performance and Policy*, ed. James E. Post (Greenwich, Conn.: JAI Press, 1986), 9, 103–122; and Keith Davis, William C. Frederick, and Robert L. Blostrom, *Business and Society: Concepts and Policy Issues* (New York: McGraw-Hill, 1979).

26 Douglas S. Sherwin, "The Ethical Roots of the Business System," *Harvard Business Review* 61 (November–December 1983), 183–192.

27 Nancy C. Roberts and Paula J. King, "The Stakeholder Audit Goes Public," *Organizational Dynamics* (winter 1989), 63–79; and Thomas Donaldson and Lee E. Preston, "The Stakeholder Theory of the Corporation: Concepts, Evidence, and Implications," *Academy of Management Review* 20, no. 1 (1995), 65–91.

28 Max B. E. Clarkson, "A Stakeholder Framework for Analyzing and Evaluating Corporate Social Performance," *Academy of Management Review* 20, no. 1 (1995), 92–117.

29 Joseph Weber, "Meet DuPont's 'In-house' Conscience," *Business Week*, June 29, 1991, 62–65.

30 Caleb Solomon, "Big Payoff: How a Neighborhood Talked Fina Refinery into Buying It Out," *The Wall Street Journal*, January 10, 1991, A1, A8.

31 Mark A. Cohen, "Management and the Environment," *The Owen Manager* 15, no. 1 (1993), 2–6.

32 Laura M. Litvan, "Going 'Green' in the '90s," *Nation's Business*, February 1995, 30–32; and "Buy Recycled and Save," Environmental Defense Fund and McDonald's Corporation, 1994.

33 Laura Litvan, Going "Green" in the 90's," *Nation's Business*, Feb, 1995, 30–32.

34 Based on Litvan, "Going 'Green' in the '90s," 31.

35 Mark Starik, *Management and the Natural Environment* (Fort Worth, Texas: The Dryden Press, 1994), 1.

36 Kathleen Dechant and Barbara Altman, "Environmental Leadership: From Compliance to Competitive Advantage," *Academy of Management Executive* 8, no. 3 (1994), 7–20; and "The Sixth Annual Business Ethics Awards," *Business Ethics*, November–December 1994, 29.

37 Mary Scott, "Interview: Yvon Chouinard," *Business Ethics*, May–June 1995, 31–34.

38 Archie B. Carroll, "A Three-Dimensional Conceptual Model of Corporate Performance," *Academy of Management Review* 4 (1979), 497–505.

39 Milton Friedman, *Capitalism and Freedom* (Chicago: University of Chicago Press, 1962), 133; and Milton Friedman and Rose Friedman, *Free to Choose* (New York: Harcourt Brace Jovanovich, 1979).

40 Bruce Hager, "What's behind Business' Sudden Fervor for Ethics?" *Business Week*, September 23, 1991, 65.

41 Eugene W. Szwajkowski, "Organizational Illegality: Theoretical Integration and Illustrative Application," *Academy of Management Review* 10 (1985), 558–567.

42 David J. Fritzsche and Helmut Becker, "Linking Management Behavior to Ethical Philosophy—An Empirical Investigation," *Academy of Management Journal* 27 (1984), 165–175.

43 Don L. Boroughs, "The Bottom Line on Ethics," *U.S. News & World Report*, March 20, 1995, 61–66.

44 Elizabeth Gatewood and Archie B. Carroll, "The Anatomy of Corporate Social Response: The Rely, Firestone 500, and Pinto Cases," *Business Horizons* 24 (September–October 1981), 9–16.

45 John Kenneth Galbraith, "Behind the Wall," *New York Review of Books*, April 10, 1986, 11–13.

46 Milton R. Moskowitz, "Company Performance Roundup," *Business and Society Review* 53 (spring 1985), 74–77.

47 Chris Welles, "What Led Beech-Nut down the Road to Disgrace," *Business Week*, February 22, 1988, 124–128; Joe Queenan, "Juicemen: Ethics and the Beech-Nut Sentences," *Barron's*, June 20, 1988, 37–38; and Paine, "Managing for Organizational Integrity."

48 Saul W. Gellerman, "Managing Ethics from the Top Down," *Sloan Management Review* (winter 1989), 73–79.

49 "Corporate Ethics: A Prime Business Asset," The Business Roundtable, 200 Park Avenue, Suite 2222, New York, New York 10166, February 1988.

50 Joseph L. Badaracco, Jr., and Allen P. Webb, "Business Ethics: A View from the Trenches," *California Management Review* 37, no. 2 (winter 1995), 8–28.

51 "Corporate Ethics."

52 Ibid.

53 Carolyn Wiley, "The ABC's of Business Ethics: Definitions, Philosophies, and Implementation," *IM*, January–February 1995, 22–27; Badaracco and Webb, "Business Ethics: a View from the Trenches"; and Ronald B. Morgan, "Self- and Co-Worker Perceptions of Ethics and Their Relationships to Leadership and Salary," *Academy of Management Journal* 36, no. 1 (February 1993), 200–214.

54 Patrick E. Murphy, "Creating Ethical Corporate Structure," *Sloan Management Review* (winter 1989), 81–87; and Wiley, "The ABC's of Business Ethics."

55 John A. Byrne, "The Best Laid Ethics Programs . . . ," *Business Week*, March 9, 1992, 67–69.

56 Marcia Parmarlee Miceli and Janet P. Near, "The Relationship among Beliefs, Organizational Positions, and Whistle-Blowing Status: A Discriminant Analysis," *Academy of Management Journal* 27 (1984), 687–705.

57 Eugene Garaventa, "An Enemy of the People by Henrik Ibsen: The Politics of Whistle-Blowing," *Journal of Management Inquiry* 3, no. 4 (December 1994), 369–374; Marcia P. Miceli and Janet P. Near, "Whistleblowing: Reaping the Benefits," *Academy of Management Executive* 8, no. 3 (1994), 65–74.

58 Kurt Eichenwald, "He Told. He Suffered. Now He's a Hero." *The New York Times*, May 29, 1994, Section 3, 1.

59 Philip L. Cochran and Robert A. Wood, "Corporate Social Responsibility and Financial Performance," *Academy of Management Journal* 27 (1984), 42–56.

60 Jean B. McGuire, Alison Sundgren, and Thomas Schneeweis, "Corporate Social Responsibility and Firm Financial Performance," *Academy of Management Journal* 31 (1988), 854–872; and Robert McGarvey, "Doing the Right Thing," *Training*, July 1993, 35–38.

61 "The Sixth Annual Business Ethics Awards," *Business Ethics*, November–December 1994, 29–31.

62 Roger Ricklefs, "Christian-Based Firms Find Following Principles Pays," *The Wall Street Journal*, December 8, 1989, B1; Jo David and Karen File, "Saintly Companies That Make Heavenly Profits," *Working Woman*, October 1989, 122–126, 169–175; and Tom Chappell, "The Soul of a Business," *Executive Female*, January–February 1994, 38–77.

The Environment of Entrepreneurship and Small-Business Management

LEARNING OBJECTIVES

After studying this chapter, you should be able to

- Describe the importance of entrepreneurship to the U.S. economy.

- Define personality characteristics of a typical entrepreneur.

- Describe the planning necessary to undertake a new business venture.

- Discuss decision tactics and sources of help that increase chances for new business success.

- Describe the five stages of growth for an entrepreneurial company.

- Explain how the management functions of planning, organizing, leading, and controlling apply to a growing entrepreneurial company.

- Discuss how to facilitate intrapreneurship in established organizations.

MANAGEMENT PROBLEM

In 1978, Brenda French started a scarf-making company in a spare bedroom of her home. Ten years later, leading department stores were showcasing her expanded line of knitwear. French Rags seemed like a booming success, but French knew better. Her business was beset by a multitude of problems. Most of the department stores refused repeated requests to fold rather than hang the clothing to prevent distortion of shapes and sizes. Thus, hundreds of products were returned to the factory each month. Store buyers would select only limited styles, sizes, and colors, and French knew that most of the clothes that shoppers wanted weren't getting through the system. Like most garment manufacturers, French relied on a factor who paid her accounts receivable invoices for a percentage of the take, an arrangement that compensates for the notoriously slow payment by retail outlets. When the factor dropped French Rags without warning, French found herself drawing on her personal savings to pay creditors. French Rags retrenched, closing showrooms and supplying only to the few stores willing to pay COD. Gross sales disappeared almost overnight. Brenda French watched with despair as the business she had carefully and lovingly woven together came unraveled.[1]

• What advice would you give Brenda French? Can a small custom-made knitwear company remain competitive against mass manufacturers with greater resources selling at lower prices?

Most people dream of having their own business. In the local bookstore, titles such as *How to Run a Small Business, Entrepreneurial Life: How to Go for It and Get It*, and *Keeping the Family Business Healthy* outnumber books on how to get rich in stocks or real estate. The enormous growth of franchising gives beginners an escorted route into a new business. Some 500 incubators for new companies have sprung up. So have self-help clubs through which entrepreneurs aid one another. Computers have given big-business power to little companies. The environment in the United States is favorable for entrepreneurs because of a market economy and the hero status of successful entrepreneurs such as Bill Gates and Ross Perot.[2]

But Brenda French's story represents a fact of life for entrepreneurs. Running a small business is difficult and risky. Two out of three small businesses fail within the first five years. Those that survive the beginning period continue to face tremendous challenges. Despite the risks, Americans are entering the world of entrepreneurship at an unprecedented rate. Small business is booming, and most analysts think the trend is likely to continue.[3]

WHAT IS ENTREPRENEURSHIP?

Entrepreneurship is the process of initiating a business venture, organizing the necessary resources, and assuming the associated risks and rewards.[4] An entrepreneur is someone who engages in entrepreneurship. An **entrepreneur** recognizes a viable idea for a business product or service and carries it out. This means finding and assembling necessary resources—money, people, machinery, location—to undertake the business venture. The entrepreneur also assumes the risks and reaps the rewards of the business. He or she assumes the financial and legal risks of ownership and receives the business's profits.

For example, Nancy Friedman launched the Telephone Doctor as a one-woman business operating out of a desk drawer after she was treated so rudely during a routine call to her insurance agent that she canceled all her policies. Friedman recognized a need among businesses for training employees in good telephone manners. The first seminar Friedman advertised and ran in St. Louis generated a 38-cent profit. Today, the Telephone Doctor is a global corporation with annual sales of $2 million, 23 people on the payroll, and clients on five continents. Nancy Friedman took the risks and is now reaping the rewards of entrepreneurship.[5] Practically everyone has heard of Federal Express, but perhaps not Frederick Smith, who started the company after he got a C on a term paper spelling out the idea for a nationwide overnight parcel delivery service. He borrowed money, acquired an initial fleet of 14 French-built Falcon jets, and on the first night delivered 16 packages. After two years of losses, the company took off like a rocket and spawned a new industry.[6]

Entrepreneurship as an Option

For decades, half the working population has been confiding secretly to pals and pollsters the desire to leave corporate America and go it alone or with a few partners, but until recently such dreams were often squashed in their infancy by worried parents, friends, and spouses. Times have clearly changed. After growing steadily since the 1950s, America's largest manufacturers began cutting their payrolls. Downsizing throughout the corporate world has forced many employees to consider other options. In addition, more and more people are beginning to seek the better quality of life that comes from working on their own and the sense of being in control of their own security rather than leaving it in the hands of a large company.[7]

Women and minorities, who have found their opportunities limited in the corporate world, are often seeing entrepreneurship as the only way to go. Fran Green recalls that five years ago she was "female and facing 50, which is death in the corporate world."

entrepreneurship
The process of initiating a business venture, organizing the necessary resources, and assuming the associated risks and rewards.

entrepreneur
Someone who recognizes a viable idea for a business product or service and carries it out.

After 25 years with a big electronics-components supplier, Green struck out on her own to start Sun State Electronics, a distribution company selling high-tech gear to the aerospace and defense industries. Victoria Bondoc, the daughter of Philippine immigrants, is legally blind, but she didn't let that stop her from using $1,500 in personal savings to start an information services and facilities management firm at the age of 26. Today, Bondoc's Gemini Industries employs 100 people and operates out of six offices in Massachusetts, New York, Virginia, and the Philippines. Women are starting small businesses at twice the rate of men, and although the percentage of minority-owned businesses is still small, it is growing. In his recent book, *Banking on Black Enterprise*, Timothy Bates notes that a new generation of African American entrepreneurs is rapidly emerging.[8]

ENTREPRENEURSHIP AND THE ENVIRONMENT

Not so long ago, scholars and policymakers were worrying about the potential of small business to survive. Today, entrepreneurship and small business are increasingly important parts of the business world. According to some estimates, small businesses in the United States create two out of every three new jobs and account for more than half the sales of all goods and services. Another interesting finding is that there are approximately 20 million Americans who make their living as "solo professionals," often working out of their homes providing services to other companies. One-person offices constitute a $7.5 billion segment of the computer and office equipment markets, and marketing researchers believe solo professionals will continue to be the fastest-growing market for phone, fax, and computer makers. Some of the more common businesses for solo professionals are financial services, high-tech marketing, political consultation, and software business. As companies continue to downsize, decentralize operations, and contract out more functions, the opportunities for solo professionals will increase.[9]

The long-term trend toward ever-larger companies has reversed itself for a number of reasons.[10]

Economic Changes.   Today's economy is fertile soil for entrepreneurs. The economy changes constantly, providing opportunities for new businesses. For example, the demand for services is booming, and 97 percent of service firms are small, with fewer than 100 employees. Since government deregulation in 1980 removed restrictions that inhibited small-business formation, more than 13,000 trucking companies have been started.

Globalization and Increased Competition.   Even the largest of companies can no longer dominate their industry in a fast-changing global marketplace. Companies must cut costs, often by outsourcing work to smaller businesses or freelancers, and focus their resources on their core business, selling off extraneous operations. Globalization and increased competition also give an advantage to the flexibility and fast response small business can offer rather than to huge companies with economies of scale.

Technology.   Rapid advances and dropping prices in computer technology have spawned whole new industries as well as entirely new methods of producing goods and delivering services. Unlike technological advances of the past, these are within the reach of companies of all sizes. Using new technology in the steel industry, minimills with fewer than 100 workers can underprice giant steel manufacturers.

New Opportunities and Market Niches.   Entrepreneurs are taking advantage of the opportunity to meet changing needs in the marketplace. John Erickson founded Senior Campus Living, Inc., which specializes in building and managing communities for middle-income retirees. Taking a cue from colleges, Senior Campus Living is designed to promote a sense of community and make one's sunset years as socially stimulating as the college years. Capitalizing on two trends, a growing interest in animal welfare and the proliferation of singles looking for mates through dating services, Melanie Gross and Maureen Keene created Animal Lovers, Inc., to match singles who share a love of animals.[11]

Few people expected the entrepreneurial explosion, but there's no doubt that it is having a tremendous impact. Before further discussing the impact of small business, we must define what a small business is.

Definition of Small Business

The full definition of "small business" used by the Small Business Administration (SBA) is detailed and complex, taking up 37 pages of SBA regulations. Most people think of a business as small if it has fewer than 500 employees. This general definition works fine, but the SBA further defines it by industry. Exhibit 6.1 gives a few examples of how the SBA defines small business for a sample of industries. It also illustrates the types of businesses most entrepreneurs start—retail, manufacturing, and service. Additional types of new small businesses are construction, agriculture, and wholesaling.

Impact of Entrepreneurial Companies

The impact of entrepreneurial companies on our economy is underscored by the latest figures: approximately 700,000 businesses are incorporated in the United States each year, along with another 600,000 unincorporated start-ups—about 1.3 million new enterprises in 1991, compared to 1.2 million in 1980 and only 90,000 in 1950. Based on 1992 tax returns, there were approximately 21.3 million businesses, with only 14,000 of those businesses employing more than 500 people. The net number of companies is increasing at a rate of between 2 percent and 3 percent annually, slightly higher than the rate of growth of the general population.[12] Many recent converts to entrepreneurship are corporate refugees (often middle management victims of corporate layoffs and downsizing) and corporate dropouts (those who prefer the uncertainty of self-employment to the corporate bureaucracy). New entrepreneurs most frequently start businesses in the areas of business services and restaurants. Demographic and lifestyle trends have created new opportunities in areas such as environmental services, children's markets, fitness, and child care.[13] The

EXHIBIT 6.1
Examples of SBA Definitions of a Small Business

Industry	A Business Is Defined as Small If:
Manufacturing	
Meat packing	Its number of employees does not exceed 500.
Household laundry equipment	Its number of employees does not exceed 2,000.
Retail	
Hardware store	Average annual receipts for its preceding 3 fiscal years do not exceed $3.5 million.
Variety store	Average annual receipts for its preceding 3 fiscal years do not exceed $5.5 million.
Grocery store	Average annual receipts for its preceding 3 fiscal years do not exceed $13.5 million.
Service	
Carpet and upholstery cleaners	Average annual receipts for its preceding 3 fiscal years do not exceed $2.5 million.
Computer programmers	Average annual receipts for its preceding 3 fiscal years do not exceed $7.0 million.
Motion picture theaters	Average annual receipts for its preceding 3 fiscal years do not exceed $14.5 million.
Miscellaneous	
Banks	It has no more than $100 million in assets.

entrepreneurship miracle in the United States is an engine for job creation, innovation, and diversity.

Job Creation.   Researchers disagree over what percentage of new jobs is created by small business. A dramatic estimate by one method of measuring new job creation indicates that, from 1986 to 1990, large firms created *no* new jobs, while in the smallest businesses (those with fewer than 20 employees), there was a 170 percent increase in new jobs created. Small business (excluding farming) represents 58 percent of all U.S. business employment and directly or indirectly provides the livelihood of more than 100 million Americans.[14] Jobs created by small business give the United States an economic vitality that no other country can claim. Exhibit 6.2 shows how U.S. small business compares to the largest world economies, based on total output.

Innovation.   Entrepreneurial companies create a disproportionate number of new products and services. Among the notable products for which small businesses can be credited are cellophane, the jet engine, and the ballpoint pen. Virtually every new business represents an innovation of some sort, whether a new product or service, how the product is delivered, or how it is made.[15] Entrepreneurial innovation often spurs larger companies to try new things. Lamaur, Inc., created a new shampoo for permanent-waved hair. Soon three giant competitors launched similar products. Small-business innovation keeps U.S. companies competitive, which is especially important in today's global marketplace.

Diversity.   Entrepreneurship offers opportunities for individuals who may feel blocked in established corporations. Large firms such as McDonald's and Wendy's make special efforts to recruit and provide financing for minorities. Derrick and Dorian Malloy, twin brothers, believed that being poor, black, and from a housing project would not be barriers to entrepreneurship. They acquired experience working at Mc-

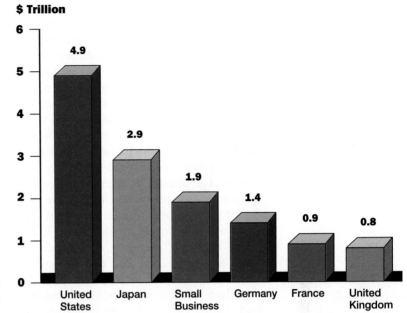

$ Trillion

**EXHIBIT 6.2
Total Output of U.S.
Small Business
Compared to World's
Largest Economies**

SOURCE: John Case, "The Wonderland Economy," *The State of Small Business*, 1995, 27.

Donald's, and now they own two Wendy's restaurants.[16] Women-owned and minority-owned businesses have tremendous potential as the "emerging growth companies of this decade."[17] Recent studies report that there are now 7.7 million women-owned businesses, which provide jobs for 15.5 million people and generate nearly $1.4 trillion in sales. Statistics for minorities are also impressive. Between 1982 and 1987, the number of black-owned businesses rose 37.6 percent, Hispanic-owned businesses rose over 80 percent, and Asian/Pacific Islander-owned businesses rose almost 90 percent.[18] However, women and minorities face special challenges in starting and running small businesses.

WHO ARE ENTREPRENEURS?

The heroes of American business—Ray Kroc, Spike Lee, Henry Ford, Sam Walton, Mary Kay Ash, Bill Gates, Ross Perot—are almost always entrepreneurs. Entrepreneurs start with a vision. Often they are unhappy with their present job and see an

internal locus of control
The belief by individuals that their future is within their control and that external forces will have little influence.

external locus of control
The belief by individuals that their future is not within their control but rather is influenced by external forces.

opportunity to bring together the resources needed for a new venture. However, the image of entrepreneurs as bold pioneers is probably overly romantic. A survey of the CEOs of the nation's fastest-growing small firms found that these entrepreneurs could be best characterized as hardworking and practical, with great familiarity with their market and industry.[19] For example, Bobby Frost worked 22 years in the mirror-manufacturing industry before leaving his employer. He started a mirror and glass fabrication business to use technology that his former employer refused to try and that Frost believed would work. It did. Eight years after its founding, Consolidated Glass & Mirror Corp. had 600 employees and $36 million in sales. Mark Bozzini, president of Pete's Brewing Company, traded a marketing job and a plush office at liquor industry giant Seagram Company for a corner of a barn and a desk made out of an old door.

A number of studies have investigated the personality characteristics of entrepreneurs and how they differ from successful managers in established organizations. Some suggest that entrepreneurs in general want something different from life than do traditional managers. Entrepreneurs seem to place high importance on being free to achieve and maximize their potential. For example, Mark Bozzini indicates that he wanted "control of my own destiny. My chances for continued personal and professional fulfillment at Seagram's were just above zero."[20] Some 40 traits have been identified as associated with entrepreneurship, but 6 have special importance.[21] These characteristics are illustrated in Exhibit 6.3.

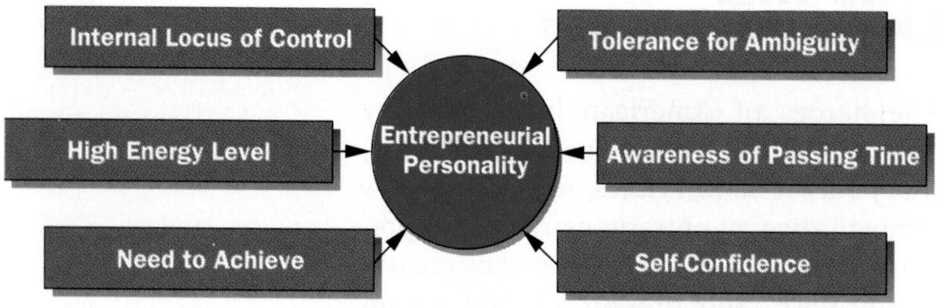

Locus of Control. The task of starting and running a new business requires the belief that you can make things come out the way you want. The entrepreneur not only has a vision but also must be able to plan to achieve that vision and believe it will happen. An **internal locus of control** is the belief by individuals that their future is within their control and that other external forces will have little influence. For entrepreneurs, reaching the future is seen as being in the hands of the individual. Many people, however, feel that the world is highly uncertain and that they are unable to make things come out the way they want. An **external locus of control** is the belief by individuals that their future is not within their control but rather is influenced by external forces. Entrepreneurs are individuals who are convinced they can make the difference between success and failure; hence they are motivated to take the steps needed to achieve the goal of setting up and running a new business.

Energy Level. A business start-up requires great effort. Most entrepreneurs report struggle and hardship. They persist and work incredibly hard despite traumas and obstacles.[22] A survey of business owners reported that half worked 60 hours or more per week. Another reported that entrepreneurs worked long hours, but that beyond 70 hours little benefit was gained. The data in Exhibit 6.4 show findings from a survey conducted by the National Federation of Independent Business. New business owners work long hours, with only 23 percent working fewer than 50 hours, which is close to a normal workweek for managers in established businesses. For example, Bobby Frost, founder of Consolidated Glass & Mirror, recalls the long hours he and other company officials put in during the early years and provides a shot of small-business work reality: "We'd all be president or whatever during the day and work in the plant at night."[23]

Need to Achieve. Another human quality closely linked to entrepreneurship is

EXHIBIT 6.3
Characteristics of Entrepreneurs

SOURCE: Adapted from Charles R. Kuehl and Peggy A. Lambing, *Small Business: Planning and Management* (Ft. Worth: The Dryden Press, 1994), 45.

the **need to achieve,** which means that people are motivated to excel and pick situations in which success is likely.[24] People who have high achievement needs like to set their own goals, which are moderately difficult. Easy goals present no challenge; unrealistically difficult goals cannot be achieved. Intermediate goals are challenging and provide great satisfaction when achieved. High achievers also like to pursue goals for which they can obtain feedback about their success.

Self-Confidence.   People who start and run a business must act decisively. They need confidence about their ability to master the day-to-day tasks of the business. They must feel sure about their ability to win customers, handle the technical details, and keep the business moving. Entrepreneurs also have a general feeling of confidence that they can deal with anything in the future; complex, unanticipated problems can be handled as they arise. Jeffrey Bezos was so sure of his new idea he quit his job and moved across the country before he even started putting the business together, as described in the Technology for Today box.

Awareness of Passing Time.   Entrepreneurs tend to be impatient; they feel a sense of urgency. They want things to progress as if there is no tomorrow. They want things moving immediately and seldom procrastinate. Entrepreneurs "seize the moment."

Tolerance for Ambiguity.   Many people need work situations characterized by clear structure, specific instructions, and complete information. **Tolerance for ambiguity** is the psychological characteristic that allows a person to be untroubled by disorder and uncertainty. This is an important trait, because few situations present more uncertainty than starting a new business. Decisions are made without clear understanding of options or certainty about which option will succeed.

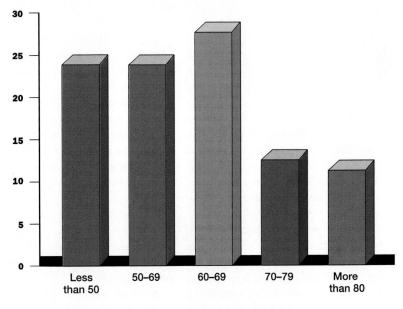

E X H I B I T   6 . 4
Reported Hours per Week Worked by Owners of New Businesses

Percent (%) of New Business Owners

Hours Worked per Week

SOURCE: National Federation of Independent Business. Reported in Mark Robichaux, "Business First, Family Second," *The Wall Street Journal,* May 12, 1989, B1.

Demographic Factors.   In addition to the six personality traits described so far, entrepreneurs often have background and demographic characteristics that distinguish them from other people. Entrepreneurs are more likely to be the first born within their families, and their parents are more likely to have been entrepreneurs. Children of immigrants also are more likely to be entrepreneurs, as are children for whom the father was absent for at least part of the childhood.[25]

In the past, most entrepreneurs launched their business between the ages of 25 and 40. However, recent research reveals an interesting trend: Eight of every ten new entrepreneurs are *over* the age of 40. Early retirement programs and corporate downsizing have created a whole new class of older entrepreneurs with high-level skills

need to achieve
A human quality linked to entrepreneurship in which people are motivated to excel and pick situations in which success is likely.

tolerance for ambiguity
The psychological characteristic that allows a person to be untroubled by disorder and uncertainty.

TECHNOLOGY FOR TODAY
AMAZON BOOKS

Whiz-kid programmer Jeffrey Bezos quit his cushy Wall Street job in 1994 when he decided to start a retail Internet business. Not one to waste time, he called the moving company and told them to load up, but he wasn't sure which city to have the stuff delivered to. As he and his wife drove west, they decided on a specific location (Seattle), he called a lawyer on his cellular phone to incorporate, and he used his laptop computer to write up a business plan.

His idea was to sell books through his Amazon Books Web site (http://www.amazon.com), which has become an underground favorite with thousands of book lovers around the world. Success came because he offers something traditional bookstores can-

not: Customers can scan through a database of 1.1 million titles, five times that of what the largest superstore offers. (He is able to do this because he does not order books until after a sale.) People can list favorite authors or topics and receive a constant flow of recommendations. Unlike other websites that flash glitzy graphics but offer not much new otherwise, Amazon truly exploits the potential of the Internet in the customer's favor. Instead of the fancy artwork that clogs many websites, Amazon instead floods the customer with information—including descriptions, reviews, "self-administered interviews"—and allows customers to share their book evaluations with each other.

As many entrepreneurs do, Bezos started his office in his garage and worried that sales would take off slowly.

But news of Amazon rapidly swept through the Internet and sales took off. Within six weeks, he moved to a spacious warehouse. Amazon now has 33 employees but no expensive furniture and no salespeople. It's open around-the-clock and has customers in some 66 countries. Strategic challenges remain, such as what to do with the massive customer database, so extensive that competitors salivate at the thought of peeking inside.

Though some bookstores seem threatened by Amazon's success, Bezos says the traditional bookstore is here to stay. He regularly hangs out at one. Like others, he loves to browse and likes how books "creak in that nice kind of way."

SOURCE: G. Bruce Knecht, "How Wall Street Whiz Found a Niche Selling Books on the Internet," *The Wall Street Journal*, May 16, 1996, A1+.

and years of experience. Many of these former managers have decided their chances are better in becoming entrepreneurs than in trying to reenter an overcrowded job market.[26] Today's successful entrepreneurs come in all ages and may have a combination of personality traits. No one should be discouraged from starting a business because he or she doesn't fit a specific profile. When R. E. Coleberd was faced with the imminent threat of losing his job at the age of 51, he considered his options and decided to start his own business.

PACIFIC WEST OIL DATA

Warnings about downsizing, restructuring, and potential layoffs had been circulating for months. Fifty-one-year-old R. E. Coleberd knew that, in 1983 in California, and to a large extent everywhere else, you were dead in the

job market at age 50. Coleberd decided to start his own business, reasoning that if he failed it would be his own fault and not the result of poor judgment at the top. His job had given him excellent experience working with petroleum industry statistical data and analysis, and Coleberd thought there might be a market among small firms that didn't have the know-how to work with statistical tables and graphs but that recognized or could be convinced that they needed sophisticated marketing intelligence in an increasingly competitive and complex industry.

On the day he was to leave his place of employment, Coleberd went into a colleague's office and told her, "You and I are going into business." Barbara Saben at first thought he was nuts, but six weeks later the two founded Pacific West Oil Data. Their extensive planning and premarketing discussions paid off. The small firms needed data to operate, but most didn't have the staff to handle it.

Eventually, even the major players were calling PacWest, saying, "[The data we need] is somewhere in the building, but it takes me two weeks to get it. . . . Sign me up."

Coleberd says he'd pick cotton in Georgia before going back to work for a large corporation. "I have felt like a kid with a new red wagon ever since I started my business."[27] ■

STARTING AN ENTREPRENEURIAL FIRM

Coleberd's story illustrates the first step in pursuing an entrepreneurial dream: Start with a viable idea for the new venture and plan like crazy. Once you have a new idea in mind, a business plan must be drawn and decisions made about legal structure, financing, and basic tactics, such as whether to start the business from scratch and whether to pursue international opportunities from the start.

New-Business Idea

To some people, the idea for a new business is the easy part. They do not even consider entrepreneurship until they are inspired by an exciting idea. Other people decide they want to run their own business and set about looking for an idea or opportunity. Exhibit 6.5 shows the most important reasons people start a new business and the source of new-business ideas, based on a survey of 500 fast-growing firms in the United States. The most important reasons people start new companies are to create something new and to be in control of their own lives. Note that 37 percent of business founders got their idea from an in-depth understanding of the industry, primarily because of past job experience. Interestingly, almost as many—36 percent—spotted a market niche that wasn't being filled. For example, Thomas Atwood founded Object Designs because he saw a niche for a new type of database that can store images, sound, or video. Regular databases handle names, numbers, and other records easily but have difficulty storing "unstructured" items into their tables and columns.[28]

The trick for entrepreneurs is to blend their own skills and experience with a need in the marketplace. Acting strictly on one's own skills may produce something no one wants to buy. On the other hand, finding a market niche that you do not have the ability to fill does not work either. Both personal skill and market need typically must be present. For example, single-parent and two-earner households have led some entrepreneurs to use their skills to provide ser-

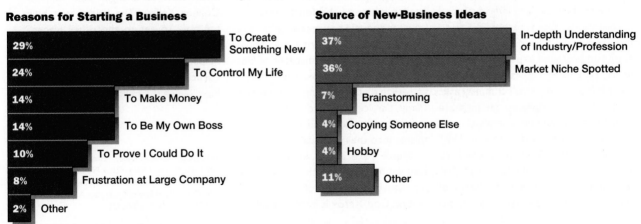

EXHIBIT 6.5
Sources of Entrepreneurial Motivation and New Business Ideas

Reasons for Starting a Business

- 29% To Create Something New
- 24% To Control My Life
- 14% To Make Money
- 14% To Be My Own Boss
- 10% To Prove I Could Do It
- 8% Frustration at Large Company
- 2% Other

Source of New-Business Ideas

- 37% In-depth Understanding of Industry/Profession
- 36% Market Niche Spotted
- 7% Brainstorming
- 4% Copying Someone Else
- 4% Hobby
- 11% Other

SOURCE: Based on Leslie Brokaw, "How To Start an *Inc. 500* Company," *Inc. 500*. 1994, 51–65.

business plan
A document specifying the business details prepared by an entrepreneur in preparation for opening a new business.

vices that meet a need for people short of time. Reunion Time, Inc., arranges high-school reunions, contracting to track down alumni. Moment's Notice Cuisine delivers meals to the homes of its customers, who are willing to pay 20 percent over the restaurant price.[29] Marlow Hotchkiss, Colleen Kelley, Robert Ott, and Gigi Cole started a unique organization called Térma to respond to growing concerns about environmental responsibility, as described in the Leading the Management Revolution box.

The Business Plan

Once an entrepreneur is inspired by a new-business idea, careful planning is crucial. A

business plan is a document specifying the business details prepared by an entrepreneur in preparation for opening a new business. Planning forces the entrepreneur to carefully think through all of the issues and problems associated with starting and developing the business. Most entrepreneurs have to borrow money, and a business plan is absolutely critical to persuading lenders and investors to participate in the business. Studies have shown that small businesses with a carefully thought-out, written business plan are much more likely to succeed than those without one.[30]

The details of business plans may vary, but a typical business plan contains much of the following.

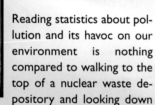

LEADING THE MANAGEMENT REVOLUTION
LIVING SYSTEMS AND THE GREENING OF CORPORATE AMERICA

Reading statistics about pollution and its havoc on our environment is nothing compared to walking to the top of a nuclear waste depository and looking down into the ugly gouge in the earth. But that is just what a small Santa Fe company had 11 research and development engineers from Xerox do recently as part of a week-long training program in the Abiquiú wilderness. Conducted by Living Systems (formerly Térma), which is dedicated to teaching individuals and corporations about responsibility to the earth and all living things, the program had profound impact on the engineers. Not using natural settings as a mere backdrop, the small company asks participants to "develop an intimate awareness with the environment."

Living Systems was started in 1991 because the four founders wanted "to address an environmental crisis that they see is at the heart of a 'crisis of spirit.'" The team spent seven years de-

veloping a training tool they call "The Box: Remembering the Gift," which is used in schools and colleges, in a women's prison, at teen centers, in church groups and seminars nationwide, and as part of Living Systems' natural systems training for businesses. The Box is divided into four stages: The first asks people to look deeply into their own life's purpose; the second asks them to reflect on life's suffering to awaken their compassion; the third invites people to discover their own healing gifts; and the fourth stage encourages people to use their gifts to revitalize the world. During the training program, Mike Tenney, manager of Electronic Systems at Xerox, says he "began to realize that everything is connected." Many participants said they left the training with a renewed sense of commitment to their spiritual roots.

Xerox executives knew that by sending managers on the training program, they ran the risk of responses like "Good God, Xerox is into spiritualism."

But project manager Ed DeJong points out that Xerox is one of the most proactive corporations in the world in terms of environmental awareness and the Living Systems training program was a tool to help the company make breakthroughs. Living Systems founders see working with companies like Xerox as a way to fight the environmental crisis threatening our planet. "One of the problems we really have today is people know we must change, but people don't know how to change," said founder Colleen Kelley. "The bridge isn't built for how to get to the other places." Small companies like Living Systems are helping to build the bridge, and large corporations like Xerox are increasingly seeing the need to cross it.

SOURCE: Colleen Kelley, "Greening the Corporate Culture: The Térma-Xerox Project," *The Ecopsychology Newsletter*, Issue 5, Spring 1996, 3; Lynn Cline, "Greening of Corporate America," *The New Mexican*, May 3, 1994, D1.

- Mission or vision of the company.
- Information about the industry and market.
- Information about suppliers.
- Information about the number and types of personnel needed.
- Financial information spelling out the sources and uses of start-up funds and operating funds.
- Plans for production of the product or service, including layout of the physical plant and production schedules.
- The business's policy for extending credit to customers.
- Legal considerations, such as information about licenses, patents, taxes, and compliance with government regulations.
- Critical risks that may threaten business success.

The business plan should indicate where the product or service fits into the overall industry and should draw on concepts that will be discussed throughout this book. For example, Chapter 7 will describe competitive strategies that entrepreneurs can use. Detailed suggestions for writing a business plan are provided in the Focus on Entrepreneurship box.

Legal Form

Before entrepreneurs have founded a business, and perhaps again as it expands, they must choose an appropriate legal structure for the company. The three basic choices are proprietorship, partnership, or corporation.

Proprietorship.   A **proprietorship** is defined as an unincorporated business owned by an individual for profit. Proprietorships make up 70 percent of the 16 million businesses in the United States. This form is popular because it is easy to start and has few legal requirements. A proprietor has total ownership and control of the company and can make all decisions without consult-

ing anyone. However, this type of organization also has drawbacks. The owner has unlimited liability for the business, meaning that if someone sues, the owner's personal as well as business assets are at risk. Also, financing can be harder to obtain because business success rests on one person's shoulders.

Partnership.   A **partnership** is an unincorporated business owned by two or more people. Partnerships, like proprietorships, are relatively easy to start. Two friends may reach an agreement to start a pet store. To avoid misunderstandings and to make sure the business is well-planned, it is wise to draw up and sign a formal partnership agreement with the help of an attorney. The agreement specifies how partners are to share responsibility and resources and how they will contribute their expertise. The disadvantages of partnerships are the unlimited liability of the partners and the disagreements that almost always occur among strong-minded people. A recent poll by *Inc.* magazine illustrated the volatility of partnerships. Fifty-nine percent of respondents considered partnerships a bad business move, citing reasons such as partner problems and conflicts. Partnerships often dissolve within five years. Respondents who liked partnerships pointed to the equality of partners (sharing of workload and emotional and financial burdens) as the key to a successful partnership.[31]

Corporation.   A **corporation** is an artificial entity created by the state and existing apart from its owners. As a separate legal entity, the corporation is liable for its actions and must pay taxes on its income. Unlike other forms of ownership, the corporation has a legal life of its own; it continues to exist regardless of whether the owners live or die. And the corporation, not the owners, is sued in the case of liability. Thus continuity and limits on owners' liability are two principal advantages of forming a corporation. For example, a physician can form a corporation so that liability for malpractice will

partnership
An unincorporated business owned by two or more people.

corporation
An artificial entity created by the state and existing apart from its owners.

proprietorship
An unincorporated business owned by an individual for profit.

FOCUS ON ENTREPRENEURSHIP
HINTS FOR WRITING THE BUSINESS PLAN

A KILLER SUMMARY
- It should have no more than three pages.
- This is the most crucial part of your plan because it must capture the reader's interest.
- Summarize what, how, why, where, etc., including market numbers.
- Complete this part *after* the finished business plan has been written.

THE BUSINESS DESCRIPTION SEGMENT
- The name of the business is stated.
- A background of the industry with history of the company (if any) should be covered here.
- The potential of the new venture should be described clearly.
- Any unique or distinctive features of the venture should be spelled out.

THE MARKETING SEGMENT
- Convince investors that sales projections and competition can be met.
- Use and disclose market studies.
- Identify target market, market position, and market share.
- Evaluate *all* competition and specifically cover "why" and "how" you will be better than the competitors.
- Identify all market sources and assistance used for this segment.
- Demonstrate pricing strategy since your price must penetrate and maintain a market share to *produce profits*. Thus "lowest" price is not necessarily the "best" price.
- Identify your advertising plans with cost estimates to validate the proposed strategy.

THE RESEARCH, DESIGN, AND DEVELOPMENT SEGMENT
- Cover the *extent* and *costs* involved in needed research, testing, or development.

- Explain carefully what has been accomplished *already* (prototype, lab testing, early development).
- Mention any research or technical assistance that has been provided for you.

THE MANUFACTURING SEGMENT
- Provide the advantages of your location (zoning, tax laws, wage rates).
- List the production needs in terms of facilities (plant, storage, office space) and equipment (machinery, furnishings, supplies).
- Describe the access to transportation (for shipping and receiving).
- Explain proximity to your suppliers.
- Mention the availability of labor in your location.
- Provide estimates of manufacturing cost. Be careful—too many entrepreneurs "underestimate" their costs.

THE MANAGEMENT SEGMENT
- Provide résumés of all key people in the management of the venture.
- Carefully describe the legal structure of the venture (sole proprietorship, partnership, or corporation).
- Cover the added assistance (if any) of advisers, consultants, and directors.
- Provide information on how everyone is to be compensated. (How much, also.)

THE CRITICAL RISKS SEGMENT
Point out potential risks *before* investors do:

- Price cutting by competitors.
- Potentially unfavorable industry-wide trends.

- Design or manufacturing costs in excess of estimates.
- Sales projections not achieved.
- Product development schedule not met.
- Difficulties or long lead times encountered in the procurement of parts or raw materials.
- Larger than expected innovation and development costs to stay competitive.
- Alternative courses of action.

THE FINANCIAL SEGMENT
- Provide statements.
- Describe the needed sources for your funds and the uses you intend for the money.
- Provide a budget.
- Create stages of financing for purposes of allowing evaluation by investors at various points.

THE MILESTONE SCHEDULE SEGMENT
- Provide a timetable to show when each phase of the venture is to be completed. This shows the relationship of events and provides a deadline for accomplishment.

PROOF OF VISION
Give enough detail so the reader will follow your ideas and see your goals are attainable. Show that you know how to sell and distribute your product and that you can hire competent people. "Vision" creates excitement for investors. Write your own plan—don't hire it out—so you really "own" it.

SOURCE: Linda Elkins, "Tips for preparing a business plan," *Nation's Business*, June 1966, 60R–61R; Donald F. Kuratko and Ray V. Montagno, *The Entrepreneur's Guide to Venture Formation* (Center for Entrepreneurial Resources, Ball State University, 1986), 33–34. Reprinted with permission from Midwest Entrepreneurial Education Center at Ball State University.

Starting an Entrepreneurial Firm

not affect his or her personal assets. The major disadvantage of the corporation is that it is expensive and complex to do the paperwork required to incorporate the business and to keep the records required by law. When proprietorships and partnerships are successful and grow large, they often incorporate to limit liability and to raise funds through the sale of stock to investors.

Financial Resources

A crucial concern for entrepreneurs is the financing of the business. An investment is usually required to acquire labor and raw materials and perhaps a building and equipment. The financing decision initially involves two options—whether to obtain loans that must be repaid (debt financing) or whether to share ownership (equity financing). A survey of successful growth businesses asked, "How much money was needed to launch the company?" Approximately one-third were started on less than $10,000, one-third needed from $10,000 to $50,000, and one-third needed more than $50,000. The primary source of this money was the entrepreneurs' own resources, but they often had to mortgage their home, borrow money from the bank, or give part of the business to a venture capitalist.[32]

Debt Financing. Borrowing money that has to be repaid at a later date in order to start a business is debt financing. One common source of **debt financing** for a start-up is to borrow from family and friends. Another common source is a bank loan. Banks provide some 25 percent of all financing for small business. Sometimes entrepreneurs can obtain money from a finance company, wealthy individuals, or potential customers.

Another form of loan financing is provided by the Small Business Administration (SBA). The SBA supplies direct loans to some entrepreneurs who are unable to get bank financing because they are considered high risk. The SBA is especially helpful for people without substantial assets, provid-

ing an opportunity for single parents, minority group members, and others with a good idea.

Equity Financing. Any money invested by owners or by those who purchase stock in a corporation is considered equity funds. **Equity financing** consists of funds that are invested in exchange for ownership in the company.

A **venture capital firm** is a group of companies or individuals that invests money in new or expanding businesses for ownership and potential profits. This is a potential form of capital for businesses with high earning and growth possibilities. Venture capital firms want new businesses with an extremely high rate of return, but in return the venture capitalist will provide assistance, advice, and information to help the entrepreneur prosper.

Tactics

There are several ways an aspiring entrepreneur can become a business owner. These include starting a new business from scratch, buying an existing business, or starting a franchise. Other entrepreneurial tactics include participation in a business incubator, being a spin-off of a large corporation, or pursuing international markets from the beginning.

Start a New Business. One of the most common ways to become an entrepreneur is to start a new business from scratch. This is exciting because the entrepreneur sees a need for a product or service that has not been filled before and then sees the idea or dream become a reality. The advantage of this approach is the ability to develop and design the business in the entrepreneur's own way. The entrepreneur is solely responsible for its success. A potential disadvantage is the long time it can take to get the business off the ground and make it profitable. The uphill battle is caused by the lack of established clientele and the many mistakes made by someone new to the

equity financing
Financing that consists of funds that are invested in exchange for ownership in the company.

venture capital firm
A group of companies or individuals that invests money in new or expanding businesses for ownership and potential profits.

debt financing
Borrowing money that has to be repaid at a later date in order to start a business.

business. Moreover, no matter how much planning is done, a start-up is risky; there is no guarantee that the new idea will work. John Peterman started several businesses and careers before one finally took off.

J. PETERMAN COMPANY

The J. Peterman Company gives a whole new meaning to the term "global market." For that is just where Peterman's "merchandisers" go to look for their catalog items, which are recognized as interesting, unique, and hard to find. Any place on the globe is seen as potential terrain for their "scouring." Not only do unusual and eye-catching pictures go into the catalog, but also such stories as: "World headquarters of conversation. Dark mahogany walls. Lean-faced men. Ruddy-faced men."—meant to simulate a pub 200 years ago and the copy for a collarless Irish pub shirt.

Though the company now sells about $70 million in merchandise a year, it started as one of a string of entrepreneurial attempts by John Peterman. A former marketing consultant, minor-league baseball player, and erstwhile beer cheese distributor, Peterman found an unusual ankle-length canvas duster coat on a trip to Wyoming. Enough people commented on it that he and a partner invested $500 in dusters and spent $3,000 on an eight-page ad spread in *The New Yorker* in 1987. That ad changed their lives, for the $29,000 in sales generated started the J. Peterman Company. Within a year they had their first catalog, with black-and-white sketches alongside the quirky ad copy.

Peterman's success, though, stems from more than imaginative catalog descriptions that blur the distinction between selling and entertaining. His business philosophy is one of customer focus. He carefully inspects each product, plans business trips, and reads customer letters. And he gives employees unusual rewards, such as St. Patrick's Day cupcakes with dollar bills inside or intimate breakfasts with eight employees—when he is not off in some corner of the globe.

But it was evidently the romance and fan-tasy of the catalog that captured the attention of the TV sitcom *Seinfeld*, where a character named J. Peterman was introduced. The real-life Peterman isn't sure whether the TV exposure has helped sales, but he says, "I'd like to believe I'm not a bore."[33] ■

Buy an Existing Business. Because of the long start-up time and the inevitable mistakes, some entrepreneurs prefer to reduce risk by purchasing an existing business. This offers the advantage of a shorter time to get started and an existing track record. The entrepreneur may get a bargain price if the owner wishes to retire or has other family considerations. Moreover, a new business may overwhelm an entrepreneur with the amount of work to be done and procedures to be established. An established business already has filing systems, a payroll tax system, and other operating procedures. Potential disadvantages are the need to pay for goodwill that the owner believes exists and the possible existence of ill will toward the business. In addition, the company may have bad habits and procedures or outdated technology, which may be why the business is for sale.

Buy a Franchise. Franchising is perhaps the most rapidly growing path to entrepreneurship. Currently, 1 out of every 12 businesses in the United States is franchised, and a new franchise business opens every eight minutes of every business day. Today, franchising employs more than 8 million people.[34] **Franchising** is an arrangement by which the owner of a product or service allows others to purchase the right to distribute the product or service with help from the owner. The franchisee invests his or her money and owns the business but does not have to develop a new product, create a new company, or test the market. The franchisee typically pays a flat fee plus a percentage of gross sales. Franchises exist for weight-loss clinics, beauty salons, computer stores, real estate offices, rental cars, and auto tune-up shops.[35] Exhibit 6.6 shows examples of some of today's fastest-growing franchises in four investment categories.

franchising
An arrangement by which the owner of a product or service allows others to purchase the right to distribute the product or service with help from the owner.

Those franchises that address today's time-pressured lives, such as Merry Maids, which sends a team of maids to clean your home in less than an hour, are expected to thrive in the coming years.[36] The powerful advantage of a franchise is that management help is provided by the owner. For example, Burger King does not want a franchisee to fail and will provide the studies necessary to find a good location. The franchisor also provides an established name and national advertising to stimulate demand for the product or service. Potential disadvantages are the lack of control that occurs when franchisors want every business managed in exactly the same way. In addition, franchises can be very expensive, running as high as several hundred thousand dollars for a McDonald's restaurant. High costs are followed with monthly payments to the franchisor that can run from 2 percent to 12 percent of sales.

Entrepreneurs who are considering a franchise should investigate the company thoroughly. The entrepreneur is legally entitled to a copy of franchisor disclosure statements, which cover 20 areas, including lawsuits. The entrepreneur should also request information regarding franchisor assistance in selection of location, set-up costs, and securing credit. Entrepreneurs should understand under what circumstances a contract can be terminated and should obtain detailed information in areas

Mini Maid Services, Inc., is a residential cleaning service *franchise* that operates in 24 states. A team can clean a house in only 55 minutes. Buying this franchise requires an initial investment of $12,500 and working capital of $18,000–$20,000. Franchisees receive three weeks of intensive training, management assistance, advertising support, and continuous follow-up. CEO Leone Ackerly reports annual growth of 20 percent and extremely favorable customer response.

E X H I B I T 6 . 6
Today's Winning Franchises

	Company	Product Category	Number of Units
$75,000 or Under	Coldwell Banker Residential Affiliates	Real Estate	2,066
	Money Mailer, Inc.	Business Services	675
	Merry Maids	Maintenance Services	810
$75,001 to $150,000	Blimpie International	Fast Food	966
	GNC Franchising	Retail	2,246
	Snap-On Inc.	Automotive Services	4,963
	Mail Boxes Etc.	Business Services	2,676
$150,001 to $250,000	Glamour Shots Licensing Inc.	Retail	323
	Sir Speedy, Inc.	Printing	887
	ExecuTrain Corp.	Computer-Related Services	135
$250,001 or More	Choice Hotels International	Lodging	3,384
	Dunkin' Donuts	Bakery Goods	3,632
	Hardee's Food Systems	Fast Food	4,060
	Ben Franklin Stores	Retail	912

SOURCE: Adapted from "Winners by Investment," *Success* 42, no. 4 (May 1995), 84

such as the management and staff training programs provided (e.g., whether "training" is limited to the distribution of manuals).[37] Answers to such questions improve the chances for choosing a successful franchise.

Participate in a Business Incubator.

An attractive innovation for entrepreneurs who want to start a business from scratch is to join a business incubator. Most incubators are sponsored by government organizations to spark job creation and business development. The **business incubator** provides shared office space, management support services, and management advice to entrepreneurs. By sharing office space with other entrepreneurs, managers share information about local business, financial aid, and market opportunities. Although this innovation has been in existence only a few years, the number of business incubators nationwide jumped from 385 in 1990 to approximately 500 by January 1993.[38] What gives incubators an edge is the expertise of the in-house mentor, who serves as adviser, role model, and cheerleader for entrepreneurs. SORRA, Inc., a drug-trial company in Birmingham, Alabama, benefited from the incubation experience. While holding down start-up costs, incubation assisted owner Vally Nance in locating capital as well as a lawyer and an accountant. Nance credits incubation for helping her company to make a "transition of competence and confidence" as it moved from her home basement to the seventh-floor offices of a clinic.[39]

Be a Spin-off.

Spin-offs, a unique form of entrepreneurial company, were previously associated with and owe their start-up to another organization. A **spin-off** is an independent company producing a product or service similar to that produced by the entrepreneur's former employer.[40] Spin-offs occur when entrepreneurs with a desire to produce a similar product quit their employers, or in some cases they produce a related product that is purchased by the former employer. The former employer may recognize that it can profit from the idea by selling patents to the spin-off and by investing in it. Employer approval is often the basis for a spin-off, although in some cases entrepreneurs start a new business because they disagree with former employers. Disagreement usually revolves around the failure of the employer to try a new idea that the entrepreneur believes in. A frustrated employee should discuss the possibility of starting a spin-off company with the support of his or her current employer. In this way, the spin-off reduces risk and has a source of management advice. The entrepreneur may also have a guaranteed customer for the spin-off's initial output.

Try Globalization.

In today's global marketplace, many new firms start out with the idea of going international immediately. Logitech, which makes mouses for personal computers, was founded in 1982 by a Swiss and two Italians who had global aspirations from the beginning. With headquarters in California and Switzerland, and R&D and manufacturing in those two locations plus Taiwan and Ireland, Logitech captured 30 percent of the worldwide market by 1989 and had revenues of $140 million.[41] Adventurous entrepreneurs are rushing to take advantage of new opportunities in Russia and Eastern Europe. Jeffrey Zieger opened a Nathan's Famous mobile unit in Moscow years ago, making hot dogs a hit in Russia before McDonald's even got off the ground. Small environmental companies, specializing in everything from wastewater treatment gear to landfill management, are finding extensive opportunities in the newly industrialized markets of South Korea, Indonesia, Malaysia, and Taiwan.[42] Many small businesses fail because the entrepreneur thinks provincially, being unaware of overseas markets. A former chief economist for the Small Business Administration, Tom Gray, has estimated that for every dollar of growth in the United States during the next decade, there will be five dollars of growth elsewhere. Small business cannot afford to ignore overseas markets.[43] Research has shown that small businesses can be quite successful by starting out with

business incubator
An innovation that provides shared office space, management support services, and management advice to entrepreneurs.

spin-off
An independent company producing a product or service similar to that produced by the entrepreneur's former employer.

international goals. It is likely that new technologies and changing market forces will lead to an increase in global start-ups over the next decade.[44]

The ability to develop an international business is enhanced by new technology that bypasses former obstacles such as language. AT&T offers a 24-hour phone line with interpreters. Phone hookups offered by AT&T, MCI, and Sprint allow direct transmission of electronic mail to distributors' computers worldwide. PC software kits, export computer services, and translation devices such as Seiko's multi-language translator assist small companies in achieving their export goals. Vita-Mix Corporation, a third-generation family-owned business, exports blenders to 20 nations. At the height of the recent recession, Vita-Mix doubled its workforce to keep up with orders pouring in to its 800 number. The owner of regional car washes in Portland, Oregon, launched his car wash system as an international business and is now selling in 71 countries and earning $100 million a year.[45]

There are a growing number of resources for small companies wishing to enter the global arena. The Service Corps of Retired Executives (SCORE) works with the Small Business Administration to match small businesses with mentors who have experience in international business. The Bankers' Association for Foreign Trade, a trade group, runs a program to help small exporters find financing. A good place for small companies to start is the U.S. Commerce Department's hot line, which can provide guidesheets on tricky exporting problems and details about the variety of federal programs designed to help new exporters tap foreign markets.[46] Many government departments offer counseling; research; assistance in finding overseas agents and sales leads; and help with export licensing, loans, export credit insurance, and other services. For example, Fred Schweser, president of Bird Corporation, received advice on test marketing his popular go-carts overseas. Today, exports account for 10 percent to 15 percent of Bird's go-cart

sales.[47] With the rapid globalization of the U.S. economy, it makes sense for new companies to target foreign markets.

Getting Help

The advice given to most entrepreneurs is to find a good accountant and attorney. They can help with the financial and legal aspects of the business. For a business that is incorporated, another great source of help is a board of directors. The entrepreneur can bring together for several meetings a year people who have needed expertise to discuss major problems. The board receives a small monthly stipend, gets a chance to help a business grow, and in some cases is given part ownership.[48]

Other sources of help are available for new entrepreneurs. For example, the Small Business Administration provides a loan program, described earlier. The government also provides financial assistance for specialized needs, such as loans for physical disasters or small-business energy loans.[49] In addition, the Small Business Administration runs several other management-assistance programs. The SBA has recently put together a free guidebook called the *Directory for Small Business Management*, which lists all SBA publications and videotapes on management issues. The National Association for the Self-Employed, founded by a few small-business owners in 1981, is a rapidly growing organization that provides benefits and services once available only to large corporations.

MANAGING A GROWING BUSINESS

Once an entrepreneurial business is up and running, how does the owner manage it? Often the traits of self-confidence, creativity, and internal locus of control lead to financial and personal grief as the enterprise grows. A hands-on entrepreneur who gave birth to the organization loves perfecting every detail. But after the start-up, continued growth requires a shift in management style. Those who fail to adjust to a growing business can be the cause of the problems rather than the solution.[50] In this section, we will look at the stages through which entrepreneurial companies move and then consider how managers should carry out their planning, organizing, leading, and controlling.

Stages of Growth

Entrepreneurial businesses go through distinct stages of growth, with each stage requiring different management skills. The five stages are illustrated in Exhibit 6.7.

1 *Existence.* In this stage, the main problems are producing the product or service and obtaining customers. Key issues facing managers are: Can we get enough customers? Will we survive? Do we have enough money?
2 *Survival.* At this stage, the business has demonstrated that it is a workable business entity. It is producing a product or service and has sufficient customers. Concerns here have to do with finances—generating sufficient cash flow to run the business and making sure revenues exceed expenses. The organization will grow in size and profitability during this period.
3 *Success.* At this point, the company is solidly based and profitable. Systems and procedures are in place to allow the owner to slow down if desired. The owner can stay involved or consider turning the business over to professional managers. Some entrepreneurs decide to sell at this point, realizing their strengths are in the start-up rather than long-term growth-building. Virginia Rogers started two successful companies and sold them both before the takeoff phase, as described below.

RELAX THE BACK

Virginia Rogers thought she had retired at age 39. By starting Ginny's Printing & Copying Services, Inc. (one of the nation's first full-service, quick-copy services in 1971) and building it to a $4 million/year business, she was ready to sell it in 1982. But six years later the itchy entrepreneur's lifelong sore back took her into a new venture. Finally seeking relief from her agonizing scoliosis, she found a tiny store in her native Austin, Texas that sold effective back-pain products.

Rather than let it go bankrupt as planned, she bought it in 1988 and introduced an array of related products and sold franchises for the company in 1989. Taking advantage of aging baby-boomers' aches and pains, the company now boasts 59 franchises selling 500 products from $1 to over $4000, including special pillows and custom-designed furniture. Relax the Back scored a public relations coup in 1995 during the O.J. Simpson trial when it offered to loan defense attorney Robert Shapiro its $1500 ergonomic chair and received national news coverage on the event.

Money has not been Rogers' main motivator, for she has already given much of her profits away to charity. She clearly loves the excitement of starting a new business. "Being an entrepreneur" is exciting, she says, because "you are taking an idea that nobody else has done and making it into something." But she knows when to move on. In late 1996, she sold Relax the Back to one of her franchisees.

"At different points in a company's growth," she says, "different people are best suited to lead it. My time has passed."[51] ■

4 *Takeoff.* Here the key problem is how to grow rapidly and finance that growth. The owner must learn to delegate, and the company must find sufficient capital to invest in major growth. This is a pivotal period in an entrepreneurial company's life. Properly managed, the company can become a big business. However, another problem for companies at this stage is how to maintain the advantages of "smallness" as the company grows.
5 *Resource maturity.* At this stage, the company has made substantial financial gains, but it may start to lose the advantages of small size, including flexibility and the entrepreneurial spirit. A com-

pany in this stage has the staff and financial resources to begin acting like a mature company with detailed planning and control systems.

Planning

In the early stage of existence, formal planning tends to be nonexistent except for the business plan described earlier in this chapter. The primary goal is simply to remain alive. As the organization grows, formal planning usually is not instituted until around the success stage. Recall from Chapter 1 that planning means defining goals and deciding on the tasks and use of resources needed to attain them. Larry Sloven and Bruce Bromberg defined a goal of carving out a niche in the volatile record industry by focusing on roots music, an eclectic mix of soulful and down-home sounds with country edges. High Tone Records is one of the few surviving profitable, independent record labels in the country.[52] Entrepreneurs sometimes strategize on an ad hoc basis. As we saw in the Technology for Today box, Jeffrey Bezos of Amazon planned his new venture while he drove across the country. Chapters 7 and 8 will describe how entrepreneurs can define goals and implement strategies and plans to meet them.

Organizing

In the first two stages of growth, the organization's structure is very informal with all employees reporting to the owner. At about stage 3—success—functional managers are often hired to take over duties performed by the owner. A functional organization structure will begin to evolve with managers in charge of finance, manufacturing, and marketing. During the latter stages of entrepreneurial growth, managers must learn to delegate and decentralize authority. If the business has multiple product lines, the owner may consider creating teams or divisions responsible for each line. The organization must hire competent managers and have sufficient management talent to handle fast growth and eliminate problems

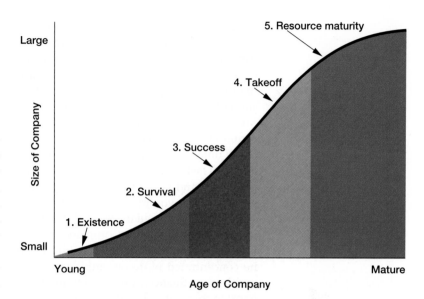

EXHIBIT 6.7
Five Stages of Growth for an Entrepreneurial Company

SOURCE: Based on Neil C. Churchill and Virginia L. Lewis, "The Five Stages of Small Business Growth," *Harvard Business Review* (May–June 1993), 30–50.

caused by increasing size. The latter growth stages are also characterized by greater use of rules, procedures, and written job descriptions.

Some of today's small companies are finding creative ways to stay small but still grow. Barbara Bobo, who turned a stove-top operation making all-natural herbal and floral soaps into a half-million-dollar company, created a network of independent contractors when demand outpaced the company's capabilities. Today, her company, Woodspirits, produces and distributes 300,000 bars of soap annually with just three employees.[53] Chapters 9–12 will discuss organizing in detail.

Leading

The driving force in the early stages of development is the leader's vision. This vision combined with the leader's personality shapes corporate culture. The leader can signal cultural values of service, efficiency, quality, or ethics. Often entrepreneurs do not have good people skills but do have excellent task skills in either manufacturing or marketing. By the success stage of growth, the owner must either learn to motivate employees or bring in managers who can. Rapid takeoff is not likely to happen without employee cooperation.

Stepping from the self-absorption of the early days of a company to the more active communication necessary for growth can be tricky for entrepreneurs. Charles Barnard, the owner of Foot Traffic, a chain of eight specialty sock stores based in Kansas City, Missouri, believes leaders should focus on communication as a company grows. "A lot of the time," Barnard says, "you get to running real fast, and you don't think about the people around you. But you can never get anywhere if you're pulling your staff around behind you all the time."[54] The president of Foreign Candy Company of Hull, Iowa, saw his company grow rapidly when he concentrated more on employee needs and less on financial growth. He made an effort to communicate with employees, conducted surveys to learn how they were feeling about the company, and found ways to involve them in decision making. His leadership style allowed the company to enter the takeoff stage with the right corporate culture and employee attitudes to sustain rapid growth.

Leadership is also important because many small firms are having a hard time hiring qualified employees. Labor shortages often hurt small firms that grow rapidly. A healthy corporate culture can help attract and retain good people.[55] You will learn more about leadership in Chapters 13–16.

Controlling

Financial control is important in each stage of the entrepreneurial firm's growth. In the initial stages, control is exercised by simple accounting records and by personal supervision. By stage 3—success—operational budgets are in place, and the owner should start implementing more structured control systems. During the takeoff stage, the company will need to make greater use of budgets and standard cost systems and perhaps acquire computers to provide statistical reports. These control techniques will become more sophisticated during the resource maturity stage.

The Sock Shop was originally a hit in New York City but eventually failed due to lack of control. Although sales progressed nicely, costs zoomed out of sight. Lack of control encouraged theft and poor decision making such as putting stores in the wrong locations. With poor financial control systems, losses led to abrupt store closings and the loss of the retailer's good name. Control will be discussed further in Chapter 17.

Coping with Chaotic Times

Small businesses operate in the same environment as larger, well-established firms and are affected by the same dramatic changes: increasingly tough global competition, rapid technological change, uncertain environments, the need to do more with less, and new challenges brought about by demographic shifts in the population and workforce. Small companies are sometimes in a better position to weather the chaos because of the speed and flexibility that smallness provides. However, many entrepreneurs are so focused on day-to-day operations that they fail to take the long-range view necessary for continued growth.

Joel Barker, whose Infinity Ltd. consulting firm has offices in Minneapolis and Orlando, says small businesses need to focus on the future in this era of rapid change. Barker advises companies to act now on the predictable changes, such as the growing diversity of the workforce, and prepare themselves to cope with the unpredictable as the world of business grows ever more turbulent. Taking a long-range view may ensure the survival of a small business in chaotic times.[56]

If a small business does not evolve, it risks failure. Burns & Russell, a family-owned business started in Baltimore in 1775, supplied the bricks for many of the structures around town, including the wharves, the B & O railroad tunnels, and Johns Hopkins Hospital. But Burns & Russell hasn't made a brick for 45 years; today the company has evolved into a high-tech manufacturer of specialty glazes for concrete blocks, along with other specialty chemicals.[57]

For some entrepreneurs, evolving may

mean turning away from their original dream. For example, Belinda Rush started V'tae to sell a line of all-natural perfumes but found the market wasn't there. So Rush started marketing a unique combination of scents and aromatherapy as well as what she calls "traditional magical use of scent" and found a hot market niche. Stephen Harper, author of *The McGraw-Hill Guide to Managing Growth in Your Emerging Business*, emphasizes that small businesses can be learning organizations, which in large part means paying attention to signals from the marketplace and changing and adapting to meet customer needs. Harper believes missing those signals is one of the biggest sins of entrepreneurs. "Too many people don't evolve, and the market just passes them by."[58]

INTRAPRENEURSHIP IN A GROWING BUSINESS

As the entrepreneurial firm grows large, it has a tendency to lose its innovative spirit with the implementation of formal control systems and bureaucratic procedures. Established firms often lose innovative ideas to entrepreneurial spin-offs from frustrated employees. The way to keep innovation within the organization is to create conditions in which intrapreneurs can flourish. **Intrapreneurship** is the process whereby an individual sees the need for innovation and promotes it within an organization. The goal for managers, who at one time were innovators themselves, is to create a climate that encourages intrapreneurs. Companies such as 3M are known for intrapreneurship. 3M intrapreneur Art Frey invented the Post-it Note as the result of personal frustration when his page markers repeatedly fell out of his church hymnal. Even the best ideas need nurturing, support, and financing in a large corporation.

The following rules provide an approach for developing the necessary atmosphere:

1 Encourage action.
2 Use informal meetings whenever possible.
3 Tolerate failure and use it as a learning experience.
4 Be persistent in getting an idea to market.
5 Reward innovation for innovation's sake.
6 Plan the physical layout of the firm to encourage informal communication.
7 Encourage clever bootlegging of ideas.
8 Organize people into small teams for future-oriented projects.
9 Strip away rigid procedures and encourage personnel to go around red tape when they find it.
10 Reward and/or promote innovative personnel.[59]

One company that maintains the innovative spirit is Hewlett-Packard.

HEWLETT-PACKARD

Charles House is an intrapreneur in Hewlett-Packard's innovative culture. He was assigned to develop a Federal Aviation Agency monitor similar to a television picture tube but with greatly enhanced capacity. It failed to meet government specifications, but House was more interested in other applications. He took a prototype to customers to learn whether it would solve their problems—in violation of HP's rules. He fought for money to support the technology despite its lack of a proven market. Finally, the project was ordered killed by Dave Packard himself. House's immediate superiors still supported him, however, and gave him one more year. House and his team succeeded, generating $10 million in annual sales simply because House persisted and would not give up. House was awarded the Medal of Defiance, shown in Exhibit 6.8. This reward signals Hewlett-Packard's fundamental values in favor of innovation.[60]

In his book *Intrapreneuring*, Gifford Pinchot argues that people like Charles House are needed in organizations. When spotted, intrapreneurs should be encouraged. Characteristics of intrapreneurs include willingness to circumvent orders aimed at stopping their dream; willingness to do any job needed to

intrapreneurship
The process of recognizing the need for innovation and promoting it within an organization.

EXHIBIT 6.8
Reward for Intrapreneurship at Hewlett-Packard

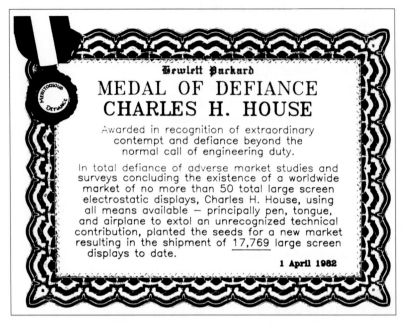

SOURCE: Courtesy of Hewlett-Packard Company.

make the project work; willingness to work underground as long as they can; willingness to be true to their goals; and willingness to remember it is easier to ask for forgiveness than for permission.[61] ■

Intrapreneurship is not always successful, however. Many companies, such as Control Data Corporation and Kodak, failed to generate profits from intrapreneur programs and dropped them. A good idea does not guarantee success. Intrapreneurs may be ill-prepared to follow through on their ideas and to make the sacrifice necessary to see the idea reach fruition. Managers may balk at the necessary capital investment or resist making exceptions to corporate policies.[62] As with any strategy, intrapreneurship is only as successful as the planning and support it receives throughout a company.

SUMMARY AND MANAGEMENT SOLUTION

This chapter explored entrepreneurship and small-business management. Entrepreneurs start new businesses, and entrepreneurship plays an important role in the economy by stimulating job creation, innovation, and opportunities for minorities and women. An entrepreneurial personality includes the traits of internal locus of control, high energy level, need to achieve, tolerance for ambiguity, awareness of passing time, and self-confidence.

Starting an entrepreneurial firm requires a new-business idea. At that point a comprehensive business plan should be developed and decisions made about legal structure and financing. Tactical decisions for the new venture include whether to start, buy, or franchise, whether to participate in a business incubator, whether to be a company spin-off, and whether to go global. After the business is started, it will typically proceed through five stages of growth—existence, survival, success, takeoff, and resource maturity. The management functions of planning, organizing, leading, and controlling should be tailored to each stage of growth. Finally, intrapreneurship, a variation of entrepreneurship, is a mechanism for encouraging innovation within a larger firm.

Small businesses must continually evolve to cope with changes in the environment and the chaos that characterizes today's business world. Returning to the management problem described at the beginning of the chapter, Brenda French was holed up at her factory contemplating her next move. The turnaround began with a stroke of luck. French Rags's loyal customers began wondering why they couldn't find the line in department stores; one customer called and said, "You bring your clothes to my house, and I know 20 people who will buy them." French knew the trip offered the possibility of around $10,000, which she sorely needed, so she agreed to the arrangement. The event grossed not $10,000 but $80,000, and French took home orders for things she didn't have but knew she could make. With renewed enthusiasm, French began looking into new technology that offered the dazzling possibility of mass customization. She invested in a German-made Stoll knitting machine that combines new technology and timeless craft. In addition, the company now uses advanced computer-aided design and manufacturing technology. French Rags can produce custom-made garments at virtually the same speed as the cookie-cutter offerings of mass producers. French created a sales force of her most affluent customers, who now sell French Rags out of their homes. Inventory costs and problems have been eliminated because everything the company makes is presold. Brenda French believes you have to constantly be prepared to change. French Rags shows the benefits small companies can gain by combining technological innovation with new ways of thinking.[63]

DISCUSSION QUESTIONS

1 Dan McKinnon started an airline with one airplane. To do so required filing more than 10,000 pages of manuals, ordering 50,000 luggage tags, buying more than $500 million in insurance, and spending more than $300,000 to train employees. A single inspection test cost $18,000. Evaluate whether you think this is a good entrepreneurial opportunity, and discuss why you think Dan McKinnon undertook it.

2 What do you think are the most important contributions of small business to our economy?

3 Why would small-business ownership have great appeal to immigrants, women, and minorities?

4 Consider the six personality characteristics of entrepreneurs. Which two traits do you think are most like those of managers in large companies? Which two are least like those of managers in large companies?

5 Why is purchasing an existing business or franchise less risky than starting a new business?

6 If you were to start a new business, would you have to search for an idea, or do you already have an idea to try? Explain.

7 Many entrepreneurs say they did little planning, perhaps scratching notes on a legal pad. How is it possible for them to succeed?

8 What is the difference between debt financing and equity financing? What are common sources of each type?

9 How does an entrepreneurial firm in the existence stage differ from one in the success stage?

10 How do the management functions of organizing and controlling differ for the existence and success stages?

11 Explain the difference between entrepreneurship and intrapreneurship. Why would entrepreneurs want intrapreneurship within their companies? Would an entrepreneur's personality tend to inhibit intrapreneurship? Discuss.

MANAGEMENT EXERCISES

MANAGER'S WORKBOOK

What Is Your Entrepreneurial Quotient?

The following questions are from a test developed by John R. Braun, psychology professor at the University of Bridgeport in Connecticut, and the Northwestern Mutual Life Insurance Company, based in Milwaukee. Simply answer yes or no to each question.

1 Are you a first-generation American?

2 Were you an honor student?

3 Did you enjoy group functions in school—clubs, team sports, even double dates?

4 As a youngster, did you prefer to be alone frequently?

5 As a child, did you have a paper route, a lemonade stand, or some other small enterprise?

6 Were you a stubborn child?

7 Were you a cautious youngster, the last in the neighborhood to try diving off the high board?

8 Do you worry about what others think of you?

9 Are you in a rut, tired of the same routine day in and day out?

10 Would you be willing to dip deeply into your "nest egg"—and possibly lose all you invested—to go it alone?

11 If your new business should fail, would you get to work immediately on another?

12 Are you an optimist?

Answers

1 Yes = 1, No = minus 1.
2 Yes = minus 4, No = 4.
3 Yes = minus 1, No = 1.
4 Yes = 1, No = minus 1.
5 Yes = 2, No = minus 2.
6 Yes = 1, No = minus 1.
7 Yes = minus 4, No = 4. If you were a particularly daring child, add another 4 points.
8 Yes = minus 1, No = 1.
9 Yes = 2, No = minus 2.
10 Yes = 2, No = minus 2.
11 Yes = 4, No = minus 4.
12 Yes = 2, No = minus 2.

Now calculate your total score. If you tallied 20 or more points, you have a strong entrepreneurial quotient. The score of 0 to 19 suggests that you have entrepreneurial possibilities. If you scored between 0 and minus 10, your chance of successfully starting an entrepreneurial business is marginal. A score below minus 11 suggests you are not the entrepreneurial type.

Go back over each question, thinking about changes you might make to become more or less entrepreneurial, depending on your career interests.

SOURCE: Peter Lohr, "Should You Be in Business for Yourself?" *Reader's Digest,* July 1989, 49–52.

MANAGER'S WORKSHOP

Start-up

1 Divide into groups of five to seven members. You are the partners of a new start-up company. Decide what type of company you want to start that you are able to with an initial investment of $10,000. It can be a manufacturing or service business.
2 Use the information under the section "Business Plan," and the box "Hints for Writing the Business Plan." Write your own business plan.
3 (Optional) Share your business plan with another group. Your instructor may ask you to "round robin" the business plans, as if you were all sitting in a circle and you passed your plan to the group on your right and received one from the group on the left. You should evaluate the group's business plan in terms of
a. Creativity and reasonableness of idea;
b. Thoroughness of data and plan;
c. Overall execution of business plan.

Copyright 1996 Dorothy Marcic.

MANAGER'S WORKBOOK

Are You an Intrapreneur?

Answer "yes" or "no" to the following questions:

1 Does your desire to make things work better occupy as much of your time as fulfilling your duty to maintain them the way they are?
2 Do you get excited about what you are doing at work?
3 Do you think about new business ideas while driving to work or taking a shower?
4 Can you visualize concrete steps for action when you consider ways to make a new idea happen?
5 Do you get in trouble from time to time for doing things that exceed your authority?
6 Are you able to keep your ideas under cover, suppressing your urge to tell everyone about them until you have tested them and developed a plan for implementation?
7 Have you successfully pushed through bleak times when something you were working on looked like it might fail?
8 Do you have more than your share of both fans and critics?
9 Do you have a network of friends at work whom you can count on for help?
10 Do you get easily annoyed by others' incompetent attempts to execute portions of your ideas?
11 Can you consider trying to overcome a natural perfec-

tionist tendency to do all the work yourself and share responsibility for your ideas with a team?

12 Would you be willing to give up some salary in exchange for the chance to try out your business idea if the rewards for success were adequate?

Scoring

If you answered "yes" more times than "no," chances are you are already behaving like an intrapreneur.

The Intrapreneur's Ten Commandments

1 Do any job needed to make your project work, regardless of your job description.
2 Share credit wisely.
3 Remember, it is easier to ask for forgiveness than permission.
4 Come to work each day willing to be fired.
5 Ask for advice before asking for resources.
6 Follow your intuition about people; build a team of the best.
7 Build a quiet coalition for your idea; early publicity triggers the corporate immune system.
8 Never bet on a race unless you are running in it.
9 Be true to your goals, but realistic about ways to achieve them.
10 Honor your sponsors.

SOURCE: Reprinted by permission of *The Wall Street Journal,* © 1996 Dow Jones & Company, Inc. All Rights Reserved Worldwide.

SURF THE 'NET

Visit at least 20 Web sites for small companies. Try to determine what role the Web site plays in the success of the companies.

1 How long has each company been in operation (if you can find out)? How long has the Web site been up? How many "hits" have there been since the start of the Web site?

2 What information is on the Web site? What kinds of graphics?

3 Can you see any pattern in terms of the type of Web site, its availability to various Web browsers, services on the Internet it offers, and how successful the company seems?

ETHICAL DILEMMA

To Grow or Not to Grow?

Chuck Campbell is the founder of Expeditions Unlimited, a specialty travel service that researches and arranges trips to unlikely places. He is famous for his unconventional approach to business in everything from his trademark blue jeans and ball caps as working attire to his personal relationships with all clients. He is the type of entrepreneur who makes deep commitments to his employees, with generous educational allowances, family leaves, and profit sharing for all of his staff. The office atmosphere is casual but professional. People dress any way they choose and music plays continually, but everyone works long hours, and customer satisfaction is the ultimate goal. For example, a 24-hour answering service relays messages to agents at home if their clients have emergencies during a booked trip.

Five years ago, Campbell consented to acquiring a computer system when his agents insisted it would help them in their jobs, but he doesn't use it. He pays two receptionists to work full-time, rather than have an automated phone system with voice mail. He believes his clients should be able to talk to a person whenever they call. The company has grown steadily, and he knows that at least two of his senior employees are ready to start branches on their own. They want his consent and his supervision, but Campbell isn't sure he wants or can handle such a radical expansion. He knows he'll need to compromise his level of contact with clients and embrace the new technology to make it work, and he's not sure that he will still enjoy his job after the transition. He also worries that the unique nature of this highly personal business may change with the growth. Campbell says employee satisfaction and growth are important. Does his commitment to employee development demand he expose his business and his personal job satisfaction to the risk of new business arrangements?

What Do You Do?

1 Refuse to expand your business. Stay within your comfort zone, but give your blessings to the senior employees who want to quit and start their own travel service in other cities.

2 Expand the business in its present location: delegate the bulk of the company and expedition management to the senior agents, with the rest doing the research and arrangements. Step back into a supervisory and client contact position only. Agents receive more responsibility, and you stay in control.

3 Train the senior agents to open branches under your corporate identity, trusting that your long association will ensure that they run the branches with the corporate values you instilled. Then let go and give them only as much supervision as you can comfortably afford to give.

CASE FOR CRITICAL ANALYSIS

TelePizza

Although Cuban-born Leo Fernandez started his pizza delivery store in Spain as a hobby, within a year he had left the corporate world for full-time entrepreneurship. Sales from TelePizza's 210 stores (60 percent franchised) in eight countries were projected to reach $100 million by the end of 1994. Fernandez had witnessed the fast-food craze while living in the United States and knew it was going to happen worldwide. He admits that he copied a lot of the successful practices of giants like McDonald's and Burger King—"If the wheel has been invented, why reinvent it?" Fernandez also gives credit to former employer Johnson & Johnson, which puts a lot of emphasis on hiring high-caliber people. Ninety percent of TelePizza's store supervisors have college degrees, an industry rarity.

Fernandez has not only hired the best, he has turned his front-line people into a band of highly motivated entrepreneurs. All of TelePizza's deliverers work part-time, between 10 and 20 hours a week depending on their study schedules, and each has responsibility for a small geographical area. They get paid not only to zoom around on mopeds delivering pizzas but also to build new business by handing out flyers and coupons at least two hours

a week. Bonuses are paid to those employees responsible for thriving areas. Gerry Durnell, executive director of the National Association of Pizza Operators in New Albany, Indiana, believes the biggest difference between TelePizza and its competitors is that Fernandez has given up a slice of his pie to reward and motivate employees. As Durnell puts it, "The entrepreneurial approach all the way down to the lowest levels of the company is the reason he's done so well."

As competition from Domino's, Pizza Hut, and Spain's Pizza World heats up, the entrepreneurial spirit at TelePizza will become even more important in keeping the business flourishing.

Questions

1 Do you think this start-up is typical of entrepreneurial companies? Discuss.
2 In what stage of growth is TelePizza now? Explain.
3 Discuss how leadership has contributed to TelePizza's success.

SOURCE: Niklas von Daehne, "A Piece of the Pie," *Success*, December 1994, 12.

ENDNOTES

1 Hal Plotkin, "Riches from Rags," *Inc. Technology,* summer 1995, 62–67.
2 Glenn Rifkin, "Inventing Heroes for the Twenty-First Century," *The New York Times,* February 14, 1993, F10; Jeremy Main, " A Golden Age for Entrepreneurs," *Fortune,* February 12, 1990, 120–125; and Keith H. Hammonds, "What B-School Doesn't Teach You about Startups," *Business Week,* July 24, 1989, 40–41.

3 Brian O'Reilly, "The New Face of Small Business," *Fortune*, May 2, 1994, 82–88.

4 Donald F. Kuratko and Richard M. Hodgetts, *Entrepreneurship: A Contemporary Approach* (Chicago: The Dryden Press, 1989).

5 Cheryl Jarvis, "Prescribing Good Manners," *Nation's Business*, May 1994, 18.

6 Eugene Carlson, "Federal Express Wasn't an Overnight Success," *The Wall Street Journal*, June 6, 1989, B2.

7 O'Reilly, "The New Face of Small Business."

8 Wendy Zellner, with Resa W. King, Veronica N. Byrd, Gail De-George, and Jane Birnbaum, "Women Entrepreneurs," *Business Week*, April 18, 1994, 104–110; Harriet Webster, "The 'Expert' Beginner," *Nation's Business*, January 1995, 16; Barbara Presley Noble, "A Few Thousand Women, Networking," *The New York Times*, March 27, 1994, 4F; and "Black Entrepreneurs: A New Generation," *Inc.*, June 1994, 32.

9 Richard M. Hodgetts and Donald F. Kuratko, *Effective Small Business Management*, 5th ed. (Fort Worth, Texas: The Dryden Press, 1995), 96–97.

10 Based on John Case, "The Wonderland Economy," *The State of Small Business*, 1995, 14–29; and Richard L. Daft, *Management*, 3d ed. (Fort Worth, Texas: The Dryden Press, 1992).

11 Jenny C. McCune, "The Entrepreneur Express," *Management Review*, March 1995, 13–19; and Mary Beth Sammons, "Pets a New Leash on Your Love Life," *The Tennessean*, July 23, 1995, 3F.

12 Case, "The Wonderland Economy."

13 Thomas McCarroll, "Entrepreneurs: Starting Over," *Time*, January 6, 1992, 62–63; Susan Caminiti, "Look Who Likes Franchising Now," *Fortune*, September 23, 1991, 125–130; David L. Birch, "The Truth about Start-Ups," *Inc.*, January 1988, 14–15; and Carl H. Vesper, *Entrepreneurship and National Policy* (Chicago: Heller Institute, 1983).

14 Case, "The Wonderland Economy"; and Hodgetts and Kuratko, *Effective Small Business Management*, 8.

15 "100 Ideas for New Businesses," *Venture*, November 1988, 35–74.

16 Leon E. Wynter, "How Two Black Franchisees Owe Success to McDonald's," *The Wall Street Journal*, July 25, 1989, B1–B2.

17 Bradford McKee and Sharon Nelton, "Building Bridges to Minority Firms," *Nation's Business*, December 1992, 29–33.

18 Bureau of Census Statistics as reported in "Black Entrepreneurship: By the Numbers," *The Wall Street Journal*, April 3, 1992, R4; and "Women-Owned Businesses Outpace All U.S. Firms," *Self-Employed America*, July–August 1995, 7.

19 John Case, "The Origins of Entrepreneurship," *Inc.*, June 1989, 51–63.

20 Ellen A. Fagenson, "Personal Value Systems of Men and Women Entrepreneurs versus Managers, *Journal of Business Venturing* 8, no. 5 (September 1993), 409–430; and McCune, "The Entrepreneur Express."

21 This discussion is based on Charles R. Kuehl and Peggy A. Lambing, *Small Business: Planning and Management*, 3d ed. (Chicago: The Dryden Press, 1994).

22 Roger Ricklefs and Udayan Gupta, "Traumas of a New Entrepreneur," *The Wall Street Journal*, May 10, 1989, B1.

23 Case, "The Origins of Entrepreneurship."

24 David C. McClelland, *The Achieving Society* (New York: Van Nostrand, 1961).

25 Robert D. Hisrich, "Entrepreneurship-Intrapreneurship," *American Psychologist*, February 1990, 209–222.

26 "Downsized Chickens Come Home to Roost," *Managing Office Technology*, January 1994, 68.

27 R. E. Coleberd, "The Business Economist at Work: The Economist as Entrepreneur," *Business Economics*, October 1994, 54–57.

28 Leslie Brokaw, "How to Start an *Inc.* 500 Company," *Inc. 500 1994*, 51–65; McCune, "The Entrepreneur Express."

29 Roger Ricklefs, "Pros Dare to Go Where Amateurs No Longer Bother," *The Wall Street Journal*, March 31, 1989, B2.

30 Paul Reynolds, "The Truth about Start-ups," *Inc.*, February 1995, 23; O'Reilly, "The New Face of Small Business."

31 The INC. FAXPOLL, *Inc.*, February 1992, 24.

32 "Venture Capitalists' Criteria," *Management Review* (November 1985), 7–8.

33 Lori Bongiorno, "Thanks for the Plug, I Guess," *Business Week*, February 12, 1996, 8; Rachel Beck, "Quirky Catalog on Air," *The Tennessean*, November 14, 1996, 1E, 4E; Arthur Salm, "Public Eye," *San Diego Union Tribune*, August 22, 1995, E2; Diane Cyr, "In Pursuit of Peterman," *Catalog Age*, V. 10, no. 7, July 1993, 131–136.

34 Echo Montgomery Garrett, "The Twenty-First-Century Franchise," *Inc.*, January 1995, 79–88.

35 Meg Whittemore, "Four Paths to Franchising," *Nation's Business*, October 1989, 75–85; and Nancy Croft Baker, "Franchising into the '90s," *Nation's Business*, March 1990, 61–68.

36 Garrett, "The Twenty-First-Century Franchise."

37 Kuehl and Lambing, *Small Business: Planning and Management*, Chapter 5.

38 Alessandra Bianchi, "New Businesses: Incubator Update," *Inc.*, January 1993, 49.

39 Bradford McKee, "Managing Your Small Business: Using Incubators as Steppingstones to Growth," *Nation's Business*, October 1991, 8.

40 Thomas S. Bateman and Carl P. Zeithaml, *Management Function and Strategy* (Homewood, Ill.: Irwin, 1990).

41 Benjamin M. Oviatt and Patricia Phillips McDougall, "Global Start-ups: Entrepreneurs on a Worldwide Stage," *Academy of Management Executive* 9, no. 2 (1995), 30–44.

42 Richard Poe and Duncan Anderson, "Gold Rush," *Success*, September 1990, 33–47; and Amy Barrett, "It's a Small (Business) World," *Business Week*, April 17, 1995, 96–101.

43 Carla A. Fried, "Nine Ways to Boost Your Profits," *Money*, Money Guide 1994 edition, January 1994, 8.

44 Oviatt and McDougall, "Global Start-ups."

45 William J. Holstein and Kevin Kelly, "Little Companies, Big Exports," *Business Week*, April 13, 1992, 70–72; and Albert G. Holzinger, "Reach New Markets," *Nation's Business*, December 1990, 18–35.

46 "Want to Go Global? Here's Where to Find Help," *Business Week*, April 17, 1995, 101.

47 Albert G. Holzinger, "Paving the Way for Small Exporters," *Nation's Business*, June 1992, 42–43.

48 Elizabeth Conlin, "Unlimited Partners," *Inc.*, April 1990, 71–79.

49 Kuehl and Lambing, *Small Business*.

50 Carrie Dolan, "Entrepreneurs Often Fail as Managers," *The Wall Street Journal*, May 15, 1989, B1.

51 "Profiting from Pain," *Success*, February 1, 1996, 28; Linda Deutsch, "Fuhrman Says He Never Met Accuser," *The Fort Worth Star-Telegram*, March 10, 1995, 1; "Local Business News in Review," *Austin American-Statesman*, September 7, 1996, 5; R. Michelle Breyer, Austinite Sells Relax the Back," *Austin American-Statesman*, September 5, 1996, D1.

52 Bruce Schoenfeld, "Hit Men," *Your Company*, spring 1995, 24–28.

53 Barbara Bobo, "Building a Business Using Contractors," *Nation's Business*, June 1995, 6.

54 Michael Barrier, "The Changing Face of Leadership," *Nation's Business*, January 1995, 41–42.

55 Udayan Gupta and Jeffrey A. Tannenbaum, "Labor Shortages Force Changes at Small Firms," *The Wall Street Journal*, May 22, 1989, B1, B2; "Harnessing Employee Productivity," *Small Business Report*, November 1987, 46–49; and Molly Klimas, "How to Recruit a Smart Team," *Nation's Business*, May 1995, 26–27.

56 Dale D. Buss, "Coping with Faster Change," *Nation's Business*, March 1995, 27–29.

57 Shu Shu Costa, "100 Years and Counting," *American Management Association*, December 1994, 32–34.

58 Minda Zetlin, "Off the Beaten Path," *American Management Association*, December 1994, 28–31.

59 Kuratko and Hodgetts, *Entrepreneurship*.

60 Gifford Pinchot III, *Intrapreneuring* (New York: Harper & Row, 1985).

61 Ibid.

62 James S. Hirsch, "Kodak Effort at 'Intrapreneurship' Fails," *The Wall Street Journal*, August 17, 1990, B1.

63 Plotkin, "Riches from Rags."

Contributing to the Community—La Madeleine

What is a socially responsible corporation? How do the concepts of corporate vision and community contribution fit? Patrick Esquerré states that his French bakeries are not part of a restaurant chain. Rather he describes each of them as "a French bakery on the corner" that provides a homey place to eat for its "guests."

Esquerré's vision of la Madeleine is "to be as close as possible to our guests, and to our associates—the people working inside the company—in order to inspire whatever needs to be done to make them feel good, to make each person feel special." What does this mean in terms of actions? Esquerré actually designed the first la Madeleine bakery and restaurant by listening to people who walked by as construction began. When they commented that they hoped there would be a wood burning stove, he made sure there was. When he asked passersby about what they thought a French bakery should have and they answered "wood beams in the ceiling," these were installed as well.

Esquerré sees his guests as the leaders of the organization. His customers decide what they want, how they want it, and even at what price. How does he view his own job? "My job is to listen to these leaders; to adapt to their tastes as much as I can without compromising on key issues; and, to surprise them by going beyond what they expect."

This unique leader sees his "guests" and associates (employees) as part of his family. One of Esquerré's priorities is to make sure that his associates are recognized for their good work as often as possible. It is important to him, for example, that associates know there is a chance for advancement and promotion within their firm. In addition, he uses a bonus plan to reward excellent performance and to increase motivation. Perhaps even more important is the fact that as part of the "orientation" program, all managers who begin a career at la Madeleine are taken to France to be given an opportunity to experience French life. This experience helps to guide them in their jobs. Managers-of-the-Year are rewarded with a free trip to France with their spouses. The managers at la Madeleine are those very people who must listen, adapt, and surprise their guests!

Esquerré also pays attention to the needs of the communities in which the bakeries are located. He and his associates regularly participate in local fundraising activities. Bill Buchanan, one of Esquerré's managers, commented, "The environment that Patrick Esquerré provides for everyone is one in which you can be successful, care for others, and give back to the community in particular—this has made an impact on my own management style, as well as how I conduct my life."

One of the company's programs is a joint effort between the local Public Broadcasting Service station, la Madeleine, and the local food bank. Esquerré makes a fresh food donation to the neighborhood food bank equivalent to 50 percent of total PBS pledges. This tends to increase overall giving to PBS as people understand that the value of their donations is increased through the program. The company has donated over $200,000 of food in a given year.

Contributions, however, are not the only way that la Madeleine is involved in community efforts. Esquerré, along with other managers, frequently takes truckloads of baked goods into the streets to feed the homeless. One manager noted that he had gone with Patrick Esquerré on a weekend to the parking lot right behind City Hall in Dallas to hand out food, coffee, and orange juice to people "who have no other means."

Does la Madeleine have no concern about its bottom line? The corporate philosophy is that you worry about the bottom line by focusing on the top—building sales and maintaining strong involvement with the community, making sure that people want to come to your bakery. Rather than focusing on the short run, la Madeleine and Patrick Esquerré focus on community and the long run—in doing so, he has developed a highly successful and growing enterprise.

QUESTIONS

1 Describe the way in which Esquerré's vision for la Madeleine affects the way he views stakeholders—customers, associates, and the local communities.

2 Describe the corporate culture at la Madeleine. How would your behavior as a manager be affected by this organization's culture?

3 Can you think of any examples of firms in your own community that are recognized as socially responsible? How has this affected their success in their location?

REFERENCES

L. Stones and K. Lynn, "Entrepreneurism + Customer Service = Success," *Management Review* (November 1993), 38–44.

VIDEO CASE

The Environment at the Center of EC Policy

The European Community (EC) was created after World War II to peacefully unite nations of Europe in their efforts to recover economically and to grow. In mid-February 1992, approximately 40 years after the birth of the European Community, the twelve member nations signed the Treaty on European Union, often called the Maastricht Treaty. This document calls for the establishment of a common European currency by 1999, introduces important citizens' rights, gives new powers to the European Parliament, and introduces common environmental, foreign, and security policies. On the first of January, 1993, in accordance with the Single European Act, Europe formally became a single market with no internal barriers. The hope of this group of nations is that by joining together to form a single market, they will be more able to compete on a worldwide basis.

How will these European nations, and others that want to join the EC, create a united market? Each member must adopt EC legislation regarding economic issues, monetary policy, labor policies, the sharing of research and technological development, as well as environmental protection. The growth in the production and movement of goods, in addition to the relocation of industries has significant effects on the environment. Firms already face new demands as a result of the need for better environmental protection. One example is the EC's eco-labeling regulation.

Environmental issues have risen to the top of the agenda for both European governments and business. The Fifth Action Programme of the European Community on the Environment deals with the issue of the sustainability of a healthy environment. A major policy development is the Council Regulation concerning a Community Award Scheme for an Eco-Label (1992). The Fifth Action Programme shows a shift in EC policy toward market-based, voluntary methods that will motivate a shared responsibility between the European Commission, business, and consumer interests. For these policies to work, both businesses and consumers must be educated about environmental policy.

What is an eco-label? This scheme builds on the idea of green purchasing—that consumers will support those businesses who manufacture products that do not harm the environment. The eco-labeling process includes:

- Identification of specific product categories
- Selection of criteria on which the products will be evaluated
- Testing to see if products are ecologically sound
- Awarding an "eco-label" to products that meet or exceed the standards

The EC's goals for this program are to provide consumers with "green guidance," and to encourage European firms to incorporate the environmental factor into their strategies with the hope of improving their competitive position in the world market. Will this type of voluntary, educational program work? Clearly, the agencies involved must have some credibility with both European businesses and their consumers. What consumers want is a simple symbol that indicates the "eco-friendliness" of the products. The benefit for business is that they have the freedom and incentives to design products in ways that will improve their attractiveness to at least one part of their market. From the EC's perspective, a program such as eco-labeling moves away from regulation of business by government and instead provides government support for business self-regulation.

Many questions remain unanswered about this type of program. Because each nation will have its own board that awards eco-labels, will consistent decisions be made by the EC members? Will small businesses be discriminated against because of their lesser in-house research capabilities? Will the eco-labels have the desired impact on consumers' purchasing patterns? These questions will be answered in 1997 when the EC begins evaluating for the eco-labeling program.

QUESTIONS

1 What kinds of environmental uncertainties exist for the EC as it moves towards a more unified market?
2 Does the level of concern the European Community demonstrates for the environment fit with current trends in the behavior of consumers?
3 What particular challenges do you believe will be most difficult for the EC to overcome as it works to implement its eco-labeling practice?

REFERENCES

Commission of the European Communities, ed., *The European Community 1992 and Beyond,* Luxembourg: Office for Official Publications of the European Communities (1992).

N. Watts, "The Eco-Labeling Regulation," *EIU European Trends,* no. 2 (1992), 68–74.

VIDEO CASE

Two Artists or Two Executives?
The Story of Two Women Boxing

In 1983, a new venture was born when artist Linda Finnell was commissioned by a non-profit photography gallery to make boxes to be used as artists' portfolios. With her best friend and fellow artist, Julie Cohn, these two women handmade each box while sitting in the middle of Linda's living room. For three more years, the two friends worked together making and selling boxes, cards, and small books before deciding to hire a small number of employees and expand into a retail business. However, hiring employees was a big step. As Julie remarked, "We never thought it would be the way it is right now. I think we really thought it would be the Julie and Linda club forever."

As artists, both women had experienced the challenges, frustrations, and rewards of creating art and then negotiating with galleries for its display and sale. In the mid-80s, Julie and Linda decided that by focusing their joint energy on a business, they could create the life they wanted. They would be the design force behind the art products made by their company, and from the business, they would attain stable, and later, growing incomes. Starting with a capital infusion of only $400, by the early 1990s, the company was grossing nearly half a million dollars.

The early years meant a lot of hard selling as well as finding contract sales representatives to handle additional geographic regions and trade shows at which their company's work was displayed. Once a part-time office manager was hired along with more women in production, Julie and Linda increased the amount of time they spent on designing new products. Still, the day-to-day business details demanded their attention.

Because of the small, family-like nature of Two Women Boxing, policies regarding employees tended to be set with the employees' needs in mind. The women on the production line have always worked at their own pace and set their own schedules. This, in part, fits well with the nature of one-of-a-kind handicrafts. On the other hand, as the demand for higher volume and rapid delivery has increased, this type of flexibility is more costly to the business. A new piece rate pay system provides an incentive for helping to meet the production schedule. Currently, the production manager is working to create production jobs with more autonomy. This means that the employees are beginning to handle the ordering of materials, shipping, and some design elements. This new system clearly demands a fairly high level of cross-training, something that has always been part of this small firm. But it also demands more of the employees. As Julie noted, "The people who will work out well are the self-starters."

The pull between a completely employee-centered work environment and the needs of the business has at times created tension for the owners. "That's been one of the hardest things in the business—to be an employer and to try to play out both sides of what it must be like to be the person who's trying not to hand down rules, but to create a working structure," according to Julie.

By 1996, Two Women Boxing and its founders had hired a small staff of professional managers: two full-time office managers and a production manager. Still, as long as the company maintained a production orientation, Julie and Linda were called upon to handle management, marketing, supplier, and financial concerns. And that's not what they want any longer. These two entrepreneurs "started the business to support their art," and that's what they are working to get back to. Julie and Linda are consciously moving the business away from manufacturing and toward the design side. They are licensing their designs to companies, like Fitz and Floyd of Dallas and Sylvestrie, that make china, giftware, and other "tabletop" items. Although they are proud of their company's work in manufacturing—the competition and costs make it less fun—the design side is their joy. Julie and Linda have been forward thinking over the years and have continuously analyzed the direction of their business. They are therefore well-prepared to move forward on this repositioning of their business.

QUESTIONS

1 At which stage of growth of an entrepreneurial business is Two Women Boxing?

2 How do Julie Cohn and Linda Finnell fulfill the management functions? Give examples. Do these women fit the typical entrepreneur profile?

3 Given the direction that Julie and Linda have chosen to pursue, what planning do you see as necessary in order to increase the likelihood of their success?

VIDEO CASE

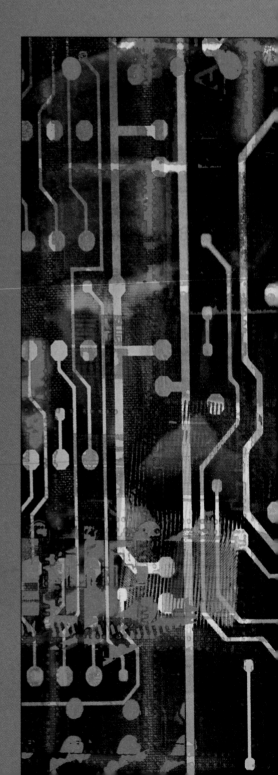

Of all the functions managers perform, without a doubt planning is the most fundamental. Uncertainties in organizational environments—new competition, new technology, and new opportunities—make it critical for managers to set clear goals and plan for alternative courses of action. This does not mean that all plans come to fruition, however. Unless organizations and their managers know where they are headed, they can never achieve their objectives. So, planning is critical for organizations in today's fast-paced business world.

In Chapter 7 we discuss the role of planning in reaching organizational goals. We explore the nature of goals, types of planning, and the importance of strategic management in achieving goals. Chapter 8 extends the discussion of planning by focusing on problem solving and decision making. It also discusses information systems and the ways they assist in daily, as well as strategic, management decisions.

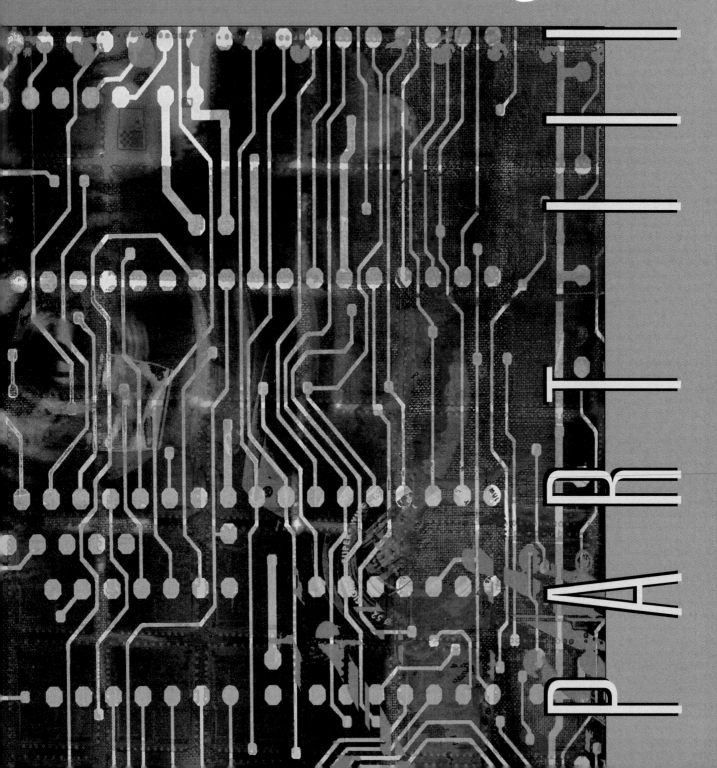

Planning

PART I

Organizational Goal Setting and Planning

LEARNING OBJECTIVES

After studying this chapter, you should be able to

- Define goals and plans and explain the relationship between them.

- Explain the concept of organizational mission and how it influences goal setting and planning.

- Describe the types of goals an organization should have and why they resemble a hierarchy.

- Define the characteristics of effective goals.

- Describe the four essential steps in the MBO process.

- Explain the difference between single-use plans and standing plans.

- Define the components of strategic management.

- Describe the strategic planning process and SWOT analysis.

- Describe business-level strategies, including competitive strategies and product life cycle.

- Enumerate the organizational dimensions used for implementing strategy.

MANAGEMENT PROBLEM

You might have one of their products on your finger, but you probably don't own any of their software. That's because Minneapolis-based Jostens Inc. forgot what business it was in. Somehow the well-known class ring and yearbook maker's planning and strategy went haywire in 1989, when it launched Jostens Learning Corporation. Its 34-year record of continually increasing sales and earnings crashed in 1993 when the bubble burst.

Planners thought the move was smart. After all, they already had excellent distribution channels. Why not expand into educational software, right? The next step was to buy up their biggest competitor and own 60 percent of the market. Foolproof strategy, so it seemed.

But what the planners neglected to consider were the needs of the customers. Jostens' integrated learning software linked all computers to a file system, thus requiring a high start-up cost for schools. Modular step-by-step integration was offered by competitors. By 1993, they had run up a $12 million loss.

Their lack of thoughtful planning and strategy was a recipe for disaster. As one analyst put it, "These were wonderful guys sitting in Minneapolis who went into a business they didn't know and seemed to have to call on the corporate treasury."[1]

• If you were developing the strategy and goals for Jostens, what would you recommend doing now? How can companies avoid this kind of expensive mistake? What should Jostens consider for the future?

It is sometimes difficult for employees and top executives to see the need to contemplate future developments when a company is as successful as Jostens had been. Yet CEO Robert Buhrmaster knows that one of the primary responsibilities of a leader is to decide where he or she wants the company to be in the future and how to get it there.

In some organizations, typically small ones, planning is informal. In others, managers follow a well-defined planning framework. The company establishes a basic mission and develops formal goals and strategic plans for carrying it out. Shell, IBM, Royal LaPaige, Mazda, and United Way undertake a strategic planning exercise each year—reviewing their missions, goals, and plans to meet environmental changes or the expectations of important stakeholders such as the community, owners, or stockholders.

Of the four management functions—planning, organizing, leading, and controlling—described in Chapter 1, planning is considered the most fundamental. Everything else stems from planning. Yet planning is also the most controversial management function. Planning cannot read an uncertain future. Planning cannot tame a turbulent environment. A statement by General Colin Powell offers a warning for managers: "No battle plan survives contact with the enemy." Consider the following comment by a noted authority on planning:

> Most corporate planning is like a ritual rain dance; it has no effect on the weather that follows, but it makes those who engage in it feel that they are in control. Most discussions of the role of models in planning are directed at improving the dancing, not the weather.[2]

In this chapter, we are going to explore the process of planning and whether it can help bring needed rain.

Special attention is given to goals and goal setting, for that is where planning starts. Then the types of plans organizations can use to achieve those goals are discussed. Finally, we will discuss new approaches to planning that emphasize the involvement of

all employees in strategic thinking and execution. The last part of the chapter will look at strategic planning in depth and examine a number of strategic options managers can use in a competitive environment. In Chapter 8, we look at management decision making. Proper decision-making techniques are crucial to selecting the organization's goals, plans, and strategic options.

OVERVIEW OF GOALS AND PLANS

Goals and plans have become general concepts in our society. A **goal** is a desired future state that the organization attempts to realize.[3] Goals are important because organizations exist for a purpose, and goals define and state that purpose. A **plan** is a blueprint for goal achievement and specifies the necessary resource allocations, schedules, tasks, and other actions. Goals specify future ends; plans specify today's means. The word **planning** usually incorporates both ideas; it means determining the organization's goals and defining the means for achieving them. Consider Compaq Computer. When Eckhard Pfeiffer became CEO of Compaq, he set the company on course toward a new goal—to transform itself from a supplier of PCs to corporations into a maker of machines for every market, from small pocket communicators to home computers, all at a highly competitive price. To achieve this outcome, Compaq's plan included both organization and technology components.[4]

Compaq squeezed costs, began running factories around the clock, changed the entire manufacturing system to a "build-on-order" model, and added thousands of retailers, including Wal-Mart, to the distribution scheme. Compaq began working with Microsoft and Novell to become the biggest maker of servers to anchor office networks. In early 1994, Compaq launched the Contura Aero subnotebook, a category of portable PCs, and is heavily involved in new technology for handheld computer devices. By investing in both new organiza-

goal
A desired future state that the organization attempts to realize.

plan
A blueprint specifying the resource allocations, schedules, and other actions necessary for attaining goals.

planning
The act of determining the organization's goals and the means for achieving them.

tion and new technology, Pfeiffer engineered a stunning turnaround at Compaq in only two years.

Exhibit 7.1 illustrates the levels of goals and plans in an organization. The planning process starts with a formal mission that defines the basic purpose of the organization, especially for external audiences. The mission is the basis for the strategic (company) level of goals and plans, which in turn shapes the tactical (divisional) level and the operational (departmental) level.[5] Planning at each level supports the other levels.

The Importance of Goals and Plans[6]

Developing explicit goals and plans at each level illustrated in Exhibit 7.1 is important because of the external and internal messages they send. These messages go to both external and internal audiences and provide important benefits for the organization.

Legitimacy. An organization's mission describes what the organization stands for and its reason for existence. It symbolizes legitimacy to external audiences such as

"Leadership through Exceptional Customer Service"—the *mission statement* for Lennox International, Inc.—tells the world what the company stands for and symbolizes its *legitimacy*—the reason for its existence. It also serves as a *motivational* tool for employees, each of whom carries an embossed card bearing the mission statement as a reminder of the goal. Lennox knows effective service to the external environment is the result of an effective, confident, and goal-oriented workforce such as the employees pictured here.

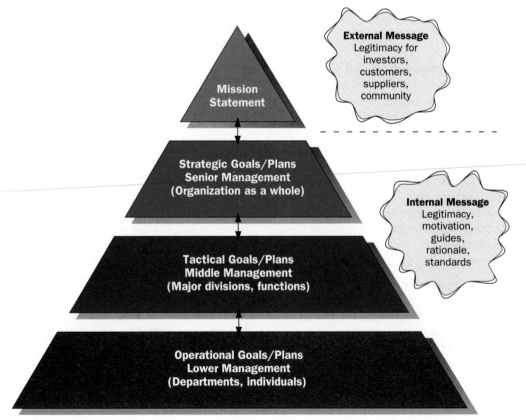

EXHIBIT 7.1
Levels of Goals/Plans and Their Importance

investors, customers, and suppliers. The mission helps them and the local community look on the company in a favorable light and, hence, accept its existence. A strong mission also has an impact on employees, enabling them to become committed to the organization because they can identify with its overall purpose and reason for existence. Consider the situation at Main Street Muffins. Things went great when the company first began branching out into new lines of business. However, new opportunities turned into problems when employee morale sank so low that bakers were calling in sick at 3 A.M. or walking off the job with no notice. The company took a nosedive toward bankruptcy before the owners developed a mission statement to remind themselves that the main goal of Main Street Muffins was "to profitably improve an organization that overwhelms the food industry with its devotion to high-quality products and services." With the new mission statement as a guide, employee morale gradually improved, and the company became profitable again within three months.[7]

Source of Motivation and Commitment. A goal statement describes the purpose of the organization or subunit to employees. A goal provides the "why" of an organization's or subunit's existence. A plan tells employees what actions to undertake. A plan tells "how" to achieve the goal. Goals and plans facilitate employees' identification with the organization and help motivate them by reducing uncertainty and clarifying what they should accomplish.

Guides to Action. Goals and plans provide a sense of direction. They focus attention on specific targets and direct employee efforts toward important outcomes.

Diane White's initial goal to provide goods that reflected African-American heritage only later became a compelling vision to become an entrepreneur.

BLACKBERRY STORES

Because her friend could not find an African-American doll, World Bank financial analyst Diane White saw a market failure. Maybe she could open a store, she reasoned. As a start, she got a part-time job in a gift store specializing in African items. By 1989 she and a friend put together $12,000 and opened the small Blackberry store in Prince George's County, Maryland mall. Within a month, they had more than recouped their investment cost.

By 1992 she opened her second store, but was evicted soon because the mall owners did not think her merchandise was "upscale" enough. Diane decided to fight. Some of her customers were connected to the media and before long she got coverage on radio, TV, and newspapers, causing the mall owners to rescind her eviction. Other locations, including prime space in the Manhattan Macy's, gave White $1 million in 1995 revenues.

After four years in the business, White finally sees herself as an entrepreneur and is pursuing it full time. Her goal is to make Blackberry a national chain with $100 million annual revenues. She doesn't miss the security of her 9–5 World Bank job, for she loves the entrepreneur's "power to have a vision and execute it." She says, "If you're lucky, you can have a few things in life that you really feel passionate about."[8] ■

Rationale for Decisions. Through goal setting and planning, managers learn what the organization is trying to accomplish. They can make decisions to ensure that internal policies, roles, performance, structure, products, and expenditures will be made in accordance with desired outcomes. Decisions throughout the organization will be in alignment with the plan.

Standard of Performance. Because goals define desired outcomes for the organization, they also serve as performance criteria. They provide a standard of assessment. If an organization wishes to

grow by 15 percent, and actual growth is 17 percent, managers will have exceeded their prescribed standard. Ed Woolard defined a goal at Du Pont of nurturing high-potential businesses while strengthening old-line businesses to produce an average return on equity of 16 percent. However, formerly fast-growing electronics businesses fell flat, and return on equity plunged to 8.3 percent. Du Pont did not meet its standard of performance for this goal.[9]

The overall planning process prevents managers from thinking merely in terms of day-to-day activities. When organizations drift away from goals and plans, they typically get into trouble. This occurred at Amex Life Assurance, an American Express subsidiary based in San Rafael, California. A new president implemented a strong planning system that illustrates the power of planning to improve organizational performance.

AMEX LIFE ASSURANCE

Sarah Nolan knew that the chairman of American Express was a self-professed maniac on quality. But when Nolan arrived as the new president of Amex Life Assurance, she found a paperwork assembly line that served customers at a snail's pace. A simple change of address took two days; sending out a new policy took at least ten. Training of new employees took three months. Nolan's primary goal was to get everyone at Amex working together while keeping the focus on the customer. She sent five managers representing different specialties to an empty office park and told them to imagine they were setting up an entirely new business. Nolan gave the group only three rules to follow in their task of redesigning the operation:

1 Put the customer first.
2 Don't copy anything we do here.
3 Be ready to process applications yourselves in six months.

Karen Gideon, vice president of strategic marketing, wasn't thrilled when she heard that she'd be keying in applications. But Nolan knew that if the managers were going to put customers first, they would have to think differently about front-line clerical workers.

When the planning group returned, ten layers of personnel had been collapsed into three, each of which would deal directly with the public. Fewer employees were needed, so more than one-third were transferred to other divisions. Expenses were cut in half and profitability increased sixfold. Nolan used planning to help managers break out of their focus on day-to-day activities and reorient the company toward its strategic goal of customer satisfaction.[10] ■

GOALS IN ORGANIZATIONS

Setting goals starts with top managers. The overall planning process begins with a mission statement and strategic goals for the organization as a whole.

Organizational Mission

At the top of the goal hierarchy is the **mission**—the organization's reason for existence. The mission describes the organization's values, aspirations, and reason for being. A well-defined mission is the basis for development of all subsequent goals and plans. Without a clear mission, goals and plans may be developed haphazardly and not take the organization in the direction it needs to go. Recall that Main Street Muffins found itself being pulled in so many directions it was coming apart until managers began examining whether goals were consistent with the company's mission. By one estimate, more than half of all companies in the United States now have a formal statement of some kind. Entrepreneurs sometimes have more informal mission statements. When Jerry Yang and David Filo started Yahoo!, their mission was to become "titans of the new media," as described in the Technology for Today box.

mission
The organization's reason for existence.

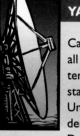

TECHNOLOGY FOR TODAY
YAHOO!

Called the "granddaddy of all search engines," the Internet directory Yahoo! was started by two Stanford University graduate students, Jerry Yang, 27, and David Filo, 30, who now say their motivation was procrastination. They looked for a fun way to consume time and avoid studying, ending up compiling a computerized list of favorite online destinations. Using Stanford's mainframe computer, they shared their list with fellow students. Without any advertisements, "hits" or visitors to their workstation in the engineering department doubled every month from the beginning. After a while, Stanford administrators' frustration level peaked as the workstation traffic kept crashing the university computer, and the students were told to get their "thing" off campus.

Without much effort, the two students found a venture capitalist who easily saw the commercial value of their endeavor, which was already logging one million visitors a week in 1994. Spurning lucrative offers from Netscape and America Online, the two partners decided to become mammoth media giants or "titans."

Campus populations are turning out more online entrepreneurs and becoming part of the U.S. "metaphysical resource" development. In fact, as Williams College economics professor Dick Sabot says, a Web venture without young people involved makes potential investors think "you don't know what you're talking about." Sabot conducted a class survey which showed that 85 percent of students feel that college is not preparing them for the future. Seeing an opportunity, two students, Bo Peabody, 25, and Brett Hershey, 24, located willing investors. They launched Tripod, an Internet site offering complete résumé and job-hunting services for those 18 to 34. With already 50,000 members, the future looks even more positive. Peabody explains that seniors "spend 20 percent of their free time on the Web, but freshmen report spending 80 percent."

SOURCE: Adapted from Hal Plotkin, "Student Uprising," *Inc.*, August 1996, 30–38; and Takuma Amano and Robert Blohm, "The Internet Economy," *Wall Street Journal Europe*, October 23, 1996, 6.

mission statement
A broadly stated definition of the organization's basic business scope and operations that distinguishes it from similar types of organizations.

The formal **mission statement** is a broadly stated definition of basic business scope and operations that distinguishes the organization from others of a similar type.[11] The content of a mission statement often focuses on the market and customers and identifies desired fields of endeavor. Some mission statements describe company characteristics such as corporate values, product quality, location of facilities, and attitude toward employees. Mission statements often reveal the company's philosophy as well as purpose. The mission statement for a Vermont-based construction company is presented in Exhibit 7.2. Bread Loaf Construction Company devised its three-sentence mission statement as a way to spur continued growth and to close the communication gap between management and employees. A group of 20 employees—hourly and salaried—was given responsibility for devising the mission statement. Each group member interviewed three coworkers. Armed with this information, the team joined company founders on a weekend retreat. The group envisioned the company's future, its potential as a global player, and members' own personal futures. The simple statement relays to both employees and customers Bread Loaf's vision of who it is. The mission statement challenges the status quo, demonstrates a commitment to excellence, focuses on day-to-day priorities, reinforces values, and balances priorities.[12]

Such short, straightforward mission statements describe basic business activities and purposes as well as the values that guide the company. Another example of this type of mission statement is that of Lunar Productions, a Memphis, Tennessee, corporate-video producer with $800,000 in annual sales. Lunar's president, Geordy Wells, is a spiritual man who wanted to reflect Lunar's commitment to honest, ethical business practices:

Honor God in all we do.

Provide excellent and affordable corpo-

rate-video, audio/visual, and broadcast production services to our valued clients.

Communicate with our clients and fellow employees as effectively as we communicate with our audiences.

Make a fair profit.[13]

Because of mission statements such as those of Bread Loaf and Lunar Productions, employees as well as customers, suppliers, and stockholders know the company's stated purpose and values.

Goals and Plans

Broad statements describing where the organization wants to be in the future are called **strategic goals.** They pertain to the

Look who's helping Owens Corning reach its *strategic goal* of becoming a $5 billion global company by the year 2000. Owens Corning recently acquired the global rights to the Pink Panther to help the company build a unified marketing campaign around the world. In addition to the target of $5 billion in sales, the company's long-range plan, referred to as OC 2000, sets forth other goals, including achieving 40 percent of sales outside the United States and attracting and maintaining a diverse workforce.

organization as a whole rather than to specific divisions or departments. Strategic goals are often called *official* goals, because they are the stated intentions of what the organization wants to achieve. Several management scholars have suggested that business organizations' goals must encompass more than profits and that businesses actually suffer when profit and shareholder value become the primary goals. Peter Drucker suggests that organizations focus on eight content areas in developing goals: market standing, innovation, productivity, physical and financial resources, profitability, managerial performance and development, worker performance and attitude, and public responsibility.[14]

Strategic plans define the action steps by which the company intends to attain strategic goals. The strategic plan is the blueprint that defines the organizational activities and resource allocations—in the form of cash, personnel, space, and facilities—required for meeting these targets. Strategic planning tends to be long term and may define organizational action steps from two to five years in the future. The purpose of strategic plans is to turn organizational goals into realities within that time period.

As an example, a small company wanted to improve its market share from 15 percent to 20 percent over the next three years. This strategic goal was pursued through the following strategic plans: (1) allocate resources

strategic goals
Broad statements of where the organization wants to be in the future; pertain to the organization as a whole rather than to specific divisions or departments.

strategic plans
The action steps by which an organization intends to attain its strategic goals.

EXHIBIT 7.2
Mission Statement for Bread Loaf Construction Co.

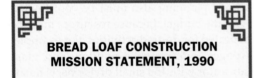

BREAD LOAF CONSTRUCTION MISSION STATEMENT, 1990

WE ARE BREAD LOAF, A FAMILY OF BUILDING PROFESSIONALS DEDICATED TO AND EMPOWERED BY THE STRENGTH OF OUR PEOPLE

WE SEEK CHALLENGES TO CREATE INNOVATIVE SOLUTIONS WHICH MAKE STATEMENTS DEMONSTRATING OUR COMMITMENT TO EXCELLENCE

AS WE GROW INTO THE 21st CENTURY, WE SHALL CONTINUALLY FOCUS UPON EMPLOYEE WELLNESS, COMMUNITY RESPONSIBILITY AND A SENSITIVE BALANCE BETWEEN PERSONAL AND PROFESSIONAL FULFILLMENT.

SOURCE: Used with permission of Bread Loaf Construction Co.

for the development of new, competitive products with high growth potential; (2) improve production methods to achieve higher output at lower costs; and (3) conduct research to develop alternative uses for current products and services.[15]

The results that major divisions and departments within the organization intend to achieve are defined as **tactical goals.** These goals apply to middle management and describe what major subunits must do in order for the organization to achieve its overall goals. For example, Lunar Productions might have a tactical goal of "communicating in writing with clients and customers via newsletter once a month." This tactical goal is one part of achieving the strategic goal of communicating effectively with clients and employees.

Tactical plans are designed to help execute major strategic plans and to accomplish a specific part of the company's strategy.[16] Tactical plans typically have a shorter time horizon than strategic plans—over the next year or so. The word *tactical* comes from the military. For example, strategic weapon systems, such as intercontinental ballistic missiles or the B-2 Stealth Bomber, are designed to deliver major blows to the enemy. These weapon systems reflect the country's overall strategic plan. Tactical weapon systems, such as fighter airplanes, are used to achieve just one part of the overall strategic plan. Tactical plans define what the major departments and organizational subunits will do to implement the overall strategic plan. Normally, it is the middle manager's job to take the broad strategic plan and identify specific tactical actions.

The specific results expected from departments, work groups, and individuals are the **operational goals.** They are precise and measurable. "Process 150 sales applications each week," "achieve 90 percent of deliveries on time," "reduce overtime by 10 percent next month," and "develop two new elective courses in accounting" are examples of operational goals.

Operational plans are developed at the lower levels of the organization to specify action steps toward achieving operational goals and to support tactical plans. The operational plan is the department manager's tool for daily and weekly operations. Goals are stated in quantitative terms, and the department plan describes how goals will be achieved. Operational planning specifies plans for supervisors, department managers, and individual employees. For example, Du Pont has a program called Individual Career Management that involves a series of discussions that define what each manager's new goals should be and whether last year's operational goals were met. At Du Pont the goals are set as high as possible to stretch the employee to ensure continued improvement. These year-end discussions also provide the basis for rewards to those who have excelled.[17]

Schedules are an important component of operational planning. Schedules define precise time frames for the completion of each operational goal required for the organization's tactical and strategic goals. Operational planning also must be coordinated with the budget, because resources must be allocated for desired activities. For example, Apogee Enterprises, a window and glass fabricator with 150 small divisions, is fanatical about operational planning and budgeting. Committees are set up that require inter- as well as intradivisional review and challenge of budgets, profit plans, and proposed capital expenditures. Assigning the dollars makes the operational plan work for everything from hiring new salespeople to increasing travel expenses.

Hierarchy of Goals

Effectively designed organizational goals fit into a hierarchy; that is, the achievement of goals at low levels permits the attainment of high-level goals. This is called a *means-ends chain* because low-level goals lead to accomplishment of high-level goals. Operational goals lead to the achievement of tactical goals, which in turn lead to the attainment of strategic goals. Strategic goals are traditionally considered the responsibility of top

---

tactical goals
Goals that define the outcomes that major divisions and departments must achieve in order for the organization to reach its overall goals.

tactical plans
Plans designed to help execute major strategic plans and to accomplish a specific part of the company's strategy.

operational goals
Specific, measurable results expected from departments, work groups, and individuals within the organization.

operational plans
Plans developed at the organization's lower levels that specify action steps toward achieving operational goals and that support tactical planning activities.

management, tactical goals that of middle management, and operational goals that of first-line supervisors and workers. However, as we will discuss later in the chapter, the shrinking of middle management combined with a new emphasis on employee empowerment has led to a greater involvement of all employees in goal setting and planning at each level.

An example of a goal hierarchy is illustrated in Exhibit 7.3. Note how the strategic goal of "Excellent service to customers"

translates into "Open one new sales office" and "Respond to customer inquiries within two hours" at lower management levels.

CRITERIA FOR EFFECTIVE GOALS

To ensure goal-setting benefits for the organization, certain characteristics and guidelines should be adopted. The characteristics

EXHIBIT 7.3
Hierarchy of Goals for a Manufacturing Organization

Mission

Manufacture both standard and custom metal products for various applications in the machine tool industry

Strategic Goals

President
12% return on investment
5% growth
No employee layoffs
Excellent service to customers

Tactical Goals

Finance V.P.	**Production V.P.**	**Marketing V.P.**
Keep outstanding accounts below $500,000	Manufacture 1,200,000 products at average cost of $19	Sell 1,200,000 units at average price of $27
Keep borrowing below $1,250,000	Scrap rate of 3% or less	Introduce 1 new product line
Provide monthly budget statements for departments	Increase manufacturing productivity by 2%	Increase sales by 5% in new market areas
Have delinquent accounts of no more than 2% of total	Resolve employee grievances within 3 working days	Open 1 new sales office
		Attain market share of 19%

Operational Goals

Accounts Receivable Manager	**Supervisor—Automatic Machines**	**Sales Manager—Region 1**
Issue invoices within 5 days of sale	Produce 150,000 standard units at average cost of $16	Respond to customer inquiries within 2 hours
Check new customers' credit within 1 working day	Have machine downtime of less than 7%	Meet sales quota of 120,600 units
Allow no account to be overdue more than 5 months	Achieve scrap rate of 3% or less	Work with salespeople to:
Call delinquent accounts weekly	Respond to employee grievances within 24 hours	Visit 1 new customer each day
		Call on each customer every 4 weeks

of both goals and the goal-setting process are listed in Exhibit 7.4.

Goal Characteristics

The following characteristics pertain to organizational goals at the strategic, tactical, and operational levels.

Specific and Measurable. When possible, goals should be expressed in quantitative terms, such as increasing profits by 2 percent, decreasing scrap by 1 percent, or increasing average teacher effectiveness ratings from 3.5 to 3.7. Not all goals can be expressed in numerical terms, but vague goals have little motivating power for employees. Granite Rock, which was discussed in Chapter 2, believes in setting lofty goals but emphasizes measurement as a way to anchor those goals in reality, as described in the Focus on Quality box. At the top of the organization, goals often are qualitative as well as quantitative. In July 1992, H. Laurance Fuller, chief executive of Amoco, defined both quantitative and qualitative goals for his organization, including trimming the workforce by 8,500, decentralizing into smaller units, targeting proven energy reserves while cutting wildcatting, and developing and marketing products, such as Amoco's Crystal Clear Ultimate (a cleaner gasoline).[18] Each goal is precisely defined and allows for measurable progress.

Cover Key Result Areas. Goals cannot be set for every aspect of employee behav-

ior or organizational performance; if they were, their sheer number would render them meaningless. Instead, managers should identify a few key result areas—perhaps up to four or five for any organizational department or job. Key result areas are those activities that contribute most to company performance.[19] For example, the marketing department at ALLTEL, a telephone company covering several regions in the United States, identified the following key result areas for which goals were specified: Identify emerging areas of service opportunities, assist regions with meaningful information to support current marketing programs, improve marketing of existing products, and develop a strategic market plan based on customer needs, competitive studies, and market trends.[20]

Challenging but Realistic. Goals should be challenging but not unreasonably difficult. One newly hired manager discovered that his staff would have to work 100-hour weeks to accomplish everything expected of them. When goals are unrealistic, they set employees up for failure and lead to decreasing employee morale.[21] However, if goals are too easy, employees may not feel motivated. Tom Peters, co-author of *In Search of Excellence,* believes that the best quality programs start with extremely ambitious goals that challenge employees to meet high standards. Companies like Rubbermaid and 3M bring out the best in their employees by making goals ever more challenging. 3M's CEO has decreed that 30 percent of sales must come from products introduced in the past four years; the old standard was 25 percent.[22] Managers should, however, make sure that goals are set within the existing resource base, not beyond departments' time, equipment, and financial resources.

Defined Time Period. Goals should specify the time period over which they will be achieved. A time period is a deadline specifying the date on which goal attainment will be measured. A goal of revising a com-

EXHIBIT 7.4
Characteristics of Effective Goal Setting

Goal Characteristics
■ Specific and measurable
■ Cover key result areas
■ Challenging but realistic
■ Defined time period
■ Linked to rewards

FOCUS ON QUALITY
GRANITE ROCK

Granite Rock believes measurement is what it's all about. The volume and accuracy of Granite Rock's measurements helped this small, family-owned manufacturer of construction materials win a Malcolm Baldrige National Quality Award in 1992. Measurement is mandated throughout the company, both inside as well using "report cards" from customers to measure their satisfaction. In the aggregate division, mixtures of different kinds of rock are subjected to statistical process control, a quality-management technique used to ensure that each batch is as nearly identical to every other batch as possible. The company measures not only its profit performance but also its market share. Granite Rock sets baseline goals each year in key result areas. Because surveys revealed that on-time delivery is the customer's highest priority, Granite

Rock measures delivery of every load and carefully tracks the results. Managers emphasize that all this measurement is done for a reason—it makes the company's goals come alive and "organizes the quality process for the entire company."

Far from viewing measurement as a means of controlling employees, Granite Rock believes data can set people free. The company measures processes, not people, and presents the measurements to employees in easily understandable graph formats. "Once they realize that they can affect that graph by their own actions and that there's no stigma attached to making a mistake, they'll try things, and if it goes in the wrong direction, they'll correct it in a hurry," says Val Verutti, Granite Rock's quality-support manager. The company's Individual Personal Development Plan (IPDP), which tracks the progress of workers in meeting individual work-

related goals, is mandatory only for salaried personnel and voluntary for the approximately 380 unionized workers. Nonetheless, overall participation is at 85 percent. One reason participation is so high is that the IPDP is not used to evaluate employees but instead to help them improve. As CEO Bruce Woolpert put it, "If managers are viewed as evaluators, as opposed to people who encourage other people to be better, it's real hard for someone to come up and say, 'I can't read.'" One of Granite Rock's drivers admitted just that to Woolpert, and the company helped him begin attending a class for adult dyslexics once a week. "It turned my life around," said the driver. "It convinced me that I could learn almost anything."

SOURCE: "Granite Rock: A Family Operation Nears Its Centennial," *Stone Review*, October 1996, 6–7; David Franceschi, Quality Director, 1996; Michael Barrier, "Learning the Meaning of Measurement," *Nation's Business*, June 1994, 72–74.

pany's job classification system could have a deadline such as June 30, 1999. If a strategic goal involves a two-to-three-year time horizon, specific dates for achieving parts of it can be set up. For example, strategic sales goals could be established on a three-year time horizon, with a $100 million target in year one, a $129 million target in year two, and a $165 million target in year three.

Linked to Rewards. The ultimate impact of goals depends on the extent to which salary increases, promotions, and awards are based on goal achievement. People who attain goals should be rewarded. Rewards give meaning and significance to goals and help commit employees to achieving goals. Failure to attain goals often is due to factors outside employees' control.

Failure to achieve a financial goal may be associated with a drop in market demand due to industry recession; thus, an employee could not be expected to reach it. Nevertheless, a reward may be appropriate if the employee partially achieved goals under difficult circumstances.[23]

PLANNING TYPES AND MODELS

Once strategic, tactical, and operational goals have been determined, managers may select a planning approach most appropriate for their situation. Critical to successful planning are *flexibility* and *adaptability* to changing environments. Managers use a number of planning approaches. Among

the most popular are management by objectives, single-use plans, standing plans, and contingency (or scenario) plans.

Management by Objectives

Management by objectives (MBO) is a method whereby managers and employees define goals for every department, project, and person and use them to monitor subsequent performance.[24] A model of the essential steps of the MBO process is presented in Exhibit 7.5. Four major activities must occur in order for MBO to be successful:[25]

1 *Setting goals.* This is the most difficult step in MBO. Setting goals involves employees at all levels and looks beyond day-to-day activities to answer the question "What are we trying to accomplish?" A good goal should be concrete and realistic, provide a specific target and time frame, and assign responsibility. Goals may be quantitative or qualitative, depending on whether outcomes are measurable. Quantitative goals are described in numerical terms, such as "Salesperson Jones will obtain 16 new accounts in December." Qualitative goals use statements such as "Marketing will reduce complaints by improving customer service next year." Goals should be jointly derived. Mutual agreement between employee and supervisor creates the strongest commitment to achieving goals. In the case of teams, all team members may participate in setting goals.
2 *Developing action plans.* An *action plan* defines the course of action needed to achieve the stated goals. Action plans are made for both individuals and departments.
3 *Reviewing progress.* A periodic progress review is important to ensure that action plans are working. These reviews can occur informally between managers and subordinates, where the organization may wish to conduct three-, six-, or nine-month reviews during the year.

This periodic checkup allows managers and employees to see whether they are on target or whether corrective action is necessary. Managers and employees should not be locked into predefined behavior and must be willing to take whatever steps are necessary to produce meaningful results. The point of MBO is to achieve goals. The action plan can be changed whenever goals are not being met.

4 *Appraising overall performance.* The final step in MBO is to carefully evaluate whether annual goals have been achieved for both individuals and departments. Success or failure to achieve goals can become part of the performance appraisal system and the designation of salary increases and other rewards. The appraisal of departmental and overall corporate performance shapes goals for the next year. The MBO cycle repeats itself on an annual basis. The specific application of MBO must fit the needs of each company. An example of how one company used MBO to solve safety problems follows.

■ PRODUCERS GAS AND TRANSMISSION

Producers Gas and Transmission Company is a medium-sized refinery and distributor of gasoline and other refinery products. A major concern of top management was an unusually high employee accident rate during the previous year. Ten employees had minor injuries, four were severely injured, and one was killed. The company lost 112 employee days of work due to accidents. Top management discussed the accident rate with department heads and decided on a corporate goal of a 50 percent reduction in all accidents for 1991.

Middle managers developed an action plan that included (1) the establishment of an employee safety training program, (2) the creation of a company-wide safety committee, and (3) a new system of safety recognition. Also, (4) line supervisors were asked to

EXHIBIT 7.5
Model of the MBO Process

develop safety training sessions for their departments within 60 days, and (5) middle managers were given 30 days to nominate supervisors to the safety committee. Finally, (6) the safety committee had 30 days in which to design a safety recognition program, including awards.

Progress was reviewed through the compilation of quarterly safety reports measuring percentage of accidents compared to the previous year. The action plan could be revised if obstacles were discovered. The safety committee appraised the safety performance of each department every 90 days and posted the results for all employees to see. Letters of commendation were given to departments that met or exceeded the 50 percent reduction goal.

At the end of the year, an overall performance appraisal was held for individuals, departments, and the corporation as a whole. Departments that had successfully reduced accidents by 50 percent were given awards (wall plaques). Information about safety procedures and accident rates was used to set a new safety goal for 1992. Delinquent departments were given stringent goals. Most important, the company achieved its 1991 goal of reducing accidents by 50 percent. The MBO system en-

ergized employee actions companywide toward a goal deemed critical by top management. MBO got all employees working toward the same end.[26] ∎

Benefits and Problems with MBO.

Many companies, such as Intel, Tenneco, Black & Decker, and Du Pont, have adopted MBO, and most managers believe that MBO is an effective management tool.[27] Managers believe they are better oriented toward goal achievement when MBO is used. Like any system, MBO achieves benefits when used properly but results in problems when used improperly. Benefits and problems are summarized in Exhibit 7.6.

The benefits of the MBO process can be many. Corporate goals are more likely to be achieved when they focus manager and employee efforts. Performance is improved because employees are committed to attaining the goal, are motivated because they help decide what is expected, and are free to be resourceful. Goals at lower levels are aligned with and enable the attainment of goals at top management levels.

Problems with MBO occur when the company faces rapid change. The environment and internal activities must have some

EXHIBIT 7.6
MBO Benefits and
Problems

Benefits of MBO	Problems with MBO
1 Manager and employee efforts are focused on activities that will lead to goal attainment. 2 Performance can be improved at all company levels. 3 Employees are motivated. 4 Departmental and individual goals are aligned with company goals.	1 Constant change prevents MBO from taking hold. 2 An environment of poor employer–employee relations reduces MBO effectiveness. 3 Strategic goals may be displaced by operational goals. 4 Mechanistic organizations and values that discourage participation can harm the MBO process. 5 Too much paperwork saps MBO energy.

Shewhart Cycle
A planning cycle used in companies that have instituted quality management; also called PDCA—plan, do, check, act—cycle.

single-use plans
Plans that are developed to achieve a set of goals that are unlikely to be repeated in the future.

standing plans
Ongoing plans used to provide guidance for tasks performed repeatedly within the organization.

stability for performance to be measured and compared against goals. When new goals must be set every few months, there is no time for action plans and appraisal to take effect. Also, poor employer–employee relations reduce effectiveness because there is an element of distrust between managers and workers. Sometimes goal "displacement" occurs if employees focus exclusively on their operational goals to the detriment of other teams or departments. Overemphasis on operational goals can harm the attainment of overall goals. Another problem arises in mechanistic organizations characterized by rigidly defined tasks and rules that may not be compatible with MBO's emphasis on mutual determination of goals by employee and supervisor. In addition, when participation is discouraged, employees will lack the training and values to jointly set goals with employers. Finally, if MBO becomes a process of filling out annual paperwork rather than energizing employees to achieve goals, it becomes an empty exercise. Once the paperwork is completed, employees forget about the goals, perhaps even resenting the paperwork in the first place.

Single-Use and Standing Plans

Single-use plans are developed to achieve a set of goals that are not likely to be repeated in the future. **Standing plans** are ongoing plans that are used to provide guidance for tasks performed repeatedly within the organization. Exhibit 7.7 outlines the major types of single-use and standing plans. Single-use plans typically include both programs and projects. The primary standing plans are organizational policies, rules, and procedures. Standing plans generally pertain to such matters as employee illness, absences, smoking, discipline, hiring, and dismissal.

Quality Planning and the Shewhart Cycle. Many companies have instituted standing plans for quality improvement, often based on W. Edwards Deming's 14 points of quality management. Employees are encouraged to participate in the continuous improvement of product and service quality. TQM (total quality management) will be discussed in more detail in Chapter 17. These companies often use the **Shewhart Cycle** of continuous improvement (sometimes called the PDCA—Plan, Do, Check, Act—Cycle), as illustrated in Exhibit 7.8 on page 211. Managers first *plan* a test or change in a specific process, then *do* the test or carry out the change, *check* the results, and finally *act* to improve the process based upon what they learn. A number of cycle iterations may be needed before satisfactory results are achieved. The cycle repeats itself continuously, planning is an ongoing activity, and everyone in the organization can learn from experience and help the company improve.[28]

Single-Use Plans	Standing Plans
Program	***Policy***
■ Plans for attaining a one-time organizational goal ■ May take several years to complete ■ Large in scope; may be associated with several projects **Examples:** Boeing's 777 aircraft NASA space station	■ Broad in scope—a general guide ■ Based on organization's overall goals/strategic plan ■ Defines boundaries within which to make decisions **Examples:** Sexual harassment policies Continuous Improvement Shewhart Cycle
Project	***Rule***
■ Also a set of plans for attaining a one-time goal ■ Smaller in scope and complexity than a program; shorter time horizon ■ Often one part of a larger program **Example:** Development of a rocket booster for NASA space station	■ Narrow in scope ■ Describes how a specific action is to be performed ■ May apply to specific setting **Example:** No-smoking rule in areas of plant where hazardous materials are stored
	Procedure
	■ Sometimes called a standard operating procedure ■ Defines a precise series of steps to attain certain goals **Examples:** Procedures for issuing refunds Grievance procedures

EXHIBIT 7.7
Major Types of Single-Use and Standing Plans

Contingency Plans

Contingency plans, sometimes referred to as *scenarios*, define company responses to be taken in the case of emergencies or setbacks. To develop contingency plans, planners identify uncontrollable factors, such as recession, inflation, technological developments, or safety accidents. To minimize the impact of these potential factors, a planning team can forecast the worst-case scenarios. For example, if sales fall 20 percent and prices drop 8 percent, what will the company do? Contingency plans can then be defined for possible layoffs, emergency budgets, and sales efforts.[29] Studies estimate that fewer than one-fourth of all small businesses survive the loss of their most important manager—the founder. Developing a contingency plan for such a circumstance could help other employees in the business know what to do and keep the company going.[30]

Royal Dutch/Shell Oil has used scenario planning since the 1970s and has been consistently better in its oil forecasts than other major oil companies. Several years ago, contingency planning was used at Shell for dealing with a potential drop in oil prices

contingency plans
Plans that define company responses to specific situations, such as emergencies or setbacks.

EXHIBIT 7.8
The Shewhart Cycle of Continuous Improvement

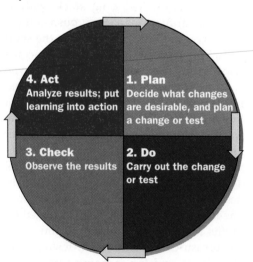

4. Act Analyze results; put learning into action

1. Plan Decide what changes are desirable, and plan a change or test

3. Check Observe the results

2. Do Carry out the change or test

SOURCE: Based on Thomas F. Rienzo, "Planning Deming Management for Service Organizations," *Business Horizons* 36, no. 3 (May–June 1993), 19–29.

that could be catastrophic. Oil was $28 a barrel and rising, but the planning group challenged Shell managers to consider what they would do in the unlikely event that oil suddenly dropped to $15 a barrel. As it turned out, the price of oil *did* drop to $15 a barrel within a few months, and Shell executives were ready because they had developed contingency plans.[31]

PLANNING TIME HORIZON

Organizational goals and plans are associated with specific time horizons. The time horizons are long term, intermediate term, and short term, as illustrated in Exhibit 7.9. *Long-term planning* includes strategic goals and plans and may extend as far as five years into the future. *Intermediate-term planning* includes tactical goals and has a time horizon of from one to two years. *Short-term planning* includes operational goals for specific departments and individuals and has a time horizon of one year or less.

One of the major problems in companies today is the emphasis on *short-term results*. Long-term planning is difficult because the world is so uncertain. Moreover, the financial community, including stock analysts and mutual-fund managers, push companies for strong financial results in the short term. This pressure fits the natural inclination of many result-oriented managers, who are concerned with outcomes for today and next week, not next year and for sure not five years out. These pressures tend to reward short-term performance and undercut long-range planning. For example, a Tennessee manufacturer of temperature control devices badly needed new plants and facilities that required massive expenditures. The managers' bonuses were calculated on profits for a one-year period. In this case, the pressures for short-term results took precedence, and the managers did not invest money in new facilities because short-term profits would suffer.

Focusing too heavily on short-term profitability as a goal has handicapped many U.S. and other Western businesses competing internationally. Japanese companies, by contrast, often take a long-term view and have multiple goals, giving equal weight to market share, profitability, and innovation.[32] Consider Matsushita Electric, the world's largest producer of consumer electronics, VCRs, color televisions, and video cameras. Sixty years ago, Konosuke Matsushita foresaw the day when the United States would provide both major markets and manufacturing centers for his company's small appliances. In 1932 he announced an ambitious 250-year plan for the company, perhaps an all-time record for long-range planning.[33] Long-term planning need not resort to such extremes. Today, senior executives are redirecting Matsushita into four areas where future growth is expected: semiconductors, factory automation, office automation, and audiovisual products. These products generate only 13 percent of sales but are expected to do well in the twenty-first century and so today are receiving 70 percent of the company's research expenditures.[34]

The New Paradigm

Today, some companies are taking decentralized planning to the point of involving workers at every level of the organization in the planning process. In this new paradigm, middle managers and planning staff become facilitators and supporters, working with line managers and front-line workers to develop dynamic plans that meet the organization's needs. In a complex and competitive business environment, traditional planning done by a select few no longer works. Strategic thinking and execution become the expectation of every employee.[35] For an example of a company that is finding hidden sources of ideas and innovation by involving all its workers in planning, consider Springfield Remanufacturing, described in the Focus on Teamwork box.

EXHIBIT 7.9
Planning Time Horizon

Today	1 Year	2 Years	3 Years	4 Years	5 Years and Beyond

Short-Term Planning
(Operational Goals)

Intermediate-Term Planning
(Tactical Goals)

Long-Term Planning
(Strategic Goals)

Start with a Strong Mission. Employee commitment and involvement are critical to helping companies compete in today's rapidly changing world. Some researchers believe a mission or philosophy that permeates daily organizational life is the beginning point. A compelling vision often serves to increase employee commitment and motivation as well as provide a guide for planning and decision making.[36] In a six-year study of exceptional companies that have stood the test of time, including Wal-Mart, 3M, General Electric, and Johnson & Johnson, James C. Collins and Jerry Porras identified a number of timeless fundamentals that helped make these com-

FOCUS ON TEAMWORK
SPRINGFIELD REMANUFACTURING CORPORATION

Jack Stack, chairman and CEO of Springfield Remanufacturing Corp. (SRC), believes companies can thrive by tapping into people's universal desire to win. SRC, which was a division of International Harvester before an employee buyout, is a business Stack calls tough, loud, and dirty—a place "where people work with plugs in their ears and leave the factory every day covered in grease." Stack has built a highly successful company based on the philosophy that "the best, most efficient, most profitable way to operate a business is to give everybody a voice in how the company is run and a stake in the financial outcome, good or bad."

Stack involves every employee in the planning process and uses a bonus system based on hitting the plan's tar-gets. SRC's planning officially kicks off when Stack and other top executives meet with the sales and marketing managers of SRC's 15 divisions in a formal two-day event. But before that meeting, the sales and marketing managers have done their homework by meeting with managers, supervisors, and front-line workers throughout their divisions. If a manager's plan is beyond the plant's capacity, the workers suggest workable alternatives. By the time managers present their plans to the top brass, everyone in the various divisions has had a say and has thus developed a sense of ownership in the plan.

All employees have access to the company's financial data and can compare performance to the plan. SRC has invested heavily in financial education for all workers—everyone learns what's at risk and what's to be gained, and everyone knows how to make a difference. Kevin Dotson, an ex-Marine who works in the Heavy Duty warehouse, says he learns something new about the financial statements every time he goes to a meeting. "It's not like you have just one meeting and learn everything. . . . But you do understand the lines on the statement that you actually affect. That's how you see how you can be more efficient or how we as a small team within a large team can improve so the next group can take the handoff more smoothly. We all have different jobs, but we're all pulling for the same goals."

SOURCE: Michael Kinsman, "CEO Says Layoffs a Sign of Management Failure," *San Diego Union-Tribune*, May 24, 1996, C-1; Jay Finegan, "Everything According to Plan," *Inc.*, March 1995, 78–85.

panies great. They found one of the key factors to be that these companies were guided by a "core ideology"—values and a sense of purpose that go beyond just making money and that provide a guide for behavior. For example, a lot of the faith Johnson & Johnson executives place in decentralized managers can be traced to the well-known Johnson & Johnson Credo, a code of ethics that tells managers what to care about and in what order. Interestingly, in this complex $15 billion organization that has never lost money since going public in 1944, the Credo puts profits dead last on the list of things managers should care about.[37]

Collins and Porras point out that the core ideology must also be balanced with a relentless drive for progress, and they identify ways companies can bring about that drive.[38]

Set BHAGs (Big Hairy Audacious Goals).

BHAGs are outrageously ambitious goals, sometimes called "stretch" goals, that are so clear, compelling, and imaginative that they fuel progress. With his first dime store in 1945, Sam Walton, founder of Wal-Mart, set the BHAG to "make my little Newport store the best, most profitable in Arkansas within five years." Walton set BHAG after BHAG, including the still-pending goal of becoming a $125 billion company by the year 2000. At Compaq Computer, Eckhard Pfeiffer set a BHAG of becoming number one in PC and workstation market share by 1996.[39]

Create an Environment that Encourages People to Experiment and Learn.

Walton valued change, experimentation, and constant improvement, and he implemented concrete mechanisms to encourage it. He gave department managers the authority and freedom to set goals and plans for their own departments as if it were their own business. He gave cash awards and public recognition to employees who contributed valuable ideas that could be reproduced at other stores. He created contests to encourage employees to try creative experiments.

Make Continuous Improvement a Way of Life.

Highly successful companies often make their best moves through constant experimentation and improvement. 3M is a classic example. The company encourages employees to try just about anything and gives them 15 percent of their time to do it. Involving everyone in planning encourages employees to constantly experiment, learn, and grow. At 3M's dental products division, nonmanagement employees attend strategic planning meetings, held town-hall style with the division vice president presiding.[40]

THINKING STRATEGICALLY

The stories of Kmart and Wal-Mart illustrate the importance of strategic planning. They both started in 1962. They looked alike, sold the same products, and even had similar names. The Troy, Michigan-based Kmart stores sat on expensive urban real estate and successfully competed with other big discounters, while Wal-Mart's stores sat in pastures outside small towns and picked off the customers of declining mom-and-pop shops. As recently as 1987, Kmart was way ahead—it had twice as many discount stores, and sales of $25.63 billion far outpaced Wal-Mart's $15.96 billion. The differing fates of Wal-Mart and Kmart can be attributed to corporate strategy.[41] Sam Walton and his successors formulated and implemented strategies that have made Wal-Mart one of America's most successful companies, while Kmart failed to cope with increased competition and changing customer expectations. Kmart's new CEO and other top executives must carefully analyze the situation to formulate a strategy that will suit the organization's strengths as well as fit changing economic times if the chain is to survive in today's competitive environment.

Every organization is concerned with strategy. Hershey developed a new strategy of being a fierce product innovator to com-

pete with Mars in the candy wars. Hershey has scored big with the introduction of such products as "Hugs," a white-chocolate version of the Hershey's Kiss, and "NutRageous," a new candy bar.[42] In the early 1990s, the American Red Cross was forced to reevaluate strategy in the face of the AIDS scare and concerns about tainted blood supplies, government charges of poor record-keeping, and criticism of its preparedness for major disasters such as Hurricane Hugo.[43] Cummins Engine Company's former CEO, Henry B. Schacht, anticipated a decline in the demand for heavy-duty diesel engines and pushed his company into new ventures and new technology. Schacht also adjusted his company's strategy by drastically cutting prices, a step that enabled the company to go toe-to-toe with Japanese competitors while most other American companies in the industry were in full retreat.[44]

All of these organizations are involved in strategic management. They are finding ways to respond to competitors, cope with difficult environmental changes, and effectively use available resources. Research has shown that strategic planning positively affects a firm's performance and financial success.[45] In this section, we focus on the topic of strategic management. First we define components of strategic management and then discuss a model of the strategic management process. Next we examine several models of strategy formulation. Finally, we discuss the tools managers use to implement their strategic plans.

The first part of this chapter provided an overview of the types of goals and plans that organizations use. In this section, we will explore strategic management, which is considered one specific type of planning. Strategic planning in for-profit business organizations typically pertains to competitive actions in the marketplace. In not-for-profit organizations like the Red Cross, strategic planning pertains to events in the external environment. Strategic thinking means to take the long-term view and to see the big picture, including the organization and the competitive environ-

ment, and how they fit together. Understanding the strategy concept, the purpose of strategy, and strategy formulation versus implementation is an important start toward strategic thinking.

What Is Strategic Management?

Strategic management is the set of decisions and actions used to formulate and implement strategies that will provide a competitively superior fit between the organization and its environment so as to achieve organizational goals.[46] Strategic management is a process used to help managers answer strategic questions such as "Where is the organization now? Where does the organization want to be? What changes and trends are occurring in the competitive environment? What courses of action will help us achieve our goals?" Through strategic management, executives define an overall direction for the organization, which is the firm's grand strategy.

strategic management
The set of decisions and actions used to formulate and implement strategies that will provide a competitively superior fit between the organization and its environment so as to achieve organizational goals.

Purpose of Strategy

Within the overall grand strategy of an organization, executives define an explicit **strategy,** which is the plan of action that describes resource allocation and activities for dealing with the environment and attaining the organization's goals. Through this strategy, executives try to develop within the organization a core competence and synergy, thus creating value for their customers.

strategy
The plan of action that prescribes resource allocation and other activities for dealing with the environment and helping the organization attain its goals.

Core Competence.   A company's **core competence** is something the organization does especially well in comparison to its competitors. A core competence represents a competitive advantage because the company acquires expertise that competitors do not have. A core competence may be in the area of superior research and development, mastery of a technology, manufacturing efficiency, or customer service.[47] For example, James River Corporation invested in

core competence
A business activity that an organization does particularly well in comparison to competitors.

state-of-the-art automation that has given it the core competence of being able to produce paper towels and tissues more cheaply than Scott Paper Company and Procter & Gamble. Johnson & Johnson excels at finding new ideas, developing them quickly, and continually improving them. By focusing on its core competence of developing great products, J&J's Vistakon division captured 25 percent of the contact lens market with its Acuvue disposable lenses. Home Depot has achieved a competitive advantage through outstanding customer service from patient, knowledgeable sales clerks.[48]

Synergy.   When organizational parts interact to produce a joint effect that is greater than the sum of the parts acting alone, **synergy** occurs. The organization may attain a special advantage with respect to cost, market power, technology, or management skill. For example, AT&T is attempting to develop synergy between communication services and hardware. Sparked by its 1991 acquisition of NCR, AT&T hopes to fuse voice and data capabilities with sophisticated equipment, enabling corporations to "one-stop shop" for communication services and hardware needed for globalization.[49] Synergy can also be obtained by good relations between suppliers and customers and by strong alliances among companies. Erie Bolt, a small Erie, Pennsylvania, company, teamed up with 14 other area companies to give itself more muscle in tackling competitive markets. Team members share equipment, customer lists, and other information that enables these small companies to go after more business than they ever could have without the team approach.[50] Hammond Enterprises, a seven-employee firm in Marietta, Georgia, designs and produces promotional caps, mugs, and T-shirts for major corporations such as Coca-Cola and Lockheed. Synergy develops because Hammond relieves the corporate giants of the hassle of research, paperwork, and design of logo-bearing promotional items, enabling them to obtain the items at less cost than if they produced the items themselves.[51] Synergy was created between

synergy
The condition that exists when the organization's parts interact to produce a joint effect that is greater than the sum of the parts acting alone.

design talent and love for snowboarding by two entrepreneurs, Erik Anderson and Jeff Sand, of Switch Manufacturing.

■ SWITCH MANUFACTURING

What makes an entrepreneur unique is the ability to turn a nuisance into a business. The nuisance in this case was sitting on their butts in the cold snow. Avid snowboarders Erik Anderson and Jeff Sand were tired of the laborious process of removing their boots from the large, bear-trap bindings and realized there *had* to be a better way.

With over a decade of design experience, they spent two years of evenings and weekends developing a better binding and launched a new business financed by loans from family and friends. Switch Manufacturing patented the design of the Autolock bindings and designed companion boots, as well.

Right after these two moonlighting designers brought Autolock to market in 1995, other, larger companies followed suit with similar systems. Switch was first, but had little time to exploit the time advantage. Their biggest challenge has been to convince consumers of the superiority of their product, no mean feat when up against industry giants with deep advertising pockets.

Switch's strategy became to license its binding, and finally its boot design, as well, in hopes it would become the industry standard. "Once we achieve the critical mass," says Anderson, "everything will work out." Switch was offered $3 million in 1996 to buy 25 percent of the company, and some analysts think it was a mistake to turn it down. The company needs a lot of cash to ward off the competition. The nine patent lawyers employed by the company eat up resources, too.

Still, Switch has advanced beyond the bunny slopes and graduated to the black-diamond trails. Even though 1996 sales are projected at $9 million, the two owners realize they have a long way to catch up with the heavily-resourced competition. But by being in an industry expected to grow 40 percent in the next three years, they may never have to sit on their cold butts again.[52] ■

Value Creation. Exploiting core competencies and attaining synergy help companies create value for their customers. *Value* can be defined as the combination of benefits received and costs paid by the customer.[53] A product that is low in cost but does not provide benefits is not a good value. For example, People Express Airlines initially made a splash with ultra-low prices, but travelers couldn't tolerate the airline's consistently late takeoffs at any price.[54] Delivering value to the customer should be at the heart of strategy. Managers need to understand which parts of the company's operation create value and which do not—a company can be profitable only when the value it creates is greater than the cost of resources. When a company does not accurately appraise its value-creating potential, it may become complacent. McDonald's made a thorough study of how to use its core competencies to create better value for customers, resulting in the introduction of "Extra Value Meals" and the decision to open restaurants in different locations, such as inside Wal-Mart and Sears stores.[55]

Strategy Formulation versus Implementation

The final aspect of strategic management involves the stages of formulation and implementation. **Strategy formulation** includes the planning and decision making that lead to the establishment of the firm's goals and the development of a specific strategic plan.[56] Strategy formulation may include assessing the external environment and internal problems and integrating the results into goals and strategy. This is in contrast to **strategy implementation,** which is the use of managerial and organizational tools to direct resources toward accomplishing strategic results.[57] Strategy implementation is the administration and execution of the strategic plan. Managers may use persuasion, new equipment, changes in organization structure, or a reward system to ensure that employees and resources are used to make formulated strategy a reality.

THE STRATEGIC MANAGEMENT PROCESS

The overall strategic management process is illustrated in Exhibit 7.10. It begins when executives evaluate their current position with respect to mission, goals, and strategies. They then scan the organization's internal and external environments and identify strategic factors that may require change. Internal or external events may indicate a need to redefine the mission or goals or to formulate a new strategy at either the corporate, business, or functional level. The final stage in the strategic management process is implementation of the new strategy.

Situation Analysis

Situation analysis typically includes a search for SWOT—strengths, weaknesses, opportunities, and threats that affect organizational performance. Situation analysis is important to all companies but is crucial to those considering globalization because of the diverse environments in which they will operate. External information about opportunities and threats may be obtained from a variety of sources, including customers, government reports, professional journals, suppliers, bankers, friends in other organizations, consultants, or association meetings. Many firms hire special scanning organizations to provide them with newspaper clippings and analyses of relevant domestic and global trends. Some firms use more subtle techniques to learn about competitors, such as asking potential recruits about their visits to other companies, hiring people away from competitors, debriefing former employees or customers of competitors, taking plant tours posing as "innocent" visitors, and even buying competitors' garbage.[58]

Executives acquire information about internal strengths and weaknesses from a variety of reports, including budgets, financial ratios, profit and loss statements, and surveys of employee attitudes and satisfaction. Managers spend 80 percent of their time

situation analysis
Analysis of the strengths, weaknesses, opportunities, and threats (SWOT) that affect organizational performance.

strategy formulation
The stage of strategic management that involves the planning and decision making that lead to the establishment of the organization's goals and of a specific strategic plan.

strategy implementation
The stage of strategic management that involves the use of managerial and organizational tools to direct resources toward achieving strategic outcomes.

EXHIBIT 7.10
The Strategic Management Process

giving and receiving information from others. Through frequent face-to-face discussions and meetings with people at all levels of the hierarchy, executives build an understanding of the company's internal strengths and weaknesses.

Internal Strengths and Weaknesses.
Strengths are positive internal characteristics that the organization can exploit to achieve its strategic performance goals. *Weaknesses* are internal characteristics that may inhibit or restrict the organization's performance. Some examples of what executives evaluate to interpret strengths and weaknesses are given in Exhibit 7.11. The information sought typically pertains to specific functions such as marketing, finance, production, and R&D. Internal analysis also examines overall organization structure, management competence and quality, and human resource characteristics. Based on their understanding of these areas, managers can determine their strengths or weaknesses vis-à-vis other companies. For example, Marriott Corporation has been able to grow rapidly because of its financial strength. It has a strong fi-

nancial base, enjoys an excellent reputation with creditors, and has always been able to acquire financing needed to support its strategy of constructing hotels in new locations.[59]

External Opportunities and Threats.
Threats are characteristics of the external environment that may prevent the organization from achieving its strategic goals. *Opportunities* are characteristics of the external environment that have the potential to help the organization achieve or exceed its strategic goals. Executives evaluate the external environment with information about the nine sectors described in Chapter 3. The task environment sectors are the most relevant to strategic behavior and include the behavior of competitors, customers, suppliers, and the labor supply. The general environment contains those sectors that have an indirect influence on the organization but nevertheless must be understood and incorporated into strategic behavior. The general environment includes technological developments, the economy, legal-political and international events, and sociocultural changes. Additional areas that might reveal

Management and Organization	Marketing	Human Resources
Management quality	Distribution channels	Employee experience, education
Staff quality	Market share	Union status
Degree of centralization	Advertising efficiency	Turnover, absenteeism
Organization charts	Customer satisfaction	Work satisfaction
Planning, information, control systems	Product quality	Grievances
	Service reputation	
	Sales force turnover	
Finance	**Production**	**Research and Development**
Profit margin	Plant location	Basic applied research
Debt-equity ratio	Machinery obsolescence	Laboratory capabilities
Inventory ratio	Purchasing system	Research programs
Return on investment	Quality control	New-product innovations
Credit rating	Productivity/efficiency	Technology innovations

EXHIBIT 7.11
Checklist for Analyzing Organizational Strengths and Weaknesses

SOURCES: Based on Howard H. Stevenson, "Defining Corporate Strengths and Weaknesses," *Sloan Management Review* 17 (spring 1976), 51–68; and M. L. Kastens, *Long-Range Planning for Your Business* (New York: American Management Association, 1976).

opportunities or threats include pressure groups, interest groups, creditors, natural resources, and potentially competitive industries.

An example of how external analysis can uncover a threat occurred in Kellogg Company's cereal business. Scanning the environment revealed that Kellogg's once-formidable share of the U.S. cold-cereal market had dropped nearly 10 percent. Information from the competitor and customer sectors indicated that major rivals were stepping up new-product innovations and cutting prices. In addition, private-label versions of such standbys as cornflakes were cutting into Kellogg's sales. Kellogg executives used knowledge of this threat as a basis for a strategic response. As a first step, the company boosted national advertising to build its brand names.[60]

The value of situation analysis in helping executives formulate the correct strategy is illustrated by Eastman Kodak Company.

EASTMAN KODAK COMPANY

Blessed with a powerhouse brand name, Kodak was rich, proud, and much admired by consumers. But things haven't been so bright at Kodak lately. In the 1980s, Kodak restructured five times in search of greater efficiency, yet the company earned less in 1993 than it had in 1982. When George M. C. Fisher took over as CEO in late 1993, he developed a new strategic direction for the ailing company that can be explained with SWOT analysis.

Despite its problems, Fisher knew Kodak still had enormous *strengths*, beginning with the trusted brand name and a 70 percent share of the traditional photography market. In addition, Kodak is blessed with technological genius. Over the years, the company has spent billions on research into digital imaging technologies that will almost certainly edge out traditional film in the future.

Kodak also had many visible *weaknesses*, including a dispirited workforce and a stodgy culture focused on protecting current businesses rather than seeking new frontiers. The company was torn between its imaging business and its health-care and household products units, unsure of which businesses it should be pursuing. Product development and marketing ability for Kodak's digital effort were ill-focused and scattered among numerous divisions.

Opportunities arose primarily from Kodak's technological strength. Digital imaging will be a fast-growing market as the traditional photography business continues to slow. In addition, opportunities in Asia plus expansion into barely developed markets such as Russia, India, and Brazil can keep the traditional business moving for at least the next decade. "Half the people in the world have yet to take their

first picture," says Fisher. "The opportunity is huge, and it's nothing fancy. We just have to sell yellow boxes of film."

The biggest *threat* for Kodak is increased competition. Fuji and private-brand film marketers have already cut into Kodak's traditional business. In the digital imaging arena, Kodak faces global competition from giants such as Canon, Casio, Fujitsu, Sony, and Hewlett-Packard as well as hundreds of smaller competitors gearing up for the emerging digital market.

What does SWOT analysis suggest for Kodak's future strategy? To capitalize on the company's strengths and opportunities, Fisher immediately sold the health-care and household products divisions to focus on the core imaging business. Improved communication and stronger leadership have improved morale, and Fisher's emphasis on accountability, quality, quick decision making, enhanced product cycle time, and tying pay to performance is beginning to transform the slow-moving culture. To prepare for the digital future, Fisher has brought together the disjointed talent into a single autonomous division and hired a former computer marketing executive to head it. Moreover, Kodak has begun negotiating a series of alliances with companies such as IBM, Hewlett-Packard, Sprint, and Microsoft so the new division can develop new products in partnership with major powers and be more competitive on a global basis.[61] ■

Business-Level Strategy

Now we turn to strategy formulation within the strategic business unit, in which the concern is how to compete. The same three generic strategies—core competence, synergy, and value creation—apply at the business level, and they are accomplished through competitive actions. Two models for formulating strategy are Porter's competitive strategies and the product life cycle. Each provides a framework for business unit competitive action.

Porter's Competitive Forces and Strategies

Michael E. Porter studied a number of business organizations and proposed that business-level strategies are the result of five competitive forces in the company's environment.[62]

Five Competitive Forces. Exhibit 7.12 illustrates the competitive forces that exist in a company's environment. These forces help determine a company's position vis-à-vis competitors in the industry environment.

1 *Potential new entrants.* Capital requirements and economies of scale are examples of two potential barriers to entry that can keep out new competitors. It is far more costly to enter the automobile industry, for example, than to start a specialized mail-order business.

2 *Bargaining power of buyers.* Informed customers become empowered customers. As advertising and buyer information educate customers about the full range of price and product options available in the marketplace, their influence over a company increases. This is especially true when a company relies on one or two large, powerful customers for the majority of its sales.

3 *Bargaining power of suppliers.* The concentration of suppliers and the availability of substitute suppliers are significant factors in determining supplier power. The sole supplier of engines to a manufacturer of small airplanes will have great power. Other factors include whether a supplier can survive without a particular purchaser, or whether the purchaser can threaten to self-manufacture the needed supplies.

4 *Threat of substitute products.* The power of alternatives and substitutes for a company's product may be affected by cost changes or trends such as increased health consciousness that will deflect buyer loyalty to companies. Companies in the sugar industry suffered from the

growth of sugar substitutes; manufacturers of aerosol spray cans lost business as environmentally conscious consumers chose other products.

5 *Rivalry among competitors.* The scrambling and jockeying for position is often exemplified by what Porter called the "advertising slugfest." As illustrated in Exhibit 7.12, these rivalries are influenced by the preceding four forces as well as by cost and product differentiation. A famous example of competitive rivalry is the battle between Pepsi and Coke. Rivalry between Federal Express and United Parcel Service is becoming almost as fierce as the two companies grapple for dominance of the express delivery business. UPS has rolled out a new 8:30 A.M. delivery, two hours earlier than Federal Express. When Federal Express introduced FedEx Ship, offering a free PC-based system that lets even the smallest customers order pickups, print shipping labels, and track delivery without ever using a telephone, UPS fired back by unveiling a new alliance to enable customers to book orders through Prodigy online services.[63]

Merck has a *business-level strategy* of competing through product innovation. Merck researchers like Amy Cheung and Thomas Rano, using advanced technology, are producing more new compounds in less time than has ever been possible. Merck spends nearly $1.3 billion on research and development and uses every means possible to reduce by months the drug discovery, development, and application processes. Merck maintains a competitive edge by having innovative products in many therapeutic categories for human and animal health.

Competitive Strategies.   In finding its competitive edge within these five forces, Porter suggests that a company can adopt one of three strategies: differentiation, cost leadership, and focus. The organizational characteristics typically associated with each strategy are summarized below.

1 *Differentiation.* The **differentiation** strategy involves an attempt to distinguish the firm's products or services from others in the industry. The organization may use advertising, distinctive product features, exceptional service, or new technology to achieve a product perceived as unique. The differentiation strategy can be profitable because customers are loyal and will pay high prices for the product. Examples of products that have benefited from a differentiation strategy include Mercedes-

Benz automobiles, Maytag appliances, and Tylenol, all of which are perceived as distinctive in their markets. Companies that pursue a differentiation strategy typically need strong marketing abilities, a creative flair, and a reputation for leadership.[64]

A differentiation strategy can reduce rivalry with competitors if buyers are loyal to a company's brand. For example, successful differentiation reduces the bargaining power of large buyers because other products are less attractive, and this also helps the firm fight off threats of substitute products. Differentiation also erects entry barriers in the form of customer loyalty that a new entrant into the market would have difficulty overcoming. Chris Zane worked on differentiating his bicycle business as one with the best service and lowest cost (which also uses Porter's Cost Leadership strategy), as described in the Leading the Management Revolution box.

differentiation
A type of competitive strategy with which the organization seeks to distinguish its products or services from competitors'.

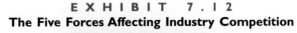

E X H I B I T   7 . 1 2
The Five Forces Affecting Industry Competition

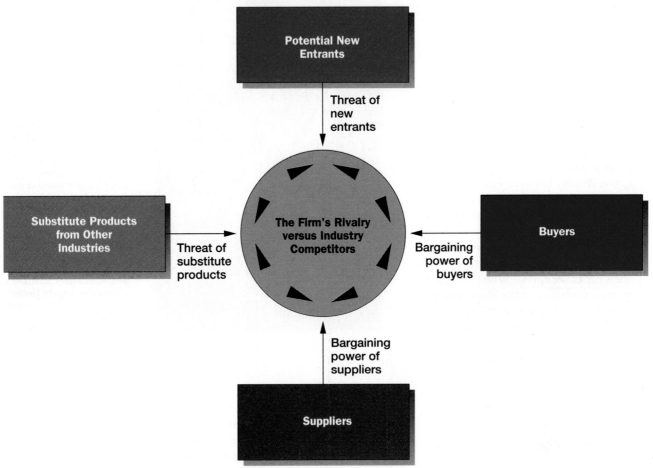

SOURCE: Based on Michael E. Porter, *Competitive Strategy: Techniques for Analyzing Industries and Competitors* (New York: Free Press, 1980).

cost leadership
A type of competitive strategy with which the organization aggressively seeks efficient facilities, cuts costs, and employs tight cost controls to be more efficient than competitors.

2 *Cost Leadership.* With a **cost leadership** strategy, the organization aggressively seeks efficient facilities, pursues cost reductions, and uses tight cost controls to produce products more efficiently than competitors. A low-cost position means that the company can undercut competitors' prices and still offer comparable quality and earn a reasonable profit. Scottish Inns and Motel 6 are low-priced alternatives to Holiday Inn and Ramada Inn. Compaq Computer used a cost-leadership strategy to reach its goal of overtaking IBM as the world's number-one PC supplier. CEO Eckhard Pfeiffer's first priority was to cut costs and prices, not come up with new engi-neering feats. A just-in-time supply chain cuts inventory and manufacturing costs, and Compaq personal computers fly off the production line at a rate of one every ten seconds. Compaq has been cutting costs better than anyone else in the business and is therefore able to supply price-busting products that are creating a huge demand from consumers.[65]

Being a low-cost producer provides a successful strategy to defend against the five competitive forces in Exhibit 7.12. For example, the most efficient, low-cost company is in the best position to succeed in a price war while still making a profit. Likewise, the low-cost producer

LEADING THE MANAGEMENT REVOLUTION
ZANE'S CYCLES

Chris Zane learned the secret of competitive strategies when fixing bikes as a 12-year-old. If you deliver what you promise and put customers first, you can make out pretty well.

As the largest independent bicycle dealer in New Haven, Connecticut, the 30-year-old college-educated Zane will do anything to attract and keep customers in this cut-throat market. Unlike most small operators, his business is growing 25 percent a year. He has turned intimacy and ingenuity into competitive advantages.

His first assault on the competition began ten years ago when he offered one-year service guarantees and he recently shocked the industry by giving

lifetime (of the bike) free service, observing that most free service is done during the first year anyway. Other techniques he has learned are:
1. No more nickel and diming. They stopped charging for any part that costs less than $1. Zane's cost is virtually nil, but the customer loyalty it generates is high, and people usually leave with larger purchases, as well.
2. Community-service marketing. The Zane Foundation, funded by an initial investment and 50 Zane Foundation-labeled candy machines, awards college scholarships to area high school seniors. And never missing a chance to talk to school kids about bike safety, Zane helps the community and gets more exposure.
3. Acting bigger than you really are. A

few years ago he made the strategic decision to commit one-fourth of the advertising budget to a glossy catalog, and he has an 800 number, which is inexpensive to run but gives big impact.
4. Coffee bar and toy corner. In order to maintain the original intimacy of his store, Zane built a play area and coffee bar into his new, larger facility.
5. Former competitors are marketers. By paying the phone company a nominal fee to transfer calls from out-of-business bike shops, Zane fields hundreds of extra calls a month.

SOURCE: Donna Fenn, "Leader of the pack," *Inc.*, February 1996, 31–38.

---

is protected from powerful customers and suppliers, because customers cannot find lower prices elsewhere, and other buyers would have less slack for price negotiation with suppliers. If substitute products or potential new entrants occur, the low-cost producer is better positioned than higher-cost rivals to prevent loss of market share. The low price acts as a barrier against new entrants and substitute products.[66]

3 *Focus*. With a **focus** strategy, the organization concentrates on a specific regional market or buyer group. The company will use either a differentiation or low-cost approach, but only for a narrow target market. Enterprise Rent-A-Car has made its mark by focusing on a market the major companies like Hertz and Avis don't even play in—the low-budget insurance replacement market. Drivers whose cars have been wrecked or stolen have one less thing to worry about when Enterprise delivers a car

right to their driveway. By using a focus strategy, Enterprise has been able to grow rapidly and was named number one in the United States by *Auto Rental News* in late 1994.[67]

Porter found that some businesses did not consciously adopt one of these three strategies and were stuck with no strategic advantage. Without a strategic advantage, businesses earned below-average profits compared with those that used differentiation, cost leadership, or focus strategies.

Product Life Cycle

The **product life cycle** is a series of stages that a product goes through in its market acceptance, as illustrated in Exhibit 7.13. First, a product is developed within the laboratories of selected companies and then is introduced into the marketplace. If the product succeeds, it enjoys rapid growth as consumers accept it. Next is the maturity stage,

focus
A type of competitive strategy that emphasizes concentration on a specific regional market or buyer group.

product life cycle
The stages through which a product or service goes: (1) development and introduction into the marketplace, (2) growth, (3) maturity, and (4) decline.

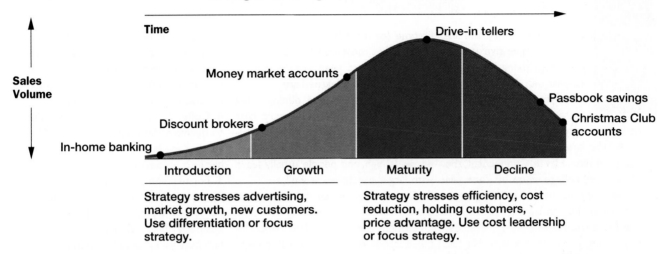

EXHIBIT 7.13
Strategies and Stages of Product Life Cycle

in which widespread product acceptance occurs but growth peaks. Gradually the product grows out of favor or fashion and enters the decline stage.[68]

The life-cycle concept also applies to services, as the banking example in Exhibit 7.13 shows. In-home banking is a new product, and discount broker services is in the rapid growth stage. Money market accounts have been around for a while and are approaching maturity, which is where drive-in tellers are. Passbook savings accounts are in decline, being replaced by money market accounts and certificates of deposit. The Christmas Club accounts are in

serious decline and are available at only a few banks.

Banks and other organizations can tailor strategy to product life-cycle stages.[69] During the introduction and growth stages, differentiation strategy is appropriate, because it stresses advertising, attracting new customers, and market growth. After the product reaches maturity, a low-cost strategy is important, because competitors will have developed products that look and perform similarly. Company strategy for a mature product or service should stress efficiency, reduce overhead costs, and seek a price advantage over competitors.

SUMMARY AND MANAGEMENT SOLUTION

This chapter described several important ideas about organizational planning. Organizational planning involves defining goals and developing a plan with which to achieve them. An organization exists for a single, overriding purpose known as its mission—the basis for strategic goals and plans. Goals within the organization are defined in a hierarchical fashion, beginning with strategic goals followed by tactical and operational goals. Plans are defined similarly, with strategic, tactical, and operational plans

used to achieve the goals. Other goal concepts include characteristics of effective goals and goal-setting behavior.

Several types of plans were described, including strategic, tactical, operational, single-use, standing, and contingency plans, and management by objectives. The Shewhart or PDCA Cycle is used by many companies that have instituted quality management. In the Shewhart Cycle, planning is continuous and everyone can learn and help the company improve. Long-term, intermediate-

term, and short-term plans have time horizons of from five years down to six months.

This chapter also described important concepts of strategic management. Strategic management begins with an evaluation of the organization's current mission, goals, and strategy. This evaluation is followed by situation analysis (called SWOT analysis), which examines opportunities and threats in the external environment as well as strengths and weaknesses within the organization. Situation analysis leads to the formulation of explicit strategic plans, which then must be implemented.

For example, Bill Gates at Microsoft understands the importance of strategy and vision for the company's long-term health. Microsoft employees are inspired by Gates's expansive long-term strategic goal, in which the company's software will be interwoven into the fabric of everyday American life. Gates encourages employee involvement in reaching for the future. In product development meetings, he challenges employees on meeting goals and encourages them to look at new ways of doing things. Microsoft's generous company stock options, combined with Gates's leadership abilities, have helped make employees feel like partners in the firm, and they are committed to helping the company reach its goals.

In the past, planning was almost always done entirely by top managers, but some of today's companies involve workers at all levels in the planning process. However, planning always begins with the support and commitment of top management. At the opening, we discussed Jostens Inc., which had imploded after a 34-year earnings rise. The executives ought to get rid of the hemorrhaging software company and "stick to the knitting" of their main business. Jostens Learning Corp., the bleeding unit that lost $54 million in 1994, was indeed sold in June of 1995. By late 1995, stock prices were up 40 percent from the previous year. Jostens could have avoided this mistake by looking more carefully at its own core competencies. Simply having a distribution system in schools was not enough. They knew virtually nothing about computers and software and should have realized their lack of expertise. Jostens needs to do a long-term strategy development, where they seriously evaluate their core competencies and then determine if there are other products they can competently develop and market.

DISCUSSION QUESTIONS

1 What types of planning would have helped Exxon respond more quickly to the oil spill from the Exxon *Valdez* near Alaska?

2 Write a brief mission statement for a local business. Can the purpose and values of a small organization be captured in a written statement?

3 What strategies could the college or university at which you are taking this management course adopt to compete for students in the marketplace? Would these strategies depend on the school's goals?

4 If you were a top manager of a medium-sized real estate sales agency, would you use MBO? If so, give examples of goals you might set for managers and sales agents.

5 A new business venture has to develop a comprehensive business plan to borrow money to get started. Companies such as Federal Express, Nike, and Rolm Corporation say they did not follow the original plan very closely. Does that mean that developing the plan was a waste of time for these eventually successful companies?

6 A famous management theorist proposed that the time horizons for all strategic plans are becoming shorter because of the rapid changes in organizations' external environments. Do you agree? Would the planning time horizon for IBM or Ford Motor Company be shorter than it was 20 years ago?

7 What are the characteristics of effective goals? Would it be better to have no goals at all than to have goals that do not meet these criteria?

8 Assume Southern University decides to (1) raise its admission standards and (2) initiate a business fair to which local townspeople will be invited. What types of plans would it use to carry out these two activities?

9 Assume you are the general manager of a large hotel and have formulated a strategy of renting banquet facilities to corporations for big events. At a monthly management meeting, your sales manager informed the head of food operations that a big reception in one week will require converting a large hall from a meeting room to a banquet facility in only 60 minutes—a difficult but doable operation that will require precise planning and extra help. The food operations manager is furious about not being informed earlier. What is wrong here?

10 Which is more important—strategy formulation or strategy implementation? Do they depend on each other? Is it possible for strategy implementation to occur first?

11 Perform a situation (SWOT) analysis for the university you attend. Do you think university administrators consider these factors when devising their strategy?

12 What is meant by the core competence and synergy components of strategy? Give examples.

13 Using Porter's competitive strategies, how would you describe the strategies of Wal-Mart, Bloomingdale's, and Kmart?

14 As administrator for a medium-sized hospital, you and the board of directors have decided to change to a drug dependency hospital from a short-term, acute-care facility. Which strategy concepts would you use to implement this strategy?

15 How would functional strategies in marketing, research and development, and production departments differ if a business changed from a differentiation to a low-cost strategy?

MANAGEMENT EXERCISES

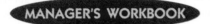

MANAGER'S WORKBOOK

Goal Setting

Consider goals for yourself regarding doing well in this course. What do you need to do in order to get a good grade? Goals should be according to the "Criteria for Effective Goals" in the chapter on pages 206–207. In addition, you need a system to monitor your progress, such as the table below, which shows the types of goals you may choose to select for yourself.

Goals			Class weeks			
	How will you measure and monitor?	First week (from now)	Second week	Third week	Fourth week	
1. 100 percent attendance						
2. Class notes						
3. Read assigned chapters						
4. Outline chapters						
5. Define vocabulary words						
6. Answer end of chapter questions						
7. Complete "Workbook" assignments						
8. Class participation						
9.						
10.						

Your instructor may ask you to turn in your monitor sheets at the end of the course.

I According to goal-setting theory, using and monitoring goals is supposed to help performance. Did do you better as a result of your goals?

2 What did you learn from this that could help you in other classes?

SOURCE: Nancy C. Morey, "Applying goal setting in the classroom," *The Organizational Behavior Teaching Review*, Vol. 11, no 4, 1986–87, 53–59.

MANAGER'S WORKSHOP

Company Crime Wave

Senior managers in your organization are concerned about internal theft. Your department has been assigned the task of writing an ethics policy that defines employee theft and prescribes penalties. Stealing goods is easily classified as theft, but other activities are more ambiguous. Before writing the policy, go through the following list, and decide which behaviors should be defined as stealing and whether penalties should apply. Discuss the items with your department members until agreement is reached. Classify each item as an example of (1) theft, (2) acceptable behavior, or (3) in between with respect to written policy. Is it theft when an employee

• Gets paid for overtime not worked?
• Takes a longer lunch or coffee break than authorized?
• Punches a time card for another?
• Comes in late or leaves early?

• Fakes injury to receive workers' compensation?
• Takes care of personal business on company time?
• Occasionally uses company copying machines or makes long-distance telephone calls for personal purposes?
• Takes a few stamps, pens, or other supplies for personal use?
• Takes money from the petty cash drawer?
• Uses company vehicles or tools for own purposes but returns them?
• Damages merchandise so a cohort can purchase it at a discount?
• Accepts a gift from a supplier?

Now consider those items rated "in between." Do these items represent ethical issues as defined in Chapter 5? How should these items be handled in the company's written policy?

MANAGER'S WORKSHOP

Developing Strategy for a Small Business

Instructions:

I Divide into groups of four to six members. Select a local business with which your group members are familiar.
2 Complete the following activities.

Activity 1—Perform a SWOT analysis for the business.

Activity 2—Write a statement of the business's current strategy.
Activity 3—Decide on a goal you would like the business to achieve in two years, and write a statement of proposed strategy for achieving that goal.
Activity 4—Write a statement describing how the proposed strategy will be implemented.
Activity 5—What have you learned from this exercise?

SWOT Analysis for ____ (name of company)

	Internal (within company)	External (outside company)
Positive	Strengths	Opportunities
Negative	Weaknesses	Threats

SURF THE 'NET

Choose three companies, either in the same industry or three different industries. Search the Internet for information on the companies, including annual reports. In each company, look particularly at the goals expressed. Refer back to the goals shown in Exhibit 7.1 and also Porter's competitive strategies.

	Goals from Exhibit 7.1 articulated	Strategies from Porter used
Company #1		
Company #2		
Company #3		

Questions

1 Which goals seem most important?
2 Look for differences in the goals and strategies of the three companies, and develop an explanation for those differences.
3 Which of the goals or strategies should be changed? Why?

Optional: Compare your table with other students and look for common themes. Which companies seem to articulate and communicate their goals and strategies the best?

ETHICAL DILEMMA

Repair or Replace?

After only a few months in sales at ComputerSource, a full-service computer business, Sam Nolan realized there were serious problems in the software department. Most of the complaints from customers were related to the incorrect selection or installation of the software needed to meet their needs. He discussed the problem with his sales manager, who was part-owner and partner with the head of service for ComputerSource. They were both aware of the problem, but they were facing an industry-wide shortage of qualified software engineers.

Nolan received an urgent call from Katherine Perry, operations manager for Ross & Lindsey, a fast-growing financial management firm that was becoming one of his best accounts. She was calling to report that they were having daily network problems that were interfering with her staff's productivity and morale. She needed an immediate solution to the problem. Like many firms, Ross & Lindsey had a hodge-podge of computer equipment and software on their network. They had bought from a series of vendors, with a patchwork approach to problems.

Nolan realized it would take an expert software engineer days or weeks of work to fix all the bugs in their existing system, which ComputerSource could not afford. A costlier alternative was to recommend a system upgrade, replacing the older hardware and loading a newer software version on the entire network. Perry had already confided that she had pushed her bosses as far as they wanted to go on computer expenditures this year, but Nolan knew she was desperate. He didn't want to risk losing her business, but he didn't trust the software engineers to fix the problems. He was also pretty sure Perry would face the same dilemma at any computer retailer in town.

What Do You Do?

1 Gamble on the service department to fix their existing system, within the limits of their budget and their frustration. If it doesn't work, it is their problem.
2 Recommend a system upgrade to correct the problem, even though it will cost the clients more than they want to pay and may jeopardize future sales.
3 Confide in the clients about your perception of the problem, give them the chance to make an informed choice, and risk having them take their business elsewhere.

CASE FOR CRITICAL ANALYSIS

H.I.D.

Dave Collins, president of H.I.D., sat down at the conference table with his management team members, Karen Setz, Tony Briggs, Dave King, and Art Johnson. H.I.D. owns ten Holiday Inns in Georgia, eight hotels of different types in Canada, and one property in the Caribbean. It also owns two Quality Inns in Georgia. Dave Collins and his managers got together to define their mission and goals and to set strategic plans. As they began their strategic planning session, the consultant they had hired suggested that each describe what he or she wanted for the company's domestic operations in the next ten years— how many hotels it should own, where to locate them, and who the target market was. Another question he asked them to consider was what the driving force of the company should be—that is, the single characteristic that would separate H.I.D. from other companies.

The team members wrote their answers on flip-charts, and the consultant summarized the results. Dave Collins's goal included 50 hotels in ten years, with the number increasing to 26 or 27 in five years. All the other members saw no more than 20 hotels in ten years and a maximum of 15 or 16 within five years. Clearly there was disagreement among the top managers about long-term goals and the desirable growth rate.

With the consultant's direction, the team members began to critique their growth targets. Dave King, director of operations and development, observed, "We just can't build that many hotels in that time period, certainly not given our current staffing, or any reasonable staffing we could afford. I don't see how we could achieve that goal." Art Johnson, the accountant, agreed. Karen Setz then asked, "Could we build them all in Georgia? You know we've centered on the medium-priced hotel in smaller towns. Do we need to move to bigger towns now, such as Jacksonville, or add another to the one we have in Atlanta?" Dave Collins responded, "We have an opportunity out in California, we may have one in New Jersey, and we are looking at the possibility of going to Jacksonville."

The consultant attempted to refocus the discussion: "Well, how does this all fit with your mission? Where are you willing to locate geographically? Most of your operation is in Georgia. Can you adequately support a national building effort?"

Tony Briggs responded, "Well, you know we have always looked at the smaller-town hotels as being our niche, although we deviated from that for the hotel in Atlanta. But we generally stay in smaller towns where we don't have much competition. Now we are talking about an expensive hotel in California."

Dave Collins suggested, "Maybe it's time we changed our target market, changed our pricing strategy, and went for larger hotels in urban areas across the whole country. Maybe we need to change a lot of factors about our company."

Questions

1 What is H.I.D.'s mission at the present time? How may this mission change?

2 What do you think H.I.D.'s mission, strategic goals, and strategic plans are likely to be at the end of this planning session? Why?

3 What goal-setting behavior is being used here to reach agreement among H.I.D.'s managers? Do managers typically disagree about the direction of their organization?

SOURCE: This case was provided by James Higgins.

ENDNOTES

1 Kenneth Labich, "Why Companies Fail," *Fortune*, November 14, 1995, 52–68; and Neal St. Anthony, "'Dutch Auction' is Josten's Ploy To Bolster Its Stock in the Long Term," *Minneapolis Star-Tribune*, August 13, 1995, 1D.

2 Russell L. Ackoff, "On the Use of Models in Corporate Planning," *Strategic Management Journal* 2 (1981), 353–359; and Oren Harari, "Good/Bad News about Strategy," *Management Review*, July 1995, 29–31.

3 Amitai Etzioni, *Modern Organizations* (Englewood Cliffs, N.J.: Prentice-Hall, 1984), 6.

4 Stephanie Losee, "How Compaq Keeps the Magic Going," *Fortune*, February 21, 1994, 90–92.

5 Max D. Richards, *Setting Strategic Goals and Objectives*, 2d ed. (St. Paul, Minn.: West, 1986).

6 This discussion is based on Richard L. Daft and Richard M. Steers, *Organizations: A Micro/Macro Approach* (Glenview, Ill.:

Scott, Foresman, 1986), 319–321; Herbert A. Simon, "On the Concept of Organizational Goals," *Administrative Science Quarterly* 9 (1964), 1–22; and Charles B. Saunders and Francis D. Tuggel, "Corporate Goals," *Journal of General Management* 5 (1980), 3–13.

7 Steven L. Marks, "Say When," *Inc.*, February 1995, 19–20.

8 Robert Maynard, "Cultural Connections," *Nation's Business*, September 1996, 16.

9 Joseph Weber, "Du Pont's Trailblazer Wants to Get Out of the Woods," *Business Week*, August 31, 1992, 70–71.

10 Frank Rose, "Now Quality Means Service Too," *Fortune*, April 22, 1991, 99–108.

11 Mary Klemm, Stuart Sanderson, and George Luffman, "Mission Statements: Selling Corporate Values to Employees," *Long-Range Planning* 24, no. 3 (1991), 73–78; John A. Pearce II and Fred David, "Corporate Mission Statements: The Bottom Line," *Academy of Management Executive* (1987), 109–116; Jerome H. Want, "Corporate Mission: The Intangible Contributor to Performance," *Management Review* (August 1986), 46–50; and Alan Farnham, "Brushing Up Your Vision Thing," *Fortune*, May 1, 1995, 129.

12 Teri Lammers, "The Effective and Indispensable Mission Statement," *Inc.*, August 1992, 75–77.

13 Sharon Nelton, "Put Your Purpose in Writing," *Nation's Business*, February 1994, 61–64.

14 Peter F. Drucker, *The Practice of Management* (New York: Harper & Brothers, 1954), 65–83; and Peter Doyle, "Setting Business Objectives and Measuring Performance," *Journal of General Management* 20, no. 2 (winter 1994), 1–19.

15 "Strategic Planning: Part 2," *Small Business Report* (March 1983), 28–32.

16 Paul Meising and Joseph Wolfe, "The Art and Science of Planning at the Business Unit Level," *Management Science* 31 (1985), 773–781.

17 Kenneth Labich, "Making Over Middle Managers," *Fortune*, May 8, 1989, 58–64.

18 Lois Therrien, "AMOCO: Running Smoother on Less Gas," *Business Week*, February 15, 1993, 110–112.

19 John O. Alexander, "Toward Real Performance: The Circuit-Breaker Technique," *Supervisory Management* (April 1989), 5–12.

20 "Positioning for the 1990s," *Intercom: A Monthly Publication for ALLTEL Employees and Friends*, September 1988, 1–2.

21 Joy Riggs, "Empowering Workers by Setting Goals," *Nation's Business*, January 1995, 6.

22 A. J. Vogl, "Noble Survivors," *Across the Board*, June 1994, 25–30; and Rahul Jacob, "Corporate Reputations," *Fortune*, March 6, 1995, 54–67.

23 Edwin A. Locke, Garp P. Latham, and Miriam Erez, "The Determinants of Goal Commitment," *Academy of Management Review* 13 (1988), 23–39.

24 George S. Odiorne, "MBO: A Backward Glance," *Business Horizons* 21 (October 1978), 14–24.

25 Jan P. Muczyk and Bernard C. Reimann, "MBO as a Complement to Effective Leadership," *The Academy of Management Executive* 3 (1989), 131–138; and W. Giegold, *Objective Setting and the MBO Process*, vol. 2 (New York: McGraw-Hill, 1978).

26 "Delegation," *Small Business Reports* (July 1986), 71–75; and R. Henry Migliore, Constance A. Pogue, and Jeffrey S. Horvath, "Planning for the Future," *Small Business Reports* (July 1991), 53–63.

27 John Ivancevich, J. Timothy McMahon, J. William Streidl, and Andrew D. Szilagyi, "Goal Setting: The Tenneco Approach to

Personnel Development and Management Effectiveness," *Organizational Dynamics* (winter 1978), 48–80.

28 Richard A. Luecke, *Scuttle Your Ships before Advancing* (New York: Oxford University Press, 1994), 64–68; Thomas F. Rienzo, "Planning Deming Management for Service Organizations," *Business Horizons* 36, no. 3 (May–June 1993), 19–29; and Gregory M. Bounds, Gregory H. Dobbins, and Oscar S. Fowler, *Management: A Total Quality Perspective* (Cincinnati: South-Western College Publishing, 1995), 219–220.

29 "Corporate Planning: Drafting a Blueprint for Success," *Small Business Report* (August 1987), 40–44.

30 J. Michael Alford, "Contingency Planning Should Be Operationalized," *IM*, March–April 1995, 5–8.

31 Paul J. H. Schoemaker, "Scenario Planning: A Tool for Strategic Thinking," *Sloan Management Review* (winter 1995), 25–40; Christopher Knowlton, "Shell Gets Rich by Beating Risk," *Fortune*, August 21, 1991, 79–82; and Arie P. de Geus, "Planning as Learning," *Harvard Business Review* (March–April 1988), 70–74.

32 Peter Doyle, "Setting Business Objectives and Measuring Performance," *Journal of General Management* 20, no. 2 (winter 1994), 1–19.

33 Anne B. Fisher, "Is Long-Range Planning Worth It?" *Fortune*, April 23, 1990, 281–284.

34 Andrew Tanzer, "We Do Not Take a Short-Term View," *Forbes*, July 13, 1987, 372–374.

35 Harari, "Good News/Bad News about Strategy."

36 Gerald E. Ledford, Jr., Jon R. Wendenhof, and James T. Strahley, "Realizing a Corporate Philosophy," *Organizational Dynamics* (winter 1995), 5–18.

37 James C. Collins, "Building Companies to Last," *The State of Small Business*, 1995, 83–86; and Brian O'Reilly, "J&J Is on a Roll," *Fortune*, December 26, 1994, 178–191.

38 Based on Collins, "Building Companies to Last"; James C. Collins and Jerry I. Porras, "Building a Visionary Company," *California Management Review* 37, no. 2 (winter 1995), 80–100; and James C. Collins and Jerry I. Porras, "The Ultimate Vision," *Across the Board*, January 1995, 19–23.

39 Losee, "How Compaq Keeps the Magic Going."

40 Rahul Jacob, "Corporate Reputations," *Fortune*, March 6, 1995, 54–67.

41 Christina Duff and Bob Ortega, "How Wal-Mart Outdid a Once-Touted Kmart in Discount-Store Race," *The Wall Street Journal*, March 24, 1995, A1, A6.

42 Bill Saporito, "The Eclipse of Mars," *Fortune*, November 28, 1994, 82–92.

43 Pamela Sebastian, "Tough Times: Red Cross Is Strained by Disasters Even as It Revamps Its Programs," *the Wall Street Journal*, September 15, 1992, A1, A10.

44 Kevin Kelly, "A CEO Who Kept His Eyes on the Horizon," *Business Week*, August 1, 1994.

45 C. Chet Miller and Laura B. Cardinal, "Strategic Planning and Firm Performance: A Synthesis of More than Two Decades of Research," *Academy of Management Journal* 37, no. 6 (1994), 1649–1665.

46 John E. Prescott, "Environments as Moderators of the Relationship between Strategy and Performance," *Academy of Management Journal* 29 (1986), 329–346; John A. Pearce II and Richard B. Robinson, Jr., *Strategic Management: Strategy, Formulation, and Implementation*, 2d ed. (Homewood, Ill.: Irwin, 1985); and David J. Teece, "Economic Analysis and Strategic Management," *California Management Review* 26 (spring 1984), 87–110.

47 Arthur A. Thompson, Jr., and A. J. Strickland III, *Strategic Management: Concepts and Cases*, 6th ed. (Homewood, Ill.: Irwin, 1992).

48 Michael Treacy and Fred Wiersema, "How Market Leaders Keep Their Edge," *Fortune*, February 6, 1995, 88–98.

49 Peter Coy, "Twin Engines: Can Bob Allen Blend Computers and Telecommunications at AT&T?" *Business Week*, January 20, 1992, 56–63.

50 John S. DeMott, "Company Alliances for Market Muscle," *Nation's Business*, February 1994, 52–53.

51 Bradford McKee, "Ties That Bind Large and Small," *Nation's Business*, February 1992, 24–26.

52 Christopher Caggiano, "Kings of the Hill," *Inc.*, August 1996, 47–53.

53 Gregory M. Bounds, Gregory H. Dobbins, and Oscar S. Fowler, *Management: A Total Quality Perspective* (Cincinnati: South-Western College Publishing, 1995), 244.

54 Michael Treacy, "You Need a Value Discipline—But Which One?" *Fortune*, April 17, 1995, 195.

55 Hitt, Ireland, and Hoskisson, *Strategic Management*.

56 Milton Leontiades, "The Confusing Words of Business Policy," *Academy of Management Review* 7 (1982), 45–48.

57 Lawrence G. Hrebiniak and William F. Joyce, *Implementing Strategy* (New York: Macmillan, 1984).

58 James E. Svatko, "Analyzing the Competition," *Small Business Reports* (January 1989), 21–28; and Brian Dumaine, "Corporate Spies Snoop to Conquer," *Fortune*, November 7, 1988, 68–76.

59 Steve Swartz, "Basic Bedrooms: How Marriott Changes Hotel Design to Tap Mid-Priced Market," *The Wall Street Journal*, September 18, 1985, 1.

60 James B. Treece with Greg Burns, "The Nervous Faces around Kellogg's Breakfast Table," *Business Week*, July 18, 1994, 33.

61 Mark Maremont, "Kodak's New Focus: An Inside Look at George Fisher's Strategy," *Business Week*, January 30, 1995, 62–68; and Peter Nulty, "Digital Imaging Had Better Boom before Kodak Film Busts," *Fotrune*, May 1, 1995, 80–83.

62 Michael E. Porter, *Competitive Strategy* (New York: Free Press, 1980), 36–46; Danny Miller, "Relating Porter's Business Strategies to Environment and Structure: Analysis and Performance Implementations," *Academy of Management Journal* 31 (1988), 280–308; and Michael E. Porter, "From Competitive Advantage to Corporate Strategy," *Harvard Business Review* (May–June 1987), 43–59.

63 David Greising, "Watch Out for Flying Packages," *Business Week*, November 14, 1994, 40.

64 Thomas L. Wheelen and J. David Hunger, *Strategic Management and Business Policy* (Reading, Mass.: Addison-Wesley, 1989).

65 Peter Burrows, "Compaq Stretches for the Crown," *Business Week*, July 11, 1994, 140–142.

66 Thompson and Strickland, *Strategic Management*.

67 Greg Burns, "It Only Hertz When Enterprise Laughs," *Business Week*, December 12, 1994, 44.

68 George W. Potts, "Exploit Your Product's Service Life Cycle," *Harvard Business Review* (September–October 1988), 32–36; and C. R. Wasson, *Dynamic Competitive Strategy and Product Life Cycles*, 3d ed. (Austin, Tex.: Austin Press, 1978).

69 Carl R. Anderson and Carl P. Zeithaml, "Stage of the Product Life Cycle, Business Strategy, and Business Performance," *Academy of Management Journal* 27 (1984), 5–24.

70 Richard Brandt with Amy Cortese, "Bill Gates's Vision," *Business Week*, June 27, 1994, 57–62; Robert D. Gatewood, Robert R. Taylor, and O. C. Ferrell, *Management: Comprehension, Analysis, and Application* (Burr Ridge, Ill.: 1995), 520–521.

Managerial Decision Making and Information Technology

LEARNING OBJECTIVES

After studying this chapter, you should be able to

- Explain why decision making is an important component of good management.

- Explain the difference between programmed and nonprogrammed decisions and the decision characteristics of risk, uncertainty, and ambiguity.

- Describe the classical and administrative models of decision making and their applications.

- Identify the six steps of managerial decision making.

- Discuss the advantages and disadvantages of participative decision making.

- Describe the importance of information technology for organizations and the attributes of quality information.

- Identify different types of information systems.

- Explain how information systems support daily operations and decision making for low-level management.

- Explain how networks are transforming the way companies operate and the services they offer.

MANAGEMENT PROBLEM

There wasn't much sun in late 1996 at ailing Sunbeam Corporation, when new CEO Albert J. Dunlap came on board. Too many people knew of "Chainsaw Al's" reputation for corporate bloodletting at such companies as Scott Paper Company, where he slashed 11,000 jobs and made deep cuts in R&D and staff training, leaving many wondering how the company could ever achieve the "synergies and cost reductions" Wall Street expected. At the end of his 18-month tenure, his paycheck was a cool $100 million.

Though stock prices initially went up at Scott after Dunlap's chainsaw massacre, some analysts say he left the company in worse shape, that most changes were merely cosmetic and new packaging. U.S. and British market share has declined for Scott. Former executives said he cut a lot of muscle along with the fat, inflating short-term profits at the expense of long-term health. Wharton Professor Peter D. Cappelli warns that Dunlap is changing acceptable corporate behavior, "persuading others that shareholder value is the be all and end all. . . . He isn't creating value, he is redistributing income from the employees and the community to the shareholders." Other critics say his firings mostly affect lower income and minorities. Dunlap brushes off such comments by saying, "Stakeholders are total rubbish."

Shortly after he arrived at Sunbeam in mid-1996, *Business Week* magazine entreated Dunlap to put away his chainsaw and take out a scalpel. What Sunbeam

needed, the authors said, was to invest in new product development, improve relationships with top retailers, and boost manufacturing efficiency. It was uncertain, though, whether Dunlap could change his style of quick cut and cut out quick. "His sentence," noted a departed Scott executive, "should be to run the company as it is for five years," which he couldn't do, as it had become just a "hollow core."[1]

• If you were in charge, what would you recommend doing at Sunbeam? Do you think Dunlap was the best CEO to bring in? What decision criteria were used to hire him? What decision criteria should be used to resolve Sunbeam's problems?

Another example of a controversial decision was the Pentium crisis at Intel. With more than 70 percent of the microprocessor market, Intel Corporation has come to define IBM-compatible PCs far more than IBM itself. The company has sales of $11.5 billion, and CEO Andrew Grove is one of the world's most admired business leaders. But Grove made a serious blunder when news surfaced about minor flaws in Intel's new Pentium chip. Faced with demands that the chips be replaced, Grove refused, calmly asserting that tests showed the problem occurred only in rare instances. Only after IBM launched an embarrassing broadside—announcing that it would stop selling Pentium-based PCs and releasing its own test results showing a higher failure rate than Intel claimed—did Grove agree to a replacement policy on the faulty chips. This public relations disaster would never have happened had Grove decided at the beginning to replace Pentium chips with no questions asked. Although Intel was not seriously damaged in the short run, the black mark against its customer service reputation won't fade easily. In addition, the poor decision may reflect deeper problems that could limit Intel's ability to remain competitive in a rapidly changing industry.[2]

Intel is clearly not in the same kind of trouble as Sunbeam, but the decisions Andy Grove and Al Dunlap make today will affect the future of their businesses. Every organization grows, prospers, or fails as a result of decisions by its managers.

Managers often are referred to as *decision makers*. Although many of their important decisions are strategic, managers also make decisions about every other aspect of an organization, including structure, control systems, responses to the environment, and human resources. Managers scout for problems, make decisions for solving them, and monitor the consequences to see whether additional decisions are required. Good decision making is a vital part of good management, because decisions determine how the organization solves its problems, allocates resources, and accomplishes its goals.

Decision making is not easy. It must be done amid ever-changing factors, unclear information, and conflicting points of view. For example, Intel was propelled to its current dominance of the market because of a smart decision Grove made in the mid-1980s to get out of the DRAM memory-chip business—a technology Intel had invented—and focus relentlessly on microprocessors. As Japanese memory-chip makers drove prices so low they crushed U.S. rivals, many U.S. memory-chip makers entered joint ventures with the Japanese to survive. Over the objections of several executives, Grove decided to axe the DRAM business, along with thousands of employees. The decision ultimately served the corporation well, but the outcome was not clear in 1985. Coca-Cola thought it had a surefire winner in its BreakMate, a miniature soda fountain designed for office use. However, the machines attracted roaches and ants in some offices, especially in the South, and distributors often found drip trays growing so much mold they "looked like a science project." After pumping some $30 million into the biggest development project in its history, Coke never saw a profit, and BreakMate fountains now sit gathering dust in storage sheds.[3]

Kay Koplovitz worked her way up to CEO of the successful USA Network and recently launched The Sci-Fi Network. This is a nail-biting gamble as Washington stalks

the cable industry with new regulations to cap charges to the public, and an FCC ruling allows phone companies, such as Bell Atlantic, to experiment with "video dial tones," which would bring video movies and other materials into homes by phone rather than cable. Still, Koplovitz and many corporate sponsors believe there are enough fans of ghouls and monsters and Martians to risk the plunge into an area where no network has gone before.[4]

Chapter 7 described strategic planning. This chapter explores the decision process that underlies strategic planning. Plans and strategies are arrived at through decision making; the better the decision making, the better the strategic planning. However, solid decisions depend on complete and accurate information. Later in the chapter, information technology will be examined. First we will examine decision characteristics. Then we will look at decision-making models and the steps executives should take when making important decisions. We will also examine participative decision making and discuss techniques for improving decision making in organizations. Finally, we will look at how information technology is changing the way business is conducted and the types of information systems available and those emerging.

TYPES OF DECISIONS AND PROBLEMS

A **decision** is a choice made from available alternatives. For example, an accounting manager's selection among Bill, Nancy, and Joan for the position of junior auditor is a decision. Many people assume that making a choice is the major part of decision making, but it is only a part.

Decision making is the process of identifying problems and opportunities and then resolving them.[5] Decision making involves effort both before and after the actual choice. Thus, the decision as to whether to select Bill, Nancy, or Joan requires the accounting manager to ascertain whether a

new junior auditor is needed, determine the availability of potential job candidates, interview candidates to acquire necessary information, select one candidate, and follow up with the socialization of the new employee into the organization to ensure the decision's success.

Programmed and Nonprogrammed Decisions

Management decisions typically fall into one of two categories: programmed and nonprogrammed. **Programmed decisions** involve situations that have occurred often enough to enable decision rules to be developed and applied in the future.[6] Programmed decisions are made in response to recurring organizational problems. The decision to reorder paper and other office supplies when inventories drop to a certain level is a programmed decision. Other programmed decisions concern the types of skills required to fill certain jobs, the reorder point for manufacturing inventory, exception reporting for expenditures 10 percent or more over budget, and selection of freight routes for product deliveries. Once managers formulate decision rules, subordinates and others can make the decision, freeing managers for other tasks.

Nonprogrammed decisions are made in response to situations that are unique, are poorly defined and largely unstructured, and have important consequences for the organization. The question of how to deal with charges of faulty Pentium chips was a nonprogrammed decision. Intel had never faced this type of problem and did not have rules for dealing with it. Many nonprogrammed decisions involve strategic planning, because uncertainty is great and decisions are complex. Decisions to build a new factory, develop a new product or service, enter a new geographical market, or relocate headquarters to another city are all nonprogrammed decisions. When Goodyear CEO Stanley Gault decided to launch four new tires at once and sell through new distribution channels, such as

programmed decision A decision made in response to a situation that has occurred often enough to enable decision rules to be developed and applied in the future.

nonprogrammed decision A decision made in response to a situation that is unique, is poorly defined and largely unstructured, and has important consequences for the organization.

decision A choice made from available alternatives.

decision making The process of identifying problems and opportunities and then resolving them.

Wal-Mart, Kmart, and Sears, he made a nonprogrammed decision. Gault and other top executives had to analyze complex problems, evaluate alternatives, and make a choice about how to revive the failing company.[7] With a real risk of going out of business, Marmot Mountain Works had to make some tough decisions in order to survive. The new president altered the previous decision style, which sought perfection, and instead worked on one or two things at a time, as described in the Leading the Management Revolution box.

Certainty, Risk, Uncertainty, and Ambiguity

In a perfect world, managers would have all the information necessary for making decisions. In reality, however, some things are unknowable; thus, some decisions will fail to solve the problem or attain the desired outcome. Managers try to obtain information about decision alternatives that will reduce decision uncertainty. Every decision situation can be organized on a scale according to the availability of information and the possibility of failure. The four positions on the scale are certainty, risk, uncertainty, and ambiguity, as illustrated in Exhibit 8.1.

Certainty. Certainty means that all the information the decision maker needs is fully available.[8] Managers have information on operating conditions, resource costs or

risk
A decision has clear-cut goals, and good information is available, but the future outcomes associated with each alternative are subject to chance.

certainty
All the information the decision maker needs is fully available.

uncertainty
Managers know what goal they wish to achieve, but information about alternatives and future events is incomplete.

EXHIBIT 8.1
Conditions That Affect the Possibility of Decision Failure

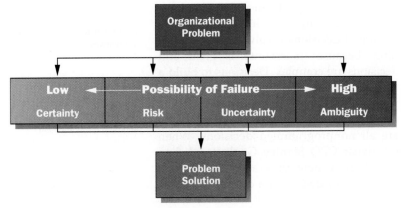

constraints, and each course of action and possible outcome. For example, if a company considers a $10,000 investment in new equipment that it knows for certain will yield $4,000 in cost savings per year over the next five years, managers can calculate a before-tax rate of return of about 40 percent. If managers compare this investment with one that will yield only $3,000 per year in cost savings, they can confidently select the 40 percent return. However, few decisions are certain in the real world. Most contain risk or uncertainty.

Risk. Risk means that a decision has clear-cut goals and that good information is available, but the future outcomes associated with each alternative are subject to chance. However, enough information is available to allow the probability of a successful outcome for each alternative to be estimated.[9] Statistical analysis might be used to calculate the probabilities of success or failure. The measure of risk captures the possibility that future events will render the alternative unsuccessful. Some oil companies use a quantitative simulation approach to estimate hydrocarbon reserves, enabling oil executives to evaluate the variation in risk at each stage of exploration and production and make better decisions. Apple Computer took a calculated risk by launching a new line of Macintoshes using the speedy PowerPC chip. The computer maker's future may hinge on the new, more powerful line, but too aggressive a transition could devastate sales of the company's older, core products.[10]

Uncertainty. Uncertainty means that managers know which goals they wish to achieve, but information about alternatives and future events is incomplete.[11] Managers do not have enough information to be clear about alternatives or to estimate their risk. Factors that may affect a decision, such as price, production costs, volume, or future interest rates, are difficult to analyze and predict. Managers may have to make assumptions from which to forge the decision even though it will be wrong if the assump-

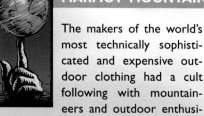

LEADING THE MANAGEMENT REVOLUTION
MARMOT MOUNTAIN WORKS

The makers of the world's most technically sophisticated and expensive outdoor clothing had a cult following with mountaineers and outdoor enthusiasts, who cherished their Marmot gear. But the company had not shown a profit in its 20-year history. Business operations were in a miserable state. The obsession with quality resulted in delayed production and delivery when the "perfect" material was unavailable.

Marmot was pushed to the brink of non-existence in 1993, when their new parent company went bankrupt. After six months of loan rejections, employees bought out the company. Startling everyone, they became the third-largest selling outdoor clothing manufacturer, after Patagonia and North Face.

The new success is attributed to new president Steve Crisafulli's decision to develop a battle plan of "concentrating on one or two small things." First was to solve delivery problems. "Anything that negatively impacts on delivery has to wait," he asserted. To avoid delays, the ten-member management team met daily, identifying and resolving potential conflicts. Growth was restrained for 18 months, to allow Marmot to service its loyal customers.

"The choice to have a single goal looming taints or filters all small decisions," says vice-president of marketing John Cooley. If anything threatened delivery time, whether resizing a jacket or developing a new product, it was not done.

Within one-and-a-half years of the bankruptcy, Marmot was making a profit for the very first time and is predicted to grow 40 percent a year. After three seasons of on-time deliveries, the moratorium on new customers was lifted.

Marmot is continuing to work on its problems, one at a time. Each February, a strategic meeting is held and the management agrees on the coming year's primary goal. Crisafulli is convinced of his "prioritizing to a fault" strategy, which hasn't failed yet. "I think that if everyone in a small business focuses on one thing," he says, "it will happen."

SOURCE: David Goodman, "One Step at a Time," *Inc.,* August 1995, 64–68.

---

tions are incorrect. Managers may have to come up with creative approaches to alternatives and use personal judgment to determine which alternative is best.

For example, Boeing faced great uncertainty in the decision to build the twenty-first-century airplane. Bypassing the traditional design route of building mock-ups, Boeing decided to build the new 777 plane, making the radical jump directly from computer image to finished product. Despite the collapse of air carriers such as Eastern and Pan Am, Boeing is gambling that its 777 will secure its future by filling the gap between the 218-passenger 767 and the 419-passenger 747.[12]

Many decisions made under uncertainty do not produce the desired results, but managers face uncertainty every day. They must find creative ways to cope with uncertainty in order to make effective decisions.

Ambiguity. Ambiguity is by far the most difficult decision situation. **Ambiguity** means that the goals to be achieved or the problem to be solved is unclear, alternatives are difficult to define, and information about outcomes is unavailable.[13] Ambiguity is what students would feel if an instructor created student groups, told each group to write a paper, but gave the groups no topic, direction, or guidelines whatsoever. Ambiguity has been called a "wicked" decision problem. Managers have a difficult time coming to grips with the issues. Wicked problems are associated with manager conflicts over goals and decision alternatives, rapidly changing circumstances, fuzzy information, and unclear linkages among decision elements.[14] Fortunately, most decisions are not characterized by ambiguity. But when they are, managers must conjure up goals and develop reasonable scenarios for decision alternatives in the absence of information. When reports surfaced several years ago that syringes and hypodermic needles had been found in cans of Pepsi, Pepsi-Cola executives faced ambiguity

ambiguity
The goals to be achieved or the problem to be solved is unclear, alternatives are difficult to define, and information about outcomes is unavailable.

classical model
A decision-making model based on the assumption that managers should make logical decisions that will be in the organization's best economic interests.

squarely in the face. After carefully analyzing the situation, the managers believed syringes could not appear in unopened cans of Pepsi. They decided not to issue a recall but rather to respond quickly and openly to consumer fears with a massive public relations and education campaign. Nationwide ad campaigns explained the decision not to issue a recall and assured consumers that there had been no injuries and not a single confirmed case of a needle found in an unopened can of Pepsi. By allying itself with the FDA and responding quickly and openly to public fears, Pepsi weathered the syringe-scare crisis with little damage.[15]

Another example of ambiguity is in the movie industry—one of the most difficult in which to make decisions because so many new movies are flops. At Warner Brothers, studio executives build personal relationships with top stars, so they will want to do pictures with the studio. Another approach is to provide stars with a percentage of gross revenues rather than a huge salary. For *Mission Impossible*, actor/producer Tom Cruise got no upfront money but received 15 percent of gross for his acting and 5 percent for producing. Paramount Pictures ended up paying him and his producing partner about $60 million for their work on the movie. Similarly, Warner Brothers paid Arnold Schwarzenegger 15 percent of gross on *Eraser*, which will end up being in excess of $15 million. These stars made millions because the movies were so successful, but they would have made little if the pictures had failed. Paramount and Warner Brothers use these approaches to reduce the financial risks of ambiguity when making new movies.[16]

normative
An approach that defines how a decision maker should make decisions and provides guidelines for reaching an ideal outcome for the organization.

DECISION-MAKING MODELS

The approach managers use to make decisions usually falls into one of two types—the classical model or the administrative model. The choice of model depends on the manager's personal preference, whether the decision is programmed or nonpro-

grammed, and the extent to which the decision is characterized by risk, uncertainty, or ambiguity.

Classical Model

The **classical model** of decision making is based on economic assumptions. This model has arisen within the management literature because managers are expected to make decisions that are economically sensible and in the organization's best economic interests. The assumptions underlying this model are as follows:

1 The decision maker operates to accomplish goals that are known and agreed upon. Problems are precisely formulated and defined.

2 The decision maker strives for conditions of certainty, gathering complete information. All alternatives and the potential results of each are calculated.

3 Criteria for evaluating alternatives are known. The decision maker selects the alternative that will maximize the economic return to the organization.

4 The decision maker is rational and uses logic to assign values, order preferences, evaluate alternatives, and make the decision that will maximize the attainment of organizational goals.

The classical model of decision making is considered to be **normative,** which means it defines how a decision maker *should* make decisions. It does not describe how managers actually make decisions so much as it provides guidelines on how to reach an ideal outcome for the organization. The value of the classical model has been its ability to help decision makers be more rational. For example, many senior managers rely solely on intuition and personal preferences for making decisions.[17] In recent years, the classical approach has been given wider application because of the growth of quantitative decision techniques that use computers. Quantitative techniques include such things as decision trees, payoff matrices, break-even analysis, linear programming, forecasting, and operations research

models. The use of computerized information systems and databases has increased the power of the classical approach.

In many respects, the classical model represents an "ideal" model of decision making that is often unattainable by real people in real organizations. It is most valuable when applied to programmed decisions and to decisions characterized by certainty or risk, because relevant information is available and probabilities can be calculated. One example of the classical approach is the model developed by a Canadian organization for scheduling ambulance services.

■ URGENCES SANTÉ

Urgences Santé, a public agency responsible for coordinating ambulance service in the Montreal area, schedules vehicle time and working hours for approximately 80 ambulances and 700 technicians. Since Urgences Santé does not own its vehicles or hire technicians but instead rents these from private companies, agency managers wanted to optimize the schedule to avoid unnecessary rental costs.

Two types of calls require ambulance service—emergency calls from the public, which occur randomly throughout the day and require immediate attention, and calls from hospitals, which are concentrated in specific time periods and are generally not urgent. In addition, demand for ambulance service is usually higher in the winter but with more emergency calls on weekends during the summer months. Besides meeting shifting demand, a number of other constraints governed the design of a new schedule.

Urgences Santé applied mathematical formulations and techniques to first build workday schedules for each type of day (weekend or weekday) for each season, then equitably assign workdays to the 15 or so private service companies, and finally build individual schedules for the 700 technicians. More than 85 percent of the individual schedules can now be created automatically. The new system has had two positive effects. First, the agency is able to meet demand while cutting rental

hours per week by up to 110 hours, thus saving approximately $250,000 per year. Second, the quality of technicians' schedules has been dramatically improved, leading to a decrease in turnover for the service companies.[18] ■

Administrative Model

The **administrative model** of decision making describes how managers actually make decisions in difficult situations, such as those characterized by nonprogrammed decisions, uncertainty, and ambiguity. Many management decisions are not sufficiently programmable to lend themselves to any degree of quantification. Managers are unable to make economically rational decisions even if they want to.[19]

Bounded Rationality and Satisficing. The administrative model of decision making is based on the work of Herbert A. Simon. Simon proposed two concepts that were instrumental in shaping the administrative model: bounded rationality and satisficing. **Bounded rationality** means that people have limits, or boundaries, on how rational they can be. The organization is incredibly complex, and managers have the time and ability to process only a limited amount of information with which to make decisions.[20] Because managers do not have the time or cognitive ability to process complete information about complex decisions, they must satisfice. **Satisficing** means that decision makers choose the first solution alternative that satisfies minimal decision criteria. Rather than pursuing all alternatives to identify the single solution that will maximize economic returns, managers will opt for the first solution that appears to solve the problem, even if better solutions are presumed to exist. The decision maker cannot justify the time and expense of obtaining complete information.[21]

An example of both bounded rationality and satisficing occurs when a junior executive on a business trip stains her blouse just before an important meeting. She will run to a nearby clothing store and buy the first satisfactory replacement she finds. Having

administrative model
A decision-making model that describes how managers actually make decisions in situations characterized by nonprogrammed decisions, uncertainty, and ambiguity.

bounded rationality
The concept that people have the time and cognitive ability to process only a limited amount of information on which to base decisions.

satisfice
To choose the first solution alternative that satisfies minimal decision criteria regardless of whether better solutions are presumed to exist.

neither the time nor the opportunity to explore all the blouses in town, she satisfices by choosing a blouse that will solve the immediate problem. In a similar fashion, managers generate alternatives for complex problems only until they find one they believe will work. For example, several years ago then-Disney chairman Ray Watson and chief operating officer Ron Miller attempted to thwart takeover attempts, but they had limited options. They satisficed with a quick decision to acquire Arivda Realty and Gibson Court Company. The acquisition of these companies had the potential to solve the problem at hand; thus, they looked no further for possibly better alternatives.[22]

The administrative model relies on assumptions different from those of the classical model and focuses on organizational factors that influence individual decisions. It is more realistic than the classical model for complex, nonprogrammed decisions. According to the administrative model,

1 Decision goals often are vague, conflicting, and lack consensus among managers. Managers often are unaware of problems or opportunities that exist in the organization.
2 Rational procedures are not always used, and, when they are, they are confined to a simplistic view of the problem that does not capture the complexity of real organizational events.
3 Managers' search for alternatives is limited because of human, information, and resource constraints.
4 Most managers settle for a satisficing rather than a maximizing solution. This is partly because they have limited information and partly because they have only vague criteria for what constitutes a maximizing solution.

The administrative model is considered to be **descriptive,** meaning that it describes how managers actually make decisions in complex situations rather than dictating how they *should* make decisions according to a theoretical ideal. The administrative model recognizes the human and environ-mental limitations that affect the degree to which managers can pursue a rational decision-making process.

Intuition.   Another aspect of administrative decision making is intuition. **Intuition** represents a quick apprehension of a decision situation based on past experience but without conscious thought.[23] Intuitive decision making is not arbitrary or irrational, because it is based on years of practice and hands-on experience that enable managers to quickly identify solutions without going through painstaking computations. Managers rely on intuition to determine when a problem exists and to synthesize isolated bits of data and experience into an integrated picture. They also use their intuitive understanding to check the results of rational analysis. If the rational analysis does not agree with their intuition, managers may dig further before accepting a proposed alternative.[24]

Intuition helps managers understand situations characterized by uncertainty and ambiguity that have proven impervious to rational analysis. The movie *M*A*S*H* and the television programs "All in the Family," "Hill Street Blues," and "Cheers" would have been squashed in their infancy if producers Robert Altman, Norman Lear, and Stephen Bochco hadn't gone with their gut feelings and pushed the projects. Speaking of the movie and television spinoff that made more than $1 billion for 20th Century Fox, Altman summed it up this way: "I always say that *M*A*S*H* wasn't released, it escaped." Some years later, George Lucas, the creator of *Star Wars*, attempted to sell this concept to 12 major studios before going to Fox. In each case, the concept was rejected. All 13 studios saw the same numbers, but only Alan Ladd and his associates at Fox had the right "feel" for the decision. Their intuition told them that *Star Wars* would be a success. In addition, George Lucas was told by many experts that the title *Star Wars* would turn away crowds at the box office. His intuition said the title would work. The rest is history.[25]

intuition
The immediate comprehension of a decision situation based on past experience but without conscious thought.

descriptive
An approach that describes how managers actually make decisions rather than how they should.

Coalition Building. The uncertainty of administrative decision making often requires coalition building. A **coalition** is an informal alliance among managers who support a specific goal. *Coalition building* is the process of forming alliances among managers. In other words, a manager who supports a specific alternative, such as increasing the corporation's growth by acquiring another company, talks informally to other executives and tries to persuade them to support the decision. When the outcomes are not predictable, managers gain support through discussion, negotiation, and bargaining. Without a coalition, a powerful individual or group could derail the decision-making process. Coalition building gives several managers an opportunity to contribute to decision making, enhancing their commitment to the alternative that is ultimately adopted.[26]

The successful coalition building of former president George Bush in response to Saddam Hussein's invasion of Kuwait in 1990 was an example for both business and political decision makers. Bush successfully built a coalition among the heads of several countries by first having a clear understanding of the need for a coalition, then targeting his message to each coalition member by explaining why Hussein's action threatened each nation's future, and finally by constant communication with the head of each country in the coalition, Congress, and the American public.[27]

The key dimensions of the classical and administrative models are listed in Exhibit 8.2. Managers may walk a fine line between two extremes: making arbitrary decisions without careful study versus relying obses-sively on numbers and rational analysis. One entrepreneur, aware of the need to more carefully analyze decision problems as his business grew, turned to outside consultants. However, by totally relying on their rational analysis of problems and failing to listen to his intuition, he made a series of bad decisions that eventually forced him to sell the company.[28] Recent research into decision-making procedures has found rational, classical procedures to be associated with high performance for organizations in stable environments. However, administrative decision-making procedures and intuition have been associated with high performance in unstable environments in which decisions must be made rapidly and under more difficult conditions.[29]

DECISION-MAKING STEPS

Whether a decision is programmed or nonprogrammed and regardless of managers' choice of the classical or administrative model of decision making, six steps typically are associated with effective decision processes. These are summarized in Exhibit 8.3.

Recognition of Decision Requirement

Managers confront a decision requirement in the form of either a problem or an opportunity. A **problem** occurs when organizational accomplishment is less than established goals. Some aspect of performance is unsatisfactory. An **opportunity** exists when managers see potential

coalition
An informal alliance among managers who support a specific goal.

problem
A situation in which organizational accomplishments have failed to meet established goals.

opportunity
A situation in which managers see potential organizational accomplishments that exceed current goals.

Classical Model	Administrative Model
Clear-cut problem and goals	Vague problem and goals
Condition of certainty	Condition of uncertainty
Full information about alternatives and their outcomes	Limited information about alternatives and their outcomes
Rational choice by individual for maximizing outcomes	Satisficing choice for resolving problem using intuition and coalitions

EXHIBIT 8.2
Characteristics of Classical and Administrative Decision-Making Models

EXHIBIT 8.3
Six Steps in the Managerial Decision-Making Process

accomplishment that exceeds specified current goals. Managers see the possibility of enhancing performance beyond current levels.

Awareness of a problem or opportunity is the first step in the decision sequence and requires surveillance of the internal and external environment for issues that merit executive attention.[30] This resembles the military concept of gathering intelligence. Managers scan the world around them to determine whether the organization is satisfactorily progressing toward its goals.

Some information comes from periodic accounting reports, MIS reports, and other sources that are designed to discover problems before they become too serious. For example, while reading a routine internal company report, Becky Roloff, a vice-president for IDS Financial Services (now American Express Financial Advisors), noted a high level of employee turnover that was not being addressed by the company. Although IDS was extremely profitable and growing rapidly, Roloff knew the high attrition could eventually threaten IDS's ability to beat back a growing host of competitors. Her discovery of the problem eventually led to a comprehensive redesign of the company, including better training programs, more emphasis on teamwork, and stronger efforts to hire minorities.[31] Managers also take advantage of informal sources. They talk to other managers, gather opinions on how things are going, and seek advice on which problems should be tackled or which opportunities embraced.[32]

Recognizing decision requirements is difficult, because it often means integrating bits and pieces of information in novel ways. For example, toy maker Worlds of Wonder, Inc., worked regularly with 1,000

diagnosis
The step in the decision-making process in which managers analyze underlying causal factors associated with the decision situation.

families chosen at random to learn about problems and opportunities in the marketplace for toys. This early recognition contributed directly to the success of Lazer Tag, a toy geared for the young-adult market.[33]

Diagnosis and Analysis of Causes

Once a problem or opportunity has come to a manager's attention, the understanding of the situation should be refined. **Diagnosis** is the step in the decision-making process in which managers analyze underlying causal factors associated with the decision situation. Managers make a mistake here if they jump right into generating alternatives without first exploring the cause of the problem more deeply.

Kepner and Tregoe, who have conducted extensive studies of manager decision making, recommend that managers ask a series of questions to specify underlying causes, including the following:

■ What is the state of disequilibrium affecting us?

■ When did it occur?

■ Where did it occur?

■ How did it occur?

■ To whom did it occur?

■ What is the urgency of the problem?

■ What is the interconnectedness of events?

■ What result came from which activity?[34]

Such questions help specify what actually happened and why. Consider how failure to analyze the situation and diagnose causes led to a disaster at Greyhound Lines.

GREYHOUND LINES INC.

Everyone agreed that Greyhound Lines had problems. The company was operating on paper-thin margins and could not afford to dispatch nearly empty vehicles or have buses and drivers on call to meet surges in demand. In the terminals, employees could be observed making fun of passengers, ignoring them, and handling their baggage haphazardly. To reduce operating costs and improve customer service, Greyhound's top executives put together a reorganization plan that called for massive cuts in personnel, routes, and services, along with the computerization of everything from passenger reservations to fleet scheduling.

Technicians urged delaying introduction of the computerized reservations system, called Trips, to work out bugs in the highly complex software. The software wasn't the only problem with Trips. Terminal workers often had less than a high school education and would need extensive training before they could be expected to use the system effectively. Some managers warned that many of Greyhound's low-income passengers did not have credit cards or even telephones to use Trips. Executives went ahead with the rollout, promising that it would improve customer service, make ticket buying more convenient, and allow customers to reserve space on specific trips. What resulted was a nightmare. The time Greyhound operators spent responding to phone calls dramatically increased. Many callers couldn't even get through because of problems in the new switching mechanism. Most passengers arrived to buy their tickets and get on the bus just like they always had, but the computers were so swamped that it sometimes took 45 seconds to respond to a single keystroke and five minutes to print a ticket. Customers stood in long lines, were separated from their luggage, missed connections, and were left to sleep in terminals overnight. Discourtesy to customers increased as a downsized workforce struggled to cope with a system they were ill-trained to operate. Ridership plunged sharply.

Greyhound executives failed to carefully analyze the causes of their decision problem

Seizing *opportunity*, this bunny (a symbol of rapid growth) is hopping off to conquer the world for PepsiCo, Inc. In identifying opportunities for the soft-drink industry, PepsiCo recognizes that the international market represents 95 percent of the population and only 25 percent of sales. PepsiCo has now targeted international expansion as the long-term growth opportunity for the future. Global plans include introduction of vending machines, expansion of diet products, and encouragement of bigger package purchases, such as cartons, over the traditional single bottle.

before jumping in with a solution. As regional rivals continue to pick off Greyhound's dissatisfied customers, the future of the huge bus company remains uncertain.[35] ■

Development of Alternatives

Once the problem or opportunity has been recognized and analyzed, decision makers begin to consider taking action. The next stage is to generate possible alternative solutions that will respond to the needs of the situation and correct the underlying causes.

For a programmed decision, feasible alternatives are easy to identify and in fact usually are already available within the organization's rules and procedures. Nonprogrammed decisions, however, require developing new courses of action that will meet the company's needs. For decisions made under conditions of high uncertainty, managers may develop only one or two custom solutions that will satisfice for handling the problem.

Decision alternatives can be thought of as the tools for reducing the difference between the organization's current and desired performance. Consider how Gateway 2000 handled the problem of competing in the turbulent and risky computer industry.

■ GATEWAY 2000

The decision to start a business that would vie with 400 computer-sales companies looked suicidal. With the competition demonstrating computers in stores and offering many goodies, Gateway 2000 co-founder and twentysomething CEO Ted Waitt chose the alternative—selling only by mail order and not including any special technology or support service. Predictions of the company's death were greatly exaggerated. Within a few years, sales were at $275 million. By 1996 its growth was one of the highest in the industry.

From the beginning, Waitt and his partner, Arthur Lazere, decided to run the North Sioux City, North Dakota, firm with low overhead and have been flinty-eyed about costs from day one. Understanding value from the customer's point of view was part of their success formula as well. Their competitors were selling either stripped-down PCs or ones technology-overloaded to the point of unaffordability. Waitt decided to target the middle of the road, believing business is about value, not price. Even now, he hasn't veered from his strategy of giving customers more for less. He maintained value in the company in the early days by doing such things as giving employees cash bonuses, which reduced turnover costs.

Though Waitt has been thus far successful in his decisions, it is not certain how long that will last in the cut-throat computer market. Can he continue to expand and still remain flexible? Gateway's 1995 acquisition of an Australian computer company and its 1996 entry into retail stores signal changes in direction. Will his as-yet-stellar decision making continue as the company's focus expands? Still only in his early 30s, Waitt has many years ahead of choosing alternatives and decision making.[36] ■

risk propensity
The willingness to undertake risk with the opportunity of gaining an increased payoff.

implementation
The step in the decision-making process that involves using managerial, administrative, and persuasive abilities to translate the chosen alternative into action.

Selection of Desired Alternative

Once feasible alternatives have been developed, one must be selected. The decision choice is the selection of the most promising of several alternative courses of action. The best alternative is one in which the solution best fits the overall goals and values of the

organization and achieves the desired results using the fewest resources.[37] The manager tries to select the choice with the least amount of risk and uncertainty. Because some risk is inherent for most nonprogrammed decisions, managers try to gauge prospects for success. Under conditions of uncertainty, they may have to rely on their intuition and experience to estimate whether a given course of action is likely to succeed. Basing choices on overall goals and values can also effectively guide selection of alternatives. Johnson & Johnson's values-based decision making became evident when the company spent $100 million pulling Tylenol from store shelves after cyanide was discovered in some of the capsules. It was an expensive alternative in the short run but one that worked wonders for J&J's image and probably helped save Tylenol as a consumer product.[38]

Making choices depends on managers' personality factors and willingness to accept risk and uncertainty. For example, **risk propensity** is the willingness to undertake risk with the opportunity of gaining an increased payoff. The level of risk a manager is willing to accept will influence the analysis of cost and benefits to be derived from any decision. Consider the situations in Exhibit 8.4. In each situation, which alternative would you choose? A person with a low risk propensity would tend to take assured moderate returns by going for a tie score, building a domestic plant, or pursuing a career as a physician. A risk taker would go for the victory, build a plant in a foreign country, or embark on an acting career.

Implementation of Chosen Alternative

The **implementation** stage involves the use of managerial, administrative, and persuasive abilities to ensure that the chosen alternative is carried out. This is similar to the idea of strategic implementation described in Chapter 7. The ultimate success of the chosen alternative depends on whether it can be translated into action. Sometimes an alternative never becomes reality because

For each of the following decisions, which alternative would you choose?

1. In the final seconds of a game with the college's traditional rival, the coach of a college football team may choose a play that has a 95 percent chance of producing a tie score or one with a 30 percent chance of leading to victory or to sure defeat if it fails.

2. The president of a Canadian company must decide whether to build a new plant within Canada that has a 90 percent chance of producing a modest return on investment or to build it in a foreign country with an unstable political history. The latter alternative has a 40 percent chance of failing, but the returns would be enormous if it succeeded.

3. A college senior with considerable acting talent must choose a career. She has the opportunity to go on to medical school and become a physician, a career in which she is 80 percent likely to succeed. She would rather be an actress but realizes that the opportunity for success is only 20 percent.

EXHIBIT 8.4
Decision Alternatives with Different Levels of Risk

---

managers lack the resources or energy needed to make things happen. Implementation may require discussion with people affected by the decision. Communication, motivation, and leadership skills must be used to see that the decision is carried out.

One reason Lee Iacocca succeeded in turning Chrysler around was his ability to implement decisions. Iacocca personally hired people from Ford to develop new auto models. He hired people who shared his vision and were eager to carry out his decisions. By contrast, Tandy Corporation's decision to become a major supplier to businesses by setting up 386 computer centers to support a new direct sales force foundered. Tandy had great success selling to consumers through its Radio Shack stores but simply did not know how to sell computers to businesses. The results were disappointing, and many of the computer centers had to be closed. Tandy lacked the ability to implement the decision to go after business customers.[39]

Evaluation and Feedback

In the evaluation stage of the decision process, decision makers gather information that tells them how well the decision was implemented and whether it was effective in achieving its goals. For example, Tandy executives' evaluation of and feedback on the decision to open computer centers revealed poor sales performance. Feedback indicated that implementation was unsuccessful, so computer centers were closed and another approach was tried.

Feedback is important because decision making is a continuous, never-ending process. Decision making is not completed when an executive or board of directors votes yes or no. Feedback provides decision makers with information that can precipitate a new decision cycle. The decision may fail, thus generating a new analysis of the problem, evaluation of alternatives, and selection of a new alternative. Many big problems are solved by trying several alternatives in sequence, each providing modest improvement. Feedback is the part of monitoring that assesses whether a new decision needs to be made.

An illustration of the overall decision-making process, including evaluation and feedback, was Coca-Cola's decision to introduce a "new" Coke flavor.

COCA-COLA COMPANY

"Dear Chief Dodo: What ignoramus decided to change the formula of Coke?" This was one of thousands of letters sent to Coca-Cola chairman Roberto Goizueta after the introduction of the new Coke flavor in 1985. Coca-Cola had made its decision via a cautious, rational decision process. The problem leading to the decision was clear: Pepsi was increasing market share at Coke's expense through supermarket sales. Pepsi was slightly sweeter and tended to beat Coke in blind taste tests. And the enormous success of Diet Coke—sweeter than regular Coke—reinforced the idea of changing the Coke formula.

The problem led to a diagnosis and the development of several alternatives. Coca-Cola spent $4 million to taste-test the new flavor on nearly 200,000 consumers in 30 cities. Coca-Cola identified the flavor people most preferred: 35 percent chose the new Coke over the old, and 52 percent chose it over Pepsi.

Yet within three months after the decision was implemented, old Coke was back in the supermarkets. Why? Because feedback revealed that brand loyalty is an elusive quality that cannot be measured. People had an emotional attachment to the original Coca-Cola from childhood. Millions of advertising dollars could not swing enough people to the new Coke flavor.

Why did the decision fail? It was a bold decision—and bold decisions are inherently risky. Coca-Cola could not measure intangible emotional attachments. On the other hand, thanks to evaluation and feedback, the decision should not be considered a total failure. Coke's near fiasco rejuvenated sagging product loyalty as customers contemplated the loss of their old favorite. After the old Coke was reintroduced under the name Coca-Cola Classic, there were two Coke brands with which to battle Pepsi. Canadian management scholar Glen Whyte once referred to this turn of events as "a good example of a sow's ear of a decision becoming a silk purse."[40] ■

Coca-Cola's decision to introduce a new flavor illustrates all the decision steps, and the process ultimately ended in success. Strategic decisions always contain some risk. In this case, feedback and follow-up decisions got Coke back on track.

Evaluation and feedback also helped get Intel back on track after the faulty Pentium chip decision described at the beginning of this chapter. Some observers believe Andrew Grove's doggedly analytical style hampered his ability to consider all sides of the situation to determine the true nature of the Pentium chip problem and carefully consider decision alternatives. Grove also failed to listen to employees who had a better feel for the situation, such as many of the company's 2,000 employees who had expressed disagreement with the harsh initial

policy. Intuition is not highly valued at Intel—as Grove puts it, "Intuition is not going to get you a three-million-transistor microprocessor." Evaluation and feedback led Grove to implement a replacement policy and decide that Intel needs to be closer to consumers. The company opened a hot line staffed by engineers to cut through the layers between chip designers and consumers. Intel could benefit from more participative decision making, particularly in regard to customer relations problems.[41] Participative decision making will be discussed in more detail later in the chapter.

Decision Biases to Avoid

At a time when decision making is so important, many corporate executives do not know how to make a good choice among alternatives. They may rely on computer analyses or personal intuition without realizing that their own cognitive biases affect their judgment. The complexities of modern corporate life make good judgment more critical than ever. Many errors in judgment originate in the human mind's limited capacity and in the natural biases most executives display during decision making. Awareness of the following six biases can help managers make more enlightened choices:

1 *Ignoring the laws of randomness.* Randomness means that the outcome of one event has nothing to do with the outcome of another. Managers often ignore this principle in making business decisions. For example, even though retail sales should be expected to fluctuate each month, a businessperson decides that a slight sales dip is the beginning of a downward trend and takes significant action, such as increasing the advertising budget. If sales rise the following month—which would be expected even without a change in advertising—the executive attributes it to the new advertising strategy. Trends should not be interpreted from a single, random event.

2 *Hindsight bias.* Hindsight bias means

that people tend to overestimate after the fact the degree to which they could have predicted an event. This is sometimes called the "I-knew-it-all-along effect." One example occurs when you are traveling in an unfamiliar area with your spouse behind the wheel. You reach an unmarked fork in the road, and your spouse decides to turn left. Twenty minutes later you are hopelessly lost, and you exclaim, "I knew you should have turned right at the fork!" Research on hindsight demonstrates that people are not very good at recalling or reconstructing how an uncertain situation appeared beforehand. Managers should be cautious about evaluating decision errors made by themselves and subordinates, because uncertainty may have been greater before the decision than they recall.

3 *Clinging to what worked in the past.* Managers often base decisions on what has worked in the past and fail to explore new options, dig for additional information, or investigate new technologies. For example, Du Pont clung to its cash cow, nylon, despite growing evidence in the scientific community that a new product, polyester, was superior for tire cords. Celanese, a relatively small competitor, blew Du Pont out of the water by exploiting this new evidence, quickly capturing 75 percent of the tire market.

4 *Being influenced by problem framing.* The decision response of a manager can be influenced by the mere wording of a problem. For example, consider whether a new product decision is framed to emphasize job savings or job losses. If managers are given the option of approving (A) a modified product that will mean a 100 percent chance of saving 200 manufacturing jobs or (B) a new product that has a one-third chance of saving 600 positions and a two-thirds chance of saving zero positions, most managers choose option A. The same problem with a negative frame would give managers the choice of selecting (C) a modified product that had a 100 percent chance of los-

ing 200 jobs, or (D) a totally new product that had a one-third chance of losing 600 jobs and a two-thirds chance of losing zero jobs. With this negative frame, most managers choose D. Because both problems are identical, the difference in decision choice is accountable strictly by how the problem is framed.

5 *Misconception of chance.* When a series of similar events occurs, managers may incorrectly gauge the probability of their future recurrence. For example, a manager who is hiring the fifth sales director in two years may feel that the person should work out well. After all, the first four did not work out, and the odds against five failures is small. In truth, the four people who failed have no bearing on the potential performance of the fifth. Each failure was a separate event, and the chance of success on the fifth try should not be overestimated.

6 *Overconfidence.* One of the interesting research findings on decision-making biases is that most people overestimate their ability to predict uncertain outcomes. Before making a decision, managers have unrealistic expectations of their ability to understand the risk and make the right choice. Overconfidence is greatest when answering questions of moderate to extreme difficulty. For example, when a group of people were asked to define quantities about which they had little direct knowledge ("What was the dollar value of Canadian lumber exports in 1977?" "What was the amount of taxes collected by the U.S. Internal Revenue Service in 1970?"), they overestimated their accuracy. Evidence of overconfidence is illustrated in cases where subjects were so certain of an answer that they felt 99.9 percent certain but in fact were correct only about 85 percent of the time. These findings are especially important for strategic decision making in which uncertainty is high, because managers may unrealistically expect that they can successfully predict outcomes and hence select the wrong alternative.[42]

INCREASING PARTICIPATION IN DECISION MAKING

Decision making is something that individual managers often do, but decision makers in the business world also operate as part of a group. Many of today's managers are including lower-level employees in the decision-making process whenever possible. In addition, some decisions require a greater degree of subordinate participation. Decisions may be made through a committee, a task group, departmental participation, or an informal coalition. We will begin our discussion of participative decision making with the Vroom–Jago model, which helps identify the correct amount of participation by subordinates in making a particular decision.

Vroom–Jago Model

Vroom–Jago model
A model designed to help managers gauge the amount of subordinate participation in decision making.

Victor Vroom and Arthur Jago developed a model of participation in decision making that provides guidance for practicing managers.[43] The **Vroom–Jago** model helps the manager gauge the appropriate amount of participation for subordinates. It has three major components: leader participation styles, a set of diagnostic questions with which to analyze a decision situation, and a series of decision rules.

Leader Participation Styles. The model employs five levels of subordinate participation in decision making ranging from highly autocratic to highly democratic, as illustrated in Exhibit 8.5. Autocratic leadership styles are represented by AI and AII, consulting styles by CI and CII, and a group decision by G. The five styles fall along a continuum, and the manager should select one depending on the situation. If the situation warrants, the manager could make the decision alone (AI), share the problem with subordinates individually (CI), or let group members make the decision (G).

Diagnostic Questions. How does a manager decide which of the five decision

styles to use? The appropriate degree of decision participation depends on the responses to eight diagnostic questions. These questions deal with the problem, the required level of decision quality, and the importance of having subordinates commit to the decision.

1 *Quality Requirement* **(QR):** *How important is the quality of this decision?* If a high-quality decision is important for group performance, the leader has to be actively involved.

2 *Commitment Requirement* **(CR):** *How important is subordinate commitment to the decision?* If implementation requires that subordinates commit to the decision, leaders should involve the subordinates in the decision process.

3 *Leader's Information* **(LI):** *Do I have sufficient information to make a high-quality decision?* If the leader does not have sufficient information or expertise, the leader should involve subordinates to obtain that information.

4 *Problem Structure* **(ST):** *Is the decision problem well-structured?* If the problem is ambiguous and poorly structured, the leader will need to interact with subordinates to clarify the problem and identify possible solutions.

5 *Commitment Probability* **(CP):** *If I were to make the decision by myself, is it reasonably certain that my subordinates would be committed to the decision?* If subordinates typically go along with whatever the leader decides, their involvement in the decision process will be less important.

6 *Goal Congruence* **(GC):** *Do subordinates share the organizational goals to be attained in solving this problem?* If subordinates do not share the goals of the organization, the leader should not allow the group to make the decision alone.

7 *Subordinate Conflict* **(CO):** *Is conflict over preferred solutions likely to occur among subordinates?* Disagreement among subordinates can be resolved by allowing their participation and discussion.

8 *Subordinate Information* **(SI):** *Do subordinates have enough information to make a*

EXHIBIT 8.5
Five Leader Decision Styles

	Decision Style		Description
Highly Autocratic		AI	You solve the problem or make the decision yourself using information available to you at the time.
		AII	You obtain the necessary information from your subordinates and then decide on the solution to the problem yourself.
		CI	You share the problem with relevant subordinates individually, getting their ideas and suggestions without bringing them together as a group. Then you make the decision.
		CII	You share the problem with your subordinates as a group, collectively obtaining their ideas and suggestions. Then you make the decision.
Highly Democratic		G	You share a problem with your subordinates as a group. Your role is much like that of chairman. You do not try to influence the group to adopt "your" solution, and you are willing to accept and implement any solution that has the support of the entire group.

NOTE: A = autocratic; C = consultative; G = group.

SOURCE: Reprinted from Victor H. Vroom and Arthur G. Jago, *The New Leadership: Managing Participation in Organizations* (Englewood Cliffs, N.J.: Prentice-Hall, 1988). Copyright 1987 by V. H. Vroom and A. G. Jago. Used with permission of the authors.

high-quality decision? If subordinates have good information, then more responsibility for the decision can be delegated to them.

These questions seem detailed, but they quickly narrow the options available to managers and point to the appropriate level of group participation in the decision.

Selecting a Decision Style. The decision flowchart in Exhibit 8.6 allows a leader to adopt a participation style by answering the questions in sequence. The leader begins at the left side of the chart with question QR: How important is the quality of the decision? If the answer is high, then the leader proceeds to question CR: How important is subordinate commitment to the decision? If the answer is high, the next question is LI: Do I have sufficient information to make a high-quality decision? If the answer is yes, the leader proceeds to answer question CP because question ST is irrelevant if the leader has sufficient information to make a high-quality decision. Managers can quickly learn to use the basic model to adapt their leadership styles to fit their decision problem and the situation.

Several decision styles are equally acceptable in many situations. When this happens, Vroom and Jago note that the autocratic style saves time without reducing decision quality or acceptance. However, in today's changing workplace, where employees are often demanding more participation, managers should try to involve subordinates in decision making whenever possible.

The decision tree model has been criticized as being less than perfect,[44] but it is useful to decision makers, and the body of supportive research is growing.[45] Managers make timely, high-quality decisions when following the model. One application of the model occurred at Barouh-Eaton Allen Corporation.

KO-REC-TYPE

Barouh-Eaton Allen started prospering when owner Vic Barouh noticed that a typist kept a piece of white chalk by her machine. To erase an error, she would lightly rub over it with the chalk. It took several passes, but the correction was neatly made. Barouh's company already

E X H I B I T   8 . 6

Vroom–Jago Decision Tree for Determining an Appropriate Decision-Making Method—Group Problems

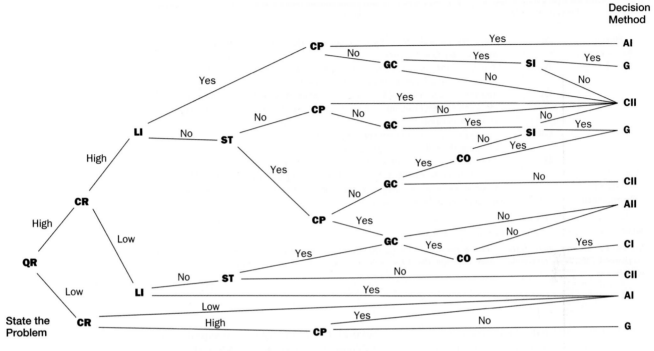

QR How important is the quality of this decision?

CR How important is subordinate commitment to the decision?

LI Do you have sufficient information to make a high-quality decision?

ST Is the problem well structured?

CP If you were to make the decision by yourself, is it reasonably certain that your subordinates would be committed to it?

GC Do subordinates share the organization goals to be attained in solving this problem?

CO Is conflict among subordinates over preferred solutions likely?

SI Do subordinates have sufficient information to make a high-quality decision?

SOURCE: Reprinted from Victor H. Vroom and Arthur G. Jago, *The New Leadership: Managing Participation in Organizations* (Englewood Cliffs, N.J.: Prentice-Hall, 1988). Copyright 1987 by V. H. Vroom and A. G. Jago. Used with permission of the authors.

made carbon paper, so he tried rubbing chalk on one side of a sheet of paper, putting the paper between the error and typewriter, and striking the same key. Most of the error disappeared under a thin coating of chalk dust. Thus, Ko-Rec-Type was born. Demand for the product was enormous, and the company prospered.

Then IBM invented the self-correcting typewriter. Within two days after IBM's announcement, nearly 40 people told Barouh that the company was in trouble. Nobody was going to buy Ko-Rec-Type again.

Barouh bought a self-correcting typewriter, took it to the plant, called everybody together, and told them what they had to do. To survive, the company had to learn to make this ribbon. They also had to learn to make the cartridge that held the ribbon, because cartridges could not be purchased on the market. They also had to learn to make the spools that held the tape. They had to learn to make the ink, the machine that puts on ink, injection molding to make the spools, and so on. It was an enormous challenge. Barouh got everyone involved regardless of position or education.

To everyone's astonishment, the company produced its first self-correcting ribbon in only six months. Moreover, it was the only company in the world to produce that product. Barouh

later learned that it took IBM six years to make its self-correcting ribbon. With the new product, sales remained high, and the company avoided disaster.[46] ■

The Vroom–Jago model shows that Vic Barouh used the correct decision style. Moving from left to right in Exhibit 8.6, the questions and answers are as follows. (QR) *How important is the quality of this decision?* Definitely high. (CR) *How important is subordinate commitment to the decision?* Importance of commitment is probably low, because subordinates had a great deal of respect for Barouh and would do whatever he asked. (LI) *Did Barouh have sufficient information to make a high-quality decision?* Definitely no. (ST) *Is the problem well-structured?* Definitely no. The remaining questions are not relevant because at this point the decision tree leads directly to the CII decision style. Barouh should have used a consultative decision style by having subordinates participate in problem discussions as a group—which he did.

Group Participation Formats

The Vroom–Jago model illustrates that managers can select the amount of group participation in decision making. They can also select decision format. Three formats generally can be used: the interactive group, the nominal group, and the Delphi group. Each format has unique characteristics that make it more suitable for certain decisions. Most task forces, committees, and work groups fall into the category of interactive groups. Nominal and Delphi groups normally are convened for the purpose of increasing creativity during group decision making.

Interactive Groups. Research on the Vroom–Jago model indicates that having subordinates meet as an interactive group leads to more effective decisions than having the group leader meet with each member individually.[47] An **interactive group** simply means that members are brought together face-to-face and have a specific

agenda and decision goals. Interactive groups typically begin with a group leader stating a problem and asking for input from members. Discussion is unorganized. The group may meander through problem identification and may require some problem redefinition. Alternatives are generated and evaluated. Eventually, participants will vote or perhaps discuss alternatives until they reach a consensus on a desired solution. A staff meeting or departmental meeting formed to discuss next year's goals is a good example of interactive group decision making. Interactive groups will be described in more detail in Chapter 15.

Nominal Groups. Because some participants may talk more and dominate group discussions in interactive groups, the **nominal group** technique was developed to ensure that every group participant has equal input in the decision-making process.[48] The nominal group is structured in a series of steps to equalize participation:

1 Each participant writes down his or her ideas on the problem to be discussed. These ideas usually are suggestions for a solution.
2 A round robin in which each group member presents his or her ideas to the group is set up. The ideas are written on a chalkboard for all members to see. No discussion of the ideas occurs until every person's ideas have been presented and written down for general viewing.
3 After all ideas have been presented, there is an open discussion of the ideas for the purpose of clarification and evaluation. This part of the discussion tends to be spontaneous and unstructured.
4 After the discussion, a secret ballot is taken in which each group member votes for preferred solutions. The adopted decision is the one that receives the most votes.

Delphi Groups. Developed by the Rand Corporation, the **Delphi group** technique is used to combine expert opinions from dif-

nominal group
A group decision-making format that emphasizes equal participation in the decision process by all group members.

interactive group
A group decision-making format in which group members are brought together face-to-face and have a specific agenda and decision goals.

Delphi group
A group decision-making format that involves the circulation among participants of questionnaires on the selected problem, sharing of answers, and continuous recirculation/refinement of questionnaires until a consensus has been obtained.

ferent perspectives about an ambiguous problem.[49] Unlike interactive and nominal groups, Delphi group participants do not meet face-to-face—in fact, they never see one another. This technique calls for a group leader to solicit and collate written, expert opinions on a topic through the use of questionnaires. After the answers are received, a summary of the opinions is developed and distributed to participants. Then a new questionnaire on the same problem is circulated. In this second round, participants have the benefit of knowing other people's opinions and can change their suggested answers to reflect this new information. The process of sending out questionnaires and then sharing the results continues until a consensus is reached.

Advantages and Disadvantages of Participative Decision Making

Whatever group techniques managers use for decision making, there are clear advantages and disadvantages compared with individual decision making.[50] Because managers often have a choice between making a decision by themselves or including others, they should understand the advantages and disadvantages of participative decision making, which are summarized in Exhibit 8.7.

Advantages.   Groups have an advantage over individuals because they bring together a broader perspective for defining

the problem and diagnosing underlying causes and effects. In addition to enriching problem diagnosis, groups offer more knowledge and facts with which to identify potential solutions and produce more decision alternatives. Moreover, people who participate in decision making are more satisfied with the decision and more likely to support it, thereby facilitating implementation. Group discussion also can help reduce uncertainty for decision makers who may be unwilling to undertake a big risk by themselves. Finally, group discussion enhances member satisfaction and produces support for a possibly risky decision.

Disadvantages.   Group decisions tend to be time-consuming. People must be consulted, and they jointly diagnose problems and discuss solutions. Moreover, groups may reach a compromise solution that is less than optimal for the organization. Another problem is groupthink. **Groupthink** is a "mode of thinking that people engage in when they are deeply involved in a cohesive in-group, and when the members' strivings for unanimity override their motivation to realistically appraise alternative courses of action."[51] Groupthink means that people are so committed to the group that they are reluctant to disagree with one another; thus, the group loses the diversity of opinions essential to effective decision making. For example, many of the people involved in making the movie *The Bonfire of the Vanities,* which bombed at the box office, had doubts about casting decisions and changes in the storyline, but no one was

groupthink
A phenomenon in which group members are so committed to the group that they are reluctant to express contrary opinions.

EXHIBIT 8.7
Advantages and Disadvantages of Participative Decision Making

Advantages	Disadvantages
1 Broader perspective for problem definition and analysis.	1 Time-consuming; wasted resources if used for programmed decisions.
2 More knowledge, facts, and alternatives can be evaluated.	2 Compromise decisions may satisfy no one.
3 Discussion clarifies ambiguous problems and reduces uncertainty about alternatives.	3 Groupthink: Group norms may reduce dissent and opinion diversity.
4 Participation fosters member satisfaction and support for decision.	4 No clear focus for decision responsibility.

willing to voice these opinions. Director Brian DePalma says he had some reservations as well, but because everyone else seemed to be in agreement, he convinced himself that making the changes was the right decision.[52] Finally, there is no clear focus of decision responsibility, because the group rather than any single individual makes the decision.

One example of the disadvantages of group decision making occurred when a coalition at Citibank refused to change the practice of "parking"—the bogus transfer of foreign exchange deposits to shift bank profits to countries with low tax rates. The line between illegal and legal activities was hazy, and groupthink appeared—people were unwilling to disagree with the current practice because group norms supported high profits and reduced taxes. Group members were willing to compromise their values, groupthink reduced dissent, and there was no clear focus of responsibility because everyone had agreed to the potentially illegal practice.[53]

IMPROVING DECISION-MAKING BREADTH AND CREATIVITY

Encouraging employee thinking and participation in solving problems can improve decision quality. Frontline workers who are in touch with the needs and concerns of customers can have a clearer insight into how to solve problems that directly concern those customers. For example, soliciting the input of terminal workers at Greyhound Lines might have helped Greyhound executives avoid some of the costly mistakes they made with the Trips reservation system. At Chrysler, the team manager for the new Dodge Neon asked for line workers' input regarding specific problems and got more than 4,000 ideas, many of which were implemented.[54]

In today's fast-changing world, decisions must often be made quickly, and an organization's ability to stimulate the creativity and innovativeness of its employees is becoming increasingly important. Competitive pressures are challenging managers to create environments that foster and support creative thinking and sharing of diverse opinions. An environment in which bosses make all the decisions and hand them down to frontline workers is becoming not only inappropriate but inefficient. As organizations seek to take full advantage of all workers' abilities and make the best use of everyone's time, it makes sense to have those who are closest to a problem involved in solving it.[55] The Leading the Management Revolution box earlier in this chapter describes how creative, participative decision making helped Marmot meet its deadlines.

How can managers pursue the advantages of participation and overcome some of the disadvantages? A number of techniques have been developed to help individual managers as well as groups make better decisions. These techniques are often used in the interactive and nominal group formats discussed in the previous section.

A **devil's advocate** is assigned the role of challenging the assumptions and assertions made by the group.[56] The devil's advocate forces the group to rethink its approach to the problem and to avoid reaching premature consensus or making unreasonable assumptions before proceeding with problem solutions. One management scholar has recommended that companies create "an institutionalized devil's advocate" by appointing teams to act as perpetual challengers of others' ideas and proposals. This forces managers and others to examine and explain the risks associated with a particular decision alternative.[57]

This approach would be similar to **multiple advocacy,** a technique that involves several advocates and multiple points of view. Minority opinions and unpopular viewpoints are assigned to forceful representatives, who then debate before the decision makers. Former president Bush was renowned for using multiple advocacy in his decision making. The proposal for

devil's advocate
A decision-making technique in which an individual is assigned the role of challenging the assumptions and assertions made by the group to prevent premature consensus.

multiple advocacy
A decision-making technique that involves several advocates and presentation of multiple points of view, including minority and unpopular opinions.

clean-air legislation in 1989 was a textbook case, because White House aides staged debates they called "Scheduled Train Wrecks" to help Bush think through the issue. These were live scrimmages with Bush asking questions back and forth during the debate. The result was a decision based on solid argument and understanding of all perspectives.[58]

brainstorming
A decision-making technique in which group members present spontaneous suggestions for problem solution, regardless of their likelihood of implementation, in order to promote freer, more creative thinking within the group.

Brainstorming uses a face-to-face, interactive group to spontaneously suggest ideas for problem solution.[59] Brainstorming is perhaps the best-known decision aid; its primary role is to supply additional creative solutions. Kodak encourages continuous brainstorming and has created a "humor room" where workers can relax and have creative brainstorming sessions. The room is filled with videotapes of comedians, joke books, stress-reducing toys, and software for creative decision making.[60] The brainstorming technique encourages group members to suggest alternatives regardless of their likelihood of being implemented. No critical comments of any kind are allowed until all suggestions have been listed. Members are encouraged to brainstorm possible solutions out loud, and freewheeling is welcomed. The more novel and unusual the idea, the better. The object of brainstorming is to promote freer, more flexible thinking and to enable group members to build on one another's creativity. The typical session begins with a warmup wherein definitional issues are settled, proceeds through the freewheeling idea-generation stage, and concludes with an evaluation of feasible ideas.[61]

Using Information Technology for Decision Making

Sometimes technology becomes the hoped-for savior in companies. But sometimes it fails and becomes a "black hole of expenditures and resources." Take the case of FoxMeyer Drug Company, the Carrollton, Texas, wholesaler described in the following example.

FOXMEYER DRUG COMPANY

In 1994 FoxMeyer Drug Company unveiled its multimillion dollar plan for a computerized system to manage critical operations. The hope was for improved efficiency and thus, decreased operation costs. As a small player in wholesale drug distribution, FoxMeyer wanted to be one of the survivors in the rapidly consolidating industry. Then-CEO Thomas Anderson promised the technology drive would accelerate sales growth without an increase in costs. As then-chief information officer Robert R. Brown said, "We're betting our company on this."

Well, they lost. In August 1996 the wholesale distributor filed for bankruptcy. This case illustrates the minefield managers can step on if they are too careless in introducing technology. Here's what when wrong. FoxMeyer managers were naive, believing what salespeople told them about the relatively new SAP software, which hadn't been used with a wholesale distributor. Difficult to implement, it would require hiring expensive consultants. Executives were so overoptimistic about computerization that they underbid on projects, expecting their own costs to be lowered. They tried too hard to be cutting-edge—but instead just got cut. The current chief information officer now says there are cheaper and better ways to do it that "aren't quite as technologically advanced."[62] And maybe not as hazardous. ■

On the other hand, there have been many success stories, such as UPS. In 1985, UPS's information systems group was comprised of 118 people; ten years later, information systems staff totals 4,000. With this increased staff UPS created the first nationwide mobile data service, linking 70 commercial carriers; 53,000 vehicles now have handheld data collection computers. Last year UPS became the first package deliverer to offer online order services through CompuServe and Prodigy.[63]

The information technology transformation at UPS has not been without problems. Will UPS's $40 million investment in information technology pay off? The challenges

faced by FoxMeyer and UPS capture the themes remaining in this chapter. We will explore developments in information technology, the various types of information systems available to organizations, and the benefits and challenges for implementing these systems. UPS was faced with expanding its information capacities because Federal Express, its major competitor, was racing to offer customers new services—services that UPS could not provide without adopting new information technology.[64]

The use of information technology may be one of the most defining aspects of organizational success in the upcoming years, as it has been for UPS. It is thus important to develop some appreciation for the changes information technology brings to organizations. Managing information technology is about managing change and uncertainty. It is about managing change and uncertainty under time duress. In order to understand these challenges, let us begin by developing an understanding of information technology and the attributes of quality information.

INFORMATION TECHNOLOGY

Information technology can be defined as the hardware, software, telecommunications, database management, and other information-processing technologies used to store, process, and deliver information.[65] These technologies allow managers to generate and access complex databases of customer and organizational information. They enable employees throughout the organization to communicate in ways previously not possible. The availability and increasingly accessible costs of information technology place pressure on organizations to invest in new hardware, software, and other information-processing technologies lest they lose their market position.

By providing managers with more information more quickly than ever before, information technology improves efficiency

and effectiveness at each stage of the strategic decision process. Whether through computer-aided manufacturing, real-time dialogues with customers, or intercity inventory control, information technology aids operational processes and decision making.[66] Consider Tokyo-based Kao Corporation, rival to Procter & Gamble and maker of floppy disks, consumer products, and specialty chemicals. Kao Corporation reported spending $27,000 per employee last year to produce a global information network. This network will allow Kao to gather more detailed information on customers and better meet customer demands for quick-response production and logistics.[67]

Data versus Information

The trade-off for generating more information presents a serious challenge to information technicians and managers. They must sort through overwhelming amounts of data to identify only necessary information for a particular purpose.[68] **Data** are raw facts and figures that in and of themselves may not be useful to managers. To be useful, data must be processed into finished information products that have relevance and purpose for the recipient. An increasing challenge for managers is being able to effectively identify and access useful information. **Information** is data that has been converted into a meaningful and useful context for specific users.[69]

The magnitude of this job is reflected in organizations' introduction of the chief information officer (CIO) position. CIOs are responsible for managing organizational databases and implementing new information technology. The purchase options in hardware, software, networking, and telecommunications products can be overwhelming to information officers. The enormity of data that combinations of this technology can produce is equally overwhelming. Decisions involving the adoption and management of new technologies often fall to the chief information officer.

data
Raw, unsummarized, and unanalyzed facts and figures.

information technology
The hardware, software, telecommunications, database management, and other technologies used to store, process, and distribute information.

information
Data that has been converted into a meaningful and useful context for the receiver.

management information system (MIS)
A form of computer-based information system that collects, organizes, and distributes the data managers use in performing their management functions.

operations information system
A computer-based information system that supports a company's day-to-day operations.

The CIO must integrate old and new technology to support organizational decision making, operational processes, and communication. The CIO must manage the infrastructure that will place the necessary information in the right place at the right time.[70]

Characteristics of Useful Information

Organizations depend on high-quality information to develop strategic plans, support employees, identify problems, and interact with other organizations. One way of viewing information is to think of it in terms of characteristics that are important to the organization. Important information attributes include time, content, and form. These information attributes are described in Exhibit 8.8.

TYPES OF INFORMATION SYSTEMS

Information systems are computer-based systems that draw on hardware, software, and human resources to support organizational information and communication needs. These systems can be classified in many ways. One way to distinguish among the many types of information systems is to focus on the functions they perform and the people they serve in an organization. **Management information systems** typically support strategic decision-making needs of top management. **Operations information systems** support information-processing needs of a business's day-to-day operations as well as low-level operations management functions.

The relationship of management information systems and operations information systems to business operations and typical level of management is depicted in Exhibit 8.9. A discussion of each of these types of systems follows.

Operations Information Systems

Transaction-processing systems, process control systems, and office automation systems are classified as operations information systems since they support daily operations and decision making for low-level management.

EXHIBIT 8.8
Characteristics of High-Quality Information

Time Dimension
Information is provided when needed. — **Timeliness**
Information is up-to-date when provided. — **Currency**
Information is provided for the past, present, or future. — **Time Period**

Content Dimension
Information is free of error. — **Accuracy**
Information suits the needs of a particular recipient. — **Relevance**
All necessary information is provided. — **Completeness**
Only needed information is provided. — **Conciseness**

Form Dimension
Information is provided in an easily understandable form. — **Clarity**
Information can be provided in detail or summary. — **Detail**
Information can be presented in narrative, numeric, or spatial form. — **Presentation**

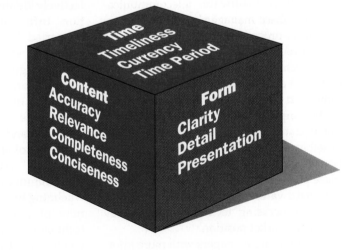

SOURCE: Adapted from James A. O'Brien, *Introduction to Information Systems*, 7th ed. (Burr Ridge, Ill.: Irwin, 1994), 309–310. Reproduced with permission.

EXHIBIT 8.9
**The Management-
Level Application of
Information Systems**

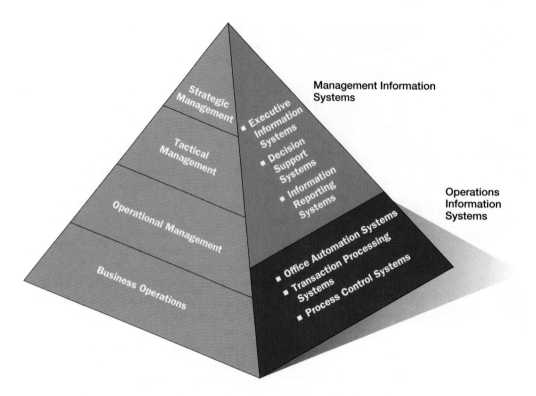

Management Information
Systems

- Executive Information Systems
- Decision Support Systems
- Information Reporting Systems

Strategic Management

Tactical Management

Operational Management

Business Operations

Operations Information Systems

- Office Automation Systems
- Transaction Processing Systems
- Process Control Systems

SOURCE: James A. O'Brien, *Introduction to Information Systems,* 7th ed. (Burr Ridge, Ill.: Irwin, 1994), 25.

Transaction-processing systems (TPSs) record and process data resulting from business operations. Information systems that record sales to customers, purchases from suppliers, inventory changes, and wages to employees are considered transaction-processing systems. These systems feed organizational databases that allow for the production of information products, such as customer statements, employee paychecks, and financial reports. Transaction-processing systems identify, collect, and organize the fundamental building blocks of information from which an organization operates. Most organizational reports are generated from these databases.[71]

In addition to the tasks of recording and processing, operations information systems can make routine decisions that control operational processes. For example, petroleum refineries, pulp and paper mills, food manufacturing plants, and electric power plants use process control systems. **Process control systems** monitor and control ongoing physical processes. Special sensing devices monitor physical phenomena such as temperature or pressure change and convert these measurements. The measurements or sensor-detected data are then relayed to a computer for processing and real-time adjustment.[72]

Office automation systems, such as word processors, desktop publishers, E-mail, and teleconferencing, are also classified as operations information systems. These systems transform traditional manual procedures to electronic media. Chevron, for example, makes more than 5,800 electronic payments a month to suppliers, nearly 14 percent of the checks it once wrote.[73] Office automation systems allow companies like Chevron to streamline accounting departments, reduce errors, and improve customer relations.

Operations information systems aid organizational decision makers in many ways and across various settings. At Northrop Corporation, for example, 400,000 pieces of paper were required to build each F/A-18 jet fighter fuselage. When Northrop converted to a computerized information system, the ten-foot-high pile of paper for each

transaction-processing system (TPS)
A type of operations information system that records and processes the organization's routinely occurring transactions, such as daily sales or purchases of supplies.

office automation systems
Systems such as word processors, desktop publishing, and E-mail that transform manual procedures to electronic media.

process control system
A computer system that monitors and controls ongoing physical processes, such as temperature or pressure changes.

Ryder Transportation Resources uses a *decision support system* called RyderLinc, a cross-functional, integrated computer system that allows computers throughout the company to interact with each other as well as with those of customers and suppliers. The new information system can give customers precise information on virtually every aspect of their transportation and distribution services on a daily or even hourly basis, thus lending support to Ryder's excellent on-time, 99 percent damage-free delivery record. RyderLinc also supports sales by giving potential customers access to global data and market information and allowing them to compare the financial implications of different distribution and transportation alternatives.

information reporting system

A system that organizes information in the form of prespecified reports that managers use in day-to-day decision making.

decision support system (DSS)

An interactive, computer-based system that uses decision models and specialized databases to support organization decision makers.

executive information system (EIS)

A decision support system that retrieves, manipulates, and displays information tailored to the needs of top-level managers.

fuselage was put on one laser disc. Employees now consult a computer for instructions, and supervisors can make instant changes in procedures across the factory, avoiding the inconvenience and confusion of paper shuffling. The new system at Northrop saved $20 million on the fuselage project.[74]

Until the 1960s, information systems were used primarily for transaction processing, accounting, and record keeping. In 1964, however, a new generation of computers was introduced that used silicon chip circuitry. This change allowed for more processing power per dollar. As computer manufacturers promoted these systems to justify new equipment costs and managers began visualizing ways in which the computers could help them make important decisions, management information systems were born.[75]

Management Information Systems

Management information systems (MISs) are computer-based systems that provide information and support for effective managerial decision making. Like operations in-

formation systems, these systems are comprised of software, hardware, and human resources. When a production manager needs to make a decision about production scheduling, he or she may need data on the anticipated number of orders in the coming month based on trends, inventory levels, and availability of computers and personnel. The MIS can provide these data. In fact, **information reporting systems,** the most common form of MIS, provide managers and decision makers with reports that support day-to-day decision-making needs. These reports typically provide managers with prespecified information for use in making structured decisions. The Technology for Today box describes how management information systems helped Buckman Laboratories employees stay close to the customer.

Decision support systems (DSSs) are interactive, computer-based information systems that rely on decision models and specialized databases to support decision makers. For example, electronic spreadsheets and other decision support software allow users to pose a series of what-if questions and receive interactive responses to ad hoc inquiries. Through DSSs, managers can explore various alternatives and receive tentative information based on different sets of assumptions.[76]

Executive information systems (EISs) are management information systems that facilitate the highest levels of strategic decision making.[77] They are typically comprised of software that provides easy access to large amounts of complex data and can analyze, present, and communicate that data in a timely fashion.[78] EISs provide top management with quick access to relevant internal and external information and, if designed properly, can help them diagnose problems as well as develop solutions. The EIS at Mississauga City, Ontario, for example, allows the city manager to travel vertically or horizontally through the city's data by jumping from graph to graph within his own department or comparing figures with other departments' data.[79]

Other Information Systems

Other categories of information systems may support either operations or management applications and are thus used at different levels of an organization. These technologies redefine collaboration in organizations through group support systems or clone expert decision-making models for nonexpert users.

A **group decision support system (GDSS)** is an interactive computer-based system that facilitates group decision making. Also called *collaborative work systems*, GDSSs are designed to allow team members to interact and at the same time take advantage of computer-based support data. Participating managers may sit around a conference table equipped with a computer terminal at each position or may sit thousands of miles apart and, through live television, use team conferencing to view one another and share data displays. The 1991 Advantage Auckland Meetings, for example, brought together 250 senior executives to develop opportunities for enhancing New Zealand's competitiveness in world markets. Through use of a group decision support system, the meetings fostered interorganizational learning and served as catalysts for change across industries previously characterized by dysfunctional conflict.[80]

Artificial Intelligence (AI) is an information technology whose ultimate goal is to make computers think, see, talk, listen, and feel like humans. The area of AI that has had the greatest impact on organizations is the expert system. An **expert system (ES)** attempts to duplicate the thinking process that professionals and managers use when making decisions.

An expert system is developed by codifying a specialist's knowledge into decision rules that are written into a computer

group decision support system (GDSS)
An interactive computer-based system that facilitates group communication and decision making; also called *collaborative work system*.

expert system (ES)
Information technology that programs a computer to duplicate an expert's decision-making and problem-solving strategies.

program to mimic the expert's problem-solving strategy. An expert system is very similar to a decision support system. In fact, both provide a high level of problem-solving support to their users. However, expert systems tend to address repetitive problems for narrow domain areas and offer recommendations, whereas DSSs typically treat ad hoc or unique problems that are more complex in nature. Export Development Corporation's GAMBLE system is referred to as a DSS but probably functions more as an ES.

Export Development Corporation (EDC) developed a computerized database several years ago when its short-term insurance group was drowning in paper. Case approval for insurance was averaging 11 days, with up to 30 handoffs among employees before approval. The database reduced paper files from 75,000 to 500 for severe risk cases. Next, EDC linked its computer to Dun & Bradstreet's Dunslink service. This allowed corporate profiles to be downloaded in seconds versus days of compilation. The resulting system, GAMBLE, calculates risk for straightforward cases in minutes, approving insurance requests of up to $5 million. GAMBLE can also make recommendations, highlight points for a credit analyst to consider, or note missing information for more complex cases.[81]

Emerging Information Systems

Exhibit 8.10 summarizes the major categories of information systems discussed so far in this chapter.

A number of new information technologies move the meeting room from down the hall to cyberspace, offer new ways for visualizing information, or draw on multiple technologies to diagnose problems and aid complex decision making. Groupware, geographic information systems, integrated information systems, and networks are irreversibly changing the work world as we know it.

Groupware, a new area of software technology, supports routine organizational collaboration as well as the kind of lateral collaboration used at the Auckland meetings described earlier. The most common form of groupware is E-mail, electronic mail messaging. Through electronic messaging, communication and geographic barriers disappear. As exemplified by the communications received from Tiananmen Square, Beijing, China, during the 1989 uprising there, E-mail may even surpass governmental control.

A **geographic information system (GIS)** is a type of DSS that provides users with

groupware
Software that enables employees on a network to interact with one another; the most common form of groupware is E-mail.

geographic information system (GIS)
A type of decision support system that provides layers of information expressed visually through the use of maps; used for distribution planning, site selection, and trade area analysis.

EXHIBIT 8.10
Major Categories of Information Systems

Operations information systems	Management information systems	Other information systems
process data generated by business operations.	provide information and support for effective managerial decision making.	■ *Group decision support systems* are interactive, computer-based systems that facilitate group decision making.
■ *Transaction-processing systems* process data resulting from business transactions, update operational databases, and produce business documents.	■ *Information reporting systems* provide information in the form of prespecified reports and displays to managers.	■ *Expert systems* address repetitive decision problems for narrow domains and offer recommendations.
■ *Process control systems* monitor and control industrial processes.	■ *Decision support systems* provide interative ad hoc support for the decision-making process of managers.	
■ *Office automation systems* automate office procedures and enhance office communications and productivity.	■ *Executive information systems* provide critical information tailored to specific information needs of top management.	

SOURCE: Adapted from James A. O'Brien, *Introduction to Information Systems*, 7th ed. (Burr Ridge, Ill.: Irwin, 1994), 309–310. Reproduced with permission.

layers of information expressed visually through the use of maps. GISs support analytical decision making for business as well as for the management of defense troops, species management, emergency management, land use planning, redistricting, and demographics, among many other applications. Although GISs have been used predominantly for environmental and municipal planning, industry has recently begun to embrace GISs as powerful tools for identifying problems and solutions. Jack Dangermond of Environmental Systems Research Institute (ESRI) believes GISs are fueling a revolution in how most information will be used and analyzed. He predicts that GISs will be embedded in most computer applications and on most desktop computers by the year 2000. Currently, GISs help decision makers in business perform distribution planning, site selection, trade area analysis, and regulatory compliance.[82] Exhibit 8.11 displays output from ArcView software, the desktop GIS software from ESRI. In this marketing view of the Atlanta, Georgia, market, ArcView software is providing a new and powerful context to perform comprehensive demographic, consumer, or product performance analysis. These views are created by integrating and visualizing both internal customer data and a variety of available external GIS data sources. ArcView software can then be used to identify and target available customers from the lowest levels (i.e., household, block, group, sales territory) to the broadest of marketing levels (i.e., distribution, market, national).

No one knows for certain where the so-called information highway will take us, but Interval Research Corporation hopes to be there first.

EXHIBIT 8. 11
Output from ArcView® GIS Software

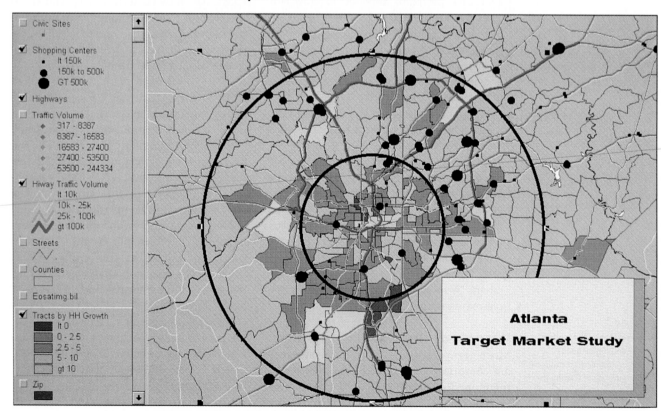

▪ INTERVAL RESEARCH CORPORATION

In 1992, Silicon Valley visionary David Liddle created Interval Research Corporation, which then disappeared off the computer world's monitor until 1994 when it went on a 33-city bus tour, displaying a circus tent full of techno-gadgets to underwhelmed crowds. So much for Liddle's goal of mapping out tomorrow.

But late 1996 saw some discernible action from Interval, which had spent its time role-playing hypothetical scenarios of a wired future and creating prototypes. Now they have three spinoff companies and a number of products designed primarily for non-work times. The original plan for Interval was to live off its initial seed money and later to be supported by licensing fees paid for its discoveries. The actual developed products are closely guarded secrets, but they involve "software systems for Internet publishing"; interactive programming for girls ages 7–12; and sophisticated signal processing technology for interactive programs designed to draw kids ages 6–11 into new and creative realms of play, involving tumbling and waving around, not just sitting and clicking a mouse.

Interval believes its artists are as essential as engineers. "In the first five minutes with a piece of technology," says Liddle, "artists push it to the edge of what's possible. . . . You need unreasonable people doing things for reasons they can't verbalize."

Other research centers have office workers developing things their counterparts would need, such as laser printers. Their research can be done on-site, but Interval's employees go out and study real people in normal daily situations to see how information technology can improve their lives. Liddle explains why they spend so much time out in the field, watching others. "We study individuals—everyday people. We can't do that by introspection."[83] ▪

network
A system that links together people and departments within or among organizations for the purpose of sharing information resources.

Integrated Information Systems.

Most organizational information systems are comprised of several of the previously mentioned systems. Integrated information systems draw on two or more technologies to provide more support to the organization than could be obtained through the use of an individual technology. For example, throughout the 1992 Los Angeles riots and the 1994 Northridge earthquake, computer resources were maintained by a help desk where a computerized multimedia/expert system continued to operate. Los Angeles has integrated these two technologies to meet client technical support needs. The integrated system, AWESOME, uses video imaging and an expert system to diagnose and coach users through computer problems. For example, if a client requests assistance with a cabling problem, the technician accesses images of the cabling connection and describes these images to the client with more speed and accuracy than a technical support manual could provide. AWESOME allows for computer problem diagnosis for the L.A. Police Department, the L.A. Fire Department, the city council and mayor, all PC users and AS/400 users across dozens of departments, and those who access the city's mainframe. AWESOME has allowed technical specialists to quickly and more accurately communicate specific solutions for a variety of client requests and to reduce average diagnostic time by almost 50 percent.[84]

Networking. Currently, considerable energy surrounds network computing or network centric computing. Lou Gerstner, CEO of IBM, has recently suggested that the arrival of low-cost digital networks is remaking the computer business and reshaping organizations in the same way the low-cost power of the microprocessor overwhelmed mainframes and minicomputers in the 1980s.[85] Gerstner defines network centric computing as computing that is driven by powerful networked technologies that provide inexpensive and high-speed digital transmission.[86]

Networks take many forms. They may link people and departments within a particular building or across corporate offices. They may also allow company representatives to interact globally with one another and with customers. Exhibit 8.12 illustrates a simplified network used by an automaker.

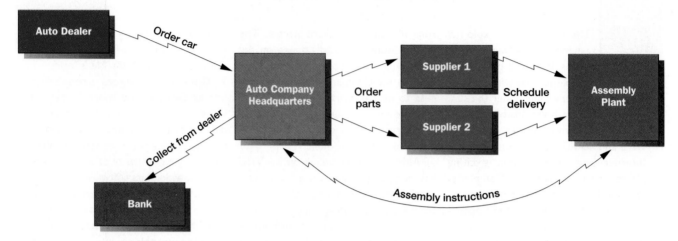

SOURCE: Based on Joel Dreyfuss, "Networking: Japan's Latest Computer Craze," *Fortune*, July 7, 1986, 95.

The computer at the auto company head-quarters electronically receives a car order specifying model, color, and options. The computer automatically orders the required parts from suppliers and then issues instructions for building the car at the assembly plant. The computer at company headquarters can also electronically invoice the dealer and pay suppliers through the network linkage to the bank.

When mainframe computing dummy terminals were used to access large databases, complex programming was required to retrieve data and convert it to user-friendly information. With the introduction of PCs and high-powered software, employees could access information readily and easily. Initially, however, these PCs could not communicate with one another; thus, information could not be easily shared among users. Networking allows organizations to establish channels of communication among employees, across companies, and between employees and customers, regardless of their geographic location.

A new category of software called *middleware*, which mediates among myriad types of hardware and software, makes global networking possible. Even within a single company, all sizes and brands of computers

and software may exist, requiring middleware to help them communicate on a network. On a global scale, middleware is essential. Middleware paves over incompatibilities among computers and accommodates the shifting complexities of today's large networks.[87]

Companies can establish their own local area network (LAN) or wide area network (WAN) or communicate directly via the Internet. For Sterling Software, Inc., a $434 million Dallas software maker, the Internet enables 3,600 employees across 75 worldwide offices to keep in touch with headquarters and customers. The company uses the Internet to distribute mail, to connect sales offices with research and development labs, and to perform interactive demonstrations of software for clients.[88] The Focus on Change box describes the Internet in more detail.

River Hills West Healthcare Center in Pewaukee, Wisconsin, uses a local area network (LAN) to simplify its drug prescription system and reduce errors. Nurses write the first three letters of the drug name on an electronic notepad, which then provides a series of boxes to check off for dosage amounts and times. The notepad automatically sends the information over a wireless link to River Hills's network server.

FOCUS ON CHANGE
BUSINESS SUCCESS ON THE INTERNET

The Internet has exploded as the techno-fad of the 1990s. It allows millions of people to chat with one another about every topic under the sun, browse through thousands of online libraries, and play new games. New software and services are also making the Internet one of the most exciting places ever to do business. Companies are quickly discovering this new way to establish networks linking their operations with distant suppliers, customers, and even employees.

WHAT IS THE INTERNET?
The Internet is the barely controlled chaos of an amorphous, rapidly growing web of corporate, educational, and research computer networks around the world. It evolved from a communications network designed by the Defense Department in 1969 to survive nuclear attack.

THE WORLD WIDE WEB
New graphical interfaces have led to stratospheric growth in the use of the World Wide Web, where browser programs such as Mosaic or Yahoo! allow you to jump from one Web computer to another effortlessly, creating the illusion of using one giant computer. The arcane codes and addresses once required to "surf the 'Net" are buried under user-friendly screens and lively graphics.

THE WEB MARKETPLACE
The uses of the Web for business are as varied as the companies. Tupperware runs virtual Tupperware parties. The Rolling Stones Voodoo Lounge on the Web plugs the group's records. J. P. Morgan and Company offers clients access to its risk-management database. IBM presents an electronic version of its magazine, with articles about the company and its products.

Although direct selling on the Web has not yet proven to be highly successful for large corporations, small companies are reaping big benefits. The Web can transform a small outfit into a global distributor. Virtual Vineyards, a Los Altos, California, company, sells tens of thousands of dollars of wine on the Web each month, amounting to around $100,000 in 1995. Hot Hot Hot, a Pasadena specialty shop, sold more than $60,000 worth of hot sauce over the Web, nearly a quarter of its total business.

However, since the Internet wasn't designed for electronic commerce, it still lacks effective security measures, and many businesses are wary of trusting the Internet with credit card numbers or sensitive company information. Companies like Trusted Information Systems and Digital Equipment Corporation are leading the way as corporate America tries to plug the security gaps and make the Internet an even friendlier place to do business.

RULES FOR SUCCESS ON THE INTERNET
1. Net routes around greed. The Internet detects and subverts excess. Remember Microsoft's attempt to establish a proprietary online service? It failed because the me-first business logic does not work with the Net's logic.

2. Generosity begets prosperity. Just as Gillette sold more blades 70 years ago after it gave away razors, so did Netscape become one of the fastest-growing software startups after its strategic generosity of letting users freely download its software.

3. There's safety in speed. As more people sample a product, excitement is generated. The "whoosh factor" is how Netscape was able to enter the market in late 1994 and hold a 75 percent market share by the following April. All this was done without fleets of trucks, elaborate advertising, or hustling for retail shelf space.

4. There is no control of anything. Monarch butterflies or schools of fish move about without any one creature in charge. Success on the Internet comes to those (Netscape, Sun, Yahoo!) applying the power of distributed intelligence who are possessed with meeting performance goals and are thoroughly decentralized.

5. No one is as smart as everyone. The Internet allows users to share and shape information. No one is a leader or in charge, and nearly everyone can find something of value.

SOURCES: Larry Keeley, "Ten Commandments for Success on the Net," *Fast Company*, June/July 1996, 60–62; Bart Ziegler, "In the Net," *The Wall Street Journal*, Nov. 18, 1996, R21; John W. Verity and Robert D. Hof, "The Internet," *Business Week*, November 14, 1994; Rick Tetzeli, "The Internet and Your Business," *Fortune*, March 7, 1994; and Kate Maddox, Mitch Wagner, and Clinton Wilder, "Making Money on the Web," *Tech Web*, 1995.

Records are instantly updated, eliminating five stages of paperwork and reducing the potential for mistakes. Previously, every prescription ordered by a doctor had to be transcribed by a secretary to a phone order, a pharmacy sheet, and several patient forms, which were then checked by nurses and entered into a three-ring binder.[89]

STRATEGIC USE OF INFORMATION TECHNOLOGY

Information technology is dramatically changing the processes and possibilities for doing business. Upgrading a computer system to include middleware, networking office computers, and providing sales representatives with mobile phones appear to be minimum strategies for remaining competitive. Information technology allows organizations to improve operational efficiency and control, as well as compete in a rapidly changing environment.

Operational Efficiency and Control

Many companies adopt information technology in an effort to speed work processes, cut costs, and improve coordination. The appropriate use of technology can greatly increase an organization's efficiency.

Efficiency. Information technology is altering how products and services are delivered and thus the speed at which they can be delivered. Recall how Northrop saved 400,000 pieces of paper on each fuselage it built and how EDC used an expert system to enable insurance underwriters to generate quotes to clients within minutes rather than days. Through investment in operations and other information systems, a company increases its operational efficiency and potentially lowers costs. This increased efficiency better enables a company to lock in customers and broaden market reach.

The efficiency of information technology is realized in many companies by the appointment of a chief information officer. CIOs are increasingly being folded into high-level strategic decision making so companies can better align their information resources with strategic needs.[90] More than anything else, CIOs must manage technological change for the organization that may involve high-level decisions with regard to investment, product, and service.

Improved Coordination and Flexibility. Another efficiency of information technology is the reduction of time and geographic barriers. With global networks and mobile computing, these barriers are dissolving. Time and place are becoming less and less important communication variables. A management team can work throughout the day on a project in Switzerland and, while they sleep, a team in the United States can continue where the Swiss team left off. With E-mail and voice mail, managers no longer have to arrive at 4 A.M. to communicate with personnel abroad.

Through a new organizational form, the **cluster organization,** teams can be brought together in infinite combinations.[91] Digital Equipment Corporation, for example, brings new teams face-to-face for a week or more to develop closeness and friendship. Then members return to their regular locations around the world and communicate by electronic mail and group decision support systems. When a problem is solved, the team disbands, and individuals are formed into new teams.

Mobile computers allow employees all over the world to reach databases at any time of the day or night and to share new information. "Wired executives" can increasingly abandon the confines of corporate offices while staying on top of business through technology. Portable computers, E-mail, cellular phones, voice mail, and faxes have freed executives and led to greater productivity. Manville Corporation CEO W. Thomas Stephens sees the computer as mind extension. "It gives you opportunity to be a lot more powerful and to focus on being creative, rather than spending your time making charts and that sort of thing."[92]

Competitive Strategy

Organizations are competing in a new era, an era characterized by global movement of weightless bits at the speed of light, an era that brings irrevocable changes in information technology and the ways for doing business.[93] Information processing will

cluster organization
An organizational form in which team members from different company locations use E-mail and group decision support systems to solve problems.

increasingly shape many companies' strategic competitive advantage. Competitive advantage will be gained by shortening the distance between customers and the organization. For example, UPS will soon provide customers with the exact tracking location for packages.[94] VF Corp., a leader in computerized "market response systems," can replace a pair of jeans sold at Wal-Mart on Tuesday by Thursday and may eventually be able to ship custom-order jeans directly to your home.[95] This transformation from moving atoms to moving bits, described by Nicholas Negroponte in *Being Digital*, will present new strategic alternatives for organizations and entrepreneurs alike.[96]

Changes in business strategy usually precede structural change, job design, and technology adoption. Sometimes, however, adoption of information technology serves as the catalyst for change and is followed by restructuring of positions and different management processes. So, while many companies adopt technology to meet strategic goals, others learn from technological introduction. Business competitiveness thus occurs through a series of tactical as well as strategic decisions.[97]

SUMMARY AND MANAGEMENT SOLUTION

This chapter made several important points about the process of organizational decision making. The study of decision making is important because it describes how managers make successful strategic and operational decisions. Managers must confront many types of decisions, including programmed and nonprogrammed, and decisions differ according to the amount of risk, uncertainty, and ambiguity in the environment.

Two decision-making approaches were described: the classical model and the administrative model. The classical model explains how managers should make decisions so as to maximize economic efficiency. The administrative model describes how managers actually make nonprogrammed, uncertain decisions with skills that include intuition and coalition building.

Decision making should involve six basic steps: problem recognition, diagnosis of causes, development of alternatives, choice of an alternative, implementation of the alternative, and feedback and evaluation.

This chapter also explained the Vroom–Jago model, which managers can use to determine when a decision calls for group participation. Managers may use several types of groups, including interactive groups, nominal groups, and Delphi groups. As competitive pressures force today's organizations to shift toward forms of decision making that encourage creativity and sharing of diverse views, managers need to maximize the advantages of group decision making and overcome the disadvantages. Useful techniques include devil's advocate, multiple advocacy, and brainstorming. These techniques can help managers and groups define problems and develop more creative solutions.

Organizations are evolving into information cultures where managers and employees alike can share information, where the same information can be accessed at the same time by many people, and where decision making can be automated through the use of expert models. These emerging information cultures will not be bound by physical space. Satellite relays, fiber optic devices, and microwave transmissions will allow future workers to be completely mobile yet in constant touch. High-speed digital computers will replace portables to connect workers with any computer network around the world at any time and place.[98] Information technology allows companies to generate new services and products but also creates demand for quality, low cost, and speedy delivery.

In this chapter the importance of information technology and systems has been addressed. Information systems produce huge amounts of data and transform them into useful information for decision makers. These systems should be designed to generate information with appropriate time, content, and form attributes. The array of information systems available and the multitude of data they produce can be overwhelming. Many organizations are creating chief information officer positions to help manage decisions regarding investment and integration of old and new information system products.

Information systems can be categorized based on who

they serve and the functions they perform. Operations information systems support daily business operations and the needs of low-level managers, whereas management information systems provide information for middle and upper management. Other information systems support users down the organizational hierarchy or clone expert decision-making models for nonexpert users. Emerging technologies of groupware, geographic information systems, and networks serve organizations in new and exciting ways. Information technology influences operational efficiency and control, organizational structure, and the degree to which employees can be empowered.

At Sunbeam, Al Dunlap's habitual style of cut-and-slash hampered his ability to consider all sides of the situation to work toward the long-term health of Sunbeam. In November 1996, Chainsaw Al eliminated 50 percent of all jobs, making it the largest percentage cutback in medium- or large-sized business in the United States. Dunlap claimed it was needed for the ailing, one-time popular, small appliance maker. Besides the layoffs, Dunlap closed over half its factories and warehouses and scrapped 87 percent of its product line. It would seem that shareholder value were the prime criteria both in hiring Dunlap and in Dunlap's decisions. However, when that type of decision is made, often there are long-term problems created. Observers worry that the recent Sunbeam cutbacks are just too drastic and will ravage worker morale, efficiency, and productivity. Warned consultant Alan Downs, "You don't cut that dramatically without creating chaos inside the company." A more productive strategy likely would have been to consider the long-term well-being of the company, and therefore its need for worker loyalty, competency, and trust, as well as the reputation of Sunbeam as a "good citizen." This would not preclude some reorganization and fat-cutting, but it would mean such steps would be taken with more care and with the consideration of a prolonged time frame to reap benefits.[99]

DISCUSSION QUESTIONS

1 You are a busy partner in a legal firm, and an experienced secretary complains of continued headaches, drowsiness, dry throat, and occasional spells of fatigue and flu. She tells you she believes air quality in the building is bad and would like something done. How would you respond?

2 Why is decision making considered a fundamental part of management effectiveness?

3 Explain the difference between risk and ambiguity. How might decision making differ for each situation?

4 Analyze three decisions you made over the past six months. Which of these were programmed and which were nonprogrammed?

5 Why are many decisions made by groups rather than by individuals?

6 The Vroom–Jago model describes five decision styles. How should a manager go about choosing which style to use?

7 What are three types of decision-making groups? How might each be used to help managers make a decision to market a product in a new geographical territory?

8 What is meant by *satisficing* and *bounded rationality?* Why do managers not strive to find the economically best solution for many organizational decisions?

9 What techniques could you use to improve your own creativity and effectiveness in decision making?

10 Which of the six steps in the decision-making process do you think is most likely to be ignored by a manager? Explain.

11 How do information systems serve the needs of employees at different decision-making levels in the organization? Provide examples.

12 Review the attributes of quality information. How might these attributes appear in guidelines that you receive for an exam and in the exam itself?

13 How is your life impacted by changes in the availability and use of new information technology?

14 What does Nicholas Negroponte mean when he says that the post-information age is characterized by the movement of bits rather than atoms?

15 Describe a scenario for which groupware would be useful.

16 How is information technology changing the ways companies are structured and the ways jobs are designed?

17 What kinds of new products and services do you envision the information age producing over the next 15 years?

MANAGEMENT EXERCISES

MANAGER'S WORKBOOK

Decision Styles

Think of some recent decisions which have influenced your life. Choose two significant decisions which you made and two which other people made. Then fill out the table below. Use Exhibit 8.1 on decision situations to choose which situation it was (Column B). Decide how bounded rationality worked (column C), and use the information on decision biases to fill in column D.

Column A	B	C	D	E
	Decision situation relevant	Bounded rationality: Was there satisficing?	Which decision biases were working?	Outcomes— recommendations for improvement?
Your decisions				
1.				
2.				
Decisions by others				
1.				
2.				

SOURCE: Adapted by Dorothy Marcic from "Action Assignment" in Jennifer M. Howard and Lawrence M. Miller, *Team Management*, Miller Consulting Group, 1994, 205.

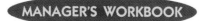

MANAGER'S WORKBOOK

What Is Your Management Information-Processing Style?

Following are 14 statements. Circle the number that indicates how much you agree that each statement is characteristic of you. The questions refer to how you use information and make decisions.

	Disagree Strongly				**Agree Strongly**
1 I like to wait until all relevant information is examined before deciding something.	1	2	3	4	5
2 I prefer information that can be interpreted in several ways and leads to different but acceptable solutions.	1	2	3	4	5
3 I like to keep gathering data until an excellent solution emerges.	1	2	3	4	5

	Disagree Strongly				Agree Strongly
4 To make decisions, I often use information that means different things to different people.	1	2	3	4	5
5 I want just enough data to make a decision quickly.	1	2	3	4	5
6 I act on logical analysis of the situation rather than on my "gut feelings" about the best alternative.	1	2	3	4	5
7 I seek information sources or people that will provide me with many ideas and details.	1	2	3	4	5
8 I try to generate more than one satisfactory solution for the problem faced.	1	2	3	4	5
9 When reading something, I confine my thoughts to what is written rather than search for additional understanding.	1	2	3	4	5
10 When working on a project, I try to narrow, not broaden, the scope so it is clearly defined.	1	2	3	4	5
11 I typically acquire all possible information before making a final decision.	1	2	3	4	5
12 I like to work on something I've done before rather than take on a complicated problem.	1	2	3	4	5
13 I prefer clear, precise data.	1	2	3	4	5
14 When working on a project, I like to explore various options rather than maintain a narrow focus.	1	2	3	4	5

Total Score _____

The *odd-numbered* questions pertain to the "amount of information" you like to use. A score of 28 or more suggests you prefer a large amount. A score of 14 or less indicates you like a small amount of information.

The *even-numbered* questions pertain to the "focus of information" you prefer. A score of 28 or more suggests you are comfortable with ambiguous, multifocused information, while a score of 14 or less suggests you like clear, unifocused data.

Your information-processing style determines the extent to which you will benefit from computer-based information systems. If you are a person who likes a large amount of information and clear, focused data, you will tend to make effective use of management information systems. You could be expected to use and benefit from an EIS or MIS in your company. If you are a person who prefers a small amount of data and data that are multifocused, you would not get the information you need to make decisions through formal information systems. You probably won't utilize EIS or MIS to a great extent, preferring instead to get decision data from other convenient sources, including face-to-face discussions.

SOURCES: This questionnaire is adapted from Richard L. Daft and Norman B. Macintosh, "A Tentative Exploration into the Amount and Equivocality of Information Processing in Organizational Work Units," *Administrative Science Quarterly* 26 (1981), 207–224; and Dorothy Marcic, *Organizational Behavior: Experiences and Cases,* 4th ed. (St. Paul, Minn.: West, 1995).

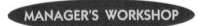

MANAGER'S WORKSHOP

The Desert Survival Situation

The situation described in this exercise is based on more than 2,000 actual cases in which men and women lived or died depending on the survival decisions they made. Your "life" or "death" will depend on how well your group can share its present knowledge of a relatively un-familiar problem so that the team can make decisions that will lead to your survival.

This exercise will challenge your ability to take advantage of a participative approach to decision making and to apply decision steps such as developing alternatives

and selecting the correct alternative. When instructed, read about the situation and do Step 1 without discussing it with the rest of the group.

The Situation It is approximately 10:00 A.M. in mid-August, and you have just crash landed in the Sonora Desert in the southwestern United States. The light twin-engine plane, containing the bodies of the pilot and the copilot, has completely burned. Only the air frame remains. None of the rest of you has been injured.

The pilot was unable to notify anyone of your position before the crash. However, he had indicated before impact that you were 70 miles south-southwest from a mining camp that is the nearest known habitation and that you were approximately 65 miles off the course that was filed in your VFR Flight Plan.

The immediate area is quite flat and, except for occasional barrel and saguaro cacti, appears to be rather barren. The last weather report indicated the temperature would reach 110° that day, which means that the temperature at ground level will be 130°. You are dressed in lightweight clothing: short-sleeved shirts, pants, socks, and street shoes. Everyone has a handkerchief. Collec-

tively, your pockets contain $2.83 in change, $85 in bills, a pack of cigarettes, and a ballpoint pen.

Your Task Before the plane caught fire, your group was able to salvage the 15 items listed in the following table. Your task is to rank these items according to their importance to your survival, starting with 1, the most important, to 15, the least important.

You may assume the following:

1. The number of survivors is the same as the number on your team.
2. You are the actual people in the situation.
3. The team has agreed to stick together.
4. All items are in good condition.

Step 1 Each member of the team is to individually rank each item. Do not discuss the situation or problem until each member has finished the individual ranking.

Step 2 After everyone has finished the individual ranking, rank order the 15 items as a team. Once discussion begins, do not change your individual ranking. Your instructor will inform you how much time you have to complete this step.

Items	Step 1: Your Individual Ranking	Step 2: The Team's Ranking	Step 3: Survival Expert's Ranking*	Step 4: Difference between Steps 1 and 3	Step 5: Difference between Steps 2 and 3
Flashlight (4-battery size)	————	————	————	————	————
Jackknife	————	————	————	————	————
Sectional air map of the area	————	————	————	————	————
Plastic raincoat (large size)	————	————	————	————	————
Magnetic compass	————	————	————	————	————
Compress kit with gauze	————	————	————	————	————
.45 caliber pistol (loaded)	————	————	————	————	————
Parachute (red and white)	————	————	————	————	————
Bottle of salt tablets (1,000 tablets)	————	————	————	————	————
1 quart of water per person	————	————	————	————	————
A book titled *Edible Animals of the Desert*	————	————	————	————	————
A pair of sunglasses per person	————	————	————	————	————
2 quarts of 180-proof vodka	————	————	————	————	————
1 topcoat per person	————	————	————	————	————
A cosmetic mirror	————	————	————	————	————
Totals (the lower the score, the better)	————	————	————	————	————
				Your Score, Step 4	Team Score, Step 5

*Instructor will provide

	Team Number					
	1	2	3	4	5	6
Step 6: Average Individual Score Add up all the individual scores (Step 4) on the team, and divide by the number on the team.	————	————	————	————	————	————

	Team Number					
	1	**2**	**3**	**4**	**5**	**6**
Step 7: Team Score	————	————	————	————	————	————
Step 8: Gain Score The difference between the Team Score and the Average Individual Score. If the Team Score is lower than Average Individual Score, then gain is "1." If Team Score is higher than Average Individual Score, then gain is "2."	————	————	————	————	————	————
Step 9: Lowest Individual Score on the Team	————	————	————	————	————	————
Step 10: Number of Individual Scores Lower than the Team Score	————	————	————	————	————	————

SOURCE: J. Clayton Lafferty, Patrick M. Eady, and Alonzo W. Pond, "The Desert Survival Situation: A Group Decision Making Experience for Examining and Increasing Individual and Team Effectiveness," 8th ed. Copyright © 1974 by Experiential Learning Methods, Inc., 15200 E. Jefferson, Suite 107, Grosse Pointe Park, MI 48230, (313) 823-4400.

SURF THE 'NET

Find one article from each of the Web pages below. In addition, find another five news sources on Web pages and get one article from each. Then list each of the 15 articles by author, name, date and source. Include an annotation or short description of each article.

1 *The Wall Street Journal.* http://www.wsj.com
2 *Business Week.* http://www.businessweek.com
3 *Fortune* magazine. http://www.fortune.com
4 Lead Story. Top story of the day, from AT&T. http://www.leadstory.com
5 *The Washington Post.* http://www.washingtonpost.com
6 New York Public Library. http://gopher.nypl.org
7 Hotwired. http://www.hotwired.com
8 IGUIDE. Internet guide. http://www.iguide.com
9 Personalized start page. Zooms to sites. http://www.msn.com
10 MSNBC 24-hour news. NBC and Microsoft link up. http://www.msnbc.com

SOURCE: Jack Pleunneke, "Old Newshound, New Web Tricks," *Business Week,* Aug. 5, 1996, 16.

ETHICAL DILEMMA

The Unhealthy Hospital

When Bruce Reid was hired as Blake Memorial Hospital's new CEO, the mandate had been clear: Improve the quality of care, and set the financial house in order.

As Reid struggled to finalize his budget for approval at next week's board meeting, his attention kept returning to one issue—the future of six off-site clinics. The clinics had been set up six years earlier to provide primary health care to the community's poorer neighborhoods. Although they provided a valuable service, they also diverted funds away from Blake's in-house services, many of which were underfunded. Cutting hospital personnel and freezing salaries could affect Blake's quality of care, which was al-

ready slipping. Eliminating the clinics, on the other hand, would save $256,000 without compromising Blake's internal operations.

However, there would be political consequences. Clara Bryant, the recently appointed commissioner of health services, repeatedly argued that the clinics were an essential service for the poor. Closing the clinics could jeopardize Blake's access to city funds. Dr. Susan Russell, the hospital's director of clinics, was equally vocal about Blake's responsibility to the community, although Dr. Winston Lee, chief of surgery, argued forcefully for closing the off-site clinics and having shuttle buses bring patients to the hospital weekly. Dr. Russell argued for an entirely new way of delivering health care—"A hospital is not a building," she said, "it's a service. And wherever the service is needed, that is where the hospital should be." In Blake's case, that meant funding more clinics. Russell wanted to create a network of neighborhood-based centers for all the surrounding neighborhoods, poor and middle income. Besides improving health care, the network would act as an inpatient referral system for hospital services. Reid considered the proposal: If a clinic network could tap the paying public and generate more

inpatient business, it might be worth looking into. Blake's rival hospital, located on the affluent side of town, certainly wasn't doing anything that creative.

What Do You Do?

1 Close the clinics and save a quick $256,000, then move on to tackle the greater problems that threaten Blake's long-term future.

2 Gradually abandon the neighborhood altogether and open free-standing clinics in more affluent suburbs, at the same time opening a minihospital in the poor neighborhood for critical care.

3 Tighten up internal efficiency to deal with immediate financial problems. Keep the clinics open for now, bring Clara Bryant into the decision-making process, and begin working with community groups to explore unmet health-care needs and develop innovative options for meeting them.

SOURCE: Based on Anthony R. Kovner, "The Case of the Unhealthy Hospital," *Harvard Business Review,* September–October 1991, 12–25.

CASE FOR CRITICAL ANALYSIS

United Way

In the summer of 1992, Jeremy Ramsey, director of a university computer center, was working at his desk when the phone rang. On the line was Susan Williams, an executive in charge of evaluation at the local United Way. She wondered if Ramsey would help design a consolidated information system that would help center directors cut paperwork and give more objective performance data for agency evaluation and control. Williams explained that in light of the recent controversy involving the national United Way organization, local agencies faced critical donation shortfalls. "It's more important than ever," she explained, "for local agencies to save money. We must find new cost-cutting methods to ensure the best value for the donations we receive."

Ramsey indicated that he was interested in helping. A week later he had his first meeting with the directors of eight neighborhood centers and executives from three

funding agencies. The directors all faced similar problems. Most of the centers had evolved from local settlement houses to neighborhood centers that provided a number of services to local residents. Services varied widely but usually included housing, employment, recreation, food, clothing, child care, health services, and referrals and transportation to other agencies. Each had its own unique variety of funding sources, and each was inundated with paperwork.

During the discussion of a potential information system, Ramsey explained what might be done to reduce the paperwork. He pointed out that the current narrative reports written by the caseworkers and the wide variety of forms could be reduced to several standardized forms. From the information on the standardized forms, the computer could produce summaries that would eliminate 80 percent of the paperwork that the directors were do-

ing. The presentation generated considerable enthusiasm, and it was agreed that Ramsey's staff would begin to wade through the numerous forms used in each of the agencies.

After three months, the computer staff had conducted more than 100 interviews with people from all levels of the eight agencies and had gathered 190 forms that were currently in use. At a follow-up meeting with the eight center directors, however, it was clear that completion of the project would be impossible until the directors understood the system and how computerization could benefit them. Agency directors voiced the usual concerns about staff training on the new machines and the potential for "losing" information. In addition, they were uncertain about their own needs—which information should be transferred to the computer and whether they could continue to use the paperwork as backup to the computer. Ramsey and his staff saw the need to work with agency directors and computer staff to design the system to fit the agency.

Questions

1 What type of information system will be most appropriate for the United Way agency?

2 Do the United Way agencies truly need a computer-based information system? What limitations do you see in the ability of a CBIS to meet their information needs?

3 How would you characterize the procedure being used to design and implement the information system? What techniques should Ramsey's staff use to help managers define their information needs and overcome their resistance?

SOURCES: Robert E. Quinn, "Computers, People, and the Delivery of Services: How to Manage the Management Information System," in John E. Diettrich and Robert A. Zawacki, *People & Organizations,* 2d ed. (Plano, Tex.: Business Publications, 1985), 226–232; and Ron Stodgill II, "United They Stand?" *Business Week,* October 19, 1992, 40.

ENDNOTES

1 Robert Frank and Joann S. Lublin, "Dunlap's Ax Falls—6,000 Times—at Sunbeam," *The Wall Street Journal,* Nov. 13, 1996, B1 & B12; John A. Byrne and Gail DeGeorge, "Dear Al: Put Away the Chainsaw," *Business Week,* Aug. 5, 1996, 28; John A. Byrne, "The Making of a Corporate Tough Guy," *Business Week,* Jan. 15, 1996, 61; John A. Byrne, "Did CEO Dunlap Save Scott Paper—or Just Pretty It Up?" *Business Week,* Jan. 15, 1996, 56.

2 Robert D. Hof, "The Education of Andrew Grove," *Business Week,* January 16, 1995, 60–62.

3 Ibid.; and John R. Emshwiller and Michael J. McCarthy, "Coke's Soda Fountain for Offices Fizzles, Dashing High Hopes," *The Wall Street Journal,* June 14, 1993, A1, A6.

4 Mark Landler, "People of Earth, We Are a Friendly Channel," *Business Week,* October 5, 1992, 50; and Joseph Weber and Peter Coy, "Look Ma, No Cable: It's Video-by-Phone," *Business Week,* November 14, 1992, 86.

5 Ronald A. Howard, "Decision Analysis: Practice and Promise," *Management Science* 34 (1988), 679–695.

6 Herbert A. Simon, *The New Science of Management* (Englewood Cliffs, N.J.: Prentice-Hall, 1977), 47.

7 Peter Nulty, "The Bounce Is Back at Goodyear," *Fortune,* September 7, 1992, 70–72.

8 Samuel Eilon, "Structuring Unstructured Decisions," *Omega* 13 (1985), 369–377; and Max H. Bazerman, *Judgment in Managerial Decision Making* (New York: Wiley, 1986).

9 James G. March and Zur Shapira, "Managerial Perspectives on Risk and Risk Taking," *Management Science* 33 (1987), 1404–1418;

and Inga Skromme Baird and Howard Thomas, "Toward a Contingency Model of Strategic Risk Taking," *Academy of Management Review* 10 (1985), 230–243.

10 J. G. Higgins, "Planning for Risk and Uncertainty in Oil Exploration," *Long Range Planning* 26, no. 1 (February 1993), 111–122; and Kathy Rebello with Neil Gross, "A Juicy New Apple?" *Business Week,* March 7, 1994, 88–90.

11 Eilon, "Structuring Unstructured Decisions"; and Philip A. Roussel, "Cutting Down the Guesswork in R&D," *Harvard Business Review* 61 (September–October 1983), 154–160.

12 Jeremy Main, "Betting on the Twenty-First Century," *Fortune,* April 20, 1992, 102–117.

13 Michael Masuch and Perry LaPotin, "Beyond Garbage Cans: An AI Model of Organizational Choice," *Administrative Science Quarterly* 34 (1989), 38–67; and Richard L. Daft and Robert H. Lengel, "Organizational Information Requirements, Media Richness and Structural Design," *Management Science* 32 (1986), 554–571.

14 David M. Schweiger, William R. Sandberg, and James W. Ragan, "Group Approaches for Improving Strategic Decision Making: A Comparative Analysis of Dialectical Inquiry, Devil's Advocacy, and Consensus," *Academy of Management Journal* 29 (1986), 51–71; and Richard O. Mason and Ian I. Mitroff, *Challenging Strategic Planning Assumptions* (New York: Wiley Interscience, 1981).

15 Michael J. McCarthy, "Pepsi Faces Problem in Trying to Contain Syringe Scare," *The Wall Street Journal,* June 17, 1993, B1; Eliza-

beth Lesly and Laura Zinn, "The Right Moves, Baby," *Business Week*, July 5, 1993, 30–31; and "The Pepsi Hoax: What Went Right?" The Pepsi-Cola Company Public Affairs Office, 1993.

16 Claudia Eller, "As Summer Winds Down, Studios Tally Profits, Losses," *Los Angeles Times*, Aug. 16, 1996, p. D1.

17 Boris Blai, Jr., "Eight Steps to Successful Problem Solving," *Supervisory Management* (January 1986), 7–9; and Earnest R. Archer, "How to Make a Business Decision: An Analysis of Theory and Practice," *Management Review* 69 (February 1980), 54–61.

18 Jean Aubin, "Scheduling Ambulances," *Interfaces* 22 (March–April 1992), 1–10.

19 Herbert A. Simon, *The New Science of Management Decision* (New York: Harper & Row, 1960), 5–6; and Amitai Etzioni, "Humble Decision Making," *Harvard Business Review* (July–August 1989), 122–126.

20 James G. March and Herbert A. Simon, *Organizations* (New York: Wiley, 1958).

21 Herbert A. Simon, *Models of Man* (New York: Wiley, 1957), 196–205; and Herbert A. Simon, *Administrative Behavior*, 2d ed. (New York: Free Press, 1957).

22 John Taylor, "Project Fantasy: A Behind-the-Scenes Account of Disney's Desperate Battle against the Raiders," *Manhattan* (November 1984).

23 Weston H. Agor, "The Logic of Intuition: How Top Executives Make Important Decisions," *Organizational Dynamics* 14 (winter 1986), 5–18; and Herbert A. Simon, "Making Management Decisions: The Role of Intuition and Emotion," *Academy of Management Executive* 1 (1987), 57–64.

24 Daniel J. Isenberg, "How Senior Managers Think," *Harvard Business Review* 62 (November–December 1984), 80–90.

25 Annetta Miller and Dody Tsiantar, "A Test for Market Research," *Newsweek*, December 28, 1987, 32–33; David Frost and Michael Deakin, *David Frost's Book of the World's Worst Decisions* (New York: Crown, 1983), 60–61; and Oren Harari, "The Tarpit of Market Research," *Management Review* (March 1994), 42–44.

26 William B. Stevenson, Jon L. Pierce, and Lyman W. Porter, "The Concept of 'Coalition' in Organization Theory and Research," *Academy of Management Review* 10 (1985), 256–268.

27 Ann Reilly Dowd, "George Bush as Crisis Manager," *Fortune*, September 10, 1990, 55–56; and "How Bush Decided," *Fortune*, February 11, 1991, 45–46.

28 Ann Langley, "Between 'Paralysis by Analysis' and 'Extinction by Instinct,'" *Sloan Management Review* (spring 1995), 63–76; and Gregory G. Braendel, "How I Lost It," *Inc.*, July 1994, 21–22.

29 James W. Fredrickson, "Effects of Decision Motive and Organizational Performance Level on Strategic Decision Processes," *Academy of Management Journal* 28 (1985), 821–843; James W. Fredrickson, "The Comprehensiveness of Strategic Decision Processes: Extension, Observations, Future Directions," *Academy of Management Journal* 27 (1984), 445–466; James W. Dean, Jr., and Mark P. Sharfman, "Procedural Rationality in the Strategic Decision-Making Process," *Journal of Management Studies* 30, no. 4 (July 1993), 587–610; Nandini Rajagopalan, Abdul M. A. Rasheed, and Deepak K. Datta, "Strategic Decision Processes: Critical Review and Future Directions," *Journal of Management Studies* 19, no. 2 (1993), 349–384; and Paul J. H. Schoemaker, "Strategic Decisions in Organizations: Rational and Behavioral Views," *Journal of Management Studies* 30, no. 1 (January 1993), 107–129.

30 Marjorie A. Lyles and Howard Thomas, "Strategic Problem For-

mulation: Biases and Assumptions Embedded in Alternative Decision-Making Models," *Journal of Management Studies* 25 (1988), 131–145; and Susan E. Jackson and Jane E. Dutton, "Discerning Threats and Opportunities," *Administrative Science Quarterly* 33 (1988), 370–387.

31 David Greising, "Rethinking IDS from the Bottom Up," *Business Week*, February 8, 1993, 110–112.

32 Richard L. Daft, Juhani Sormumen, and Don Parks, "Chief Executive Scanning, Environmental Characteristics, and Company Performance: An Empirical Study" (unpublished manuscript, Texas A&M University, 1988).

33 Jerry Jakuvovics, "Rising Stars in Toys and Togs," *Management Review* (May 1987), 19–20.

34 C. Kepner and B. Tregoe, *The Rational Manager* (New York: McGraw-Hill, 1965).

35 Robert Tomsho, "How Greyhound Lines Re-Engineered Itself Right into a Deep Hole," *The Wall Street Journal*, October 30, 1994, A1.

36 "Gateway 2000 Profit Rose 48% in Quarter; Revenue Climbed 35%," *The Wall Street Journal*, October 25, 1996, B4; "Gateway 2000 Inc: Mail-Order Concern to Sell New PC through Retailers," *The Wall Street Journal*, August 21, 1996, B2; "Gateway 2000 Acquisition," *The Wall Street Journal*, August 4, 1995, Joshua Hyatt, "Betting the Farm," *Inc.*, December 1991, 36–45; "Clone King," *Business Week*, January 13, 1992, 134.

37 Peter Mayer, "A Surprisingly Simple Way to Make Better Decisions," *Executive Female*, March–April 1995, 13–14; and Ralph L. Keeney, "Creativity in Decision-Making with Value-Focused Thinking," *Sloan Management Review* (summer 1994), 33–41.

38 Brian O'Reilly, "J&J Is on a Roll," *Fortune*, December 26, 1994, 178–191.

39 Todd Mason, "Tandy Finds a Cold, Hard World outside the Radio Shack," *Business Week*, August 31, 1987, 68–70.

40 Glen Whyte, "Decision Failures: Why They Occur and How to Prevent Them," *Academy of Management Executive* 5, no. 3 (1991), 23–31; Betsy D. Gelb and Gabriel M. Gelb, "New Coke's Fizzle—Lessons for the Rest of Us," *Sloan Management Review* (fall 1986), 71–76; and Shona McKay, "When Good People Make Bad Choices," *Canadian Business* (February 1994), 52–55.

41 Hof, "The Education of Andrew Grove."

42 David E. Vell, Howard Raiffa, and Amos Tversky, *Decision Making* (Cambridge: Cambridge University Press, 1988); John McCormick, "The Wisdom of Solomon," *Newsweek*, August 17, 1987, 62–63; Max H. Bazerman, *Judgment in Managerial Decision Making* (New York: Wiley, 1990); Oren Harari, "The Thomas Lawson Syndrome," *Management Review*, February 1994, 58–61; and Gary Belsky, "Why Smart People Make Major Money Mistakes," *Money* (July 1995), 76–85.

43 V. H. Vroom and Arthur G. Jago, *The New Leadership: Managing Participation in Organizations* (Englewood Cliffs, N.J.: Prentice-Hall, 1988).

44 R. H. G. Field, "A Test of the Vroom–Yetton Normative Model of Leadership," *Journal of Applied Psychology* (October 1982), 523–532; and R. H. G. Field, "A Critique of the Vroom–Yetton Contingency Model of Leadership Behavior," *Academy of Management Review* 4 (1979), 249–257.

45 Jennifer T. Ettling and Arthur G. Jago, "Participation under Conditions of Conflict: More on the Validity of the Vroom–Yetton Model," *Journal of Management Studies* 25 (1988), 73–83; Madeline E. Heilman, Harvey A. Hornstein, Jack H. Cage, and Judith

K. Herschlag, "Reactions to Prescribed Leader Behavior as a Function of Role Perspective: The Case of the Vroom–Yetton Model," *Journal of Applied Psychology* (February 1984), 50–60; and Arthur G. Jago and Victor H. Vroom, "Some Differences in the Incidence and Evaluation of Participative Leader Behavior," *Journal of Applied Psychology* (December 1982), 776–783.

46 Tom Richman, "One Man's Family," *Inc.*, November 1983, 151–156.

47 Ettling and Jago, "Participation under Conditions of Conflict."

48 Andre Delbecq, Andrew Van de Ven, and D. Gustafson, *Group Techniques for Program Planning* (Glenview, Ill.: Scott, Foresman, 1975); and William M. Fox, "Anonymity and Other Keys to Successful Problem-Solving Meetings," *National Productivity Review* 8 (spring 1989), 145–156.

49 "Group Decision Making: Approaches to Problem Solving," *Small Business Reports* (July 1988), 30–33; and N. Delkey, *The Delphi Method: An Experimental Study of Group Opinion* (Santa Monica, Calif.: Rand Corporation, 1969).

50 John L. Cotton, David A. Vollarth, Kirk L. Froggatt, Mark L. Lengnick-Hall, and Kenneth R. Jennings, "Employee Participation: Diverse Forms and Different Outcomes," *Academy of Management Review* 13 (1988), 8–22; and Walter C. Swap, "Destructive Effects of Groups on Individuals," in *Group Decision Making*, ed. Walter C. Swap and Associates (Beverly Hills, Calif.: Sage, 1984).

51 Irving L. Janis, *Groupthink*, 2d ed. (Boston: Houghton Mifflin, 1982), 9; Glen Whyte, "Groupthink Reconsidered," *Academy of Management Review* 14 (1989), 40–56; and Brian Mullen, Tara Anthony, Eduardo Salas, and James E. Driskell, "Group Cohesiveness and Quality of Decision Making: An Integration of Tests of the Groupthink Hypothesis," *Small Group Research* 25, no. 2 (May 1994), 189–204.

52 Aimee L. Stern, "Why Good Managers Approve Bad Ideas," *Working Woman*, May 1992, 75, 104.

53 Roy Rowan, "The Maverick Who Yelled Foul at Citibank," *Fortune*, January 10, 1983, 46–56.

54 David Woodruff with Karen Lowry Miller, "Chrysler's Neon," *Business Week*, May 3, 1993, 116–126.

55 Robert Kreitner and Angelo Kinicki, *Organizational Behavior*, 3d ed. (Chicago: Irwin, 1995), 320, 323; and Gregory M. Bounds, Gregory H. Dobbins, and Oscar S. Fowler, *Management: A Total Quality Perspective* (Cincinnati: Southwestern College Publishing, 1995), 209.

56 David M. Schweiger and William R. Sandberg, "The Utilization of Individual Capabilities in Group Approaches to Strategic Decision-Making," *Strategic Management Journal* 10 (1989), 31–43; and "The Devil's Advocate," *Small Business Report* (December 1987), 38–41.

57 Stern, "Why Good Managers Approve Bad Ideas."

58 Michael Duffy, "Mr. Consensus," *Time*, August 21, 1989, 16–22.

59 "Group Decision-Making," *Small Business Report* (July 1988), 30–33.

60 Kreitner and Kinicki, *Organizational Behavior*, 323.

61 A. Osborn, *Applied Imagination* (New York: Scribner, 1957).

62 William M. Bulkeley, "When Things Go Wrong," *The Wall Street Journal*, Nov. 18, 1996, R25, R26.

63 Geoffrey Smith, "The New Realism in Office Systems," *Business Week*, June 15, 1992, 128–133.

64 Joseph Maglitta, "United Parcel Service," *Computerworld*, May 1, 1995, 15.

65 Steve Molloy and Charles R. Schwenk, "The Effects of Information Technology on Strategic Decision Making," *Journal of Management Studies* 32, no. 3 (May 1995), 283–311.

66 Regis McKenna, "Real-Time Marketing," *Harvard Business Review* 73, no. 4 (July–August 1995), 87–95.

67 Bruce Rayner, "All Roads Lead to IT," *Computerworld*, May 1, 1995, 6–8.

68 Rick Tetzeli, "Surviving Information Overload," *Fortune*, July 11, 1994, 60–62.

69 James A. O'Brien, *Introduction to Information Systems*, 7th ed. (Burr Ridge, Ill.: Irwin, 1994), 19.

70 Edward Wakin, "Multifaceted CIO," *Beyond Computing*, May 1995, 37–40.

71 O'Brien, *Introduction to Information Systems*, 195.

72 Ibid., 197.

73 Fred R. Bleakley, "Electronic Payments Now Supplant Checks at More Large Firms," *The Wall Street Journal*, April 13, 1994, 1, 5.

74 Frances Seghres, "A Search and Destroy Mission—Against Paper," *Business Week*, February 6, 1989, 91, 95.

75 Raymond McLeod, Jr., *Management Information Systems: A Study of Computer-Based Information Systems*, 6th ed. (Englewood Cliffs, N.J.: Prentice-Hall, 1995), 18.

76 O'Brien, *Introduction to Information Systems*, 207.

77 Fess Crockett, "Revitalizing Executive Information Systems," *Sloan Management Review* (summer 1992), 39–47.

78 Robin Matthews and Anthony Shoebridge, "EIS—A Guide for Executives," *Long Range Planning* 25, no. 6 (1992), 94–101.

79 Joyce Hampton, "Friends of the People," *Canadian Productivity* (November 1994), 43.

80 Jim Sheffield and Brent R. Gallupe, "Using Group Support Systems to Improve the New Zealand Economy—Part II: Followup Results," *Journal of Management Information Systems* 11, no. 3 (winter 1994/1995), 135–153.

81 Harvey Schachter, "Risk and Reward," *Canadian Productivity* (November 1994), 35.

82 ESRI Map Book, vol. 10, "Creating a New World," Environmental Systems Research Institute, Inc., 1995.

83 Janet Rae-Dupree, "Interval Hatches First Three Spinoffs," Mercury News Service, Nov. 13, 1996; David Kirkpatrick, "A Look Inside Allen's Think Tank," *Information Technology*, special report of *Fortune*, July 11, 1994, 78.

84 William L. Fuerst, James M. Ragusa, and Efraim Turban, "Expert Systems and Multimedia: Examining the Potential for Integration," *Journal of Management Information Systems* 11, no. 3 (winter 1994/1995), 155–179.

85 Ira Sager, "The View from IBM," *Business Week*, October 30, 1995, 142–150.

86 Ira Sager, "Lou Gerstner on Catching the Third Wave," *Business Week*, October 30, 1995, 152.

87 Peter Nulty, "When to Murder Your Mainframe," *Fortune*, November 1, 1993, 109–120; and John W. Verity, "Cyber-Networks Need a Lot of Spackle," *Business Week*, June 26, 1995, 92.

88 Rick Tetzeli, "The Internet and Your Business," *Fortune*, March 7, 1994, 86–96.

89 Neil Gross, "Kiss That Old Patient Logbook Goodbye," *Business Week*, June 26, 1995, 108.

90 Wakin, "Multifaceted CIO."

91 Lynda M. Applegate, James I. Cash, Jr., and D. Quinn Mills, "Information Technology and Tomorrow's Management," *Harvard Business Review* (November–December 1988), 128–136.

92 Gene Bylinsky, "Saving Time with New Technology," *Fortune*, December 30, 1991, 98–104.

93 Nicholas Negroponte, *Being Digital* (New York: Alfred A. Knopf, 1995), 12.

94 Smith, "The New Realism in Office Systems."

95 Joseph Weber, "Just Getting It to the Stores on Time," *Business Week*, March 6, 1995, 66–67.

96 Negroponte, *Being Digital*, 12.

97 Philip W. Yetton, Kim D. Johnston, and Jane F. Craig, "Computer-Aided Architects: A Case Study of IT and Strategic Change," *Sloan Management Review* (summer 1994), 57–67.

98 Liz Thach and Richard W. Woodman, "Organizational Change and Information Technology: Managing on the Edge of Cyberspace," *Organizational Dynamics* (Summer 1994), 30–46.

99 Frank and Lublin, "Dunlap's Ax Falls"; Byrne and DeGeorge, "Dear Al: Put Away the Chainsaw"; Byrne, "The Making of a Corporate Tough Guy."

Where'd Ya Get That Hat?—Drew Pearson Companies

When Drew Pearson, wide receiver for the Dallas Cowboys, played in his third Super Bowl, he had no idea that a decade later he would be the CEO of one of the top designers and manufacturers of sports caps. "When I left professional football, it was hard to imagine that my earning power would one day eclipse my earning power on the field. But for the last two years, DPC (Drew Pearson Companies) has doubled its revenues. Of course, our success hasn't been without challenges, but by focusing keen attention on every aspect of our operations, we've been able to grow and to differentiate ourselves from our competitors."

DPC is one of only six companies to have negotiated licenses with the NFL, NBA, Major League Baseball and the National Hockey League, and it is the only company to have rights with the Walt Disney Company worldwide. In 1995, DPC shipped 30 million trend-setting caps with names like "the jagged edge" to 7,500 retailers across the U.S. That's an increase of 1,500 retailers since 1994.

These results have been attained because DPC has evolved a carefully crafted set of strategies over its lifetime. Ken Shead, President of DPC, describes the early steps the company took. "When Drew Pearson Enterprises began in 1985, we had a very specific strategy. We wanted to participate in the apparel industry with the high schools of the great state of Texas. . . . We were able to learn very quickly at this beginning stage, and move very rapidly to the professional team ranks. That is what has given us the credibility we now have with retailers around the world. When you go into a retail account with the list of licensors that we have—the NFL, Major League Baseball, the NBA, Hockey, the Walt Disney Company as well as Warner Brothers—you attract the attention of the major buyers in most organizations. So following through on that credibility with the delivery of well-designed products that are priced right turned us into the company we are now."

Building and maintaining good relationships with their licensors and customers certainly has not been ignored by DPC management. Mike Russell, Executive Vice-President of Marketing, comments that "We try to . . . focus upon the particular needs of the licensors (NFL or Walt Disney) and major retail clients (Kmart or Foot Locker) to determine what their objectives are and how we can serve them best. In trying to serve their needs, that is how you build the relationship."

In the mid-eighties, DPC was already looking ahead to a strategy that would separate them from their competition—character licensing, with Mickey Mouse as the future highest selling design. With this dual strategy in place (sports logos and character designs), product design was the biggest challenge, and ultimately has become DPC's chief competitive advantage. While the competition was sticking with the same designs for sports caps from year to year, DPC chose to make unique products, progressive headwear with very colorful, intricate designs. Additionally, DPC changes the design of their caps quickly.

What does it take to create enough designs to replace caps, even caps selling at high volume, every 3 to 6 months? DPC brought in sophisticated computer technology that would allow its young designers to generate 3-dimensional designs that can be rotated on the computer screen in order to more easily develop "forward looks and backward looks." With most DPC caps manufactured outside of the U.S., this same computer technology allows new designs to be communicated to manufacturing facilities instantaneously. By carefully choosing and monitoring manufacturers, DPC can change factories quickly when needed, change designs rapidly, retool equipment and generally avoid any elements of manufacturing obsolescence.

Drew Pearson Companies has become known as a leader in the sports headwear industry, and it continues to pursue new directions. In order to prolong the shelf life of their unique designs and to expand their business, three years ago they made the decision to focus on the international market. With a product line that transcends national borders (Mickey Mouse in California is Mickey Mouse in Munich), and a growing demand for U.S. products in other countries, the international facet of DPC's business is strengthening the company's sales significantly.

QUESTIONS

1 Describe the corporate-level and business-level strategies of the Drew Pearson Companies. What is their primary core competence?

2 Analyze the competitive forces that exist in the environment for the Drew Pearson Companies.

3 How does the life cycle of Drew Pearson products affect their choice of strategy and functional implementation?

VIDEO CASE

"Baby Boomers and Beyond"— Centex Corporation Looks Forward

The March 4, 1996 Fortune magazine showed Centex Corporation once again ranked in the engineering and construction industry as one of the most admired corporations in the United States. The "admiration index" ranked Centex 118th among all U.S. corporations. These rankings are based upon a poll of more than 10,000 senior executives, outside directors, and financial analysts.

What makes Centex so special? It is the nation's largest and most geographically diverse home builder, as well as the fifth largest general building contractor in this country. The company also produces and distributes cement, ready-mix concrete, gypsum wallboard, and other building materials. Founded in Dallas in 1950, the company went public in 1969 and due to dramatic growth, by 1995 had become a multi-industry conglomerate operating in four related business segments: home building, financial services, contracting and construction services, and within a limited partnership, real estate development.

Centex operates in over 40 metropolitan areas and over 20 states. The houses Centex builds range in size from 1,000 to 6,000 square feet with a similarly diverse range in price. Despite its size, Centex Corporation's operations account for less than 1 percent of the housing starts in the U.S. In addition to single-family units, Centex has also been responsible for such projects as the Orlando International Airport, the Clorox Company headquarters, and the Dallas Museum of Art.

The response Centex made to the increasing interest rates in 1995 illustrates their contingency planning ability. Centex found their ability to raise prices, increase volume, and achieve higher profit margins diminished. Given their experience in other similar business cycles, Centex adapted by controlling inventories, reducing overhead, and deferring expansion plans.

Certainly, contingency planning is a Centex strength. It appears that planning for the more distant future is as well. In 1995, a number of Centex employees participated in a unique series of focus group meetings entitled "Baby Boomers and Beyond—Products, Services, and Ideas." The meetings were an attempt to develop ideas that would lead to possible new business opportunities for Centex.

The primary purposes of the meetings were: (1) to engage in a Centex creative exercise; (2) to generate information for Centex about unsatisfied desires of people aged 30 and up that would be used to formulate new products and services; and (3) to have fun! Participating employees gathered in breakout groups for discussion and brainstorming. First, groups developed a list of universal desires and determined which of those desires were not being adequately satisfied. In the second session, participants took their lists of "least satisfied desires" and explored ways to create more time in which people could satisfy those desires, and identified those things that most people would prefer to have others do for them. Finally, in the third session, the previous issues were used as a basis for brainstorming ideas for new products or services that could be developed to meet the unsatisfied desires.

Product and service ideas the groups developed included a concept one group labeled "The Total Living Community" in which vertical, multi-family housing would provide essential services such as on-site medical and dental care, shopping and food services, pools, and recreational and entertainment areas. Additionally, traditional yards that demand attention and care were replaced with a communal rooftop garden for those who were interested. One other group chose to explore products and services for the "Home Office."

Planning for the future is a characteristic of Centex. With financial strength generated by a fairly conservative approach to debt and other financial practices, Centex has the luxury to take a long-term view. They are currently examining the potential for expansion into international markets.

QUESTIONS

1 Does Centex seem to fit better into traditional planning approaches or into more contemporary approaches to planning? Justify your response.

2 Given what you know about Centex from this case, prepare a short mission statement for the organization.

3 As an employee of the company, how would you view the opportunity to participate in focus groups such as those described in the above case? Why? What benefits do you see Centex gaining from encouraging employees to go through that type of experience?

REFERENCES

Centex Some Times, Employee Newsletter, Centex Corporation. Vol. 7, No. 1, March 7, 1995 and Vol. 7, No. 2, July 1, 1995.

M.F. Van Breda and D. Jobe, *Centex,* American Institute of Certified Public Accountants, Case No. 92-12.

VIDEO CASE

Planning for Worldwide Growth—Pier 1 Imports

According to Everen Securities' investment report, by mid-1996, Pier 1 Imports was on its way to experiencing a record year for both revenue and earnings. With a better mix of merchandise, as well as the company's first television advertising campaign in place, store traffic had increased significantly. How did Pier 1 achieve this level of success?

While in the early 1980s Pier 1 had struggled with both its merchandise selection and its image, by the mid-80s, a new President and CEO, Clark Johnson, had been brought in to introduce needed change. Based upon a strategic plan developed in 1985, an ambitious program to double the number of stores was launched, along with other changes.

The focus of the 1985 plan was on target customer marketing, the upgrading and expansion of merchandise, and the development and implementation of major new corporate systems. Since 1985, over $27 million has been invested by Pier 1 Imports in a variety of such systems. For example, the company was able to reduce inventory levels because of improved systems in the stores and distribution centers. Customer service has been greatly enhanced by a more intelligent cash register system that facilitates price look-up, credit card processing, and communication with local area stores. But nowhere has the investment in systems had a greater payoff than in the logistics area. Beginning with order entry in foreign countries, through shipment from the company's six massive distribution centers to company stores, merchandise is monitored each step of the way, providing a significant increase in cost-effectiveness.

Has Pier 1's growth been a smooth process? Hardly! In 1990, as the U.S. economy slowed down, so did consumer buying. Like other retailers, Pier 1 focused on controlling costs and increasing the efficiency of its operations. By 1992, however, on Pier 1's 30th anniversary, record earnings were again reported. During the early 1990s, Pier 1 once again invested in an extensive strategic planning process.

What are management's current plans for their organization? In a corporate document entitled "A Strategy for Profitable Worldwide Growth," management states that "Pier 1 Imports will expand its North American retail operations to 900 stores by the year 2000 and enter new worldwide retail markets through direct investment and partnerships." Other strategic goals for the year 2000 include:

- Achieve $1.25 billion in sales and produce $75 million in net income.

- Introduce Pier 1 Imports stores internationally with direct investment in selected countries.
- Expand Pier 1 Imports' market presence in Southeast Asia, Mexico, and Central and South America through Master Franchise agreements and joint ventures.
- Enter new specialty retail markets in North America to be chosen using several specific and consistent criteria.
- Establish a major procurement, logistics, and distribution presence in Singapore to reinforce the company's international sourcing capacity.

With goals and a strategic plan in place, Pier 1 Imports' management believes that the company's focus is clear for the 1990s. "When 2000 arrives, our goal is to look back and verify:

- We defined a clear strategy and executed it well through the end of the 1990s.
- We produced long-term financial results that exceeded expectations.
- We identified global opportunities along the way, moved decisively, and increased the intrinsic value of Pier 1 Imports.
- We remained sensitive to each market area and adapted readily to customer wants and needs.
- We focused clearly on our basic strategy of profitable growth through market expansion, new store openings, maximizing profitability of existing units, motivating our associates, and remaining dedicated to our customers."

Building on their past successes, Pier 1 Imports is committed to achieving these goals.

QUESTIONS

1 What are some of Pier 1 Imports' functional strategies as described in the case? Do you see any that reflect corporate core competencies?
2 Given the corporate level goals stated in the case, what lower level goals—say at the regional level or within the functional areas—must be developed in order to assure that corporate goals are attained by the year 2000? Give several examples.

VIDEO CASE

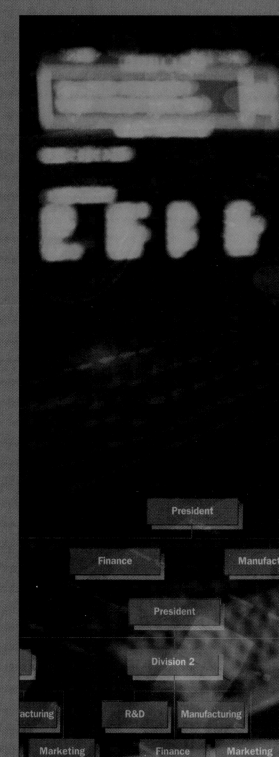

aily news stories discuss corporate reorganizations and buyouts. The structure of organizations has been one of the most closely scrutinized features of business in recent times. Why? In addition to its impact on employees, structure is the most visible manifestation of an organization's strategy.

Chapter 9 presents the basics of organization—the factors that affect overall structure, the organization of work and chain of command, and functional approaches to organization. In Chapter 10 we discuss the importance of innovation and change to the work environment, including ways to initiate and implement change. Chapter 11 highlights the role of human resource management in staff recruiting, hiring, training and development, and performance appraisal. Finally, in Chapter 12 we focus on diversity in the workplace and discuss the importance of the varied backgrounds and experiences of a diverse workforce.

Organizing

P A R T I V

Marketing

Division 3

Manufacturing

Finance   Marketing

Structure and Fundamentals of Organizing

LEARNING OBJECTIVES

After studying this chapter, you should be able to

- Describe how structure can be used to achieve an organization's strategic goals.

- Describe four stages of the organizational life cycle and explain how size and life cycle influence the correct structure.

- Explain the fundamental characteristics of organizing, including such concepts as work specialization, chain of command, line and staff, and task forces.

- Explain when specific structural characteristics such as centralization, span of management, and formalization should be used within organizations.

- Compare the functional approach to structure with the divisional approach.

- Explain the matrix approach to structure and its application to both domestic and international organizations.

- Explain the contemporary team and network structures and why they are being adopted by organizations.

CHAPTER 9

MANAGEMENT PROBLEM

Frank Fulkerson was watching the business his grandfather founded 50 years earlier slowly fall apart. Vortex Industries of Costa Mesa, California, is a 130-employee family-owned business that repairs and replaces warehouse doors. By the early 1990s, high costs and stagnant sales were threatening the company's viability. New commercial construction was down sharply due to the deepening recession, and companies that might once have been installing warehouse doors were now repairing them, in direct competition with Vortex. Although the company served customers in six counties, most of its people and equipment were bunched at one location near downtown Los Angeles. Work specialization meant that each employee handled a single, specific task. Vortex's bureaucratic procedures, combined with its high prices, had customers turning to competitors for cheaper and faster service. Employee morale was sinking with the company's fortunes, because employees felt their individual actions made little difference. Fulkerson was faced with a desperate situation. He knew that for Vortex to survive, it had to cut costs and prices, build employee morale, and serve customers better and faster.[1]

• If you were Frank Fulkerson, how would you transform Vortex to serve customers faster with lower prices? What advice would you give him about using organization structure to achieve this goal?

organizing
The deployment of organizational resources to achieve strategic goals.

Managers in companies like Vortex frequently must rethink structure and may reorganize to meet new competitive conditions in the environment. In this chapter, we examine the fundamentals of structure that apply to all organizations. We then focus more precisely on structure as a tool, especially on how managers can use such concepts as departmentalization and chain of command to achieve specific goals. In recent years, many corporations, including American Express, Apple, IBM, Amex Corporation, and Bausch & Lomb, have realigned departmental groupings, chains of command, and teams and task forces to attain new strategic goals. Structure is a powerful tool for reaching strategic goals, and a strategy's success often is determined by its fit with organization structure. By the end of this chapter, the problem at Vortex will be easily identified as a mismatch of Vortex's structure with its technology and competitive situation. Frank Fulkerson's solution to achieve better coordination called for a new structural approach.

Every firm wrestles with the problem of how to organize. Reorganization often is necessary to reflect a new strategy, changing market conditions, or innovative production technology. Companies throughout the world are restructuring to become leaner, more efficient, and more nimble in today's highly competitive global environment.

Xerox Corporation has restructured itself from one large, hierarchical company into nine independent product divisions. The new structure allows collaboration within each division that helps provide fast transition of new technology into new products for the marketplace.[2] Eastman Chemical Company replaced its senior vice presidents for administration, manufacturing, and research and development with self-directed work teams.[3] AT&T stunned the telecommunications industry by breaking into three decentralized businesses to go after growth opportunities in every part of the global information industry.[4] To reduce administrative overhead, Brunswick Corporation chopped out many of its headquarters' staff departments and one layer of management.[5]

Each of these organizations is using fundamental concepts of organizing. **Organizing** is the deployment of organizational resources to achieve strategic goals. The deployment of resources is reflected in the organization's division of labor into specific departments and jobs, formal lines of authority, and mechanisms for coordinating diverse organization tasks.

Organizing is important because it follows from planning strategy—the topic of Part 3. Strategy defines *what* to do; organizing defines *how* to do it. Organization structure is a tool that managers use to harness resources for getting things done. Part 4 explains the variety of organizing principles and concepts used by managers. This chapter covers fundamental concepts that apply to all organizations and departments. We look at how structural designs are tailored to the organization's situation. Chapter 10 discusses how organizations can be structured to facilitate innovation and change. Chapter 11 examines how to utilize human resources to the best advantage within the organization's structure.

Elements of structure such as chain of command, centralization/decentralization, formal authority, teams, and coordination devices fit together to form an overall structural approach. In some organizations, the formal, vertical hierarchy is emphasized as the way to achieve control and coordination. In other organizations, decision making is decentralized, cross-functional teams are implemented, and employees are given great freedom to pursue their tasks as they see fit. In many organizations, a trade-off occurs, because an emphasis on vertical structure means less opportunity for horizontal coordination and vice versa.

The balance between vertical and horizontal structure reflects the trend toward greater employee empowerment and is similar to the concepts of mechanistic and organic organizations introduced in Chapter 3.[6] When the vertical structure is very tight, as in traditionally designed organizations,

Traditional
Tight, Mechanistic Organization

Contemporary
Loose, Organic Organization

Dominant
Structural
Approach

Horizontal structure is dominant.

1. Shared tasks
2. Relaxed hierarchy, authority by expertise, few rules
3. Horizontal communication, face-to-face
4. Many teams, task forces, and integrators
5. Informal, decentralized decision making

Vertical structure is dominant.

1. Specialized tasks
2. Strict hierarchy of authority, many rules
3. Vertical communication and reporting systems
4. Few teams, task forces, or integrators
5. Centralized decision making

EXHIBIT 9.1
Differences in Mechanistic versus Organic Organizations

the structure is *mechanistic*. The organization emphasizes vertical control. Tasks are broken into routine jobs and are rigidly defined. Voluminous rules exist, and the hierarchy of authority is the major form of control. Decision making is centralized, and communication is vertical.

When horizontal structures dominate, as in contemporary empowered companies, the structure is *organic*.[7] Tasks are frequently redefined to fit employee and environmental needs. There are few rules, and authority is based on expertise rather than hierarchy. Decision making is decentralized. Communication is horizontal and is facilitated through the use of task forces, teams, and integrators as well as through new computer information systems that enable employees to share information. An organic organization may not have job descriptions or even an organization chart. A comparison of mechanistic versus organic organizations is presented in Exhibit 9.1. Debi Fields used a sophisticated computer system to maintain a flat structure in her expanding organization.

 MRS. FIELDS COOKIES

Debi Fields discovered the secret ingredient for success in her first cookie store, opened in 1977 in Palo Alto, California. Though there are now 617 cookie emporiums and bakeries worldwide, she has maintained that element of flat structure to keep her organization viable.

When starting out, Debi set sales quotas for herself and baked daily inventory based on her experiences. Early on, she developed an enduring policy of not selling any product more than two hours old. But how to maintain that on-top-of-hourly-sales approach once she expanded was a challenge.

Soon after her second store opened in 1984, Debi's husband, Randy, and the MIS vice president, Paul Quinn, developed an innovative software system called Retail Operations Intelligence (ROI) to do just that. ROI links all the emporiums and bakeries with the Park City, Utah, company headquarters and allows store managers and regional directors to have daily computer contact with Debi and any other administrator. The system includes, then, not only E-mail, but also an automatic electronic flow of operating results and information, from inventory and production planning to sales reporting and analysis and even interviewing protocol. As a result, Debi's management skills are spread throughout the company to help everyone sell lots of cookies.

For example, the production planning module tells store managers how many cookies they can expect to sell hour to hour and

then how much dough of each kind to prepare, as well as when to bake in order to maximize sales and minimize losses. Hourly progress versus projections are charted and suggestions are given on how to sell more cookies.

The technology frees the employees to be with customers and gives managers more time with staff and customer. Plus it gives Debi the closeness she desires. She often calls stores in the morning with the performance test results to congratulate them. Says Quinn, "It makes them feel . . . that she cares."[8] ■

FACTORS AFFECTING STRUCTURE

How do managers know whether to design a tight or loose structure? The answer lies in the contingency factors that influence organization structure. Recall from Chapter 2 that contingency pertains to those factors on which structure depends. Research on organization structure shows that the emphasis given to loose or tight structure depends on such contingency factors as stage of maturity, technology, and environment. The right structure is designed to "fit" the contingency factors as illustrated in Exhibit 9.2. Let us look at the relationship between each contingency factor and organization structure in more detail to see how structure should be designed.

Contingency Factor: Stages of Maturity

The organization's **size** is its scope or magnitude and frequently is measured by number of employees. A considerable body of research findings has shown that large organizations are structured differently from small ones. Small organizations are informal and have little division of labor, few rules and regulations, ad hoc budgeting and performance systems, and small professional and clerical support staffs. Large organizations such as IBM necessarily have an extensive division of labor, large professional staffs, numerous rules and regulations, and internal systems for control, rewards, and innovation.[9]

Organizations evolve from small to large by going through stages of a life cycle. Within the **organization life cycle,** organizations follow predictable patterns through major developmental stages that are sequential in nature. This is similar to the product life cycle described in Chapter 7 except that it applies to the organization as a whole. Each stage involves changes in the range of organization activities and overall structure.[10] Every organization progresses through the life cycle at its own pace, but most encounter the four stages defined in Exhibit 9.3: birth, youth, midlife, and maturity.

Birth Stage. In the **birth stage,** the organization is created. The founder is an entrepreneur, who alone or with a handful of employees performs all tasks. The organization is very informal, and tasks are overlapping. There are no professional staff, no rules and regulations, and no internal systems for planning, rewards, or coordination. Decision authority is centralized with the owner. Apple Computer was in the birth stage when it was created by Steven Jobs and Stephen Wozniak in Wozniak's parents' garage. Jobs and Wozniak sold their own belongings to raise money to personally build 200 Apple computers. Kentucky Fried Chicken was in the birth stage when Colonel Harlan Sanders was running a combination gas station/restaurant in Corbin, Kentucky, before the popularity of his restaurant began to spread.

Youth Stage. In the **youth stage,** the organization has more employees and a product that is succeeding in the marketplace.

---

organization life cycle
The organization's evolution through major developmental stages.

birth stage
The phase of the organization life cycle in which the company is created.

size
The organization's scope or magnitude, typically measured by number of employees.

youth stage
The phase of the organization life cycle in which the organization is growing rapidly and has a product enjoying some marketplace success.

EXHIBIT 9.2
Contingency Factors That Influence Organization Structure

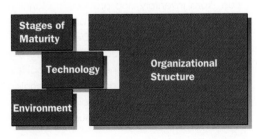

E X H I B I T   9 . 3
Structural Characteristics during Organization Life-Cycle Stages

	Birth Stage	Youth Stage	Midlife Stage	Maturity Stage
Size	Small	Medium	Large	Very large
Bureaucracy	Nonbureaucratic	Prebureaucratic	Bureaucratic	Very bureaucratic
Division of labor	Overlapping tasks	Some departments	Many departments, well-defined tasks, organization chart	Extensive—small jobs, written job descriptions
Centralization	One-person rule	Top leaders rule	Decentralization to department heads	Enforced decentralization, top management overloaded
Formalization	No written rules	Few rules	Policy and procedures manuals	Extensive—most activities covered by written manuals
Administrative intensity	Secretary, no professional staff	Increasing clerical and maintenance, little professional staff	Increasing professional support staff	Large—multiple professionals and clerical staff departments
Internal systems (information, budget, planning, performance)	Nonexistent	Crude budget and information system	Control systems in place—budget, performance, operational reports	Extensive—planning, financial, and personnel systems added
Lateral teams, task forces for coordination	None	Top leaders only	Some use of integrators and task forces	Frequent at lower levels to break down barriers of bureaucracy

SOURCES: Based on Robert E. Quinn and Kim Cameron, "Organizational Life Cycles and Some Shifting Criteria of Effectiveness: Some Preliminary Evidence," *Management Science* 29 (1983), 31–51; and Richard L. Daft and Richard M. Steers, *Organizations: A Micro/Macro Approach* (Glenview, Ill.: Scott, Foresman, 1986).

The organization is growing rapidly. The owner no longer has sole possession. A few trusted colleagues share in the decision making, although control is still relatively centralized. A division of labor is emerging, with some designation of task responsibility to newly created departments. Internal systems remain informal. A few formal rules and policies appear, and there are a few professional and administrative personnel. Apple Computer was in the youth stage during the years of rapid growth from 1978 to 1981, when the major product line was established and more than 2,000 dealers signed on to sell Apple computers. Kentucky Fried Chicken was in the youth stage when Colonel Sanders convinced more than 400 franchises in the United States and Canada to use his original recipe. Although both organizations were growing rapidly, they were still being run in a very informal fashion. Any company goes through these stages. The following example shows how toymaker Georgetown Collection, Inc., is coping with its youth stage.

 MAGIC ATTIC CLUB

Christmas wasn't jingling all the way in 1995, when 40,000 dolls arrived in Westbrook, Maine, from the factory in China with a not-so-minor flaw—their arms were falling off. For thousands of hopeful girls, Christmas was in jeopardy. But the stakes were higher for Georgetown Collection, Inc., a hot maker of the porcelain dolls that bet its future on this new Magic Attic Club line. If the dolls could not be fixed and shipped out, Georgetown faced a certain death.

So the 100 employees—secretaries, accountants, everyone—worked into the nights reassembling the 80,000 little arms onto the dolls, figuring out how to do it in 24 hours. The hard work paid off and Georgetown now sees skyrocketing demand, more than the capital-poor company can handle. Such problems are common to entrepreneurial firms who pass the first stages of growth. After some success, they often end up with overwhelming problems from rapid expansion, including telephone

maturity stage
The phase of the organization life cycle in which the organization has become exceedingly large and mechanistic.

ordering systems, warehousing, distribution, and staffing problems, as well as foreign outsourcing headaches. "This is the point where companies grow or fail," notes marketing vice president Gretchen Springer.

Owner and founder Jeffrey H. McKinnon had worked in the toy industry and struck out on his own with his collectible-doll business, Georgetown Collection, in 1987. His previous experience of working with Chinese factories helped him negotiate economical production deals, so the high-quality dolls could sell for only $59. He went from nothing to a 19 percent market share.

Georgetown introduced the new "Chronicles of Narnia"-inspired dolls in 1994 and sold out by distributing more than 100,000 Magic Attic catalogs. Sales in 1995 were $3 million and doubled in 1996.[11]

The company, though, still struggles and can't count on happy endings just yet. But those happy little girls who got the dolls would never know it. ■

midlife stage
The phase of the organization life cycle in which the firm has reached prosperity and grown substantially large.

Midlife Stage. By the **midlife stage,** the organization has prospered and grown quite large. At this point, the organization begins to look like a more formalized bureaucracy. An extensive division of labor appears, with statements of policies and responsibilities. Rules, regulations, and job descriptions are used to direct employee activities. Professional and clerical staff are hired to undertake specialized activities in support of manufacturing and marketing. Reward, budget, and accounting control systems are put in place. Top management decentralizes many responsibilities to functional departments, but flexibility and innovation may decline. Apple Computer is now well into the midlife stage because it has adopted a host of procedures, internal systems, and staff departments to provide greater control over the organization. Kentucky Fried Chicken moved into the midlife stage when Colonel Sanders sold his company to John Y. Brown, who took the company through a national promotion and building campaign.

Maturity Stage. In the **maturity stage,** the organization is large and mechanistic—indeed, the vertical structure often becomes too strong. Budgets; control systems; rules; policies; large staffs of engineering, accounting, and finance specialists; and a refined division of labor are in place. Decision making is centralized. At this point, the organization is in danger of stagnation. To offset the rigid vertical hierarchy, inspire innovation, and shrink barriers among departments, the organization may reorganize. To regain flexibility and innovation, managers may decentralize and create teams, task forces, and integrator positions. This is especially true for such mature organizations as Procter & Gamble, Sears, Westinghouse, John Deere, and General Motors, which have experienced major changes in the external environment and found that the mature vertical structure inhibited flexible responses. Many companies decide to reengineer business processes as a way to revitalize, as we will discuss later in the chapter. Reengineering may also lead to downsizing—the planned elimination of positions, jobs, functions, hierarchical levels, or business units.[12]

Moving Through the Life Cycle. Organizations do not progress through the four life-cycle stages in a logical, orderly fashion. Stages may lead or lag in a given organization. The transition from one stage to the next is difficult and often promotes crises. Employees who were present at the organization's birth often long for the informal atmosphere and resist the formalized procedures, departmentalization, and staff departments required in maturing organizations. Organizations that prematurely emphasize a rigid vertical structure or that stay informal during later stages of the life cycle have the wrong structure for their situation. Performance suffers. The failure of People Express airline occurred because the firm never grew up. Despite its being the fifth largest airline, top management ran it informally without a strong vertical structure. The structure fit neither People Express's size nor life-cycle stage.

Contingency Factor: Manufacturing and Service Technologies

Technology includes the knowledge, tools, techniques, and activities used to transform organizational inputs into outputs.[13] Technology includes machinery, employee skills, and work procedures. A useful way to think about technology is as "work flow." The production work flow may be to produce steel castings, television programs, or computer software.

Production technology is significant because it has direct influence on the organization structure. Structure must be designed to fit the technology as well as to accommodate the external environment and organization size. Technologies vary between manufacturing and service organizations. In the following paragraphs, we discuss each characteristic of technology and the structure that best fits it.

Woodward's Manufacturing Technology. The most influential research into the relationship between manufacturing technology and organization structure was conducted by Joan Woodward, a British industrial sociologist.[14] She gathered data from 100 British firms to determine whether basic structural characteristics, such as administrative overhead, span of control, centralization, and formalization, were different across firms. She found that manufacturing firms could be categorized according to three basic types of work flow technology:

1 *Small batch and unit production.* **Small batch production** firms produce goods in batches of one or a few products designed to customer specification. Each customer orders a unique product. This technology also is used to make large, one-of-a-kind products, such as computer-controlled machines. Small batch manufacturing is close to traditional skilled-craft work, because human beings are a large part of the process; they run machines to make the product. Examples of items produced through small batch manufacturing include custom clothing, special-order machine tools, space capsules, satellites, and submarines.

2 *Large batch and mass production.* **Mass production** technology is distinguished by standardized production runs. A large volume of products is produced, and all customers receive the same product. Standard products go into inventory for sale as customers need them. This technology makes greater use of machines than does small batch production. Machines are designed to do most of the physical work, and employees complement the machinery. Examples of mass production are automobile assembly lines and the large batch techniques used to produce Macintosh computers, tobacco products, and textiles.

3 *Continuous process production.* In **continuous process production,** the entire work flow is mechanized. This is the most sophisticated and complex form of production technology. Because the process runs continuously, there is no starting and stopping. Human operators are not part of actual production because machinery does all of the work. Human operators simply read dials, fix machines that break down, and manage the production process. Examples of continuous process technologies are chemical plants, distilleries, petroleum refineries, and nuclear power plants.

The important conclusion about manufacturing technology was described by Woodward as follows: "Different technologies impose different kinds of demands on individuals and organizations, and these demands have to be met through an appropriate structure."[15] Woodward found that the relationship between structure and technology was directly related to company performance. Low-performing firms tended to deviate from the preferred structural form, often adopting a structure appropriate for another type of technology. High-performing organizations had characteristics very similar to those listed in Exhibit 9.4.

technology
The knowledge, tools, techniques, and activities used to transform the organization's inputs into outputs.

mass production
A type of technology characterized by the production of a large volume of products with the same specifications.

continuous process production
A type of technology involving mechanization of the entire work flow and nonstop production.

small batch production
A type of technology that involves the production of goods in batches of one or a few products designed to customer specifications.

EXHIBIT 9.4
Relationship between Manufacturing Technology and Organization Structure

	Manufacturing Technology		
	Small Batch	*Mass Production*	*Continuous Process*
Technical Complexity of Production Technology	Low	Medium	High
Organization structure:			
Formalization	Low	High	Low
Centralization	Low	High	Low
Top administrator ratio	Low	Medium	High
Indirect/direct labor ratio	1/9	1/4	1/1
Supervisor span of control	23	48	15
Communication:			
Written (vertical)	Low	High	Low
Verbal (lateral)	High	Low	High
Overall structure	Organic	Mechanistic	Organic

SOURCE: Based on Joan Woodward, *Industrial Organizations: Theory and Practice* (London: Oxford University Press, 1965).

flexible manufacturing
A manufacturing technology using computers to automate and integrate manufacturing components such as robots, machines, product design, and engineering analysis.

service technology
Technology characterized by intangible outputs and direct contact between employees and customers.

Flexible Manufacturing. The most recent development in manufacturing technology is called **flexible manufacturing,** which uses computers to automate and integrate manufacturing components such as robots, machines, product design, and engineering analysis. Companies such as John Deere, General Motors, Intel, and Illinois Tool Works use flexible manufacturing in a single manufacturing plant to do small batch and mass production operations *at the same time.* Bar codes enable machines to make instantaneous changes—such as putting a larger screw in a different location—as different batches flow down the automated assembly line. Sunrise Medical uses flexible manufacturing to make wheelchairs tailored to an individual customer's exact specifications.[16] Flexible manufacturing is considered to be at a higher level of technical complexity than the three manufacturing technologies studied by Woodward. The structures associated with the new technology tend to have few rules, decentralization, a small ratio of administrators to workers, face-to-face lateral communication, and a team-oriented, organic approach.[17]

Service Technology. Service organizations are becoming increasingly important in North America. Since 1982, more employees have been employed in service organizations than in manufacturing organizations. Thus, new research has been undertaken to understand the structural characteristics of service organizations. **Service technology** can be defined as follows:

1 *Intangible output.* The output of a service firm is intangible. Services are perishable and, unlike physical products, cannot be stored in inventory. The service is either consumed immediately or lost forever. Manufactured products are produced at one point in time and can be stored until sold at another time.

2 *Direct contact with customers.* Employees and customers interact directly to provide and purchase the service. Production and consumption are simultaneous. Service firm employees have direct contact with customers. In a manufacturing firm, technical employees are separated from customers, and hence no direct interactions occur.[18]

The output of service organizations is frequently intangible; that of manufacturing organizations is tangible. Examples of service firms include consulting companies, law firms, brokerage houses, airlines, hotels, advertising firms, public relations firms, amusement parks, and educational organizations. Service technology also characterizes many departments in large corporations, even manufacturing firms. In a manufacturing organization such as Ford Motor Company, the legal, human resources, finance, and market research departments provide service. Thus, the

structure and design of each of these departments reflect its own service technology rather than the manufacturing plant's technology. Service technology concepts therefore can be used to structure both service organizations and the many large service departments within manufacturing organizations.

One distinct feature of service technology that directly influences structure is the need for employees to be close to the customer.[19] Structural characteristics are similar to those for continuous manufacturing technology, shown in Exhibit 9.4 (on page 290). Service firms tend to be organic, informal, and decentralized. Lateral communication is high because employees must share information and resources to serve customers and solve problems. Services are also dispersed; hence each unit is often small and located geographically close to customers. For example, banks, hotels, fast-food franchises, and doctors' offices disperse their facilities into regional and local offices.

Although service firms in general tend to be more organic and decentralized, some, such as McDonald's, develop set rules and procedures for customer service. When services can be standardized, a mechanistic, centralized structure can be very effective, as revealed by the Marriott Corporation.

At Marriott, the hotel itself is the main service, and a mind-boggling system is used to make the right impression every time. Top managers make no apologies for the tightly centralized system of policies, procedures, and controls for operational details. Room attendants have 66 things to do in cleaning a room, from dusting the tops of pictures (number 7) to keeping the telephone book and Bibles in a neat condition (number 37). Bill Marriott says, "The more the system works like the Army, the better." The cooks have 6,000 recipes available to them, and they are not allowed to deviate. One rule for chefs says, "Deviations from the standard written specifications may not be made without prior approval and written consent of the vice president of food and beverages."

Marriott Corporation plans to add new hotels each year. It routinizes the service and builds luxury into the physical structure to ensure that guests are treated the same way every time. The most recent program is First 10, which focuses on making a lasting impression of great service on customers during the first ten minutes of their hotel stay. Marriott was rated as one of the five best-managed companies, and Bill Marriott and four executive vice presidents spend half the year on the road visiting company facilities. The close, personal supervision and careful reading of customer suggestions help Bill Marriott give business travelers the service they expect and deserve.[20] ■

MARRIOTT CORPORATION

Marriott Corporation is now the nation's largest hotel operator, and the president, Bill Marriott, plans to make it even larger. Marriott's success has come from two strategies: Put hotels where the customers are and provide excellent service. Putting hotels where the customers are means building hotels downtown and at airports. Convention centers, such as Atlantic City, are another target. Marriott also searches for new niches. The Courtyard is a new type of garden apartment hotel aimed at the moderate-priced segment of the market. Courtyards are scattered around major metropolitan areas.

Contingency Factor: The Environment

In Chapter 3, we discussed the nature of environmental uncertainty. Environmental uncertainty means that decision makers have difficulty acquiring good information and predicting external changes. Uncertainty occurs when the external environment is rapidly changing and complex. An uncertain environment causes three things to happen within an organization.

I *Increased differences occur among departments.* In an uncertain environment, each major department—marketing,

E X H I B I T   9 . 5
Relationship between Environment and Structure

STRUCTURE

	Mechanistic	Organic
Uncertain (Unstable)	**Incorrect Fit:** Mechanistic structure in uncertain environment Structure too tight	**Correct Fit:** Organic structure in uncertain environment
Certain (Stable)	**Correct Fit:** Mechanistic structure in certain environment	**Incorrect Fit:** Organic structure in certain environment Structure too loose

ENVIRONMENT (label at left, between the two rows)

manufacturing, research and development—focuses on the task and environmental sectors for which it is responsible and hence distinguishes itself from the others with respect to goals, task orientation, and time horizon.[21] Departments work autonomously. These factors create barriers among departments.

2 *The organization needs increased coordination to keep departments working together.* Additional differences require more emphasis on lateral coordination to link departments together and overcome differences in departmental goals and orientations.

3 *The organization must adapt to change.* The organization must maintain a flexible, responsive posture toward the environment. Changes in products and technology require cooperation among departments, which means additional emphasis on coordination through the use of teams, task forces, and lateral information processing.[22]

The contingency relationship between environmental uncertainty and structural approach is illustrated in Exhibit 9.5. When the external environment is more stable, the organization should have a mechanistic structure that emphasizes vertical control. There is little need for change, flexibility, or intense coordination. The structure can em-

phasize specialization, centralized decision making, and wide spans of control. When environmental uncertainty is high, an organic structure that emphasizes lateral relationships such as teams and task forces is appropriate. Vertical structure characteristics such as specialization, centralization, and formalized procedures should be downplayed. In an uncertain environment, the organization figures things out as it goes along, departments must cooperate, and decisions should be decentralized to the teams and task forces working on specific problems.

When managers use the wrong structure for the environment, reduced performance results. A rigid, mechanistic structure in an uncertain environment prevents the organization from adapting to change. Likewise, a loose, organic structure in a stable environment is inefficient. Too many resources are devoted to meetings and discussions when employees could be more productive focusing on specialized tasks.

ORGANIZING THE VERTICAL STRUCTURE

The organizing process leads to the creation of organization structure, which defines how tasks are divided and resources deployed. **Organization structure** is defined

organization structure The framework in which the organization defines how tasks are divided, resources are deployed, and departments are coordinated.

EXHIBIT 9.6
Organization Chart for a Textile Company

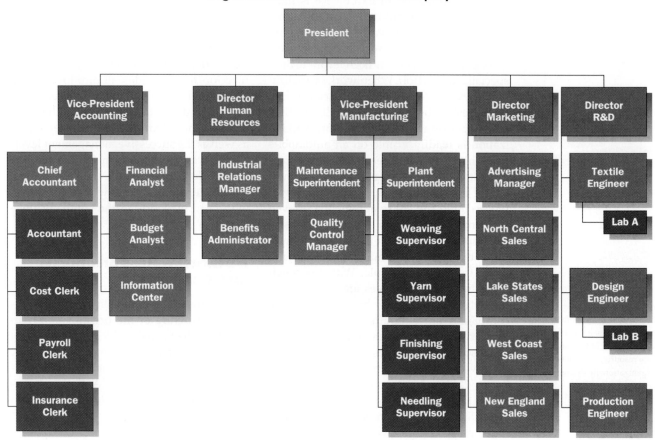

as (1) the set of formal tasks assigned to individuals and departments; (2) formal reporting relationships, including lines of authority, decision responsibility, number of hierarchical levels, and span of managers' control; and (3) the design of systems to ensure effective coordination of employees across departments.[23]

The set of formal tasks and formal reporting relationships provides a framework for vertical control of the organization. The characteristics of vertical structure are portrayed in the **organization chart,** which is the visual representation of an organization's structure.

A sample organization chart for a textile mill is illustrated in Exhibit 9.6. The mill has five major departments—accounting, human resources, manufacturing, marketing,

and research and development. The organization chart delineates the chain of command, indicates departmental tasks and how they fit together, and provides order and logic for the organization. Every employee has an appointed task, line of authority, and decision responsibility. The following sections discuss several important features of vertical structure in more detail.

Work Specialization

Organizations perform a wide variety of tasks. A fundamental principle is that work can be performed more efficiently if employees are allowed to specialize.[24] **Work specialization,** sometimes called *division of labor,* is the degree to which organizational

organization chart
The visual representation of an organization's structure.

work specialization
The degree to which organizational tasks are subdivided into individual jobs; also called *division of labor.*

tasks are subdivided into separate jobs. Work specialization in Exhibit 9.6 is illustrated by the separation of manufacturing tasks into weaving, yarn, finishing, and needling. Employees within each department perform only the tasks relevant to their specialized function. When work specialization is extensive, employees specialize in a single task. Jobs tend to be small, but they can be performed efficiently. Work specialization is readily visible on an automobile assembly line where each employee performs the same task over and over again. It would not be efficient to have a single employee build the entire automobile or even perform a large number of unrelated jobs.

Despite the apparent advantages of specialization, many organizations are moving away from this principle. With too much specialization, employees are isolated and do only a single, tiny, boring job. Many companies are enlarging jobs to provide greater challenges or assigning teams to tasks so that employees can rotate among the several jobs performed by the team. At Sony Corporation's factory in Kohda, Japan, the assembly line for camcorders has been dismantled and replaced with small, four-person shops, where workers walk through a spiral line and assemble an entire camera themselves, doing everything from soldering to testing. U.S. companies are taking similar paths. Production increased 51 percent after Compaq Computer's Scotland and Texas plants switched from assembly lines to four-worker manufacturing teams.[25] Productivity increases were even higher at Lantech after it got rid of its division-of-labor system, as well as some unnecessary high-tech equipment, as explained in the Technology for Today box. The team approach to organization design will be discussed later in this chapter, and approaches to designing jobs to fit employee needs are described in Chapters 14 and 16.

authority
The formal and legitimate right of a manager to make decisions, issue orders, and allocate resources to achieve organizationally desired outcomes.

chain of command
An unbroken line of authority that links all individuals in the organization and specifies who reports to whom.

Chain of Command

The **chain of command** is an unbroken line of authority that links all persons in an organization and shows who reports to whom. It is associated with two underlying principles. *Unity of command* means that each employee is held accountable to only one supervisor. *The scalar principle* refers to a clearly defined line of authority in the organization that includes all employees. Authority and responsibility for different tasks should be distinct. All persons in the organization should know to whom they report as well as the successive management levels all the way to the top. In Exhibit 9.6, the payroll clerk reports to the chief accountant, who in turn reports to the vice president, who in turn reports to the company president.

Authority, Responsibility, and Delegation

The chain of command illustrates the authority structure of the organization. **Authority** is the formal and legitimate right of a manager to make decisions, issue orders, and allocate resources to achieve organizationally desired outcomes. Authority is distinguished by three characteristics:[26]

1 *Authority is vested in organizational positions, not people.* Managers have authority because of the positions they hold, and other people in the same positions would have the same authority.
2 *Authority is accepted by subordinates.* Although authority flows top down through the organization's hierarchy, subordinates comply because they believe that managers have a legitimate right to issue orders. The acceptance theory of authority argues that a manager has authority only if subordinates choose to accept his or her commands. If subordinates refuse to obey because the order is outside their zone of acceptance, a manager's authority disappears.[27] For example, Richard Ferris, the former chairman of United Airlines, resigned because few people accepted his strategy of acquiring hotels, a car rental company, and other organizations to build a travel empire. When key people refused to

TECHNOLOGY FOR TODAY
WHEN HIGH-TECH IS SLOW

By all accounts, Lantech Inc., manufacturer of industrial packaging equipment, was a decently run, thriving company, relying heavily on automation and a succession of ever-more powerful mainframe computers—until 1989 when it lost a key design patent. New competitors attacked with aggressive pricing strategies and the company foundered, losing the patent-edge that had given them a 50 percent market share. Committees worked on improving productivity. Just turning up the speed didn't seem to do much, though, and in the end, members spent most of their time bickering with each other.

Lantech was similar to other factories that were run on the old Henry Ford-prototype process, where core processes define a strict division of labor and departmentalization. Produc-tivity was increased by speeding up the core processes. Founder and owner Pat Lancaster began reading about "whole cycle-management," originally developed by Toyota, a system of continuous improvement for the entire factory. Its focus is on continually finding better and more efficient ways to manufacture. Relying on the line worker to spot most problems and to propose solutions, it would mean nothing less than a complete revolution in the company's culture.

Lancaster knew something had to change or the company would be doomed. New vice-president Ron Hicks assembled transition teams to evaluate and redesign every aspect of production. The shift was made from a division-of-labor approach to a generalized-labor approach. Mass production turned into a "one-piece flow line." Increased worker involvement helped identify some problems unseen before, resulting in a great reduction of excess inventory. As workers adapted to the microlines, it became obvious that Lantech's sophisticated automation was not compatible with the new system, for they assumed an uninformed and under-responsible workforce. Now, the non-automated machines, or "hand tools," make the microlines much more flexible.

Lantech discovered what a small number of companies are realizing. High-tech isn't for everyone. Lancaster never started out to be a low-tech prophet, but the 100 percent increase in productivity realized by using four-decade-old technology is hard to ignore.

SOURCE: Fred Hapgood, "Keeping It Simple," *Inc. Technology*, 1996, no. 1, 66–72.

accept his direction, his authority was lost, and he resigned.

3 *Authority flows down the vertical hierarchy.* Positions at the top of the hierarchy are vested with more formal authority than are positions at the bottom.

Responsibility is the flip side of the authority coin. **Responsibility** is the duty to perform the task or activity an employee has been assigned. Typically, managers are assigned authority commensurate with responsibility. When managers have responsibility for task outcomes but little authority, the job is possible but difficult. They rely on persuasion and luck. When managers have authority exceeding responsibility, they may become tyrants, using authority toward frivolous outcomes.[28]

Accountability is the mechanism through which authority and responsibility are brought into alignment. **Accountability** means that the people with authority and responsibility are subject to reporting and justifying task outcomes to those above them in the chain of command.[29] Subordinates must be aware that they are accountable for a task and accept the responsibility and authority for performing it. Accountability can be built into the organization structure. For example, at Whirlpool incentive programs provide strict accountability. Performance of all managers is monitored, and bonus payments are tied to successful outcomes.

Another concept related to authority is delegation.[30] **Delegation** is the process managers use to transfer authority and responsibility to positions below them in the hierarchy. Most organizations today encourage managers to delegate authority to the lowest possible level to provide

accountability
The fact that the people with authority and responsibility are subject to reporting and justifying task outcomes to those above them in the chain of command.

responsibility
The duty to perform the task or activity an employee has been assigned.

delegation
The process managers use to transfer authority and responsibility to positions below them in the hierarchy.

maximum flexibility to meet customer needs and adapt to the environment. Managers are encouraged to delegate authority, although they often find it difficult. Techniques for delegation are discussed in the Focus on Management box. The trend toward increased delegation begins in the chief executive's office in companies such as USX, PPG Industries, Johnsonville Foods, Ford, and General Electric. At Johnsonville, a committee of employees from the shop floor has been delegated authority to formulate the manufacturing budget.

Span of Management

The **span of management** is the number of employees reporting to a supervisor. Sometimes called the *span of control*, this characteristic of structure determines how closely a supervisor can monitor subordinates. Traditional views of organization design recommended a span of management of about seven subordinates per manager. However, many lean organizations today have spans of management as high as 30, 40, and even higher. Research on the Lockheed Missile and Space Company and other manufacturing companies has suggested that span of management can vary widely and that several factors influence the span.[31] Generally, when supervisors must be closely involved with subordinates, the span should be small, and when supervisors need little involvement with subordinates, it can be large. The following factors are associated with less supervisor involvement and thus larger spans of control:

1 Work performed by subordinates is stable and routine.
2 Subordinates perform similar work tasks.
3 Subordinates are concentrated in a single location.
4 Subordinates are highly trained and need little direction in performing tasks.
5 Rules and procedures defining task activities are available.
6 Support systems and personnel are available for the manager.

7 Little time is required in nonsupervisory activities such as coordination with other departments or planning.
8 Managers' personal preferences and styles favor a large span.

Tall versus Flat Structure. The average span of control used in an organization determines whether the structure is tall or flat. A **tall structure** has an overall narrow span and more hierarchical levels. A **flat structure** has a wide span, is horizontally dispersed, and has fewer hierarchical levels.

The trend in the 1980s and 1990s has been toward wider spans of control as a way to facilitate delegation.[32] Exhibit 9.7 illustrates how an international metals company was reorganized. The multilevel set of managers shown in panel *a* was replaced with ten operating managers and nine staff specialists reporting directly to the CEO, as shown in panel *b*. The CEO welcomed this wide span of 19 management subordinates because it fit his style, his management team was top quality and needed little supervision, and they were all located on the same floor of an office building.

Centralization and Decentralization

Centralization and decentralization pertain to the hierarchical level at which decisions are made. **Centralization** means that decision authority is located near the top of the organization. With **decentralization,** decision authority is pushed downward to lower organization levels. Organizations may have to experiment to find the correct hierarchical level at which to make decisions.

In the United States and Canada, the trend over the past 30 years has been toward greater decentralization of organizations. Decentralization is believed to relieve the burden on top managers, make greater use of workers' skills and abilities, ensure that decisions are made close to the action by well-informed people, and permit more rapid response to external changes.

tall structure
A management structure characterized by an overall narrow span of management and a relatively large number of hierarchical levels.

flat structure
A management structure characterized by an overall broad span of control and relatively few hierarchical levels.

span of management
The number of employees who report to a supervisor; also called *span of control.*

centralization
The location of decision authority near top organizational levels.

decentralization
The location of decision authority near lower organizational levels.

FOCUS ON MANAGEMENT
HOW TO DELEGATE

The attempt by top management to decentralize decision making often gets bogged down because middle managers are unable to delegate. Managers may cling tightly to their decision-making and task responsibilities. Failure to delegate occurs for a number of reasons: Managers are most comfortable making familiar decisions; they feel they will lose personal status by delegating tasks; they believe they can do a better job themselves; or they have an aversion to risk—they will not take a chance on delegating because performance responsibility ultimately rests with them.

Yet decentralization offers an organization many advantages. Decisions are made at the right level, lower-level employees are motivated, and employees have the opportunity to develop decision-making skills. Overcoming barriers to delegation in order to gain these advantages is a major challenge. The following approach can help each manager delegate more effectively:

1. *Delegate the whole task.* A manager should delegate an entire task to one person rather than dividing it among several people. This gives the individual complete responsibility and increases his or her initiative while giving the manager some control over the results. If more than one person is needed on a project, at least limit the number involved.

2. *Select the right person.* Not all employees have the same capabilities and degree of motivation. Managers must match talent to task if delegation is to be effective. They should identify subordinates who have made independent decisions in the past and have shown a desire for more responsibility.

3. *Ensure that authority equals responsibility.* Merely assigning a task is not effective delegation. Managers often load subordinates with increased responsibility but do not extend their decision-making range. In addition to having responsibility for completing a task, the worker must be given the authority to make decisions about how best to do the job.

4. *Give thorough instruction.* Successful delegation includes information on what, when, why, where, who, and how. The subordinate must clearly understand the task and the expected results. It is a good idea to write down all provisions discussed, including required resources and when and how the results will be reported.

5. *Maintain feedback.* Feedback means keeping open lines of communication with the subordinate to answer questions and provide advice, but without exerting too much control. Open lines of communication make it easier to trust subordinates. Feedback keeps the subordinate on the right track.

6. *Evaluate and reward performance.* Once the task is completed, the manager should evaluate results, not methods. When results do not meet expectations, the manager must assess the consequences. When they do meet expectations, the manager should reward employees for a job well done with praise, financial rewards when appropriate, and delegation of future assignments.

ARE YOU A POSITIVE DELEGATOR?

Positive delegation is the way an organization implements decentralization. Do you help or hinder the decentralization process? If you answer yes to more than three of the following questions, you may have a problem delegating:

- ◆ I tend to be a perfectionist.
- ◆ My boss expects me to know all the details of my job. No one seems to do things as carefully as I do.
- ◆ I don't have the time to explain clearly and concisely how a task should be accomplished.
- ◆ I often end up doing tasks myself.
- ◆ My subordinates typically are not as committed as I am.
- ◆ I get upset when other people don't do the task right.
- ◆ I really enjoy doing the details of my job to the best of my ability.
- ◆ I like to be in control of task outcomes.

SOURCES: "Delegate Your Way to Success," *Successful Meetings*, vol. 45 no. 8, July 1996, 32; Thomas R. Horton, "Delegation and Team Building: No Solo Acts Please," *Management Review*, September 1992, 58–61; Andrew E. Schwartz, "The Why, What, and to Whom of Delegation," *Management Solutions* (June 1987), 31–38; "Delegation," *Small Business Report* (June 1986), 38–43; and Max E. Douglas, "How to Delegate Safely," *Training and Development Journal*, February 1987, 8.

However, this trend does not mean that every organization should decentralize all decisions. Managers should diagnose the organizational situation and select the decision-making level that will best meet the organization's needs. Factors that typically influence centralization versus decentralization are as follows:

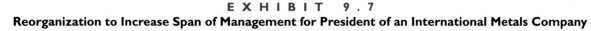

EXHIBIT 9.7
Reorganization to Increase Span of Management for President of an International Metals Company

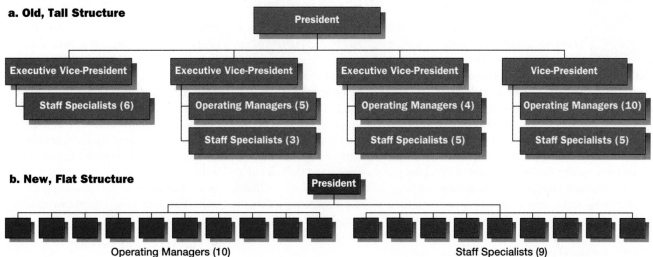

a. Old, Tall Structure

President

Executive Vice-President — Staff Specialists (6)

Executive Vice-President — Operating Managers (5) — Staff Specialists (3)

Executive Vice-President — Operating Managers (4) — Staff Specialists (5)

Vice-President — Operating Managers (10) — Staff Specialists (5)

b. New, Flat Structure

President

Operating Managers (10)   Staff Specialists (9)

1 Greater change and uncertainty in the environment are usually associated with decentralization. A good example of how decentralization can help cope with rapid change and uncertainty occurred during Operation Desert Shield, when the highly decentralized U.S. Tactical Air Command deployed double the number of squadrons expected during the first week while other centralized U.S. forces fell behind their deployment schedules.[33] Today, most companies feel greater uncertainty because of intense global competition; hence, many have decentralized.

2 The amount of centralization or decentralization should fit the firm's strategy. For example, Johnson & Johnson gives almost complete authority to its 168 operating companies to develop and market their own products. Decentralization fits the corporate strategy of empowerment that gets each division close to customers so it can speedily adapt to their needs.[34] As new technology and competition changed the banking industry, BancOne Chairman John B. McCoy switched to centralization to cut costs, speed decision making, and move faster with new products and services.[35]

3 In times of crisis or risk of company failure, authority may be centralized at the top. When Honda could not get agreement among divisions about new car models, President Nobuhiko Kawamoto made the decision himself.[36]

Sometimes, an organization has to find the right balance between centralization and decentralization to meet different strategic needs. Consider the example of VeriFone, Inc.

VERIFONE, INC.

Responding quickly to customer needs was a high priority for William R. Pape, when 14 years ago he founded VeriFone, Inc., an equipment supplier for credit card verification and automated payments. Being completely centralized would mean slower reactions and sensitivities to clients. Pape also realized technology would have to play a big part. Structuring a company to be "virtual," that is, with heavy use of E-mail, online data bases, and LANs (local area networks), requires decentralization.

Still, being *completely* decentralized didn't seem right either, for that can easily turn into anarchy. Getting the proper balance is tricky.

VeriFone has learned to have some "corporate" policies for their 40-plus locations, with each business unit allowed a great deal of latitude in how to implement them. With their corporate compensation standards, each unit can decide how to reward its members as long as it meets its target performance level and operates with certain standard procedures (such as open communication, workplace ethics, and following any corporate standards).

Each situation is handled separately. Managers ask, would this process be better served if it were centralized or decentralized? Which structure will help solve problems, stay close to customers, and reach a wider range of new customers? (For these questions it is usually decentralization.) Which structure helps choose a computer system or react to an emergency? (centralization)

Decentralization can increase motivation and sales, but, warns Pape, managers need new skills to utilize it effectively. They must learn to trust their staff. That means no more phone calls to "check up" on workers. Greater skill in communication is required, too. Sometimes E-mail works and, other times, it is not the best medium.

Pape's years at VeriFone have given him a great deal of wisdom, for he says, "Dividing work is the best way to unify the whole."[37] ■

COORDINATION

As organizations grow and evolve, two things happen. First, new positions and departments are added to deal with factors in the external environment or with new strategic needs.[38] For example, Raytheon established a new-products center to facilitate innovation in its various divisions. Korbel Champagne Cellars created a Department of Romance, Weddings, and Entertaining to enhance the linkage between romance and champagne consumption among potential customers. Exhibit 9.8 shows an ad for Korbel's Director of Romance that generated more than 800 applications.[39] Comerica created a position of corporate quality manager to form a department that would be responsible for

EXHIBIT 9.8
Example of a Position Created to Deal with Environment and Strategy

SOURCE: Courtesy of Korbel Champagne Cellars.

Comerica's Managing Total Quality program. Employees in this new department help people understand and implement the quality process within their area. As companies add positions and departments to meet changing needs, they grow more complex, with hundreds of positions and departments performing incredibly diverse activities.

Second, senior managers have to find a way to tie all of these departments together. The formal chain of command and the supervision it provides is effective, but it is not enough. The organization needs systems to process information and enable communication among people in different departments and at different levels. **Coordination** refers to the quality of collaboration across departments. Without coordination, a company's left hand will not act in concert with the right hand, causing problems and conflicts. Coordination is required regardless of what type of structure the organization uses. Employees identify with their immediate department or team, taking its interest to heart, and may not want to compromise with other units for the good of the organization as a whole.

In the international arena, coordination is especially important. How can managers ensure that needed coordination will take place in their company, both domestically and globally? Coordination is the outcome

coordination
The quality of collaboration across departments.

The Engineering Division of Rohm and Haas Company used *business process reengineering* to achieve radical goals of building new plants faster and with dramatically lower costs. At one critical stage, existing processes were "mapped" using symbols so that inefficiencies could be identified and eliminated. Rohm and Haas, long recognized as an innovative leader in the specialty chemicals business, has committed itself to reanalyzing its work processes so the company can meet the higher expectations of today's customers, employees, and shareholders.

reengineering
The radical redesign of business processes to achieve dramatic improvements in cost, quality, service, and speed.

of information and cooperation. Managers can design systems and structures to promote communication. The most important methods for achieving coordination are reengineering, task forces and teams, and integrating managers.

Reengineering

One of the most popular management concepts sweeping through corporate America is **reengineering,** the radical redesign of business processes to achieve dramatic improvements in cost, quality, service, and speed. Sometimes called *business process reengineering,* this approach involves a complete rethinking and transformation of key business processes, leading to strong coordination across functional areas and greater flexibility in responding to changes in the environment.[40] A recent survey found that 21 percent of companies of all sizes are undergoing corporate-wide reengineering.[41] Union Carbide, Pacific Bell, Chemical Bank, and J. P. Morgan have all achieved breakthroughs in speed, flexibility, innovation, and quality through reengineering.

Reengineering basically means starting over, throwing out all the notions of how

work *was* done, and deciding how it can best be done now. It requires identifying customer needs and then designing processes and aligning people to meet those needs. Liquid Carbonic Industries, an Oak Brook, Illinois, industrial gas company, reengineered to improve customer service. The two-year effort dramatically changed the company, transforming it into an enterprise operating along process lines instead of the traditional business units. Operations are mapped around long-term customer relationships; sales employees, who once competed with one another, now cooperate to sell a range of products rather than specialize in one product.[42]

Organizing around key business processes often means that work is handled by small, cross-functional work teams, and many companies are redesigning their information systems to cut across departmental lines. Managers are finding ways to share information throughout the organization to make their companies more competitive and more responsive to customers. To speed up order cycle time and improve service to giant customers like Wal-Mart, the Gillette Company of Boston changed from a mainframe computer to a client–server system that can draw information from around the company and be accessed by any team member who needs it. Bow Valley Energy cut layers of management and redesigned its computer information system so that geologists, geophysicists, production engineers, and contract managers can now consolidate information and share data worldwide.[43]

Reengineering can lead to stunning results, but, like all business ideas, it has its drawbacks. Simply defining the organization's key business processes can be mind-boggling. AT&T's Network Systems division started with a list of 130 processes and then began working to pare them down to 13 core ones.[44] Because reengineering is expensive, time consuming, and usually painful, it seems best suited to companies that are facing serious competitive threats.

Task Forces and Teams

A **task force** is a temporary team or committee designed to solve a short-term problem involving several departments.[45] Task force members represent their departments and share information that enables coordination.

The Shawmut National Corporation created two task forces in the human resources department to consolidate all employment services into a single area. The task force looked at job banks, referral programs, employment procedures, and applicant tracking systems; found ways to perform these functions for all Shawmut's divisions in one human resource department; and then disbanded.[46] General Motors uses task forces to solve temporary problems in its manufacturing plants. When a shipment of car doors arrived from a fabricating plant with surface imperfections, the plant manager immediately created a task force to solve the problem: "I got the vice-president of manufacturing—who is my boss—the plant manager of the stamping plant, the die engineers, the quality engineers, the United Auto Workers representatives from both plants, the Olds guy from Lansing, a Cadillac guy, and the Fisher Body guy from the Tech Center. So I had everybody right out there on the floor looking at the exact part that is giving us the problem, and the problem was resolved in about two hours."[47]

In addition to creating task forces, companies also set up teams. As used for coordination, a **team** is a group of participants from several departments who meet regularly to solve ongoing problems of common interest.[48] The permanent team is similar to a task force except that it works with continuing rather than temporary problems and may exist for several years. For example, to improve coordination at Simplicity Pattern Company, CEO Louis Morris set up a Creative Committee, made up of the heads of the sales, finance, marketing, and creative departments. Snap-On Tools gained a competitive edge by creating engineering teams to work with marketing and customer-focus groups to discuss ideas and define new products. Team cooperation helps new-product projects sail smoothly through the design and development cycle.[49]

Integrating Managers

An **integrating manager** is a person in a full-time position created for the purpose of coordinating the activities of several departments.[50] The distinctive feature of the integrating position is that the person is not a member of one of the departments being coordinated. These positions often have such titles as product manager, project manager, program manager, or branch manager. The coordinator is assigned to coordinate departments on a full-time basis to achieve desired project or product outcomes.

task force
A temporary team or committee formed to solve a specific short-term problem involving several departments.

team
A group of participants from several departments who meet regularly to solve ongoing problems of common interest.

integrating manager
An individual responsible for coordinating the activities of several departments on a full-time basis to achieve specific project or product outcomes.

EXHIBIT 9.9
Example of Integrating Manager Relationships to Other Departments

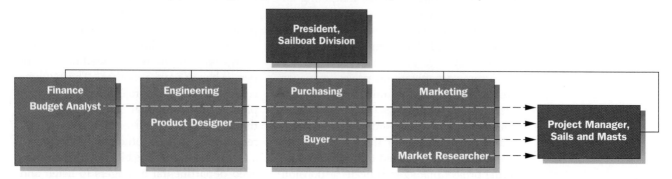

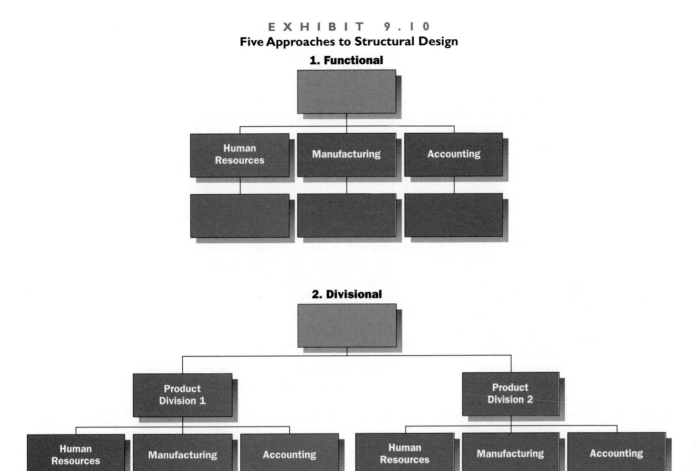

EXHIBIT 9.10
Five Approaches to Structural Design

1. Functional

2. Divisional

General Mills, Procter & Gamble, and General Foods all use product managers to coordinate their product lines. A manager is assigned to each line, such as Cheerios, Bisquick, and Hamburger Helper. Product managers set budget goals, marketing targets, and strategies and obtain the cooperation from advertising, production, and sales personnel needed for implementing product strategy.

In some organizations, project managers are included on the organization chart, as illustrated in Exhibit 9.9. The project manager is drawn to one side of the chart to indicate authority over the project but not over the people assigned to it. Dashed lines to the project manager indicate responsibility for coordination and communication with assigned team members, but department managers retain line authority over functional employees.

An interesting variation of the integrator role was developed at Florida Power & Light Company. To keep the construction of a nuclear power plant on schedule, several project managers were assigned the role of "Mothers." The philosophy of the person in charge was "If you want something to happen, it has to have a mother." The Mothers could nurture their projects to timely completion. This unusual label worked. Although departmental employees did not report directly to a Mother, the Mothers had a great deal of responsibility, which encouraged departmental managers to listen and cooperate.[51]

EXHIBIT   9.10
Five Approaches to Structural Design

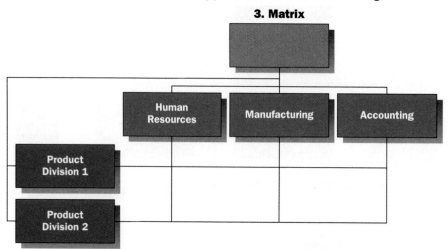

3. Matrix

Human Resources   Manufacturing   Accounting

Product Division 1

Product Division 2

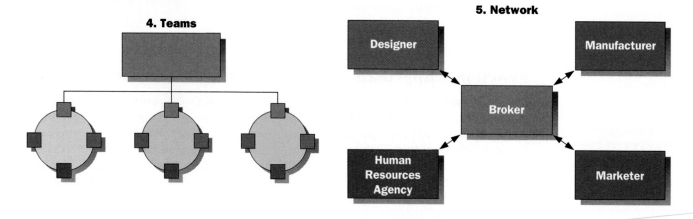

4. Teams

5. Network

Designer   Manufacturer

Broker

Human Resources Agency   Marketer

DEPARTMENTALIZATION

Another fundamental characteristic of organization structure is **departmentalization,** which is the basis for grouping positions into departments and departments into the total organization. Managers make choices about how to use the chain of command to group people together to perform their work. There are five approaches to structural design that reflect different uses of the chain of command in departmentalization. The functional, divisional, and matrix are traditional approaches that rely on the chain of command to define departmental groupings and reporting relationships along the hierarchy. Two contemporary approaches

are the use of teams and networks. These newer approaches have emerged to meet organizational needs in a highly competitive global environment. A brief illustration of the five structural alternatives is presented in Exhibit 9.10.

Each approach to structure serves a distinct purpose for the organization, and each has advantages and disadvantages. The basic difference among structures is the way in which employees are departmentalized and to whom they report. The differences in structure illustrated in Exhibit 9.10 have major consequences for employee goals and motivation. Let us now turn to each of the five structural designs and examine their implications for managers.[52]

departmentalization
The basis on which individuals are grouped into departments and departments into total organizations.

EXHIBIT 9.11
Functional Structure for American Airlines

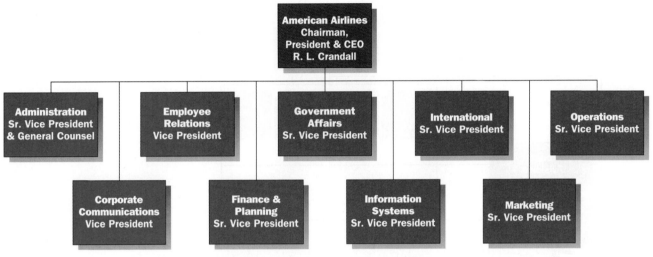

SOURCE: Used with permission of American Airlines.

Functional Approach

functional structure
An organization structure in which positions are grouped into departments based on similar skills, expertise, and resource use.

divisional structure
An organization structure in which departments are grouped based on similar organizational outputs.

Functional structure is the grouping of positions into departments based on similar skills, expertise, and resource use. A functional structure can be thought of as departmentalization by organizational resources, because each type of functional activity—human resources, engineering, manufacturing—represents specific resources for performing the organization's task. People and facilities representing a common organizational resource are grouped together into a single department.

An example of a functional structure for American Airlines is presented in Exhibit 9.11. The major departments under the chairman are groupings of similar expertise and resources, such as employee relations, government affairs, operations, information systems, and marketing. Each of the functional departments at American Airlines is concerned with the airline as a whole. The employee relations vice president is concerned with human resources issues for the entire airline, and the marketing department is responsible for all sales and marketing.

Divisional Approach

In contrast to the functional approach, in which people are grouped by common skills and resources, the **divisional structure** occurs when departments are grouped together based on organizational outputs. Functional and divisional structures are illustrated in Exhibit 9.12. In the divisional structure, divisions are created as self-contained units for producing a single product. Each functional department resource needed to produce the product is assigned to one division. For example, in a functional structure, all engineers are grouped together and work on all products. In a divisional structure, separate engineering departments are established within each division. Each department is smaller and focuses on a single product line. Departments are duplicated across product lines.

The divisional structure is sometimes called a *product structure, program structure,* or *self-contained unit structure.* Each of these terms means essentially the same thing: Diverse departments are brought together to produce a single organizational output, whether it be a product, a program, or a service to a single customer.

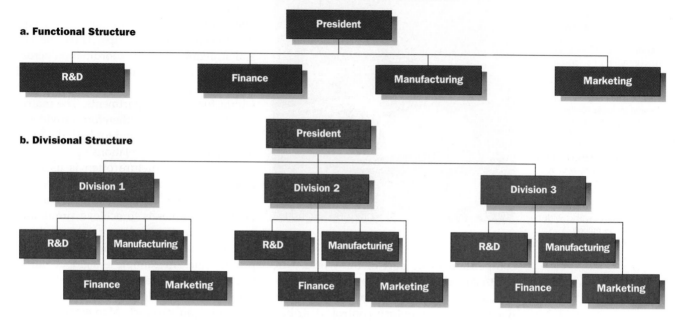

EXHIBIT 9.12
Functional versus Divisional Structures

In very large companies, a divisional structure is essential. Most large corporations have separate business divisions that perform different tasks, serve different clients, or use different technologies. When a huge organization produces products for different markets, the divisional structure works because each division is an autonomous business. For example, PepsiCo uses a divisional structure. Frito-Lay, Pizza Hut, Taco Bell, North American Van Lines, and Wilson's Sporting Goods are stand-alone divisions within PepsiCo. Time Warner, Inc., also uses a divisional structure. Divisions include Warner Brothers, the world's largest record company; HBO, the leading pay cable television channel; *Time* magazine; and Little, Brown, a book publisher. Each of these companies is run as a separate business under the guidance of Time Warner corporate headquarters.

A major difference between divisional and functional structures is that the chain of command from each function converges lower in the hierarchy. In an organization such as the one in Exhibit 9.12, differences of opinion among research and development, marketing, manufacturing, and finance would be resolved at the divisional level rather than by the president. Thus, the divisional structure encourages decentralization. Decision making is pushed down at least one level in the hierarchy, freeing the president and other top managers for strategic planning.

Geographic-Based Divisions.   An alternative for assigning divisional responsibility is to group company activities by geographic region, as illustrated in Exhibit 9.13. In this structure, all functions in a specific country or region report to the same division manager. This structure focuses company activities on local market conditions. For example, competitive advantage may come from the production or sale of a product adapted to a given country. For example, at LSI Logic Corporation, management's strategy is to divide the world into three geographic markets—Japan, the United States, and Europe. Each division has all the resources to focus on the fierce

Gaylord Entertainment Company utilizes *the divisional approach* in entertainment, cable networks, broadcasting, and cable television systems. Gaylord successfully achieves synergy among its various divisions that focus on country music and country lifestyle. The entertainment division includes Nashville-based properties such as Opryland U.S.A., the Grand Ole Opry (pictured here), the Opryland Hotel, and the General Jackson Showboat. The cable networks division includes the Nashville Network, one of the nation's largest cable networks with more than 54 million subscribers.

competition in its part of the world.[53] In North America, Sears, Roebuck & Co. is organized into five regions, each with its own warehousing, inventory control, distribution system, and stores. This geographic structure enables close coordination of activities to meet the needs of customers within each region.

Matrix Approach

matrix approach

An organization structure that utilizes functional and divisional chains of command simultaneously in the same part of the organization.

The **matrix approach** utilizes functional and divisional chains of command simultaneously in the same part of the organization.[54] The matrix actually has dual lines of author-

ity. In Exhibit 9.14, the functional hierarchy of authority runs vertically, and the divisional hierarchy of authority runs laterally. The lateral chain of command formalizes the divisional relationships. Thus, the lateral structure provides coordination across functional departments while the vertical structure provides traditional control within functional departments. The matrix approach to structure therefore provides a formal chain of command for both the functional and divisional relationships.

The matrix structure often is used by global corporations such as Dow Corning or Asea Brown Boveri. The problem for global companies is to achieve simultaneous coordination of various products within each country or region and for each product line. An example of a global matrix structure is illustrated in Exhibit 9.15 on page 308. The two lines of authority are geographic and product. Managers of local affiliate companies within a country such as Germany report to two superiors. As noted in Exhibit 9.15, for example, the general manager of a plant producing plastic containers in Germany reports to both the head of the plastics products division and the head of German operations. The German boss coordinates all the affiliates within Germany, and the plastics products boss coordinates the manufacturing and sale of plastics products around the world.

E X H I B I T   9 . 1 3
Geographic-Based Global Organization Structure

Chief Executive Officer

Corporate Staff

| Western U.S. Division | Eastern U.S. Division | Latin American Division | Asian Division |

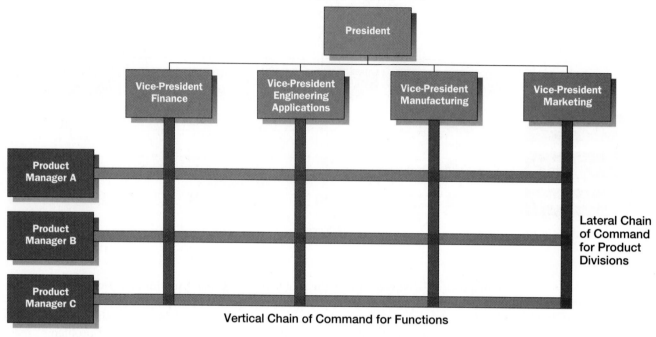

EXHIBIT 9.14
Dual-Authority Structure in a Matrix Organization

The dual authority structure causes confusion, but after managers learn to use it, the matrix provides excellent coordination simultaneously for each geographic region and product line.

Key Relationships. The success of the matrix structure depends on the abilities of people in key matrix roles. Exhibit 9.16 provides a close-up of the reporting relationships in the dual chain of command for a domestic company. The senior engineer in the medical products division reports to both the medical products vice president and the engineering director. This violates the unity-of-command concept described earlier in this chapter but is necessary to give equal emphasis to both functional and divisional lines of authority. Confusion is reduced by separating responsibilities for each chain of command. The functional boss is responsible for technical and personnel issues, such as quality standards, providing technical training, and assigning technical personnel to projects. The divisional boss is responsible for programwide issues, such as overall design decisions, schedule deadlines, and coordinating technical specialists from several functions.

The senior engineer is called a **two-boss employee** because he or she reports to two supervisors simultaneously. Two-boss employees must resolve conflicting demands from the matrix bosses. They must confront senior managers and reach joint decisions. They need excellent human relations skills with which to confront managers and resolve conflicts. The **matrix boss** is the product or functional boss, who in Exhibit 9.16 is the engineering director and the medical products vice-president. The matrix boss is responsible for one side of the matrix. The top leader is responsible for the entire matrix. The **top leader** oversees both the product and functional chains of command. His or her responsibility is to maintain a power balance between the two sides of the matrix.

two-boss employee
An employee who reports to two supervisors simultaneously.

matrix boss
A product or functional boss, responsible for one side of the matrix.

top leader
The overseer of both the product and the functional chains of command, responsible for the entire matrix.

EXHIBIT 9.15
Global Matrix Structure

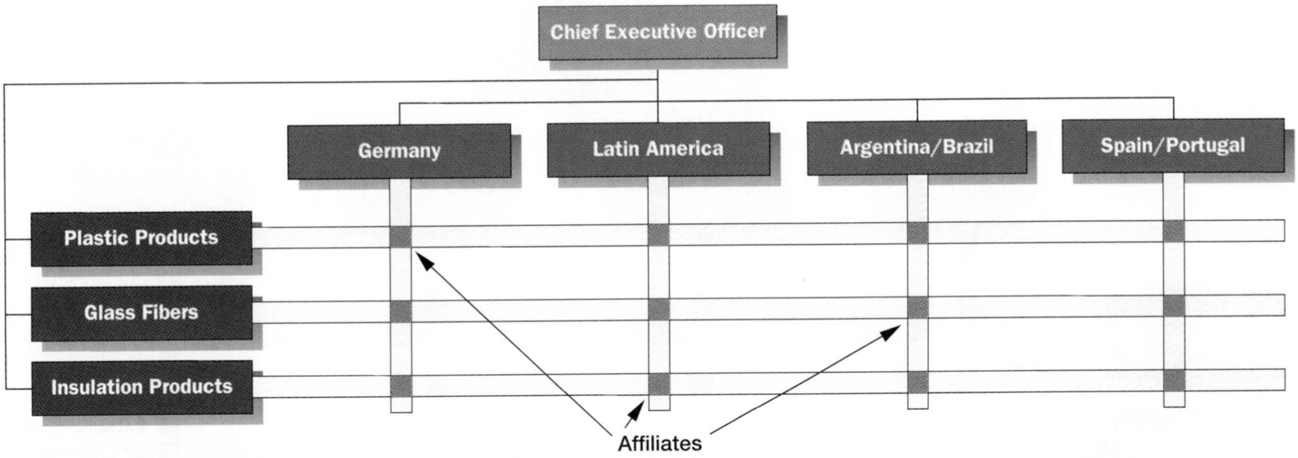

Affiliates

cross-functional team
A group of employees assigned to a functional department that meets as a team to resolve mutual problems.

If disputes arise between them, the problem will be kicked upstairs to the top leader.[55]

Matrix bosses and two-boss employees often find it difficult to adapt to the matrix. The matrix boss has only half of each employee. Without complete control over employees, bosses must consult with their counterparts on the other side of the matrix. This necessitates frequent meetings and discussions to coordinate matrix activities. The two-boss employee experiences problems of conflicting demands and expectations from the two supervisors.

Team Approach

Probably the most widespread trend in departmentalization has been the effort by companies to implement team concepts. The vertical chain of command is a powerful means of control, but passing all decisions up the hierarchy takes too long and keeps responsibility at the top. Companies in the 1990s are trying to find ways to delegate authority, push responsibility to low levels, and create participative teams that engage the commitment of workers. This approach enables organizations to be more flexible and responsive in the competitive global environment. Chapter 16 will discuss teams in detail.

permanent team
A group of participants from several functions who are permanently assigned to solve ongoing problems of common interest.

Cross-functional teams consist of employees from various functional departments who are responsible to meet as a team and resolve mutual problems. Team members typically still report to their functional departments, but they also report to the team, one member of whom may be the leader. Computer-based companies such as Lanier Technology Corporation, Compaq Computer Corporation, Quantum Corporation, and AST Research are obsessed with creating a team atmosphere using cross-functional teams.[56] Cross-functional teams helped Modicon Inc., a small Massachusetts company, bring six software products to market in one-third the time it would normally take. Modicon is structured by function, but many of the 900 employees are involved in up to 30 teams that span departments.[57]

Some organizations have created **permanent teams,** groups of employees who are brought together as a formal department. The permanent-team approach resembles the divisional approach described earlier, except that teams are much smaller. Teams may consist of only 20 to 30 members, each bringing a functional specialty to the team. For example, Kollmorgen Corporation, a manufacturer of electronic circuitry and other goods, divided its organization into

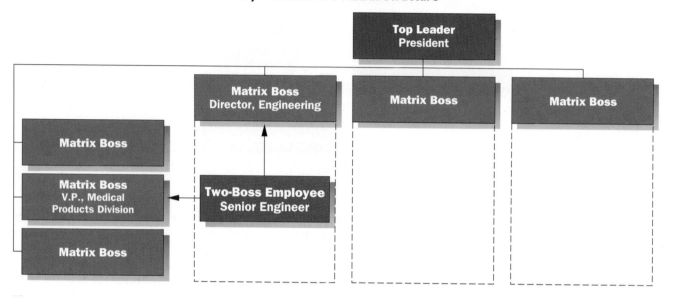

EXHIBIT 9.16
Key Positions in a Matrix Structure

teams that average 75 employees.[58] Even at this size, employees think of themselves as a team. Performance jumped dramatically after Kollmorgen shifted to this concept.

Many companies reorganize into permanent teams after going through a process called reengineering, which was described earlier in the chapter. Because the focus is on process rather than function, reengineering often leads to a shift away from a vertical structure to one emphasizing teamwork and empowerment.[59]

At Hallmark, reengineering led to a new team approach to greeting-card development.

 HALLMARK CARDS

Hallmark used to be organized by functional departments and designed cards in a step-by-step process—artists and writers rarely spoke to one another, and the employees who created the lettering worked in a building a quarter-mile away. Because of delays and rework, it sometimes took the company more than two years to create and produce a new greeting card.

Now Hallmark puts teams of employees from every department in the same room and empowers each team to take charge of cards for a particular holiday. Artists, lithographers, writers, designers, and photographers share ideas, critique their own work, and make decisions without waiting for management permission. The cycle time for getting new cards to market has been cut in half. For employees, the change has brought more responsibility and greater job satisfaction. Not satisfied with the status quo of this success, Hallmark has gone on to a factory-wide business process redesign, involving a "competency dictionary" for employees. For a company that lives or dies on new products, the team and competency approaches mean dramatically faster development, leading to big savings in time and money.[60] ■

Network Approach

The newest approach to departmentalization has been called a "dynamic network" organization.[61] The **network structure** means that the organization disaggregates

network structure
An organization structure that disaggregates major functions into separate companies that are brokered by a small headquarters organization.

EXHIBIT 9.17
Network Approach to Departmentalization

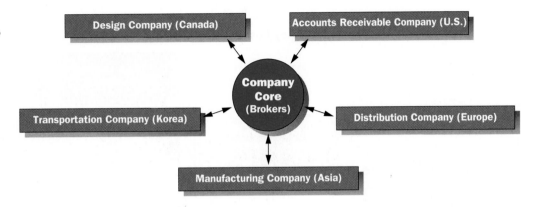

major functions into separate companies that are brokered by a small headquarters organization. Rather than manufacturing, engineering, sales, and accounting being housed under one roof, these services are provided by separate organizations working under contract and connected electronically to the central office.[62] An illustration of a hypothetical network organization is shown in Exhibit 9.17.

The network approach is revolutionary, because it is difficult to answer the question "Where is the organization?" in traditional terms. For example, a firm may contract for expensive services such as training, transportation, legal, and engineering, so these functions are no longer part of the organization. Or consider a piece of ice hockey equipment that is designed in Scandinavia, engineered in the United States, manufactured in Korea, and distributed in Canada by a Japanese sales organization. These pieces are drawn together contractually and coordinated electronically, creating a new form of organization.

This organizational approach is especially powerful for international operations. For example, Just Toys Inc.'s products are manufactured by factories in China, Taiwan, and Hong Kong. A New York importer of leather goods handles back office operations and helps with overseas transactions. Cigna Corporation took over an unused factory in Ireland and hired workers to process medical claims more cheaply and efficiently

than could be done in the United States. McGraw-Hill has people working at computer terminals in Ireland also, maintaining worldwide circulation files for its magazines. These departments are tied electronically to the home offices in the United States.[63] High-tech firms such as Apple, IBM, and Dell Computer are working with contractors around the world to manufacture products. Sun Microsystems relies so heavily on outside manufacturers and distributors that its own employees never touch one of its computers.[64] Tomima Edmark built TopsyTail, Inc., into an $80 million company with only two full-time employees. TopsyTail's production partners include a toolmaker, two injection molders, a package designer, a logo designer, freelance photographers, and a printer. The company also outsources packaging and shipping to three fulfillment houses, television commercials to a video production company, customer mailings to a mailing list firm, and publicity to a public relations firm. Four distributing companies sell TopsyTail products in the United States, Canada, Mexico, the Pacific Rim, Europe, and South Africa.[65]

Small entrepreneurial firms find they can save money and reach a larger market for their products by using outside manufacturers and distributors.[66] The Leading the Management Revolution box describes how the founders of Nu Skin International used the network structure to grow.

LEADING THE MANAGEMENT REVOLUTION
NU SKIN INTERNATIONAL

Nu Skin International has soared from zero to $500 million in sales in a decade. It began with a line of skin and hair care products made by an Arizona company and hand-spooned by the three founders into used jars and containers. Today, Nu Skin has added a division with vitamin supplements, nutrition bars, and a sports drink and has expanded into Canada, Hong Kong, Taiwan, Australia, New Zealand, Japan, and Mexico.

Nu Skin's visionary use of technology to support a marketing and distribution network made the growth possible. Each day, detailed distributor and sales order information pours into Nu Skin's Provo, Utah, headquarters from every corner of the world via satellite and fiber optics. The company's mainframe computer calculates commissions for every one of the 250,000 active distributors and transmits the results back to each Nu Skin market, where checks are cut in the local currency. The company also invested in a software application that translates screen prompts into each country's native language so that distributors can easily access needed information. Nu Skin's Voice Information Program (VIP) enables distributors to keep track of thousands of current and prospective customers as well as maintain close contact with headquarters. The exhibit below illustrates Nu Skin's distributor network.

One executive says Nu Skin will be in at least six new countries within the next three years. Since the technological infrastructure enables Nu Skin to open a new market in just 90 days, the company is well positioned for continued international expansion.

SOURCE: Niklas von Daehne, "Techno-Boom," *Success,* December 1994, 43–46.

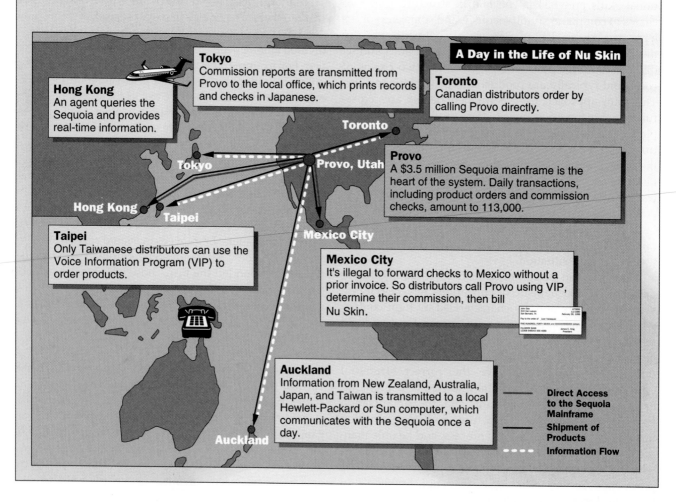

A Day in the Life of Nu Skin

Tokyo
Commission reports are transmitted from Provo to the local office, which prints records and checks in Japanese.

Hong Kong
An agent queries the Sequoia and provides real-time information.

Toronto
Canadian distributors order by calling Provo directly.

Provo
A $3.5 million Sequoia mainframe is the heart of the system. Daily transactions, including product orders and commission checks, amount to 113,000.

Taipei
Only Taiwanese distributors can use the Voice Information Program (VIP) to order products.

Mexico City
It's illegal to forward checks to Mexico without a prior invoice. So distributors call Provo using VIP, determine their commission, then bill Nu Skin.

Auckland
Information from New Zealand, Australia, Japan, and Taiwan is transmitted to a local Hewlett-Packard or Sun computer, which communicates with the Sequoia once a day.

——— **Direct Access to the Sequoia Mainframe**

——— **Shipment of Products**

- - - - **Information Flow**

SUMMARY AND MANAGEMENT SOLUTION

This chapter introduced a number of important organizing concepts. Fundamental characteristics of organization structure include work specialization, chain of command, authority and responsibility, span of management, and centralization and decentralization. These dimensions of organization represent the vertical hierarchy and indicate how authority and responsibility are distributed along the hierarchy.

The other major concept is departmentalization, which describes how organization employees are grouped. Three traditional approaches are functional, divisional, and matrix; contemporary approaches are team and network structures. The functional approach groups employees by common skills and tasks. The opposite structure is divisional, which groups people by organizational output such that each division has a mix of functional skills and tasks. The matrix structure uses two chains of command simultaneously, and some employees have two bosses. The two chains of command in a domestic organization typically are functional and product division, and, for international firms, the two chains of command typically are product and geographic regions. The team approach uses permanent teams and cross-functional teams to achieve better coordination and employee commitment than is possible with a pure functional structure. The network approach represents the newest form of organization structure. Departmental tasks are subcontracted to other organizations, so the central organization is simply a broker that coordinates several independent organizations to accomplish its goal. Each organization form has advantages and disadvantages and can be used by managers to meet the needs of the competitive situation.

Managers can design organizations to be organic or mechanistic. Mechanistic organizations rely heavily on vertical structure and are characterized by tight control, whereas organic organizations are loosely structured and rely heavily on lateral coordination mechanisms. Contingency factors of environment, size and life cycle, and production technology influence the correct structural approach. When environmental uncertainty is high, lateral coordination is important, and the organization should have an organic structure. For manufacturing firms, small batch, continuous process, and flexible manufacturing technologies tend to be structured organically, whereas a mechanistic structure is appropriate for mass production. Service technologies are people oriented, and firms are located geographically close to dispersed customers. Some services can be broken down into explicit steps where employees follow objective, standardized procedures for serving customers and solving problems, and these may be controlled with a mechanistic structure. However, in general, services tend to be organically structured, with decentralized decision making.

At Vortex Industries, described at the beginning of the chapter, the highly centralized, mechanistic structure was preventing the company from providing the level of customer service needed to fend off new competition. High overhead costs meant the company had to charge higher prices. Vortex also suffered because its services were not located geographically close to customers. Frank Fulkerson set out to reengineer his company, although he didn't call it by that name. As an experiment, he split off one branch of the company in one of the six counties Vortex served and rearranged the duties of everyone who worked there. The branch manager served as team leader and handled several functions that had previously been divided among people in rigid categories at the central office. For example, the manager became responsible not only for quoting the customer a price on repairing a door but also for getting the service trucks there on time. To encourage team spirit, Fulkerson set up a profit-sharing plan. Business at the branch went through the roof, so Fulkerson reorganized the company into six independent branches, with only a lightly staffed home office. Fulkerson also flipped the organization chart, from a pyramid with him at the top to a cone with him at the bottom. Now, he sees his job as helping the staff at the home office. In turn, their job is to help the field teams, whose job is to help the customers. Employees mastered several skills instead of just one. Although some employees didn't like the changes and left the firm, those who remained enjoy the increased job variety and responsibility. Fulkerson's structural changes set Vortex on the right path and led to a $1.5 million increase in sales. The company has expanded to ten branches in Southern California and one in Denver.[67]

As organizations increase in size, they require greater vertical control. Organizations in the birth and youth stages typically are loosely structured. In the midlife stage, a strong vertical structure emerges. In a mature organization, such as Vortex, the vertical structure may be too strong, necessitating the installation of teams, task forces, and other horizontal devices to achieve greater cooperation across departments.

DISCUSSION QUESTIONS

1 Sonny Holt, manager of Electronics Assembly, asked Hector Cruz, his senior technician, to handle things in the department while Sonny worked on the budget. Sonny needed peace and quiet for at least a week to complete his figures. After ten days, Sonny discovered that Hector had hired a senior secretary, not realizing that Sonny had promised interviews to two other people. Evaluate Sonny's approach to delegation.

2 Many experts note that organizations have been making greater use of teams in recent years. What factors might account for this trend?

3 Contrast centralization with span of management. Would you expect these characteristics to affect each other in organizations? Why?

4 An organizational consultant was heard to say, "Some aspect of functional structure appears in every organization." Do you agree? Explain.

5 The divisional structure is often considered almost the opposite of a functional structure. Do you agree? Briefly explain the major differences in these two approaches to departmentalization.

6 What are important skills for matrix bosses and two-boss employees in a matrix organization?

7 Some people argue that the matrix structure should be adopted only as a last resort because the dual chains of command can create more problems than they solve. Do you agree or disagree? Why?

8 What is the network approach to structure? Is the use of authority and responsibility different compared with other forms of departmentalization? Explain.

9 Why are divisional structures frequently used in large corporations? Does it make sense for a huge corporation such as American Airlines to stay in a functional structure?

10 An international matrix structure tends to be organized by product divisions and geographic regions. Why would these two chains of command be used rather than product and function as in domestic companies? Explain.

11 What is the difference between a task force and an integrating manager? Which would be more effective in achieving coordination?

12 Discuss why an organization in an uncertain environment requires more horizontal relationships than one in a certain environment.

13 Explain the difference between assembly line and continuous process production. How do these two technologies influence structural characteristics such as the indirect/direct labor ratio and span of control?

14 What is the difference between manufacturing and service technology? How would you classify a university, a local discount store, a nursery school? How would you expect the structure of a service organization to differ from that of a manufacturing organization?

MANAGEMENT EXERCISES

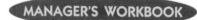

MANAGER'S WORKBOOK

Loose versus Tight Organization Structure

Interview an employee at your university, such as a department head or secretary. Have the employee answer the following thirteen questions about his or her job and organizational conditions.

	Disagree Strongly				Agree Strongly
1 Your work would be considered routine.	5	4	3	2	1
2 There is a clearly known way to do the major tasks you encounter.	5	4	3	2	1
3 Your work has high variety and frequent exceptions.	1	2	3	4	5
4 Communications from above consist of information and advice rather than instructions and directions.	1	2	3	4	5

	Disagree Strongly				Agree Strongly
5 You have the support of peers and supervisors to do your job well.	1	2	3	4	5
6 You seldom exchange ideas or information with people doing other kinds of jobs.	5	4	3	2	1
7 Decisions relevant to your work are made above you and passed down.	5	4	3	2	1
8 People at your level frequently have to figure out for themselves what their jobs are for the day.	1	2	3	4	5
9 Lines of authority are clear and precisely defined.	5	4	3	2	1
10 Leadership tends to be democratic rather than autocratic in style.	1	2	3	4	5
11 Job descriptions are written and up-to-date for each job.	5	4	3	2	1
12 People understand each other's jobs and often do different tasks.	1	2	3	4	5
13 A manual of policies and procedures is available to use when a problem arises.	5	4	3	2	1

Total Score _____

A score of 52 or above suggests that the employee is working in a "loosely structured" organization. The score reflects an organic structure that is often associated with uncertain environments, organizational flexibility, and small-batch technology. People working in this structure feel empowered. Many organizations today are moving in the direction of organic structures and empowerment.

A score of 26 or below suggests a mechanistic or "tight structure." This structure utilizes traditional control and functional specialization, which often occurs in a certain environment, a stable organization, and routine or mass-production technology. People in this structure may feel controlled and constrained.

Discuss the pros and cons of loose versus tight structure. Does the structure of the employee you interviewed fit the nature of the organization's environment, size, strategic goals, and technology? How might you redesign the structure to make the work organization more effective?

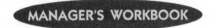

MANAGER'S WORKBOOK

You and Organization Structure

In order to better understand the importance of organization structure in your life, do the following assignment. Select one of the following situations to organize:

a. the registration process at your university or college;

b. a new fast-food franchise;

c. a sports rental in an ocean resort area, such as Jet Ski, etc.;

d. a bakery.

Background

Organization is a way of gaining some power against an unreliable environment. The environment provides the organization with inputs, which include raw materials, human resources, and financial resources. There is a service or product to produce that involves technology. The output goes to clients, a group that must be nurtured. The complexities of the environment and the technology determine the complexity of the organization.

Planning your organization

1. Write down the mission or purpose of the organization in a few sentences.
2. What are the specific things to be done to accomplish the mission?
3. Based on the specifics in #2, develop an organization chart. Each position in the chart will perform a specific task or is reponsible for a certain outcome.
4. Add duties to each job position in the chart. These will be the job descriptions.

5 How can you make sure people in each position will work together?

6 What level of skill and abilities is required at each position and level in order to hire the right persons?

7 Make a list of the decisions that would have to be made as you developed your organization.

8 Who is responsible for customer satisfaction? How will you know if customers' needs are met?

9 How will information flow within the organization?

SOURCE: *Action in Organizations* 2/e by Donald D. White and William H. Vroman, © 1982. Reprinted by permission of Prentice-Hall, Inc., Upper Saddle River, NJ.

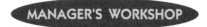

MANAGER'S WORKSHOP

Bistro Technology

You will be analyzing the technology used in three different restaurants—McDonald's, Burger King, and a typical family restaurant. Your instructor will tell you whether to do this assignment as individuals or in a group.

You must visit all three restaurants and infer how the work is done, according to the criteria below. However, you are not allowed to "interview" any employees, but instead be an observer. Take lots of notes when you are there.

	McDonald's	Burger King	Family restaurant
Organization goals: speed, service, atmosphere, etc.			
Authority structure			
Type of technology using Woodward's model			
Organization structure: mechanistic or organic			
Team vs. individual—do people work together or alone?			
Tasks: routine vs. non-routine			
Specialization of tasks by employees (division of labor)			
Expertise required: technical vs. social			
Decision making: centralized vs. decentralized			

1 Is the technology used the best one for each restaurant, considering its goals and environment?

2 From the data above, determine if the structure and other characteristics fit the technology.

3 If you were part of a consulting team assigned to improve the operations of each organization, what recommendations would you make?

SOURCE: Copyright 1996 by Dorothy Marcic. Adapted loosely from "Hamburger Technology," in Douglas T. Hall, et al., *Experiences in Management and Organizational Behavior*, 2e, John Wiley & Sons, 1982, 244–247, as well as "Behavior, Technology, and Work Design" in A. B. Shani and James B. Lau, *Behavior in Organizations*. Chicago: Irwin, 1996, M16-23 to M16-26.

SURF THE 'NET

Locate Web sites for at least 10 companies and find evidence of how they use or handle the following:

Work specialization, chain of command, authority, responsibility and delegation, span of management, centralization and decentralization, coordination, reengineering, task forces, and teams.

ETHICAL DILEMMA

A Matter of Giving

Renee Washington was proud to have been recruited out of college to work at Standol Corporation. In addition to a spotless reputation in environmental responsibility, Standol was famous for its active part in supporting various civic and cultural organizations in the community. When the opportunity came to participate in the Helping Hands drive, Washington quickly volunteered. She soon had reason to regret her decision.

A memo was issued to the volunteer coordinator in each department, indicating the expected donation from each employee. It was Washington's job to collect a "pledge" to be withdrawn from each payroll check, or a lump sum payment. The memo indicated Standol expected each volunteer coordinator to collect the suggested amount or make up the difference out of their own pockets. Washington found herself listening to countless hard-luck stories as she applied pressure to fellow employees for their contributions. As she enlisted the aid of managers in the coercion, Washington felt her pride and excitement in the project diminishing.

She began to question whether a sterling reputation in community charities was worth the embarrassment and resentment it caused Standol employees. She wondered if people might give more freely if they felt they weren't being ordered to give at levels set by top management. She wanted to make suggestions for changes but feared doing so would threaten her future at Standol.

What Do You Do?

1 Comply with the traditional fund-raising approach, blaming the company for putting you in the position of the bad guy.
2 Collect only the funds that are genuinely donated, without making up the difference out of pocket. If you are criticized, expose the coercive practices to Helping Hands officials and the press.
3 Propose changes for coordinating fund-raising across departments that emphasize teamwork and come from within the organization, rather than from the top down.

SOURCE: Based on Doug Wallace, "A Twisted Arm," *What Would You Do? Business Ethics*, vol. II (January–February 1994), 17–18.

CASE FOR CRITICAL ANALYSIS

Malard Manufacturing Company

Malard Manufacturing Company produces control valves that regulate flows through natural gas pipelines. Malard has approximately 1,400 employees and has successfully produced a standard line of control valves that are price competitive in the industry. However, whenever the production of a new control valve is required,

problems arise. Developments in electronics, metallurgy, and flow control theory require the introduction of new products every year or two. These new products have been associated with interdepartmental conflict and disagreement.

Consider the CV305, which is in process. As usual, the research and development group developed the basic design, and the engineering department converted it into a

prototype control valve. Now the materials department must acquire parts for the prototype and make plans for obtaining parts needed for production runs. The production department is to manufacture and assemble the product, and marketing is responsible for sales.

Department heads believe that future work on the CV305 should be done simultaneously instead of sequentially. Marketing wants to provide input to research and development so that the design will meet customer needs. Production insists that the design fit machine limitations and be cost efficient to manufacture—indeed, it wants to speed up development of the final plans so that it can acquire tooling and be ready for standard production. Engineering, on the other hand, wants to slow down development to ensure that specifications are correct and have been thoroughly tested.

All of these controversies with the CV305 exist right now. Department managers are frustrated and becoming uncommunicative. The research and development and engineering departments are keeping their developmental plans secret, causing frustration for the other departments. Moreover, several department managers are new and inexperienced in new-product development. Ms. Crandell, the executive vice president, likes to keep tight control over the organization. Department managers must check with her before making major decisions. However, with the CV305, she has been unable to keep

things running smoothly. The span of control is so large that Crandell has no time to personally shepherd the CV305 through the system.

On November 1, Crandell received a memo from the marketing department head. It said, in part,

> The CV305 must go to market immediately. This is urgent. It is needed now because it provides the precision control our competitors' products already have. Three of our salespeople reported that loyal customers are about to place orders with competitors. We can keep this business if we have the CV305 ready for production in 30 days.

Questions

1 What is the balance between vertical and horizontal structure in Malard Manufacturing? Is it appropriate that department managers always turn to the executive vice president for help rather than to one another?

2 If you were Ms. Crandell, how would you resolve this problem? What could you do to facilitate production of the CV305 over the next 30 days?

3 What structural changes would you recommend to prevent these problems in future new-product developments? Would a smaller span of control help? An integrating manager with responsibility for coordinating the CV305? A task force?

ENDNOTES

1 Michael Barrier, "Re-engineering Your Company," *Nation's Business,* February 1994, 16–22.

2 Lisa Driscoll, "The New, New Thinking at Xerox," *Business Week,* June 22, 1992.

3 John A. Byrne, "The Horizontal Corporation," *Business Week,* December 20, 1993, 76–81.

4 Evan Ramstad, "AT&T Remakes Itself," *The Tennessean,* September 21, 1995, 2E, 4E.

5 "A Slimmed-Down Brunswick Is Proving Wall Street Wrong," *Business Week,* May 28, 1984, 90–98; and J. Vettner, "Bowling for Dollars," *Forbes,* September 12, 1983, 138.

6 Tom Burns and G. M. Stalker, *The Management of Innovation* (London: Tavistock, 1961).

7 Frank Shipper and Charles C. Manz, "An Alternative Road to Empowerment," *Organizational Dynamics* 20 (winter 1992), 48–61.

8 "Mrs. Fields Cookies to Nearly Triple International Outlets," *PR Newswire,* 1995; Jack Schember, "Mrs Fields' Secret Weapon," *Personnel Journal,* 70, no. 9, September 1991, 56–58.

9 W. Graham Astley, "Organization Size and Bureaucratic Structure," *Organization Studies* 6 (1985), 201–228; John B. Cullen, Kenneth S. Anderson, and Douglas D. Baker, "Blau's Theory of

Structural Differentiation Revisited: A Theory of Structural Change or Scale?" *Academy of Management Journal* 29 (1986), 203–229; and Daft, *Organization Theory and Design.*

10 Robert E. Quinn and Kim Cameron, "Organizational Life Cycles and Shifting Criteria of Effectiveness: Some Preliminary Evidence," *Management Science* 29 (1983), 33–51; and John R. Kimberly, Robert H. Miles, and associates, *The Organizational Life Cycle* (San Francisco: Jossey-Bass, 1980).

11 Glenn Collins, "Growing Pains for a Doll Maker," *The New York Times,* September 17, 1996, C1, C19.

12 Manganelli and Klein, "A Framework for Reengineering"; and Wayne F. Cascio, "Downsizing: What Do We Know? What Have We Learned?" *Academy of Management Executive* 7, no. 1 (1993), 95–103.

13 Denise M. Rousseau and Robert A. Cooke, "Technology and Structure: The Concrete, Abstract, and Activity Systems of Organizations," *Journal of Management* 10 (1984), 345–361; Charles Perrow, "A Framework for the Comparative Analysis of Organizations," *American Sociological Review* 32 (1967), 194–208; and Denise M. Rousseau, "Assessment of Technology in Organizations: Closed versus Open Systems Approaches," *Academy of Management Review* 4 (1979), 531–542.

14 Joan Woodward, *Industrial Organizations: Theory and Practice* (London: Oxford University Press, 1965); and Joan Woodward, *Management and Technology* (London: Her Majesty's Stationery Office, 1958).

15 Woodward, *Industrial Organizations*, vi.

16 Barrier, "Re-engineering Your Company."

17 Raghavan Parthasarthy and S. Brakash Sethi, "The Impact of Flexible Automation on Business Strategy and Organizational Structure," *Academy of Management Review* 17 (1992), 86–111; Patricia L. Nemetz and Louis W. Fry, "Flexible Manufacturing Organizations: Implementation for Strategy Formulation and Organization Design," *Academy of Management Review* 13 (1988), 627–638; and Paul S. Adler, "Managing Flexible Automation," *California Management Review* (spring 1988), 34–56.

18 Peter K. Mills and Thomas Kurk, "A Preliminary Investigation into the Influence of Customer–Firm Interface on Information Processing and Task Activity in Service Organizations," *Journal of Management* 12 (1986), 91–104; Peter K. Mills and Dennis J. Moberg, "Perspectives on the Technology of Service Operations," *Academy of Management Review* 7 (1982), 467–478; and Roger W. Schmenner, "How Can Service Businesses Survive and Prosper?" *Sloan Management Review* 27 (spring 1986), 21–32.

19 Richard B. Chase and David A. Tansik, "The Customer Contact Model for Organization Design," *Management Science* 29 (1983), 1037–1050; and Gregory B. Northcraft and Richard B. Chase, "Managing Service Demand at the Point of Delivery," *Academy of Management Review* 10 (1985), 66–75.

20 Maryfran Johnson, "Marriott Rests on RS/6000," *Computerworld*, October 5, 1992, 6; and Thomas Moore, "Marriott Grabs for More Rooms," *Fortune*, October 31, 1983, 107–122.

21 Paul R. Lawrence and Jay W. Lorsch, *Organization and Environment* (Homewood, Ill.: Irwin, 1969).

22 Robert B. Duncan, "Characteristics of Organizational Environments and Perceived Environmental Uncertainty," *Administrative Science Quarterly* 17 (1972), 313–327; W. Alan Randolph and Gregory G. Dess, "The Congruence Perspective of Organization Design: A Conceptual Model and Multivariate Research Approach," *Academy of Management Review* 9 (1984), 114–127; and Masoud Yasai-Ardekani, "Structural Adaptations to Environments," *Academy of Management Review* 11 (1986), 9–21.

23 John Child, *Organization: A Guide to Problems and Practice*, 2d ed. (London: Harper & Row, 1984).

24 Adam Smith, *The Wealth of Nations* (New York: Modern Library, 1937).

25 Michael Williams, "Some Plants Tear Out Long Assembly Lines, Switch to Craft Work," *The Wall Street Journal*, October 24, 1994, A1, A6.

26 This discussion is based on Richard L. Daft, *Organization Theory and Design*, 4th ed. (St. Paul, Minn.: West, 1992), 387–388.

27 C. I. Barnard, *The Functions of the Executive* (Cambridge, Mass.: Harvard University Press, 1938).

28 Thomas A. Stewart, "CEOs See Clout Shifting," *Fortune*, November 6, 1989, 66.

29 Michael G. O'Loughlin, "What Is Bureaucratic Accountability and How Can We Measure It?" *Administration & Society* 22, no. 3 (November 1990), 275–302.

30 Carrie R. Leana, "Predictors and Consequences of Delegation," *Academy of Management Journal* 29 (1986), 754–774.

31 Paul D. Collins and Frank Hull, "Technology and Span of Control: Woodward Revisited," *Journal of Management Studies* 23 (March 1986), 143–164; David D. Van Fleet and Arthur G. Bedeian, "A History of the Span of Management," *Academy of Management Review* 2 (1977), 356–372; and C. W. Barkdull, "Span of Control—A Method of Evaluation," *Michigan Business Review* 15 (May 1963), 25–32.

32 Brian Dumaine, "What the Leaders of Tomorrow See," *Fortune*, July 3, 1989, 48–62.

33 James Kitfield, "Superior Command," *Government Executive* (October 1993), 18–23.

34 Brian O'Reilly, "J&J Is on a Roll," *Fortune*, December 26, 1994, 178–191; and Joseph Weber, "A Big Company That Works," *Business Week*, May 4, 1992, 124–132.

35 Saul Hansell, "Banc One Lives Up to Its Name," *The New York Times*, May 12, 1995, C1, C4.

36 Clay Chandler and Paul Ingrassia, "Just as U.S. Firms Try Japanese Management, Honda Is Centralizing," *The Wall Street Journal*, April 11, 1991, A1, A10.

37 William R. Pape, "Divide and Conquer," *Inc. Technology* (1996), no. 2, 25–27.

38 Richard L. Daft, *Organization Theory and Design*, 5th ed. (Minneapolis, Minn.: West, 1995).

39 Bruce Buursma, "Wanted: Romance Executive," *Chicago Tribune*, July 19, 1989.

40 This discussion is based on Richard L. Daft, *Organization Theory and Design*, 5th ed. (Minneapolis, Minn.: West Publishing Company, 1995), 238; Raymond L. Manganelli and Mark M. Klein, "A Framework for Reengineering," *Management Review* (June 1994), 9–16; and Barbara Ettorre, "Reengineering Tales from the Front," *Management Review* (January 1995), 13–18.

41 Lori Calabro, "The Numbers Don't Lie," *CFO* (October 1994), 15.

42 Ettorre, "Reengineering Tales from the Front."

43 Bob Lindgren, "Going Horizontal," *Enterprise* (April 1994), 20–25.

44 John A. Byrne, "The Horizontal Corporation," *Business Week*, December 20, 1993, 76–81.

45 William J. Altier, "Task Forces: An Effective Management Tool," *Management Review* (February 1987), 52–57.

46 "Task Forces Tackle Consolidation of Employment Services," *Shawmut News*, Shawmut National Corporation, May 3, 1989, 2.

47 Michael Brody, "Can GM Manage It All?" *Fortune*, July 8, 1985, 22–28.

48 Henry Mintzberg, *The Structure of Organizations* (Englewood Cliffs, N.J.: Prentice-Hall, 1979).

49 Barbara Ettorre, "Simplicity Cuts a New Pattern," *Management Review* (December 1993), 25–29; and Joyce Hoffman, ed., *Reflections* 10 (1989), 12–15.

50 Paul R. Lawrence and Jay W. Lorsch, "New Managerial Job: The Integrator," *Harvard Business Review* (November–December 1967), 142–151.

51 Ron Winslow, "Utility Cuts Red Tape, Builds Nuclear Plant Almost on Schedule," *The Wall Street Journal*, February 22, 1984, 1, 18.

52 The following discussion of structural alternatives draws heavily on Jay R. Galbraith, *Designing Complex Organizations* (Reading, Mass.: Addison-Wesley, 1973); Jay R. Galbraith, *Organization Design* (Reading, Mass.: Addison-Wesley, 1977); Robert Duncan, "What Is the Right Organization Structure?" *Organizational Dynamics* (winter 1979), 59–80; and J. McCann and Jay R. Galbraith, "Interdepartmental Relations," in *Handbook of Organizational Design*, ed. P. Nystrom and W. Starbuck (New York: Oxford University Press, 1981), 60–84.

53 Mike Tharp, "LSI Logic Corp. Does as the Japanese Do," *The Wall Street Journal*, April 17, 1986, 6.

54 Lawton R. Burns, "Matrix Management in Hospitals: Testing Theories of Matrix Structure and Development," *Administrative Science Quarterly* 34 (1989), 349–368.

55 Stanley M. Davis and Paul R. Lawrence, *Matrix* (Reading, Mass.: Addison-Wesley, 1977).

56 Joel Kotkin, "The 'Smart-Team' at Compaq Computer," *Inc.* (February 1986), 48–56.

57 Byrne, "The Horizontal Corporation."

58 Lucien Rhodes, "The Passion of Robert Swiggett," *Inc.* (April 1984), 121–140.

59 Michael Hammer with Steven Stanton, "The Art of Change," *Success* (April 1995), 44A–44H; and Byrne, "The Horizontal Corporation."

60 Gillian Flynn, "Hallmark Cares," *Personnel Journal* 75, no. 3, March 1996, 50–53+; John Hillkirk, "Challenging Status Quo Now in Vogue," *USA Today*, November 9, 1993; and Thomas A. Stewart, "The Search for the Organization of Tomorrow," *Fortune*, May 18, 1992, 92–98; company sources.

61 Charles C. Snow, Raymond E. Miles, and Henry J. Coleman, Jr., "Managing Twenty-First Century Network Organizations," *Organizational Dynamics* 20 (winter 1992), 5–20; Miles, "Adapting to Technology and Competition"; and Raymond E. Miles and Charles C. Snow, "The New Network Firm: A Spherical Structure Built on a Human Investment Philosophy," *Organizational Dynamics* (spring 1995), 5–18.

62 Raymond E. Miles and Charles C. Snow, "Organizations: New Concepts for New Forms," *California Management Review* 28 (spring 1986), 62–73; and "Now, The Post-Industrial Corporation," *Business Week*, March 3, 1986, 64–74.

63 Jenny C. McCune, "Thin Is In," *Small Business Reports*, May 1993, 30–40; and Bernard Wysocki, Jr., "American Firms Send Office Work Abroad to Use Cheaper Labor," *The Wall Street Journal*, August 14, 1991, A1, A4.

64 Gianni Lorenzoni and Charles Baden-Fuller, "Creating a Strategic Center to Manage a Web of Partners," *California Management Review* 37, no. 3 (spring 1995), 146–163; Shawn Tully, "You'll Never Guess Who Really Makes . . . ," *Fortune*, October 3, 1994, 124–128; and G. Pascal Zachary, "High-Tech Firms Find It's Good to Line Up Outside Contractors," *The Wall Street Journal*, July 29, 1992, A1, A5.

65 Echo Montgomery Garrett, "Innovation + Outsourcing = Big Success," *Management Review* (September 1994), 17–20.

66 Julie Candler, "You Make It, They Distribute It," *Nation's Business* (March 1994), 46–48; and Barbara Bobo, "Building a Business Using Contractors," *Nation's Business* (June 1995), 6.

67 Barrier, "Re-engineering Your Company."

Innovation and Change

LEARNING OBJECTIVES

After studying this chapter, you should be able to

- Define organizational change and explain the forces for change.

- Describe the sequence of four change activities that must be performed in order for change to be successful.

- Explain the techniques managers can use to facilitate the initiation of change in organizations, including idea champions and new-venture teams.

- Define sources of resistance to change.

- Explain force field analysis and other implementation tactics that can be used to overcome resistance to change.

- Explain the difference among technology, product, structure, and culture/people changes.

- Explain the change process—bottom up, top down, horizontal—associated with each type of change.

- Define organizational development and organizational revitalization.

MANAGEMENT PROBLEM

When Saby Behar co-founded General Stair Corp. in 1987, he developed plans so that the Opa-Locka, Florida, maker of prefabricated stairs and railings would produce a quality product and keep raising its market share, which it had—currently up to about 30 percent. Within seven years, he had a "vertical transportation of people" business of 35 employees with wobbly margins and the real threat of an ugly price war with the increasing competition. The problem was: How to sell a commodity without being in a constant price war? Stairs, after all, were not particularly distinct from one another. They all go up and they all go down. He needed to keep his merchant–builder customers (who worked on 30 houses at a time) less focused on price. Despite his good quality, there were plenty of competitors ready to underbid.

Feeling desperate by April 1994, he called his three managers together to discuss necessary changes in the company. General Stair needed to lead the market in some unique way or get lost in the shuffle. Behar noted that the one thing, besides a quality product, that General Stair was really good at was delivery. He proposed the company offer a money-back delivery guarantee. The managers were aghast. How could he risk losing the business, considering the liabilities this could possibly entail? Not to mention the cost of upgrading the company, which was conservatively estimated at $50,000 to improve only communications.[1]

• If you were one of General Stair's managers, would you support Behar's proposal? What changes would be needed in the company in order to achieve his goal? What should General Stair do to prepare for those changes?

Managers at General Stair are not alone. Every organization experiences stress and difficulty in coping with change. Resistance to innovation from within is widely recognized as one of the critical problems facing business today in the United States and Canada. To be successful, organizations must embrace many types of change. Businesses must develop improved production technologies, create new products desired in the marketplace, implement new administrative systems, and upgrade employees' skills. Companies such as Westinghouse, Black & Decker, and Merck implement all of these changes and more.

How important is organizational change? Consider this: The parents of today's college students grew up without cable television, voice mail, stain-resistant carpet, personal computers, VCRs, electronic games, CDs, cellular phones, video stores, or laser checkout systems in supermarkets. Companies that produce the new products have prospered, but many companies caught with outdated products and technologies have failed. Organizations that change successfully, such as General Electric, Hewlett-Packard, and Motorola, are both profitable and admired.

Organizational change is defined as the adoption of a new idea or behavior by an organization.[2] In this chapter, we will look at how organizations can be designed to respond to the environment through internal change and development. First we will examine the basic forces for organizational change. Then we will look closely at how managers facilitate two change requirements: initiation and implementation. Finally, we will discuss the four major types of change—technology, new product, structure, and culture/people—and how the organization can be designed to facilitate each.

learning organization
An organization in which everyone is engaged in identifying and solving problems, enabling the organization to continuously improve and increase its capability.

organizational change
The adoption of a new idea or behavior by an organization.

THE LEARNING ORGANIZATION

In today's highly complex world, organizations need to continuously adapt to new situations if they are to survive and prosper. The current trend is toward development of the **learning organization,** which engages everyone in problem solving and continuous improvement based on the lessons of experience.[3]

The interacting systems that make up the learning organization resemble a web in which each element responds to and influences every other element. *Leadership* provides vision for development of strategies and serves as a crucial support function for empowerment of employees, the determination of organizational design, and the extent of openness in information sharing. *Empowerment* liberates employees but also places upon them the added responsibilities of working collaboratively, accepting greater leadership roles, and participating in strategy to benefit the entire organization. Redefining *culture* demands the rethinking of roles, processes, and values, breaking down barriers that have separated departments so that everyone shares information and works together. *Information sharing* requires adjustments on the part of managers for the inclusion of employees, suppliers, and customers, often necessitating cultural and structural changes. *Strategy* is likewise linked to structure and culture as the organization changes its fundamental way of doing business and allows strategic initiatives to flow bottom up as well as top down. The *horizontal structure,* which replaces the familiar hierarchical pyramid, incorporates empowerment and information sharing and relies on employees as team members and managers as facilitators.

The learning organization simultaneously embraces two types of planned change: *operational change,* based on organizational efforts to improve basic work and organizational processes in different areas of the business; and *transformational change,* which involves redesign and renewal of the

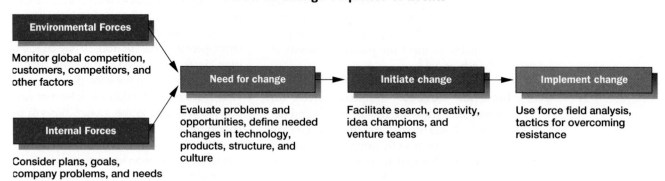

EXHIBIT   10.1
Model of Change Sequence of Events

total organization.[4] We will be discussing operational change in this chapter. The learning organization was discussed in detail in Chapter 2.

MODEL OF PLANNED ORGANIZATIONAL CHANGE

Change can be managed. By observing external trends, patterns, and needs, managers use planned change to help the organization adapt to external problems and opportunities.[5] When organizations are caught flat-footed, failing to anticipate or respond to new needs, management is at fault.

An overall model for planned change is presented in Exhibit 10.1. Four events make up the change sequence: (1) Internal and external forces for change exist; (2) organization managers monitor these forces and become aware of a need for change; and (3) the perceived need triggers the initiation of change, which (4) is then implemented. How each of these activities is handled depends on the organization and managers' styles.

We now turn to a brief discussion of the specific activities associated with the first two events—forces for change and the perceived need for the organization to respond.

Forces for Change

Forces for organizational change exist both in the external environment and within the organization.

Environmental Forces. As described in Chapters 3 and 4, external forces originate in all environmental sectors, including customers, competitors, technology, economic forces, and the international arena. For example, many North American companies have been blindsided by global competition. Consider General Electric, which built a new factory to produce microwave ovens. As GE's plans were being made, Yun Soo Chu was working 80 hours per week for Samsung in Korea to perfect a microwave oven. About the time the GE plant came on stream, Samsung started exporting thousands of microwaves to the United States at one-third the cost of GE microwaves. Today, Samsung has 25 percent of the U.S. market, and GE is one of its best customers. GE closed its microwave plant, preferring to buy the cheaper Samsung ovens to sell under the GE label.[6] After three engineers started Ensoniq Corporation to produce home computers, they experienced an external force of low consumer demand and switched product lines to electronic keyboards. Using innovative technologies, Ensoniq's founders produced an affordable Mirage keyboard, enabling people with

musical talents (as well as the untalented) to make music. Ensoniq responded to other environmental needs by producing the Sound Selector hearing aid, which is programmable to meet the particular needs of each individual.[7]

Internal Forces. Internal forces for change arise from internal activities and decisions. If top managers select a goal of rapid company growth, internal actions will have to be changed to meet that growth. New departments or technologies will be created. General Motors' senior management, frustrated by poor internal efficiency, designed the Saturn manufacturing plant to solve this internal need. Demands by employees, labor unions, and production inefficiencies can all generate a force to which management must respond with change.

Need for Change

As indicated in Exhibit 10.1, external or internal forces translate into a perceived need for change within the organization.[8] Managers sense a need for change when there is a **performance gap**—a disparity between existing and desired performance levels. The performance gap may occur because current procedures are not up to standard or because a new idea or technology could improve current performance. Recall from Chapter 8 that management's responsibility is to monitor threats and opportunities in the external environment as well as strengths and weaknesses within the organization to determine whether a need for change exists. Juliette Engel saw the need for change in a broader social context and developed a company to meet that need.

CRUISE WITH A CAUSE

Radiologist Juliette Engel was not in the social-betterment business—until she traveled to Russia in 1990 for a conference and was transformed. Russia was a country desperately in need of basic health care. Maternity clinics were appalling for their lack of basic sanita-

tion. Abandoned children lived 150 to small orphanage houses, often with no shoes and little food. Villages throughout the entire, huge country (it has 12 time zones) were without clinics, prenatal care, doctors, or any basic services. So Engel opened a maternal clinic in Moscow. But that was not enough.

She quit her $250,000 job later that year and found herself in the tourism business by starting MiraMed International to help support the clinics. She hired the relatively inexpensive and underused Russian tourist boats and set up "Cruise with a Cause" trips, in order to support their maternity clinics. Participants pay money to go on the 12-day river cruises. They stop along the way at clinics and orphanages, where they bring a suitcase filled with supplies, which might be school materials, aspirin, cough syrup, toothpaste and toothbrushes, or clothing.

About 70 percent of the tourists are women ages 40 and over, many of whom have never traveled before. At the end, there is a deep sense of fulfillment and of touching others' lives. Many of them keep in touch with the orphanages and continue to make donations. MiraMed has expanded to 17 tours in various countries.

Engel is clear about the advantages of helping people to serve others. Not only does this make the world a better place, but it also fills the participants' deeper needs for meaning in their lives. "People can make a difference by being there and giving back," she says. Her business is about "the power of the individual to effect change."[9] ■

Managers in every company must be alert to problems and opportunities, because the perceived need for change is what sets the stage for subsequent actions that create a new product or technology. Big problems are easy to spot. Sensitive monitoring systems are needed to detect gradual changes that can fool managers into thinking their company is doing fine. An organization may be in greater danger when the environment changes slowly, because managers may fail to trigger an organizational response. Failing to use planned change to meet small needs can place the organization

performance gap
A disparity between existing and desired performance levels.

in hot water, as illustrated in the following passage:

> When frogs are placed in a boiling pail of water, they jump out—they don't want to boil to death. However, when frogs are placed in a cold pail of water, and the pail is placed on a stove with the heat turned very low, over time the frogs will boil to death.[10]

INITIATING CHANGE

After the need for change has been perceived, the next part of the change process is initiating change, a truly critical aspect of change management. This is where the ideas that solve perceived needs are developed. Responses that an organization can make are to search for or create a change to adopt.

Search

Search is the process of learning about current developments inside or outside the organization that can be used to meet the perceived need for change. Search typically uncovers existing knowledge that can be applied or adopted within the organization. Managers talk to friends and colleagues, read professional reports, or hire consultants to learn about ideas used elsewhere.

Many needs, however, cannot be resolved through existing knowledge but require that the organization develop a new response. Initiating a new response means that managers must design the organization so as to facilitate creativity of both individuals and departments, encourage innovative people to initiate new ideas, or create new-venture departments. These techniques have been adopted with great success by such corporations as GE and Hallmark.

Creativity

Creativity is the development of novel solutions to perceived problems.[11] Creative individuals develop ideas that can be adopted by the organization. People noted for their creativity include Edwin Land, who invented the Polaroid camera; Frederick Smith, who came up with the idea for Federal Express's overnight delivery service during an undergraduate class at Yale; and Swiss engineer George de Mestral, who created Velcro after noticing the tiny hooks on the burrs caught on his wool socks. Each of these people saw unique and creative opportunities in a familiar situation. Ideas for encouraging creative thinking are listed in the Focus on Innovation box.

Each of us has the capacity to be creative. Characteristics of highly creative people are illustrated in the left-hand column of Exhibit 10.2. Creative people often are known for originality, open-mindedness, curiosity, a focused approach to problem solving, persistence, a relaxed and playful attitude, and receptivity to new ideas.[12]

Creativity can also be designed into organizations. Companies or departments within companies can be organized to be creative and initiate changes. The characteristics of creative organizations correspond to those of individuals, as illustrated in the right-hand column of Exhibit 10.2. Creative organizations are loosely structured. People find themselves in a situation of ambiguity, assignments are vague, territories overlap, tasks are poorly defined, and much work is done through teams.[13] Creative organizations have an internal culture of playfulness, freedom, challenge, and grass-roots participation.[14] They harness all potential sources of new ideas from within. Many participative management programs are born out of the desire to enhance creativity for initiating changes. People are not stuck in the rhythm of routine jobs.

The most creative companies encourage employees to make mistakes. Jim Read, president of the Read Corporation, says, "When my employees make mistakes trying to improve something, I give them a round of applause. No mistakes mean no new products. If they ever become afraid to make one, my company is doomed."[15]

Open channels of communication, overlapping jobs, discretionary resources, decentralization, and employees' freedom to

search
The process of learning about current developments inside or outside the organization that can be used to meet a perceived need for change.

creativity
The development of novel solutions to perceived organizational problems.

FOCUS ON INNOVATION
NURTURING CREATIVITY

Experts generally agree on some basic principles to apply in order to create a climate of innovation: an environment where workers' creativity is enhanced, rather than stifled as it is too often done. Follow these tips and watch creative juices flow.

1. Cultivate a culture based on curiosity.

2. Make this motto stick: "Give it a try—and quick!"

3. Encourage and insist on continual learning.

4. Flood the organization with information.

5. Hold internal "trade show" or "show and tell" sessions to share new ideas in a supportive environment.

6. Recognize the innovator, especially at a public demonstration. Monetary rewards don't hurt, either.

7. Leaders should mentor and coach innovative-nurturing behavior, suspending the "critical eye" during initial stages of idea development.

8. Develop a culture of cooperation, where people can call on one another to brainstorm or solve problems when implementing an idea.

9. Recruit and reward innovative people.

10. Break down organizational barriers, whether it be tight departmental divisions, limiting job descriptions, or confining notions of policy. New ideas have a hard time blooming in restricted places.

SOURCES: Marshall Loeb, "Ten Commandments for Managing Creative People," *Fortune,* January 6, 1996, 135–36; Timothy D. Schellhardt, "David and Goliath," *The Wall Street Journal,* May 23, 1996, R14; Robert D. Russell, "The Role of Organizational Culture in Fostering Innovation in a Small Business," *Entrepreneurial Edge Magazine,* #2755, 1996; Oren Harari, "Turn Your Organization into a Hotbed of Ideas," *Management Review,* December 1995, 37–39.

---

choose problems and make mistakes can generate unexpected benefits for companies. Creative organizational conditions such as those described in Exhibit 10.2 enable more than 200 new products a year to bubble up from 3M's research labs.

The same creative conditions enabled the solution to the following problem: How do you pack many potato chips into a small space without crushing them? A small company used the analogy in nature of stacking dry leaves and wet leaves. Through the use of such creative thinking, the obvious solution emerged: Mold the chips into uniform,

---

EXHIBIT 10.2
Characteristics of Creative People and Organizations

SOURCES: Based on Gary A. Steiner, ed., *The Creative Organization* (Chicago: University of Chicago Press, 1965), 16–18; Rosabeth Moss Kanter, "The Middle Manager as Innovator," *Harvard Business Review* (July–August 1982), 104–105; and James Brian Quinn, "Managing Innovation: Controlled Chaos," *Harvard Business Review* 63 (May–June 1985), 73–84.

The Creative Individual	The Creative Organization or Department
1 Conceptual fluency Open-mindedness	1 Open channels of communication Contact with outside sources Overlapping territories Suggestion systems, brainstorming, nominal group techniques
2 Originality	2 Assignment of nonspecialists to problems Eccentricity allowed Use of teams
3 Less authority Independence	3 Decentralization, loosely defined positions, loose control Acceptance of mistakes Risk-taking norms
4 Playfulness Undisciplined exploration Curiosity	4 Freedom to choose and pursue problems Not a tight ship, playful culture Freedom to discuss ideas, long time horizon
5 Persistence Commitment Focused approach	5 Resources allocated to creative personnel and projects without immediate payoff Reward system encourages innovation Absolution of peripheral responsibilities

stackable shapes *before* they dry. Armed with this innovation, the company sold its idea to Procter & Gamble, and the canned chip Pringles was born.[16]

Idea Champions and New-Venture Teams

If creative conditions are successful, new ideas will be generated that must be carried forward for acceptance and implementation. This is where idea champions come in. The formal definition of an **idea champion** is a person who sees the need for and champions productive change within the organization. For example, Bonnie McKeever of Federal Express championed the idea of a coalition of companies to combat mounting medical fees. The Memphis Business Group on Health was created, saving its members an estimated tens of millions of dollars through competitive bidding and discounts.[17] Wendy Black of Best Western International championed the idea of coordinating the corporate mailings to the company's 2,800 hoteliers into a single packet every two weeks. Some hotels were receiving three special mailings a day from different departments. Her idea saved $600,000 a year for five years in postage alone.[18]

Remember: Change does not occur by itself. Personal energy and effort are required to successfully promote a new idea. Often a new idea is rejected by management. Champions are passionately committed to a new product or idea despite rejection by others.

Championing an idea successfully requires roles in organizations, as illustrated in Exhibit 10.3. Sometimes a single person may play two or more of these roles, but successful innovation in most companies involves an interplay of different people, each adopting one role. The *inventor* develops a new idea and understands its technical value but has neither the ability nor the interest to promote it for acceptance within the organization. The *champion* believes in the idea, confronts the organizational realities of costs and benefits, and gains the political and financial support needed to bring it to reality. The *sponsor* is a high-level manager who approves the idea, protects the idea, and removes major organizational barriers to acceptance. The *critic* counterbalances the zeal of the champion by challenging the concept and providing a reality test against hard-nosed criteria. The critic prevents people in the other roles from adopting a bad idea.[19]

Managers can directly influence whether champions will flourish. When Texas Instruments studied 50 of its new-product introductions, a surprising fact emerged: Without exception, every new product that had failed had lacked a zealous champion. In contrast, most of the new products that succeeded had a champion. Texas Instruments' managers made an immediate decision: No new product would be approved unless someone championed it.

A recent idea for facilitating corporate innovation is known as a new-venture team. A **new-venture team** is a unit separate from the rest of the organization and is responsible for developing and initiating a major innovation.[20] New-venture teams give free reign to members' creativity because their separate facilities and location free them from organizational rules and procedures. These teams typically are small, loosely structured, and organic, reflecting the characteristics of creative organizations described in Exhibit 10.2. Peter Drucker advises organizations that wish to innovate to use a separate team or department:

> For the existing business to be capable of innovation, it has to create a structure that allows people to be entrepreneurial. . . . This means, first, that the entrepreneurial, the new, has to be organized separately from the old and the existing. Whenever we have tried to make an existing unit the carrier of the entrepreneurial project, we have failed.[21]

The new-venture team is quite different from the horizontal relationships or the matrix structure described in Chapter 9. In those structures, employees remain members of their everyday departments and

idea champion
A person who sees the need for and champions productive change within the organization.

new-venture team
A unit separate from the mainstream of the organization that is responsible for developing and initiating innovations.

E X H I B I T   1 0 . 3
Four Roles in Organizational Change

Inventor	**Champion**	**Sponsor**	**Critic**
Develops and understands technical aspects of idea	Believes in idea	High-level manager who removes organizational barriers	Provides reality test
Does not know how to win support for the idea or make a business of it	Visualizes benefits	Approves and protects idea within organization	Looks for shortcomings
	Confronts organizational realities of cost, benefits		Defines hard-nosed criteria that idea must pass
	Obtains financial and political support		
	Overcomes obstacles		

SOURCES: Based on Harold L. Angle and Andrew H. Van de Ven, "Suggestions for Managing the Innovation Journey," in *Research in the Management of Innovation: The Minnesota Studies*, ed. A. H. Van de Ven, H. L. Angle, and Marshall Scott Poole (Cambridge, Mass.: Ballinger/Harper & Row, 1989); and Jay R. Galbraith, "Designing the Innovating Organization," *Organizational Dynamics* (winter 1982), 5–25.

simply work on a project part-time while reporting to their regular boss. Under the new-venture team concept, employees no longer report through the normal structure.[22] New-venture teams are kept small and separate to ensure that no bureaucracy will intrude.

For a giant corporation such as IBM, new-venture teams free people from the constraints of the large organization. IBM's biggest success—the personal computer—was built by a new-venture group. The PC new-venture team was so appealing that 5,000 employees applied for the initial 50 positions.[23] The most recent successful new-venture team at IBM is a small group that built the Power Visualization System, a graphics supercomputer introduced after a mere two years in development. The supercomputer lets scientists and engineers literally "see" the billions of pieces of data their experiments generate.[24]

Other companies that have created new-venture units are Monsanto, Levi Strauss, and Exxon. 3M utilizes action teams to create new products. The action team concept allows individuals with new product ideas to recruit team members from throughout the company. These people may end up running the newly created division if the idea is successful.[25]

One variation of new-venture teams is the **new-venture fund,** which provides resources from which individuals and groups can draw to develop new ideas, products, or businesses. For example, Teleflex, a producer of many technical and consumer products, allocates one-half of 1 percent of sales to a new-venture fund. More than $1 million was allocated to employees in one year to explore new ideas.[26]

IMPLEMENTING CHANGE

Creative culture, idea champions, and new-venture teams are ways to facilitate the initiation of new ideas. The other step to be managed in the change process is implementation. A new, creative idea will not benefit the organization until it is in place and being fully utilized. One frustration for managers is that employees often seem to resist change for no apparent reason. To effectively manage the implementation process, managers should be aware of the reasons for employee resistance and be prepared to use techniques for obtaining employee cooperation.

Resistance to Change

Idea champions often discover that other employees are unenthusiastic about their new ideas. Members of a new-venture group may be surprised when managers in

new-venture fund
A fund providing resources from which individuals and groups draw to develop new ideas, products, or businesses.

the regular organization do not support or approve their innovations. Managers and employees not involved in an innovation often seem to prefer the status quo. Employees appear to resist change for several reasons, and understanding them helps managers implement change more effectively.

Self-Interest. Employees typically resist a change they believe will take away something of value. A proposed change in job design, structure, or technology may lead to a perceived loss of power, prestige, pay, or company benefits. The fear of personal loss is perhaps the biggest obstacle to organizational change.[27] When Mesa Oil Corporation tried to buy Phillips Petroleum, Phillips employees started a campaign to prevent the takeover. Employees believed that Mesa would not treat them well and that they would lose financial benefits. Their resistance to change was so effective that the merger failed to take place.

Lack of Understanding and Trust. Employees often do not understand the intended purpose of a change or distrust the intentions behind it. If previous working relationships with an idea champion have been negative, resistance may occur. One manager had a habit of initiating a change in the financial reporting system about every 12 months and then losing interest and not following through. After the third time, employees no longer went along with the change because they did not trust the manager's intention to follow through to their benefit.

Uncertainty. *Uncertainty* is the lack of information about future events. It represents a fear of the unknown. Uncertainty is especially threatening for employees who have a low tolerance for change and fear the novel and unusual. They do not know how a change will affect them and worry about whether they will be able to meet the demands of a new procedure or technology.[28] Union leaders at General Motors' Steering Gear Division in Saginaw, Michigan, resisted the introduction of employee partici-

pation programs. They were uncertain about how the program would affect their status and thus initially opposed it.

Different Assessments and Goals. Another reason for resistance to change is that people who will be affected by innovation may assess the situation differently from an idea champion or new-venture group. Often critics voice legitimate disagreements over the proposed benefits of a change. Managers in each department pursue different goals, and an innovation may detract from performance and goal achievement for some departments. For example, if marketing gets the new product it wants for its customers, the cost of manufacturing may increase, and the manufacturing superintendent thus will resist. Resistance may call attention to problems with the innovation. At a consumer products company in Racine, Wisconsin, middle managers resisted the introduction of a new employee program that turned out to be a bad idea. The managers truly believed that the program would do more harm than good. One manager bluntly told his boss, "I've been here longer than you, and I'll be here after you've gone, so don't tell me what really counts at this company."[29]

These reasons for resistance are legitimate in the eyes of employees affected by the change. The best procedure for managers is not to ignore resistance but to diagnose the reasons and design strategies to gain acceptance by users.[30] Strategies for overcoming resistance to change typically involve two approaches: the analysis of resistance through the force field technique and the use of selective implementation tactics to overcome resistance.

Force Field Analysis

Force field analysis grew from the work of Kurt Lewin, who proposed that change was a result of the competition between *driving* and *restraining forces*.[31] When a change is introduced, some forces drive it and other forces resist it. To implement a change, management should analyze the change forces.

force field analysis
The process of determining which forces drive and which resist a proposed change.

EXHIBIT 10.4
Using Force Field Analysis to Change from Traditional to Just-in-Time Inventory System

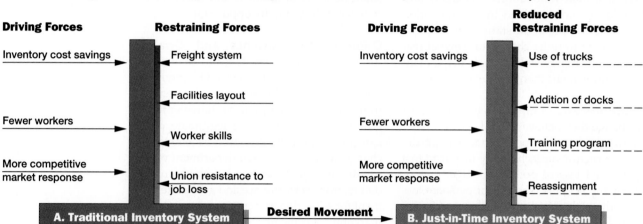

By selectively removing forces that restrain change, the driving forces will be strong enough to enable implementation, as illustrated by the move from A to B in Exhibit 10.4. As restraining forces are reduced or removed, behavior will shift to incorporate the desired changes.

Just-in-time (JIT) inventory control systems schedule materials to arrive at a company just as they are needed on the production line. In an Ohio manufacturing company, management's analysis showed that the driving forces associated with the implementation of JIT were (1) the large cost savings from reduced inventories, (2) savings from needing fewer workers to handle the inventory, and (3) a quicker, more competitive market response for the company. Restraining forces discovered by managers were (1) a freight system that was too slow to deliver inventory on time, (2) a facility layout that emphasized inventory maintenance over new deliveries, (3) worker skills inappropriate for handling rapid inventory deployment, and (4) union resistance to loss of jobs. The driving forces were not sufficient to overcome the restraining forces.

To shift the behavior to JIT, managers attacked the restraining forces. An analysis of the freight system showed that delivery by truck provided the flexibility and quickness needed to schedule inventory arrival at a specific time each day. The problem with facility layout was met by adding four new loading docks. Inappropriate worker skills were attacked with a training program to instruct workers in JIT methods and in assembling products with uninspected parts. Union resistance was overcome by agreeing to reassign workers no longer needed for maintaining inventory to jobs in another plant. With the restraining forces removed, the driving forces were sufficient to allow the JIT system to be implemented.

Implementation Tactics

The other approach to managing implementation is to adopt specific tactics to overcome employee resistance. For example, resistance to change may be overcome by educating employees or inviting them to participate in implementing the change. Methods for dealing with resistance to change have been studied by researchers. The following five tactics, summarized in Exhibit 10.5, have proven successful.[32]

Communication and Education.
Communication and *education* are used when solid information about the change is needed by users and others who may resist implementation. Education is especially im-

Approach	When to Use
Communication, education	■ Change is technical. ■ Users need accurate information and analysis to understand change.
Participation	■ Users need to feel involved. ■ Design requires information from others. ■ Users have power to resist.
Negotiation	■ Group has power over implementation. ■ Group will lose out in the change.
Coercion	■ A crisis exists. ■ Initiators clearly have power. ■ Other implementation techniques have failed.
Top management support	■ Change involves multiple departments or reallocation of resources. ■ Users doubt legitimacy of change.

EXHIBIT 10.5
Tactics for Overcoming Resistance to Change

SOURCE: Based on J. P. Kotter and L. A. Schlesinger, "Choosing Strategies for Change," *Harvard Business Review* 57 (March–April 1979), 106–114.

portant when the change involves new technical knowledge or when users are unfamiliar with the idea. Canadian Airlines International spent a year and a half preparing and training employees before changing its entire reservations, airport, cargo, and financial systems as part of a new "Service Quality" strategy. Smooth implementation resulted from this intensive training and communications effort, which involved 50,000 tasks, 12,000 people, and 26 classrooms around the world.[33]

Participation. *Participation* involves users and potential resisters in designing the change. This approach is time-consuming, but it pays off because users understand and become committed to the change. Participation also helps managers determine potential problems and understand the differences in perceptions of change among employees.[34] When General Motors tried to implement a new management appraisal system for supervisors in its Adrian, Michigan, plant, it met with immediate resistance. Rebuffed by the lack of cooperation, top managers proceeded more slowly, involving supervisors in the design of the new appraisal system. Through participation in system design, managers understood what the new approach was all about and dropped their resistance to it. Preston Trucking Company used participation to effectively bring about a much-needed change.

PRESTON TRUCKING COMPANY

Several years ago, top managers at Maryland-based Preston Trucking Company started to fear for the future of their organization. Deregulation was making the trucking industry more competitive, and a survey of employees uncovered 40 negative comments for every positive comment about the company. Rather than help the company become more efficient, employees were unhappy and often hostile. One truck driver stayed parked on a customer's lot for two hours to show Preston managers who ran the company. Top managers at Preston were frustrated, because creating a culture that fostered innovation and commitment seemed so difficult. Preston, hammered by deregulation and unhappy employees, decided to revise its corporate culture and encourage bottom-up change in its production process. The survey results indicating how bad things were unfroze management. Consultants were brought in, and meetings were held to determine the best way to proceed and to gain employee participation. A new mind-set was introduced that made employees equal partners in the trucking business. Improved production efficiency occurred through weekly idea meetings from which suggestions flowed from lower-level employees. In one year, more than 4,000 money-making ideas were proposed, worth about $1.5 million. One idea helped decrease truck service maintenance from 23 hours to 11

hours. With both a new corporate culture and a steady bottom-up flow of modifications in production technology, Preston has become the darling of the trucking industry. Growth is rapid, sales and profits are up, and grievances are way down.[35] ■

Negotiation. Negotiation is a more formal means of achieving cooperation. *Negotiation* uses formal bargaining to win acceptance and approval of a desired change. For example, if the marketing department fears losing power if a new management structure is implemented, top managers may negotiate with marketing to reach a resolution. General Motors, General Electric, and other companies that have strong unions frequently must formally negotiate change with the unions. The change may become part of the union contract reflecting the agreement of both parties.

Coercion. *Coercion* means that managers use formal power to force employees to change. Resisters are told to accept the change or lose rewards or even their jobs. Coercion is necessary in crisis situations when a rapid response is urgent. When middle managers at TRW, Inc.'s Valve Division in Cleveland refused to go along with a new employee involvement program, top management reassigned several first-line supervisors and managers. The new jobs did not involve supervisory responsibility. Further, other TRW managers were told that future pay increases depended on their adoption of the new procedures. The coercive techniques were used as a last resort because managers refused to go along with the change any other way.[36]

Top Management Support. The visible support of top management also helps overcome resistance to change. *Top management support* symbolizes to all employees that the change is important for the organization. Top management support is especially important when a change involves multiple departments or when resources are being reallocated among departments. Without top management support, these changes can get bogged down in squabbling among departments. Moreover, when top managers fail to support a project, they can inadvertently undercut it by issuing contradictory orders. This happened at Flying Tiger Lines before it was acquired by Federal Express. The airborne freight hauler came up with a plan to eliminate excessive paperwork by changing the layout of offices so that two agents rather than four could handle each shipment. No sooner had part of the change been implemented than top management ordered another system; thus, the office layout was changed again. The new layout was not as efficient, but it was the one that top management supported. Had middle managers informed top managers and obtained their support earlier, the initial change would not have been defeated by a new priority.[37]

TYPES OF PLANNED CHANGE

Now that we have explored how the initiation and implementation of change can be carried out, let us look at the different types of change that occur in organizations. We will address two issues: what parts of the organization can be changed and how managers can apply the initiation and implementation ideas to each type of change.

The types of organizational change are strategy, technology, products, structure, and culture/people, as illustrated in Exhibit 10.6. Organizations may innovate in one or more areas, depending on internal and external forces for change. In the rapidly changing toy industry, a manufacturer has to introduce new products frequently. In a mature, competitive industry, production technology changes are adopted to improve efficiency. The arrows connecting the types of change in Exhibit 10.6 show that a change in one part may affect other parts of the organization: A new product may require changes in technology, and a new technology may require new people skills or a new structure. For example, when Shenandoah Life Insurance Company computerized pro-

cessing and claims operations, the structure had to be decentralized, employees required intensive training, and a more participative culture was needed. Related changes were required for the new technology to increase efficiency.

Technology Changes

A **technology change** is related to the organization's production process—how the organization does its work. Technology changes are designed to make the production of a product or service more efficient. For example, the adoption of robotics to improve production efficiency at General Motors and Chrysler is an example of a technology change, as is the adoption of laser-scanning checkout systems at supermarkets. At IBM's manufacturing plant in Charlotte, North Carolina, an automated miniload storage and retrieval system was installed to handle production parts. This change provided an efficient method for handling small-parts inventory and changed the technology of the IBM plant.

How can managers encourage technology change? The general rule is that technology change is bottom up.[38] The *bottom-up approach* means that ideas are initiated at lower organization levels and channeled upward for approval. Lower-level technical experts act as idea champions—they invent and champion technological changes. Employees at lower levels understand the technology and have the expertise needed to propose changes. For example, at Kraft General Foods, employees have proposed several hundred cost-saving projects. One that can save $3.5 million a year is simply to improve the accuracy of machines that weigh product portions.[39]

Managers can facilitate the bottom-up approach by designing creative departments as described earlier in this chapter. A loose, flexible, decentralized structure provides employees with the freedom and opportunity to initiate continuous improvements. A rigid, centralized, standardized structure stifles technology innovation. Anything managers can do to involve the grass

roots of the organization—the people who are experts in their parts of the production process—will increase technology change. Managers at Johnson Controls started a worker-idea program to help develop technological innovations in the factory.

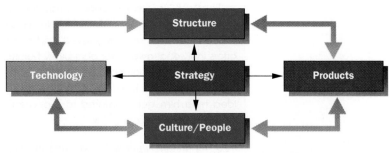

EXHIBIT 10.6
Types of Organizational Change

SOURCE: Based on Harold J. Leavitt, "Applied Organizational Change in Industry: Structural, Technical, and Human Approaches," in *New Perspectives in Organization Research*, ed. W. W. Cooper, H. J. Leavitt, and M. W. Shelly II (New York: Wiley, 1964), 55–74.

technology change
A change that pertains to the organization's production process.

JOHNSON CONTROLS FOAMECH

Putting up a scorecard on the factory floor might not sound like technological innovation, but it helped Johnson Controls FoaMech reduce machine downtime by 75 percent. As part of the company's program to encourage the 230 workers to offer efficiency-oriented ideas, this was one of 631 suggestions from the Georgetown, Kentucky, plant during the past year.

Previously, maintenance specialist Russ Harrod spent too much time trying to figure out which machines needed repair, while team leader Kim Darnell spent a lot of time yelling, trying to locate Harrod. With all the loud factory noise, the system did not work well. Harrod and Darnell realized they needed something different and developed FoaMech's own version of an outfield scoreboard.

Instead of the typical flashing scores, they posted the status of all 50 machines. Various color lights indicated that a machine needed either maintenance or repair, or they might mean team leaders were needed.

Other ideas from FoaMech workers included an innovative way to handle seat foam for cushions. Larry Hacker figured out a way to eliminate the use of forklifts, using instead returnable carts, at a yearly savings of over $300,000.

FoaMech is serious about encouraging workers' ideas and rewards the whole group based on amount of money saved, and it also offers individual awards for particularly helpful suggestions. And perhaps an award may include a promotion. Did Hacker's money-saving idea help him get promoted to supervisor? "Couldn't hurt," he said.[40] ■

A *top-down approach* to technology change usually does not work.[41] Top managers are not close to the production process and lack expertise in technological developments. Mandating technology change from the top produces fewer rather than more technology innovations. The spark for a creative new idea comes from people close to the technology. The rationale behind Motorola's "participative management program," Data General's "pride teams," and Honeywell's "positive action teams" is to encourage new technology ideas from people at lower levels of the organization.

New-Product Changes

A **product change** is a change in the organization's product or service output. New-product innovations have major implications for an organization, because they often are an outcome of a new strategy and may define a new market.[42] Examples of new products are Frito-Lay's introduction of O'Grady's potato chips and GE's development at its Medical Division of a device for monitoring patients' heart cycles.

The introduction of a new product is difficult, because it not only involves a new technology but also must meet customers' needs. In most industries, only about one in eight new-product ideas is successful.[43] Companies that successfully develop new products usually have the following characteristics:

1 People in marketing have a good understanding of customer needs.
2 Technical specialists are aware of recent technological developments and make effective use of new technology.
3 Members from key departments—research, manufacturing, marketing—

cooperate in the development of the new product.[44]

These findings mean that the ideas for new products typically originate at the lower levels of the organization just as they do for technology changes. The difference is that new-product ideas flow horizontally among departments. Product innovation requires expertise from several departments simultaneously. A new-product failure is often the result of failed cooperation.[45] Rebecca and Dan Matthias used their joint expertise in engineering to help create and develop a successful clothing company. Much of their success can be attributed to the inventory information system they developed, as described in the Technology for Today box.

One approach to successful new-product innovation is called the **horizontal linkage model,** which is illustrated in Exhibit 10.7.[46] The model shows that research, manufacturing, and marketing must simultaneously develop new products. People from these departments meet frequently in teams and task forces to share ideas and solve problems. Research people inform marketing of new technical developments to learn whether they will be useful to customers. Marketing people pass customer complaints to research to use in the design of new products. Manufacturing informs other departments whether a product idea can be manufactured within cost limits. When the horizontal linkage model is used, the decision to develop a new product is a joint one.

Today's increasingly sophisticated consumer is demanding an ever-increasing role in product development and marketing. Empowerment in today's competitive environment goes beyond employees to include suppliers and customers in the product development process. Entire industries, such as automakers, are actively soliciting consumer feedback for new products and are including consumer participation from the beginning of the design process.

Horizontal linkages are being adopted in the computer industry to overcome new-

horizontal linkage model
An approach to product change that emphasizes shared development of innovations among several departments.

product change
A change in the organization's product or service output.

TECHNOLOGY FOR TODAY
MOTHERS WORK INC.

How does a pregnant architect/engineer with no fashion-business experience create a company that is now the dominant player in maternity wear? Rebecca Matthias and her engineer-husband started Mothers Work Inc. in 1982 when Mrs. Matthias couldn't find any decent maternity clothes to wear to business meetings. Starting a small mail-order business, they hit a vein of need for baby boomer career women. But the beginning was anything but easy.

Advertising in major publications, they got 100 catalog requests, but no orders. Not one to give up, Mrs. Matthias personally called all 100 potential customers to find out why they weren't buying and used that information to improve. That intense need to understand customers has been a driving force in the ultimate success of the company.

Having master's degrees in engineering helped them create an innovative inventory information system called TrendTrack, which is Mothers Work's competitive edge. The system tracks the current 450 retail shops daily, noting which styles are selling. Mrs. Matthias passes this information to the designers and merchants, so that customers are better served. None of her stores has ever run out of stock.

The Matthiases aren't afraid to admit they use numbers when making merchandise-stock decisions. Hard experience has taught them that gut instinct alone is not enough. "Every merchant we hire wants to expand into colored blouses," says Mrs. Matthias. "But I know the most important thing our customers want is a white shirt."

Success has no secret formula, believes Mrs. Matthias, other than persistence and ingenuity. "You have to overcome every obstacle that's thrown at you," she says. "I can't tell you how many times I wanted to walk away. . . . [But] there's always a way out of the box. You almost never get it the first time."

SOURCE: Laura Bird, "High-tech Inventory System Coordinates Retailer's Clothes with Customers' Taste," *The Wall Street Journal*, June 12, 1996, B1; Martha Mangelsdorf, "The Hottest Entrepreneurs in America," *Inc.*, Dec. 1992, vol. 14, no. 13, 88-103; Stephanis Campbell, "Growth-Controlled Chaos," *Entrepreneurial Edge Magazine*, #6412, 1996.

product problems. For example, at Convergent Technologies, Workslate, a portable computer, received accolades when it was introduced. One year later, Workslate was dead. Production problems with the new product had not been worked out. Marketing people had not fully analyzed customer needs. The idea had been pushed through without sufficient consultation among research, manufacturing, and marketing. At Lotus Development Corporation, the delays in new software ran on for months and years, earning the name "vaporware" because they never appeared. New senior vice president Frank King enforced a regime of daily and weekly meetings involving programmers and code writers, and monthly gatherings of all employees to update one another. These enforced linkages gradually reduced product development time.[47]

Innovation is becoming a major strategic weapon in the global marketplace. One example of innovation is the use of **time-based competition,** which means delivering products and services faster than competitors, giving companies a significant strategic advantage. For example, Hewlett-Packard reduced the time to develop a new printer from 4.5 years to 22 months. Lenscrafters jumped from 3 to 300 stores based on its ability to provide quality eyeglasses in one hour. Dillard's department stores went to an automatic reorder system that replenishes stocks in 12 days rather than 30, providing retail goods to customers more quickly.[48] Sprinting to market with a new product requires a *parallel approach,* or

time-based competition
A strategy of competition based on the ability to deliver products and services faster than competitors.

EXHIBIT 10.7
Horizontal Linkage Model for New-Product Innovation

simultaneous linkage among departments. This is similar to a rugby match wherein players run together, passing the ball back and forth as they move downfield. The teamwork required for the horizontal linkage model is a major component of using rapid innovation to beat the competition with speed.[49]

Structural Changes

structural change
Any change in the way in which the organization is designed and managed.

Structural changes involve the hierarchy of authority, goals, structural characteristics, administrative procedures, and management systems.[50] Almost any change in how the organization is managed falls under the category of structural change. At General Telephone & Electronics Corporation, structural changes included a structural reorganization, new pay incentives, a revised performance appraisal system, and affirmative action programs. IBM's change from a functional to a product structure was a structural change. The implementation of a no-smoking policy is usually considered a structural or an administrative change.

Successful structural change is accomplished through a top-down approach, which is distinct from technology change (bottom up) and new products (horizontal).[51] Structural change is top down because the expertise for administrative improvements originates at the middle and upper levels of the organization. The champions for structural change are middle and top managers. Lower-level technical specialists have little interest or expertise in administrative procedures. If organization structure causes negative consequences for lower-level employees, complaints and dissatisfaction alert managers to a problem. Employee dissatisfaction is an internal force for change. The need for change is perceived by higher managers, who then take the initiative to propose and implement it.

The top-down process does not mean that coercion is the best implementation tactic. Implementation tactics include education, participation, and negotiation with employees. Unless there is an emergency, managers should not force structural

culture/people change
A change in employees' values, norms, attitudes, beliefs, and behavior.

change on employees. They may hit a resistance wall, and the change will fail. This is exactly what happened at the company for which Mary Kay Ash worked before she started her own cosmetics business. The owner learned that even a top-down change in commission rate needs to incorporate education and participation to succeed:

> I worked for a company whose owner decided to revise the commission schedule paid to his sales managers. . . . To an audience of 50 sales managers he announced that the 2 percent override they were presently earning on their units' sales production was to be reduced to 1 percent. "However," he said, "in lieu of that 1 percent, you will receive a very nice gift for each new person you recruit and train."
>
> At that point a sales manager stood up and let him have it with both barrels. "How dare you do this to us? Why, even 2 percent wasn't enough. But cutting our overrides in half and offering us a crummy gift for appeasement insults our intelligence." With that she stormed out of the room. And every other sales manager for that state followed her—all 50 of them. In one fell swoop the owner had lost his entire sales organization in that region—the best in the country. I had never seen such an overwhelming rejection of a change of this kind in my entire life![52]

Top-down change means that initiation of the idea occurs at upper levels and is implemented downward. It does not mean that lower-level employees are not educated about the change or allowed to participate in it.

CULTURE/PEOPLE CHANGES

A **culture/people change** refers to a change in employees' values, norms, attitudes, beliefs, and behavior. Changes in culture and people pertain to how employees think; these are changes in mind-set rather than

technology, structure, or products. People change pertains to just a few employees, such as when a handful of middle managers is sent to a training course to improve their leadership skills. Culture change pertains to the organization as a whole, such as when Union Pacific Railroad changed its basic mind-set by becoming less bureaucratic and focusing employees on customer service and quality through teamwork and employee participation.[53] The Leading the Management Revolution box describes one company's innovative approach to culture change within an industry. Robert McDonald set out to change not just his business, but the way insurance companies operate. Training is the most frequently used tool for changing the organization's mind-set. A company may offer training programs to large blocks of employees on subjects such as teamwork, listening skills, quality circles, and participative management. Training programs will be discussed further in Chapter 11 on human resource management.

Another major approach to changing people and culture is organizational development. This has evolved as a separate field that is devoted to large-scale organizational change.

Organizational Development

Organizational development (OD) is the application of behavioral science knowledge to improve an organization's health and effectiveness through its ability to cope with environmental changes, improve internal relationships, and increase problem-solving capabilities.[54] Organizational development improves working relationships among employees.

The following are three types of current problems that OD can help managers address.[55]

1 *Mergers/acquisitions.* The disappointing financial results of many mergers and acquisitions are caused by the failure of executives to determine whether the administrative style and corporate culture of the two companies "fit." Executives

Weirton Steel Corporation is breaking away from the traditional mind-set in the tough steel industry. Four hundred employee-owners created Weirton's "Vision for Success" that encourages empowerment and employee participation in problem solving and decision making. This change in *culture and people values* empowers employees to respond quickly to changes in automation and market demand. The 120 Employee Participation Groups eagerly take advantage of the cross-functional workshops such as the one pictured here and free computer skills courses offered by West Virginia Community College.

may concentrate on potential synergies in technology, products, marketing, and control systems but fail to recognize that two firms may have widely different values, beliefs, and practices. These differences create stress and anxiety for employees, and these negative emotions affect future performance. Cultural differences should be evaluated during the acquisition process, and OD experts can be used to smooth the integration of two firms.

2 *Organizational decline/revitalization.* Organizations undergoing a period of decline and revitalization experience a variety of problems, including a low level of trust, lack of innovation, high turnover, and high levels of conflict and stress. The period of transition requires opposite behaviors, including confronting stress, creating open communication, and fostering creative innovation to emerge with high levels of productivity. OD techniques can contribute greatly to cultural revitalization by managing conflicts, fostering commitment, and facilitating communication.

organizational development (OD)
The application of behavioral science techniques to improve an organization's health and effectiveness through its ability to cope with environmental changes, improve internal relationships, and increase problem-solving capabilities.

LEADING THE MANAGEMENT REVOLUTION
LIFEUSA

Robert McDonald started Minneapolis-based LifeUSA in the late 1980s not to build another life insurance business, but rather to "create a new way of business." "We're trying to revolutionize this industry," he said, with a "completely different approach in terms of both products and culture." His vision is for LifeUSA to do for insurance what Federal Express did for deliveries.

Despite LifeUSA's growth from nothing to $1 billion in 1995 premiums, it has remained remarkably lean, with a youthful workforce of about 400. Changing the rules of the game, his business model is defined by the three principles of shared ownership, organizational transparency, and speed. Employees who help grow the company share in the value they create, with an industry-innovative 20 percent of agent commissions offered in stock options. President Maggie Hughes says it takes 18 months for workers to "get it" that they own the company. LifeUSA teaches "people to think for themselves," as well as teaching employees about financial statistics, wealth creation, investment strategies, and customer service.

Transparency means that all information is passed up and down the company. But workers don't rely as much on the often-isolating E-mail as they do on voice mail, because it "creates more personal relationships." E-mail is used for bulletin boards and discussion groups.

LifeUSA wants to be a literally *fast* company and guarantees agents' commissions to be paid within 24 hours, customer policies issued within 24 hours, and agents' questions answered within 48 minutes.

McDonald is careful to realize the tenuousness of the company. "We've made a good start," he says. "The key is to maintain the openness and the candor as we get larger."

SOURCE: Kate A. Kane, "LifeUSA's Number One Policy—Speed," *Fast Company,* Aug./Sept. 1996, 22–24.

---

team building
A type of OD intervention that enhances the cohesiveness of departments by helping members learn to function as a team.

survey feedback
A type of OD intervention in which questionnaires on organizational climate and other factors are distributed among employees and the results are reported back to them by a change agent.

3 *Conflict management.* Conflict can occur at any time and place within a healthy organization. For example, a product team for the introduction of a new software package was formed at a computer company. Made up of strong-willed individuals, the team made little progress because members would not agree on project goals. At a manufacturing firm, salespeople promised delivery dates to customers that were in conflict with shop supervisor priorities for assembling customer orders. In a publishing company, two managers disliked each other intensely. They argued at meetings, lobbied politically against each other, and hurt the achievement of both departments. Organizational development efforts can help solve these kinds of conflicts.

Organizational development can be used to solve the types of problems just described and many others. Specialized OD techniques have been developed for these applications.

OD Activities. A number of OD activities have emerged in recent years. Some of the most popular and effective are as follows.

1 *Team-building activities.* **Team building** enhances the cohesiveness and success of organizational groups and teams. For example, a series of OD exercises can be used with members of cross-departmental teams to help them learn to act and function as a team. An OD expert can work with team members to increase their communication skills, facilitate their ability to confront one another, and accept common goals.

2 *Survey-feedback activities.* **Survey feedback** begins with a questionnaire distributed to employees on values, climate, participation, leadership, and group cohesion within their organization.[56] After the survey is completed, an OD consultant meets with groups of employees to provide feedback about their responses and the problems identified.[57] Employees are engaged in problem solving based on the data.

3 *Intergroup activities.* These activities include retreats and workshops to improve the effectiveness of groups or departments that must work together. The focus is on helping employees develop the skills to resolve conflicts, increase coordination, and develop better ways of working together.

4 *Process-consultation activities.* Organizational development consultants help managers understand the human processes within their organization and how to manage them. Managers learn to think in terms of cultural values, leadership, communication, and intergroup cooperation.

5 *Symbolic leadership activities.* This approach helps managers learn to use the techniques for cultural change described in Chapter 3, including public statements, symbols, ceremonies, and slogans. For example, public statements that define a pathfinding vision and cultural values account for the success of such companies as Disney, Dana, and Wal-Mart. Managers can signal appropriate behavior through symbols and ceremonies, such as when Roy Ash had several of AM International's copying machines removed to signal the need for less paperwork. Harold Geneen, president of ITT, captured the new value for his corporation with the slogan: "Search for the Unshakeable Facts," which helped do away with smoke screens and political games.

OD Steps. Consider the cultural change at Westinghouse Canada's manufacturing facility at Airdrie, Alberta. Cycle time for made-to-order motor-controlled devices was reduced from 17 weeks to 1 week. One major requirement for reducing the time was to change the mind-set of both managers and workers to give workers more discretion. Instead of waiting for approval from superiors, production employees now talk directly with customers and suppliers to solve their problems.[58]

Organizational development experts acknowledge that corporate culture and human behavior are relatively stable and that company-wide changes, such as those at Westinghouse Canada, require major effort. The theory underlying organizational development proposes three distinct steps for achieving behavioral and attitudinal change: (1) unfreezing, (2) changing, and (3) refreezing.[59]

In the first step, **unfreezing,** participants must be made aware of problems and be willing to change. This step is often associated with *diagnosis,* which uses an outside expert called a *change agent.* The **change agent** is an OD specialist who performs a systematic diagnosis of the organization and identifies work-related problems. He or she gathers and analyzes data through personal interviews, questionnaires, and observations of meetings. The diagnosis helps determine the extent of organizational problems and helps unfreeze managers by making them aware of problems in their behavior.

The second step, **changing,** occurs when individuals experiment with new behavior and learn new skills to be used in the workplace. This is sometimes known as *intervention,* during which the change agent implements a specific plan for training managers and employees. This plan may include team-building, survey feedback, intergroup, process-consultation, and symbolic leadership activities as described earlier.

The third step, **refreezing,** occurs when individuals acquire new attitudes or values and are rewarded for them by the organization. The impact of new behaviors is evaluated and reinforced. The change agent supplies new data that show positive changes in performance. Senior executives can reward positive behavioral changes by employees. Managers and employees also participate in refresher courses to maintain and reinforce the new behaviors.

The spirit of what OD tries to accomplish with culture/people change was illustrated in Honeywell's use of OD to change the corporate culture from an autocratic to a participative mind-set.

unfreezing
A step in the diagnosis stage of organizational development in which participants are made aware of problems in order to increase their willingness to change their behavior.

change agent
An OD specialist who contracts with an organization to facilitate change.

changing
A step in the intervention stage of organizational development in which individuals experiment with new workplace behavior.

refreezing
A step in the reinforcement stage of organizational development in which individuals acquire a desired new skill or attitude and are rewarded for it by the organization.

HONEYWELL

For many years, a Honeywell division had been an authoritarian entity. Then top managers believed that individuals could contribute to effectiveness if middle- and lower-level managers would allow them to participate more fully:

> Many organizations today want to break out of the beat-'em-up school of management and move toward a more participative management style. But like abused children who grow up to become abusive parents, managers raised in a less enlightened manner may have difficulty operating under a new set of rules.
>
> At Honeywell, we have been working to change from what I call the Patton style of management to a more collaborative way of operating. The way we manage people is still less than perfect. But now our employees can have a real share of the action rather than feeling blocked or frustrated by a rigid bureaucracy.[60]

The implementation of this new way of thinking was not easy. Managers and employees alike had to think in a different way and approach one another with respect and a desire for a positive working relationship. The new values that Honeywell wished to inculcate included the following management principles, published and circulated among all of its employees:

1 Productivity is a responsibility shared by both management and employees.
2 Broadened employee participation in the decision-making process will be fostered.
3 Teamwork, mutual respect, and a sense of ownership will be promoted at all divisional levels.
4 A positive climate for career growth will be supported throughout the division.
5 Work life and personal life have interacting requirements that will be recognized.

Through OD, Honeywell created a higher level of participation for employees. Managers learned to think of employees as whole people, not as instruments of production. ■

SUMMARY AND MANAGEMENT SOLUTION

Change is inevitable in organizations. This chapter discussed the techniques available for managing the change process. The trend today is toward the learning organization, which embraces continuous learning and change. Managers should think of change as having four elements—the forces for change, the perceived need for change, the initiation of change, and the implementation of change. Forces for change can originate either within or outside the firm, and managers are responsible for monitoring events that may require a planned organizational response. Techniques for initiating changes include designing the organization for creativity, encouraging change agents, and establishing new-venture teams. The final step is implementation. Force field analysis is one technique for diagnosing restraining forces, which often can be removed. Managers also should draw on the implementation tactics of communication, participation, negotiation, coercion, or top management support.

This chapter also discussed specific types of change. Technology changes are accomplished through a bottom-up approach that utilizes experts close to the technology. Successful new-product introduction requires horizontal linkage among marketing, research and development, manufacturing, and perhaps other departments. Structural changes tend to be initiated in a top-down fashion, because upper managers are the administrative experts and champion these ideas for approval and implementation. Culture/people change pertains to the skills, behaviors, and attitudes of employees. Organizational development is an important approach to changes in people's mind-set and corporate culture. The OD process entails three steps—unfreezing (diagnosis of the problem),

the actual change (intervention), and refreezing (reinforcement of new attitudes and behaviors). Popular OD techniques include team building, survey feedback, intergroup activities, and process consultation.

These concepts apply to the General Stair company discussed in the chapter opening problem. Saby Behar and his three managers needed to make important changes in the company or risk losing market share or worse. Behar suggested a money-back guarantee. In this business, on-time delivery was important, for the builders could not go on to other things such as second floors or some bathrooms until the stairs were complete. Learning from Domino's Pizza's promise to deliver within 30 minutes or pay the customer, Behar decided to offer a guarantee that required payment from the company if it goofs. Consultant Christopher W. L. Hart says that such an *extraordinary* guarantee can "transform the company from bottom to top . . . [and] is like turning up the power on a hose. Suddenly, you see leaks you never saw before." When there is a money-back guarantee, ironically, operating costs usually go down, as it focuses efforts to empower employees to make sure the guarantee is met. Knowing that such a plan would create resistance to change, Behar spent several meetings just talking about change and what it would mean for the company. "I tried to preempt some of their emotions," he said. They asked

one another questions such as: What will it feel like to change? Where will the gains be either professionally or personally? Though these discussions did not remove the qualms about the guarantee, they at least helped the managers begin to talk about whether a guarantee might work. In order to do this, they realized, they would need to revamp the communications between field reps, giving them cellular phones, two-way radios, and voice mail/beeper capabilities. Faxes would be used more, to validate promises and progress with builders. Within a month, they brought in the rest of the employees to the change discussions. What they learned was that the whole company had to change—distribution, compensation, as well as communication. Meetings were spent asking a lot of questions and hammering out the details of needed changes. Rather than a complete money-back guarantee, they settled on a fine of $50 per day for late stairs. The employees suggested going from salary to piecework. Did all this employee involvement pay off? When the new guarantee was in place by September, labor costs were slashed 30 percent, but workers were earning 60 percent more. Productivity was up 300 percent. And by May 1995, after nine months, they had only paid out five $50 vouchers. General Stair is a model on how to change effectively.[61]

DISCUSSION QUESTIONS

1 A manager of an international chemical company said that very few new products in her company were successful. What would you advise the manager to do to help increase the company's success rate?

2 What are internal and external forces for change? Which force do you think is the major cause of organizational change?

3 Carefully planned change often is assumed to be effective. Do you think unplanned change can sometimes be beneficial to an organization? Discuss.

4 Why do organizations experience resistance to change? What techniques can managers use to overcome resistance?

5 Explain force field analysis. Analyze the driving and restraining forces for a change with which you have been associated.

6 Define the roles associated with an idea champion. Why are idea champions so essential to the initiation of change?

7 To what extent would changes in technology affect products and vice versa? Compare the process for changing technology and that for product change.

8 Given that structural change is often made top down, should coercive implementation techniques be used?

9 Do the underlying values of organizational development differ from assumptions associated with other types of change? Discuss.

10 Compare and contrast team-building and survey-feedback techniques for OD intervention.

MANAGEMENT EXERCISES

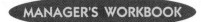

MANAGER'S WORKBOOK

Innovation Climate

In order to examine differences in level of innovation encouragement in organizations, you will be asked to rate two different organizations. You may choose one in which you have worked or the university. The other should be someone else's workplace, either a family member, friend, or acquaintance. Therefore, you will have to interview that person to answer the questions below. You should put your own answers in column A, your interviewee's answers in column B, and finally, what you think would be the "ideal" in column C.

Use the following scale of 1–5: 1 = don't agree at all to 5 = agree completely

Innovation Measures

Item of measure	Column A Your organization	Column B Other organization	Column C Your ideal
1 Creativity is encouraged here.*			
2 People are allowed to solve the same problems in different ways.*			
3 I get free time to pursue creative ideas.#			
4 The organization publicly recognizes and also rewards those who are innovative.#			
5 Our organization is flexible and always open to change.*			
Below score items on the opposite scale: 1 = agree completely through 5 = don't agree at all			
6 The primary job of people here is to follow orders which come from the top.*			
7 The best way to get along here is to think and act like the others.*			
8 This place seems to be more concerned with the status quo than with change.*			
9 People are rewarded more if they don't rock the boat.#			
10 New ideas are great, but we don't have enough people or money to carry them out.#			

NOTE: * items indicate the organization's innovation climate.
items show "resource support."

1 What comparisons about innovation climates can you make from these two organizations?
2 How might productivity differ when there is either a climate that supports innovation versus a climate that does not support innovation?

3 Which type of place would you rather work at? Why?

SOURCE: Adapted from Susanne G. Scott and Reginald A. Bruce, "Determinants of Innovative Behavior: A Path Model of Individual Innovation in the Workplace," *Academy of Management Journal* 37 (3), 1994, 580–607.

MANAGER'S WORKBOOK

Adaptors and Innovators

1 Complete the creative style assessment. Then read the background on A-I Theory and answer the questions at the end of that section.

2 Based on assessment scores, instructor divides class into groups of four to eight persons based on their A-I scores. Students will be grouped with those of similar range on the A-I scale.

3 Each group completes the following assignment: Develop a two- or three-minute presentation (depending on the number of groups—if there are more groups, the two-minute limit may be reasonable) for a product or process that would make some major improvement in the world or for some company. This may be an organization where one of your members works or it may be a fictitious organization. This is all the instruction you will receive on this assignment.

4 Each group gives its presentation to the class.

5 Instructor leads a discussion on adaptors and innovators and the differences, as well as how the various groups exhibited characteristics of their style.

Creative Style Assessment
Circle a or b, depending on which answer is generally more descriptive of your behavior.

1 When I am working on a task, I tend to
   a. go along with a consistent level of work.
   b. work with high energy at times, with periods of low energy.

2 If there is a problem, I usually am the one who thinks of
   a. a number of solutions, some of which are unusual.
   b. one or two solutions that are methods other people would generally accept.

3 When keeping records, I tend to
   a. be very careful about documentation.
   b. be more haphazard about documentation.

4 In meetings, I am often seen as one who
   a. keeps the group functioning well and maintains order.
   b. challenges ideas or authority.

5 My thinking style could be most accurately described as
   a. linear thinker, going from a to b to c.
   b. thinking like a grasshopper, going from one idea to another.

6 If I have to run a group or a project, I
   a. have the general idea and let people figure out how to do the tasks.
   b. try to figure out goals, time lines, and expected outcomes.

7 If there are rules to follow, I tend to
   a. generally follow them.
   b. question whether those rules are meaningful or not.

8 I like to be around people who are
   a. stable and solid.
   b. bright, stimulating, and change frequently.

9 In my office or home, things are
   a. here and there in various piles.
   b. laid out neatly or at least in a reasonable order.

10 I usually feel the way people have done things in the past
   a. must have some merit and comes from accumulated wisdom.
   b. can almost always be improved upon.

Score one point for "I" and "A" as follows:

I	A
1b	1a
2a	2b
3b	3a
4b	4a
5b	5a
6a	6b
7b	7a
8b	8a
9a	9b
10b	10a

Total for I: **Total for A:**

Circle I or A below, depending on which score is higher.

If A is higher, you are adaptive (A).

If I is higher, you are innovative (I).

Subtract I from A.
Take the absolute value and place it here: _____

Scoring styles:

If you are I or A and the difference between A and I is 1 or less, you are a MID **I/A** STYLE.

If you are A and the difference between A and I is 2–4, you are a MODERATE **A** STYLE.

If you are A and the difference between the two is 5–7, you are a MID-RANGE **A** STYLE.

If you are A and the difference between A and I is 8–10, you are a STRONG **A** STYLE.

If you are an I and the difference between A and I is 2–4, you are a MODERATE **I** STYLE.

If you are an I and the difference is 5–7, you are a MID-RANGE **I** STYLE.

If you are an I and the difference is 8–10, you are a STRONG **I** STYLE.

Background on A-I Theory

A-I theory measures creative style. Until recently, most work on creativity defined it as one type of behavior, that of a preponderance of many new and unusual ideas. However, Kirton (1976) developed an instrument to measure two styles of creativity—adaptive and innovative. Those with an adaptive style work within the situation as it is given and try to make it more efficient, reliable, and precise. People with the innovative style, though, are paradigm breakers and are always looking for a new way to do something. As a result, they often rock the boat and may have more difficulty being part of an ongoing team.

Therefore, both adaptors and innovators are creative, only in different ways, with different styles. Adaptors ask the question, "How can I make this better?" while innovators ask the question, "How can I make this different?"

Below are listed some characteristics of adaptors and innovators. See if the characteristics match how you see yourself and others.

SOURCE: Dorothy Marcic, *Organizational Behavior: Experiences and Cases* 4/e (South-Western Publishing, 1995), 378–381. Reproduced with permission.

Behavior Descriptions of Adaptors and Innovators

Adaptors	Innovators
Characterized by precision, reliability, efficiency, methodicalness, prudence, discipline, conformity.	Seen as undisciplined, thinking tangentially, approaching tasks from unsuspected angles.
Concerned with resolving problems rather than finding them. Seeks solutions in tried and understood ways.	Could be said to discover problems and discover avenues of solution.
Reduces problems by improvement, greater efficiency, with maximum continuity, stability.	Queries problems' concommitant assumptions; manipulates problems.
Seen as sound, conforming, safe, dependable.	Is catalyst to settled groups, irreverent of their consensual views; seen as abrasive, creating dissonance.
Liable to make goals of means.	In pursuit of goals, treats accepted means with little regard.
Seems impervious to boredom, seems able to maintain routine (systems maintenance) high accuracy in long spells of detailed work.	Capable of detailed work only for short bursts. Quick to delegate routine tasks.
Is an authority within given structures.	Tends to take control in unstructured situations.
Challenges rules rarely, cautiously when assured strong support.	Often challenges rules, has little respect for customs.
Tends to have self-doubt. Needs consensus to maintain certitude and authority; compliant. Vulnerable to social pressure.	Appears to have low self-doubt when generating ideas, not outwardly conforming.
Is essential in the functioning of the institution all the time, but occasionally needs to be "dug out."	In the institution, is ideal in unscheduled crises, or better still to help avoid them if she or he can be controlled.
When collaborating with innovators, supplies stability and order.	When collaborating with adaptors, supplies task orientations, continuity to the partnership.
Sensitive to people, maintains group cohesion and cooperation.	Insensitive to people, often threatens group cohesion and cooperation.
Provides a safe base for the innovator's riskier operations.	Provides the dynamics to bring about periodic radical change, without which institutions tend to ossify.

SOURCE : Copyright © 1976 by the American Psychological Association. Reprinted with permission.

MANAGER'S WORKSHOP

An Ancient Tale

1. *Read the introduction and case study and answer the questions.*
2. *In groups of three or four, discuss your answers.*
3. *Groups report to the whole class and the instructor leads a discussion on the issues raised.*

Introduction

To understand, analyze, and improve organizations, we must carefully think through the issue of who is responsible for what activities in different organizational settings. Often we hold responsible someone who has no control over the outcome, or we fail to teach or train someone who could make the vital difference.

To explore this issue, the following exercise could be conducted on either an individual or group basis. It provides an opportunity to see how different individuals assign responsibility for an event. It is also a good opportunity to discuss the concept of organizational boundaries (what is the organization, who is in or out, etc.).

Case Study

You should read the short story and respond quickly to the first three questions. Then take a little more time on questions four through six. The results, criteria, and implications could then be discussed in groups.

Long ago in an ancient kingdom there lived a princess who was very young and very beautiful. The princess, recently married, lived in a large and luxurious castle with her husband, a powerful and wealthy lord. The young princess was not content, however, to sit and eat strawberries by herself while her husband took frequent and long journeys to neighboring kingdoms. She felt neglected and soon became quite unhappy. One day, while she was alone in the castle gardens, a handsome vagabond rode out of the forest bordering the castle. He spied the beautiful princess, quickly won her heart, and carried her away with him.

Following a day of dalliance, the young princess found herself ruthlessly abandoned by the vagabond. She then discovered that the only way back to the castle led through the bewitched forest of the wicked sorcerer. Fearing to venture into the forest alone, she sought out her kind and wise godfather. She explained her plight, begged forgiveness of the godfather, and asked his assistance in returning home before her husband returned. The godfather, however, surprised and shocked at her behavior, refused forgiveness and denied her any assistance. Discouraged but still determined, the princess disguised her identity and sought the help of the most noble of all the kingdom's knights. After hearing the sad story, the knight pledged his unfailing aid—for a modest fee. But alas, the princess had no money and the knight rode away to save other damsels.

The beautiful princess had no one else from whom she might seek help, and decided to brave the great peril alone. She followed the safest path she knew, but when she was almost through the forest, the wicked sorcerer spied her and caused her to be devoured by the fire-breathing dragon.

1. Who was inside the organization and who was outside? Where were the boundaries?
2. Who is most responsible for the death of the beautiful princess?
3. Who is next most responsible? Least responsible?
4. What are your criteria for the above decisions?

Check one character in each column.

Character	Most Responsible	Next Most Responsible	Least Responsible
Princess			
Husband			
Vagabond			
Godfather			
Knight			
Sorcerer			

5 What interventions would you suggest to prevent a recurrence?

6 What are the implications for *organizational development and change?*

SOURCE: J. B. Ritchie and Paul Thompson, *Organization and People: Readings, Cases and Exercises in Organizational Behavior.* (South-Western Publishing, 1980), 68–70. Reproduced with permission.

SURF THE 'NET

In order to be part of the innovation of the Internet, you should begin to think about having your own Web page. Before you do so, read the list of "DOs" and "DON'Ts" below. Then find examples on the Web of people who have done either a Do or a Don't. Find at least one example for each Do and Don't. One Web page may have more than one example. Fill out the table below.

Rules for URLs

DON'T:

I Use graphics or pictures of your family members or pets—BORING!

2 Forget to give users navigational cues such as site map, table of contents, or some search help. Don't assume they know anything about your site.

3 Overdo extraneous information. Keep the top of the page to 40K. Just remember most people aren't as interested in the details of your life as you are (or maybe your mother is).

4 Abandon your page for months. Remember, we are living in an age where nanoseconds are the unit of time measure. If you leave your page untouched more than a month, it spells STALE and GHOST TOWN.

DO:

I Make sure your content is engaging, which will vary according to your interests. But the more you can narrow your focus, the better to attract people who share it.

2 Keep your graphics usable. Focus on issues like bandwidth, rather than snazzy and large images. Think of the user rather than your own fun.

3 Let people know how to contact you, to ask questions, give feedback. Include an E-mail address.

4 Put in the effort to provide fresh links, so that regulars will come back—with their friends.

Rule	Description and address of Web page that is example of DON'T or DO
DON'T:	
I Use family or pets	
2 Forget navigational cues	
3 Use extraneous information	
4 Leave page untouched for long periods	
DO:	
I Have interesting content	
2 Have usable graphics	
3 Give E-mail address	
4 Provide fresh links	

SOURCE: Gina Imperato, "You are your URL," *Fast Company,* Aug./Sept. 1996, 44–46.

ETHICAL DILEMMA

Research for Sale

Lucinda Jackson walked slowly back to R&D Laboratory 4 at Reed Pharmaceuticals. She was stunned. Top management was planning to sell her entire team project to Trichem Industries in an effort to raise the capital Reed needed to buy a small, competing drug company. Two years ago, when she was named project administrator for the cancer treatment program, Jackson was assured that the program was the highest priority at Reed. She was allowed to recruit the best and the brightest in the research center in their hunt for an effective drug to treat lung cancer. There had been press releases and personal appearances at stockholder meetings.

When she first approached a colleague, Len Rosen, to become head chemist on the project, he asked her whether Reed was in cancer research for the long haul or if they were just grabbing headlines. Based on what she had been told by the vice president in charge of R&D, Jackson assured him that their project was protected for as long as it took. Now, a short two years later, she learned that not only was Reed backing out but also that the project was being sold as a package to an out-of-state firm. There were no jobs at Reed being offered as alternatives for the team. They were only guaranteed jobs if they moved with the project to Trichem.

Jackson felt betrayed, but she knew it was nothing compared to what the other team members would feel.

Rosen was a ten-year veteran at Reed, and his wife and family had deep roots in the local community. A move would be devastating to them. Jackson had a few friends in top management, but she didn't know if any would back her if she fought the planned sale.

What Do You Do?

1 Approach top management with the alternative of selling the project and sending the team temporarily to train staff at Trichem but allowing them to return to different projects at Reed after the transition. After all, they promised a commitment to the project.
2 Wait for the announcement of the sale of the project and then try to secure as much support as possible for the staff and families in their relocation: moving expense reimbursement, job placement for spouses, etc.
3 Tell a few people, such as Rosen, and then combine forces with them and threaten to quit if the project is sold. Make attempts to scuttle the sale to Trichem before it happens, and perhaps even leak the news to the press. Perhaps the threat of negative publicity will cause top management to reconsider.

SOURCE: Reprinted with permission from *Business Ethics Magazine*, 52 South 10th Street #10, Minneapolis, MN 55403. 612-962-4700

CASE FOR CRITICAL ANALYSIS

United Electric Controls Company

Maker of industrial temperature and pressure controls, United Electric Controls Company was a conservative, 60-year-old, family-run company. United Electric's autocratic management style and old manufacturing methods seemed adequate to meet market needs. But in 1987, the company suffered its worst-ever sales loss, shaking everyone up.

How did United Electric respond? Chairman Robert Reis and President David Reis launched a massive cultural revamping. The first step was to abandon the old manufacturing approach and give new emphasis to Japanese methods of *pakayoke* (mistake proofing) and *kanban* (inventory control). For the centerpiece of their new

program, the Reis brothers launched a program to encourage employees to champion their own ideas. Vice president Bruce Hamilton admitted, "We had developed a structure, over time, that was designed to resist employee participation." The new structure was based on the concept that employees are the company's best resource and was designed to empower those employees.

Management devised a program that actively sought, supported, and rewarded employee ideas. The idea-harvesting plans included (1) a value-ideas program that offers a $100 cash bonus for each usable idea and awards chances in a drawing for unused suggestions; (2) action centers involving employee-initiated formation of short-term groups that meet during work hours in conference

rooms to find solutions to specific problems; and (3) CEDAC (cause and effect diagram with the addition of cards), a problem-solving method using long-term teams to analyze and determine causes of major problems that affect several departments. All possible causes were charted and subjected to rigorous study over a period of months.

The results of these efforts were astonishing. The innovative culture is working, as indicated by a tidal wave of innovative ideas. In 1990 alone, 90 percent of the Watertown, Massachusetts, employees submitted ideas, compared to a mere 20 employee suggestions in the entire 20 years prior to the program. By 1991 United Electric's sales had risen by $8 million over 1987 sales. The experience of United Electric illustrates the power of management-facilitated innovation.

Questions

1 Did the changes taking place at United Electric follow the four stages of forces, need, initiation, and implementation? Explain.

2 What was the major type of change—technology, product, structure, or culture/people—in this case? To what extent does the primary change have secondary effects on other types of change at United Electric?

3 What techniques were used for change implementation? Would you recommend additional techniques to implement the new culture and philosophy at United Electric?

SOURCE: Based on Joshua Hyatt, "Ideas at Work," *Inc.,* May 1991, 59–66.

ENDNOTES

1 Joshua Hyatt, "Guaranteed Growth," *Inc.,* Sept. 1995, 69–78.

2 Richard L. Daft, "Bureaucratic vs. Nonbureaucratic Structure in the Process of Innovation and Change," in *Perspectives in Organizational Sociology: Theory and Research,* ed. Samuel B. Bacharach (Greenwich, Conn.: JAI Press, 1982), 129–166.

3 This discussion is based on Richard L. Daft, *Organization Theory and Design,* 5th ed. (St. Paul, Minn.: West, 1995); and Don Hellriegel and John W. Slocum, Jr., *Management,* 7th ed. (Southwestern, 1996).

4 Tom Broersma, "In Search of the Future," *Training and Development,* January 1995, 38–43.

5 Andre L. Delbecq and Peter K. Mills, "Managerial Practices That Enhance Innovation," *Organizational Dynamics* 14 (summer 1985), 24–34.

6 Ira Magaziner and Mark Tatinkin, *The Silent War: Inside the Global Business Battles Shaping America's Future* (New York: Random House, 1989).

7 Sharon Nelton, "How a Pennsylvania Company Makes the Sweet Sounds of Innovation," *Nation's Business,* December 1991, 16.

8 Andrew H. Van de Ven, Harold Angle, and Marshall Scott Poole, *Research on the Management of Innovation* (Cambridge, Mass.: Ballinger, 1989).

9 Virginia de Leon, "Cruise Russia—For the Kids," *The Seattle Times,* April 3, 1996; Ed Fischbein, "Practicing Peaceful Medicine," *Hemispheres Magazine,* Nov. 1996, 27–30.

10 Attributed to Gregory Bateson in Andrew H. Van de Ven, "Central Problems in the Management of Innovation," *Management Science* 32 (1986), 595.

11 Charles Pearlman, "A Theoretical Model for Creativity," *Education* 103 (1983), 294–305; and Robert R. Godfrey, "Tapping Employees' Creativity," *Supervisory Management* (February 1986), 16–20.

12 Gordon Vessels, "The Creative Process: An Open-Systems Conceptualization," *Journal of Creative Behavior* 16 (1982), 185–196; and Pearlman, "A Theoretical Model."

13 James Brian Quinn, "Managing Innovation: Controlled Chaos," *Harvard Business Review* 63 (May–June 1985), 73–84; Howard H. Stevenson and David E. Gumpert, "The Heart of Entrepreneurship," *Harvard Business Review* 63 (March–April 1985), 85–94; and Marsha Sinetar, "Entrepreneurs, Chaos, and Creativity—Can Creative People Really Survive Large Company Structure?" *Sloan Management Review* 6 (winter 1985), 57–62.

14 Cynthia Browne, "Jest for Success," *Moonbeams,* August 1989, 3–5; and Rosabeth Moss Kanter, *The Change Masters* (New York: Simon and Schuster, 1983).

15 "Hands On: A Manager's Notebook," *Inc.,* January 1989, 106.

16 Magaly Olivero, "Some Wacko Ideas That Worked," *Working Woman,* September 1990, 147–148.

17 Bonnie McKeever, "How I Did It: Teaming Up to Cut Medical Costs," *Working Woman,* July 1992, 23–24.

18 Katy Koontz, "How to Stand Out from the Crowd," *Working Woman,* January 1988, 74–76.

19 Harold L. Angle and Andrew H. Van de Ven, "Suggestions for Managing the Innovation Journey," in *Research in the Management of Innovation: The Minnesota Studies,* ed. A. H. Van de Ven, H. L. Angle, and Marshall Scott Poole (Cambridge, Mass.: Ballinger/Harper & Row, 1989).

20 Christopher K. Bart, "New Venture Units: Use Them Wisely to Manage Innovation," *Sloan Management Review* (summer 1988), 35–43.

21 Peter F. Drucker, *Innovation and Entrepreneurship* (New York: Harper & Row, 1985).

22 Michael Tushman and David Nadler, "Organizing for Innovation," *California Management Review* 28 (spring 1986), 74–92.

23 Carl E. Larson and Frank M. J. LaFasto, *TeamWork* (Newbury Park, Calif.: Sage, 1989); and "How the PC Changed the Way IBM Thinks," *Business Week,* October 3, 1983, 86–90.

24 John Markoff, "Abe Peled's Secret Start-Up at IBM," *The New York Times,* December 8, 1991, 3–1, 6.

25 Russell Mitchell, "Masters of Innovation: How 3M Keeps Its New Products Coming," *Business Week*, April 10, 1989, 58–63.

26 "Teleflex Incorporated Annual Report," 1988, Limerick, Penn.

27 John P. Kotter and Leonard A. Schlesinger, "Choosing Strategies for Change," *Harvard Business Review* 57 (March–April 1979), 106–114.

28 G. Zaltman and Robert B. Duncan, *Strategies for Planned Change* (New York: Wiley Interscience, 1977).

29 Leonard M. Apcar, "Middle Managers and Supervisors Resist Moves to More Participatory Management," *The Wall Street Journal*, September 16, 1985, 25.

30 Dorothy Leonard-Barton and Isabelle Deschamps, "Managerial Influence in the Implementation of New Technology," *Management Science* 34 (1988), 1252–1265.

31 Kurt Lewin, *Field Theory in Social Science: Selected Theoretical Papers* (New York: Harper & Brothers, 1951).

32 Paul C. Nutt, "Tactics of Implementation," *Academy of Management Journal* 29 (1986), 230–261; Kotter and Schlesinger, "Choosing Strategies"; Richard L. Daft and Selwyn Becker, *Innovation in Organizations: Innovation Adoption in School Organizations* (New York: Elsevier, 1978); and Richard Beckhard, *Organization Development: Strategies and Models* (Reading, Mass.: Addison-Wesley, 1969).

33 Rob Muller, "Training for Change," *Canadian Business Review*, (spring 1995), 16–19.

34 Taggart F. Frost, "Creating a Teamwork-Based Culture within a Manufacturing Setting," *IM*, May–June 1994, 17–20.

35 Patty Watts, "Preston and the Teamsters Keep On Trucking," *Management Review* (March 1988), 22–24; and Alan Farnham, "The Trust Gap," *Fortune*, December 4, 1989, 56–78.

36 Apcar, "Middle Managers."

37 Jeremy Main, "The Trouble with Managing Japanese-Style," *Fortune*, April 2, 1984, 50–56.

38 Daft, *Organization Theory and Design*; and Tom Burns and G. M. Stalker, *The Management of Innovation* (London: Tavistock Publications, 1961).

39 Stratford P. Sherman, "How Philip Morris Diversified Right," *Fortune*, October 23, 1989, 120–129.

40 Robert Rose, "Kentucky Plant Workers Are Cranking Out Good Ideas," *The Wall Street Journal*, Aug. 13, 1996, B1.

41 Richard L. Daft, "A Dual-Core Model of Organizational Innovation," *Academy of Management Journal* 21 (1978), 193–210; and Kanter, *The Change Masters*.

42 Harold J. Leavitt, "Applied Organizational Change in Industry: Structural, Technical, and Human Approaches," in *New Perspectives in Organization Research*, ed. W. W. Cooper, H. J. Leavitt, and M. W. Shelly II (New York: Wiley, 1964), 55–74.

43 Edwin Mansfield, J. Rapoport, J. Schnee, S. Wagner, and M. Hamburger, *Research and Innovation in Modern Corporations* (New York: Norton, 1971).

44 Andrew H. Van de Ven, "Central Problems in the Management of Innovation," *Management Science* 32 (1986), 590–607; Daft, *Organization Theory*; and Science Policy Research Unit, University of Sussex, *Success and Failure in Industrial Innovation* (London: Centre for the Study of Industrial Innovation, 1972).

45 William L. Shanklin and John K. Ryans, Jr., "Organizing for High-Tech Marketing," *Harvard Business Review* 62 (November–December 1984), 164–171; and Arnold O. Putnam, "A Redesign for Engineering," *Harvard Business Review* 63 (May–June 1985), 139–144.

46 Daft, *Organization Theory*.

47 Keith H. Hammonds, "Teaching Discipline to Six-Year-Old Lotus," *Business Week*, July 4, 1988, 100–102.

48 Susan Caminiti, "A Quiet Superstar Rises in Retailing," *Fortune*, October 23, 1989, 167–174.

49 Brian Dumaine, "How Managers Can Succeed through Speed," *Fortune*, February 13, 1989, 54–59; and George Stalk, Jr., "Time—The Next Source of Competitive Advantage," *Harvard Business Review* (July–August 1988), 41–51.

50 Fariborz Damanpour, "The Adoption of Technological, Administrative, and Ancillary Innovations: Impact of Organizational Factors," *Journal of Management* 13 (1987), 675–688.

51 Daft, "Bureaucratic vs. Nonbureaucratic Structure."

52 Mary Kay Ash, *Mary Kay on People Management* (New York: Warner, 1984), 75.

53 Edgar H. Schein, "Organizational Culture," *American Psychologist* 45 (February 1990), 109–119; and Andrew Kupfer, "An Outsider Fires Up a Railroad," *Fortune*, December 18, 1989, 133–146.

54 Marshall Sashkin and W. Warner Burke, "Organization Development in the 1980s," *General Management* 13 (1987), 393–417; and Edgar F. Huse and Thomas G. Cummings, *Organization Development and Change*, 3d ed. (St. Paul, Minn.: West, 1985).

55 Paul F. Buller, "For Successful Strategic Change: Blend OD Practices with Strategic Management," *Organizational Dynamics* (winter 1988), 42–55; and Robert M. Fulmer and Roderick Gilkey, "Blending Corporate Families: Management and Organization Development in a Postmerger Environment," *The Academy of Management Executive* 2 (1988), 275–283.

56 David A. Nadler, *Feedback and Organizational Development: Using Data-Based Methods* (Reading, Mass.: Addison-Wesley, 1977).

57 Wendell L. French and Cecil H. Bell, Jr., *Organization Development: Behavioral Science Interventions for Organization Improvement*, 3d ed. (Englewood Cliffs, N.J.: Prentice-Hall, 1984).

58 Buller, "For Successful Strategic Change."

59 Kurt Lewin, "Frontiers in Group Dynamics: Concepts, Method, and Reality in Social Science," *Human Relations* 1 (1947), 5–41; and Huse and Cummings, *Organization Development*.

60 Richard J. Boyle, "Wrestling with Jelly Fish," *Harvard Business Review* (January–February 1984), 74–83.

61 Hyatt, "Guaranteed Growth."

Human Resource Management

LEARNING OBJECTIVES

After studying this chapter, you should be able to

■ Explain the role of human resource management in organizational strategic planning.

■ Describe federal legislation and societal trends that influence human resource management.

■ Describe how human resource professionals work with line managers to attract, develop, and maintain human resources in the organization.

■ Explain how organizations determine their future staffing needs through human resource planning.

■ Describe the tools managers use to recruit and select employees.

■ Describe how organizations develop an effective workforce through training and performance appraisal.

■ Explain how organizations maintain a workforce through the administration of wages and salaries, benefits, and terminations.

MANAGEMENT PROBLEM

His 24 years as a *Fortune* 100 executive gave Tom Melohn no direct manufacturing experience. Yet he bought financially troubled North American Tool & Die, hoping to turn it around. It would not be easy. The metal stamping and subassembly small business used older, labor-intensive machines, whereas its well-heeled, offshore competitors used highly automated technology to achieve efficiency and quality. Other domestic job shops were going out of business left and right, so Melohn needed a strategy to regain his company's competitiveness. North American's profits were marginal, its workforce unenthusiastic, and its prospects dim. Employee turnover was 27 percent annually. Absenteeism was at 10 percent, while a full 7 percent of production output was rejected. CEO Melohn agonized over how to change this debilitated company and realized his top priority was to find and keep good people.[1]

• What should Tom Melohn do to attract and retain high-quality employees? How can human resources be part of the strategy to restore North American's competitiveness?

human resource management (HRM)
Activities undertaken to attract, develop, and maintain an effective workforce within an organization.

As a vital player in corporate strategy, *HRM activities* include attracting, developing, and maintaining an effective workforce. One way The Stride Rite Corporation attracts and keeps good workers is by offering innovative *benefits*, such as the intergenerational, on-site day-care program pictured here. These unique day-care facilities bring together elderly people and children in a loving environment, relieving Stride Rite workers of the burden of finding quality day-care services for children or aging parents. In addition, the reading, play, and conversation bring special joy to participants at the center.

Tom Melohn's problem at North American Tool & Die illustrates the need for managing human resources. Melohn must develop the company's ability to recruit, train, and keep first-quality employees, as well as its ability to train and motivate seasonal workers. Without effective human resource management, company growth will be restricted and performance will continue to suffer. The term **human resource management (HRM)** refers to activities undertaken to attract, develop, and maintain an effective workforce within an organization. Companies such as General Electric and Hewlett-Packard have become famous for their philosophy about human resource management, which is the foundation of their success. HRM is equally important for not-for-profit organizations. For example, the Catholic church must address the crisis of the sharply declining number of priests. Unless the church can find ways to attract and keep priests, a mere 17,000 priests will be serving 75 million U.S. Catholics by the year 2005.[2]

Over the past decade, human resource management has shed its old "personnel" image and gained recognition as a vital player in corporate strategy. Despite its importance, company employees often do not understand HRM functions. For example, at Transamerica surveys indicated employees were not aware of the full range of human resource services or their access to those services. Effective education about HRM functions is essential.[3]

Human resource management consists of three parts. First, all managers are human resource managers. For example, at IBM every manager is expected to pay attention to the development and satisfaction of subordinates. Line managers use surveys, career planning, performance appraisal, and compensation to encourage commitment to IBM.[4] Second, employees are viewed as assets. Employees, not buildings and machinery, give a company a competitive advantage. In today's brutally competitive business environment, how a company manages its workforce may be the single most important factor in sustained competitive success.[5] Third, human resource management is a matching process, integrating the organization's goals with employees' needs. Employees should receive satisfaction equal to that of the company.

STRATEGIC GOALS OF HRM

In this chapter, we will examine the three primary goals of HRM as illustrated in Exhibit 11.1. These goals, which take place within the organizational environment, include competitive strategy, federal legislation, and societal trends. The three goals are to attract an effective workforce to the organization, develop the workforce to its potential, and maintain the workforce over the long term.[6] Achieving these goals requires skills in planning, forecasting, training, performance appraisal, wage and salary administration, benefit programs, and even termination. Each of the activities in Exhibit 11.1 will be discussed in this chapter. Most organizations employ human resource professionals to perform these functions. *Human resource specialists* focus on one of the

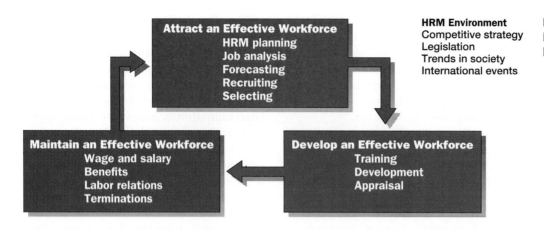

EXHIBIT 11.1
Human Resource Management Goals

HRM areas, such as recruitment of employees or administration of wage or benefit programs. *Human resource generalists* have responsibility in more than one HRM area.

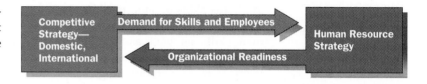

EXHIBIT 11.2
Interdependence of Organizational and Human Resource Strategy

SOURCE: Adapted from Cynthia A. Lengnick-Hall and Mark L. Lengnick-Hall, "Strategic Human Resources Management: A Review of the Literature and a Proposed Typology," *Academy of Management Review* 13 (1988), 454–470.

ENVIRONMENTAL INFLUENCES ON HRM

"Our strength is the quality of our people." "Our people are our most important resource."

These often-repeated statements by executives emphasize the importance of HRM. Human resource managers must find, recruit, train, nurture, and retain the best people. Human resource programs are designed to fit organizational needs, core values, and strategic goals. Without the proper personnel, the brightest idea or management fad—whether teams, quality circles, or flexible compensation—is doomed to failure. For these reasons, it is important that human resource executives be involved in competitive strategy. Human resource executives also interpret federal legislation and help detect issues and trends both in society and internationally.[7]

Competitive Strategy

The human resource management function has changed enormously over the years. In the 1920s, HRM was a low-level position charged with ensuring that procedures were developed for hiring and firing employees and with implementing benefit plans. By the 1950s unions were a major force, and the HRM manager was elevated to a senior position as chief negotiator. During the 1980s, unions began to decline, and top HRM managers became directly involved in corporate strategic management.[8]

Exhibit 11.2 illustrates the interdependence between company and human resource strategy. The organization's competitive strategy may include mergers and acquisitions, downsizing to increase efficiency, international operations, or the acquisition of automated production technology. These strategic decisions determine the demand for skills and employees. The human resource strategy, in turn, must include the correct employee makeup to implement the organization's strategy. In the 1990s strategic decisions more than ever have to be based on human resource considerations. For example, **downsizing** is the systematic reduction in the number of managers and employees to make a company more cost efficient and competitive.[9] When Boeing CEO Frank Shrontz predicted 1993

downsizing
The systematic reduction in the number of managers and employees to make a company more cost efficient and competitive.

discrimination
The hiring or promoting of applicants based on criteria that are not job relevant.

affirmative action
A policy requiring employers to take positive steps to guarantee equal employment opportunities for people within protected groups.

price wars and increased competition, the company targeted 25 percent to 30 percent cost reduction goals. Shrontz focused on the Defense & Space Group, eliminating 16,000 of 53,000 workers through attrition and transfers to other units, making effective use of human resource strategy.[10]

As another example, the introduction of flexible manufacturing systems such as those described in Chapter 9 have dramatically changed the need for workforce skill. These new machines require a highly skilled workforce, including interpersonal skills and the ability to work as a team. To make the strategic change to automated technology, the HRM department must upgrade the skills of shop machine operators and recruit new employees who have human skills as well as technical skills.[11] Chrysler spent a million hours training workers, many without a high school education, to run its new, highly automated Detroit plant using self-directed work teams. As aging factory workers retire, the company is recruiting workers with more education to replace them. Chrysler and other American automakers striving to create a workforce better suited to fierce global competition and rapid technological change want workers who can learn new skills quickly and require less supervision.[12]

Federal Legislation

Over the past 30 years, several federal laws have been passed to ensure equal employment opportunity (EEO). Key legislation and executive orders are summarized in Exhibit 11.3. The point of the laws is to stop discriminatory practices that are unfair to specific groups and to define enforcement agencies for these laws. EEO legislation attempts to balance the pay given to men and women; provide employment opportunities without regard to race, religion, national origin, and sex; ensure fair treatment for employees of all ages; and avoid discrimination against disabled individuals. More recent legislation pertains to illegal aliens.

The Equal Employment Opportunity Commission (EEOC) created by the Civil Rights Act of 1964 initiates investigations in response to complaints concerning discrimination. The EEOC is the major agency involved with employment discrimination. **Discrimination** occurs when some applicants are hired or promoted based on criteria that are not job relevant. For example, refusing to hire a black applicant for a job he is qualified to fill and paying a woman a lower wage than a man for the same work are discriminatory acts. When discrimination is found, remedies include providing back pay and taking affirmative action. **Affirmative action** requires that an employer take positive steps to guarantee equal employment opportunities for people within protected groups. An affirmative action plan is a formal document that can be reviewed by employees and enforcement agencies. The goal of organizational affirmative action is to reduce or eliminate internal inequities among affected employee groups.

However, in recent years, the perception of affirmative action as a means for "leveling the playing field" has been replaced by complaints of the program as a way of imposing quotas. Even the intended beneficiaries of affirmative action are divided on the need for continuation. For example, a 1995 poll revealed that 49 percent of women favor continuation of affirmative action while 41 percent oppose it.[13]

Failure to comply with equal employment opportunity legislation can result in substantial fines and penalties for employers. For example, Shoney's was accused of discrimination against black employees and job applicants. The class-action suit charged that company policy conspired to limit the number of black employees working in public areas of the restaurant. In 1992 the company agreed to pay $105 million to victims of its hiring, promotion, and firing policies, dating back to 1985.[14] Suits for discriminatory practices can cover a broad range of employee complaints, including "potty parity." One company, Pro-Line Cap

EXHIBIT 11.3
Major Federal Laws Related to Human Resource Management

Federal Law	Year	Provisions
Equal Opportunity/Discrimination Laws		
Civil Rights Act	1991	Provides for possible compensatory and punitive damages plus traditional back pay for cases of intentional discrimination brought under Title VII of the 1964 Civil Rights Act. Shifts the burden of proof to the employer.
Americans with Disabilities Act	1990	Prohibits discrimination against qualified individuals by employers on the basis of disability and demands that "reasonable accommodations" be provided for the disabled to allow performance of duties.
Immigration Reform and Control Act	1986	Prohibits employers from knowingly hiring illegal aliens and prohibits employment on the basis of national origin or citizenship.
Vietnam-Era Veterans Readjustment Act	1974	Prohibits discrimination against disabled veterans and Vietnam-era veterans and requires affirmative action.
Vocational Rehabilitation Act	1973	Prohibits discrimination based on physical or mental disability and requires that employees be informed about affirmative action plans.
Age Discrimination in Employment Act (ADEA)	1967 (amended 1978, 1986)	Prohibits age discrimination and restricts mandatory retirement.
Executive Orders 11246 and 11375	1965	Requires federal contractors to eliminate employment discrimination through affirmative action.
Civil Rights Act, Title VII	1964	Prohibits discrimination in employment on the basis of race, religion, color, sex, or national origin.
Compensation/Benefits Laws		
Family and Medical Leave Act	1993	Requires employers to provide up to 12 weeks unpaid leave for childbirth, adoption, or family emergencies.
Older Workers Benefit Protection Act	1990	Requires that waivers of ADEA (Age Discrimination in Employment) rights be voluntary and codifies the "equal benefit or equal cost" principle.
Pregnancy Discrimination Act	1978	Requires that women affected by pregnancy, childbirth, or related medical conditions be treated as all other employees for employment-related purposes, including benefits.
Employee Retirement Income Security Act (ERISA)	1974	Prescribes eligibility rules, vesting standards, and an insurance program for private pension plans.
Equal Pay Act	1963	Prohibits sex differences in pay for substantially equal work.
Workers Compensation Laws	Various	State-by-state laws that establish insurance plans to compensate workers injured on the job.
Health/Safety Laws		
Consolidated Omnibus Budget Reconciliation Act (COBRA)	1985	Requires continued health insurance coverage (paid by employee) following termination.
Health Maintenance Organization Act	1973	Requires companies with 25 or more employees to provide an HMO alternative to regular group insurance if an HMO is available in the area.
Occupational Safety and Health Act (OSHA)	1970	Establishes mandatory safety and health standards in organizations.

of Fort Worth, Texas, was forced to provide almost $117,000 in back pay to 30 female workers the company had fired in order to avoid providing additional toilet facilities. Female workers in Oxnard, California, brought a similar class-action suit against Nabisco. The women accused the company of giving male workers restroom access throughout the day, while limiting 200 female workers to three scheduled seven-minute breaks, during which they scrambled to use 12 toilets.[15]

One thing concerning human resource legislation is clear: The scope of equal employment opportunity legislation is increasing at federal, state, and municipal levels. The working rights and conditions of women, minorities, older employees, and

the disabled will receive increasing legislative attention in the future. Also, most cases in the past have concerned low-level jobs, but the 1990s will see more attention given to equal employment opportunity in upper-level management positions.

Trends in Society

The complexity of demands on human resource executives often seems overwhelming. Just as human resource managers learn to insert themselves into corporate strategy making and learn the subtleties of such federal regulations as the Americans with Disabilities Act, other trends that surface raise new problems for staffing the firm. These trends include everything from court decisions that rule against companies that fire employees to dramatic changes in the makeup of the labor force. A few of the important current trends are as follows.

Globalization. As companies of every size enter the global marketplace and expand operations, HR executives must deal with such staffing concerns as whether to send expatriate managers or hire local managers for foreign operations.

Workforce Diversity. The ethnic and gender makeup of the people filling jobs in the year 2000 will be different from that of current employees. The implications of this trend are so important that Chapter 12 is devoted to discussing them.

Labor Supply Fluctuations. Changing demographics and economic conditions affect labor supply. In the late 1980s, predictions of severe labor shortages proved untrue because of the persistent recession in the early 1990s and the end of the Cold War. The massive reduction in the nation's defense needs and widespread corporate downsizing reversed the labor "shortage" as millions of white-collar and blue-collar Americans joined the ranks of the unemployed. The future labor supply may fluctuate further between shortage and oversupply as economic or demographic

conditions change, such as the beginning of baby-boomer retirement in the year 2000.

Employment at Will. Employers no longer enjoy the undisputed right to fire employees. Many discharged employees are filing lawsuits with almost 80 percent of the verdicts favoring the employee and damage awards exceeding $100,000. The *employment-at-will* rule traditionally permitted an employer to fire an employee for just cause or even no cause. Now 40 states have written employment laws to severely limit the "at will" doctrine and to protect against wrongful firing of employees who refuse to violate a law or who expose an illegal action by their employers. Although termination is generally accepted by the courts when employers can show employee incompetence or changing business requirements, many employers remain confused about their rights regarding termination. Employers now avoid terms such as *permanent employment*, and many employers are now spelling out their termination policy to employees, asking them to acknowledge that the employment agreement can be terminated at any time, thereby avoiding an implied long-term employment contract.[16] A portion of Apple Computer Inc.'s written employment contract is shown in Exhibit 11.4.

Employee Flexibility. One of the clearest trends is the increased effort to obtain quality employees and at the same time reduce excess employee costs so that firms can remain competitive in the global marketplace. This means that employers will be making greater use of part-time employees, work schedules that allow employees to work other than the traditional hours during the day, employee leasing and temporary employees, and employees who work under contract only for specific hours and tasks, thereby allowing employers to get exactly what they need and avoiding the necessity of providing offices and benefits on a full-time basis. Companies such as Hallmark, Pacific Bell, and Worthington Industries have turned to employee flexibility to reduce costs without having to lay off val-

ued employees. One study predicts that by the year 2000, 50 percent of the American workforce will be made up of contingent workers who are hired for short-term work as the need arises.[17] The trend toward officeless workers scattered geographically is described in the Technology for Today box.

Unionization. The general trend in North America is away from unionization, but many employees belong to unions, and labor continues to unionize new companies. The National Labor Relations Act of 1935 provides that employees may elect to be represented by unions in negotiations with employers over wages, hours, and other terms and conditions of employment. Currently, about one-fourth of all workers are covered by collective bargaining agree-

EXHIBIT 11.4
Apple Computer's Written Employment Contract

An "Apple Deal"

Here's the deal Apple will give you; and here's what we want from you. We're going to give you a really neat trip while you're here. We're going to teach you stuff you couldn't learn anywhere else. In return . . . we expect you to work like hell, buy the vision as long as you're here. . . . We're not interested in employing you for a lifetime, but that's not the way we are thinking about this. It's a good opportunity for both of us that is probably finite.

SOURCE: Barbara Ettorre, "The Contingency Workforce Moves Mainstream," *Management Review*, February 1994, 9–16.

TECHNOLOGY FOR TODAY
VIRTUAL HRM

William Herndon's choice to give up his office in 1996 is part of a growing trend toward the virtual office. By streamlining work space and bulking up on technology such as a laptop computer, wireless modem, cellular phone, and a personal 800 number, he can turn planes, hotels, and boardrooms into his personal office, from which he directs his personal staff.

Technology has allowed a stark change in the way we work together. A company can have employees in far-flung locations and still get the job done. Canadian Dorothy Millman started a technical support company (DMS) from her home and gradually grew it to its status as the largest outsourcing call center in Canada, with 1,200 employees across the entire country.

Companies benefit from alternative office arrangements through reduced real estate costs, forcing employees to have more face-to-face time with customers, and by helping workers create a better balance between work and family.

But these changes create new problems for HR managers. How do you hire and evaluate people you will rarely see? Virtual workers need to have initiative, proficient self-management skills, a strong work ethic, be familiar with the job, be technically self-sufficient, be able problem solvers, be results oriented, and be good communicators with a sense of humor. HR managers also should design means for supporting virtual workers by developing guidelines to determine the best types of "virtual" employees, evaluating whether current orientation programs are relevant, and using focus groups and surveys to find out what employees need for greater productivity. Other ways HR managers can assist virtual workers are by writing policies on who pays for computers

and other equipment, phone lines, and online services, and by setting up online means for expense invoices and administrative matters. They can also examine benefits eligibility as more people move back and forth between full- and part-time work, train managers who supervise off-site employees, adjust performance planning and review, and nurture ongoing feedback from customers, employees, and managers.

Technology has allowed many workers, such as those at Millman's DMS, to work from home—just like in the beginning, pre-industrial revolution. Says Millman, "Now it's come full circle."

SOURCE: Sandra E. O'Connell, "The Virtual Workplace Moves at Warp Speed," *HRM Magazine*, March 1996, 51–54; William R. Pape, "Hire Power," *Inc. Technology*, 1996, no. 4, 23; Dean Takahashi, "Road Warrior," *The Wall Street Journal*, Nov. 18, 1996, R27, R31; Tamsen Tillson, "Call Moll," *Canadian Business*, Sept. 1996, 57.

One of the recent *trends in society* is the new responsiveness of unions to changes in competition. At Federal-Mogul Corporation's Lititz, Pennsylvania, plant, unions and management joined hands to successfully launch production of green rings, a component previously outsourced to suppliers. Here, union-management cooperation is celebrated and recognized by state government officials.

matching model
An employee selection approach in which the organization and the applicant attempt to match each other's needs, interests, and values.

ments. In companies where unions represent workers, union officials research the needs of members, the elements of the pay package, and the employers' financial condition. When a contract expires, union officials negotiate on behalf of the members of the bargaining unit for desired pay components and other issues relevant to workers.[18]

One current area of concern is the cooperation between management and unions regarding employee participation programs. Back-to-back rulings by the National Labor Relations Board in cases involving *Electromation vs. The International Brotherhood of Teamsters* and *Du Pont vs. the Chemical Workers Association* found such programs in violation of the 1935 National Labor Relations Act. For companies with labor unions, it is important to ensure that the union is involved in the process of establishing employee participation programs. Nonunionized companies face a dilemma, because such programs legally fall under the act's prohibition of "unfair labor practices by management," which could prevent employees from voluntarily forming their own

union. A bill pending in Congress would amend the 1935 law to allow U.S. businesses to "establish, without the presence of a labor union, workplace groups consisting of both labor and management to address such issues as productivity, quality control, and safety."[19]

In general, unions have been responsive to new competitive conditions affecting U.S. business. The need for cross-training, employee participation, and new compensation systems to meet global competition have brought unions into closer collaboration with management.

Within this context of trends in society, human resource managers must achieve the three primary goals described earlier in this chapter: attracting, developing, and maintaining an effective workforce for the organization. Let us now review some of the established techniques for accomplishing these goals.

ATTRACTING AN EFFECTIVE WORKFORCE

The first goal of HRM is to attract individuals who show signs of becoming valued, productive, and satisfied employees. The first step in attracting an effective workforce involves human resource planning, in which managers or HRM professionals predict the need for new employees based on the types of vacancies that exist, as illustrated in Exhibit 11.5. The second step is to use recruiting procedures to communicate with potential applicants. The third step is to select from the applicants those persons believed to be the best potential contributors to the organization. Finally, the new employee is welcomed into the organization.

Underlying the organization's effort to attract employees is a matching model. With the **matching model,** the organization and the individual attempt to match the needs, interests, and values that they offer each other. The organization offers "inducements," and the employee offers "contribu-

EXHIBIT 11.5
Attracting an Effective Workforce

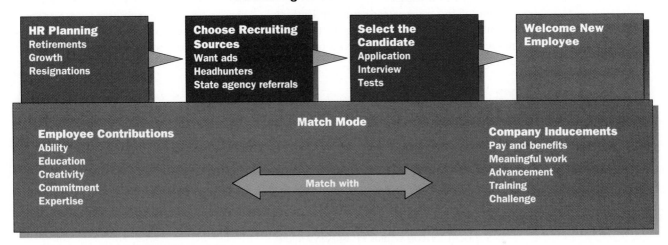

HR Planning	Choose Recruiting Sources	Select the Candidate	Welcome New Employee
Retirements	Want ads	Application	
Growth	Headhunters	Interview	
Resignations	State agency referrals	Tests	

Match Mode

Employee Contributions
Ability
Education
Creativity
Commitment
Expertise

Match with ⟷

Company Inducements
Pay and benefits
Meaningful work
Advancement
Training
Challenge

tions."[20] HRM professionals attempt to identify a correct match. For example, a small software developer may require long hours from creative, technically skilled employees. In return, it can offer freedom from bureaucracy, tolerance of idiosyncrasies, and potentially high pay. A large manufacturer can offer employment security and stability, but it may have more rules and regulations and require greater skills for "getting approval from the higher-ups." The individual who would thrive working for the software developer might feel stymied and unhappy working for a large manufacturer. Both the company and the employee are interested in finding a good match.

Human Resource Planning

Human resource planning is the forecasting of human resource needs and the projected matching of individuals with expected vacancies. Human resource planning begins with several questions:

- What new technologies are emerging, and how will these affect the work system?
- What is the volume of the business likely to be in the next five to ten years?

- What is the turnover rate, and how much, if any, is avoidable?

The responses to these questions are used to formulate specific questions pertaining to HRM activities, such as the following:

- How many senior managers will we need during this time period?
- What types of engineers will we need, and how many?
- Are persons with adequate computer skills available for meeting our projected needs?
- How many administrative personnel—technicians, secretaries—will we need to support the additional managers and engineers?[21]

Answers to these questions help define the direction for the organization's HRM strategy. For example, if forecasting suggests that there will be a strong need for more technically trained individuals, the organization can (1) define the jobs and skills needed in some detail, (2) hire and train recruiters to look for the specified skills, and/or (3) provide new training for existing employees. By anticipating future HRM needs, the organization can prepare itself to meet competitive challenges more effec-

human resource planning
The forecasting of human resource needs and the projected matching of individuals with expected job vacancies.

tively than organizations that react to problems only as they arise.

One of the most successful applications of human resource planning is the Tennessee Valley Authority's development of an eight-step system.

TVA

In the confusion and uncertainty following a period of reorganization and downsizing, a crucial role for HRM is balancing the need for future workforce planning with the creation of a climate of stability for the remaining workers. TVA created an eight-step plan that can serve as a model for companies in assessing future HR needs and formulating actions to meet those needs. The first step is laying the groundwork for later implementation of the program by creating planning and oversight teams within each business unit. Step two involves assessing processes and functions that can be benchmarked. Step three involves the projection of skills and employee numbers (demand data) necessary to reach goals within each business unit. Once these numbers are in place, step four involves projection of the current employee numbers (supply data) over the "planning horizon" without new hires and taking into consideration the normal attrition of staff through death, retirement, resignation, and so forth. Comparison of the difference between supply and demand (step five) gives the "future gap" or "surplus situation." This knowledge enables HR to develop strategies and operational plans (step six). Step seven involves communication of the action plan to employees. The final step is to periodically evaluate and update the plan as the organization's needs change.

Although, in a small organization, developing demand and supply data could be handled with a pad and a calculator, TVA uses a sophisticated automated system to update and revise the plan as needed to meet new competitive situations. Determining skills-gap and surplus information (step five) helped TVA develop a workforce plan to implement cross-organizational placement and retraining as alternatives to further employee cutbacks in the

individual business units, thereby providing a greater sense of stability for workers. If needs change and TVA faces a demand for additional employees, this process will enable the company to recruit workers with the skills needed to help meet organizational goals.[22] ■

HRM Forecasting Techniques. A variety of HRM forecasting techniques are in use today. These can be classified as short range and long range.

Short-range forecasting frequently uses the following steps:

■ The demand for the organization's product or service is predicted. Major expected external changes (such as increased demand for a new line of products) are accounted for in this estimation.

■ The overall sales forecast is estimated; anticipated internal changes (for example, the conversion to word processors from typewriters) are considered.

■ Working budgets to reflect the expected workloads of every department are estimated.

■ Personnel requirements are determined through conversion of dollars or units into numbers of people.

■ Forecasts of labor market conditions or internal organization factors (such as turnover rate) that may affect the future labor supply are considered.

An example of short-range forecasting is USAir's introduction of the first Boeing 737-300 into scheduled service. Introducing a new aircraft into an airline operation required careful planning and coordination, beginning with a forecast of the number of pilots needed. Then 737-300 flight simulators had to be obtained and set up in a classroom. Pilots had to be trained before the new aircraft was introduced. New pilots with qualifications fitting the 737-300 also had to be hired.

Long-range forecasting ranges from the intuitive to the sophisticated. As described in Chapter 8, some forecasting techniques are

based on mathematical extrapolation from past trends. Others involve group decision-making techniques, such as the Delphi method, wherein groups of top managers or other experts use their judgment to make forecasts. Statistical data are also used to project the impact of future employment levels, sales activity, employee turnover, and other variables on the organization's future labor needs.

The need for long-range planning was illustrated by General Electric when top executives realized that corporate human resources did not fit new products and technologies. General Electric's chairman said, "We were a company with 30,000 electromechanical engineers becoming a company that needed electronics engineers. We didn't plan for this change . . . and it caused us big problems. . . ." Without planning, a company such as GE could be forced to drain engineers and managers from a stable division to support a growing division, which would propel people into positions above their competence and necessitate a costly rapid-hiring effort.[23]

Recruiting

Recruiting is defined as "activities or practices that define the characteristics of applicants to whom selection procedures are ultimately applied."[24] An important lesson in recruiting is shown below in the example of an entrepreneur seeking clerical help.

■ SANDAL TREE

Former retail-chain buyer Paula Sussex decided to buy for her own business and opened her first Sandal Tree store on the Hawaiian Island of Maui. It was seven days from the time she was offered the purchase of the already existing store until she opened—little time for the business plan and bank loan she needed. On the first day, sales were $1,000 and the location was profitable after the second month.

One thing led to another and within four years the Hawaiian entrepreneur found herself the owner of three stores, which was far more overwhelming than running only one. Sussex worked seven days a week and was desperate for clerical help in her office. Like many other managers, she placed an ad that offered an attractive position. Within a year she had hired and lost six people. Only then did she see the important lesson—be honest in your advertisements. She ran an ad painting a candid—if not boring—picture of the job and ended up hiring an older woman who actually enjoyed working alone.

"I learned something there," Sussex says. "Don't make a job look glamorous if it's not. If what you want is just an ordinary person to do ordinary work, say so."[25] ■

Although we frequently think of campus recruiting as a typical recruiting activity, many organizations use *internal recruiting*, or "promote-from-within" policies, to fill their high-level positions.[26] At Mellon Bank, for example, current employees are given preference when a position opens. Open positions are listed in Mellon's career opportunity bulletins, which are distributed to employees. Internal recruiting has several advantages: It is less costly than an external search, and it generates higher employee commitment, development, and satisfaction, because it offers opportunities for career advancement to employees rather than outsiders.

Frequently, however, *external recruiting*—recruiting newcomers from outside the organization—is advantageous. Applicants are provided by a variety of outside sources including newspaper advertising, state employment services, private employment agencies ("headhunters"), job fairs, and employee referrals. Some employers even provide cash awards for employees who submit names of people who subsequently accept employment, because referral is one of the cheapest and most reliable methods for external recruiting.[27]

Realistic Job Previews. One approach to enhancing recruiting effectiveness is called a *realistic job preview*. A **realistic job preview (RJP)** gives applicants all pertinent and realistic information—positive and

recruiting
The activities or practices that define the desired characteristics of applicants for specific jobs.

realistic job preview (RJP)
A recruiting approach that gives applicants all pertinent and realistic information about the job and the organization.

negative—about the job and the organization.[28] RJPs enhance employee satisfaction and reduce turnover, because they facilitate matching individuals, jobs, and organizations. Individuals have a better basis on which to determine their suitability to the organization and "self-select" into or out of positions based on full information. When employees choose positions without RJPs, unmet expectations may cause initial job dissatisfaction and increased turnover. For example, Linda McDermott left a good position in an accounting firm to become an executive vice-president of a new management consulting company. She was told she would have a major role in helping the business grow. As it turned out, her boss relegated her to administrative duties, so she quit after a few months, causing the company to initiate another lengthy search and sidetracking her career for a year or two.[29]

Legal Considerations. Organizations must ensure that their recruiting practices conform to the law. As discussed earlier in this chapter, equal employment opportunity (EEO) laws stipulate that recruiting and hiring decisions cannot discriminate on the basis of race, national origin, religion, or sex. *Affirmative action* refers to the use of goals, timetables, or other methods in recruiting to promote the hiring, development, and retention of "protected groups"—persons historically underrepresented in the workplace. For example, companies adopting an affirmative action policy may recruit at colleges with large enroll-

ments of black students. A city may establish a goal of recruiting one black firefighter for every white firefighter until the proportion of black firefighters is commensurate with the black population in the community.

Most large companies try to comply with affirmative action and EEO guidelines. Prudential Insurance Company's policy is presented in Exhibit 11.6. Prudential actively recruits employees and takes affirmative action steps to recruit individuals from all walks of life.

Another legal consideration is company liability in connection with hiring employees who later commit crimes in the workplace, such as an employee who goes berserk and shoots fellow workers. An increasing number of court cases cite employer negligence in hiring people without careful background checks. As a result, HR departments are increasingly looking beyond personal references and personnel records to investigate prospective employees through past immediate supervisors, credit bureaus, criminal court records, and driver's license records. Careful hiring practices are important, but they must be implemented without discriminating against applicants or violating the individual's right to privacy.[30]

Selecting

The next step for managers is to select desired employees from the pool of recruited applicants. In the **selection** process, em-

selection
The process of determining the skills, abilities, and other attributes a person needs to perform a particular job.

EXHIBIT 11.6
Prudential's Corporate Recruiting Policy

An Equal Opportunity Employer
Prudential recruits, hires, trains, promotes, and compensates individuals without regard to race, color, religion or creed, age, sex, marital status, national origin, ancestry, liability for service in the armed forces of the United States, status as a special disabled veteran or veteran of the Vietnam era, or physical or mental handicap.
This is official company policy because:
- we believe it is right
- it makes good business sense
- it is the law

We are also committed to an ongoing program of affirmative action in which members of under-represented groups are actively sought out and employed for opportunities in all parts and at all levels of the company. In employing people from all walks of life, Prudential gains access to the full experience of our diverse society.

SOURCE: Prudential Insurance Company.

ployers attempt to determine the skills, abilities, and other attributes a person needs to perform a particular job. Then they assess applicants' characteristics in an attempt to determine the "fit" between the job and applicant characteristics.

Job Descriptions. A good place to start in making a selection decision is the job description. Human resource professionals or line managers who make selection decisions may have little direct experience with the job to be filled. If these persons are to make a good match between job and candidate, they should read the job description before they review applications.

A **job description** typically lists job duties as well as desirable qualifications for a particular job. An example of a job description for American Airlines appears in Exhibit 11.7.

job description
A listing of duties as well as desirable qualifications for a particular job.

EXHIBIT 11.7
A Sample Job Description

AmericanAirlines

JOB DESCRIPTION

Title:	Associate - Corporate Development
Department:	Corporate Development
Location:	Corporate Headquarters Dallas/Fort Worth Airport, Texas
Reports To:	Managing Director - Corporate Development

American Airlines is seeking an Associate for its Corporate Development Department. This position supports the growing diversification activities of AMR Corporation, American Airlines and other subsidiaries.

Functional Description:

Responsibilities include identifying, analyzing and negotiating merger and acquisition transactions in a diverse group of industries. Position involves interaction with senior management as well as the Legal, Tax and operating departments.

Qualifications:

MBA degree required. The successful applicant will have excellent communication and analytical skills. Prior experience in mergers and acquisition and knowledge of PC financial modeling techniques are preferred.

P.O. BOX 619616, DALLAS FORT WORTH AIRPORT, TEXAS 75261-9616, CABLE ADDRESS AMAIR

SOURCE: Used with permission of American Airlines.

Selection Devices. Several devices are used for assessing applicant qualifications. The most frequently used are the application form, interview, paper-and-pencil test, and assessment center. Human resource professionals may use a combination of these devices to obtain a valid prediction of employee job performance. **Validity** refers to the relationship between one's score on a selection device and one's future job performance. A valid selection procedure will provide high scores that correspond to subsequent high job performance.

validity
The relationship between an applicant's score on a selection device and his or her future job performance.

Application Form. The **application form** is used to collect information about the applicant's education, previous job experience, and other background characteristics. Research in the life insurance industry shows that biographical information inventories can validly predict future job success.[31]

application form
A device for collecting information about an applicant's education, previous job experience, and other background characteristics.

One pitfall to be avoided is the inclusion of questions that are irrelevant to job success. In line with affirmative action, the application form should not ask questions that will create an adverse impact on "protected groups" unless the questions are clearly related to the job.[32] For example, employers should not ask whether the applicant rents or owns his or her own home because (1) an applicant's response might adversely affect his or her chances at the job, (2) minorities and women may be less likely to own a home, and (3) home ownership is probably unrelated to job performance. On the other hand, the CPA exam is relevant to job performance in a CPA firm; thus, it is appropriate to ask whether an applicant for employment has passed the CPA exam even if only one-half of all female or minority applicants have done so versus nine-tenths of male applicants.

Interview.[33] The interview is used in the hiring process in almost every job category in virtually every organization. The *interview* serves as a two-way communication channel that allows both the organization and the applicant to collect information that would otherwise be difficult to obtain.

paper-and-pencil test
A written test designed to measure a particular attribute such as intelligence or aptitude.

Although widely used, the interview as generally practiced is not a valid predictor of later job performance. Researchers have identified many reasons for this. Interviewers frequently are unfamiliar with the job. They tend to make decisions in the first few minutes of the interview before all relevant information has been gathered. They also may base decisions on personal biases (such as against minority groups or physically unattractive persons and in favor of those similar to themselves). The interviewer may talk too much and spend time discussing matters irrelevant to the job.[34]

Organizations will continue to use interviews in spite of the pitfalls. Thus, researchers have identified methods for increasing their validity. Advice for effective interviewing—as well as some unusual interview experiences—is summarized in the Focus on Employees box.

Paper-and-Pencil Test. Many companies use **paper-and-pencil tests** such as intelligence tests, aptitude and ability tests, and personality inventories, particularly those shown to be valid predictors.[35] For example, a 109-question personality test has been used by independent insurance agents to hire clerical and customer service employees. The test is designed to measure such traits as "motivation to please others" and "people orientation." The insurance agencies believe they need something to accurately gauge applicants' strengths and weaknesses. The test has been successful,

FOCUS ON EMPLOYEES
THE RIGHT WAY TO INTERVIEW A JOB APPLICANT

A so-so interview usually nets a so-so employee. Many hiring mistakes can be prevented during the interview. The following techniques will ensure a successful interview:

1. *Know what you want.* Before the interview, prepare questions based on your knowledge of the job to be filled. If you do not have a thorough knowledge of the job, read a job description. If possible, call one or more job holders, and ask them about the job duties and what is required to succeed. Another idea is to make up a list of traits and qualifications for the ideal candidate. Use behavior-based interviewing techniques to analyze behaviors needed for job success and develop interview questions for three or four crucial "core competencies." Talk to present job holders ahead of time to have complete information on the job in question. You may decide, as Microsoft does, to nearly

ignore skills and go for the smartest people, realizing that today's skills have a short half-life in this rapidly changing world. Be specific about what it will take to get the job done.

2. *Prepare a road map.* Develop questions that will reveal whether the candidate has the correct background and qualifications. The questions should focus on previous experiences that are relevant to the current job. If the job requires creativity and innovation, ask a question such as, "What do you do differently from other sales reps?"

3. *Use open-ended questions in which the right answer is not obvious.* Ask the applicant to give specific examples of previous work experiences. For example, don't ask, "Are you a hard worker?" or "Tell me about yourself." Instead ask, "Can you give me examples from your previous work history that reflect your level of motivation?" or "How did you go about getting your current job?"

4. *Do not ask questions that are irrelevant to the job.* This is particularly important when the irrelevant questions might adversely affect minorities or women. Questions that are considered objectionable are the same as those considered objectionable on application forms. Avoid questions related to date or place of birth, whether the person owns a home (minorities are statistically less likely to own one), or whether that person has ever filed a worker's compensation claim (impermissible under the Americans with Disabilities Act, until a firm job offer is made).

5. *Listen; don't talk.* You should spend most of the interview listening. If you talk too much, the focus will shift to you, and you may miss important cues. Listen carefully to tone of voice as well as content. Body language also can be revealing; for example, failure to make eye contact is a danger signal.

. . . continued

because candidates hired have displayed strong tendencies to provide service to customers.[36]

Assessment Center. First developed by psychologists at AT&T, assessment centers are used to select individuals with high potential for managerial careers by such organizations as AT&T, IBM, General Electric, and JCPenney.[37] **Assessment centers** present a series of managerial situations to groups of applicants over, say, a two- or three-day period. One technique is the "in-basket" simulation, which requires the applicant to play the role of a manager who must decide how to respond to ten memos in his or her in-basket within a two-hour period. Panels of two or three trained judges observe the applicant's decisions and assess the extent to which they reflect interpersonal, communication, and problem-solving skills.

Assessment centers have proven to be valid predictors of managerial success, and some organizations now use them for hiring technical workers.[38] At Kimberly-Clark's newest plants, for example, applicants for machine operator jobs are put through a simulation in which they are asked to play the role of a supervisor. The idea is to see whether candidates have sufficient "people skills" to fit into the participative work atmosphere. Assessment centers are important because they provide a more valid measure of interpersonal skills than do paper-and-pencil tests.

assessment center
A technique for selecting individuals with high managerial potential based on their performance on a series of simulated managerial tasks.

6. *Allow enough time so that the interview will not be rushed.* Leave time for the candidate to ask questions about the job. The types of questions the candidate asks can be an important clue to his or her interest in the job. Try to delay forming an opinion about the applicant until after the entire interview has been completed.

7. *Avoid reliance on your memory.* Request the applicant's permission to take notes; then do so unobtrusively during the interview or immediately after. If several applicants are interviewed, notes are essential for remembering what they said and the impressions they made.

Even a well-planned interview may be disrupted by the unexpected. When asked to describe the most unusual thing that they were aware of ever happening during a job interview, human resource directors told of applicants who:

◆ "Wore a Walkman and said she could listen to me and the music at the same time."
◆ "Announced she hadn't had lunch and proceeded to eat a hamburger and french fries in the interviewer's office."
◆ "Declared she would like to convert employees to her brand of religion." (This was at an organization committed to diversity.)
◆ "Wore a jogging suit to interview for a position as a vice president."
◆ "Said he was so well-qualified that if he didn't get the job, it would prove that the company's management was incompetent."

Other bizarre HR stories include:
◆ "A balding candidate abruptly excused himself. He returned to the office a few minutes later wearing a hairpiece."
◆ "Not only did he ignore the 'No Smoking' sign in my office, he lit up the wrong ends of several filter-tip cigarettes."
◆ "She chewed bubble gum and constantly blew bubbles."
◆ "Job applicant challenged the interviewer to arm wrestle."
◆ "He stretched out on the floor to fill out the job application."
◆ "He interrupted to telephone his therapist for advice on answering specific interview questions."
◆ "He dozed off and started snoring during the interview."
◆ "He said that if he were hired, he would demonstrate his loyalty by having the corporate logo tattooed on his forearm."

SOURCES: Reprinted by permission of the publisher, from *Management Review* (October 1989), © 1989. American Management Association, New York. All rights reserved.

Companies such as Toyota rely heavily on a combination of selection techniques to fill jobs at a higher than 90 percent success rate.

■ TOYOTA MOTOR CORPORATION

To land a production job at a North American Toyota plant takes at least 18 hours. First, prospective employees must pass a literacy and general knowledge exam as well as a test of their attitudes toward work. Applicants go in groups of 12 to an assessment center where they must demonstrate skills in areas such as communication, mental flexibility, problem solving, and teamwork. Applicants may go through a manufacturing exercise in which they are expected to improve the method of assembling plastic pipes. Or they may be told that a lawn mower manufacturer has production problems to see which applicants ask the right questions and can work cooperatively to find a solution. Finally, intense interviews help weed out those who appear to have bad attitudes. Only 10 percent of applicants make it through the tests for reading, math, manual dexterity, job fitness, technical knowledge, hypothetical production problems, interpersonal skills, and attitude. The resulting Toyota team members are a spirited elite who love their jobs and are devoted to Toyota.[39] ■

DEVELOPING AN EFFECTIVE WORKFORCE

Following selection, the major goal of HRM is to develop employees into an effective workforce. Development includes training and performance appraisal.

Training and Development

Training and development represent a planned effort by an organization to facilitate employees' learning of job-related behaviors.[40] Some authors distinguish the two forms of intervention by noting that the term *training* usually refers to teaching low-level or technical employees how to do their present jobs, whereas *development* refers to teaching managers and professionals the skills needed for both present and future jobs. For simplicity, we will refer to both interventions as *training*.

Organizations spend nearly $100 billion each year on training. In 1987 IBM reported spending more than $750 million a year on corporate schooling, more than the entire budget of Harvard University.[41] Training may occur in a variety of forms. The most common method is on-the-job training. In **on-the-job training (OJT),** an experienced employee is asked to take a new employee "under his or her wing" and show the newcomer how to perform job duties. OJT has many advantages, such as few out-of-pocket costs for training facilities, materials, or instructor fees and easy transfer of learning back to the job. The learning site is the work site.

Other frequently used training methods include:

- *Orientation training,* in which newcomers are introduced to the organization's "culture," standards, and goals.
- *Classroom training,* including lectures, films, audiovisual techniques, and simulations.
- *Programmed and computer-assisted instruction,* in which the employee works at his or her own pace to learn material from a text that includes exercises and quizzes to enhance learning.
- *Conference and case discussion groups,* in which participants analyze cases or discuss topics assisted by a training leader.

Motorola provides all employees with 40 hours of training annually. The company has rededicated itself to the concept of lifelong training and plans to quadruple the annual training hours by the turn of the century. Great Plains Software of Fargo, North Dakota, replaced its one-day orientation with an intense three-month training pro-

on-the-job training (OJT)
A type of training in which an experienced employee "adopts" a new employee to teach him or her how to perform job duties.

gram. A new employee is paired with a personal "coach" and completes a roster of classes on a wide range of topics, from employee benefits to technology training.[42]

Companies are not only increasing training budgets but also experimenting with a variety of new training approaches. One of the most popular is "cross-training," which teaches employees multiple skills so they can perform a number of different jobs, thus providing variety for employees and enabling companies to quickly adjust to changes in staffing needs. Another approach, "integrative learning," uses team exercises to establish and reinforce effective teamwork habits.[43] Described below are two organizations that use a blend of OJT, classroom training, and cross-training, all of which helped them to become more successful.

NORTON MANUFACTURING/TACO INC.

Success can bring more problems, as Fostoria, Ohio, Norton Manufacturing found out in the past five years when its niche as the superior crankshaft maker meant a need to increase its workforce from 40 to the present 400. The result: an urgent need for employee training and testing. Norton has to do this "because the schools are not getting it done for us." Machine operators, who rely heavily on math, tested out at a seventh-grade math level. After 20 hours of classes, though, low scorers were rated at a college freshman level.

After that success, Norton contracted with a local community college to have an instructor at the plant for all three shifts, offering weekly classes on such subjects as "machine-shop math," basic blueprint reading, statistical process control, and Total Quality Management. Workers gain immediately from this training because "they can apply it to the job," says Ralph Toscano, former HR director. "It's not theory-based education, it's application-based education."

Small companies often avoid training, not only because of its cost, but due to the fear of developing more skilled workers who then leave for better jobs. Cranston, Rhode Island, Taco Inc. has proved this myth wrong. By investing in all kinds of on-company-time courses, in "almost anything where there is an interest," including job skills (marketing, sales, quality control) with cross-training and personal life competencies (such as music appreciation, gardening, aerobics, and government), the heating and cooling equipment manufacturer created a more committed workforce. Ninety-five percent of workers attended courses in the first year and employee turnover shrank to less than one percent.

Executive vice president John White, Jr. credits the Learning Center for helping Taco change from a no-growth company in the '80s to one of current annual 20 percent growth. Employees will give more "the more they feel you're trying to help them," he says. "The payback is incredible."[44] ■

Promotion from Within. Promotion from within helps companies retain and develop productive employees. It provides challenging assignments, prescribes new responsibilities, and helps employees grow by developing their abilities.

One approach to promotion from within is *job posting*, which means that positions are announced on bulletin boards or in company publications as openings occur. Interested employees notify the human resource department, which then helps make the fit between employees and positions.

Another approach is the *employee resource chart*, which is designed to identify likely successors for each management position. The chart looks like a typical organization chart with every employee listed. Every key position includes the names of top candidates to move into that position when it becomes vacant. Candidates are rated on a five-point scale reflecting whether they are ready for immediate promotion or need additional experience. These charts show the potential flow of employees up through the hierarchy and provide motivation to employees who have an opportunity for promotion.

Performance Appraisal

performance appraisal
The process of observing and evaluating an employee's performance, recording the assessment, and providing feedback to the employee.

360-degree feedback
A process that uses multiple raters, including self-rating, to appraise employee performance and guide development.

Performance appraisal is another important technique for developing an effective workforce. **Performance appraisal** comprises the steps of observing and assessing employee performance, recording the assessment, and providing feedback to the employee. Managers use performance appraisal to describe and evaluate the employees' performances. During performance appraisal, skillful managers give feedback and praise concerning the acceptable elements of the employee's performance. They also describe performance areas that need improvement. Employees can use this information to change their job performance. Performance appraisal can also reward high performers with merit pay, recognition, and other rewards.

For example, Northern Telecom's Raleigh, North Carolina, Installation Center uses a performance appraisal system as part of a skills-based pay program to encourage field technicians to stay abreast of new technologies and to reward them for increasing skill levels. Employees demonstrating proficiency in a skill receive certification from a committee made up of the employee's immediate supervisor, an HRM representative, and a coworker. The performance appraisal system forms the basis of promotion and compensation; as employees become certified in higher-level skills, they move up the salary range.[45]

Generally, HRM professionals concentrate on two things to make performance appraisal a positive force in their organization: (1) the accurate assessment of performance through the development and application of assessment systems such as rating scales and (2) training managers to effectively use the performance appraisal interview, so managers can provide feedback that will reinforce good performance and motivate employee development.

Assessing Performance Accurately.

To obtain an accurate performance rating, managers must acknowledge that jobs are multidimensional and performance thus may be multidimensional as well. For example, a sports broadcaster may perform well on the job-knowledge dimension; that is, she or he may be able to report facts and figures about the players and describe which rule applies when there is a questionable play on the field. But the same sports broadcaster may not perform as well on another dimension, such as communication. She or he may be unable to express the information in a colorful way that interests the audience or may interrupt the other broadcasters.

If performance is to be rated accurately, the performance appraisal system should require the rater—usually the supervisor—to assess each relevant performance dimension. A multidimensional form increases the usefulness of the performance appraisal for giving rewards and facilitates employee growth and development.

A recent trend in performance appraisal is called **"360-degree feedback,"** a process that uses multiple raters, including self-rating, as a way to increase awareness of strengths and weaknesses and guide employee development. Members of the appraisal group may include supervisors, coworkers, and customers, as well as the individual, thus providing appraisal of the employee from a variety of perspectives.[46] The following example describes how one company uses 360-degree feedback as part of a performance appraisal system that treats employees and managers as partners.

SOUTHERN CALIFORNIA EDISON

Like many other companies in these turbulent times, Rosemead, California-based Southern California Edison (SCE) has been redefining its corporate culture to be more adaptive to changing needs. SCE's new values stress empowerment and teamwork, but the human resources department discovered that the performance appraisal system worked in direct opposition to those values. In the spirit of empowerment, corporate HR left it up to each department to design its own new appraisal system.

Ron Juliff, head of the health and employee services department, created a task force made up of volunteers from all functions, processes, and hierarchical levels of his department. As they worked to create a new system, task force members regularly solicited the advice and suggestions of other employees. To reflect and reinforce the new system's positive, egalitarian approach, the task force scrapped the old "performance appraisal" label in favor of Performance Enhancement Process (PEP). In the new system, employee and supervisor work together to improve one another's performance. The PEP process begins with discussions between the two about the company's mission, values, and customers. Then, employee and supervisor together define goals that lead to accomplishing company strategies. These may be measurable with time limits, productivity gauges, or desired outcomes. Once goals have been collaboratively defined and agreed upon, the employee suggests the best people to assess how well he or she is doing in meeting the goals. The list may include supervisors, coworkers, customers, suppliers, or colleagues from other departments. Employee and supervisor determine the final list of reviewers, decide who they will interview about the employee's performance, and come up with the list of questions to be used in the interviewing. These sources are contacted throughout the year, and feedback on performance becomes a part of day-to-day work life. At the follow-up session at the end of the year, employee and supervisor compare notes, share ideas, and define what each of them must do to change problem areas.

Employees praise the new system for giving them more control. As one put it, "This process makes me feel more accountable to myself and the company. I'm aware that I actually have goals, that they're in sync with the company goals, and that I need to be monitoring them, not just doing my job by rote."

By working together to improve performance, employees and supervisors have eliminated the "us versus them" feeling of traditional performance appraisals and have become true partners in working to improve their company.[47] ∎

Although we would like to believe that every manager carefully assesses employees' performances, researchers have identified several rating problems.[48] For example, **halo error** occurs when an employee receives the same rating on all dimensions even if his or her performance is good on some dimensions and poor on others. **Homogeneity** occurs when a rater gives all employees a similar rating even if their performances are not equally good.

One approach to overcome management performance evaluation errors is to use a behavior-based rating technique, such as the behaviorally anchored rating scale. The **behaviorally anchored rating scale (BARS)** is developed from critical incidents pertaining to job performance. Each job performance scale is anchored with specific behavioral statements that describe varying degrees of performance. By relating employee performance to specific incidents, raters can more accurately evaluate an employee's performance.[49]

Exhibit 11.8 illustrates the BARS method for evaluating a production line supervisor. The production supervisor's job can be broken down into several dimensions, such as equipment maintenance, employee training, or work scheduling. A behaviorally anchored rating scale should be developed for each dimension. The dimension in Exhibit 11.8 is work scheduling. Good performance is represented by a 7, 8, or 9 on the scale and unacceptable performance as a 1, 2, or 3. If a production supervisor's job has eight dimensions, the total performance evaluation will be the sum of the scores for each of eight scales.[50]

Performance Appraisal Interview. Most corporations provide formal feedback in the form of an annual **performance appraisal interview** with the employee. Too often, however, this meeting between boss and subordinate does not stimulate better job performance.[51] Managers may be unaware of the true causes of performance problems, because they have not carefully observed employee job activities. They may have a number of useful ideas for subordi-

halo error
A type of rating error that occurs when an employee receives the same rating on all dimensions regardless of his or her performance on individual ones.

homogeneity
A type of rating error that occurs when a rater gives all employees a similar rating regardless of their individual performances.

behaviorally anchored rating scale (BARS)
A rating technique that relates an employee's performance to specific job-related incidents.

performance appraisal interview
A formal review of an employee's performance conducted between the superior and the subordinate.

EXHIBIT 11.8
Example of a Behaviorally Anchored Rating Scale

Job: Production Line Supervisor
Work Dimension: Work Scheduling

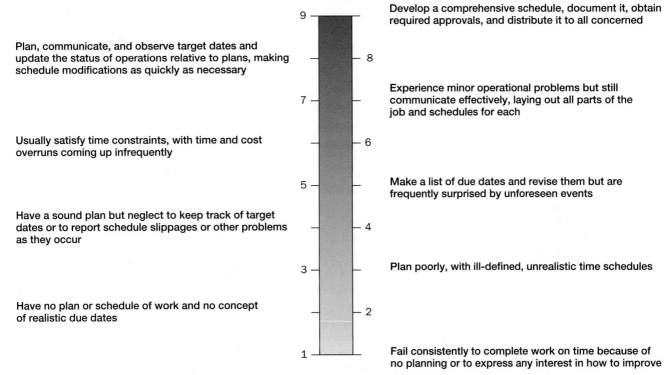

Develop a comprehensive schedule, document it, obtain required approvals, and distribute it to all concerned — 9

Plan, communicate, and observe target dates and update the status of operations relative to plans, making schedule modifications as quickly as necessary — 8

Experience minor operational problems but still communicate effectively, laying out all parts of the job and schedules for each — 7

Usually satisfy time constraints, with time and cost overruns coming up infrequently — 6

Make a list of due dates and revise them but are frequently surprised by unforeseen events — 5

Have a sound plan but neglect to keep track of target dates or to report schedule slippages or other problems as they occur — 4

Plan poorly, with ill-defined, unrealistic time schedules — 3

Have no plan or schedule of work and no concept of realistic due dates — 2

Fail consistently to complete work on time because of no planning or to express any interest in how to improve — 1

SOURCES: Based on J. P. Campbell, M. D. Dunnette, R. D. Arvey, and L. V. Hellervik, "The Development and Evaluation of Behaviorally Based Rating Scales," *Journal of Applied Psychology* 57 (1973), 15–22; and Francine Alexander, "Performance Appraisals," *Small Business Reports* (March 1989), 20–29.

nates but present them in a threatening manner. As a result, employees may feel defensive and reject suggestions for improvement.

Research into the performance appraisal interview suggests a number of steps that will increase its effectiveness.[52]

1 Raters (usually supervisors) should be knowledgeable about the subordinates' jobs and performance levels.
2 Raters should welcome employee participation during the interview rather than "tell and sell" their views by lecturing to subordinates. This is particularly true when the employee is knowledgeable and accustomed to participating with the supervisor.
3 A flexible approach to feedback based on the characteristics of the subordinate,

the job, and his or her performance level is useful. For example, newer employees need more frequent feedback than other employees do.
4 Training is used to help supervisors devise interview strategies for different situations. Role-playing that involves practice appraisal interviews is helpful for this purpose.

Performance feedback is more effective when it includes specific examples of good and bad performance. For example, "Your attendance record shows that you were here on time nearly every day this month, and this is a great improvement over last month" is more specific and helpful than "You seem to have a much better attitude these days about your work." Some experts suggest that managers keep diaries of em-

ployee performance so that they will not have to rely on memory to generate specific examples. However, managers should keep in mind that feedback is a daily responsibility. It is not fair for managers to "save up" a list of criticisms with which to hit workers in the performance appraisal interview. This interview should be used as an opportunity for constructive communication between manager and employee.

One of the most recent appraisal innovations is to involve peers in performance review. Companies such as General Electric and Eastman Kodak have found that this *peer review* process dramatically increases openness, commitment, and trust within the organization and prevents problems that sometimes occur with a one-on-one interview. Managers learn that employees have good opinions about performance, and soliciting opinions from other employees provides a group approach to problem solving around important performance issues.[53] YSI Inc., a Yellow Springs, Ohio, instrumentation device producer, assigned peer review duties to each of its 25 manufacturing teams. Each team member is assessed on performance, and individual corrective plans are devised for specific problem areas. If necessary, team members advise the manager and HR department of the need to let a problem employee go.[54] A few forward-looking companies are even experimenting with a bottom-up performance appraisal process in which subordinates provide a performance appraisal of their boss. Granite Rock Company maintains a competitive advantage through its people by using a mix of performance review, goal development, good solid communication, and lots of training and development, as shown in the Leading the Management Revolution box.

MAINTAINING AN EFFECTIVE WORKFORCE

Now we turn to the topic of how managers and HRM professionals maintain a workforce that has been recruited and developed. Maintenance of the current workforce involves compensation, wage and salary structure, benefits, and occasional terminations.

Compensation

The term **compensation** refers to (1) all monetary payments and (2) all goods or commodities used in lieu of money to reward employees.[55] An organization's compensation structure includes wages and/or salaries and benefits such as health insurance, paid vacations, or employee fitness centers. A company's compensation structure does not just happen. It is designed to fit company strategy and to provide compensation equity.

Compensation Strategy.   Ideally, management's strategy for the organization should be a critical determinant of the features and operations of the pay system.[56] For example, managers may have the goal of maintaining or improving profitability or market share by stimulating employee performance. Thus, they should design and use a merit pay system rather than a system based on other criteria such as seniority. As another example, managers may have the goal of attracting and retaining desirable employees. Here they can use a pay survey to determine competitive wages in comparable companies and adjust pay rates to meet or exceed the going rates.

Pay-for-performance systems are becoming extremely popular in both large and small businesses, including Caterpillar, Aluminum Company of America, and Au Bon Pain. These systems are usually designed as a form of profit sharing to reward employees when profitability goals are met. At Alcoa, payouts to employees equal 7 percent of each worker's salary. Caterpillar employees each received an $800 bonus, and Ford employees received an average $3,700 per employee. Employees have an incentive to make the company more efficient and profitable, because if goals are not met, no bonuses are paid. Jim Bernstein, CEO of General Health, Inc., a small business,

compensation
Monetary payments (wages, salaries) and nonmonetary goods/commodities (benefits, vacations) used to reward employees.

LEADING THE MANAGEMENT REVOLUTION
GRANITE ROCK COMPANY

Granite Rock Company discovered that aggressively developing its human resources would ultimately lead to better customer responsiveness. In Chapter 2, we discussed how Co-CEO Bruce Woolpert transformed the company into a learning organization to gain a competitive advantage in the increasingly difficult market. Through implementing a new management system, he brought back into focus the company's greatest asset—its people.

Instead of the more common job descriptions and performance reviews, Granite Rock uses the Individual Professional Development Plan, where workers meet annually with supervisors to plot goals on everything from skill development to job advancement. Enhancements result from managers seeing a clearer picture of employee aspirations, while input and advice from

superiors regarding goal achievement helps engender worker loyalty. Supervisors follow up the feedback with round-table sessions to discuss the education and training needed to help employees reach goals.

The asphalt and concrete company's quality emphasis led to the creation of Granite Rock University, where employees use company time to study such diverse topics as leadership, statistical process controls, or more than 50 different industry-training courses. The company funds 40 annual hours of training at $2,300 per worker, a substantial investment for such a small business. Still, this may be a bargain, considering that poor workmanship, refunds, and lost customers can cost companies up to 30 percent of sales.

Such company-wide training brings two other obvious benefits: an improved customer responsiveness and increased initiative in problem solving.

Many of the 535 unionized employees are cross-trained, performing more than one job and also serving on 50 quality teams. Woolpert believes the time to correct problems is now and the place is at the source. A state-of-the-art information system helps track competitive forces, highlights operational flaws, and identifies market shifts before competitors are aware of them. Well-trained and motivated employees keep this all working optimally.

From the early days until now, Granite Rock's credo has been, "We want to learn the latest methods of thinking about business as quickly as we can. We want to know."

SOURCE: "Granite Rock: A Family Operation Nears Its Centennial," *Stone Review*, October 1996, 6–7; David Franceschi, Quality Director, 1996; Edward Welles, "How're We Doing?" *Inc.*, May 1991, 80–83; John Case, "The Change Masters," *Inc.*, March 1992, 58–70; company sources, 1996.

---

promised all 30 employees they would get an extra month's pay if the company hit the sales target. Sales shot up, going far beyond the target, showing how powerful the correct incentive can be.[57]

Compensation Equity. Managers often wish to maintain a sense of fairness and equity within the pay structure and thereby fortify employee morale. **Job evaluation** refers to the process of determining the value or worth of jobs within an organization through an examination of job content. Job evaluation techniques enable managers to compare similar and dissimilar jobs and to determine internally equitable pay rates—that is, pay rates that employees believe are fair compared with those for other jobs in the organization. Managers also may want to provide income security so that

their employees need not be overly concerned with the financial consequences of disability or retirement.

Wage and Salary Structure

Large organizations typically employ HRM compensation specialists to establish and maintain a pay structure. They may also hire outside consultants, such as the Hay Group or PAQ (Position Analysis Questionnaire) Associates, whose pay systems have been adopted by many companies and government organizations. The majority of large public- and private-sector U.S. employers use some formal process of job evaluation.[58]

The most commonly used job evaluation system is the **point system**.[59] First, compensation specialists must ensure that job de-

job evaluation
The process of determining the value of jobs within an organization through an examination of job content.

point system
A job evaluation system that assigns a predetermined point value to each compensable job factor in order to determine the worth of a given job.

scriptions are complete, up to date, and accurate. Next, top managers select compensable job factors (such as skill, effort, and responsibility) and decide how each factor will be weighed in establishing job worth. These factors are described in a point manual, which is used to assign point values to each job. For example, the characteristic of "responsibility" could receive from 0 to 5 points depending on whether job responsibility is "routine work performed under close supervision" (0 points) or "complete discretion with errors having extreme consequences to the organization and public safety" (5 points).

The compensation specialist then compares each job factor in a given job description to that specified in the point manual. This process is repeated until the job has been evaluated on all factors. Then the compensation specialist evaluates a second job and repeats the process until all jobs have been evaluated.

The job evaluation process can establish an internal hierarchy of job worth. However, to determine competitive market pay rates, most organizations obtain one or more pay surveys. **Pay surveys** show what other organizations pay incumbents in jobs that match a sample of "key" jobs selected by the organization. Pay surveys are available from many sources, including consulting firms and the U.S. Bureau of Labor Statistics.

The compensation specialist then compares the survey pay rates for key jobs with their job evaluation points by plotting them on a graph as illustrated in Exhibit 11.9. The **pay-trend line** shows the relationship between pay and total point values. The compensation specialist can use the pay-trend line to determine the pay values of all jobs for which point values have been calculated. Ranges of pay for each job class are established, enabling a newcomer or low performer to be paid less than other people in the same job class. The organization must then specify how individuals in the same job class can advance from the low to the high end of the range. For example, the organization can reward merit, seniority, or a combination of both.

Benefits

The wage and salary structure is an important part of the compensation package that maintains a productive workforce, but equally important are the benefits offered by the organization. Benefits were once called "fringe" benefits, but this term is no longer accurate because they are now a central rather than peripheral part of the pay structure. A U.S. Chamber of Commerce

pay-trend line
A graph that shows the relationship between pay and total job point values for determining the worth of a given job.

pay survey
A study of what other companies pay employees in jobs that correspond to a sample of key positions selected by the organization.

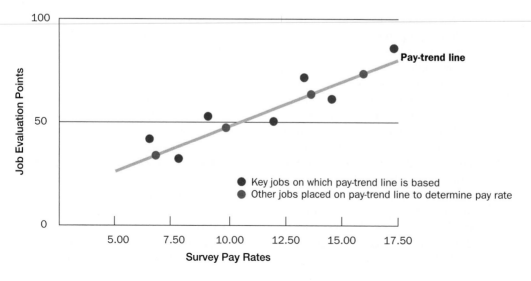

EXHIBIT 11.9
Pay-Trend Line

Job Evaluation Points

100

50

0

Pay-trend line

● Key jobs on which pay-trend line is based
● Other jobs placed on pay-trend line to determine pay rate

5.00   7.50   10.00   12.50   15.00   17.50

Survey Pay Rates

survey has revealed that benefits in general compose more than one-third of labor costs and in some industries nearly two-thirds.[60]

A major reason that benefits make up such a large portion of the compensation package is that health-care costs have been increasing so quickly. Because employers frequently provide health-care insurance as an employee benefit, these costs are important in the management of benefits. Between 1983 and 1993, annual corporate spending on health care tripled to $225 billion.[61] The federal government has been struggling to reform health care, and many companies are reviewing health plans.

Organizations that want to provide cost-effective benefits should be sensitive to changes in employee lifestyles. One to two decades ago, benefits were based on the assumption that the typical worker was a married man with a dependent wife and two school-age children. The benefits packages provided life insurance coverage for the worker, health insurance coverage for all family members, and no assistance with child-care expenses. But today fewer than 10 percent of American workers fit the description of the so-called typical worker.[62] Increased workforce diversity means that far more workers are single; in addition, both spouses in most families are working. These workers are not likely to value the traditional benefits package. In response, some companies are establishing *cafeteria-plan benefits packages* that allow employees to select the benefits of greatest value to them.[63] Other companies use surveys to determine which combination of fixed benefits is most desirable. The benefits packages provided by large companies attempt to meet the needs of all employees. Hallmark Cards, Inc., created a "family-friendly" benefits package, including the following: parental leave of up to six months; unpaid maternal/paternal leave; partial reimbursement for adoption expenses; assistance with finding child- and elder-care facilities; flextime and job-sharing options; lunchtime seminars on parenting and family-care topics; and sick-child services through six area hospitals.[64]

St. Paul Companies found flextime a solution to the problem of a tight labor market for information systems employees.

ST. PAUL COMPANIES

Labor shortages are the brutal reality of information systems departments, with some skilled workers getting two calls a day from headhunters. Insurer St. Paul Companies' flextime solution has given it a mere 3 percent turnover compared to the average 20 percent elsewhere. When other companies discarded their flexible schedules during the 1990s layoffs and cost reductions, St. Paul instead spent 18 months reengineering its program for better effectiveness.

St. Paul now has a state-of-the-art program instrumental in keeping the company well-staffed in the tight labor market. Any staff member (about half males and half females) who can show good reason has access to flextime. But St. Paul had to overcome some obstacles to make the program work well.

First, the previous "entitlement mentality" meant workers felt they never had to vary their attractive schedules. A volunteer employee committee worked on a program where employees must "give flexibility to get flexibility," when the work demands changes. Next, under the old program, core requirement days were Monday through Thursday, while Friday became a "ghost" (fewer personnel) day. There are no more core days now and schedules are based on business and personal needs. One worker prefers Wednesdays off, for example, so he can rollerblade when the paths aren't crowded. Employees also moved beyond the "this is not fair" stage and saw flextime was not only for parents. Finally, managers could not handle vacation requests before, since everyone was on a nonstandard schedule. The only solution was to create an easy-to-change, online system for tracking time off based on hours worked and that adjusts oddball schedules with benefit plans.

Flexibility is as important to these information systems workers as extra money. A programmer told a headhunter recently that he

would have to make $10,000 more per year to compensate for the loss of his compressed work week. Even though St. Paul is not known as a high-paying employer, it is seen as "a great place to work," says David Healy, a veteran Minneapolis recruiter.[65] ■

Termination

Despite the best efforts of line managers and HRM professionals, the organization will lose employees. Some will retire, others will depart voluntarily for other jobs, and still others will be forced out through mergers and cutbacks or for poor performance. The value of termination for maintaining an effective workforce is twofold. First, employees who are poor performers can be dismissed. Productive employees often resent disruptive, low-performing employees who are allowed to stay with the company and receive pay and benefits comparable to theirs. Second, employers can use exit interviews. An **exit interview** is an interview conducted with departing employees to determine why they are leaving.[66] The value of the exit interview is to provide an excellent and inexpensive tool for learning about pockets of dissatisfaction within the organization and hence for reducing future turnover.

With so many companies experiencing downsizing through mergers or because of global competition, often a large number of managers and workers are terminated at the same time. In these cases, enlightened companies try to find a smooth transition for departing employees. For example, General Electric laid off 900 employees in three gradual steps. It also set up a reemployment center to assist employees in finding new jobs or in learning new skills. It provided counseling in how to write a résumé and conduct a job search. An additional step General Electric took was to place an advertisement in local newspapers saying that these employees were available. When Rhino Foods had to make temporary layoffs, the company president went directly to his employees to ask for their input concerning possible alternatives. The solution was "employee swapping"—contracting out workers on a temporary basis to other companies, such as Gardener's Supply and Ben & Jerry's. During the job swap, Rhino's laid-off workers received pay from the temporary employers while maintaining Rhino health and other benefits.[67] By showing genuine concern in helping place laid-off employees, a company communicates the value of human resources and helps maintain a positive corporate culture.[68]

exit interview
An interview conducted with departing employees to determine the reasons for their termination.

SUMMARY AND MANAGEMENT SOLUTION

This chapter described several important points about human resource management in organizations. All managers are responsible for human resources, and most organizations have a human resource department that works with line managers to ensure a productive workforce. The human resource department is responsible for interpreting and responding to the large human resource environment. The HR department must be part of the organization's competitive strategy, implement procedures to reflect federal and state legislation, and respond to trends in society. Within this context, the HR department tries to achieve three goals for the organization. The first goal of the human resource department is to attract an effective workforce through human resource planning, recruiting, and employee selection. The second is to develop an effective workforce. Newcomers are introduced to the organization and to their jobs through orientation and training programs. Moreover, employees are appraised through performance appraisal programs. The third goal is to maintain an effective workforce. Human resource managers retain employees with wage and salary systems, benefits packages, and termination procedures.

Thomas Melohn, president of North American Tool & Die, used these ideas when he was faced with low profits, an unenthusiastic workforce, a 7 percent customer reject

rate, 10 percent absenteesim, and a 27 percent turnover rate. First, he got the word out to generate a large pool of applicants, thoroughly screening the completed forms from the company's thoughtful job application (he calls it a "little window to the soul"). Only 10 percent made it to the formal interview stage, which focused on finding employees with similar values and looked for neatness, completeness, and outside interests, while carefully checking references. Melohn was cautious about employees who didn't ask questions (they may be too fearful or unprepared for interview); those who said, "Let me be completely honest with you"; or those always saying "my" and "me." Before hiring, he brought in recruits for a paid trial day and kept the good ones for a one-month trial pe-

riod. After employees were completely on board, Melohn continued to nurture them through recognition, complete information, ownership in the company, pay for performance, acts of caring, and trustful relationships between employer and employee. All of this took a great deal of time, but acquiring and retaining the right people has produced impressive results. Employee turnover plummeted to less than 4 percent, absenteeism went to nearly zero, while the customer reject rate dropped to 0.1 percent. Employees became enthusiastic and productivity increased nearly 500 percent, while pretax earnings went up by 2,400 percent. Human resources have enabled this small company to beat well-heeled foreign competitors at price, quality, and delivery.[69]

DISCUSSION QUESTIONS

1 It is the year 2010. In your company, central planning has given way to frontline decision making, and bureaucracy has given way to teamwork. Shop floor workers use computers and robots. There is a labor shortage for many job openings, and the few applicants lack skills to work in teams, make decisions, or use sophisticated technology. As vice president of human resource management since 1990, what did you do to prepare for this problem?

2 If you were asked to advise a private company about its equal employment opportunity responsibilities, what two points would you emphasize as most important?

3 How can the human resource activities of planning, recruiting, performance appraisal, and compensation be related to corporate strategy?

4 Think back to your own job experience. What human resource management activities described in this chap-

ter were performed for the job you filled? Which ones were absent?

5 Why are planning and forecasting necessary for human resource management? Discuss.

6 How "valid" do you think the information obtained from a personal interview versus a paper-and-pencil test versus an assessment center would be for predicting effective job performance for a college professor? An assembly-line worker in a team-oriented plant? Discuss.

7 What techniques can managers adopt to improve their recruiting and interviewing practices?

8 How does affirmative action differ from equal employment opportunity in recruiting and selection?

9 How can exit interviews be used to maintain an effective workforce?

10 Describe the procedure used to build a wage and salary structure for an organization.

MANAGEMENT EXERCISES

MANAGER'S WORKBOOK

Test Your Human Resources Knowledge

This quiz will test your knowledge of human resources issues affecting today's workplace. The quiz was designed by the Council on Education in Management, a Walnut Creek, California, firm that conducts human resources and employment law seminars nationwide.

1 If you receive an unsolicited résumé in the mail, you must keep it for two years. **T F**

2 Time-management principles are pretty much the same in any administrative job. **T F**

3 Regardless of the type of business or the various laws

that may apply, there is a core of common practices for keeping personnel records and files that makes sense for almost any organization. **T F**

4 Every employer must have an affirmative action plan. **T F**

5 An employer must investigate an allegation of sexual harassment even if the victim asks to remain anonymous. **T F**

6 An employer is not obligated to pay overtime to a nonexempt employee who works more than 40 hours in a week after being asked not to put in overtime. **T F**

7 If your company is found guilty of discrimination, the Equal Employment Opportunity Commission will be more lenient if your records show that the violation was unintentional. **T F**

8 Americans with Disabilities Act regulations require companies to maintain written job descriptions. **T F**

9 Reference checking is an important procedure, despite the fact that many companies won't release this information. **T F**

10 Your employee orientation and handbook should help assure new employees that they will be a part of the team as long as they do a good job. **T F**

Answers: 1. F; 2. F; 3. T; 4. F; 5. T; 6. F; 7. F; 8. F; 9. T; 10. F.

MANAGER'S WORKSHOP

Hiring and Evaluating Using Core Competencies

1 Form groups of four to seven members. Develop a list of "core competencies" for the job of student in this course. (Or alternately, you may choose a job in one of the group members' organizations). List the core competencies below.
1.   5.
2.   6.
3.   7.
4.   8.

2 Which four of the above are the most important?
1.   3.
2.   4.

3 What questions would you ask a potential employee/student to determine if that person could be successful in this class, based on the four most important core competencies? (interviewing)
1.
2.
3.
4.

4 What learning experiences would you develop to enhance those core competencies? (training and development)
1.
2.
3.
4.

5 How would you evaluate or measure the success of a student in this class, based on the four core competencies? (performance evaluation)
1.
2.
3.
4.

SOURCE: Copyright 1996 by Dorothy Marcic. All rights reserved.

SURF THE 'NET

1 In Chapter 10, you were asked to evaluate various Web pages. Now, you should create your own Web page. Consider it as another type of résumé. Before you do this, though, find ten personal Web pages where people are looking for jobs. Complete the table to identify each page's strengths and weaknesses.

Name of person	URL address	Web page strengths	Web page weaknesses
1.			
2.			
3.			
4.			
5.			
6.			
7.			
8.			
9.			
10.			

2 Now develop your own Web page. Include—at minimum—the following:

Name   E-mail address

Type of work you want   Qualifications

3 Your instructor may ask you to print out your Web page and turn it in.

ETHICAL DILEMMA

A Conflict of Responsibilities

As director of human resources, Tess Danville was asked to negotiate a severance deal with Terry Winston, the Midwest regional sales manager for Cyn-Com Systems. Winston's problems with drugs and alcohol had become severe enough to precipitate his dismissal. His customers were devoted to him, but top management was reluctant to continue gambling on his reliability. Lives depended on his work as the salesman and installer of Cyn-Com's respiratory diagnostic technology. Winston had been warned twice to clean up his act, but had never succeeded. Only his unique blend of technical knowledge and high-powered sales ability had saved him before.

But now the vice president of sales asked Danville to offer Winston the option of resigning rather than be fired if he would sign a noncompete agreement and agree to go into rehabilitation. Cyn-Com would also extend a guarantee of confidentiality on the abuse issue and a good work reference as thanks for the millions of dollars of business that Winston had brought to Cyn-Com. Winston agreed to take the deal. After his departure, a series of near disasters was uncovered as a result of Winston's mismanagement. Some of his maneuvers to cover up his mistakes bordered on fraud.

Today Danville received a message to call the human resources director at a cardiopulmonary technology company to give a personal reference on Terry Winston. From the area code, Danville could see that he was not in violation of the noncompete agreement. She had also heard that Winston had completed a 30-day treatment program as promised. Danville knew she was expected to honor the confidentiality agreement, but she also knew that if his shady dealings had been discovered before his departure, he would have been fired without any agreement. Now she was being asked to give Winston a reference for another medical sales position.

What do you do?

1 Honor the agreement, trusting Winston's rehabilitation is complete on all levels and that he is now ready for a responsible position. Give a good recommendation.

2 Contact the vice-president of sales and ask him to release you from the agreement or to give the reference himself. After all, he made the agreement. You don't want to lie.

3 Without mentioning specifics, give Winston such an unenthusiastic reference that you hope the other human resources director can read between the lines and believe that Winston will be a poor choice.

CASE FOR CRITICAL ANALYSIS

MONY

Senior executives at Mutual of New York (MONY) decided to relocate its operations division from Manhattan to nearby Westchester County. Although MONY's headquarters remained in New York City, many economies could be achieved by moving the operations division to another location.

The human resource environment in Westchester County was different from that in Manhattan, and Sue Garbey, director of human resources, had her work cut out for her. More than 50 percent of the needed 1,000 employees would relocate from Manhattan, thanks to a generous relocation package. However, as the corporate newcomer in the area, MONY was a small competitor compared with neighbors IBM, General Foods, PepsiCo, and Reader's Digest and would have to be innovative to recruit and retain quality employees. Members of the human resource department realized that they were facing a labor shortage due to the baby bust, made even more difficult by recruiting competition from MONY's corporate neighbors. Moreover, the pool of potential workers was affluent, had many choices, and was considered selective about employers.

In response, MONY's HR department decided to experiment with nontraditional programs such as flexible hours, summer hours, job sharing, variable work sites, and child-care assistance. Flexible hours means that each department must have coverage during the core business hours of 8:30 A.M. to 4:30 P.M., but individual staff members can work anytime from 7:30 A.M. to 9:00 P.M. Some 25 employees are involved in job sharing, which means that the position is filled by 2 people, each working less than 40 hours. Part-time employees receive prorated benefits. Variable work sites allow many people to work at home at least part of the time. These employees do computer work and can log on anytime of the day or night. Child-care assistance includes six months of unpaid leave and guarantee of the same job upon return. MONY also offers flexible spending accounts as part of the benefits package that can help reimburse for dependent care.

MONY's philosophy is "What's good for the individual is also good for business." Top management and HR professionals believe the use of innovative means to recruit and retain people will enable high productivity and a successful division.

Questions

1 Evaluate the extent to which the recruiting and retention policies reflect the environment within which the human resource department works.

2 Would you like to work for MONY's operations division? Why?

3 What suggestions would you make about additional programs MONY might undertake to recruit and retain employees in this environment?

ENDNOTES

1 Thomas H. Melohn, "Build Trust with Team Members," *Executive Excellence* 12, no. 6, June 1995, 11–12; John Brandt, "The Flip Side of Corporate," *Industry Week* 243, no. 17 (September 19, 1994), 12–16; Thomas Melohn, "Screening for the Best Employees," *Inc.* 9, no. 1 (January 1987), 104–106; Joshua Hyatt, "How to Hire Employees," *Inc.* 12, no. 3, (March 1990), 106–108; Tom Melohn,

The New Partnership: Profit by Bringing Out the Best in People. New York: John Wiley & Sons, 1994.

2 R. Gustav Niebuhr, "Mass Shortage: Catholic Church Faces Crisis as Priests Quit and Recruiting Falls," *The Wall Street Journal*, November 13, 1990, A1, A13.

3 David E. Bowen and Edward E. Lawler III, "Total Quality-Ori-

ented Human Resource Management," *Organizational Dynamics* (spring 1992), 29–41.

4 D. Kneale, "Working at IBM: Intense Loyalty in a Rigid Culture," *The Wall Street Journal*, April 7, 1986, 17.

5 Jeffrey Pfeffer, "Producing Sustainable Competitive Advantage through the Effective Management of People," *Academy of Management Executive* 9, no. 1 (1995), 55–72.

6 Cynthia D. Fisher, "Current and Recurrent Challenges in HRM," *Journal of Management* 15 (1989), 157–180.

7 Lloyd Baird and Iian Meshoulam, "Getting Payoff from Investment in Human Resource Management," *Business Horizons* (January–February 1992), 60–75; and Donna Brown, "HR: Survival Tool for the 1990s," *Management Review* (March 1991), 10–14.

8 Cynthia A. Lengnick-Hall and Mark L. Lengnick-Hall, "Strategic Human Resources Management: A Review of the Literature and a Proposed Typology," *Academy of Management Review* 13 (1988), 454–470; and "Human Resources Managers Aren't Corporate Nobodies Any More," *Business Week*, December 2, 1985, 58–59.

9 Steven H. Appelbaun, Roger Simpson, and Barbara T. Shapiro, "The Tough Test of Downsizing," *Organizational Dynamics* (Autumn 1987), 68–79.

10 Shawn Tully, "Can Boeing Reinvent Itself?" *Fortune*, March 8, 1993, 66–73.

11 Richard E. Walton and Gerald I. Susman, "People Policies for the New Machines," *Harvard Business Review* 87 (March–April 1987), 98–106; and Randall S. Schuler and Susan E. Jackson, "Linking Competitive Strategies with Human Resource Management Practices," *The Academy of Management Executive* 1 (1987), 207–219.

12 Neal Templin, "Auto Plants, Hiring Again, Are Demanding Higher-Skilled Labor," *The Wall Street Journal*, March 11, 1994, A1, A4.

13 Joanne L. Symons, "Is Affirmative Action in America's Interest?" *Executive Female* (May–June 1995), 52; and David M. Alpern, "Why Women Are Divided on Affirmative Action," *Working Woman*, July 1995, 18.

14 Deidre A. Depke, "Picking Up the Tab for Bias at Shoney's," *Business Week*, November 6, 1992, 50.

15 Nina Schuyler, "No Rest Room for the Weary," *Working Woman* (July 1995), 13.

16 William E. Fulmer and Ann Wallace Casey, "Employment at Will: Options for Managers," *Academy of Management Executive* 4 (May 1990), 102–107; Aaron Bernstein, "More Dismissed Workers Are Telling It to the Judge," *Business Week*, October 17, 1988, 68–69; and Michael Goldblatt, "Preserving the Right to Fire," *Small Business Report* (December 1986), 87.

17 Barbara Ettorre, "The Contingency Workforce Moves Mainstream," *Management Review* (February 1994), 10–16.

18 Rod Willis, "Can American Unions Transform Themselves?" *Management Review* (February 1988), 12–21.

19 Ross L. Fink, Robert K. Robinson, and Ann Canty, "DuPont vs. Chemical Workers Association: Further Limits on Employee Participation Programs," *Industrial Management* (March–April 1994), 3–5; Scott Seegert and Brian H. Kleiner, "The Future of Labor-Management Relations," *Industrial Management* (March–April 1993), 15–16; and "Washington Week," *The Tennessean*, October 1, 1995, 18A.

20 James G. March and Herbert A. Simon, *Organizations* (New York: Wiley, 1958).

21 Dennis J. Kravetz, *The Human Resources Revolution* (San Francisco, Calif.: Jossey-Bass, 1989).

22 David E. Ripley, "How to Determine Future Workforce Needs," *Personnel Journal* (January 1995), 83–89.

23 D. Quinn Mills, "Planning with People in Mind," *Harvard Business Review* 63 (July–August 1985), 97–105; and USAir, 1985 Annual Report, 5.

24 J. W. Boudreau and S. L. Rynes, "Role of Recruitment in Staffing Utility Analysis," *Journal of Applied Psychology* 70 (1985), 354–366.

25 Roberta Maynard, "If the Shoe Fits . . ." *Nation's Business*, Oct. 1996, 18.

26 Brian Dumaine, "The New Art of Hiring Smart," *Fortune*, August 17, 1987, 78–81.

27 P. Farish, "HRM Update: Referral Results," *Personnel Administrator* 31 (1986), 22.

28 J. P. Wanous, *Organizational Entry* (Reading, Mass.: Addison-Wesley, 1980).

29 Larry Reibstein, "Crushed Hopes: When a New Job Proves to Be Something Different," *The Wall Street Journal*, June 10, 1987, 25.

30 Jacquelyn Denalli, "Negligent Hiring: Are You Liable When Employees Do Wrong?" *Self-Employed America* (January–February 1995), 10–11; and William S. Saling, "The Worth of Another's Words," *Self-Employed America* (January–February 1995), 11.

31 P. W. Thayer, "Somethings Old, Somethings New," *Personnel Psychology* 30 (1977), 513–524.

32 J. Ledvinka, *Federal Regulation of Personnel and Human Resource Management* (Boston: Kent, 1982); and Civil Rights Act, Title VII, 42 U.S.C. Section 2000e et seq. (1964).

33 The material in this section is largely drawn from R. D. Arvey and J. E. Campion, "The Employment Interview: A Summary and Review of Recent Research," *Personnel Psychology* 35 (1982), 281–322.

34 James M. Jenks and Brian L. P. Zevnik, "ABCs of Job Interviewing," *Harvard Business Review* (July–August 1989), 38–42.

35 A. Brown, "Employment Tests: Issues without Clear Answers," *Personnel Administrator* 30 (1985), 43–56.

36 Larry Reibstein, "More Firms Use Personality Tests for Entry-Level, Blue-Collar Jobs," *The Wall Street Journal*, January 16, 1986, 25.

37 "Assessment Centers: Identifying Leadership through Testing," *Small Business Report* (June 1987), 22–24; and W. C. Byham, "Assessment Centers for Spotting Future Managers," *Harvard Business Review* (July–August 1970), 150–167.

38 G. F. Dreher and P. R. Sackett, "Commentary: A Critical Look at Some Beliefs about Assessment Centers," in *Perspectives on Employee Staffing and Selection*, ed. G. F. Dreher and P. R. Sackett (Homewood, Ill.: Irwin, 1983), 258–265.

39 Bruce McDougall, "The Thinking Man's Assembly Line," *Canadian Business* (November 1991), 40–44; Louis Kraar, "Japan's Gung-Ho U.S. Car Plants," *Fortune*, January 30, 1989, 98–108; and Richard Koenig, "Toyota Takes Pains, and Time, Filling Jobs at Its Kentucky Plant," *The Wall Street Journal*, December 1, 1987, 129.

40 Bernard Keys and Joseph Wolfe, "Management Education and Development: Current Issues and Emerging Trends," *Journal of Management* 14 (1988), 205–229.

41 Michael Brody, "Helping Workers to Work Smarter," *Fortune*, June 8, 1987, 86–88.

42 Kevin Kelly and Peter Burrows, "Motorola: Training for the Millennium," *Business Week*, March 28, 1994, 158–163; and Nancy K. Austin, "Giving New Employees a Better Beginning," *Working Woman* (July 1995), 20–21, 74.

43 Pfeffer, "Producing Sustainable Competitive Advantage"; McCune, "On the Train Gang"; Max Messmar, "Cross-Discipline

Training: A Strategic Method to Do More with Less," *Management Review* (May 1992), 26–28; and Robert Cournoyer, "Integrative Learning Speeds Teamwork," *Management Review* (December 1991), 43–44.

44 Michael Barrier, "Closing the Skills Gap," *Nation's Business* (March 1996), 26–28.

45 Shari Caudron, "Skill-based Pay Program Improves Customer Service," *Personnel Journal*, June 1993, 64.

46 Walter W. Tornow, "Editor's Note: Introduction to Special Issue on 360-Degree Feedback," *Human Resource Management* 32, no. 2/3 (summer/fall 1993), 211–219; and Brian O'Reilly, "360 Feedback Can Change Your Life," *Fortune*, October 17, 1994, 93–100.

47 Milan Moravec, Ron Juliff, and Kathleen Hesler, "Partnerships Help a Company Manage Performance," *Personnel Journal*, January 1995, 104–108.

48 V. R. Buzzotta, "Improve Your Performance Appraisals," *Management Review* (August 1988), 40–43; and H. J. Bernardin and R. W. Beatty, *Performance Appraisal: Assessing Human Behavior at Work* (Boston: Kent, 1984).

49 Ibid.

50 Francine Alexander, "Performance Appraisals"; *Small Business Reports* (March 1989), 20–29.

51 D. Cederblom, "The Performance Appraisal Interview: A Review, Implications, and Suggestions," *Academy of Management Review* 7 (1982), 219–227.

52 Buzzotta, "Improve Your Performance Appraisals"; and Alexander, "Performance Appraisals."

53 Andrea Gabor, "Take This Job and Love It," *The New York Times*, January 26, 1992, F1, F6; and Steve Ventura and Eric Harvey, "Peer Review: Trusting Employees to Solve Problems," *Management Review* (January 1988), 48–51.

54 "Management Solutions: Peer Reviews: From Hiring to Firing," *Executive Management Forum* (April 1994), 1.

55 Richard I. Henderson, *Compensation Management: Rewarding Performance*, 4th ed. (Reston, Va.: Reston, 1985).

56 Renée F. Broderick and George T. Milkovich, "Pay Planning, Organization Strategy, Structure and 'Fit': A Prescriptive Model of Pay" (paper presented at the 45th Annual Meeting of the Academy of Management, San Diego, August 1985).

57 Michael Schroeder, "Watching the Bottom Line Instead of the Clock," *Business Week*, November 7, 1988, 134–136; and Bruce G.

Posner, "You Get What You Pay For," *Inc.* (September 1988), 91–92.

58 L. R. Burgess, *Wage and Salary Administration* (Columbus, Ohio: Merrill, 1984); and E. J. McCormick, *Job Analysis: Methods and Applications* (New York: AMACOM, 1979).

59 B. M. Bass and G. V. Barrett, *People, Work, and Organizations: An Introduction to Industrial and Organizational Psychology*, 2d ed. (Boston: Allyn & Bacon, 1981); and D. Doverspike, A. M. Carlisi, G. V. Barrett, and R. A. Alexander, "Generalizability Analysis of a Point-Method Job Evaluation Instrument," *Journal of Applied Psychology* 68 (1983), 476–483.

60 U.S. Chamber of Commerce, *Employee Benefits 1983* (Washington, D.C.: U.S. Chamber of Commerce, 1984).

61 Christopher Farrell, Paul Magnusson, and Wendy Zellner, "The Scary Math of New Hires," *Business Week*, February 22, 1993, 70–71.

62 J. A. Haslinger, "Flexible Compensation: Getting a Return on Benefit Dollars," *Personnel Administrator* 30 (1985), 39–46, 224.

63 Robert S. Catapano-Friedman, "Cafeteria Plans: New Menu for the '90s," *Management Review* (November 1991), 25–29.

64 James H. Donnelly, Jr., James L. Gibson, and John M. Ivancevich, "Management Focus: Hallmark," *Fundamentals of Management*, 9th ed. (Homewood, Ill.: Irwin, 1995), 447.

65 Sue Schellenbarger, "Insurance Firm Cracks Tight Labor Market with Flexible Hours," *The Wall Street Journal*, November 13, 1996, B1.

66 "Exit Interviews: An Overlooked Information Source," *Small Business Report* (July 1986), 52–55.

67 Michael P. Cronin, "Managing People: Employee Swapping," *Inc.* (December 1993), 165.

68 Rod Willis, "What's Happening to America's Middle Managers," *Management Review* (January 1987), 23–26; and Yvette Debow, "GE: Easing the Pain of Layoffs," *Management Review* (September 1987), 15–18.

69 Thomas H. Melohn, "Build Trust with Team Members," *Executive Excellence* 12, no. 6 (June 1995), 11–12; John Brandt, "The Flip Side of Corporate," *Industry Week*, Vol. 243, no. 17, Sept. 19, 1994, 12–16; Thomas Melohn, "Screening for the Best Employees," *Inc.* 9, no. 1 (January 1987), 104–106; Joshua Hyatt, "How to Hire Employees," *Inc.* 12, no. 3 (March 1990), 106–108; Tom Melohn, *The New Partnership: Profit by Bringing Out the Best in People* (New York: John Wiley & Sons, 1994).

Diversity in the Workplace

LEARNING OBJECTIVES

After studying this chapter, you should be able to

- Explain the dimensions of employee diversity and why ethnorelativism is the appropriate attitude for today's corporations.

- Discuss the changing workplace and the management activities required for a culturally diverse workforce.

- Explain affirmative action and why factors such as the glass ceiling have kept it from being more successful.

- Describe how to change the corporate culture, structure, and policies and how to use diversity awareness training to meet the needs of diverse employees.

- Explain what people expect in organizations, including the addressing of issues such as invisible minorities and sexual harassment.

- Describe benefits that accrue to companies that value diversity and the cost to companies that ignore it.

MANAGEMENT PROBLEM

In 1989, Phil Kosak, owner of Carolina Fine Snacks (CFS), was asked by the State Department of Rehabilitation to attend a job fair that placed disabled adults in the workforce. Kosak and his two partners, tired of dealing with an 80 percent employee turnover every six months, decided to explore this underutilized labor source. At the fair, David Bruton, who suffered from a severe learning disability, impressed Kosak with his optimism, honesty, and sincere desire to work. Kosak decided to give him a chance, hiring him on the spot as a packer and shipper. Bruton recalls, "Being the first handicapped person [hired by the company] was a great challenge to me." Kosak's decision to hire Bruton—and, later, seven other disabled people—was also a challenge to CFS's other employees, who were expected to train the new workers. Some were concerned about these workers' abilities to do the job or unsure of how employing disabled workers might affect company benefits programs. Others feared the disabled workers would have higher rates of absenteeism, increasing the workload of other employees. Many of the disabled employees, on the other hand, were eager to learn and work but felt uncomfortable in their new, unfamiliar surroundings and were nervous about fitting in with other employees.[1]

• Do you think disabled workers can make a genuine contribution at Carolina Fine Snacks? If you were Phil Kosak, how would you address the concerns of both the disabled employees and physically able CFS workers?

Diversity in the population, the workforce, and the marketplace is a fact of life no manager can afford to ignore today. All managers—those in small organizations such as Carolina Fine Snacks as well as those in giant corporations such as PepsiCo and Du Pont—daily face the challenge of managing employee diversity. The management of employee diversity entails recruiting, training, and fully utilizing workers who reflect the broad spectrum of society in all areas—gender, race, age, disability, ethnicity, religion, sexual orientation, education, and economic level.

Companies such as Xerox, AT&T, Burger King, Avon, Levi Strauss, and Hoechst Celanese all have established programs for increasing diversity. These programs teach current employees to value ethnic, racial, and gender differences, direct their recruiting efforts, and provide development training for females and minorities. These companies value diversity and are enforcing this value in day-to-day recruitment and promotion decisions.

Companies are beginning to reflect the U.S. image as a melting pot, but with a difference. In the past, the United States was a place where people of different national origins, ethnicities, races, and religions came together and blended to resemble one another. Opportunities for advancement were limited to those workers who fit easily into the mainstream of the larger culture. Some immigrants chose desperate measures to fit in, such as abandoning their native language, changing their last name, and sacrificing their own unique cultures. In essence, everyone in workplace organizations was encouraged to share similar beliefs, values, and lifestyles despite differences in gender, race, and ethnicity.[2]

Now organizations recognize that everyone is not the same and that the differences people bring to the workplace are valuable.[3] Rather than expecting all employees to adopt similar attitudes and values, companies are learning that these differences enable them to compete globally and to acquire rich sources of new talent. Although

diversity in North America has been a reality for many years, genuine efforts to accept and *manage* diverse people are a phenomenon of the 1990s.

This chapter introduces the topic of diversity, its causes and consequences. Ways to deal with workforce diversity are discussed, and organizational responses to diversity are explored. The negative consequences of ignoring diversity in today's world are identified, and the benefits of successfully maintaining a diverse workforce are discussed.

VALUING DIVERSITY

A Digital Equipment Corporation factory near Boston produces keyboards for Digital's computers. The factory employs 350 people, who come from 44 countries and speak 19 languages. When plant managers issue written announcements, they are printed in English, French, Spanish, Chinese, Portuguese, Vietnamese, and Haitian Creole.[4] This astonishing diversity is becoming typical in many companies.

Most managers, from any ethnic background, are ill-prepared to handle these multicultural differences. Many Americans attended segregated schools, lived in racially unmixed neighborhoods, and were unexposed to people substantially different from themselves.[5] A typical manager, schooled in traditional management training, easily could make the following mistakes.[6]

■ To reward a Vietnamese employee's high performance, her manager promoted her, placing her at the same level as her husband, who also worked at the factory. Rather than being pleased, the worker became upset and declined the promotion because Vietnamese husbands are expected to have a higher status than their wives.

■ A manager, having learned that a friendly pat on the arm or back would make workers feel good, took every

chance to touch his subordinates. His Asian employees hated being touched and thus started avoiding him, and several asked for transfers.

■ A manager declined a gift offered by a new employee, an immigrant who wanted to show gratitude for her job. He was concerned about ethics and explained the company's policy about not accepting gifts. The employee was so insulted she quit.

These issues related to cultural diversity are difficult and real. But before discussing how companies handle them, let's define diversity and explore people's attitudes toward it.

Dimensions of Diversity

Workforce diversity means the hiring and inclusion of people with different human qualities or who belong to various cultural groups. From the perspective of individuals, diversity means including people different from themselves along dimensions such as age, ethnicity, gender, or race.

Several important dimensions of diversity are illustrated in Exhibit 12.1. The inner circle represents primary dimensions of diversity, which include inborn differences or differences that have ongoing impact throughout one's life.[7] These are age, ethnicity, gender, physical abilities, race, and sexual orientation. These dimensions are core elements through which people shape their self-image and worldview.

Secondary dimensions of diversity, illustrated in the outer ring of Exhibit 12.1, can be acquired or changed throughout one's lifetime. These dimensions tend to have less impact than those of the core but nevertheless have impact on a person's self-definition and worldview. For example, Vietnam veterans may be perceived differently from other people and may have been profoundly affected by their military experience. Married people may be perceived differently and have somewhat different attitudes from people who are single. Like-

wise, work experience, education, and geographic location add dimensions to the way people define themselves and are defined by others.

A 55-year-old white male, an M.B.A. from Harvard and the father of two grown children, who is vice-president of a *Fortune* 500 company, may be perceived very differently from a female clerical worker, age 25, who is a single mother of two children and is attending evening classes to earn a college degree. Based on this information, can you predict the personal priorities and career expectations each person may have of the organization? The challenge for companies today is to recognize these differences and to value and use the unique strengths each person brings to the workplace.[8]

Attitudes toward Diversity

Valuing diversity by welcoming, recognizing, and cultivating differences among people so they can develop their unique talents and be effective organizational members is difficult to achieve. **Ethnocentrism** is the belief that one's own group and subculture are inherently superior to other groups and cultures. Ethnocentrism makes it difficult to value diversity. Viewing one's own culture as the best culture is a natural tendency

Consumers Gas (CG), Canada's largest natural-gas distribution utility, is one example of a company that *values diversity*. CG's commitment to diversity is evidenced by a long-term program, including in-house surveys to determine cultural diversity, efforts to attract a diverse workforce through an aggressive ad campaign, and participation in BRIDGES, a City-of-Toronto-sponsored program to increase skills for women in nontraditional careers. Here, some of the CG employees representing 22 countries celebrate cultural diversity at CG's 1992 Consumers Caravan.

workforce diversity
Hiring people with different human qualities who belong to various cultural groups.

ethnocentrism
The belief that one's own group or subculture is inherently superior to other groups or cultures.

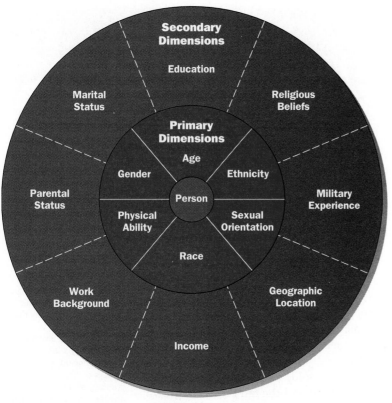

EXHIBIT 12.1

Primary and Secondary Dimensions of Diversity

SOURCE: Marilyn Loden and Judy B. Rosener, *Workforce America!* (Burr Ridge, IL: Irwin), 20. Reproduced with permission.

ethnorelativism

The belief that groups and subcultures are inherently equal.

pluralism

The organization accommodates several subcultures, including employees who would otherwise feel isolated and ignored.

monoculture

A culture that accepts only one way of doing things and one set of values and beliefs.

among most people.[9] Moreover, the business world tends to reflect the values, behaviors, and assumptions based on the experiences of a rather homogeneous, white, middle-class, male workforce.[10] Indeed, most theories of management presume that workers share similar values, beliefs, motivations, and attitudes about work and life in general. As discussed in the Focus on Diversity box, this is a false supposition, even when dealing with workers who share the same cultural background. These theories presume there is one set of behaviors that best help an organization to be productive and effective and therefore should be adopted by all employees.[11] This one-best-way approach explains why a manager may cause a problem by touching Asian employees or by not knowing how to handle a gift from an immigrant.

Ethnocentric viewpoints and a standard set of cultural practices produce a **monoculture**, a culture that accepts only one way of doing things and one set of values and be-

liefs. Exhibit 12.2 illustrates the assumptions that produce a monoculture and the type of monoculture that exists in many U.S. organizations. The assumption that people who are different are somehow deficient hampers efforts to take advantage of unique talents and abilities. Assumptions that diversity threatens smooth organizational functioning, that people who complain are oversensitive, or that people should not call attention to differences all support the status quo. These assumptions discourage analysis of organizational subcultures and allow managers to ignore the changes occurring in the workplace.

These assumptions of equality as sameness typically produce an "ideal" employee, qualities of which are listed in the center of Exhibit 12.2. When qualities such as being married, competitive, and Protestant become the norm for everyone, many people feel as if they do not fit into the organization. People of color, women, gay people, the disabled, the elderly, and other diverse employees may feel undue pressure to conform, may be victims of stereotyping attitudes, and may be presumed deficient because they are different. White, heterosexual men, many of whom themselves do not fit the notions of the "ideal" employee, may also feel uncomfortable with the monoculture and resent stereotypes that label all white males as racists and sexists. Valuing diversity means ensuring that all people are given equal opportunities in the workplace.[12]

The goal for organizations seeking cultural diversity is pluralism rather than a monoculture and ethnorelativism rather than ethnocentrism. **Ethnorelativism** is the belief that groups and subcultures are inherently equal. **Pluralism** means that an organization accommodates several subcultures. Movement toward pluralism seeks to fully integrate into the organization the employees who otherwise would feel isolated and ignored. As the workforce changes, organizations will come to resemble a global village.

Most organizations must undertake conscious efforts to shift from a monoculture

FOCUS ON DIVERSITY
DO WOMEN AND MEN COMMUNICATE DIFFERENTLY?

In recent years, researchers and writers have captured the public imagination with descriptions of gender differences in communication and moral development. Carol Gilligan's *In a Different Voice* describes how women's sense of morality and right versus wrong is different (though not necessarily better or worse) than men's. In decision making, then, men are more concerned with abstract concepts, rules, and hierarchy, while women focus on connections with other human beings and the quality of relationships. Similarly, Deborah Tannen's *You Just Don't Understand* identifies the tendency for women to be more relationship oriented. Hence, they tend to be better communicators and try to be supportive and inclusive without offending others. Men, on the other hand, have a more competitive communication style that is outcome oriented. In relationships, women often want to share and process, while men want to give advice and offer solutions.

It should be pointed out that no one is ever purely "male" or "female" in style. However, the following chart shows some basic gender differences in communication.

Male style *Emphasis is on*	*Female style* *Emphasis is on*
Superiority or uniqueness	Understanding
Work accomplishments	Personal needs of self or others
Content	Process
Asking directly for needs	Hinting about needs
Acting businesslike with others at work	Making others feel comfortable and included
Raising voice	Speaking politely
Rules, procedures, and techniques to solve problems	Relying on the strength of relationships to resolve issues
Showing power with position in organization	Showing power with respect to others

Gilligan found that the differences begin early in life. Young boys tend to play games with elaborate rules and a lot of competition; when there is a problem, the rules are used to solve it. Girls' games, on the other hand, are more relationship oriented and have few rules, being designed to make other players feel included. When they have problems, girls often end the game rather than jeopardize the friendship. Gilligan believes adult male and female style differences are based on these early divergent approaches.

As to where these differences come from, the debate over whether boys and girls are born different or socialized to be different rages on. As shown in the following chart from an actual kindergarten class, girls are often taught different values, motivations, and attitudes at an early age and carry these into adulthood.

Chart of Kindergarten Awards

Boys' Awards	*Girls' Awards*
Very best thinker	All-around sweetheart
Most eager learner	Sweetest personality
Most imaginative	Cutest personality
Most enthusiastic	Best sharer
Most scientific	Best artist
Best friend	Biggest heart
Mr. Personality	Best manners
Hardest worker	Best helper
Best sense of humor	Most creative

SOURCES: Carol Gilligan, *In a Different Voice* (Cambridge, Mass.: Harvard University Press, 1982); Deborah Tannen, *You Just Don't Understand* (New York: Morrow Books, 1990); Nancy Langton, "Gender Difference in Communication," in *Organizational Behavior: Experiences and Cases*, ed. Dorothy Marcic, 4th ed. (St. Paul, Minn.: West, 1995), 265–268; and Kathleen Deveny, "Chart of Kindergarten Awards," *The Wall Street Journal*, December 5, 1994, B1.

---

perspective to one of pluralism. Employees in a monoculture may not be aware of culture differences, or they may have acquired negative stereotypes toward other cultural values and assume that their own culture is superior. Through effective training, employees can be helped to accept different ways of thinking and behaving, the first step away from narrow, ethnocentric thinking. Ultimately, employees are able to integrate diverse cultures, which means that judgments of appropriateness, goodness, badness, and morality are no longer applied to cultural differences. Cultural differences are experienced as essential, natural, and joyful, enabling an organization to enjoy true pluralism and take advantage of diverse human resources.[13]

For example, IBM has made a firm commitment to break out of monoculture thinking. To defuse tensions among diverse employees at IBM's System Storage Division in San Jose, the company launched an annual diversity day, where employees

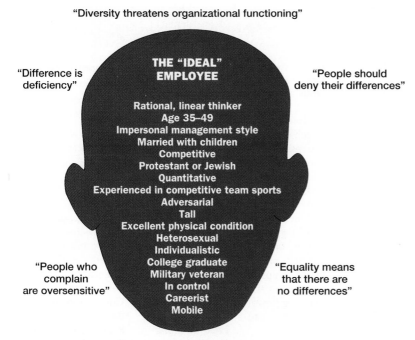

"Diversity threatens organizational functioning"

"Difference is deficiency"

THE "IDEAL" EMPLOYEE

"People should deny their differences"

Rational, linear thinker
Age 35–49
Impersonal management style
Married with children
Competitive
Protestant or Jewish
Quantitative
Experienced in competitive team sports
Adversarial
Tall
Excellent physical condition
Heterosexual
Individualistic
College graduate
Military veteran
In control
Careerist
Mobile

"People who complain are oversensitive"

"Equality means that there are no differences"

"Different people must change, not the organization"

EXHIBIT 12.2
Cultural Assumptions Associated with a White, Male Monoculture

SOURCE: Marilyn Loden and Judy B. Rosener, *Workforce America!* (Burr Ridge, IL: Irwin), 43. Reproduced with permission.

dress in ethnic costumes, perform traditional dances, and prepare authentic ethnic dishes to share with fellow workers. Videos featuring a different culture each month are played in key gathering spots throughout the plant.[14] By helping employees develop greater sensitivity and acceptance of cultural difference, IBM moves away from an ethnocentric attitude and is able to accept and integrate people from diverse cultural backgrounds.

THE CHANGING WORKPLACE

The importance of cultural diversity and employee attitudes that welcome cultural differences will result from the inevitable changes taking place in the workplace, in our society, and in the economic environment. These changes include globalization and the changing workforce.[15] Earlier chapters described the impact of global competition on business in North America. Competition is intense. About 70 percent of

all U.S. businesses are engaged directly in competition with companies overseas. Companies that succeed in this environment need to adopt radical new ways of doing business, with sensitivity toward the needs of different cultural practices. For example, approximately 18 car companies, especially those from Japan and Germany, have established design centers in Los Angeles. Southern California is viewed as a melting pot, an Anglo-Afro-Latino-Asian ethnic mix. Companies that need to sell cars all over the world love the diverse values in this multicultural proving ground.[16]

Other companies, such as Gillette and Motorola, are building plants overseas, not only to obtain inexpensive labor but also to develop a presence in rapidly growing markets. The international diversity must be integrated into the overall company to allow it to work effectively. To encourage workers at a plant in Boynton Beach, Florida, to collaborate with a sister plant in Singapore, Motorola flew most of them to a Colorado resort for bonding exercises.[17]

The single biggest challenge facing companies is the changing composition of the workforce. The average worker is older now, and many more women, people of color, and immigrants are entering the workforce. Indeed, white males, the majority of workers in the past, compose less than half the workforce, and white, native-born males are expected to contribute only 15 percent of new entrants to the workforce through the year 2000.[18]

Exhibit 12.3 illustrates the management activities required for dealing with a culturally diverse workforce. For example, consider the increased career involvement of women. By the year 2000, it is estimated that 61 percent of the women in the United States will be employed, constituting 47 percent of the workforce, almost equaling the percentage of male workers.[19] This change represents an enormous opportunity to organizations, but it also means that organizations must deal with issues such as work–family conflicts, dual-career couples, and sexual harassment. Since seven of ten women in the labor force have children, or-

E X H I B I T   1 2 . 3
Management Activities for a Culturally Diverse Workforce

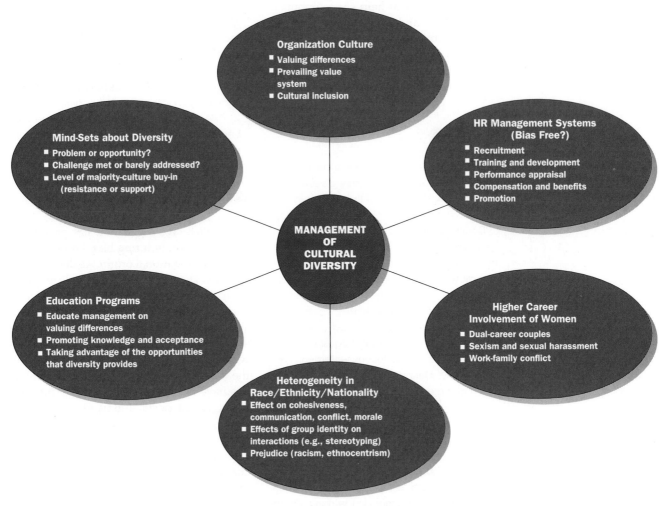

SOURCE: Taylor H. Cox and Stacy Blake, "Managing Cultural Diversity: Implications for Organizational Competitiveness," *Academy of Management Executive* 5, no. 3 (1991), 45–56.

ganizations should prepare to take more of the responsibility for child care.

Moreover, can human resource management systems operate bias free, dropping the perception of a middle-aged, white male as the ideal employee? People of African, Asian, and Hispanic descent make up 21 percent of the American population today, and that figure will grow to 25 percent in ten years. Already more than 30 percent of New York City's residents are foreign-born. Miami is two-thirds Hispanic American; Detroit is two-thirds African American; and San Francisco is one-third Asian American.[20] Whereas in previous generations most foreign-born immigrants came from Western Europe, 84 percent of recent immigrants come from Asia and Latin America.[21] These immigrants come to the United States with a wide range of backgrounds, often without adequate skills in using English. Organizations must not only face the issues of dealing with race, ethnicity, and nationality to provide a prejudice-free workplace but also develop sufficient educational programs to help immigrants

acquire the technical and customer service skills required in a service economy.

Top managers can help shape organizational values and employee mind-sets about cultural differences. In addition, training programs can promote knowledge and acceptance of diverse cultures and educate managers on valuing the differences.

 DENNY'S

Restaurant-chain Denny's has shown how a worst-offender status in minority discrimination can be changed to one of the leaders in multicultural sensitivity through strong leadership.

Denny's restaurants in 1993 were seen as the epitome of big-business bigotry. Class action suits for discrimination towards minority customers were filed and the public found out there were no minority top-managers and only one out of 512 franchisees was a minority. Another distinction it claimed around that time was the payout of the largest ($54 million) public accommodations settlement ever.

To many, Denny's looked pretty hopeless. And many are now surprised by its quick turnaround in just a few years' time. By 1996, minority officers made up 11% of the group and African American franchisees rose to 27. Even the lawyer for the black customers said that Denny's has "jumped out in front and taken a positive approach to solving its problems, unlike most companies that do the minimum required by law."

In order to bring about these massive changes, Denny's brought in a new CEO and its parent company also got a new leader. Together the two new CEOs revamped the old culture, taking an offensive and proactive approach. CEO Adamson said he would do everything possible to "provide better jobs for women and minorities. And I will fire you if you discriminate. Anyone who doesn't like the direction this train is moving had better jump off now."

Within a few months, eight of the twelve officers left. Some of the replacements include Hispanics and women.

Adamson's changes included four parts: (a) loosen up the hierarchy, (b) use diversity as a performance criterion for managers, (c) send everyone to diversity training, and (d) never miss a chance to preach the gospel of diversity. In addition, Denny's now has a fast-track program for aspiring minorities and is aggressively recruiting and assisting potential minority franchisees. In order to facilitate these changes, Adamson hired Rachelle Hood-Phillips as head of diversity affairs. Perhaps Denny's new success in diversity is attributable to her attitude.

"We want to help people to change their hearts, their perspectives, and their behavior," she says.[22] ■

AFFIRMATIVE ACTION

Since 1964, civil legislation has prohibited discrimination in hiring based on race, religion, sex, or national origin. As described in Chapter 11 of the text, these policies were designed to facilitate recruitment, retention, and promotion of minorities and women. To some extent, these policies have been successful, opening organization doors to women and minorities. However, despite the job opportunities, women and minorities have not succeeded in getting into top management posts. Today, affirmative action is being hotly debated in the states, Congress, the Supreme Court, and corporate America, and there are likely to be changes in affirmative action programs over the next few years. [23]

Current Debates about Affirmative Action

Affirmative action was developed in response to conditions 30 years ago. Adult white males dominated the workforce, and economic conditions were stable and improving. Because of widespread prejudice and discrimination, legal and social coercion was necessary to allow women, people of color, immigrants, and other minorities to become part of the economic system.[24]

Today, the situation has changed. More than half the U.S. workforce consists of women and minorities; the economic situation is changing rapidly as a result of international competition.

Within this fluid situation, many companies actively recruited women and minorities to comply with affirmative action guidelines. Companies often succeeded in identifying a few select individuals who were recruited, trained, and given special consideration. These people carried great expectations and pressure. They were highly visible role models for the newly recruited groups. It was generally expected that these individuals would march right to the top of the corporate ladder.

Within a few years, it became clear that few of these people would reach the top. Management typically was frustrated and upset because of the money poured into the affirmative action programs. The individuals were disillusioned about how difficult it was to achieve and felt frustrated and alienated. Managers were unhappy with the program failures and may have doubted the qualifications of people they recruited. Did they deserve the jobs at all? Were women and minority candidates to blame for the failure of the affirmative action program? Should companies be required to meet federally mandated minority-hiring targets?

In recent years, outspoken opponents of affirmative action have brought the debate into the public consciousness. Washington has sent mixed messages to women and minorities. President George Bush's firm "no quotas" position stood in sharp contrast to the passage of the 1990 Americans with Disabilities Act or the 1991 Civil Rights Act. Each issue stirred debate about cultural bias versus increasing government interference in business. More recently, leading Republican presidential candidates made statements opposing racial hiring preferences, and California Governor Pete Wilson issued an executive order dismantling some of that state's affirmative action programs. For the first time since its inception, President Clinton publicly ordered an internal review of affirmative action, signaling a less-than-firm commitment on the part of Democratic leaders as well.[25] Californian Jack Ybarra is an example of someone directly affected by the changes in affirmative action.

TRANSMETRICS INC.

The son of immigrant fruit-pickers, Mexican American Jack Ybarra launched his transportation-engineering company, Transmetrics Inc., in 1982 with a home equity loan and almost called it quits. Contracts were few and far between. Just as he was about to give up, he got a big contract from Bechtel Corp., who hired Ybarra partly because of his minority status.

Because California-based Transmetrics could qualify for preferred disadvantaged-minority status, Ybarra got more contracts, enabling him to earn revenues of more than $3 million in recent years. Now the company is too big and no longer gets preferential treatment. But Ybarra expects 1997 to hit $4 million. Still, about 88 percent of contracts are affirmative action holdovers, even though he is now proud of the competent work record and satisfied clients.

With California's recent repeal of affirmative action preference programs, Ybarra believes minority contractors will have hard times ahead. "It [will be] rough," he says.[26] ∎

Some companies are arguing the need for broader diversity strategies intended to foster a bias-free workplace, rather than strict head counts of women or minorities hired. At Pacific Gas & Electric, long a proponent of affirmative action, one vice-president says downsizing has made it almost impossible for the San Francisco-based utility to meet its minority hiring targets. PG&E is asking Washington to approve a pilot program that would count mentoring and leadership development seminars for minorities as part of its affirmative action program.[27] Social justice activists, on the other hand, argue that this is just a way for companies to put on a show of virtue without having to do anything concrete about affirmative action issues. Al Jackson, director of diversity and staff development at *Scholastic Magazine,* echoes the sentiments of many when he notes that most firms do not hire and promote women and minorities as readily as they do white males, no matter how much they talk about valuing diversity.[28]

Ultimately, the problem with affirmative action boils down to an unspoken and often unintended sexism and racism in organizations. Top managers find it hard to understand just how white and male their corporate culture is and how forbidding it seems to those who are obviously different.[29] The affirmative action cycle fails when women, people of color, and immigrants are brought into a monoculture system and the burden of adaptation falls on the candidates coming through the system rather than on the organization itself. Part of the reason for the failure may be attributed to what is called the *glass ceiling.*

The Glass Ceiling

The **glass ceiling** is an invisible barrier that separates women and minorities from top management positions. They can look up through the ceiling and see top management, but prevailing attitudes are invisible obstacles to their own advancement. A recent study suggested the additional existence of "glass walls," which serve as invisible barriers to important lateral movement within the organization. Glass walls bar experience in areas such as line supervisor positions that would enable women and minorities to advance vertically.[30]

Evidence of the glass ceiling is the distribution of women and minorities, who are clustered at the bottom levels of the corporate hierarchy. A recent study shows that 97 percent of the top managers in the United States are white, and at least 95 percent of them are male.[31] Women and minorities also earn substantially less. As shown in Exhibit 12.4, black, male employees earn 24 percent to 27 percent less than what their white counterparts earn, even when educational levels are similar. Women earn considerably less than their male peers, with black women earning the least. As women move up the career ladder, the wage gap widens; at the level of vice-president, a woman's average salary is 42 percent less than her male counterpart.[32]

In particular, women who leave the corporate world to care for young children have a difficult time moving up the hierarchy when they return. One term used to describe this is the *mommy track,* which implies that women's commitment to their children limits their commitment to the company or their ability to handle the rigors of corporate management. These women risk being treated as beginners when they return, no matter how vast their skills and experience, and they continue to lag behind in salary, title, and responsibility.[33]

Another current issue related to the glass ceiling is homosexuals in the workplace. Many gay men and lesbians believe they will not be accepted as they are and risk losing their jobs or their chances for advancement. The director of human resources for a large Midwestern hospital would like to be honest about her lesbianism but says she knows of almost no one at her level of the corporate hierarchy who has taken that step—"It's just not done here."[34] Thus, gays and lesbians often fabricate heterosexual identities to keep their jobs or avoid running into the glass ceiling they see other employees encounter.

Why does the glass ceiling persist? The monoculture at top levels is the most frequent explanation. Top-level corporate culture evolves around white, heterosexual, American males, who tend to hire and promote people who look, act, and think like them. Compatibility in thought and behavior plays an important role at higher levels of organizations.[35] Of the people moving up the corporate ladder, white men tend to be more compatible with those already at the top.

Another reason for the persistent glass ceiling is the relegation of women and minorities to less visible positions and projects so that their work fails to come to the attention of top executives. Stereotyping by male middle managers may lead to the assumption that a woman's family life will interfere with her work or that minorities lack competence for important assignments. Women and minorities often believe that they must work harder and perform at higher levels than their white male counterparts in order to be noticed, recognized, fully accepted,

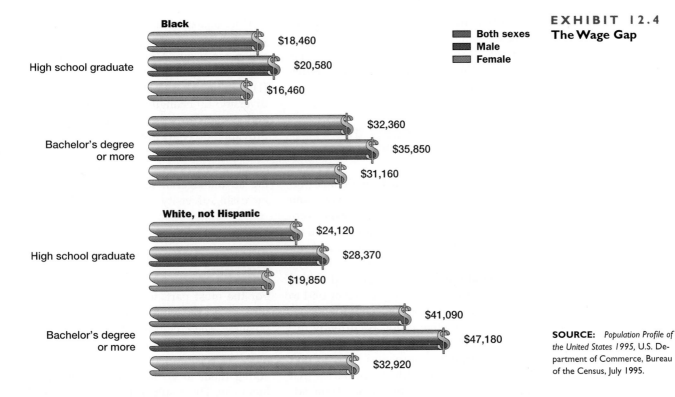

EXHIBIT 12.4
The Wage Gap

SOURCE: *Population Profile of the United States 1995*, U.S. Department of Commerce, Bureau of the Census, July 1995.

and promoted. Even when women or minorities are promoted into supervisory positions, they often fail to move farther up the hierarchy because of subtle sexism and racism in the workplace.

For example, African Americans have found that racism in the workplace often shows up in subtle ways—the disregard by a subordinate for an assigned chore; a lack of urgency in completing an important assignment; the ignoring of comments or suggestions made at a meeting. Black managers struggle on a daily basis with the problem of delegating authority and responsibility to employees who show them little respect. This often results from tension or jealousy by white employees who have never before been supervised by a minority manager; what's more, many of these employees may not even be aware of what they're doing. "We certainly don't want to imply that everyone is consciously running around being racist," says Jacqueline Dickins, coauthor with her husband of *The Black Manager: Making It in the Corporate World*. "These attitudes are so ingrained in our society that we don't often realize we are practicing the behavior."

With the increased number of women and minorities in the workplace, many companies have put diversity training at the top of the corporate agenda. Xerox Corporation, for example, offers seminars on sensitive topics such as race relations, including white backlash. Still, some black managers question the commitment of corporate America to diversity and believe their prospects for future advancement are bleak.

Recent problems with alleged racism and discrimination at such companies as Texaco Inc., prove what these black managers have been saying: We have a long way to go. One reason diversity training achieves only mild success is that executives rarely pursue diversity strategy with the same passion as company initiatives believed to be more directly relevant to the proverbial bottom line. Diversity program budgets get squeezed, managers rush through their canned speeches to the "troops," and workers view off-the-shelf videos. It's no surprise that little happens.

"There aren't that many of us," said one black manager, "[and] the limitations are blatant. I can't say that one day I will become the CEO of this company. There is definitely a glass ceiling."[36]

NEW RESPONSES TO CULTURAL DIVERSITY

Affirmative action opened the doors of organizations in this country to women and minorities. However, the path toward promotion to top ranks has remained closed for the most part, with many women and minorities hitting the glass ceiling.[37] Although the federal government responded to this problem with the Civil Rights Act of 1991 to amend and strengthen the Civil Rights Act of 1964, affirmative action is currently under attack. As the debate over affirmative action continues, companies need to find new ways to deal with the obstacles that prevent women and minorities from advancing to senior management positions in the future.

How can managers prepare their organizations to accommodate diversity in the future? First, organization leaders and managers must come to terms with their own definitions of diversity and should be encouraged to think beyond race and gender issues to consider such factors as education, background, and personality differences.

Once a vision for a diverse workplace has been created and defined, the organization can analyze and assess the current culture and systems within the organization. This assessment is followed by a willingness to change the status quo in order to modify current systems and ways of thinking. Throughout this process, people need support in dealing with the many challenges and inevitable conflicts they will face. Training and support are important for the people in pioneering roles. Finally, managers should not de-emphasize affirmative action programs, because these are critical for giving minorities and women access to jobs in the organization.

Once managers accept the need for a program to develop a truly diverse workplace, action can begin. A program to implement such a change involves three major steps: (1) building a corporate culture that values diversity; (2) changing structures, policies, and systems to support diversity; and (3) providing diversity awareness training. For each of these efforts to succeed, top management support is critical, as well as holding all managerial ranks accountable for increasing diversity.

Changing the Corporate Culture

For the most part, today's corporate cultures reflect the white male model of doing business. These cultures are not conducive to including women and minorities in important decision-making processes or enabling them to go high in the corporate hierarchy. The result of this mismatch between the dominant culture and the growing employee population of minorities and women is that many employees' talents will be underutilized, and the corporation will be less competitive.

Chapters 3 and 10 describe approaches for changing corporate culture. Managers can start by actively using symbols for the new values, such as encouraging and celebrating the promotion of minorities. To promote positive change, executives must change their own assumptions and recognize that employee diversity is real, is good, and must be valued. Executives must lead the way in changing from a white male monoculture to a multiculture in which differences among people are valued.

To accomplish this, managers must be willing to examine the unwritten rules and assumptions. What are the myths about minorities? What are the values that exemplify the existing culture? Are unwritten rules communicated from one person to another in a way that excludes women and minorities? For example, many men may not discuss unwritten rules with women and minorities because they assume everyone is

aware of them and they do not want to seem patronizing.[38]

Companies are addressing the issue of changing culture in a variety of ways. Some are using surveys, interviews, and focus groups to identify how the cultural values affect minorities and women. Others have set up structured networks of people of color, women, and other minority groups to explore the issues they face in the workplace and to recommend changes to senior management. Corning, Inc., appointed a task force to tackle the problem of how to recruit, retain, and develop talented minority workers.

CORNING, INC.

In the mid-1980s, Corning was losing female and African American professionals at twice the rate of white males. As part of a corporate-wide total quality effort, top management appointed a task force to examine the problem of how to retain and develop talented women and African Americans. The task force was part of a top-down initiative with the goal of ensuring that each employee had the opportunity "to participate fully, to grow professionally, and to develop to his or her highest potential." The task force study led to the following interventions:

◆ Race and gender awareness training, in which aspects of corporate culture that inhibit flexibility and diversity are addressed. One outcome is that new employees are no longer encouraged to adopt the dress, style, and social activities of the white male culture.
◆ Company child-care services and expanded family-care leaves for all workers who need them.
◆ Career-planning seminars for all employees, plus more widely disseminated information about the processes for promotion.
◆ Community projects that make the geographical area more attractive to minority families.
◆ Incorporation of workplace flexibility and diversity issues into management performance reviews.

Since Corning began making these changes, the recruitment, retention, and advancement of women and African Americans have all improved, and the company is now turning its attention to other minority groups. Corning's culture has gradually begun to change; diverse styles are seen as a strength that helps the company relate to the varied styles of its customers.[39] ■

Many companies have discovered, as did Corning, that people will choose companies that are accepting, inviting, and friendly and that help them meet personal goals.[40] Successful companies, like Corning, carefully assess their cultures and make changes from the top down because the key to productivity is a loyal, trained, capable workforce. New cultural values mean that the exclusionary practices of the past must come to an end.

Changing Structures and Policies

Many policies within organizations originally were designed to fit the stereotypical male employee. Now leading companies are changing structures and policies to facilitate the recruitment and career advancement of diverse employee groups.

Recruitment. A good way to revitalize the recruiting process is for the company to examine employee demographics, the composition of the labor pool in the area, and the composition of the customer base. Managers then can work toward a workforce composition that reflects the labor pool and the customer base. Moreover, the company can look at dimensions of diversity other than race and gender, including age, ethnicity, physical abilities, and sexual orientation. For example, workers age 55 and over are the fastest growing segment of America's labor force, and concern over age discrimination is an increasingly important issue.[41]

For many organizations, a new approach to recruitment will mean recruiting more effectively than today. This could mean

making better use of formal recruiting strategies, offering internship programs to give people opportunities, and developing creative ways to draw upon previously unused labor markets.

Career Advancement. The successful advancement of diverse group members means that organizations must find ways to eliminate the glass ceiling. One of the most successful structures to accomplish this is the mentoring relationship. A mentor is a higher ranking, senior organizational member who is committed to providing upward mobility and support to a protégé's professional career.[42] Mentoring provides minorities and women with direct training and inside information on the norms and expectations of the organization. A mentor also acts as a friend or counselor, enabling the employee to feel more confident and capable.

Research indicates that women and minorities are less likely than men to develop mentoring relationships.[43] In the workplace where people's backgrounds are diverse, forging these relationships may be more difficult. Women often do not seek mentors because they feel job competency is enough to succeed, or they may fear that initiating a mentoring relationship could be misunderstood as a romantic overture. Male mentors may feel uncomfortable with minority male protégés. Their backgrounds and interests may differ, leaving them with nothing but work in common. Male mentors may stereotype women as mothers, wives, or sisters rather than as executive material. The few minorities and women who have reached the upper ranks often are overwhelmed with mentoring requests from people like themselves, and they may feel uncomfortable in highly visible minority–minority or female–female mentoring relationships, which isolate them from the white male status quo.

The solution is for organizations to overcome some of the barriers to mentor relationships between white males and minorities. When organizations can institutionalize the value of white males actively seeking women and minority protégés, the benefits will mean that women and minorities will be steered into pivotal jobs and positions critical to advancement. Mentoring programs also are consistent with the Civil Rights Act of 1991 that requires the diversification of middle and upper management.

Accommodating Special Needs. Many people have special needs of which male top managers are unaware. For example, if a number of people entering the organization at the lower level are single parents, the company can reassess job scheduling and opportunities for child care. If a substantial labor pool is non-English-speaking, training materials and information packets can be provided in another language.

In many families today, both parents work, which means that the company may provide structures to deal with child care, maternity or paternity leave, flexible work schedules, home-based employment, and perhaps part-time employment or seasonal hours that reflect the school year. The key to attracting and keeping elderly or disabled workers may include long-term-care insurance and special health or life benefits. Alternative work scheduling also may be important for these groups of workers.

In the United States, racial/ethnic minorities and immigrants have fewer educational opportunities than most other groups. Many companies have started working with high schools to provide fundamental skills in literacy and arithmetic, or they provide these skills within the company to upgrade employees to appropriate educational levels. The movement toward increasing educational services for employees can be expected to increase for immigrants and the economically disadvantaged in the years to come.

Diversity Awareness Training

Many organizations, including Monsanto, Xerox, and Mobil Oil, provide special training, called **diversity awareness training,** to help people become aware of their own cul-

diversity awareness training
Special training designed to make people aware of their own prejudices and stereotypes.

tural boundaries, their prejudices and stereotypes, so they can learn to work and live together. Working or living within a multicultural context requires a person to use interaction skills that transcend the skills typically effective when dealing with others from one's own in-group.[44] Diversity awareness programs help people learn how to handle conflict in a constructive manner, which tends to reduce stress and negative energy in diverse work teams.

People vary in their sensitivity and openness to other cultures. Exhibit 12.5 shows a model of six stages of diversity awareness. The continuum ranges from a total lack of awareness to a complete understanding and acceptance of people's differences. This model is useful in helping diversity awareness trainers assess participants' openness to change. People at different stages may require different kinds of training. A basic aim of awareness training is to help people recognize that hidden and overt biases direct their thinking about specific individuals and groups. If people can come away from a training session recognizing that they prejudge people and that this needs to be consciously addressed in communications with and treatment of others, an important goal of diversity awareness training has been reached.

Many diversity awareness programs used today are designed to help people of varying backgrounds communicate effectively with one another and to understand the language and context used in dealing with people from other groups. The point of this training is to help people be more flexible in their communications with others, to treat each person as an individual, and not to rely on stereotypes. Effective programs move people toward being open in their relationships with others. For example, if you were a part of such a program, it would help you develop an explicit awareness of your own cultural values, your own cultural boundaries, and your own cultural behaviors. Then you would be provided the same information about other groups, and you would be given the opportunity to learn about and communicate with people

from other groups. One of the most important elements in diversity training is to bring together people of differing perspectives so that they can engage in learning new interpersonal communication skills with one another.

DEFINING NEW RELATIONSHIPS IN ORGANIZATIONS

Men, women, people of color, whites, older people, younger people, the physically able, the physically disabled, and others are all struggling to define new ways of relating in the workplace. In the past, ways of relating to other groups were defined outside the workplace, in the family or community. The stereotypes and role expectations that define traditional ways of relating often did not allow these groups to develop their unique strengths at work. Diverse organizations have the potential to meet the wants of all groups, including "invisible" minorities, while fostering balanced priorities and psychological intimacy and preventing sexual harassment.

What People Want

People in all groups are struggling to identify how to relate to people who are different from themselves. Most employees genuinely want to learn how to handle work relationships without being affected by stereotypes and prejudices, and they are becoming more sensitive to what others need and want in work relationships.

Questions for understanding what people want and for avoiding stereotypes are illustrated in Exhibit 12.6. Men have needs as well as women, whites as well as blacks.[45] Exhibit 12.6 illustrates factors that would increase comfort levels in organizations and decrease tension among people of diverse backgrounds. Understanding what people want enables them to relate to one another with authenticity and acceptance. Understanding these needs helps managers to respect and accept others on their own terms.

EXHIBIT 12.5
Stages of Diversity Awareness

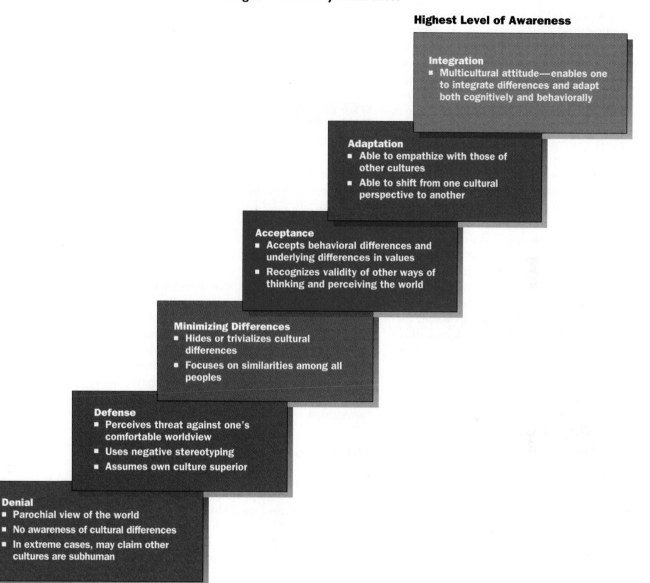

Highest Level of Awareness

Integration
- Multicultural attitude—enables one to integrate differences and adapt both cognitively and behaviorally

Adaptation
- Able to empathize with those of other cultures
- Able to shift from one cultural perspective to another

Acceptance
- Accepts behavioral differences and underlying differences in values
- Recognizes validity of other ways of thinking and perceiving the world

Minimizing Differences
- Hides or trivializes cultural differences
- Focuses on similarities among all peoples

Defense
- Perceives threat against one's comfortable worldview
- Uses negative stereotyping
- Assumes own culture superior

Denial
- Parochial view of the world
- No awareness of cultural differences
- In extreme cases, may claim other cultures are subhuman

Lowest Level of Awareness

SOURCE: Based on M. Bennett, "A Developmental Approach to Training for Intercultural Sensitivity," *International Journal of Intercultural Relations* 10 (1986), 179–196.

Everyone, not just minorities, has needs and wants that can be met in a workplace that acknowledges and values diversity.

Invisible Minorities

Considerable focus has been placed on the problems, rights, and working conditions of visible minorities—women, blacks, Asians, Hispanics, the aged, the disabled—but members of "invisible minorities" continue suffering prejudice, alienation, and isolation. **Invisible minorities** include individuals who share a social stigma that is not visibly recognizable.[46] Concerns about unmasking the stigma so that it becomes visi-

invisible minorities
Individuals who share a social stigma that is not visibly recognizable.

EXHIBIT 12.6
**Building a
Multiculture: What
Do People Want?**

Younger and Older Employees Want
To have more respect for their life experiences
To be taken seriously
To be challenged by their organizations, not patronized

Women Want
To be recognized as equal contributors
To have active support of male colleagues
To have work and family issues actively addressed by organizations

Men Want
To have the same freedom to grow/feel that women have
To be perceived as allies, not the enemy
To bridge the gap with women at home and at work

People of Color Want
To be valued as unique individuals, as members of ethnically diverse groups, as people of different races, and as equal contributors
To establish more open, honest working relationships with people of other races and ethnic groups
To have the active support of white people in fighting racism

White People Want
To have their ethnicity acknowledged
To reduce discomfort, confusion, and dishonesty in dealing with people of color
To build relationships with people of color based on common goals, concerns, and mutual respect for differences

Disabled People Want
To have greater acknowledgment of and focus on abilities, rather than on disabilities
To be challenged by colleagues and organizations to be their best
To be included, not isolated

Able-Bodied People Want
To develop more ease in dealing with physically disabled people
To give honest feedback and appropriate support without being patronizing or overprotective

Gay Men and Lesbians Want
To be recognized as whole human beings, not just sexual beings
To have equal employment protection
To have increased awareness among people regarding the impact of heterosexism in the workplace

Heterosexuals Want
To become more aware of lesbian and gay issues
To have a better understanding of the legal consequences of being gay in America
To increase dialogue about heterosexist issues with lesbians and gay men

SOURCE: Marilyn Loden and Judy B. Rosener, *Workforce America!* (Burr Ridge, IL: Irwin), 76–78. Reproduced with permission.

ble become the major social dynamic for these groups. We all have so-called skeletons in our closets, but the potential social stigma toward invisible minorities dominates their working and social relationships. For example, gays and lesbians, unwed parents, atheists, children of gays and lesbians, family members of people with AIDS, and members of 12-step recovery programs for alcohol, drugs, or eating disorders often feel they must carefully guard their "real" lives. Members of invisible minorities wonder "Should I tell?" "Whom should I tell?" "Will they find out?" "How will they react?"

As companies increasingly focus on diversity issues and establish programs dealing with various groups and subcultures, management can also develop an awareness of, and sensitivity to, the experiences of people in less visible minority groups.

Balancing Family Priorities

With 8.7 million single moms and 1.4 million single dads in the workforce, managers

are discovering that family programs are no longer a luxury but a necessity for competitive companies. Many companies have come to believe that successful family policies will increasingly attract and retain the most talented workers.[47]

Family-friendly companies such as Johnson & Johnson, IBM, Aetna, Corning, and AT&T have established a variety of programs—family-care leave, on-site child- and elder-care centers, health care for part-timers, flexible schedules, job sharing, subsidies and grants for child care, work at home, and children's after-school or summer programs—to meet changing family needs and values. Despite the programs and policies of some companies, however, business in general has not been able to respond to family needs or to assist employees trying to balance work and family responsibilities. Family issues have become a topical corporate issue, but only a small percentage of businesses actually have strong family programs to address them. The pressure for developing these programs is mounting, but companies attempting to implement them should avoid acting precipitously. They must carefully analyze employee needs as well as company resources in responding to this pressure. One expert on work and family issues states that to be successful, family programs must be seen as a central part of the company's business mission.[48] However, many women are finding that starting their own companies often gives them even more flexibility. Of the 5.9 million U.S. small enterprises, women own one-third and represent the fastest-growing segment. It isn't only family flexibility: these women often attain high salary and corporate levels but hit the "glass ceiling" before realizing their talents are better spent in their own ventures.[49]

Emotional Intimacy

Another outcome of diversity is a greater incidence of close friendships between men and women in the workplace. Close relationships between men and women often have been discouraged in companies for fear that they would disrupt the balance of power and threaten organizational stability.[50] This opinion grew out of the assumption that organizations are designed for rationality and efficiency, which were best achieved in a nonemotional environment. Close relationships between men and women could become romantic or sexual in nature, upsetting the stable working relationships.

A recent study of friendships in organizations sheds interesting light on this issue.[51] Managers and workers responded to a survey about emotionally intimate relationships with both male and female coworkers. Many men and women reported having close relationships with an opposite-sex coworker. Called "nonromantic love relationships," the friendships resulted in trust, respect, constructive feedback, and support in achieving work goals. Intimate friendships did not necessarily become romantic, and they affected each person's job and career in a positive way. Rather than causing problems, nonromantic love relationships, according to the study, affected work teams in a positive manner because conflict was reduced. Indeed, men reported somewhat greater benefit than women from these relationships, perhaps because the men had fewer close relationships outside the workplace upon which to depend.

In any event, the evidence suggests that close psychological and emotional relationships between men and women at work are healthy and helpful. The challenge is for people to learn to cultivate these relationships and thus benefit themselves and their organizations.

Sexual Harassment

While psychological closeness between men and women in the workplace may be a positive experience, sexual harassment is not. Sexual harassment is illegal. As a form of sexual discrimination, sexual harassment in the workplace is a violation of Title VII of the 1964 Civil Rights Act. Sexual harassment in the classroom is a violation of Title VIII of the Education Amendment of 1972.

The following categorize various forms of sexual harassment as defined by one university:

- *Generalized.* This form involves sexual remarks and actions that are not intended to lead to sexual activity but that are directed toward a coworker based solely on gender and reflect on the entire group.

- *Inappropriate/offensive.* Though not sexually threatening, it causes discomfort in a coworker, whose reaction in avoiding the harasser may limit his or her freedom and ability to function in the workplace.

- *Solicitation with promise of reward.* This action treads a fine line as an attempt to "purchase" sex, with the potential for criminal prosecution.

- *Coercion with threat of punishment.* The harasser coerces a coworker into sexual activity by using the threat of power (through recommendations, grades, promotions, and so on) to jeopardize the victim's career.

- *Sexual crimes and misdemeanors.* The highest level of sexual harassment, these acts would, if reported to the police, be considered felony crimes and misdemeanors.[52]

The Anita Hill–Clarence Thomas hearings focused national attention on the problem of sexual harassment. Sexual harassment claims increased 50 percent in the months following the 1991 hearings.[53] More recently, the movie version of Michael Crichton's *Disclosure,* about a female boss sexually harassing a male subordinate, made sexual harassment a hot topic of public discussion, consequently broadening the focus to include harassment of men by female supervisors as well as same-sex harassment.[54] Eight men, former employees of Jenny Craig Inc., have sued the company charging that female bosses made lewd comments or that they were denied promotions because of their sex. A male worker at a hot tub manufacturer won a $1 million court decision after claiming that his female boss made sexual overtures to him almost daily. These are among a growing number of men urging recognition that sexual harassment is not just a woman's problem.[55]

Because the corporate world is dominated by a male culture, however, sexual harassment affects women to a much greater extent. Women who are moving up the corporate hierarchy by entering male-dominated industries report a high frequency of harassment. Surveys report an increase in sexual harassment programs, but female employees also report a lack of prompt and just action by executives to incidents of sexual harassment. However, companies are discovering that "an ounce of prevention really is worth a pound of cure." Top executives are seeking to address problems of harassment through company diversity programs, revised complaint systems and grievance procedures, written policy statements, workshops, lectures, and role-playing exercises to increase employee sensitivity and awareness to the issue.[56]

GLOBAL DIVERSITY

One of the most rapidly increasing sources of diversity in North American companies is globalization, which means hiring employees in many countries. Some estimate that by the year 2000, half of the world's assets will be controlled by multinational corporations.[57] Globalization means that companies must apply diversity management across a broader stage than North America. This means that managers must develop new skills and awareness to handle the unique challenges of global diversity: cross-cultural understanding, the ability to build networks, and the understanding of geopolitical forces. Two significant aspects of global diversity programs involve employee selection and training and the understanding of the communication context.

Selection and Training

Expatriates are employees who live and work in a country other than their own.

expatriates
Employees who live and work in a country other than their own.

The children in this Avezzano, Italy, school share cultures and learn firsthand the dynamics of *global diversity*. The school was established by Texas Instruments for the families of U.S. and Japanese employees involved in T.I.'s six-nation team that is building Europe's largest semiconductor. Such efforts, along with Minority Procurement programs, demonstrate T.I.'s commitment to a diverse, multinational corporate environment.

high-context culture
A culture in which communication is used to enhance personal relationships.

low-context culture
A culture in which communication is used to exchange facts and information.

Careful screening, selection, and training of employees to serve overseas increase the potential for corporate global success. Human resource managers consider global skills in the selection process. In addition, expatriates receive cross-cultural training that develops language skills and cultural and historical orientation. Career-path counseling is often available.[58]

Equally important, however, is honest self-analysis by overseas candidates and their families. Before seeking or accepting an assignment in another country, a candidate should ask himself or herself such questions as the following:

- Is your spouse interrupting his or her own career path to support your career? Is that acceptable to both of you?

- Is family separation for long periods involved?

- Can you initiate social contacts in a foreign culture?

- Can you adjust well to different environments and changes in personal comfort or quality of living, such as the lack of television, gasoline at $5 per gallon, limited hot water, varied cuisine, national phone strikes, and warm beer?

- Can you manage your future reentry into the job market by networking and

maintaining contacts in your home country?[59]

Employees working overseas must adjust to all of these conditions. Managers going global may find that their own management "style" needs adjustment to succeed in a foreign country. One aspect of this adjustment is learning the communication context of a foreign location.

Communication Differences

People from some cultures tend to pay more attention to the social context (social setting, nonverbal behavior, social status) of their verbal communication than Americans do. For example, General Norman Schwarzkopf soon realized that social context was of considerable importance to leaders of Saudi Arabia. During the initial buildup for the Persian Gulf War, he suppressed his own tendency toward impatience and devoted hours to "philosophizing" with members of the Saudi royal family. Schwarzkopf realized it was *their* way of making decisions.[60]

Exhibit 12.7 indicates how the emphasis on social context varies among countries. In a **high-context culture,** people are sensitive to circumstances surrounding social exchanges. People use communication primarily to build personal social relationships; meaning is derived from context—setting, status, nonverbal behavior—more than from explicit words; relationships and trust are more important than business; and the welfare and harmony of the group are valued. In a **low-context culture,** people use communication primarily to exchange facts and information; meaning is derived primarily from words; business transactions are more important than building relationships and trust; and individual welfare and achievement are more important than the group.[61]

To understand how differences in cultural context affect communications, consider the U.S. expression "The squeaky wheel gets the grease." It means that the loudest person will get the most attention, and attention is assumed to be favorable.

Equivalent sayings in China and Japan are "Quacking ducks get shot" and "The nail that sticks up gets hammered down," respectively. Standing out as an individual in these cultures clearly merits unfavorable attention. The Leading the Management Revolution box describes how J. D. Hokoyama started an organization to help Asian and Asian American workers who have been held back because of this difference in communication style.

High-context cultures include Asian and Arab countries. Low-context cultures tend to be American and Northern European. Even within North America, cultural subgroups vary in the extent to which context counts, explaining why differences among groups make successful communication difficult. White females, Native Americans, and African Americans all tend to prefer higher context communication than do white males. A high-context interaction requires more time because a relationship has to be developed, and trust and friendship must be established. Furthermore, most male managers and most people doing the hiring in organizations are from low-context cultures, which conflicts with people entering the organization from a background in a higher context culture. Overcoming these differences in communication is a major goal of diversity awareness training.

BENEFITS AND COSTS OF DIVERSITY

As a rule, organizations have not been highly successful in managing women and minorities, as evidenced by higher turnover rates, higher absenteeism, lower job satisfaction, and general frustration over career development for these groups. Moreover, the fact that women and minorities are clustered at lower organization levels indicates they are not progressing as far as they might and are not developing their full potential.[62] Valuing diversity provides distinct benefits to organizations, and ignoring diversity has specific costs. These are summarized in Ex-

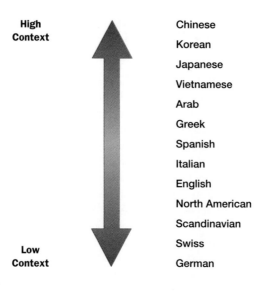

EXHIBIT 12.7
Arrangement of High- and Low-Context Cultures

High Context

Chinese
Korean
Japanese
Vietnamese
Arab
Greek
Spanish
Italian
English
North American
Scandinavian
Swiss
German

Low Context

SOURCES: Edward T. Hall, *Beyond Culture* (Garden City, N.Y.: Anchor Press/Doubleday, 1976); and J. Kennedy and A. Everest, "Put Diversity in Context," *Personnel Journal* (September 1991), 50–54.

hibit 12.8. Although it is clear that valuing diversity is desirable for today's organizations, it also presents a paradox for top managers.

The Paradox of Diversity

Diversity in the workplace is inevitable and, as we will discuss in the following section, provides numerous benefits; yet top managers face a challenge in simultaneously promoting diversity and maintaining a strong, unified corporate culture.[63] Although companies with a homogeneous workforce are limited because of the lack of diverse views and values, homogeneous cultures do provide a firmer basis for building a strong corporate culture. Diversity within the workplace means managers must work harder to unite employees around a common purpose while also allowing individual differences among employees to flourish.

Diverse ethnic groups within a work environment can be competitive with and even antagonistic toward one another. To overcome these problems, managers use diversity awareness training and other methods discussed throughout this chapter. The time and energy a manager spends dealing with interpersonal issues may dramatically

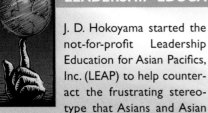

LEADING THE MANAGEMENT REVOLUTION
LEADERSHIP EDUCATION FOR ASIAN PACIFICS, INC.

J. D. Hokoyama started the not-for-profit Leadership Education for Asian Pacifics, Inc. (LEAP) to help counteract the frustrating stereotype that Asians and Asian Americans are hard workers but not management material. Those who aspire to management positions are often perceived as too quiet and not assertive enough. One Chinese American woman says her boss claimed she was not strong enough for management because she didn't raise her voice in discussions as he did. Japanese American Hokoyama runs workshops to alert Asian Americans to the ways in which their communication styles may hold them back in the American workplace.

While American culture regards face-to-face confrontation and competition as ways to motivate people, in Asian cultures there is more emphasis on group harmony. Workshop participants are taught to use more eye contact, start more sentences with "I," and use more assertive body language.

Some Asian Americans believe people of other races should also attend the workshops, and they question whether they should abandon their cultural values to succeed. Hokoyama, however, looks at it as a way for Asian Americans to understand how the stereotype affects them and then adjust their styles as needed to get more Asian Americans into leadership positions. Pauline Ho, a senior technical staff member at Sandia National Laboratories, agrees. She has seen the obstacles her parents and other immigrants faced: "They want to get ahead, but they don't understand what they should be doing."

Hokoyama does not believe Asian Americans should give up their cultural values, but he recognizes that overcoming differences in communication is a start toward breaking down barriers in a culture that is still dominated by white, American-born males.

SOURCE: Kenneth Brown and Lyle Sussman, "Phong Siu-Ming vs. Burgers-R-Us," *Business Horizons*, March 1, 1995, 51; Vivian Louie, "For Asian-Americans, a Way to Fight a Maddening Stereotype," *The New York Times*, August 8, 1993, 9.

increase in a diverse environment. In a company made up of diverse individuals with differing beliefs, ideas, and ways of thinking and behaving, creating and communicating a shared vision and values for the organization as a whole becomes even more critical. Uniting diverse employees around a core vision can be a powerful competitive force. To do this, managers should make sure all employees understand the vision, have the opportunity to contribute fully to achieving the vision, and are rewarded for their commitment to fulfilling the organization's purpose.

Benefits of Valuing Diversity

Hal Burlingham, AT&T senior vice-president for human resources, said, "Valuing diversity is not only the right thing to do, it's the right business thing to do. Companies that do a good job of valuing and effectively managing diversity in the 1990s will have a competitive advantage over the ones that don't."[64] Paying attention to the diverse workforce has become an economic imperative. There is no question that the workforce is changing and that U.S. organizations have to change to reflect the new workforce composition.

The first benefit of valuing diversity is the opportunity to develop employee and organizational potential. This means higher morale, because people feel valued for what they bring to the organization. It also produces better relationships at work, because people acquire the skills to recognize, understand, and accept cultural differences. Developing employee skills and valuing diversity have become a bottom-line business issue.

Second, companies that treat women and racial/ethnic minorities well will be able to recruit the best employees, both those new to the workforce and experienced employees from other organizations. Retaining these employees means a qualified, trained workforce for the future. Demographics tell us that the labor market is slowly tightening, and those organizations that boast a

Benefits of Valuing Diversity	Costs of Ignoring Diversity
1 Increased opportunity to develop employee and organizational potential 2 Enhanced recruiting and retention 3 Successful interaction with clients/marketplace 4 Increased creativity and problem solving	1 Reduced individual and organizational productivity 2 Tarnished corporate image 3 Substantial monetary cost 4 Limited creativity and new ideas

EXHIBIT 12.8
Benefits and Costs of Diversity Issues

healthy environment for women and minorities will be in the best competitive position to attract and retain scarce employees.

An enhanced ability to meet the needs of diverse customers is the third benefit of diversity. A Glass Ceiling Commission study notes that two out of every three people in the United States are females or minority-group members or both.[65] Culture plays an important part in determining the goods, entertainment, social services, and household products that people buy and use. Understanding how people live and what they need will help organizations adapt to changing consumer populations. This understanding comes in part from including representatives from that population in the workforce.

Finally, organizations can expect enhanced creativity and problem solving from a diverse workforce. Research has shown that diverse groups tend to be more creative than homogeneous groups, in part because people with diverse backgrounds bring different perspectives to problem solving. The presence of cultural and gender diversity in a group reduces the risk of "groupthink" when people contribute freely to a discussion.

Costs of Ignoring Diversity

The costs associated with high turnover and absenteeism are well understood. When organizations can adapt to the needs of a diverse workforce, rather than expect the workforce to adapt to the organization, absenteeism and turnover can be turned around and satisfaction increased.[66] The consequences of not valuing diversity include loss of productivity, a poor image for

the organization, and the monetary cost of unhappy employees.

Reduced individual and organizational productivity occurs when women and minorities experience prejudice and nonacceptance. They feel unappreciated, do not expect to advance, and feel resentment that saps energy and productivity for the organization. People who feel excluded do not take risks for the organization, are less innovative, and are less aggressive in pressing their ideas or in assuming leadership. They will not voice disagreement, because they want to be accepted and included.

Second, a less obvious cost is the tarnished corporate image and reputation developed around employee dissatisfaction. If a corporation becomes known as one that alienates nontraditional employees, that corporation will have a hard time finding qualified workers and managers in a period of limited labor supply.

The third important cost is financial. A company loses all the money invested in recruiting and training when a dissatisfied employee leaves. At Corning, Inc., described earlier in the chapter, high turnover among female and minority workers cost the company between $3.5 and $4 million annually. This wasted money may include fees for Equal Employment Opportunity disputes, the cost of recruiting replacement employees, the wasted training for those who left, and the cost of additional training for those who stay.[67]

With the anticipated tight job market, corporations that want to be successful must embrace diversity. A number of innovative companies are already responding. A recent survey found that 56 percent of all U.S. organizations with more than 100

employees conducted some kind of diversity training program in 1994.[68] Apple Computer has appointed a multicultural and affirmative action manager, Avon has established a cultural network, and Honeywell, Procter & Gamble, and Security Pacific Bank have established mentoring programs, advisory counsels, and minority networks. Burger King, which has expanded the percentage of minority employees at headquarters to 28 percent, uses "The Diversity Game," a board game that raises awareness of diversity issues and stimulates discussion among employees from diverse backgrounds.[69] The near-full-employment economy means new attitudes are required for the diverse workforce making up low-wage workers.

LOW-WAGE WORKERS

Try to manage employees, one-fourth of whom do not read and who together speak 65 different languages. Such is the typical environment for companies such as ConAgra Cos. and Marriott Corporation, which rely on low-wage workers. Made up largely of immigrants and under-educated Americans, this 30 percent of the U.S. workforce can no longer be ignored in these times of a full-employment economy. Other problems brought by the low-paid workers are poor work habits, culture clashes, financial woes, inadequate child care, and domestic violence—for starters.

ConAgra Refrigerated Food Cos.' problems with immigrant workers resulted in turnover rates of 100 percent. The company started housing projects, prenatal care, and on-site child care, all of which drastically reduced the attrition rate. "The burden is on us, not the employee, to change," says company HR manager Charles H. Romeo. "For many of us, that is a new recognition."

Other strategies are being tried elsewhere. Aramark gives conflict resolution classes, JCPenney allows flexible work hours and Opryland USA Hotel offers company housing, free bus rides, one free meal a day, and subsidized child care for its low-wage workers. Marriott offers company-time ESL and money-management classes, while managers report 15 percent of time spent as "social workers."

Does all this "care" benefit the company? If you count lower turnover, increased motivation, less distraction, then yes, it does help. Consider the case of Thong Lee, a Marriott bartender for 16 years, who learned English from the hotel courses. He will never forget that a previous boss, Sandy Olson, shut down department operations for a day so the entire staff could attend Lee's mother's funeral. Now Lee is loyal for life. "Every day I put on this uniform," he says with pride, "I feel just like an NBA player."[70] ■

As one senior executive said, "In a country seeking competitive advantage in a global economy, the goal of managing diversity is to develop our capacity to accept, incorporate, and empower the diverse human talents of the most diverse nation on earth. It is our reality. We need to make it our strength."[71]

SUMMARY AND MANAGEMENT SOLUTION

Several important ideas pertain to workforce diversity, which is the inclusion of people with different human qualities and from different cultural groups. Dimensions of diversity are both primary, such as age, gender, and race, and secondary, such as education, marital status, and income. Ethnocentric attitudes generally produce a monoculture that accepts only one way of doing things and one set of values and beliefs, thereby excluding non-traditional employees from full participation.

Acceptance of workforce diversity is becoming especially important because of sociocultural changes and the changing workforce. Diversity in the workplace reflects

diversity in the larger environment. Innovative companies are initiating a variety of programs to take advantage of the diverse workforce.

Affirmative action programs have been successful in gaining employment for women and minorities, but the glass ceiling has kept many women and minorities from obtaining top management positions. The Civil Rights Act of 1991 amends and strengthens the Civil Rights Act of 1964.

Breaking down the glass ceiling ultimately means changing the corporate culture within organizations; changing internal structures and policies toward employees, including accommodating special needs; and providing diversity awareness training to help people become aware of their own cultural boundaries and prejudices. This training also helps employees learn to communicate with people from other cultural contexts.

The increased diversity in organizations has produced unexpected benefits, such as enabling all groups to define what they want from the company; it has enabled women who use an interactive leadership style to succeed and has provided opportunities for emotional intimacy and friendship between men and women that are beneficial to all parties. Increasing diversity also means that organizations must develop programs to deal with global as well as domestic diversity and with potential conflicts, such as sexual harassment, that arise.

Valuing diversity has many benefits, such as developing employees to their full potential and allowing successful interaction with diverse clients in the marketplace. Organizations that ignore diversity reduce productivity, suffer tarnished corporate images, and suffer substantial financial costs associated with turnover, training, and EEO disputes.

At Carolina Fine Snacks, described in the chapter opening, Phil Kosak expanded his recruitment efforts to tap into a previously unused labor source. David Bruton, the first disabled adult hired by CFS, not only could do the job, he ran circles around the other workers and has now been promoted twice. Workers initially reluctant to teach disabled employees were impressed by the new employees' sincere desire to learn. Because the disabled workers were never late, always showed up for work, and took great pride in their jobs, the attitudes of other workers began to change for the better. To help disabled workers feel included and give all employees a chance to interact with one another, CFS holds weekly meetings that educate workers about the different jobs at the plant. All employees also have direct contact with clients, who are brought to the plant for guided tours. The human resources manager learned sign language to ease communication with the hearing impaired. Overall, production has increased to 95 percent of capacity, from 60 percent in 1989. Employee turnover has shrunk to only 5 percent. "These folks have changed everybody's life," Kosak says. "Everyone here works hard as part of a team."[72]

DISCUSSION QUESTIONS

1 If you were a senior manager at a company such as PepsiCo, how would you resolve the concerns of current middle managers when female or minority senior managers are hired from outside?

2 Some people argue that social class is a major source of cultural differences, yet social class is not listed as a primary or secondary dimension in Exhibit 12.1. Discuss reasons for this.

3 Have you been associated with an organization that made assumptions associated with a monoculture? Describe the culture.

4 Do you think any organization can successfully resist diversity today? Discuss.

5 What is the glass ceiling, and why do you think it has proved to be such a barrier to women and minorities?

6 In preparing an organization to accept diversity, do you think it is more important to change the corporate culture or to change structures and policies? Explain.

7 If a North American corporation could choose either high-context or low-context communications, which do you think would be best for the company's long-term health? Discuss.

8 What do you think the impact on an organization would be for diversity within its own country versus international diversity? Discuss.

9 Many single people meet and date people from their work organization because the organization provides a context within which to know and trust another person. How do you think this practice affects the potential for emotional intimacy? Sexual harassment?

MANAGEMENT EXERCISES

MANAGER'S WORKBOOK

Are You Diversity Aware?

Answer the following questions to test your awareness of diversity issues. Circle T if you believe the statement is true, F if you believe the statement is false.

1 In addition to age, gender, nationality, and race, diversity includes such things as education, physical ability, mental capacity, personality, and culture.   **T   F**

2 By the year 2000, the average age of U.S. workers is expected to be 35.   **T   F**

3 Women make up about 65% of new workers entering the labor force.   **T   F**

4 People of color make up 15% of new workers entering the labor force.   **T   F**

5 By the year 2000, immigrants are expected to comprise almost 25% of new hires.   **T   F**

6 The management group most affected by the changing mix of new workers in the workforce is middle management.   **T   F**

7 Before 1970, most immigrants to the U.S. were from Canada and Europe; since 1970, most immigrants have been from Latin America and Asia.   **T   F**

8 The U.S. values individuality more than any other country.   **T   F**

9 The individual is valued more than the group in most of the world.   **T   F**

10 Approximately 15% of new workers coming into the workforce are white males.   **T   F**

The answers to questions 1, 3, 5, 7, 8, and 10 are true. Question 2 is false because the average age is 40. In 1970, the average age was 28. Number 4 is false because people of color make up 20% of new workers. Number 6 is false because the changing mix of new workers most strongly impacts front-line supervisors. Number 9 is false because the group is valued over the individual in 70% of the world; the U.S. is in the minority.

If you answered eight to ten of the above questions correctly, consider yourself exceptionally well informed about matters of diversity. If you answered six or seven correctly, consider yourself well informed. If you answered five or fewer correctly, more reading and awareness of diversity may be a good thing for your career.

How do you feel about the changing nature of the workforce, with more new workers coming from minority groups and immigrants? Discuss how this can be good for organizations. Will organizations have to change to accommodate increasing diversity? Discuss.

SOURCE: J. W. Pfeiffer (ed.), *The 1994 Annual* (Pfeiffer & Company, 1994), 65–66. Reproduced with permission.

MANAGER'S WORKSHOP

Stereotypes

1 Individually complete the questions in column A of the table on page 409.

2 Divide into groups of four to six members and discuss each question, coming up with some "group responses" for column B.

3 The instructor will lead a discussion on the origins of prejudice and its effects. How can you change yourself and others to remove prejudices?

Questions	Column A Your own answers	Column B Group responses
a. List some common stereotypes you are familiar with (you do not have to agree with the stereotypes) regarding ethnic, racial, social class, sexual preference, religious, gender or other differences.		
b. Describe one or two situations where you were the target of a stereotype. What happened and how did you feel?		
c. List some of your own prejudices. Where do you think they came from? Do other family members share these prejudices?		
d. What effects do prejudices have in the workplace?		

SOURCE: Adapted from Anne McKee and Susan Schorr, "Confronting Prejudice and Stereotypes: A Teaching Model," *Journal of Management Education,* Vol. 18, no. 4, Nov. 1994, 447–467.

SURF THE 'NET

Find Web pages for at least 15 small-to-medium-sized companies. One third of these should be minority-owned, one third woman-owned, and one third remaining.

1. What differences, similarities did you find in relation to:
   a. Type of business.
   b. Evidence of diversity in their employment.
   c. Information in the Web page.
   d. Other differences or similarities.

2 How easy or difficult was it to find minority- or women-owned businesses on the Web?

3 List the fifteen businesses with the name, type of business, and Web address for each.

ETHICAL DILEMMA

Promotion or Not?

You are the president of CrownCutters, Inc. You have worked closely with Bill Smith for several years now. In many situations, he has served as your *de facto* right-hand person.

Due to a retirement, you have an opening in the position of executive vice-president. Bill is the natural choice—and this is obvious to the other mid- and senior-level managers at CrownCutters. Bill is popular with most of the managers in the company. Of course, he also has his share of detractors.

Prior to announcing the appointment of Bill Smith, you receive a memo from Jane Jones, your controller. Jane's memo indicates that she was subjected to sporadic sexual

harassment by Bill starting ten years ago when she first joined the company and was working for him. Her memo indicates that the harassment essentially stopped six years ago when she moved to a position in which Bill was no longer her superior. She requests that this information be kept totally confidential.

You have never heard of any allegations like this about Bill before.

What Do You Do?

1 Move ahead with the promotion because, even if true, this is an isolated incident that is a part of Bill's past and is not his current behavior.

2 Stop the promotion because Bill is not the type of person who should help lead the company and shape its values.

3 Put the promotion on hold until you can discuss the situation extensively with Bill and Jane, although this means the accusation probably will become public knowledge.

SOURCE: This case was provided by Professor David Scheffman, Owen Graduate School of Management, Vanderbilt University, Nashville, Tennessee.

CASE FOR CRITICAL ANALYSIS

Nordstrom, Inc.

Nordstrom, Inc., is one of the nation's leading retailers. It made diversity a corporate goal after several minority employees at its downtown Seattle store filed discrimination complaints with the Equal Employment Opportunity Commission.

A consultant who helps companies deal with multicultural workplaces created the following composite in 1987 that represented the Nordstrom look: "She was young, blond and light-skinned. She had a slim, athletic build. She came from a middle- to upper-class background, and she projected an image of sorority-girl enthusiasm." This composite emerged after asking employees to describe Nordstrom's shoppers, corporate culture, and personal traits required to rise in the employee ranks.

Top managers were stunned by the narrowness of the composite and suddenly understood why they had failed to hire outstanding minority candidates. Nordstrom was sending a subliminal culture message that a person of color wouldn't fit in the organization.

Since that finding, Nordstrom has created a new human resource department charged with the hiring and promotion of people of color. Nordstrom has begun to use models from various ethnic backgrounds in its catalogs and to advertise in publications such as *Ebony* and *Jet* that target minority groups. Nordstrom has solicited minority-owned companies as its suppliers.

Today, nearly one-third of its employees, including 17 percent of its department managers, are people of color. Three of its vice-presidents are people of color, and the president is female. This is a good record in an industry largely dominated by white men. As Nordstrom opens new stores, its human resource directors make sure employees hired reflect a range of races and ethnic backgrounds. Although a few minority people still complain about discrimination, Nordstrom believes that it has come a long way in four years.

Consultants tell Nordstrom that minorities are shopping there more frequently and feel more identification with the chain.

Questions

1 Do you believe the changes made by Nordstrom were necessary, considering the workforce and marketplace? Explain.
2 Was Nordstrom's change primarily that of corporate culture or structures and policies? Should the focus of change be redirected? Why?
3 Do you believe Nordstrom has successfully shattered the glass ceiling? Discuss.

SOURCE: From Himanee Gupta, "Nordstrom Retools Image for More Inclusive Market," *Dallas Morning News*, February 2, 1992, Section H, 1, 18. Reprinted with permission of The *Dallas Morning News*.

ENDNOTES

1 Tom Peters, *The Pursuit of Wow!: Every Person's Guide to Topsy-Turvy Times* (New York: Vintage, 1994), 92–93.

2 M. Fine, F. Johnson, and M. S. Ryan, "Cultural Diversity in the Workforce," *Public Personnel Management* 19 (1990), 305–319.

3 Taylor H. Cox, "Managing Cultural Diversity: Implications for Organizational Competitiveness," *Academy of Management Executive* 5, no. 3 (1991), 45–56; and Faye Rice, "How to Make Diversity Pay," *Fortune,* August 8, 1994, 78–86.

4 Joel Dreyfuss, "Get Ready for the New Workforce," *Fortune,* April 29, 1990, 165–181.

5 Lennie Copeland, "Valuing Diversity, Part I: Making the Most of Cultural Differences at the Workplace," *Personnel,* June 1988, 52–60.

6 Lennie Copeland, "Learning to Manage a Multicultural Workforce," *Training,* May 25, 1988, 48–56; and D. Farid Elashmawi, "Culture Clashes: Barriers to Business," *Managing Diversity* 2, no. 11 (August 1993), 1–3.

7 Marilyn Loden and Judy B. Rosener, *Workforce America!* (Homewood, Ill.: Business One Irwin, 1991).

8 N. Songer, "Workforce Diversity," *B & E Review,* April–June 1991, 3–6.

9 G. Haight, "Managing Diversity," *Across the Board* 27, no. 3 (1990), 22–29.

10 Songer, "Workforce Diversity."

11 Robert Doktor, Rosalie Tung, and Mary Ann von Glinow, "Future Directions for Management Theory Development," *Academy of Management Review* 16 (1991), 362–365; and Mary Munter, "Cross-Cultural Communication for Managers," *Business Horizons,* May–June 1993, 69–78.

12 Renee Blank and Sandra Slipp, "The White Male: An Endangered Species?" *Management Review,* September 1994, 27–32; Michael S. Kimmel, "What Do Men Want?" *Harvard Business Review,* November–December 1993, 50–63; and Sharon Nelton, "Nurturing Diversity," *Nation's Business,* June 1995, 25–27.

13 M. Bennett, "A Developmental Approach to Training for Intercultural Sensitivity," *International Journal of Intercultural Relations* 10 (1986), 179–196.

14 Rice, "How to Make Diversity Pay."

15 C. Keen, "Human Resource Management Issues in the '90s," *Vital Speeches* 56, no. 24 (1990), 752–754.

16 Kurt Anderson, "California Dreamin'," *Time,* September 23, 1991, 38–42.

17 Paula Dwyer, Pete Engardio, Zachary Schiller, and Stanley Reed, "Tearing Up Today's Organization Chart," *Business Week/21st Century Capitalism,* November 18, 1994, 80–90.

18 W. B. Johnston and A. H. Packer, *Workforce 2000* (Indianapolis, Ind.: Hudson Institute, 1987).

19 United States Department of Labor, *Opportunity 2000: Creative Affirmative Action Strategies for a Changing Workforce* (Indianapolis, Ind.: Hudson Institute, 1988).

20 Copeland, "Valuing Diversity, Part I: Making the Most of Cultural Differences at the Workplace."

21 S. Hutchins, Jr., "Preparing for Diversity: The Year 2000," *Quality Process* 22, no. 10 (1989), 66–68.

22 Faye Rice, "Denny's Changes It Spots," *Fortune,* May 13, 1996, 133.

23 Catherine Yang, Maria Mallory, and Alice Cuneo, "A 'Race-Neutral' Helping Hand?" *Business Week,* February 27, 1995, 120–121.

24 Roosevelt Thomas, Jr., "From Affirmative Action to Affirming Diversity," *Harvard Business Review* (March–April 1990), 107–117; and Nicholas Lemann, "Taking Affirmative Action Apart," *The New York Times Magazine,* July 11, 1995, 36–43.

25 Lemann, "Taking Affirmative Action Apart."

26 Benjamin Holden, "When a Minority Business 'Graduates,'" *The Wall Street Journal,* Nov. 25, 1996, B1, B2.

27 Yang, Mallory, and Cuneo, "A 'Race-Neutral' Helping Hand?"

28 Jack Gordon, "Different from What? Diversity as a Performance Issue," *Training,* May 1995, 25–33; and Leon E. Wynter, "Diversity Is Often All Talk, No Affirmative Action," *The Wall Street Journal,* December 21, 1994, B1.

29 B. Geber, "Managing Diversity," *Training* 27, no. 7 (1990), 23–30.

30 Julie Amparano Lopez, "Study Says Women Face Glass Walls as Well as Ceilings," *The Wall Street Journal,* March 3, 1992, B1, B2.

31 Nelton, "Nurturing Diversity."

32 C. Soloman, "Careers under Glass," *Personnel Journal* 69, no. 4 (1990), 96–105.

33 Deborah L. Jacobs, "Back from the Mommy Track," *The New York Times,* October 9, 1994, F1, F6.

34 Barbara Presley Noble, "A Quiet Liberation for Gay and Lesbian Employees," *The New York Times,* June 13, 1993, F4.

35 Soloman, "Careers under Glass."

36 Ron Stodgill II, "Get Serious about Diversity Training," *Business Week,* Nov. 25, 1996, p. 39; Veronica Byrd, "The Struggle for Minority Managers," *The New York Times,* March 7, 1993, F27.

37 Anne B. Fisher, "When Will Women Get to the Top?" *Fortune,* September 21, 1992, 44–56.

38 Copeland, "Learning to Manage a Multicultural Workforce."

39 Douglas T. Hall and Victoria A. Parker, "The Role of Workplace Flexibility in Managing Diversity," *Organizational Dynamics* (summer 1993), 5–18.

40 Geber, "Managing Diversity."

41 Loden and Rosener, *Workforce America!;* and Genevieve Capowski, "Ageism: The New Diversity Issue," *Management Review,* October 1994, 10–15.

42 B. Ragins, "Barriers to Mentoring: The Female Manager's Dilemma," *Human Relations* 42, no. 1 (1989), 1–22.

43 Mary Zey, "A Mentor for All," *Personnel Journal,* January 1988, 46–51.

44 J. Black and M. Mendenhall, "Cross-Cultural Training Effectiveness: A Review and a Theoretical Framework for Future Research," *Academy of Management Review* 15 (1990), 113–136.

45 Loden and Rosener, *Workforce America!;* and Marc Hequet, "Men at Work," *Training,* January 1995, 38–42.

46 David Shallenberger, "Invisible Minorities: Coming Out of the Classroom Closet," *Journal of Management Education* (August 1991), 325–334.

47 Aaron Bernstein, "When the Only Parent Is Daddy," *Business Week,* November 23, 1992, 122–127; Keith H. Hammonds and William C. Symonds, "Taking Baby Steps toward a Daddy Track," *Business Week,* April 15, 1991, 90–92; and Sue Shellenbarger, "More Job Seekers Put Family Needs First," *The Wall Street Journal,* November 15, 1991, B1, B12.

48 Aaron Bernstein, Joseph Weber, Lisa Driscoll, and Alice Cuneo, "Corporate America Is Still No Place for Kids," *Business Week,* November 21, 1991, 234–238.

49 Stephanie N. Mehta, "More Women Quit Lucrative Jobs to Start Their Own Businesses," *The Wall Street Journal,* Nov. 11, 1996, A1, A5.

50 E. G. Collins, "Managers and Lovers," *Harvard Business Review* 61 (1983), 142–153.

51 Sharon A. Lobel, Robert E. Quinn, Lynda St. Clair, and Andrea Warfield, "Love without Sex: The Impact of Psychological Intimacy between Men and Women at Work,"*Organizational Dynamics* (summer 1994), 5–16.

52 "Sexual Harassment: Vanderbilt University Policy" (Nashville: Vanderbilt University, 1993).

53 Troy Segal, Kevin Kelly, and Alisa Solomon, "Getting Serious about Sexual Harassment," *Business Week,* November 9, 1992, 78–82.

54 Jennifer J. Laabs, "Sexual Harassment: HR Puts Its Questions on the Line," *Personnel Journal,* February 1995, 36–45.

55 Barbara Carton, "At Jenny Craig, Men Are Ones Who Claim Sex Discrimination," *The Wall Street Journal,* November 29, 1994, A1, A11.

56 Laabs, "Sexual Harassment"; Sharon Nelton, "Sexual Harassment: Reducing the Risks," *Nation's Business,* March 1995, 24–26; and Gary Baseman, "Sexual Harassment: The Inside Story," *Working Woman,* June 1992, 47–51, 78.

57 Joel Dreyfuss, "Get Ready for the New Work Force," *Fortune,* April 23, 1990, 165–181; and Ronald E. Dulek, John S. Fielden, and John S. Hill, "International Communication: An Executive Primer," *Business Horizons,* January–February 1991, 20–25.

58 Joann S. Lublin, "Companies Use Cross-Cultural Training to Help Their Employees Adjust Abroad," *The Wall Street Journal,* August 4, 1992, B1, B9.

59 Gilbert Fuchsberg, "As Costs of Overseas Assignments Climb, Firms Select Expatriates More Carefully," *The Wall Street Journal,* January 9, 1992, B3, B4.

60 Brian Dumaine, "Management Lessons from the General," *Fortune,* November 2, 1992, 143.

61 J. Kennedy and A. Everest, "Put Diversity in Context," *Personnel Journal,* September 1991, 50–54.

62 Cox, "Managing Cultural Diversity."

63 Based on Nicholas Imparato and Oren Harari, *Jumping the Curve: Innovation and Strategic Choice in an Age of Transition* (San Francisco: Jossey-Bass, 1994), 186–203.

64 J. Castelli, "Education Forms Common Bond," *HRMagazine* 35, no. 6 (1990), 46–49.

65 Nelton, "Nurturing Diversity."

66 Cox, "Managing Cultural Diversity."

67 S. Caudron, "Monsanto Response to Diversity," *Personnel Journal* 69, no. 11 (1990), 72–80; and Hall and Parker, "The Role of Workplace Flexibility in Managing Diversity."

68 Gordon, "Different from What?"

69 Suzanne B. Laporte, "12 Companies That Do the Right Thing," *Working Woman,* January 1991, 57–59; and Lena Williams, "Scrambling to Manage a Diverse Work Force," *The New York Times,* December 15, 1992, C1, C2.

70 Catherine Yang, "Low-Wage Lessons," *Business Week,* Nov. 11, 1996, 109–116.

71 Thomas, "From Affirmative Action to Affirming Diversity."

72 Peters, *The Pursuit of Wow!*

Growth and Change at Paradigm Simulation

As the defense industry began to shrink, Paradigm Simulation had to reconsider both its products and its markets. As a start-up company, Paradigm developed and sold very expensive, high-end 3-D graphic simulation software. Flight simulators, for example, were priced in the $1 million range. A few years later, according to Dave Gatchel, VP of Entertainment, Silicon Graphics equipment has reduced the cost to closer to $100,000. In an industry in which technology and price are moving rapidly, change is inevitable.

The entertainment industry was the market that quickly became the most lucrative for Paradigm's technology. "It's the same techniques whether you're a million dollar simulator or you're a $250 console device in somebody's home," says Gatchel. An example of the cascading of product from defense to entertainment industry is Viper, a combat simulation originally designed by Paradigm for military training, currently featured in Magic Edge, an entertainment theme park in Mountain View, California. With Nintendo and Disney among its new clients, growth and change have become constant for Paradigm.

In the first few years of Paradigm's life, the company had an employee roster of between five and ten people. It was easy to have all-company meetings—everyone in one office at lunchtime. With a small group of highly creative and technically proficient people, the atmosphere, dress, and communications were informal and relaxed. Friday lunch gatherings provided a means of reviewing the week's work and deciding on what had to happen next.

As Paradigm Simulation has grown to approximately 70 people, it has been a challenge to maintain the small company atmosphere. Co-founder Wes Hoffman comments: "Obviously, a lot of the reason we decided to start a company was because we all worked at large companies and were sick of the bureaucratic nonsense. But maintaining that kind of creative thinking in a large company where people start becoming kind of political and then develop some bureaucracy—these dynamics tend to start inhibiting really creative thinking because people just want to avoid making waves."

Paradigm has changed its organizational structure so that people are now grouped into teams and the teams communicate with each other. "We have to be a little bit more active in how we get people together, to communicate, and logistically handle problems," says VP of Finance Ron Paige. The structure of the company and the way in which its people communicate have become more formal, with a not unexpected reliance on e-mail for spreading the word quickly on product and market issues. In fact, the organizational structure now used by Paradigm looks more like a matrix structure, in which quality control or customer advocacy groups support all the different product teams. Paradigm now relies on individual business managers who are responsible for markets in their areas.

When Paradigm was a start-up company, little job specialization existed—people contributed in any way they could to the organization's needs. With the organization's growth to mid-size, the company's founders work to maintain the flexibility of the earlier days. According to Mike Engledinger, co-founder, "Our creative people and engineers are sort of one and the same—some people may favor engineering over the creative side, but in general, we have a pretty well-rounded staff for dealing with both creative and technical issues at the same time."

Perhaps as a function of the rapid success that Paradigm has achieved, the company's founders are deeply concerned with continuing to nurture the organization's culture. With growth and change constant for this firm, the tension between creativity and freedom and formality and structure will need to be kept in balance. "We don't feel bad about communicating when we are not hitting the mark on culture," comments Paige. "We have to be able to share with all the managers that 'Hey, this isn't where we want to be, this isn't how we want things to happen . . .' But when we get a letter in from a customer that says, 'We can't believe you; you appeared to be a member of our *own* team'—then we know we are hitting on all eight cylinders."

QUESTIONS

1 What issues for Paradigm has growth in the size of their workforce posed?

2 How have the co-founders managed the organizational change process at Paradigm? What strategies do they appear to use to support employee adjustment to change and development?

3 Do you believe that adaptation to change is built into the culture at Paradigm? Why or why not?

VIDEO CASE

Managing Cultural Diversity—JCPenney

In 1902, James Cash Penney opened his first store in Kemmerer, Wyoming, and named it "The Golden Rule." Penney's pledge to his customers was that they would find the best quality merchandise at the lowest possible prices. He insisted that customers always be served with courtesy and respect. Penney said, "If there is a secret of good management in the business of living, it lies in the partnerships we make, for no man is sufficient unto himself. I say partners because we believe that all our associates work together as partners."

Today, JCPenney is known not only as a major national department store retailer, but also for its mail-order catalog operations. Penney's operates over 1,246 stores in all 50 states and in Puerto Rico. These stores account for about 75 percent of sales. The catalog operation contributes 17 percent to overall corporate sales, and the company's Thrift Drug stores provide around 10 percent. JCPenney's primary competitive advantage is that it has 113 million square feet of prime retail space in malls.

In the 1990s, there are nearly 200,000 associates at JCPenney stores serving nearly 98 million customers each year. Mary Rostad, Vice President of Human Resources, states that "we really believe that our associates should have an opportunity to be part of the business strategies and the development of business opportunities." More than the increase in the size of the company, the changing demographics of the workforce and the marketplace have affected the JCPenney organization.

Charles Brown, Vice President and Director of Credit Operations, maintains that the JCPenney Company places a great emphasis on diversity by trying to understand it and by valuing the differences it brings to the workplace. "When you look at our associate population and our consumer base, you see mirrored what is happening in the U.S. as a whole. We understand that demographics are changing and that different types of people are entering the workplace. There are more women in the workplace, more minorities, more seniors. All these groups are part of our need to understand and value diversity. We see a connection with the bottom line because they represent our customer, and the differences among our customers represent opportunities for us to fill their needs."

JCPenney associates participate in a one-and-a-half-day workshop, "Valuing Cultural Differences," designed to create an awareness of diversity. Management developed a position statement on diversity that is given to every associate so that they clearly understand the company's commitment to diversity. Part of this understanding is that it is everyone's responsibility to value diversity.

In 1989, the company backed its formal commitment to diversity with the formation of the minority advisory team and later, the women's advisory team. The charge to these teams was to explore and identify roadblocks to advancement for their constituents within JCPenney.

Recommendations from the minority and women's advisory teams resulted in the establishment of the company's mentoring programs. These programs were designed to increase the likelihood that minority associates would stay with the company and also to help them gain an understanding of the company's culture more quickly. The development of a career pathing program was the second major recommendation from the advisory teams. Making advancement opportunities more visible and providing assistance with career planning helps not only to set realistic expectations, but to increase the speed of advancement. The third priority set by the advisory teams was to recruit top minority and female candidates.

Has JCPenney gained tangible benefits from its commitment to and investment in managing diversity? According to Charles Brown, because of the increasing awareness of diversity, the company is now targeting specific market segments. Minority and female associates are in leadership positions throughout the organization in increased numbers. But perhaps more important, Brown suggests, is that associates within the company now discuss sensitive issues that used to be avoided. Whether it's child care or race relations, the issues can be aired more openly and effectively.

QUESTIONS

1 Discuss Charles Brown's remarks about the connection between valuing diversity and the bottom line. In what ways can a diverse workforce at JCPenney aid the company in terms of growth in sales and revenue?

2 What strategies can JCPenney's human resource professionals utilize in order to increase their success in hiring more minority associates?

3 Evaluate JCPenney's use of minority and women's advisory teams to improve diversity. How do these teams help build a corporate culture that values diversity? Are there any potential costs from using teams such as these?

VIDEO CASE

How Does Nonprofit Status Affect What We Do?—North Texas Public Broadcasting

The Public Broadcasting Service (PBS) was established in 1970 and since that time has made it possible for every person in the United States to have access to education, world travel, music, art, science, and exposure to the leaders in the field of public affairs. Headquartered in Dallas, North Texas Public Broadcasting, Inc. is a community-based nonprofit organization that holds the licenses for two vital PBS stations, KERA Channel 13, and KDTN Channel 2. KERA/KDTN broadcasts high-quality programs to more than two million viewers and listeners (there is a KERA radio station also) in North, East and West Texas as well as parts of Oklahoma and Louisiana.

How do KERA and KDTN, nonprofit PBS stations, differ from commercial television stations? The mission of KERA/KDTN is to serve their communities by excelling in the production, presentation, and distribution of television and radio programming and related activities that educate, inspire, enrich, inform and entertain. KERA/KDTN reach nearly 100 percent of the TV households in the Dallas/Fort Worth/Denton area with their broadcast signals. As public television stations, Channel 13's and Channel 2's programming is available without additional charge to viewers.

Viewers in more than 1.3 million homes turn to Channel 13 every week, making the station one of the top five most-watched PBS stations in the country. Bill Young, Director of Programming at the station, says, "While ratings are an important part of our formula, they are not our sole purpose for being on the air." The Vice President of Broadcasting, Michael Seymour, adds that, "...we're not driven by the commercial sell ... we can take risks and do some things that other stations won't do, like Town Hall Meetings and the Metropolitan Opera."

However, ratings are important in that they represent the viewers from whom funds will have to be raised during drives. "The more viewers we have," says Bill Young, "the more possible members we have. It's not, however, the only basis that an overall program schedule is measured against. Programs that serve a unique mission or purpose can have very low ratings, but if they provide a mission or voice to an underserved audience, then they can be considered successful (i.e., election coverage, children's programming, etc.). Outreach programs become very important locally in that they 'make a difference.'"

The programs that air on Channel 13 are some of the most respected programs on TV today, including *The News-Hour with Jim Lehrer, Frontline, Masterpiece Theater, National Geographic Specials,* and, of course, *Sesame Street.* Channel 2's schedule is devoted to educational and public affairs programming. Channel 2 broadcasts more than 120 series to over 300,000 students in their classrooms.

KERA/KDTN membership drives provide a nearly continuous barometer of whether people feel that public television is important and whether they will support it. Program underwriters and corporations who may be more driven by visibility still come to public television, says Seymour. "Not for the segmentation of the audience, but they come because they believe in who the audience is and they believe in public broadcasting." Additionally, while members of the KERA/KDTN management may view money as a "necessary evil," they pay attention to which programs touch individuals enough to pledge and recognize the importance of PBS.

It's not just station management who consider their jobs to be "mission driven," either. Hoyt Neal, KERA/KDTN Manager of Personnel, says, "Although there is a wide diversity of opinions among our 100+ staff, several people have commented that their careers have been mission-driven and they have great opportunity to serve their community. There is a strong perception that while the compensation might be lower in public broadcasting, the atmosphere is friendlier and provides a more stable work environment."

Susan Harmon, Vice President for Finance and Radio, suggests that nonprofit organizations frequently offer tremendous opportunities, "because you get to do a lot of different things. You have to like the rough and tumble of small business, and most nonprofits are really small businesses. It's not so hierarchical; it's freer."

QUESTIONS

1 What level of interdependence would you expect to exist between staff responsible for fund-raising and the pledge campaign, and the programming staff at KERA/KDTN? Why?

2 Draw a brief organizational chart for KERA/KDTN based on the case. Be sure to note the position titles given in the case.

3 Would the contemporary team approach fit the needs and culture of KERA/KDTN? If yes, give an example of where or how it might work well.

VIDEO CASE

ften the most effective leaders are people who can inspire and motivate others.

There are many kinds of leaders: coaches, parents, religious leaders, government and community officials, corporate CEOs. No one leadership style is right for all situations. Each leader requires different skills and knowedge to succeed, but all leaders have the ability to influence people to reach objectives.

Chapter 13 discusses the nature of leadership and explains the difference between leadership and management, traits and types of leaders, and behavioral, contingency, and new approaches to leadership. Chapter 14 discusses the impact of leaders in organizations—motivation of the workforce. Chapter 15 defines communications, explores the different types of communication, and presents ways of managing communication. Chapter 16 focuses on teams, their characteristics, and team development.

Leading

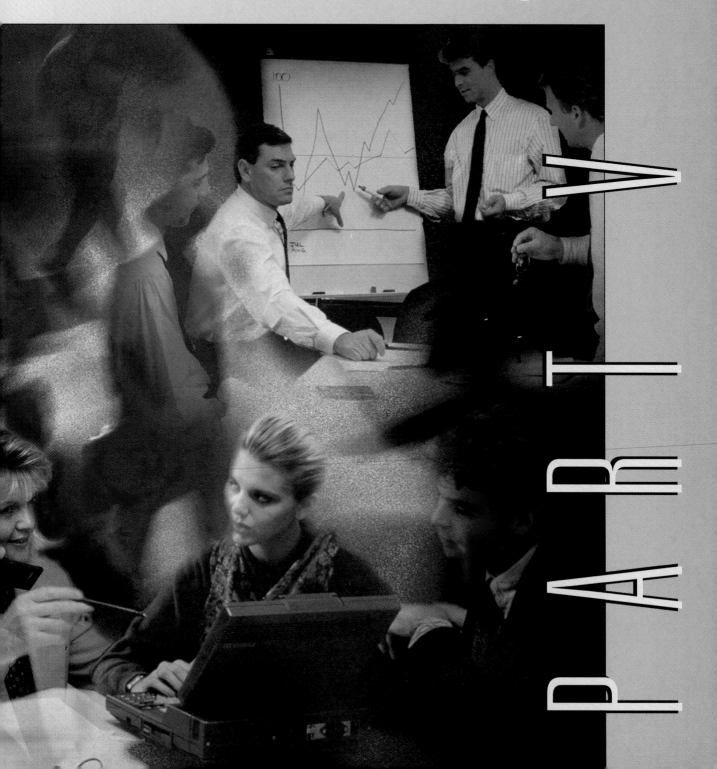

Leadership in Organizations

LEARNING OBJECTIVES

After studying this chapter, you should be able to

- Define leadership and explain its importance for organizations.

- Identify personal characteristics associated with effective leaders.

- Explain the five sources of power and how each causes different subordinate behavior.

- Describe the leader behaviors of initiating structure and consideration and when they should be used.

- Describe Hersey and Blanchard's situational theory and its application to subordinate participation.

- Explain the path–goal model of leadership.

- Explain how leadership fits the organizational situation and how organizational characteristics can substitute for leadership behaviors.

- Describe transformational leadership and when it should be used.

MANAGEMENT PROBLEM

"More losses. I don't know how much more we can take," sighed Steve Silverman to his wife and business partner, Robin. As owners of the Grand Forks, North Dakota, clothing store, Silverman's, they knew they would go out of business if they stayed downtown for another year rather than move to the malls that customers now preferred. In the past three years Silverman's sales had plummeted 30 percent and they were overloaded in inventory and personnel.

Moving, though, seemed out of the question, since the 83-year-old business had purchased the building it had been in for 40 years. Robin knew she and Steve could not manage to take care of everything required for a move, either. Counting on their employees to pitch in and help was impossible. The company was still managed according to the vision of Steve's grandfather, that is, excellent customer service and a "carefree" employee family. Carefree was the operant word here, for the employees lacked initiative to take responsibility or problem-solve. The owners set and enforced the rules of the working "household," making sure at least one of them approved every decision made.

With red ink threatening their store's existence, Robin and Steve leased mall space equal to one-half their current square footage. It wouldn't be just a move. They knew it would require a complete makeover of the physical space, as well as the way they ran the business.[1]

• Do you think Robin and Steve need a new leadership

style? What should they change? What is wrong with the way they have been leading?

The leadership style of Steve and Robin Silverman kept their small, family-owned business successful for many years, but new situations may call for new ways of leading. For example, in 1990, CEO Paul B. Kazarian was instrumental in rescuing Sunbeam-Oster Company from Chapter 11 after its parent, Allegheny International, slid into bankruptcy. A former investment banker, Kazarian chose to tightly control operations and inventory. Although this style helped turn the company around, executives soon began complaining that Kazarian's interference with daily operations and his unwillingness to commit to new plants and products were limiting growth. In January 1993, Kazarian was ousted and replaced by Roger W. Schipke, whose contrasting leadership style includes aggressive development of new products and liberal delegation of authority to line managers.[2] Many styles of leadership can be successful in organizations depending on the leader and the situation. Consider the leadership style of Irish pop star Bob Geldof, who mobilized aid for Ethiopia's famine-stricken population in the 1980s. Geldof threaded together diverse international forces to create two historical music events, Band Aid and Live Aid. Alternatively stroking, coaxing, and prodding, Geldof successfully coordinated communication technology and delicate star egos into a "collective individualism." Today, executives for global companies study Geldof's multinational coordination techniques.[3]

This chapter explores one of the most widely discussed and researched topics in management—leadership. Here we will define leadership, explore the differences between a leader and a manager, and discuss the sources of leader power. We will examine trait, behavioral, and contingency theories of leadership effectiveness. We will also discuss new leadership styles, such as transformational, charismatic, and interactive approaches. Chapters 14 through 16 deal with many of the functions of leadership,

leadership
The ability to influence people toward the attainment of organizational goals.

including employee motivation, communication, and leading groups.

THE NATURE OF LEADERSHIP

There is probably no topic more important to business success today than leadership. The concept of leadership continues to evolve as the needs of organizations change. Among all the ideas and writings about leadership, three aspects stand out—people, influence, and goals. Leadership occurs among people, involves the use of influence, and is used to attain goals.[4] *Influence* means that the relationship among people is not passive. Moreover, influence is designed to achieve some end or goal. Thus, **leadership** as defined here is the ability to influence people toward the attainment of goals. This definition captures the idea that leaders are involved with other people in the achievement of goals.

Leadership is reciprocal, occurring *among* people.[5] Leadership is a "people" activity, distinct from administrative paper shuffling or problem-solving activities. Leadership is dynamic and involves the use of power.

LEADERSHIP VERSUS MANAGEMENT

Much has been written in recent years about the difference between management and leadership. Management and leadership are both important to organizations. Because management power comes from organizational structure, it promotes stability, order, and problem solving within the structure. Leadership power, on the other hand, comes from personal sources that are not as invested in the organization, such as personal interests, goals, and values. Leadership power promotes vision, creativity, and change in the organization. Exhibit 13.1 illustrates the different qualities attributed to leaders and managers, although it is impor-

tant to remember that some people can exhibit a combination of leader/manager qualities.

One of the major differences between the leader and the manager relates to their source of power and the level of compliance it engenders within followers. **Power** is the potential ability to influence the behavior of others.[6] Power represents the resources with which a leader effects changes in employee behavior. Within organizations, there are typically five sources of power: legitimate, reward, coercive, expert, and referent.[7] Sometimes power comes from a person's position in the organization, while other sources of power are based on personal characteristics.

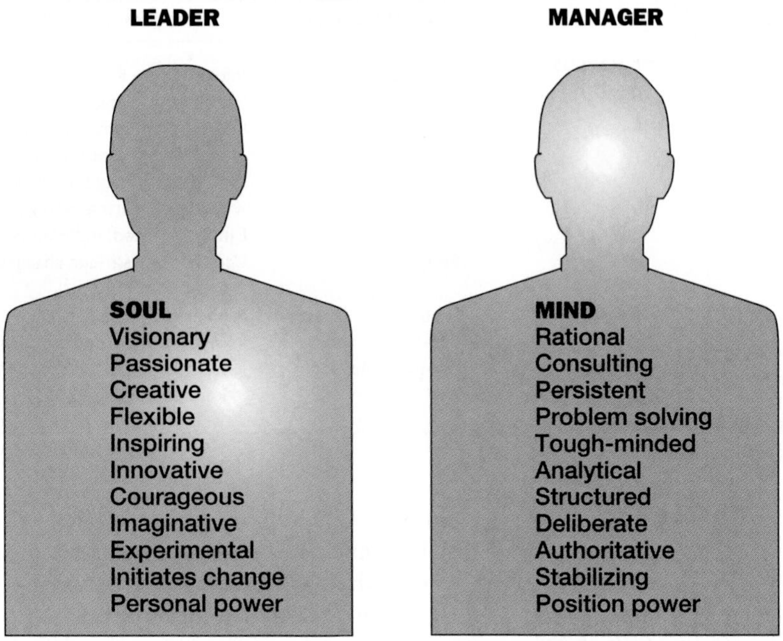

Position Power

The traditional manager's power comes from the organization. The manager's position gives him or her the power to reward or punish subordinates in order to influence their behavior. Legitimate power, reward power, and coercive power are all forms of position power used by managers to change employee behavior.

Legitimate Power. Power coming from a formal management position in an organization and the authority granted to it is called **legitimate power.** For example, once a person has been selected as a supervisor, most workers understand that they are obligated to follow his or her direction with respect to work activities. Subordinates accept this source of power as legitimate, which is why they comply.

Reward Power. Another kind of power, **reward power,** stems from the authority to bestow rewards on other people. Managers may have access to formal rewards, such as pay increases or promotions. They also have at their disposal such rewards as praise, attention, and recognition. Managers can use rewards to influence subordinates' behavior.

Coercive Power. The opposite of reward power is **coercive power.** It refers to the authority to punish or recommend punishment. Managers have coercive power when they have the right to fire or demote employees, criticize, or withdraw pay increases. For example, if Paul, a salesman, does not perform as expected, his supervisor has the coercive power to criticize him, reprimand him, put a negative letter in his file, and hurt his chance for a raise.

Different types of position power elicit different responses in followers.[8] Legitimate power and reward power are most likely to generate follower compliance. *Compliance* means that workers will obey orders and carry out instructions, although they may personally disagree with them and may not be enthusiastic. Coercive power most often generates resistance. *Resistance* means that workers will deliberately try to avoid carrying out instructions or will attempt to disobey orders. How power is used can also depend on whether the leader is in an established corporation or the start-up of a new venture, as illustrated in Exhibit 13.2.

LEADER

SOUL
Visionary
Passionate
Creative
Flexible
Inspiring
Innovative
Courageous
Imaginative
Experimental
Initiates change
Personal power

MANAGER

MIND
Rational
Consulting
Persistent
Problem solving
Tough-minded
Analytical
Structured
Deliberate
Authoritative
Stabilizing
Position power

EXHIBIT 13.1
Leader versus Manager Qualities

SOURCE: Genevieve Capowski, "Anatomy of a Leader: Where Are the Leaders of Tomorrow?" *Management Review,* March 1994, 12.

power
The potential ability to influence others' behavior.

legitimate power
Power that stems from a formal management position in an organization and the authority granted to it.

reward power
Power that results from the authority to reward others.

coercive power
Power that stems from the authority to punish or recommend punishment.

EXHIBIT 13.2
Professional Management versus Entrepreneurial Management

SOURCE: NATION'S BUSINESS (December 1996), p. 56. The Cohn Financial Group Inc., Phoenix, AZ. Reproduced with permission.

Area of Activity	Entrepreneurial Management	Professional Management
Organization	Informal; plan as you go	Formal, systematic planning
Leadership	Varies from dictatorial to laissez-faire	Consultative, participative
Control	Informal structure with overlapping and undefined responsibilities	Formal, well-defined structure
Management development	Individual training for specific needs at the time; learn as you go	Training, education integrated with goals
Culture	Family-oriented, tradition-bound	Well-defined corporate identity
Budgeting	Usually not clear-cut; changes as needs arise	Based on industry standards and corporate goals
Profit	Seen as a by-product	Seen as an important goal
Information and communication	Information guarded and shared on a need-to-know basis; communication informal, on-the-fly	Open, shared information; regularly scheduled interactive forums

Thomas C. Graham, chairman of AK Steel, is a believer in position power. Unimpressed with new ideas about empowering workers, he prefers a military-style management, where cost cutting is rewarded and mistakes are quickly disciplined. His blunt views suggest that management in the steel industry has failed to push people and equipment hard enough. Graham's tough hierarchical approach has resulted in turnarounds for mills at LTV, U.S. Steel, and Washington Steel but has also caused him to be ousted or passed over for promotion in the midst of his successes.[9]

Personal Power

In contrast to the external sources of position power, personal power most often comes from internal sources, such as a person's special knowledge or personality characteristics. Personal power is the tool of the leader. Subordinates follow a leader because of the respect, admiration, or caring they feel for the individual and his or her ideas. Two types of personal power are expert power and referent power.

Expert Power. Power resulting from a leader's special knowledge or skill regarding the tasks performed by followers is referred to as **expert power.** When the leader is a true expert, subordinates go along with recommendations because of his or her superior knowledge. Leaders at supervisory

levels often have experience in the production process that gains them promotion. At top management levels, however, leaders may lack expert power because subordinates know more about technical details than they do.

Referent Power. The last kind of power, **referent power,** comes from leader personality characteristics that command subordinates' identification, respect, and admiration so they wish to emulate the leader. When workers admire a supervisor because of the way she deals with them, the influence is based on referent power. Referent power depends on the leader's personal characteristics rather than on a formal title or position and is most visible in the area of charismatic leadership, which will be discussed later in this chapter.

The follower reaction most often generated by expert power and referent power is commitment.[10] *Commitment* means that workers will share the leader's point of view and enthusiastically carry out instructions. Needless to say, commitment is preferred to compliance or resistance. It is particularly important when change is the desired outcome of a leader's instructions, because change carries risk or uncertainty. Commitment assists the follower in overcoming fear of change.

An example of expert power is Bill Gates of Microsoft Corporation. His visionary leadership style, combined with his own

referent power
Power that results from characteristics that command subordinates' identification with, respect and admiration for, and desire to emulate the leader.

expert power
Power that stems from special knowledge of or skill in the tasks performed by subordinates.

expertise, has led his company to the top of the computer software industry. Current explorations into network computing, online services, office equipment, and biotechnology promise to keep Microsoft on the leading edge of technology and its employees committed to constant change.[11]

Empowerment

A significant recent trend in corporate America is for top executives to *empower* lower employees. Fully 74 percent of executives in a survey claimed that they are more participatory, more concerned with consensus building, and more reliant on communication than on command compared with the past. Executives no longer hoard power.

At Steiner/Bressler Advertising, when the deaths of the president and account-services chief left John Zimmerman as boss, he mobilized his colleagues into a team to completely redefine the autocratic culture. He brought in a financial expert, opened the books to employees, and placed 40 percent of after-tax profits into a companywide bonus pool. Five teams became the structure, completely organized and driven by customer needs. The results were a 25 percent drop in expenses and new business that doubled billings to $18 million.[12]

Empowering employees works because total power in the organization seems to increase. Everyone has more say and hence contributes more to organizational goals. The goal of senior executives in many corporations today is not simply to wield power but also to give it away to people who can get jobs done.[13] For entrepreneurs, giving away power is often more difficult than starting a company. Casey Cowell, though, was able to empower and continue to run his ever-growing company.

U.S. ROBOTICS

Casey G. Cowell and some college buddies decided to start a company in honor of a shared hero, science fiction writer Isaac Asimov. The only problem was: What should their new U.S. Robotics manufacture? Knowing nothing about biotechnology, they decided on computers and, through a fluke, ended up with modems. But it wasn't until the Internet took off that their company could move away from threatened bankruptcy.

Now the North American modem leader, Skokie, Illinois-based USR has 6,000 employees and is doubling every 12 months, as new generations of modems are needed almost that quickly.

Cowell is the rare entrepreneur who is able to start a company and later manage a multi-billion dollar corporation. The essence of his success is his willingness to hand over responsibility to talented executives. An example is R&D head Dale Walsh, who took a chance in 1983 on the then-tiny USR because Cowell told him he could run his own show, and who is largely responsible for USR's jump on its competitors with cutting-edge technology. Cowell's leadership of USR has now taken it international and into diversification by selling network communication systems.

A former championship hockey goalie, Cowell insists on teamwork at USR, where performance goals for salespeople to managers alike are based on "pooled" goals, rather than individual ones. He pushes for aggressive targets and wears out some employees, but his light personal touch often saves the day and may be seen by his office guitar-playing, riding a bike, or commandeering his Range Rover.

Cowell's advice to entrepreneurs struggling to develop: "Build teams and let them run the business, go global as soon as you can, develop diverse product lines from competitive strengths," and know what being a leader means. "You want to have veto power," he says.[14] ∎

LEADERSHIP TRAITS

Early efforts to understand leadership success focused on the leader's personal characteristics or traits. **Traits** are the distinguishing personal characteristics of a leader, such as intelligence, values, and appearance. The early research focused on leaders who had achieved a level of

traits
Distinguishing personal characteristics, such as intelligence, values, and appearance.

greatness and hence was referred to as the *great man* approach. The idea was relatively simple: Find out what made these people great, and select future leaders who already exhibited the same traits or could be trained to develop them. Generally, research found only a weak relationship between personal traits and leader success.[15] For example, football coaches Tom Osborne at Nebraska and Joe Paterno at Penn State have different personality traits, but both are successful leaders of their football programs.

In addition to personality traits, physical, social, and work-related characteristics of leaders have been studied. Exhibit 13.3 summarizes the physical, social, and personal leadership characteristics that have received the greatest research support.[16] However, these characteristics do not stand alone. The appropriateness of a trait or set of traits depends on the leadership situation. The same traits do not apply to every organization.

Another example from football is Joe Montana, retired quarterback for the Kansas City Chiefs. Montana was sometimes called the ultimate turnaround specialist, with his last-minute plays that led to victory. Although his physical attributes dimmed over time, his cool concentration on the task at hand, his ability to spontaneously spot opportunities and use them, his discipline and experience in executing sophisticated game plans, and the quiet pride he communicated to teammates made him a leader of winning teams.[17]

Further studies have expanded the understanding of leadership beyond the personal traits of the individual to focus on the dynamics of the relationship between leaders and followers.

AUTOCRATIC VERSUS DEMOCRATIC LEADERS

One way to approach leader characteristics is to examine autocratic and democratic leaders. An **autocratic leader** is one who tends to centralize authority and rely on legitimate, reward, and coercive power. A **democratic leader** delegates authority to others, encourages participation, and relies on expert and referent power to influence subordinates.

The first studies on these leadership characteristics were conducted at Iowa State University by Kurt Lewin and his associates.[18] These studies compared autocratic and democratic leaders and produced some interesting findings. The groups with autocratic leaders performed highly so long as the leader was present to supervise them. However, group members were displeased with the close, autocratic style of leadership, and feelings of hostility frequently arose. The performance of groups who were assigned democratic leaders was almost as good, and these were characterized by positive feelings rather than hostility. In addition, under the democratic style of leadership, group members performed well even when the leader was absent and left the group on its own.[19] The participative

autocratic leader
A leader who tends to centralize authority and rely on legitimate, reward, and coercive power to manage subordinates.

democratic leader
A leader who delegates authority to others, encourages participation, and relies on expert and referent power to manage subordinates.

EXHIBIT 13.3
Personal Characteristics of Leaders

Physical characteristics	Personality	Social characteristics
Activity	Alertness	Ability to enlist cooperation
Energy	Originality, creativity	Cooperativeness
Social background	Personal integrity, ethical conduct	Popularity, prestige
Mobility	Self-confidence	Sociability, interpersonal skills
Intelligence and ability	**Work-related characteristics**	Social participation
Judgment decisiveness	Achievement drive, desire to excel	Tact, diplomacy
Knowledge	Drive for responsibility	
Fluency of speech	Responsibility in pursuit of goals	
	Task orientation	

SOURCE: Adapted from Bernard M. Bass, *Stogdill's Handbook of Leadership*, rev. ed. (New York: Free Press, 1981), 75–76. This adaptation appeared in R. Albanese and D. D. Van Fleet, *Organizational Behavior: A Managerial Viewpoint* (Hinsdale, Ill.: The Dryden Press, 1983).

techniques and majority rule decision making used by the democratic leader trained and involved group members such that they performed well with or without the leader present. These characteristics of democratic leadership explain why the empowerment of lower employees is a popular trend in companies today.

This early work suggested that leaders were either autocratic or democratic in their approach. However, further work by Tannenbaum and Schmidt indicated that leadership could be a continuum reflecting different amounts of employee participation.[20] Thus, one leader might be autocratic (boss-centered), another democratic (subordinate-centered), and a third a mix of the two styles. The leadership continuum is illustrated in Exhibit 13.4.

Leaders may adjust their styles depending on the situation. Recall the Vroom–Jago model from Chapter 8, which assists the leader in determining the appropriate participation level of subordinates in the decision-making process. Tannenbaum and Schmidt also suggested that the extent to which leadership is boss-centered or subordinate-centered depends on organizational circumstances. For example, if there is time pressure on a leader or if it takes too long for subordinates to learn how to make decisions, the leader will tend to use an autocratic style. When subordinates are able to learn decision-making skills readily, a par-

ticipative style can be used. Another situational factor is the skill difference between subordinates and the leader. The greater the skill difference, the more autocratic the leader approach, because it is difficult to bring subordinates up to the leader's expertise level.[21]

For example, Stephen Fleming uses an autocratic style as a marketing manager in an oil products company. He is being groomed for a higher position because his marketing department has performed so well. However, this has meant time spent at meetings away from his group, and their performance has declined because the subordinates have not learned to function independently. In contrast, Dorothy Roberts, CEO of Echo Scarves, believes that people are managed best by showing them respect and courtesy. Decision making is shared by representatives of design, sales, marketing, and operations. In the traditionally tough fashion industry, her nice-guy leadership style permeates the entire company, creating a unique corporate culture that is open, honest, and supportive of employees. Company prosperity is centered on treating people well. Roberts's leadership style creates satisfied employees who in turn create satisfied customers, which may be more difficult with an autocratic leadership style.[22] Working around an autocratic leadership style takes great ingenuity, as illustrated in the Technology for Today box.

EXHIBIT 13.4
Leadership Continuum

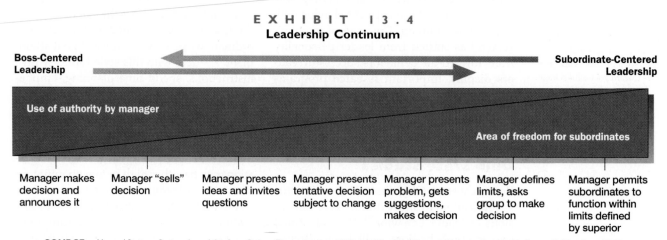

SOURCE: *Harvard Business Review.* An exhibit from Robert Tannenbaum and Warren Schmidt, "How to Choose a Leadership Pattern" (May–June 1973). Copyright © 1973 by the president and Fellows of Harvard College.

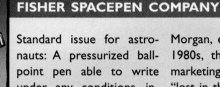

TECHNOLOGY FOR TODAY
FISHER SPACEPEN COMPANY

Standard issue for astronauts: A pressurized ballpoint pen able to write under any conditions, including zero gravity and vacuum, manufactured by Fisher SpacePen Company. The NASA seal of approval gave the company a bonanza (not unlike Tang's) in the 1970s when millions of yearly revenues came in.

So how did a new-invention company become stuck in a time-warp with flat sales, sickly profits, and Sputnik-era technology? Because the 82-year-old pen inventor and gadget lover Paul Fisher couldn't launch into the information-intensive technologies necessary to keep the company merely even with its competitors.

By the time Fisher's sons, Cary and Morgan, entered the business in the 1980s, they realized the company's marketing and finance approaches were "lost in the Sixties," while their father spent all his time perfecting ink formulas. So the company languished for years with stone-age operations until an old SpacePen fan, Jim Jobin, came on board as marketing and technology consultant. Nothing was automated, including a clumsy sales system of notebook and scraps of paper. Preferring to manage a small company, Jobin knew he could not persuade Fisher by big plans. Instead, Jobin wooed him by establishing trust through numerous tennis games and then sold him on the idea of new "gadgetry."

With only a $35,000 budget, Jobin and Cary studied network technology and spent weekends wiring the office themselves. They set up Act!, a contact management program, tracking every sales lead, and connected a 1-800-number database with salespeople's laptops. Sales productivity increased over 100 percent, so the elder Fisher was convinced to hire 53 new salespeople and boost international sales. Selling a Web site to him, though, was as difficult as explaining the Internet to your grandparents.

Jobin's work has paid off. Sales have leaped up like an astronaut jumping on the moon—by an increase of 65 percent. Even 82-year-old Fisher is finally booting up. He had a PC installed next to the astronaut memorabilia.

SOURCE: Sarah Schafer, "A SpacePen Odyssey," *Inc. Technology*, No. 2, 1996, 74–79.

---

consideration
A type of leader behavior that describes the extent to which a leader is sensitive to subordinates, respects their ideas and feelings, and establishes mutual trust.

initiating structure
A type of leader behavior that describes the extent to which a leader is task oriented and directs subordinates' work activities toward goal achievement.

BEHAVIORAL APPROACHES

The autocratic and democratic styles suggest that it is the "behavior" of the leader rather than a personality trait that determines leadership effectiveness. Perhaps any leader can adopt the correct behavior with appropriate training. The focus of recent research has shifted from leader personality traits toward the behaviors successful leaders display. Important research programs on leadership behavior were conducted at Ohio State University, the University of Michigan, and the University of Texas.

Ohio State Studies

Researchers at Ohio State University surveyed leaders to study hundreds of dimensions of leader behavior.[23] They identified two major behaviors, called *consideration* and *initiating structure*.

Consideration is the extent to which the leader is mindful of subordinates, respects their ideas and feelings, and establishes mutual trust. Considerate leaders are friendly, provide open communication, develop teamwork, and are oriented toward their subordinates' welfare.

Initiating structure is the extent to which the leader is task-oriented and directs subordinate work activities toward goal attainment. Leaders with this style typically give instructions, spend time planning, emphasize deadlines, and provide explicit schedules of work activities.

Consideration and initiating structure are independent of each other, which means that a leader with a high degree of consideration may be either high or low on initiating structure. A leader may have any of four styles: high initiating structure–low consideration, high initiating structure–high consideration, low initiating structure–low consideration, or low initiating

structure–high consideration. The Ohio State research found that the high consideration–high initiating structure style achieved better performance and greater satisfaction than the other leader styles. However, new research has found that effective leaders may be high on consideration and low on initiating structure or low on consideration and high on initiating structure, depending on the situation. Thus, the "high–high" style is not always the best.[24]

Michigan Studies

Studies at the University of Michigan at about the same time took a different approach by comparing the behavior of effective and ineffective supervisors.[25] The most effective supervisors were those who focused on the subordinates' human needs in order to "build effective work groups with high performance goals." The Michigan researchers used the term *employee-centered leaders* for leaders who established high performance goals and displayed supportive behavior toward subordinates. The less effective leaders were called *job-centered leaders*; these tended to be less concerned with goal achievement and human needs in favor of meeting schedules, keeping costs low, and achieving production efficiency.

The Leadership Grid

Blake and Mouton of the University of Texas proposed a two-dimensional leadership theory called **leadership grid** that builds on the work of the Ohio State and Michigan studies.[26] The two-dimensional model and five of its seven major management styles are depicted in Exhibit 13.5. Each axis on the grid is a 9-point scale, with 1 meaning low concern and 9 high concern.

Team management (9,9) often is considered the most effective style and is recommended for managers because organization members work together to accomplish tasks. *Country club management* (1,9) occurs when primary emphasis is given to people rather than to work outputs. *Authority-*

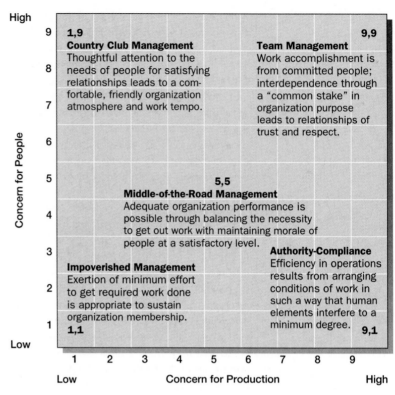

EXHIBIT 13.5
The Leadership Grid® Figure

SOURCE: The Leadership Grid® Figure from Robert R. Blake and Anne Adams McCanse, *Leadership Dilemmas—Grid Solutions* (Houston: Gulf, 1991), 29. Copyright © 1991 by Scientific Methods, Inc.

compliance management (9,1) occurs when efficiency in operations is the dominant orientation. *Middle-of-the-road management* (5,5) reflects a moderate amount of concern for both people and production. *Impoverished management* (1,1) means the absence of a management philosophy; managers exert little effort toward interpersonal relationships or work accomplishment. Consider these examples.

M/A-COM AND TENNECO

In a world of constant stress and change, the humane leader must balance, and help others balance, the tremendous pressures of work with demands from the rest of their lives. No one knows that better than Rick Hess, the CEO of M/A-Com, a company that manufactures microwave communications equipment for the defense industry. He and his staff typically spend 12-hour days at work, and he knows helping everyone avoid burnout is one of his

leadership grid
A two-dimensional leadership theory that measures a leader's concern for people and concern for production.

most important jobs. He stays close to employees, taking them to lunch, playing ball with them one night a week, finding out what's going on in their lives. If someone's wife is having a baby, Hess doesn't give him an assignment that requires working an 80-hour week. "The worst thing I can do is give someone an assignment he's bound to fail," he asserts. Hess motivates people to challenge themselves, to extend their reach. "Don't trap people in cubbies," he says. "Let a technical guy go and talk with customers and grow."

Compare the style of Rick Hess with that of former West Point professor Dana G. Mead, CEO of Tenneco, Inc. His motto, adapted from General George Patton, is "Plan deliberately; execute violently." His hard-driving management style is to set ambitious goals for division presidents on everything from return on capital investments to workplace safety. If the executives already know how to meet these goals, Mead says they were set too low to call forth true creativity. And if they can't? Before his executives prevailed upon him to remove it, Mead had a noose hanging in his office. "The first division president that walks in here and hasn't made his numbers is going to try it on for size," he used to say.[27] ■

The leadership style of Rick Hess is characterized by high people concern and moderate concern for production. Dana Mead, in contrast, is high on concern for costs and production and low on concern for people. Both leaders are successful because of their different situations. The next group of theories builds on the leader–follower relationship of behavioral approaches to explore how organizational situations affect the leader's approach.

CONTINGENCY APPROACHES

Several models of leadership that explain the relationship between leadership styles and specific situations have been developed. These are termed **contingency approaches** and include the leadership model

developed by Fiedler and his associates, the situational theory of Hersey and Blanchard, the path–goal theory presented by Evans and House, and the substitutes-for-leadership concept.

Fiedler's Contingency Theory

An early, extensive effort to combine leadership style and organizational situation into a comprehensive theory of leadership was made by Fiedler and his associates.[28] The basic idea is simple: Match the leader's style with the situation most favorable for his or her success. By diagnosing leadership style and the organizational situation, the correct fit can be arranged.

Leadership Style. The cornerstone of Fiedler's contingency theory is the extent to which the leader's style is relationship-oriented or task-oriented. A *relationship-oriented leader* is concerned with people, as in the consideration style described earlier. A *task-oriented leader* is primarily motivated by task accomplishment, which is similar to the initiating structure style described earlier.

Leadership style was measured with a questionnaire known as the least preferred coworker (LPC) scale. The **LPC scale** has a set of 16 bipolar adjectives along an 8-point scale. Examples of the bipolar adjectives used by Fiedler on the LPC scale follow:

open _ _ _ _ _ _ _	guarded
quarrelsome _ _ _ _ _ _ _	harmonious
efficient _ _ _ _ _ _ _	inefficient
self-assured _ _ _ _ _ _ _	hesitant
gloomy _ _ _ _ _ _ _	cheerful

If the leader describes the least preferred coworker using positive concepts, he or she is considered relationship-oriented: that is, a leader who cares about and is sensitive to other people's feelings. Conversely, if a leader uses negative concepts to describe the least preferred coworker, he or she is considered task-oriented: that is, a leader who sees other people in negative terms and places greater value on task activities than on people.

LPC scale
A questionnaire designed to measure relationship-oriented versus task-oriented leadership style according to the leader's choice of adjectives for describing the "least preferred coworker."

contingency approach
A model of leadership that describes the relationship between leadership styles and specific organizational situations.

Situation.   Leadership situations can be analyzed in terms of three elements: the quality of leader–member relationships, task structure, and position power.[29] Each of these elements can be described as either favorable or unfavorable for the leader.

1 *Leader–member relations* refers to group atmosphere and members' attitude toward and acceptance of the leader. When subordinates trust, respect, and have confidence in the leader, leader–member relations are considered good. When subordinates distrust, do not respect, and have little confidence in the leader, leader–member relations are poor.

2 *Task structure* refers to the extent to which tasks performed by the group are defined, involve specific procedures, and have clear, explicit goals. Routine, well-defined tasks, such as those of assembly-line workers, have a high degree of structure. Creative, ill-defined tasks, such as research and development or strategic planning, have a low degree of task structure. When task structure is high, the situation is considered favorable to the leader; when low, the situation is less favorable.

3 *Position power* is the extent to which the leader has formal authority over subordinates. Position power is high when the leader has the power to plan and direct the work of subordinates, evaluate it, and reward or punish them. Position power is low when the leader has little authority over subordinates and cannot evaluate their work or reward them. When position power is high, the situation is considered favorable for the leader; when low, the situation is unfavorable.

Combining the three situational characteristics yields a list of eight leadership situations, which are illustrated in Exhibit 13.6. Situation I is most favorable to the leader because leader–member relations are good, task structure is high, and leader position power is strong. Situation VIII is most unfavorable to the leader because leader–member relations are poor, task structure is low, and leader position power is weak. All other octants represent intermediate degrees of favorableness for the leader.

Contingency Theory.   When Fiedler examined the relationships among leadership style, situational favorability, and group task performance, he found the pattern shown in Exhibit 13.7. Task-oriented leaders are more effective when the situation is either highly favorable or highly unfavorable. Relationship-oriented leaders are more effective in situations of moderate favorability.

The task-oriented leader excels in the favorable situation because everyone gets along, the task is clear, and the leader has power; all that is needed is for someone to take charge and provide direction. Similarly, if the situation is highly unfavorable to the leader, a great deal of structure and task direction is needed. A strong leader defines task structure and can establish authority over subordinates. Because leader–member relations are poor anyway, a strong task orientation will make no difference in the leader's popularity.

The relationship-oriented leader performs better in situations of intermediate favorability because human relations skills are important in achieving high group performance. In these situations, the leader may be moderately well liked, have some power, and supervise jobs that contain some ambiguity. A leader with good interpersonal skills can create a positive group atmosphere that will improve relationships, clarify task structure, and establish position power.

A leader, then, needs to know two things in order to use Fiedler's contingency theory. First, the leader should know whether he or she has a relationship- or task-oriented style. Second, the leader should diagnose the situation and determine whether leader–member relations, task structure, and position power are favorable or unfavorable.

E X H I B I T   1 3 . 6
Fiedler's Classification of Situation Favorableness

	Very Favorable		Intermediate				Very Unfavorable	
Leader-Member Relations	Good	Good	Good	Good	Poor	Poor	Poor	Poor
Task Structure	High		Low		High		Low	
Leader Position Power	Strong	Weak	Strong	Weak	Strong	Weak	Strong	Weak
Situations	I	II	III	IV	V	VI	VII	VIII

SOURCE: Reprinted from "The Effects of Leadership Training and Experience: A Contingency Model Interpretation," by Fred E. Fiedler published in *Administrative Science Quarterly* Vol. 17, No. 4 by permission of *Administrative Science Quarterly*.

E X H I B I T   1 3 . 7
How Leader Style Fits the Situation

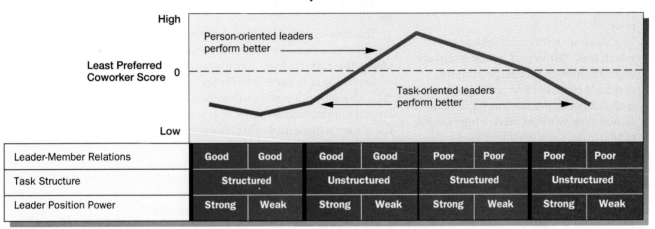

Leader-Member Relations	Good	Good	Good	Good	Poor	Poor	Poor	Poor
Task Structure	Structured		Unstructured		Structured		Unstructured	
Leader Position Power	Strong	Weak	Strong	Weak	Strong	Weak	Strong	Weak

SOURCE: Reprinted from "The Effects of Leadership Training and Experience: A Contingency Model Interpretation," by Fred E. Fiedler published in *Administrative Science Quarterly* Vol. 17, No. 4 by permission of *Administrative Science Quarterly*.

Fitting leader style to the situation can help a company transform itself successfully. Consider the situation of Corsair Communications, Inc.

■ CORSAIR COMMUNICATIONS, INC.

A tiny blond woman stood in front of the 60 engineers, jettisoned from a large Silicon Valley defense contractor and now employees of Corsair Communications, Inc., reporting to Mary Ann Byrnes. The engineers were skeptical and Byrnes was nervous.

They had developed a technology capable of identifying the "fingerprint" of a particular Soviet submarine, with commercial value in in-

hibiting illegal cellular phone use, which could save cellular providers $1 billion per year.

Byrnes had to change Corsair's culture from one where work was done on assigned tasks according to established procedures and where employees never talked to customers because competition wasn't even an issue.

The new culture, though, had to deliver real products to real customers and beat the competition. In place of the engineers' relative isolation, the new culture would need to communicate a sense of community, encouraging a customer focus and a sense of urgency.

Corsair is based on cross-functional teams with a continual sharing of information, highlighted by Friday pizza lunches where anything

and everything is discussed. Because employees now focus on customer needs and hold company stock, they value the work differently. "It's important for me not to make certain decisions," she says, "otherwise they won't get follow-through."

Corsair's culture is its "principal competitive weapon." If the company succeeds, it will be because Byrnes created an environment that's more instrumental in motivating and allowing the engineers to get the job done. So far, the company is succeeding, with stellar financial performance in its first year.

What Byrnes set out to do was take some of the smartest scientists in the world and to make them productive, to assist them in swiftly perfecting what they had been unable to deliver before. One proof of her effectiveness is how the previously skeptical engineers see her. Her leadership has let them feel part of the decision making and the rewards. As one of them said, "She trusts us."[30] ■

Mary Ann Byrnes's experience at Corsair illustrates Fiedler's model; a relationship-oriented leadership style was correct for a new, unstructured situation.

An important contribution of Fiedler's research is that it goes beyond the notion of leadership styles to show how styles fit the situation to improve organizational effectiveness. On the other hand, the model has also been criticized.[31] Using the LPC score as a measure of relationship- or task-oriented behavior seems simplistic, and how the model works over time is unclear. For example, if a task-oriented leader is matched with an unfavorable situation and is successful, the organizational situation is likely to improve and become more favorable to the leader. The leader might need to change his style or go to a new situation to find the same challenge for his task-oriented leader style.

Hersey and Blanchard's Situational Theory

The **situational theory** of leadership is an interesting extension of the behavioral theories described earlier and summarized in

the leadership grid (Exhibit 13.5). More than previous theories, Hersey and Blanchard's approach focuses a great deal of attention on the characteristics of employees in determining appropriate leadership behavior. The point of Hersey and Blanchard is that subordinates vary in readiness level. People low in task readiness, because of little ability or training, or insecurity, need a different leadership style than those who are high in readiness and have good ability, skills, confidence, and willingness to work.[32]

The relationships between leader style and follower readiness are summarized in Exhibit 13.8. The upper part of the exhibit indicates style of leader, which is based on a combination of relationship behavior and task behavior. The bell-shaped curve is called a prescriptive curve, because it indicates when each leader style should be used. The four styles—telling (S1), selling (S2), participating (S3), and delegating (S4)—depend on the readiness of followers, indicated in the lower part of Exhibit 13.8. R1 is low readiness and R4 represents high readiness. The telling style is for low-readiness subordinates, because people are unable and unwilling to take responsibility for their own task behavior. The selling and participating styles work for followers with moderate readiness, and delegating is appropriate for employees with high readiness.

This contingency model is easier to understand than Fiedler's model, but it incorporates only the characteristics of followers, not those of the situation. The leader should evaluate subordinates and adopt whichever style is needed. If one or more followers are at low levels of readiness, the leader must be very specific, telling them exactly what to do, how to do it, and when. For followers high in readiness, the leader provides a general goal and sufficient authority to do the task as they see fit. Leaders must carefully diagnose the readiness level of followers and then tell, sell, participate, or delegate.

Phil Hagans is a leader who understands how follower readiness determines leadership style. As the owner of two McDonald's franchises in northeast Houston, Hagans

situational theory
A contingency approach to leadership that links the leader's behavioral style with the task readiness of subordinates.

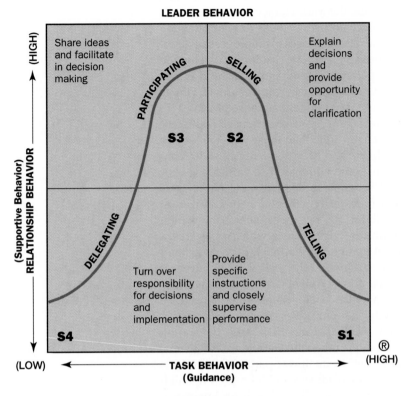

LEADER BEHAVIOR

(HIGH)

(Supportive Behavior)
RELATIONSHIP BEHAVIOR

Share ideas and facilitate in decision making

PARTICIPATING

S3

SELLING

Explain decisions and provide opportunity for clarification

S2

DELEGATING

Turn over responsibility for decisions and implementation

S4

TELLING

Provide specific instructions and closely supervise performance

S1

(LOW) ◄──── TASK BEHAVIOR ────► (HIGH)
(Guidance)

FOLLOWER READINESS

HIGH	MODERATE		LOW
R4	R3	R2	R1
Able and Willing or Confident	Able but Unwilling or Insecure	Unable but Willing or Confident	Unable and Unwilling or Insecure

FOLLOWER DIRECTED | LEADER DIRECTED

EXHIBIT I3.8
The Situational Theory of Leadership

path–goal theory
A contingency approach to leadership specifying that the leader's responsibility is to increase subordinates' motivation by clarifying the behaviors necessary for task accomplishment and rewards.

gives many of his young employees their first job as well as an introduction to the culture of work as he received it, moving up through the ranks. Starting with instruction on every detail of the job from how to dress to how to clean the grill, he coaches them through their first days. As they grow in ability and confidence, he uses a more participatory style but continues to mentor them with financial planning and educational assistance. Because many of his employees have never held a job before, Hagans knows to guide them through each

level of readiness.[33] A leader would need to use a different style with a part-time worker who was retired after 40 years in the business world.

Path–Goal Theory

Another contingency approach to leadership is called the path–goal theory.[34] According to the **path–goal theory,** the leader's responsibility is to increase subordinates' motivation to attain personal and organizational goals. As illustrated in Exhibit 13.9, the leader increases their motivation by either (1) clarifying the subordinates' path to the rewards that are available or (2) increasing the rewards that they value and desire. Path clarification means that the leader works with subordinates to help them identify and learn the behaviors that will lead to successful task accomplishment and organizational rewards. Increasing rewards means that the leader talks with subordinates to learn which rewards are important to them—that is, whether they desire intrinsic rewards from the work itself or extrinsic rewards such as raises or promotions. The leader's job is to increase personal payoffs to subordinates for goal attainment and to make the paths to these payoffs clear and easy to travel.[35] The Leading the Management Revolution box illustrates how George Sztykiel's leadership style as "number-one servant" has created a motivated workforce and successful company.

This model is called a contingency theory because it consists of three sets of contingencies—leader behavior and style, situational contingencies, and the use of rewards to meet subordinates' needs.[36] Whereas in the Fiedler theory described earlier the assumption would be to switch leaders as situations change, in path–goal theory leaders switch their behaviors to match the situation.

Leader Behavior. The path–goal theory suggests a fourfold classification of leader behaviors.[37] These classifications are the types of leader behavior the leader can

Leader Roles in the Path–Goal Model

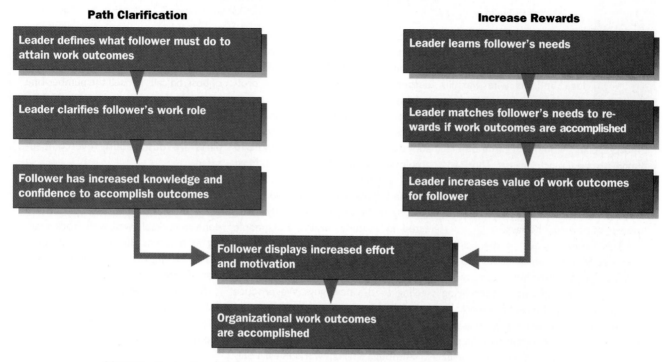

SOURCE: Based on Bernard M. Bass, "Leadership: Good, Better, Best," *Organizational Dynamics* 13 (winter 1985), 26–40.

adopt and include supportive, directive, achievement-oriented, and participative styles.

Supportive leadership involves leader behavior that shows concern for subordinates' well-being and personal needs. Leadership behavior is open, friendly, and approachable, and the leader creates a team climate and treats subordinates as equals. Supportive leadership is similar to the consideration leadership described earlier.

Directive leadership occurs when the leader tells subordinates exactly what they are supposed to do. Leader behavior includes planning, making schedules, setting performance goals and behavior standards, and stressing adherence to rules and regulations. Directive leadership behavior is similar to the initiating-structure leadership style described earlier.

Participative leadership means that the leader consults with his or her subordinates about decisions. Leader behavior includes asking for opinions and suggestions, en-couraging participation in decision making, and meeting with subordinates in their workplaces. The participative leader encourages group discussion and written suggestions.

Achievement-oriented leadership occurs when the leader sets clear and challenging goals for subordinates. Leader behavior stresses high-quality performance and improvement over current performance. Achievement-oriented leaders also show confidence in subordinates and assist them in learning how to achieve high goals.

The four types of leader behavior are not considered ingrained personality traits as in the Fiedler theory; rather, they reflect types of behavior that every leader is able to adopt, depending on the situation.

Situational Contingencies. The two important situational contingencies in the path–goal theory are (1) the personal characteristics of group members and (2) the work environment. Personal characteristics

LEADING THE MANAGEMENT REVOLUTION
SPARTAN MOTORS

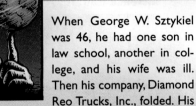

When George W. Sztykiel was 46, he had one son in law school, another in college, and his wife was ill. Then his company, Diamond Reo Trucks, Inc., folded. His reaction was to take out a second mortgage and, along with three others, build his first truck chassis. Thus was Spartan Motors born. Sztykiel believes the "luxury" of those traumas led to their ultimate success. "We had the power of poverty," he says.

This novel principle is the guiding force at Spartan, which builds chassis for fire trucks, motor homes, and, more recently, transit and school buses. Being driven by poverty forces hard work, he believes, which in turn builds value and creates wealth. The complacent die, and so does the company if the hunger ever fades.

Austerity and function are also integral values, as shown by the company's threadbare industrial building in Charlotte, Michigan. Sztykiel has no secre-tary, and there are no budgets. Three department heads have final say over expenditures, which are justified by desperate need and potential for prof-itability.

Spartan's workforce demonstrates the essence of the company. Only about 2 percent of the company's 510 employees have college degrees. Most of the "engineers" began on the assem-bly line before being promoted to the drafting table. Sztykiel is strictly inter-ested in attitude, brains, and people who are not afraid to work. "Building trucks is not a science, it is an art," he says. "The old engineers pass on the feeling to the new guys. We produce ten times faster than bigger companies, where they have lost the feeling, so all they can do is apply science."

Although Spartan workers earn only 80 percent of what their union coun-terparts earn at GM, they stay because of the family atmosphere, profit shar-ing, and job security. In an industry fraught with plant closings and worker-shedding, Spartan has never had to lay off an employee and Sztykiel vows it will never happen. Disdaining the title of boss, he calls himself the number-one servant of the corporation. Making $100,000, or four times the lowest-paid worker, Sztykiel believes his counter-parts are outrageously overcompen-sated.

Though the heavy-truck industry has been in a quasi-depression for much of the past decade, Spartan has done remarkably well, with stock soar-ing as much as 800 percent in some years. Earnings in 1996 were double that of 1995.

Spartan's growth has been based on old-fashioned values and strong leader-ship. GM executives may need to learn about the power of poverty.

SOURCES: "Investor's Information," Spartan Motors, August 1996; 1995 Annual Report of Spartan Motors, 1996; Edward O. Welles, "The Shape of Things to Come," *Inc.*, Feb. 1992, 66–74; and Richard S. Teitelbaum, "Spartan Motors," *Fortune*, Dec. 28, 1992, 55. Company sources.

---

of subordinates are similar to Hersey and Blanchard's readiness level and include such factors as ability, skills, needs, and mo-tivations. For example, if an employee has a low level of ability or skill, the leader may need to provide additional training or coaching in order for the worker to improve performance. If a subordinate is self-cen-tered, the leader must use rewards to moti-vate him or her. Subordinates who want clear direction and authority require a di-rective leader who will tell them exactly what to do. Craftworkers and professionals, however, may want more freedom and au-tonomy and work best under a participative leadership style.

The work environment contingencies in-clude the degree of task structure, the na-ture of the formal authority system, and the work group itself. The task structure is sim-ilar to the same concept described in Fiedler's contingency theory; it includes the extent to which tasks are defined and have explicit job descriptions and work proce-dures. The formal authority system in-cludes the amount of legitimate power used by managers and the extent to which poli-cies and rules constrain employees' behav-ior. Work group characteristics are the educational level of subordinates and the quality of relationships among them.

Use of Rewards. Recall that the leader's responsibility is to clarify the path to re-wards for subordinates or to increase the amount of rewards to enhance satisfaction

and job performance. In some situations, the leader works with subordinates to help them acquire the skills and confidence needed to perform tasks and achieve rewards already available. In others, the leader may develop new rewards to meet the specific needs of a subordinate.

Exhibit 13.10 illustrates four examples of how leadership behavior is tailored to the situation. In the first situation, the subordinate lacks confidence; thus, the supportive leadership style provides the social support with which to encourage the subordinate to undertake the behavior needed to do the work and receive the rewards. In the second situation, the job is ambiguous, and the employee is not performing effectively. Directive leadership behavior is used to give instructions and clarify the task so that the follower will know how to accomplish it and receive rewards. In the third situation, the subordinate is unchallenged by the task; thus, an achievement-oriented behavior is used to set higher goals. This clarifies the path to rewards for the employee. In the fourth situation, an incorrect reward is given to a subordinate, and the participative leadership style is used to change this. By discussing the subordinate's needs, the leader is able to identify the correct reward for task accomplishment. In all four cases, the outcome of fitting the leadership behavior to the situation produces greater employee effort by either clarifying how subordinates can receive rewards or changing the rewards to fit their needs.

In some organizations, such as McArthur-Glen Group, leaders display complementary leadership styles to meet subordinates' needs.

McARTHUR-GLEN GROUP

The leadership of Cheryl McArthur and Alan Glen, co-founders of a company that developed and manages 13 outlet malls, illustrates the strengths that differing leadership styles can bring to an organization.

McArthur's management style stresses interactive characteristics often displayed by women managers. Empowerment is a priority, and McArthur willingly shares information and strives to keep the lines of communication open. McArthur's people skills enable her to convey the company vision to each of the 125 employees, clarify tasks, and provide the

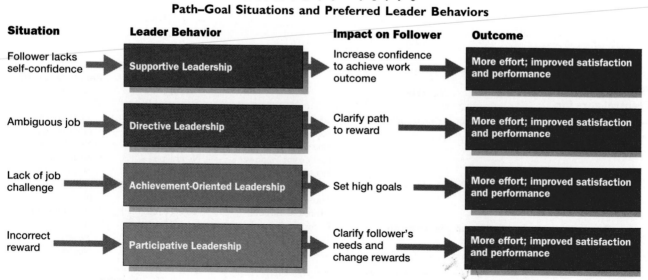

EXHIBIT 13.10
Path–Goal Situations and Preferred Leader Behaviors

Situation	Leader Behavior	Impact on Follower	Outcome
Follower lacks self-confidence	Supportive Leadership	Increase confidence to achieve work outcome	More effort; improved satisfaction and performance
Ambiguous job	Directive Leadership	Clarify path to reward	More effort; improved satisfaction and performance
Lack of job challenge	Achievement-Oriented Leadership	Set high goals	More effort; improved satisfaction and performance
Incorrect reward	Participative Leadership	Clarify follower's needs and change rewards	More effort; improved satisfaction and performance

SOURCE: Adapted from Gary A. Yukl, *Leadership in Organizations* (Englewood Cliffs, N.J.: Prentice-Hall, 1981), 146–152.

supportive leadership necessary to help the individual employee perform effectively under deadline pressure.

Glen, by contrast, focuses on the creative end. His experience enables the company to set deadlines and realistic timetables and to get the malls up and running with a minimum of hassle. Glen prefers to focus on the big picture and leave the daily organizational and staff details to McArthur. However, Glen credits his partner with the "ambition" that drives the company forward and makes his vision a reality. Each partner appreciates the strengths of the other, and the two contrasting styles are complementary. Employees, too, appreciate these leadership styles of McArthur and Glen, remarking, "they fit together like a zipper."[38] ■

Although Glen's leadership style is achievement oriented, McArthur's style is considered supportive leadership behavior, which gives Glen the support to overcome obstacles and achieve higher performance.

Path–goal theorizing can be complex, but much of the research on it has been encouraging.[39] Using the model to specify precise relationships and make exact predictions about employee outcomes may be difficult, but the four types of leader behavior and the ideas for fitting them to situational contingencies provide a useful way for leaders to think about motivating subordinates.

substitute
A situational variable that makes a leadership style redundant or unnecessary.

neutralizer
A situational variable that counteracts a leadership style and prevents the leader from displaying certain behaviors.

Substitutes for Leadership

The contingency leadership approaches considered so far have focused on the leaders' style, the subordinates' nature, and the situation's characteristics. The final contingency approach suggests that situational variables can be so powerful that they actually substitute for or neutralize the need for leadership.[40] This approach outlines those organizational settings in which a leadership style is unimportant or unnecessary.

Exhibit 13.11 shows the situational variables that tend to substitute for or neutralize leadership characteristics. A **substitute** for leadership makes the leadership style unnecessary or redundant. For example, highly professional subordinates who know how to do their tasks do not need a leader who initiates structure for them and tells them what to do. A **neutralizer** counteracts the leadership style and prevents the leader from displaying certain behaviors. For example, if a leader has absolutely no position power or is physically removed from subordinates, the leader's ability to give directions to subordinates is greatly reduced.

Situational variables in Exhibit 13.11 include characteristics of the group, the task, and the organization itself. For example, when subordinates are highly professional and experienced, both leadership styles are less important. The employees do not need

EXHIBIT 13.11
Substitutes and Neutralizers for Leadership

Variable		Task-Oriented Leadership	People-Oriented Leadership
Organizational variables:	Group cohesiveness	Substitutes for	Substitutes for
	Formalization	Substitutes for	No effect on
	Inflexibility	Neutralizes	No effect on
	Low positional power	Neutralizes	Neutralizes
	Physical separation	Neutralizes	Neutralizes
Task characteristics:	Highly structured task	Substitutes for	No effect on
	Automatic feedback	Substitutes for	No effect on
	Intrinsic satisfaction	No effect on	Substitutes for
Group characteristics:	Professionalism	Substitutes for	Substitutes for
	Training/experience	Substitutes for	No effect on
	Low value of rewards	Neutralizes	Neutralizes

much direction or consideration. With respect to task characteristics, highly structured tasks substitute for a task-oriented style, and a satisfying task substitutes for a people-oriented style. With respect to the organization itself, group cohesiveness substitutes for both leader styles. Formalized rules and procedures substitute for leader task orientation. Physical separation of leader and subordinate neutralizes both leadership styles.

The value of the situations described in Exhibit 13.11 is that they help leaders avoid leadership overkill. Leaders should adopt a style with which to complement the organizational situation. For example, the work situation for bank tellers provides a high level of formalization, little flexibility, and a highly structured task. The head teller should not adopt a task-oriented style, because the organization already provides structure and direction. The head teller should concentrate on a people-oriented style. In other organizations, if group cohesiveness or previous training meet employees' social needs, the leader is free to concentrate on task-oriented behaviors. The leader can adopt a style complementary to the organizational situation to ensure that both task needs and people needs of the work group will be met.

NEW LEADERSHIP APPROACHES

In Chapter 1, we defined management to include the functions of leading, planning, organizing, and controlling. But recent work on leadership has begun to distinguish leadership as something more: a quality that inspires and motivates people beyond their normal levels of performance.

Transactional Leaders

The traditional management function of leading has been called *transactional leadership*.[41] **Transactional leaders** clarify the role and task requirements of subordinates, ini-

Disney CEO Michael Eisner is considered a *charismatic leader*. Disney's uniqueness stems from having a creative executive in charge rather than a financier or lawyer. He shapes the corporate value system by inducing creativity in others and calls himself the "head cheerleader." Freewheeling and wildly creative brainstorming sessions are typical of what Eisner will do to get creative energy flowing. His vision of creativity extends the corporate culture founded by Walt Disney and fuels Disney's current growth and competitiveness.

tiate structure, provide appropriate rewards, and try to be considerate to and meet the social needs of subordinates. The transactional leader's ability to satisfy subordinates may improve productivity. Transactional leaders excel at management functions. They are hardworking, tolerant, and fair-minded. They take pride in keeping things running smoothly and efficiently. Transactional leaders often stress the impersonal aspects of performance, such as plans, schedules, and budgets. They have a sense of commitment to the organization and conform to organizational norms and values.

Charismatic Leaders

Charismatic leadership goes beyond transactional leadership techniques. The **charismatic leader** has the capacity to motivate people to do more than normally expected. The impact of charismatic leaders is normally from (1) stating a lofty vision of an imagined future that employees identify with, (2) shaping a corporate value system for which everyone stands, and (3) trusting subordinates and earning their complete trust in return.[42] Charismatic leaders raise subordinates' consciousness about new outcomes and motivate them to transcend their own interests for the sake of the department

charismatic leader
A leader who has the ability to motivate subordinates to transcend their expected performance.

transactional leader
A leader who clarifies subordinates' role and task requirements, initiates structure, provides rewards, and displays consideration for subordinates.

or organization. Charismatic leaders tend to be less predictable than transactional leaders. They create an atmosphere of change, and they may be obsessed by visionary ideas that excite, stimulate, and drive other people to work hard. Charismatic leaders have an emotional impact on subordinates. They stand for something, have a vision of the future, are able to communicate that vision to subordinates, and motivate them to realize it.[43] The Focus on Leadership box provides a short quiz to help you determine whether you have the potential to be a charismatic leader.

Charismatic leaders include Mother Teresa; Martin Luther King, Jr.; and Adolf Hitler. The true charismatic leader often does not fit within a traditional organization and may lead a social movement rather than a formal organization. H. Ross Perot is an example of how charismatic leadership can provide the foundation for a successful business or a political movement.

Transformational Leaders

Critics of the state of business today charge that most U.S. companies have a tendency to be "overmanaged and underled." Managers deal with "organizational complexity"; leaders initiate "productive change."[44] Transformational leaders balance the demands of both. **Transformational leaders** are similar to charismatic leaders but are distinguished by their special ability to bring about innovation and change.[45]

Transformational leaders emerge to take an organization through major strategic change, such as revitalization. They have the ability to lead changes in the organization's mission, structure, and human resource management. Transformational leaders do not analyze or control specific transactions with followers using only rules, directions, or financial incentives. They focus on intangible qualities, such as vision, shared values, and ideas, to build relationships, give larger meaning to separate activities, and provide common ground to enlist their followers in the changes.[46]

Interactive Leaders

As women move into higher positions in organizations, it has been perceived that they often possess a different leadership style that is very effective in today's turbulent corporate environment. Leadership qualities traditionally associated with white, American males have included aggressiveness or assertiveness, taking initiative, and a "take charge" attitude. Men tend to be competitive and individualistic and prefer working in vertical hierarchies. They often describe their leadership style as transactional and are likely to use position power in their dealings with subordinates.

Although women in leadership may also share these qualities, they tend to demonstrate and stress leadership behaviors that are interactive. An **interactive leader** is concerned with consensus building, inclusiveness, participation, and caring.[47] Interactive leadership promotes the idea that striving to reach organizational goals enables employees to reach their personal goals. Female leaders such as Linda Johnson Rice, president and CEO of Johnson Publishing Company, which owns *Ebony, Jet*, and Fashion Fair Cosmetics, are often more willing to share power and information, to empower their employees, and to strive to enhance workers' self-worth. As Rice puts it, "It is the creative process that I find stimulating, sitting down and letting ideas flow among the different groups. I love the interaction with people. To me, that's the best part."[48]

The interactive leadership style is not limited to women. Many male managers are learning to adopt this style by developing their skills in attention to nonverbal behavior, empathy, cooperation, collaboration, and listening.[49] Another leadership style that builds on the interactive principle is servant or steward leadership.

Servant Leaders

The concept of leadership as stewardship or service is a bottom-up approach to leadership that starts with the follower's needs. It

interactive leader
A leader who is concerned with consensus building, is open and inclusive, and encourages participation.

transformational leader
A leader distinguished by a special ability to bring about innovation and change.

FOCUS ON LEADERSHIP
ARE YOU A CHARISMATIC LEADER?

If you were the head of a major department in a corporation, how important would each of the following activities be to you? Answer yes or no to indicate whether you would strive to perform each activity.

1. Help subordinates clarify goals and how to reach them.
2. Give people a sense of mission and overall purpose.
3. Help get jobs out on time.
4. Look for the new product or service opportunities.
5. Use policies and procedures as guides for problem solving.
6. Promote unconventional beliefs and values.
7. Give monetary rewards in exchange for high performance from subordinates.

8. Command respect from everyone in the department.
9. Work alone to accomplish important tasks.
10. Suggest new and unique ways of doing things.
11. Give credit to people who do their jobs well.
12. Inspire loyalty to yourself and to the organization.
13. Establish procedures to help the department operate smoothly.
14. Use ideas to motivate others.
15. Set reasonable limits on new approaches.
16. Demonstrate social nonconformity.

The even-numbered items represent behaviors and activities of charismatic leaders. Charismatic leaders are personally involved in shaping ideas, goals, and direction of change. They use

an intuitive approach to develop fresh ideas for solving old problems and seek new directions for the department or organization. The odd-numbered items are considered more traditional management activities, or what would be called *transactional leadership*. Managers respond to organizational problems in an impersonal way, make rational decisions, and coordinate and facilitate the work of others. If you answered yes to more even-numbered than odd-numbered items, you may be a potential charismatic leader.

SOURCES: Based on Bernard M. Bass, *Leadership and Performance beyond Expectations* (New York: Free Press, 1985); and Lawton R. Burns and Selwyn W. Becker, "Leadership and Managership," in *Health Care Management*, ed. S. Shortell and A. Kaluzny (New York: Wiley, 1986).

operates from the assumption that work exists for the development of the worker as much as the worker exists to do the work.[50] **Servant leaders** operate on two levels: for the fulfillment of their subordinates' goals and needs and for the realization of the larger purpose or mission of their organization.[51] The purpose of servant leadership is to bring the followers' higher motives to the work and connect them to the organization's mission and goals. Wal-Mart's corporate culture, developed by Sam Walton, was

to lead from the top but run from the bottom. His view of servant leadership was to provide workers with whatever they needed to serve the customers, in terms of merchandise, capital, information, and inspiration, and then get out of the way.[52]

Servant leadership is particularly useful in the learning organization, which was discussed in Chapter 2, because it unleashes followers' creativity, full commitment, and natural impulse to learn.

servant leader
A leader who works to fulfill subordinates' needs and goals as well as to achieve the organization's larger mission.

SUMMARY AND MANAGEMENT SOLUTION

This chapter covered several important ideas about leadership. The early research on leadership focused on personal traits such as intelligence, energy, and appearance.

Later, research attention shifted to leadership behaviors that are appropriate to the organizational situation. Behavioral approaches dominated the early work in this

area; consideration and initiating structure were suggested as behaviors that lead work groups toward high performance. The Ohio State and Michigan approaches and the leadership grid are in this category. Contingency approaches include Fiedler's theory, Hersey and Blanchard's situational theory, the path–goal model, and the substitutes-for-leadership concept.

Leadership concepts have evolved from the transactional approach to charismatic, transformational, interactive, and servant leadership behaviors. Charismatic leadership is the ability to articulate a vision and motivate followers to make it a reality. Transformational leadership extends charismatic qualities to guide and foster dramatic organizational change. Interactive leadership, typical of many women leaders, involves consensus building, empowerment, and sharing of information and resources. Servant leadership facilitates the growth, goals, and empowerment of followers first in order to liberate their best qualities in pursuing organizational goals.

Robin and Steve Silverman, from the chapter opening, had to change their way of doing business in order for their clothing store to survive. It was losing so much money they had to move to a mall and take on a new leadership style. Robin and Steve decided to let the staff lead them for a change. They took the staff to the new mall

space and said, "You're about to see your future." The tailors were excited about their new and larger alterations shop and the sales staff admired the brightness of the selling floor. Within two days, all staff had divided themselves into three teams: one to organize the moving sale, one to arrange for the actual move, and the last to oversee opening the new store. Robin and Steve were pleasantly surprised at the skills that emerged. A quiet secretary became a phone-system research dynamo, calling vendors to find the best deals. The marketing manager took on the new store decoration with an intense passion, and a salesman who never seemed to know mannequins even existed suddenly began dressing the forms like an old pro. Three staff members, though, could not make the transition to the new "culture" and quit or were fired. The moving sale paid off old debts and the move was made on time. The new location has helped them create more streamlined inventory and improved working conditions. Sales are increasing. Most important, Robin and Steve decided never to manage by themselves again. They do everything teaming with various managers, talking over problems and creating a new vision. Solutions developed are cost-effective and have the support of the whole staff. After a year in the new location, Silverman's has "new" leaders, a committed staff, and plenty of sales.[53]

DISCUSSION QUESTIONS

1 Rob Martin became manager of a forklift assembly plant and believed in participative management, even when one supervisor used Rob's delegation to replace two competent line managers with his own friends. What would you say to Rob about his leadership style in this situation?

2 Suggest some personal traits that you believe would be useful to a leader. Are these traits more valuable in some situations than in others?

3 What is the difference between trait theories and behavioral theories of leadership?

4 Suggest the sources of power that would be available to a leader of a student government organization. To be

effective, should student leaders keep power to themselves or delegate power to other students?

5 Would you prefer working for a leader who has a consideration or an initiating-structure leadership style? Discuss the reasons for your answer.

6 Consider Fiedler's theory as illustrated in Exhibit 13.6. How often do very favorable, intermediate, or very unfavorable situations occur in real life? Discuss.

7 What is transformational leadership? Differentiate between transformational leadership and transactional leadership. Give an example of each.

8 One critic argued that women should not be stereotyped as having a leadership style different from that

of men. Do you agree? Do you think that women, on average, have a more interactive style of leadership than men? Discuss.

9 Do you think leadership style is fixed and unchangeable for a leader or flexible and adaptable? Discuss.

10 Consider the leadership position of a senior partner in a law firm. What task, subordinate, and organizational factors might serve as substitutes for leadership in this situation?

MANAGEMENT EXERCISES

MANAGER'S WORKBOOK

T–P Leadership Questionnaire: An Assessment of Style

Some leaders deal with general directions, leaving details to subordinates. Other leaders focus on specific details with the expectation that subordinates will carry out orders. Depending on the situation, both approaches may be effective. The important issue is the ability to identify relevant dimensions of the situation and behave accordingly. Through this questionnaire, you can identify your relative emphasis on two dimensions of leadership: task orientation (T) and people orientation (P). These are not opposite approaches, and an individual can rate high or low on either or both.

Directions: The following items describe aspects of leadership behavior. Respond to each item according to the way you would most likely act if you were the leader of a work group. Circle whether you would most likely behave in the described way: always (A), frequently (F), occasionally (O), seldom (S), or never (N).

1 I would most likely act as the spokesperson of the group. A F O S N
2 I would encourage overtime work. A F O S N
3 I would allow members complete freedom in their work. A F O S N
4 I would encourage the use of uniform procedures. A F O S N
5 I would permit members to use their own judgment in solving problems. A F O S N
6 I would stress being ahead of competing groups. A F O S N
7 I would speak as a representative of the group. A F O S N
8 I would needle members for greater effort. A F O S N

9 I would try out my ideas in the group. A F O S N
10 I would let members do their work the way they think best. A F O S N
11 I would be working hard for a promotion. A F O S N
12 I would tolerate postponement and uncertainty. A F O S N
13 I would speak for the group if there were visitors present. A F O S N
14 I would keep the work moving at a rapid pace. A F O S N
15 I would turn the members loose on a job and let them go to it. A F O S N
16 I would settle conflicts when they occur in the group. A F O S N
17 I would get swamped by details. A F O S N
18 I would represent the group at outside meetings. A F O S N
19 I would be reluctant to allow the members any freedom of action. A F O S N
20 I would decide what should be done and how it should be done. A F O S N
21 I would push for increased production. A F O S N
22 I would let some members have authority which I could keep. A F O S N
23 Things would usually turn out as I had predicted. A F O S N
24 I would allow the group a high degree of initiative. A F O S N
25 I would assign group members to particular tasks. A F O S N
26 I would be willing to make changes. A F O S N

27 I would ask the members to work harder.   A F O S N

28 I would trust the group members to exercise good judgment.   A F O S N

29 I would schedule the work to be done.   A F O S N

30 I would refuse to explain my actions.   A F O S N

31 I would persuade others that my ideas are to their advantage.   A F O S N

32 I would permit the group to set its own pace.   A F O S N

33 I would urge the group to beat its previous record.   A F O S N

34 I would act without consulting the group.   A F O S N

35 I would ask that group members follow standard rules and regulations.   A F O S N

T _____   P _____

The T–P Leadership Questionnaire is scored as follows:

a. Circle the item number for items 8, 12, 17, 18, 19, 30, 34, and 35.

b. Write the number 1 in front of a *circled item number* if you responded *S* (seldom) or *N* (never) to that item.

c. Also write a number 1 in front of *item numbers not circled* if you responded *A* (always) or *F* (frequently).

d. Circle the number 1s that you have written in front of the following items: 3, 5, 8, 10, 15, 18, 19, 22, 24, 26, 28, 30, 32, 34, and 35.

e. *Count the circled number 1s.* This is your score for concern for people. Record the score in the blank following the letter *P* at the end of the questionnaire.

f. *Count uncircled number 1s.* This is your score for concern for task. Record this number in the blank following the letter *T.*

SOURCE: Copyright 1969 by the American Educational Research Association. Adapted by permission of the publisher.

MANAGER'S WORKSHOP

The Many Faces of Leadership

1 Think of examples of leaders who used their leadership abilities as a positive force, and those who used leadership as a negative force. Fill in the table below.

Leaders with positive force (Name)	General leadership characteristics	List characteristics according to Fiedler's contingency and path–goal theory	Results/outcome of their leadership
1.			
2.			
3.			
4.			
Leaders with negative force (Name)			
1.			
2.			
3.			
4.			

2 Divide into groups of four to seven members. Develop a "group list" of positive and negative leaders, having about five positive and five negative. Complete the second table as you answer each question.

3 What were the similarities between the positive and negative? What were the characteristics of leadership that were comparable?

4 What was it about the positive and negative leaders that made their outcomes so very different? Can you identify one or two critical elements that distinguish positive leaders from negative ones?

5 Refer back to information in Chapter 5 on ethics. Look at Exhibit 5.2 and see if you can find what levels of moral development the positive and negative leaders were operating out of.

6 Refer to the Focus on Leadership Box on charismatic leadership in this chapter. What similarities can you find with those characteristics and the leaders you identified?

Question 2	Question 3	Question 4	Question 5	Question 6
Positive leader names	**Characteristics identified that have commonality with other leaders**	**What makes positive leader outcomes positive?**	**Level of moral development for each**	**Similarities to charismatic leaders**
1.				
2.				
3.				
4.				
5.				
Negative leader names		**What makes negative leader outcomes negative?**		
1.				
2.				
3.				
4.				
5.				

SURF THE 'NET

Surf through various company and personal Web sites. Find evidence for autocratic and democratic leadership styles, as well as people-oriented and task-oriented leadership.

List the evidence you discovered and why you think it is proof of each of these four leadership styles.

ETHICAL DILEMMA

Does Wage Reform Start at the Top?

Preston Smith has just been offered the opportunity of a lifetime. The chairman of the board of Resitronic Corporation has just called to ask him to take the job as director of the troubled audio equipment manufacturing subsidiary. The first question Smith asked was "Will the board give me the autonomy to turn this company around?" The answer was yes. Resitronic's problems were so severe that the board was desperate for change and ready to give Smith whatever it took to save the company.

Smith knows that cost-cutting is the first place he needs to focus. Labor expenses are too high, and product quality and production times are below industry standards. He sees that labor and management at Resitronic are two armed camps, but he needs cooperation at all levels to achieve a turnaround. Smith is energized. He knows he finally has the autonomy to try out his theories about an empowered workforce. He knows he must ask managers and workers to take a serious pay cut, with the promise of incentives to share in any improvements they might make. He also knows that everyone will be looking at his own salary as an indication of whether he walks his talk.

Smith is torn. He realizes he faces a year or two of complete hell, with long hours, little time for his family or outside interests, bitter resistance in subordinates, and no guarantees of success. Even if he comes in at the current director's salary, he will be taking a cut in pay. But if he takes a bigger cut coming in, with the promise of bonuses

and stock options tied to his own performance, he sends a strong message to the entire subsidiary that they rise or fall together. He wonders what might happen if he fails. Many influences on the audio equipment subsidiary are beyond his control. Resitronic itself is in trouble. From his current vantage point, Smith believes he can turn things around, but what will he discover when he gets inside? What if the board undercuts him? Doesn't he owe it to himself and his family to be compensated at the highest possible level for the stress and risk they will be enduring? Can he afford to risk his own security to send a message of commitment to the plan he is asking others to follow?

What Do You Do?

1 Take the same salary as the current director for one year. Circulate the information that although you are taking a cut to come to Resitronic, you are confident that you can make a difference. Build in pay incentive bonuses for the following years if the subsidiary succeeds.

2 Take a bigger cut in pay with generous incentive bonuses. Ask the board and the entire workforce to do the same. Open the books and let the whole company know exactly where they stand.

3 Ask for the same salary you are making now. You know you are going to be worth it, and you don't want to ask your family to suffer monetarily as well as in their quality of life during this transition.

CASE FOR CRITICAL ANALYSIS

Technical Services Division

When DGL International, a manufacturer of refinery equipment, brought in John Terrill to manage its Technical Services division, company executives informed him of the urgent situation. Technical Services, with 20 engi-

neers, was the highest-paid, best-educated, and least-productive division in the company. The instructions to Terrill: Turn it around. Terrill called a meeting of the engineers. He showed great concern for their personal welfare and asked point blank: "What's the problem? Why can't

we produce? Why does this division have such turnover?"

Without hesitation, employees launched a hail of complaints. "I was hired as an engineer, not a pencil pusher." "We spend over half our time writing asinine reports in triplicate for top management, and no one reads the reports."

After a two-hour discussion, Terrill concluded he had to get top management off the engineers' backs. He promised the engineers, "My job is to stay out of your way so you can do your work, and I'll try to keep top management off your backs too." He called for the day's reports and issued an order effective immediately that the originals be turned in daily to his office rather than mailed to headquarters. For three weeks, technical reports piled up on his desk. By month's end, the stack was nearly three feet high. During that time no one called for the reports. When other managers entered his office and saw the stack, they usually asked, "What's all this?" Terrill answered, "Technical reports." No one asked to read them.

Finally, at month's end, a secretary from finance called and asked for the monthly travel and expense report. Terrill responded, "Meet me in the president's office tomorrow morning."

The next morning the engineers cheered as Terrill walked through the department pushing a cart loaded with the enormous stack of reports. They knew the showdown had come.

Terrill entered the president's office and placed the stack of reports on his desk. The president and the other senior executives looked bewildered.

"This," Terrill announced, "is the reason for the lack of productivity in the Technical Services division. These are the reports you people require every month. The fact that they sat on my desk all month shows that no one reads this material. I suggest that the engineers' time could be used in a more productive manner, and that one brief monthly report from my office will satisfy the needs of other departments."

Questions

1 What leadership style did John Terrill use? What do you think was his primary source of power?
2 Based on the Hersey–Blanchard theory, should Terrill have been less participative? Should he have initiated more task structure for the engineers? Explain.
3 What leadership approach would you have taken in this situation?

ENDNOTES

1 Robin Landew Silverman, "A Moving Experience," *Inc.* (August 1996) 23–24.
2 Gail DeGeorge, "Why Sunbeam Is Shining Brighter," *Business Week,* August 29, 1994, 74–75.
3 David C. Limerick, "Managers of Meaning: From Bob Geldof's Band Aid to Australian CEOs," *Organizational Dynamics* (spring 1990), 22–23.
4 Gary Yukl, "Managerial Leadership: A Review of Theory and Research," *Journal of Management* 15 (1989), 251–289.
5 James M. Kouzes and Barry Z. Posner, "The Credibility Factor: What Followers Expect from Their Leaders," *Management Review* (January 1990) 29–33.
6 Henry Mintzberg, *Power in and around Organizations* (Englewood Cliffs, N.J.: Prentice-Hall, 1983); and Jeffrey Pfeffer, *Power in Organizations* (Marshfield, Mass.: Pitman, 1981).
7 J. R. P. French, Jr., and B. Raven, "The Bases of Social Power," in *Group Dynamics,* ed. D. Cartwright and Alvin F. Zander (Evanston, Ill.: Row, Peterson, 1960), 607–623.
8 G. A. Yukl and T. Taber, "The Effective Use of Managerial Power," *Personnel* (March–April 1983), 37–44.
9 Erle Norton, "Chairman of AK Steel Tries to Shake Off Tag of 'Operating Man,'" *The Wall Street Journal,* November 25, 1994, A1, A5.
10 Yukl and Taber, "The Effective Use of Managerial Power."
11 Mark Maremont, "Bill Gates' Vision," *Business Week,* June 27, 1994, 56–62.
12 Patricia Sellers, "When Tragedy Forces Change," *Fortune,* January 10, 1994, 114.
13 Thomas A. Stewart, "New Ways to Exercise Power," *Fortune,* November 6, 1989, 52–64; and Thomas A. Stewart, "CEOs See Clout Shifting," *Fortune,* November 6, 1989, 66.

14 Peter Elstrom, "Casey Cowell's Modem Operandi," *Business Week,* November 11, 1996, 104, 107.

15 G. A. Yukl, *Leadership in Organizations* (Englewood Cliffs, N.J.: Prentice-Hall, 1981); and S. C. Kohs and K. W. Irle, "Prophesying Army Promotion," *Journal of Applied Psychology* 4 (1920), 73–87.

16 R. Albanese and D. D. Van Fleet, *Organizational Behavior: A Managerial Viewpoint* (Hinsdale, Ill.: The Dryden Press, 1983).

17 Doron P. Levin, "Joe Montana, Case Study in Leadership Excellence," *The Tennessean,* January 23, 1994, 3E.

18 K. Lewin, "Field Theory and Experiment in Social Psychology: Concepts and Methods," *American Journal of Sociology* 44 (1939), 868–896; K. Lewin and R. Lippitt, "An Experimental Approach to the Study of Autocracy and Democracy: A Preliminary Note," *Sociometry* 1 (1938), 292–300; and K. Lewin, R. Lippitt, and R. K. White, "Patterns of Aggressive Behavior in Experimentally Created Social Climates," *Journal of Social Psychology* 10 (1939), 271–301.

19 R. K. White and R. Lippitt, *Autocracy and Democracy: An Experimental Inquiry* (New York: Harper, 1960).

20 R. Tannenbaum and W. H. Schmidt, "How to Choose a Leadership Pattern," *Harvard Business Review* 36 (1958), 95–101.

21 F. A. Heller and G. A. Yukl, "Participation, Managerial Decision Making and Situational Variables," *Organizational Behavior and Human Performance* 4 (1969), 227–241.

22 Patricia O'Toole, "How Do You Build a $44 Million Company? By Saying 'Please,'" *Working Woman* (April 1990) 88–92.

23 C. A. Schriesheim and B. J. Bird, "Contributions of the Ohio State Studies to the Field of Leadership," *Journal of Management* 5 (1979), 135–145; and C. L. Shartle, "Early Years of the Ohio State University Leadership Studies," *Journal of Management* 5 (1979), 126–134.

24 P. C. Nystrom, "Managers and the High-High Leader Myth," *Academy of Management Journal* 21 (1978), 325–331; and L. L. Larson, J. G. Hunt, and Richard N. Osborn, "The Great High-High Leader Behavior Myth: A Lesson from Occam's Razor," *Academy of Management Journal* 19 (1976), 628–641.

25 R. Likert, "From Production- and Employee-Centeredness to Systems 1–4," *Journal of Management* 5 (1979), 147–156.

26 Robert R. Blake and Jane S. Mouton, *The Managerial Grid III* (Houston: Gulf, 1985).

27 Brian Dumaine, "The New Non-Manager Managers," *Fortune,* February 22, 1993, 80–84; and Allen R. Myerson, "West Pointer Commands Tenneco," *The New York Times,* May 15, 1994, F4.

28 Fred E. Fiedler, "Assumed Similarity Measures as Predictors of Team Effectiveness," *Journal of Abnormal and Social Psychology* 49 (1954), 381–388; F. E. Fiedler, *Leader Attitudes and Group Effectiveness* (Urbana, Ill.: University of Illinois Press, 1958); and F. E. Fiedler, *A Theory of Leadership Effectiveness* (New York: McGraw-Hill, 1967).

29 Fred E. Fiedler and M. M. Chemers, *Leadership and Effective Management* (Glenview, Ill.: Scott, Foresman, 1974).

30 Alessandra Bianchi, "Mission Improbable," *Inc.* (September 1996) 69–75.

31 R. Singh, "Leadership Style and Reward Allocation: Does Least Preferred Co-worker Scale Measure Tasks and Relation Orientation?" *Organizational Behavior and Human Performance* 27 (1983), 178–197; and D. Hosking, "A Critical Evaluation of Fiedler's Contingency Hypotheses," *Progress in Applied Psychology* 1 (1981), 103–154.

32 Paul Hersey and Kenneth H. Blanchard, *Management of Organizational Behavior: Utilizing Human Resources,* 4th ed. (Englewood Cliffs, N.J.: Prentice-Hall, 1982).

33 Jonathon Kaufman, "A McDonald's Owner Becomes a Role Model for Black Teenagers," *The Wall Street Journal,* August 23, 1995, A1, A6.

34 M. G. Evans, "The Effects of Supervisory Behavior on the Path–Goal Relationship," *Organizational Behavior and Human Performance* 5 (1970), 277–298; M. G. Evans, "Leadership and Motivation: A Core Concept," *Academy of Management Journal* 13 (1970), 91–102; and B. S. Georgopoulos, G. M. Mahoney, and N. W. Jones, "A Path–Goal Approach to Productivity," *Journal of Applied Psychology* 41 (1957), 345–353.

35 Robert J. House, "A Path–Goal Theory of Leader Effectiveness," *Administrative Science Quarterly* 16 (1971), 321–338.

36 M. G. Evans, "Leadership," in *Organizational Behavior,* ed. S. Kerr (Columbus, Ohio: Grid, 1974), 230–233.

37 Robert J. House and Terrence R. Mitchell, "Path–Goal Theory of Leadership," *Journal of Contemporary Business* (autumn 1974), 81–97.

38 Sharon Nelton, "Men, Women, & Leadership," *Nation's Business* (May 1991) 16–22.

39 Charles Greene, "Questions of Causation in the Path–Goal Theory of Leadership," *Academy of Management Journal* 22 (March 1979), 22–41; and C. A. Schriesheim and Mary Ann von Glinow, "The Path–Goal Theory of Leadership: A Theoretical and Empirical Analysis," *Academy of Management Journal* 20 (1977), 398–405.

40 S. Kerr and J. M. Jermier, "Substitutes for Leadership: Their Meaning and Measurement," *Organizational Behavior and Human Performance* 22 (1978), 375–403; and Jon P. Howell and Peter W. Dorfman, "Leadership and Substitutes for Leadership among Professional and Nonprofessional Workers," *Journal of Applied Behavioral Science* 22 (1986), 29–46.

41 The terms *transactional* and *transformational* come from James M. Burns, *Leadership* (New York: Harper & Row, 1978); and Bernard M. Bass, "Leadership: Good, Better, Best," *Organizational Dynamics* 13 (winter 1985), 26–40.

42 Jay A. Conger and Rabindra N. Kanungo, "Toward a Behavioral Theory of Charismatic Leadership in Organizational Settings," *Academy of Management Review* 12 (1987), 637–647; Walter Kiechel III, "A Hard Look at Executive Vision," *Fortune,* October 23, 1989, 207–211; and Allan Cox, "Focus on Teamwork, Vision, and Values," *The New York Times,* February 26, 1989, F3.

43 Robert J. House, "Research Contrasting the Behavior and Effects of Reputed Charismatic vs. Reputed Non-Charismatic Leaders" (paper presented as part of a symposium, "Charismatic Leadership: Theory and Evidence," Academy of Management, San Diego, 1985).

44 John P. Kotter, "What Leaders Really Do," *Harvard Business Review* (May–June 1990), 103–111.

45 Noel M. Tichy and David O. Ulrich, "The Leadership Challenge–A Call for the Transformational Leader," *Sloan Management Review* 26 (fall 1984), 59–68.

46 Richard L. Daft and Robert H. Lengel, *The Fourth Way: A New Leadership Covenant to Unshackle Your Organization* (Berett-Koehler, 1998).

47 Judy Rosener, "Ways Women Lead," *Harvard Business Review* (November–December 1990), 119–125; and Nelton, "Men, Women, & Leadership."

48 Dawn Hill, "Women Leaders Doing It Their Way," *New Woman* (January 1994) 78.

49 M. Fine, F. Johnson, and M. S. Ryan, "Cultural Diversity in the Workforce," *Public Personnel Management* 19 (1990), 305–319; and Hill, "Women Leaders Doing It Their Way."

50 Daft and Lengel, *The Fourth Way*.

51 Peter M. Senge, "The Leader's New Work: Building Learning Organizations," *Sloan Management Review* 32, no. 1 (fall 1990), 12–13.

52 Bill Saporito, "And the Winner Is Still . . . Wal-Mart," *Fortune*, May 2, 1994, 62–70.

53 Silverman, "A Moving Experience."

Motivation in Organizations

LEARNING OBJECTIVES

After studying this chapter, you should be able to

- Define *motivation* and explain the difference between current approaches and traditional approaches to motivation.

- Identify and describe content theories of motivation based on employee needs.

- Identify and explain process theories of motivation.

- Describe reinforcement theory and how it can be used to motivate employees.

- Discuss major approaches to job design and how job design influences motivation.

- Discuss new management applications of motivation theories.

MANAGEMENT PROBLEM

Frustrated and bored—that describes Gary Aronson's general attitude about his work in the gourmet fast-food business. As the 30-year-old manager of an Au Bon Pain store, he made a meager $26,000 per year and wondered what he was doing in this business. Not known as a whiner and complainer, his heart was not in this dead-end job, and it seemed his employees felt the same way. The best he could hope for was an additional $3,000 in income over the next five years, so he spent a lot of energy deciding what to do next with his life. The sad story is that Gary Aronson was typical of managers in all 40 Au Bon Pain stores.[1]

• If you were president of Au Bon Pain, how would you motivate managers like Gary Aronson to give their all to the company? Is high motivation even possible in this kind of service business? What encourages improved performance?

The problem for Au Bon Pain is that unmotivated managers mean unmotivated employees, all doing the minimum amount of work and causing the company to lose its competitive edge. One secret for success in small and medium-sized businesses is motivated and enthusiastic employees. The challenge for Au Bon Pain and other companies is to keep employee motivation consistent with organizational goals. Motivation is a challenge for managers because motivation arises from within employees and typically differs for each employee. For example, Janice Rennie makes a staggering $350,000 a year selling residential real estate in Toronto; she attributes her success to the fact that she likes to listen carefully to clients and then find a house to meet their needs. Greg Storey is a skilled machinist who is challenged by writing programs for numerically controlled machines. After dropping out of college, he swept floors in a machine shop and was motivated to learn to run the machines. Frances Blais sells *World Book Encyclopedia.* She is a top salesperson, but she does not care about the $50,000-plus commissions: "I'm not even thinking money when I'm selling. I'm really on a crusade to help children read well." In stark contrast, Rob Michaels gets sick to his stomach before he goes to work. Rob is a telephone salesperson who spends all day trying to get people to buy products they do not need, and the rejections are painful. His motivation is money; he earned $120,000 in the past year and cannot make nearly that much doing anything else.[2]

Rob is motivated by money, Janice by her love of listening and problem solving, Frances by the desire to help children read, and Greg by the challenge of mastering numerically controlled machinery. Each person is motivated to perform, yet each has different reasons for performing. With such diverse motivations, it is a challenge for managers to motivate employees toward common organizational goals.

This chapter reviews theories and models of employee motivation. First we will review several perspectives on motivation

and cover models that describe the employee needs and processes associated with motivation. Then, we will discuss how *job design*—changing the structure of the work itself—can affect employee satisfaction and productivity. Finally, we will examine the new trend of *empowerment,* where authority and decision making are delegated to subordinates to increase employee motivation.

THE CONCEPT OF MOTIVATION

Most of us get up in the morning, go to school or work, and behave in ways that are predictably our own. We respond to our environment and the people in it with little thought as to why we work hard, enjoy certain classes, or find some recreational activities so much fun. Yet all these behaviors are motivated by something. **Motivation** refers to the forces either within or external to a person that arouse enthusiasm and persistence to pursue a certain course of action. Employee motivation affects productivity, and part of a manager's job is to channel motivation toward the accomplishment of organizational goals.[3] The study of motivation helps managers understand what prompts people to initiate action, what influences their choice of action, and why they persist in that action over time.

A simple model of human motivation is illustrated in Exhibit 14.1. People have basic *needs,* such as for food, achievement, or monetary gain, that translate into an internal tension that motivates specific behaviors with which to fulfill the need. To the extent that the behavior is successful, the person is rewarded in the sense that the need is satisfied. The reward also informs the person that the behavior was appropriate and can be used again in the future.

Rewards are of two types: intrinsic and extrinsic. **Intrinsic rewards** are the satisfactions a person receives in the process of performing a particular action. The completion of a complex task may bestow a pleasant feeling of accomplishment, or solving a

motivation
The arousal, direction, and persistence of behavior.

intrinsic reward
The satisfaction received in the process of performing an action.

EXHIBIT 14.1
A Simple Model of Motivation

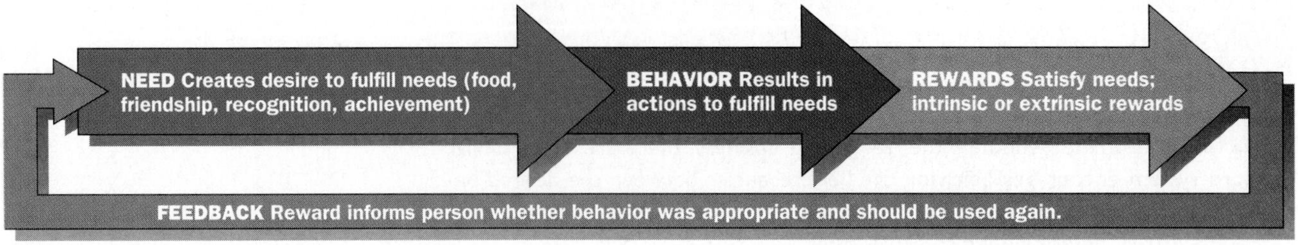

NEED Creates desire to fulfill needs (food, friendship, recognition, achievement) ➔ **BEHAVIOR** Results in actions to fulfill needs ➔ **REWARDS** Satisfy needs; intrinsic or extrinsic rewards

FEEDBACK Reward informs person whether behavior was appropriate and should be used again.

problem that benefits others may fulfill a personal mission. For example, Frances Blais sells encyclopedias for the intrinsic reward of helping children read well. **Extrinsic rewards** are given by another person, typically a manager, and include promotions and pay increases. They originate externally, as a result of pleasing others. Rob Michaels, who hates his sales job, nevertheless is motivated by the extrinsic reward of high pay.

The importance of motivation as illustrated in Exhibit 14.1 is that it can lead to behaviors that reflect high performance within organizations.[4] Managers can use motivation theory to help satisfy employees' needs and simultaneously encourage high work performance. When workers are not motivated to achieve organizational goals, managers may need to evaluate the reward system, as discussed in the Focus on Motivation box.

FOUNDATIONS OF MOTIVATION

A manager's assumptions about employee motivation and use of rewards depend on his or her perspective on motivation. Three distinct perspectives on employee motivation that have evolved are the traditional approach, the human relations approach, and the human resource approach.[5] The most recent theories about motivation represent a fourth perspective called *contemporary approaches.*

Traditional Approach

The study of employee motivation really began with the work of Frederick W. Taylor on scientific management. Recall from Chapter 2 that scientific management pertains to the systematic analysis of an employee's job for the purpose of increasing efficiency. Economic rewards are provided to employees for high performance. The emphasis on pay evolved into the perception of workers as *economic people*—people who would work harder for higher pay. This approach led to the development of incentive pay systems, in which people were paid strictly on the quantity and quality of their work outputs.

Human Relations Approach

The economic man was gradually replaced by a more sociable employee in managers' minds. Beginning with the landmark Hawthorne studies at a Western Electric plant, noneconomic rewards, such as congenial work groups who met social needs, seemed more important than money as a motivator of work behavior.[6] For the first time, workers were studied as people, and the concept of *social man* was born. Further study led researchers to conclude that simply paying attention to workers could change their behavior for the better—this was called the *Hawthorne effect.*

Human Resource Approach

The human resource approach carries the concepts of economic man and social man

extrinsic reward
A reward given by another person.

FOCUS ON MOTIVATION
ON THE FOLLY OF REWARDING *A* WHILE HOPING FOR *B*

Managers who complain about the lack of motivation in workers might do well to examine whether the reward system encourages behavior different from what they are seeking. People usually determine which activities are rewarded and then seek to do those things, to the virtual exclusion of activities not rewarded. Nevertheless, there are numerous examples of fouled-up systems that reward unwanted behaviors, while the desired actions are not being rewarded at all.

In sports, for example, most coaches stress teamwork, proper attitude, and one-for-all spirit. However, rewards are usually distributed according to individual performance. The college basketball player who passes the ball to teammates instead of shooting will not compile impressive scoring statistics and will be less likely to be drafted by the pros. The big-league baseball player who hits to advance the runner rather than to score a home run is less likely to win the titles that guarantee big salaries. In universities, a primary goal is the transfer of knowledge from professors to students; yet professors are rewarded primarily for research and publication, not for their commitment to good teaching. Students are rewarded for making good grades, not necessarily for acquiring knowledge,

and may resort to cheating rather than risk a low grade on their college transcript.

In business, there are often similar discrepancies between the desired behaviors and those rewarded. For example:

Managers hope for:	But they reward:
Teamwork and collaboration	The best individual performers
Innovative thinking and risk taking	Proven methods and not making mistakes
Development of people skills	Technical achievements and accomplishments
Employee involvement and empowerment	Tight control over operations and resources
High achievement	Another year's routine effort
Commitment to quality	Shipping on time, even with defects
Long-term growth	Quarterly earnings

What do a majority of managers see as the major obstacles to dealing with fouled-up reward systems?

1 *The inability to break out of old ways of thinking about reward and recognition.* This includes entitlement mentality in workers and resistance by management to revamp performance review and reward systems.

2 *Lack of an overall system view of performance and results.* This is particularly true of systems that promote subunit results at the expense of the total organization.

3 *Continuing focus on short-term results by management and shareholders.*

Motivation theories must be sound because people do what they are rewarded for. But when will organizations learn to reward what they say they want?

SOURCE: Steven Kerr, "An Academy Classic: On the Folly of Rewarding A, while Hoping for B," and "More on the Folly," *Academy of Management Executive* 9, no. 1 (1995), 7–16.

farther to introduce the concept of the *whole person.* Human resource theory suggests that employees are complex and motivated by many factors. For example, the work by McGregor on Theory X and Theory Y described in Chapter 2 argued that people want to do a good job and that work is as natural and healthy as play. Proponents of the human resource approach believed that earlier approaches had tried to manipulate employees through economic or social rewards. By assuming that employees are competent and able to make major contributions, managers can enhance organizational performance. The human resource approach laid the groundwork for contemporary perspectives on employee motivation. Consider the case of an entrepreneur who had to motivate not only employees, but also independent distributors.

MAGNET, INC.

"The average person visits the refrigerator 11 times a day. In one year, that's 16,000 times your business logo will be recognized by the average family of four," customers are told by Bill Wood, founder and chairman of Magnet, Inc., of small-town Washington, Missouri, near St. Louis.

Wood began the "world's largest magnet supplier" in 1984 when he bought an old car wash and invested in $500 of magnet manufacturing equipment. Pizza Hut was his first big customer and helped him work toward his current annual sales of $33 million. Now he has a large office and manufacturing plant in a new industrial park. In order to keep growing past the current 150 million magnets per year, Wood has had to recently add two more plants in Missouri and Illinois.

Working with a network of 8,000 independent distributors is a challenge for Wood, trying to communicate to them the company spirit and keep them motivated to sell his magnets rather than the pens or golf balls of other vendors.

Much of Magnet, Inc.'s success, says Wood, is due to the incredibly hard-working and loyal 610 employees. But Wood has influenced that commitment through his "gain-sharing" plan, where employees get bonuses when production quotas are exceeded. And through a company program called Education Pays, where university instructors come to the factory and workers are paid to earn college credits in various business courses. Those benefits extend to the 80 part-time retirees, which only adds to the climate of motivation. As one thankful 82-year-old said, Magnet, Inc. "gives me a reason to get up in the morning."[7] ■

Contemporary Approaches

Contemporary approaches to employee motivation are dominated by three types of theories, each of which will be discussed in the following sections. The first are *content theories*, which stress the analysis of underlying human needs. Content theories provide insight into the needs of people in organizations and help managers understand how needs can be satisfied in the workplace. *Process theories* concern the thought processes that influence behavior. They focus on how employees seek rewards in work circumstances. *Reinforcement theories* focus on employee learning of desired work behaviors. Referring to Exhibit 14.1, content theories focus on the concepts in the first box, process theories on those in the second, and reinforcement theories on those in the third.

CONTENT PERSPECTIVES ON MOTIVATION

Content theories emphasize the needs that motivate people. At any point in time, people have basic needs such as those for food, achievement, or monetary reward. These needs translate into an internal drive that motivates specific behaviors in an attempt to fulfill the needs. An individual's needs are like a hidden catalog of the things he or she wants and will work to get. To the extent that managers understand worker needs, the organization's reward systems can be designed to meet them and reinforce employees for directing energies and priorities toward attainment of organizational goals.

content theories
A group of theories that emphasize the needs that motivate people.

Hierarchy of Needs Theory

Probably the most famous content theory was developed by Abraham Maslow.[8] Maslow's **hierarchy of needs theory** proposes that humans are motivated by multiple needs and that these needs exist in a hierarchical order as illustrated in Exhibit 14.2. Maslow identified five general types of motivating needs in order of ascendance:

1. *Physiological needs.* These are the most basic human physical needs, including food, water, and sex. In the organizational setting, these are reflected in the needs for adequate heat, air, and base salary to ensure survival.
2. *Safety needs.* These are the needs for a safe and secure physical and emotional

hierarchy of needs theory
A content theory that proposes that people are motivated by five categories of needs—physiological, safety, belongingness, esteem, and self-actualization—that exist in a hierarchical order.

Many companies are finding that "fun" is a great, high-level motivator. A regular infusion of silliness, such as the antics of the "Joy Gang" at Ben & Jerry's Ice Cream who initiate fun activities, lightens up the daily routine and creates a feeling of belonging.[9] Blue Fish Clothing and Amy's Ice Creams use fun and other unusual means to encourage creativity and filling some deeper needs of employees.

Need hierarchy theory helps explain why organizations find ways to recognize employees through awards and ceremonies. The "Lend a Helping Hand" contest, sponsored by GMAC Albany's Quality Council, judged employees for their helpfulness to other workers. The winners' smiles reflect appreciation not only for the award of gift certificates but also for the company's recognition of their efforts. Public recognition helps motivate workers by fulfilling high-level *belongingness* and *esteem needs.*

environment and freedom from threats—that is, for freedom from violence and for an orderly society. In an organizational workplace, safety needs reflect the needs for safe jobs, fringe benefits, and job security.

3 *Belongingness needs.* These needs reflect the desire to be accepted by one's peers, have friendships, be part of a group, and be loved. In the organization, these needs influence the desire for good relationships with coworkers, participation in a work group, and a positive relationship with supervisors.

4 *Esteem needs.* These needs relate to the desire for a positive self-image and to receive attention, recognition, and appreciation from others. Within organizations, esteem needs reflect a motivation for recognition, an increase in responsibility, high status, and credit for contributions to the organization.

5 *Self-actualization needs.* These represent the need for self-fulfillment, which is the highest need category. They concern developing one's full potential, increasing one's competence, and becoming a better person. Self-actualization needs can be met in the organization by providing people with opportunities to grow, be creative, and acquire training for challenging assignments and advancement.

BLUE FISH CLOTHING/AMY'S ICE CREAMS

As an art school freshman in 1984, Jennifer Barclay hand-printed a T-shirt with a linoleum block. She liked the product so much she invested $100 in plain T-shirts and sold the blocked ones for $450 dollars at a crafts fair. By 1986, she launched Blue Fish Clothing, which sells funky, oversized women's clothing.

Her management style may seem as whimsical as her clothing. But her purpose is to motivate employees and fill deeper needs. "We spend our lives at work," she says. "We might as well really enjoy what we do and who we work with, and that's all I've really wanted—just that."

She keeps her employees motivated and committed by building a sense of community and helping employees realize their dreams. Workers are given the freedom to identify what they do best, defining their own jobs and titles, such as "Spiritkeeper," "Dreams to Reality," or "Seeking and Guidance." Even if you think this is too wishy-washy, it's hard to argue with her success. Blue Fish now sells to 500 U.S. stores and has 217 employees.

Other companies are discovering the motivational power of creative expression, even for routine jobs. Amy Miller's seven-store ice-cream chain keeps customer focus, prevents the product from becoming another commodity, and makes the potentially boring ice-cream dipper job fun by encouraging employee performances. Amy's Ice Creams' servers toss scoops of ice cream, juggle their serving spades, pop trivia questions, and offer free ice cream to customers who will sing or recite poems. Careful recruiting is important in

EXHIBIT 14.2
Maslow's Hierarchy of Needs

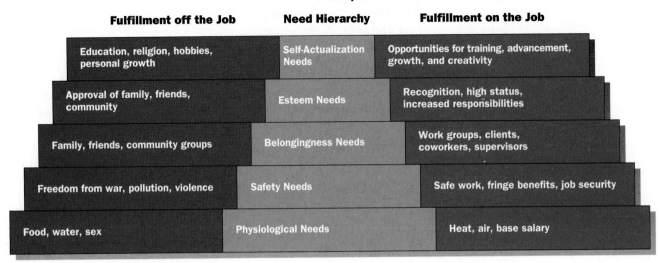

Fulfillment off the Job	Need Hierarchy	Fulfillment on the Job
Education, religion, hobbies, personal growth	Self-Actualization Needs	Opportunities for training, advancement, growth, and creativity
Approval of family, friends, community	Esteem Needs	Recognition, high status, increased responsibilities
Family, friends, community groups	Belongingness Needs	Work groups, clients, coworkers, supervisors
Freedom from war, pollution, violence	Safety Needs	Safe work, fringe benefits, job security
Food, water, sex	Physiological Needs	Heat, air, base salary

such environments, and Miller does it by asking applicants to change a plain paper bag into a work of art, and then hiring the most creative.

Jennifer Barclay's clothing may be a metaphor for the changes occuring around us. Going from the constricting suit signifying the "business as usual" profit-only motive, her line offers more creativity, a process that cocoons people and dreams, still making money, but not binding to the waistline—or the soul.[10] ■

According to Maslow's theory, low-order needs take priority—they must be satisfied before higher-order needs are activated. The needs are satisfied in sequence: Physiological needs come before safety needs, safety needs before social needs, and so on. A person desiring physical safety will devote his or her efforts to securing a safer environment and will not be concerned with esteem needs or self-actualization needs. Once a need is satisfied, it declines in importance and the next higher need is activated. When a union wins good pay and working conditions for its members, basic needs are met; union members may then desire to have belongingness and esteem needs met in the workplace.

ERG Theory. Clayton Alderfer proposed a modification of Maslow's theory in an effort to simplify it and respond to criticisms of its lack of empirical verification.[11] His **ERG theory** identified three categories of needs:

1 *Existence needs.* These are the needs for physical well-being.
2 *Relatedness needs.* These pertain to the need for satisfactory relationships with others.
3 *Growth needs.* These focus on the development of human potential and the desire for personal growth and increased competence.

The ERG model and Maslow's need hierarchy are similar because both are in hierarchical form and presume that individuals move up the hierarchy one step at a time. However, Alderfer reduced the number of need categories to three and proposed that movement up the hierarchy is more complex, reflecting a **frustration–regression principle,** namely, that failure to meet a high-order need may trigger a regression to an already fulfilled lower-order need. Thus, a worker who cannot fulfill a need for personal growth may revert to a lower-order social need and redirect his or her efforts toward making a lot of money. The ERG model therefore is less rigid than Maslow's need hierarchy, suggesting that individuals

ERG theory
A modification of the needs hierarchy theory that proposes three categories of needs: existence, relatedness, and growth.

frustration–regression principle
The idea that failure to meet a high-order need may cause a regression to an already satisfied lower-order need.

may move down as well as up the hierarchy, depending on their ability to satisfy needs.

Need hierarchy theory helps explain why organizations find ways to recognize employees and encourage their participation in decision making. Employees at Federal Express receive "Bravo Zulu" awards for outstanding performance, and the recognition letter is more important to recipients than the money. The importance of filling higher-level belongingness and esteem needs on the job was illustrated by a young manager who said, "If I had to tell you in one sentence why I am motivated by my job, it is because when I know what is going on and how I fit into the overall picture, it makes me feel important." No company knows more about the importance of recognition than Mary Kay Cosmetics.

hygiene factors
Factors that involve the presence or absence of job dissatisfiers, including working conditions, pay, company policies, and interpersonal relationships.

motivators
Factors that influence job satisfaction based on fulfillment of high-level needs such as achievement, recognition, responsibility, and opportunity for growth.

■ MARY KAY COSMETICS

"Desire for recognition is a powerful motivator," says Mary Kay Ash, founder and chairwoman emeritus of Mary Kay Cosmetics. "Our legacy will be that we have helped hundreds of thousands of women find out how great they really are."

Making full use of equal measures of enthusiasm and rewards, the company realizes that recognition is as important to the "beauty consultants" as compensation. Their annual Dallas seminar includes coronations, bauble bequests, and kissy-face, all to the delight of participants. For this group, nothing matters but performance, and producers enjoy plaudits not only from peers, but from Mary Kay herself. She crowns four outstanding performers and poignantly tells of her early direct-sales days at Stanley Products, when she was *not* crowned queen. High achievers are awarded the legendary pink Cadillacs and everyone works hard to do well.

Mary Kay Cosmetics rejects rigid hierarchy, understanding it tends to de-motivate workers. The basic management philosophy is founded on the Golden Rule—management by sharing and caring. Current leadership of the company continues with Mary Kay's vision. As

Vice President Richard C. Bartlett said, "Loving what you do is a more powerful motivation than money.[12] ■

Two-Factor Theory

Frederick Herzberg developed another popular theory of motivation called the *two-factor theory*.[13] Herzberg interviewed hundreds of workers about times when they were highly motivated to work and other times when they were dissatisfied and unmotivated at work. His findings suggested that the work characteristics associated with dissatisfaction were quite different from those pertaining to satisfaction, which prompted the notion that two factors influence work motivation.

The two-factor theory is illustrated in Exhibit 14.3. The center of the scale is neutral, meaning that workers are neither satisfied nor dissatisfied. Herzberg believed that two entirely separate dimensions contribute to an employee's behavior at work. The first, called **hygiene factors,** involves the presence or absence of job dissatisfiers, such as working conditions, pay, company policies, and interpersonal relationships. When hygiene factors are poor, work is dissatisfying. However, good hygiene factors simply remove the dissatisfaction; they do not in themselves cause people to become highly satisfied and motivated in their work.

The second set of factors does influence job satisfaction. **Motivators** are high-level needs and include achievement, recognition, responsibility, and opportunity for growth. Herzberg believed that when motivators are absent, workers are neutral toward work, but when motivators are present, workers are highly motivated and satisfied. Thus, hygiene factors and motivators represent two distinct factors that influence motivation. Hygiene factors work only in the area of dissatisfaction. Unsafe working conditions or a noisy work environment will cause people to be dissatisfied; their correction will not lead to a high level of motivation and satisfaction. Motivators such as challenge, responsibility, and recognition must be in place before employees

will be highly motivated to excel at their work.

The implication of the two-factor theory for managers is clear. Providing hygiene factors will eliminate employee dissatisfaction but will not motivate workers to high achievement levels. On the other hand, recognition, challenge, and opportunities for personal growth are powerful motivators and will promote high satisfaction and performance. The manager's role is to remove dissatisfiers—that is, provide hygiene factors sufficient to meet basic needs—and then use motivators to meet higher-level needs and propel employees toward greater achievement and satisfaction. Consider the manager's role at Outback Steakhouse.

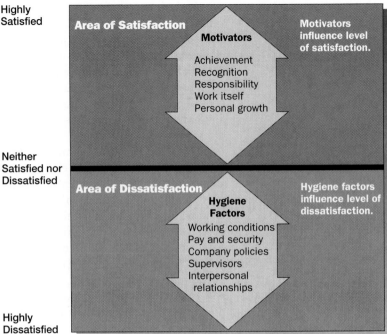

EXHIBIT 14.3
Herzberg's Two-Factor Theory

OUTBACK STEAKHOUSE

With their years of experience in the restaurant business, Robert Basham, Timothy Gannon, and Chris Sullivan, founders of Outback Steakhouse, were acutely aware of the hygiene factors in the food-service industry. While the average restaurant is designed to maximize the number of customers at the expense of the food preparation area, Outback puts the emphasis on providing the best possible spaces for servers and kitchen staff to do their jobs effectively, even at peak business times. Outback's dinner-only policy and maximum five-day workweek give managers and staff time for a life outside the restaurant, which cuts down on employee turnover. Each server handles only three tables at a time, ensuring first-class service to customers and higher tips for servers.

To motivate managers, Outback provides ownership. After making a $25,000 investment and signing a five-year contract, Outback managers receive 10 percent of the earnings of their restaurants each month. This provides the average manager with a total income of about $118,600 per year, far above the rest of the industry. In addition, managers receive about 4,000 shares of stock that are vested at the end of five years. Hourly staff also participate in a stock ownership plan.

Managers are further motivated by the

level of responsibility Outback bestows on them. Restaurant managers have the authority to make their own decisions rather than merely implement decisions dictated by headquarters.

Has Outback's motivational approach worked? In December 1994, six years after its launch, there were 210 Outbacks, with revenues estimated at $544 million, up from $347.5 million the year before. As Timothy Gannon put it, "We believe if you treat employees as if you were one of them and give them the right environment, they will blow you away with their performance."[14] ∎

Acquired Needs Theory

The final content theory was developed by David McClelland. The *acquired needs theory* proposes that certain types of needs are acquired during the individual's lifetime. In other words, people are not born with these needs but may learn them through their life experiences.[15] The three needs most frequently studied are these:

I *Need for achievement:* the desire to accomplish something difficult, attain a high

standard of success, master complex tasks, and surpass others.

2 *Need for affiliation:* the desire to form close personal relationships, avoid conflict, and establish warm friendships.

3 *Need for power:* the desire to influence or control others, be responsible for others, and have authority over others.

Early life experiences determine whether people acquire these needs. If children are encouraged to do things for themselves and receive reinforcement, they will acquire a need to achieve. If they are reinforced for forming warm human relationships, they will develop a need for affiliation. If they get satisfaction from controlling others, they will acquire a need for power.

For more than 20 years, McClelland studied human needs and their implication for management. People with a high need for achievement tend to be entrepreneurs. They like to do something better than competitors and take sensible business risks. On the other hand, people who have a high need for affiliation are successful "integrators," whose job is to coordinate the work of several departments in an organization.[16] Integrators include brand managers and project managers who must have excellent people skills. People high in need for affiliation are able to establish positive working relationships with others.

A high need for power often is associated with successful attainment of top levels in the organizational hierarchy. For example, McClelland studied managers at AT&T for 16 years and found that those with a high need for power were more likely to follow a path of continued promotion over time. More than half of the employees at the top levels had a high need for power. In contrast, managers with a high need for achievement but a low need for power tended to peak earlier in their careers and at a lower level. The reason is that achievement needs can be met through the task itself, but power needs can be met only by ascending to a level at which a person has power over others.

In summary, content theories focus on people's underlying needs and label those particular needs that motivate people to behave. The hierarchy of needs theory, the ERG theory, the two-factor theory, and the acquired needs theory all help managers understand what motivates people. In this way, managers can design work to meet needs and hence elicit appropriate and successful work behaviors. Looking at people's deeper, and perhaps unnoticed, need for achievement as well as need for esteem (from Maslow's theory) can be a force for social good, as Dorothy Balsis Thompson proved.

STREETLIGHTS

Can you motivate high performance from a group of former convicts, welfare recipients, and homeless people? Dorothy Balsis Thompson tried. After the 1992 L.A. riots, the 46-year-old "Alice in Wonderland" look-alike wanted to help ease racial tensions. Quitting her cushy TV-commercial-producer job and investing all her savings, she started Streetlights in an effort to combat the entertainment industry's disinterest in fighting the frustration, unemployment, and violence of inner-city minority youth.

Initially, movie companies were reluctant to hire former gang members and thieves, but by the fourth year, she has placed 62 "graduates" as production assistants on such movies as *The Nutty Professor, The Truth About Cats and Dogs,* and *The Juror.*

Thompson looks for deprived youth who want a chance to work. Many of them were gang leaders, such as Robert "Crazy Ace" Leon, an intensely tattooed, convicted felon at the top of the gang hierarchy because of his social skills and flair for leadership. People like Ace want to "be somebody," and Thompson has capitalized on that ambition, using it for positive, rather than violent, outcomes.

Motivation for them is the chance to work in one of the world's most glamorous industries. Thompson requires that recruits attend a six-week training program of set etiquette, film-crew hierarchy, work habits, and money management, attaining vital self-confidence in the process.

Another success story is Maurice "Moe" Freeman, previously living with his welfare mother and working a minimum-wage warehouse job. Friends said he was crazy trying to make it in the "white people's world," but he has since worked on *Dangerous Minds* and with Whoopi Goldberg. He learned "success depends most on the strength of one's will."

Thompson knows that a person without hope is dangerous. Streetlights motivates through bringing hope. "I used to dream about a good future," said Ace. "But I couldn't see it. Now I can see it."[17] ■

PROCESS PERSPECTIVES ON MOTIVATION

Process theories explain how workers select behavioral actions to meet their needs and determine whether their choices were successful. There are two basic process theories: equity theory and expectancy theory.

Equity Theory

Equity theory focuses on individuals' perceptions of how fairly they are treated compared with others. Developed by J. Stacy Adams, equity theory proposes that people are motivated to seek social equity in the rewards they expect for performance.[18]

According to equity theory, if people perceive their compensation as equal to what others receive for similar contributions, they will believe that their treatment is fair and equitable. People evaluate equity by a ratio of inputs to outcomes. Inputs to a job include education, experience, effort, and ability. Outcomes from a job include pay, recognition, benefits, and promotions. The input-to-outcome ratio may be compared to another person in the work group or to a perceived group average. A state of **equity** exists whenever the ratio of one person's outcomes to inputs equals the ratio of another's outcomes to inputs.

Inequity occurs when the input/outcome ratios are out of balance, such as when a person with a high level of education or experience receives the same salary as a new, less-educated employee. Perceived inequity also occurs in the other direction. Thus, if an employee discovers she is making more money than other people who contribute the same inputs to the company, she may feel the need to correct the inequity by working harder, getting more education, or considering lower pay. Perceived inequity creates tensions within individuals that motivate them to bring equity into balance.[19]

The most common methods for reducing a perceived inequity are these:

- *Change inputs.* A person may choose to increase or decrease his or her inputs to the organization. For example, underpaid individuals may reduce their level of effort or increase their absenteeism. Overpaid people may increase effort on the job.

- *Change outcomes.* A person may change his or her outcomes. An underpaid person may request a salary increase or a bigger office. A union may try to improve wages and working conditions in order to be consistent with a comparable union whose members make more money.

- *Distort perceptions.* Research suggests that people may distort perceptions of equity if they are unable to change inputs or outcomes. They may artificially increase the status attached to their jobs or distort others' perceived rewards to bring equity into balance.

- *Leave the job.* People who feel inequitably treated may decide to leave their jobs rather than suffer the inequity of being under- or overpaid. In their new jobs, they expect to find a more favorable balance of rewards.

The implication of equity theory for managers is that employees indeed evaluate the perceived equity of their rewards compared to others'. An increase in salary or a promotion will have no motivational effect if it is perceived as inequitable relative to that of other employees. Some organizations, for example, have created a two-tier

process theories
A group of theories that explain how employees select behaviors with which to meet their needs and determine whether their choices were successful.

equity theory
A process theory that focuses on individuals' perceptions of how fairly they are treated relative to others.

equity
A situation that exists when the ratio of one person's outcomes to inputs equals that of another's.

Some companies, such as Science Applications International Corporation (SAIC), a high-tech research and engineering firm, use *expectancy theory* principles by designing incentive systems that identify desired outcomes and give all employees the same opportunity to attain rewards. SAIC's employee stock ownership plans allow employees to buy stock directly as well as acquire stock through bonuses and options given as recognition for achievements. SAIC believes the people who build the company should share in its success. Employees are motivated to perform well because the potential for financial reward is great—*Fortune* magazine cited one production technician retiring with $300,000 in stock.

E → P expectancy
Expectancy that putting effort into a given task will lead to high performance.

P → O expectancy
Expectancy that successful performance of a task will lead to the desired outcome.

expectancy theory
A process theory that proposes that motivation depends on individuals' expectations about their ability to perform tasks and receive desired rewards.

wage system to reduce wage rates. New employees make far less than experienced ones, which creates a basis for inequity. Flight attendants at American Airlines are determined to topple the two-tier structure under which they are paid. Chris Boschert, who sorts packages for United Parcel Service, was hired after the two-tier wage system took effect. "It makes me mad," Boschert said. "I get $9.68 an hour, and the guy working next to me makes $13.99 doing exactly the same job."[20] Inequitable pay puts pressure on employees that is sometimes almost too great to bear. They attempt to change their work habits, try to change the system, or leave the job.[21]

Smart managers try to keep feelings of equity in balance in order to keep their workforces motivated.

Expectancy Theory

Expectancy theory suggests that motivation depends on individuals' expectations about their ability to perform tasks and receive desired rewards. Expectancy theory is associated with the work of Victor Vroom, although a number of scholars have made contributions in this area.[22] Expectancy theory is concerned not with identifying types

of needs but with the thinking process that individuals use to achieve rewards. Consider Bill Bradley, a university student with a strong desire for a B in his accounting course. Bill has a C+ average and one more exam to take. Bill's motivation to study for that last exam will be influenced by (1) the expectation that hard study will lead to an A on the exam and (2) the expectation that an A on the exam will result in a B for the course. If Bill believes he cannot get an A on the exam or that receiving an A will not lead to a B for the course, he will not be motivated to study exceptionally hard.

Expectancy theory is based on the relationship among the individual's *effort*, the individual's *performance*, and the desirability of *outcomes* associated with high performance. These elements and the relationships among them are illustrated in Exhibit 14.4. The keys to expectancy theory are the expectancies for the relationships among effort, performance, and outcomes with the value of the outcomes to the individual.

E → P expectancy involves whether putting effort into a task will lead to high performance. For this expectancy to be high, the individual must have the ability, previous experience, and necessary machinery, tools, and opportunity to perform. For Bill Bradley to get a B in the accounting course, the E → P expectancy is high if Bill truly believes that with hard work, he can get an A on the final exam. If Bill believes he has neither the ability nor the opportunity to achieve high performance, the expectancy will be low, and so will be his motivation.

P → O expectancy involves whether successful performance will lead to the desired outcome. In the case of a person who is motivated to win a job-related award, this expectancy concerns the belief that high performance will truly lead to the award. If the P → O expectancy is high, the individual will be more highly motivated. If the expectancy is that high performance will not produce the desired outcome, motivation will be lower. If an A on the final exam is likely to produce a B in the accounting

EXHIBIT 14.4
Major Elements of Expectancy Theory

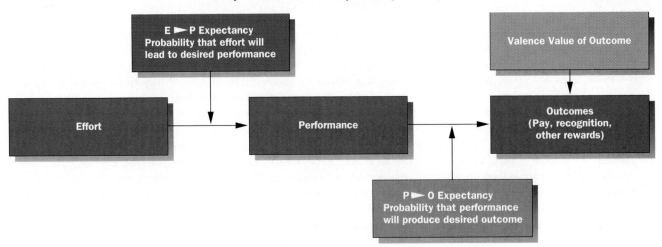

course, Bill Bradley's P → O expectancy will be high. Bill may talk to the professor to see whether an A will be sufficient to earn him the B in the course. If not, he will be less motivated to study hard for the final exam.

Valence is the value of outcomes, or attraction for outcomes, for the individual. If the outcomes that are available from high effort and good performance are not valued by employees, motivation will be low. Likewise, if outcomes have a high value, motivation will be higher.

Expectancy theory attempts not to define specific types of needs or rewards but only to establish that they exist and may be different for every individual. One employee may want to be promoted to a position of increased responsibility, and another may have high valence for good relationships with peers. Consequently, the first person will be motivated to work hard for a promotion and the second for the opportunity for a team position that will keep him or her associated with a group.

A simple sales department example will explain how the expectancy model in Exhibit 14.4 works. If Jane Anderson, a salesperson at the Diamond Gift Shop, believes that increased selling effort will lead to higher personal sales, we can say that she has a high E → P expectancy. Moreover, if Jane also believes that higher personal sales

will lead to a bonus or pay raise, we can say that she has a high P → O expectancy. Finally, if Jane places a high value on the bonus or pay raise, valence is high and Jane will have a high motivational force. On the other hand, if either the E → P or P → O expectancy is low, or if the money or promotion has low valence for Jane, the overall motivational force will be low. For an employee to be highly motivated, all three factors in the expectancy model must be high.[23]

Implications for Managers. The expectancy theory of motivation is similar to the path–goal theory of leadership described in Chapter 13. Both theories are personalized to subordinates' needs and goals. Managers' responsibility is to help subordinates meet their needs and at the same time attain organizational goals. Managers must try to find a match between a subordinate's skills and abilities and the job demands. To increase motivation, managers can clarify individuals' needs, define the outcomes available from the organization, and ensure that each individual has the ability and support (namely, time and equipment) needed to attain outcomes.

Some companies use expectancy theory principles by designing incentive systems that identify desired organizational outcomes

valence
The value or attraction an individual has for an outcome.

FOCUS ON EMPLOYEES
BONUS PLANS

In Steve Wilson's contract-engineer staffing company, the problem was how to keep his 37 employees enthused about placing the maximum number of technical people in client firms. So, his Davenport, Iowa, Mid-States Technical Staffing Services started a "bucket" plan. When a "bucket" is full (a certain level of profit is reached), then a percentage of that profit is distributed to employees. And the best part is that the more buckets filled, the higher the percentage payout to employees, with a possible double-bonus. Last year employees filled nine $75,000 profit buckets, with eight being double-bonus. Sales manager David Mc-Cracken believes the company's incredible growth in the past ten years is largely due to the "bucket" plan. "When the bucket is getting close to full," he says, "it's exciting time around here. Everybody is keyed up."

Paul Silvis's Bellefonte, Pennsylvania, Restek company had a different dilemma. The laboratory testing supply manufacturer was hiring too many people, keeping costs high. "It seemed any problem was solved by adding more bodies," said Silvis. To reverse the trend, Silvis set up a bonus program that made employees cautious about hiring. The first part of the program pays bonuses based on gross payroll dollars divided by the number of employees. Therefore, more employees means a smaller bonus. But too few employees is not good, either. So Silvis's Part II connects company performance to the bonus, as well, where staffers share in the semi-annual profits. The sheer complexity of these programs begs for computer and spreadsheet solutions.

Another type of bonus plan is the contest, which has given Paul Abraham's Bernardi Honda–Audi–Volkswagen dealership a new spirit and more excitement. Points are awarded for new customers and achieving self-targeted sales goals, with cash awards paid out periodically. John Spomar, Jr. of Norco Cleaners solved his absenteeism problem by playing "poker" with employees, who get a new card each day of the week—if they show up and on time. On Friday, whoever has the best hand wins. Now tardiness and absenteeism are down 30 percent.

Restek's program is doing so well that last year the company paid out bonuses worth one-fifth of the total payroll budget. Silvis is pleased with the results. Before, any problem generated interest in adding staff. Now, he says, employees "think of how they can solve the issue by using existing resources, because it means money in their pockets."

But the biggest benefit of these motivating programs is probably the trust created between management and workers.

SOURCE: Howard Scott, "Bonus Programs with a Motive," *Nation's Business*, Dec. 1995, 46R–47R; Howard Scott, "Contest Can Rev Up Employees," *Nation's Business*, July 1996, 38.

---

reinforcement theory
A motivation theory based on the relationship between a given behavior and its consequences.

behavior modification
The set of techniques by which reinforcement theory is used to modify human behavior.

law of effect
The assumption that positively reinforced behavior tends to be repeated and unreinforced or negatively reinforced behavior tends to be inhibited.

and give everyone the same shot at getting the rewards. The trick is to design a system that fits with employees' abilities and needs. Consider the changes made by Mid-States Technical Staffing, Restek, and an auto dealer and how a good system is crucial in such changes, as described in the Focus on Employees box.

REINFORCEMENT PERSPECTIVE ON MOTIVATION

The reinforcement approach to employee motivation sidesteps the issues of employee needs and thinking processes described in the content and process theories. **Reinforcement theory** simply looks at the relationship between behavior and its consequences. It focuses on changing or modifying the employees' on-the-job behavior through the appropriate use of immediate rewards and punishments.

Reinforcement Tools

Behavior modification is the name given to the set of techniques by which reinforcement theory is used to modify human behavior. The basic assumption underlying behavior modification is the **law of effect,** which states that behavior that is positively reinforced tends to be repeated, and behav-

ior that is not reinforced tends not to be repeated. **Reinforcement** is defined as anything that causes a certain behavior to be repeated or inhibited. The four reinforcement tools are positive reinforcement, avoidance learning, punishment, and extinction.[24] Each type of reinforcement is a consequence of either a pleasant or unpleasant event being applied or withdrawn following a person's behavior. The four types of reinforcement are summarized in Exhibit 14.5.

Positive Reinforcement. *Positive reinforcement* is the administration of a pleasant and rewarding consequence following a desired behavior. A good example of positive reinforcement is immediate praise for an employee who arrives on time or does a little extra in his or her work. The pleasant consequence will increase the likelihood of the excellent work behavior occurring again.

Avoidance Learning. *Avoidance learning* is the removal of an unpleasant consequence following a desired behavior.

Avoidance learning is sometimes called *negative reinforcement*. Employees learn to do the right thing by avoiding unpleasant situations. Avoidance learning occurs when a supervisor stops harassing or reprimanding an employee once the incorrect behavior has stopped.

Punishment. *Punishment* is the imposition of unpleasant outcomes on an employee. Punishment typically occurs following undesirable behavior. For example, a supervisor may berate an employee for performing a task incorrectly. The supervisor expects that the negative outcome will serve as a punishment and reduce the likelihood of the behavior recurring. The use of punishment in organizations is controversial and often criticized because it fails to indicate the correct behavior.

Extinction. *Extinction* is the withdrawal of a positive reward, meaning that behavior is no longer reinforced and hence is less likely to occur in the future. If a perpetually tardy employee fails to receive praise and pay raises, he or she will begin to realize

reinforcement
Anything that causes a given behavior to be repeated or inhibited.

EXHIBIT 14.5
Changing Behavior with Reinforcement

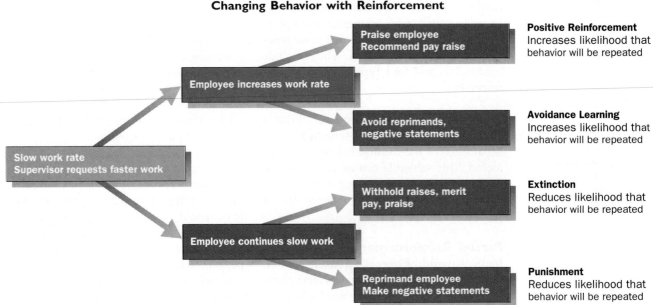

Positive Reinforcement
Increases likelihood that behavior will be repeated

Avoidance Learning
Increases likelihood that behavior will be repeated

Extinction
Reduces likelihood that behavior will be repeated

Punishment
Reduces likelihood that behavior will be repeated

SOURCE: Based on Richard L. Daft and Richard M. Steers, *Organizations: A Micro/Macro Approach* (Glenview, Ill.: Scott, Foresman, 1986), 109.

that the behavior is not producing desired outcomes. The behavior will gradually disappear if it is continually nonreinforced.

Some executives use reinforcement theory very effectively to shape employees' behavior. Jack Welch, chairman of General Electric, always made it a point to reinforce behavior. As an up-and-coming group executive, Welch reinforced purchasing agents by having someone telephone him whenever an agent got a price concession from a vendor. Welch would stop whatever he was doing and call the agent to say, "That's wonderful news; you just knocked a nickel a ton off the price of steel." He would also sit down and scribble out a congratulatory note to the agent. The effective use of positive reinforcement and the heightened motivation of purchasing employees marked Jack Welch as executive material in the organization.[25]

Schedules of Reinforcement

A great deal of research into reinforcement theory suggests that the timing of reinforcement has an impact on the speed of employee learning. **Schedules of reinforcement** pertain to the frequency with which and intervals over which reinforcement occurs. A reinforcement schedule can be selected to have maximum impact on employees' job behavior. There are five basic types of reinforcement schedules, which include continuous and four types of partial reinforcement.

Continuous Reinforcement.   With a **continuous reinforcement schedule,** every occurrence of the desired behavior is reinforced. This schedule can be very effective in the early stages of learning new types of behavior, because every attempt has a pleasant consequence.

Partial Reinforcement.   However, in the real world of organizations, it is often impossible to reinforce every correct behavior. With a **partial reinforcement schedule,** the reinforcement is administered only after some occurrences of the correct behavior.

There are four types of partial reinforcement schedules: fixed interval, fixed ratio, variable interval, and variable ratio.

Fixed-Interval Schedule.   The *fixed-interval schedule* rewards employees at specified time intervals. If an employee displays the correct behavior each day, reinforcement may occur every week. Regular paychecks or quarterly bonuses are examples of a fixed-interval reinforcement.

Fixed-Ratio Schedule.   With a *fixed-ratio schedule*, reinforcement occurs after a specified number of desired responses, say, after every fifth. For example, paying a field hand $1.50 for picking ten pounds of peppers is a fixed-ratio schedule. Most piece-rate pay systems are considered fixed-ratio schedules.

Variable-Interval Schedule.   With a *variable-interval schedule*, reinforcement is administered at random times that cannot be predicted by the employee. An example would be a random inspection by the manufacturing superintendent of the production floor, at which time he or she commends employees on their good behavior.

Variable-Ratio Schedule.   The *variable-ratio schedule* is based on a random number of desired behaviors rather than on variable time periods. Reinforcement may occur sometimes after 5, 10, 15, or 20 displays of behavior. One example is the attraction of slot machines for gamblers. People anticipate that the machine will pay a jackpot after a certain number of plays, but the exact number of plays is variable.

The schedules of reinforcement available to managers are illustrated in Exhibit 14.6. Continuous reinforcement is most effective for establishing new learning, but behavior is vulnerable to extinction. Partial reinforcement schedules are more effective for maintaining behavior over extended time periods. The most powerful is the variable-ratio schedule, because employee behavior will persist for a long time due to the administration of reinforcement only after a long interval.[26]

schedule of reinforcement
The frequency with which and intervals over which reinforcement occurs.

continuous reinforcement schedule
A schedule in which every occurrence of the desired behavior is reinforced.

partial reinforcement schedule
A schedule in which only some occurrences of the desired behavior are reinforced.

EXHIBIT 14.6
Schedules of Reinforcement

Schedule of Reinforcement	Nature of Reinforcement	Effect on Behavior When Applied	Effect on Behavior When Withdrawn	Example
Continuous	Reward given after each desired behavior	Leads to fast learning of new behavior	Rapid extinction	Praise
Fixed-interval	Reward given at fixed time intervals	Leads to average and irregular performance	Rapid extinction	Weekly paycheck
Fixed-ratio	Reward given at fixed amounts of output	Quickly leads to very high and stable performance	Rapid extinction	Piece-rate pay system
Variable-interval	Reward given at variable times	Leads to moderately high and stable performance	Slow extinction	Performance appraisal and awards given at random times each month
Variable-ratio	Reward given at variable amounts of output	Leads to very high performance	Slow extinction	Sales bonus tied to number of sales calls, with random checks

One example of a small business that successfully uses reinforcement theory is Parsons Pine Products.

 ## PARSONS PINE PRODUCTS

Parsons Pine Products has only 75 employees, but it is the world's largest manufacturer of slats for louvered doors and shutters. Managers have developed a positive reinforcement scheme for motivating and rewarding workers. The plan includes the following:

1 *Safety pay.* Every employee who goes for a month without a lost-time accident receives a bonus equal to four hours' pay.
2 *Retro pay.* If the company saves money when its worker's compensation premiums go down because of a lower accident rate, the savings are distributed among employees.
3 *Well pay.* Employees receive monthly well pay equal to eight hours' wages if they have been neither absent nor tardy.
4 *Profit pay.* All company earnings above 4 percent after taxes go into a bonus pool, which is shared among employees.

The plan for reinforcing correct behaviors has been extraordinarily effective. Parsons's previous accident rate had been 86 percent above the state average; today it is 32 percent below it. Turnover and tardiness are mini-

mal, and absenteeism has dropped to almost nothing. The plan works because the reinforcement schedules are strictly applied, with no exceptions. Owner James Parsons has said, "One woman called to say that a tree had fallen, and she couldn't get her car out. She wanted me to make an exception. If I did that, I'd be doing it all the time."[27] ∎

Reinforcement also works at such organizations as Campbell Soup Co., Emery Air Freight, Michigan Bell, and General Electric, because managers reward appropriate behavior. They tell employees what they can do to receive reinforcement, tell them what they are doing wrong, distribute rewards equitably, tailor rewards to behaviors, and keep in mind that failure to reward deserving behavior has an equally powerful impact on employees.

Indeed, reinforcement as well as the content and process perspectives of motivation described earlier are now being adopted in Eastern European countries as well as in Russia and China.

JOB DESIGN FOR MOTIVATION

A *job* in an organization is a unit of work that a single employee is responsible for performing. A job could include writing

job rotation

A job design that systematically moves employees from one job to another to provide them with variety and stimulation.

job design

The application of motivational theories to the structure of work for improving productivity and satisfaction.

job simplification

A job design whose purpose is to improve task efficiency by reducing the number of tasks a single person must perform.

tickets for parking violators in New York City or doing long-range planning for ABC television. Jobs are important because performance of their components may provide rewards that meet employees' needs. An assembly line worker may install the same bolt over and over, whereas an emergency room physician may provide each trauma victim with a unique treatment package. Managers need to know what aspects of a job provide motivation as well as how to compensate for routine tasks that have little inherent satisfaction. **Job design** is the application of motivational theories to the structure of work for improving productivity and satisfaction. Approaches to job design are generally classified as job simplification, job rotation, job enlargement, and job enrichment.

Job Simplification

Job simplification pursues task efficiency by reducing the number of tasks one person must do. Job simplification is based on principles drawn from scientific management and industrial engineering. Tasks are designed to be simple, repetitive, and standardized. As complexity is stripped from a job, the worker has more time to concentrate on doing more of the same routine task. Workers with low skill requirements can perform the job, and the organization achieves a high level of efficiency. Indeed, workers are interchangeable, because they need little training or skill and exercise little

judgment. As a motivational technique, however, job simplification has failed. People dislike routine and boring jobs and react in a number of negative ways, including sabotage, absenteeism, and unionization. Job simplification is compared with job rotation and job enlargement in Exhibit 14.7.

Job Rotation

Job rotation systematically moves employees from one job to another, thereby increasing the number of different tasks an employee performs without increasing the complexity of any one job. For example, an autoworker may install windshields one week and front bumpers the next. Job rotation still takes advantage of engineering efficiencies, but it provides variety and stimulation for employees. Although employees may find the new job interesting at first, the novelty soon wears off as the repetitive work is mastered.

Companies such as National Steel, Motorola, and Dayton Hudson have built on the notion of job rotation to train a flexible workforce. As companies break away from ossified job categories, workers can perform several jobs, thereby reducing labor costs. One employee might shift among the jobs of drill operator, punch operator, and assembler, depending on the company's need at the moment. Some unions have resisted the idea, but many now go along, realizing that it helps the company be more competitive.[28]

E X H I B I T   1 4 . 7
Types of Job Design

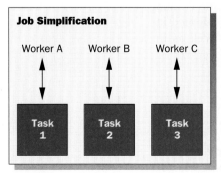

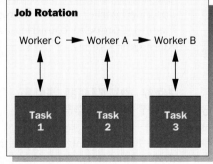

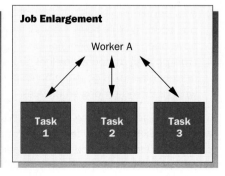

Job Enlargement

Job enlargement combines a series of tasks into one new, broader job. This is a response to the dissatisfaction of employees with oversimplified jobs. Instead of only one job, an employee may be responsible for three or four and will have more time to do them. Job enlargement provides job variety and a greater challenge for employees. At Maytag, jobs were enlarged when work was redesigned such that workers assembled an entire water pump rather than doing each part as it reached them on the assembly line. In General Motors' new assembly plants, the assembly line is gone. In its place is a freewheeling, motorized carrier that transports each car independently through the assembly process. The carrier moves to a workstation, where it stops for a group of workers to perform a coordinated block of tasks, such as installing an engine and its accessories. Thus the workers perform an enlarged job on a stationary automobile, rather than a single task on a series of automobiles moving past them.

Job Enrichment

Recall the discussion of Maslow's need hierarchy and Herzberg's two-factor theory. Rather than just changing the number and frequency of tasks a worker performs, **job enrichment** incorporates high-level motivators into the work, including job responsibility, recognition, and opportunities for growth, learning, and achievement. In an enriched job, employees have control over the resources necessary for performing it, make decisions on how to do the work, experience personal growth, and set their own work pace. Many companies, including AT&T, IBM, and General Foods, have undertaken job enrichment programs to increase employees' motivation and job satisfaction.

Half-Price books took job enrichment to the limit by basing its planning and expansion on satisfying valued employees' managerial aspirations.

HALF-PRICE BOOKS

What's a CEO of a $50 million company doing driving a 1986 Volkswagen and earning only $50,000 per year? Sharon Wright, daughter of the founder of Dallas's Half-Price Books, is following in her late mother's footsteps by keeping costs low in order to make the business flourish.

Everything in the first store in 1972 was homemade or secondhand, and employees were hired for their eccentricities as well as their love of books, meaning they were educated and often had gifts in display and promotion. Pat Anderson, Wright's mother, had a knack for pricing books low enough so that they flew off the shelves at a profit.

Half-Price Books has a number of unusual practices; perhaps the one which defies common business practice most was its stubborn refusal to grow intentionally through a systematic plan or analysis of optimum market conditions. Instead, the company opened new stores mostly to reward valuable employees who wanted to be managers. When Dallas became saturated with Half-Price stores, expansion took place in cities where employees had a desire to relocate. By 1997, Half-Price books had 55 stores in eight states.

After Pat Anderson died in 1995, many employees assumed Wright would sell off the business and start to live the good life. But Sharon never thought of that. "Why would I want to sell?" she asks. "My family and friends all work here!"[29] ∎

Job Characteristics Model

The most recent work on job design is the job characteristics model developed by Richard Hackman and Greg Oldham.[30] Hackman and Oldham's research concerned **work redesign,** which is defined as altering jobs to increase both the quality of employees' work experience and their productivity. Hackman and Oldham's research into the design of hundreds of jobs yielded the **job characteristics model,** which is

job enlargement
A job design that combines a series of tasks into one new, broader job to give employees variety and challenge.

job enrichment
A job design that incorporates achievement, recognition, and other high-level motivators into the work.

work redesign
The altering of jobs to increase both the quality of employees' work experience and their productivity.

job characteristics model
A model of job design that comprises core job dimensions, critical psychological states, and employee growth-need strength.

illustrated in Exhibit 14.8. The model consists of three major parts: core job dimensions, critical psychological states, and employee growth-need strength.

Core Job Dimensions.   Hackman and Oldham identified five dimensions that determine a job's motivational potential:

1 *Skill variety* is the number of diverse activities that compose a job and the number of skills used to perform it. A routine, repetitive, assembly line job is low in variety, whereas an applied research position that entails working on new problems every day is high in variety.
2 *Task identity* is the degree to which an employee performs a total job with a recognizable beginning and ending. A chef who prepares an entire meal has more task identity than a worker on a cafeteria line who ladles mashed potatoes.
3 *Task significance* is the degree to which the job is perceived as important and having impact on the company or consumers. People who distribute penicillin and other medical supplies during times of emergencies would feel they have significant jobs.
4 *Autonomy* is the degree to which the worker has freedom, discretion, and self-determination in planning and carrying out tasks. A house painter can determine how to paint the house; a paint sprayer on an assembly line has little autonomy.
5 *Feedback* is the extent to which doing the job provides information back to the employee about his or her performance. Jobs vary in their ability to let workers see the outcomes of their efforts. A football coach knows whether the team won or lost, but a basic research scientist may have to wait years to learn whether a research project was successful.

The job characteristics model says that the more these five core characteristics can be designed into the job, the more the employees will be motivated and the higher will be performance quality and satisfaction.

Critical Psychological States.   The model posits that core job dimensions are more rewarding when individuals experience three psychological states in response

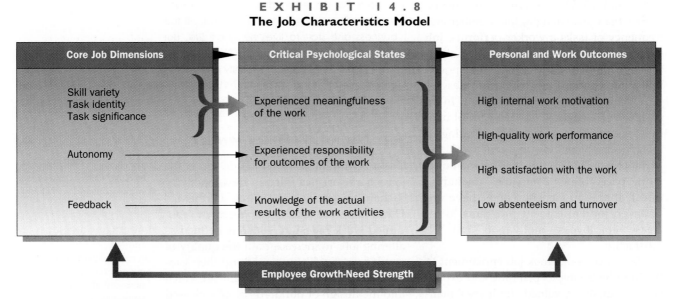

E X H I B I T   1 4 . 8
The Job Characteristics Model

SOURCE: Adapted from J. Richard Hackman and G. R. Oldham, "Motivation through the Design of Work: Test of a Theory," *Organizational Behavior and Human Performance* 16 (1976), 256.

TECHNOLOGY FOR TODAY
SEQUINS INTERNATIONAL

Every little glitter you see on the stars' gowns at the Oscars or Grammys comes with pain. Or at least it did in the past, when garment workers at Woodside, NY-based Sequins International, Inc. applied the sequins through a technology called spooling, where the 40 female workers sat on rigid chairs and used their right hands to turn a tire-sized wheel crank, while they used their left hands to pinch sequin-thread to feel for defects. Because of stiff global competition from cheap-wage countries such as China and India, the factory has tried to keep costs low and still uses 1940s technology.

Not surprisingly, two-thirds of the workers reported right shoulder pain, with prospects only of becoming worse. This condition is so common in industry it now has a name: repetitive motion disorder.

Enter Ladies' Garment Workers' Union health and safety specialist Lau-

rie Kellogg, who became concerned when she got complaints from workers at Sequins International. During a visit to the factory, she reported she "had a cow" when she saw the $7.13 per hour women hunched over the old equipment.

Rather than decree changes, Kellogg worked with the plant manager and set up the more empowering structure of a five-worker committee, to come up with more ergonomic equipment requirements. Despite worker conflicts and some plant layoffs, the new spooling device was ready to roll some months later. Gone was the crank, replaced with a mechanized foot pedal. Chairs became adjustable. Gauges were moved so that workers would not have to strain their necks to read them.

Since the new technology, right shoulder pain decreased from 66 percent of the workers to 35 percent. In addition, the factory has recently started job rotation, to further reduce the repetitive nature of the jobs, and

has therefore increased skill variety into the workers' days. Because most workers are Hispanic with poor English skills, English classes are offered during lunchtime. Workers also have the opportunity to be part of two teams, one for product quality and the other for customer support.

Because of the improvements in job design and motivation, worker satisfaction has dramatically increased, absenteeism is down over 200 percent, and the cost of producing goods is down by 30 percent.

Now Mardi Gras or ballet costumers will not necessarily bring pain to those women's lives. Technology helped turn pain into gain.

SOURCE: Pamela Mendels, "The Workplace Gain from Pain," *Newsday*, March 5, 1995, 1; Barbara Ettorre, "Retooling People and Processes," *Management Review*, June 1995, 19–23.

to job design. In Exhibit 14.8, skill variety, task identity, and task significance tend to influence the employee's psychological state of *experienced meaningfulness of work.* The work itself is satisfying and provides intrinsic rewards for the worker. The job characteristic of autonomy influences the worker's *experienced responsibility.* The job characteristic of feedback provides the worker with *knowledge of actual results.* The employee thus knows how he or she is doing and can change work performance to increase desired outcomes.

Personal and Work Outcomes. The impact of the five job characteristics on the psychological states of experienced meaningfulness, responsibility, and knowledge of actual results leads to the personal and work outcomes of high work motivation, high work performance, high satisfaction, and low absenteeism and turnover.

Employee Growth-Need Strength. The final component of the job characteristics model is called *employee growth-need strength,* which means that people have different needs for growth and development. If a person wants to satisfy low-level needs, such as safety and belongingness, the job characteristics model has less effect. When a person has a high need for growth and development, including the desire for personal challenge, achievement, and challenging work, the model is especially effective. People with a high need to grow

and expand their abilities respond very favorably to the application of the model and to improvements in core job dimensions.

One application of the job characteristics model that worked extremely well took place at Sequins International Inc., as described in the Technology for Today box.

EMPOWERMENT AND NEW MOTIVATIONAL PROGRAMS

Organizations have adopted a number of new programs in recent years that apply motivational theory to improve employees' satisfaction and performance. Exhibit 14.9 summarizes several methods of incentive pay and employee involvement. The newest trend in motivation is **empowerment,** the delegation of power or authority to subordinates in an organization.[31] Increasing employee power heightens motivation for task accomplishment because people improve their own effectiveness, choosing how to do a task and using their creativity.[32] Most people come into an organization with the desire to do a good job, and empowerment releases the motivation that is already there.

Ralph Stayer, CEO of Johnsonville

Foods, believes a manager's strongest power comes from committed and motivated employees: "Real power comes from giving it up to others who are in a better position to do things than you are."[33] The manager who shares power with employees receives motivation and creativity in return.

Empowering employees means giving them four elements that enable them to act more freely to accomplish their jobs: information, knowledge, power, and rewards.[34]

Employees receive information about company performance. In companies where employees are fully empowered, such as Com-Corp Industries, no information is secret. At Com-Corp, every employee has access to all financial information, including executive salaries.

Employees have knowledge and skills to contribute to company goals. Companies use training programs to help employees acquire the knowledge and skills they need to contribute to organizational performance. At Tellabs, Inc., a maker of sophisticated telephone equipment, CEO Grace Pastiak personally leads workshops for about a dozen factory workers each month, enabling them to solve problems and make quality improvements on their own.[35]

Employees have the power to make substantive decisions. Workers have the authority to

empowerment
The delegation of power and authority to subordinates.

EXHIBIT 14.9
New Motivational Compensation Programs

Program Name	Purpose
Pay for Performance	Rewards individual employees in proportion to their performance contributions. Also called merit pay.
Gain Sharing	Rewards all employees and managers within a business unit when predetermined performance targets are met. Encourages teamwork.
Employee Stock Ownership Plan (ESOP)	Gives employees part ownership of the organization, enabling them to share in improved profit performance.
Lump-Sum Bonuses	Rewards employees with a one-time cash payment based on performance.
Pay for Knowledge	Links employee salary with the number of task skills acquired. Workers are motivated to learn the skills for many jobs, thus increasing company flexibility and efficiency.
Flexible Work Schedules	Flextime allows workers to set their own hours. Job sharing allows two or more part-time workers to jointly cover one job.

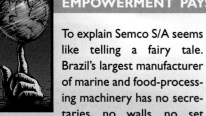

LEADING THE MANAGEMENT REVOLUTION
EMPOWERMENT PAYS AT SEMCO S/A

To explain Semco S/A seems like telling a fairy tale. Brazil's largest manufacturer of marine and food-processing machinery has no secretaries, no walls, no set hours, and no dress codes. Managers set their own salaries and are regularly evaluated by subordinates, whose responses are tabulated and posted on bulletin boards. Company financial books are open to anyone, anytime, and employees are given courses in reading balance sheets and cash-flow statements. Workers set their own production goals and share 22 percent of the profits. Managers do their own faxing, phoning and fetching guests. The policy is to have no policies nor organization charts because "structure creates hierarchy and hierarchy creates restraints." And no one knows exactly how many

employees work there (maybe 300?) because work is shared between in-house workers and company-supported satellite production.

Though it seems like chaos, it is now one of the most successful companies in Brazil, despite severe economic conditions. When Ricardo Semler took over the moribund company in 1980, it was near bankruptcy. Because of his revolutionary policies, Semco has increased productivity 700 percent and growth 900 percent in the past ten years.

Semler believes in hiring adults and treating them as such, and then "getting out of their way and let them do their jobs." Employees are not expected to abuse their freedom, but rather to achieve maximum and beneficial results to the company, customer, co-workers and themselves. Semler's methods are

based on three principles: "**participation** gives them control of their work; **profit-sharing** gives them a reason to do it; and **information** tells them what's working and what's not."

At Semco there is "little control, less organization and virtually no discipline," notes Semler. "Does it make me feel I have given up power? You bet it does. But I probably sleep better at night than the manufacturer who runs his business with an iron hand and whose employees leave their trouble in his lap every night."

SOURCE: Mary M. Crossan et al., "The Improvising Organization," *Organizational Dynamics*, March 1, 1996, 20; "Empowering Employees—Maverick Style," Institute of Personnel and Development, M2 Presswire, Nov. 1, 1996; Ricardo Semler, *Maverick*. New York: Warner Books, 1993; Ricardo Semler, Managing without Managers, in "Managing with People in Mind," *Harvard Business Review*, Boston: Harvard Business School, 1991, 144–52.

directly influence work procedures and organizational performance, often through quality circles or self-directed work teams. At Compaq Computer, salespeople now work out of their homes and set their own schedules. The company provides a fully equipped networked computer so workers can share information with colleagues and access comprehensive databases. Under the new system, Compaq's sales force has set new records for productivity.[36] The Leading the Management Revolution box describes how empowering workers to make decisions made Semco S/A wildly successful, even in the unstable economy of Brazil.

Employees are rewarded based on company performance. Organizations that empower workers often reward them based on the results shown in the company's bottom line. Johnsonville Foods instituted a "company performance share," a fixed percentage of pretax profits to be divided every six months among employees. Individual shares are based on a performance appraisal system designed and administered by a volunteer team of line workers.[37] Organizations may also use other motivational programs described in Exhibit 14.9 to tie employee efforts to company performance.

SUMMARY AND MANAGEMENT SOLUTION

This chapter introduced a number of important ideas about the motivation of people in organizations. The content theories of motivation focus on the nature of underlying employee needs. Maslow's hierarchy of needs, Alderfer's ERG theory, Herzberg's two-factor theory, and McClelland's acquired needs theory all suggest that people are motivated to meet a range of needs. Process theories examine how people go about selecting rewards with which to meet needs. Equity theory says that people compare their contributions and outcomes with others' and are motivated to maintain a feeling of equity. Expectancy theory suggests that people calculate the probability of achieving certain outcomes. Managers can increase motivation by treating employees fairly and by clarifying employee paths toward meeting their needs. Still another motivational approach is reinforcement theory, which says that employees learn to behave in certain ways based on the availability of reinforcements.

The application of motivational ideas is illustrated in job design and other motivational programs. Job design approaches include job simplification, job rotation, job enlargement, job enrichment, and the job characteristics model. Managers can change the structure of work to meet employees' high-level needs. The recent trend toward empowerment motivates by giving employees more information and authority to make decisions in their work while connecting compensation to the results. Other motivational programs include pay for performance, gain sharing, ESOPs, lump-sum bonuses, pay for knowledge, and flexible work schedules. A highly successful application of motivational ideas occurred for factory managers at Au Bon Pain.

Recall from the chapter opening that Gary Aronson was an unmotivated store manager at Au Bon Pain, making a mere $26,000 a year. Thanks to a new incentive system called The Partner/Manager Program, Aronson's salary went up to $80,000. He throws his heart and soul into his work, putting in a minimum of 65 hours per week, and he loves it. The dramatic motivation began when top executives created a 50–50 split with store managers on controllable profits, or those which managers have some control over. To save on overhead, Aronson got rid of one assistant manager and then reorganized the store to increase seating capacity. He motivated the staff through monetary and other rewards, as well as getting to know them all personally, in order to ensure prompt and friendly service. Though there were loose controls on the system, such as overhead costs, there were tight controls on outputs, such as customer satisfaction. Aronson and other store managers solved problems they had previously dumped on the company. Under the new system, stores ran 40 percent ahead of their profit goals, showing that incentives and a sense of ownership are effective. Au Bon Pain continues to grow, with the current number of stores at 282. In 1995, it was rated as having one of the most productive workforces in the Boston area by the *Boston Globe*.[38] Perhaps the best explanation for the sharply improved performance is expectancy theory, because managers saw how to link effort and performance to the outcomes they desired. They also received positive reinforcement, and their job responsibilities were enriched, thereby satisfying higher-level needs.

DISCUSSION QUESTIONS

1 Low-paid service workers represent a motivational problem for many companies. Consider the ill-trained and poorly motivated X-ray machine operators trying to detect weapons in airports. How might these people be motivated to reduce boredom and increase their vigilance?

2 One small company recognizes an employee of the month, who is given a parking spot next to the president's space near the front door. What theories would explain the positive motivation associated with this policy?

3 Campbell Soup Company reduces accidents with a lottery. Each worker who works 30 days or more without losing a day for a job-related accident is eligible to win prizes in a raffle drawing. Why has this program been successful?

4 One executive argues that managers have too much safety because of benefit and retirement plans. He rewards his managers for taking risks and has removed many guaranteed benefits. Would this approach motivate managers? Why?

5 If an experienced secretary discovered that she made less money than a newly hired janitor, how would she react? What inputs and outcomes might she evaluate to make this comparison?

6 Would you rather work for a supervisor high in need for achievement, need for affiliation, or need for power? Why? What are the advantages and disadvantages of each?

7 A survey of teachers found that two of the most important rewards were the belief that their work was important and a feeling of accomplishment. Is this consistent with Hackman and Oldham's job characteristics model?

8 The teachers in question 7 also reported that pay and fringe benefits were poor, yet they continued to teach. Use Herzberg's two-factor theory to explain this finding.

9 Many organizations use sales contests and motivational speakers to motivate salespeople to overcome frequent rejections and turndowns. How would these devices help motivate salespeople?

10 What characteristics of individuals determine the extent to which work redesign will have a positive impact on work satisfaction and work effectiveness?

11 Do you think an empowerment program of increased employee authority and responsibility would succeed without being tied to a motivational compensation program, such as gain sharing or ESOPs? Discuss.

MANAGEMENT EXERCISES

MANAGER'S WORKBOOK

Motivation Questionnaire

You are to indicate how important each characteristic is to you. Answer according to your feelings about the most recent job you had or about the job you currently hold. Circle the number on the scale that represents your feeling—1 (very unimportant) to 7 (very important).

When you have completed the questionnaire, score it as follows:

Rating for question 5 = ____.
    Divide by 1 = ____ security.
Rating for questions 9 and 13 = ____.
    Divide by 2 = ____ social.
Rating for questions 1, 3, and 7 = ____.
    Divide by 3 = ____ esteem.

Rating for questions 4, 10, 11, and 12 = ____.
    Divide by 4 = ____ autonomy.
Rating for questions 2, 6, and 8 = ____.
    Divide by 3 = ____ self-actualization.

The instructor has national norm scores for presidents, vice presidents, and upper middle-level, lower middle-level, and lower-level managers with which you can compare your mean importance scores. How do your scores compare with the scores of managers working in organizations?

1 The feeling of self-esteem a person gets from being in that job	1	2	3	4	5	6	7
2 The opportunity for personal growth and development in that job	1	2	3	4	5	6	7
3 The prestige of the job inside the company (that is, regard received from others in the company)	1	2	3	4	5	6	7
4 The opportunity for independent thought and action in that job	1	2	3	4	5	6	7
5 The feeling of security in that job	1	2	3	4	5	6	7
6 The feeling of self-fulfillment a person gets from being in that position (that is, the feeling of being able to use one's own unique capabilities, realizing one's potential)	1	2	3	4	5	6	7
7 The prestige of the job outside the company (that is, the regard received from others not in the company)	1	2	3	4	5	6	7
8 The feeling of worthwhile accomplishment in that job	1	2	3	4	5	6	7
9 The opportunity in that job to give help to other people	1	2	3	4	5	6	7

10 The opportunity in that job for participation in the setting of goals	1 2 3 4 5 6 7
11 The opportunity in that job for participation in the determination of methods and procedures	1 2 3 4 5 6 7
12 The authority connected with the job	1 2 3 4 5 6 7
13 The opportunity to develop close friendships in the job	1 2 3 4 5 6 7

SOURCE: Lyman W. Porter, *Organizational Patterns of Managerial Job Attitudes* (New York: American Foundation for Management Research, 1964), 17, 19.

MANAGER'S WORKSHOP

My Absolute Worst Job

1 By yourself, complete the table below, except for the "group" row answers.

2 Divide into groups of four to seven members. Groups discuss individual answers and complete the row for your group.

Reasons for job being so awful

	Title and duties	Working conditions?	Supervision? Boss?	Work itself, lack of rewards, co-workers?	Other?	Compare to best job
Your worst job						
Groups— member #1						
Member #2						
#3						
#4						
#5						
#6						

3 The instructor asks for a show of hands on the number of people whose worst jobs fit into the following categories:
  a. Factory
  b. Restaurant
  c. Manual labor
  d. Driving or delivery
  e. Professional
  f. Health care
  g. Phone sales or communications
  h. Other

4 Instructor gathers data from each group on worst jobs and asks groups to answer:
  a. What are any common characteristics of the worst jobs in your group?

  b. How did your co-workers feel about their jobs?
  c. What happens to morale and productivity when a worker hates the job?
  d. What was the difference in your own morale/productivity in your worst job versus a job you really enjoyed?
  e. Why do organizations continue to allow unpleasant working conditions to exist?
  f. What motivation theories are relevant for understanding how to prevent these "worst" jobs?

SOURCE: Copyright 1988 Dorothy Marcic. All rights reserved. Thanks to Georgann Bohlig-Nirva for sparking the original idea.

SURF THE 'NET

Surf through company (numbers 1–3) and individual (numbers 4–6)
Web sites, finding good examples to complete the table below:

Name and address of Web site	For company, types of incentives offered to employees	For individual, types of incentives, perks wanted in a job	Which motivation theories are relevant for each incentive? Why?	If company, would you want to work there? If individual, would you hire? Why?
1.				
2.				
3.				
4.				
5.				
6.				

ETHICAL DILEMMA

Compensation Showdown

When Suzanne Lebeau, human resources manager, received a call from Bert Wilkes, comptroller of Farley Glass Works, she anticipated hearing good news to share with the Wage and Bonus Committee. She had already seen numbers to indicate that the year-end bonus plan, which was instituted by her committee in lieu of the traditional guaranteed raises of the past, was going to exceed expectations. It was a real relief to her, because the plan, devised by a committee representing all levels of the workforce, had taken eleven months to complete. It had also been a real boost to morale at a low point in the company's history. Workers at the glass shower production plant were bringing new effort and energy to their jobs, and Lebeau wanted to see them rewarded.

She was shocked to see Wilkes's face so grim when she arrived for her meeting. "We have a serious problem, Suzanne," Wilkes said to open the meeting. "We ran the numbers from third quarter to project our end-of-the-year figures and discovered that the executive bonus objectives, which are based on net operating profit, would not be met if we paid out the employee bonuses first. The executive bonuses are a major source of their income. We can't ask them to do without their salary to insure a bonus for the workers."

Lebeau felt her temper rising. After all their hard work, she was not going to sit by and watch the employees be disappointed because the accounting department had not structured the employee bonus plan to work with the executive plan. She was afraid they would undo all the good that the bonus plan had done in motivating the plant workers. They had kept their end of the bargain, and the company's high profits were common knowledge in the plant.

What Do You Do?

1 Ask to appear before the executive committee to argue that the year-end bonus plan for workers be honored. Executives could defer their bonuses until the problem in the structure of the compensation plan is resolved.
2 Go along with the comptroller. It isn't fair for the executives to lose so much money. Begin to prepare the workers to not expect much this first year of the plan.
3 Go to the board of directors and ask for a compromise plan that splits the bonuses between the executives and the workers.

SOURCE: Reprinted with permission from *Business Ethics Magazine*, 52 South 10th Street #10, Minneapolis, MN 55403. 612-962-4700.

CASE FOR CRITICAL ANALYSIS

Bloomingdale's

Bloomingdale's is at the forefront of a quiet revolution sweeping department store retailing. Thousands of hourly sales employees are being converted to commission pay. Bloomingdale's hopes to use commissions to motivate employees to work harder, to attract better salespeople, and to enable them to earn more money. For example, under the old plan, a Bloomingdale's salesclerk in women's wear would earn about $16,000 a year, based on $7 per hour and 0.5 percent commission on $500,000 sales. Under the new plan, the annual pay would be $25,000 based on 5 percent commission on $500,000 sales.

John Palmerio, who works in the men's shoe salon, is enthusiastic about the changeover. His pay has increased an average of $175 per week. But in women's lingerie, employees are less enthusiastic. A target of $1,600 in sales per week is difficult to achieve but is necessary for salespeople to earn their previous salary and even to keep their jobs. In previous years, the practice of commission pay was limited to big-ticket items such as furniture, appliances, and men's suits, where extra sales skill pays off. The move into small-item purchases may not work as well, but Bloomingdale's and other stores are trying anyway.

One question is whether Bloomingdale's can create more customer-oriented salespeople when they work on commission. They may be reluctant to handle complaints, make returns, and clean shelves, preferring instead to chase customers. Moreover, it cost Bloomingdale's about $1 million per store to install the commission system because of training programs, computer changes, and increased pay in many departments. If the overall impact on service is negative, the increased efficiency may not seem worthwhile.

Questions

1 What theories about motivation underlie the switch from salary to commission pay?
2 Are high-level needs met under the commission system?
3 As a customer, would you prefer to shop where employees are motivated to make commissions?

SOURCES: Based on Francine Schwadel, "Chain Finds Incentives a Hard Sell," *The Wall Street Journal*, July 5, 1990, B4; and Amy Dunkin, "Now Salespeople Really Must Sell for Their Supper," *Business Week*, July 31, 1989, 50–52.

ENDNOTES

1 "Au Bon Pain Cools Unit Growth as It Works on Performance," *Nation's Restaurant News* 30, no. 1, January 1, 1996, 12; "Most Productive Employees," *Boston Globe*, May 23, 1995, 61; Bruce G. Posner, "May the Force Be with You," *Inc.* (July 1987), 70–75.

2 David Silburt, "Secrets of the Super Sellers," *Canadian Business* (January 1987), 54–59; "Meet the Savvy Supersalesmen," *Fortune*, February 4, 1985, 56–62; Michael Brody, "Meet Today's Young American Worker," *Fortune*, November 11, 1985, 90–98; and Tom Richman, "Meet the Masters. They Could Sell You Anything . . . ," *Inc.* (March 1985), 79–86.

3 Richard M. Steers and Lyman W. Porter, eds., *Motivation and Work Behavior*, 3d ed. (New York: McGraw-Hill, 1983); Don Hellriegel, John W. Slocum, Jr., and Richard W. Woodman, *Organizational Behavior*, 7th ed. (St. Paul, Minn.: West, 1995), 170; and Jerry L. Gray and Frederick A. Starke, *Organizational Behavior: Concepts and Applications*, 4th ed. (New York: Macmillan, 1988), 104–105.

4 Kenneth A. Kovach, "What Motivates Employees? Workers and Supervisors Give Different Answers," *Business Horizon* 30 (September–October), 58–65.

5 Steers and Porter, *Motivation*.

6 J. F. Rothlisberger and W. J. Dickson, *Management and the Worker* (Cambridge, Mass.: Harvard University Press, 1939).

7 "Adapted from Claire Buhl, "Stick-to-itiveness Pays," *Nation's Business* (January 1996), 22–24.

8 Abraham F. Maslow, "A Theory of Human Motivation," *Psychological Review* 50 (1943), 370–396.

9 Julia Lawlor, "Employees Encouraged to Lighten Up," *USA Today*, September 23, 1991, A1, B1; and Everett T. Suters, "Show and Tell," *Inc.* (April 1987), 111–112.

10 Mardelle Feigenbaum, "Blue Fish Clothing Company," *Greenmoney Journal* (Spring 1996); "Designing Woman," *People*, Dec. 16, 1996, 98; John Case, "Corporate Culture," *Inc.* (November 1996), 42–51.

11 Clayton Alderfer, *Existence, Relatedness and Growth* (New York: Free Press, 1972).

12 Sandra Mardenfeld, "Mary Kay Ash," *Incentive Magazine*, (January 1996), 170, no. 1, 54–55; Richard C. Bartlett, "Mary Kay's Foundation," *Journal of Business Strategy* (July/August 1995), 16, no. 4, 16–19; Alan Farnham, "Mary Kay's Lessons in Leadership," *Fortune* (September 20, 1993), 128, no. 6, 68–77.

13 Frederick Herzberg, "One More Time: How Do You Motivate Employees?" *Harvard Business Review* (January–February 1968), 53–62.

14 Jay Finegan, "Unconventional Wisdom," *Inc.* (December 1994), 44–58.

15 David C. McClelland, *Human Motivation* (Glenview, Ill.: Scott, Foresman, 1985).

16 David C. McClelland, "The Two Faces of Power," in *Organizational Psychology*, ed. D. A. Colb, I. M. Rubin, and J. M. McIntyre (Englewood Cliffs, N.J.: Prentice-Hall, 1971), 73–86.

17 Celest Fremon, "His Life is a Movie," *Los Angeles Times Magazine*, October 6, 1996, 8; Allison Lynn and Michelle Keller, "Lighting the Way," *People*, December 16, 1996, 65–69.

18 J. Stacy Adams, "Injustice in Social Exchange," in *Advances in Experimental Social Psychology*, 2d ed., ed. L. Berkowitz (New York: Academic Press, 1965); and J. Stacy Adams, "Toward an Understanding of Inequity," *Journal of Abnormal and Social Psychology* (November 1963), 422–436.

19 Ray V. Montagno, "The Effects of Comparison to Others and Primary Experience on Responses to Task Design," *Academy of Management Journal* 28 (1985), 491–498; and Robert P. Vecchio, "Predicting Worker Performance in Inequitable Settings," *Academy of Management Review* 7 (1982), 103–110.

20 "The Double Standard That's Setting Worker against Worker," *Business Week*, April 8, 1985, 70–71.

21 James E. Martin and Melanie M. Peterson, "Two-Tier Wage Structures: Implications for Equity Theory," *Academy of Management Journal* 30 (1987), 297–315.

22 Victor H. Vroom, *Work and Motivation* (New York: Wiley, 1964); B. S. Gorgopoulos, G. M. Mahoney, and N. Jones, "A Path–Goal Approach to Productivity," *Journal of Applied Psychology* 41 (1957), 345–353; and E. E. Lawler III, *Pay and Organizational Effectiveness: A Psychological View* (New York: McGraw-Hill, 1981).

23 Richard L. Daft and Richard M. Steers, *Organizations: A Micro/Macro Approach* (Glenview, Ill.: Scott, Foresman, 1986).

24 H. Richlin, *Modern Behaviorism* (San Francisco: Freeman, 1970); and B. F. Skinner, *Science and Human Behavior* (New York: Macmillan, 1953).

25 Tom Peters and Nancy Austin, *A Passion for Excellence: The Leadership Difference* (New York: Random House, 1985), 267.

26 L. M. Sarri and G. P. Latham, "Employee Reaction to Continuous and Variable Ratio Reinforcement Schedules Involving a Monetary Incentive," *Journal of Applied Psychology* 67 (1982), 506–508; and R. D. Pritchard, J. Hollenback, and P. J. DeLeo, "The Effects of Continuous and Partial Schedules of Reinforcement on Effort, Performance, and Satisfaction," *Organizational Behavior and Human Performance* 25 (1980), 336–353.

27 "Creating Incentives for Hourly Workers," *Inc.* (July 1986), 89–90.

28 Norm Alster, "What Flexible Workers Can Do," *Fortune*, February 13, 1989, 62–66.

29 Thomas Petzinger, Jr. "Sharon Wright Follows Her Mother's Legacy Down to the Letter," *The Wall Street Journal*, January 17, 1996, B1.

30 J. Richard Hackman and Greg R. Oldham, *Work Redesign* (Reading, Mass.: Addison-Wesley, 1980); and J. Richard Hackman and Greg Oldham, "Motivation through the Design of Work: Test of a Theory," *Organizational Behavior and Human Performance* 16 (1976), 250–279.

31 Edwin P. Hollander and Lynn R. Offermann, "Power and Leadership in Organizations," *American Psychologist* 45 (February 1990), 179–189.

32 Jay A. Conger and Rabindra N. Kanungo, "The Empowerment Process: Integrating Theory and Practice," *Academy of Management Review* 13 (1988), 471–482.

33 Thomas A. Stewart, "New Ways to Exercise Power," *Fortune* 6 (November 1989), 52–64.

34 David E. Bowen and Edward E. Lawler III, "The Empowerment of Service Workers: What, Why, How, and When," *Sloan Management Review* (spring 1992), 31–39; and Ray W. Coye and James A. Belohav, "An Exploratory Analysis of Employee Participation," *Group and Organization Management* 20, no. 1 (March 1995), 4–17.

35 John Holusha, "Grace Pastiak's 'Web of Inclusion,'" *The New York Times*, May 5, 1991, F1, F6.

36 Arno Penzias, "New Paths to Success," *Fortune*, June 12, 1995, 90–94.

37 Ralph Stayer, "How I Learned to Let My Workers Lead," *Harvard Business Review* (November–December 1990), 66–83.

38 "Au Bon Pain Cools Unit Growth as It Works on Performance," *Nation's Restaurant News*, 30, no. 1, January 1, 1996, 12; "Most Productive Employees," *Boston Globe*, May 23, 1995, 61; Bruce G. Posner, "May the Force Be with You," *Inc.* (July 1987), 70–75.

Communicating in Organizations

CHAPTER OUTLINE

Communication and the Manager's Job
What Is Communication?
The Communication Process

Communicating among People
Perception and Communication
Communication Channels
Nonverbal Communication
Listening

Organizational Communication
Formal Communication Channels
Informal Communication Channels

Communicating in Teams

Managing Organizational Communication
Barriers to Communication
Overcoming Communication Barriers

LEARNING OBJECTIVES

After studying this chapter, you should be able to

- Explain why communication is essential for effective management.

- Define the basic elements of the communication process.

- Describe how perception, nonverbal behavior, and listening affect communication among people.

- Describe the concept of channel richness, and explain how communication channels influence the quality of communication among managers.

- Explain the difference between formal and informal organizational communications and the importance of each for organization management.

- Describe team communication and how structure influences communication outcomes.

- Discuss how open communication and dialogue can enhance team spirit and effectiveness.

- Describe barriers to organizational communication, and suggest ways to avoid or overcome them.

MANAGEMENT PROBLEM

From its beginnings, Wild Oats Market was offbeat, serving up health foods in a tiny market in Boulder, Colorado. Owners Libby Cook, Michael Gilliland and Randy Clapp rang up sales and stocked the shelves themselves. It was easy back then to stay in touch with employees and customers. After four years, though, their success had exacted a price. With 11 stores scattered across three states, they found themselves managing a corporation rather than a tiny market. Employee training and performance reviews had deteriorated. Back when they worked side by side with shelf stockers and produce clerks, they could gauge employee morale, important information for them. As Cook said, "In our business we need to keep our staff happy because they're the first line of defense when customers come into the store." But now they not only could not work alongside them, they couldn't even visit them all. The three owners knew they had to devise some means of knowing what was happening in each store, to get feedback from each worker, so they could prevent potential problems before customers shopped elsewhere.[1]

• If you were in charge of Wild Oats, what would you use to reestablish the lines of communication with employees? Do you think the barriers to communication can be overcome?

The owners of Wild Oats Market believed in communication but faced problems in breaking down communication barriers. In today's intensely competitive environment, top managers at most companies are trying to improve communication. The president of Syntex Corporation, a pharmaceuticals maker, eats breakfast at 7:30 each morning in the employee cafeteria exchanging information with workers. The president and CEO of Windham Hill Records holds weekly one-hour meetings with rank-and-file employees, giving each the opportunity to discuss the week ahead. This formula keeps all employees informed about activities and problems in other departments.[2] Dial-A-Mattress founder and president Napoleon Barragan insists on a "no secrets" culture, believing that a lack of communication is the root of almost every organizational problem. Up-to-the-minute financial, telemarketing, and sales information is relayed to employees daily. Regular meetings serve as forums for cross-departmental communication. The company also solicits ideas and suggestions from customers, suppliers, and even competitors.[3]

These executives are interested in staying connected with employees and customers and with shaping company direction. To do so, they must be in touch; hence they excel at personal communications. Nonmanagers often are amazed at how much energy successful executives put into communication. Consider the comment about Robert Strauss, former chairman of the Democratic National Committee and former ambassador to Russia:

> One of his friends says, "His network is everywhere. It ranges from bookies to bank presidents. . . ."
>
> He seems to find time to make innumerable phone calls to "keep in touch"; he cultivates secretaries as well as senators; he will befriend a middle-level White House aide whom other important officials won't bother with. Every few months, he sends candy to the White House switchboard operators.[4]

This chapter explains why executives such as Robert Strauss, Napoleon Barragan, and the presidents of Windham Hill Records and Syntex Corporation are effective communicators. First we will see how managers' jobs require communication. Next, we will define *communication* and describe a model of the communication process. Then we will consider the interpersonal aspects of communication, including perception, channels, and listening skills, that affect managers' ability to communicate. Next, we will look at the organization as a whole and consider formal upward and downward communications as well as informal communications. Finally, we will examine barriers to communication and how managers can overcome them.

COMMUNICATION AND THE MANAGER'S JOB

How important is communication? Consider this: Managers spend at least 80 percent of every working day in direct communication with others. In other words, 48 minutes of every hour is spent in meetings, on the telephone, or talking informally while walking around. The other 20 percent of a typical manager's time is spent doing desk work, most of which is also communication in the form of reading and writing.[5] Exhibit 15.1 illustrates the crucial position of management in the information network. Managers gather important information from both inside and outside the organization and then distribute appropriate information to others who need it.

Communication permeates every management function described in Chapter 1.[6] For example, when managers perform the planning function, they gather information; write letters, memos, and reports; and then meet with other managers to explain the plan. When managers lead, they communicate with subordinates to motivate them. When managers organize, they gather information about the state of the organization and communicate a new structure to

others. Communication skills are a funda-mental part of every managerial activity.

What Is Communication?

Before going farther, let us determine what communication is. A professor at Harvard once asked a class to define communication by drawing pictures. Most students drew a manager speaking or writing. Some placed "speech balloons" next to their characters; others showed pages flying from a type-writer. "No," the professor told the class, "none of you has captured the essence of communication." He went on to explain that communication means to "share"—not "to speak" or "to write."

Communication thus can be defined as the process by which information is ex-changed and understood by two or more people, usually with the intent to motivate or influence behavior. Communication is not just sending information. This distinc-tion between *sharing* and *proclaiming* is cru-cial for successful management. A manager who does not listen is like a used-car sales-person who claims, "I sold a car—they just did not buy it." Management communica-tion is a two-way street that includes listen-ing and other forms of feedback. Effective communication, in the words of one expert, is as follows:

> When two people interact, they put themselves into each other's shoes, try to perceive the world as the other per-son perceives it, try to predict how the other will respond. Interaction involves reciprocal role-taking, the mutual em-ployment of empathetic skills. The goal of interaction is the merger of self and other, a complete ability to anticipate, predict, and behave in accordance with the joint needs of self and other.[7]

It is the desire to share understanding that motivates executives to visit employees on the shop floor or eat breakfast with them. The things managers learn from direct com-munication with employees shape their un-derstanding of the corporation.

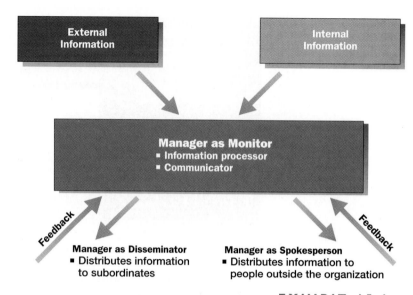

EXHIBIT 15.1
The Manager as Information Nerve Center

SOURCE: Adapted from Henry Mintzberg, *The Nature of Manager-ial Work* (New York: Harper & Row, 1973), 72.

The Communication Process

Many people think communication is sim-ple because they communicate without conscious thought or effort. However, com-munication is usually complex, and the op-portunities for sending or receiving the wrong messages are innumerable. How of-ten have you heard someone say, "But that's not what I meant"? Have you ever received directions you thought were clear and yet still got lost? How often have you wasted time on misunderstood instructions?

To more fully understand the complexity of the communication process, note the key elements outlined in Exhibit 15.2. Two com-mon elements in every communication situ-ation are the sender and the receiver. The *sender* is anyone who wishes to convey an idea or concept to others, to seek informa-tion, or to express a thought or emotion. The *receiver* is the person to whom the message is sent. The sender **encodes** the idea by se-lecting symbols with which to compose a message. The **message** is the tangible for-mulation of the idea that is sent to the re-ceiver. The message is sent through a **channel,** which is the communication car-rier. The channel can be a formal report, a telephone call, or a face-to-face meeting. The receiver **decodes** the symbols to inter-pret the meaning of the message. Encoding

communication
The process by which informa-tion is exchanged and under-stood by two or more people, usually with the intent to mo-tivate or influence behavior.

encode
To select symbols with which to compose a message.

message
The tangible formulation of an idea to be sent to a receiver.

channel
The carrier of a communica-tion.

decode
To translate the symbols used in a message for the purpose of interpreting its meaning.

EXHIBIT 15.2
A Model of the Communication Process

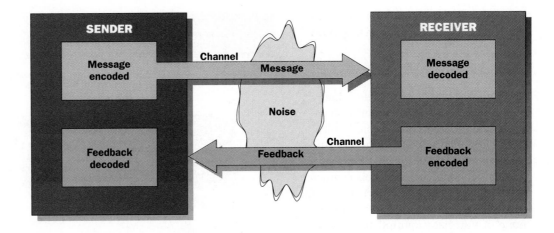

and decoding are potential sources for communication errors, because knowledge, attitudes, and background act as filters and create "noise" when translating from symbols to meaning. Finally, **feedback** occurs when the receiver responds to the sender's communication with a return message. Without feedback, the communication is *one-way*; with feedback, it is *two-way*. Feedback is a powerful aid to communication effectiveness, because it enables the sender to determine whether the receiver correctly interpreted the message.

Managers who are effective communicators understand and use the circular nature of communication. For example, James Treybig of Tandem Computers, Inc., widened the open-door policy in order to communicate with employees. Treybig appears on a monthly television program broadcast over the company's in-house television station. Employees around the world watch the show and call in their questions and comments. The television is the channel through which Treybig sends his encoded message. Employees decode and interpret the message and encode their feedback, which is sent through the channel of the telephone hookup. The communication circuit is complete. Similarly, Tom Monaghan, president of Domino's Pizza, maintains communication channels with employees when he fields complaints for two hours during a monthly "call-in." Monaghan also maintains toll-free numbers on which em-

feedback
A response by the receiver to the sender's communication.

ployees call him directly. Treybig and Monaghan understand the elements of communication and have developed systems that work.[8] More sophisticated systems for communicating between locations or franchisees are described in the Technology for Today box.

COMMUNICATING AMONG PEOPLE

The communication model in Exhibit 15.2 illustrates the components that must be mastered for effective communication. Communications can break down if sender and receiver do not encode or decode language in the same way.[9] The selection of communication channels can determine whether the message is distorted by noise and interference. The listening skills of both parties can determine whether a message is truly shared. Thus, for managers to be effective communicators, they must understand how interpersonal factors such as perception, communication channels, nonverbal behavior, and listening all work to enhance or detract from communication.

Perception and Communication

The way we perceive people is the starting point for how we communicate. When one person wishes to share an idea with another, the message is formulated based on

TECHNOLOGY FOR TODAY
ENTREMKT

The startup of EntreMkt was based on a core belief—we are in a time of great change for American business, and in the future there will be only two types of companies: "those that use database marketing and those that are out of business."

Intending to fill the needs generated by those socioeconomic changes, Paul Carter, Monte Hamilton, and Richard Rennick started the Palm Springs, California, EntreMkt in 1995. It is a specialized Internet service designed to help franchises develop a presence on the World Wide Web in order to attract new franchisees. The company also offers an intranet service, so that franchise groups can communicate with one another about sales, orders, or problems. EntreMkt educates its clients about Internet bulletin boards, mailing lists, and download directories.

Digging for the best ways to exploit technology and the Internet, Hamilton is always searching for new knowledge to pass along to clients. One of the best ways to get information, he says, is on-line databases, whether it is Dun and Bradstreet's Million Dollar Directory, CompuServe's "Biz" File database, or the multitude of databases available on the Internet, using search engines such as Yahoo!, Alta Vista, or others. Hamilton believes Java software, purported to be the coming wave for companies to access huge databases using their own search engines, represents the most exciting part of the Internet's future.

His newest tool for clients is making telephone calls over the Internet, using VocalTec Inc.'s Internet Phone. Working particularly well with international operations, the two units merely connect via the Internet and have a private, voice phone call, paying only for the local phone charge. "It's a way to connect with franchisees all over the world," says Hamilton, "and it's less expensive."

Sylvan Learning Systems connects its franchisees through satellite. Even though the child and adult supplemen-tal-education company must pay $800 for each location's dish, and $1,000 an hour of airtime for its franchisee-training programs, this is much cheaper than the previous method of copying and mailing videotapes.

Accounting firm Padgett Business Services realized its real product was information and saw that more real-time information to its franchisees means more revenues. Changes in tax law have wide implications for their business. In 1995, chairman Dan Sautner ended up calling all 350 franchises about an 11th-hour tax change. But Sautner balked at last year's $50,000 bid to hook up his franchisees with a bulletin board, E-mail, and a chat room. Along came EntreMkt, offering a bulletin board and private E-mail for only $3,000. "At that cost," says Sautner, "you can't *not* do it."

SOURCE: Kristin Dunlap Godsey, "The New CEO: Online Addict," *Success*, Sept. 1996, 57–58; Carol Steinberg, "Wired for Growth," *Success*, March 1996, 69–73; company sources.

references constructed from past events, experiences, expectations, and current motivations. When a receiver hears a message, he or she relies on a particular frame of reference for decoding and understanding it. The more similar the frames of reference between people, the more easily they can communicate.

Perception is the process people use to make sense out of the environment. However, perception in itself does not always lead to an accurate picture of the environment.[10] **Perceptual selectivity** is the process by which individuals screen and select the various objects and stimuli that vie for their attention. Certain stimuli catch their attention, and others do not. Once a stimulus is recognized, individuals organize or catego-rize it according to their frame of reference, that is, **perceptual organization.** Only a partial cue is needed to enable perceptual organization to take place. For example, all of us have spotted an old friend from a long distance and, without seeing the face or other features, recognized the person from the body movement.

The most common form of perceptual organization is stereotyping. A **stereotype** is a widely held generalization about a group of people that assigns attributes to them solely on the basis of one or a few categories, such as age, race, or occupation. For example, young people may assume that older people are old-fashioned or conservative. Students may stereotype professors as absentminded or as political liberals.

perceptual organization
The categorization of an object or stimulus according to one's frame of reference.

perception
The process of making sense out of one's environment.

stereotype
A widely held generalization about a group of people that assigns attributes to them solely on the basis of a limited number of categories.

perceptual selectivity
The screening and selection of objects and stimuli that compete for one's attention.

How do perceptual selectivity and organization affect manager behavior? Consider the following comment from Joe, a staff supervisor, on his expectations about the annual budget meeting with his boss Charlie:

About a month before the meetings are to begin, I find myself waking up around 4:00 A.M., thinking about Charlie and the arguments I'm going to have with him. I know he'll accuse me of trying to "pad" my requests and, in turn, I'll accuse him of failing to understand the nature of my department's needs. I'll be trying to anticipate every little snide remark he can generate and every argument that he's likely to propose, and I'll be getting ready with snide remarks and arguments of my own. This year, as always, I've got to be sure to get him before he gets me.[11]

Selective perception may cause a manager to immediately recognize any cues that reinforce stereotypes. The manager will organize these cues to fit his belief, thus preventing open and honest communication.

Perceptual differences and perceptual mistakes also occur when people perceive simple objects in dissimilar ways. Typical examples are illustrated in Exhibit 15.3. In panel *a*, many people see a sad old woman, but others see a beautiful young lady with a large head covering. In panel *b*, the top airplane looks larger to most people because of perceptual organization. The background lines provide a frame of reference that distorts the actual size of the airplanes.

An important point for managers to understand is that perceptual differences are natural but can distort messages and interfere with communications. Each person has a distinct personality and perceptual style; hence each interprets messages in a personal way. Managers should remember that words can mean different things to different people and should not assume that they already know what the other person or the communication is about.

Communication Channels

Managers have a choice of many channels through which to communicate to other managers or employees. A manager may discuss a problem face-to-face, use the telephone, write a memo or letter, or put an item in a newsletter, depending on the nature of the message. Recent research has attempted to explain how managers select communication channels to enhance communication effectiveness.[12] The research has found that channels differ in their capacity to convey information. Just as a pipeline's physical characteristics limit the kind and amount of liquid that can be pumped through it, a communication channel's physical characteristics limit the kind and amount of information that can be conveyed among managers. The channels available to managers can be classified into a hierarchy based on information richness. **Channel richness** is the amount of information that can be transmitted during a communication episode. The hierarchy of channel richness is illustrated in Exhibit 15.4.

The capacity of an information channel is influenced by three characteristics: (1) the ability to handle multiple cues simultaneously; (2) the ability to facilitate rapid, two-way feedback; and (3) the ability to establish a personal focus for the communication. Face-to-face discussion is the richest medium, because it permits direct experience, multiple information cues, immediate feedback, and personal focus. Face-to-face discussions facilitate the assimilation of broad cues and deep, emotional under-

channel richness
The amount of information that can be transmitted during a communication episode.

EXHIBIT 15.3
Perception: What Do You See?

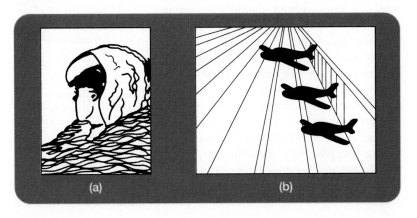

(a)   (b)

EXHIBIT 15.4
Hierarchy of Channel Richness and Application to Messages

Richest Channel ←————————————————→ **Leanest Channel**

Physical presence (face-to-face talk)	Interactive channels (telephone, electronic media)	Personal static channels (memos, letters)	Impersonal static channels (fliers, bulletins, general reports)

Best for nonroutine, ambiguous, difficult messages ←————————————————→ Best for routine, clear, simple messages

standing of the situation. For example, Tony Burns, CEO of Rider Systems, Inc., likes to handle things face-to-face: "You can look someone in the eyes, and you can tell by the look in his eyes or the inflection in his voice what the real problem or question or answer is."[13] Telephone conversations and interactive electronic media, such as voice mail and electronic mail, while increasing the *speed* of communication, lack the element of "being there." Eye contact, gaze, blush, posture, and body language cues are eliminated. In recognition of the need for channel richness, interactive communication is taking on the immediacy of "being there" through increased use of video conferencing. Written media that are personalized, such as memos, notes, and letters, can be personally focused, but they convey only the cues written on paper and are slow to provide feedback. Impersonal written media, including fliers, bulletins, and standard computer reports, are the lowest in richness. These channels are not focused on a single receiver, use limited information cues, and do not permit feedback.

It is important for managers to understand that each communication channel has advantages and disadvantages, and that each can be an effective means of communication in the appropriate circumstances.[14] Channel selection depends on whether the message is routine or nonroutine. *Nonroutine messages* typically are ambiguous, concern novel events, and impose great potential for misunderstanding. Nonroutine messages often are characterized by time pressure and surprise. Managers can communicate nonroutine messages effec-

tively only by selecting rich channels. On the other hand, routine communications are simple and straightforward. *Routine messages* convey data or statistics or simply put into words what managers already agree on and understand. Routine messages can be efficiently communicated through a channel lower in richness. Written communications also should be used when the audience is widely dispersed or when the communication is "official" and a permanent record is required.[15] Aspen Home Health Services found the most effective means for communicating with various members was through high-tech methods.

ASPEN HOME HEALTH SERVICES

Four years ago, Kristen Gunsay started a business to help senior citizens remain self-sufficient and receive health care in the privacy of their own homes. High-tech solutions were the only way for communications to link the home office of the Utah-based Aspen Home Health Services Agency with its network of nurses, medical technicians, doctors, and field case managers—who also need instant access to patient records.

She began with only a fax machine, digital answering machine, and a pager. But as her business grew, she added more computers, modems, cellular phones, and now all five locations are linked together through a Novell network. Field case managers have laptop computers for charting patients' progression, updating patient needs, and for contacting drug databases online. Recent network improvements mean they can now bill Medicare

automatically, avoiding the cost of a medical typist.

Even though Gunsay will spend $100,000 this year on technological improvements, the money is an investment in higher efficiency. For example, they will soon be able to have a caller's patient record onscreen before the telephone is even answered, which means a nurse can handle 33 percent more calls.

High-tech communications have helped Aspen grow to revenues of $3.5 million. One advantage is working in "real time," where an EKG report done in the home can be sent by modem immediately to the physician for evaluation. As Gunsay says, "It links the patient to the doctor without having to leave home."[16] ■

Aspen Home Health Services' high-tech system supports both routine and nonroutine communication. Managers have to determine the appropriate communication channels. Consider a CEO trying to work out a press release with public relations people about a plant explosion that injured 15 employees. If the press release must be ready in three hours, the communication is truly nonroutine and forces a rich information exchange. The group will meet face-to-face, brainstorm ideas, and provide rapid feedback to resolve disagreement and convey the correct information. If the CEO has three days to prepare the release, less information capacity is needed. The CEO and public relations people might begin developing the press release with an exchange of memos and telephone calls.

Nonverbal Communication

nonverbal communication
A communication transmitted through actions and behaviors rather than through words.

Nonverbal communication refers to messages sent through human actions and behaviors rather than through words.[17] Although most nonverbal communication is unconscious or subconscious on our part, it represents a major portion of the messages we send and receive. Most managers are astonished to learn that words themselves carry little meaning. Major parts of the shared understanding from communication come from the nonverbal messages of facial expression, voice, mannerisms, posture, and dress.

Nonverbal communication occurs mostly face-to-face. One researcher found three sources of communication cues during face-to-face communication: the verbal, which are the actual spoken words; the vocal, which include the pitch, tone, and timbre of a person's voice; and facial expressions. According to this study, the relative weights of these three factors in message interpretation are as follows: verbal impact, 7 percent; vocal impact, 38 percent; and facial impact, 55 percent.[18]

This research strongly implies that "it's not what you say but how you say it." Nonverbal messages convey thoughts and feelings with greater force than do our most carefully selected words. Body language often communicates our real feelings eloquently. Thus, while the conscious mind may be formulating vocal messages such as "I'm happy" or "Congratulations on your promotion," the body language may be signaling true feelings through blushing, perspiring, glancing, crying, or avoiding eye contact. When the verbal and nonverbal messages are contradictory, the receiver may be confused and usually will give more weight to behavioral actions than to verbal messages.[19]

A manager's office also sends powerful nonverbal cues. For example, what do the following seating arrangements mean if used by your supervisor? (1) She stays behind her desk, and you sit in a straight chair on the opposite side. (2) The two of you sit in straight chairs away from her desk, perhaps at a table. (3) The two of you sit in a seating arrangement consisting of a sofa and easy chair. To most people, the first arrangement indicates "I'm the boss here" or "I'm in authority." The second arrangement indicates "This is serious business." The third indicates a more casual and friendly "Let's get to know each other."[20] Nonverbal messages can be a powerful asset to communication if they complement and support verbal messages. Managers should pay close attention to nonverbal behavior when communicating. They must learn to coordinate their verbal and nonverbal messages and at the same

EXHIBIT 15.5
Ten Keys to Effective Listening

Keys	Poor Listener	Good Listener
1 Listen actively	Is passive, laid back	Asks questions, paraphrases what is said
2 Find areas of interest	Tunes out dry subjects	Looks for opportunities, new learning
3 Resist distractions	Is easily distracted	Fights or avoids distractions; tolerates bad habits; knows how to concentrate
4 Capitalize on the fact that thought is faster than speech	Tends to daydream with slow speakers	Challenges, anticipates, mentally summarizes; weighs the evidence; listens between the lines to tone of voice
5 Be responsive	Is minimally involved	Nods; shows interest, give and take, positive feedback
6 Judge content, not delivery	Tunes out if delivery is poor	Judges content; skips over delivery errors
7 Hold one's fire	Has preconceptions, starts to argue	Does not judge until comprehension is complete
8 Listen for ideas	Listens for facts	Listens to central themes
9 Work at listening	Shows no energy output; faked attention	Works hard, exhibits active body state, eye contact
10 Exercise one's mind	Resists difficult material in favor of light, recreational material	Uses heavier material as exercise for the mind

SOURCES: Adapted from Sherman K. Okum, "How to Be a Better Listener," *Nation's Business* (August 1975), 62; and Philip Morgan and Kent Baker, "Building a Professional Image: Improving Listening Behavior," *Supervisory Management* (November 1985), 34–38.

time be sensitive to what their peers, subordinates, and supervisors are saying nonverbally.

Listening

Managers who believe that giving orders is the important communication requirement are in for a surprise. The new skill is *listening*, both to customers and to employees. Most executives now believe that important information flows from the bottom up, not the top down, and managers had better be tuned in.[21] In the communication model in Exhibit 15.2, the listener is responsible for message reception, which is a vital link in the communication process. **Listening** involves the skill of receiving messages to accurately grasp facts and feelings to interpret the message's genuine meaning. Only then can the receiver provide the feedback with which to complete the communication circuit. Listening requires attention, energy, and skill.

Many people do not listen effectively. They concentrate on formulating what they are going to say next rather than on what is being said to them. Our listening efficiency, as measured by the amount of material understood and remembered by subjects 48 hours after listening to a ten-minute message, is, on average, no better than 25 percent.[22]

What constitutes good listening? Exhibit 15.5 gives ten keys to effective listening and illustrates a number of ways to distinguish a bad from a good listener. A good listener finds areas of interest, is flexible, works hard at listening, and uses thought speed to mentally summarize, weigh, and anticipate what the speaker says.

Merrill Lynch superbroker Richard F. Green explained the importance of listening to organizational success: "If you talk, you'll like me. If I talk, I'll like you—but if I do the talking, my business will not be served."[23] Tom Peters, the famous management author and consultant, says that executives can become good listeners by observing the following: Effective listening is engaged listening; ask dumb questions, break down barriers by participating with employees in casual get-togethers, force yourself to get out and about, provide listening forums, take notes, promise feedback—and deliver.[24]

listening
The skill of receiving messages to accurately grasp facts and feelings to interpret the genuine meaning.

EXHIBIT 15.6
Downward, Upward, and Horizontal Communication in Organizations

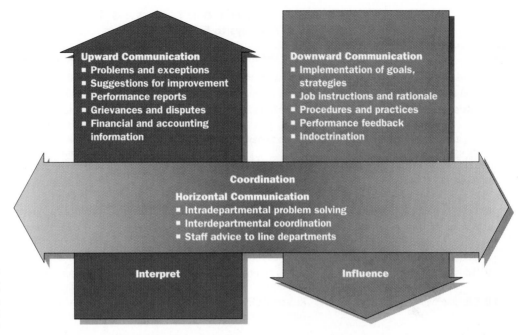

SOURCE: Adapted from Richard L. Daft and Richard M. Steers, *Organizations: A Micro/ Macro Approach*, 538. Copyright © 1986 by Scott, Foresman and Company. Used by permission.

ORGANIZATIONAL COMMUNICATION

Another aspect of management communication concerns the organization as a whole. Organization-wide communications typically flow in three directions—downward, upward, and horizontally. Managers are responsible for establishing and maintaining formal channels of communication in these three directions. Managers also use informal channels, which means they get out of their offices and mingle with employees.

Formal Communication Channels

formal communication channel
A communication channel that flows within the chain of command or task responsibility defined by the organization.

Formal communication channels are those that flow within the chain of command or task responsibility defined by the organization. The three formal channels and the types of information conveyed in each are illustrated in Exhibit 15.6.[25]

downward communication
Messages sent from top management down to subordinates.

Downward Communication. The most familiar and obvious flow of formal communication, **downward communication,** refers to the messages and information sent from top management to subordinates in a downward direction. For example, Mike Olson, plant manager at Ryerson Midwest Coil Processing, holds monthly meetings to discuss financial data and performance analyses with all employees. He also uses other forms of communication. Because workers were continuously dropping expensive power tools, Olson hung price tags on the tools to show the replacement cost; workers solved the problem by finding a way to hook up the tools so they wouldn't be dropped. Olson's communication helps workers see how their actions affect the entire company and creates a climate of working *together* for solutions.[26]

Managers can communicate downward to employees through speeches, messages in company publications, electronic mail, information leaflets tucked into pay envelopes, material on bulletin boards, and policy and procedure manuals. When Gerald M. Lieberman, senior human resources officer at Citicorp, launched the company's Choices '91 flexible benefits plan, he communicated options to 56,000 employees using several information channels: workbooks, videos, seminars, software, and a hot line. Lieberman understands that different

employees are responsive to different kinds of communication. A computer whiz may like information software better than reading a benefits booklet. A secretary may enjoy the give-and-take of an information seminar. Lieberman's communication strategy enabled individual employees to study their options and make wise choices.[27]

Downward communication in an organization usually encompasses the following topics:

1 *Implementation of goals and strategies.* Communicating new strategies and goals provides information about specific targets and expected behaviors. It gives direction for lower levels of the organization. Example: "The new quality campaign is for real. We must improve product quality if we are to survive."

2 *Job instructions and rationale.* These are directives on how to do a specific task and how the job relates to other organizational activities. Example: "Purchasing should order the bricks now so the work crew can begin construction of the building in two weeks."

3 *Procedures and practices.* These are messages defining the organization's policies, rules, regulations, benefits, and structural arrangements. Example: "After your first 90 days of employment, you are eligible to enroll in our company-sponsored savings plan."

4 *Performance feedback.* These messages appraise how well individuals and departments are doing their jobs. Example: "Joe, your work on the computer network has greatly improved the efficiency of our ordering process."

5 *Indoctrination.* These messages are designed to motivate employees to adopt the company's mission and cultural values and to participate in special ceremonies, such as picnics and United Way campaigns. Example: "The company thinks of its employees as family and would like to invite everyone to attend the annual picnic and fair on March 3."

The major problem with downward communication is *drop off*, the distortion or loss of message content. Although formal communications are a powerful way to reach all employees, much information gets lost—25 percent or so each time a message is passed from one person to the next. In addition, the message can be distorted if it travels a great distance from its originating source to the ultimate receiver. A tragic example is the following:

A reporter was present at a hamlet burned down by the U.S. Army 1st Air Cavalry Division in 1967. Investigations showed that the order from the Division headquarters to the brigade was: "On no occasion must hamlets be burned down."

The brigade radioed the battalion: "Do not burn down any hamlets unless you are absolutely convinced that the Viet Cong are in them."

The battalion radioed the infantry company at the scene: "If you think there are any Viet Cong in the hamlet, burn it down."

The company commander ordered his troops: "Burn down that hamlet."[28]

Information drop off cannot be completely avoided, but the techniques described in the previous sections can reduce it substantially. Using the right communication channel, consistency between verbal and nonverbal messages, active listening, and aligning messages with the perception of users can maintain communication accuracy as it moves down the organization. Pat Kelly worked really hard to communicate openness and honesty at PSS, and to reduce the drop off.

 PSS

Pat Kelly started PSS in 1983 and within four years it was profitable. The Jacksonville, Florida-based Physician Sales and Service soon became the premier service provider and could charge higher rates as a result. The future was rosy—until managed care came and costs were squeezed everywhere. No one cared

anymore for paying higher rates, no matter how great the service.

Realizing the only viable change was to become the low-cost supplier, Pat Kelly knew it would be a hard sell with employees. How do you keep a motivated workforce when commissions and bonuses were going to fall? In many cases you don't. Employees grumble and quit. But not at PSS. After a really tough year, the company recovered and is now once again the industry's national leader.

What's the incentive? To have a culture that values openness and honesty. Hire enthusiastic and smart people, then train them endlessly, promoting from within. Give them a piece of the company in terms of stock options. But doing this *after* the change would be less effective. Kelly's key was that he had developed this culture from the beginning. Workers trusted him and knew there were no secrets. So when Kelly leveled with them about the problems and the new strategy, they didn't have to second-guess him and wonder what the real motives were. PSS was then able to get the extraordinary devotion and commitment needed to make the painful change, emerging again on top.

The company remains successful also because Pat Kelly knows the importance of minimizing bureaucracy, letting employees have fun, yet still firing them up with his message: "You'll have to work harder than you ever imagined. But you're part of a company with a future, and we'll put no barriers in the way of your success."[29] ■

Upward Communication.   Formal **upward communication** includes messages that flow from the lower to the higher levels in the organization's hierarchy. Most organizations take pains to build in healthy channels for upward communication. Employees need to air grievances, report progress, and provide feedback on management initiatives. Coupling a healthy flow of upward and downward communication ensures that the communication circuit between managers and employees is complete.[30] Five types of information communicated upward are the following:

upward communication
Messages transmitted from the lower to the higher levels in the organization's hierarchy.

1 *Problems and exceptions.* These messages describe serious problems with and exceptions to routine performance in order to make senior managers aware of difficulties. Example: "The printer has been out of operation for two days, and it will be at least a week before a new one arrives."

2 *Suggestions for improvement.* These messages are ideas for improving task-related procedures to increase quality or efficiency. Example: "I think we should eliminate step 2 in the audit procedure because it takes a lot of time and produces no results."

3 *Performance reports.* These messages include periodic reports that inform management how individuals and departments are performing. Example: "We completed the audit report for Smith & Smith on schedule but are one week behind on the Jackson report."

4 *Grievances and disputes.* These messages are employee complaints and conflicts that travel up the hierarchy for a hearing and possible resolution. Example: "The manager of operations research cannot get the cooperation of the Lincoln plant for the study of machine utilization."

5 *Financial and accounting information.* These messages pertain to costs, accounts receivable, sales volume, anticipated profits, return on investment, and other matters of interest to senior managers. Example: "Costs are 2 percent over budget, but sales are 10 percent ahead of target, so the profit picture for the third quarter is excellent."

Many organizations make a great effort to facilitate upward communication. Mechanisms include suggestion boxes, employee surveys, open-door policies, management information system reports, and face-to-face conversations between workers and executives.

William J. O'Brien, CEO of Hanover Insurance Company, points out: "The fundamental movement in business in the next 25 years will be in the dispersing of power, to give meaning and fulfillment to employees

in a way that avoids chaos and disorder." Power sharing means inviting upward communication. At Pacific Gas & Electric, CEO Richard A. Clark keeps employee communication lines open with employee surveys, biannual video presentations, and monthly brown-bag lunches to hear questions and complaints.[31]

Despite these efforts, however, barriers to accurate upward communication exist. Managers may resist hearing about employee problems, or employees may not trust managers sufficiently to push information upward.[32] One innovative attempt at ensuring that information gets to the top managers without distortion was developed by John Strazzanti, who also made sure employees would get accurate information from above as well.

■ COM-CORP INDUSTRIES

John Strazzanti wanted a different kind of company when he became president of Com-Corp Industries, a $1.3 million metal stamp shop specializing in headlight parts for autos. Strazzanti began his career like many of his employees—on the shop floor as press operator. Over the years, he had learned valuable lessons about what management should and should not do, and he was ready to apply those lessons to create a culture of participation at Com-Corp.

Central to Strazzanti's strategy was the notion that much of the resentment between workers and managers could be removed if workers were informed about how and why the company operated as it did. He began with a series of workshops addressing a myriad of employee concerns and questions, such as how the value of goods is determined in the open market, how long-range organizational planning can help the company meet employee needs, or, on the personal side, how to develop personalized money-management programs.

Strazzanti also gave employees a greater voice in matters that directly concerned them, such as compensation, job security, and the potential for personal improvement and ad-

vancement. A committee of workers sets compensation rates. The committee first determines the going market rate for each job. Employee performance is then measured according to specific criteria, such as safety record, achievement of deadlines, attendance, and parts per hour. Employees who score 80 percent on the review are paid 80 percent of the highest industry pay rate for that job. Since implementation of the program, negative employee turnover (those who leave the company for a higher-paying position elsewhere) has dropped to a mere 2 percent.

The problem of job security was especially important to Strazzanti who, when he worked on the shop floor, was outraged by the lack of company concern for employees' years of dedicated service. Borrowing from the world of academia, he instituted a program of employee "tenure." Full-time workers are eligible after three years' service and, as in academia, must be voted on by those with tenure, requiring a two-thirds vote. Achievement of tenure does not mean employees can loaf on the job, however. If the tenured employee slacks off, so does his or her pay.

Finally, Com-Corp addressed employee concerns for ongoing training and development by creating educational benefits packages for those wishing to continue their education. Approximately 10 percent of Com-Corp's full-time employees are enrolled in educational programs.

Strazzanti is constantly looking for ways to make the management of Com-Corp more democratic. By designing a workplace that treats all workers fairly, he has created a culture based on trust, participation, and a commitment to quality and service.[33] ■

Horizontal Communication. Horizontal communication is the lateral or diagonal exchange of messages among peers or coworkers. It may occur within or across departments. The purpose of horizontal communication is not only to inform but also to request support and coordinate activities. Horizontal communication falls into one of three categories:

horizontal communication
The lateral or diagonal exchange of messages among peers or coworkers.

Valassis Communication, Inc.'s "On the M.O.V.E." committee (which stands for Motivate Our Valassis Employees) researches and implements programs like flexible hours, job sharing, and suggestion review systems, as well as plans a variety of "lighten up" events that contribute to high employee morale and a strong corporate culture. Valassis formed the committee to improve *horizontal communication* and create positive energy across the entire organization. It's one of many techniques VCI uses to stimulate ideas, promote teamwork, and encourage ongoing communication.

informal communication channel
A communication channel that exists outside formally authorized channels without regard for the organization's hierarchy of authority.

management by wandering around (MBWA)
A communication technique in which managers interact directly with workers to exchange information.

1 *Intradepartmental problem solving.* These messages take place among members of the same department and concern task accomplishment. Example: "Betty, can you help us figure out how to complete this medical expense report form?"

2 *Interdepartmental coordination.* Interdepartmental messages facilitate the accomplishment of joint projects or tasks. Example: "Bob, please contact marketing and production and arrange a meeting to discuss the specifications for the new subassembly. It looks like we may not be able to meet their requirements."

3 *Staff advice to line departments.* These messages often go from specialists in operations research, finance, or computer services to line managers seeking help in these areas. Example: "Let's go talk to the manufacturing supervisor about the problem he's having interpreting the computer reports."

Recall from Chapter 9 that many organizations build in horizontal communications in the form of task forces, committees, or even a matrix structure to encourage coordination. For example, Carol Taber, former publisher of *Working Woman,* was bothered by the separation of departments at her magazine. She instituted frequent meetings among department heads and a monthly report to keep everyone informed and involved on a horizontal basis.[34]

Informal Communication Channels

Informal communication channels exist outside the formally authorized channels and do not adhere to the organization's hierarchy of authority. Informal communications coexist with formal communications but may skip hierarchical levels, cutting across vertical chains of command to connect virtually anyone in the organization. For example, to improve communications at SafeCard Services of Jacksonville, Florida, Paul Kahn propped open the door to the executive wing, made the "executives-only" fitness center available to all employees, and began scheduling regular breakfasts and lunches for employees and managers to get together in a relaxed, informal atmosphere. Providing greater opportunities for informal communications helped Kahn turn the struggling company around.[35] An illustration of both formal and informal communications is given in Exhibit 15.7. Note how formal communications can be vertical or horizontal, depending on task assignments and coordination responsibilities.

Two types of informal channels used in many organizations are "management by wandering around" and the "grapevine."

Management by Wandering Around.
The communication technique known as **management by wandering around (MBWA)** was made famous by the books *In Search of Excellence* and *A Passion for Excellence.*[36] These books describe executives who talk directly with employees to learn what is going on. MBWA works for managers at all levels. They mingle and develop positive relationships with employees and learn directly from them about their department, division, or organization. For example, the president of ARCO had a habit of visiting a district field office. Rather than schedule a big strategic meeting with the district supervisor, he would come in unannounced and chat with the lowest-level employees. Andy Pearson of PepsiCo started

his tours from the bottom up: He went directly to a junior assistant brand manager and asked, "What's up?" In any organization, both upward and downward communication are enhanced with MBWA. Managers have a chance to describe key ideas and values to employees and in turn learn about the problems and issues confronting employees.

When managers fail to take advantage of MBWA, they become aloof and isolated from employees. For example, Peter Anderson, president of Ztel, Inc., a maker of television switching systems, preferred not to personally communicate with employees. He managed at arm's length. As one manager said, "I don't know how many times I asked Peter to come to the lab, but he stayed in his office. He wasn't that visible to the troops." This formal management style contributed to Ztel's troubles and eventual bankruptcy.[37] Golden Corral modified MBWA to be Management by Working Down.

GOLDEN CORRAL RESTAURANT

It's too easy for managers to become far removed from the day-to-day operations of their business. The more layers of hierarchy between them means they have to rely on "surrogates"—sophisticated feedback, often from supervisors.

Golden Corral restaurant implemented a solution for this problem. One weekend a year, the 50 top managers work hands-on restaurant duties, so that the chain's decision makers will remember what the business is all about. For example, chief financial officer Lamar Bell spent his weekend setting tables, cutting steaks, and taking out the garbage.

A small-company competitive edge is their quick reaction to marketplace changes, resulting from the closer connection between front-line employees and top management. Now larger companies are seeing the advantages and sending out senior managers to wait on customers. Even an operation with as few as three locations should start this practice, be-

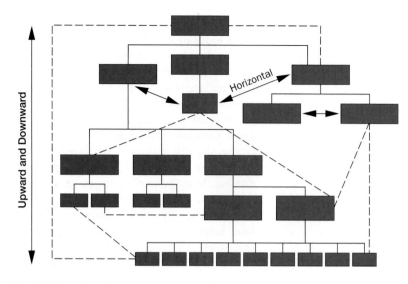

EXHIBIT 15.7
Formal and Informal Organizational Communication Channels

lieves Professor Rollie Tillman, Jr. of the University of North Carolina at Chapel Hill. Otherwise, he says, "you start getting too many pieces of paper and too much to keep track of."

Bell has been working his yearly weekends for all the 11 years he has been with Golden Corral. He has learned a lot, including the fact that store managers may be completing their paperwork at 2 A.M. after working a full day and night in the restaurant. Now he is more careful about the kinds of things he requests of them. "Those managers are serving the customers first," he says. "Anything we require of them is secondary."[38] ∎

Formal channels ———
Informal channels - - - - -

The Grapevine. The **grapevine** is an informal, person-to-person communication network of employees that is not officially sanctioned by the organization.[39] The grapevine links employees in all directions, ranging from the president through middle management, support staff, and line employees. The grapevine will always exist in an organization, but it can become a dominant force when formal channels are closed. In such cases, the grapevine is actually a service because the information it provides helps makes sense of an unclear or uncer-

grapevine
An informal, person-to-person communication network of employees that is not officially sanctioned by the organization.

tain situation. Employees use grapevine rumors to fill in information gaps and clarify management decisions. The grapevine tends to be more active during periods of change, excitement, anxiety, and sagging economic conditions. For example, when Jel, Inc., an auto supply firm, was under great pressure from Ford and GM to increase quality, rumors circulated on the shop floor about the company's possible demise. Management changes to improve quality—learning statistical process control, introducing a new compensation system, buying a fancy new screw machine from Germany—all started out as rumors, circulating days ahead of the actual announcements, and were generally accurate.[40]

Research suggests that a few people are primarily responsible for the grapevine's success. Exhibit 15.8 illustrates the two most typical grapevines.[41] In the *gossip chain*, a single individual conveys a piece of news to many other people. In a *cluster chain*, a few individuals each convey information to several others. Having only a few people conveying information may account for the accuracy of grapevines. If every person told one other person in sequence, distortions would be greater.

Surprising aspects of the grapevine are its accuracy and its relevance to the organization. About 80 percent of grapevine communications pertain to business-related topics rather than personal, vicious gossip. Moreover, from 70 to 90 percent of the details passed through a grapevine are accurate.[42] Many managers would like the grapevine to be destroyed because they consider its rumors to be untrue, malicious, and harmful to personnel. Typically this is not the case; however, managers should be aware that almost five of every six important messages are carried to some extent by the grapevine rather than through official channels. When official communication channels are closed, destructive rumors can occur. Particularly in times of crisis, top executives need to manage communications effectively so that the grapevine is not the only source of information about the company.[43]

COMMUNICATING IN TEAMS

The importance of teamwork in organizations, discussed in more detail in Chapter 16, emphasizes the need for team communication. Team members work together to accomplish tasks, and the team's communication structure influences both team performance and employee satisfaction. Research into team communication has focused on two characteristics: the extent to which team communications are centralized and the nature of the team's task.[44] The relationship between these characteristics is illustrated in Exhibit 15.9. In a **centralized network,** team members must communicate through one individual to solve problems or make decisions. In a **decentralized network,** individuals can communicate freely with other team members. Members process information equally among themselves until all agree on a decision.[45]

In laboratory experiments, centralized communication networks achieved faster solutions for simple problems. Members could simply pass relevant information to a central person for a decision. Decentralized communications were slower for simple problems because information was passed

centralized network
A team communication structure in which team members communicate through a single individual to solve problems or make decisions.

decentralized network
A team communication structure in which team members freely communicate with one another and arrive at decisions together.

EXHIBIT 15.8
Two Grapevine Chains in Organizations

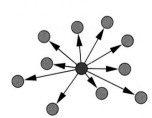

Gossip Chain
(One tells many)

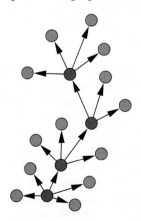

Cluster Chain
(A few tell selected others)

SOURCE: Based on Keith Davis and John W. Newstrom, *Human Behavior at Work: Organizational Behavior,* 7th ed. (New York: McGraw–Hill, 1985).

among individuals until someone finally put the pieces together and solved the problem. However, for more complex problems, the decentralized communication network was faster. Because all necessary information was not restricted to one person, a pooling of information through widespread communications provided greater input into the decision. Similarly, the accuracy of problem solving was related to problem complexity. The centralized networks made fewer errors on simple problems but more errors on complex ones. Decentralized networks were less accurate for simple problems but more accurate for complex ones.[46]

The implication for organizations is as follows: In a highly competitive global environment, organizations use teams to deal with complex problems. When team activities are complex and difficult, all members should share information in a decentralized structure to solve problems. Teams need a free flow of communication in all directions.[47] However, teams who perform routine tasks spend less time processing information, and thus communications can be centralized. Data can be channeled to a supervisor for decisions, freeing workers to spend a greater percentage of time on task activities.

Two recent trends in team communication that reflect management's growing concern for empowering employees and enhancing productivity are open communication and dialogue. **Open communication** means sharing all types of information throughout the company, across functional and hierarchical levels. Many companies, such as Springfield Remanufacturing Corporation and Globe Metallurgical, are opening the financial books to workers at all levels so they understand how and why the company operates as it does. Team approaches that bring together people from different departments require broader information sharing. At Cypress Semiconductor Corporation, which organizes most of its work around projects rather than by strict functional lines, CEO T. J. Rodgers says information is collected and shared in so much detail that the company can be con-

EXHIBIT 15.9
Effectiveness of Team Communication Network

SOURCE: Adapted from A. Bavelas and D. Barrett, "An Experimental Approach to Organization Communication." *Personnel* 27 (1951), 366–371; M. E. Shaw, *Group Dynamics: The Psychology of Small Group Behavior* (New York: McGraw-Hill, 1976); and E. M. Rogers and R. A. Rogers, *Communication in Organizations* (New York: Free Press, 1976).

sidered "transparent."[48] Much of Cypress's open communication is dependent on computer technology, which enables all employees to easily access the information they need to do their jobs effectively. Rykodisc, described in the Leading the Management Revolution box, also illustrates how new technology can enhance communication and help create a sense of community and teamwork even across thousands of miles.

Another means of creating team spirit is **dialogue**, a group communication process aimed at creating a culture based on collaboration, fluidity, trust, and commitment to shared goals.[49] A useful way to describe dialogue is to contrast it with discussion. The intent of discussion, generally, is to deliver one's point of view and to persuade others to adopt it, thus leading to divisiveness and polarization in groups. Dialogue, on the other hand, asks that participants suspend their attachments to a particular viewpoint so that a deeper level of listening, synthesis, and meaning can evolve from the group. Individual differences are acknowledged and respected, but, rather than trying to figure out who is right or wrong, the group searches for an expanded collective perspective. To help them gain a better understanding of their collective challenges and priorities, a human resources group at a successful company undergoing rapid, almost daily, change was introduced to dialogue at a staff retreat. When they returned to their day-to-day activities, employees continued to use dialogue in their meetings.

dialogue
A group communication process aimed at creating a culture based on collaboration, fluidity, trust, and commitment to shared goals.

open communication
Sharing all types of information throughout the company, across functional and hierarchical levels.

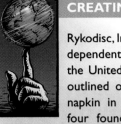

LEADING THE MANAGEMENT REVOLUTION
CREATING COMMUNITY AT RYKODISC

Rykodisc, Inc., the largest independent record label in the United States, was first outlined on the back of a napkin in 1983, when the four founders decided to kick around ideas about U.S. production of compact discs, which at that time were produced solely in Japan and Germany. The biggest problem was that the partners were spread all over the country—from Los Angeles to Philadelphia, from Minneapolis to Salem, Massachusetts—and no one intended to move.

The solution from the beginning was constant information sharing as the cornerstone of the organizational culture. The founders attribute Rykodisc's success to the company's obsession with keeping every type of information constantly flowing among all employees, no matter where they're situated geographically, functionally, or hierarchically. All Rykodisc employees, from the mailroom clerk to the chief financial officer, write and circulate short weekly memos, so that everyone knows what everyone else in the company is doing. Armed with information, Rykodisc employees consistently outproduce larger competitors. The founders and department heads also hold weekly conference calls to talk about specific problems or opportunities.

At first, Rykodisc built its communications primarily around phone calls, faxes, and airline schedules, avoiding networks and E-mail because of a fear that less personal communications might erode the sense of community. Yet it was new technology that led to the birth of Rykodisc, and the founders soon realized that technology could serve as another tool to keep far-flung employees communicating. "Technology itself is a cool medium," says founder Dan Rose, "[but] the way we use it we make it a warm process." He's found that some employees are more comfortable leaving an E-mail message than walking into his office or calling him on the phone. Rose answers all internal E-mail personally and now corresponds regularly with some employees he'd had little interaction with before the company networked.

Rykodisc turned to its own employees rather than to outside talent to make sure its high-tech systems are developed and used in a way that brings people together rather than keeping them apart. One highly motivated employee, Lars Murray, is now responsible for maintaining the Rykodisc Web home page. Visitors to the site can download art and listen to music samples from the Rykodisc catalog. The company is gearing up for the day when music will be distributed online. Rykodisc knows that connection to the customer is a vital part of information flow.

For a company intent on sharing information as broadly as possible, high technology is another tool to maintain a sense of community and keep employees working toward the common goal of "delivering music to the customer."

SOURCE: Hal Plotkin, "Spin Doctors," *Inc. Technology* 2 (1995), 60–64.

As a result, they reported an enhanced ability to work collaboratively, stay focused on goals, and cope with rapid organizational change.[50]

MANAGING ORGANIZATIONAL COMMUNICATION

Many of the ideas described in this chapter pertain to barriers to communication and how to overcome them. Barriers can be categorized as those that exist at the individual level and those that exist at the organizational level. First we will examine communication barriers; then we will look at techniques for overcoming them. These barriers and techniques are summarized in Exhibit 15.10.

Barriers to Communication

Barriers to communication can exist within the individual or as part of the organization.

Individual Barriers.   First, there are interpersonal barriers; these include problems with emotions and perceptions held by employees. For example, rigid perceptual labeling or categorizing of others prevents modification or alteration of opinions. If a

E X H I B I T   1 5 . 1 0
Communication Barriers and Ways to Overcome Them

Barriers	How to Overcome
Individual	
Interpersonal dynamics	Active listening
Channels and media	Selection of appropriate channel
Semantics	Knowledge of other's perspective
Inconsistent cues	MBWA
Organizational	
Status and power differences	Climate of trust
Departmental needs and goals	Development and use of formal channels
Communication network unsuited to task	Changing organization or group structure to fit communication needs
Lack of formal channels	Encouragement of multiple channels, formal and informal

person's mind is made up before the communication starts, communication will fail. Moreover, people with different backgrounds or knowledge may interpret a communication in different ways.

Second, selecting the wrong channel or medium for sending a communication can be a problem. For example, when a message is emotional, it is better to transmit it face-to-face rather than in writing. On the other hand, writing works best for routine messages but lacks the capacity for rapid feedback and multiple cues needed for difficult messages.

Third, semantics often causes communication problems. **Semantics** pertains to the meaning of words and the way they are used. A word such as *effectiveness* may mean achieving high production to a factory superintendent and employee satisfaction to a human resources staff specialist. Many common words have an average of 28 definitions; thus, communicators must take care to select the words that will accurately encode ideas.[51]

Fourth, sending inconsistent cues between verbal and nonverbal communications will confuse the receiver. If one's facial expression does not match one's words, the communication will contain noise and uncertainty. The tone of voice and body language should be consistent with the words, and actions should not contradict words.

Organizational Barriers. Organizational barriers pertain to factors for the organization as a whole. First is the problem of status and power differences. Low-power people may be reluctant to pass bad news up the hierarchy, thus giving the wrong impression to upper levels.[52] High-power people may not pay attention or may feel that low-status people have little to contribute.

Second, differences across departments in terms of needs and goals interfere with communications. Each department perceives problems in its own terms. The production department is concerned with production efficiency and may not fully understand the marketing department's need to get the product to the customer in a hurry.

Third, the communication flow may not fit the team's or organization's task. If a centralized communication structure is used for nonroutine tasks, there will not be enough information circulated to solve problems. The organization, department, or team is most efficient when the amount of communication flowing among employees fits the task.

Fourth, the absence of formal channels reduces communication effectiveness. Organizations must provide adequate upward, downward, and horizontal communication in the form of employee

semantics
The meaning of words and the way they are used.

Employees at Mobil Oil Singapore have fine-tuned their listening skills in a program called EARS, which Mobil managers designed to *overcome communication barriers* and encourage positive, effective communication. As part of the program, employees attend training sessions to show them what to expect when they leave their office to meet customers. The results have improved total quality management because of greater customer loyalty and employees who learn about the ultimate results of their work.

other's perspective. Managers can sensitize themselves to the information receiver so that they will be better able to target the message, detect bias, and clarify missed interpretations. By communicators understanding others' perspectives, semantics can be clarified, perceptions understood, and objectivity maintained.

The fourth individual skill is management by wandering around. Managers must be willing to get out of the office and check communications with others. For example, John McDonnell of McDonnell Douglas always eats in the employee cafeteria when he visits far-flung facilities. Through direct observation and face-to-face meetings, managers develop an understanding of the organization and are able to communicate important ideas and values directly to others.

surveys, open-door policies, newsletters, memos, task forces, and liaison personnel. Without these formal channels, the organization cannot communicate as a whole.

Overcoming Communication Barriers

Managers can design the organization so as to encourage positive, effective communication. Designing involves both individual skills and organizational actions.

Individual Skills   Perhaps the most important individual skill is active listening. Active listening means asking questions, showing interest, and occasionally paraphrasing what the speaker has said to ensure that one is interpreting accurately. Active listening also means providing feedback to the sender to complete the communication loop.

Second, individuals should select the appropriate channel for the message. A complicated message should be sent through a rich channel, such as face-to-face discussion or telephone. Routine messages and data can be sent through memos, letters, or electronic mail, because there is little chance of misunderstanding.

Third, senders and receivers should make a special effort to understand each

Organizational Actions.   Perhaps the most important thing managers can do for the organization is to create a climate of trust and openness. This will encourage people to communicate honestly with one another. Subordinates will feel free to transmit negative as well as positive messages without fear of retribution. Efforts to develop interpersonal skills among employees can be made to foster openness, honesty, and trust.

Second, managers should develop and use formal information channels in all directions. Scandinavian Design uses two newsletters to reach employees. GM's Packard Electric plant is designed to share all pertinent information—financial, future plans, quality, performance—with employees. Bank of America uses programs called Innovate and Idea Tap to get ideas and feedback from employees. Other techniques include direct mail, bulletin boards, and employee surveys.

Third, managers should encourage the use of multiple channels, including both formal and informal communications. Multiple communication channels include written directives, face-to-face discussions, MBWA, and the grapevine. For example, managers at GM's Packard Electric plant

use multimedia, including a monthly newspaper, frequent meetings of employee teams, and an electronic news display in the cafeteria. Sending messages through multiple channels increases the likelihood that they will be properly received.

Fourth, the structure should fit communication needs. For example, Harrah's created the Communication Team as part of its structure at the Casino/Holiday Inn in Las Vegas. The team includes one member from each department. It deals with urgent company problems and helps people think beyond the scope of their own departments to communicate with anyone and everyone to solve those problems. An organization can be designed to use teams, task forces, integrating managers, or a matrix structure as needed to facilitate the horizontal flow of information for coordination and problem solving. Structure should also reflect information needs. When team or department tasks are difficult, a decentralized structure should be implemented to encourage discussion and participation. Dialogue can help team members arrive at collective solutions to complex problems.

SUMMARY AND MANAGEMENT SOLUTION

This chapter described several important points about communicating in organizations. Communication takes up 80 percent of a manager's time. Communication is a process of encoding an idea into a message, which is sent through a channel and decoded by a receiver. Communication among people can be affected by perceptions, communication channels, nonverbal communication, and listening skills.

At the organizational level, managers are concerned with managing formal communications in a downward, upward, and horizontal direction. Informal communications also are important, especially management by wandering around and the grapevine. Moreover, research shows that communication structures in teams and departments should reflect the underlying tasks. Open communication and dialogue can develop a sense of trust and team spirit.

Finally, several barriers to communication were described. These barriers can be overcome by active listening, selecting appropriate channels, engaging in MBWA, developing a climate of trust, using formal channels, and designing the correct structure to fit communication needs. A good example of overcoming barriers to communication occurred at Wild Oats Market, which was described in the chapter's opening management problem.

Because Wild Oats staffers were known for their free-spirited attitudes, Cook, Gilliland, and Clapp developed a questionnaire to evaluate employee morale and satisfaction using potential measures of "awful," and "remarkably bad," to "wonderful," and "terrific." Their "Happiness Index" rated respondents' sentiments from "giddy" to "suicidal." Gilliland discovered that store managers were taking negative criticisms hard, even if they had a lot of "terrifics." To prevent this, he began reviewing the questionnaires to remove gratuituous or nonconstructive carping comments before going over them personally with each manager. The feedback has not only given a clear idea of workforce morale, but has also resulted in employee solutions to specific problems, such as employee participation in a stock option program and a $200 per worker wellness program allowance. Since the program began, turnover has dramatically decreased. Communication and management practices at Wild Oats continue to be successful, for the company now operates 37 stores in eight states and is up to yearly revenues of $100 million.[53]

DISCUSSION QUESTIONS

1 ATI Medical, Inc., has a "no-memo" policy. The 300 employees must interact directly for all communications. What impact do you think this policy would have on the organization?

2 Describe the elements of the communication process. Give an example of each part of the model as it exists in the classroom during communication between teacher and students.

3 How might perception influence communication accuracy? Is perception more important for ambiguous or unambiguous messages? Explain.

4 Should the grapevine be eliminated? How might managers control information that is processed through the grapevine?

5 What do you think are the major barriers to upward communication in organizations? Discuss.

6 What is the relationship between group communication and group task? For example, how should communications differ in a strategic planning group and a group of employees who stack shelves in a grocery store?

7 Some senior managers believe they should rely on written information and computer reports because these yield more accurate data than do face-to-face communications. Do you agree?

8 Why is management by wandering around considered effective communication? Consider channel richness and nonverbal communications in formulating your answer.

9 Is speaking accurately or listening actively the more important communication skill for managers? Discuss.

10 Assume that you have been asked to design a training program to help managers become better communicators. What would you include in the program?

MANAGEMENT EXERCISES

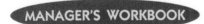

MANAGER'S WORKBOOK

Do You Love Your Company?

Open, honest, and authentic communication can help create the kind of organization that employees love. Here's an instrument to determine which of five key principles your company does best.

	Strongly agree	Somewhat agree	Neutral	Somewhat disagree	Strongly disagree
Capture the Heart					
1 We have a written vision that is known to all and lived every day.	1	2	3	4	5
2 We seek creative, low-cost ways to balance work and family.	1	2	3	4	5
3 We love to celebrate and find innovative ways to inject fun into the workplace.	1	2	3	4	5
Open Communication					
1 It is obvious that management considers internal listening a priority.	1	2	3	4	5
2 Attention is given to using multiple communication channels— more than just using memos and E-mail.	1	2	3	4	5
3 Employees receive feedback in real time (immediate, direct, positive) rather than merely occasional performance appraisals.	1	2	3	4	5
Create Partnerships					
1 There are few, if any, status barriers between employees (i.e., reserved parking, bonuses only for top management, special benefits).	1	2	3	4	5
2 We actively share financial numbers, ratios, and company performance measures with all employees.	1	2	3	4	5

	Strongly agree	Somewhat agree	Neutral	Somewhat disagree	Strongly disagree
3 Management visibly serves the front-line, customer-contact employee first (providing tools, resources, and training) before asking the front-line employee to serve management with reports, paperwork, etc.	1	2	3	4	5
Drive Learning					
1 We guarantee lifelong employability (rather than lifetime employment) through offering extensive training, cross-training, and work variety.	1	2	3	4	5
2 Special attention is given to creating visible, activity-filled programs that help drive learning through all levels of the organization—up, down, and laterally.	1	2	3	4	5
3 We actively support a philosophy of lifelong learning for our employees that goes beyond focusing only on today's job needs.	1	2	3	4	5
Emancipate Action					
1 We allow employees the freedom to fail and try again.	1	2	3	4	5
2 Constant attention is given to creating freedom from bureaucracy, unnecessary sign-offs, outdated procedures, and office politics.	1	2	3	4	5
3 All employees are encouraged to openly challenge the status quo to help find better, faster, more profitable ways to serve our customers.	1	2	3	4	5

Summary score: The higher the score (on any of the five principles), the more you believe this principle is alive and well in your organization. The lower the score, the more your organization needs to address this principle

MANAGER'S WORKBOOK

Listening Self-Inventory

Instructions: Go through the following questions, checking yes or no next to each question. Mark it as truthfully as you can in the light of your behavior in the last few meetings or gatherings you attended.

	Yes	No
1 I frequently attempt to listen to several conversations at the same time.	___	___
2 I like people to give me only the facts and then let me make my own interpretation.	___	___
3 I sometimes pretend to pay attention to people.	___	___
4 I consider myself a good judge of nonverbal communications.	___	___
5 I usually know what another person is going to say before he or she says it.	___	___
6 I usually end conversations that don't interest me by diverting my attention from the speaker.	___	___
7 I frequently nod, frown, or whatever to let the speaker know how I feel about what he or she is saying.	___	___

	Yes	No
8 I usually respond immediately when someone has finished talking.	——	——
9 I evaluate what is being said while it is being said.	——	——
10 I usually formulate a response while the other person is still talking.	——	——
11 The speaker's "delivery" style frequently keeps me from listening to content.	——	——
12 I usually ask people to clarify what they have said rather than guess at the meaning.	——	——
13 I make a concerted effort to understand other people's points of view.	——	——
14 I frequently hear what I expect to hear rather than what is said.	——	——
15 Most people feel that I have understood their point of view when we disagree.	——	——

The correct answers according to communication theory are as follows: No for questions 1, 2, 3, 5, 6, 7, 8, 9, 10, 11, 14. Yes for questions 4, 12, 13, 15. If you missed only one or two questions, you strongly approve of your own listening habits, and you are on the right track to becoming an effective listener in your role as manager. If you missed three or four questions, you have uncovered some doubts about your listening effectiveness, and your knowledge of how to listen has some gaps. If you missed five or more questions, you probably are not satisfied with the way you listen, and your friends and coworkers may not feel you are a good listener either. Work on improving your active listening skills.

MANAGER'S WORKSHOP

Ugli Orange Case

1 Form groups of three members. One person will be Dr. Roland, one will be Dr. Jones, and the third will be an observer.
2 Roland and Jones read only their own roles, while the observer reads both.
3 Role play: Instructor announces: "I am Mr. Cardoza. The owner of the remaining Ugli oranges. My fruit-export firm is based in South America. My country does not have diplomatic relations with your country, although we do have strong trade relations."

Groups spend about 10 minutes meeting with the other firm's representative and decide on a course of action. Be prepared to answer the following questions:
  a What do you plan to do?
  b If you want to buy the oranges, what price will you offer?
  c To whom and how will the oranges be delivered?
4 Observers report the solutions reached. Groups describe decision-making process used.
5 The instructor will lead a discussion on the exercise addressing the following questions:
  a Which groups had the most trust? How did that influence behavior?
  b Which groups shared more information? Why?
  c How are trust and disclosure important in negotiations?

Role of "Dr. Jones"

You are Dr. John W. Jones, a biological research scientist employed by a pharmaceutical firm. You have recently developed a synthetic chemical useful for curing and preventing Rudosen. Rudosen is a disease contracted by pregnant women. If not caught in the first four weeks of pregnancy, the disease causes serious brain, eye, and ear damage to the unborn child. Recently there has been an outbreak of Rudosen in your state, and several thousand women have contracted the disease. You have found, with volunteer patients, that your recently developed synthetic serum cures Rudosen in its early stages. Unfortunately, the serum is made from the juice of the Ugli orange, which is a very rare fruit. Only a small quantity (approximately 4,000) of these oranges were produced last season. No additional Ugli oranges will be available until next season, which will be too late to cure the present Rudosen victims. You've demonstrated that your synthetic serum is in no way harmful to pregnant women. Consequently, there are no side effects. The Food and Drug Administration has approved production and dis-

tribution of the serum as a cure for Rudosen. Unfortunately, the present outbreak was unexpected, and your firm had not planned on having the compound serum available for six months. Your firm holds the patent on the synthetic serum, and it is expected to be a highly profitable product when it is generally available to the public.

You have recently been informed on good evidence that Mr. R. H. Cardoza, a South American fruit exporter, is in possession of 3,000 Ugli oranges in good condition. If you could obtain the juice of all 3,000 you would be able to both cure present victims and provide sufficient inoculation for the remaining pregnant women in the state. No other state currently has a Rudosen threat.

You have recently been informed that Dr. P. W. Roland is also urgently seeking Ugli oranges and is also aware of Mr. Cardoza's possession of the 3,000 available. Dr. Roland is employed by a competing pharmaceutical firm. He has been working on biological warfare research for the past several years. There is a great deal of industrial espionage in the pharmaceutical industry. Over the past several years, Dr. Roland's firm and yours have sued each other for infringement of patent rights and espionage law violations several times.

You've been authorized by your firm to approach Mr. Cardoza to purchase 3,000 Ugli oranges. You have been told he will sell them to the highest bidder. Your firm has authorized you to bid as high as $250,000 to obtain the juice of the 3,000 available oranges.

Role of "Dr. Roland"

You are Dr. P. W. Roland. You work as a research biologist for a pharmaceutical firm. The firm is under contract with the government to do research on methods to combat enemy uses of biological warfare.

Recently several World War II experimental nerve gas bombs were moved from the United States to a small island just off the U.S. coast in the Pacific. In the process of transporting them, two of the bombs developed a leak. The leak is presently controlled by government scientists, who believe that the gas will permeate the bomb chambers within two weeks. They know of no method of preventing the gas from getting into the atmosphere and spreading to other islands, and very likely to the West Coast as well. If this occurs, it is likely that several thousand people will incur serious brain damage or die.

You've developed a synthetic vapor that will neutralize the nerve gas if it is injected into the bomb chamber before the gas leaks out. The vapor is made with a chemical taken from the rind of the Ugli orange, a very rare fruit. Unfortunately, only 4,000 of these oranges were produced this season.

You've been informed on good evidence that a Mr. R. H. Cardoza, a fruit exporter in South America, is in possession of 3,000 Ugli oranges. The chemicals from the rinds of all 3,000 oranges would be sufficient to neutralize the gas if the vapor is developed and injected efficiently. You have also been informed that the rinds of these oranges are in good condition.

You have also been informed that Dr. J. W. Jones is also urgently seeking purchase of Ugli oranges, and he is aware of Mr. Cardoza's possession of the 3,000 available. Dr. Jones works for a firm with which your firm is highly competitive. There is a great deal of industrial espionage in the pharmaceutical industry. Over the years, your firm and Dr. Jones' have sued each other for violations of industrial espionage laws and infringement of patent rights several times. Litigation on two suits is still in process.

The federal government has asked your firm for assistance. You've been authorized by your firm to approach Mr. Cardoza to purchase 3,000 Ugli oranges. You have been told he will sell them to the highest bidder. Your firm has authorized you to bid as high as $250,000 to obtain the rind of the oranges.

Before approaching Mr. Cardoza, you have decided to talk to Dr. Jones to influence him so that he will not prevent you from purchasing the oranges.

SOURCE: Dr. Robert House, The Wharton School of the University of Pennsylvania. Reprinted by permission.

SURF THE 'NET

Surf the 'Net and find examples of companies that offer services to enhance communications for individuals or organizations. Find examples of 10 *different* technologies or services offered.

ETHICAL DILEMMA

The Voice of Authority

When Gehan Rasinghe was hired as an account assistant at Werner and Thompson, a business and financial management firm, he was very relieved. He was overqualified for the job with his degree in accounting, but the combination of his accented English and his quiet manner had prevented him from securing any other position. Beatrice Werner, one of the managing partners of the firm, was impressed by his educational credentials and his courtly manner. She assured him he had advancement potential with the firm, but the account assistant position was the only one available. After months of rejections in his job hunt, Rasinghe accepted the position. He was committed to making his new job work at all costs.

Account Manager Cathy Putnam was Rasinghe's immediate superior. Putnam spoke with a heavy Boston accent, speaking at a lightning pace to match her enormous workload. She indicated to Rasinghe that he would need to get up to speed as quickly as possible to succeed in working with her. It was soon apparent that Putnam and Rasinghe were at odds. She resented having to repeat directions more than once to teach him his responsibilities. He also seemed resistant to making the many phone calls asking for copies of invoices, disputing charges on credit cards, and following up with clients' staff to get the information necessary to do his job. His accounting work was impeccable, but the public contact part of his job was in bad shape. Even his quiet answer of "No problem" to all her requests was starting to wear thin on Putnam. Before giving Rasinghe his three-month review, Putnam appealed to Beatrice Werner for help. Putnam was frustrated at their communication problems and didn't know what to do.

Werner had seen the problem coming. Although she had found Rasinghe's bank reconciliations and financial report preparations to be first-rate, she knew that phone work and client contact were a big part of any job in the firm. But as the daughter of German immigrants, Werner also knew that language and cultural barriers could be overcome with persistence and patience. Diversity was one of her ideals for her company, and it was not always easy to achieve. She felt sure that Rasinghe could become an asset to the firm in time. She worried that the time it would take was more than they could afford to give him.

What Do You Do?

1. Give Rasinghe his notice, with the understanding that a job that is primarily paperwork would be a better fit for him. Make the break now rather than later.
2. Place him with an account manager who has more time to help him develop his assertiveness and telephone skills and appreciates his knowledge of accounting.
3. Create a new position for him, where he could do the reports and reconciliations for several account managers, while their assistants concentrated on the public contact work. He would have little chance of future promotion, however.

CASE FOR CRITICAL ANALYSIS

Atlanta Tool and Die, Inc.

The president of Atlanta Tool and Die, Inc., Rich Langston, wanted to facilitate upward communication. He believed an open-door policy was a good place to start. He announced that his own door was open to all employees and encouraged senior managers to do the same. He felt this would give him a way to get early warning signals that would not be filtered or redirected through the formal chain of command. Langston found that many employees who used the open-door policy had been with the company for years and were comfortable talking to the president. Sometimes messages came through about inadequate policies and procedures. Langston would raise these issues and explain any changes at the next senior managers' meeting.

The most difficult complaints to handle were those from people who were not getting along with their bosses. One employee, Leroy, complained bitterly that his manager had overcommitted the department and put everyone under too much pressure. Leroy argued that long hours and low morale were major problems. But he would not allow Rich Langston to bring the manager into the discussion nor to seek out other employees to confirm the complaint. Although Langston suspected that Leroy might be right, he could not let the matter sit and blurted out, "Have you considered leaving the company?" This made Leroy realize that a meeting with his immediate boss was unavoidable.

Before the three-party meeting, Langston contacted Leroy's manager and explained what was going on. He insisted that the manager come to the meeting willing to listen and without hostility toward Leroy. During the meeting, Leroy's manager listened actively and displayed no ill will. He learned the problem from Leroy's perspective and realized he was over his head in his new job. After the meeting, the manager said he was relieved. He had been promoted into the job from a technical position just a few months earlier and had no management or planning experience. He welcomed Rich Langston's offer to help him do a better job of planning.

Questions

1 What techniques increased Rich Langston's communication effectiveness? Discuss.
2 Do you think that an open-door policy was the right way to improve upward communications? What other techniques would you suggest?
3 What problems do you think an open-door policy creates? Do you think many employees are reluctant to use it? Why?

SOURCE: Based on Everett T. Suters, "Hazards of an Open-Door Policy," *Inc.,* January 1987, 99–102.

ENDNOTES

1 Michele Conklin, "Wild Oats to Sow Expansion," *Rocky Mountain News,* October 9, 1996, 2b; Michele Conklin, "Store Sows Wild Oats in Wash Park," *Rocky Mountain News,* May 3, 1995, 45a; Phaedra Hise, "The Motivational Employee-Satisfaction Questionnaire," *Inc.* (February 1994), 73–75.

2 "Hands On: Tell Us about It," *Inc.* (June 1990), 101; and Thomas F. O'Boyle and Carol Hymowitz, "More Corporate Chiefs Seek Direct Contact with Staff, Customers," *The Wall Street Journal,* February 27, 1985, 1, 12.

3 Jenny C. McCune, "The Open Corporation," *Management Review,* (August 1994), 22.

4 Elizabeth B. Drew, "Profile: Robert Strauss," *The New Yorker,* May 7, 1979, 55–70.

5 Henry Mintzberg, *The Nature of Managerial Work* (New York: Harper & Row, 1973).

6 Fred Luthans and Janet K. Larsen, "How Managers Really Communicate," *Human Relations* 39 (1986), 161–178; and Larry E. Penley and Brian Hawkins, "Studying Interpersonal Communication in Organizations: A Leadership Application," *Academy of Management Journal* 28 (1985), 309–326.

7 D. K. Berlo, *The Process of Communication* (New York: Holt, Rinehart and Winston, 1960), 24.

8 Nelson W. Aldrich, Jr., "Lines of Communication," *Inc.* (June 1986), 140–144.

9 Bruce K. Blaylock, "Cognitive Style and the Usefulness of Information," *Decision Sciences* 15 (winter 1984), 74–91.

10 Richard L. Daft and Richard M. Steers, *Organizations: A Micro/Macro Approach* (Glenview, Ill.: Scott, Foresman, 1986).

11 James R. Wilcox, Ethel M. Wilcox, and Karen M. Cowan, "Communicating Creatively in Conflict Situations," *Management Solutions* (October 1986), 18–24.

12 Robert H. Lengel and Richard L. Daft, "The Selection of Communication Media as an Executive Skill," *Academy of Management Executive* 2 (August 1988), 225–232; and Richard L. Daft and Robert H. Lengel, "Organizational Information Requirements, Media Richness and Structural Design," *Managerial Science* 32 (May 1986), 554–572.

13 Ford S. Worthy, "How CEOs Manage Their Time," *Fortune,* January 18, 1988, 88–97.

14 Ronald E. Rice, "Task Analyzability, Use of New Media, and Effectiveness: A Multi-Site Exploration of Media Richness," *Organizational Science* 3, no. 4 (November 1992), 475–500; and M. Lynne Markus, "Electronic Mail as the Medium of Managerial Choice," *Organizational Science* 5, no. 4 (November 1994), 502–527.

15 Richard L. Daft, Robert H. Lengel, and Linda Klebe Trevino, "Message Equivocality, Media Selection and Manager Performance: Implication for Information Systems," *MIS Quarterly* 11 (1987), 355–368.

16 Kristen Dunlap Godsey, "House Calls," *Success* (April 1996), 50–52.

17 I. Thomas Sheppard, "Silent Signals," *Supervisory Management* (March 1986), 31–33.

18 Albert Mehrabian, *Silent Messages* (Belmont, Calif.: Wadsworth, 1971); and Albert Mehrabian, "Communicating without Words," *Psychology Today* (September 1968), 53–55.

19 Sheppard, "Silent Signals."

20 Arthur H. Bell, *The Complete Manager's Guide to Interviewing* (Homewood, Ill.: Richard D. Irwin, 1989).

21 C. Glenn Pearce, "Doing Something about Your Listening Ability," *Supervisory Management* (March 1989), 29–34; and Tom Peters, "Learning to Listen," *Hyatt Magazine* (spring 1988), 16–21.

22 Gerald M. Goldhaber, *Organizational Communication,* 4th ed. (Dubuque, Iowa: Wm. C. Brown, 1980), 189.

23 Monci Jo Williams, "America's Best Salesman," *Fortune,* October 26, 1987, 122–134.

24 Peters, "Learning to Listen."

25 Daft and Steers, *Organizations;* and Daniel Katz and Robert Kahn, *The Social Psychology of Organizations,* 2d ed. (New York: Wiley, 1978).

26 Roberta Maynard, "It Can Pay to Show Employees the Big Picture," *Nation's Business* (December 1994), 10.

27 Claudia H. Deutsch, "Managing: The Multimedia Benefits Kit," *The New York Times,* October 14, 1990, Sec. 3, 25.

28 J. G. Miller, "Living Systems: The Organization," *Behavioral Science* 17 (1972), 69.

29 John Case, "Corporate Culture," *Inc.,* (November 1996), 42–53; John Case, "The 10 Commandments of Hypergrowth," *Inc.* October 1995, 32.

30 Michael J. Glauser, "Upward Information Flow in Organizations: Review and Conceptual Analysis," *Human Relations* 37 (1984), 613–643; and "Upward/Downward Communication: Critical Information Channels," *Small Business Report* (October 1985), 85–88.

31 Anne B. Fisher, "CEO's Think That Morale Is Dandy," *Fortune,* November 18, 1991, 83–84.

32 Mary P. Rowe and Michael Baker, "Are You Hearing Enough Employee Concerns?" *Harvard Business Review* 62 (May–June 1984), 127–135; W. H. Read, "Upward Communication in Industrial Hierarchies," *Human Relations* 15 (February 1962), 3–15; and Daft and Steers, *Organizations.*

33 Teri Lammers Prior, "If I Were President," *Inc.* (April 1995), 56–61.

34 Jacqueline Kaufman, "Carol Taber, Working Woman," *Management Review* (October 1986), 60–61.

35 Nancy K. Austin, "The Skill Every Manager Must Master," *Working Woman* (May 1995), 29–30.

36 Thomas J. Peters and Robert H. Waterman Jr., *In Search of Excellence* (New York: Harper & Row, 1982); and Tom Peters and Nancy Austin, *A Passion for Excellence: The Leadership Difference* (New York: Random House, 1985).

37 Lois Therrien, "How Ztel Went from Riches to Rags," *Business Week,* June 17, 1985, 97–100.

38 Roberta Maynard, "Back to the Basics," *Nation's Business* (December 1996), 38–39.

39 Keith Davis and John W. Newstrom, *Human Behavior at Work: Organizational Behavior,* 7th ed. (New York: McGraw-Hill, 1985).

40 Joshua Hyatt, "The Last Shift," *Inc.* (February 1989), 74–80.

41 Goldhaber, *Organizational Communication;* and Philip V. Louis, *Organizational Communication,* 3d ed. (New York: Wiley, 1987).

42 Donald B. Simmons, "The Nature of the Organizational Grapevine," *Supervisory Management* (November 1985), 39–42; and Davis and Newstrom, *Human Behavior.*

43 Timothy Galpin, "Pruning the Grapevine," *Training and Development* (April 1995), 28–33.

44 E. M. Rogers and R. A. Rogers, *Communication in Organizations* (New York: Free Press, 1976); and A. Bavelas and D. Barrett, "An Experimental Approach to Organization Communication," *Personnel* 27 (1951), 366–371.

45 This discussion is based on Daft and Steers, *Organizations*.

46 Bavelas and Barrett, "An Experimental Approach"; and M. E. Shaw, *Group Dynamics: The Psychology of Small Group Behavior* (New York: McGraw-Hill, 1976).

47 Richard L. Daft and Norman B. Macintosh, "A Tentative Exploration into the Amount and Equivocality of Information Processing in Organizational Work Units," *Administrative Science Quarterly* 26 (1981), 207–224.

48 D. Keith Denton, "Open Communication," *Business Horizons* (September–October 1993), 64–69.

49 The discussion is based on Glenna Gerard and Linda Teurfs, "Dialogue and Organizational Transformation," in *Community Building: Renewing Spirit and Learning in Business*, ed. Kazinierz Gozdz (New Leaders Press, 1995), 142–153; and Edgar H. Schein, "On Dialogue, Culture, and Organizational Learning," *Organizational Dynamics* (autumn 1993), 40–51.

50 Gerard and Teurfs, "Dialogue and Organizational Transformation."

51 James A. F. Stoner and R. Edward Freeman, *Management*, 4th ed. (Englewood Cliffs, N.J.: Prentice-Hall, 1989).

52 Janet Fulk and Sirish Mani, "Distortion of Communication in Hierarchical Relationships," in *Communication Yearbook*, vol. 9, ed. M. L. McLaughlin (Beverly Hills, Calif.: Sage, 1986), 483–510.

53 Conklin, "Wild Oats to Sow Expansion"; Conklin, "Store Sows Wild Oats in Wash Park"; Hise, "The Motivational Employee-Satisfaction Questionnaire."

Teamwork in Organizations

CHAPTER OUTLINE

LEARNING OBJECTIVES

After studying this chapter, you should be able to

- Identify the types of teams in organizations.

- Discuss new applications of teams to facilitate employee involvement.

- Identify roles within teams and the type of role you could play to help a team be effective.

- Explain the general stages of team development.

- Explain the concepts of team cohesiveness and team norms and their relationship to team performance.

- Understand the causes of conflict within and among teams and how to reduce conflict.

- Discuss the assets and liabilities of organizational teams.

MANAGEMENT PROBLEM

Tom Huber, president of Hearing Technology, Inc., founded his hearing-aid company to provide a flexible response to dealers. His six employees could provide a rapid three-day response to dealers for custom hearing aids. The sales, production, and credit people had the right attitude to make things happen. But when the company quickly grew to 80 employees, response times for orders stretched to eight days, enough to cause dealers to try other manufacturers. Moreover, the dealers complained about the sluggish credit department, its poor coordination with production and sales, and the slowness with which suggestions were implemented. Huber tried to refocus everyone's efforts by one-on-one sessions and speeches, but sluggishness remained. Huber started to wonder if his company, at 80 employees, had grown so inflexible and unresponsive that it could not be competitive.[1]

• What would you recommend to Tom Huber to recapture flexibility and responsiveness in his growing company? How might the formation of teams help solve this problem?

The problems facing a small business like Hearing Technology also confront large companies. How can they be more flexible and responsive in an increasingly competitive global environment? A quiet revolution is taking place in corporate America as more companies try using teams as a solution. The notion of teamwork is changing the look of organizations. Teams are replacing individuals as the basic building block of organizations. The significance of teamwork is reflected by the results of a *Wall Street Journal* survey of 200 *Fortune* 500 companies that found that teamwork was the most frequent topic to be taught in company training programs.[2] In an article called "The Team as Hero," the author argues that

> if we are to compete in today's world, we must begin to celebrate collective entrepreneurship, endeavors in which the whole of the effort is greater than the sum of individual contributions. We need to honor our teams more, our aggressive leaders and maverick geniuses less.[3]

Teams are popping up in the most unexpected places. At Mattel, a team of artists, toy designers, computer experts, and automobile designers slashed 13 months from the usual toy design process, creating Top Speed toy cars in only 5 months. Volvo uses teams of hourly workers to assemble a complete car, abandoning the assembly line. Hecla Mining Company uses teams for company goal-setting; a major telecommunications company uses teams of salespeople to deal with big customers with complex purchasing requirements; and Lassiter Middle School in Jefferson County, Kentucky, uses teams of teachers to prepare daily schedules and handle student discipline problems. Multinational corporations are now using international teams composed of managers from different countries. Ford uses teams to spot quality problems and improve efficiency, and other manufacturers use teams to master sophisticated new production technologies.[4] And as we saw in Chapter 8, teams are often used to make important decisions, and many orga-

nizations are now run by top management teams under the title of Office of the CEO.

As we will see in this chapter, teams have emerged as a powerful management tool, because they involve and empower employees. Teams can cut across organizations in unusual ways. Hence workers are more satisfied, and higher productivity and product quality typically result. Moreover, managers discover a more flexible organization in which workers are not stuck in narrow jobs.

This chapter focuses on teams and their new applications within organizations. We will define various types of teams, explore their stages of development, and examine such characteristics as size, cohesiveness, and norms. We will discuss how individuals can make contributions to teams and review the benefits and costs associated with teamwork. Teams are an important aspect of organizational life, and the ability to manage them is an important component of manager and organization success.

TEAMS AT WORK

In this section, we will first define teams and then discuss a model of team effectiveness that summarizes the important concepts.

What Is a Team?

A **team** is a unit of two or more people who interact and coordinate their work to accomplish a specific goal.[5] This definition has three components. First, two or more people are required. Teams can be quite large, running to as many as 75 people, although most have fewer than 15 people. Second, people in a team have regular interaction. People who do not interact, such as when standing in line at a lunch counter or riding in an elevator, do not compose a team. Third, people in a team share a performance goal, whether it be to design a new type of hand calculator or write a textbook. Students often are assigned to teams to do classwork assignments, in which case

team
A unit of two or more people who interact and coordinate their work to accomplish a specific goal.

the purpose is to perform the assignment and receive an acceptable grade.

Although a team is a group of people, the two terms are not interchangeable. An employer, a teacher, or a coach can put together a *group* of people and never build a *team*. The team concept implies a sense of shared mission and collective responsibility. Exhibit 16.1 lists the primary differences between groups and teams. Coaches such as Grambling's Eddie Robinson or Indiana's Bobby Knight can testify that their most successful teams may have less individual talent and fewer stars but achieve higher levels of success through shared leadership, purpose, and responsibility by all members working toward a common goal.[6]

Model of Work Team Effectiveness

Some of the factors associated with team effectiveness are illustrated in Exhibit 16.2. Work team effectiveness is based on two outcomes—productive output and personal satisfaction.[7] *Satisfaction* pertains to the team's ability to meet the personal needs of its members and hence maintain their membership and commitment. *Productive output* pertains to the quality and quantity of task outputs as defined by team goals.

The factors that influence team effectiveness begin with the organizational context.[8] The organizational context in which the group operates is described in other chapters and includes such factors as structure, strategy, environment, culture, and reward systems. Within that context, managers define teams. Important team characteristics are the type of team, the team structure, and team composition. Managers must decide when to create permanent teams within the formal structure and when to use a temporary task team. Team size and roles also are important. Managers must also consider whether a team is the best way to do a task. If costs outweigh benefits, managers may wish to assign an individual employee to the task. St. Luke's advertising agency has created an organization structure that looks

more like a team than a hierarchical structure, for the founders feel it fits most closely with their mission and values.

■ ST. LUKE'S

If Quest sounds to you like a medieval computer game, think again. It doubles in meaning as a "QUalifying Employee Shareholder Trust" or communal-type ownership, and as the name of decision makers at the rebellious young British ad agency of St. Luke's.

All 55 employees own equal share in the agency, governed by the five-member council, the Quest. "Board" sounded too pinstripy and identified with "privilege." Founders Andy Law and David Abraham want to remove organizational barriers. "There's no rule about who's got the greatest ability to contribute," says Law. "The idea is king."

But St. Luke's is on a greater mission than testing shared ownership. Rather, it seeks to be advertising's new role model: "honest, ethical

Teams are emerging as a *powerful management tool* and are popping up in the most unexpected places, such as this manufacturing cell at TRINOVA's Aeroquip Inoac facility in Fremont, Ohio. The facility uses more than 40 teams that cross operations and job functions, helping the company eliminate non-value-added activities, lower costs, improve customer responsiveness, and increase quality. Toyota recently selected the Fremont facility, a joint venture between Aeroquip and Japan's Inoac Corporation, to participate in its prestigious Toyota Production System Strategic Program.

advertising that represents a company's Total Role in Society," or TRS. Hung about its hallways is the mission: "Profit Is Like Health. You Need It, But It Is Not What You Live For . . . "

They have a hard road ahead. Gallup's 1995 American survey of ethical occupations placed advertising down near the bottom, ahead of only congressmembers and used-car salespeople.

Last year the group left en masse from another agency and decided to name itself after a St. Luke gospel parable. Convinced of systemic industry problems needing attention, the members see twenty-first-century companies being required to apply the sorts of principles, namely ethics, proposed millennia ago by Aristotle.

As the fastest-growing ad agency in London, it already has annual billings of $72 million. To Law and Abraham, though, the primary purpose is a general restoration of commerce. Unlike agencies that build up a business and then milk its profits later during decline, the two have a more lasting purpose. Says Law, "We've created this company to live beyond us. We're just renting resources." Since the company is a collective, everyone is equal. "What's disappeared are ego and greed, the two major driving forces behind the advertising business."[9] ■

The team characteristics listed in Exhibit 16.2 influence processes internal to the team, which in turn affect output and satisfaction. Leaders must understand and manage stages of development, cohesiveness, norms, and conflict in order to establish an effective team. These processes are influenced by team and organizational characteristics and by the ability of members and leaders to direct these processes in a positive manner.

The model of team performance in Exhibit 16.2 is the basis for this chapter. In the following sections, we will examine types of organizational teams, team structure, internal processes, and team benefits and costs.

TYPES OF TEAMS

Many types of teams can exist within organizations. The easiest way to classify teams is in terms of those created as part of the organization's formal structure and those created to increase employee participation.

Formal Teams

Formal teams are created by the organization as part of the formal organization structure. Two common types of formal teams are vertical and horizontal, which typically represent vertical and horizontal structural relationships, as described in Chapter 9. These two types of teams are illustrated in Exhibit 16.3 on page 514. A third type of formal team is the special-purpose team.

---

formal team
A team created by the organization as part of the formal organization structure.

EXHIBIT 16.1
Differences between Groups and Teams

Group	Team
Has a designated strong leader	Shares or rotates leadership roles
Individual accountability	Individual and mutual accountability (accountable to each other)
Identical purpose for group and organization	Specific team vision or purpose
Individual work products	Collective work products
Runs efficient meetings	Meetings encourage open-ended discussion and problem solving
Effectiveness measured indirectly by influence on business (such as financial performance)	Effectiveness measured directly by assessing collective work
Discusses, decides, delegates work to individuals	Discusses, decides, shares work

SOURCE: Adapted from Jon R. Katzenbach and Douglas K. Smith, "The Discipline of Teams," *Harvard Business Review* (March April 1995), 111–120.

EXHIBIT 16.2
Work Team Effectiveness Model

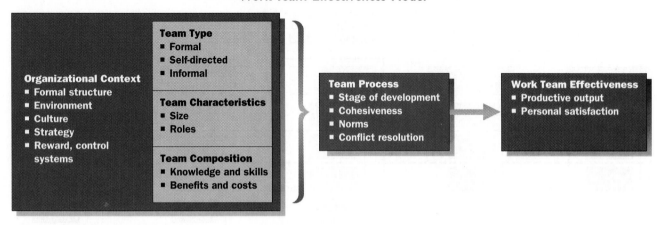

Vertical Team. A **vertical team** is composed of a manager and his or her subordinates in the formal chain of command. Sometimes called a *functional team* or a *command team,* the vertical team may in some cases include three or four levels of hierarchy within a functional department. Typically, the vertical team includes a single department in an organization. The third-shift nursing team on the second floor of St. Luke's Hospital is a vertical team that includes nurses and a supervisor. A financial analysis department, a quality control department, an accounting department, and a human resource department are all command teams. Each is created by the organization to attain specific goals through members' joint activities and interactions.

Horizontal Team. A **horizontal team** is composed of employees from about the same hierarchical level but from different areas of expertise.[10] A horizontal team is drawn from several departments, is given a specific task, and may be disbanded after the task is completed. The two most common types of horizontal teams are task forces and committees.

As described in Chapter 9, a *task force* is a group of employees from different departments formed to deal with a specific activity and existing only until the task is completed. Sometimes called a *cross-functional team,* the task force might be used to create a new product in a manufacturing organization or a new history curriculum in a university. Several departments are involved, and many views have to be considered, so these tasks are best served with a horizontal team. IBM used a large task force to develop the System 360. Contact among team members was intense, and principal players met every day.

A **committee** is generally long-lived and may be a permanent part of the organization's structure. Membership on a committee is usually decided by a person's title or position rather than by personal expertise. A committee often needs official representation, compared with selection for a task force, which is based on personal qualifications for solving a problem. Committees typically are formed to deal with tasks that recur regularly. For example, a grievance committee handles employee grievances; an advisory committee makes recommendations in the areas of employee compensation and work practices; a worker-management committee may be concerned with work rules, job design changes, and suggestions for work improvement.[11]

As part of the horizontal structure of the organization, task forces and committees offer several advantages: (1) They allow

vertical team
A formal team composed of a manager and his or her subordinates in the organization's formal chain of command.

committee
A long-lasting, sometimes permanent team in the organization structure created to deal with tasks that recur regularly.

horizontal team
A formal team composed of employees from about the same hierarchical level but from different areas of expertise.

E X H I B I T   1 6 . 3
Horizontal and Vertical Teams in an Organization

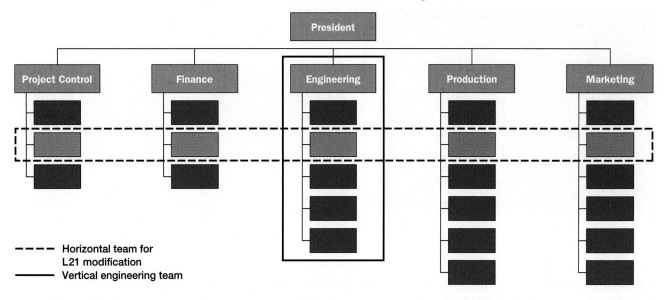

organization members to exchange information; (2) they generate suggestions for coordinating the organizational units that are represented; (3) they develop new ideas and solutions for existing organizational problems; and (4) they assist in the development of new organizational practices and policies.

special-purpose team
A team created outside the formal organization to undertake a project of special importance or creativity.

Special-Purpose Team. Special-purpose teams are created outside the formal organization structure to undertake a project of special importance or creativity. McDonald's created a special team to create the Chicken McNugget. E. J. (Bud) Sweeney was asked to head up a team to bring bits of batter-covered chicken to the marketplace. The McNugget team needed breathing room and was separated from the formal corporate structure to give it the autonomy to perform successfully. A special-purpose team is still part of the formal organization and has its own reporting structure, but members perceive themselves as a separate entity.[12] Birkenstock uses special-purpose teams to interview job candidates and finds this helps keep its distinctive culture.

■ **BIRKENSTOCK**

Birkenstock human resource manager Mary Pischke remembers wondering who would ever wear *those* shoes. That is, until she got hired by the company, after which she bought 27 pairs. The podiatrically positive shoes were introduced from Europe to the United States in 1964 by Margot Fraser, who wanted to build a company with a heart and a soul, embracing "kindness, integrity, and respect for the earth" as daily business practices. She uses the company to create "positive, harmonious relationships with employees, customers, and vendors."

Sound too touchy-feely for Real Business? Then consider their success over the years. After minute growth over decades, revenues were $50 million for 1992 and $100 million for 1995. Still, the company knows the competition is intense. Managers and employees must stretch and learn in order to react to marketplace changes.

Part of the Novato, California, organization's success is due to finding the kind of people who share Fraser's positive and holistic

business vision. In the early days, it was not hard finding workers who were essentially the "nonprofit" type but could fit in a for-profit business. Nowadays, the process is more difficult, and the company had to develop a system to identify the right people. With only 130 employees, any "rotten apple" could damage the work environment.

Candidates are interviewed by 3- to 12-member employee teams, who meet first to develop a list of questions. After the interview, the team decides whether to hire or if another interview is needed. Teams decide by consensus. Greater involvement in the hiring also empowers current employees, further strengthening the company.

Such a process takes more time and therefore money, but Pischke believes it is a worthwhile investment, as they see the payoffs later on. Now employees take more responsibility for the new recruit, and hiring is done more thoughtfully than before. Vice-president Mary Jones says that getting the right "fit" in hiring is important. "Today's market makes maintaining our culture real tough."[13] ■

Self-Directed Teams

Employee involvement through teams is designed to increase the participation of low-level workers in decision making and the conduct of their jobs, with the goal of improving performance. Employee involvement represents a revolution in business prompted by the success of teamwork in Japanese companies. Hundreds of companies, large and small, are jumping aboard the bandwagon, including Boeing, LTV Steel, Cummins Engine, and Tektronix. Employee involvement started out simply with techniques such as information sharing with employees or asking employees for suggestions about improving the work. Gradually, companies moved toward greater autonomy for employees, which led first to problem-solving teams and then to self-directed teams.[14]

Problem-solving teams typically consist of 5 to 12 hourly employees from the same department who voluntarily meet to discuss ways of improving quality, efficiency, and the work environment. Recommendations are proposed to management for approval. Problem-solving teams are usually the first step in a company's move toward greater employee participation. The most widely known application is quality circles, initiated by the Japanese, in which employees focus on ways to improve quality in the production process. USX has adopted this approach in several of its steel mills, recognizing that quality takes a team effort. Under the title All Product Excellence program (APEX), USX set up 40 APEX teams of up to 12 employees at its plant in West Mifflin, Pennsylvania. These teams meet several times a month to solve quality problems. The APEX teams have since spread to mills in Indiana, Ohio, and California.[15]

As a company matures, problem-solving teams can gradually evolve into self-directed teams, which represent a fundamental change in how employee work is organized. **Self-directed teams** consist of 5 to 20 multiskilled workers who rotate jobs and produce an entire product or service. Self-directed teams are permanent teams that typically include the following elements:

- The team includes employees with several skills and functions, and the combined skills are sufficient to perform a major organizational task. A team may include members from the foundry, machining, grinding, fabrication, and sales departments, with each member cross-trained to perform one another's jobs. The team eliminates barriers among departments, enabling excellent coordination to produce a product or service.

- The team is given access to resources such as information, equipment, machinery, and supplies needed to perform the complete task.

- The team is empowered with decision-making authority, which means that members have the freedom to select new members, solve problems, spend money, monitor results, and plan for the future.[16]

self-directed team
A team consisting of 5 to 20 multiskilled workers who rotate jobs to produce an entire product or service, often supervised by an elected member.

problem-solving team
Typically 5 to 12 hourly employees from the same department who meet to discuss ways of improving quality, efficiency, and the work environment.

In a self-directed team, team members take over managerial duties such as scheduling work or vacations or ordering materials. They work with minimum supervision, perhaps electing one of their own as supervisor, who may change each year. At AT&T Credit Corporation, teams of 10 to 15 workers make their own decisions about how to deal with customers, schedule their time off, reassign work when people are absent, and interview prospective employees. The teams are able to process up to 800 credit applications a day, versus 400 previously, and are often able to reach a final answer in 24 hours rather than the three or four days it once took.[17]

Self-directed teams can be highly effective. Service companies like Federal Express and IDS have boosted productivity up to 40 percent by adopting self-directed teams. Volvo uses self-directed teams of 7 to 10 hourly workers to assemble four cars per shift. However, there is still a reluctance among management to entrust workers with managerial responsibilities and duties. A survey conducted by the University of Southern California's Center for Effective Organizations found that, although 68 percent of *Fortune* 1000 companies report using self-directed teams, only 10 percent of workers are involved.[18]

One type of self-directed team, the virtual team, has resulted from globalization and advances in technology. **Virtual teams** use computer technology and groupware to tie together geographically distant members working toward a common goal. Virtual teams can be formed within an organization whose plants and offices are scattered across the nation or around the world. A company may also use virtual teams in partnership with suppliers or, in many cases, with competitors to pull together the best minds to complete a project or speed a new product to market. Leadership among team members is shared or altered, depending on the area of expertise needed at each point in the project. The success of virtual teams is dependent upon several crucial elements, including careful selection of partners and team members,

virtual team
A team that uses computer technology and groupware so that geographically distant members can collaborate on projects and reach common goals.

strong management support of the team and its goals, clear goals, utilization of the best communications tools and procedures, the development of trust among all members, and information sharing.[19] Virtual teams can be used by groups of entrepreneurs, as well, to help them improve their business practices, as described in the Technology for Today box.

WORK TEAM CHARACTERISTICS

Teams in organizations take on characteristics that are important to internal processes and team performance. Two characteristics of concern to managers are team size and member roles.

Size

The ideal size of work teams is often thought to be 7, although variations of from 5 to 12 are typically associated with good team performance. These teams are large enough to take advantage of diverse skills, enable members to express good and bad feelings, and aggressively solve problems. They are also small enough to permit members to feel an intimate part of the group.

In general, as a team increases in size, it becomes harder for each member to interact with and influence the others. A summary of research on group size suggests the following:

1 Small teams (2 to 4 members) show more agreement, ask more questions, and exchange more opinions. Members want to get along with one another. Small teams report more satisfaction and enter into more personal discussions. They tend to be informal and make few demands on team leaders.

2 Large teams (12 or more) tend to have more disagreements and differences of opinion. Subgroups often form, and conflicts among them occur, ranging from protection of "turf" to trivial matters such as "what kind of coffee is brewing

TECHNOLOGY FOR TODAY
LEARNING THROUGH BUSINESS IMPROVEMENT GROUPS

Entrepreneurs and small businesses often lack concrete information or standards to evaluate which parts of their businesses are doing well and which parts are not. Such data would give them the freedom to concentrate on the poorly performing areas and leave the adequate parts alone.

Business Improvement Groups (BIG) were started for small business owners through Marshall University in West Virginia by John B. Wallace and George G. Stollings. As a group, members compared performance, shared tricks of the trade, and were supportive while others implemented changes. After the trial period, members reported benefits to their company of ten times what the program had cost.

Though the pilot program was conducted with solo practice dentists, Wallace and Stollings believe this model would work equally well for any professional group, be it doctors, lawyers, veterinarians, or architects, for none of these groups received regular course work in becoming an entrepreneur. Managing the business, they found, is not merely spending money, it is a matter of "how you make money, how you market your practice, how to advertise," and how to get referrals.

Using the technology of Interfirm Comparison (IFC), the "learning cycle" starts with each business's problems and goals, with the long-term strategy of "self-directed learning" and "action learning." IFC systems do not work unless the indicators are for similar businesses with similar conditions, the information is held in confidence, and the top partners in the business are the members. Lower-level associates rarely have much influence on policy. By joining the BIG, "Dr. Tom" saw that his profits and growth were low, even though he worked as many hours as his colleagues. Changing *how* he was working was the answer, rather than merely putting in more hours. It was obvious from looking at the data that his ability to achieve financial independence was less than others', for he was investing less in his business. BIG indicators also helped him see he was not service-oriented enough.

After analyzing problems and making changes, "Dr. Tom" went from a monthly gross of $13,000 to $30,000. Before BIG, he was so disgusted with dentistry, he almost quit. Now he realizes it wasn't dentistry he hated. His own poor management had caused his near-exit from the field in which he now does so well.

SOURCE: Adapted from John B. Wallace and George G. Stollings, "Business Improvement Groups: A Basis for SBI Strategic Alliances?" Edward Lowe Foundation, SBANET #1228.

---

in the pot." Demands on leaders are greater because there is more centralized decision making and less member participation. Large teams also tend to be less friendly. Turnover and absenteeism are higher in a large team, especially for blue-collar workers. Because less satisfaction is associated with specialized tasks and poor communication, team members have fewer opportunities to participate and feel an intimate part of the group.[20]

As a general rule, large teams make need satisfaction for individuals more difficult; thus, there is less reason for people to remain committed to their goals. Teams of from 5 to 12 seem to work best. If a team grows larger than 20, managers should divide it into subgroups, each with its own members and goals.

Member Roles

For a team to be successful over the long run, it must be structured so as to both maintain its members' social well-being and accomplish its task. In successful teams, the requirements for task performance and social satisfaction are met by the emergence of two types of roles: task specialist and socioemotional.[21]

People who play the **task specialist role** spend time and energy helping the team reach its goal. They often display the following behaviors:

■ *Initiation:* Propose new solutions to team problems.

■ *Give opinions:* Offer opinions on task solutions; give candid feedback on others' suggestions.

task specialist role
A role in which the individual devotes personal time and energy to helping the team accomplish its task.

dual role
A role in which the individual both contributes to the team's task and supports members' emotional needs.

nonparticipator role
A role in which the individual contributes little to either the task or members' socioemotional needs.

socioemotional role
A role in which the individual provides support for team members' emotional needs and social unity.

■ *Seek information:* Ask for task-relevant facts.

■ *Summarize:* Relate various ideas to the problem at hand; pull ideas together into a summary perspective.

■ *Energize:* Stimulate the team into action when interest drops.[22]

People who adopt a **socioemotional role** support team members' emotional needs and help strengthen the social entity. They display the following behaviors:

■ *Encourage:* Are warm and receptive to others' ideas; praise and encourage others to draw forth their contributions.

■ *Harmonize:* Reconcile group conflicts; help disagreeing parties reach agreement.

■ *Reduce tension:* May tell jokes or in other ways draw off emotions when group atmosphere is tense.

■ *Follow:* Go along with the team; agree to other team members' ideas.

■ *Compromise:* Will shift own opinions to maintain team harmony.[23]

Exhibit 16.4 illustrates task specialist and socioemotional roles in teams. When most individuals in a team play a social role, the team is socially oriented. Members do not criticize or disagree with one another and do not forcefully offer opinions or try to accomplish team tasks, because their primary interest is to keep the team happy. Teams with mostly socioemotional roles can be very satisfying, but they also can be unproductive. At the other extreme, a team made up primarily of task specialists will tend to have a singular concern for task accomplishment. This team will be effective for a short period of time but will not be satisfying for members over the long run. Task specialists convey little emotional concern for one another, are unsupportive, and ignore team members' social and emotional needs. The task-oriented team can be humorless and unsatisfying.

As Exhibit 16.4 illustrates, some team members may play a dual role. People with **dual roles** both contribute to the task and meet members' emotional needs. Such people may become team leaders because they satisfy both types of needs and are looked up to by other members. Exhibit 16.4 also shows the final type of role, called the *nonparticipator role*. People in the **nonparticipator role** contribute little to either the task or the social needs of team members. They typically are held in low esteem by the team.

EXHIBIT 16.4
Team Member Roles

	Member Social Behavior	
High — Member Task Behavior	**Task Specialist Role** — Focuses on task accomplishment over human needs — Important role, but if adopted by everyone, team's social needs won't be met	**Dual Role** — Focuses on task and people — May be a team leader — Important role, but not essential if members adopt task specialist and socioemotional roles
Low — Member Task Behavior	**Nonparticipator Role** — Contributes little to either task or people needs of team — Not an important role—if adopted by too many members, team will disband	**Socioemotional Role** — Focuses on people needs of team over task — Important role, but if adopted by everyone, team's tasks won't be accomplished
	Low ——— Member Social Behavior ——— High	

The important thing for managers to remember is that effective teams must have people in both task specialist and socioemotional roles. Humor and social concern are as important to team effectiveness as are facts and problem solving. Managers also should remember that some people perform better in one type of role; some are inclined toward social concerns and others toward task concerns. A well-balanced team will do best over the long term because it will be personally satisfying for team members and permit the accomplishment of team tasks.

TEAM PROCESSES

Now we turn our attention to internal team processes. Team processes pertain to those dynamics that change over time and can be influenced by team leaders. In this section, we will discuss the team processes of stages of development, cohesiveness, and norms. The fourth type of team process, conflict, will be covered in the next section.

Stages of Team Development

After a team has been created, there are distinct stages through which it develops.[24] New teams are different from mature teams. Recall a time when you were a member of a new team, such as a fraternity or sorority pledge class, a committee, or a small team formed to do a class assignment. Over time the team changed. In the beginning, team members had to get to know one another, establish roles and norms, divide the labor, and clarify the team's task. In this way, members became parts of a smoothly operating team. The challenge for leaders is to understand the stage of the team's development and take action that will help the group improve its functioning.

Research findings suggest that team development is not random but evolves over definitive stages. Several models describing these stages exist; one useful model is shown in Exhibit 16.5. The five stages typi-

cally occur in sequence. In teams that are under time pressure or that will exist for only a few days, the stages may occur rapidly. Each stage confronts team leaders and members with unique problems and challenges.[25]

Forming. The **forming** stage of development is a period of orientation and getting acquainted. Members break the ice and test one another for friendship possibilities and task orientation. Team members find which behaviors are acceptable to others. Uncertainty is high during this stage, and members usually accept whatever power or authority is offered by either formal or informal leaders. Members are dependent on the team until they find out what the ground rules are and what is expected of them. During this initial stage, members are concerned about such things as "What is expected of me?" "What is acceptable?" "Will I fit in?" During the forming stage, the team leader should provide time for members to get acquainted with one another and encourage them to engage in informal social discussions.

Storming. During the **storming** stage, individual personalities emerge. People become more assertive in clarifying their roles and what is expected of them. This stage is marked by conflict and disagreement. People may disagree over their perceptions of the team's mission. Members may jockey for positions, and coalitions or subgroups based on common interests may form. One subgroup may disagree with another over the total team's goals or how to achieve them. The team is not yet cohesive and may be characterized by a general lack of unity. Unless teams can successfully move beyond this stage, they may get bogged down and never achieve high performance. During the storming stage, the team leader should encourage participation by each team member. Members should propose ideas, disagree with one another, and work through the uncertainties and conflicting perceptions about team tasks and goals.

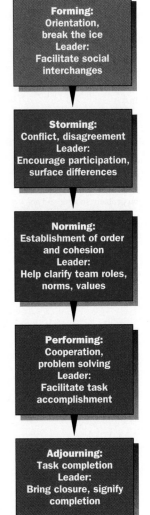

EXHIBIT 16.5
Five Stages of Team Development

Forming:
Orientation, break the ice
Leader: Facilitate social interchanges

Storming:
Conflict, disagreement
Leader: Encourage participation, surface differences

Norming:
Establishment of order and cohesion
Leader: Help clarify team roles, norms, values

Performing:
Cooperation, problem solving
Leader: Facilitate task accomplishment

Adjourning:
Task completion
Leader: Bring closure, signify completion

forming
The stage of team development characterized by orientation and acquaintance.

storming
The stage of team development in which individual personalities and roles, and resulting conflicts, emerge.

norming
The stage of team development in which conflicts developed during the storming stage are resolved and team harmony and unity emerge.

team cohesiveness
The extent to which team members are attracted to the team and motivated to remain in it.

performing
The stage of team development in which members focus on problem solving and accomplishing the team's assigned task.

adjourning
The stage of team development in which members prepare for the team's disbandment.

Norming. During the **norming** stage, conflict is resolved, and team harmony and unity emerge. Consensus develops on who has the power, who is the leader, and members' roles. Members come to accept and understand one another. Differences are resolved, and members develop a sense of team cohesion. This stage typically is of short duration. During the norming stage, the team leader should emphasize oneness within the team and help clarify team norms and values.

Performing. During the **performing** stage, the major emphasis is on problem solving and accomplishing the assigned task. Members are committed to the team's mission. They are coordinated with one another and handle disagreements in a mature way. They confront and resolve problems in the interest of task accomplishment. They interact frequently and direct discussion and influence toward achieving team goals. During this stage, the leader should concentrate on managing high task performance. Both socioemotional and task specialists should contribute.

Leadership plays an important role in determining whether a team successfully evolves to the performing stage. Westrum Development Co.'s employees began to act and perform as a team after John Westrum developed a system of measurable goals, as described in the Focus on Leadership box.

Adjourning The **adjourning** stage occurs in committees, task forces, and teams that have a limited task to perform and are disbanded afterward. During this stage, the emphasis is on wrapping up and gearing down. Task performance is no longer a top priority. Members may feel heightened emotionality, strong cohesiveness, and depression or even regret over the team's disbandment. They may feel happy about mission accomplishment and sad about the loss of friendship and associations. At this point, the leader may wish to signify the team's disbanding with a ritual or ceremony, perhaps giving out plaques and awards to signify closure and completeness.

Team Cohesiveness

Another important aspect of the team process is cohesiveness. **Team cohesiveness** is defined as the extent to which members are attracted to the team and motivated to remain in it.[26] Members of highly cohesive teams are committed to team activities, attend meetings, and are happy when the team succeeds. Members of less-cohesive teams are less concerned about the team's welfare. High cohesiveness is normally considered an attractive feature of teams.

Determinants of Team Cohesiveness.
Characteristics of team structure and context influence cohesiveness. First is *team interaction.* The greater the amount of contact among team members and the more time spent together, the more cohesive the team. Through frequent interactions, members get to know one another and become more devoted to the team.[27] Second is the concept of *shared goals.* If team members agree on goals, they will be more cohesive. Agreeing on purpose and direction binds the team together. Third is *personal attraction to the team,* meaning that members have similar attitudes and values and enjoy being together.

Two factors in the team's context also influence group cohesiveness. The first is the presence of competition. When a team is in moderate competition with other teams, its cohesiveness increases as it strives to win. Whether competition is among sales teams to attain the top sales volume or among manufacturing departments to reduce rejects, competition increases team solidarity and cohesiveness.[28] Finally, team success and the favorable evaluation of the team by outsiders add to cohesiveness. When a team succeeds in its task and others in the organization recognize the success, members feel good, and their commitment to the team will be high.

Chaparral Steel, an amazingly successful steel company in Midlothian, Texas, encourages team cohesiveness through promotion of the "Chaparral Process." The steelmaker strives to create super teams in

FOCUS ON LEADERSHIP
WESTRUM DEVELOPMENT CO.

So what's wrong with 700 percent growth in three years and revenues soaring to the millions? For John Westrum's homebuilding company, it meant unhappy customers, screaming contractors, and a collapsed system for invoicing and payments. It also meant the Blue Bell, Pennsylvania, Westrum Development Co. had gotten away from its four founding principles: "quality construction, customer satisfaction, on-time delivery, and on-budget performance."

Westrum and his 30 employees went on a retreat to develop measurable goals based on those four principles. They ended up with a measurement for customer satisfaction, an 11-point plan addressing length of construction time, and a 178-point checklist for measuring construction-job quality. Westrum started a bonus-pool incentive equal to roughly $1,000 per house built to be paid out quarterly depending on level of goal achievement.

Westrum knew they had to start slowly. "If you set unrealistic goals in the beginning," he said, "people will get discouraged." Everyone agreed that when intermediate goals were fulfilled, bonuses would be paid and the next higher level of goals would kick in. But the first year was tough, even "demoralizing," as employees worked for higher and higher goals. Only 20 percent of the bonus pool was paid out that year. Westrum persisted, by putting company performance on spreadsheets and posting them. People started attending to results rather than dollars. During the third year, 80 percent was paid out, with individuals receiving up to $20,000 each.

As for the original principles, customer satisfaction increased by 80 percent, margins are up, and home quality inspection scores are much higher, too. The goals became the incentive to work harder and become more of a team. "Anytime we weren't meeting an objective," said Westrum, "people would rally behind the person who needed help . . . the effect was phenomenal."

SOURCE: Donna Fenn, "Goal-Driven Incentives," *Inc.,* August 1996, 91.

---

which each member sees his or her job in relation to the entire organization and its goals. Commitment to cohesiveness and efficiency enables Chaparral teams to perform amazing tasks. The purchase and installation of new mill equipment is a highly complicated task for any steel company, and calibrating and fine-tuning the steelmaking process can take years. However, a Chaparral team of four completed the worldwide search, purchase negotiations, shipment, and installation in one year.[29]

Consequences of Team Cohesiveness.
The outcome of team cohesiveness can fall into two categories—morale and productivity. As a general rule, morale is higher in cohesive teams because of increased communication among members, a friendly team climate, maintenance of membership because of commitment to the team, loyalty, and member participation in team decisions and activities. High cohesiveness has almost uniformly good effects on the satisfaction and morale of team members.[30]

With respect to team performance, research findings are mixed, but cohesiveness may have several effects.[31] First, in a cohesive team, members' productivity tends to be more uniform. Productivity variance among members is small because the team exerts pressure toward conformity. Noncohesive teams do not have this control over member behavior and therefore tend to have wider variation in member productivity.

With respect to the productivity of the team as a whole, research findings suggest that cohesive teams have the potential to be productive, but the degree of productivity depends on the relationship between management and the working team. Thus, team cohesiveness does not necessarily lead to higher team productivity. One study surveyed more than 200 work teams and correlated job performance with their cohesiveness.[32] Highly cohesive teams were more productive when team members felt

This "trust fall" during a team-building session at Gilbane Building Company helps strengthen team cohesiveness by leading to increased communication, trust, and a friendly team atmosphere. High *team cohesiveness* has almost uniformly good effects on the satisfaction and morale of team members. Team building and project partnering is a major component of Gilbane's culture, and the company is now extending the team concept to include clients, customers, and subcontractors.

norm
A standard of conduct that is shared by team members and guides their behavior.

management support and less productive when they sensed management hostility and negativism. Management hostility led to team norms and goals of low performance, and the highly cohesive teams performed poorly, in accordance with their norms and goals.

The relationship between performance outcomes and cohesiveness is illustrated in Exhibit 16.6. The highest productivity occurs when the team is cohesive and also has a high performance norm, which is a result of its positive relationship with management. Moderate productivity occurs when cohesiveness is low, because team members are less committed to performance norms. The lowest productivity occurs when cohesiveness is high and the team's performance norm is low. Thus, cohesive teams are able to attain their goals and enforce their norms, which can lead to either very high or very low productivity. Southwest Airlines provides an excellent example of team cohesiveness combined with a high performance norm.

SOUTHWEST AIRLINES

When research conducted jointly by the National Aeronautics and Space Administration (NASA) and Boeing Co. indicated that 60 percent of air-carrier accidents were attributable to human error, the aviation industry responded with implementation of CRM (Crew Resource Management). The program was derided by nonpilot employees as *Cockpit* Resource Management, since the attitude of most airlines is that flight safety is in the hands of the pilot.

Not at Southwest. The successful, slightly "off-center" airline, led by the colorful, charismatic Herbert D. Kelleher, expanded CRM training and the responsibility for flight safety to all members of the Southwest team—from pilots and flight attendants to ground crews and baggage handlers.

A steering committee created Southwest's program after grilling CRM specialists and examining programs at other airlines. Their findings were then fine-tuned to fit Southwest's unique culture and create a special training program. The emphasis is on communication and mutual understanding of each employee's role in ensuring a safe flight. Informal training sessions encourage interaction so that crew members understand the regulations, time constraints, expectations, and particular problems of other workers. For example, dispatchers observe pilots in cockpit simulation training. Pilots gain insight to the safety and time concerns of baggage handlers. The combination of team cohesiveness and management support has made Southwest's workers the most productive in the industry and the company a benchmark for flight safety.[33]   ■

Team Norms

A team **norm** is a standard of conduct that is shared by team members and guides their behavior.[34] Norms are informal. They are not written down as are rules and procedures. Norms are valuable because they define boundaries of acceptable behavior. They make life easier for team members by providing a frame of reference for what is

EXHIBIT 16.6
Relationship among Team Cohesiveness, Performance Norms, and Productivity

High	**Moderate Productivity** Weak norms in alignment with organization goals	**High Productivity** Strong norms in alignment with organization goals
Team Performance Norms		
Low	**Low/Moderate Productivity** Weak norms in opposition to organization goals	**Low Productivity** Strong norms in opposition to organization goals
	Low Team Cohesiveness **High**	

right and wrong. Norms identify key values, clarify role expectations, and facilitate team survival. For example, union members may develop a norm of not cooperating with management because they do not trust management's motives. In this way, norms protect the group and express key values.

Norms begin to develop in the first interactions among members of a new team.[35] Norms that apply to both day-to-day behavior and employee output and performance gradually evolve. Norms thus tell members what is acceptable and direct members' actions toward acceptable productivity or performance. Four common ways in which norms develop for controlling and directing behavior are illustrated in Exhibit 16.7.[36]

Critical Events. Often *critical events* in a team's history establish an important precedent. One example occurred when Arthur Schlesinger, despite his serious reservations about the Bay of Pigs invasion, was pressured by Attorney General Robert Kennedy not to raise his objections to President Kennedy. This critical incident helped create a norm in which team members refrained from expressing disagreement with the president.

Any critical event can lead to the creation of a norm. In one organization, a department head invited the entire staff to his house for dinner. The next day people discovered that no one had attended, and this resulted in a norm prohibiting outside entertaining.[37]

Primacy. *Primacy* means that the first behaviors that occur in a team often set a precedent for later team expectations. For example, when the president of Sun Company set up teams in the Dallas-based exploration division, top managers made sure the initial meetings involved solving genuine company problems. The initial success created a norm that team members carried into other work. "Suddenly we had two hundred evangelists," said Sun President McCormick.[38]

Carryover Behaviors. *Carryover behaviors* bring norms into the team from outside. One current example is the strong norm against smoking in many management teams. Some team members sneak around, gargling with mouthwash, and fear expulsion because the team culture believes everyone should kick the habit. At such companies as Johnson & Johnson, Dow Chemical, and Aetna Life & Casualty, the norm is "If you want to advance, don't smoke."[39] Carryover behavior also influences small teams of college students assigned by instructors to do class work. Norms brought into the team from outside suggest that students should participate equally and help members get a reasonable grade.

Explicit Statements. With *explicit statements*, leaders or team members can initiate norms by articulating them to the team. Explicit statements symbolize what counts and thus have considerable impact. Making

EXHIBIT 16.7
Four Ways Team Norms Develop

conflict
Antagonistic interaction in which one party attempts to thwart the intentions or goals of another.

explicit statements is probably the most effective way for managers to change norms in an established team. For example, Richard Boyle of Honeywell wrote a memo relaxing the company's excessive formality and creating a new norm. Called "Loosening Up the Tie," the memo said in part:

> I wish to announce a relaxed wearing apparel policy, and loosen my tie for the summer. Let's try it starting on May 15th and tentatively ending on September 15th. Since departments vary in customer contact and, depending on location, may even vary slightly in temperature, Department Heads are hereby given authority to allow variations. . . .
>
> This change requires each of us to use good judgment. On the one extreme it means you do not have to wear a tie; on the other, tennis shoes, shorts, and a t-shirt is too relaxed. Have a comfortable, enjoyable summer. I hope to.[40]

The tie memo helped demonstrate management's interest in developing a relaxed, more casual atmosphere at Honeywell.

MANAGING TEAM CONFLICT

The final characteristic of team process is conflict. Of all the skills required for effec-

tive team management, none is more important than handling the conflicts that inevitably arise among members. Whenever people work together in teams, some conflict is inevitable. Conflict can arise among members within a team or between one team and another. **Conflict** refers to antagonistic interaction in which one party attempts to block the intentions or goals of another.[41] Competition, which is rivalry among individuals or teams, can have a healthy impact because it energizes people toward higher performance.[42] However, too much conflict can be destructive, tear relationships apart, and interfere with the healthy exchange of ideas and information.[43]

Causes of Conflict

Several factors can cause people to engage in conflict:[44]

Scarce Resources. Resources include money, information, and supplies. In their desire to achieve goals, individuals may wish to increase their resources, which throws them into conflict. Whenever individuals or teams must compete for scarce or declining resources, conflict is almost inevitable.

Jurisdictional Ambiguities. Conflicts also emerge when job boundaries and responsibilities are unclear. When task responsibilities are well-defined and predictable, people know where they stand. When they are unclear, people may disagree about who has responsibility for specific tasks or who has a claim on resources. The conflict between owners' and players' associations in both professional football and baseball is often a struggle to see which organization has jurisdiction over such things as drug testing.[45]

Communication Breakdown. Communication, as described in Chapter 15, is sometimes faulty. Poor communications result in misperceptions and misunderstandings of other people and teams. In some

cases, information may be intentionally withheld, which can jeopardize trust among teams and lead to long-lasting conflict.

Personality Clashes. A personality clash occurs when people simply do not get along with one another and do not see eye to eye on any issue. Personality clashes are caused by basic differences in personality, values, and attitudes. Often it's a good idea to simply separate the parties so that they need not interact with one another.

Power and Status Differences. Power and status differences occur when one party has disputable influence over another. Low-prestige individuals or departments may resist their low status. People may engage in conflict to increase their power and influence in the team or organization.

Goal Differences. Conflict often occurs simply because people are pursuing conflicting goals. Goal differences are natural in organizations. Individual salespeople's targets may put them in conflict with one another or with the sales manager. Moreover, the sales department may have goals that conflict with those of manufacturing. One conflict emerged within the United Auto Workers (UAW) because one subgroup is against teamwork, believing that it exploits workers and does nothing but make them work harder. Other factions in the UAW believe it is beneficial for both workers and the organization. These opposing goals are causing major clashes among these UAW subgroups.[46]

An interesting example of conflict occurred within a product marketing team at Salvo, a designer of computer software programs.

SALVO, INC.

Product marketing teams at Salvo develop demonstration tapes of its new games and programs for use in dealer stores. The tapes are filled with sound, color, and clever graphics that are successful sales tools. The marketing person on the team works up an outline for a tape based on product content. The outline is then submitted to the team member from the information systems department to work out the displays and graphics.

Larry from marketing is energetic, has a good sense of humor, and has a high standard for excellence. He knows what a computer can do, but he is not a programmer. Larry submitted an outline of a new videotape to Eric in information systems for development. Eric, a new member of the team, is serious and somewhat introverted. He sent a highly technical memo to Larry explaining why the project wouldn't work as requested. Larry was upset, because he didn't understand the memo or why Eric had written a memo instead of talking to him face-to-face.

Larry and Eric had a blowup at their first meeting because of their different goals and personalities. Miscommunication further aggravated the situation. Also, it was unclear who was responsible for each task in the development of the demonstration tapes, because Eric was new and unaccustomed to taking orders from another team member. Although both Eric and Larry supposedly had the same team goal, the problems with personality, communication, jurisdictional ambiguity, and individual goals caused an almost explosive conflict between them.[47] ■

Styles to Handle Conflict

Teams as well as individuals develop specific styles for dealing with conflict, based on the desire to satisfy their own concern versus the other party's concern. A model that describes five styles of handling conflict is in Exhibit 16.8. The two major dimensions are the extent to which an individual is assertive versus cooperative in his or her approach to conflict.

Effective team members vary their style of handling conflict to fit a specific situation. Each style is appropriate in certain cases.

| The *competing style*, which reflects assertiveness to get one's own way, should be used when quick, decisive action is vital on important issues or unpopular

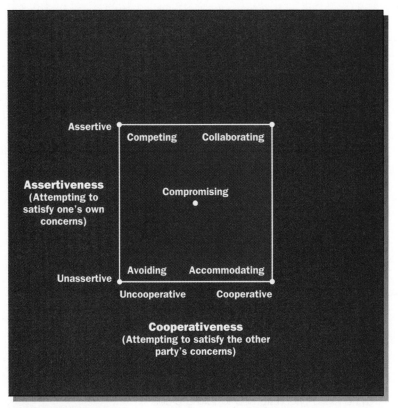

EXHIBIT 16.8
A Model of Styles to Handle Conflict

SOURCE: Adapted from Kenneth Thomas, "Conflict and Conflict Management," in *Handbook of Industrial and Organizational Behavior*, ed. M. D. Dunnette (New York: John Wiley, 1976), 900.

superordinate goal
A goal that cannot be reached by a single party.

actions, such as during emergencies or urgent cost cutting.

2 The *avoiding style*, which reflects neither assertiveness nor cooperativeness, is appropriate when an issue is trivial, when there is no chance of winning, when a delay to gather more information is needed, or when a disruption would be very costly.

3 The *compromising style* reflects a moderate amount of both assertiveness and cooperativeness. It is appropriate when the goals on both sides are equally important, when opponents have equal power and both sides want to split the difference, or when people need to arrive at temporary or expedient solutions under time pressure.

4 The *accommodating style* reflects a high degree of cooperativeness, which works best when people realize that they are wrong, when an issue is more important to others than to oneself, when building social credits for use in later discussions,

and when maintaining harmony is especially important.

5 The *collaborating style* reflects both a high degree of assertiveness and cooperativeness. The collaborating style enables both parties to win, although it may require substantial bargaining and negotiation. The collaborating style is important when both sets of concerns are too important to be compromised, when insights from different people need to be merged into an overall solution, and when the commitment of both sides is needed for a consensus.[48]

The various styles of handling conflict can be used when an individual disagrees with others. But what does a manager or team member do when a conflict erupts among others within a team or among teams for which the manager is responsible? Research suggests that several techniques can be used as strategies for resolving conflicts among people or departments. These techniques might also be used when conflict is formalized, such as between a union and management.

Superordinate Goals. The larger mission that cannot be attained by a single party is identified as a **superordinate goal**.[49] A superordinate goal requires the cooperation of the conflicting parties for achievement. People must pull together. To the extent that employees can be focused on team or organization goals, the conflict will decrease because they see the big picture and realize they must work together to achieve it. GE Plastics division needed a superordinate goal to eliminate hostilities from employees in a new acquisition, as described in the Leading the Management Revolution box.

Bargaining/Negotiation. Bargaining and negotiation mean that the parties engage one another in an attempt to systematically reach a solution. They attempt logical problem solving to identify and correct the conflict. This approach works well if the individuals can set aside personal animosities and deal with the conflict in a businesslike way.

How can a dilapidated YMCA in a gang- and drug-infested neighborhood bring unity between two former archrival business competitors? GE Plastics division had recently bought out its old competitor, Borg-Warner Chemicals. Not only were there strong negative feelings between the two groups, but their cultures were vastly different. Nearly everyone thought the merger would be troublesome. Morale sunk low.

Joel Hurt was responsible for the upcoming GE Plastics corporate meeting. But how could he create trust in Borg-Warner employees and win back their own workers from cynicism? Instead of planning the regular golf tournament, Hurt got permission to try something new and innovative.

"Share to Gain" got into full swing as the 470 employees sat in the ballroom at a swank San Diego resort. Hurt got on stage and asked if they were willing to do something constructive, to create lasting value, after which he showed a film on the run-down Copley YMCA. In its rough neighborhood, it was an alternative for kids. But deteriorating resources showed up in serious disrepair of building and grounds. "The director of this Y says fixing this place up will cost $500,000 and take years," he told the employees. "But I am here tonight to tell you it's not going to take years. This GE army is going to attack this place. We're going to do it in eight hours, and we're going to do it tomorrow!"

The 30 preselected and division-mixed teams were given detailed instructions and spent the remainder of the evening on intense logistical planning. When they piled off the buses the next morning, they eagerly started their tasks, using materials already waiting. Teams pulled up carpet, removed old lockers, laid tile, repaired decaying ceilings, built a retaining wall, replaced an irrigation system, fixed basketball backboards, landscaped grounds, and even restored an old mural with 34 paint colors. Olympic gold-medal-winning diver Greg Louganis, who had learned to swim at the Copley Y, stopped by and told them how important their work was to the community.

At the end of 12 hours, the teams had successfully completed all their work. What's more, a new feeling of camaraderie emerged, leaving the old rivalries behind. To some, it felt like a modern version of a barn-raising. The teams were drawn together by working toward leaving something behind of lasting value.

"We didn't invent this concept," says Hurt. "People are doing projects to help people all the time. What we did is apply it to the business meeting."

SOURCE: David Bollier, "Building Corporate Loyalty while Rebuilding the Community," *Management Review*, October 1, 1996, 1; David Bollier, *Aiming Higher*. New York: AMACOM, 1996.

Mediation. Using a third party to settle a dispute involves **mediation.** A mediator could be a supervisor, higher-level manager, or someone from the human resource department. The mediator can discuss the conflict with each party and work toward a solution. If a solution satisfactory to both sides cannot be reached, the parties may be willing to turn the conflict over to the mediator and abide by his or her solution.

Providing Well-Defined Tasks. When conflict is a result of ambiguity, managers can reduce it by clarifying responsibilities and tasks. In this way, all parties will know the tasks for which they are responsible and the limits of their authority.

Facilitating Communication. Managers can facilitate communication to ensure that conflicting parties hold accurate perceptions. Providing opportunities for the disputants to get together and exchange information reduces conflict. As they learn more about one another, suspicions diminish and improved teamwork becomes possible.

For example, the conflict between Larry and Eric at Salvo, Inc., over the demonstration tape was eventually resolved by improved communication, clear definition of their respective tasks, and stronger commitment to the superordinate goal of finishing the tape. Part of the problem was that Larry was using a competing style and Eric an

mediation
The process of using a third party to settle a dispute.

avoiding style in dealing with this issue. Larry went to see Eric and discussed the problem with him. The discussion revealed that they were pursuing different goals because Larry wanted the tape right away and Eric wanted to keep it until he could perfect it. Discussing each point of view was a collaborative style that was a key to their solution. Debbie, another team member, agreed to help them so that the tape could be of high quality and still be finished in two weeks. Larry and Eric also worked out a clear schedule that specified their respective responsibilities and tasks.

BENEFITS AND COSTS OF TEAMS

social facilitation
The tendency for the presence of others to influence an individual's motivation and performance.

In deciding whether to use teams to perform specific tasks, managers must consider both benefits and costs. Teams may have positive impact on both the output productivity and satisfaction of members. On the other hand, teams may also create a situation in which motivation and performance are actually decreased.

Potential Benefits of Teams

Teams come closest to achieving their full potential when they enhance individual productivity through increased member effort, members' personal satisfaction, integration of diverse abilities and skills, and increased organizational flexibility.

Level of Effort. Employee teams often unleash enormous energy and creativity from workers who like the idea of using their brains as well as their bodies on the job. Companies such as Kimberly-Clark have noticed this change in effort among employees as they switched to team approaches.[50] The shift to a team approach at Northern Telecom's (Nortel) Nashville facility unleashed employee energy and enthusiasm that may have prevented the company from going out of business. Director of operations Burgess Oliver took his job the day after a 75 percent workforce layoff,

leaving just 200 employees remaining. Believing the company would fold, the remaining 200 workers were demoralized and unmotivated. Oliver started teamwork programs, beginning with extensive training in problem solving, conflict resolution, customer service, and team leadership. Finally, members took over the responsibilities of management while the managers themselves became consultants. Today Nortel's Nashville Facility sports one of the highest customer satisfaction ratings, while sales are up 12 percent and absenteeism has dropped dramatically.[51]

One explanation for this motivation is the research finding that working in a team increases an individual's motivation and performance. **Social facilitation** refers to the tendency for the presence of others to enhance an individual's motivation and performance. Simply being in the presence of other people has an energizing effect.[52]

Satisfaction of Members. As described in Chapter 14, employees have needs for belongingness and affiliation. Working in teams can help meet these needs. Participative teams reduce boredom and often increase employees' feeling of dignity and self-worth because the whole person is employed. People who have a satisfying team environment cope better with stress and enjoy their jobs.

Expanded Job Knowledge and Skills. The third major benefit of using teams is the empowerment of employees to bring greater knowledge and ability to the task. For one thing, multiskilled employees learn all of the jobs that the team performs. Teams gain the intellectual resources of several members who can suggest shortcuts and offer alternative points of view for team decisions.

Organizational Flexibility. Traditional organizations are structured so that each worker does only one specific job. But when employee teams are used, from 5 to 15 people work next to one another and are able to exchange jobs. Work can be reorganized

and workers reallocated as needed to produce products and services with great flexibility. The organization is able to be responsive to rapidly changing customer needs. One company that has discovered the benefits of teams is General Motors.

SATURN

Corporations are trying to integrate a variety of team approaches into their production plants. For example, when designing the Saturn automobile, General Motors had a blank slate on which to design the plant structure as it wished and gave high priority to teams, which was believed to offer more worker satisfaction, among other benefits.

At GM's Saturn facility in Tennessee, work teams are trained to operate without bosses. GM reduced the traditional six levels of authority to four. Work Unit Teams (6–15 employees) are each led by an elected counselor. Team members hire workers, assign jobs, maintain equipment, order supplies, and keep tabs on everything from budgets and production schedules to freight deliveries and auto quality. At the top level of the plant, decisions are also made in teams that include top managers and UAW representatives.

Saturn's methods are seen as the wave of the future and have been studied and copied by others.[53] Saturn quality is luring U.S. consumers away from foreign brands, and dealer sales for July 1992 topped 22,000, an average of 115 car sales per dealer—twice that of the closest competitor (Toyota). However, Saturn's success breeds new problems. As demand outstrips supply, parts suppliers repeatedly hold the popular auto "hostage" with labor strikes that halt or slow Saturn production. The team concept at Saturn faces new challenges in responding to these problems.[54] ■

Potential Costs of Teams

When managers decide whether to use teams, they must assess certain costs or liabilities associated with teamwork. When teams do not work very well, the major reasons usually are power realignment, free riding, coordination costs, or legal hassles.

Power Realignment. When companies form shop workers into teams, the major losers are low- and middle-level managers. These managers are reluctant to give up power. Indeed, when teams are successful, fewer supervisors are needed. This is especially true for self-directed teams, because workers take over supervisory responsibility. The adjustment is difficult for managers who fear the loss of status or even their job and who have to learn new, people-oriented skills to survive.[55]

Free Riding. The term **free rider** refers to a team member who attains benefit from team membership but does not do a proportionate share of the work.[56] Free riding is sometimes called *social loafing*, because members do not exert equal effort. In large teams, some people are likely to work less. For example, research found that the pull exerted on a rope was greater by individuals working alone than by individuals in a group. Similarly, people who were asked to clap and make noise made more noise on a per person basis when working alone or in small groups than they did in a large group.[57] The problem of free riding has been experienced by people who have participated in student project groups. Some students put more effort into the group project than others, and often it seems that no members work as hard for the group as they do for their individual grades.

Coordination Costs. The time and energy required to coordinate the activities of a group to enable it to perform its task are called **coordination costs.** Groups must spend time getting ready to do work and lose productive time in deciding who is to do what and when.[58] Once again, student project groups illustrate coordination costs. Members must meet after class just to decide when they can meet to perform the task. Schedules must be checked, telephone calls made, and meeting times arranged in order to get down to business. Hours may

free rider
A person who benefits from team membership but does not make a proportionate contribution to the team's work.

coordination costs
The time and energy needed to coordinate the activities of a team to enable it to perform its task.

be devoted to the administration and coordination of the group. Students often feel they could do the same project by themselves in less time.

Legal Hassles. As more companies utilize teams, new questions of legality surface. A 1990 National Labor Relations Board judgment against management's use of union-member teams at Electromation, Inc., has set a confusing precedent. The Wagner Act of 1935 was enacted to prevent companies from forming organizations or employee committees to undercut legitimate unions. Union leaders today support the formation of problem-solving teams but may balk when management takes an active role in the formation and direction of such teams. As union membership and power decline, increasingly vocal critics charge that the team concept is a management ploy to kill unions. Autoworkers especially are challenging team approaches because union jobs continue to disappear despite repeated concessions. Although few experts expect the courts to halt teams altogether, most believe that strict new guidelines will be implemented to control the formation and use of teams.[59]

SUMMARY AND MANAGEMENT SOLUTION

Several important concepts about teams were described in this chapter. Organizations use teams both to achieve coordination as part of the formal structure and to encourage employee involvement. Formal teams include vertical teams along the chain of command and horizontal teams such as cross-functional task forces and committees. Special-purpose teams are used for special, large-scale, creative organization projects. Employee involvement via teams is designed to bring low-level employees into decision processes to improve quality, efficiency, and satisfaction. Companies typically start with problem-solving teams, which may evolve into self-directed teams that take on responsibility for management activities.

For example, Hearing Technology, Inc., described at the beginning of this chapter, grew rapidly to 80 employees and became sluggish in its response to hearing-aid dealers. President Tom Huber was frustrated because the three-day response time increased to eight days, provoking complaints from dealers. Huber's attempt to reenergize the company failed, and he tried a drastic restructuring into employee teams. Huber implemented three things that made the team approach work: Regular meetings of employee teams were held, usually every week; departments were encouraged to talk with one another and work together through cross-functional teams; and power was shared with employees. Four longtime employees supervised manufacturing as a team, reinforcing the team approach. With teams, the response time for custom orders was halved to four days, and dealers were happy again. Employees began enjoying themselves, too.[60]

Most teams go through systematic stages of development: forming, storming, norming, performing, and adjourning. Team characteristics that can influence organizational effectiveness are size, cohesiveness, norms, and members' roles. All teams experience some conflict because of scarce resources, ambiguous responsibility, communication breakdown, personality clashes, power and status differences, and goal conflicts. Techniques for resolving these conflicts include superordinate goals, bargaining, clear definition of task responsibilities, mediation, and communication. Advantages of using teams include increased motivation, diverse knowledge and skills, satisfaction of team members, and organizational flexibility. Potential costs of using teams are power realignment, free riding, coordination costs, and legal hassles.

DISCUSSION QUESTIONS

1 Volvo went to self-directed teams to assemble cars because of the need to attract and keep workers in Sweden, where pay raises are not a motivator (high taxes) and many other jobs are available. Is this a good reason for using a team approach? Discuss.

2 During your own work experience, have you been part of a formal vertical team? A task force? A committee? An employee involvement team? How did your work experience differ in each type of team?

3 What are the five stages of team development? What happens during each stage?

4 How would you explain the emergence of problem-solving and self-directed teams in companies throughout North America? Do you think implementation of the team concept is difficult in these companies? Discuss.

5 Assume that you are part of a student project team and one member is not doing his or her share. Which conflict resolution strategy would you use? Why?

6 Do you think a moderate level of conflict might be healthy for an organization? Discuss.

7 When you are a member of a team, do you adopt a task specialist or socioemotional role? Which role is more important for a team's effectiveness? Discuss.

8 What is the relationship between team cohesiveness and team performance?

9 Describe the advantages and disadvantages of teams. In what situations might the disadvantages outweigh the advantages?

10 What is a team norm? What norms have developed in teams to which you have belonged?

11 One company had 40 percent of its workers and 20 percent of its managers resign during the first year after reorganizing into teams. What might account for this dramatic turnover? How might managers ensure a smooth transition to teams?

MANAGEMENT EXERCISES

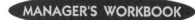

MANAGER'S WORKBOOK

Is Your Group a Cohesive Team?

Think about a student group with which you have worked. Answer the questions below as they pertain to the functioning of that group.

	Disagree Strongly				Agree Strongly
1 Group meetings were held regularly and everyone attended.	1	2	3	4	5
2 We talked about and shared the same goals for group work and grade.	1	2	3	4	5
3 We spent most of our meeting time talking business, but discussions were open-ended and active.	1	2	3	4	5
4 We talked through any conflicts and disagreements until they were resolved.	1	2	3	4	5
5 Group members listened carefully to one another.	1	2	3	4	5

	Disagree Strongly				Agree Strongly
6 We really trusted each other, speaking personally about what we really felt.	1	2	3	4	5
7 Leadership roles were rotated and shared, with people taking initiative at appropriate times for the good of the group.	1	2	3	4	5
8 Each member found a way to contribute to the final work product.	1	2	3	4	5
9 I was really satisfied being a member of the group.	1	2	3	4	5
10 We freely gave each other credit for jobs well done	1	2	3	4	5
11 Group members gave and received feedback to help the group do even better.	1	2	3	4	5
12 We held each other accountable; each member was accountable to the group.	1	2	3	4	5
13 Group members really liked and respected each other.	1	2	3	4	5

Total Score _____

The questions here are about team cohesion. If you scored 52 or greater, your group experienced authentic teamwork. Congratulations. If you scored between 39 and 51, there was a positive group identity that might have been developed even further. If you scored between 26 and 38, group identity was weak and probably not very satisfying. If you scored below 26, it was hardly a group at all, resembling a loose collection of individuals.

Remember, teamwork doesn't happen by itself. Individuals like you have to understand what a team is and then work to make it happen. What can you do to make a student group more like a team? Do you have the courage to take the initiative?

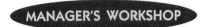

MANAGER'S WORKSHOP

Boyberik: Team Problem-Solving

Background

The new country of Boyberik has requested help from the World Bank to develop its economic system. One project approved is to develop a reasonable pricing system for its products, in order for it to compete in the global marketplace. The main industry in Boyberik produces babkizzes of high quality. In Boyberik, quantities are measured by bunches and gaggles. Paper currency is called bani-bani, while the four types of coins are groshen, mezuma, penizay, and fluce.

Goal

Your task is to determine the price each babkiz should sell for. The instructor will give each group a set of cards with information on each one. You are allowed to tell other group members what your cards say, but you *cannot* show the cards to anyone else.

1 Divide the class into groups of five to eight members. Each group goes to a different part of the room, after which the instructor gives a set of cards to each group.

One person in the group "deals" the cards out to each person, trying to give an equal amount (or near equal) to each member. Members may not show cards to anyone else, but may share information orally. Cards should not leave "owners" hands during playing.
2 Each group tries to solve the problem of what should be the price of each babkiz.
3 Instructor announces solution to the groups.

4 Observers give feedback on the level of teamwork. This can be done either within individual groups, after which there is a general discussion, or there can be general feedback given in the whole class.

Source: Copyright 1994 by Gedaliahu Harel, Technion University, Haifa, Israel, and Dorothy Marcic. All rights reserved.

SURF THE 'NET

On the Internet, look for examples in company Web sites, periodical databases, and other locations for examples of:

1 team effectiveness
2 team ineffectiveness
3 formal teams
4 vertical, horizontal, or special-purpose teams
5 self-directed teams
6 stages of team development
7 team cohesiveness

Make sure you have at least two sources from company Web sites and two or more from periodical databases.

ETHICAL DILEMMA

Consumer Safety or Team Commitment?

Nancy was part of a pharmaceutical team developing a product called loperamide, a liquid treatment for diarrhea for people unable to take solid medicine, namely infants, children, and the elderly. Loperamide contained 44 times the amount of saccharin allowed by the FDA in a 12-ounce soft drink, but there were no regulations governing saccharin content in medication.

Nancy was the only medical member of the seven-person project team. The team made a unanimous decision to reduce the saccharin content before marketing loperamide, so the team initiated a three-month effort for reformulation. In the meantime, management was pressuring the team to allow human testing with the original formula until the new formula became available. After a heated team debate, all the team members except Nancy voted to begin testing with the current formula.

Nancy believed it was unethical to test on old people and children a drug she considered potentially dangerous. As the only medical member of the team, she had to sign the forms allowing testing. She refused and was told that unless she signed, she would be removed from the project, demoted, and seen as a poor team player, nonpromotable, lacking in judgment, and unable to work with marketing people. Nancy was aware that no proof existed that high saccharin would be directly harmful to potential users of loperamide.

What Do You Do?

1 Refuse to sign. As a medical doctor, Nancy must stand up for what she believes is right.
2 Resign. There is no reason to stay in this company and be punished for ethically correct behavior. Testing the drug will become someone else's responsibility.

3 Sign the form. The judgment of other team members cannot be all wrong. The loperamide testing is not illegal and will move ahead anyway, so it would preserve team unity and company effectiveness to sign.

SOURCE: Based on Tom L. Beauchamp, *Ethical Theory and Business*, 2d ed. (Englewood Cliffs, N.J.: Prentice-Hall, 1983).

CASE FOR CRITICAL ANALYSIS

A. O. Smith Corp.

A. O. Smith Corporation's Milwaukee plant had bored workers repeating the same robotlike task every 20 seconds, welding and riveting car and truck frames for supply to General Motors. Beginning in the early 1980s, General Motors shifted some of its business elsewhere. Later, GM and other automakers forced Smith and other suppliers to cut prices.

With resources getting tight, Smith tried a quality circle program as a way to introduce teamwork. Quality improved, but the union refused to be involved. As external threats became greater, the union president began to support widespread application of the teamwork concept. The union pressed for five- to seven-member teams, letting workers rotate jobs and elect team leaders. Smith's management went along, turning the control of the shops over to employees. The ratio of supervisors to workers was reduced from 1 supervisor to 10 workers to 1 supervisor to 34 workers.

Smith's executives moved slowly because a consultant argued that self-directed teams would not work until workers wanted them to happen; teams must evolve from their own experience. With the support of the union, Smith undertook the rare transformation from a traditional manufacturing plant with rigid work rules and labor-management warfare to a new culture with participation and equality. All the problems are not yet resolved, because the plant still has not reached its potential. However, observers believe an obsolete production system has been transformed into a competitive one.

Questions

1 What types of teams discussed in the chapter are represented in this case?
2 Do you agree that workers must want the teamwork concept before it can be imposed by management? Explain.
3 What might be a next step to further improve the employee involvement climate at A. O. Smith?

SOURCE: Based on John Hoerr, "The Cultural Revolution at A. O. Smith," *Business Week*, May 29, 1989, 66–68.

ENDNOTES

1 Bruce G. Posner, "Divided We Fall," *Inc.* (July 1989), 105–106.
2 "Training in the 1990s," *The Wall Street Journal*, March 1, 1990, B1.
3 Robert B. Reich, "Entrepreneurship Reconsidered: The Team as Hero," *Harvard Business Review* (May–June 1987), 77–83.

4 Eric Schine, "Mattel's Wild Race to Market," *Business Week*, February 21, 1994, 62–63; Frank V. Cespedes, Stephen X. Dole, and Robert J. Freedman, "Teamwork for Today's Selling," *Harvard Business Review* (March–April 1989), 44–55; Victoria J. Marsick,

Ernie Turner, and Lars Cederholm, "International Managers as Team Leaders," *Management Review* (March 1989), 46–49; and "Team Goal-Setting," *Small Business Report* (January 1988), 76–77.

5 Carl E. Larson and Frank M. J. LaFasto, *TeamWork* (Newbury Park, Calif.: Sage, 1989).

6 Jon R. Katzenbach and Douglas K. Smith, "The Discipline of Teams," *Harvard Business Review* (March–April 1993), 111–120.

7 Eric Sundstrom, Kenneth P. De Meuse, and David Futrell, "Work Teams," *American Psychologist* 45 (February 1990), 120–133.

8 Deborah L. Gladstein, "Groups in Context: A Model of Task Group Effectiveness," *Administrative Science Quarterly* 29 (1984), 499–517.

9 Steven Alburty, "The Ad Agency to End All Ad Agencies," *Fast Company* (December/January 1997), 116–124.

10 Thomas Owens, "Business Teams," *Small Business Report* (January 1989), 50–58.

11 "Participation Teams," *Small Business Report* (September 1987), 38–41.

12 Larson and LaFasto, *TeamWork*.

13 Rebecca Simmons, "Clunky, Comfy Birkies Have Loyal Following," *St. Louis Post-Dispatch*, December 12, 1996, 9; Brenda Paik Sunoo, "Birkenstock Braces to Fight the Competition," *Personnel Journal* (August 1994), 73. no 7, 68–75; Leslie Brokaw, "Feet Don't Fail Me Now," *Inc.* (May 1994), 70.

14 James H. Shonk, *Team-Based Organizations* (Homewood, Ill.: Business One Irwin, 1992); and John Hoerr, "The Payoff from Teamwork," *Business Week*, July 10, 1989, 56–62.

15 Gregory L. Miles, "Suddenly, USX Is Playing Mr. Nice Guy," *Business Week*, June 26, 1989, 151–152.

16 Thomas Owens, "The Self-Managing Work Team," *Small Business Report* (February 1991), 53–65.

17 John Hoerr, "Benefits for the Back Office, Too," *Business Week*, July 10, 1989, 59.

18 Brian Dumaine, "The Trouble with Teams," *Fortune*, September 5, 1994, 86–92; and Brian Dumaine, "Who Needs a Boss?" *Fortune*, May 7, 1990, 52–60.

19 Dumaine, "The Trouble with Teams"; and Beverly Geber, "Virtual Teams," *Training* (April 1995), 36–40.

20 For research findings on group size, see M. E. Shaw, *Group Dynamics*, 3d ed. (New York: McGraw-Hill, 1981); and G. Manners, "Another Look at Group Size, Group Problem-Solving and Member Consensus," *Academy of Management Journal* 18 (1975), 715–724.

21 George Prince, "Recognizing Genuine Teamwork," *Supervisory Management* (April 1989), 25–36; K. D. Benne and P. Sheats, "Functional Roles of Group Members," *Journal of Social Issues* 4 (1948), 41–49; and R. F. Bales, *SYMLOG Case Study Kit* (New York: Free Press, 1980).

22 Robert A. Baron, *Behavior in Organizations*, 2d ed. (Boston: Allyn & Bacon, 1986).

23 Ibid.

24 Kenneth G. Koehler, "Effective Team Management," *Small Business Report*, July 19, 1989, 14–16; and Connie J. G. Gersick, "Time and Transition in Work Teams: Toward a New Model of Group Development," *Academy of Management Journal* 31 (1988), 9–41.

25 Bruce W. Tuckman and Mary Ann C. Jensen, "Stages of Small-Group Development Revisited," *Group and Organizational Studies* 2 (1977), 419–427; and Bruce W. Tuckman, "Developmental Sequences in Small Groups," *Psychological Bulletin* 63 (1965), 384–399. See also Linda N. Jewell and H. Joseph Reitz, *Group Effectiveness in Organizations* (Glenview, Ill.: Scott, Foresman, 1981).

26 Shaw, *Group Dynamics*.

27 Daniel C. Feldman and Hugh J. Arnold, *Managing Individual and Group Behavior in Organizations* (New York: McGraw-Hill, 1983).

28 Ricky W. Griffin, *Management* (Boston: Houghton Mifflin, 1990).

29 Dumaine, "Who Needs a Boss?"

30 Dorwin Cartwright and Alvin Zander, *Group Dynamics: Research and Theory*, 3d ed. (New York: Harper & Row, 1968); and Elliot Aronson, *The Social Animal* (San Francisco: W. H. Freeman, 1976).

31 Peter E. Mudrack, "Group Cohesiveness and Productivity: A Closer Look," *Human Relations* 42 (1989), 771–785.

32 Stanley E. Seashore, *Group Cohesiveness in the Industrial Work Group* (Ann Arbor, Mich.: Institute for Social Research, 1954).

33 Connie Bovier, "Teamwork: The Heart of the Airline," *Training* (June 1993), 53–58.

34 J. Richard Hackman, "Group Influences on Individuals," in *Handbook of Industrial and Organizational Psychology*, ed. M. Dunnette (Chicago: Rand McNally, 1976).

35 Kenneth Bettenhausen and J. Keith Murnighan, "The Emergence of Norms in Competitive Decision-Making Groups," *Administrative Science Quarterly* 30 (1985), 350–372.

36 The following discussion is based on Daniel C. Feldman, "The Development and Enforcement of Group Norms," *Academy of Management Review* 9 (1984), 47–53.

37 Hugh J. Arnold and Daniel C. Feldman, *Organizational Behavior* (New York: McGraw-Hill, 1986).

38 Kenneth Labich, "Making Over Middle Managers," *Fortune*, May 8, 1989, 58–64.

39 Alix M. Freedman, "Cigarette Smoking Is Growing Hazardous to Career in Business," *The Wall Street Journal*, April 23, 1987, 1, 14.

40 Reprinted by permission of the *Harvard Business Review*. Excerpts from "Wrestling with Jellyfish" by Richard J. Boyle (January–February 1984). Copyright © 1984 by the President and Fellows of Harvard College; all rights reserved.

41 Stephen P. Robbins, *Managing Organizational Conflict: A Nontraditional Approach* (Englewood Cliffs, N.J.: Prentice-Hall, 1974).

42 Daniel Robey, Dana L. Farrow, and Charles R. Franz, "Group Process and Conflict in System Development," *Management Science* 35 (1989), 1172–1191.

43 Koehler, "Effective Team Management"; and Dean Tjosvold, "Making Conflict Productive," *Personnel Administrator* 29 (June 1984), 121.

44 This discussion is based in part on Richard L. Daft, *Organization Theory and Design* (St. Paul, Minn.: West, 1992), Chapter 13.

45 Brian Bremner, "That Head-Banging You Hear Is the NFL Owners," *Business Week*, September 4, 1989, 36.

46 Wendy Zeller, "The UAW Rebels Teaming Up against Teamwork," *Business Week*, March 27, 1989, 110–114; and Wendy Zeller, "Suddenly, the UAW Is Raising Its Voice at GM," *Business Week*, November 6, 1989, 96–100.

47 Based on Mary Jean Parson, "The Peer Conflict," *Supervisory Management* (May 1986), 25–31.

48 This discussion was based on K. W. Thomas, "Towards Multidimensional Values in Teaching: The Example of Conflict Behaviors," *Academy of Management Review* 2 (1977), 487.

49 Robbins, *Managing Organizational Conflict*.

50 Gary Jacobson, "A Teamwork Ultimatum Puts Kimberly-Clark's Mill Back on the Map," *Management Review* (July 1989), 28–31.

51 John Southerst, "Now Everyone Can Be a Boss," *Canadian Business* (May 1994), 48–50.

52 R. B. Zajonc, "Social Facilitation," *Science* 149 (1965), 269–274.

53 John Hoerr, "Is Teamwork a Management Plot? Mostly Not," *Business Week,* February 20, 1989, 70.

54 David Woodruff, James B. Treece, Sunita Wadekar Bhargava, and Karen Lowry, "Saturn," *Business Week,* August 17, 1992, 87–91.

55 Aaron Bernstein, "Detroit vs. the UAW: At Odds over Teamwork," *Business Week,* August 24, 1987, 54–55.

56 Robert Albanese and David D. Van Fleet, "Rational Behavior in Groups: The Free-Riding Tendency," *Academy of Management Review* 10 (1985), 244–255.

57 Baron, *Behavior in Organizations.*

58 Harvey J. Brightman, *Group Problem Solving: An Improved Managerial Approach* (Atlanta: Georgia State University, 1988).

59 Aaron Bernstein, "Putting a Damper on That Old Team Spirit," *Business Week,* May 4, 1992, 60; and Hoerr, "Is Teamwork a Management Plot? Mostly Not," 70.

60 Posner, "Divided We Fall."

Leading Through Empowerment at Southwest Airlines

Southwest Airlines has achieved its success by choosing to follow a radically different strategy from its competitors. Begun in the late 1960s as a low-fare, low-frills, high-frequency, short-haul, point-to-point, single-class, irreverent airline, it has grown and increased its astounding success by doing the same thing at each new airport to which it expands. While many airline industry analysts would give Herb Kelleher, the founder and CEO of Southwest, the primary credit for this, Kelleher himself would be more likely to give credit to his employees, whom he describes as people who thrive on competition and who marshal their vigor to prevail.

Southwest Airlines has built its business and corporate cultures around three key tenets: focus on the customer, empower and involve all employees in decision-making and innovation, and make improvements at every opportunity. These are not just slogans on posters. Take for example the Southwest customer service agent who was approached by a near-panicked customer who was desperately trying to check his dog onto his flight to California. Because Southwest does not fly animals, he very well might have missed connecting with his vacationing family. The service agent volunteered to take the dog home, care for it, and bring the dog back two weeks later, upon the man's return! A torn-up back lawn along with a very appreciative customer were the outcomes.

How does an organization instill in its employees willingness to make decisions, to take risks, and in essence, to be leaders? Libby Sartain, Vice-President of People, describes the culture at Southwest as one ". . . designed to avoid complacency, to encourage high spirits." Bureaucracy and rules tend to be kept to a minimum, with employees encouraged "to do what they think is the right thing to do when it comes to servicing our customers."

With little emphasis on hierarchy and lots of emphasis on breaking the rules when it makes sense, employees at Southwest Airlines are carefully selected and trained to be successful in such an organizational culture. "Southwest Airlines does a lot of things to foster pride and a sense of ownership among our employees," claims VP Sartain. Southwest starts by selecting people who show the ability to develop a high degree of commitment to a team.

From the day employees join the company, they take part in a continuous learning process, from orientation to the company to leadership training for all employees. "Leadership begins at Southwest Airlines from the minute you walk in the door as an employee. We don't just view leaders as being the top leadership, and, in fact, our culture allows no elitism at all. Since we work as one big team," Sartain states, "we start employees from the moment they are hired training them to be good leaders. Since we promote from within, that's always worked well for us because leadership develops as the person progresses in his or her career."

The corporate culture at Southwest consistently fosters ownership, pride, and involvement of its employees in their jobs, in Southwest Airlines and even in the community. Employees are given many opportunities to get involved at Southwest, even beyond their job descriptions. Sherry Phelps claims that "you make your job what you want it to be." In order to make the feeling and reality of ownership even higher, Southwest Airlines implemented a profit-sharing and employee stock ownership program from its earliest days.

"We tell our people that we value inconsistency," Kelleher explains. Employees have to be trained and ready to make decisions. As Kelleher says, "What we tell our people is, 'Hey, we can't anticipate all of these things; you handle them the best way possible. You make a judgment and use your discretion; we trust you'll do the right thing. If we think you've done something erroneous, we'll let you know— without criticism, without backbiting.'"

QUESTIONS

1 Referring to the contingency leadership approaches described in the chapter, describe the situational variables and the subordinates' characteristics at Southwest Airlines. What do these elements say about the most appropriate leadership style for the organization?

2 What substitutes for leadership appear to exist at Southwest Airlines?

3 Think about the places you have worked. How was leadership practiced in these organizations? How did it compare to what has been described about Southwest Airlines? What impact did the differences have on your workplace(s)?

REFERENCES

A. Bryant, "United's Bid to Rule Western Skies," *The New York Times,* September 16, 1994, C1.

C.A. Jaffe, "Moving Fast By Standing Still," *Nation's Business,* October 1991, 59.

VIDEO CASE

When Employees Are Part of the Family—La Madeleine

Nancy Cain, a culinary critic for *Business Horizons,* insists that visitors to Dallas put a meal at one of the six local la Madeleine bakeries and cafes on their itineraries. "You might just be greeted by one of the funniest and friendliest international entrepreneurs you will have the pleasure of meeting anywhere—Patrick Esquerré himself."

In the early 1980s, Esquerré founded la Madeleine. Although he knew little about running either a restaurant or bakery, he had grown up in the Loire Valley of France with a love for good food, good wine, and good life. As a promotion director with Young & Rubicam advertising agency in Paris, he was introduced to American culture. After moving to the U. S. to pursue various business ventures, he met Neiman Marcus founder, Stanley Marcus, who advised him to "build an authentic French country bakery near SMU."

By 1996, la Madeleine had expanded to more than 30 neighborhood bakeries, each with a staff of somewhere between 25 and 75. Each bakery is built on the concept that it should be home-like, with customers viewed as "guests." Like many entrepreneurs, Esquerré is dedicated to his customers, answering suggestion cards with personal notes and real action. This dedication also extends to his staff. Esquerré refers to members of his staff as "associates" because he believes that all are working together to make the company a success. "They are family members," he says. "If something happens to one of them or their families, we are there to help them." He is convinced that this is the best way to run a business, and this attitude pervades his management policies.

Jeremy Hartley, President of la Madeleine, confirms the strong feeling of family culture within the organization. "Strong, open, free communication is very important here . . . feeling like they belong to something a little bigger than their own bakery—that their contributions are respected and appreciated." Hartley sees these elements, along with good training and trips to France, as essential to making sure that associates are focused on pleasing their "guests."

Praise and recognition of good performance, including the ability of managers to "surprise" their guests, are used frequently in the company. Formal opportunities for associates to talk and make suggestions—while management really listens—have been developed. These meetings are called associate forums. Led by managers, Esquerré and Hartley included, associates are asked what can be done better, and how.

Are communication and sense of family the only sources of motivation at la Madeleine? Although Esquerré has disdain for the notion of "corporation" and "employees" and works hard to maintain a more informal organization, there are structured reward programs in place. The la Madeleine French Franc Program gives "redeemable" francs to associates who go above and beyond guest expectations. Multiple Christmas parties are given to which all the associates, not just managers in the company, are invited. Bonus programs and stock option plans are provided for managers who stay with la Madeleine.

Under Esquerré's leadership, the focus on the well-being of associates has created a fairly stable group of managers. Unlike some restaurant organizations, managers' personal lives are respected with a normal workweek of perhaps 50 hours. One la Madeleine manager commented that in other food service firms he had worked for, the norm was 70, 75, and even 80 hours a week. Healthier, happier people are more easily able to have fun at work and to communicate this to the people they serve.

With the rapid growth la Madeleine continues to experience, and because of Esquerré's dedication to the concept of promotion from within, even entry-level associates often find that there is a future for them as a shift leader and eventually a manager.

Is the la Madeleine family culture working? With more than 30 bakeries and continual expansion, it certainly seems to be!

QUESTIONS

1 What elements of the various theories of motivation has Esquerré built into his associate relations?
2 Describe the expectations Esquerré most likely holds for his managers and staff. What, if anything, does this type of organization share with those built on team structures?
3 Is la Madeleine the type of company for which you might like to work? What elements of the organization do you find most attractive? Least attractive? Explain.

REFERENCES

L. Stones and K. Lynn, "Entrepreneurism + Customer Service = Success," *Management Review* (November, 1993), 38–44.

VIDEO CASE

Building Community Through Communications—Centex Corporation

Corporations send messages in many ways. At Centex, videos, employee newsletters, and annual reports are just a few of the media used to emphasize the message that the largest builder of single family housing in the United States recognizes the importance of planning, financial strength, and people to both its past and continued successes.

Given the size and visibility of Centex, a large number of investment analysts and shareholders follow the company's financial health closely. Members of senior management at Centex meet directly with investment managers several times a year in order to provide information and to answer questions. With approximately 35,000 Centex annual reports distributed each year, the financial reporting process at Centex begins with a careful targeting of its audiences. Potential segments include shareholders, financial analysts, institutional investors and brokers, potential individual investors, potential and current customers and employees, members of the media, students, and others.

Although the particular corporate objectives for the annual report vary each year, Centex's primary intention is to communicate the "state of the company." As in most Centex communications, the two themes—Centex people as the corporation and fiscal conservatism—were emphasized in the *1995 Annual Report*. The introductory letter to stockholders, for example, opens with, "In fiscal 1995, Centex people again demonstrated their ability to manage effectively amid volatile economic conditions and intense industry competition." The introduction to the *Annual Report* goes on to explain the results for the year as well as the strategic initiatives begun.

The Centex video, "Building Community," produced in 1994, provides another example of Centex communication efforts. Tim Eller, President and CEO of Centex Homes, tells the viewer that although Centex is a very large company, "...it's also in the eyes of our customers a very small company because Centex, to our customers, is the people in our company and the people represent Centex." David Quinn, Executive Vice President and CFO of Centex Corporation, adds, "Since becoming publicly held in 1969, Centex has not reported a quarterly or annual loss—or major write-off. This is primarily a result of our people following very conservative accounting and financial policies, consistent financial strategies, and maintaining a focus on keeping a strong, healthy balance sheet." The video also showcases a number of the building projects that Centex has completed, particularly in the health care field.

Centex Some Times, the employee newsletter, contains several different types of information. When Centex is visible in the press, or receives an award, this is communicated to employees in a front page article. Financial results of the Corporation also receive consistent coverage. In the spring of 1995, when Centex Homes entered into a joint venture in the UK, this first international expansion was announced and described in the newsletter. However, it's not only corporate accomplishments that are covered in the *Some Times*. When employees from the Dallas/Fort Worth area participated in a series of future-oriented focus groups for Centex products, a full description of the process, as well as the names of employees who participated, was featured. The last several pages of each newsletter report on employee accomplishments and awards, volunteer work, and reminders about employee benefits issues.

While Centex pursues increased growth and profitability, the organization continues to put substantial effort and care into communicating with their many stakeholders.

QUESTIONS

1 This case describes a number of vehicles that Centex management uses in order to maintain communications with various target audiences. What other channels of communication must be present in order for Centex to maintain a high level of effectiveness as an organization?

2 Review the communication process as described in your textbook. What element of the communication process is not described in this case? How do you think Centex manages this other element of communication?

3 Have you ever worked for an organization with an employee newsletter? Did you read it? Why or why not? What about the newsletter made it a successful or unsuccessful means of communication?

REFERENCES

Centex Some Times, Employee Newsletter, Centex Corporation, Vol. 7, No. 1, March 7, 1995 and Vol. 7, No. 2, July 1, 1995.

M.F. Van Breda and D. Jobe, *Centex,* American Institute of Certified Public Accountants, Case No. 92-12.

1995 Centex Corporation Annual Report, Centex Corporation, Dallas, Texas.

VIDEO CASE

ike many other functions in organizations, the concept of organizational control has changed dramatically in recent years. From the former philosophy of inspecting work that empoyees do and then correcting errors, we have now moved into an era of empowering employees to do things correctly from the start. Control, like teamwork, is increasingly the business of every employee in an organization and it happens continually. But management still needs to ensure that performance standards and goals are met and budgets and finances are controlled.

Chapter 17 closes the text with a look at the importance of control in organizations. It discusses the importance of strategic planning and quality control; proactive, concurrent, and reactive feedback; and total quality management. We also present budgeting approaches and trends in financial control. Control of quality and financial resources is a cornerstone of success for the future.

Controlling

Atlanta
Target Marke

P A R T

P A R T V I

Productivity through Management and Quality Control Systems

CHAPTER OUTLINE

LEARNING OBJECTIVES

After studying this chapter, you should be able to

- Define organizational control and explain why it is a key management function.

- Describe how organizational control relates to strategic planning.

- Explain the four steps in the control process.

- Describe differences in control focus, including feedforward, concurrent, and feedback control.

- Describe the concept of total quality management.

- Describe the TQM techniques of quality circles, empowerment, benchmarking, reduced cycle time, outsourcing, and continuous improvement.

- Explain the advantages of top-down versus bottom-up budgeting.

- Describe zero-based budgeting and how it applies to organizations.

- Describe new trends in financial control and their impact on organizations.

- Describe the trends in effective organizational control.

MANAGEMENT PROBLEM

Environmentalist Roger Telschow earned money part-time by setting up a tiny press in his Silver Spring, Maryland, basement, where he printed brochures and fliers. Within five years he found himself a full-time printer with one employee. His main goal had been for Ecoprint to have the "most environmentally responsible printing anywhere," but instead he found himself in the uncomfortable position of manager. Soon he had three workers. Heeding advice from colleagues, he insisted the three employees call him "Mr. Telschow" and never even had lunch with them. Trying to get things done right, he alternated between harsh ultimatums and "being nice," neither of which worked. The only way he could ensure good quality service and profits was to work long hours, doing nearly everything himself. When this proved too much for him, he decided to sell Ecoprint. But, like other entrepreneurs, he found it difficult to let it go and wondered if there were some other alternative.[1]

• If you were a consultant to Telschow, what would you recommend he do? How can he maintain quality control without overseeing every aspect of the business himself?

CHAPTER 17

Entrepreneurs like Roger Telschow frequently face problems when their businesses grow beyond their ability to personally oversee everything, and many small businesses fail because of a lack of control.

Control, especially quality control, is an issue facing every manager in every organization today. Newspaper articles during the early 1990s about the savings and loan scandal and about the enormous overdrafts by members of Congress at the House of Representatives Bank are about control. The time needed to resupply merchandise in stores, the length of time that customers must wait in checkout lines, and the number of steps to process and package a roll of film are all control concerns. Merrill Lynch's huge losses from loosely supervised traders, its 9,000-employee workforce reduction, and its strategic refocus on customer service and profits are also about control. Control, including quality control, also involves office productivity, such as improved customer service, elimination of bottlenecks, and reduction in paperwork mistakes.[2]

organizational control
The systematic process through which managers regulate organizational activities to make them consistent with expectations established in plans, targets, and standards of performance.

THE IMPORTANCE OF CONTROL

Here is a true story: Ken Jones, president of the Ontario Centre for Advanced Manufacturing, said that a few years ago IBM Canada Ltd. ordered some parts from a new supplier in Japan. The company stated in its order that acceptable quality allowed for 1.5 percent defects—a high standard in North America at that time. The Japanese sent the order, with a few parts packaged separately in plastic. Their letter said, "We don't know why you want 1.5 percent defective parts, but for your convenience we have packaged them separately."[3]

This story crystalizes the problems with control in North America. First is complacency, the assumption that our management techniques are the best in the world. Second is a top-down, pyramidal control style that is almost feudal in nature. Top management expects to control everything, making all decisions, while middle and lower managers implement decisions, and production workers do only as they are told.

This philosophy is now being stood on its head as a new control philosophy emerges. As we saw in the chapters on leadership, structure, motivation, and teams, low-level employees are being included in management and control decisions. Top management no longer decides the "right" way to do something. More and more, the people who are in control of a particular work setting are those who work within 50 feet of it. Thus at IBM Canada Ltd., all 11,000 employees have now been organized into participation groups. A 1.5 percent defect standard is no longer tolerable.[4]

Organizational control is defined as the systematic process through which managers regulate organizational activities to make them consistent with the expectations established in plans, targets, and standards of performance.[5] To effectively control an organization, managers (or workers) must plan and set performance standards, implement an information system that will provide knowledge of actual performance, and take action to correct deviations from the standard. In addition, every organization needs basic systems for allocating financial resources, approving and developing human resources, analyzing financial performance, and evaluating operational productivity. In long-established organizations such as Cummins Engine, Lever Brothers, and Mack Trucks, the challenge for managers is to know how to use these control systems and improve them. In new, entrepreneurial firms—especially those that have grown rapidly—managers must design and implement new control systems.

STRATEGIC PLANNING AND QUALITY CONTROL

To exert effective control for the organization, management must integrate quality control with the strategic planning ideas described in Part III. If control simply moni-

tors internal activities, it may not help the organization achieve its strategic goals. The linkage of strategy to control is important because strategy reflects changes in the problems and opportunities that appear in the external environment.

Environmental Change

Environments create uncertainty for organizations because of change. As we discussed in Chapter 3, social, economic, technological, and political forces all influence an organization.[6] Sometimes environmental change is gradual, permitting organizations to shift internal controls in an incremental fashion. At other times, changes are **environmental discontinuities,** which are large changes over a short time period. Organizations may need to respond almost overnight. The banking business, for example, used to be straightforward. Interest rates and the number of banks were determined by the government. Suddenly—within a few months—the financial services industry spewed forth new organizations. Banks now compete with insurance companies and stockbrokers.

What do environmental discontinuities mean for organizational control? The firm adapts to these events through strategic planning. As described in the chapters on planning, the organization scans the environment and develops strategic plans that reflect opportunities and potential threats. Internal control systems must change to reflect new strategic goals and new standards of performance. The internal control system should be flexible to accommodate factors considered uncontrollable.[7]

As illustrated in Exhibit 17.1, uncontrollable events lead to the creation of new strategic plans, which in turn lead to new standards of performance, activities, and feedback systems. Control flexibility usually requires employee involvement. Thus, the control cycle, which establishes standards, measures performance, and takes corrective action, is continuously changing. If managers do not carefully link control to strategy, the organization may exert tight control over current tasks—which are the wrong tasks for successful performance.

American Standard developed an innovative manufacturing system in order to fulfill its strategy of being more globally competitive.

■ AMERICAN STANDARD

It's enough to make you flush with excitement. American Standard's success in selling toilets in China, that is. Competing head-on with premier manufacturer Toto Ltd. of Japan could have drained the company's coffers, but the two rivals were essentially on an even playing field with no clogging from protectionist policies. With China as one of the biggest growth markets for commodes, a lot was at stake.

Toto has the seeming advantage of quicker, computerized design from the Japanese home office engineers, while American Standard designers sketch and craft the models by hand. In this case, though, the high-tech Japanese method obstructs quality, for it limits creativity and neglects foreign preferences, blocking Toto's entry into new markets

Second, the turbulent 1980s' painful restructuring left American Standard lean and flexible. They can easily fill any kind of odd-sized order that Toto finds hard to even think about filling. Because American Standard employs a made-to-order manufacturing system known as "Demand Flow"—which reduces inventory/overhead cost—they fill new orders by

environmental discontinuity
A large change in the organization's environment over a short period.

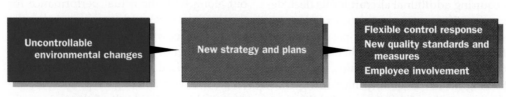

SOURCE Based on Peter Lorange, Michael F. Scott Morton, and Sumantra Ghoshal, *Strategic Control* (St. Paul, MN: West, 1986), Chapter 1.

EXHIBIT 17.1
Relationship of Organizational Control to Strategic Planning

making the toilets rather than using their inventory, as Toto does. Since most of China has used the traditional "squat" facilities, adapting to the old outlet ports is anything but standard and must be continuously customized.

Finally, American Standard excels by offering greater variety. Toto has prided itself in selling what Japanese consumers demand, namely, high-quality, flawless products, which are way too expensive for most Chinese buyers. American Standard is now the top importer of toilets to China, owning almost 40 percent of the market, compared to Toto's 12 percent. Until recently, Toto had stable Japanese demand and no worries about foreign competition, and therefore little reason to adjust its rigid business style. "We know we must change," says a Toto manager. "But it won't happen overnight."

Until then, American Standard is the Commode King of China.[8] ■

Steps in the Traditional Control Process

Based on our definition of organizational control, a well-designed control system consists of four key steps, which are illustrated in Exhibit 17.2.

Establish Standards of Performance. Within the organization's overall strategic plan, managers define goals for organizational departments in specific, operational terms that include a *standard of performance* against which to compare organizational activities. A standard of performance could include "reducing the reject rate from 15 percent to 3 percent," "increasing the corporation's return on investment to 7 percent," or "reducing the number of accidents to one per each 100,000 hours of labor." American Airlines sets standards for such activities as acquiring additional aircraft for its fleet, designing discount fares to attract price-conscious travelers, improving passenger load factors, and increasing freight business. Motorola, a global leader in quality, established Six Sigma as its quality measuring standard, targeting 3.4 defects per million for every Motorola product or service.[9] Standards must be defined in a precise way so that managers and workers can determine whether activities are on target. Standards can then be understood by the people in the organization responsible for achieving them.

Measure Actual Performance. Many organizations develop quantitative measurements of performance that can be reviewed on a daily, weekly, or monthly basis. For example, Robert McDermott, CEO of USAA (an insurance and investment group), blamed his company's system of measurement, rather than employee ability, for a drop in productivity growth. A complete overhaul of USAA's measurement system resulted in creation of the family of measures (FOM), which charts and evaluates employees in four target areas: quality, quantity, timeliness, and customer service. Evaluations under the FOM system determine promotions and bonuses. USAA productivity was soon back on track and growing.[10] In most companies, however, managers do not rely exclusively on quantitative measures. They get out into the organization to see how things are going, especially for such goals as increasing employee participation and personal growth. Managers have to observe for themselves whether employees are participating in decision making and are being offered challenging opportunities for personal growth.

Compare Performance to Standards. The third step is the explicit comparison of actual activities to performance standards. Managers take time to read computer reports or walk through the plant and thereby compare actual performance to standards. In many companies, targeted performance standards are right on the computer printout along with the actual performance for the previous week and year. This makes the comparison easy for managers. A. O. Smith, manufacturer of heavy metal frames for automobiles, used comparison to determine whether it was meeting its plans to diversify products as a result of the changes in

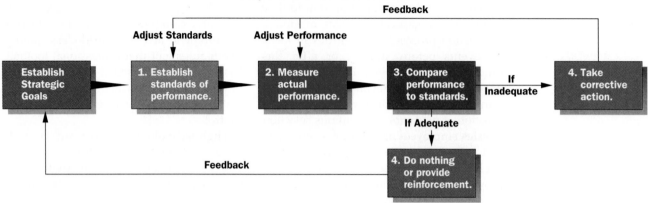

E X H I B I T   1 7 . 2
Steps in the Control Process

the design of automobiles. Smith's managers obtained data revealing that 20 percent of sales were from products not made five years earlier, indicating they were on target for diversification.

However, when performance falls below standard, remember that interpreting the comparison between standards and actual performance is not always easy. Managers are expected to dig beneath the surface and find the cause of the problem. If the sales goal is to increase the number of sales calls by 10 percent and a salesperson achieved an increase of 8 percent, where did she fail to achieve her goal? Perhaps several businesses on her route closed, additional salespeople were assigned to her area by competitors, or she needs training in making cold sales calls. Management should take an inquiring approach to deviations in order to gain a broad understanding of factors that influenced performance. Effective management control involves subjective judgment and employee discussions as well as objective analysis of performance data.

Feedback. *Corrective action* should follow changes in work activities in order to bring them back to acceptable performance standards. In a traditional top-down control approach, managers exercise their formal authority to make necessary changes. Managers may encourage employees to work

harder, redesign the production process, or fire employees. One Friday night, the night shift at the Toledo, Ohio, AMC Jeep plant had a 15 percent no-show rate for workers, which is above the acceptable absenteeism standard of 10 percent. Management's corrective action was to shut the plant down and send the other 85 percent of workers home without pay. In the newer, participative control approach, managers and employees together would determine the corrective action necessary, perhaps through problem-solving teams or quality circles. Positive feedback can be given when performance is satisfactory.

In some cases, managers may take corrective action to change performance standards. They may realize that standards are too high or too low if departments continuously fail to meet or exceed standards. If contingency factors that influence organizational performance change, performance standards may need to be altered to be more realistic and provide positive motivation for employees.

Managers may wish to provide positive reinforcement when performance meets or exceeds targets. They may reward a department that has exceeded its planned goals or congratulate employees for a job well done. Managers should not ignore high-performing departments in favor of taking corrective actions elsewhere.

When managers design and implement the preceding four steps of control, on which part of the organization should they focus? The organization exists around a production process, and control can focus on events before, during, or after this process.[11] For example, a local automobile dealer can focus control on activities before, during, or after sales of new cars. Careful inspection of new cars and cautious selection of sales employees are examples of control that occur before sales take place. Monitoring how salespeople act with customers and providing rules and procedures for guiding the sales process would be considered control during the sales task. Counting the number of new cars sold during the month or telephoning buyers about their satisfaction with sales transactions would constitute control after sales have taken place. These three types of control are formally called *feedforward, concurrent,* and *feedback* and are illustrated in Exhibit 17.3.

ORGANIZATIONAL CONTROL FOCUS

Feedforward Control

Feedforward control focuses on human, material, and financial resources that flow into the organization. Sometimes called *preliminary* or *preventive quality control,* its purpose is to ensure that input quality is sufficiently high to prevent problems when the organization performs its tasks.[12] Feedforward control is anticipatory and attempts to identify and prevent deviations before they occur.

Feedforward controls are evident in the selection and hiring of new employees. Westinghouse selects only 5 percent of job applicants for its College Station, Texas, plant, because only a certain type of person fits the plant's culture. Tandem Computer subjects potential middle managers to 20 grueling hours of interviews with both top-level managers and prospective peers to ensure that no problems will occur after hiring.[13] Before McDonald's could open its restaurant in Moscow, experts had to spend

time in Russia helping farmers learn to grow high-quality potatoes and bakers to bake high-quality bread. These preventive control techniques enabled the Moscow restaurant to achieve world-class quality. The requirement that professional football, basketball, and baseball players pass a physical exam before their contracts are validated is still another form of feedforward control.

High-technology feedforward controls were used on Doug Hartford's farm to achieve maximum crop productivity, as explained in the Technology for Today box.

Concurrent Control

Concurrent control monitors ongoing employee activities to ensure that they are consistent with quality standards. Concurrent control is a common form of control because it assesses current work activities. It relies on performance standards and includes rules and regulations for guiding employee tasks and behaviors. Concurrent control is designed to ensure that employee work activities produce the correct results.

At a construction company, the construction superintendent may hire laborers with little screening. Employees are given a chance to perform, and the superintendent monitors their behavior. If employees obey the rules and work effectively, they are allowed to stay; if they do not, they are let go. In a manufacturing firm, it is not unusual for production managers to have a series of quality checkpoints to see whether the production steps have been completed satisfactorily. As another example of concurrent control, Frito-Lay uses handheld computers to monitor daily sales activities in every store across the country. Data are immediately relayed to headquarters, enabling managers to rapidly respond to a decline in sales.

Feedback Control

Feedback control focuses on the organization's outputs. Sometimes called *postaction* or *output control,* it focuses on the quality of

concurrent control
Control that consists of monitoring ongoing employee activities to ensure their consistency with established standards.

feedforward control
Control that focuses on human, material, and financial resources flowing into the organization; also called *preliminary* or *preventive quality control.*

feedback control
Control that focuses on the organization's outputs; also called *postaction* or *output control.*

E X H I B I T   1 7 . 3
Organizational Control Focus

the end product or service after the organization's task is completed. An intensive final inspection of a refrigerator at a General Electric assembly plant is an example of feedback control in the manufacturing department. Caterpillar Tractor Company uses feedback control when it surveys customers after 300 and 500 hours of product use. In the National Basketball Association, feedback control is used when team managers focus on games won or lost. If a basketball team wins the targeted number of games for the season, the organization is considered to have met quality standards.

The Mall of America hired a new kind of security guard to control rambunctious teens, and the numbers of teens arrested were used as an evaluation tool to determine the effectiveness of this new type of security guard.

MALL OF AMERICA

You might not listen to your own mother, but you might to someone else's. That's the principle behind the Minnesota Mall of America's new program to subdue unruly gangs of teens

TECHNOLOGY FOR TODAY
PRECISION FARMING

Doug Hartford walks through his fields with a backpack on his back. Not so unusual for a farmer. But this year is different. In his backpack is a Geographic Information System (GIS) unit. Carrying a small computer with a blinking cursor for his field position and data from the most recent planting serving as an overlay, the GIS software coordinates information and tells him, on the spot, what should be done. Coming up: A wireless modem will send the information to the local farm supply store, which will convert the data into an order.

Welcome to American farmland in the 1990s, no longer the bastion of the stereotyped "yokels" in bib overalls. Modern farms, losing their long-held price supports, are now subject to the same influences as other businesses—foreign competition, need for better marketing, restructuring, outsourcing.

A pioneer in "precision farming," the executive-looking Hartford works the 1,500-acre Illinois farm like his ancestors did as another kind of pioneer more than 100 years ago. In 1992 he took his first laptop and a global positioning system (GPS) receiver, using 21 different satellites to ascertain the precise geographic coordinates of his combine or tractor from moment to moment and fixing that with a software-driven analysis of yield monitoring to know how every square meter of

his farm performs. GPS was developed by the Defense Department to track missiles and has been available for civilian use since 1983.

The cost is not as bad as it might seem. Hartford has spent only $20,000 since 1992 on the technology and upgrades. Is it worth it? In just one year, 1995, he saved $18,000 by using seed, fertilizer, and herbicides more wisely. However, the system has its limits. "We have the ability to control everything," says Hartford, "but the weather."

SOURCE: Ronald E. Yates, "High-Tech Farming Sows Success," *Chicago Tribune*, May 12, 1996, 5-1, 5-6.

---

who would too often harass customers. The recent evening curfew, requiring those under age 16 to be supervised by an adult, was instituted because as many as 5,000 unsupervised teens would be in the nation's largest mall (annual visitors: 40 million) on a typical Saturday night.

Added to the 150-member security force were 20 mothers, armed only with "verbal judo" and their "Mighty Mom" baseball caps, who are paid $20 an hour for a five-hour shift. Whether these new security personnel are pregnant or grandmotherly, teens tend to listen better to the "Mighty Moms," who seem less onerous than someone in a uniform. One of the mall's managers, Virgil Heatwole, got the idea when he saw a basketball player being interviewed on TV who said, "Hi mom." He realized everyone listens to and respects mothers.

In fact, teens are less likely to mouth off to Mighty Moms, who have proven effective in diffusing potentially heated incidents through friendly chats rather than threats and showdowns.

It seems to be working. Before the program started, there were 10 teens arrested every night of the weekend and now there are none. Plus the local police department has reduced on-duty officers from 12 to 6.

One potentially difficult situation was softened by Mighty Mom Lynn Jones, who reduced tension with a teen by asking about how she got her hair that particular shade of pink. "It's hard to be a jerk to a mom," says Jones.[14] ■

Decentralized Control

Decentralized control (or Modern Management Control) relies on social values, traditions, shared beliefs, and trust to foster compliance with organizational goals. Employees are trusted, and managers believe that employees are willing to perform correctly without extensive rules or supervision. Given minimal direction and standards, employees are assumed to perform well—indeed, they participate in setting standards and designing the control system.

decentralized control
The use of social values, traditions, common beliefs, and trust to generate compliance with organizational goals.

In decentralized control, technology is used to empower employees by giving them the information they need to make effective decisions. Through networked information systems, workers throughout the company can access data that was once available only to a select few. At Hewlett-Packard, a company that thrives on decentralized control, 97,000 employees exchange 20 million E-mail messages a month; share nearly 3 trillion characters of data, such as engineering specs; and execute more than one-quarter of a million electronic transactions with customers and suppliers. "With the ability to share information broadly and fully without filtering it through a hierarchy," HP's chief information officer Robert Walker says, "we can manage the way we always wanted to."[15] When managers share information and power, control can no longer be exercised using the traditional bureaucratic approach. Decentralized control is usually implemented in the following areas.

Corporate Culture.   Corporate culture was described in Chapter 3 as the norms and values shared by organization members. If the organization has a strong corporate culture and the established values are consistent with its goals, corporate culture will be a powerful control device. The organization is like a large family, and each employee is committed to activities that will best serve it. Corporate traditions such as the HP Way and Mary Kay's pink Cadillac awards instill values in employees that are consistent with the goals and behaviors needed for corporate success.

Peer Group.   In Chapter 16, we saw that norms evolve in working teams and that cohesive teams influence employee behavior. If peer control is established, less top-down bureaucratic control is needed. Employees are likely to pressure coworkers into adhering to team norms and achieving departmental goals.

Self-Control.   No organization can control employees 100 percent of the time. Self-discipline and self-control are what keep employees performing their tasks up to standard. Most employees bring to the job a belief in doing high-quality work and a desire to contribute to the organization's success in return for rewards and fair treatment. To the extent that managers can take greater advantage of employee self-control, bureaucratic controls can be reduced. Often, employees high in self-control are those who have had several years of experience and training and hence have internal standards of performance. The experience, training, and socialization of professionals provide these internal standards of performance that allow for self-control.[16] Empowering employees can also contribute to stronger self-control. When employees have the power and information to make decisions that affect their work, they develop a greater sense of responsibility and pride and feel less like a "cog in the corporate wheel."[17] For example, a Saturn worker featured in a recent television commercial relays the sense of responsibility and pride he felt the day he made the decision to "pull the rope" and halt production until a problem he'd discovered was solved.

Employee Selection and Socialization.   With decentralized control, managers rely on a careful selection process to choose employees who will fit in with the company's culture and show a strong desire to contribute to the organization's success. For example, companies often subject employment candidates to a rigorous selection process that relies more on personal evaluations than formal testing procedures. For an entry-level position at Procter & Gamble, each candidate is interviewed at length by line managers who have been trained to probe deeply into such issues as the person's ability to work as part of a team or attitudes toward individual responsibility. Then there is a full day of one-on-one interviews at corporate headquarters and a group interview over lunch. After candidates are hired, they are subjected to intensive training in company values, standards,

and traditions. Rigorous selection and socialization activities are an effective way to ensure that candidates buy into the company's values, goals, and quality traditions and hence need few rules and little supervision for control.

In summary, decentralized control utilizes methods different from those of bureaucratic control. The important point is that both methods provide organizational control. It is a mistake to assume that decentralized control is weak or represents the absence of control simply because visible rules, procedures, and supervision are absent. Indeed, some people believe that the decentralized approach is the stronger form of control because it engages employees' commitment and involvement. Decentralization is the wave of the future, with more companies adopting it as part of a strong corporate culture that encourages employee involvement.

Exhibit 17.4 compares bureaucratic and decentralized methods. Bureaucratic control is concerned with compliance and decentralized control with employee commitment.[18] Bureaucratic methods define explicit standards that translate into minimum performance and use top-down

control. Compensation is based on individual performance. Employees rarely participate in the control process. With decentralized methods, employees strive to achieve standards beyond explicitly stated goals. Influence is mutual, with employees having a say in how tasks are performed and even in determining standards of performance and design of control systems. Shared goals and values replace rules and procedures. Compensation is based on group, departmental, and organizational success rather than on individual performance. This induces individuals to help each other improve quality rather than compete against one another. Employees participate in a wide range of areas, including quality governance, goal setting, and performance standards.

An example of how far decentralized control can go is Marquette Electronics.

MARQUETTE ELECTRONICS

Marquette Electronics makes sophisticated medical devices that doctors use to make life-or-death decisions. Considering the seriousness of its task, it is surprising to see the company

E X H I B I T   1 7 . 4
Bureaucratic and Decentralized Methods of Control

	Bureaucratic	**Decentralized**
Purpose	Employee compliance with rules	Employee commitment to quality
Techniques	Rules, formal control systems, hierarchy, QC inspectors, selection and training, and technology	Corporate culture, peer group, self-control, selection, and socialization
Performance expectations	Measurable standards define minimum performance; fixed indicators	Emphasis on higher performance and oriented toward dynamic marketplace
Organization structure	Tall structure, top-down controls	Flat structure, mutual influence
	Rules and procedures for coordination and control	Shared goals, values, and traditions for coordination and control
	Authority of position; QC department monitors quality	Authority of knowledge and expertise; everyone monitors quality
Rewards	Based on employee's achievement in own job	Based on group achievement and equity across employees
Participation	Formalized and narrow (e.g., grievance procedures)	Informal and broad, including quality control, system design, and organizational governance

SOURCE   Based on Richard E. Walton, "From Control to Commitment in the Workplace," *Harvard Business Review* (March–April 1985), 76–84.

characterized by disorder. Some employees wear Hawaiian shirts and have a boom box playing in the background. In the company cafeteria, employees may enjoy a beer. The day-care center takes care of employees' children, and employees can take time off to play with them. Managers at Marquette Electronics do not overcontrol. "The truth is, we're all quite bad managers," says the engineering vice-president. "Maybe we're not managers at all."

The company is well-managed, but management consciously delegates important responsibilities to employees. Marquette's approach scorns policies and procedures and eschews memos and directives. The guiding philosophy, as expressed by President Mike Cudahy, follows: "People want to love their job, their boss, and their company. They want to perform. You've got to give people a voice in their jobs. You've got to give them a piece of the action and a chance to excel."

The Marquette culture is fluid and informal, but that does not mean a lack of control. People are not bound by traditional rules, but the group norms and the company culture encourage a high standard of quality. Everyone shares a simple but strong expectation: Make quality products, give good customer service, and do it all fast. This may seem an unusual approach to management, but as one former employee said, "Boy, does it work."[19] ■

TOTAL QUALITY MANAGEMENT

About ten years ago, a *Wall Street Journal* survey confirmed the fears of U.S. managers by revealing that three-fourths of all Americans consider foreign-made products equal or superior in quality to products made in the United States. An NBC documentary titled "If Japan Can . . . Why Can't We?" also challenged U.S. quality standards. Executives saw the task of improving service and product quality as the most critical challenge facing their companies. Throughout the 1980s and into the 1990s, the quality revolution spread as U.S. executives saw quality improvement as the route to restoring global competitiveness, and

many companies recommitted themselves to quality.[20]

The term used to describe this approach is *total quality management (TQM)*, which infuses quality throughout every activity in a company. This approach was successfully implemented by Japanese companies that earned an international reputation for high quality. As we saw in Chapter 2, much of the foundation for the Japanese system was laid by U.S. educators and consultants following World War II. The Japanese eagerly adopted the quality ideas of Americans such as Deming, Juran, and Feigenbaum.[21] The sounding of the quality alarm in North America and the publication of such books as *Quality Is Free: The Art of Making Quality Certain* by Philip Crosby and *The Deming Management Method* by Mary Walton helped reawaken managers to the need for quality throughout U.S. companies.[22]

Total quality management (TQM) is a philosophy of organization-wide commitment to continuous improvement, with the focus on teamwork, increasing customer satisfaction, and lowering costs. TQM works through horizontal collaboration across functions and departments and extends to include customers and suppliers.[23] Teams of workers are trained and empowered to make decisions that help the organization achieve high standards of quality.

Cost reduction, a 15 percent rise in productivity, and on-time delivery helped these Campbell Soup Company employees at Maxton, North Carolina, win their second company-sponsored "World Class Manufacturing Award." By embracing the philosophy of *total quality management*, Campbell is reaping rewards in areas such as continuous-flow manufacturing, continuous product replenishment, and just-in-time delivery—all of which improve productivity, keep Campbell competitive, and propel the company's global consumer crusade, springing from the vision of "Campbell Brands Preferred around the World."

total quality management (TQM)

A philosophy of organization-wide commitment to continuous improvement, focusing on teamwork, customer satisfaction, and lowering costs.

This is a revolution in managerial thinking, because quality control departments and formal control systems no longer have primary control responsibility. Companies that really want to improve quality are urged to stop inspecting every part and to get rid of their quality control departments. These companies are then told to train the workers and trust them to take care of quality.

This approach can give traditional executives several sleepless nights as their traditional means of control vanish. Total quality control means a shift from a bureaucratic to a decentralized method of control.

Company-wide participation in quality control requires quite a change in corporate culture values as described in Chapter 10. The mind-set of both managers and employees must shift. Companies traditionally have practiced the Western notion of achieving an "acceptable quality level." This allows a certain percentage of defects and engenders a mentality that imperfections are okay. Only defects caught by a quality control department need be corrected. Total quality control not only engages the participation of all employees but has a target of zero defects. Everyone strives for perfection. A rejection rate of 2 percent will lead to a new quality target of 1 percent. This approach instills a habit of continuous improvement rather than the traditional Western approach of attempting to meet the minimum acceptable standard of performance.

Recent books and articles advocating a systematic quality effort suggest that to be successful, company-wide quality control programs:

1 Reflect total *commitment* to quality by management.
2 Be devoted to *prevention* rather than appraisal and correction.
3 Focus on quality *measurement* (using feedback).
4 *Reward* quality (employing incentives and penalties).
5 Focus on quality *training* at all levels.
6 Stress problem identification and *solution* (using teams).

7 Promote *innovation* and continuous *improvement.*
8 Promote total *participation.*
9 Stress high performance *standards* with zero defects.
10 Provide *calculations* and *reports* of cost savings.[24]

Quality control thus becomes part of the day-to-day business of every employee. Management needs to evaluate quality in terms of lost sales and total company performance rather than as some percentage indicator from a management control system. Each employee must internalize the value of preventing defects. When handled properly, the total quality approach really works. Standout companies using these techniques include Ford Motor Company, Motorola, Westinghouse, and Florida Power & Light.[25]

The implementation of total quality control is similar to that of other control methods. Targets must be set for employee involvement and for new quality standards. Employees must be trained to think in terms of prevention, not detection, and they must be given the responsibility and power to correct their own errors and expose any quality problems they discover. Top management should provide the training, information, and support employees need to meet quality standards.

One impetus for total quality management in the United States is the growing awareness of cost savings in this increasingly competitive global economy. Some companies are using technology-driven "paperless" management systems to cut budgets, as described in the Focus on Quality box.

TQM Techniques

The implementation of total quality management involves the use of many techniques. Most companies that have adopted TQM have incorporated quality circles, empowerment, benchmarking, outsourcing, reduced cycle time, and continuous improvement.

FOCUS ON QUALITY
PAPERLESS CONTROL

Consistent quality and performance are a major part of competitive strategy for such companies as Federal Express, McDonald's, Disney, and Levi-Strauss. However, the cost of building and maintaining consistency through traditional control approaches has been high, and these and other companies are now adopting paperless management systems to keep costs low and quality top-notch.

Organizations as diverse as Owens Corning and Mrs. Fields Cookies are using today's advanced technology to operate more effectively. At Owens Corning, 20 percent of the company's square footage was previously devoted to storing paper files. Automated systems not only save on storage space but also decrease the time spent on administrative tasks and provide better and faster information to top managers. A time and attendance software package enabled Mrs. Fields Cookies to save $200,000 a year by reducing corporate staff. At Chaparral Steel, two full-time accounts-payable clerks now handle thousands of transactions previously divided among numerous employees.

Automation is also being used on the shop floor, where it reduces time and errors in the manufacturing process as well as in such systems as receiving and accounting. Technology such as bar coding and portable data collection devices replace the cost of paper supplies and worker-hours once required for identification of incoming goods. Automation is also linking the manufacturing and financial systems so that inventory records, management accounts, and the purchase ledger are simultaneously updated, thus removing non-value-added steps.

A totally paper-free work environment may be unrealistic. As Ronald Bullock of Mrs. Fields says, "People are reassured to have something in their hands." However, top managers are finding that by reducing the paper pileup, they can run more productive, cost-efficient businesses.

SOURCES: Based on Don L. Boroughs, "Paperless Profits," *U.S. News & World Report*, July 17, 1995, 40–42; Alan Keene, "Automatic Data," *Manufacturing Engineer*, June 1995, 131–133; and Randall Fields and Nicholas Imparato, "Cost, Competition and Cookies," *Management Review*, April 1995, 57–61.

Quality Circles. One approach to implementing a total quality philosophy and engaging the workforce in a decentralized approach is that of quality circles (QCs). A **quality circle** is a group of from 6 to 12 volunteer employees who meet regularly to discuss and solve problems affecting their common work activities.[26] Time is set aside during the workweek for these groups to meet, identify problems, and try to find solutions. The key idea is that people who do the job know it better than anyone else and can make recommendations for improved performance. QCs also push control decision making to a lower organizational level. Circle members are free to collect data and take surveys. In many companies, team members are given training in team building, problem solving, and statistical quality control to enable them to confront problems and find solutions more readily. The groups do not focus on personal gripes and problems. Often a facilitator is present to help guide the discussion. Quality circles use many of the teamwork concepts described in Chapter 16. The quality circle process as used in most U.S. companies is illustrated in Exhibit 17.5, which begins with a selected problem and ends with a decision given back to the team.

The quality circle concept spread to the United States and Canada from Japan. It had been developed by Japanese companies as a method of gaining employee commitment to high standards. The success of quality circles impressed executives visiting Japan from Lockheed, the first company to adopt this practice. Many other North American companies, including Westinghouse, Digital Equipment, and Baltimore Gas & Electric Company, have since adopted quality circles. In several of these companies, managers attest to the improved performance and cost savings. Westinghouse has more than 100 quality circles; a single innovation proposed by one group saved the company $2.4 million. To build on these successes, Westinghouse

quality circle (QC)
A group of 6 to 12 volunteer employees who meet regularly to discuss and solve problems that affect their common work activities.

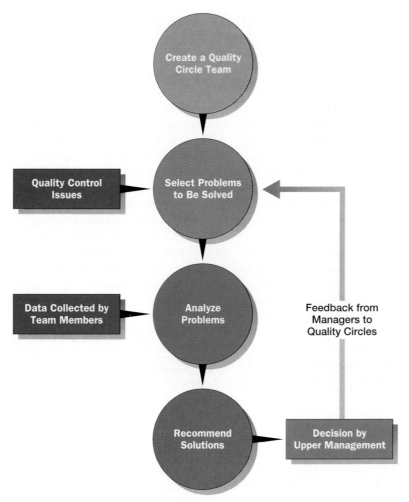

EXHIBIT 17.5
The Quality Circle Process

SOURCE Adapted from Burlington Industries, Inc., *1985 Annual Report*, 9.

benchmarking
The continuous process of measuring products, services, and practices against the toughest competitors or those companies recognized as industry leaders.

created the Productivity and Quality Center that assists departments throughout the company. It acts as a SWAT team of sorts to help divisions do the same work in half the time with better quality results.[27]

An alternative to the quality circle, which can be established within the traditional hierarchical structure, is the *web*, which utilizes today's primary technology (integrated computer networks) and better serves the structural integrity of today's decentralized organization. Solutions are achieved through the inclusive sharing of information throughout the organization and across functions, departments, and even regions. As technology speeds the need for instant decision making and as decision making is increasingly pushed down

to frontline workers, it is crucial that individual authority be enhanced with the best, up-to-the-minute information.[28]

Empowerment. A significant trend within organizations adopting TQM is the empowerment of employees, suppliers, and customers in the decision-making process, reflecting dramatic changes in technology and environment. As companies reduce staff and layers of management, offer alternative work options (such as telecommuting, job sharing, or the creation of a mobile workforce), or shift tasks to suppliers or outside organizations, managers need to share rather than hoard information. Likewise, as customers increase their product sophistication levels and their demands for higher quality, organizations are recognizing the need for customer inclusion in the information loop by providing product and service information and developing interactive relationships between the company and the customer. For example, companies are discovering the wisdom of empowerment through customization. Automakers such as Volvo and BMW are abandoning finished-product inventories in favor of build-to-order. Customers order a customized car with options designed to meet their needs and personal taste. The information is instantly relayed to the factory, where the car is assembled and shipped within two to three days.[29]

Benchmarking. Introduced by Xerox in 1979, benchmarking is now a major TQM component. **Benchmarking** is defined by Xerox as "the continuous process of measuring products, services, and practices against the toughest competitors or those companies recognized as industry leaders."[30] The key to successful benchmarking lies in analysis. Starting with its own mission statement, a company must honestly analyze its current procedures and determine areas for improvement. As a second step, a company must *carefully* select competitors worthy of copying. For example, Xerox studied the order fulfillment techniques of L. L. Bean and learned ways to

reduce warehouse costs by 10 percent. Companies can emulate internal processes and procedures of competitors, but with caution. For example, a small company may court failure by copying the "big boys" such as Ford or Xerox, whose methods are incompatible with a small-company situation. Once a strong, compatible program is found and analyzed, the benchmarking company can then devise a strategy for implementing a new program.[31]

Cementos Mexicanos could not figure out how to adapt to its wildly chaotic environment until it benchmarked practices at Federal Express and the Houston Fire Department.

CEMENTOS MEXICANOS

With every load of cement in rotating cylinders just 90 minutes away from spoiling, delivering on time is crucial to a company's well-being. In Mexico this is complicated by labor disputes, unexpected government inspections, unpredictable weather, traffic gridlocks, and labor disruptions. As expected, Cementos Mexicanos (Cemex) was long ruled by bedlam and telling the customer the proverbial lie of "the truck is almost there." Cemex tried to reduce the 50 percent cancellation/change rate of orders by requiring a 24-hour notice from customers. Even so, Cemex itself still couldn't promise its delivery closer than a three-hour range, often holding an entire construction crew hostage, like waiting all morning for the telephone guy.

Finally, Cemex decided to benchmark and sent a team to Federal Express in Memphis, where they were stunned by logistics, and another crew to the Houston Fire Department, which gracefully responded to many unpredictable crises.

As a result, Cemex's computer expert Homero Resendez launched the new project's "dynamic synchronization of operations," switching trucks from plant managers' control to a huge pool for citywide dispatch. Orders coming in are matched against customer site, mixing-plant locale, and truck location, selecting the best combination based on pouring

conditions, traffic, and order pattern. But the technology would not work without a change in attitudes. Dispatchers were informed, "You are no longer scheduling, you are committing." Grade-school educated drivers were sent to hundreds of hours of computer and customer service training. Cumbersome work rules were discarded, with union agreement coming from the expectation of more efficient trucks bringing higher pay. Driver Salvador Lamas believes this is better for the company and "for us. As a matter of fact, we are the company."

Today, standard service includes same-day delivery, even with order changes, and the office bedlam is replaced with calm, as dispatchers and drivers communicate via software and satellite. And if an order is more than 20 minutes late, Cemex pays a penalty to the builder.[32] ∎

Outsourcing. One of the fastest-growing trends in U.S. business is **outsourcing,** the farming out of a company's in-house operation to a preferred vendor with a high quality level in the particular task area. Companies such as B. F. Goodrich and Glacxo Pharmaceuticals have latched on to outsourcing as a route to almost immediate savings and quality improvement. Traditional in-house operations can be farmed out to save costs on employee benefits, to reduce personnel, and to free existing personnel for other duties. For example, banks have outsourced the processing of credit cards to companies that can do it more cheaply. Large oil companies have outsourced the cleaning and maintenance of refineries. Eastman Kodak outsourced its computer operations to IBM. Manufacturing companies have outsourced the designing of new plants, and service organizations have outsourced mailrooms, warehousing, and delivery services. Outsourcing has also become a viable option for city and state governments trying to slash costs and improve efficiency. In Scottsdale, Arizona, Rural/Metro Company contracts with the city to run fire departments and emergency medical services and is able to provide better service at a fraction of the cost of

outsourcing
The farming out of a company's in-house operation to a preferred vendor.

FOCUS ON CHANGE
PLAYING WITH THE BIG BOYS

When is the manufacturer *not* the manufacturer?

The whole concept of manufacturing and brand names is undergoing a dramatic paradigm shift on the eve of the twenty-first century as more and more companies farm out manufacturing tasks to suppliers and specialists.

Under the concept of outsourcing, intricate collaborations are worked out between major corporations and small factories to produce everything from the tiniest component to near-finished products that, by the time they reach the "mother plant," need little more than bolting together and slapping on the company logo.

A number of economic factors contributed to this growing trend. First, rising costs for maintaining huge manufacturing facilities and large numbers of employees forced many companies to downsize by selling off production facilities and slashing jobs. Second, the rise of small, specialized companies with skilled craftspeople, using state-of-the-art equipment, meant large companies could obtain quality products and parts without the high cost of retooling, updating technology, or retraining employees.

Computers, food and beverages, and autos are among the industries most inclined toward this trend. Your Apple Power PC is built, packaged, and shipped from a California company called Solectron. Computer giant Dell doesn't even have a factory; by using contract manufacturing, Dell can boast $50 in sales for every dollar in plant and equipment compared to IBM's $3.50 figure.

Led by low-cost champion Chrysler, the auto industry has also latched on to the concept of utilizing independent suppliers. Automakers are increasingly focusing on core processes and farming out other tasks. For example, Mercedes and BMW maintain control over world-famous engines, transmissions, and suspensions, but suppliers provide other parts for end-product modular assembly. The lower costs for nonunion suppliers located outside high-income areas appeal to the big automakers facing angry unions, skyrocketing wage and benefits packages as more workers near retirement, and aging plant facilities. Companies such as Eaton, United Technologies Automotive, Prince Corp., and Magna International are finding lucrative niches in the once-impossible-to-tap auto industry.

SOURCES: Shawn Tully, "You'll Never Guess Who Really Makes . . . ," *Fortune*, October 3, 1994, 124–128; Alex Taylor III, "The Auto Industry Meets the New Economy," *Fortune*, September 5, 1994, 52–60; and Shawn Tully, "Auto Supplier with an Attitude," *Fortune*, September 5, 1994, 60.

---

traditional government-run services. As with other quality systems, outsourcing is successful when care is taken in selecting the operations that can be accomplished with greater quality elsewhere and in finding the best outsourcing partners.[33] As described in the Focus on Change box, the trend toward outsourcing is widespread.

Reduced Cycle Time. In the book *Quality Alone Is Not Enough*, the authors refer to cycle time as the "drivers of improvement." **Cycle time** refers to the steps taken to complete a company process, such as teaching a class, publishing a textbook, or designing a new car. The simplification of work cycles, including the dropping of barriers between work steps and among departments and the removal of worthless steps in the process, is what enables a TQM program to succeed. Even if an organization decides not to use quality circles, substantial improvement is possible by focusing on improved responsiveness and acceleration of activities into a shorter time. Reduction in cycle time improves overall company performance as well as quality.[34]

For example, L. L. Bean, Inc., the Freeport, Maine, mail-order firm, is a recognized leader in cycle time control. Workers have used flowcharts to track their movements and pinpoint wasted motions, shifting high-volume merchandise closer to the packing station. Improvements such as these have enabled L. L. Bean to respond with a correct shipment rate of 99.9 percent within only a few hours after the order is received.[35] Reducing cycle time has helped homebuilder Doyle Wilson become successful.

cycle time
The steps taken to complete a company process.

DOYLE WILSON HOMEBUILDER, INC.

Doyle Wilson put himself through the University of Texas by starting a roofing company. By graduation, it was the largest roofing company in Austin, and he then expanded to home building. He owes his big success, though, to a car dealership where he saw Deming's customer-satisfaction principles at work back in 1991. That led him to attend a Deming seminar and later read about Toyota's "lean production system."

What he learned changed his attitude toward business, and he told his managers, "This is what has to be done; you guys lead the charge." Despite some initial resistance, Wilson instituted a number of TQM changes, such as the well-known "flag system," where the person involved with each step hoists a flag while working—green for going well, red for delay. Realizing delays are not only on the building site, Wilson researched the permit process and was able to decrease permit-issue time from 14 days down to 36 hours. He reduced suppliers from 100 to 40, working closely with each one to reduce lead times.

His push for improvement has grown the company to building 430 homes in 1996 at up to $300,000 each. Last year it took 165 days to build a house and now the average construction time is just 124 days—a reduction of 25 percent. Still, Wilson is not satisfied. "We operate under the principles of continual improvement," he says. "And continual improvement is all about continuing."[36] ■

Continuous Improvement. In North America, crash programs and grand designs have been the preferred method of innovation. Yet the finding from Japanese success is that continuous improvement produces an even more effective result. **Continuous improvement** is the implementation of a large number of small, incremental improvements in all areas of the organization on an ongoing basis. In a successful TQM program, all employees learn that they are expected to contribute by initiating changes in their own job activities. The basic philosophy is that improving

things a little bit at a time, all the time, has the highest probability of success. Find one small way to improve the job today and act on it. That improvement will suggest another useful piece tomorrow. No improvement is too small to implement—activities are fine-tuned all the time. In this way, innovations can start simple, and employees can run with their ideas. There is no end to the process. Improvements occur all the time, and the resulting changes give a company a significant competitive advantage.[37]

The continuous improvement concept applies to all departments, products, services, and activities throughout an organization. At South Carolina Baptist Hospital in Columbia, South Carolina, 2,500 employees have been trained in continuous improvement techniques. Managers learn a coaching role, empowering employees to recognize and act on their contributions. Baptist has learned that countless improvements require a long-term approach to building quality into the very fiber of the organization. Over time, project by project, human activity by human activity, quality through continuous improvement has become the way the hospital's employees do their work.[38]

TQM Success Factors

Despite its promise, total quality management does not always work. A few firms have had disappointing results. A recent survey of 500 executives showed that only about one-third of the respondents believed that quality programs truly improved their competitiveness. In another survey of 300 companies, two-thirds reported that a quality program had not reduced defects by more than 10 percent.

Many organizational contingency factors can influence the success of a quality circle or TQM program (see Exhibit 17.6).[39] For example, one positive contingency factor is the task skill demands on employees in the quality circle. When skill demands are great, the quality circle can further enhance productivity. When tasks are simple and require low skills, improved skills from TQM

continuous improvement
The implementation of a large number of small, incremental improvements in all areas of the organization on an ongoing basis.

EXHIBIT 17.6
Quality Program Success Factors

Positive Factors	Negative Factors
• Tasks make high skill demands on employees. • TQM serves to enrich jobs and motivate employees. • Problem-solving skills are improved for all workers. • Participation and teamwork are used to tackle significant problems. • Continuous improvement is a way of life.	• Management expectations are unrealistically high. • Middle managers are dissatisfied about loss of authority. • Workers are dissatisfied with other aspects of organizational life. • Union leaders are left out of QC discussions. • Managers wait for big, dramatic innovations.

training will have little impact on output. TQM or QC success also increases when the program serves to enrich jobs and improve employee motivation. In addition, when the quality program improves workers' problem-solving skills, productivity is likely to increase. When the participation and teamwork aspects of TQM are used to tackle significant problems, such as how to keep metal parts free of oil film, the outcome is better. TQM or quality circles should not be used to tackle simple, routine problems. Finally, a quality program has the greatest chance of success in a corporate culture that stresses continuous improvement as a way of life.

Quality programs often have trouble when senior management's expectations are too high. Managers quickly become disaffected if they are expecting immediate jumps in quality. Quality success comes through a series of small, incremental gains. Moreover, middle and upper-level managers sometimes are dissatisfied because problem-solving opportunities are taken from them and given to employees on the shop floor. Also, when workers are dissatisfied with their organizational lives, quality programs have a smaller chance of success. Union leaders can also upset the quality program if they feel left out of the discussions between workers and management. Finally, if the corporate culture stresses big, dramatic innovations rather than continu-

ous improvement, the quality program has less chance of adding significant improvements to productivity and output.

When correctly applied, quality programs generate enormous savings. At Lockheed, savings of $3 million were documented. At the Norfolk Naval Shipyard, savings of $3.41 for every dollar invested in a QC program were reported over an 18-month period. Another company that succeeded with a total quality control program is Florida Power & Light Company, the first company outside Japan to win a Deming Prize—Japan's prestigious award for quality.

FLORIDA POWER & LIGHT

Who would believe that a regulated monopoly with little pressure to excel would become a benchmark of business excellence? The judges for the Deming Prize believed it after spending 18 months scrutinizing Florida Power & Light's management techniques and delivery of services.

How did FPL do it? The story of quality management began with quality circles. Thousands of employees served on about 1,900 volunteer teams. It was not unusual for a team of meter readers or lineworkers to pause from their daily work to diagram and analyze a particular service problem. But employees loved the challenge, and they produced startling re-

sults. A power-line team devised a plastic pipe to make line installation faster and easier. Meter readers were the most injury-prone employees because of dog bites, so a team devised a way to program handheld computers to beep a warning at residences with a dog on the premises. One team even devised a way to reduce power outages caused by lightning strikes.

The hundreds of team suggestions produced dramatic payoffs. The best quality indicator is customer satisfaction. Customers are delighted because FPL has not sought a rate increase in five years. The number of complaints to the Public Service Commission dropped 75 percent, the best record of any utility in Florida. Another measure is service outages, which used to average 100 minutes per customer per year, similar to the national average—not a bad record. The average of outages was reduced to 43 minutes and continued declining.

Nearly 1,000 companies have made pilgrimages to FPL, and the company developed a how-we-do-it seminar to spread the word that total quality management works.[40] ■

TQM programs work well with the decentralized approach to control. Yet, whether an organization emphasizes the bureaucratic or decentralized approach or focuses on feedforward, concurrent, or feedback activities, quality control is an important part of managing. Another concern for managers is financial control. Every organization needs basic systems for allocating financial resources and analyzing financial performance. One primary financial control device is the budget.

THE BUDGETING PROCESS

The budgeting process is an integral part of the planning process and is concerned with how budgets are actually formulated and implemented in an organization. Budgets are allocated during the strategic planning process commensurate with agreed-upon goals. In this section, we will briefly describe the procedure many companies use to develop the budget for the coming year.

Top-Down or Bottom-Up Budgeting

Many traditional companies use **top-down budgeting,** which is consistent with a more bureaucratic or centralized control approach described in Exhibit 17.4. The budgeted amounts for the coming year are literally imposed on middle and lower-level managers.[41] The top-down process has certain advantages: Top managers have information on overall economic projections; they know the financial goals and forecasts; and they have reliable information about the amount of resources available in the coming year. Thus, the top-down process enables managers to set budget targets for each department to meet the needs of overall company revenues and expenditures.

The problem with the top-down budgeting process is that lower managers often are not committed to achieving budget targets. They are excluded from the budgeting process and resent their lack of involvement in deciding the resources available to their departments in the coming year.[42]

In response to these negative outcomes, many organizations adopt **bottom-up budgeting,** which is in line with the decentralized approach to control. Lower managers anticipate their departments' resource needs, which are passed up the hierarchy and approved by top management. The advantage of the bottom-up process is that lower managers are able to identify resource requirements about which top managers are uninformed, have information on efficiencies and opportunities in their specialized areas, and are motivated to meet the budget because the budget plan is their responsibility.[43]

However, the bottom-up approach also has problems. Because managers are evaluated on their performance against the budget, they may not be motivated to make their budget submissions very challenging, striving instead for the most conservative budget that can get approval.[44] Another

top-down budgeting
A budgeting process in which middle and lower-level managers set departmental budget targets in accordance with overall company revenues and expenditures specified by top management.

bottom-up budgeting
A budgeting process in which lower-level managers budget their departments' resource needs and pass them up to top management for approval.

zero-based budgeting (ZBB)
A budgeting process in which each responsibility center calculates its resource needs based on the coming year's priorities rather than on the previous year's budget.

problem is that managers' estimates of future expenditures may be inconsistent with realistic economic projections for the industry or with company financial forecasts and goals. A university accounting department may plan to increase the number of professors by 20 percent, which is too much if the university plans to increase accounting student enrollment by only 10 percent.

The result of these advantages and disadvantages is that many companies use a joint process. Top managers and the controller define economic projections and financial goals and forecasts and then inform lower managers of the anticipated resources available to them. Once these overall targets (for example, a resource increase of 4 percent to 7 percent) are made available, department managers can develop their budgets within them. Each department can take advantage of special information, resource requirements, and opportunities. The budget is then passed up to the next management level, where inconsistencies across departments can be removed.

The combined top-down and bottom-up process is illustrated in Exhibit 17.7. Top managers begin the cycle. They also end it by giving final approval to all departmental budgets. Departmental budgets fall within the guidelines provided by top management, and the overall company budget reflects the specific knowledge, needs, and opportunities within each department.

Zero-Based Budgeting

In most organizations, the budgeting process begins with the previous year's ex-

penditures; that is, managers plan future expenditures as an increase or decrease over the previous year. This procedure tends to lock departments into a stable spending pattern that lacks flexibility to meet environmental changes. **Zero-based budgeting (ZBB)** was designed to overcome this rigidity by having each department start from zero in calculating resource needs for the new budget period.[45] ZBB assumes that the previous year's budget is not a valid base from which to work. Rather, based on next year's strategic plans, each responsibility center justifies its work activities and needed personnel, supplies, and facilities for the next budget period. Responsibility centers that cannot justify expenditures for the coming year will receive fewer resources or be disbanded altogether. In zero-based budgeting, each year is viewed as bringing a new set of goals. It forces department managers to thoroughly examine their operations and justify their departments' activities based on their direct contribution to the achievement of organizational goals.[46]

The zero-based budgeting technique was originally developed for use in government organizations as a way to justify cost requests for the succeeding year. The U.S. Department of Agriculture was the first to use zero-based budgeting in the 1960s. ZBB was adopted by Texas Instruments in 1970 and by many government and business organizations during the 1970s and 1980s. Companies such as Ford, Westinghouse, Owens-Illinois, and New York Telephone as well as government agencies at both the federal and state levels use zero-based budgeting.

E X H I B I T 17.7
Top-Down and Bottom-Up Budgeting

SOURCE Based on Neil C. Churchill, "Budget Choice: Planning vs. Control," *Harvard Business Review* (July–August 1984), 150–164.

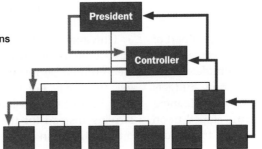

Top-Down
- Provides overall economic projections
- Conveys corporate financial goals and forecast
- Tells resource availability and range of budget amounts

Bottom-Up
- Identifies specific resource requirements
- Includes economies and opportunities in specialized areas
- Resolves resource inconsistencies among departments
- Increases employee commitment

The specific steps used in zero-based budgeting are as follows:

1 Managers develop a *decision package* for their responsibility centers. The decision package includes written statements of the department's goals, activities, costs, and benefits; alternative ways of achieving goals; consequences of not performing each activity; and personnel, equipment, and resources required during the coming year. Managers then assign a rank order to the activities in their department for the coming year.

2 The decision package is then forwarded to top management for review. Senior managers rank the decision packages from the responsibility centers according to their degree of benefit to the organization. These rankings involve widespread management discussions and may culminate in a voting process in which managers rate activities from "essential" to "would be nice to have" to "not needed."

3 Top management allocates organizational resources based on activity rankings. Budget resources are distributed according to the activities rated as essential to meeting organizational goals. Some departments may receive large budgets and others nothing at all.

Zero-based budgeting demands more time and energy than conventional budgeting. Because it forces management to abandon traditional budget practices, top management should develop a consensus among participants that ZBB will have a positive influence on both the company and its employees.

TRENDS IN FINANCIAL CONTROL

Today, companies are responding to changing economic realities and global competition by reassessing organizational management and processes—including the way they control their finances. Some of the major trends in financial control include

open-book management, economic value-added (EVA) systems, and activity-based costing (ABC).

These trends have emerged from changing organizational structures and the resulting management methods that stress information sharing, employee participation, and teamwork. The realities of higher quality demands from consumers, together with the need to cut costs while improving product and service, also require new approaches to financial control.

Open-Book Management

In the changing organizational environment that touts information sharing, teamwork, and managers as facilitators rather than bosses, top executives do not hoard financial data. Employees throughout the organization are admitted into the loop of financial control and responsibility to encourage active participation and commitment to organizational goals.

Open-book management provides employees with the "why" to reorganization, cost cutting, customer service, and other organizational strategies.[47] First, open-book management allows employees to see for themselves—through charts, computer

Praxair, Inc., a provider of industrial gases and high-performance surface coatings, uses a training program called "Becoming the Best—Business Basics" (a.k.a. "Apples & Oranges") created by Celemi, Inc., Simsbury, CT, to teach employees the basics of financial management. Through a relaxed, hands-on approach and direct references to Praxair's own situation, employees learn the meaning of financial terms and understand how and why business decisions are made. Praxair's *open-book management* enables workers to see how their own jobs and decisions affect company success as well as their own compensation through programs such as the Performance Incentive Plan.

open-book management
Sharing financial information and results with all employees in the organization.

printouts, meetings, and so forth—the financial condition of the company. Second, open-book management shows the individual employee how his or her job fits into the picture and affects the financial future of the organization. Finally, open-book management ties employee rewards to the company's overall success. As employees see the interdependence and importance of each function, cross-functional communication and cooperation are enhanced.

The goal of open-book management is to get every employee thinking and acting like a business owner rather than like a hired hand. To get employees to think like owners, they are provided with the same information as owners and given responsibility and authority to act on what they know.[48] Top management support and regular communication with employees throughout the company are essential to the success of open-book management, as illustrated by Globe Metallurgical, described in the Leading the Management Revolution box.

Economic Value-Added Systems

Some companies, including Coca-Cola, AT&T, Quaker Oats, and Briggs & Stratton, have set up **economic value added (EVA) measurement systems** as a new way to gauge financial performance. EVA can be defined as a company's net operating profit after taxes and after deducting the cost of capital.[49] EVA measurement captures all the things a company can do to add value from its activities, such as run the business more efficiently, satisfy customers, and reward shareholders. Each job, department, or process in the organization is measured by the value added.

To be successful, EVA should be central to the financial management system and integrated throughout company policies and procedures. In addition, employees throughout the organization should be trained, because even the smallest jobs can help create value for the company. For example, Variety, a farm equipment manufacturer based in Buffalo, provided EVA training to all 3,500 of its European employees, including those who tighten bolts on tractors.[50] When implemented properly, EVA systems can effectively measure and help control a company's financial performance.

Activity-Based Costing (ABC)

In recent years, the dramatic rise in production concepts such as just-in-time manufacturing and total quality management (TQM) created a financial dilemma for corporate accountants. Their information was *precise* but often irrelevant. The traditional costing system assumed that products consume resources in preset amounts.[51] Often a product would cost far more to manufacture than it could be sold for, but costing systems hid this fact, losing the company a lot of money.

The relationship between labor and overhead has changed. Increased automation has resulted in less employee labor. Total product costs are driven to a degree by higher overhead costs for setup, distribution, and maintenance of sophisticated machinery. In addition, small-batch production to meet changing consumer desires drives up costs.[52]

Activity-based costing (ABC) assumes that true costs are reflected by a formula under which products consume activities and activities consume resources. The crucial step is identifying various activities needed to produce a product and determining the costs of those activities. Costs are then allocated to products accordingly. For example, a manufacturing division may develop three cost pools:[53]

1 *Procurement overhead*, including incoming documentation, storage, inspection, and logistics.
2 *Production overhead*, including various steps in the production process, such as start-up stations, soldering, and testing and defect analysis.
3 *Support overhead*, including production and process engineering and data processing.

In the mid-1980s, Globe Metallurgical, a Cleveland, Ohio-based manufacturing company, underwent a leveraged buyout and extensive restructuring. Staff was reduced by half, but costs still needed to be cut. Top managers realized they needed to do a better job of communicating with employees throughout the company so that workers would understand the need for cost cutting and how they could help.

Globe now has regular daily, weekly, monthly, and quarterly meetings to discuss operational costs and the overall productivity of the corporation and the plants. Quarterly meetings, attended by all Globe employees, are run by the president, the head of finance, and the executive vice-president of administration. They provide ongoing financial and operational results to employees, complete with definitions, and present the information in terms of what it means to workers. "This never happened before," says Globe's director of quality, Norman Jennings. "In the past the attitude was, 'You do your job, we'll pay you.' Now we pay them and we offer them an opportunity to get more. They're interested in how to get more, and to do this they need to be aware of cost structure."

A key element in the success of the program is that Globe's meetings go to the workers rather than expecting the workers to come to the meetings. Meetings are held right in the plants during regular shift hours. That means Globe's top managers deliver the same information dozens of times, at all hours of the day and night.

Globe hoped that open-book management would enable the company to weather downturns in the economy. It worked. Costs are down, productivity is up, and Globe hasn't had to lay off a single worker since it began the program in 1988.

SOURCE: Catherine Romano, "When Money Talks," *Management Review*, November 1994, 44–47.

For each pool, overhead costs are measured and allocated according to the true cost of specific products.

The ABC process can provide an accurate reflection of product costs by measuring specific cost factors. The key is the selection of appropriate activities and selection of an allocation base that best reflects each activity. Activity-based costing is appealing because implementation does not interfere with the financial accounting system, and it can be tailored to specific company needs. For example, Siemens focuses on key business activities while the Fort Worth division of General Dynamics uses ABC for analysis of factory modification and product innovation.[54]

SIGNS OF INADEQUATE BUDGET CONTROL SYSTEMS

Activity-based costing, open-book management, and budgets are designed to provide adequate control for the organization. Often, however, management control systems are not working properly. Then they must be examined for possible clarification, revision, or overhaul. Indicators of the need for a more effective control approach or revised management control systems are as follows:[55]

- Deadlines missed frequently.
- Poor quality of goods and services.
- Declining or stagnant sales or profits.
- Loss of leadership position or market share within the industry.
- Inability to obtain data necessary to evaluate employee or departmental performance.
- Low employee morale and high absenteeism.
- Insufficient employee involvement and management–employee communications.
- Excessive company debts, uncertain cash flow, or unpredictable borrowing requirements.
- Inefficient use of human and material resources, equipment, and facilities.

Management control systems help achieve overall company goals. They help ensure that operations progress satisfactorily by identifying deviations and correcting problems. Properly used, controls help management respond to unforeseen developments and achieve strategic plans. Improperly designed and used, management control systems can lead a company into bankruptcy.

SUMMARY AND MANAGEMENT SOLUTION

This chapter introduced a number of important concepts about organizational control. Organizational control is the systematic process through which managers regulate organizational activities to meet planned standards of performance. The implementation of control includes four steps: establishing standards of performance, measuring actual performance, comparing performance to standards, and taking corrective action. Control should be linked to strategic planning. Changes in the environment require that internal control systems adapt to strategic changes; control systems must not continue measuring what was important in the past.

The focus of organizational control can be on resource input, the production process, or product and service outputs. These forms of control are called, respectively, feedforward, concurrent, and feedback. Most organizations use all three types simultaneously but emphasize the form that most closely corresponds to their strategic goals.

A new approach to control being widely adopted in Canada and the United States is total quality management, which reflects decentralized control ideas rather than traditional bureaucratic control. TQM involves everyone in the organization who is committed to the control function. Six major TQM techniques are quality circles, empowerment, benchmarking, reduced cycle time, outsourcing, and continuous improvement. Quality circles, which are teams of 6 to 12 employees who identify quality problems and discuss solutions, are one means of implementing a quality control philosophy in an organization.

Financial control is another important component of an organization's overall control system. The budget process can be either top down or bottom up, but a budget system that incorporates both seems most effective. Zero-based budgeting is a variation of the budget process and requires that managers start from zero to justify budget needs for the coming year. Recent trends in financial control include open-book management, economic value-added measurement systems, and activity-based costing.

Recall from the management problem that the owner of Ecoprint could only maintain quality control by overseeing every aspect of the business himself. Instead of selling the company, Roger Telschow decided to try satisfying customers by working as a team with his employees. He told them he wanted them to manage their own jobs and he would help in any way he could. And he added, "Just call me Roger." They all started talking about how to meet customer requirements. After a while it was obvious they had unwittingly instituted a total quality management program. Telschow started providing more training, being more open to his workers, and asking for their help and ideas. To give his employees a stake in the company, he began a quarterly profit-sharing bonus and paid $5 cash on the spot to any employee who found a mistake in a work order (which he figures saved him $100 each time by reducing wastage). Another successful TQM concept he implemented is a "frustration log" that allows employees to note any problems they have getting the printing done. Now customer satisfaction tops 95 percent and nearly 100 percent of jobs are delivered on time, all without Telschow doing most of the work himself. His (now) 10 employees are 50 percent more productive than industry averages and sales volume has increased six times as fast as competitors. Ecoprint won awards in 1991, 1994, 1995, and 1996 for productivity. But Telschow is clear that the secret is not in the usual high-tech solutions, but rather in something more human. "Our principal competitive edge is our people," he says. While most people think of TQM as a computerized scientific process, he explains, it is not about "robotics and advanced technology. It's about employees and how they feel and how the customer feels."[56]

DISCUSSION QUESTIONS

1 Federal policy is to take blood tests of operators after a train crash. Would it be more effective to take regular tests of operators on a random basis? What types of control do these different tests represent?

2 Why is control an important management function? How does it relate to the other management functions of planning, organizing, and leading?

3 Briefly describe the four steps of control. Give an example of each step from your own organizational work experience.

4 What does it mean to say that organizational control should be linked to strategic planning?

5 How might organizations use reduced cycle time, benchmarking, or outsourcing to improve the quality of products and services?

6 Which three concepts associated with successful total quality programs do you consider most essential? Explain.

7 The theme of total quality control is "The burden of quality proof rests . . . with the makers of the part." How does this differ from traditional North American approaches to quality?

8 What is a quality circle? How can it be used to improve organizational quality control?

9 What are the advantages of top-down versus bottom-up budgeting? Why is it better to combine the two approaches?

10 According to zero-based budgeting, a department that cannot justify a budget will cease to exist. Do you think this actually happens under zero-based budgeting? Discuss.

11 Would you like to work in a company that uses open-book management? Why or why not?

MANAGEMENT EXERCISES

MANAGER'S WORKBOOK

Quality Improvement Questionnaire

For each item circle the number that best describes your attitude or behavior on the job or at school.

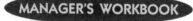

	Agree				Disagree
1 I recognize the practical constraints of existing conditions when someone proposes an improvement idea.	5	4	3	2	1
2 I like to support change efforts, even when the idea may not work.	5	4	3	2	1
3 I believe that many small improvements are usually better than a few big improvements.	5	4	3	2	1
4 I encourage other people to express improvement ideas, even if they differ from mine.	5	4	3	2	1
5 There is truth to the statement, "If it isn't broke, don't fix it."	5	4	3	2	1
6 I work at the politics of change to build agreement for my improvement ideas.	5	4	3	2	1
7 I study suggestions carefully to avoid change just for the sake of change.	5	4	3	2	1

	5	4	3	2	1
8 I like to have clear goals that support improvement, even if changes upset my efficiency.	5	4	3	2	1
9 I constantly talk about ways to improve what I'm doing.	5	4	3	2	1
10 I am able to get higher-ups to support my ideas for improvement.	5	4	3	2	1

Total Score _____

Your score indicates the extent to which you are a positive force for quality improvement. The questions represent behaviors associated with the Japanese approach to companywide continuous improvement of quality.

- 40–50: Great. A dynamo for quality improvement.
- 30–40: Good. A positive force.
- 20–30: Adequate. You have a typical North American attitude.
- 10–20: Poor. You may be dragging down quality efforts.

Go back over the questions on which you scored lowest, and develop a plan to improve your approach toward quality. Discuss your ideas with other students.

MANAGER'S WORKSHOP

Management Control and Organizational Effectiveness

1 Divide into groups of four to six members.
2 Consider the four organizational settings along the top of the table. As a group, discuss how you would measure the effectiveness of your efforts in each control/outcome. List two measurements under each control/outcome for each of the four settings. Therefore, you will have eight measurement techniques for each setting.

Type of control or outcome	Small manufacturing plant	Counseling center (univ. or other)	Local courier service	College basketball team
Quality	1.			
	2.			
Feedback	1.			
	2.			
Feedforward	1.			
	2.			
Productivity	1.			
	2.			

3 How will applying these measurements help the organization become more effective? Which measures could be given more weight than others? Why?

4 Present your chart to the rest of the class. Each group should explain why it chose those particular measures and which are more important. Be prepared to defend your position to the other groups, which are encouraged to question your choices.

SOURCE: Adapted loosely from Jennifer Howard and Larry Miller, *Team Management*, The Miller Consulting Group, 1994, 92.

SURF THE 'NET

Surf through a number of company Web sites, as well as articles from online journals, newspapers, or magazines. Find evidence for at least six kinds of management controls. You should find three of these from company Web sites and three from online publications. Complete the table.

Type of Management Control	Where found: description and Web address	Company name and division or department if applicable	How does control work? Recommendations for improvement of control
1.			
2.			
3.			
4.			
5.			
6.			

ETHICAL DILEMMA

Aide or Abuser?

Elizabeth Lopez, nursing supervisor at Richland Rehabilitation Center, faced a problem. A granddaughter of Libby Simpson, one of the geriatric patients at Richland, had filed a complaint of abuse by a night-shift nursing aide, Susan Johnson. Simpson, like many of the elderly clients, had been in the geriatric wing at Richland for years. She had Alzheimer's disease and was also crippled by rheumatoid arthritis. Lopez reviewed Simpson's file and found that she and her family had filed numerous complaints over the years, although never as serious as this one. Several people on the staff had labeled Simpson a "problem" patient, who was hard to work with, was a complainer, and who sometimes struck out at attendants.

Lopez also reviewed the personnel file of Susan Johnson. Johnson was a three-year veteran in geriatrics. She had voluntarily selected the night shift, because she and her husband covered their child-care responsibilities by

working opposite shifts. Richland Center was owned and operated by Healthcare International, and, by the standards of productivity Healthcare demanded, Johnson was a model employee. Her normal shift put her in charge of 23 patients, and there were no complaints by day-shift workers that her work was not done. On the other hand, the charge nurse at night admitted to Lopez that Johnson could be rough and impatient at times, and, although she had never witnessed any real abuse, she had warned Johnson about her manner a few times.

Lopez was surprised to discover no background check in Johnson's file, although that was procedure. She was concerned that either Johnson might be approaching burnout or that she might abuse a patient who would not be a credible witness against her. But Lopez was aware that geriatric aides were always difficult to find, particularly on the night shift. Replacing Johnson would not be easy, especially with the client load she could handle. Lopez's budget in geriatrics was already stretched to the maximum.

What Do You Do?

1 Dismiss Susan Johnson, because patient welfare is always the first concern. This is not an isolated incident. You must take action now.

2 Investigate the complaint further, ask for a background check on Johnson, and wait for the results to make a decision.

3 Talk to Johnson and give her a warning to be gentle. She will know you are watching. Her immediate superior has never seen any abuse, this is the first complaint against her, and she will be nearly impossible to replace. Care that is slightly rough is better than none.

CASE FOR CRITICAL ANALYSIS

University Microfilms, Inc.

The situation at University Microfilms, Inc. (UMI), was desperate. Because of a worsening economy and job market for several years, many college graduates had decided to postpone the job hunt and pursue master's and Ph.D. degrees, and a requirement of these degree programs is a dissertation. As the nation's top publisher of dissertations, UMI saw its business booming, and booming, and BOOMING. With increased volume came the nightmare of increased backlog. Despite the use of the newest technology, UMI was drowning under a sea of dissertations, with backlogs running in the thousands each year and irate customers screaming over delays. By 1988, UMI backlogs had reached a whopping 8,000 dissertations, and the customer complaint rate hit 20 percent.

UMI set up quality teams to investigate the problem. The teams discovered that only 2 of the 150 days needed for publication of the average thesis were used working on the manuscript. Managers were shocked. What was going on during the other 148 days? The teams also discovered that although technology had changed, the publication process itself remained stagnant, stuck in the same sequence of steps that had always been followed. Workers in each department believed that each step in the process must be completed before moving on to the next stage. So the work on copyrights, indexing, and so on was postponed until after lengthy correspondence with the author had worked out some minor detail. After analyzing the process, the quality team recommended more flexible editing standards that reduced the 150-day holding time by half.

Questions

1 Which TQM concepts best describe the improvements made at UMI?

2 If you were a consultant to UMI's senior management, what advice would you give them about launching a total quality management effort?

3 In a typical company, do you think more quality gains can be achieved in administrative functions or in the technical functions such as manufacturing?

SOURCE: Aaron Bernstein, "Quality Is Becoming Job One in the Office, Too," *Business Week*, April 29, 1991, 52–56.

ENDNOTES

1 Rod Greig, "Pure Gold: 1996 National Association of Printers and Lithographers Management Plus Competition Awards," *American Printer,* June 1, 1996, 42; "Blueprints for Success," *Printing Impressions,* August 1, 1995, 32; Roger Telschow, "Quality Begins at Home," *Nation's Business* (January 1993), 6.

2 Richard J. Schonberger, "Total Quality Management Cuts a Broad Swath—through Manufacturing and Beyond," *Organizational Dynamics* (spring 1992), 16–28; Leah Nathans Spiro, "Raging Bull," *Business Week,* November 25, 1991, 218–221; and Ronald Henkoff, "Make Your Office More Productive," *Fortune,* February 25, 1991, 72–84.

3 "Quality: The Soul of Productivity, the Key to Future Business Growth," *Interview,* Inter-City Gas Corporation, vol. 3 (autumn 1988), 3–5. The story was originally related by Patrick Lush in *The Globe & Mail,* Toronto, June 15, 1988.

4 Ibid.; and T. K. Das, "Organizational Control: An Evolutionary Perspective," *Journal of Management Studies* 26 (1989), 459–475.

5 Stephen G. Green and M. Ann Welsh, "Cybernetics and Dependence: Reframing the Control Concept," *Academy of Management Review* 13 (1988), 287–301; and Kenneth A. Merchant, *Control in Business Organizations* (Marshfield, Mass.: Pitman, 1985).

6 Peter Lorange, Michael F. Scott Morton, and Sumantra Ghoshal, *Strategic Control* (St. Paul, Minn.: West, 1986), Chapter 1.

7 Scott S. Cowen and J. Kendall Middaugh II, "Matching an Organization's Planning and Control System to Its Environment," *Journal of General Management* 16 (autumn 1990), 69–84.

8 Steve Glain, "Top Toilet Makers from U.S. and Japan Vie for Chinese Market," *Wall Street Journal Europe,* December 19, 1996, 1, 8.

9 Barbara Ettorre, "How Motorola Closes Its Books in Two Days," *Management Review,* March 1995, 40–44; and Ronald Henkoff, "Keeping Motorola on a Roll," *Fortune,* April 18, 1994, 67–78.

10 Henkoff, "Make Your Office More Productive."

11 William H. Newman, *Constructive Control* (Englewood Cliffs, N.J.: Prentice-Hall, 1975).

12 Edward P. Gardner, "A Systems Approach to Bank Credential Management and Supervision: The Utilization of Feedforward Control," *Journal of Management Studies* 22 (1985), 1–24.

13 Myron Magnet, "Managing by Mystique at Tandem Computers," *Fortune,* June 28, 1982, 84–91.

14 Neal Karlen, "Tapping 'Mom' Power to Police a Huge Mall," *The New York Times,* December 19, 1996, C2.

15 Thomas A. Stewart, "Managing in a Wired Company," *Fortune,* July 11, 1994, 44–56.

16 Beverly H. Burris, "Technocratic Organization and Control," *Organization Studies* 10 (1989), 1–22.

17 Paul Pence and Kris Lunderman, "Controlling and Managing Empowerment," *The Total Quality Review* (July–August 1995), 33–38.

18 Richard E. Walton, "From Control to Commitment in the Workplace," *Harvard Business Review* (March–April 1985), 76–84.

19 Ellen Wojahn, "Will the Company Please Come to Order," *Inc.* (March 1986), 78–86; "Honor Roll of U.S. Exporters," *Business America,* March 12, 1990, 20.

20 John Lorinc, "Dr. Deming's Traveling Quality Show," *Canadian Business* (September 1990), 38–42; Nancy K. Austin, "Dr. Deming and the 'Q' Factor," *Working Woman* (September 1991), 31–34; and Ross Johnson and William O. Winchell, "Management and Quality," American Society for Quality Control, 1989.

21 A. V. Feigenbaum, *Total Quality Control: Engineering and Management* (New York: McGraw-Hill, 1961).

22 Philip B. Crosby, *Quality Is Free: The Art of Making Quality Certain* (New York: McGraw-Hill, 1979); and Mary Walton, *The Deming Management Method* (New York: Dodd-Meade & Co., 1986).

23 John R. Schermerhorn, Jr., James G. Hunt, and Richard N. Osborne, *Managing Organizational Behavior,* 5th ed. (New York: John Wiley & Sons, Inc., 1994), 5; James W. Dean, Jr., and David E. Bowen, "Management Theory and Total Quality: Improving Research and Practice through Theory Development," *Academy of Management Review* 19, no. 3 (1994), 392–418; and Gregory M. Bounds, Gregory H. Dobbins, and Oscar S. Fowler, *Management: A Total Quality Perspective* (Cincinnati: South-Western College Publishing, 1995).

24 Donna Brown, "Ten Ways to Boost Quality," *Management Review,* January 1991, 5; Schonberger, "Total Quality Management Cuts a Broad Swath—through Manufacturing and Beyond"; and Michael Barrier, "Small Firms Put Quality First," *Nation's Business* (May 1992), 22–32.

25 Richard J. Schonberger, "Production Workers Bear Major Quality Responsibility in Japanese Industry," *Industrial Engineering* (December 1982), 34–40.

26 Johnson and Winchell, "Management and Quality"; and Edward E. Lawler III and Susan A. Mohrman, "Quality Circles after the Fad," *Harvard Business Review* (January–February 1985), 65–71.

27 Thomas A. Stewart, "Westinghouse Gets Respect at Last," *Fortune,* July 3, 1989, 92–98.

28 Sally Helgesen, "Beyond Teams . . . ," *Across the Board* (September 1995), 43–48.

29 Linda R. Logan and Linda S. Wing, "Quality, Empowerment, and the Mobile Workforce," *The Total Quality Review* (July–August 1995), 15–20.

30 Howard Rothman, "You Need Not Be Big to Benchmark," *Nation's Business* (December 1992), 64–65.

31 Otis Port and Geoffrey Smith, "Beg, Borrow and Benchmark," *Business Week,* November 30, 1992, 74–75.

32 Thomas Petzinger, Jr. "Mexican Cement Firm Decides to Mix Chaos into Company Strategy." *The Wall Street Journal,* December 13, 1996.

33 Donna Brown, "Outsourcing: How Companies Take Their Business Elsewhere," *Management Review* (February 1992), 16–18; David Kirkpatrick, "Why Not Farm Out Your Computing?" *Fortune,* September 23, 1991, 103–112; and Eric Schine, Richard S. Dunham, and Christopher Farrell, "America's New Watchword: If It Moves, Privatize It," *Business Week,* December 12, 1994, 39.

34 Philip R. Thomas, Larry J. Gallace, and Kenneth R. Martin, "Quality Alone Is Not Enough," *AMA Management Briefing* (New York: American Management Association, 1992).

35 Otis Port, John Carey, Kevin Kelly, and Stephanie Anderson Forest, "Quality: Small and Midsize Companies Seize the Challenge Not a Moment Too Soon," *Business Week,* November 30, 1992, 68–72.

36 Christina Novicki, "Meet the Best Little House Builder in Texas," *Fast Company* (September 1996), 38–40.

37 "Beyond Total Quality," *Success* (October 1990), 48–49.

38 Robert W. Haney and Charles D. Beaman, Jr., "Management Leadership Critical to CQI Success," *Hospitals*, July 20, 1992, 64.

39 Rick Tetzeli, "News/Trends: Making Quality More than a Fad," *Fortune*, May 18, 1992, 12–13; Thomas et al., "Quality Alone Is Not Enough"; David E. Bowen and Edward E. Lawler III, "Total Quality-Oriented Human Resources Management," *Organizational Dynamics* (spring 1992), 29–41; Robert Wood, Frank Hull, and Koya Azumi, "Evaluating Quality Circles: The American Application," *California Management Review* 26 (fall 1983), 37–53; and Gregory P. Shea, "Quality Circles: The Danger of Bottled Change," *Sloan Management Review* 27 (spring 1986), 33–46.

40 Jeremy Main, "Quality Fever at Florida Power," *Fortune*, July 1, 1991, 65; and Donald C. Bacon, "A Pursuit of Excellence," *Nation's Business* (January 1990), 27–28.

41 Anthony, Dearden, and Bedford, *Management Control Systems*, Chapter 4.

42 Participation in budget setting has been described in a number of studies, including Peter Brownell, "Leadership Style, Budgetary Participation and Managerial Behavior," *Accounting Organizations and Society* 8 (1983), 307–321; and Paul J. Carruth and Thurrell O. McClandon, "How Supervisors React to 'Meeting the Budget' Pressure," *Management Accounting* 66 (November 1984), 50–54.

43 Neil C. Churchill, "Budget Choice: Planning vs. Control," *Harvard Business Review* (July–August 1984), 150–164.

44 Finney, "Budgeting: From Pain to Power."

45 "Zero-Based Budgeting," *Small Business Report* (April 1988), 52–57; and Peter A. Pyhrr, *Zero-Based Budgeting: A Practical Management Tool for Evaluating Expense* (New York: Wiley, 1973).

46 "Zero-Based Budgeting: Justifying All Business Activity from the Ground Up," *Small Business Report* (November 1983), 20–25; and M. Dirsmith and S. Jablonsky, "Zero-Based Budgeting as a Management Technique and Political Strategy," *Academy of Management Review* 4 (1979), 555–565.

47 John Case, "The Open Book Revolution," *Inc.* (June 1995), 26–43.

48 Catherine Romano, "When Money Talks," *Management Review* (November 1994), 44–47.

49 G. Bennett Stewart III, "EVA Works—But Not If You Make These Mistakes," *Fortune*, May 1, 1995, 117.

50 Ibid.

51 Vidya N. Awasthi, "ABCs of Activity-Based Costing," *Industrial Management* (July–August 1994), 8–11; and William M. Baker, "Understanding Activity-Based Costing," *Industrial Management* (March–April 1994), 28–30.

52 Awasthi, "ABCs of Activity-Based Costing."

53 Ibid.

54 Ibid.

55 Based on "Controlling with Standards," *Small Business Report* (August 1987), 62–65.

56 Greig, "Pure Gold: 1996 National Association of Printers and Lithographers Management Plus Competition Awards;" "Blueprints for Success;" Telschow, "Quality Begins at Home."

Paradigm Simulation—Managing Technology and Assuring Product Quality

Although founded as recently as 1990, Paradigm Simulation is a mid-size company that has already established credibility within the simulation and virtual reality industry. At the core of its success has been a product called VEGA, says Dave Gatchel, VP of Entertainment. "Our VEGA product was revolutionary because it provides not only an application interface to engineers. . . but also provides a graphical user interface—a point-and-click environment that less technical users can utilize to manipulate and run applications. These people could visualize and construct a simulation without having to write software, without being a software engineer."

Paradigm's success in developing innovative, user-friendly tools has allowed them to forge a lucrative strategic alliance with Silicon Graphics, a computer hardware company. SGI uses Paradigm's software to demonstrate the performance of its new, powerful, and yet affordable desktop workstation. As a result of this association, a number of important clients have been attracted to Paradigm, including Nintendo. According to Gatchel, Nintendo was looking for firms that could help them bring 3-D games to the home market. "After seven months of contract negotiations, we established a contract to build a game for Nintendo," commented Ron Toupal, co-founder and CEO of Paradigm. The game, Pilot Wings, has led to deals with Disney and other clients.

Paradigm's evolving strategy has been to decrease costs on 3-D simulation software to the point that it is accessible to an increasingly broad market. This strategy co-exists with "listening to the voice of the customer" in designing products. According to Ron Paige, Paradigm VP of Finance, customers are impressed with the feeling that Paradigm becomes part of the customers' team—that Paradigm's job does not stop as soon as they sell the product.

Paradigm gets direct customer interaction through their training programs developed specifically for their customers. During these programs, "Meet the Maker" sessions are scheduled in which the Paradigm employees who have designed a certain software module are brought into the classroom to give hints on how to use "product idiosyncrasies" to the customer's advantage. This shows customers that they have access to the entire organization, not just a trainer.

Although Paradigm's success is clearly dependent upon state-of-the-art technologies expertly applied to customer needs, VP Paige states that "We could have the greatest product in the world, but if we can't process an order correctly, if we can't communicate what our product does, if we can't make sure that when there are problems that we satisfy the customers' concerns successfully, we wouldn't sell anything. We wouldn't be in business! So, people are an es-*sential* component of our success."

Standards of performance, as well as actual measures of performance, must be communicated throughout the company. Elizabeth Smith, Director of Human Resources, suggests that as the company has grown larger, there is an increasing need to document what has been done, to develop more formal procedures for doing so, and to make sure that everyone has access to that information who needs it. Dave Gatchel comments, "With our growth, there are now a number of different projects and an expanded customer base. So from the standpoint of dealing with personnel, or engineering development, we need procedures in place for making sure that there is some review cycle for people's work—we need to maintain controls which allow us to ensure that we're being responsive to our customers. This means that we've had to evolve a more structured management process."

Ron Toupal takes a continuous improvement approach to the business. "Improving the quality of your software, producing it and developing it—that's all done by people. The success of our software business is, to a large extent, based upon the continual commitment of individuals to improve and to better what they have done in the past. In that sense, in this particular business, our people are everything."

QUESTIONS

1 Does Paradigm Simulation appear to be following the four steps in the control process as described in Chapter 17?

2 Are Paradigm's control approaches more bureaucratic or decentralized in nature? Do you think this best fits the organization? Why or why not?

3 In what ways does Paradigm practice TQM and/or Continuous Improvement? Are there elements of these that you believe Paradigm should examine more carefully and perhaps implement? Why?

VIDEO CASE

Finding and Maintaining Quality Merchandise—
International Vendor Relations at Pier 1 Imports

Over 200,000 pieces of stainless steel flatware are just sitting in a Pier 1 Imports warehouse. Where did these come from? Most recently they were stocked in Pier 1 stores—that is until a couple of customers informed store managers that the stainless steel pieces rusted. The company response? After a very rapid testing process that confirmed the customers' observations, the offending product was pulled from all stores and sent to its "resting place"—all within a two-week period.

The people in merchandising at company headquarters in Fort Worth, Texas, and the local Pier 1 agent in China now have ascertained that while there are 47 different types of stainless steel, only one—referred to as 18-8—can be used to make serviceable flatware that won't rust. This newly recognized quality specification has been quickly communicated to all other company agents who purchase flatware assuring that this product quality issue will not arise again.

It is John Baker's responsibility to oversee the network of corporate buyers and on-site agents who are directly responsible for finding, choosing, and assuring the quality of merchandise imported from around the world. Baker, the Senior Manager of Merchandise Compliance, accepted a position at Pier 1 Imports over 20 years ago after working for various department stores purchasing "table-top" and kitchen wares. When he first came on board as a buyer, he spent nearly 6 months of the year on the road, working with the agent network and finding new vendors for Pier 1 merchandise. Today, Baker also handles the increasingly complex area of government regulations of merchandise.

Because such a high percentage of Pier 1 Imports' merchandise is imported (over 85 percent), it is especially critical that U.S. government regulations regarding various product categories be studied and communicated to the manufacturers in other countries. These government regulations form one of the two measures of quality assurance for Pier 1 products. The second is that the products must conform to aesthetic standards that guarantee that the product fits the Pier 1 image and Pier 1 customer desires. It is in large part the buyer's expertise that assures that these standards are met.

What is the process for finding and selecting vendors in countries other than the United States? First of all, Pier 1 depends upon a well- and long-established network of agents in every country from which they import. In some lesser-developed regions, Pier 1 agents work with governments to help locate professional exporters. Some exporters are found at international trade fairs as well. The bulk of Pier 1 agents are native to the country in which they work, and some have been in place for as long as 30 years with their children now taking over the local positions.

The agents' jobs include finding local producers of handcrafted items that fit the Pier 1 customer needs. Buyers look for new sources of products at local craft fairs and even flea markets. Right now, for example, local agents in several countries are looking for sources of wooden furniture—primarily chests and tables—because Pier 1 would like to add to this in-store category. Based upon the location of raw materials, in this case in Italy, South America, Indonesia, and Thailand, agents are searching for just the right manufacturers to be brought to the buyers' attention.

Because it is the agents based within the various exporting countries who must enforce quality requirements, it is critical that John Baker and his colleagues carefully communicate both governmental and aesthetic product requirements to the agents. The agents can then "sit down at the table" with the manufacturers and work out the quality issues. If misunderstandings occur, Pier 1 is always ready to accept some of the responsibility because they view their manufacturers and agents as their partners in this business.

Because Pier 1 Imports has carefully carved out a unique niche in the specialty retail store industry, buyers are hard to hire from outside the company. As Baker noted, "The bulk of our staff has come out of our stores. It is easy for a buyer to move from Macy's to Hudson's—the products are the same as are most of the vendors. The Pier 1 buyer, however, must understand the Pier 1 store in order to be able to effectively and efficiently buy for it." These Pier 1 buyers, along with their agents onsite around the globe, serve as the company's primary link to product quality.

QUESTIONS

1 Review the elements of effective organizational control and then rate the quality control methods used by Pier 1 Imports to assure imported product quality.

2 What advantages does Pier 1 Imports have in working with a network of product suppliers that they would not have if they manufactured their own products? Think about this question primarily from the perspective of ensuring quality and conformance to standards.

VIDEO CASE

Financial Planning and Control— North Texas Public Broadcasting

After 35 years of operation in a Dallas studio that was once abandoned by a commercial television station, KERA Channel 13, and its sister public broadcasting stations, KERA 90.1 and KDTN Channel 2, celebrated the grand opening of the Mary Nell and Ralph B. Rogers Telecommunications Center with a ribbon-cutting ceremony broadcast live on all three stations. Funds for the construction of the 62,400 square-foot facility were contributed by individuals, corporations, and foundations during a capital campaign that began in 1993 and raised $8.6 million by the end of 1995.

The new facility allows the stations to increase production of public television and public radio specials and series about the Southwest, doing much of the work in-house that formerly had to be assigned to outside contractors. Channel 13 and Channel 2 have also enhanced their educational television programming and outreach activities, providing better service to more than 300,000 Texas kindergarten-through-high-school students and tens of thousands of adult learners who turn to the stations for instructional television, college-credit telecourses, and adult literacy programs.

Headquartered in Dallas, North Texas Public Broadcasting, Inc., is a community-based nonprofit organization that holds the licenses for KERA, KDTN, and the KERA radio station. Guided by a volunteer board of directors who represent a cross-section of the communities served by the stations, KERA/KDTN broadcast high quality programs to more than two million viewers and listeners in North, East, and West Texas, as well as parts of Oklahoma and Louisiana. How has this nonprofit organization managed to plan for, raise funds for, and build a major capital project? Additionally, what type of financial planning and budgeting do they do?

"In terms of our recently completed capital campaign, I'd say that the starting point was that the Board and management of this organization have always been very fiscally conservative. For years, we've run in the black and have carried no debt. We own the land where our current facility exists and where we decided to build the new one.... Additionally, for over ten years we've been planning for this new facility. We did a year's worth of very careful studying about what the facility would look like, about the budget we would need, and about how we would go about raising the money." This is how Susan Harmon, Vice President of Administration, Finance and Radio, describes the lead up to the capital campaign. Additionally, the company paid to have a feasibility study conducted during which community leaders were interviewed to determine their level of support. Harmon commented that " ... the feasibility study was one of the best things we did. Then, we had tremendous leadership of the fund-raising campaign itself."

While the KERA/KDTN capital campaign was a hands-down success, yearly budgeting and fundraising is an ongoing activity. Financial resources come from the contributions of the stations' members and donors, including 72,000 individual and family members who provide nearly half of KERA/KDTN's revenue. With a fiscal year operating budget of over $12 million, the underwriting by over 275 corporations, businesses, and foundations is a substantial amount as well (20 percent of revenue). Additional revenue is raised through special fund-raising efforts such as concerts, program production and sales, and other sources.

What happens when a fund-raising goal is not met? Harmon explained that management keeps monthly tabs on expenditures and income streams. The company as a whole has a conservative approach to financial matters and attempts, particularly in the early part of the year, to come in under budget in order to provide for contingencies that may occur later in the year. Like any organization, if fund-raising or other revenue sources do not meet expectations, expenses are reduced where possible.

Richie Meyer, President and CEO of North Texas Broadcasting, says that while his organization is a business, its purpose is not to make money. "We're a business to serve the public and serve our audiences. We run as if we are a business, in the sense that we are fiscally stable... We operate with a balanced budget and any end-of-year excess is plowed right back into programming." In some very real sense, with a PBS station, if the audience is happy, so are the 'stockholders.' Our stockholders are the audience, and they are also the ones who receive our services."

QUESTIONS

1 Describe the various types of budgeting systems used by North Texas Broadcasting as illustrated in the case.
2 Which type of budgeting process—top-down or bottom-up—would most likely have the most advantages for an organization like North Texas Broadcasting? Explain.
3 Assess the adequacy of the budget control systems at North Texas Broadcasting. Does fiscal conservatism most likely help or hurt fund-raising efforts? Explain.

VIDEO CASE

Insights Into Individual Behavior

Do you ever "see" an assignment differently from others at work or at school? When discussing a movie? Have you ever felt that your work associates or your classmates just can't seem to get their message across to you? Or that they don't fully understand your point of view? Have you ever wondered why some people around you want to be told what to do, while others bristle at authority? If you answered "yes" to any of these questions, you have already experienced what practicing managers describe as their most time-consuming task: *people problems*. People problems are based on the complex and unique qualities people bring to the workplace.

Leading is defined in the text as the management function that involves using influence to motivate employees to achieve organizational goals. Three basic skills associated with *leading* are at the core of dealing with people problems: (1) *diagnosing*, or gaining insight into the situation you as a manager are trying to influence; (2) *adapting* your behavior and other resources at your disposal to meet the needs of the situation; and (3) *communicating* in a way that others can understand and accept. Skill at dealing with people problems begins with *diagnosing* the situation. You have to have insight about individual differences to understand what a behavioral situation is now and what it will be in the future. The discrepancy between the situation now and the desired future behavior is the problem to be solved.[1]

This appendix has been written with two purposes. One is to help you understand what makes you "you." With an awareness of what influences your behavior, you will gain insight both into yourself and into the behavior of others. The second purpose is to help you improve your management skill of *diagnosing*. By increasing your knowledge of individual differences in the areas of personality, problem-solving styles, perception, and learning styles, you will be able to understand and manage the behaviors of your associates in various workplace situations.

Note: Contributed by Susan Halfhill.

PERSONALITY

When we talk about an individual's personality as pleasant or bubbly or stubborn, we are describing specific traits. When researchers talk about an individual's *personality*, they are referring to a set of characteristics that underlie a relatively stable pattern of behavior in response to ideas, objects, or people in the environment. Understanding an individual's personality can be useful in predicting how he or she will react in a particular situation.

Let's take a look at three specific work-related personality dimensions: locus of control, authoritarianism/dogmatism, and Machiavellianism.

Locus of Control

Some people believe that their actions can strongly influence what happens to them. They feel in control of their own fate. These individuals have a high *internal locus of control* (internals). Other people believe that events in their lives occur because of chance, luck, or outside people and events. They feel more like pawns of their fate. These individuals have a high *external locus of control* (externals).

Research on locus of control has shown real differences in behavior between internals and externals across a wide range of settings. Internals are easier to motivate because they believe the rewards are the result of their behavior. Internals are better able to handle complex information and problem solving, are more achievement oriented, but are also more independent and therefore more difficult to lead. On the other hand, externals are harder to motivate, less involved in their jobs, more likely to blame others when faced with a poor performance evaluation, but more compliant and conforming and, therefore, easier to lead than internals.[2]

Do you believe luck plays an important role in your life, or do you feel you control your fate? To find out more about your locus of control, read the instructions and complete the questionnaire called Measuring Locus of Control that appears in Exhibit A.1.[3]

Authoritarianism and Dogmatism

Authoritarianism is the belief that power and status differences *should* exist within the organization. Individuals high in authoritarianism tend to be concerned with power and toughness, obey recognized authority above them, stick to conventional values, critically judge others, and oppose the use of subjective feelings.[4] This has important implications for managers in their formal use of authority in organizations. Consider for a minute how authoritarianism relates to the Chapter 9 discussion of authority and how authoritarianism would be related to organizational decentralization or empowerment.

Dogmatism is a closely related term that refers to an individual's receptiveness to new ideas and opinions. A highly dogmatic person is closed-minded and not receptive to new ideas. Research shows that highly dogmatic individuals see the world as a threatening place, readily accept orders from superiors, and may even prefer superiors who are highly directive in their leadership styles. Dogmatic individuals tend to make decisions quickly based on a minimum of information, and they are unreceptive to information that conflicts with their decisions.[5] Imagine the impact this personality trait could have on the quality of decision making, especially under conditions of risk, uncertainty, or ambiguity as described in Chapter 8.

Think for a few moments about people you know—friends, family members, co-workers, instructors—and how they differ on the personality dimensions of authoritarianism and dogmatism. What type of person on these dimensions would you like to have working for you? What type would you like to have as your manager? Discuss your conclusions with other people and see whether they agree.

Machiavellianism

Machiavellianism is a personality dimension characterized by acquisition of power and by manipulation of other people for purely

EXHIBIT A.1
Measuring Locus of Control

The questionnaire below is designed to measure locus-of-control beliefs. Researchers using this questionnaire in a recent study of college students found a mean of 51.8 for men and 52.2 for women, with a standard deviation of 6 for each. The higher your score on this questionnaire, the more you tend to believe that you are generally responsible for what happens to you; in other words, higher scores are associated with internal locus of control. Low scores are associated with external locus of control. Scoring low indicates that you tend to believe that forces beyond your control, such as powerful other people, fate, or chance, are responsible for what happens to you.

For each of these ten questions, indicate the extent to which you agree or disagree using the following scale:

1 = strongly disagree   5 = slightly agree
2 = disagree   6 = agree
3 = slightly disagree   7 = strongly agree
4 = neither disagree nor agree

_____ 1 When I get what I want, it's usually because I worked hard for it.
_____ 2 When I make plans, I am almost certain to make them work.
_____ 3 I prefer games involving some luck over games requiring pure skill.
_____ 4 I can learn almost anything if I set my mind to it.
_____ 5 My major accomplishments are entirely due to my hard work and ability.
_____ 6 I usually don't set goals, because I have a hard time following through on them.
_____ 7 Competition discourages excellence.
_____ 8 Often people get ahead just by being lucky.
_____ 9 On any sort of exam or competition, I like to know how well I do relative to everyone else.
_____ 10 It's pointless to keep working on something that's too difficult for me.

To determine your score, reverse the values you selected for questions 3, 6, 7, 8, and 10 (1 = 7, 2 = 6, 3 = 5, 4 = 4, 5 = 3, 6 = 2, 7 = 1). For example, if you strongly disagreed with the statement in question 3, you would have given it a value of 1. Change this value to a 7. Reverse the scores in a similar manner for questions 6, 7, 8, and 10. Now add the point values from all ten questions together.

Your score: _____

SOURCE: Adapted from J. M. Burger, *Personality: Theory and Research* (Belmont, Calif.: Wadsworth, 1986), 400–401, cited in D. Hellriegel, J. W. Slocum, Jr., and R. W. Woodman, *Organizational Behavior*, 6th ed. (St. Paul, Minn.: West, 1992), 97–100.

personal gain. The dimension is named after Niccolo Machiavelli, a sixteenth-century author who wrote *The Prince*, a book for noblemen of the day on how to acquire and use power.[6] Psychologists have developed instruments to measure a person's Machiavellianism (Mach) orientation.[7] Research shows that high Machs are predisposed to being pragmatic, are capable of lying to achieve personal goals, are more likely to win in win-lose situations, and are more likely to persuade than be persuaded. In loosely structured situations, high Machs actively take control, while low Machs accept the direction given by others. On the other hand, low Machs thrive in highly structured situations, while high Machs perform in a detached, disinterested way. High Machs are particularly good in jobs that require bargaining skills or that involve substantial rewards for winning.[8]

Do you think you are closer to a high Mach or a low Mach? You can assess your score by completing the Mach Assessment Instrument that appears in Exhibit A.2.[9] Discuss your score with classmates.

PROBLEM-SOLVING STYLES[10]

Individuals differ in the way they go about gathering and evaluating information for problem solving and decision making. Four psychological functions have been identified by Carl Jung as related to this process: sensation, intuition, thinking, and feeling.[11]

Before you read further, complete the

EXHIBIT A.2
Mach Assessment Instrument

For each of the following statements, circle the number that most closely resembles your attitude.

	Disagree			Agree	
Statement	A lot	A little	Neutral	A little	A lot
1 The best way to handle people is to tell them what they want to hear.	1	2	3	4	5
2 When you ask someone to do something for you, it is best to give the real reason for wanting it rather than reasons that might carry more weight.	1	2	3	4	5
3 Anyone who completely trusts someone else is asking for trouble.	1	2	3	4	5
4 It is hard to get ahead without cutting corners here and there.	1	2	3	4	5
5 It is safest to assume that all people have a vicious streak, and it will come out when they are given a chance.	1	2	3	4	5
6 One should take action only when it is morally right.	1	2	3	4	5
7 Most people are basically good and kind.	1	2	3	4	5
8 There is no excuse for lying to someone else.	1	2	3	4	5
9 Most people forget more easily the death of their father than the loss of their property.	1	2	3	4	5
10 Generally speaking, people won't work hard unless forced to do so.	1	2	3	4	5

Scoring Key and Interpretation

This assessment is designed to compute your Machiavellianism (Mach) score. Mach is a personality characteristic that taps people's power orientation. The high-Mach personality is pragmatic, maintains emotional distance from others, and believes that ends can justify means. To obtain your Mach score, add up the numbers you checked for questions 1, 3, 4, 5, 9, and 10. For the other four questions, reverse the numbers you have checked so that 5 becomes 1, 4 is 2, and 1 is 5. Then total both sets of numbers to find your score. A random sample of adults found the national average to be 25. Students in business and management typically score higher.

The results of research using the Mach test have found (1) men are generally more Machiavellian than women; (2) older adults tend to have lower Mach scores than younger adults; (3) there is no significant difference between high Machs and low Machs on educational level or marital status; and (5) high Machs tend to be in professions that emphasize the control and manipulation of people—for example, managers, lawyers, psychiatrists, and behavioral scientists.

SOURCE: Adapted from R. Christie and F. Geis, *Studies in Machiavellianism* (New York: Academic Press, 1970), cited in J. R. Schermerhorn, J. G. Hunt, and Richard N. Osborn, *Managing Organizational Behavior*, 4th ed. (New York: John Wiley, 1991), 453–455.

Problem-Solving Diagnostic Questionnaire and then the scoring key that appears in Exhibit A.3.[12] There are no right or wrong answers; just read each item carefully, and then respond with your answer.

According to Jung, gathering information and evaluating information are separate activities. People gather information either by *sensation* or *intuition*, but not by both simultaneously. *Sensation-type* people would rather work with known facts and hard data and prefer routine and order in gathering information. *Intuitive-type* people would rather look for possibilities than work with facts and prefer solving new problems and using abstract concepts.

Information evaluation involves making judgments about the information a person has gathered. People evaluate information by *thinking* or *feeling*. These represent the extremes in orientation. *Thinking-type* individuals base their judgments on impersonal analysis, using reason and logic rather than personal values or emotional aspects of the situation. *Feeling-type* individuals base their judgments more on personal feelings such as harmony and tend to make decisions that result in approval from others.

According to Jung, only one of the four functions—sensation, intuition, thinking, or feeling—is dominant in an individual. However, the dominant function is usually backed up by one of the functions from the other set of paired opposites. Exhibit A.4 shows the four problem-solving styles that result from these matchups.[13]

Look back at your scores. What is your personal problem-solving style? Read the

Your personality is what you are. You have similarities and differences from other people. The differences measured here are not better or worse, merely different. Complete and score the inventory below to find out your personality type.

Personality Inventory
For each item, circle either "a" or "b." If you feel both "a" and "b" are true, decide which one is more like you, even if it is only slightly more true.

1 When making a decision, the most important considerations are
  a. Rational thoughts, ideas and data.
  b. People's feelings and values.
2 When discussing a problem with colleagues, it is easy for me
  a. To see "the big picture."
  b. To grasp the specifics of the situation.
3 When I am working on an assignment, I tend to
  a. Work steadily and consistently.
  b. Work in bursts of energy with "down time" in between.
4 When I listen to someone talk on a subject, I usually try to
  a. Relate it to my own experience and see if it fits.
  b. Assess and analyze the message.
5 In work, I prefer spending a great deal of time on issues of
  a. Ideas.
  b. People.
6 In meetings I am most often annoyed with people who
  a. Come up with many sketchy ideas.
  b. Lengthen meetings with many practical details.
7 I would rather work for an organization where
  a. My job was intellectually stimulating.
  b. I was committed to its goals and mission.
8 I would rather work for a boss who is
  a. Full of new ideas.
  b. Practical.

In the following, choose the word in each pair that appeals to you more:

9 a. Social
  b. Theoretical
10 a. Ingenuity
  b. Practicality

action tendencies. Do they fit? Studies show that the sensation-thinking (ST) combination characterizes many managers in Western, industrialized societies. Do you think the ST style is the best fit for most jobs in today's society? Exhibit A.4 also matches the four problem-solving styles with their occupational preferences. Is there a good fit between your individual style and your desired occupation?

PERCEPTION[14]

Remember the opening question about whether you ever "see" assignments differently from others at work or at school? Most people answer "yes" to that question because "seeing" things differently is the essence of perception. *Perception* is the process we use to make sense out of our environment by selecting, organizing, and interpreting information from the environment.

We are all aware of our environment, but not everything in it is equally important to our perception of it. We tune in to some data (e.g., a familiar voice off in the distance) and tune out other data (e.g., footsteps and paper shuffling next to us). Individual perceptual awareness varies widely. Recognizing the difference between what is perceived and what is real is a key element in *diagnosing* a situation.

EXHIBIT A.3
Continued

SOURCE: Adapted from I. Myers, *The Myers-Briggs Type Indicator* (Princeton, N.J.: Educational Testing Service, 1962). © Consulting Psychologist Press, Palo Alto, CA.

Scoring Key

Count one point for each item listed below which you circled in the inventory.

Score for S	Score for N
2b	2a
3a	3b
6a	6b
8b	8a
10b	10a

Total

Circle the one with more points: S   or   N

Score for T	Score for F
1a	1b
4b	4a
5a	5b
7a	7b
9b	9a

Total

Circle the one with more points: T   or   F

Your Score is:

S or N _____   T or F _____

We can think of perception as a step-by-step process. First, we observe information (sensory data) from the environment through our senses: taste, smell, hearing, sight, and touch. Next, our mind screens the data and will select only the items we will process further. Third, we *organize* the selected data into meaningful patterns for interpretation and response. Most differences in perception among people at work are related to how they select (perceptual selectivity) and organize (perceptual organization) sensory data.

Perceptual Selectivity

Imagine standing on a busy street corner with cars honking, signs flashing, traffic lights changing, and a bus whizzing by just as a dog bites the cuff of your pants. Is it any wonder you never noticed the person tugging on your sleeve asking for directions? We are bombarded by so much sensory data that we cannot process it all. Our solution is to run the data through a perceptual filter that retains some parts (selective attention) and eliminates other parts.

Perceptual selectivity is defined as the screening and selecting of sensory data (objects and stimuli) that compete for one's attention. Exactly what we screen and select depends on a number of factors, some of which relate to the sensory data being perceived and some of which relate to the perceiver. Certain characteristics of the sensory data or of the object being perceived can enhance the chance it will be selected. Relevant characteristics of the object being perceived include *contrast, novelty, familiarity, intensity, motion, repetition,* and *size.* Descriptions of these characteristics are summarized in Exhibit A.5.

An organizational example of the influence of data characteristics on the perceptual process comes from an employment interview. Interviewers often compare a job applicant to other applicants interviewed for the same job instead of against a predetermined standard. Based on the characteristic of *contrast,* an applicant might be scored too low if preceded by an outstanding applicant or too high if preceded by a poor applicant. This is also an example of a perceptual error that can occur without awareness by the perceiver.

Several characteristics of the perceiver

EXHIBIT A.4
Four Problem-Solving Styles

Personal Style	Action Tendencies	Likely Occupations
Sensation-thinking	■ Emphasizes details, facts, certainty ■ Is decisive, applied thinker ■ Focuses on short-term, realistic goals ■ Develops rules and regulations for judging performance	■ Accounting ■ Production ■ Computer programming ■ Market research ■ Engineering
Intuitive-thinking	■ Shows concern for current, real-life human problems ■ Is creative, progressive, perceptive thinker ■ Emphasizes detailed facts about people rather than tasks ■ Focuses on possibilities using interpersonal analysis	■ Systems design ■ Systems analysis ■ Law ■ Middle/Top management ■ Teaching business, economics
Sensation-feeling	■ Prefers dealing with theoretical or technical problems ■ Is pragmatic, analytical, methodical, and conscientious ■ Focuses on possibilities using interpersonal analysis ■ Is able to consider a number of options and problems simultaneously	■ Directing supervisor ■ Counseling ■ Negotiating ■ Selling ■ Interviewing
Intuitive-feeling	■ Avoids specifics ■ Is charismatic, participative, people-oriented, and helpful ■ Focuses on general views, broad themes, and feelings ■ Decentralizes decision making, develops few rules and regulations	■ Public Relations ■ Advertising ■ Personnel ■ Politics ■ Customer services

can also influence the selection of sensory data. These include *needs* and *motivation*, *values* and *beliefs*, *personality*, *learning*, and *primacy* and *recency*. Descriptions of the perceiver's characteristics are contained in Exhibit A.6.

One example of the influence a perceiver's characteristics can have on perception relates to "first impressions." Most of us try to look our best when we are meeting someone for the first time, whether in an interview, at a meeting, or on a blind date. We have been told repeatedly (often by our parents) that first impressions really count. In fact, studies support that conclusion. The *primacy* characteristic can cause us to form impressions quickly that are rather hard to change. Unfortunately, this could lead to a perceptual error. We also tend to be more attentive at the beginning and at the end of an activity, a tendency that is a common problem during job interviews. What you say to an interviewer during the middle of the interview may not be retained as well or carry as much weight as what you say at the beginning or the end.

From these examples, we should recognize that *perceptual selectivity* is not a simple process of reducing data down to an amount that is easy to perceive. It is a complex filtering process that determines which sensory data will receive our attention. Characteristics of the object and of ourselves are clues about why we "see" things differently from those around us.

Perceptual Organization

Once people have selected the sensory data to be perceived, they begin grouping the data into recognizable patterns. *Perceptual organization* is the categorization of sensory data (stimuli or objects) according to our personal frame of reference. We have learned to simplify and make sense out of our perceptions through a gradual process of organizing sensory data as we experience life.

For example, all of us have a mental picture of an object with the following properties: wood, four legs, a seat, a back, and an arm rest. This is our image

EXHIBIT A.5
Perceptual Selectivity: Characteristics of the Perceived Object that Enhance Selection

Contrast	The extent to which an object stands out against other objects in the background
Novelty	The extent to which an object is new or different from objects perceived previously
Familiarity	The extent to which an object is known or familiar to the perceiver
Intensity	The extent to which an object is more intense (e.g., brighter, louder) than objects surrounding it
Motion	The extent of movement of the object
Repetition	The number of times an object is repeated
Size	The larger the size of the object

of a chair. When we see an object that has all these properties, we recognize it as a chair. We have organized the incoming information into a meaningful whole.[15]

Several factors in perceptual organization contribute to individual differences among people in the work setting.

Perceptual grouping is the organizing of sensory data into patterns by using mechanisms such as closure, continuity, proximity, and similarity.

Closure is the tendency to perceive incomplete data in its whole, complete form. What do you see in part *a* of Exhibit A.7? Most people see this series of spots as a dog, but others see 20 unrelated ink blobs.

Continuity is the tendency to perceive sensory data in continuous patterns, even if they are not. Read aloud the message in part *b* of Exhibit A.7. Do you see any discontinuity in the sentence? Read it again carefully. *The* appears at the end of the first line and is repeated at the beginning of the second line. Many people read this as a continuous sentence with only one *the*.

Proximity is the tendency to perceive sensory data as related because of close physical location. For example, people working on the same floor of a large office building may be perceived as a unit even though they represent portions of several departments of the company.

Similarity is the tendency to perceive sensory data as a common group because they are alike in some way. Similarity is valued at some private schools; thus, all students wear uniforms. The similarity provided by uniforms also diminishes attention to other differences among students. As another example, read the following sentence carefully.

> Finished files are the result of years of scientific study combined with the experience of many years.

Read the sentence several times *before reading any farther.*

Now, go back and count the number of times the letter *F* appears in the sentence.

How many did you count? Three? Six? Most people count only three the first time. If you counted three, go back and try again. The correct answer is six. The most common error is to overlook the word *of* because it has a *v* sound, not an *f* sound. Only the *f* sounds fall into a similar group for most people; hence, a perceptual mistake is made because the *f*s with a *v* sound are not recognized.

Figure-ground is another factor in perceptual organization. *Figure-ground* is the tendency to perceive the sensory data you are most attentive to as standing out against the background of sensory data to which you are less attentive. Look at part *c* of Exhibit A.7. How many blocks do you see, six or seven? Some people have to turn the figure upside down before they can see seven blocks. Although this is just a reversible figure-ground pattern, it shows us that once we have "seen" something one way, it is difficult for us to "see" it differently. Exhibit 15.3 in the text shows another figure-ground pattern. What do you see first, a young girl or an old woman? What does that tell you about the sensory data you are most attentive to?

Perceptual distortions are errors in our perceptual judgment. Errors can arise from

Needs and motivation	People notice sensory data that will potentially satisfy their important needs.
Values and beliefs	People filter out sensory data that are inconsistent with their values and beliefs.
Personality	Personality traits (e.g., Machiavellianism or locus of control) cause people to filter out or actively select sensory data based on their orientation.
Learning	People notice sensory data based on their past experience with the same or similar data.
Primacy and recency	People notice sensory data that occur toward the beginning of an event and toward the end of the event.

EXHIBIT A.6
Perceptual Selectivity: Characteristics of the Perceiver that Influence Selection

inaccuracies in any part of the perception process. Some types of errors are so common that managers should become familiar with them.

Stereotyping is the tendency to assign an individual to a group or broad category (e.g., female, black, elderly or male, white, disabled) and then to attribute widely held generalizations about the group to the individual (e.g., "females are emotional" or "males are stubborn"). Stereotyping clouds individual differences, and inappropriate stereotyping based on race, ethnicity, gender, and age contributes to hidden barriers limiting the advancement of individuals who are members of those categories.

Halo effect occurs when the perceiver develops an overall impression of a person or situation based on one attribute, either favorable or unfavorable. In other words, a halo blinds the perceiver to other attributes that should be used in generating a more complete assessment. The halo effect can play a significant role in performance appraisal. For example, a person with an outstanding attendance record may be assessed as responsible, industrious, and highly productive; another person with less-than-average attendance may be assessed as a poor performer. Either assessment may be true, but it is the manager's job to be sure the assessment is based on complete information about all job-related attributes and not just his or her preferences for good attendance.

Projection is the tendency of perceivers to see their own personal traits in other people; that is, they project their own needs, feelings, values, and attitudes into their judgment of others. For example, a manager who is achievement oriented may assume that her subordinates are as well. This may cause her to restructure jobs in her department to be less routine and more challenging. However, subordinates might have been quite satisfied with the jobs that the manager saw as routine. Self-awareness and empathy are the best guards against errors based on projection.

Perceptual defense is the tendency of perceivers to protect themselves against ideas, objects, or people that are threatening. People perceive things that are satisfying and pleasant but tend to disregard things that are disturbing and unpleasant. In essence, people develop blind spots in the perceptual process so that negative sensory data do not hurt them. For example, a manager who suppressed the memory of his own sexual abuse as a child may avoid listening to and may not be sympathetic to a story of abuse to others. Recognizing these perceptual blind spots will help people develop a clearer picture of reality.

The point was made at the start of this section on perception that effective *diagnosing* in a situation was predicated on recognizing the difference between what is perceived and what is real. If you have increased your knowledge and understanding of the perceptual process, you will have improved your ability to recognize reality.

LEARNING[16]

Years of schooling have conditioned many students to think that learning is rather

EXHIBIT A.7
Perceptual Objects

(a)

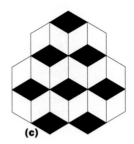

(c)

(b)
Read this sentence out loud.

A BIRD IN THE
THE HAND IS WORTHLESS.

passive. Good teachers tell us what we need to know. Learning is the process of acquiring and remembering abstract ideas and concepts. Textbooks are important. And learning is an activity separate from the real world—after all, it takes place in a classroom. With this view, in the managerial world of time deadlines and concrete action, learning seems remote, even irrelevant. However, today's successful managers need specific knowledge and skills as well as the ability to adapt to changes in the world around them. Managers have to learn.

Learning is a change in behavior or performance that occurs as the result of one's experience. Learning is a person's way of adapting to events in the outside world. It is also linked to perception because learning depends on the ability to perceive sensory data. Think about what you read in the previous section concerning perception. If two individuals experience the same action— for example, they are transferred to a department in a foreign country—are they likely to adapt their behaviors (that is, learn) to the experience in the same way? Probably not. Let's take a closer look at the learning process and how individuals differ in this activity.

One model of the learning process is

shown in Exhibit A.8.[17] In this model learning is conceived as a four-stage cycle. A concrete experience we encounter is followed by thinking and reflective observation, which lead to abstract conceptualizations and in turn to active experimentation, which in turn leads to new experiences as the cycle repeats.

The arrows in this model are meant to imply that the learning cycle is continuously recurring. We continuously test our conceptualizations and adapt them as a result of our personal reflections and observations about the experience.

For example, while working on a term paper, you might see (concrete experience) the need for a textbook used two years ago that provides a conceptual definition you cannot recall. After thinking (reflective observation) for a moment, you remember putting it on your bedroom shelf (abstract conceptualization), and you go there to find it (active experimentation). It is not there (concrete experience). You start the process again, this time looking in the garage. Success. You learned where the book was and found the definition.

Although this example is simple, the learning model in Exhibit A.8 is important because each of us develops a personal learning style that may place much more

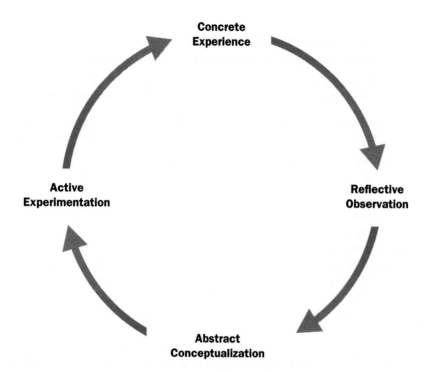

emphasis on one or two of the stages while skipping the other stages in the cycle. These differences occur because the learning process is directed by our individual needs and goals. For example, an engineer may place greater emphasis on abstract concepts, while a salesperson may place greater emphasis on concrete experiences. Personal learning styles typically have strong and weak points because of these preferences.

The Learning Style Inventory (LSI) is a self-description test based on the learning model in Exhibit A.8. It is designed to assess a person's strong and weak points as a learner in the learning cycle by measuring the relative emphasis on each of the four learning stages. In the LSI the learning stages are called "learning modes." The four modes are concrete experience (CE), reflective observation (RO), abstract conceptualization (AC), and active experimentation (AE).

Before you read farther, complete the Learning Style Inventory in Exhibit A.9. There are no right and wrong answers; just follow the instructions, and think about the way you learn or the way you deal with day-to-day

situations in your life as you read the four word sets in the questionnaire.

You can get an indication of the learning modes you tend to emphasize by plotting your scores on the "target" graph in Exhibit A.9. This graph gives norms on CE, RO, AC, and AE for approximately 2,000 adults ranging from 18 to 60 years of age. The raw scores for each of the four scales are listed on the crossed lines of the target. Circle your raw score for each scale, and connect the points with straight lines to create a graphic representation of your learning style profile. Percentile scores for the population of respondents are represented by the concentric circles on the target graph.

Which learning modes do you tend to emphasize? Are you surprised? Few of us take the time to think about how we actually prefer to learn. How balanced is your learning style profile? Of concern is a very high score on one mode because that may indicate a tendency to overemphasize that stage of the learning process, or a very low score on one mode because that may indicate a tendency to avoid that aspect of learning. Not many people have totally balanced

E X H I B I T   A . 9
Learning Style Inventory (LSI)

Instructions

There are nine sets of four words listed below. Rank the words in each set by assigning a *4* to the word that best characterizes your learning style, a *3* to the word that next best characterizes your learning style, a *2* to the next most characteristic word, and a *1* to the word that is least characteristic of you as a learner.

You may find it hard to choose the words that best characterize your learning style. Nevertheless, keep in mind that there are no right or wrong answers—all the choices are equally acceptable. The aim of the inventory is to describe how you learn, not to evaluate your learning ability.

Be sure to assign a different rank number to each of the four words in each set; do not make ties.

1	____discriminating	____tentative	____involved	____practical
2	____receptive	____relevant	____analytical	____impartial
3	____feeling	____watching	____thinking	____doing
4	____accepting	____risk taker	____evaluative	____aware
5	____intuitive	____productive	____logical	____questioning
6	____abstract	____observing	____concrete	____active
7	____present oriented	____reflecting	____future oriented	____pragmatic
8	____experience	____observation	____conceptualization	____experimentation
9	____intense	____reserved	____rational	____responsible

Scoring

The four columns of words above correspond to the four learning style scales: CE, RO, AC, and AE. To compute your scale scores, write your rank numbers in the boxes below only for the designated items. For example, in the third column (AC), you would fill in the rank numbers you have assigned to items 2, 3, 4, 5, 8, and 9. Compute your scale scores by adding the rank numbers for each set of boxes.

Score items:	Score items:	Score items:	Score items:
2 3 4 5 7 8	1 3 6 7 8 9	2 3 4 5 8 9	1 3 6 7 8 9
□□□□□□	□□□□□□	□□□□□□	□□□□□□
CE = ____	RO = ____	AC = ____	AE = ____

To compute the two combination scores, subtract CE from AC and subtract RO from AE. Preserve negative signs if they appear.

AC   CE   AE   RO

AC–CE: □ – □ =   AE–RO: □ – □ =

SOURCE: D. A. Kolb, I. M. Rubin, and J. M. McIntyre, *Organizational Psychology: An Experimental Approach*, 3d ed. (Englewood Cliffs, N.J.: Prentice-Hall, 1984).

profiles, which is fine. The key to effective learning is being competent in each of the four modes when it is needed.

Because each person's learning style is a combination of the four learning modes, it is useful to describe your style by a single concept that combines the scores of all four modes. You can determine your learning style type by plotting the two combination scores, AC–CE and AE–RO, on the Learning Style Type Grid in Exhibit A.9. By marking your raw scores on the two lines (AC–CE on the vertical and AE–RO on the horizontal) and plotting their points of intersection, you can see which of the four learning style quadrants you fall into. The four quadrants—labeled diverger, assimila-

tor, converger, and accommodator—represent the four dominant learning style types. Descriptions and characteristics of these learning styles are summarized in Exhibit A.10.

It is important for each of us to be aware of our personal learning style so that we understand how we approach problems and issues, our learning strengths and weaknesses, and how we react to coworkers, students, or professors who have different styles. It is also important to recognize the necessity of continuous learning for both the individual and the organization. We need to stop from time to time and ask ourselves and those around us, "What can we learn from this experience?"

EXHIBIT A.9
Continued

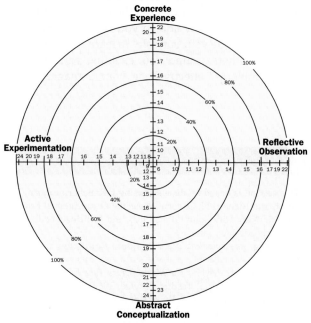

(a) The Learning Style Profile Norms for the Learning Style Inventory (Copyright 1976 by David A. Kolb)

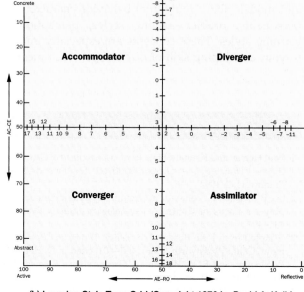

(b) Learning Style Type Grid (Copyright 1976 by David A. Kolb)

EXHIBIT A.10
Learning Style Types

Learning Style Type	Dominant Learning Abilities	Learning Characteristics	Likely Occupations
Converger	■ Abstract conceptualization ■ Active experimentation	■ Is good at decisiveness, practical application of ideas, and hypothetical deductive reasoning ■ Prefers dealing with technical tasks rather than interpersonal issues	■ Engineering ■ Production
Diverger	■ Concrete experience ■ Reflective observation	■ Is good at generating ideas, seeing a situation from multiple perspectives, and being aware of meaning and value ■ Tends to be interested in people, culture, and the arts	■ Human resource management ■ Counseling ■ Organization development specialist
Assimilator	■ Abstract conceptualization ■ Reflective observation	■ Is good at inductive reasoning, creating theoretical models, and combining disparate observations into an integrated explanation ■ Tends to be less concerned with people than ideas and abstract concepts	■ Research ■ Strategic planning
Accommodator	■ Concrete experience ■ Active experimentation	■ Is good at implementing decisions, carrying out plans, and getting involved in new experiences ■ Tends to be at ease with people but may be seen as impatient or pushy	■ Marketing ■ Sales

SUMMARY

This appendix has tried to sensitize you to a few examples of individual differences that can be important in the workplace. Exhaustive research exists on the concepts and models about individual behavior characterized as personality, problem-solving styles, perception, and learning styles. These concepts are especially important to your developing skill of *diagnosing*, which means understanding what a behavioral situation is now and knowing what you can expect in the future. The material presented will not only add to your base of knowledge but may also pique your curiosity to learn more about the behavior of others around you, enabling you to handle "people problems" effectively in your management career.

ENDNOTES

1 Paul Hersey and Kenneth Blanchard, *Management of Organizational Behavior: Utilizing Human Resources,* 6th ed. (Englewood Cliffs, N.J.: Prentice-Hall, 1993), 5–6.

2 See P. E. Spector, "Behavior in Organizations as a Function of Employee's Locus of Control," *Psychological Bulletin* (May 1982), 482–497.

3 Adapted from J. M. Burger, *Personality: Theory and Research* (Belmont, Calif.: Wadsworth, 1986), 400–401, cited in D. Hellriegel, J. W. Slocum, and R. W. Woodman, *Organizational Behavior,* 6th ed. (St. Paul, Minn.: West, 1992), 97–100.

4 This section is based on a discussion by Hellriegel et al., *Organizational Behavior,* 84.

5 Ibid.

6 Niccolo Machiavelli, *The Prince,* trans. George Bull (Middlesex: Penguin, 1961).

7 Richard Christie and Florence Geis, *Studies in Machiavellianism* (New York: Academic Press, 1970).

8 Ibid.; and J. R. Schermerhorn, J. G. Hunt, and R. N. Osborn, *Managing Organizational Behavior,* 4th ed. (New York: John Wiley, 1991), 123.

9 Adapted from Christie and Geis, *Studies in Machiavellianism,* cited in Schermerhorn et al., *Managing Organizational Behavior,* 453–455.

10 This section is based on discussions by J. R. Schermerhorn, J. G. Hunt, and Richard N. Osborn, *Managing Organizational Behavior,* 2nd ed. (New York: John Wiley, 1982); and Hellriegel et al., *Organizational Behavior,* 140–163.

11 Carl Jung, *Psychological Types* (London: Routledge and Kegan Paul, 1923).

12 Adapted from I. Myers, *The Myers-Briggs Type Indicator* (Princeton, N.J.: Educational Testing Service, 1962), cited in D. Hellriegel, J. W. Slocum, and R. W. Woodman, *Organizational Behavior,* 3d ed. (St. Paul, Minn.: West, 1983), 128, 143.

13 Adapted from Schermerhorn et al., *Managing Organizational Behavior,* 1982 and 1991.

14 This section is based on discussions by Mel Schnake, *Organizational Behavior Supplement* (Chicago: The Dryden Press, 1991); and Hellriegel et al., *Organizational Behavior,* 1992.

15 Hellriegel et al., *Organizational Behavior,* 1992, 110.

16 This section is based on a discussion and exercise by D. A. Kolb, I. M. Rubin, and J. M. McIntyre, *Organizational Psychology: An Experiential Approach,* 3d ed. (Englewood Cliffs, N.J.: Prentice-Hall, 1984), 27–54.

17 David A. Kolb, "Management and the Learning Process," *California Management Review* 18, no. 3 (spring 1976), 21–31.

Management Science
Aids for Planning and
Decision Making

In Chapters 7 and 8 we saw how good managers are distinguished from poor ones by how effectively they set goals, develop plans with which to meet those goals, and make the necessary decisions. This appendix introduces quantitative techniques that can serve as valuable decision aids and planning tools. Management science techniques are especially effective when many factors affect a problem, when problems can be quantified, when relationships among factors can be defined, and when the decision maker can control the key factors affecting performance outcomes.[1] For example, management science techniques are invaluable to American Airlines. Its Decision Technologies unit develops quantitative models to enhance efficiency of the reservations division. The results: $1.4 billion in savings over three years.[2] American likewise schedules more than 8,300 pilots for 16,200 flights through development of TRIP (Trip Re-evaluation and Improvement Program), which is now considered a standard for the industry and is being implemented by other transportation companies.[3]

This appendix describes some of the more common management science techniques that are applicable to managerial planning and decision making. It discusses quantitative approaches to forecasting, break-even analysis, linear programming, PERT charting, and the decision aids of payoff matrix and decision tree. These techniques are not covered in depth; managers need to understand only the basic approach and be able to communicate with management science experts.

THE NATURE AND ROLE OF MANAGEMENT SCIENCE

Management science techniques are designed to supplement managerial planning and decision making. For many decisions, management science leads to better answers. For example, in today's organizations, it is not uncommon to find experts who use mathematical and statistical analyses to help managers make capital budgeting decisions; decide whether to open a new factory; predict economic trends or customer demands; determine whether to rent or buy a new computer system; schedule trucks, ships, or aircraft; decide among several proposals for research and development projects; and assess whether a new-product introduction is likely to be profitable.

Management science is defined as a set of quantitatively based decision models used to assist management decision makers. There are three key components in this definition.

First, *management science is a set of quantitative tools*. Mathematically based procedures impart a systematic rigor to the decision process. Certain types of data must be gathered, put into a specific format, and analyzed according to stringent mathematical rules.

Second, *management science uses decision models*. A *model* is a simplified representation of a real-life situation. For example, small-scale physical models were constructed for every set in the movie *Raiders of the Lost Ark* to diagnose filming problems before constructing the real sets. In a mathematical model, key elements are represented by numbers. Mathematical models are difficult for many students and managers because they use a language that is abstract and unfamiliar. However, outcomes from mathematical models can still aid in decision making.

Third, *quantitative models assist decision makers; they cannot substitute for or replace a manager.*[4] Management science models are simply one of many tools in a manager's tool kit. The manager's role is to provide information for use in the models, interpret the information they provide, and carry out the final plan of action.

Sometimes proponents of management science techniques oversell their value for managerial decision making. Conversely, managers who are unfamiliar with mathematics may resist the use of management science techniques and hence fail to take advantage of a powerful tool. The best management approach is to attempt to understand the types of problems to which management science aids apply and then work with specialists to formulate the necessary data and analytical procedures. For example, using models, a severity index was developed to enable physicians to predict survival time for persons diagnosed with AIDS. The index enables hospital administrators to anticipate necessary resources for patients, including beds, and to assess the effectiveness of the care program.[5]

Exhibit B.1 lists some of the more common management problems and applicable management science techniques. These techniques apply to problems in production, product distribution, new-product decisions, and sales force assignment. Scores of management science techniques are available. The remainder of this chapter will describe some of the most important management science tools and illustrate their use in managerial planning and decision making.

FORECASTING

Managers look into the future through forecasts. *Forecasts* are predictions about future organizational and environmental circumstances that will influence plans, decisions, and goal attainment. Forecasts are a basic part of the SWOT analysis described in Chapter 7. Virtually every planning decision depends on assumptions about future conditions.

Four types of forecasts are frequently used by managers.

I **Sales forecasts** predict future company sales. Sales forecasting is critical, be-

management science
A set of quantitatively based decision models used to assist management decision makers.

sales forecast
A forecast of future company sales based on projected customer demand for products or services.

Management Problem	Applicable Management Science Tool
Production mix	Linear programming
Scheduling and sequencing	PERT network
Distribution	Simulation
New-product decision	Payoff matrix
	Decision tree
Pricing decisions	Payoff matrix
	Decision tree
Sales force assignment	Assignment models
Forecasting	Time series
	Regression series
	Econometric models

EXHIBIT B.1
Management Problems and Applicable Management Science Tools

cause it defines customers' demands for products or services. Sales forecasts determine production levels for three months, six months, or one year into the future. Managers use them to hire necessary personnel, buy needed raw materials, make plans to finance an expansion, and arrange needed transportation services. Medium- and large-sized companies such as Sound Warehouse, Paychex, Wallace Computer Services, and Monsanto use sales forecasts to plan production activities.

2 **Technological forecasts** attempt to predict the advent of technological changes, especially major technological breakthroughs that could alter an organization's way of doing business. Companies forecast technological changes to avoid building plants or acquiring equipment that is out of date and noncompetitive. General Motors has been forecasting the use of robotics in automobile manufacturing so as to remain competitive with other American and Japanese automobile producers. Watch manufacturers tracked developments from a company called AT&E Corporation that found a high-tech way to transform a standard wristwatch into a paging device.

3 **Demographic forecasts** pertain to the characteristics of society, including birthrates, educational levels, marriage rates, and diseases. For example, the baby boomlet of the 1980s enabled managers in schools and companies that make children's clothing and toys to plan for increased product demand.

4 **Human resources forecasts** predict the organization's future personnel needs.[6] When AT&T predicted a decrease of several thousand employees during the late 1980s, its human resources department arranged for early retirements and helped displaced employees find jobs elsewhere. Likewise, companies in rapidly growing industries must initiate employee recruitment programs and urge the location of new plants in areas where employees are available.

Forecasts provide information that reduces uncertainty in decision making. Several specific techniques, both quantitative and qualitative, help managers derive forecasts for use in their planning and decision making. Exhibit B.2 illustrates some of the forecasting techniques, their possible applications, and their degree of accuracy.

Let us now examine both the quantitative and qualitative techniques more closely.

Quantitative Forecasting Techniques

Quantitative forecasts start with a series of past data values and then use a set of mathematical rules with which to predict future values.[7] Quantitative techniques have become widely used by managers for two reasons. First, the techniques have repeatedly demonstrated accuracy, especially in the short and intermediate term, thus earning managers' confidence as a planning aid.

human resources forecast
A forecast of the organization's future personnel needs.

technological forecast
A forecast of the occurrence of technological changes that could affect an organization's way of doing business.

quantitative forecast
A forecast that begins with a series of past data values and then applies a set of mathematical rules with which to predict future values.

demographic forecast
A forecast of societal characteristics such as birthrates, educational levels, marriage rates, and diseases.

E X H I B I T   B . 2
Forecasting Techniques Used by Organizations

		Accuracy		
Quantitative Techniques	**Sample Application**	**Short Term**	**Intermediate Term**	**Long Term**
Times series analysis	Sales, earnings, inventory control	Excellent	Good	Good
Regression analysis	Sales, earnings	Excellent	Excellent	Fair
Economic models	GNP, sales, demographics, economic shifts	Excellent	Good	Fair
Qualitative Techniques				
Delphi	Product development, technological predictions	Good	Good	Good
Sales force composite	Sales projections, future customer demand	Fair	Fair	Poor
Jury of opinion	Sales, new-product development, earnings	Good	Fair	Poor

SOURCE: Adapted from J. Chambers, S. Mullick, and D. Smith, "How to Choose the Right Forecasting Technique," *Harvard Business Review* (July–August 1971), 55–64.

Second, improvements in computer hardware and software have increased the efficiency and decreased the expense of using quantitative techniques. A large number of variables can be incorporated into the analysis, and statistical refinements have improved the techniques' ability to meet the forecasting needs of company managers.

Quantitative forecasting techniques can be subdivided into two categories: time series analysis and causal models. Time series analysis projects past behavior into the future. Causal modeling attempts to unearth past causes of behavior as a way of projecting into the future.[8]

Time Series Analysis The forecasting technique called **time series analysis** examines the patterns of movement in historical data. It defines patterns in terms of one of four categories:

1 Secular trends   3 Seasonal variation
2 Cyclic patterns   4 Random variation

A *secular trend* is the general behavior of a variable over a long period of time. Panel *a* of Exhibit B.3 shows a set of data with an upward trend in unit sales each year. The demand for this company's sales is growing regularly, and managers project sales for 1997 based on this growth.

A *cyclic pattern* involves a recurring up-and-down movement that is periodic in nature. The pattern extends over several years

and cannot always be counted on to repeat with precise regularity. Cyclic patterns are related to general business cycles of growth and recession, which managers find extremely valuable to predict. Panel *b* of Exhibit B.3 shows units sold over a typical business cycle of several years.

Seasonal variation is a regular variation in behavior that recurs within a period of one year or less. Climatic changes and social and religious customs can cause seasonal variation. For example, the coordinator for Montreal ambulances found seasonal variance in ambulance use, with higher winter demand for increased emergency use and hospital transfers but a substantial decrease in the summer.[9]

In another example, bicycle sales normally peak in November and December—prior to Christmas—decline in the winter months, rise in the spring and summer, and decline again in the fall. Panel *c* of Exhibit B.3 shows a seasonal pattern of units sold that would help a manager predict future sales.

Random variation is not a pattern at all. *Random variation* means that there are changes in units sold, but they are unpredictable. These movements might be caused by random factors such as a strike, natural disaster, or changes in government regulations. Panel *d* of Exhibit B.3 shows data that have random variation. Managers are unable to use random variation to predict the future.

Time series analysis is used to predict both

time series analysis
A forecasting technique that examines the patterns of movement in historical data.

EXHIBIT B.3
Examples of Time Series Forecasting Patterns

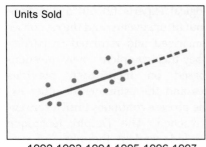

(a) Secular Trend

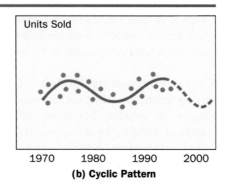

(b) Cyclic Pattern

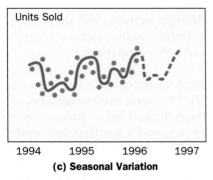

(c) Seasonal Variation

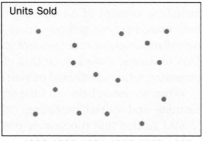

(d) Random Variation

━━━━ Historical trend
▬ ▬ ▬ Forecast

short-term and intermediate-term behavior. Its power is its ability to account for seasonal changes as well as long-run trends. Time series analysis works best when the business environment is relatively stable, that is, when the past is a good indicator of the future. In environments in which consumer tastes change radically or random occurrences have a great impact on sales, time series models tend to be inaccurate and of little value.

One company that was able to take advantage of time series forecasting is Huffy Corporation.

HUFFY CORPORATION

Huffy Corporation is the largest U.S. producer of bicycles. In the early 1980s, Huffy's plants were producing at maximum capacity in several of its product lines. Huffy executives were concerned about whether they should undertake plans to increase future capacity. Because a major corporate goal was 100 percent customer satisfaction, managers realized that an accurate sales forecasting system was important.

The internal accounting and financial group was commissioned to develop a forecasting system with the following characteristics:

1 Be usable by managers responsible for all product lines and divisions.
2 Use data from the current management information system database.
3 Be cost efficient.
4 Be easily maintained and readily understood by nontechnical managers.
5 Base forecasts on available sales data.
6 Produce forecasts accurate within ±5 percent for divisions, ±10 percent for each product, and ±10 percent for each brand.

After studying many forecasting techniques, Huffy's managers selected a time series model. They found it easy to use because it

avoided complex statistics. The final model predicted future sales based on both cyclical and seasonal variation projected from six months of sales history. The time series model was easy to understand and accurate, meeting Huffy's forecasting objective.[10] ■

Causal Forecasting Models   The forecasting technique called **causal modeling** attempts to predict behavior, called the *dependent variable,* by analyzing its causes, called *independent variables.* Thus, causal modeling may attempt to predict sales (the dependent variable) by examining those factors that cause sales to increase or decrease, including amount of advertising expenditure, unit price, competitors' prices, and the overall inflation rate (independent variables). This technique differs from that of simply projecting future sales based on past sales.[11]

When choosing between time series predictions and causal modeling, managers should realize that time series predictions are better at describing seasonal sales variations and predicting changes in sales direction, and causal models provide better information on how to influence a dependent variable such as units sold. Both time series and causal forecasting approaches can produce reliable forecasts if they start with proper data and assumptions. Managers using causal or time series models may wish to work closely with management science experts for maximum benefit.

Qualitative Forecasting Techniques

Qualitative techniques are used when quantitative historical data are unavailable. **Qualitative forecasts** rely on experts' judgment. Three useful forms of qualitative forecasting are the Delphi technique, sales force composite, and jury of opinion.

Delphi Technique.   A process whereby experts come to a consensus about future events without face-to-face discussion is called the **Delphi technique.**[12] The Delphi procedure was described in Chapter 8 as a means of group decision making. It is especially effective for technological forecasts, because precise data for predicting technological breakthroughs are not available. Technological experts fill out a questionnaire about future events, and the responses are summarized and returned to participants. They then complete a new questionnaire based on their own previous responses and the estimates of other experts. The process continues until a consensus is reached. The Delphi technique promotes independent thought and precludes direct confrontations and participants' defensiveness about their ideas. Its biggest advantage is that experts with widely different opinions can share information with one another and reach agreement about future predictions.[13]

Sales Force Composite.   Another technique, called the **sales force composite,** relies on the combined expert judgments of field sales personnel. Experienced salespeople know their customers and generally sense fluctuations in customers' needs and buying patterns before these changes are reflected in quantitative data. Salespeople are polled about their customers' expected purchases in the coming time period. Each estimate is reviewed by a district or regional sales manager, who combines these estimates and makes adjustments for expected changes in economic conditions. Findings by Dun and Bradstreet suggest that businesspeople are good forecasters except in times of unexpected or deep recession. During especially bad periods, both managers and salespeople tend to be overly optimistic about the future.[14]

Jury of Opinion.   A third technique is the **jury of opinion,** sometimes called the *jury of executive opinion,* which averages the opinions of managers from various company divisions and departments. It is similar to a Delphi procedure in that jury members need not meet face-to-face. Because opinions come from several people, the forecast is less risky than it would be if conducted by a single individual. The method is quick and inexpensive and does

---

causal modeling
A forecasting technique that attempts to predict behavior (the dependent variable) by analyzing its causes (independent variables).

sales force composite
A type of qualitative forecasting that relies on the combined expert opinions of field sales personnel.

qualitative forecast
A forecast based on the opinions of experts in the absence of precise historical data.

jury of opinion
A method of qualitative forecasting based on the average opinions of managers from various company divisions and departments.

Delphi technique
A qualitative forecasting method in which experts reach consensus about future events through a series of continuously refined questionnaires rather than through face-to-face discussion.

not require elaborate statistical analysis. It takes advantage of management's knowledge of the environment based on past experience and good judgment. Jury of opinion was used to forecast the 1990s glut of new automobiles. Experts saw that new plants built in the United States by Japanese and American carmakers would lead to overcapacity by 6 million units. Based on this forecast, some companies curtailed expansion plans.[15]

All forecasting is based on historical patterns, and qualitative techniques are used when precise, historical data are unavailable. If managers feel that experts' biases are affecting forecast accuracy, they can correct future forecasts through instructional feedback. As managers or other experts see that their forecasts are too high or too low, they learn to forecast more accurately in future periods.[16]

QUANTITATIVE APPROACHES TO PLANNING

Once a sales forecast is developed, managers incorporate that information into their planning for the firm's future actions.

Many quantitative techniques are available to help managers plan. Three of these techniques tell managers how many units must be sold before a product is profitable (break-even analysis), which combination of products can minimize costs (linear programming), and how to schedule complex projects to be completed in the shortest amount of time (PERT). The following discussion illustrates how these techniques assist planning in some situations.

Break-even Analysis

Break-even analysis is a quantitative technique that helps managers determine the levels of sales at which total revenues equal total costs and, hence, the firm breaks even.[17] Break-even analysis portrays the relationships among units of output, sales revenue, and costs, as illustrated in Exhibit B.4. This analysis is an important tool for small business and can answer such questions as What would happen to sales volume and profits if fixed costs rise 10 percent and prices are held constant? What can we do if our competitor cuts prices 10 percent and our sales volume drops 5 percent? What increase in sales volume must be gained to justify a 15 percent increase in the advertising

break-even analysis
A quantitative technique that helps managers determine the level of sales at which total revenues equal total costs.

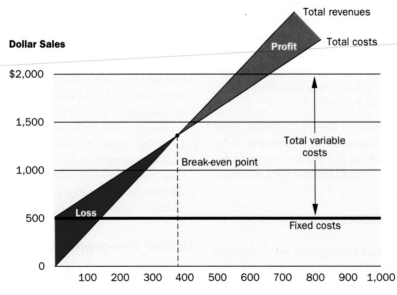

EXHIBIT B.4
Break-Even Model

budget? At what point should company operations simply be shut down?[18] These questions can be answered using the following variables of break-even analysis:

1 *Fixed costs.* Costs that remain the same regardless of the level of production, such as the payment on the building's mortgage. Fixed costs, represented by the horizontal line in Exhibit B.4, remain at $500 whether production is low or high.

2 *Variable costs.* Costs that vary with the number of units produced, such as the cost of raw material. These costs increase as production increases and are the difference between total costs and fixed costs in Exhibit B.4.

3 *Total costs.* The sum of fixed and variable costs, illustrated by the diagonal line in Exhibit B.4.

4 *Total revenues.* Total revenue dollars for a given unit of production, as illustrated by the steep diagonal line in Exhibit B.4. Total revenues are calculated as units sold times unit price.

5 *Break-even point.* The production volume at which total revenues equal total costs, illustrated by the crossover of the two diagonal lines in Exhibit B.4. As the dashed line indicates, the break-even point in this particular case is about 380 units.

6 *Profit.* The amount by which total revenues exceed total costs. In Exhibit B.4, profit occurs at a production volume greater than the break-even point.

7 *Loss.* The amount by which total costs exceed total revenues, which occurs at a production volume less than the break-even point in Exhibit B.4.

The application of these concepts to an organizational situation can be illustrated by the computation of the break-even point for CCC Bakeries, a small business in California.

CCC BAKERIES

The cookie wars have gotten hot in Canada and the United States because profits are terrific. Cookie shops are small and normally have one of the highest sales per square foot

of any kind of retail shop. Companies such as the Original Great American Chocolate Chip Cookie Company in Atlanta, Mrs. Fields Cookies, which originated in Park City, Utah, David's Cookies in New York City, and the Original Cookie Company in Cleveland are four rapidly expanding cookie chains.[19]

Jan Smith started the Chocolate Chip Cookies Bakeries in northern California. She has two shops and is considering a third in a San Francisco mall. Before opening the shop, she wants to calculate the cost of the operation and the sales volume required for profitability. She has contacted the owners of the San Francisco mall about the cost of rent and equipment rental, and she has a good idea from her other two shops about salary and raw material costs.

Following are her figures:

Fixed costs:	
Rent	$ 700
Salaries:	
Manager	800
Part-timers	300
Equipment rental	500
Total fixed costs	$2,300
Variable costs:	
Cookie mixture	$0.25/cookie
Paper bags and tissue	0.01/cookie
Total variable costs	$0.26/cookie
Estimated revenue	$0.53/cookie

Exhibit B.5 shows the break-even analysis for the proposed cookie store. The horizontal line reflects the fixed costs of $2,300. The total cost line is computed by adding the variable costs to the fixed costs. The total revenue line reflects the $0.53 income per cookie. The analysis shows that Jan must sell 8,518 cookies to break even. At this point, Jan's revenue and costs both will be approximately $4,515. If Jan can sell 10,000 cookies a month, she will make a profit of $400. The cookie business has high fixed costs relative to variable costs. Exhibit B.5 shows that once the break-even point is reached, profits will increase rapidly. High profits can be earned as volume increases to a high level. ▪

Linear Programming

Linear programming applies to such planning problems as allocating resources across competing demands or mixing

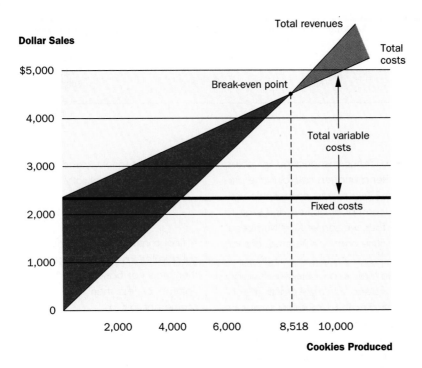

things together efficiently. Farmers want to blend the cheapest feeds to provide enough nutrition to fatten chickens. Oil companies must decide whether to make more jet fuel or heating oil at a refinery, depending on the costs of crude oil and market prices. Airlines must decide what mix of planes to put on routes, depending on fuel costs and passenger loads. Manufacturing managers must decide whether their profits can be maximized by producing more of product A and less of product B, or vice versa. Linear programming is a technique for solving these kinds of problems.[20] For example, linear programming was used to model the planning and management of New Zealand forest, including the amounts and types of trees to harvest, trees to replace, and estimated cash flow.[21]

Linear programming is a mathematical technique that allocates resources to optimize a predefined objective. Moreover, linear programming assumes that the decision maker has limited resources with which to attain the objective.

The nontechnical manager needs to understand only the three basic steps in formulating a linear programming problem:

- **Step 1:** Define the relevant decision variables. These variables must be controllable by the manager.
- **Step 2:** Define the objective in terms of the decision variables. There can be only one objective; thus, it must be chosen carefully.
- **Step 3:** Define the resource restrictions or constraints *first* as word statements and then as mathematical statements.

The following example demonstrates the three steps used in formulating a linear programming model.

 WICKER CLASSICS

Wicker Classics makes wicker baskets and seats. Both products must be processed by soaking, weaving, and drying. A basket has a profit margin of $3.25 and a seat a profit margin of $5. Exhibit B.6 summarizes the number of hours available for soaking, weaving, and drying and the number of hours required to complete each task. The question confronting Wicker Classics' managers is How many baskets and seats should Wicker make per day to maximize profits?

linear programming
A quantitative technique that allocates resources to optimize a predefined organizational objective.

EXHIBIT B.6
Resource Requirements for Wicker Classics

	Soaking Time (Hours)	Weaving Time (Hours)	Drying Time (Hours)	Profit
Per basket	0.2	0.4	0.3	$3.25
Per seat	0.4	0.4	0.8	$5.00
Available hours	60.0	90.0	108.0	

Step 1 is to define the decision variables. What can Wicker managers control in the production process? Two readily controllable variables are the number of baskets and seats to be produced. Thus, we can let X_1 = Number of baskets to produce and X_2 = Number of seats to produce.

Step 2 is to define an objective function. The objective is clear: Maximize profits. This objective can be described mathematically by using the two decision variables. The profit for each basket is $3.25, or 3.25X_1$. Similarly, the profit for each seat produced is $5, or 5.00X_2$. Total profits for the firm will be the sum of these two components:

Maximize profits = 3.25X_1$ + 5.00X_2$

Step 3 is to define resource constraints. This is the most difficult step in formulating a linear programming model. Wicker is constrained by three scarce resources, expressed in words as follows.

1 Soaking time cannot exceed 60 hours.
2 Weaving time cannot exceed 90 hours.
3 Drying time cannot exceed 108 hours.

These constraints enable us to state in mathematical terms that total soaking time must be less than or equal to 60 hours. Every basket takes 0.2 hours of soaking time and every seat 0.4 hours. The total production of baskets and seats cannot exceed 60 hours; therefore, our mathematical statement can be

$$0.2X_1 + 0.4X_2 \leq 60$$

The remaining constraints can be described in similar fashion. Weaving time cannot exceed 90 hours, which is expressed as

$$0.4X_1 + 0.4X_2 \leq 90$$

Drying time cannot exceed 108 hours, which is expressed mathematically as

$$0.3X_1 + 0.8X_2 \leq 108$$

A final constraint for keeping the mathematical calculations in the correct range is that neither seats nor baskets can be produced in a volume of less than zero. This is expressed mathematically as

$$X_1 \geq 0$$
$$X_2 \geq 0$$

The completed problem formulation looks like this:

◆ Maximize profits = $3.25X_1 + 5.00X_2$
◆ Subject to
  Soaking time: $0.2X_1 + 0.4X_2 \leq 60$
  Weaving time: $0.4X_1 + 0.4X_2 \leq 90$
  Drying time: $0.3X_1 + 0.8X_2 \leq 108$
  Nonnegativity: $X_1 \geq 0, X_2 \geq 0$

Exhibit B.7 graphs the constraints for Wicker Classics. Each constraint defines a boundary called the *feasibility region,* which is that region bounded by a resource restriction. The optimal solution for maximizing profits is found at the intersection of two or more constraints at the edge of the feasibility region. Those intersections are at points A, B, C, or D.

Management science specialists use computers and sophisticated software to solve linear programming problems. For a simple problem such as Wicker Classics, the solution can be defined on the graph in Exhibit B.7. Profit maximization is formally defined as the point (A, B, C, or D) that lies farthest from the origin (O) and through which a line can be drawn that has only one point in common with the feasibility region. In Exhibit B.7 this is point C, because it is farthest from the origin, and the

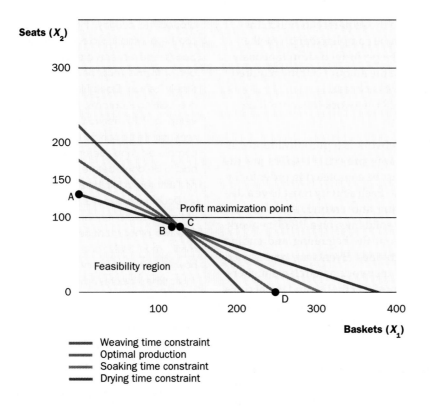

Seats (X_2)

Profit maximization point

Feasibility region

Baskets (X_1)

- —— Weaving time constraint
- —— Optimal production
- —— Soaking time constraint
- —— Drying time constraint

dark green line drawn through point C touches the feasibility region at only one point. Thus, the production mix to maximize profits is 125 baskets and 85 seats.[22] ∎

Personal Computers. Linear programming may seem complicated, but it has many applications in small business. With the advent of personal computers and new software, small businesses can use this powerful tool for planning and decision making. A user simply sets up the information on costs and other constraints on the Lotus 1-2-3 spreadsheet, and the computer will calculate what should be optimized. The cost for software is inexpensive, ranging from $200 to $1,000 depending on complexity. Hawley Fuel Corporation, for example, uses a personal computer to make the cheapest blend of coal that meets utility customers' demands for a particular sulfur content, ash content, and heating value. Even small-business managers who do not understand the underlying mathematics can use PCs and linear programming software for decision making.[23]

PERT

Organizations often confront a situation in which they have a large project to complete for which a complicated, single-use plan is developed. A large project may consist of many interrelated activities. In 1958, the U.S. Navy was confronted with the enormous task of coordinating thousands of contractors to build the Polaris nuclear submarine. The Program Evaluation and Review Technique (PERT) was developed to manage the building of submarines.

PERT allows managers to decompose a project into specific activities and to plan far in advance when it is to be completed. PERT can pinpoint bottlenecks and indicate whether resources should be reallocated. It also provides a map of the project and allows managers to control its execution by determining whether activities are completed on time and in the correct sequence.

There are four basic steps required in the use of PERT:

1 Identify all major activities (tasks) to be performed in the project.

PERT

The Program Evaluation and Review Technique; consists of breaking down a project into a network of specific activities and mapping out their sequence and necessary completion dates.

2 Determine the sequence in which the tasks must be completed and whether tasks can be performed simultaneously.

3 Determine the amount of time required to complete each task.

4 Draw a PERT network for controlling the project.

A PERT network is a graphical representation of a large project. *Activities* are the tasks that must be completed in order to finish the project. Each activity must have a discrete beginning and ending. Activities are illustrated as solid lines on a PERT network. *Events* represent the beginning and ending of specific activities. Events are represented on the PERT network as circled numbers. *Paths* are strings of activities and events on a network diagram. Project managers determine the sequence of activities that must be performed in order to complete the entire project. A *critical activity* is one that if delayed will cause a slowdown in the entire project. The path with the longest total time is called the **critical path** and represents the total time required for the project.[24]

The application of PERT can best be seen through an illustration.

CAREER RESOURCES, INC.

Career Resources, Inc., is a consulting firm that provides training seminars for companies all around the country. Planning these seminars can be a difficult project, because each company's requirements are different, and a number of factors must be brought together in a timely fashion. Doug Black is director of Executive Training Programs, and he decided to develop a PERT network for the next training seminar. He began by listing all activities to be completed and determined whether each had to be done before or after other activities, as illustrated in Exhibit B.8.

Doug's next step was to determine the length of time required for each activity. To do this, he and two other managers decided on an optimistic, most likely, and pessimistic estimate of how long each activity would take. The optimistic time indicates how quickly the activity will be completed if there are no problems or obstacles. The pessimistic time indicates the amount of time required if everything goes wrong. The most likely time is the estimate assuming that only a few routine problems will occur.

The expected time is a weighted average of the three estimates. The most likely time is weighted by four. The estimated time is calculated as shown in the following formula.

$$\text{Estimated time} = \frac{\text{Optimistic} + (4)\,\text{Most likely} + \text{Pessimistic}}{6}$$

The expected time for completing each activity is shown in the right-hand column of Exhibit B.8.

critical path
The path with the longest total time; represents the total time required for the project.

EXHIBIT B.8
Activities Required for Designing a Training Program

Activity	Description	Immediate Predecessor(s)	Estimated Time (Weeks)			
			Optimistic	Likely	Pessimistic	Expected
A	Determine topic	—	3.0	4.0	5.0	4.0
B	Locate speakers	A	4.0	5.0	12.0	6.0
C	Find potential meeting sites	—	2.0	4.0	6.0	4.0
D	Select location	C	3.0	4.0	5.0	4.0
E	Arrange speaker travel plans	B, D	1.0	2.0	3.0	2.0
F	Finalize speaker plans	E	2.0	4.0	6.0	4.0
G	Prepare announcements	B, D	2.0	4.0	12.0	5.0
H	Distribute announcements	G	2.0	3.0	4.0	3.0
I	Take reservations	H	6.0	8.0	10.0	8.0
J	Attend to last-minute details	F, I	3.0	4.0	5.0	4.0

EXHIBIT B.9
PERT Network for Designing a Training Program

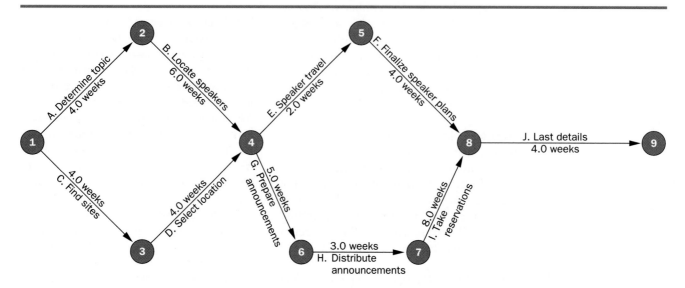

Based on the information listed in Exhibit B.8, Doug drew the PERT network illustrated in Exhibit B.9. This network shows when activities must be completed in order to move on to the next activity. The critical path is the longest path through the network, which for Doug's project is A-B-G-H-I-J. Thus, the project is expected to take 4 + 6 + 5 + 3 + 8 + 4 = 30 weeks to complete. ∎

Personal Computers. Doug Black of Career Resources, Inc., drew the PERT chart by hand, but microcomputers have made PERT charting much easier. More than two dozen project-planning software packages are now on the market. These packages provide an easy method of charting and following any kind of task. For example, Rick Gehrig, production coordinator at Westuff Tool & Die, St. Louis, can coordinate 80 different projects at once, printing out charts and schedules for each one, on his IBM PC. He even links the projects together in one big schedule to show resource needs for the whole plant. Nuvatec, Inc., located in Downers Grove, Illinois, manages 50 consulting projects with a microcomputer. The tasks and times required for each step in a consulting project are plugged into the computer, which provides a nice method for reporting the status of consulting projects to customers as well as forestalling unpleasant surprises.[25]

QUANTITATIVE APPROACHES TO DECISION MAKING

Now we turn to quantitative techniques that help managers make choices under conditions of risk and uncertainty. Recall from Chapter 8 that managerial decision making follows six steps: problem definition, diagnosis, development of alternatives, selection of an alternative, implementation, and evaluation/feedback. Decision aids focus on the fourth step—selecting an alternative. First we will examine two quantitative decision approaches: the payoff matrix and the decision tree. Then we will discuss simulation models, an extension of the two decision approaches.

Payoff Matrix

To use the **payoff matrix** as an aid to decision making, a manager must be able to define four variables.

payoff matrix
A decision-making aid comprising relevant strategies, states of nature, probability of occurrence of states of nature, and expected outcome(s).

Strategies. *Strategies* are the decision alternatives. There can be two strategies or ten, depending on the number of alternatives available. For example, a manager wanting to open a new store might consider four different locations, or a university considering an expansion of its football stadium might consider three expansion alternatives of 8,000, 15,000, and 20,000 seats.

States of Nature. Future events or conditions that are relevant to decision outcomes are called **states of nature.** For example, the states of nature for a new store location could be the anticipated sales volume at each site, and those for expanding the football stadium could be the number of additional paying fans at football games.

Probability. *Probability* represents the likelihood, expressed as a percentage, that a given state of nature will occur. Thus, the store owner may calculate the probability of making a profit in location 1 as 20 percent, in location 2 as 30 percent, and in location 3 as 50 percent. A probability of 50 percent would be listed in the payoff matrix as 0.5. University administrators would estimate the probability of filling the stadium under each condition of 8,000, 15,000, and 20,000 additional seats. The probabilities associated with the states of nature must add up to 100 percent.

Outcome. The outcome is the payoff calculated for each strategy given the probabilities associated with each state of nature. The outcome is called the **expected value,** which is the weighted average of each possible outcome for a decision alternative. For example, the store owner could calculate the expected profit from each store location, and the university administrators could calculate the expected returns associated with each construction alternative of 8,000, 15,000, and 20,000 seats.

To illustrate the payoff matrix in action, let us consider the problem facing Sanders Industries' managers, who are trying to decide how to finance the construction of a new plant and its equipment.

state of nature
A future event or condition that is relevant to a decision outcome.

expected value
The weighted average of each possible outcome for a decision alternative.

■ SANDERS INDUSTRIES

The senior managers at Sanders Industries wish to raise funds to finance the construction and new machinery for a new plant to be located in Alberta, Canada. They have determined that they have three alternative funding sources: to issue common stock, bonds, or preferred stock. The desired decision outcome is the net dollars that can be raised through each financing vehicle. The state of nature that affects the decision is the interest rate at the time the securities are issued, because interest rates influence the firm's ability to attract investment dollars. If interest rates are high, investors prefer bonds; if interest rates are low, they prefer stocks. Sanders's financial experts have advised that if interest rates are high, a common stock issue will bring $1 million, bonds $5 million, and preferred stock $3 million. If interest rates are moderate, common stocks will yield $3.5 million, bonds $3.5 million, and preferred stock $3 million. If interest rates are low, common stock will return $7.5 million, bonds $2.5 million, and preferred stock $4 million. The financial experts also have estimated the likelihood of low interest rates at 10 percent, of moderate interest rates at 40 percent, and of high interest rates at 50 percent.

Sanders's senior managers want to use a logical structure to make this decision, and the payoff matrix is appropriate. The three decision alternatives of stock, bonds, and preferred stock are shown in Exhibit B.10. The three states of nature—low, moderate, and high interest rates—are listed across the top of the exhibit. The listing of strategy on one side and of states of nature on the other side composes the payoff matrix. The probability associated with each interest rate is also included in the exhibit.

The decision outcome as defined by the managers is to gain the highest expected monetary value from issuing a security. Thus, the managers must calculate the expected monetary return associated with each decision alternative. The calculation of expected value for each decision alternative is performed by multiplying each dollar amount by the probability of occurrence. For the figures in Exhibit B.10, the expected value of each strategy is calculated as follows:

EXHIBIT B.10
Payoff Matrix for Sanders Industries

| Strategy (Decision Alternative) | Event (Interest Rate Level/State of Nature) | | |
	Low (0.1)	Moderate (0.4)	High (0.5)
Common Stock	$7,500,000	$3,500,000	$1,000,000
Bonds	2,500,000	3,500,000	5,000,000
Preferred Stock	4,000,000	3,000,000	3,000,000

Expected value of
common stock = (0.1)(7.5 million)
+ (0.4)(3.5 million)
+ (0.5)(1 million)
= $2,650,000

Expected value of
bonds = (0.1)(2.5 million)
+ (0.4)(3.5 million)
+ (0.5)(5 million)
= $4,150,000

Expected value of
preferred stock = (0.1)(4 million)
+ (0.4)(3 million)
+ (0.5)(3 million)
= $3,100,000

From this analysis, the best decision clearly is to issue bonds, which have an expected value of $4,150,000. Although managers cannot be certain about which state of nature will actually occur, the expected-value calculation weights each possibility and indicates the choice with the highest likelihood of success. ■

Decision Tree

Management problems often require that several decisions be made in sequence. As the outcome of one decision becomes obvious or as additional information becomes available, another decision is required to correct past mistakes or take advantage of new information. For instance, a production manager analyzing the company's product line may decide to add a new product on a trial basis. If customers buy the product, the manager must then decide how to increase production to meet demand. Conversely, if the new product fails to generate sufficient demand, the manager must then decide whether to drop the product.

This type of decision is difficult to structure into a payoff matrix because of the decision sequence. **Decision trees** are an alternative to payoff tables for decision situations that occur in sequence. The objective of decision tree analysis is the same as for payoff tables: to select the decision that will provide the greatest return to the company. The decision tree approach requires the following variables:

1 The decision tree, which is a pictorial representation of decision alternatives, states of nature, and the outcomes of each course of action.
2 The estimated probabilities of each outcome occurring.
3 The payoff (profit or loss) associated with each outcome.
4 The expected value, which is calculated based on the probabilities and conditional payoffs along each branch of the decision tree.

The decision tree consists of a series of nodes and connecting lines. A square node, called a *decision fork,* represents the alternative strategies available to the decision maker *at that time.* From a decision fork, the decision maker must choose one branch to follow. A round node, called a *chance fork,* represents states of nature over which the decision maker has no control. For branches emanating from a chance fork, the decision maker cannot choose which path to follow and must wait until after the decision has been made to see which state of nature occurred.

The use of a decision tree for decision making can be illustrated by the risks and uncertainties associated with the decision to use fire in contemporary forest management.

decision tree
A decision-making aid used for decision situations that occur in sequence; consists of a pictorial representation of decision alternatives, states of nature, and outcomes of each course of action.

NATIONAL FOREST SERVICE

Forest management personnel often use fires under controlled conditions to reduce natural fire hazards and enhance the wildlife habitat. However, decision uncertainties are inherent in the use of fire. For example, the decision to commit personnel and equipment to the burn site and to actually initiate the burn must be made before weather conditions and fire behavior can be determined with certainty.

A specific burn has two basic alternatives, as illustrated in Exhibit B.11. Decision fork 1 shows that forest managers can either (1) commit resources to the burn or (2) postpone the burn. Two uncertainties are central to this decision. The first is the actual weather conditions on the day of the burn, illustrated in chance fork A. There is a 50 percent likelihood that the weather will be poor, in which case the burn will have to be canceled. The second results from the decision to carry out the burn: Will the objectives be met, or will the burn be only marginally successful? This decision is illustrated by chance fork B in Exhibit B.11. The experts have estimated a 60 percent probability of a successful burn and a 40 percent probability of a marginal burn in that situation.

Given the uncertainties facing National Forest Service managers, should they decide to commit the resources or postpone the burn to await better information? The payoff value of each outcome is listed on the far right in Exhibit B.11. If everything is successful, the benefit to the forest service will be $2,800. If a marginal burn occurs, there will be a loss of $200. If the

burn is canceled after resources have been committed, there will be a loss of $1,200. If the burn is postponed indefinitely, there will be a loss of $300 in management costs.

The way to choose the best decision is through a procedure known as *rollback.* The rollback procedure begins with the end branches and works backward through the tree by assigning a value to each decision fork and chance fork. A fork's value is the expected return from the branches emanating from the fork. Applying the rollback procedure to the data in Exhibit B.11 produces the following outcomes: The expected value (EV) of chance fork B is $(0.6)(2,800) + 0.4(-200) = \$1,600$; the expected value of chance fork A is $(0.5)(1,600) + 0.5(-1,200) = \$200$.

These figures provide the information needed for the decision. If the managers decide to commit resources, there is a positive expected value of $200. If they postpone the burn, there is a certain loss of $300. Thus, it is worthwhile to go ahead with the planned burn despite management's uncertainty about the weather and possible outcomes.[26] ■

Decision tree analysis is one of the most widely used decision analysis techniques.[27] As with linear programming and PERT charting described earlier, excellent software programs are available. General managers and small-business managers can use decision tree analysis without hiring a staff specialist. This technique can be used for any decision situation in which probabilities can be estimated and decisions occur in sequence, such as those concerning new-

EXHIBIT B.11
Decision Tree for Controlled Forest Fire

SOURCE: David Cohan, Stephen M. Haas, David L. Radloff, and Richard F. Yancik, "Using Fire in Forest Management: Decision Making under Uncertainty," *Interfaces* 14 (September–October 1984), 8–19. © 1984 The Institute of Management Sciences. Reprinted with permission.

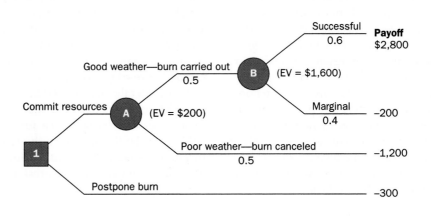

product introduction, pricing, plant expansion, advertising campaigns, or even acquiring another firm.

Simulation Models

Another useful tool for management decision makers is a simulation model. **Simulation models** are mathematical representations of the relationships among variables in real-life organizational situations.[28] For example, simulations are popular for the risky business of new-product innovations. For, say, a new bar of soap, managers can feed data into a computer about where the soap will be introduced, how much money will be spent on advertising, and what kind of promotion will be done. Data from past new products are in the computer, providing comparisons. The simulation model can predict the new soap's yearly sales. Simulation would take no more than 90 days and cost around $50,000, compared with a minimum 9 months and $1 million dollars to test a real product. Simulations will not always be accurate, however, especially for highly innovative products that have no historical base, but simulations have become very accurate where firms have compiled new-product case histories.[29]

Simulations have many applications, and because they typically are done by computer, many options can be tried. For example, Monsanto Corporation has one oceangoing chemical tanker, and managers wished to have a model that would help them determine the number of trips per year that would provide the most income. A simulation model provided the answer. The model included nine ports, fuel prices, operating charges for the tanker, voyage time, amount of fuel used, time in port, time steaming, and voyage itinerary. The simulation model gave operating managers an ongoing decision tool. If vessel managers needed to evaluate the impact of taking on an additional load, they simply simulated the current trip using the model. By inserting the data for the additional load and expenses for the extra stop, they could also ask the model if the steaming speed for the voyage could be increased so that the additional stop would not increase total voyage time. They could also calculate the cost increase from making the additional stop and simply charge the additional cost plus a reasonable profit to the customer. Using the simulation model to assist management decisions on scheduling the tanker has saved Monsanto an estimated $20,000 per year.[30]

STRENGTHS AND LIMITATIONS OF MANAGEMENT SCIENCE AIDS

When selectively applied, management science techniques provide information for improving both planning and decision making. Many businesses have operations research departments in which experts apply management science techniques to organizational problems. And with the use of microcomputers and the many available software programs, management science aids can also be used by small-business managers. Whether using these techniques in small businesses or large businesses, however, managers should be aware of their basic strengths and limitations, which are summarized in Exhibit B.12.

Strengths

The primary strength of management science aids is their ability to enhance decision effectiveness in many situations. For example, time series forecasting helps predict seasonal sales variations. Causal models help managers understand the reasons for future sales increases or decreases. Decision trees, payoff matrices, and PERT networks are valuable when data can be organized into the framework the model requires.

Another strength of management science techniques is that they provide a systematic way of thinking about and organizing complex problems. Managers may use these models intuitively, perhaps sketching things out to clarify their thinking. Moreover, new software packages ask all the right questions so managers will provide

simulation model
A mathematical representation of the relationships among variables in real-world organizational situations.

**Strengths and
Limitations of
Management Science
Techniques**

Strengths	Limitations
■ Enhance decision effectiveness in many situations ■ Provide a framework for handling complex problems ■ Promote rationality ■ Are inexpensive compared with alternatives	■ Do not fit many situations ■ May not reflect reality ■ Require overhead costs ■ Are given too much legitimacy

the correct data. The computer helps managers organize their thinking and reach the best decision.

Still another strength is that the models promote management rationality when fully applied. They help managers define a problem, select alternatives, gauge probabilities of alternatives' success, and understand the trade-offs and potential payoffs. Managers need not rely on hunch or intuition to make a complicated, multidimensional decision.

Finally, management science aids are inexpensive compared with alternatives such as organizational experiments. If an organization actually had to build a new plant to learn whether it would increase profits, a failure would be enormously expensive. Management science models provide a way to experiment with the decision without having to build the plant.

Limitations

The growth of management science has led to some problems. First—and perhaps most important—management science techniques do not yet fit many decision situations. Many management decisions are too

ambiguous and subjective. For example, management science techniques have little impact on the poorly structured strategic problems at the top levels of corporations.

A second limitation is that they may not reflect the reality of the organizational situation. The management science model is a simplification, and the outcome can be no better than the numbers and assumptions fed into the model. If these numbers are not good or important variables are left out, the outcome will be unrealistic.

A third limitation is overhead costs. The organization may hire management science specialists and provide computer facilities. If these specialists are not frequently used to help solve real problems, they will add to the organization's overhead costs while providing little return.[31]

Finally, management science techniques can be given too much legitimacy. When managers are trying to make a decision under uncertainty, they may be desperate for a clear and precise answer. A management science model may produce an answer that is taken as fact even though the model is only a simplification of reality and the decision needs the interpretation and judgment of experienced managers.

SUMMARY

This appendix described several important points about management science aids for managerial planning and decision making. Forecasting is the attempt to predict behavior in the future. Forecasting techniques can be either quantitative or qualitative. Quantitative techniques include time series analysis and causal modeling. Qualitative techniques include the Delphi method, sales force composite, and jury of opinion.

Quantitative aids to management planning include

break-even analysis, linear programming, and PERT. Break-even analysis indicates the volume at which a new product will earn enough revenues to cover costs. Linear programming helps managers decide which product mix will maximize profits or minimize costs. PERT helps managers plan, monitor, and control project progress.

Management science aids to decision choices also were described. The payoff matrix helps managers determine the expected value of various alternatives. The decision

tree is a similar procedure that is used for decisions made in sequence. Simulation models use mathematics to evaluate the impact of management decisions. Microcomputers and new software make all of these techniques accessible to managers, but managers should remember that management science aids have limitations as well as strengths.

ENDNOTES

1 David R. Anderson, Dennis J. Sweeney, and Thomas A. Williams, *Quantitative Methods for Business*, 4th ed. (St. Paul, Minn.: West, 1989); and H. Watson and P. Marett, "A Survey of Management Science Implementation Problems," *Interfaces* 9 (August 1979), 124–128.

2 Barry C. Smith, John F. Leimkuhler, and Ross M. Darrow, "Yield Management at American Airlines," *Interfaces* (January–February 1992), 8–31.

3 Ranga Anbil, Eric Gelman, Bruce Patty, and Rajan Tanga, "Recent Advances in Crew-Pairing Optimization at American Airlines," *Interfaces* 21 (January–February 1991), 62–74.

4 For further explanation of management science techniques, see B. Render and R. Stair, *Quantitative Analysis for Management*, 2d ed. (Boston: Allyn & Bacon, 1985); and S. Lee, L. Moore, and B. Taylor, *Management Science* (Dubuque, Iowa: W. C. Brown, 1981).

5 Farrokh Alemi, Barbara Turner, Leona Markson, Richard Szorady, and Tom McCarron, "Prognosis after AIDS: A Severity Index Based on Expert's Judgments," *Interfaces* 21 (May–June 1991), 109–116.

6 Thomas H. Stone and Jack Fiorito, "A Perceived Uncertainty Model of Human Resource Forecasting Technique Use," *Academy of Management Review* 11 (1986), 635–642.

7 S. C. Wheelwright and S. Makridakis, *Forecasting Methods for Management* (New York: Wiley, 1973).

8 Ibid.

9 Jean Aubin, "Scheduling Ambulances," *Interfaces* 22 (March–April 1992), 1–10.

10 Robert F. Reilly, "Developing a Sales Forecasting System," *Managerial Planning* (July–August 1981), 24–30.

11 Dexter Hutchins, "And Now, the Home-Brewed Forecast," *Fortune,* January 20, 1986, 53–54.

12 N. Dalkey, *The Delphi Method: An Experimental Study of Group Opinion* (Santa Monica, Calif.: Rand Corporation, 1969).

13 Bruce Blaylock and L. Reese, "Cognitive Style and the Usefulness of Information," *Decision Sciences* 15 (winter 1984), 74–91.

14 J. Duncan, "Businessmen Are Good Sales Forecasters," *Dun's Review* (July 1986).

15 Alex Taylor III, "Who's Afraid in the World Auto War," *Fortune,* November 9, 1987, 74–88.

16 M. Moriarty, "Design Features of Forecasting Systems Involving Management Judgments," *Journal of Marketing Research* 22 (November 1985), 353–364; and D. Kahneman, B. Slovic, and A. Tversky, eds., *Judgment under Uncertainty: Heuristics and Biases* (Cambridge, Mass.: Cambridge Press, 1982).

17 M. Anderson and R. Lievano, *Quantitative Management: An Introduction*, 2d ed. (Boston: Kent, 1986).

18 "Break-Even Analysis: Analyzing the Relationship between Costs and Revenues," *Small Business Report* (August 1986), 22–24.

19 Kevin McManus, "The Cookie Wars," *Forbes,* November 7, 1983, 150–152.

20 Anderson and Lievano, *Quantitative Management;* J. Byrd and L. Moore, "The Application of a Product Mix Linear Programming Model in Corporate Policy Making," *Management Science* 24 (September 1978), 1342–1350; and D. Darnell and C. Lofflin, "National Airlines Fuel Management and Allocation Model," *Interfaces* 7 (February 1977), 1–16.

21 Bruce R. Manley and John A. Threadgill, "LP Used for Valuation and Planning of New Zealand Plantation Forests," *Interfaces* 21 (November–December 1991), 66–79.

22 P. Williams, "A Linear Programming Approach to Production Scheduling," *Production and Inventory Management* 11 (3d quarter 1970), 39–49.

23 William M. Bulkeley, "The Right Mix: New Software Makes the Choice Much Easier," *The Wall Street Journal,* March 27, 1987, 25.

24 W. J. Erikson and O. P. Hall, *Computer Models for Management Science* (Reading, Mass.: Addison-Wesley, 1986).

25 Nancy Madlin, "Streamlining the PERT Chart," *Management Review* (September 1986), 67–68.

26 David Cohan, Stephen M. Haas, David L. Radloff, and Richard F. Yancik, "Using Fire in Forest Management: Decision Making under Uncertainty," *Interfaces* 14 (September–October 1984), 8–19.

27 J. W. Ulvila and R. V. Brown, "Decision Analysis Comes of Age," *Harvard Business Review* (September–October 1982), 130–141.

28 B. Render and Stair, *Quantitative Analysis for Management.*

29 Toni Mack, "Let the Computer Do It," *Forbes,* August 10, 1987, 94.

30 Raymond F. Boykin and Reuven R. Levary, "An Interactive Decision Support System for Analyzing Ship Voyage Alternatives," *Interfaces* 15 (March–April 1985), 81–84.

31 T. Naylor and H. Schauland, "A Survey of Users of Corporate Planning Models," *Management Science* 22 (1976), 927–937.

GLOSSARY

360-degree feedback A process that uses multiple raters, including self-rating, to appraise employee performance and guide development.

accommodative response A response to social demands in which the organization accepts—often under pressure—social responsibility for its actions to comply with the public interest.

accountability The fact that the people with authority and responsibility are subject to reporting and justifying task outcomes to those above them in the chain of command.

activity-based costing (ABC) A control system that identifies the various activities needed to produce a product or service, determines the cost of those activities, and allocates financial resources according to the true cost of each product or service.

adjourning The stage of team development in which members prepare for the team's disbandment.

administrative model A decision-making model that describes how managers actually make decisions in situations characterized by nonprogrammed decisions, uncertainty, and ambiguity.

administrative principles A subfield of the classical management perspective that focused on the total organization rather than the individual worker, delineating the management functions of planning, organizing, commanding, coordinating, and controlling.

affirmative action a policy requiring employers to take positive steps to guarantee equal employment opportunities for people within protected groups.

ambiguity The goals to be achieved or the problem to be solved is unclear, alternatives are difficult to define, and information about outcomes is unavailable.

application form A device for collecting information about an applicant's education, previous job experience, and other background characteristics.

assessment center A technique for selecting individuals with high managerial potential based on their performance on a series of simulated managerial tasks.

authority The formal and legitimate right of a manager to make decisions, issue orders, and allocate resources to achieve organizationally desired outcomes.

autocratic leader A leader who tends to centralize authority and rely on legitimate, reward, and coercive power to manage subordinates.

behavior modification The set of techniques by which reinforcement theory is used to modify human behavior.

behavioral sciences approach A subfield of the humanistic management perspective that applies social science in an organizational context, drawing from economics, psychology, sociology, and other disciplines.

behaviorally anchored rating scale (BARS) A rating technique that relates an employee's performance to specific job-related incidents.

benchmarking The continuous process of measuring products, services, and practices against the toughest competitors or those companies recognized as industry leaders.

birth stage The phase of the organization life cycle in which the company is created.

bottom-up budgeting A budgeting process in which lower-level managers budget their departments' resource needs and pass them up to top management for approval.

boundary-spanning roles Roles assumed by people and/or departments that link and coordinate the organization with key elements in the external environment.

bounded rationality The concept that people have the time and cognitive ability to process only a limited amount of information on which to base decisions.

brainstorming A decision-making technique in which group members present spontaneous suggestions for problem solution regardless of their likelihood of implementation, in order to promote freer, more creative thinking within the group.

bureaucratic organizations A subfield of the classical management perspective that emphasizes management on an impersonal, rational basis through such elements as clearly defined authority and responsibility, formal recordkeeping, and separation of management and ownership.

business incubator An innovation that provides shared office space, management support services, and management advice to entrepreneurs.

business plan A document specifying the business details prepared by an entrepreneur in preparation for opening a new business.

centralization The location of decision authority near top organizational levels.

centralized network A team communication structure in which team members communicate through a single individual to solve problems or make decisions.

ceremony A planned activity that makes up a special event and is conducted for the benefit of an audience.

certainty All the information the decision maker needs is fully available.

chain of command An unbroken line of authority that links all individuals in the organization and specifies who reports to whom.

change agent An OD specialist who contracts with an organization to facilitate change.

changing A step in the intervention stage of organizational development in which individuals experiment with new workplace behavior.

channel richness The amount of information that can be transmitted during a communication episode.

channel The carrier of a communication.

charismatic leader A leader who has the ability to motivate subordinates to transcend their expected performance.

classical model A decision-making model based on the assumption that managers should make logical decisions that will be in the organization's best economic interests.

classical perspective A management perspective that emerged during the nineteenth and early twentieth centuries that emphasized a rational, scientific approach to the study of management and sought to make organizations efficient operating machines.

closed systems A system that does not interact with the external environment.

cluster organization An organizational form in which team members from different company locations use E-mail and group decision support systems to solve problems.

coalition An informal alliance among managers who support a specific goal.

code of ethics A formal statement of the organization's values regarding ethics and social issues.

coercive power Power that stems from the authority to punish or recommend punishment.

collectivism A preference for a tightly knit social framework in which individuals look after one another and organizations protect their members' interests.

committee A long-lasting, sometimes permanent team in the organization structure created to deal with tasks that recur regularly.

communication The process by which information is exchanged and understood by two or more people, usually with the intent to motivate or influence behavior.

compensation Monetary payments (wages, salaries) and nonmonetary goods/commodities (benefits, vacations) used to reward employees.

compensatory justice The concept that individuals should be compensated for the cost of their injuries by the party responsible and also that individuals should not be held responsible for matters over which they have no control.

competitors Other organizations in the same industry or type of business that provide goods or services to the same set of customers.

conceptual skill The cognitive ability to see the organization as a whole and the relationship among its parts.

concurrent control Control that consists of monitoring ongoing employee activities to ensure their consistency with established standards.

conflict Antagonistic interaction in which one party attempts to thwart the intentions or goals of another.

consideration A type of leader behavior that describes the extent to which a leader is sensitive to subordinates, respects their ideas and feelings, and establishes mutual trust.

content theories A group of theories that emphasize the needs that motivate people.

contingency approach A model of leadership that describes the relationship between leadership styles and specific organizational situations.

contingency plans Plans that define company responses to specific situations, such as emergencies or setbacks.

contingency view An extension of the humanistic perspective in which the successful resolution of organizational problems is thought to depend on managers' identification of key variables in the situation at hand.

continuous improvement The implementation of a large number of small, incremental improvements in all areas of the organization on a ongoing basis.

continuous process production A type of technology involving mechanization of the entire work flow and nonstop production.

continuous reinforcement schedule A schedule in which every occurrence of the desired behavior is reinforced.

controlling The management function concerned with monitoring employees' activities, keeping the organization on track toward its goals, and making corrections as needed.

coordination costs The time and energy needed to coordinate the activities of a team to enable it to perform its task.

coordination The quality of collaboration across departments.

core competence A business activity that an organization does particularly well in comparison to competitors.

corporation An artificial entity created by the state and existing apart from it owners.

cost leadership A type of competitive strategy with which the organization aggressively seeks efficient facilities, cuts costs, and employs tight cost controls to be more efficient than competitors.

countertrade The barter of products for other products rather than their sale for currency.

creativity The development of novel solutions to perceived organizational problems.

cross-functional team A group of employees assigned to a functional department that meets as a team to resolve mutual problems.

culture gap The difference between an organization's desired cultural norms and values and actual norms and values.

culture/people change A change in employees' values, norms, attitudes, beliefs, and behavior.

culture The set of key values, beliefs, understandings, and norms that members of an organization share.

culture The shared knowledge, beliefs, values, behaviors, and ways of thinking among members of a society.

customers People and organizations in the environment who acquire goods or services from the organization.

cycle time The steps taken to complete a company process.

data Raw, unsummarized, and unanalyzed facts and figures.

debt financing Borrowing money that has to be repaid at a later date in order to start a business.

decentralization The location of decision authority near lower organizational levels.

decentralized control The use of social values, traditions, common beliefs, and trust to generate compliance with organizational goals.

decentralized network A team communication structure in which team members freely communicate with one another and arrive at decisions together.

decision A choice made from available alternatives.

decision making The process of identifying problems and opportunities and then resolving them.

decision support system (DSS) An interactive, computer-based system that uses decision models and specialized databases to support organization decision makers.

decode To translate the symbols used in a message for the purpose of interpreting its meaning.

defensive response A response to social demands in which the organization admits to some errors of commission or omission but does not act obstructively.

delegation The process managers use to transfer authority and responsibility to positions below them in the hierarchy.

Delphi group A group decision-making format that involves the circulation among participants of questionnaires on the selected problem, sharing of answers, and continuous recirculation/refinement of questionnaires until a consensus has been obtained.

democratic leader A leader who delegates authority to others, encourages participation, and relies on expert and referent power to manage subordinates.

departmentalization The basis on which individuals are grouped into departments and departments into total organizations.

descriptive An approach that describes how managers actually make decisions rather than how they should.

devil's advocate A decision-making technique in which an individual is assigned the role of challenging the assumptions and assertions made by the group to prevent premature consensus.

diagnosis The step in the decision-making process in which managers analyze underlying causal factors associated with the decision situation.

dialogue A group communication process aimed at creating a culture based on collaboration, fluidity, trust, and commitment to shared goals.

differentiation A type of competitive strategy with which the organization seeks to distinguish its products or services from competitors'.

direct investing An entry strategy in which the organization is involved in managing its production facilities in a foreign country.

discretionary responsibility Organizational responsibility that is voluntary and guided by the organization's desire to make social contributions not mandated by economics, law, or ethics.

discrimination The hiring or promoting of applicants based on criteria that are not job relevant.

distributive justice The concept that different treatment of people should not be based on arbitrary characteristics. In the case of substantive differences, people should be treated differently in proportion to the differences among them.

diversity awareness training Special training designed to make people aware of their own prejudices and stereotypes.

divisional structure An organization structure in which departments are grouped based on similar organizational outputs.

downsizing The systematic reduction in the number of managers and employees to make a company more cost efficient and competitive.

downward communication Messages sent from top management down to subordinates.

dual role A role in which the individual both contributes to the team's task and supports members' emotional needs.

E→P expectancy Expectancy that putting effort into a given task will lead to high performance.

economic dimension The dimension of the general environment representing the overall economic health of the country or region in which the organization functions.

economic forces The availability, production, and distribution of resources in a society.

economic value-added system (EVA) A control system that captures all the things a company can do to add value from its activities and measures each job, department, or process by the value added.

effectiveness The degree to which the organization achieves a stated goal.

efficiency The use of minimal resources—raw materials, money, and people—to produce a desired volume of output.

empowerment The delegation of power and authority to subordinates.

encode To select symbols with which to compose a message.

entrepreneur Someone who recognizes a viable idea for a business product or service and carries it out.

entrepreneurship The process of initiating a business venture, organizing the necessary resources, and assuming the associated risks and rewards.

entropy The tendency for a system to run down and die.

environmental discontinuity A large change in the organization's environment over a short period.

equity financing Financing that consists of funds that are invested in exchange for ownership in the company.

equity theory A process theory that focuses on individuals' perceptions of how fairly they are treated relative to others.

equity A situation that exists when the ratio of one person's outcomes to inputs equals that of another's.

ERG theory A modification of the needs hierarchy theory that proposes three categories of needs: existence, relatedness, and growth.

ethical dilemma A situation that arises when all alternative choices or behaviors have been deemed undesirable because of potentially negative ethical consequences, making it difficult to distinguish right from wrong.

ethics committee A group of executives assigned to oversee the organization's ethics by ruling on questionable issues and disciplining violators.

ethics ombudsman An official given the responsibility of corporate conscience who hears and investigates ethics complaints and points out potential ethical failures to top management.

ethics The code of moral principles and values that govern the behaviors of a person or group with respect to what is right or wrong.

ethnocentrism A cultural attitude marked by the tendency to regard one's own culture as superior to others.

ethnocentrism The belief that one's own group or subculture is inherently superior to other groups or cultures.

ethnorelativism The belief that groups and subcultures are inherently equal.

executive information system (EIS) A decision support system that retrieves, manipulates, and displays information tailored to the needs of top-level managers.

exit interview An interview conducted with departing employees to determine the reasons for their termination.

expatriates Employees who live and work in a country other than their own.

expectancy theory A process theory that proposes that motivation depends on individuals' expectations about their ability to perform tasks and receive desired rewards.

expert power Power that stems from special knowledge of or skill in the tasks performed by subordinates.

expert system (ES) Information technology that programs a computer to duplicate an expert's decision-making and problem-solving strategies.

exporting An entry strategy in which the organization maintains its production facilities within its home country and transfers its products for sale in foreign markets.

external locus of control The belief by individuals that their future is not within their control but rather is influenced by external forces.

extrinsic reward A reward given by another person.

feedback A response by the receiver to the sender's communication.

feedback control Control that focuses on the organization's outputs; also called postaction or output control.

feedforward control Control that focuses on human, material, and financial resources flowing into the organization; also called preliminary or preventive quality control.

femininity A cultural preference for cooperation, group decision-making, and quality of life.

first-line manager A manager who is at the first or second management level and is directly responsible for the production of goods and services.

flat structure A management structure characterized by an overall broad span of control and relatively few hierarchical levels.

flexible manufacturing A manufacturing technology using computers to automate and integrate manufacturing components such as robots, machines, product design, and engineering analysis.

focus A type of competitive strategy that emphasizes concentration on a specific regional market or buyer group.

force field analysis The process of determining which forces drive and which resist a proposed change.

formal communication channel A communication channel that flows within the chain of command or task responsibility defined by the organization.

formal team A team created by the organization as part of the formal organization structure.

forming The stage of team development characterized by orientation and acquaintance.

franchising A form of licensing in which an organization provides its foreign franchisees with a complete assortment of materials and services.

franchising An arrangement by which the owner of a product or service allows others to purchase the right to distribute the product or service with help from the owner.

free rider A person who benefits from team membership but does not make a proportionate contribution to the team's work.

frustration-regression principle The idea that failure to meet a high-order need may cause a regression to an already satisfied lower-order need.

functional manager A manager who is responsible for a department that performs a single functional task and has employees with similar training and skills.

functional structure An organization structure in which positions are grouped into departments based on similar skills, expertise, and resource use.

general environment The layer of the external environment that affects the organization indirectly.

general manager A manager who is responsible for several departments that perform different functions.

geographic information system (GIS) A type of decision support system that provides layers of information expressed visually through the use of maps; used for distribution planning, site selection, and trade area analysis.

glass ceiling Invisible barrier that separates women and minorities from top management positions.

global outsourcing Engaging in the international division of labor so as to obtain the cheapest sources of labor and supplies regardless of country; also called global sourcing.

goal A desired future state that the organization attempts to realize.

grapevine An informal, person-to-person communication network of employees that is not officially sanctioned by the organization.

greenfield venture The most risky type of direct investment, whereby a company builds a subsidiary from scratch in a foreign country.

group decision support system (GDSS) An interactive computer-based system that facilitates group communication and decision making; also called *collaborative work system.*

groupthink A phenomenon in which group members are so committed to the group that they are reluctant to express contrary opinions.

groupware Software that enables employees on a network to interact with one another; the most common form of groupware is E-mail.

halo error A type of rating error that occurs when an employee receives the same rating on all dimensions regardless of his or her performance on individual ones.

Hawthorne Studies A series of experiments on worker productivity begun in 1924 at the Hawthorne plant of Western Electric Company in Illinois; attributed employees' increased output to managers' better treatment of them during the study.

hero A figure who exemplifies the deeds, character, and attributes of a corporate culture.

hierarchy of needs theory A content theory that proposes that people are motivated by five categories of needs—physiological, safety, belongingness, esteem, and self-actualization—that exist in a hierarchical order.

high-context culture A culture in which communication is used to enhance personal relationships.

homogeneity A type of rating error that occurs when a rater gives all employees a similar rating regardless of their individual performances.

horizontal communication The lateral or diagonal exchange of messages among peers or coworkers.

horizontal linkage model An approach to product change that emphasizes shared development of innovations among several departments.

horizontal team A formal team composed of employees from about the same hierarchical level but from different areas of expertise.

humanistic perspective A management perspective that emerged around the late nineteenth century that emphasized understanding human behavior, needs and attitudes in the workplace.

human relations movement A movement in management thinking and practice that emphasized satisfaction of employees' basic needs as the key to increased worker productivity.

human resource management (HRM) Activities undertaken to attract, develop, and maintain an effective workforce within an organization.

human resource planning The forecasting of human resource needs and the projected matching of individuals with expected job vacancies.

human resources perspective A management perspective that suggests jobs should be designed to meet higher-level needs by allowing workers to use their full potential.

human skill The ability to work with and through other people and to work effectively as a group member.

hygiene factors Factors that involve the presence or absence of job dissatisfiers, including working conditions, pay, company policies, and interpersonal relationships.

idea champion A person who sees the need for and champions productive change within the organization.

implementation The step in the decision-making process that involves using managerial, administrative, and persuasive abilities to translate the chosen alternative into action.

individualism approach The ethical concept that acts are moral when they promote the individual's best long-term interests, which ultimately leads to the greater good.

individualism A preference for a loosely knit social framework in which individuals are expected to take care of themselves.

informal communication channel A communication channel that exists outside formally authorized channels without regard for the organization's hierarchy of authority.

information Data that has been converted into a meaningful and useful context for the receiver.

information reporting system A system that organizes information in the form of prespecified reports that managers use in day-to-day decision making.

information technology The hardware, software, telecommunications, database management, and other technologies used to store, process, and distribute information.

infrastructure A country's physical facilities that support economic activities.

initiating structure A type of leader behavior that describes the extent to which a leader is task oriented and directs subordinates' work activities toward goal achievement.

integrating manager An individual responsible for coordinating the activities of several departments on a full-time basis to achieve specific project or product outcomes.

interactive group A group decision-making format in which group members are brought together face-to-face and have a specific agenda and decision goals.

interactive leader A leader who is concerned with consensus building, is open and inclusive, and encourages participation.

internal environment The environment within the organization's boundaries.

internal locus of control The belief by individuals that their future is within their control and that external forces will have little influence.

international dimension Portion of the external environment that represents events originating in foreign countries as well as opportunities for American companies in other countries.

international management The management of business operations conducted in more than one country.

intrapreneurship The process of recognizing the need for innovation and promoting it within an organization.

intrinsic reward The satisfaction received in the process of performing an action.

intuition The immediate comprehension of a decision situation based on past experience but without conscious thought.

invisible minorities Individuals who share a social stigma that is not visibly recognizable.

job characteristics model A model of job design that comprises core job dimensions, critical psychological states, and employee growth-need strength.

job description A listing of duties as well as desirable qualifications for a particular job.

job design The application of motivational theories to the structure of work for improving productivity and satisfaction.

job enlargement A job design that combines a series of tasks into one new, broader job to give employees variety and challenge.

job enrichment A job design that incorporates achievement, recognition, and other high-level motivators into the work.

job evaluation The process of determining the value of jobs within an organization through an examination of job content.

job rotation A job design that systematically moves employees from one job to another to provide them with variety and stimulation.

job simplification A job design whose purpose is to improve task efficiency by reducing the number of tasks a single person must perform.

joint venture A strategic alliance or program by two or more organizations.

joint venture A variation of direct investment in which an organization shares costs and risks with another firm to build a manufacturing facility, develop new products, or set up a sales and distribution network.

justice approach The ethical concept that moral decisions must be based on standards of equity, fairness, and impartiality.

labor market The people available for hire by the organization.

law of effect The assumption that positively reinforced behavior tends to be repeated and unreinforced or negatively reinforced behavior tends to be inhibited.

leadership The ability to influence people toward the attainment of organizational goals.

leadership grid A two-dimensional leadership theory that measures a leader's concern for people and concern for production.

leading The management function that involves the use of influence to motivate employees to achieve the organization's goals.

learning organization An organization in which everyone is engaged in identifying and solving problems, enabling the organization to continuously experiment, improve, and increase its capability.

legal-political dimension The dimension of the general environment that includes federal, state, and local government regulations and political activities designed to control company behavior.

legitimate power Power that stems from a formal management position in an organization and the authority granted to it.

licensing An entry strategy in which an organization in one country makes certain resources available to companies in another in order to participate in the production and sale of its products abroad.

listening The skill of receiving messages to accurately grasp facts and feelings to interpret the genuine meaning.

low-context culture A culture in which communication is used to exchange facts and information.

LPC scale A questionnaire designed to measure relationship-oriented versus task-oriented leadership style according to the leader's choice of adjectives for describing the "least preferred coworker."

management The attainment of organizational goals in an effective and efficient manner through planning, organizing, leading, and controlling organizational resources.

management by objectives A method of management whereby managers and employees define goals for every department, project, and person and use them to monitor subsequent performance.

management by wandering around (MBWA) A communication technique in which managers interact directly with workers to exchange information.

management information system (MIS) A form of computer-based information system that collects, organizes, and distributes the data managers use in performing their management functions.

management science perspective A management perspective that emerged after World War II and applied mathematics, statistics, and other quantitative techniques to managerial problems.

market entry strategy An organizational strategy for entering a foreign market.

masculinity A cultural preference for achievement, heroism, assertiveness, work centrality, and material success.

mass production A type of technology characterized by the production of a large volume of products with the same specifications.

matching model An employee selection approach in which the organization and the applicant attempt to match each other's needs, interests, and values.

matrix approach An organization structure that utilizes functional and divisional chains of command simultaneously in the same part of the organization.

matrix boss A product or functional boss, responsible for one side of the matrix.

maturity stage The phase of the organization life cycle in which the organization has become exceedingly large and mechanistic.

mechanistic structure An organizational structure characterized by rigidly defined tasks, many rules and regulations, little teamwork, and centralized decision making.

mediation The process of using a third party to settle a dispute.

merger The combination of two or more organizations into one.

message The tangible formulation of an idea to be sent to a receiver.

middle manager A manager who works at the middle levels of the organization and is responsible for major departments.

midlife stage The phase of the organization life cycle in which the firm has reached prosperity and grown substantially large.

mission statement A broadly stated definition of the organization's basic business scope and operations that distinguishes it from similar types of organizations.

mission The organization's reason for existence.

monoculture A culture that accepts only one way of doing things and one set of values and beliefs.

moral-rights approach The ethical concept that moral decisions are those that best maintain the rights of those people affected by them.

most favored nation A term describing a GATT clause that calls for member countries to grant other member countries the most favorable treatment they accord any country concerning imports and exports.

motivation The arousal, direction, and persistence of behavior.

motivators Factors that influence job satisfaction based on fulfillment of high-level needs such as achievement, recognition, responsibility, and opportunity for growth.

multinational corporation (MNC) An organization that receives more than 25 percent of its total sales revenues from operations outside the parent company's home country; also called global corporation or transnational corporation.

multiple advocacy A decision-making technique that involves several advocates and presentation of multiple points of view, including minority and unpopular opinions.

need to achieve A human quality linked to entrepreneurship in which people are motivated to excel and pick situations in which success is likely.

network A system that links together people and departments within or among organizations for the purpose of sharing information resources.

network structure An organization structure that disaggregates major functions into separate companies that are brokered by a small headquarters organization.

neutralizer A situational variable that counteracts a leadership style and prevents the leader from displaying certain behaviors.

new-venture fund A fund providing resources from which individuals and groups draw to develop new ideas, products, or businesses.

new-venture team A unit separate from the mainstream of the organization that is responsible for developing and initiating innovations.

nominal group A group decision-making format that emphasizes equal participation in the decision process by all group members.

nonparticipator role A role in which the individual contributes little to either the task or members' socioemotional needs.

nonprogrammed decision A decision made in response to a situation that is unique, is poorly defined and largely unstructured, and has important consequences for the organization.

nonverbal communication A communication transmitted through actions and behaviors rather than through words.

norm A standard of conduct that is shared by team members and guides their behavior.

normative An approach that defines how a decision maker should make decisions and provides guidelines for reaching an ideal outcome for the organization.

norming The stage of team development in which conflicts developed during the storming stage are resolved and team harmony and unity emerge.

obstructive response A response to social demands in which the organization denies responsibility, claims that evidence of misconduct is misleading or distorted, and attempts to obstruct investigation.

office automation systems Systems such as word processors, desktop publishing, and E-mail that transform manual procedures to electronic media.

on-the-job training(OJT) A type of training in which an experienced employee "adopts" a new employee to teach him or her how to perform job duties.

open communication Sharing all types of information throughout the company, across functional and hierarchical levels.

open systems A system that interacts with the external environment.

open-book management Sharing financial information and results with all employees in the organization.

operational goals Specific, measurable results expected from departments, work groups, and individuals within the organization.

operational plans Plans developed at the organization's lower levels that specify action steps toward achieving operational goals and that support tactical planning activities.

operations information system A computer-based information system that supports a company's day-to-day operations.

opportunity A situation in which managers see potential organizational accomplishments that exceed current goals.

organic structure An organizational structure that is free flowing, has few rules and regulations, encourages employee teamwork, and decentralizes decision making to employees doing the job.

organization chart The visual representation of an organization's structure.

organization life cycle The organization's evolution through major developmental stages.

organization structure The framework in which the organization defines how tasks are divided, resources are deployed, and departments are coordinated.

organization A social entity that is goal directed and deliberately structured.

organizational change The adoption of a new idea or behavior by an organization.

organizational control The systematic process through which managers regulate organizational activities to make them consistent with expectations established in plans, targets, and standards of performance.

organizational development(OD) The application of behavioral science techniques to improve an organization's health and effectiveness through its ability to cope with environmental changes, improve internal relationships, and increase problem-solving capabilities.

organizational environment All elements existing outside the organization's boundaries that have the potential to affect the organization.

organizing The deployment of organization resources to achieve strategic goals.

organizing The management function concerned with assigning tasks, grouping tasks into departments, and allocating resources to departments.

outsourcing The farming out of a company's in-house operation to a preferred vendor.

P→O expectancy Expectancy that successful performance of a task will lead to the desired outcome.

paper-and-pencil test A written test designed to measure a particular attribute such as intelligence or aptitude.

paradigm A mind-set that presents a fundamental way of thinking about, perceiving, and understanding the world.

partial reinforcement schedule A schedule in which only some occurrences of the desired behavior are reinforced.

partnership An unincorporated business owned by two or more people.

path-goal theory A contingency approach to leadership specifying that the leader's responsibility is to increase subordinates' motivation by clarifying the behaviors necessary for task accomplishment and rewards.

pay survey A study of what other companies pay employees in jobs that correspond to a sample of key positions selected by the organization.

pay-trend line A graph that shows the relationship between pay and total job point values for determining the worth of a given job.

perception The process of making sense out of one's environment.

perceptual organization The categorization of an object or stimulus according to one's frame of reference.

perceptual selectivity The screening and selection of objects and stimuli that compete for one's attention.

performance appraisal interview A formal review of an employee's performance conducted between the superior and the subordinate.

performance appraisal The process of observing and evaluating an employee's performance, recording the assessment, and providing feedback to the employee.

performance gap A disparity between existing and desired performance levels.

performance The organization's ability to attain its goals by using resources in an efficient and effective manner.

performing The stage of team development in which members focus on problem solving and accomplishing the team's assigned task.

permanent team A group of participants from several functions who are permanently assigned to solve ongoing problems of common interest.

plan A blueprint specifying the resource allocations, schedules, and other actions necessary for attaining goals.

planning The management function concerned with defining goals for future organizational performance and deciding on the tasks and resource use needed to attain them.

pluralism The organization accommodates several subcultures, including employees who would otherwise feel isolated and ignored.

point system A job evaluation system that assigns a predetermined point value to each compensable job factor in order to determine the worth of a given job.

political activity Organizational attempts, such as lobbying, to influence government legislation and regulation.

political forces The influence of political and legal institutions on people and organizations.

political risk A company's risk of loss of assets, earning power, or managerial control due to politically motivated events or actions by host governments.

power The potential ability to influence others' behavior.

power distance The degree to which people accept inequality in power among institutions, organizations, and people.

pressure group An interest group that works within the legal-political framework to influence companies to behave in socially responsible ways.

proactive response A response to social demands in which the organization seeks to learn what is in its constituencies' interest and to respond without pressure from them.

problem A situation in which organizational accomplishments have failed to meet established goals.

problem-solving team Typically 5 to 12 hourly employees from the same department who meet to discuss ways of improving quality, efficiency, and the work environment.

procedural justice The concept that rules should be clearly stated and consistently and impartially enforced.

process control system A computer system that monitors and controls ongoing physical processes, such as temperature or pressure changes.

process theories A group of theories that explain how employees select behaviors with which to meet their needs and determine whether their choices were successful.

product change A change in the organization's product or service output.

product life cycle The stages through which a product or service goes: (1) development and introduction into the marketplace, (2) growth, (3) maturity, and (4) decline.

programmed decision A decision made in response to a situation that has occurred often enough to enable decision rules to be developed and applied in the future.

project manager A manager responsible for a temporary work project that involves the participation of other people at a similar level in the organization.

proprietorship An unincorporated business owned by an individual for profit.

quality circle (QC) A group of 6 to 12 volunteer employees who meet regularly to discuss and solve problems that affect their common work activities.

realistic job preview (RJP) A recruiting approach that gives applicants all pertinent and realistic information about the job and the organization.

recruiting The activities or practices that define the desired characteristics of applicants for specific jobs.

reengineering The radical redesign of business processes to achieve dramatic improvements in cost, quality, service, and speed.

referent power Power that results from characteristics that command subordinates' identification with, respect and admiration for, and desire to emulate the leader.

refreezing A step in the reinforcement stage of organizational development in which individuals acquire a desired new skill or attitude and are rewarded for it by the organization.

reinforcement Anything that causes a given behavior to be repeated or inhibited.

responsibility The duty to perform the task or activity an employee has been assigned.

reward power Power that results from the authority to reward others.

risk propensity The willingness to undertake risk with the opportunity of gaining an increased payoff.

risk A decision has clear-cut goals, and good information is available, but the future outcomes associated with each alternative are subject to chance.

role A set of expectations for one's behavior.

satisfice To choose the first solution alternative that satisfies minimal decision criteria regardless of whether better solutions are presumed to exist.

schedule of reinforcement The frequency with which and intervals over which reinforcement occurs.

scientific management A subfield of the classical management perspective that emphasizes scientifically determined changes in management practices as the solution to improving labor productivity.

search The process of learning about current developments inside or outside the organization that can be used to meet a perceived need for change.

selection The process of determining the skills, abilities, and other attributes a person needs to perform a particular job.

self-directed team A team consisting of 5 to 20 multiskilled workers who rotate jobs to produce an entire product or service, often supervised by an elected member.

semantics The meaning of words and the way they are used.

servant leader A leader who works to fulfill subordinates' needs and goals as well as to achieve the organization's larger mission.

service technology Technology characterized by intangible outputs and direct contact between employees and customers.

Shewhart Cycle A planning cycle used in companies that have instituted quality management; also called PDCA—plan, do, check, act—Cycle.

single-use plans Plans that are developed to achieve a set of goals that are unlikely to be repeated in the future.

situation analysis Analysis of the strengths, weaknesses, opportunities, and threats (SWOT) that affect organizational performance.

situational theory A contingency approach to leadership that links the leader's behavioral style with the task readiness of subordinates.

size The organization's scope or magnitude, typically measured by number of employees.

slogan A phrase or sentence that succinctly expresses a key corporate value.

small batch production A type of technology that involves the production of goods in batches of one or a few products designed to customer specifications.

social facilitation The tendency for the presence of others to influence an individual's motivation and performance.

social forces Those aspects of a culture that guide and influence relationships among people.

social responsibility The obligation of organization management to make decisions and take actions that will enhance the welfare and interests of society as well as the organization.

sociocultural dimension The dimension of the general environment representing the demographic characteristics, norms, customs, and values of the population within which the organization operates.

socioemotional role A role in which the individual provides support for team members' emotional needs and social unity.

span of management The number of employees who report to a supervisor; also called *span of control.*

special-purpose team A team created outside the formal organization to undertake a project of special importance or creativity.

spin-off An independent company producing a product or service similar to that produced by the entrepreneur's former employer.

stakeholder Any group within or outside the organization that has a stake in the organization's performance.

standing plans Ongoing plans used to provide guidance for tasks performed repeatedly within the organization.

stereotype A widely held generalization about a group of people that assigns attributes to them solely on the basis of a limited number of categories.

storming The stage of team development in which individual personalities and roles, and resulting conflicts, emerge.

story A narrative based on true events that is repeated frequently and shared by organizational employees.

strategic goals Broad statements of where the organization wants to be in the future; pertain to the organization as a whole rather than to specific divisions or departments.

strategic management The set of decisions and actions used to formulate and implement strategies that will provide a competitively superior fit between the organization and its environment so as to achieve organizational goals.

strategic plans The action steps by which an organization intends to attain its strategic goals.

strategy formulation The stage of strategic management that involves the planning and decision making that lead to the establishment of the organization's goals and of a specific strategic plan.

strategy The plan of action that prescribes resource allocation and other activities for dealing with the environment and helping the organization attain its goals.

strategy implementation The stage of strategic management that involves the use of managerial and organizational tools to direct resources toward achieving strategic outcomes.

structural change Any change in the way in which the organization is designed and managed.

substitute A situational variable that makes a leadership style redundant or unnecessary.

subsystems Parts of a system that depend on one another for their functioning.

superordinate goal A goal that cannot be reached by a single party.

suppliers People and organizations who provide the raw materials the organization uses to produce its output.

survey feedback A type of OD intervention in which questionnaires on organizational climate and other factors are distributed among employees and the results reported back to them by a change agent.

symbol An object, act, or event that conveys meaning to others.

symbolic leader A manager who defines and uses signals and symbols to influence corporate culture.

synergy The condition that exists when the organization's parts interact to produce a joint effect that is greater than the sum of the parts acting alone.

system A set of interrelated parts that function as a whole to achieve a common purpose.

systems theory An extension of the humanistic perspective that describes organizations as open systems that are characterized by entropy, synergy, and subsystem interdependence.

tactical goals Goals that define the outcomes that major divisions and departments must achieve in order for the organization to reach its overall goals.

tactical plans Plans designed to help execute major strategic plans and to accomplish a specific part of the company's strategy.

tall structure A management structure characterized by an overall narrow span of management and relatively large number of hierarchical levels.

task environment The layer of the external environment that directly influences the organization's operations and performance.

task force A temporary team or committee formed to solve a specific short-term problem involving several departments.

task specialist role A role in which the individual devotes personal time and energy to helping the team accomplish its task.

team A group of participants from several departments who meet regularly to solve ongoing problems of common interest; a unit of two or more people who interact and coordinate their work to accomplish a specific goal.

team building A type of OD intervention that enhances the cohesiveness of departments by helping members learn to function as a team.

team cohesiveness The extent to which team members are attracted to the team and motivated to remain in it.

technical skill The understanding of and proficiency in the performance of specific tasks.

technological dimension The dimension of the general environment that includes scientific and technological advancements in the industry and society at large.

technology change A change that pertains to the organization's production process.

technology The knowledge, tools, techniques, and activities used to transform the organization's inputs into outputs.

Theory Z A management perspective that incorporates techniques from both Japanese and North American management practices.

time-based competition A strategy of competition based on the ability to deliver products and services faster than competitors.

tolerance for ambiguity The psychological characteristic that allows a person to be untroubled by disorder and uncertainty.

top leader The overseer of both the product and the functional chains of command, responsible for the entire matrix.

top manager A manager who is at the top of the organizational hierarchy and is responsible for the entire organization.

top-down budgeting A budgeting process in which middle and lower-level managers set departmental budget targets in accordance with overall company revenues and expenditures specified by top management.

total quality management (TQM) A concept that focuses on managing the total organization to deliver quality to customers. Four significant elements of TQM are employee involvement, focus on the customer, benchmarking, and continuous improvement.

trade association An association made up of organizations with similar interests for the purpose of influencing the environment.

traits Distinguishing personal characteristics, such as intelligence, values, and appearance.

transaction processing system A type of operations information system that records and processes the organization's routinely occurring transactions, such as daily sales or purchases of supplies.

transactional leader A leader who clarifies subordinates' role and task requirements, initiates structure, provides rewards, and displays consideration for subordinates.

transformational leader A leader distinguished by a special ability to bring about innovation and change.

two-boss employee An employee who reports to two supervisors simultaneously.

uncertainty Managers know what goal they wish to achieve, but information about alternatives and future events is incomplete.

uncertainty avoidance A value characterized by people's intolerance for uncertainty and ambiguity and resulting support for beliefs that promise certainty and conformity.

unfreezing A step in the diagnosis stage of organizational development in which participants are made aware of problems in order to increase their willingness to change their behavior.

upward communication Messages transmitted from the lower to the higher level in the organization's hierarchy.

utilitarian approach The ethical concept that moral behaviors produce the greatest good for the greatest number.

valence The value or attraction an outcome has for an individual.

validity The relationship between an applicant's score on a selection device and his or her future job performance.

venture capital firm A group of companies or individuals that invests money in new or expanding businesses for ownership and potential profits.

vertical team A formal team composed of a manager and his or her subordinates in the organization's formal chain of command.

virtual team A team that uses computer technology and groupware so that geographically distant members can collaborate on projects and reach common goals.

Vroom-Jago model A model designed to help managers gauge the amount of subordinate participation in decision making.

whistle-blowing The disclosure by an employee of illegal, immoral, or illegitimate practices by the organization.

wholly owned foreign affiliate A foreign subsidiary over which an organization has complete control.

work redesign The altering of jobs to increase both the quality of employees' work experience and their productivity.

work specialization The degree to which organizational tasks are subdivided into individual jobs; also called *division of labor.*

workforce diversity Hiring people with different human qualities who belong to various cultural groups.

youth stage The phase of the organization life cycle in which the organization is growing rapidly and has a product enjoying some marketplace success.

zero-based budgeting (ZBB) A budgeting process in which each responsibility center calculates its resource needs based on the coming year's priorities rather than on the previous year's budget.

PHOTO CREDITS

NAME INDEX

COMPANY INDEX

Sampling of Companies and Web Sites from *Understanding Management*, Second Edition

Chapter 1

Kentucky Fried Chicken
www.kentuckyfriedchicken.com
SportsGear
www.sportsgear.com
Harbor Sweets
www.harbor-sweets.com

Chapter 2

Behlen
www.behlenmfg.com
Massachusetts Department of Revenue
www.magnet.state.ma.us/dor
Xerox Corporation
www.xerox.com
Granite Rock Company
www.graniterock.com
United Parcel Service (UPS)
www.ups.com
Saturn Corporation
www.saturncars.com

Chapter 3

C/Net Online
www.cnet.com
SAS (Statistical Analysis Systems) Institute
www.sas.com
Wal-Mart
www.wal-mart.com
Woods Memorial Hospital
www.cococo.net/business/etowah/health.htm
GTO, Inc.
www.gtoinc.com

Chapter 4

Federal Express
www.fedex.com
SinoAmerican Telecom
www.sinoamtel.com
ISPAT Steel
www.ispat.co.uk/index.htm
Triad (Siemens AG, Toshiba, IBM)
www.siemens.de, www.toshiba.com, www.ibm.com
Coca-Cola
www.cocacola.com
Danube Knitwear
apparelex.com/danube

Chapter 5

Tatra, Inc.
clearlight.com/~brawicz/tatra_trucks
Yakima Products
www.yakima.com
Beech-Nut Nutrition Corporation
www.beechnut.com

Starbucks
www.starbucks.com
Texas Instruments
www.ti.com

Chapter 6

J. Peterman Company
www.jpeterman.com
Relax The Back
www.relaxtheback.com
Hewlett-Packard
www.hp.com
TelePizza
www.sektor.de/telepizza
Amazon Books
www.amazon.com

Chapter 7

Jostens, Inc.
www.jostens.com
Amex Life Assurance
www.americanexpress.com
Autolock Bindings
www.switch-sf.com/autolock/autolock_index.html
Eastman Kodak Company
www.kodak.com
Yahoo!
www.yahoo.com
Granite Rock
www.graniterock.com

Chapter 8

Greyhound Lines Inc.
www.greyhound.com
Gateway 2000
www.gw2k.com
Coca-Cola Company
www.cocacola.com
Interval Research Corporation
www.interval.com
United Way
www.unitedway.org
Marmot Mountain Works
www.marmot.com
Buckman Laboratories
www.buckman.com

Chapter 9

Vortex Industries
www.vortexdata.com/index.htm
Magic Attic Club
www.tlcdoll.com/index2.htm
Marriott Corporation
www.marriott.com/index.shtml